ENCYCLOPEDIA OF WORLD LITERATURE
in the 20th Century

ENCYCLOPEDIA OF

in the

General Editor

IN THREE VOLUMES

An enlarged and updated edition of the

WORLD LITERATURE

20th Century

Wolfgang Bernard Fleischmann

*Dean of the School of Humanities
and Professor of Comparative Literature
Montclair State College*

VOLUME 3
O - Z

Herder *Lexikon der Weltliteratur im 20. Jahrhundert*

FREDERICK UNGAR PUBLISHING CO.
NEW YORK

The General Editor thanks the Research Council of the Graduate School at the University of Massachusetts for a grant that eased the last stages of manuscript preparation for the present volume.

The material translated or adapted from
Lexikon der Weltliteratur im 20. Jahrhundert
is included by arrangement with
Verlag Herder, Freiburg

Library of Congress Catalog Card Number: 67-13615
ISBN 0-8044-3091-8 (Complete set)
ISBN 0-8044-3094-2 (Vol. 3)

Board of Advisers

v

Contributors to Volume 3

Elsie B. Adams
Zangwill

Jaakko A. Ahokas
Pekkanen
Sarkia
Vala
Viita
Waltari

Fernando Alegría
Prado Calvo

Ernst Alker
Roth, Joseph

David D. Anderson
Pakistani Literature

Enrique Anderson Imbert
Spanish-American Literature

Janis Andrups
Skalbe
Virza
Ziverts

R. K. J. E. Antonissen
Opperman

Reza Arasteh
Persian Literature

William A. Armstrong
O'Flaherty

Horst Baader
Unamuno y Jugo

J. O. Bailey
Wells

Anna Balakian
Surrealism

Leo L. Barrow
Régio

Edward Bauer
Risse

Albin Eduard Beau
Portuguese Literature
Ribeiro
Sá-Carneiro

Richard Beck
Thórðarson

George J. Becker
Society and Literature

Karl Beckson
Strachey

CONTRIBUTORS TO VOLUME 3

E. M. Beekman
Ostaijen
Pillecijn
Teirlinck

Bruno Berger
Tharaud, Jérôme Ernest and Jean Charles

William H. Biddle
Zunzunegui y Laredo

Konrad Bieber
Prévert
Rivière
Schallück
Triolet
Vercors

R. L. Blackmore
Powys, John Cowper

Theophilus E. M. Boll
Sinclair, May

B. R. Bradbrook
Wolker

Sidney D. Braun
Paulhan

Evelyn Bristol
Pilnyak

Niels C. Brøgger
Undset

David Bronsen
Polgar

Calvin S. Brown
Weinheber

Douglas Brown
Powys, Theodore Francis

Francis Bulhof
Roland Holst, Adriaan

Charles Burkhart
Robinson, Edwin Arlington

Maryvonne Butcher
Sayers

Glauco Cambon
Pascoli

James F. Carens
Waugh

Richard Cary
Stephens

Leonard Casper
Philippine Literature

Maxime Chastaing
Woolf

Edson M. Chick
Wiechert

Christen Christensen
Øverland

Alí Chumacero
Reyes

Erwin Chvojka
Preradović

Hernani Cidade
Pascoaes

Austin Clarke
Robinson, Lennox

B. Bernard Cohen
Schwartz

Ruby Cohn
Sarraute

Gustavo Correa
Quiroga

E. J. Czerwinski
Polish Literature in the 1960's

Richard L. Dauenhauer
Simonov

Vincent C. De Baun
O'Casey

Andonis Manganaris Decavalles
Prevelakis
Seferis
Terzákis

Irving Deer
Roth, Philip

L. S. Dembo
Pound

Janet Winecoff Díaz
Spanish Literature

Anton Dieterich
Pérez Galdós

Thomas Doulis
Theotókas
Venézis
Xenópoulos

John Robert Doyle, Jr.
Plomer

Leon Edel
Psychology and Literature

Thomas Eekman
Trayanov

Stefán Einarsson
Stephansson

Rolf Ekmanis
Rainis

Richard Ellmann
Yeats

Emil Engelhardt
Tagore

Alfred Garvin Engstrom
Symbolism

Alexsandr Fadayev
Socialist Realism, Part II

Doris V. Falk
O'Neill

John M. Fein
Paz

John T. Flanagan
Sandburg

John Flasher
Yáñez

Walter Fleischmann
Zuckmayer

Howard R. Floan
Saroyan

Albert M. Forcadas
Sagarra i de Castellarnau
Sánchez Ferlosio

Wallace Fowlie
Psichari
Radiguet

Charles Frank
Wilson, Edmund

Emil Frederiksen
Paludan
Pontoppidan
Rode
Rørdam

Herbert Frenzel
Quasimodo

Melvin J. Friedman
O'Connor
O'Sullivan

Erhard Friedrichsmeyer
Weiss, Peter

Edward L. Galligan
Simenon

Arthur Ganz
Wilde

Xenia Gasiorowska
Żukrowski

Albert S. Gérard
Rhodesian Literature
Rwanda Literature
Sotho Literature
Swahili Literature
Xhosa Literature
Zulu Literature

Herbert S. Gershman
Tzara

Wolfgang Gesemann
Vazov

Monk Gibbon
Russell
Synge

Morgan Gibson
Rexroth
West, Nathanael

Mirra Ginsburg
Zamyatin

Helmut Goll
Thoma

George Gömöri
Weöres

Stefan Grunwald
Zweig, Arnold

Werner Günther
Ramuz

Talat Sait Halman
Turkish Literature
Yaşar Kemal

Anne-Marie de Moret Hamburg
Roblès

George Harjan
Parandowski

William E. Harkins
Olesha

Ihab Hassan
Salinger
Styron

Donald Heiney
Vittorini

Herder staff (indicated by * * *)
Penzoldt
Prévost
Régnier, Paule
Reymont
Sternheim
Wyspiański

Christoph Hering
Stramm

Charles G. Hill
Pagnol
Peyrefitte
Queneau
Salacrou
Sartre
Soupault
Troyat
Zola

Roland Hill
Thompson

Milton Hindus
Proust

Hans Hinterhäuser
Palazzeschi
Papini

Wolfgang Hirschberg
Soloukhin
Trenev

Frederick J. Hoffman
Stein

Leon-François Hoffmann
Oldenbourg

Richard Hoggart
Thomas, Dylan

Urban T. Holmes
Provençal Literature

Eberhard Horst
Weiss, Konrad

Wilhelm Hortmann
O'Faolain

Roger David Horwitz
Thomas, Henri

Johannes Hösle
Panzini
Verga

Renée Riese Hubert
Supervielle

Claude L. Hulet
Ramos

Virgil Ierunca
Rebreanu
Sadoveanu

W. R. Irwin
Tolkien

Barry Jacobs
Swedish Literature in the 1960's

Hubert Jannach
Traven

Manly Johnson
Paton
Spender

Joseph Jones and Robert E. McDowell
South African Literature: English Language

Erich Kahler
Time in Literature

Brigitte Kahr
Renard
Rostand

Gerald Kamber
Roth, Henry

Marc Kaminsky
Wright

Sonja Karsen
Pellicer
Torres Bodet

Eli Katz
Peretz

Christopher Kent
Priestley

Elizabeth M. Kerr
Richardson, Dorothy
Wolfe

Charles L. King
Sender

M. Klimenko
Voznesenski

Karl F. Knight
Ransom

Thomas R. Knipp
Senghor

Henri Kops
Walschap

Helena Kosek
Pujmanová

Jerzy R. Krzyżanowski
Różewicz
Zawieyski

Anneliese Kuchinke-Bach
Werfel

Heinrich Kunstmann
Polish Literature
Tuwim
Vančura

Joseph E. Laggini
Zolla

Renée B. Lang
Valéry

Amanda Langemo
Sandemose

Reinhard Lauth
Péguy

Vergene F. Leverenz
Rice
Sitwell, Edith
Spark
Stafford
Wain
West, Rebecca

H. Ernest Lewald
Payró

Bernth Lindfors
Soyinka
Tutuola

Liu Wu-chi
Shen Yen-ping
Su Man-shu

Mark Liwszyc
Sienkiewicz
Żeromski

George Luckyj
Prishvin
Tolstoi, Aleksei
Ukrainian Literature

Roy MacGregor-Hastie
Romanian Literature

Charles A. Madison
Opatoshu
Pinski
Reisen
Singer, Israel Joshua
Yehoash
Yiddish Literature

Lina Mainiero
Pascarella

Augustin Maissen
Swiss Literature

Irving Malin
Singer, Isaac Bashevis

Otto Mann
Toller

Vladimir Markov
Pasternak
Selvinski
Tikhonov
Zabolotzki

Elaine Marks
Yourcenar

Jean-Claude Martin
Obaldia
Vian

Wilson Martins
Queiroz

Eudo C. Mason
Rilke

W. U. McDonald, Jr.
Welty

Frederick P. W. McDowell
Roberts

Robert E. McDowell and Joseph Jones
South African Literature: English Language

Keith A. McDuffie
Vallejo

Dorothy Tuck McFarland
Pinter
Sackville-West
Shapiro
Williams, Charles
Winters
Wouk

George R. McMurray
Usigli
Villaurrutia

Robert G. Mead, Jr.
Spanish-American Literature in the 1960's

Ulrich Melzer
Wedekind

Judica I. H. Mendels
Roelants
Sabbe

John L. Modic
Wilder

Emir Rodriguez Monegal
Rodo

Nicholas Moravcevich
Yugoslav Literature

Walter D. Morris
Vesaas

Bruce Morrissette
Robbe-Grillet

Elliott D. Mossman
Soviet Literature in the 1960's

Kenneth Muir
Shaw, G. B.

Reinhard Müller-Freienfels
Schnitzler

James T. Nardin
Sherwood

Conny Nelson
Saint-John Perse
Zilahy

Virgil Nemoianu
Petrescu, Camil
Petrescu, Cezar

Oswalt von Nostitz
Pavese
Saint-Exupéry

Harley D. Oberhelman
Reyles

Otto Oberholzer
Strindberg

Ants Oras
Tammsaare

Anna Otten
Walser, Martin

Temira Pachmuss
Tolstoi, Lev

Sergio Pacifici
Tozzi

Stanley J. Pacion
Tate
Ważyk
Wittlin

Augustus Pallotta
Piovene

Douglas Parmée
Régnier, Henri François

Richard Pearse
O'Hara
Sansom
Vidal

Thomas A. Perry
Voiculescu

Fran Petrè
Prežihov
Župančíč

Gwynedd O. Pierce
Welsh Literature: Literature in the Welsh Language

Cyrena N. Pondrom
Pritchett

John Povey
West African Literature: English Language

Cecil Price
Watkins

Olga Prjevalinskaya-Ferrer
Panova
Paustovski
Sholokhov

Sanford Radner
Powell

Olga Ragusa
Pirandello

Luciano Rebay
Ungaretti

Henry Regensteiner
Schnurre

Karel Reijnders
Roland Holst-Van der Schalk
Schendel
Verwey

M. Ricciardelli
Sciascia

Richard N. Ringler
Trausti

Piero Rismondo
Svevo

Stanley L. Rose
Oliveira

Frank Rosengarten
Pratolini

Peter Rossbacher
Solzhenitzyn

Fritz Schalk
Perez de Ayala

Brigitte Scheer-Schaezler
Pynchon
Updike

Georges Schlocker
Ponge
Saint-Pol-Roux
Trakl

Franz K. Schneider
Silone

R. Schneider
Schickele

G. C. Schoolfield
Södergran

Gertrude C. Schwebell
Sachs
Schaper

Robert Scott
Palés Matos
Rivera
Rojas

Carl Seelig
Walser, Robert

Ingo Seidler
Santayana

Jadwiga Zwolska Sell
Wierzyński

Jorge de Sena
Pessoa

Donald Sheehan
Stevens

R. Baird Shuman
Odets

Rimvydas Šilbajoris
Radauskas
Vaičiulaitis

Juris Silenieks
Schehadé

Arthur Simon
Salmon

John K. Simon
Simon

G. Singh
Saba

Giovanni Sinicropi
Pasolini
Soldati

Grover Smith
Read

Gonzalo Sobejano
Riba Bracóns
Ruyra I Oms
Salinas
Villaespesa

Richard L. Spear
Tayama
Yamamoto

Robert D. Spector
Wiesel

Thomas F. Staley
Porter

Heinrich Stammler
Voloshin-Kiriyenko

Emil Štampar
Vojnovič

Raney Stanford
Snow

Marketa Goetz Stankiewicz
Talev

William Startt
Shaw, Irwin

Robert C. Steensma
Rølvaag

Marie-Georgette Steisel
Pinget

Victor H. Strandberg
  Warren

Carl J. Stratman, C.S.V.
  Tragedy

Josef Strelka
  Plievier
  Wassermann

Gleb Struve
  Russian Literature
  Sologub

Rudolf Sturm
  Slovak Literature

Walter Sutton
  Williams, William Carlos

Joris Taels
  Swedish Literature
  Swedish-Finnish Literature
  Timmermans
  Vermeylen
  Woestijne

Oskar Jan Tauschinski
  Przybyszewski
  Rittner

Mark Temmer
  Reverdy

R. George Thomas
  Welsh Literature: Anglo-Welsh Literature

Robert D. Thornton
  Scottish Literature

Zina Tillona
  Tecchi

Frederick Ungar
  Stoessl

xvi

Ungar staff (indicated by ****)
  Palamas
  Papadat-Bengescu
  Papadiamantís
  Pardo Bazán
  Pessanha
  Petersen
  Piontek
  Plisnier
  Pourrat
  Pourtalès
  Psiháris
  Remizov
  Rolland
  Romains
  Rostworowski
  Rozanov
  Sikilianós
  Sinclair, Upton
  Sitwell, Osbert
  Sitwell, Sacheverell
  Spitteler
  Thurber
  Trilussa
  Twain
  Tzvetayeva
  Under
  Valle-Inclán
  Vrchlický
  Wharton
  Zoshchenko
  Zweig, Stefan

Alonso Zamora Vicente
  Palacio Valdés

Lauri Viljanen
  Sillanpää

Richard J. Voorhees
  Wodehouse

Wayne Warncke
  Orwell

CONTRIBUTORS TO VOLUME 3

Clifford Warren
Williams, Tennessee

Kenneth Webb
Wast

Frances Wyers Weber
Ortega y Gasset

Kurt Weinberg
Verhaeren

Samuel A. Weiss
Osborne

Dennis S. R. Welland
Owen

René Wellek
Šalda

John C. Weston
Smith
Soutar

Kenneth S. White
Tardieu

G. A. Wilkes
White

Gero von Wilpert
Socialist Realism, Part I

Verna D. Wittrock
Richardson, Henry Handel

Johanna Wolf
Olbracht

George Wolff
Roethke

Friedrich Wilhelm Wollenberg
Remarque

James Woodress
Steinbeck

Leo Zanderer
Wilson, Angus

Leon M. Zolbrod
Tanizaki

Abbreviations for Periodicals, Volume 3

AALIAM	Arcadia, Accademia Letteraria Italiana. Atti e Memorie
AL	American Literature
APh	Acta Philologica (Roma: Societas Academica Dacoromana)
AQ	American Quarterly
ArL	Archivum Linguisticum
ArQ	Arizona Quarterly
AUC	Anales de la Universidad de Chile
BA	Books Abroad
BB	Bulletin of Bibliography
BHS	Bulletin of Hispanic Studies
CathW	Catholic World
CCa	Civiltà Cattolica
CE	College English
CHA	Cuadernos Hispanoamericanos (Madrid)
ChC	Chinese Culture
ChiR	Chicago Review
CL	Comparative Literature
CLAJ	College Language Association Journal (Morgan State Coll., Baltimore)
CMLR	Canadian Modern Language Review
CPe	Castrum Peregrini
Crit	Critique: Studies in Modern Fiction
CritQ	Critical Quarterly
CS	Cahiers du Sud
DA	Dissertation Abstracts
DR	Dalhousie Review
DramS	Drama Survey (Minneapolis)
DRs	Deutsche Rundschau
DS	Danske Studier
DubR	Dublin Review (London)
DVLG	Deutsche Vierteljahrsschrift für Literaturwissenschaft und Geistesgeschichte
EA	Études Anglaises
EG	Études Germaniques
EIC	Essays in Criticism (Oxford)
EJ	English Journal
FdL	Forum der Letteren
FH	Frankfurter Hefte
FL	Figaro Littéraire
FLe	Fiera Letteraria
FR	French Review
FS	French Studies
GaR	Georgia Review
Gids	De Gids
GL&L	German Life and Letters
GQ	German Quarterly
GR	Germanic Review
GRM	Germanisch-romanische Monatsschrift, Neue Folge
HSS	Harvard Slavic Studies
HudR	Hudson Review
ICS	L'Italia che Scrive
ILA	International Literary Annual (London)
IQ	Italian Quarterly
ISS	Indiana Slavic Studies

JAAC	Journal of Aesthetics and Art Criticism		*RI*	Revista Iberoamericana
JGE	Journal of General Education		*RLI*	Rassegna della Letteratura Italiana
JGG	Jahrbuch der Grillparzer-Gesellschaft		*RLM*	La Revue des Lettres Modernes
JHI	Journal of the History of Ideas		*RMS*	Renaissance and Modern Studies (Univ. of Nottingham)
KR	Kenyon Review		*RomN*	Romance Notes (Univ. of North Carolina)
			RUL	Revue de l'Université d'Ottawa
MD	Modern Drama			
MdF	Mercure de France		*SatR*	Saturday Review
MFS	Modern Fiction Studies		*SCB*	The South Central Bulletin (Tulsa, Okla., Studies by Members of the South Central MLA)
MinnR	Minnesota Review			
ML	Modern Languages (London)			
MLJ	Modern Language Journal			
MLN	Modern Language Notes		*SEEJ*	Slavic and East European Journal
MLQ	Modern Language Quarterly		*SEER*	Slavonic and East European Review
MLR	Modern Language Review			
			SI	Svizzera Italiana
NDH	Neue Deutsche Hefte		*SlavR*	Slavic Review (Seattle)
NDQ	North Dakota Quarterly		*SLT*	Svensk Litteraturtidskrift
NL	Nouvelles Littéraires		*SoR*	Southern Review (Louisiana State Univ.)
NM	Neuphilologische Mitteilungen			
NRF	Nouvelle Revue Française		*SP*	Studies in Philology
NSammlung	Neue Sammlung		*SR*	Sewanee Review
NTg	De Nieuwe Taalgids		*SRo*	Studi Romani
NVT	Nieuw Vlaams Tijdschrift		*SS*	Scandinavian Studies
NY	The New Yorker		*SSL*	Studies in Scottish Literature (Texas Technological Coll., Lubbock)
PBA	Proceedings of the British Academy			
PMLA	Publications of the Modern Language Association of America		*TamR*	Tamarack Review (Toronto)
			TCL	Twentieth Century Literature
PolR	Polish Review (New York)		*TDR*	Tulane Drama Review
PR	Partisan Review		*TLS*	Times Literary Supplement (London)
PSA	Papeles de Son Armadans (Mallorca)			
			TM	Temps Modernes
			TR	La Table Ronde
RCB	Revista de Cultura Brasileña		*TSLL*	Studies in Literature and Language (Univ. of Texas)
RealM	Realtà del Mezzogiorno			
RESl	Revue des Études Slaves			
RFE	Revista de Filología Española		*UKCR*	University of Kansas City Review
RGB	Revue Générale Belge		*UTQ*	University of Toronto Quarterly
RHL	Revue d'Histoire Littéraire de la France		*VQR*	Virginia Quarterly Review
RHM	Revista Hispánica Moderna		*WHR*	Western Humanities Review

WPQ	Western Political Quarterly (Univ. of Utah)	*YCGL*	Yearbook of Comparative and General Literature (Indiana Univ.)
WSCL	Wisconsin Studies in Contemporary Literature	*YFS*	Yale French Studies
WuWahr	Wort und Wahrheit	*YR*	Yale Review
WZ	Wort in der Zeit (Vienna)		
WZUB	Wissenschaftliche Zeitschrift der Humboldt-Universität zu Berlin. Gesellschafts-und Sprachwissenschaftliche Reihe		

Illustrations

facing page   *facing page*

René de Obaldia	4	Salvatore Quasimodo	136
Sean O'Casey	4	Horacio Quiroga	136
Clifford Odets	10	Jānis Rainis	140
John O'Hara	10	Graciliano Ramos	140
Antônio de Oliveira	10	José Régio	148
Eugene O'Neill	18	Aleksei Remizov	148
José Ortega y Gasset	18	Alfonso Reyes	154
George Orwell	26	Carlos Reyles	154
Leopoldus van Ostaijen	26	Rainer Maria Rilke	160
Arnulf Øverland	26	Helge Rode	174
Kostis Palamás	34	Maurice Roelants	174
Luis Palés Matos	34	Adriaan Roland Holst	178
Jan Parandowski	40	Henriëtte Roland Holst-Van der Schalk	178
Teixeira de Pascoaes	40	Romain Rolland	182
Giovanni Pascoli	42	Jules Romains	182
Pier Paolo Pasolini	42	Joseph Roth	188
Boris Pasternak	44	Philip Milton Roth	188
Alan Paton	50	G. W. Russell (pseud.: A.E.)	214
Cesare Pavese	50	Nelly Sachs	214
Roberto Payró	56	Antoine de Saint-Exupéry	218
Octavio Paz	56	Saint-John Perse	218
Fernando Pessoa	68	Carl Sandburg	228
Nis Petersen	68	Aksel Sandemose	228
Filip de Pillecijn	76	George Santayana	232
Robert Pinget	76	Kaarlo Teodor Sarkia	232
Guido Piovene	76	Nathalie Sarraute	232
Luigi Pirandello	82	Jean-Paul Sartre	236
Henrik Pontoppidan	82	Dorothy Sayers	244
Ezra Pound	102	Arthur Schnitzler	244
Henri Pourrat	102	George Seferis	258
Jacques Prévert	112	Ramón Sender	258
John Priestley	112	Léopold Senghor	258
Marcel Proust	112	George Bernard Shaw	262

ILLUSTRATIONS

Robert Sherwood	262	Rodolfo Usigli	458
Mikhail Sholokhov	274	Paul Valéry	458
Frans Sillanpää	274	Ramón del Valle-Inclán	464
Ignazio Silone	274	César Vallejo	464
Claude Simon	278	Giovanni Verga	470
Konstantin Simonov	278	Émile Verhaeren	470
Isaac Bashevis Singer	288	Xavier Villaurrutia	476
Osbert, Sacheverell, and Edith Sitwell	288	Andrei Voznesenski	476
Edith Södergran	310	Mika Waltari	488
Aleksandr Solzhenitzyn	310	Robert Penn Warren	488
Stephen Spender	344	Hugo Wast	488
Carl Spitteler	344	Evelyn Waugh	494
Gertrude Stein	360	Frank Wedekind	494
Johan August Strindberg	360	H. G. Wells	500
Rabindranath Tagore	392	Franz Werfel	500
Tanizaki Jun'ichirō	392	Edith Wharton	522
Dylan Thomas	404	Oscar Wilde	528
Thórbergur Thórðarson	404	Thornton Wilder	528
Felix Timmermans	414	William Carlos Williams	532
Aleksei Tolstoi	414	P. G. Wodehouse	532
Lev Tolstoi	416	Thomas Wolfe	538
Georg Trakl	440	Virginia Woolf	538
Mark Twain	440	Richard Wright	542
Marina Tzvetayeva	448	William Butler Yeats	542
Miguel de Unamuno y Jugo	448	Juan Antonio de Zunzunegui	590
Sigrid Undset	452	Stefan Zweig	590

Acknowledgments

For permission to reproduce the illustrations in this volume,
the publishers are indebted to the following:

RENÉ DE OBALDIA	French Cultural Services, N.Y.
SEAN O'CASEY	Edizioni Paoline, Rome
CLIFFORD ODETS	Edizioni Paoline, Rome
JOHN O'HARA	Harper & Row, N.Y.
ANTÔNIO DE OLIVEIRA	Ministério da Educação e Cultura-Biblioteca Nacional, Rio de Janeiro
EUGENE O'NEILL	Bildarchiv Herder, Freiburg-in-the-Breisgau
JOSÉ ORTEGA Y GASSET	W. W. Norton & Company, Inc., N.Y.
GEORGE ORWELL	Harcourt, Brace, Jovanovich, Inc., N.Y.
LEOPOLDUS VAN OSTAIJEN	Nederlands Letterkundig Museum en Documentatie-centrum, The Hague
ARNULF ØVERLAND	Royal Norwegian Embassy Information Service, N.Y.
KOSTIS PALAMÁS	Edizioni Paoline, Rome
LUIS PALÉS MATOS	Istituto de Cultura Puertorriqueña, San Juan
JAN PARANDOWSKI	Courtesy of Mr. Parandowski
TEIXEIRA DE PASCOAES	Casa de Portugal, N.Y.
GIOVANNI PASCOLI	Istituto Italiano di Cultura, N.Y.
PIER PAOLO PASOLINI	Istituto Italiano di Cultura, N.Y.
BORIS PASTERNAK	Bildarchiv Herder, Freiburg-in-the-Breisgau
ALAN PATON	Charles Scribner's Sons, N.Y.
CESARE PAVESE	Farrar, Straus, & Giroux, Inc., N.Y.
ROBERTO PAYRÓ	Julio E. Payró and OAS Photos, Washington, D.C.
OCTAVIO PAZ	Grove Press, N.Y.
FERNANDO PESSOA	Casa de Portugal, N.Y.
NIS PETERSEN	Danish Information Office, N.Y.
FILIP DE PILLECIJN	Belgian Consulate General, N.Y.
ROBERT PINGET	French Cultural Services, N.Y.
GUIDO PIOVENE	Istituto Italiano di Cultura, N.Y.
LUIGI PIRANDELLO	Bildarchiv Herder, Freiburg-in-the-Breisgau
HENRIK PONTOPPIDAN	Danish Information Office, N.Y.
EZRA POUND	Boris De Rachewiltz and New Directions Publishing Corp., N.Y.
HENRI POURRAT	French Cultural Services, N.Y.
JACQUES PRÉVERT	French Cultural Services, N.Y.
JOHN PRIESTLEY	Mark Gerson and Harper & Row, N.Y.
MARCEL PROUST	The Bettmann Archive, N.Y.
SALVATORE QUASIMODO	Istituto Italiano di Cultura, N.Y.
HORACIO QUIROGA	OAS Photos, Washington, D.C.
JĀNIS RAINIS	Courtesy of Rolf Ekmanis
GRACILIANO RAMOS	Ministério da Educação e Cultura-Biblioteca Nacional, Rio de Janeiro
JOSÉ RÉGIO	Casa de Portugal, N.Y.
ALEKSEI REMIZOV	Edizioni Paoline, Rome
ALFONSO REYES	Mexican Government—Ministry of Foreign Relations

ACKNOWLEDGMENTS

CARLOS REYLES	Hispanic Institute, Columbia University, N.Y.
RAINER MARIA RILKE	Insel-Verlag, Wiesbaden
HELGE RODE	Danish Information Office, N.Y.
MAURICE ROELANTS	Nederlands Letterkundig Museum en Documentatie-centrum, The Hague
ADRIAAN ROLAND HOLST	Netherlands Information Service, N.Y.
HENRIËTTE ROLAND HOLST-VAN DER SCHALK	Nederlands Letterkundig Museum en Documentatie-centrum, The Hague
ROMAIN ROLLAND	French Cultural Services, N.Y.
JULES ROMAINS	Edizioni Paoline, Rome
JOSEPH ROTH	Verlag Kiepenheuer-Witsch, Cologne
PHILIP MILTON ROTH	Judy Feiffer and Random House, N.Y.
G. W. RUSSELL (pseud.: A. E.)	Edizioni Paoline, Rome
NELLY SACHS	Stockholm Riwkin and Farrar, Straus, & Giroux, Inc., N.Y.
ANTOINE DE SAINT-EXUPÉRY	Harcourt, Brace, Jovanovich, Inc., N.Y.
SAINT-JOHN PERSE	French Cultural Services, N.Y.
CARL SANDBURG	Edizioni Paoline, Rome
AKSEL SANDEMOSE	Royal Norwegian Embassy Information Service, N.Y.
GEORGE SANTAYANA	Edizioni Paoline, Rome
KAARLO TEODOR SARKIA	Consulate General of Finland, N.Y.
NATHALIE SARRAUTE	French Cultural Services, N.Y.
JEAN-PAUL SARTRE	Keystone, Munich
DOROTHY SAYERS	Edizioni Paoline, Rome
ARTHUR SCHNITZLER	Verlag Ullstein, Berlin
GEORGE SEFERIS	Edizioni Paoline, Rome
RAMÓN SENDER	Hispanic Institute, Columbia University, N.Y.
LÉOPOLD SENGHOR	Edizioni Paoline, Rome
GEORGE BERNARD SHAW	Verlag Ullstein, Berlin
ROBERT SHERWOOD	Edizioni Paoline, Rome
MIKHAIL SHOLOKHOV	*Literaturen der Völker der Sowjetunion*, edited by Dr. Harri Jünger
FRANS SILLANPÄÄ	Consulate General of Finland, N.Y.
IGNAZIO SILONE	De Biasi and Harper & Row, N.Y.
CLAUDE SIMON	French Cultural Services, N.Y.
KONSTANTIN SIMONOV	*Literaturen der Völker der Sowjetunion*, edited by Dr. Harri Jünger
ISAAC BASHEVIS SINGER	Patt Meara and Farrar, Straus, & Giroux, Inc., N.Y.
OSBERT, SACHEVERELL, AND EDITH SITWELL	Edizioni Paoline, Rome
EDITH SÖDERGRAN	Swedish Information Service, N.Y.
ALEKSANDR SOLZHENITZYN	Farrar, Straus, & Giroux, Inc., N.Y.
STEPHEN SPENDER	Camilla McGrath and Random House, N.Y.
CARL SPITTELER	Verlag Orell Füssli, Zurich
GERTRUDE STEIN	Edizioni Paoline, Rome
JOHAN AUGUST STRINDBERG	Swedish Information Service, N.Y.
RABINDRANATH TAGORE	Edizioni Paoline, Rome
TANIZAKI JUN'ICHIRŌ	Courtesy of Harold Strauss
DYLAN THOMAS	Rollie McKenna and New Directions, N.Y.
THÓRBERGUR THÓRĐARSON	Consulate General of Iceland, N.Y.
FELIX TIMMERMANS	Nederlands Letterkundig Museum en Documentatie-centrum, The Hague
ALEKSEI TOLSTOI	*Literaturen der Völker der Sowjetunion*, edited by Dr. Harri Jünger
LEV TOLSTOI	Edizioni Paoline, Rome
GEORG TRAKL	Wilfried Göpel, Berlin
MARK TWAIN	Edizioni Paoline, Rome
MARINA TZVETAYEVA	Edizioni Paoline, Rome
MIGUEL DE UNAMUNO Y JUGO	Hispanic Institute, Columbia University, N.Y.
SIGRID UNDSET	Alfred A. Knopf, Inc., N.Y.
RODOLFO USIGLI	Zbigniev Lagocki, Cracow
PAUL VALÉRY	Verlag Ullstein, Berlin

ACKNOWLEDGMENTS

RAMÓN DEL VALLE-INCLÁN	Hispanic Institute, Columbia University, N.Y.
CÉSAR VALLEJO	Juan Larrea and Grove Press, N.Y.
GIOVANNI VERGA	Edizioni Paoline, Rome
ÉMILE VERHAEREN	Verlag Ullstein, Berlin
XAVIER VILLAURRUTIA	Mexican Government—Ministry of Foreign Relations
ANDREI VOZNESENSKI	Hill & Wang, Inc., N.Y.
MIKA WALTARI	G. P. Putnam's Sons, N.Y.
ROBERT PENN WARREN	Harold Strauss and Random House, N.Y.
HUGO WAST	Hispanic Institute, Columbia University, N.Y.
EVELYN WAUGH	Verlag Ullstein, Berlin
FRANK WEDEKIND	Lolo Handke, Bad Berneck
H. G. WELLS	Edizioni Paoline, Rome
FRANZ WERFEL	S. Fischer-Verlag, Frankfurt-on-the-Main
EDITH WHARTON	Charles Scribner's Sons, N.Y.
OSCAR WILDE	Edizioni Paoline, Rome
THORNTON WILDER	Edizioni Paoline, Rome
WILLIAM CARLOS WILLIAMS	Edizioni Paoline, Rome
P. G. WODEHOUSE	Ira Rosenberg and Simon and Schuster, N.Y.
THOMAS WOLFE	Verlag Ullstein, Berlin
VIRGINIA WOOLF	Harcourt, Brace, Jovanovich, Inc., N.Y.
RICHARD WRIGHT	Harper & Row, N.Y.
WILLIAM BUTLER YEATS	Edizioni Paoline, N.Y.
JUAN ANTONIO DE ZUNZUNEGUI	Hispanic Institute, Columbia University, N.Y.
STEFAN ZWEIG	Lolo Handke, Bad Berneck

ENCYCLOPEDIA OF WORLD LITERATURE
in the 20th Century

O

OBALDIA, René de

French dramatist, novelist, and poet, b. 22 Oct. 1918, Hong Kong

The son of a Panamanian and a Frenchwoman, O. was brought to France as an infant. After attending the Lycée Condorcet, he had no further academic training. *Humaï* (1937), his first book of poems, was published when he was nineteen. During World War II, O. was a German prisoner-of-war from 1940 to 1945.

O.'s *Midi* (1949) won the Louis-Parrot poetry prize and was followed by *Les Richesses naturelles* (1952), a book of prose poems, and *Tamerlan des coeurs* (1955), a novel.

As deputy director of the Royaumont International Cultural Center, O. began writing short plays to entertain the center's guests. In 1957, several of these plays—*Le Défunt* and *Le Sacrifice du bourreau*—were performed in Paris. Turning to fiction, O. published *Fugue à Waterloo* (1956) and *Le Centenaire* (1959). In *Le Centenaire,* "senility is considered as a fine art" as an old man tells the moving and rather ridiculous details of his life.

Edouard et Agrippine (1958), an impromptu radio play, won the Grand Prix de Paris, but O.'s first important play was *Genousie* (1960; Jenousia, 1965). In it we see an eccentric snob, Madame de Tubéreuse, who delights in entertaining distinguished intellectuals. Among the latter are Hassingor, a playwright, and his beautiful wife, Irène, who speaks only "genousien," a language that nobody understands. In this play, O. contrasts the two realms in which man lives: the mundane world of reality, in which Madame de Tubéreuse's guests meet and chat; and Hassingor's world

of dreams, in which strange and wonderful things happen.

In *Le Satyre de la Villette* (1963) we are introduced to Eudoxie, an emancipated young girl in some ways similar to Queneau's (q.v.) Zazie. Though she uses language that appalls the adults around her, she is essentially innocent and lives in a child's paradise.

Du Vent dans les branches de sassafras (1965), described by O. as a "sitting-room western," combines features of the *commedia dell'arte* and the Hollywood western. In parodying the conventions of the latter—noble sentiments, heroic poses, battles with Indians, etc.—O. is actually ridiculing the conventions of all Western civilization. The play inaugurated a genre special to O.: a potpourri of other genres parodied in a style that hilariously contrasts the expected and the unexpected.

Le Cosmonaute agricole (1966) is a satire on the Space Age. In this play O. points a classic moral by presenting an astronaut who goes into space only to find a duplication of the emptiness within him. *Innocentines* (1969) is a book of poems "for children and a few adults." Calling his poems "moments of grace," O. urges a return to the innocent world of childhood.

Though many features link O.'s somewhat surrealistic plays to the theater of the absurd, he himself rejects this label. In addition to echoes of Jarry, Ionesco, and Beckett (qq.v.), his theater also shows a strong poetic element in the tradition of Giraudoux and Audiberti (qq.v.). O. not only uses situations that are poetic in themselves, but he employs language in a fanciful and amusing manner that often mixes classical quotations and advertising slogans.

Rejecting the dourness of those who complain of life's "absurdity," O. insists that life is whatever we make of it. His unique approach to language and his virtuoso use of parody have resulted in a modern theater of rare humor and tenderness.

FURTHER WORKS: *Théâtre I* (1966; includes *Genousie, Le Satyre de la Villette,* and *Le Général inconnu*); *Théâtre II* (1966; includes *L'Air du large, Du Vent dans les branches de sassafras,* and *Le Cosmonaute agricole*); *Théâtre III* (1967; includes *Sept impromptus à loisir*)

BIBLIOGRAPHY: *Dictionnaire de littérature contemporaine* (1962); Bory, J.-L., Preface to *Choix de textes de R. de O.* (1963); Poirot-Delpech, B., "Du Vent dans les branches de sassafras," *Le Monde,* 1 Dec. 1965; Nadeau, M., Afterword to *Tamerlan des coeurs* (1964); Bonnefoy, C., *Littérature de notre temps,* Vol. III (1966); Surer, P., *Cinquante Ans de théâtre* (1969)

JEAN-CLAUDE MARTIN

O'CASEY, Sean

(pseud. of *John Casey,* later Gaelicized to *Sean O'Cathasaigh*), Irish dramatist, b. 30 March 1880, Dublin; d. 18 Sept. 1964, Torquay

O., the youngest of thirteen children, was born in a slum. Because of a painful eye disease and the death of his father when O. was only six years old, he did not learn to read until he was fourteen. He then began an ambitious program of self-education.

O. went to work in his early teens as a laborer. As late as his forty-fifth year, before his first success in the theater, he was mixing cement on a road gang. Angered by the brutalization of the lower classes, he became secretary of the Citizen Army, a socialist organization that instigated a violent general strike in Dublin in 1913. He was alienated further from the world of wealth and power because he was a Protestant in a Roman Catholic city subject to strict clerical control. His memories of this pre-World War I period —and the Irish Easter Rebellion of 1916 and the civil war of the 1920's—are basic in all his early plays.

O. began writing seriously in 1918, after some of his articles appeared in labor journals. The mild success of his ballads, short pieces of fiction, patriotic narratives, and a history of the Citizen Army (*The Story of the Irish Citizen Army,* 1919) encouraged him to turn to drama.

O. had enjoyed appearing in amateur theatricals, dearly esteemed Shakespeare and Dion Boucicault (1822–90), and admired Shaw and Strindberg (qq.v.). Although his first three scripts were rejected by the Abbey Theatre, the directors showed increasing interest. Then, in 1923, *The Shadow of a Gunman* was produced at the Abbey Theatre. It was followed by *Juno and the Paycock* (1924) and *The Plough and the Stars* (1926). His fame rests securely on these two great naturalist tragicomedies, unusual mixtures of melodrama, boisterous humor, and poetic dialect.

The Plough and the Stars contains scenes showing the Irish flag in a pub frequented by a prostitute. In response the nationalist and pious middle class protested violently, inciting riots in which the actors were attacked on stage by outraged spectators. The emotions this evoked prompted O. to go to live permanently in England.

O.'s next play, *The Silver Tassie* (1928), brought changes in style and material. Although certain naturalist elements remained, O. used a powerful expressionistic sequence, reminiscent of Kaiser or Toller (qq.v.), to present a World War I battlefield. Yeats (q.v.), then the leading spirit of the Abbey Theatre, objected to this shift in method and rejected the play. It was produced in London, where it caused sharp critical controversy.

Having freed himself from specifically Irish themes and the confines of the box set, O. thereafter inventively combined expressionism and naturalism in a series of plays dealing with larger human issues, principally man's need to combat conformist, authoritarian society. *Within the Gates* (1933) is set in the Great Depression. *The Star Turns Red* (1940) shows the contending forces of communism and fascism against a background suggesting the Spanish Civil War. *Red Roses for Me* (1942) deals with the 1913 Dublin strike but is actually a play about the Irish conflict between affirming the life force and submitting to modern puritanical bleakness. *Oak Leaves and Lavender* (1946) deals heavily with the triumph of proletarian spirit over a moribund aristocracy during the Battle of Britain in World War II.

O.'s sympathy with communism is clear in all these plays, especially *The Star Turns Red*

RENÉ DE OBALDIA

SEAN O'CASEY

and *Oak Leaves and Lavender,* which is probably the weakest of his works.

In 1940, O. offered his public a comedy, *Purple Dust,* which sings of the pleasures of natural physical love. This foreshadowed *Cock-a-Doodle Dandy* (1949), *The Bishop's Bonfire* (1955), and *The Drums of Father Ned* (1960), all of which have an Irish setting. In all these plays he continues to fuse expressionism and naturalism, and he treats fantastically, with bold and slapstick ingenuity, the Irish sense of joyous life and its repression by authority, both clerical and political. The satire is telling but mellow.

Throughout his adult years O. wrote critical and personal essays. The most important are *The Flying Wasp* (1937), *The Green Crow* (1956), and *Under a Coloured Cap* (1963). Vital to an understanding of his methods and personality is his six-volume autobiography, published under the omnibus title *Mirror in My House* (1956). It synthesizes his spirit and shows, at their best and their worst, his abiding gaiety, pride, loneliness, moral sensibility, quick anger, and compassion.

FURTHER WORKS: *Songs of the Wren* (1918); *More Songs of the Wren* (1918); *The Story of Thomas Ashe* (1918); *Cathleen Listens In* (1923); *Nannie's Night Out* (1924); *Windfalls* (1934); *I Knock at the Door* (1939); *Pictures in the Hallway* (1942); *Drums under the Windows* (1945); *Inishfallen, Fare Thee Well* (1949); *Collected Plays* (4 vols., 1949–50); *Rose and Crown* (1952); *Bedtime Story* (1953); *Hall of Healing* (1954); *Time to Go* (1954); *Sunset and Evening Star* (1954); *Five One-Act Plays* (1958); *Three Plays* (includes Behind the Green Curtains, Figuro in the Night, The Moon Shines on Kylenamoe; 1961); *Feathers from the Green Crow: S. O. 1905–1925* (ed. R. Hogan; 1962)

BIBLIOGRAPHY: Starkie, W., *The Irish Theatre* (1939); Koslow, J., *The Green and the Red* (1950); Kavanagh, P., *The Story of the Abbey Theatre* (1950); Krause, D., *S. O.: The Man and His Work* (1960); Hogan, R., *The Experiments of S. O.* (1960); special O. issue: *Modern Drama,* IV (Dec. 1961), 223–91; Cowasjee, S., *S. O.: The Man Behind the Plays* (1964); Fallon, G., *S. O.* (1965); McCann, S., ed., *The World of S. O.* (1966); Armstrong, W. A., *S. O.* (1967); Krause, D., *A Self-Portrait of the Artist as a Man* (1968)

VINCENT C. DE BAUN

Mr. O.'s most recent play takes place immediately before and during the Easter Rebellion instead of during the post-war disturbances in which *Juno and the Paycock* was set. Nevertheless, it would seem to be increasingly obvious that Mr. O.'s dramatic inspiration comes almost entirely from the misfortunes of his countrymen during the last decade. Apparently he sees the sequence of revolutionary episodes as one vast drama, and from it selects for his own purposes dramatic episodes which he places against a shrewdly observed background of Irish proletarian life. This would seem to explain the very real lack of structure to be noticed in both these plays, since he conceives the frame of them to be outside of both of them, and many other plays which he has written and, it is to be hoped, will write. He himself sees so clearly a beginning, an end, and a middle in recent Irish history, that he conceives it unnecessary to stress these dramatic props in the segments of that history which he chooses to dramatise.

The Plough and the Stars is a better play than *Juno,* because there are not three distinct strings of plot to unravel—more poignant in the characters selected from Dublin's underworld as mediums for alternate passages of humour and terror. No one of the characters, perhaps, suggests the potential greatness of Captain Boyle, but none of them cheat their promise as did he....

It is my guess that, although Mr. O. will never *construct* a play so as to attain the maximum effect out of its rhythm and movement, he will in his succeeding plays increasingly eliminate such devices and other breaches of dramatic taste, with the result that we shall have greater power with no less of the entertainment which he undoubtedly affords.

Milton Waldman, in *The London Mercury*
(July 1926), p. 299

Do we imagine that in these victims of society we have at last fastened Mr. O. down to something, if only a break in the evening hate? Never were playgoers more mistaken, for the play [*Within the Gates*] has a Dreamer, the ethereal offspring of Galsworthy and Mr. Drinkwater, who at the end of the play says roundly that the Down-and-Outs are scum and ought to be down-and-outed. After which he expresses the opinion that the street-walker is the best of the lot, since she has courage, if only of the despairing sort.

It is difficult to separate one's disagreement of opinion from the place of that opinion in a work of art. That we should impatiently ask what is biting Mr. O. does not affect his right to be bitten, with, if he likes, unending objurgations; still, it would be a little boring if all Shakespeare's sonnets had been written on the theme of "Tired with all these, for restful death I cry." This play is obviously non-realistic, and therefore one must not put it to a naturalistic test. What a pity, then, that

Mr. O. should make it so difficult for us by making his characters both real and unreal, earthbound and fantastic, so that his play reads like *Alice in Wonderland* interleaved with Euclid!

But perhaps this is the new medium which the unusual rhythm of this play is said to usher in? If that is so, then there is one dramatic critic who will have to go out of business. I think I can understand park-keepers, prelates, and, at a pinch, prostitutes, and I try to grapple with symbols, sublimations, subfuscations and substantiations whereby an author shelves his characters to substitute himself. But I find it difficult to do these two things at the same time, and in my view the characters in every play should decide at the beginning whether they are going to be a metaphysical all-my-eye or a real Betty Martin. The trouble is that Mr. O. is essentially an Irishman who, while labelling his characters English and dropping the accent, still retains the Irish idiom. Take the Old Woman, for example. Any drunken old lady who is Irish has that poetry in her which befits her for Kathleen-Ni-Houlihan, whereas the capacity to soar is not in the English Mrs. Gamp. If this play were translated back into the Irish in which it was conceived one might take a very different view of it.

James Agate, *First Nights* (1934), pp. 274–75

After Synge, the deluge. The Easter Rising, the Troubles, the founding of the Free State. A more headlong period found a more headlong writer: O. He did not use the distorting mirrors of Synge, but one that permitted itself only the slight enlargements of dramatic realism. Another epoch, another class. In 1916 Yeats felt that a terrible beauty was born, but O. belonged to a class that was the victim rather than the agent of heroism, and to a generation that saw the heroes degenerate into bureaucrats. "A terrible beauty is borneo,/Republicans once so forlorneo,/ Subjected to all kinds of scorneo,/ Tophatted, frockcoated, with manifest skill/ Are well away now on Saint Patrick's steep hill/ Directing the labor of Jack and of Jill/ In the dawn of a wonderful morneo."

O. was not in reaction against Synge. He belongs to a class and a generation that can have no relation to Synge whatsoever, even that of reaction. What he is in reaction against is the heroics of the second-rate men. He does not scorn their ideals. He observes that they use these ideals for the deception of others and, sometimes, themselves. Amid the unheroic facts the heroic words are incongruous. From this incongruity spring the tears and laughter of O.'s realistic dramas.

Eric Bentley, "Heroic Wantonness" (1951), *In Search of Theater* (1953), p. 317

O. realises . . . [his] conflict with all the vitality of a man who really believes in popular theatre. Farce, pantomime, flights of wild, comic lyricism, outbursts of savage satire—he exploits them all with a zestful assurance. The struggle is both spiritual and physical.

Albert Hunt, in *Drama* (Nov.-Dec. 1959), p. 39

Even when he is in a serious mood O. is likely to be satiric not solemn, poignant not pathetic. And when the tragic events or consequences of war and poverty become most crucial he will open up the action and counterbalance the incipient tragedy with a music-hall turn or a randy ballad or a mock-battle. While everyone awaits a terrifying raid by the Black and Tans in *The Gunman* the well-oiled Dolphie Grigson parades into the house spouting songs and biblical rhetoric in drunken bravado. Just when Mrs. Tancred is on her way to bury her ambushed son in *Juno* the Boyles have launched their wild drinking and singing party. While the streets ring with patriotic speeches about heroic bloodshed in *The Plough* [*and the Stars*] the women of the tenements have a free-for-all fight about respectability in a Pub.

This pattern of ironic counterpoint is maintained as a tragicomic rhythm throughout the plays. For each tragic character there are comic foils who constantly bring the action round from the tragic to the comic mood. . . . It is this attitude which keeps his plays from becoming melancholy or pessimistic. His humour saves him and his characters from despair.

David Krause, *Sean O'Casey* (1960), pp. 71–72

What are the later plays? What are O.'s intentions? Briefly, his intentions would seem to be the destruction of dramatic realism. It is something of a paradox that the reigning convention of the modern theatre should be realism although the greatest modern dramatists in their greatest plays are not realists. Perhaps the subtle influence of the film is responsible, and perhaps it is easier to understand the Ibsen of *The Pillars of Society* than the Ibsen of *The Master Builder*. . . . Today's theatrical growth is from *Murder in the Cathedral* to *The Cocktail Party*, from poetry to prose. O., who has never attempted to come to terms with theatrical convention, has progressed from prose to poetry. . . .

O.'s work, however, has tended in the direction of freedom, of breaking down the forms and conventions of dramatic realism. He cries with Shaw that there are no rules, but this statement should be taken probably as one of narrow polemic against realism, rather than as a broad statement of dramatic theory. In his early plays O. was thought to be a realist of erratic and primitive genius, a dramatist of great original talent who, if he learned to harness and control his structure, would produce quite overpowering plays. *The Silver Tassie* and the subsequent plays, however, indicated the dramatist was getting too big for his britches, was setting himself up as an intellectual and a member of the avant garde, was throwing discipline out the window, whimsically dissipating his meager power in the slough of Expressionism and perversely biting the pale and poetic hand that fed him from the door (back door probably) of the Abbey Theatre.

Actually the early plays, like the later ones of Chekhov, seemed slovenly in form and slipshod in structure only because they were not based on the four-point traditional structure of *Protasis, Epitasis, Catastasis,* and *Catastrophe* which, under various pseudonyms, have been chewed over by critics from Donatus to Scaliger to Dryden to the latest composer of a "How to Write a Play" textbook. The early plays are far from structureless, but have a structure akin to *Bartholomew Fair* and *The Alchemist.* From the beginning, then, O. was straining against the confines of realism and by the poorly understood success of *The Plough and the Stars* reasserting the vitality of this second structure with its unique utilization of tragic irony and its broadness of scope that the conventional, four-point, single-action plays of his contemporaries denied.

Robert Hogan, *The Experiments of Sean O'Casey* (1960), pp. 10–11

Unconcerned with such things as dramatic style and construction, O. just turns the pages of his zestful Irish picture book [*The Bishop's Bonfire*]: the humor of tramps and servants, social theory, satire on the clergy, the melodrama of love with a tragic ending, Irish folklore, and Gaelic fairy tales all make their own artless effects regardless of literary form and structure. He also shows a grimly humorous defense of the liberty and happiness of ordinary life, which are so often sacrificed to slogans and bigotry.

Siegfried Kienzle, *Modern World Theater* (1970), p. 341

O'CONNOR, Flannery

American novelist and short-story writer, b. 25 March 1925, Savannah, Georgia; d. 3 Aug. 1964, near Milledgeville, Georgia

Flannery O. spent most of her life in her native Georgia, which, along with eastern Tennessee, is the setting of almost all of her fiction. In 1946 she started to publish short stories novels, and essays. Unusual as it may seem, she was championed by the *Kenyon Review–Sewanee Review* coterie, on the one hand, and by the Catholic press on the other. A victim of the blood disease that had caused her father's death and was to end her life before she reached forty, she was crippled for the last ten years of her life. Yet her dedication to literature never wavered.

Flannery O. was herself the unlikely combination of Southerner and Roman Catholic. Her two novels and two collections of stories offer an intriguing blend of what has been called Southern Gothic with a strain of prophecy and evangelism (Catholic-inspired). She always insisted on the need for Christian dogma—even if gently disguised—in a writer's work. Along with the feeling for redemption that haunted her fiction is a heightened awareness of the comic and grotesque.

Her first novel, *Wise Blood* (1952), is filled with false prophets and blind evangelists. She has aptly characterized it as "a comic novel about a Christian *malgré lui,* and as such, very serious, for all comic novels that are any good must be about matters of life and death." Hazel Motes, the main character, with the crusading urgency of a Nathanael West (q.v.) hero, preaches the gospel of the "Church without Christ." He meets a succession of mock revivalists who prepare the moral atmosphere for Motes's self-blinding and eventual death.

Tarwater, in *The Violent Bear It Away* (1960), is a religiously displaced Huck Finn who grows into a full-fledged prophet after a series of harrowing spiritual and profane experiences. Like most of Flannery O.'s heroes, he leaves his accustomed backwoods surroundings on an "evangelical" mission. His return, however, is symbolically triumphant, and the novel ends on an affirmative note.

In 1955, Flannery O. published *A Good Man Is Hard to Find.* Most of these stories are peopled by "grotesques" and are filled with moments of violence and redemption. Flannery O.'s short fiction seems to have elements in common with Sherwood Anderson's (q.v.) *Winesburg, Ohio.*

Everything That Rises Must Converge, with an affectionate, informative memoir by Robert Fitzgerald, appeared posthumously in 1965. The most ambitious story in this collection is probably "The Lame Shall Enter First," which originally appeared in the Flannery O. special issue of the *Sewanee Review* (Summer 1962). The Southern setting and the special quality of Bible Belt morality are presented in "The Lame Shall Enter First" with considerable power, a power untempered with pity and filled with anger and scorn.

Despite the eccentricities in characterization and setting, the fiction of Flannery O. is almost free from experiments in structure and technique. Her work has often been compared to that of Kafka and Nathanael West (qq.v.) for its gothic eeriness, to that of Graham Greene and Evelyn Waugh (qq.v.) for its sense of Catholic redemption and to that of Faulkner (q.v.) for its precise Southern background and its appreciation of the grotesque.

FURTHER WORKS: *Mystery and Manners: Occasional Prose* (ed. Sally and Robert Fitzgerald; 1969)

BIBLIOGRAPHY: *Crit,* special issue devoted to F. O. and J. F. Powers (Fall 1958); *Esprit,* special issue devoted to F. O., VIII (Winter 1964); Friedman, M. J., and Lawson, A., eds., *The Added Dimension: The Art and Mind of F. O.* (1966); Drake, R., *F. O.: A Critical Essay* (1966); Hyman, S. E., *F. O.* (Minnesota Pamphlets on American Writers, No. 54; 1966); Reiter, R., *F. O.* (1968); *SR,* special issue devoted to F. O., LXXVI (Spring 1968), 263–356; Martin, C. W., *The True Country: Themes in the Fiction of F. O.* (1969); *Renascence,* special issue devoted to F. O., XXII (Autumn 1969), 3–25, 34–42, 49–55; Hendin, J. G., *The World of F. O.* (1970)

MELVIN J. FRIEDMAN

ODETS, Clifford

American dramatist, director, film and television writer, b. 18 July 1906, Philadelphia, Pennsylvania; d. 14 Aug. 1963, Los Angeles, California

O. left high school at fifteen to become an actor. Essentially unsuccessful acting experiences with Theatre Guild (1923–30) and Group Theatre (1930–35) productions early caused O. to leave the stage. His subsequent career roughly coincides with important trends in American dramatic writing of the next three decades: O. wrote proletarian, social-problem plays in the 1930's, light Hollywood scenarios in the 1940's, and psychological dramas for the Broadway stage in the 1950's. In 1961, O. received the Drama Award of the American Academy of Arts and Letters.

Of O.'s three writing phases, the best dramas came out of his first period. *Waiting for Lefty* (1935), a one-act play concerned with the plight of striking taxicab drivers in a capitalist society, won first prize in the New Theatre-New Masses Theatre Contest as well as the George Pierce Baker Drama Prize at Yale. *I've Got the Blues,* later retitled *Awake and Sing!* (1935), displays at their best O.'s talents for psychological characterization and well-balanced tragicomedy. Both that play and *Paradise Lost* (1935) deal with the lives of middle-class Jewish families beset by the grave economic problems of the depression. *Till the*

Day I Die (1935), a play about the problems of communists in Nazi Germany, and *Golden Boy* (1937) round out O.'s efforts on behalf of proletarian drama. *The Big Knife* (1949), however, a bitter commentary on Hollywood's exploitation of artists, may be seen as a late addition to that phase of O.'s work.

O.'s Hollywood scenarios largely center on the theme of love and marriage. Only *Night Music* (1940) and *None but the Lonely Heart* (1943) have survived as film classics, but *Rocket to the Moon* (1938), *Clash by Night* (1941), *Humoresque* (1942), and *Deadline at Dawn* (1944) were all successful films in their time. Late in life, O. returned to screenwriting with *The Story on Page One* (1959), which he directed himself.

Of the psychological plays in O.'s third writing phase, *Country Girl* (1951), the story of an actor's conquest of alcoholism, is considered stronger than *The Flowering Peach* (1954), an allegorical treatment of the Biblical Noah story. Both plays, however, are more interesting as documents revealing the taste of Broadway audiences in the 1950's than as literature.

O.'s contributions to proletarian literature in the United States should be placed at the qualitative summit of that movement in American letters.

FURTHER WORKS: *Rifle Rule in Cuba* (with Carleton Beales; 1935); *I Can't Sleep* (1936); *The General Died at Dawn* (1937)

BIBLIOGRAPHY: McCarten, J., "Revolution's Number One Boy," *New Yorker,* 22 Jan. 1938, pp. 21–27; Clurman, H., *The Fervent Years* (1945); Dusenbury, W., *The Theme of Loneliness in American Drama* (1960); Shuman, R. B., *C. O.* (1962); Shuman, R. B., "*Waiting for Lefty:* A Problem in Structure," *Revue des Langues Vivantes,* XXVIII (1962), 521–26; Literary interview of 1961—Odets, C., "How a Playwright Triumphs," *Harpers,* CCXXXII (1966), 64–70, 73–74; Shuman, R. B., "C. O.: From Influence to Affluence," in *Modern American Drama,* ed. W. E. Taylor, 39–46

R. BAIRD SHUMAN

O'FAOLAIN, Sean

Irish short-story writer, biographer, and travel writer, b. 22 Feb. 1900, Dublin

O. studied at the National University of Ireland and at Harvard. In the late 1920's and early 1930's he taught at universities and high schools in England, North America, and Ireland. In 1933 his novel *A Nest of Simple Folk* attracted wide attention. Since then he has been known chiefly as a writer of biographies, travel books, and short stories.

O.'s loves are Ireland and its history, the problems of the youthful Free State, the Celtic renaissance, and above all the Irish people. On the one hand, as he sees it, his countrymen are priest-ridden, unrealistically caught up in a heroic vision of history, and full of faith in their country. On the other hand, they are open to the world, eager to emigrate, and steadily growing more dependent on England culturally. Thus they live in a state of conflict.

O.'s many short stories—collected in *A Purse of Coppers* (1937), *Teresa* (1947), and *The Man Who Invented Sin* (1948)—draw a realistic portrait of the Irish middle class and deal with various aspects of the "Irish problem."

O.'s biographies of Irish national heroes (such as *King of the Beggars: A Life of Daniel O'Connell*, 1938, and *The Great O'Neill*, 1942), *The Irish: A Character Study* (1949), and *An Irish Journey* (1940), show him to be a perceptive interpreter of history and a critical sociologist.

FURTHER WORKS: *The Life Story of Eamon De Valera* (1928); *A Midsummer Night Madness* (1932); *Constance Markievicz* (1934); *There's a Birdie in the Cage* (1935); *Bird Alone* (1936); *She Had to Do Something* (1938); *Come Back to Erin* (1940); *The Story of Ireland* (1943); *The Short Story* (1948); *A Summer in Italy* (1949); *Newman's Way* (1952); *South to Sicily* (1953); *The Vanishing Hero* (1956); *The Stories of S. O.* (1958); *I Remember! I Remember!* (1962); *Vive Moi!* (1964); *The Talking Trees, and Other Stories* (1970)

BIBLIOGRAPHY: Hopkins, R. H., "The Pastoral Mode of S. O.'s 'The Silence of the Valley,' " *Studies in Short Fiction*, I (1964), 93–98; Harmon, M., "The Man from Half-Moon Street," *Massachusetts Review*, VI (1965), 636–41; Saul, G., "The Brief Fiction of S. O.," *Colby Library Quarterly*, Ser. VII (1965), 46–54; Doyle, P. A., "S. O. as a Novelist," *South Atlantic Quarterly*, LXVI (1967), 566–73; Harmon, M., *S. O.: A Critical Introduction* (1967); Trautmann, J., "Counterparts: The Stories and Traditions of Frank O'Connor and S. O.," *DA*, XXVIII (1967), 2267; Doyle, P. A., *S. O.* (1968)

WILHELM HORTMANN

O'FLAHERTY, Liam

Irish novelist and short-story writer, b. 19 March 1897, Aran Islands

Educated at Jesuit colleges and at the National University in Dublin, O. was intended for the priesthood. Nevertheless, he joined the British army in 1915 and was discharged in 1917 after having been shell-shocked in Belgium. Before he turned to writing, he fought for the republicans in the Irish Civil War and traveled in South America, the Mediterranean, and North America.

O.'s autobiography, *Two Years* (1930), describes his travels, his rejection of Roman Catholicism, his interest in Marxism, and his decision to "nourish within me the germs of all vice as well as virtue, that I might stand beyond good and evil."

O.'s methods as a writer owe something to the impersonal craft of Maupassant, the naturalism of Dreiser (q.v.), the mysticism of Dostoyevski, and the primitivism of Synge and Hemingway (qq.v.); but all these influences are subordinate to his individual response to Irish life in Galway and Dublin, the two great regions of his work.

O.'s first important work was his novel *The Black Soul* (1924), an autobiographical allegory. It describes how a war-ravaged stranger loses his "black soul" of disillusion by choosing a woman who symbolizes the wildness and honesty of nature in preference to another who symbolizes the graces and inhibitions of civilization. These are persistent themes in O.'s work. Most of the short stories in *Spring Sowing* (1924), for example, reveal the harsh honesty and unconscious heroism of the struggle for existence in nature.

O.'s best novel, *The Informer* (1926), contrasts the black soul of a paranoid Marxist with the tragic soul of Gypo Nolan, a huge but inarticulate peasant who has been caught in the trammels of city life and is executed as an informer. *The Assassin* (1928) and *The Puritan* (1931) are studies of other tormented souls, against a similar Dublin background, just as the stories in *The Tent, and Other Stories* (1926) are penetrating studies of life at an animal level.

In the 1930's O. began increasingly to turn his attention to political and patriotic themes, particularly in his novels *Skerrett* (1932), *Famine* (1937), *Land* (1946), and *Insurrection* (1950). *Famine* is a brilliant evocation of the suffering, betrayal, and endurance of an Irish village during the potato famine of the 1840's.

The short story and the short novel are the forms best suited to O.'s poetic vision; *The Tent* and *The Informer* have a masterly symmetry lacking in *Famine,* his longest work. Nevertheless, O.'s achievements in fiction are hardly less impressive than those of Synge and O'Casey (qq.v.) in drama.

FURTHER WORKS: *The Neighbour's Wife* (1923); *Darkness* (1926); *Mr. Gilhooley* (1926); *The Life of Tim Healy* (1927); *The Fairy Goose* (1927); *Red Barbara* (1928); *A Tourist's Guide to Ireland* (1929); *The Return of the Brute* (1929); *The House of Gold* (1929); *The Mountain Tavern* (1929); *Joseph Conrad* (1930); *I Went to Russia* (1931); *The Ecstasy of Angus* (1931); *The Wild Swan* (1932); *The Martyr* (1933); *Shame the Devil* (1934); *Hollywood Cemetery* (1935); *The Short Stories of L. O.* (1937); *Two Lovely Beasts* (1948); *Dúil* (1953)

BIBLIOGRAPHY: Mercier, V., and Greene, D., "1000 Years of Irish Prose," *Bookman* (Jan. 1930); Saul, G. B., "A Wild Sowing: The Short Stories of L. O.," *Review of English Literature,* IV (1963), 108–13; Canedo, A., "L. O.: Introduction and Analysis," *DA,* XXVI (1965), 2744–45; Mercier, V., "Man Against Nature: The Novels of L. O.," *Wascana Review,* I (1966), 37–46; Doyle, P. A., ed., "A L. O. Checklist," *TCL,* XIII (1967), 49–51; Zneimer, J. N., "L. O.: The Pattern of Spiritual Crisis in His Art," *DA,* XXVIII (1967), 701A–02A; Murray, M. H., "L. O. and the Speaking Voice," *Studies in Short Fiction,* V (1968), 154–62

WILLIAM A. ARMSTRONG

O'HARA, John

American novelist and short-story writer, b. 31 Jan. 1905, Pottsville, Pennsylvania; d. 11 April 1970, Princeton, New Jersey

The son of a successful doctor, O. was admitted into Yale University, but his father's sudden death changed the family's financial situation and necessitated his taking newspaper and clerical work in Pennsylvania and then New York. In 1928 his first stories appeared in *The New Yorker* and were collected as *The Doctor's Son, and Other Stories* (1935). O.'s strengths were immediately apparent: an ability to record accurate dialogue, to depict a wide range of characters, to pinpoint the crucial moment in their lives, and to provide finely documented evidence that they are pri-

marily motivated by concern over social status.

These qualities are also apparent in O.'s first and best novel, *Appointment in Samarra* (1934). The study of a wealthy, upper-class businessman whose irritability and weakness for alcohol lead to social ruin and therefore (inevitably, in O.'s world) to death, the novel was both a critical and popular success.

Over the next ten years, O.'s experience as a Hollywood scriptwriter resulted in tales of the entertainment world both there and in New York. His vernacular stories of an incompetently predatory nightclub singer were collected as *Pal Joey* (1940) and made into a successful musical that same year. Though entertaining, the stories lack a comprehensive shape and point; they seem as aimless as their protagonist.

Another collection, *Pipe Night* (1945), is much more effective in its organization of details (primarily social manners) that provide a series of revelations about its characters. In "Graven Image," for example, an applicant for a high government position loses his chance when he behaves arrogantly toward an interviewer he considers his social inferior.

O.'s later novels seem to have lost in structure and perspective, though the social details of his Gibbsville world—the fictional equivalent of his native Pottsville—are as impeccably presented as ever. His most detailed account of life in eastern Pennsylvania, *A Rage to Live* (1949), concerns an unhappy marriage, but it illuminates neither of the main protagonists. *Ten North Frederick* (1955) is more successful since it focuses its study of a divided family on the remoteness of the father.

O. has also written closely of the Eastern world of society and business. *Elizabeth Appleton* (1963) depicts the course of an unequal marriage between a Long Island society girl and a college professor. But the novel's resolution of the problems presented by her sexual waywardness and his political indiscretions seems arbitrary. Paradoxically, the more O. documents his characters' lives, the more unmotivated and inexplicable those lives seem to be.

The Lockwood Concern (1965) reveals O.'s vast scope. Though this study of a family dynasty covers four generations, it nonetheless finds a sufficient center—in the inhuman character of George Lockwood—from which to examine the family's struggle for financial power and dominance over one another. Another point in the novel's favor is O.'s concern

JOHN O'HARA

ANTÔNIO DE OLIVEIRA

CLIFFORD ODETS

for that struggle and its social ramifications, even though this concern is clearly greater than his commitment to his characters as individuals.

A writer whose fascination with the intricacies of social status and financial power resembles that of Fitzgerald (q.v.) and whose interest in the documentation of the lives of characters on many social levels recalls Dreiser (q.v.), O. has also frequently been compared to Hemingway (q.v.) because of his understated, objective style. But O.'s contribution to fiction, his talent for the minutely observed detail that reveals social pretense, is quite individual in its intensity.

FURTHER WORKS: *Butterfield 8* (1935); *Hope of Heaven* (1938); *Files on Parade* (1939); *Hellbox* (1947); *The Farmers Hotel* (1951); *Pal Joey: The Libretto and the Lyrics* (1952); *A Family Party* (1956); *Selected Short Stories* (1956); *Three Views of the Novel* (with I. Stone and M. Kantor; 1957); *From the Terrace* (1958); *Ourselves to Know* (1960); *Sermons and Soda-Water* (1960); *Assembly* (1961); *Five Plays* (1961); *The Big Laugh* (1962); *The Cape Cod Lighter* (1962); *49 Stories* (1963); *The Horse Knows the Way* (1964); *Waiting for Winter* (1966); *The Instrument* (1967); *And Other Stories* (1968)

BIBLIOGRAPHY: Wilson, E., *The Boys in the Back Room* (1941); Trilling, L., "J. O. Observes Our Mores," *New York Times Book Review,* 18 March 1945, pp. 1, 9; Carson, E. R., *The Fiction of J. O.* (1961); Grebstein, S., *J. O.* (1966); Walcutt, C. C., *J. O.* (1969)

RICHARD PEARSE

OLBRACHT, Ivan
(pseud. of *Kamil Zeman*), Czech novelist and short-story writer, b. 6 Jan. 1882, Semily; d. 30 Dec. 1952, Prague

O. was the son of the writer Antal Stašek (1843–1931). After studying philosophy and law in Prague, he was editor of the communist newspaper *Rudé právo* until 1929. He also edited socialist and communist periodicals in Vienna and Prague. Unlike his father, he believed in Marx's theory of class warfare and was opposed to social reconciliation. Toward the end of World War II, during which he was forced to hide in southern Bohemia, he joined a partisan group. From 1946 until his death he served in the Czechoslovakian Parliament.

In his early stories and in his psychological novel *Žalář nejtemnější* (1916), which described the unhappiness of a blind man, O. tried to make technical innovations. By means of the *Doppelgänger* device, he broke away from traditional forms in the war novel *Podivné přátelství herce Jesenia* (1918).

In O.'s later works, *Anna proletářka* (1928), the story of a servant girl, and *Nikola Šuhaj loupežník* (1933), he openly turned to fighting for a new social order. *Nikola Šuhaj loupežník,* O.'s best novel, presents Nikola, a Ruthenian robber, as a noble and heroic figure. (*Nikolai Šuhaj, the Brigand,* an English translation of *Nikola Šuhaj loupežník,* appears in *Heart of Europe: An Anthology of Creative Writing in Europe, 1920–1940,* 1943, ed. by Klaus Mann and Hermann Kesten.)

In *Golet v údolí* (1937; The Bitter and the Sweet, 1967), a collection of short stories, O. describes the world of religious Jews.

FURTHER WORKS: *O zlých samotářích* (1913); *Obrazy ze soudobého Ruska* (1920); *Spisy* (1926 ff.); *Zamřížované zrcadlo* (1930); *Hory a staleti* (1935); *Dobyvatel* (1947); *O modrej bidpajove a jeho zvířatkách* (1947); *Sebrané spisy* (1950 ff.). **Selected English translations:** "Miracle in the Mountains" in *Hundred Towers, a Czechoslovak Anthology of Creative Writing* (ed. Franz Carl Weiskopf; 1945)

BIBLIOGRAPHY: Václavek, B., *Tvorbou k realitě* (1937); Rechcigl, M., ed., *The Czechoslovak Contribution to World Culture* (1964); Opelík, J., "I. O.," *Česka Literatúra,* XIII (1965), 273–302; Opelík, J., "Os. reife Schaffensperiode sub specie seiner Uebersetzungen aus Thomas Mann und Lion Feuchtwanger," *Zeitschrift für Slawistik,* XII (1967), 20–37; Zádor, A., *I. O.* (1967)

JOHANNA WOLF

OLDENBOURG, Zoé
French historical novelist, b. 31 March 1916, Leningrad

Zoé O. is the granddaughter of S. F. Oldenbourg, a renowned Sanskritologist, and daughter of Serge Oldenbourg, a writer and journalist. She came to Paris in 1925 and studied at the Lycée Molière and at the Sorbonne.

Zoé O.'s first novel, *Argile* (1946; later published as *Argile et Cendre*; The World Is Not Enough, 1948), is set in medieval France. Her second novel, the highly successful Prix Fémina

11

winner, *La Pierre angulaire* (1953; The Cornerstone, 1955), also has a medieval French setting.

Two later novels are set in Paris just before and just after World War II: *Réveillés de la vie* (1956; The Awakened, 1957) and *Les Irreductibles* (1958; The Chains of Love, 1959).

In 1958, Zoé O. published *Bûcher de Montségur* (Massacre at Montségur, 1962). It revolves around the Albigensian crusade and the ruthless suppression of the Cathars, whose heretical thinking had provoked the crusade. The title refers to the wholesale slaughter in 1244 of the defenders of Montségur, the last stronghold of the Albigensians.

The research done for this study inspired two subsequent novels, the setting of which is southern France at the time of this tragic war: *Les Brûlés* (1960; Destiny of Fire, 1961) and *Les Cités charnelles* (1961; Cities of the Flesh, 1963).

Zoé O.'s historical novels transcend the usual limitation of this popular genre. Her careful research makes them treasurehouses of factual information about the everyday life of medieval France. They are not for the squeamish; the chilling panoramas of cruelty and lust that characterize her fiction indicate her vital concern with man's eternal inhumanity to his fellows. Yet her portrayals of quiet heroism and steadfast abnegation are compassionate and convincing.

Zoé O. refuses to adorn her stories with local color; she carefully avoids the pseudoarchaic jargon so often found in historical novels. She sees the past not as a reservoir of material for the concoction of entertaining fiction but as a moment in the continuous adventure of man. Thus her characters, though deeply involved in the life of their times, are, in a very real sense, our contemporaries.

All of Zoé O.'s works, both fictional and historical, have been widely acclaimed both in France and abroad.

FURTHER WORKS: *Les Croisades* (1956; The Crusades, 1966); *Catherine the Great* (1965; Cathèrine de Russie, 1966)

BIBLIOGRAPHY: On *Cities of the Flesh*—Anon., *TLS,* 18 Jan. 1963, p. 37; Ascherson, N., *New Statesman,* 18 Jan. 1963, p. 87; On *Catherine the Great*—Anon., *TLS*, 9 Dec. 1965, p. 1122; Payne, R., *New York Times Book Review,* 7 Feb. 1965, p. 7; On *The Crusades*—Bergin, T. G., *SatR,* XLIX (2 July 1966), p. 26; Bryant, A., *Book Week,* 28 Aug. 1966, p. 8

LEON-FRANÇOIS HOFFMANN

OLESHA, Yurii Karlovich

Soviet-Russian novelist, short-story writer, and dramatist, b. 3 March 1899, Kirovograd; d. 10 May 1960, Moscow

O. grew up in Odessa in a family of Polish origin. In 1922 he went to Moscow, where he made his literary debut with poems published in a railway workers' newspaper. His novel *Zavist'* (1927; Envy, 1947) immediately established his reputation and made him one of the most controversial Soviet novelists. It was followed by a fairy-tale account of the revolution, *Tri tolstyaka* (1928; The Three Fat Men, 1964), a number of short stories, and several plays.

Given the increasingly restrictive atmosphere of the 1930's, O. found it more and more difficult to publish or even to write. Announcing that the building of a new Soviet order was not his theme, he pleaded at the First Congress of Soviet Writers (1934) for a greater humanism in Soviet letters. But as the 1930's advanced, his published work became more and more fragmentary, and he busied himself writing film scenarios. After 1938 O. disappeared from the literary scene almost completely.

It was not until the "thaw" (*see* Russian literature) following Stalin's death that O.'s works were again published. *Izbrannye sochineniya,* a selection of his work, appeared in 1956. *Povesti i rasskazy,* a collection of his novels and stories, was published in 1965, along with an interesting volume of reminiscences and reflections, *Ni dnya bez strochki.*

O.'s masterpiece is *Zavist',* which deals in a symbolic and expressionist style with the conflict between the old and new orders in Soviet life. Its hero, Kavalerov, longs for personal fame, success, and love, all of which he finds unattainable in Soviet society. Rejecting the new socialist order in the person of Andrei Babichev, a complacent and philistine food commissar who has perfected a new sausage and is trying to open a chain of cheap soup kitchens, Kavalerov sides with those who preach a "conspiracy of feelings" in the name of such emotions as love, ambition, and jealousy. After the conspiracy's failure, he attempts to salve his wounded ego in the suffocating embraces of a fat widow.

This comic novel has a rare freshness and originality of visual imagery. In a poet's prose rich in metaphors, similes, and conceits, O. rejects both the old and new orders—the one for its lack of progress and concern for social welfare, the other because it is too mechanical and unfeeling.

Influenced by philosopher Henri Bergson (1859–1941), O. saw an irreparable dichotomy in life between the mechanical and the biological. Such is the theme of his stories "Lyubov'" (1928; Love, in *The Heritage of European Literature,* ed. E. H. Weatherly, 1948–49) and "Vishnevaya kostochya (1930; The Cherry Stone, in *Heart of Europe,* ed. K. Mann, 1943). In the latter the possibility of a synthesis is indicated when the architects of a new steel and concrete building remember to provide in their plans for a garden.

"Liompa" (1928; Eng., in *Love, and Other Stories,* 1967) contrasts a dying man for whom the world has become a collection of meaningless names and a child for whom it is a bright chaos of nameless objects.

The first critics of O.'s work took his writing as a negative comment on Soviet reality of the 1920's and early 1930's. Though this is undoubtedly true, it becomes increasingly clear that his expressionist fiction fits into the context of Western literature of the period and that its universal theme is applicable to both Soviet and Western society.

Though O. never fulfilled the promise of his first brilliant novel, we can now see that he is one of the most vivid exponents of the European "vitalist" current of the 1920's. His profoundly philosophical work remains as readable and fresh as when it was written.

FURTHER WORK: *Spisok blagodeyanii* (1931; A List of Assets, in *Twentieth Century Russian Drama,* A. McAndrew, 1963). **Selected English translation:** *Love, and Other Stories* (1967)

BIBLIOGRAPHY: Struve, G., *Soviet Russian Literature, 1917–1950* (1951); Alexandrova, V., *A History of Soviet Literature* (1964); Nilsson, N. A., "Through the Wrong End of Binoculars: An Introduction to Y. O.," *Scando-slavica,* XI (1965), 40–68; Harkins, W. E., "The Theme of Sterility in O.'s *Envy,*" *SlavR,* XXV (Sept. 1966), 443–57

WILLIAM E. HARKINS

OLIVEIRA, Antônio Mariano Alberto de
    Brazilian poet, b. 28 April 1857 (?), Palmital de Saquarema; d. 19 Jan. 1937, Niterói

The son of a carpenter, O. was the fourth child in a family of sixteen. He graduated in pharmacy in 1884 and went on to complete three years of medical school. O. taught Portuguese language, literature, and history, and occupied various administrative posts in public education.

In 1897 O. was elected to the Brazilian Academy of Letters. The academy elected him president in 1926 but he declined the honor. The results of a poll taken from writers and poets two years before that proclaimed him the Prince of Brazilian Poets.

Although O. had grown up during the peak of romantic influence in Brazil, his first collection of poetry, *Canções românticas* (1878), showed antiromantic tendencies. Machado de Assis (q.v.) cautioned him against trying to write the sociopolitical poetry currently in vogue and encouraged him to write in a manner more consistent with his own natural mode of expression.

Following this advice, O. published *Meridionais* (1884), a volume of poems that by example defined standards for himself and for the parnassian movement that prevailed during the next decade. Even though parnassianism faded out with the coming of symbolism (q.v.), O. continued to write in the same style well into the beginning of the modernist period (1920's).

In *Meridionais* and subsequent publications, O. worked in two veins. On the one hand he wrote poetry that was a reflection of French parnassianism, with its exotic themes and aloof, impersonal tone. On the other hand he wrote descriptions of Brazilian nature in a less restrained, more emotionally involved mood.

O.'s language progressed from a rather free and imprecise expression to a very correct and complicated style with the archaisms, inversions, conceits, synaloepha, synereses, and *enjambements* so often characteristic of parnassian poetry. His best work was done in the sonnets. An accepted master of the Brazilian parnassian poets, he adhered more closely than the others to the precepts of the movement.

Because of his sensitive treatment of Brazilian nature, O. was treated favorably by the poets/critics of the Modern Art Week (São Paulo, 1922), and he escaped the opprobrium generously applied by them to other poets and writers of his generation. Since these modernist poets were successful in shaping the course of Brazilian literature into its present forms, the appreciation of O.'s poetry even during the iconoclastic beginnings of the new generation is a significant indication of the lasting qualities of his art.

FURTHER WORKS: *Sonetos e poemas* (1885); *Versos e rimas* (1895); *Poesias* (4 vols., 1900–27); *Poesias escolhidas* (1933); *Póstuma* (1944)

BIBLIOGRAPHY: Goldberg, I., *Brazilian Literature* (1922); Le Gentil, G., "L'influence parnassienne au Brèsil," *Revue de Littérature Comparée,* XI (Jan.–March 1931), i, 23–43; Bandeira, M., Preface to *Antologia dos poetas da fase parnasiana* (1940); Veríssimo, E., *Brazilian Literature: An Outline* (1945); Putnam, S., *Marvelous Journey* (1948); Silva Ramos, P. E. da, in *A Literatura no Brazil* (Vol. 2, 1955); Serpa, P., *A. de O., 1857–1957* (1957); Bandeira, M., *Brief History of Brazilian Literature* (1958)

STANLEY L. ROSE

O'NEILL, Eugene

American dramatist, b. 16 Oct. 1888, New York City; d. 27 Nov. 1953, Boston, Massachusetts

O.'s early experiences provided material for his dramas. The son of a successful actor, he, along with the rest of the family, accompanied his father on tour. From age seven to fourteen he was educated in Roman Catholic schools. Then, after renouncing Catholicism, he attended a nonsectarian preparatory school and studied for a year at Princeton.

Later, voyages as a merchant seaman were interspersed with short tours with his father's company, odd jobs, and periods of destitution in South America and, in 1911–12 (crucial years for the plays), on the New York waterfront. During this period O. suffered from emotional depression and attempted suicide as the result of marital problems. (He was married three times.)

In 1912 he went to live with his family in New London, Connecticut, and worked as a reporter and verse columnist on the local newspaper. Succumbing to tuberculosis, he lived in a sanatorium for a year. While in the sanatorium he decided to become a dramatist. He had been reading widely, especially Strindberg (q.v.)—who was to become his most important dramaturgical model—Ibsen, and Wedekind (qq.v.).

By 1914 O. had written twelve one-act plays and two full-length ones. He studied for a year at Harvard, attending George Pierce Baker's class in playwriting. In 1916 his career was launched with a performance by the Provincetown Players of *Bound East for Cardiff,* a one-

act play. *Beyond the Horizon* (completed in 1918; performed in 1920) won a Pulitzer Prize for O. and high praise from the critics, who saw the play as the harbinger of a new era of serious art in the American theater.

Critics have since disagreed as to the "art" of O.'s plays but not about his intense seriousness. He belonged to a generation in rebellion against the artificialities of a society that glorified material success, and against the romantic conventions of a theater dedicated to entertaining, but not troubling, the "tired businessman." Although O. constantly placed the hardheaded materialist and the sensitive idealist in conflict, his plays were never intended as propaganda for social reform. The negative aspects of American culture, including its puritanical backgrounds, were to him symbols of forces that inhibit universal man and cause agonizing psychological conflict within the individual. The plays represent O.'s personal conception of the "mystery" behind life. As his work progressed, the psychological struggles that he portrayed became increasingly his own, rooted in the family problems he was finally to describe in *Long Day's Journey into Night* (1940–41; pub. 1956).

O.'s technical strategy, both literary and theatrical, was designed to present this highly subjective view of life as effectively as possible. The writers, philosophers, and psychoanalysts —Dostoyevski, Conrad (q.v.), Nietzsche (q.v.), Schopenhauer, Jung, and Freud—who envisioned the forces behind life somewhat as O. did were naturally of great inspiration to him. He found his theatrical approach in the psychological but not literal realism of Ibsen and Strindberg and in the expressionistic projection of the inner lives of the characters. He became noted for such stylistic devices as the following: the monologue and the aside; symbolic masks, makeup, and costumes; thematic repetition of phrases, theatrical effects, and actions; the use of archetypal motifs drawn from mythology and religion. But O. was never above using the old devices of melodrama and theatrical realism when they served his purpose, with the result that his work evades any one of the conventional categories.

O. said that *Bound East for Cardiff* contained "the germ of the spirit, life-attitude, etc., of all [my] more important future work." Breaking with tradition, this play has no real plot. It portrays a badly injured seaman who on his deathbed reveals the simple values—friendship and courage—that have made his mundane and often sordid life worthwhile. He also talks wistfully about his hope that he will some day leave the sea and become a farmer. This theme of man's dependence upon a life-giving illusion, or pipe dream, became central to O.'s mature plays.

Beyond the Horizon is the story of two brothers, one of whom is realistic and practical, while the other is a poetic dreamer. Although the dreamer destroys himself and his family through his romanticism, he does demonstrate a transcendent human spirit by returning just before his death to faith in the ideal. The play was written in alternating indoor and outdoor scenes so as to portray, O. said, the rhythmic "alternation of longing and of loss." This play, too, like *Bound East for Cardiff,* reflected the "life-attitude" of O.'s future plays.

O.'s work falls into fairly well-defined periods according to the order of composition. The years 1913–18 were apprentice years. Of lasting value from this period are the short plays of the sea that along with *Bound East for Cardiff* form a unit: *In the Zone, The Long Voyage Home, The Moon of the Caribbees,* and *'Ile.*

In 1918, O. completed *The Straw,* a love story based on his days in the tuberculosis sanatorium. In this play the characteristic mixture of affirmation and negation of the earlier plays was expressed in the phrase "hopeless hope."

In 1920 and 1921, O. completed *Anna Christie* (1921; Pulitzer Prize, 1922), *The Emperor Jones* (1921), and *The Hairy Ape* (1922). All these reflect his increasing concern with his characters' search for individual identity as well as for a sense of belonging.

In *Anna Christie,* the ex-prostitute does find her identity when she returns to her father and the sea. Nevertheless, O. felt that the search never really ended, and the sea and the fog became for him constant symbols of the mystery of fate and the bewilderment of people.

The Emperor Jones makes more extreme use of expressionistic techniques: to the beat of a drum in pulse rhythm the Negro "emperor" is pursued by his island subjects through a jungle that is both real and symbolic. The guilt and fear that also pursue him are revealed in monologues and in a series of hallucinations projected from his mind.

The Hairy Ape portrays the search for identity on the part of a stoker on a transatlantic liner, who loses his pride in his work and in himself as the muscular representative of the force behind modern industry. The only self-image left him is that of a caged ape at a zoo. The stoker meets his death in a symbolic embrace with the ape, who escapes and leaves his victim to die in the cage. The play concludes with "and, perhaps, the Hairy Ape at last belongs."

Of the seven plays written between 1921 and 1925 most are failures. They depend too heavily upon mystical or philosophical solutions to the characters' problems, ideas derived from Nietzsche and Schopenhauer, Taoistic mysticism, and psychoanalytic analogies to these in Jung and Freud. *All God's Chillun Got Wings* (1924) created a sensation by depicting miscegenation, but it is only incidentally a play about the Negro in American society. *Marco Millions* (1927) is a masked pageant portraying Marco Polo as an American Babbitt, one who confronts the mysticism of the East with total incomprehension. *The Great God Brown* (1926), an overintricate mask-using play, extends the antithesis between materialism and idealism to include that between paganism and Christianity. The hero's search for meaning amid these conflicts results in disintegration and death. Death here, however, is proclaimed as the unifier, an affirmative step in the eternal process, the act that should be welcomed rather than feared because it restores man to his harmony with nature.

The only drama from this period that continues to be produced with popular success is *Desire under the Elms* (1925). In it O. moved away from mysticism and pseudopoetry to return to naturalism and the vernacular. His characters are rugged New England farm people, driven by violent emotion—sex, avarice, and vindictiveness. By suggesting that these people are subjected to forces comparable to the gods or fates of classic tragedy, O. sought to give tragic stature to the crimes and punishments of his characters. The battle between the materialist and the idealist now takes the form of hatred between father and son. The son takes vengeance upon his father by becoming intimate with his father's young wife, who then bears the son's child. A trace of the affirmative exultation of the other plays of this period is found at the end of *Desire under the Elms* when, after murdering the infant, the mother and her lover are reconciled in mutual love and share the guilt of the murder. The total effect of the ending, however, is ironic and inconclusive.

In *Strange Interlude* (1928; Pulitzer Prize in 1928) and *Mourning Becomes Electra* (written between 1926 and 1931) O. continued to equate physical and unconscious drives with tragic fate.

Strange Interlude was a stream-of-consciousness novel in dramatic form. It consisted of nine acts, took five hours to perform, and made continuous use of the aside, through which the characters revealed their semiconscious motives. The characters are all at the mercy of their parent complexes or other forces as described by Freud, Jung, and Schopenhauer. The central figure is Nina Leeds, who must exploit the male characters to fulfill her needs for a father, lover, husband, and son. The action of the play ceases only when Nina, all passion spent, without hope of fulfilling these needs, accepts old age.

Mourning Becomes Electra is O.'s version of the tragedy of the house of Atreus, set in 19th-c. New England. This trilogy (made up of *Homecoming, The Hunted,* and *The Haunted*) interprets the familiar story of the murder of Agamemnon and its consequences in psychoanalytic terms. The action centers around Lavinia (Electra), who secures the avenging of her father's murder by persuading Orin (Orestes) to kill Christine's (Clytemnestra's) lover; this is followed by the suicide of the mother and subsequently of Orin. Shouldering the family guilt, Lavinia locks herself in the family mansion to live with and be hounded by the ghosts of the past.

After 1932, O. became increasingly preoccupied with his own past. His next play, *Days without End,* was completed late in 1933, after many laborious drafts. It was another drama of inner conflict, in which two actors play the two selves of the protagonist. The conflict is finally resolved by the protagonist's return to the Roman Catholic Church. (Although the ending suggested to many that O. had returned to Catholicism, the reverse was true; the works that followed were anti-Christian and nihilistic.)

In a few weeks in 1932, O. wrote his only comedy, *Ah, Wilderness!* Its nostalgic portrayal of middle-class American family life was based in part on O.'s family memories of his Connecticut days. The play had immediate and lasting success.

In 1936, O. was awarded the Nobel Prize. Between that year and 1943, when a disease of the nervous system terminated his writing, he completed *The Iceman Cometh* (1939), *Long Day's Journey into Night* (written 1940–41; pub. 1956), *Hughie* (a one-act play; written 1941–42; pub. 1959), *A Moon for the Misbegotten* (written 1943; pub. 1952), and *A Touch of the Poet* (written 1943; pub. 1957). All these

plays were written in the same mood of despair that O. had previously suffered in 1911–12. Life is bearable for the characters only by virtue of their illusions or pipe dreams. Without these, existence is worthless and the only salvation is death.

The Iceman Cometh pursues this theme in the lives of a group of derelicts who live on liquor and their pipe dreams in the back room of a saloon modeled on those O. haunted in his youth. The characters come also from O.'s own past; the action is set in 1912, the year of his severe emotional depression. But while hope is lost for the characters in the play who face reality, it is not entirely gone for those who maintain their illusions; they go on living in "hope's back room."

In *Long Day's Journey into Night,* O. withdrew entirely into his personal past to tell the tragic story of his family and their ambivalent love and hate for each other, each of whom was haunted by his own guilts and by his knowledge of the mother's helpless addiction to drugs.

A Moon for the Misbegotten continues the story but focuses on O.'s older brother, an alcoholic who died shortly after his mother's death. Its contrived fictional framework, however, robs it of dramatic power.

O. had planned two long cycles of plays that his illness prevented him from writing. In one of these, "A Tale of Possessors Self-dispossessed," he hoped to present the history of an Irish-American family over a period of two hundred years. *A Touch of the Poet* is the only surviving play. The second play in the cycle sequence, *More Stately Mansions* (pub. 1964), exists only in a long, unpolished typescript, which, after considerable cutting, was produced by the Royal Dramatic Theater of Stockholm in 1962.

Of the second projected cycle, to be called "By Way of Obit," only *Hughie* survives. In it a small-time gambler with illusions about his past talks himself and a hotel clerk into believing that this past was real. But the listening clerk turns out to symbolize death, and the atmosphere is that of the hopeless paralysis that finally beset both the playwright and his work.

FURTHER WORKS: *Thirst, and Other One-Act Plays* (1914); *Before Breakfast* (1916); *The Plays of E. O.* (3 vols., 1919–55); *Gold* (1920); *Diff'rent* (in *The Emperor Jones, and Other Plays*; 1921); *The First Man* (in *The Hairy*

Ape, and Other Plays; 1922); *Welded* (in *All God's Chillun Got Wings*; 1924); *The Fountain* (in *The Great God Brown, and Other Plays*; 1926); *Lazarus Laughed* (1927); *Collected Poems* (1931); *Where the Cross Is Made* (1939); *The Lost Plays of E. O.* (1950)

BIBLIOGRAPHY: Clark, B. H., *E. O.* (1926; rev. ed., 1947); Winther, S. K., *E. O.: A Critical Study* (1934); Engel, E. A., *The Haunted Heroes of E. O.* (1953); Falk, D. V., *E. O. and the Tragic Tension* (1958); Alexander, D., *The Tempering of E. O.* (1962); Cargill, O., et al., eds., *O. and His Plays* (1962); Gelb, A., and B., *O.* (1962); Miller, J. Y., *E. O. and the American Critic* (bibliography, 1962); Gassner, J., ed., *O.: A Collection of Critical Essays* (1964); Braem, H., *E. O.* (1965); Coolidge, O., *E. O.* (1966); Long, C. C., *The Role of Nemesis in the Structure of Selected Plays by E. O.* (1968); Sheaffer, L., *O.: Son and Playwright* (1968); Tiusanen, T., *O.'s Scenic Images* (1968)

DORIS V. FALK

The Hairy Ape is not a perfect play. Felicity of any kind is not a characteristic of Mr. O. He is strong and feeble. No touch of beauty or charm ever hides the moments of failure in his work. In *The Hairy Ape* those moments are few. The drama is momentous in its vision, strength, and truth. There is something hard in its quality, but it is the hardness of the earth's rocks ; there is something of violence, but it is the violence of an intolerable suffering.

Ludwig Lewisohn, *Nation* (22 March 1922), p. 350

...The dialogue of *The First Man* ...proves in reading so tasteless and dreary that one does not see how one could sit through it.

But E. O. has another vein in which he is a literary artist of genius. When he is writing the more or less grammatical dialogue of the middle-class characters of his plays, his prose is heavy and indigestible even beyond the needs of naturalism. People say the same things to one another over and over again and never succeed in saying them any more effectively than the first time; long speeches shuffle dragging feet, marking time without progressing, for pages. But as soon as Mr. O. gets a character who can only talk some kind of vernacular, he begins to write like a poet.

Edmund Wilson, "Eugene O'Neill and the Naturalists" (1922), *The Shores of Light* (1952), pp. 99–100

Mr. O. reveals the first burst of his emotions in powerful clean-cut pictures that seem almost like simple ballads in our complex world.... His first acts impress me as being the strongest; while the last, I shall not say go to pieces but, undoubtedly, are very much weaker than the others. The close of *The Hairy Ape*, as well as that of *The Emperor Jones*, seems to me to be too direct, too simple, too expected; it is a little disappointing to a European with his complex background, to see the arrow strike the target toward which he had watched it speeding all the while.

Hugo von Hofmansthal, in *Freeman* (21 March 1923), p. 41

The two gifts that E. O. up to now has displayed are for feeling and for dramatic image. His plays have often conveyed a poignancy that is unique in the modern drama. You felt that whatever was put down was at the dramatist's own expense; he paid out of himself as he went. His great theatre gift has been in the creation of images that speak for themselves.... In *Mourning Becomes Electra* Mr. O. comes now into the full stretch of clear narrative design. He discovers that in expressive pattern lies the possibility of all that parallels life, a form in which fall infinite shadings and details, as the light with its inexhaustible nuances and elements appears on a wall. He has come to what is so rare in Northern art, an understanding of repetition and variation on the same design, as contrasted with matter that is less deep or subtle, though expressed with lively surprise, variety, or novelty.

Stark Young, in *New Republic* (11 Nov. 1931), pp. 354–5

Not only has O. tried to encompass more of life than most American writers of his time but, almost alone among them, he has persistently tried to solve it.... Not the minutiae of life, not its feel and color and smell, not its nuance and humor, but the "great inscrutable forces" are his interest. He is always moving toward the finality which philosophy sometimes, and religion always, promises. Life and death, good and evil, spirit and flesh, male and female, the all and the one, Anthony and Dionysius —O.'s is a world of these antithetical absolutes such as religion rather than philosophy conceives, a world of pluses and minuses; and his literary effort is an algebraic attempt to solve the equations.

Lionel Trilling, in *New Republic* (23 Sept. 1936), pp. 176–7

That he is the foremost dramatist in the American theatre is ... generally granted. His eminence is predicated on the fact that no other has anywhere near his ability to delve into and appraise character, his depth of knowledge of his fellow man, his sweep and pulse and high resolve, his command of a theatre stage and all its manifold workings, and his mastery of the intricacies of dramaturgy. His plays at their best have in them a real universality. His characters are not specific, individual and isolated types but active symbols of mankind in general, with mankind's virtues and faults, gropings and findings, momentary triumphs and doomed defeats. He writes not for a single theatre but for all theatres of the world.

George Jean Nathan, in *American Mercury*
(Dec. 1946), p. 718

At one time he performed a historic function, that of helping the American theatre grow up. In all his plays an earnest attempt is made to interpret life; this fact in itself places O. above his predecessors in American drama and beside his colleagues in the novel and poetry. He was a good playwright insofar as he kept within the somewhat narrow range of his own sensibility. When he stays close to a fairly simple reality and when, by way of technique, he uses fairly simple forms of realism or fairly simple patterns of melodrama, he can render the bite and tang of reality or, alternatively, he can startle and stir us with his effects.... But the more he attempts, the less he succeeds. *Lazarus Laughed* and *The Great God Brown* and *Days Without End* are inferior to *The Emperor Jones* and *Anna Christie* and *Ah, Wilderness!*

Eric Bentley, in *KR* (Summer 1952), p. 488

O. was a faulty craftsman; he was not a sound thinker.... Yet to dwell on these shortcomings ... is to confess one's own inadequate and bloodless response to the world we live in.... O. not only lived intensely but attempted with perilous honesty to contemplate, absorb and digest the meaning of his life and ours. He possessed an uncompromising devotion to the task he set himself: to present and interpret in stage terms what he had lived through and thought about—a devotion unique in our theatre.... O.'s work is more than realism. And if it is stammering—it is still the most eloquent and significant stammer of the American theatre. We have not yet developed a cultivated speech that is either superior to it or as good.

Harold Clurman, in *Nation* (3 March 1956),
pp. 182–3

OPATOSHU, Joseph

(originally, *Opatovsky*), Yiddish novelist and short-story writer, b. 24 Dec. 1886, near Mlave, Poland; d. 7 Oct. 1954, New York City

O. was educated in Hebrew and Polish schools, and studied civil engineering for a year in Nancy, France. In 1907 he emigrated to New York City. After working at odd jobs and completing his studies at Cooper Union, he turned to teaching and writing.

O. published his first story in 1910, *Fun New Yorker ghetto* in 1914, and *A roman fun a pferd-ganev* in 1917. In 1914 he became a regular contributor to the Yiddish daily *Der*

Tog and published hundreds of stories and articles in its pages. His short fiction is notable both for its acid satire and for the robustness of his characters.

O.'s first major work was *Di poilishe welder* (1921; Polish Woods, 1938). This was the middle volume of a trilogy that included *Aleyn* (1919) and *1863* (1926). This work pictures a people in a time of spiritual flux: Hasidism is in decline, enlightenment in its early stages, the factious Poles are initiating their abortive insurrection of 1863.

In *Di tentzerin* (1930), O. describes the agonized persistence of a debased Hasidism in America. *A Tog in Regensburg un Elivahu Bokher* (1933; A Day in Regensburg, 1968) treats of Jewish ghetto life in an earlier period with historical freshness and linguistic accuracy.

O.'s last major fictional work, *Der letzter oifshtand* (I, *Rabbi Akiva*, 1948 [The Story of Rabbi Akiba, 1952]; II, *Bar kokhba*, 1955), which tells of Jewish life in Palestine in 132 A.D. and the uprising against Rome, gives artistic reality to the activities of the people (from the simple to the complex) in a fine Yiddish prose, which is enhanced by Hebrew aphorisms and precepts.

FURTHER WORKS: *Unterwelt* (1918); *Morris un sejn zun* (1919); *Hebrew* (1920); *Lyncher* (1920); *Lehrer* (1922); *Arum di khurves* (1922); *Raceh, lincherai* (1923); *Mentchen un khayes* (1928); *Gezamelte werk* (14 vols., 1928–36); *Tzwishen yamen un welder* (1934); *Mlave-New York* (1939); *Wen Poilen is gefalen* (1943); *Yiddish un Yiddishkeit* (1949). **Selected English translation:** *Jewish Legends* (1951)

BIBLIOGRAPHY: Meisel, N., *Y. O.* (1937); Rivkin, B., *Y. O.* (1948); Freilich, I., *Y. O.'s Shafung-Weg* (1951); Niger, S., Shatsky, J., and others, *Lexicon fun der neier Yiddisher Literatur* (1956–68); Bickel, S., *Shreiber fun nein dor* (1958); Madison, C. A., *Yiddish Literature: Its Scope and Major Writers* (1968)

CHARLES A. MADISON

OPPERMAN, Diederik Johannes

South African poet, dramatist, and critic (writing in Afrikaans), b. 29 Sept. 1914, district of Dundee, Natal

Educated at the Universities of Natal and Cape Town, O. lectured at the latter institution from 1949 to 1959, when he was appointed professor of Afrikaans literature at the

EUGENE O'NEILL

JOSÉ ORTEGA Y GASSET

university in Stellenbosch. As chief editor of the leading South African literary periodical, *Standpunte,* from 1950 to 1955 he put on that publication the "anti-aestheticist" and "objectivist" stamp of the generation of the 1940's, to which he belongs. His doctoral thesis on the "poets of the 1930's," *Digters van Dertig* (1953), and his collected essays *Wiggelstok* (1959, "Divining-rod") similarly advance a "poetics" that differs from the more egocentric poetry of confession advocated by his immediate predecessors.

Extremely dense, concrete, metaphorical, and occasionally cryptic, O.'s poetry is sometimes in lyrical and sometimes in epic style, and often in patterns that are a subtle blend of both genres. Each volume is carefully planned to produce a kaleidoscopic image integrating the greatest possible diversity of seemingly incompatible phenomena into a complex interplay of cosmic, temporal, and surrealist perspectives. Intensely aware of mankind's precarious balance between the divine and the perverse, between animal-like instinctiveness and technological sterility, the poet tirelessly explores all forms of life and reveals the most unexpected interrelationships between good and evil, the beautiful and the ugly, the highest and the lowest creatures.

O. purposefully dispossesses the Self, in order that he may "live from within" the multifarious individuations of eternal Being and conjure up their godlike essence. As O. sees it the poet is neither a propagandist, a humanitarian prophet, nor a re-creator of things past and present: the poet, and the artist in general, asserts himself as *the* co-creator of a God who Himself establishes the play of order and chaos for the benefit of His creation. The artist appears as a being who hews the angel out of the rock, delivers the flower from amorphous nature, and discloses the evidences of God in the world.

Three verse dramas in the tragic mood, *Periandros van Korinthe* (1954), *Vergelegen* (1956), and *Voëlvry* (1968, "Outlawed"), treat basically related themes. They exemplify how dreams of the Absolute come into conflict with historical realities that inexorably bring pressure to bear on human endeavors. The structure of these plays rests on the interaction of poetical images rather than on the conflict of characters.

O. is the poet of South African actuality par excellence; at the same time he is also the most mythical of the South African writers.

The ensemble of his creative work might be characterized, paradoxically, as a powerful expression of "down-to-earth metaphysics."

FURTHER WORKS: *Heilige beeste* (1945; "Holy Beasts"); *Negester oor Ninevé* (1947; "Nine Stars over Nineveh"); *Joernaal van Jorik* (1949; "Jorik's Journal"); *Engel uit die klip* (1950; "Angel from the Stone"); *Blom en baaierd* (1956; "Flower and Chaos"); *Dolosse* (1963; "Astragali"); *Kuns-mis* (1964; "Artmanure"); *Edms. Bpk.* (1970; "Pty., Ltd.")

BIBLIOGRAPHY: Cloete, T. T., *Trekkerswee en Joernaal van Jorik* (1953); Malherbe, F. E. J., *Afrikaanse lewe en letterkunde* (1958); Antonissen, R., *Kern en tooi* (1963); Grove, A. P., *Tyn net van die woord* (1965); Grove, A. P., *D. J. O.* (1965); Antonissen, R., *Spitsberaad* (1966)

R. K. J. E. ANTONISSEN

ORSZÁGH, Pavol
See Hviezdoslav

ORTEGA Y GASSET, José
Spanish philosopher and essayist, b. 8 May 1883, Madrid; d. there, 18 Oct. 1955

O. y G. was the son of José Ortega Munilla, noted journalist and novelist, and the grandson of Eduardo Gasset, the founder of the newspaper *El Imparcial.* He attended a Jesuit school in Málaga and the University of Madrid, where he received his doctorate in 1904. In 1906 he went to Leipzig and Berlin. Later he spent a year in Marburg, where he studied with Hermann Cohen, the neo-Kantian. From 1910 to 1936 he was professor of metaphysics at the University of Madrid.

Eager to contribute to the creation in Spain of a climate suited to philosophical and systematic thought, he sought to reach the public that did not attend universities by means of newspapers, journals, and public lectures. Two of his most significant social and political works, *España invertebrada* (1922; Invertebrate Spain, 1937) and *La rebelión de las masas* (1923; The Revolt of the Masses, 1932) were first published in installments in the periodical *El Sol* (1920 and 1922). His lecture series on "What Is Philosophy?" in 1929 attracted a surprisingly large and varied audience. In 1916 he began the publication of a one-man review, *El Espectador,* whose eight volumes appeared at irregular intervals from 1916 to 1934. In 1923 he founded

19

the prestigious *Revista de Occidente,* which was decisive in the intellectual and artistic formation of many writers of his generation.

O. y G.'s first trip to Buenos Aires in 1916 marked the beginning of his influence among Latin-American writers. Throughout his life he made lecture tours to North and South America and to various European countries. O. y G. lived outside Spain during the civil war and did not return until 1949.

O. y G.'s works are extremely varied, for they reflect his constant interest in all the elements of his "circumstance." He wrote on philosophical, political, social, historical, and literary topics; he described the landscape of Castile, the phenomenology of love, the writings of Azorín, Baroja y Nessi, Proust (qq.v.), the painting of Velázquez and Goya. In his preoccupation with the problem of Spain and the changes of values in modern technological society, he continued to develop some of the themes of the "generation of 1898." Like Azorín, Antonio Machado y Ruiz, and Unamuno (qq.v.), O. y G. wanted to "save" the reality of Spain, to elevate even the humblest aspects of that world to their fullest meaning. But whereas the "generation of 1898" effected the literary transformation of the Spanish landscape, psychology, and history, O. y G.'s confrontation of these circumstances led him to his central philosophical conceptions: perspectivism and historical or vital reason.

The formula "I am myself plus my circumstances"—stated in his first book *Meditaciones del Quijote* (1914; Meditations on Quixote, 1961) and fully elaborated in *El tema de nuestro tiempo* (1923; The Modern Theme, 1933)—expresses not only the relation of the individual to his physical and cultural environment but forms the basis of the theory that the point of view is one of the components of reality. This theory must be distinguished from any purely psychological relativism; for O. y G. perspective refers not only to the subject but to reality itself. "Truth, the real, the universe, life—whatever you want to call it—breaks into innumerable facets . . . each one of which faces a certain individual" ("Verdad y perspectiva," *El Espectador,* 1916). Each point of view is unique and indispensable. Each person, nation, and historical period is an irreplaceable organ for the discovery of truth. The coincidence of two points of view can only mean that the object of focus is an abstraction and not reality; the real, the concrete, can only be grasped through infinite, diverse perspectives.

In *El tema de nuestro tiempo,* O. y G. argued in favor of a vital reason that, unlike the abstract reason of rationalism, would concern itself with the ever-changing phenomena of life. The modern theme is the need to place reason within the vital or biological sphere; thought is a biological function and it is also the tool one must use in order to live. Reason is *not* a special gift man can employ at his leisure; reason is something man must have recourse to in order to make his way in that "uncertain repertory of possibilities and difficulties" presented to him by the world (*Ideas y creencias,* 1940).

In *¿Qué es filosofía?* (1929; What Is Philosophy?, 1960) and *Historia como sistema* (1941; pub. first in English as History as a System, 1936), works which show the influence of existentialist ideas and vocabulary, O. y G. defines human life as the radical reality because all other realities occur within it. And that reality is no specific thing: it cannot be fixed and defined; it is precisely the evasion of all definition. Man himself is neither a body nor a soul (which are both "things"); instead he is a series of choices and actions—a drama. Life is not given to us already formed; on the contrary it consists of continuously deciding what we are to do and be. This constant and constitutive instability is freedom. Man is necessarily free. Since life has no stable, definable form, the only possible way of understanding anything human, whether personal or collective, is by telling a story, by relating its history.

Vital reason is the same as historical reason. "Man does not have a nature but a history." Historical reason adapts itself to the fluid course of life and situates the individual in relation to his specific environment; it is therefore more rigorous, more demanding, more "rational" than abstract reason.

Although O. y G. views life as radically problematical and uncertain, he also portrays it as an immense festive or "sporting" phenomenon. He differentiates between a primary activity that is spontaneous, disinterested, and creative, and a secondary one that responds to demands imposed from without. The first, an effort we make for the sheer delight of making it, is sport; the second, necessary, dependent, utilitarian, and mechanized, is work. Since life itself serves no ulterior purpose, its highest products—scientific and artistic creations, political and moral heroism, religious sainthood—are the result of a playful, superfluous expenditure of energy (*El Tema de nuestro tiempo*). It is in this sense that one should understand

O. y G.'s statements, in *La deshumanización del arte* (1925; The Dehumanization of Art, 1948), about the essentially ironical and playful nature of the new art, an art that claims to have no transcending consequences.

Whether considering it as insecurity or as play, O. y G. defends life's flexibility and diverseness from all rigid schemes and rules. In the name of life values he attacks the superstitious deification of reason and culture. Art, science, philosophy, ethics are interpretations or clarifications of life and should never be elevated to ends in themselves. In his political and social works—*España invertebrada, La rebelión de las masas, En torno a Galileo* (1933; Man and Crisis, 1958), *El hombre y la gente* (1957; Man and People, 1957)—O. y G. sees society as a constant threat to individual authenticity. In the social realm, originally spontaneous acts become mere customary usages, empty gestures. O. y G. often speaks of society as a fossilization of life, a mineralized excrescence of human existence. Against the danger of this degradation, O. y G. asserts the need continually to absorb one's circumstances, to retreat from the accumulated mass of cultural forms in order to make unique and personal responses (*Ensimismamiento y alteración,* 1939).

O. y G.'s simplistic and mechanical division of society into elites and masses make his sociology unacceptable. His unwillingness to integrate the various aspects of his thought into a coherent system, as well as certain important contradictions and inconsistencies, has left some of his ideas—especially those on modern art—open to misinterpretation. Outside of Spain he is known for his least impressive works (*La rebelión de las masas,* for example). O. y G.'s significant contributions to existentialism are to be found in the development of the concepts of perspectivism and historical or vital reason.

FURTHER WORKS: *Vieja y nueva política* (1914); *Personas, obras y cosas* (1916); *Ideas sobre la novela* (1925; Notes on the Novel, 1948); *La redención de las provincias y la decadencia nacional* (1931); *Rectificación de la república* (1931); *Pidiendo un Goethe desde dentro* (1932); *Misión de la universidad* (1932; Mission of the University, 1966); *Estudios sobre el amor* (1939; On Love, 1957); *Teoría de Andalucía y otros ensayos* (1942); *Del imperio romano* (1946; Concord and Liberty, 1963); *Obras completas* (6 vols., 1946 ff.; en-larged ed., 9 vols., 1957); *Papeles sobre Velázquez y Goya* (1950); *La idea de principio en Leibniz y la evolución de la teoría deductiva* (1958)

BIBLIOGRAPHY: Livingstone, L., "O. y G.'s Philosophy of Art," *PMLA,* LXVII (1952), v, 609–54; Stern, A., "O. y G., Existentialist or Essentialist?," *La Torre,* IV (1956), xv–xvi, 388–99; Mora, J. F., *O. y G.: An Outline of His Philosophy* (1957); Marías, J., *O.: Circunstancia y vocación* (1960); Gaete, A., *El sistema maduro de O.* (1962); Winecoff, J., "J. O. y G., Existentialist?," *DA,* XXII (1962), 4357; Sebastian, E. G., "J. O. y G.," *Hispania,* XLVI (1963), 490–95; Read, H., "High Noon and Darkest Night: Some Observations on O. y G.'s Philosophy of Art," *JAAC,* XXIII (1964), 43–50; Weber, F., "An Approach to O.'s Idea of Culture," *Hispanic Review,* XXXII (1964), 142–56; Prescott, E. K., "Art and Reality in the Aesthetic Theory of O. y G.," *DA,* XXVII (1966), 780A; Vita, L. W., *Triptico de Ideas* (1967); Drijoune, L., *La concepción de la historia en la obra de O. y G.* (1968); Moron Arroyo, C., *El sistema de O. y G.* (1968)

FRANCES WYERS WEBER

For those who see in history brute forces and sinister interests which no amount of enlightenment will of itself remove, O. y G. . . . is an impossible political and social philosopher. . . . The basic idea in O. y G.'s equipment is this: "The convulsive situation in Europe at the present moment is due to the fact that the average Englishman, the average Frenchman, the average German are uncultured." As if it were lack of culture and not its cause that we should attack! As if lack of culture actually were cause and not symptom!

O. y G.'s entirely justified dissatisfaction with the ordinary man grows into something entirely unjustified when he comes, as nearly all such thinkers do, to stake everything upon the extraordinary man and when, looking for him today in vain, he assumes his existence in some past era, which is thereby sentimentalized. . . . A return to which period in history? O. y G. hedges. . . . A man whose philosophy has so shaky a foundation as this is surely not to be taken very seriously.

Eric Bentley, in *Saturday Review* (23 Dec. 1944), p. 8

Thus it happens that man has no other recourse than doing something in order to maintain his existence. Before him open diverse possibilities of being and doing. These possibilities, O. y G. tells us, are not given to us. We must invent them.

"Between these possibilities I must choose. I am therefore free. But . . . unavoidably free, whether I want to be or not." What man chooses . . . is his "vital program," his "project." To exist, then, is to invent projects of doing and of being in view of the circumstances.

These ideas of O. y G.'s are purely existentialist. The best proof of this is the fact that the great master of contemporary existentialism Jean-Paul Sartre, adopted them, in every detail, and developed them in his *Being and Nothingness,* eight years after O. y G. had put them forth in *History as a System.* . . .

Sartre proclaimed, "There is no human nature." Eight years earlier O. y G. had written, "It is false to speak of a human nature . . . man has no nature." The existentialism of Sartre opposes a "*choisiste*" conception of man and O. y G. insists that "man is not a thing." . . .

O. y G. concludes, saying that man has no nature other than the one that he has made for himself. Thus man is, in a certain sense, the totality of his acts, as one can read in Hegel, in Malraux, and finally in Sartre. Explicitly he declares that man makes his own essence, which follows his existence. But this is the basic thesis of existentialism, which Sartre expressed in the famous words "existence precedes essence."

> Alfred Stern, "O. y G., Existentialist or Essentialist?," *La Torre,* IV: 15–16 (July–Dec. 1956), pp. 388–90

And in spite of the fact that O. y G. himself affirmed frequently that he was above all a writer of immediate objectives, the creator of a "circumstantial work" (to use terms that are very much his), it is evident that there always operated in him an aesthetic impulse. One could even say . . . that perhaps O. y G. the verbal artist has more than once modified, for aesthetic "reasons," the thought of O. y G. the philosopher.

> Juan Marichal, *La voluntad del estilo* (1957), p. 270

O. y G. impresses and infuriates. He was determined to turn philosophy and history into belles lettres. Half of him was prophet and rather smug on that account. He sought in prose for a Paterian radiance, and appeared to think metaphor and repetition essential to the expression of sincere thought. Most of his works—*The Revolt of the Masses* excluded—support a tribal dance of ideas, some of them huge and seminal. But his vatic repetition too often becomes erratic variation, and we have to read him with a potato-peeler. He puts nothing plainly until he's baffled us with adumbration. He is a self-celebrated writer and at his best only when he isn't trying too hard. This forefather of Malraux has much in common with Arnold Toynbee and the Algerian in Camus. Their ways

of self-conception are his, and so are most of their ideas.

> Paul West, in *Twentieth Century* (Oct. 1959), p. 241

O. y G. is certainly the greatest philosophical essayist of the first half of the twentieth century, and very likely one of its few genuinely seminal minds. O. y G.'s writings range over the whole expanse of modern culture, and there is not a single issue—from abstract art to Einstein and Freud—on which he has not said a suggestive and enlightening word. Although O. y G. never published a systematic philosophical work, he performed a rarer and perhaps more difficult task. He seized problems, issues, ideas on the fly, and, while they were still new and controversial, attempted to explore them with philosophical rigor and philosophical range.

O. y G.'s essay on *The Dehumanization of Art* is still among the best efforts to define and interpret the radical break in continuity between modern art and the whole Renaissance tradition of representation which ended in the nineteenth century. First published in 1925, this essay had a considerable influence on the brilliant younger generation of writers and artists in the Spanish-speaking world. O. y G.'s ideas have also had wide circulation elsewhere and it is impossible to consult any book on modern art without coming across a reference to his terms and ideas.

> Joseph Frank, "The Dehumanization of Art," *The New Republic* (1 June 1959), p. 16

For him, being a philosopher included being a Spaniard, a political thinker, a writer, and, of course, a modern man. Furthermore, even if O. y G. had wished to be a philosopher independently of anything else, he would not have limited himself to abstruse philosophizing. It was all right for Edmund Husserl to do practically nothing but philosophy in Göttingen or in Freiburg. But it was impossible—or rather, as O. y G. put it, "indecent" —to act as a purely technical philosopher in Madrid in 1910, 1923, or even 1931. O. y G. was expected to say something . . . on topics which philosophers as philosophers usually evade or treat only perfunctorily. He was expected to say something about love, women, Spain, the poetry of Anne de Noailles, the Roman Empire, the " population explosion," the theory of relativity, and what not. He was expected above all to say his word on political and social issues in contemporary Spain. . . . He was likely to treat such issues more deeply than any of the professional political commentators, and more specifically than any of the traditional philosophers of history. . . .

He believed that it was his task to clarify the problems that these circumstances raised and certainly not as an innocent pastime in which one may occasionally indulge, but as a full-time job. If we are ready then to understand O. y G.'s intentions, and the reasons supporting them, we will no longer deplore the fact that his philosophy was not expressed like Husserl's or Rudolf Carnap's. We will not consider it too alarming that O. y G. had a brilliant style.

José Ferrater Mora, Introduction to *The Modern Theme* (1961), pp. 4–5

When, guided by O. y G.'s finger, the most sagacious readers of *Meditations on Quixote* have found in its pages certain serious philosophical theses, they have had the impression that they were disconnected. At best, they appeared as glimpses, sudden flashes of insight, still immature or at least not elaborated. Others have considered them as mere "bright ideas," to which only a later exegesis gave philosophical scope. The truth is exactly the opposite: the philosophical doctrine which is expounded in the *Meditations* is perfectly coherent; the connection between its statements, far from being nonexistent, is closely woven, almost excessively so, because it is a real and vital connection, not merely theoretical. . . . The mere logical argument, the simple "concatenation" of elements, is replaced in this book, as in all O. y G.'s later work, by something more compact, because the effective connections between real elements are not a "chain," but the systematic and reciprocal vivification of the ingredients in a circumstantial and concrete drama. The function of the elements can only be discovered from the "argument"—characters, settings, feelings, static relationships—of any dramatic structure. The theory is just another dramatic structure.

Julián Marías, Introduction to *Meditations on Quixote* (1963), pp. 17–18

O. y G. was far too intelligent a philosopher to dismiss the extremism of modern art as an aberration of the mind, a twilight of the intellect. He realized that it is a historical phenomenon that has grown from a multitude of entangled roots, but he thought that an explanatory investigation of the kind required was too serious a task for him to attempt. He concluded his polemic with a final all-embracing charge: the modern movement is a disguised attack on Art itself—"a mask which conceals surfeit with art and hatred of it"; and he hinted that this was but one aspect of a wider phenomenon, the rankling grudge which modern Western man bears against his own historical essence.

Herbert Read, "High Noon and Darkest Night," in *Man in Art* (1965), p. 62

ORWELL, George

(pseud. of *Eric Blair*), English novelist, essayist, and social critic, b. 23 Jan. 1903, Bengal, India; d. 21 Jan. 1950, London

O., who was primarily a novelist, nevertheless accomplished some of his best writing in auto-

biographical nonfiction and the polemical essay. These forms better served his strong sociopolitical concerns and the moral temper that led his contemporaries to call him the conscience of his age.

O.'s early work of the 1930's consists of social novels, dealing largely with middle-class English life, and books of autobiographical reportage, drawn from his active involvement in the poverty and war that dominated the decade.

O.'s first book, *Down and Out in Paris and London* (1933), shows him to be a keen observer and penetrating social analyst, committed to recording accurately and imaginatively the plight of the poverty-stricken laborer and tramp on the continent and in England. O.'s point of view in this book, that of the involved and sympathetic observer, reflects O.'s life style of subjecting himself to personal hardship in the interests of championing the underdog.

The Road to Wigan Pier (1937), in which the social protest is voiced even more articulately, was written for the Victor Gollancz's Left Book Club as an exposé of the depressed living conditions of workers in the north of England. It contains a disturbingly sharp lengthy criticism of the weaknesses of contemporary socialism and socialists. Though O. belonged to the left, he remained to the end of his life an uncompromising individualist and political idealist, maintaining that the ends of socialism must be justice and freedom.

O.'s involvement in the Spanish Civil War as a common soldier attested to his need to act upon his political ideals. His experiences in Spain produced *Homage to Catalonia* (1938), still considered one of the best books in English on the Spanish war. The book records O.'s initiation into the international political turmoil of the late 1930's, and foreshadows his later political fiction.

Many of O.'s attributes as a writer are evident in this personal account of life at the front and ideological conflict behind the lines. O. captures the image of war and its absurdities in the plain and vivid prose style that was to become so highly praised. Though the book is pervaded by O.'s disillusionment in the efficacy of party politics, its theme expresses O.'s abiding faith in the decency of the common man.

O.'s fiction of the same period is less distinguished. *Burmese Days* (1934) is O.'s sole novel related to his experiences in Burma. Like *A Clergyman's Daughter* (1935), *Keep the Aspidistra Flying* (1936), *Coming Up for Air* (1939), this novel depicts protagonists that are victims of their social environments and their own inner frustrations and doubts. In these novels O. deals with lonely, unhappy, sometimes oppressed people, with people who suffer nostalgia for the past because they live in the gray world of failure, religious doubt, poverty, or boredom.

Although linked thematically with much modern fiction, the early novels are technically unimpressive and fall far short of the achievements of O.'s better-known contemporaries, such as Huxley, Lawrence, and Joyce (qq.v.). O. had not yet found the literary medium that would express his most compelling vision of society.

In the 1940's O. set out "to make political writing an art," and in two estimable works of fiction he accomplished what he spoke of as the fusion of "political purpose and artistic purpose into one whole."

Animal Farm (1945), a political satire in the form of an animal fable, depicts the revolt of barnyard animals against their farmer oppressors and the establishment of an autonomous socialistic state. The original ideals of the animals rapidly degenerate at the hands of the pigs, who assume dictatorial power and turn the society into a police state. The animals—except for the pigs of course—are returned to a bondage and misery more severe than they had initially suffered. Clearly an allegory of the Russian Revolution and particularly of the Stalinist regime, the novel avoids a narrow topicality by suggesting the disappointing aftermath of more than one revolution. O. directs his satire at a universal human condition; *i.e.,* that all political radicalisms inevitably become reactionary when based on power and power alone.

In 1949, O. published *1984,* his second political novel and last major work. This antiutopian novel was influenced by O.'s reading in Wells, Zamiatin, Koestler, and Aldous Huxley (qq.v.). Precipitated by the international phenomenon of the rise of totalitarian states and the long, hard years of World War II, *1984* is a protest against the fearful direction in which O. believed the modern world was moving. Undoubtedly O. again wrote with the Stalinist regime in mind, but the machinery of his not so imaginary society is also drawn from the English scene of the war and postwar years.

The effectiveness of *1984* derives in part from an immediately recognizable reality, one whose atmosphere extends beyond any specific totalitarian state and includes even aspects of the so-called free societies. The book exposes the horror of totalitarianism whatever the form. O.'s pessimism is apparent throughout, and the final emotional and intellectual capitulation of the protagonist, another Orwellian victim, to Big Brother and the authority of the state is depressing rather than tragic. Yet O.'s purpose was to shock his readers into an awareness of the disastrous results of absolute power. Less a prophecy than a warning, the novel exists as a continual reminder to contemporary Western man that he is dangerously close to losing not only his freedom but the very attributes that make him human.

O.'s sense of social and political responsibility is as apparent in his early essay "A Hanging" (1931) and the many periodical contributions of almost twenty years as it is in *1984.* The first extensive collection of his major essays, *Critical Essays* (1946; Am., Dickens, Dali and Others), includes some of his most perceptive commentaries on important social and cultural issues of his time.

Like Camus (q.v.), O. was convinced that the contemporary writer must become involved, must take sides, with a sincerity that becomes the *sine qua non* of literary effectiveness. Few modern writers have been as assiduous as O. in devoting their lives and creative efforts to the cause of freedom and social amelioration. This commitment is the dominant force in all of his work.

FURTHER WORKS: *Inside the Whale, and Other Essays* (1940); *The Lion and the Unicorn: Socialism and the English Genius* (1941); *The English People* (1947); *Shooting an Elephant, and Other Essays* (1950); *England, Your England* (1953; Am., Such, Such Were the Joys); *The Orwell Reader: Fiction, Essays, and Reportage* (1956); *Selected Essays* (1957); *Collected Essays* (1961); *The Collected Essays, Journalism and Letters of George Orwell* (2 vols., 1968)

BIBLIOGRAPHY: Atkins, J., *G. O.* (1954); Brander, L., *G. O.* (1954); Rieff, P., "G. O. and the Post-Liberal Imagination," *KR,* XVI (1954), 49–70; Hollis, C., *A Study of G. O.* (1956); Rees, R., *G. O.: Fugitive from the Camp of Victory* (1961); Voorhees, R., *The Paradox of G. O.* (1961); Thomas, E. M., *O.* (1965); Woodcock, G., *The Crystal Spirit* (1966); Oxley, B. T., *G. O.* (1967); Warncke, W., "The Permanence of O.," *University Review—Kansas City,* XXXIII (1967), 189–96; Wulfsberg, F., *G. O.* (1968)

WAYNE WARNCKE

OSBORNE, John

English dramatist and actor, b. 12 Dec. 1929, London

"I want to make people feel, to give them lessons in feeling. They can think afterwards." Thus O. wrote in "And They Call It Cricket" (*Declaration*, ed. T. Maschler, 1958). Two years earlier, O. had achieved sudden fame as a leading "angry young man" with his play *Look Back in Anger* (1956), the first of many plays comprising the "new wave" of British drama and including such playwrights as Pinter, Behan (qq.v.), Arnold Wesker (b. 1932), N. F. Simpson (b. 1920), and Shelagh Delaney (b. 1939).

O. was twenty-six at the time—an obscure actor born in London to a working-class mother and middle-class father—and found himself hailed as spokesman for the rebellious working-class intellectuals of his generation. His hero, Jimmy Porter, a volcanic romantic, lashes the sterility, boredom, hypocrisy, and callousness of life about him but is unable to do anything about it beyond dissipating his energies in battles of sex. Jimmy, educated above his working-class origins, nonconforming, and bitter in speech and feeling, projected a new voice into the English theater of genteel drawing-room comedies.

O.'s concern with the quality of life in postwar welfare-state England underlay *Look Back in Anger* and succeeding works. O. was angered by the H-bomb, the invasion of Suez, the irresponsibility of church and press, the folly of monarchy, and the insensitivity of the English ruling classes—all symptoms, he thought, of national decay.

In *Look Back in Anger, Epitaph for George Dillon* (1958; written earlier, with Anthony Creighton), *Luther* (1961), *Inadmissible Evidence* (1964), and *A Patriot for Me* (1965), O. dramatized the dilemma of nonconforming individuals in a decadent society. In *Plays for England* (1962), he attacked idolatrous attitudes toward the monarchy and the venal press; and in *The Entertainer* (1957) as well as in *A Patriot for Me*, he treated the subject of imperial decline.

O.'s strengths and weaknesses were already established in *Look Back in Anger*. On the one hand were the brilliant invective by the rebel suffering the world and his troubled self, the outraged social conscience and concern for a more intense, free, honest, and purposeful existence, the exposing of psychosexual elements in iconoclasm, and the courageous handling of taboo subjects.

On the other hand were a tendency toward monologue, the subordination of other characters to the protagonist and lowering of dramatic interaction, special pleading, unfocused attacks, and a failure to dramatize concretely the social forces around the hero. Thus, despite his social concerns, O. appeared more interested in the personality of his protagonists than in their surroundings. His historical plays, *Luther* and *A Patriot for Me*, which point contemporary parallels of revolt and corruption, suffer an imbalance of private and public dimensions.

Look Back in Anger and *George Dillon*, O.'s early studies of the failed rebel, are essentially realistic, well-made plays. In *The Entertainer* and *Luther*, however, O. used devices of the "epic theater": episodic structure, narrator, songs. *The Entertainer* integrates these devices with the subject matter of a music-hall entertainer's desperate yet determined existence in a declining profession. *Inadmissible Evidence*, another study of human failure, also goes beyond naturalism by projecting the anxieties and guilts of its hero expressionistically. Still O.'s basic talent is realistic, and he has yet to reconcile realism with his interest in technical experiment.

The strong response that O. evoked among members of his generation and the theater public, despite uneven work, testifies to his having touched on critical social and psychological problems. His plays are best at moments of psychological revelation and rhetorical brilliance but often do not sustain dramatic tension and balanced form. Yet, by injecting a fresh, challenging and relevant voice into midcentury English theater, O. prepared the way for a remarkable burst of new English drama, to which he has been a major contributor.

FURTHER WORKS: *The World of Paul Slickey* (1959); *A Subject of Scandal and Concern* (TV play; 1960); *Tom Jones* (film script; 1964); *A Bond Honoured* (1966); *Time Present and Hotel in Amsterdam* (1968)

BIBLIOGRAPHY: Allsop, K., *The Angry Decade* (1958); Armstrong, W. A., ed., *Experimental Drama* (1963); Bailey, S., "J. O.: A Bibliography," *TCL*, VII (1961); Brown, J. R. ed., *Modern British Dramatists* (1968); Hayman, R., *J. O.* (1968); Kitchin, L., *Mid-Century Drama* (1960); Taylor, J. R., *Anger and After* (1964); Weiss, Samuel A., "O.'s Angry Young Play," *Educational Theatre Journal*, XII (1960)

SAMUEL A. WEISS

OSTAIJEN, Leopoldus Andreas van
Belgian poet (writing in Flemish), b. 22 Feb. 1896, Antwerp; d. there, 18 March 1928

O. never finished his secondary education. While working as a clerk for the city of Antwerp, he started contributing to periodicals. Involvement with local politics forced him to flee abroad, and from 1918 to 1921 he lived in Berlin. On his return to Belgium, he managed to eke out a living from his poetry and from journalism, before dying of tuberculosis at the age of thirty-two.

O. made his literary debut with *Music-Hall* (1916), a volume of poems that were written when he was about eighteen. The book was immediately influential because its new vocabulary and rhythms were related to a new theme: the metropolis.

O.'s promise was fulfilled in his second volume of poems, *Het sienjaal* (1918). All the previous qualities, now openly joined by a strong humanist and apostolic credo, were developed into a verbal torrent so typical of the heyday of German expressionism (q.v.). Striking individual lines and images blend into the total effect of roaring in the name of humanity and of a newly blossoming earth. An important document in the development of expressionist poetry, the book set the tone for many of O.'s contemporaries.

O. seemed assured of a respectable and successful career, but during his years in Berlin, he essayed to redefine humanitarian expressionism and began writing the kind of poetry for which he is famous. Delirious with cocaine and revolution, in 1921 he wrote the tormented pages of *De feesten van angst en pijn*. Not published until 1952, the volume is a genuine and haunting farewell to the past, a witness of the turmoil and pain of the present, and a dire prophecy of the future.

Having met and studied the work of kindred dadaistic (*see* dadaism) spirits, O. published *Bezette stad* (1921), a bitter and incisive indictment of war. A highly unusual poetic document, it describes the horror and desolation of war, as well as the cowardice of terrified citizens and the cynicism of the "State, Church, and Monarchy Corporation." Typographically, the sinister texts explode from the page—poetic shrapnel of a generation that could no longer be deceived by slogans of any kind.

O.'s social criticism after 1921 was primarily continued in masterly tales that he called "grotesques." Acerbic, absurdly reasoned, these satires have lost none of their force. Reminiscent of the writings of Swift and Kafka (q.v.), they present a world out of joint and a society quite happily unaware of this condition. Some were printed during his lifetime, but most were published in posthumously issued collections that pleased few people.

O.'s poetic adventure continued in a series of texts that have become basic to modern Flemish poetry. He explained his objectives and techniques in a number of important essays, and he put his basic theory of thematic lyricism and association into practice in a series of masterful poems that were not printed in book form until the posthumously issued *Gedichten* (1928). These profoundly simple and musical poems describe the mystery of the common and the commonplace of the metaphysical. Outstripping conventions and traditions, they reflect O.'s lifelong dilemma: the limitations of expression make it impossible to capture the primordial secret of existence and of nature. Truth lies in the attempt.

O. educated his countrymen to the significant innovations of modern culture in a series of essays that included both literary topics and discussions of the plastic arts. He prepared one of the first translations of Kafka and wrote the script for the only film ever made by the dadaists.

In his quest for the pure poem, in his cerebral and vitriolic satires, and in his important essays on the arts and literature, O. showed himself always ahead of the avant-garde. A major contribution to 20th-c. literature, his accomplishments reach far beyond the confines of his native Flemish tongue to assure him a foremost and irrevocable place in the vanguard of this century. His poetry and prose are only now being accorded their proper prominence in both his native and in European literature.

FURTHER WORKS: *De trust der vaderlandsliefde* (1925); *Het bordeel van Ika Loch* (1926); *Vogelvrij* (1928); *Intermezzo* (1929); *Het eerste boek van Schmoll* (1929); *Krities Proza* (2 vols., 1929–31); *De bende van de Stronk* (1932); *Diergaarde voor Kinderen van Nu* (1932); *Self-Defense* (1933); *Verzameld Werk* (4 vols., 1952–56). **Selected English translation:** *Patriotism Incorporated, and Other Tales* (1970)

BIBLIOGRAPHY: Gilliams, M., "Een bezoek aan het Prinsengraf," *Vita Brevis. Verzamelde Werken,* III (1959); Uyttersprot, H., "Kanttekeningen bij O. en het Verzameld Werk,"

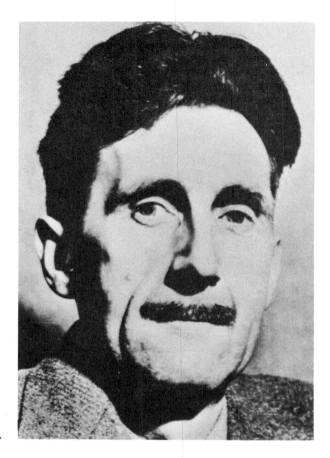

GEORGE ORWELL

LEOPOLDUS VAN OSTAIJEN   ARNULF ØVERLAND

Spiegel der Letteren, III, Nos. 3–4 (1959), pp. 225–59; Uyttersprot, H., *O. en zijn proza* (1959); Uyttersprot, H., *Uit O. Lyriek* (1964); Roover, A., *O.* (1963); Hadermann, P., *De kringen naar binnen. De dichterlijke wereld van O.* (1965); Vree, P., *O.* (1967); Beekman, E. M., *Homeopathy of the Absurd: The Grotesque in O.'s Creative Prose* (1969)

E. M. BEEKMAN

O'SULLIVAN, Seumas

(pseud. of *James Sullivan Starkey*), Irish poet, essayist, and editor, b. 1897, Dublin; d. there, 24 March 1958

O. belonged to the "Celtic twilight" group of poets. His career was launched with his contribution to *New Songs* (1904), a publication devoted to the work of the younger poets.

In 1905 he published *The Twilight People*—a collection of poems—which many critics regard as his most distinctive work. After its publication G. W. Russell (q.v.) said that O. was "the literary successor of those old Gaelic poets who were fastidious in their verse, who loved little in this world but some chance light in it which reminded them of fairyland."

Departing from the Irish fairy tale as favored subject, O. reveals a preoccupation with city life, especially that of 18th-c. Dublin, in *The Earth-lover, and Other Poems* (1909).

O.'s poetry is frequently compared to that of the early Yeats (q.v.). His concern with the musical quality of the language of poetry links him to the French symbolists (*see* symbolism). He indirectly recognized this debt with the three poems (republished in *Poems,* 1912) he wrote in the manner of Henri Régnier (q.v.).

Padraic Colum (q.v.), his contemporary and friend, appropriately called O., in *The Road round Ireland,* "the most aloof of Irish poets."

Among O.'s works in prose are *Essays and Recollections* (1944) and *The Rose and Bottle* (1946), both of which contain literary and autobiographical essays.

O.'s career was impressively rounded out by his brilliant, if short-lived, activity in the theater, his founding of the *Dublin Magazine* in 1923, and his vice-presidency of the Irish Academy of Letters.

FURTHER WORKS: *Verses Sacred and Profane* (1908); *Selected Lyrics* (1910); *Impressions* (1912); *Requiem* (1917); *Mud and Purple* (1917); *The Lamplighter* (1929); *Twenty-five Lyrics* (1933); *Personal Talk* (1936); *Dublin*

Poems (1946); *Collected Poems* (1946); *Translations and Transcriptions* (1950)

BIBLIOGRAPHY: Boyd, E. A., *Ireland's Literary Renaissance* (1923); Colum, P., *The Road Round Ireland* (1926); Howarth, H., *The Irish Writers* (1959); Skelton, R., and Clark, D. R., eds., *Irish Renaissance* (1965)

MELVIN J. FRIEDMAN

ØVERLAND, Arnulf

Norwegian poet, essayist, short-story writer, and dramatist, b. 27 April 1889, Kristiansund; d. 25 March 1968, Oslo

Ø. studied philosophy briefly. In his youth he was influenced by German intellectual life and especially by the ideas of Heine, Schopenhauer, and Nietzsche (q.v.). An *engagé* writer, Ø. supported socialism during World War I, and opposed fascism and Nazism in the 1930's. During the Nazi occupation of Norway in World War II, Ø.'s poems of defiance were secretly circulated. When this act of resistance was discovered Ø. was arrested and sent, in 1942, to the Sachsenhausen concentration camp. After World War II Ø. was the recipient of the lifetime pension that Norway grants to its most honored writers. He died at the Grotten, a government-supported residence for outstanding writers.

Ø.'s first published work was *Den ensomme fest* (1911). This was followed by *De hundrede violiner* (1912) and *Advent* (1915). His best-known volume of poetry is *Hustavler* (1929). In *Vi overlever alt* (1945), a collection of his wartime poems, patriotism is the leading theme.

Ø., an individualist, is a revolutionary and satirist. Poems of loneliness and yearning stand side by side with attacks on Christianity, the established church, and bourgeois hypocrisy.

FURTHER WORKS: *Den hårde fred* (1916); *Venner* (1917); *Brød og vin* (1919); *Deilig er jorden* (1923); *Berget det blå* (1927); *Giv mig ditt hjerte* (1930); *Gud plantet en have* (1931); *Riket er ditt* (1934); *Jeg besverger dig* (1934); *Den røde front* (1937); *Ord i alvor til det norske folk* (1940); *Tilbake til livet* (1945); *Samlede dikt* (1947); *Nordiske randstater eller atlantisk fred* (1949); *Fiskeren og hans sjel* (1950); *I beundring og forargelse* (1954); *Skerdet bak døren* (1956); *Dikte i udvalg* (1961); *På nebobjerg* (1962); *Møllerupgåsens liv og himmelfart og andre troverdige beretninger* (1964)

BIBLIOGRAPHY: Johnsen, E. E., *Livets spiral: A. Ø.* (1956); Hoel, S., ed., *Festskrift til A. Ø.* (1959); Beyer, E., "Die norwegische Literatur nach 1900," *Schweizer Monatshefte,* XLV (1965), 473–83; Haakonsen, D., *A. Ø. og den estetiske realisme 1905–40* (1966); Landquist, J., *Möten* (1966); Støverud, T., *Milestones of Norwegian Literature* (1967); Anon., "Er war immer unbequem: Zum Tode des norwegischen Dichters A. Ø.," *Ausblick,* XIX (1968), 17–20

CHRISTEN CHRISTENSEN

OWEN, Wilfred

English poet, b. 18 March 1893, Oswestry; d. 4 Nov. 1918, Landrecies, France

During World War I, O., who had enlisted in the English army in 1917, was sent to the French battlefields. Suffering a psychic collapse, he was admitted to the military hospital in Craiclockhart, England. It was here that he met Sassoon (q.v.), who encouraged his brief period of creativity. In August 1918 he was sent back to combat in France and was killed in action.

At his death O. left a small collection of poems, only four of which had been published in his lifetime. From these manuscripts his friend Sassoon compiled the collection *Poems* (1920). In 1931 a revised edition (*The Poems of W. O.*; revised ed., 1961), more inclusive and textually more accurate, with a memoir by Blunden (q.v.), was published.

Deeply shocked by the harshness of war, O. set out to communicate its true nature in his poetry. "The Show," "Dulce et decorum est," and "The Sentry" depict life in the trenches, bringing alive its brutality through imagery. These poems—like the even more terrible ones O. wrote about the soldier gone mad—are unusual in the way the description shifts abruptly to a passionate indictment of war, for which the reader is made to share some of the guilt. O.'s deep compassion raises these poems of protest to a tragic height, which is especially noticeable in the elegiac "Futility," "Anthem for Doomed Youth," and "Spring Offensive."

O.'s most significant poem is "Strange Meeting," which combines a Shelleyan romanticism with a personal religion of humanity, derived from Christianity, and a denouncing prophecy of the values of postwar society.

O.'s most important contribution to poetic technique is the "half rhyme" based on vowel dissonance and consonant assonance, which he probably adopted from French poetry (*e.g.,* "cold" and "killed").

During the 1930's O.'s work strongly influenced poets such as Auden, Spender, and Day Lewis (qq.v.).

FURTHER WORK: *The Collected Poems* (C. Day Lewis, ed., 1963)

BIBLIOGRAPHY: Welland, D., *W. O., A Critical Study* (1960); Owen, H., *Journey from Obscurity* (W. O. biography in 3 vols., 1963–65); Fletcher, J., "W. O. Re-edited," *EA,* XVII (1964), 171–78; Lewis, C. Day, ed., *The Collected Poems of W. O.,* with an "Introduction" (Am. ed., 1964); Cohen, J., "O. Agonistes," *English Literature in Transition,* VIII (1965), 253–68; Landon, G., "The Contribution of Grammar to the Poetic Style of W. O.," *DA,* XXV (1965), 6610; White, W., "W. O. . . . A Bibliography," *The Serif,* II (1965), iv, 5–16; Tomlinson, C., "O. as Correspondent," *Agenda,* VI (1968), ii, 66–70

DENNIS S. R. WELLAND

P

PAGNOL, Marcel

French dramatist and filmmaker, b. 28 Feb. 1895, Aubagne (near Marseilles), Bouches-du-Rhône

P. studied at the University of Aix-en-Provence, where in 1913 he helped found a student literary magazine *Fantasio*. Later, as *Les Cahiers du Sud*, it was to become one of the most influential literary magazines of the century. From 1915 to 1922, P. taught English in various *lycées*, and has since devoted himself to writing plays, making films, and editing *Cahiers du Cinéma*. In 1946, he became the first filmmaker to be elected to the French Academy.

Topaze (1928; Eng., 1958) was P.'s first great success. In this play, P. traces the metamorphosis of an obscure schoolteacher into a wily businessman. The lies of politicians, the venality of newspapers, the moral decline of an era in which money has become the key to success, are the principal themes of *Topaze*.

P.'s name is especially associated with his trilogy of plays: *Marius* (1929), *Fanny* (1931), and *César* (1936). The setting of this cycle of plays is the Vieux Port of Marseilles, and P. skillfully portrayed its noisy indolent life under the strong sunlight. He writes with affection about the people of Provence, their tenderness and their bravado, their dreams and their fears. The ebullient dialogue of the first two plays in particular illustrates the temperament typical of the *midi:* a sentimentality that easily becomes moralistic. An American musical adaptation of the entire cycle was called *Fanny* (1955).

In his autobiography, *Souvenirs d'enfance* (3 vols., 1958–60), P. described with simplicity and charm his early years in Marseilles and in the hills above the city. The first volume, *La Gloire de mon père* (1958), is in praise of P.'s father, who was an elementary-school teacher. In the second and third volumes, *Le Château de ma mère* (1959) and *Le Temps des secrets* (1960), P. writes about his school years and summer vacations. (*The Days Were Too Short*, 1960, is an English translation of the first two volumes; the third was published here as *The Time of Secrets*, 1962.)

Today P. is better known as a filmmaker than as a playwright. His first two films, *Marius* and *Fanny*, were actually directed by Korda and Allégret, but P. himself, as author and producer, took such an active part in the coaching of the actors (the cast of the stage productions also appeared in the films) that subsequently he took over the full responsibility of directing *César* and *Topaze*.

Besides the successful directing of movies made from his own plays, P.'s outstanding achievements are films based on texts by two other Provence writers, Giono (q.v.) and Alphonse Daudet (1840–97): *Angèle* (after *Un de Baumugnes*), *Regain,* and *La Femme du boulanger* by Giono, and a film version of three episodes from Daudet's *Lettres de mon moulin*.

The aesthetics of P.'s films is not very different from that of his plays. In both genres, he is primarily concerned with a poetic or picturesque interpretation of what is real, and not with dramatic or cinematographic experimentation. He has used in both mediums the natural settings of the city, the harbor, and the countryside as a background for the garrulous *méridional*, successfully conveying this character's petulance, gaiety, and optimism.

FURTHER WORKS: *Catulle* (1922); *Ulysse chez les Phéniciens* (1925); *Les Marchands de gloire* (1925); *Jazz* (1927); *Pirouettes* (1932); *La Petite Fille aux yeux sombres* (1933); *Merlusse* (1935); *Cigalon* (1936); *Le Schpountz* (1938); *Le Premier Amour* (1946); *Notes sur le rire* (1947); *Critique des critiques* (1949); *Maison des sources* (1953); *Œuvres dramatiques* (1954); *Judas* (1955); *Fabien* (1956); *Le Masque de fer* (1965)

BIBLIOGRAPHY: Combaluzier, I., *Le jardin de P.* (1937); Literary interview with P.—*FL*, 6–12 Aug. 1964, pp. 1 and 16, 13–19 Aug. 1964, pp. 17 and 18, 20–26 Aug. 1964, pp. 17 and 18, 27 Aug.–2 Sept. 1964, p. 18; Ages, A., "P.'s New Look at Judas," *Revue de l' Université d'Ottawa*, XXXV (1965), 314–22; Boucherat, M., "P.: Souvenirs d'Enfance," *Die Neueren Sprachen*, XVI (1967), 183–87

CHARLES G. HILL

PAKISTANI LITERATURE

Pakistani literature in the 20th c. is actually a gradual converging of English-language writing with the Islamic literatures of Urdu, Bengali, Pushto, Punjabi, Sindhi, and other regional and linguistic groups of the Indian peninsula.

Like Pakistan itself, a new country emerging out of the Islamic Indian peninsula and given its modern direction by the influences of 200 years of the British rule and of British political and social idealism, Pakistani literature was not born until 1947.

Since then a national literature has been slowly emerging as national themes reminiscent of the struggle for a national identity have become discernible in recent years. Neither the country nor its literature has yet resolved the diversity of its origins, however, and to speak of a national literature is to anticipate a philosophical and technical fusion that has not yet occurred.

Since the beginning of the 20th c., the literary heritage that was to become Pakistan's was the result of two major coexistent movements, the traditional and the modern. Essentially, the distinction between traditional and modern writing in Pakistan is that much of the literary work is dominated either by the traditional Islamic idealistic philosophy or by the naturalistic pessimism of the post-Darwinian, post-Marxian West, which did not make its major impact on Islamic writing in the Indian peninsula until the 1930's.

Although many cross-influences have been at work in these years, traditional writing has been largely in the vernaculars, and much of the modern writing, produced by those who have accepted Western-oriented education, has been in English. In the English-language writing especially, unusual literary works have resulted out of the interaction of Western genres, techniques, and influences and traditional story-telling patterns, subjects, and verse forms and rhythms. The vernacular literatures, each of which stems from Persian and Sanskrit traditional literatures, have, to a greater or lesser extent, felt the impact of 19th-c. and 20th-c. Western literary conventions and philosophies.

Urdu and Bengali writing has suffered from the emphasis both educational institutions and the government have placed on the use of English as well as from the smallness of the vernacular-reading audiences. In addition, the future role of the vernaculars in public affairs is still being disputed. Bengali, especially, has suffered from an attempt to Urduize the language, a movement which was opposed by East Pakistan, and an equivalent movement (which may have been Hindu-inspired) to purify the language. Nevertheless, both Bengali and Urdu writing are thriving today.

Few young writers today are working in the lesser vernaculars of Pakistan even though recent government subsidies have encouraged publishing in Pushto and Sindhi as well as Bengali and Urdu.

A condescending attitude toward the vernaculars, all too common in the educated elite, has led many of the Pakistani writers, both before and after partition, to write primarily in English. Because much if not all of their education has been in English and its use often provides opportunities otherwise closed to them, many present-day writers use English almost exclusively, although others write with equal facility in English and one of the vernaculars.

Pakistan continues to be a nation of poets. Prior to the 1930's serious works were usually written in verse, and it is only recently that prose fiction gained respectability in the Indian peninsula. Poetry, whether it be in English or in the vernacular, surpasses prose in quantity and often in quality as well as in popularity. The development of prose fiction in Pakistan has been hindered by the unfortunate lack of a widespread audience.

Before the 1930's serious writing was usually

steeped in traditional Islamic philosophy. In the late 19th c. it had begun to be increasingly imbued with a spirit of Islamic nationalism, a spirit that was to a great extent to be responsible for both the growth of Islamic national consciousness and the emergence of Pakistan as a sovereign nation.

In these nascent years the most significant writers in Urdu (the lingua franca of West Pakistan) were Hali (1837–1914), the poet, and Iqbal (q.v.) philosopher, nationalist, and poet. Traditionalists in their acceptance, celebration, and propagation of traditional Islamic philosophy, both were linguistic and poetic revolutionaries who made major contributions to the revitalizing of Urdu, which had stagnated under the British rule, into a viable literary language.

At the same time Hali and Iqbal pioneered a new verse style, the *nazm,* and rejected the traditional *ghazal.* The *ghazal,* embossed with traditional symbolism and highly dependent for its effects upon the intricacies of end-rhymes and its lyrical quality, was to Hali and later Iqbal inadequate for expressing their new ideas on Islamic nationalism and on the relationships between God and man. Consequently, following the leadership of Sayed Ahmed Khan (1817–98), they rejected the ornateness of classical Urdu writing in favor of straightforward language and rhythm, and they sought to use that newly freed language in the *nazm* (literally, poem), in which the old conventions were replaced by a wide variety of free forms.

Hali's contribution to revitalizing traditional Urdu writing was the simplicity of statement and the directness of sentiment expressed in the voice he evolved from the living language of the bazaars, villages, and streets. His *Mussadas* marked the direction of the new Urdu tradition in both form and philosophy as it introduced the theme of Islamic unity in new, forceful six-line stanzas that borrowed freely from the classic imagery of the West and rejected the stereotyped patterns of the Urdu classics.

Iqbal (q.v.) brought Hali's revolution to its logical culmination by uniting the twin dreams of Islamic nationalism and a viable Urdu language into literature. Iqbal (who was an equally gifted poet in the Persian language) accepted the role of literature as a medium for philosophic expression, for propaganda, and for demands for reform rather than as a conventional art form existing for its own sake.

The concept of Pakistan itself, a national entity firmly rooted in Islamic tradition, was largely Iqbal's creation. Surrounded by a nationalist myth that has grown up around his life and work, Iqbal is today considered the spiritual father of Pakistan, just as Mohammad Ali Jinnah is its political father.

In the revitalizing of the traditional Bengali language and literature of East Pakistan, Nazrul Islam (1899–1942) has been the major force. Largely a traditionalist in subject matter and philosophy and a rebel in politics, Nazrul, in his lyrics, *ghazals,* and Islamic and nationalistic poems, emphasized humanistic and romantic rather than theological and political values. Into his traditional verse he introduced Arabic, Persian, and Urdu words. In this way he endeavored to maintain a link to the past (traditionally, Islamic ideals and subjects were discussed in these languages) and to expand the literary potential of Bengali. At the same time, as a crusader for Islamic unity and independence, he provided a redirection, the effects of which are still being explored.

Currently the most outstanding Bengali vernacular writer is the poet Jasimuddin (b. 1902), who records the legends, the hopes, and the dreams of the people of the East Pakistan villages. His work, firmly rooted in the green countryside, is local rather than national. Yet though it is representative of the universal Pakistani experience—an experience that is rural, pastoral, and tragic rather than urban, mechanical, and pathetic—Jasimuddin has still to be considered a regional writer.

Younger writers in both Bengali and Urdu (especially in Urdu) are shifting emphasis from poetry to prose fiction. In both languages, social themes, romantic love, and some humor, based on Islamic tradition though carrying further the secular innovations of Iqbal and Nazrul, dominate the post-partition writings of the younger, self-consciously Pakistani writers. Prose fiction in Urdu and Bengali is still rooted in the age-old, oral storytelling still being enjoyed in the bazaars and tea shops. This heritage of the old traditions of Islamic idealism and the naïve-seeming, rambling oral literature is being fused with a sophisticated, controlled Western-inspired approach.

This can be seen in the works of such Urdu writers as Ghulam Abbas (b. 1909), a satirist who specializes in short tales, and Saadat Hasan Manto (1912–55), who explored the tragedy and irony of the independence and

31

partition movements. (Both of these writers have also written short stories in English.)

A major figure in the development of Pakistani prose fiction is Ahmed Ali (b. 1908), who has adapted the techniques of English prose to the vernacular and provided much of the impetus toward the development of Urdu fiction. Especially significant is his use of the stream-of-consciousness technique in *Mahavton Ki Ek Raat*, published in the early 1930's.

Despite these various developments most young Pakistanis writing in the vernaculars have not yet come under the influence of the naturalistic philosophies of the West.

English poetry, like vernacular poetry, surpasses prose in quantity, quality, and also popularity. Like the vernacular poets, the Pakistani English-language poets have largely sought their inspiration in the idealism of both the Islamic and the English romantic traditions. Taking their inspiration from Iqbal, Nazrul, and Jasimuddin, from poets of the West as diverse as William Wordsworth and Walt Whitman, they are also exploring the techniques of Pound and Eliot (qq.v). The result, as in the poems of Kaleem Omar, Riaz Quadir, and Syed Quamaruzzeman, is an optimistic fusion of past and present.

Generally speaking, the English-language prose writers have largely rejected traditional Islamic idealism and romanticism and emphasize in their works the harsh reality of life in present-day Pakistan. For their labors they have been accused of pessimism, lack of patriotism, and atheism, but their works, strongly critical and often satirical, have been efficacious in arousing the literate public and the government to a new social awareness.

Particularly influential in the development of Pakistani prose writing in English is the aforementioned Ahmed Ali (b. 1908), whose major work was done in prepartition India. He was one of a group of young writers who determined to throw off the shackles of tradition and write forcefully and honestly of the world around them, to the resulting displeasure of both Islamic conservatives and the British raj.

Ahmed Ali's major work, especially the novel *Twilight in Delhi* (1940), is in English. In this novel he forcefully fused the subject matter and the *Weltanschauung* of the Indian peninsula with the structure of the English novel and the tragic predicament of 20th-c. man. The result was an Asian English novel, a remarkable *tour de force* that has yet to be equaled either by Ahmed Ali or by the young writers who are emulating him.

Among the younger English-language writers are Iqbal Ahmad (b. 1921), Yunus Said, and Anwar Enayetullah. These three gifted writers illustrate the major trends current in Pakistani English-language writing. Both Iqbal Ahmad and Yunus Said, who have been strongly influenced by Western determinism and pessimism, write about the Western-educated elite of the cities. They write about the tragedy inherent in man's struggle against a hostile universe, and their outlook is grim. They insist that not only the people of Pakistan, but mankind itself, in this atomic age, is doomed. Iqbal Ahmad's vision of man's fate is truly tragic, while Yunus Said's people take refuge in the irony of their predicament.

Anwar Enayetullah, on the other hand, writes in the old tradition of romantic optimism, of confidence in the ultimate triumph of man through the virtues of Islam and of humanity.

Slowly, coincidental with the growth of national consciousness, a search for unity behind diversity in literature is taking place in Pakistan. As of 1970 the writers themselves have not yet written the works that would draw the many sources and influences together. As of now no post-partition writer has yet emerged with the talent, dedication, and insight of a Nazrul or an Iqbal, or of others who wrote under, and often in opposition to, the British raj. And as of now, Pakistani literature reflects the diversity inherent in the political, social, and economic structure of the country.

BIBLIOGRAPHY: Shahid Hosain, ed., *First Voices: Six Poets from Pakistan* (1965); Anderson, D., "Pakistani Literature Today," *Literature East and West*, X (1966), 235–44; Lewis, D., "Past and Present in Modern Indian and Pakistani Poetry," *Literature East and West*, X (1966), 69–85, and XI (1967), 301–12

DAVID D. ANDERSON

PALACIO VALDÉS, Armando

Spanish novelist, short-story writer, and essayist, b. 4 Oct. 1853, Entralgo, Asturias; d. 3 Feb. 1938, Madrid

P. V., who came from a prosperous middle-class family, was educated in Avilés and Oviedo and studied law in Madrid.

The background of P. V.'s stories is often Asturias. This is the setting of, among others,

La fé (1892; Faith, 1892), the first novel in which P. V. treats religious subjects; of *El maestrante* (1893; The Grandee, 1894), a story of extramarital love; of *Los majos de Cádiz* (1896); and of his famous novel *La hermana San Sulpicio* (1899; Sister Saint Sulpice, 1890). *La aldea perdida* (1903) describes the changes introduced into the life of Asturias by mining and industry.

As a regional novelist, P. V. has not confined himself to Asturias. He has been equally able to evoke the particular quality and atmosphere of Valencia in *La alegría del capitán Ribot* (1899; The Joy of Captain Ribot, 1900) and of Madrid in *Riverita* (1886), *Maximina* (1887; Eng., 1888), and *La espuma* (1891; Froth, 1891).

P. V.'s novels belong to the tradition of moderate realism. His characters, especially the women, are precisely outlined. The milieu in his novels is always clearly conceived. A Dickensian humor marks many works, though *Tristán o el pesimismo* (1906; Tristan, 1925) expresses a negative view of humanity.

FURTHER WORKS: *El señorito Octavio* (1881); *Marta y María* (1883; The Marquis of Peñalta, 1886); *El idilio de un enfermo* (1884); *José* (1885; Eng., 1901); *El cuarto poder* (1888; The Fourth Estate, 1901); *Obras completas* (28 vols., 1901–32); *Los papeles del Doctor Angélico* (1911); *Santa Rogelia* (1916); *Años de la juventud del Doctor Angélico* (1918); *El gobierno de las mujeres* (1918); *La novela de un novelista* (1921); *Cuentos escogidos* (1923); *La hija de Natalia* (1924); *El pájaro en la nieve y otros cuentos* (1925); *Los cármenes de Granada* (1927); *Testamento literario* (1929); *Sinfonía pastoral* (1931); *Tiempos felices* (1933); *Álbum de un viejo* (1940); *Epistolario con Clarín* (1941); *Obras completas* (2 vols., 1945)

BIBLIOGRAPHY: Cruz Rueda, A., *A. P.* (1924); Narbone, R., *A. P. o la armonía* (1941); Colangeli Romano, M., *A. P. V. romanziere* (1957); Childers, J. W., "Sources of P. V.'s *Las barbujas,*" *Hispania,* XLI (1958), 181–85; "P. V." in *Diccionario de Literatura Española* (3rd rev. ed., 1964)

ALONSO ZAMORA VICENTE

PALAMÁS, Kostís

Greek poet and journalist, b. 8 Jan. 1859, Pátras; d. 27 Feb. 1943, Athens

In 1876, P., who had spent most of his orphaned childhood in Misolóngi, went to Athens to study law at the university. His first job, however, was as a reporter for *Rambagás,* and he worked as a newspaper editor from 1879 to 1885. From 1897 to 1927 he was secretary-general of the University of Athens. In 1926 he helped to found the Academy of Science in Athens, of which he became president in 1930.

After 1888 P. was a leader in the hard-fought, successful campaign to have demotic Greek designated as the official language of modern Greece (*see* Greek literature). During these years he published poetry, short stories, art criticism, and political essays.

In 1886 his first collection of poetry, *Tragoúdia tis patrídos mou* (in demotic Greek), was published. The Greek nation alone—its life, its people, its soul, its ethnos—offered P. an inexhaustible wealth of themes for his poetry. Actually all areas of spirit and experience—science, philosophy, human emotions, the age of antiquity, nature—were the matter of poetry in his inspired hands. His poetry reveals the erudition, vision, breadth of mind, and profound understanding with which P. viewed experience. Though highly receptive throughout his life to all that was stirring in western Europe, he never subordinated his identity as a Greek to his universality.

P.'s literary achievement was the creation of lyrical, metaphor-filled, prophetic poetry in which he proved definitively that the voice of modern Greece was best articulated in demotic Greek.

P.'s well-deserved preeminence stems from his dual role: he was the spiritual and intellectual leader of modern Greece as well as its most important writer. This must have seemed natural to P., who believed that the function of a true poet was to lead as well as to write.

FURTHER WORKS: *Ímnos is tin Athenán* (1889); *Ta mátia tis psihís mou* (1892); *O táfos* (1898); *Íamvi ke anápesti* (1899); *O thánatos tou palikariú* (1901; A Man's Death, 1934); *Trisévyeni* (1903; Royal Blossom, 1923); *I asálefti zoí* (1904; Life Immovable, 1919); *O dodekálogos tou yíftou* (1907; The Twelve Words of the Gypsy, 1964); *I floyéra tou vasiliá* (1910; The King's Flute, 1967); *I politía ke i monaxiá* (1912); *I kaymí tis limnothálasas* (1912); *Ta dekatetrástiha* (1919); *Diiyímata* (1920); *O kíklos ton tetrástihon* (1929); *Pezí drómi* (3 vols., 1929–32). **Selected English translations:** *A Hundred Voices, and Other Poems* (1921); *Poems by K. P.* (1925)

BIBLIOGRAPHY: Thrílos, A., *K. P.* (1924); Psiháris, J., *K. P.* (1927); Karandónis, A., *Isagoyí sto Palamikó érgo* (1929); Tsátsos, K., *K. P.* (1936); Hourmoúsios, A., *O P. ke i epohí tou* (1943–44); Panayotópoulos, I. M., *K. P.* (1944); Demarás, K. T., *K. P.* (1947); Jenkins, R. J. H., *K. P.* (1947); Sofrónion, S. A., "The Parnassianism of K. P.," *SEER*, XXXVIII (1960), 166–77; Special P. issue, *Annales de l'Université de Paris*, XXXI (1961); Will, F., Introduction to *The King's Flute* (1967)

* * * *

PALAZZESCHI, Aldo

(pseud. of *Aldo Giurlani*), Italian poet and novelist, b. 2 Feb. 1885, Florence

Like all major representatives of the oldest generation of living Italian writers, P. came from the ranks of the futurists (*see* futurism), though he broke with them in 1914. He vented his youthful exuberance in a lampoon attacking sorrow and seriousness and praising light-heartedness.

P.'s *L'incendiario* (1910), an early volume of poems, is a technically conservative (despite its use of coarse language), maliciously humorous sideshow of 19th-c. peculiarities. His amusing novel *Il codice di Perelà* (1911, Perela, The Man of Smoke, 1936; revised ed., *Perelà, uomo di fumo*, 1954) today looks like a precursor of surrealist fiction.

After a period of silence, P. asserted himself as an accomplished writer of fiction with the publication of *Stampe dell'ottocento* (1932), which is fairly traditional in both content and form.

In 1934, at a time when it was appearing questionable whether Italian prose writers could produce anything but subjective, memory-drenched literature, P. offered another traditionally constructed, objective novel. This, his masterpiece, was *Le sorelle Materassi* (1934; The Sisters Materassi, 1953). In these grotesque fifty-year-old sisters, pathetically naïve and fiercely attached to life, desperate and impermeable in their disillusionment, one can perceive a kind of self-portrait of P.

Through these years, from 1920 to 1943, P. relentlessly opposed the fascist regime because of a variety of morally and intellectually radical ideas to which he was committed. He was described as "one of the sharpest, most reticent, and most sorrowful of the antifascists" (Luigi Russo, 1950).

After World War II, P. wrote *I fratelli Cuccoli* (1948), a thematic counterpart to *Le sorelle Materassi* that deals with vicarious fatherhood. The religious note discernible here becomes dominant in *Roma* (1953; Eng., 1965), a fluid epic novel, rooted in the antagonism between the bygone age of faith and immoral, materialistic modern times, that reflects the maturity of the sixty-eight-year-old author.

In 1957 P. was granted the highest Italian award—the Feltrinelli dei Lincei Accademia—for his work as a whole. In 1967 he published *Il Doge*, a portrait of Venice, the city which has allowed him to live his old age in serenity and solitude.

P. is one of the most attractive figures in Italian literature of the first half of the 20th c.—an individualist who neither founded a school nor belonged to one after reaching maturity.

FURTHER WORKS: *I cavalli bianchi* (1905); *Lanterna* (1907); *Poesie* (1930); *Il palio dei buffi* (1937); *Romanzi straordinari* (1943); *Tre imperi . . . mancati* (1945); *Bestie del novecento* (1951); *Viaggio sentimentale* (1955); *Scherzi di gioventù* (1956); *Tutte le novelle* (1957); *Opere giovanili* (1958); *I romanzi della maturità* (1960); *Il piacere della memoria* (1964); *Il buffo integrale* (1966)

BIBLIOGRAPHY: De Luca, J., *A. P.* (1941); Bo, C., "Rittrato di P.," *Palatina*, II (1958), v., 3–17; Sanguineti, E., "Tra libertà e crepuscolarismo," *Lettere Italiane*, XII (1961), 189–208; Chuzeville, J., "Regard étranger sur P.," special issue on P. edited by Ungaretti, *Caffé*, X (1962), iii, 23–34; Pullini, G., *A. P.* (1965); Gozzi, A., "P. e la poetica della liggerezza," *Veeri*, No. 20 (1966), pp. 82–92; Bo, C., "L'innocenza di P.," *Corriere della Sera*, 13 June 1968, p. 3

HANS HINTERHÄUSER

PALÉS MATOS, Luis

Puerto Rican poet, b. 1898, Guayma; d. 23 Feb. 1959, San Juan

P. M.'s parents were poets, and it seemed natural for him and his two younger brothers to follow in their footsteps. P. M. himself had his first verses published at the age of sixteen in a volume called *Azaleas* (1915). These were in the modernist vein and melancholic in tone. Many of them were sonnets describing tropical landscapes. The style is primarily parnassian and somewhat imitative of Herrera y Reissig and Lugones (qq.v.).

KOSTIS PALAMÁS

LUIS PALÉS MATOS

The years between 1918 and 1925 mark a transition in P. M.'s poetry and indicate a progression toward a more personal style. In 1921, with his friend José I. de Diego Padró, P. M. introduced vanguardist poetry into Puerto Rico, experimenting with onomatopoeia, imaginative metaphors, and rhythmic innovations. The movement became known as *diepalismo.*

With his poem "Pueblo Negro" (1926), P. M., while not a Negro himself, became the first poet in the Spanish language to exploit black themes poetically. His later volume, *Tuntún de pasa y grifería* (1937), portrays in a stylized manner, and often with humor, the sensual and primitive world of the Afro-Antillean. It makes use of syncopation, striking rhymes, onomatopoeia, African proper names, superstitions, and myths. While they are highly original, these poems have perhaps unfortunately overshadowed the rest of his work, which is also of the highest quality.

One of Puerto Rico's most distinguished poets, P. M. stresses in his work a disenchantment with civilization and a desire to return to the pristine, uncorrupted nature of things.

FURTHER WORKS: *Litoral* (1952); *Poesía 1915–1956* (1957)

BIBLIOGRAPHY: Labarthe, P. J., "El tema negroide en la poesía de L. P. M.," *Hispania,* XXXI (1948); Arce de Vázquez, M., *Impresiones. Notas puertorriqueñas* (1950); Blanco, T., *Sobre L. P. M.* (1950); Florit, E., "Los versos de L. P. M.," *RHM,* XXIV (1958); Onis, F. de, "L. P. M., 1: Vida y obra. 2: Bibliografía. 3: Antología," *Islas,* I (1959)

ROBERT SCOTT

PALINURUS
See Connolly, Cyril

PALUDAN, Jacob
Danish novelist and essayist, b. 7 Feb. 1896, Copenhagen

P.'s father, a very conservative literary historian, was sharply attacked by the liberals. At the age of twenty-four P. went to Ecuador and later to the United States. Dismayed by the American way of life, he returned home determined to fight American influence. His experiences were recounted in his essaylike novel *De vestlige veje* (1922).

By 1933, P. had written six novels combining psychologically sensitive description of charac-

ter and milieu with a critical treatment of the society of the 1920's.

In 1932 and 1933 he published *Jørgen Stein og hans kreds* (I, *Torden i syd;* II, *Under regnbuen;* both translated as Jørgen Stein, 1966). This well-received novel is a document of the period between the world wars. Its leading character sees himself as a representative of the generation "which stumbled at the start."

FURTHER WORKS: *Urolige sange* (1923); *Søgelys* (1923); *En vinter lang* (1924); *Fugle omkring fyret* (1925; Birds around the Light, 1928); *Markerne modnes* (1927); *F. Jansens jeremiader* (1927); *Året rundt* (1929); *Som om intet var hændt* (1938); *Søgende ånder* (1943); *Facetter* (1947); *Skribenter på yderposter* (1949); *Litterært selskab* (1956); *Røgringe* (1959)

BIBLIOGRAPHY: Hallar, S., *J. P.* (1927); Hesselaa, P., *J. P.* (1927); Lundbo, O., *J. P.* (1943); Hansen, T., *J. P.* (1947); Beyschlag, S., "J. P.," *Euphorion,* XLV (1950); Frederiksen, E., in *Ung dansk litteratur* (1951)

EMIL FREDERIKSEN

PANOVA, Vera Fiodorovna
Soviet-Russian novelist and playwright, b. 20 March 1905, Rostov-on-Don

From 1922 to 1946 Vera P. was a journalist. In her autobiographical novel *Sentimental'nyi roman* (1958) and, to some extent, *Vremena goda* (1953) she tells of the experiences of being a young reporter in Rostov.

Vera P. began writing plays in 1933: *Ilya Kosogor* (1939), *V staroi Moskve* (1940), *Metelitza* (1942–56), *Devochki* (1945), *Provody belykh nochei* (1961). However, she finds it difficult to comply with the rigid demands of the drama and prefers to write novels.

In 1944, while working in the Urals for the Perm newspapers, Vera P. was assigned by the local writers' union to edit a report (which was never published) on the work during World War II of the staff of an army hospital train. Through this experience Vera P.'s best book—*Sputniki* (1946; Am., The Traveling Companions, 1965; Eng., The Train, 1948)—came into being. The tragic and the humorous are movingly blended here in this story of the lives of those who had belonged to the unit for four years. For this she won the Stalin Prize in 1947.

In 1948, Vera P. was again awarded the Stalin

Prize, this time for *Kruzhilikha* (1947; *Looking Ahead*, 1957), a story of life in a factory—named Kruzhilikha—during World War II. Sympathetically she presents the hardships—and the ability to bear them with goodwill—of the Soviet proletariat in those years. The setting of *Yasni bereg* (1949)—winner of the 1950 Stalin Prize—is a collective farm in the postwar Soviet Union.

Shortly before the Second Congress of Soviet Writers convened (this meeting in 1954 was the first since 1934), Vera P. was one of the writers to receive a public reprimand, which was based on ideological considerations. Nevertheless, she was elected to the executive board of the Congress of Soviet Writers in 1954.

Vera P.'s tales about the youngster *Seriozha* (1955; *Times Walked*, 1959) reveal her serious and tender regard, in the Chekhov (q.v.) tradition, for childhood. This book was made into the delightful film *A Summer to Remember*.

Warmth and sincerity are the most valuable assets of Vera P.'s versatile talent. She excels in revealing a character's personality through dialogue and by means of significant or humorous short scenes. In her search for truth she has refused to be encumbered by any ready-made solutions. It is because of this attitude that the protagonists of her novels and plays are sometimes ambiguous and she is regarded as a controversial author in the Soviet Union.

FURTHER WORKS: *Pervoye puteshestviye Vali* (1955); *Valya i Volodya* (1959); *Troye malchishek u vorot i drugiye rasskazy i povesti* (1964); *Liki na zare* (1966)

BIBLIOGRAPHY: Obrazovskaya, E. N., *Tvorchestvo V. F. Panovoi: Avtoreferat kandidatskoi dissertatzii* (1952); Fradkina, S. Ya., *V mire geroyev Very Panovoi* (1961); Prjevalinskaya-Ferrer, O., "Bromas y veras en la creación literaria de Vera Panova," *Cuadernos americanos*, V (1962); Plotkin, L., *Tvorchestvo Very Panovoi* (1962); Boguslavskaya, Z., *Vera P.: Ocherk tvorchestva* (1963); Starikova, E., "Geroi Very Panovoi," *Novyi Mir*, No. 3 (1963); Moody, C., Introduction to *Serezha and Valya* (1964); Stilman, G., ed., Introduction to *Sputniki* (1964)

OLGA PRJEVALINSKAYA-FERRER

PANZINI, Alfredo

Italian novelist, b. 31 Dec. 1863, Senigallia; d. 10 April 1939, Rome

P. developed a willful, ironical prose style derived from Horace, Laurence Sterne, Heine, and Carducci. As he grew older he often parodied his own style. The fictional structure is usually of minor importance, since P.'s favorite form was the impressionistic travel sketch.

P.'s first novel, *Il libro dei morti* (1893), shows his close tie to the past. *La lanterna di Diogene* (1907) is an account of a happy bicycling vacation. In *Santippe* (1914) he vented his resentment against women and, like G. B. Shaw (q.v.), gave a comically realistic sketch of antiquity.

P.'s novel *Il mondo è rotondo* (1921), written under the stress of World War I, reveals his darkening outlook on life. Its protagonist, Beatus Renatus, can no longer find his way amidst the turmoil of modern ideas and attitudes. This suggests that the enthusiasm for classical antiquity and the joy in country life expressed in P.'s early work might have been avenues of escape from his own times.

Toward the end of his life P. wrote *Il bacio di Lesbia* (1937), a subtle, humorous sketch of the Roman Augustan age that is one of P.'s most harmonious works.

FURTHER WORKS: *La Cagna nera* (1896); *Moglie nuova* (1899); *Trionfi di donna* (1903); *Il viaggio di un povero letterato* (1919); *Io cerco moglie* (1920; *Wanted—a Wife*, 1922); *Signorine* (1921); *Il padrone sono me* (1922); *Diario sentimentale della guerra* (1923); *La pulcella senza pulcellaggio* (1925); *Sei romanzi fra due secoli* (1939); *Romanzi d'ambo i sessi* (1941); *Per amore di Biancofiore* (1948); *La cicuta, i gigli e le rose* (1950); *La mia storia* (1958); *Rose d'ogni mese* (1959)

BIBLIOGRAPHY: Baldini, G., *P.* (1942); Sorni, B., *Viaggio e divigazione* (1955); Pedicini, R., *A. P.* (1957); Nardi, T., *Sulle Orme di Santippe da Platone a P.* (1958)

JOHANNES HÖSLE

PAPADAT-BENGESCU, Hortensia

Romanian novelist, b. 1878, Iveşti, Tecuci; d. 1955

The daughter of a general, Hortensia P.-B. belonged to the "sburătorul" circle and was one of the Western-oriented Romanian writers (as opposed to those primarily interested in the Romanian folk culture).

After lyrical and dramatic experiments, Hortensia P.-B. went on to become a master of the psychological novel. She brought remarkable skill to her task, which was bold and cool dissection of the human soul. By delicate, detailed analysis she pursued the exploration of the conscious and unconscious to a point where reality becomes displaced by a facsimile of reality. Her novels, stimulated by Proust's (q.v.) work, anticipated the techniques of the *nouveau roman.*

WORKS: *Ape adânci* (1919); *Sfinxul* (1920); *Bătrânul* (1920); *Femeia în faţa oglinzii* (1921); *Bălaurul* (1923); *Romanţă provincială* (1925); *Fecioarele despletite* (1926); *Concert din muzică de Bach* (1927); *Desenuri tragice* (1927); *Drumul ascuns* (1932); *Logodnicul* (1935); Rădăcini (2 vols., 1938)

BIBLIOGRAPHY: Reichman, E., "Les lettres roumaines: Un lent apprentissage à la liberté," *Preuves*, No. 175 (1965), pp. 37–47; Philippide, A., "The Spirit and Tradition of Modern Romanian Literature," *Romanian Review*, XXI (1967), ii, 5–10; Ciopraga, C., "Arta romanului la H. P.-B.," *Viaţa Românească*, XXI (1968), v, 60–68

* * * *

PAPADIAMANTÍS, Aléxandros
Greek short-story writer, b. 3 March 1851, Skiathos; d. there, 3 Jan. 1911

P. attended gymnasiums in Chalkis and Piraeus and studied philology at the University of Athens. He was unusual among his Greek contemporaries in that his literary approach was determined by his native land rather than by foreign literary forces.

P., whose classically restrained prose is unequalled in modern Greek literature, is the master of the modern Greek short story. During his lifetime his work was published only in newspapers and magazines. In these modest, appealing short stories, he described the society of the island of Skiathos, re-creating its simple people and its old-time mores. P.'s asceticism and strongly felt Christianity lend a rich dimension to these stories.

FURTHER WORKS: *I fónisa* (1912); *Máyises; Pashalinà diiyímata, Hristouyeniátika diiyímata; Protohroniátika diiyímata; O pentárfanos; I holeriasméni; I nostalgós; Ta Hristoúyena tou tembéli* (8 vols. of collected short stories, 1912–15); *Ródina akroyaliá* (1913)

BIBLIOGRAPHY: Hesseling, D., *Histoire de la littérature grecque moderne* (1924); Katsímbalis, G. K., *A. P.* (1934); Lorentzátos, Z., *Melétes* (1966); Tomadákis, N. B., *A. P.* (1966); Vitti, M., *Poesia greca del novecento* (1966)

* * * *

PAPINI, Giovanni
Italian novelist and critic, b. 9 Jan. 1881, Florence; d. there, 8 July 1956

P. was the son of an atheistic cabinetmaker. Between 1902 and 1904 he taught Italian and worked as a museum clerk.

The story of P.'s life is the story of his intellectual shifts (and of the journals in which he from time to time proclaimed them). At the age of twenty-two, he and Giuseppe Prezzolini (b. 1882) founded *Leonardo* (1903–1907) as a turbulent protest against the times and milieu and as the forum in which a new paganism, "personalism," and pragmatism could be promulgated.

In 1909 he became the leading contributor to and temporary chief editor of the famous and influential *La Voce*. In 1913 he once again established his own journal—the militant, inflammatory, futurist (*see* futurism) *Lacerba*.

By the early 1920's P. seemingly managed to achieve some peace of mind when this series of intellectual adventures and "apostolates" was ended by his embracing of Roman Catholicism. By this turn in the road, however, he was to sacrifice his capacity to exert an influence on Italian intellectual development.

In *Un uomo finito* (1912; Am., The Failure, 1924; Eng., A Man Finished, 1924), P. told the story of his youth—his intellectual explorations, his Promethean rebellion against the limits of human existence, the way in which tradition and the region in which he was born sustained him. Here P.'s style is already fully developed; page-long outpourings of words stand beside penetrating, precise statements.

Storia di Cristo (1921; Am., The Story of Christ, 1924; Eng., Life of Christ, 1923) informed the world of P.'s acceptance of Roman Catholicism. By no means did this radical volte-face cause him to relinquish his titanism, his egocentric striving for originality, or his polemical passion.

A certain elegance and mellowing first became noticeable in *Il diavolo* (1953; The Devil, 1954). Here P. attempted a rehabilitation of the devil, trying to present him as "God's indispensable counterweight."

P.'s *Giudizio universale* (1957), which for years was announced by him as forthcoming, appeared posthumously. Artistically the work is uneven. The "setting" of this work is the Last Judgment itself. Some 350 representatives of mankind, both the historically famous and the imagined anonymous, are allowed, as a final concession of mercy, to testify to a "choir of angels" before they are called before the divine judge.

P., who until 1921 was decisively involved in all Italian literary movements, was the most controversial Italian writer of the first half of the 20th c.

FURTHER WORKS: *Il crepuscolo dei filosofi* (1906); *Il tragico quotidiano* (1906) and *Il pilota cieco* (1907; translated together as Life and Myself, 1930); *Le memorie d'Iddio* (1911; The Memoirs of God, 1926); *Parole e sangue* (1912); *24 cervelli* (1913); *Buffonate* (1914); *Cento pagine de poesia* (1915); *La paga del sabato* (1915); *Stroncature* (1916); *Opera prima* (1917); *Testimonianze* (1918); *Giorni di festa* (1918); *L'esperienza futurista* (1919); *Pane e vino* (1926); *Operai della vigna* (1929; Labourers in the Vineyard, 1930); *Sant' Agostino* (1929; Saint Augustine, 1930); *Gog* (1931; Eng., 1931); *La scala di Giacobbe* (1932); *Eresie letterarie* (1932); *Ritratti italiani* (1932); *Dante vivo* (1933, Eng., 1934); *La pietra infernale* (1934); *Storia della letteratura italiana* (1937); *I testimoni della passione* (1938); *Italia mia* (1939); *Mostra personale* (1941); *Imitazione del padre* (1942); *Saggi sul rinascimento* (1942); *Cielo e terra* (1943); *Lettere agli uomini del Papa Celestino VI* (1946; The Letters of Pope Celestine VI to All Mankind, 1948); *Santi e poeti* (1947); *Passato remoto* (1948); *Vita di Michelangeolo* (1949; Michelangelo: His Life and His Era, 1951); *Le pazzie del poeta* (1950); *Il libro nero* (1952); *Concerto fantastico* (1954); *Il bel viaggio* (1954); *La spia del mondo* (1955); *L'aurora della letteratura italiana* (1956); *La felicità dell'infelice* (1956); *La loggia dei busti* (1956); *Poesia e fantasia* (1958); *La seconda nascita* (1958); *Prose morali* (1959); *Tutte le opere* (10 vols., 1966). **Selected English translations:** *Four and Twenty Minds* (1922; containing essays from *24 cervelli, Stroncature,* and *Testimonianze*)

BIBLIOGRAPHY: Prezzolini, G., *Discorsi su G. P.* (1915); Palmiere, E., *G. P.* (1927); Apollonio, M., *G. P.* (1944); *P. ani settanta* (1951); Bargellini, P., *G. P.* (1956); Casnati, F., *P.* (1956); Caprin, G., *Reviviscenze* (1957); Franca, M. di, *G. P.* (1958); Savonarola, C., *Tempo di Sosfitica* (1959); Gullace, G., "G. P. and the Redemption of the Devil," *Personalist,* XLIII (1961), 233–52; Vintili, H., *G. P.* (1963); Gaye, V., *La critica letteraria di G. P.* (1965); Vettori, V., *G. P.* (1966)

HANS HINTERHÄUSER

PARANDOWSKI, Jan

Polish novelist, essayist, and literary historian, b. 11 May 1895, Lwów

While still attending the gymnasium in Lwów, P. began to write. His first book, a study of Rousseau, appeared in 1913. During World War I, he was interned in central Russia. In 1918 P. returned to Lwow, where he resumed his university studies and deceived a degree in philosophy and archaeology. At that time he was also active as a journalist and theater critic.

Since 1930 P. has lived in Warsaw. During the German occupation of Poland (1939–45) P. was forced into hiding. After Poland was liberated by Soviet troops, he became a professor of comparative literature at Lublin Catholic University. P. is president of the Polish P.E.N. club (since 1933) and vice-president of the International P.E.N. club (since 1962).

P. is perhaps best known as a devoted and erudite scholar of antiquity. In 1923 he published *Mitologia,* a retelling of Greek myths for young readers, and *Eros na Olimpie,* a ribald classic depicting the amorous adventures of the Greek gods. *Dwie wiosny* (1927), a magnificent historico-literary travelogue, was the result of his journeys to Greece in 1925 and to Sicily in 1926. By his translations (Caesar's *Civil War,* Longus' *Daphnis and Chloe,* Homer's *Odyssey*), P. has made a substantial contribution to Polish cultural life.

In 1932, after another trip to Greece, P. published *Dysk Olimpijski* (The Olympic Discus, 1939). Through this depiction of the Olympic Games in 476, P. has reconstructed the life of Ancient Greece. P.'s unusual ability to create the visual and his meticulous research combine to make this one of the major representations of Ancient Greece in modern fiction. For this novel P. was awarded a bronze medal at the Berlin Olympic Games in 1936 despite the protests of the Germans. It is this book, which was translated into several languages, that introduced P. to the western-European reader.

Niébo w płomieniach (1936), undoubtedly one of P.'s best works, is a psychological novel that treats a subject hitherto unknown in Polish literature—a religious crisis in the soul of a young boy. It provoked keen criticism and controversy among Roman Catholics and writers of the right. The protagonist reappears as a grown man in *Powrót do życia* (1961), but the emphasis of this novel is primarily on the Poland of World War II. *Wrześniówa noc* (1962) is P.'s account of his personal experiences during the Nazi German occupation of Poland.

Ideologically, P. occupies a detached, seemingly neutral position, and considers himself a realist; he is often called a contemporary Polish humanist. His literary style reflects his equanimity, his optimism, and his unceasing search for harmony.

FURTHER WORKS: *Aspazja* (1925); *Król życia* (1930); *Odwiedziny i spotkania* (1933); *Trzy znaki zodiaku* (1939); *Godzina śródziemnomorska* (1949); *Alchemia słowa* (1950); *Zegar słoneczny* (1952); *Pisma wybrane* (1955); *Petrarce* (1956); *Podróże literackie* (1958); *Mój Rzym* (1959); *Wspomnienia i sylwety* (1960); *Juvenilia* (1960); *Luźne kartki* (1965); *Szkice* (1968); *Akacja* (1968)

BIBLIOGRAPHY: Czachowski, K., *Obraz Współczesnej Literatury Polskiej*, Vol. III (1936); Harjan, G., "J. P.: A Contemporary Polish Humanist," *BA,* XXXIV (1960), 261–66; Wójcikowna, E., *Twórczość J. P.* (1961); Backvis, C., "J. P.," *Flambeau,* XLVIII (1966), 281–89

GEORGE HARJAN

PARDO BAZÁN, Emilia

Spanish novelist, short-story writer, and literary critic, b. 15 Sept. 1851, La Coruña; d. 15 May 1921, Madrid

The daughter of a count, Emilia P. B. showed a strong inclination to literature in her youth. After her marriage to José Quiroga in 1868, she traveled widely in Europe. In 1916 she became professor of Romance languages at the University of Madrid. Possessing broad literary knowledge, she used her position to disseminate European cultural currents in Spain.

Emilia P. B., a great admirer of Zola (q.v.), is probably to be credited with introducing into Spain French naturalism (q.v.), which she defended in *La cuestión palpitante* (1883). In practice the naturalism in her novels was colored by her Catholicism and regionalism. Her glorious descriptions of Galicia, her native province, in *Los pazos de Ulloa* (1886) and *La madre naturaleza* (1887), are an example of her unusual talent for regional fiction as well as of her tart, vigorous prose and her skill at pinpointing precise detail.

In 1887 Emilia P. B. wrote *La Revolución y la novela en Rusia* (Russia: Its People and Its Literature, 1890), in which she tried to interest her countrymen in the quality of the 19th-c. Russian novel. The significance of this venture was that by 1890 she had begun to write the psychological and spiritual novel and had moved substantially away from the naturalism she had so ardently championed at the beginning of her writing career.

Three novels of this last period—*La quimera* (1905; Midsummer Madness, 1907), *La sirena negra* (1908), and *Dulce dueño* (1911)—show the influence of the later Lev Tolstoi (q.v.) in that life's existential problems are resolved by one's relationship to God.

Although her eminence among contemporary writers was achieved mostly for her novels, Emilia P. B. also wrote poetry, travel books, literary criticism, monographs about contemporary writers (Zorrilla, Campoamor, Valera, Alarcon), as well as excellent short stories. The best of these short stories are those about Galicia that are collected in *Cuentos de Marineda* (1892) and *Un destripador de antaño* (1900).

FURTHER WORKS: *Pascual López* (1879); *Una viaje de novios* (1881; A Wedding Trip, 1891); *San Francisco de Asís* (1882); *La tribuna* (1883); *El cisne de Vilamorte* (1885; The Swan of Vilamorte, 1891); *De mi tierra* (1888; Homesickness, 1891); *Morriña* (1889); *Insolación* (1889); *Por Francia y por Alemania* (1890); *La prueba* (1890); *Una cristiana* (1890; A Christian Woman, 1891); *La piedra angular* (1891; The Angular Stone, 1892); *Adán y Eva* (1894); *Arco Iris* (1895); *Cuentos de Navidad y Reyes* (1902); *Misterio* (1902; The Mystery of the Lost Dauphin, 1906); *Novelas ejemplares* (1906); *Belcebú* (1908); *Obras completas* (46 vols., 1909 ff.); *La literatura francesa moderna* (3 vols., 1910–14); *Cuentos de la tierra* (1922). **Selected English translations:** *A Galician Girl's Romance* (1900); *The Son of the Bondwoman* (1908); *Short Stories by E. P. B.* (1933)

BIBLIOGRAPHY: Andrade Coello, A., *La

condesa de P. (1922); Brown, M. G., *La vida y las novelas de P.* (1940); Gonzales Lopez, E., *E. P.* (1944); Scone, E. L., "Cosmopolitan Attitudes in the Works of P. B.," *DA*, XX (1960), 2809

* * * *

PASCARELLA, Cesare

Italian poet and short-story writer, b. 27 April 1858, Rome; d. there, 8 May 1940

P. was a painter, especially of animals, before he turned to poetry. He traveled extensively through Europe, the Americas, and India. Though he had been a friend of Giosuè Carducci (1835–1907) and D'Annunzio (q.v.), he spent an unhappy, secluded old age, to which his deafness was a contributing factor.

In his sonnets and sonnet sequences, P. used the Roman dialect with a success approached only by Giuseppe Belli (1791–1863). By means of the dialect he was able to utilize his keen feeling for the humorous and his talent for caricature to write sometimes moving, sometimes delightful poetry. It is generally agreed that his most successful works are *Villa Gloria* (1886) and *La scoperta de l'America* (1893). *Villa Gloria*, a sequence of twenty-five sonnets, is a participant's account of an attempt to seize Rome in the pre-unification days. *La scoperta de l'America*, in a sequence of fifty delightful sonnets, tells the story of Columbus discovering America.

P. also wrote short stories and sketches of modern Roman life in literary Italian. Though his work in these genres is distinguished, it is less well-esteemed than his dialect poetry.

FURTHER WORKS: *Il morto di campagna* (1882); *La serenata* (1882); *Le memorie di uno smemorato* (1910); *Sonetti* (1911); *Viaggio in ciociaria* (1914); *Poesie disperse* (1919); *Prose* (1920); *Storia nostra* (1941); *Tutte le opere* (1955)

BIBLIOGRAPHY: Jandolo, A., *C. P.* (1940); Bizzarri, E., *C. P.* (1941); Aurigemma, M., *P.* (1959)

LINA MAINIERO

PASCOAES, Teixeira de

(pseud. of *Joaquim Pereira Teixeira de Vasconcelos*), Portuguese poet and biographer, b. 2 Nov. 1877, Amarante, Minho; d. there, 4 Dec. 1952

P. ranks as an important exponent of the

Portuguese spirit. When he was young he gave up the practice of law to live in the country as a lay brother, devoting himself to philosophy and mystical contemplation. He was at first influenced by the poetry of Abílio Manuel de Guerra Junqueiro (1850–1923) and António Nobre (1867–1900).

P.'s early poetry—*Terra proibida* (1899), *Jesus e Pan* (1903), *Para a luz* (1904), and *Vida etérea* (1906)—revealed his individual view of the world. The Marao mountains form the scenic background of many of his works, but the concrete world in all its natural beauty exists only to provide a backdrop. He is much more interested—as the poetry of *Marános* (1911) shows—in his visions of his inner world. That is, he seeks the numen behind the phenomenon. His thinking was dominated by a concept of a pantheistic evolutionism that will culminate in the complete spiritualization of the universe.

The core of P.'s *Weltanschauung* was the Portuguese *saudade*—that which is the blending of memory, desire and yearning, melancholy regret and vital hope. It also aspires to God in remembrance of and hope of union with Him.

From 1912 to 1916 P. edited *A Águia*, the journal of the Portuguese revival movement, while continuing, in various writings, to proclaim the doctrine of *saüdosismo* (*see* Portuguese literature).

Later P. wrote biographies: *São Paulo* (1934); *São Jerónimo* (1936); *Napoleao* (1940); *O Penitente* (1942), the subject of which is the Portuguese Romantic poet Camilo Castelo Branco (1825–1890); and *Santo Agostinho* (1945).

Of the many novels P. began, only two—*Empecido* (1950) and *Os dois jornalistas* (1951)—were published.

FURTHER WORKS: *Sempre* (1894); *As Sombras* (1907); *Regresso ao paraíso* (1912); *O espírito Lusitano ou o Saüdosismo* (1912); *O doido e a morte* (1913); *O gênio Português na sua expressão filosófica, poética e religiosa* (1913); *Verbo escuro* (1914); *Elegia de solidão* (1920); *Elegia de amor* (1924); *Jesus Cristo em Lisbôa* (1924); *Dom Carlos* (1925); *Livro de memorias* (1928); *O pobre tôlo* (1930); *Painel* (1935); *Obras completas* (7 vols. 1935 ff.); *Duplo passeio* (1942); *Ultimos versos* (1953)

BIBLIOGRAPHY: Prado Coelho, J. do, *A poesia de T. de P.* (1945); Sardoeira, I., *P.* (1951); Ambrósio de Pina, A., *A filosofia da*

JAN PARANDOWSKI

TEIXEIRA DE PASCOAES

saudade de T. de P. (1958); Margarido, A., *T. de P.* (1961)

HERNANI CIDADE

PASCOLI, Giovanni

Italian poet, b. 31 Dec. 1855, San Mauro; d. 18 Feb. 1912, Bologna

P. was born into a Romagna farming family. His youth was marked by the tragic murder of his father and the death several years later of his mother and sister. The farm and these early bereavements were to be important influences on P.'s poetry, which is marked by a deep love of nature and rural life as well as a constant preoccupation with death.

During his years at Bologna University (1873–82), P. was briefly involved in politically radical activities, but, more importantly, he came under the influence of Giosuè Carducci (1835–1907), the literary lion of the age. After teaching classics in various cities in southern and central Italy, P. was appointed to succeed Carducci in the Italian literature chair at Bologna. The last years of his life were spent alternately in Bologna and the Castelvecchio home he had built with the money derived from thirteen prizes won over the years for Latin poems he submitted to the Amsterdam Latin Poetry Contest. These poems were posthumously published under the title *Carmina* (1914).

P., D'Annunzio (q.v.), and their common mentor, Carducci, were the dominant Italian *fin-de-siècle* poets, and they are somewhat misleadingly known under the coverall label of classicists. However, what marks P.'s best known collection of verse, *Myricae* (1891), is the ease with which he frees himself of Carducci's rhetoric to strike his own unmistakably personal note. Even in his earliest lyrics, historical and literary reminiscence is reabsorbed into a fairy-tale landscape, and the stately sonnet form attains a playful airiness. Though there are a few isolated attempts to pattern Italian verse on Greek and Latin cadences, generally speaking, P. stays with Romance prosody and achieves effects of exquisite flexibility. For example, P. excells in his treatment of the traditional eleven-syllable line that is the Italian equivalent of English poetry's iambic pentameter.

Most of the poems in *Myricae* are short and nonnarrative, employing a vivid imagery that occasionally verges on expressionist (*see* expressionism) intensity. P.'s themes range from autobiographical elegy to rich description of rural life. His language often incorporated elements of popular speech, and his avoidance of heavily structured syntax achieves a general feeling of immediacy that is aided by the skillful echoing or insertion of folk-song motifs.

Humor, pathos, and close observations of the grace of animal life add a touch of freshness to these poems. P. seems to know the call of every bird and the name and color of every flower. Around and above these myriad manifestations of life, nature looms as a tragic, beautiful, and unfathomable force. Like his beloved Virgil, to whom he pointedly refers in his selection of the title *Myricae,* P. escapes the limitations of the georgic genre. Cosmic symbols pervade his poetry, and the atmospheric effects of some of the introspective pieces recall Paul Verlaine (1844–96), Stéphane Mallarmé (1842–98), and Maeterlinck (q.v.).

In subsequent collections of verse, P. variously develops his several strains. *Canti di Castelvecchio* (1903) continues the themes and tone of *Myricae* with bolder experiments in imagery and sound; *Primi poemetti* (1904) and *Nuovi poemetti* (1909) celebrate rural life in terza rima; *Poemi conviviali* (1904) narrates scenes from Greek and Roman mythology and history, adding to them a poignantly subtle "decadent" flavor; *Odi e inni* (1906) treats subjects of public import with broad human concern, sometimes, as in the piece on the lost polar aeronaut Andrée, adding an eerie note.

Croce (q.v.) and other critics were severe in their comments on the sentimentality and technical affectation to be found in some of P.'s work. More recently P.'s poetry has undergone a revaluation and revival. P. is now seen as an inventive experimenter, whose use of elliptical analogy and effects achieved by onomatopoeia, synesthesia, and linguistic pluralism are controlled by a well-modulated conversational tone that was to find its best embodiments first in the verse of Guido Gozzano and then in that of Montale (qq.v.). No important 20th-c. movement, from that of the *crepuscolari* to the futurists (*see* futurism) and the hermeticists, is without its debt to P.

FURTHER WORKS: *Il fanciullino* (1897); *Minerva oscura* (1898); *Sotto il velame* (1900); *La mirabile visione* (1902); *Nell'anno mille* (1902); *La messa d'oro* (1905); *Pensieri e discorsi* (1907); *Poemi italici e canzoni di Re Enzio* (1908–1911); *Poemi del Risorgimento*

(1913); *Traduzioni e riduzioni* (1913); *Antico sempre nuovo* (1925). **Selected English translations:** *Poems of G. P.* (1927); Selections in *The Penguin Book of Italian Verse* (ed. G. Kay; 1958)

BIBLIOGRAPHY: Borgese, A., *La vita e il libro* (1912); Cecchi, E., *La poesia di G. P.* (1912); Croce, B., *G. P.* (1920); Russo, L., *G. P.* (1954); Antonielli, S., *La poesia del P.* (1955); Valgimigli, M., and Vicinelli, A., eds., *Omaggio a G. P.* (1955); Getto, G., *Carducci e P.* (1957); Anceschi, L., *Barocco e novecento* (1958); Pascoli, M., *Lungo la vita di G. P.*, ed. A. Vicinelli (1962); Barberi Squarotti, G., *Simboli e strutture della poesia del P.* (1966); Mazzamuto, P., *P.* (1966). Publications from the P. anniversary symposia—*P.: Discorsi nel centenario* (Bologna, 1958), *Studi pascoliani* (Faenza, 1958), *Studi per il centenario della nascita di G. P.* (Bologna, 1958), *Atti del Convegno Nazionale di studi pascoliani* (San Mauro Pascoli, 1962), *Nuovi studi pascoliani* (Bolzano-Cesena, 1963)

GLAUCO CAMBON

PASOLINI, Pier Paolo

Italian novelist, poet, and movie director, b. 5 March 1922, Bologna

P.'s father was an army career officer, so the family moved from city to city in northern Italy. When World War II began, P. went to Casarsa, his mother's native town, where he remained until 1949. He earned a doctorate in letters and philosophy from the University of Bologna with his dissertation on Pascoli (q.v.).

During this period, P. and some friends founded the "Academiuta de Lenga Furlana" (Academy of Friulan Language). The results of his literary activity centered about the "academy" may be found in *La meglio gioventù: poesie friulane* (1954), which contains P.'s poems in the Friulan language, including those that had previously appeared in the booklet *Poesie a Casarsa* (1942). P.'s interest in Friulan (not a dialect, but one of the languages of the Romance group) came not from an inclination toward folk forms but from cultural experiences connected with the symbolist (*see* symbolism) school and Italian hermeticism, which led him to attempt a means of expression through which he might recapture an ancestral world of unspoiled purity.

L'usignuolo della chiesa cattolica (1958), a second poetry collection, contains compositions in Italian written from 1943 to 1949. Beginning with early experiments that hark back to the tradition of religious poetry, these poems move on to dramatic testimony of P.'s youthful renunciation of his faith, and then to his decisive encounter with Marx ("La scoperta di Marx," 1949), an event that brought this first period of his literary activity to a close. P.'s first novel, *Il sogno di una cosa* (written, 1949–50; published, 1962), already presupposes a Marxist sociopolitical commitment in its portrayal of the struggle between the day laborers and the large landowners of the Venetian provinces.

P.'s reflections on the texts of Marx and Antonio Gramsci (1891–1937), whom he discovered simultaneously, led him to a new apprehension of reality that lent itself more truly to his stylistic tendencies and to the moral ideals he conceived during the Resistance (1943–45), a struggle of which he was but a marginal witness.

Living in Rome, P. initiated a period of feverish activity in which his creative work was intimately connected with social and political endeavors. He focused on the world of Rome's subproletariat (*Lumpenproletariat* in Marx's scornful description), people so hopelessly immersed in misery that they lacked even the social consciousness indispensable to their redemption. From this experience came the novel *Ragazzi di vita* (1955; The Ragazzi, 1968), in which, taking up the *verismo* narrative tradition of Verga (q.v.), P. portrays this world in a prose that draws on Roman dialect and jargon and is polemically directed against the institutionalized narrative language of the bourgeoisie.

The novel led to a lawsuit on grounds of obscenity. It was followed by *Una vita violenta* (1959; A Violent Life, 1968), a closely related work in which the protagonists seem on the point of acquiring social consciousness.

The poems written during this period were collected in *Le ceneri di Gramsci* (1957) and *La religione del mio tempo* (1961). Rejecting current decadent experimental modes and resuming traditional Italian forms (radically reformed in their meters), P. strove to restore to poetry the civil and social functions announced by Gramsci's notion of "popular-national literature."

To these creative endeavors P. added a restless activity as a militant critic, debating his

GIOVANNI PASCOLI

PIER PAOLO PASOLINI

ideas in several literary journals (he was among the founders of the magazine *Officina*) and introducing both lay readers and scholars to a large repertory of folk poetry that had remained excluded from middle-class culture.

Although his collaboration with the motion picture industry started in 1954, P. directed his first film, *Accattone!*, in 1961. In this and in other films up to the time of *Il Vangelo secondo Matteo* (1964), he consistently strove to develop a personal language based on the stylistic modes inherited from neorealism. Beginning with *Uccellacci e uccellini* (1966) and including *Edipo re* (1967) and *Teorema* (1968), P.'s cinematographic language is more and more complex and symbolic, dealing with ambiguous and disquieting theological themes. An anticipation of this new existential uneasiness is to be found in the poems of *Poesia in forma di rosa* (1964).

FURTHER WORKS: *I diarii di P. P. P.* (1945); *I pianti* (1946); *Dov'è la mia patria* (1949); *Tal cour di frut* (1953); *Dal diario, 1945–47* (1954); *Sonetto primaverile, 1953* (1960); *Passione e ideologia* (1960); *L'odore dell'India* (1962); *Alì dagli occhi azzurri* (1965); *Teorema* (1968)

BIBLIOGRAPHY: Fortini, F., "Le poesie italiane di questi anni," in *Il Menabò*, Vol. II (1960); *Aut aut*, X (Jan.-March 1961), contains articles by E. Paci, G. Pampaloni, G. Bàrberi-Squarotti, E. Sanguineti, S. Pantano; Leonetti, F., "P., compte rendu," *Paragone*, XII (1961); Carella, A., "Un apôtre incroyant: P. P. P.," *TR* No. 203 (Dec. 1964); Ferretti, G. C., *Letteratura e ideologia: Bassani, Cassola, P.* (1964), pp. 163–356, 368–75; Asor-Rosa, A., *Scrittori e popolo* (1965), pp. 261–68; Stack, O., *P. on P.* (1969)

GIOVANNI SINICROPI

PASTERNAK, Boris Leonidovich

Russian poet and novelist, b. 10 Feb. 1890, Moscow; d. 30 May 1960, Peredelkino

P.'s father (a friend of Lev Tolstoi [q.v.]) was a well-known painter, his mother, a musician. P. studied law at the University of Moscow. For a time he seriously thought of a musical career, but then settled upon philosophy, which he studied both in Moscow and in Marburg, Germany, then the center of neo-Kantian idealism.

Though he was close to modernist poetic

circles after 1907, he did not start to publish his poetry until 1912. In 1913 he joined the Tsentrifuga, a group of moderate futurists (*see* futurism).

During World War I, unfit for military service, P. was a tutor for a wealthy family and later worked as a clerk in a chemical factory in the Urals. After the Russian Revolution in 1917 P. worked at the library of the People's Commissariat for Enlightenment and Education. Briefly he affiliated himself with the organization LEF (Levy Front Iskusstva—a group of futurists who wanted to reform literature and all the other arts), later breaking with it, because he did not share the LEF ideas of utilitarian art.

When P. won the Nobel Prize for Literature in 1958, he first gladly accepted it. Later, however, after he was subjected by the Soviet press to a campaign of vituperation and was expelled by his colleagues (the majority of whom had never read the novel) from the Union of Soviet Writers he dissociated himself from the prize. Despite these circumstances he lived in Peredelkino, the writer's colony near Moscow, until his death.

P.'s first book of verse, *Bliznetz v tuchakh* (1914), was followed by *Poverkh barerov* (1917; republished with addition of new poems in 1929).

P. became famous after writing, in 1917, his third book of verse *Sestra moya zhizn* (1922; Sister: My Life, 1967). The poems of P.'s *Sestra moya zhizn* are highly original in their descriptions of nature and the tranquil life, which are perceived from unusual points of view. The love theme forms a counterpoint to nature. Emotions and moods are communicated indirectly, through descriptions of rains, thunderstorms, snowfalls, and the like.

P.'s next book, *Temy i variatzii* (1923), written in a darker mood, shows greater maturity. The love theme is presented in its more dramatic aspects; here P. emphasizes the motifs of lovers' conflicts and separations. This volume includes poems about literary men such as Shakespeare, Goethe, and Pushkin. A technique similar to that of musical variation is often used.

The prose works that make up the book *Rasskazy* (1925) defy classification. Plotless and atmospheric, the subject is usually just a pretext for something else. "Il Tratto di Apelle" (written in 1915) is a humorous love story with an Italian background in which the poet Heinrich Heine is the hero. "Pis'ma iz Tuly" (written in 1918) tells about the protagonist's struggle with his conscience and of his search for the meaning of life. "Detstvo Lyuvers" (written in 1918; Am., The Adolescence of Zhanya Luvers, 1961; Eng., The Childhood of Luvers, n.d.), which is among P.'s finest works, is praised by many as a contemporary classic. In this, life is presented as it is perceived by a girl who is growing out of adolescence. (The names of Rilke and Proust (qq.v.) frequently come up when this story is talked about.) "Vozdushnyye puti" (written in 1924) is a tragic story about a lost child. (P. used this title for the second edition of these four works, published in 1933.)

Less successful were P.'s attempts to write on revolutionary topics—Leitenant Shmidt (1926) and Devyat'sot pyatyi god (1927).

Okhrannaya gramota (1931), P.'s first autobiography, starts with an account of meeting Rilke—to whom the book is dedicated—on a train. P. then tells about meetings with the composer Scriabin, Neo-Kantian philosopher Hermann Cohen (1842–1918) of Marburg University, and the poet Mayakovski (q.v.), each of which is presented as an important stage on P.'s way to poetry through music and philosophy. The book is heavily endowed with closely observed details and imagery, and the prose is exquisitely orchestrated. The narrative is frequently interrupted by lyrical and philosophical passages. (Among the latter is P.'s definition of art as "a dislocation of reality, made by emotion").

In the poems of Vtoroye rozhdeniye (1932), P. touches on the theme of the individual versus communism, but he does not treat it in the party-prescribed way. Stylistically, the book is a step toward simplicity of imagery and more traditional rhythms, a development present in all of P.'s later poetry.

Severely criticized by communist critics for his "esotericism" and "apolitical attitude" after the publication of his long autobiographical poem Spektorski (1932), P. wrote no original works for about ten years. From 1933 to 1943 he published translations only—collected in Gruzinskiye liriki and Izbrannyye perevody (1940). Among the works he translated were Shakespeare's tragedies and sonnets, Schiller's Maria Stuart, Heinrich von Kleist's Prinz von Homburg, and poems by Rilke, Verlaine, and Keats.

During World War II, P. published Na rannikh poyezdakh (1943), a slender book of new poems in the simpler idiom that he had

started to develop in the 1930's. This was followed by Zemnoi prostor (1945). Both contain poems about the war.

Then, in 1954, the literary magazine Znamya published ten poems (The Poems of Doctor Zhivago, 1965), that purported to be by one Doctor Zhivago, the protagonist of P.'s new novel. The novel itself, however, because of its ideology, has never been published in Russia, but the Soviet literary authorities could of course do little to prevent the publication of Doctor Zhivago abroad. After its first appearance in Italian translation in 1958, it was rapidly translated into other languages (Eng., 1958). (Doktor Zhivago was published in Russian in 1961 by the University of Michigan Press.) The novel quickly became a best-seller outside the Iron Curtain.

Doctor Zhivago is the account of the life of a Russian intellectual, Yurii Zhivago, a doctor and a poet, during the first three decades of the 20th c. A broad epic picture of Russia is developed as the background to Zhivago's family life, his creative ecstasies, his love for Lara (another man's wife), his emotional upheavals, wanderings, and moments of happiness. Though the novel ends with Zhivago's decline and death as a result of what P. saw as the dehumanization of life that prevailed in the postrevolution years, the epilogue is full of expectations of the freedom that is to come. The poems that end the novel are an optimistic exegi monumentum ("I built a monument").

Throughout Doctor Zhivago, the individual is juxtaposed against mechanical group thinking; and the ideas that are voiced come close to those of reverence for life. For this nonrealistic novel, P. has drawn eclectically from various novelistic traditions and techniques. Like Dante's Commedia, it can be read on different levels. Though P. has here liberally used New Testament symbols (e.g., those of Resurrection), his concept of the historical and moral essence of Christianity is highly individual. Written in a poetic prose, a lyrical undercurrent always accompanies the action. Though the novel is rich and infinitely varied in style, it indicates that P. was turning away from his previous mannered prose and was developing a new simplicity.

In 1958 there appeared in French translation a second autobiography (Eng., I Remember, 1959), written originally as a preface to a collection of P.'s poetry that was never published in Russia. In it P. makes a revaluation of his artistic past.

BORIS PASTERNAK

P.'s last poems appeared in Paris in 1959 under the title *Kogda razgulayetsya.*

P. was a lyric poet *par excellence,* an individualist, and a romantic impressionist. His poetic genealogy can be traced to Mikhail Lermontov (1814–41), Afanasii Fet (1820–92), and Fiodor Tyutchev (1803–1873), as well as to Nikolaus Lenau (1802–1850) and Heinrich von Kleist (1777–1811). He has been compared with John Donne (1572–1631) and G. M. Hopkins (1844–89). P.'s most astonishing qualities are freshness and spontaneity. (The Russian critic D. S. Mirsky wrote that P.'s poetry gave an impression of a man who is "seeing the world for the first time.") They coexist in rare combination with a sharp analytical mind, with sophistication, and with a rich, profound, Western-oriented cultural background. He treats reality with "passionate objectivity."

P. is probably the only modern Russian poet who successfully, and in an original way, blended the best contributions of three main movements in modern Russian poetry: he assimilated the subtle word magic of the Russian symbolists (see symbolism); he developed the acmeists' keen eye for details of the surrounding world; and he learned from the futurists his colloquial diction and intonation, his surrealistic (*see* surrealism) imagery, and his predilection for purely verbal effects. P., perhaps because of his study of philosophy, was consistently interested in problems of time, space, and form. In addition, the irrational is an important element in his poetry.

P.'s reputation of being a "difficult" poet and a "poet's poet" is to be attributed to his technique. His poems, often developing on two levels, give simultaneously two motifs, two sides of a theme, two *raccourcis* of one image. His elliptic verse is surcharged with contrasts in vocabulary and unexpected metaphors that follow each other in free association. Often his approach to a topic is so unusual that "realistic descriptions look like tropes" (C. M. Bowra) and familiar things take on a new and strange look. P.'s diction includes prosaicisms and even technical words. The power and variety of his rhythms are partly achieved through a capricious syntax. His dissonant rhymes are subtle and original.

As complexities of P.'s poetic devices deprived him of mass appeal and wide success, so his independent attitude made him a favored target for communist critics' attacks, who accused him of being aloof and found "decadent" even his brilliant translation of Goethe's *Faust* (1953).

In reality, P.'s poetry is indeed healthy and vigorous. It should also be affirmed that P. was always sincere in his acceptance of the revolution, and that he was never wanting in interest in or sympathy with the problems of contemporary life. He did, however, steadfastly refuse to mix poetry and politics. Moreover, he insisted on defending his own values whatever the official values handed down by the party, thus retaining his personal and creative integrity.

Whatever the current Soviet tendency to underrate or ignore P., his reputation in Soviet literary circles has always been high, and many critics, during the last decades of his lifetime, agreed in considering him the greatest living Russian poet and placing him (according to S. Schimanski) "in the forefront of contemporary European poetry—with Eliot, Rilke, Valéry, García Lorca, and Yeats [qq.v.]." P.'s influence on modern Russian poetry—e.g., Tikhonov, Bargitzki, Selvinski, Mandelstamm, Bryusov, Voznesenski, Marina Tzvetayeva (qq.v.)—is enormous.

The first complete edition of P.'s works, *Sochineniya,* was published in the United States by the University of Michigan Press in 1961. This edition consists of four volumes edited by Vladimir Veidle: *Stikhi i poemy, 1912–1932,* a collection of verses and poems; *Proza, 1915–1958,* which includes P.'s novels, short stories, and autobiographical works; *Stikhi,* verses written between 1930 and 1957, children's verses, and essays and speeches; and *Doktor Zhivago.*

FURTHER WORKS: *Stikhotvoreniya v odnom tome* (1933); *Stikhotvoreniya i poemy* (1965); *Pis'ma k gruzinskim* (n.d., Letters to Georgian Friends, 1968). **Selected English translations:** *The Collected Prose Works* (2 parts, 1945); *Selected Poems* (1946); *Selected Writings: Safe Conduct, An Autobiography, and Other Writings* (1949); *An Essay in Autobiography* (1959); *The Poetry of B. P., 1917–1959* (1959); *Poems* (1959); *Prose and Poems* (1959); *Poems, 1945–1960* (1960); *Poems, 1955–1959* (1960); *Fifty Poems* (1963); *Poems* (1964); *Three Letters from B. P.* (1967)

BIBLIOGRAPHY: Ehrenburg, I., "B. L. P.," *Portrety russkikh poetov* (1922), pp. 127–30; Tzvetayeva, M., "Svetovoi liven," *Epopeya,* No. 3 (1922); Leznev, A., "B. P.," *Sovremenniki* (1927), pp. 32–54; Schimanski, S., "The Prose

Works of B. P.," in *The Collected Prose Works* (1945), pp. 11–44; Stepun, F., "B. L. P.," *Novyi Zhurnal*, LVI (1959); Conquest, R., *Courage of Genius: The P. Affair* (1961); Payne, R., *The Three Worlds of B. P.* (1961); Plank, D. L., *P.'s Lyric* (1966); Rowland, M., and P., *P.'s Dr. Zhivago* (1967)

VLADIMIR MARKOV

P. is a great poet. At the moment he is the greatest of all: the majority of the present poets *have been,* some of them *are,* but he alone *will be.* Because, actually he does not as yet exist: mumblings, twitter, odds-and-ends—he exists entirely in the tomorrow! These are the choking incoherencies of an infant, and that infant is the World. Incoherences. Breathlessness. P. does not speak, he has no time to finish, he tears himself apart, as if his chest were too small: a--ch! He does not yet know our words: instead there is something insular-babyish-primeval and incomprehensible, and overwhelming. . . . It is not P. who is an infant, but the world in him. I would be inclined to place P. within the very first days of creation: of the first rivers, first glances, first storms. He was created *before* Adam.

Marina Tzvetayeva, commenting on Pasternak's *Sister: My Life.* As quoted by Vladimir Veidlé in *Boris Pasternak: Stikhi 1936–1959* (1961)

P's position is the position, consequently, of an idealist and formalist moving in the direction contrary to that of Soviet art. It is not surprising that he is supported by the enemies of the Soviet people. The English professor C. M. Bowra, for example, speaking of P.'s poetry, almost chokes with enthusiasm. "Remarkable receptiveness"; "a great talent at transmitting the feelings"; "a dynamic perception of life"; "the powerful poet of Russia"—the article of the highly esteemed professor is replete with such utterances. . . .

P.'s artistic work is the most blatant example of rotten decadence. He himself, apparently sensing his alienation from the people, has ceased publishing new poems.

A. Tarasenkov, in *Znamya* (Oct. 1949), p. 163

It is our view that Doctor Zhivago is, in fact, the incarnation of a definite type of Russian intellectual of that day, a man fond of talking about the sufferings of the people and able to discuss them, but unable to cure those sufferings in either the literal or the figurative sense of the word. He is the type of man consumed with a sense of his own singularity, his intrinsic value, a man far removed from the people and ready to betray them in difficult times, to cut himself off from their sufferings and their cause. His is the type of the "highly intellectual" Philistine, tame when left alone but capable in thought as well as in deed of inflicting

any wrong whatsoever on the people just as soon as he feels the slightest wrong—real or imagined —has been done to him.

You are no stranger to symbolism, and the death, or rather the passing, of Doctor Zhivago in the late 1920's is for you, we feel, a symbol of the death of the Russian intelligentsia, destroyed by the revolution. Yes, it must be admitted that for the Doctor Zhivago you depicted in the novel the climate of the revolution is deadly. And our disagreement with you is not over this but, as we have already mentioned, over something quite different.

To you, Doctor Zhivago is the peak of the spirit of the Russian intelligentsia.

To us, he is its swamp.

To you, the members of the Russian intelligentsia who took a different path from the one Doctor Zhivago took and who chose the course of serving the people, betrayed their true calling, committed spiritual suicide, and created nothing of value.

To us they found their true calling on precisely that path and continued to serve the people and to do for the people precisely the things that had been done for them—in laying the groundwork for the revolution—by the best segment of the Russian intelligentsia, which was then, and is today, infinitely remote from that conscious break with the people and ideological regnancy of which your Doctor Zhivago is the bearer.

The editors of *Literaturnaya Gazeta,* in their rejection letter. Quoted in *The Current Digest of the Soviet Press* (3 Dec. 1958), pp. 7–8, 11

Doctor Zhivago will, I believe, come to stand as one of the great events in man's literary and moral history. Nobody could have written it in a totalitarian state and turned it loose on the world who did not have the courage of genius.

Edmund Wilson, "Doctor Life and His Guardian Angel," *The New Yorker* (15 Nov. 1958)

In this novel [Doctor Zhivago] of a hundred memorable characters there is a third whose significance is central, a woman named Lara Guishar. Among the figures who converge in the opening pages are Pasha Antipov and Lara. When still a schoolgirl she is seduced by a rich lawyer, Komarovsky, a man who was also, by a coincidence, partly responsible for the death of Zhivago's father. It is difficult to speak of Lara without vulgarising the conception. She evades Komarovsky, tries to shoot him at a party where Zhivago (who doesn't yet know her) is also present, and marries Antipov, who later changes his name to Strelnikov. A union between Zhivago and Lara is written into the pattern from the start, and their life together is all hunger, illegality and anonymity, a sort of holist Resistance against revolutionary abstraction. For Lara assumes a vast burden of meaning. She is life, the principle Zhivago worships, and thence she is Russia, betrayed in different ways by the Komarovskys and the Strelnikovs; she has a simple, direct relationship with reality or God, and is capable of a beautiful repentance when her demon is exorcised. P. lovingly enlarges the Magdalen theme. None of this is as crude as I have to make it sound; there is here and elsewhere an element of parable, and P. believes that a story becomes valid only when it acquires the qualities of myth. The wholeness he tries to achieve must carry its own explanations; and he succeeds so far that the terrible history his book contains becomes, like death in tragedy, a part of the complex and irreducible beauty of the whole image.

F. Kermode, in *The Spectator*
(5 Sept. 1958), p. 315

The tumult, the wealth and grandiosity of events are certainly not the essential matter in *Doctor Zhivago*. And even less the depiction of solid, well-rounded characters, the joy of describing life and making it palpitate which fills Tolstoy with such exuberance. In P., there are on one side the events and the vicissitudes of the individual characters, on the other—as a constant counterpoint—a certain ecstasy of the spirit outside of the immediate reality, an ecstasy found in the vision of universal life and in the effort to understand in human terms that which is happening. There is, more than a religious, a mystical feeling for nature, a powerful and proud "yes" said to life, despite everything. But there is not a single smile, nor a single moment of joy, save for the joy of freedom during the first days of the revolution, and this is an impersonal rapture more than a true joy. The events are narrated in every detail, with bare simplicity; but they seem far-off and muffled, plunged in a kind of twilight; terrible as they are, they occur and pass away in a sort of strange silence and tranquillity, almost as though even their terror cannot disturb that which exists at the bottom of things and of the human spirit. As a result, they give us the feeling of memories which rise to the surface of consciousness, sharp yet insubstantial: shadows which ask to be placated by understanding. And they are shadows which also are characters: almost pure names, with nothing physical about them. What one is told about them is solely the part they play in each other's lives, the way in which they are twisted and beaten by the storm, a few of the essential expressions of their spirit, a few of their thoughts and judgments. Their existences are so disordered and torn to pieces that nothing is left to them (and, in particular, to the protagonist) but the pure distance of the spirit from circumstances, the meditative solitude in which they endure the raging of destiny. At the end, we know that all that has been told was told so as to describe this distance and this solitude: Doctor Zhivago's conscience and how it managed, by resisting death, to remain human.

N. Chiaromonte, in *Partisan Review*
(Winter 1958), p. 129

[*The Childhood of Luvers*] is a story that has no real plot, a tale of a girl who has just crossed the threshold of puberty, built up from innumerable careful observations, without definite beginning or end. This is a piece of prose which is unique in Russian literature. In method the story is related to the works of Proust. Of *The Childhood of Luvers*, and indeed of all P.'s early prose, could be said what Ortega y Gasset said of Marcel Proust, "Proust's characters are without outline: they are unsubstantial wraiths, intellectual images which change constantly in a breath of air or a ray of light. Proust is undoubtedly 'the explorer' of the human soul in the Stendhal tradition." The detailed description of environment, the psychological observation of emotions, is in P.'s case never verbose or over-protracted. On the contrary, in the concentrated intensity of his style each word is laden with deep meaning—almost overladen, in fact. This tightly packed method of presentation demands almost too much from the reader. There are no points at which he can relax and digest what he has read; there are no links, no explanations. P. tries to produce in the reader a certain definite sensation, and he omits everything that he considers superfluous to the achievement of this aim. But in spite of all these difficulties, and its strange and unusual style, *The Childhood of Luvers* was to remain, in its pure translucence and gentle charm, his most beautiful and important early work in prose. When this story appeared ... in a volume of P.'s prose, the critics praised it as one of the most important pieces of prose of the first period of Soviet art.

Gerd Ruge, *Pasternak: A Pictorial Biography* (1959), p. 41

P. surprises not only by a violent association of disparate elements, but by the even more violent dissociation of each one of them from the frame of reference to which it naturally belongs. The ripe pear which one of his poems describes while falling to the ground along with its leafy stem and torn branch can be taken as an emblem of his art. Hence the frequency in his verse of such words and ideas as "fracture" or "breach." At the end of the closing poem of the cycle "Rupture" (meaning here a lovers' quarrel, or their break), even the opening of a window is equated with the opening of a vein. In the same piece the poet transfers the trauma of life to an uncreated thing: for instance to the piano, which "licks its foam," as if it were a human being in an epileptic fit. Yet even in metaphors like these the poet transcends both pathos and bathos, reshaping the disorder of experience into a vision of his own. If he succeeds in doing so, it is because in his poetry (as he said in *The Safe-Conduct*) the author remains silent and lets the image speak. In this ability to infuse words with passion, rather than passion with words, P. has no rival among his contemporaries, and, among the poets of the previous generation, he yields only to Aleksandr Blok.

Renato Poggioli, *The Poets of Russia,*
1890–1930 (1960)

From the very beginning he possessed a very sharp and lively feeling—not for the word [the literary language], but rather for words: for their scaly or slippery, or satinlike bodies, for their objective meaning, that is, the meaning that pertains to the immediate perception of objects. This feeling possessed him entirely; it interfered with friendship or enmity between words, with their relation to thought that unifies objects, with their arrangements in sense clusters or layers. His words always interfere with his artistic language, preventing the language from expressing itself, or reducing such expression to something insignificant or accidental.

Vladimir Veidlé, "Boris Pasternak and Modernism," in *Boris Pasternak: Stikhi i poemy, 1912–1932* (1961)

From one day to the next, from one line to another, P. reiterates untiringly about the aliveness of nature that brings salvation and conquers all. Trees, grass, clouds, brooks are endowed in his verse with the exalted right to speak in the name of life itself, to turn us to the path of goodness and truth.... Landscape in the work of P. often becomes not a depicted object, but the subject of action, the main mover and protagonist of events. The entire fullness of life in the variety of its manifestations is contained in a fragment of nature which, it seems, is capable of accomplishing deeds, of feeling and of thinking.

Andrei Sinyavski, Introduction to *Boris Pasternak: Stikhotvoreniya i poemy* (1965)

PATON, Alan Stewart

South African writer, b. 11 Jan. 1903, Pietermaritzburg, Natal

P.'s writing is identified with the racial strife of South Africa, but he interprets the race struggle as a larger revolt of man against domination—against dominating and being dominated. This view marked his innovations as principal of Diep Kloof Reformatory near Johannesburg, an experience that provided the material for several short stories and moved him to political action in the apartheid-opposed Liberal Association, of which he was a founder (1953) and president. The poles of his political views and literary themes are the same: the negative, a distrust of institutionalized power; the positive, a belief in the power of love expressed as human brotherhood.

The subject of an early, uncompleted novel

—Christ's return to South Africa—anticipates the material of P.'s published novels. His first published novel, *Cry, the Beloved Country* (1948), is about racial tensions, but its primary theme is the brotherhood of man. His second, *Too Late the Phalarope* (1953), is about a man destroyed because of an affair with a native girl. Again the primary object is to indict the inhumanity of racial separateness as institutionalized in such legislation as the Immorality Act, which prohibits sexual relations between black and white.

The death of his wife in 1967 turned P. to a self-searching analysis of domination in the complex structure of marriage, *Kontakion for You Departed* (1969). In this novel P. attempted to define marital communion as the sacramental point of transition from what is at best a flawed agape existing among mankind toward the perfection of the Creator's love.

Critics often overlook this thematic preoccupation when they object that humanitarian zeal sometimes reduces P.'s fiction to the level of propaganda. The charge is in any case more applicable to the volume of short stories, *Tales from a Troubled Land* (1961; Eng. Debbie, Go Home), than to the novels.

The effectiveness of these novels derives from the language—simple, seemingly unadorned, but modified by the rhythms of African languages and Afrikaans—and an intricate symbolic interweaving of land, people, and theme.

FURTHER WORKS: *South Africa Today* (1953); *The Land and People of South Africa* (1955); *South Africa in Transition* (with Dan Weiner; 1956); *Hope for South Africa* (1959); *Hofmeyr* (1964); *South African Tragedy* (1965); *Sponono* (with Krishna Shah; 1965); *Instrument of Thy Peace* (1968); *The Long View* (1968)

BIBLIOGRAPHY: Anon., *TLS*, 23 Oct. 1948, and 28 Aug. 1953; Baker, S., "P.'s Beloved Country and the Morality of Geography," *CE*, XIX (Nov. 1957), 56–61; Callan, E., *A. P.* (1968)

MANLY JOHNSON

PAULHAN, Jean

French literary critic, essayist, novelist, b. 2 Dec. 1884, Nîmes; d. 9 Oct. 1968, Melun

After receiving his *licence-ès-lettres* at the Sorbonne, P. spent several years prospecting for gold and teaching on the island of Madagascar. Upon his return to Paris, he became a professor of Malagasy at the École des Langues Orientales. From 1925 to 1940 he worked for the *Nouvelle Revue Française,* succeeding Rivière (q.v.) as its editor in 1925. During World War II, he was instrumental in launching the clandestine *Les Lettres Françaises* and Editions de Minuit, and he cooperated with the French resistance movement. Later, however, he approved the return of those writers who had been collaborators.

P. was the recipient of the Grand Prix de Littérature de l'Académie Française in 1945 and of the Grand Prix de la Ville de Paris in 1951. In 1953 he resumed his responsibilities as editor of the *Nouvelle Nouvelle Revue Française* and as a consultant to the Gallimard publishing house. In these capacities, he exercised a profound influence on new talents, whom he discovered and encouraged. He was elected to the French Academy in 1964. It was not until the last years of his life, when his collected works (*Œuvres complètes,* 1966 ff.) began to be published, that his writing won for him the widespread recognition that he so well deserved.

P. wrote the preface to the scandalous *L'Histoire d'O.,* which was published under the pseudonym Pauline Réage, and he was for a long time presumed to be the author of the novel. The book was, however, apparently written by a woman long associated with him as friend and secretary.

P.'s interest in and exploration of the problem of language, his lifelong preoccupation, was stimulated by his sojourn as a young man in Madagascar. He brought back from there *Les Hain-Tenys* (1913), which contains the Malagasy songs and proverbs he had been collecting. Their form and brevity bring Picasso to mind.

P. continued to be dominated by the idea of language when writing *Le Guerrier appliqué* (1917), *Jacob Cow, le pirate* (1922), *Le Pont traversé* (1922), *La Guérison sévère* (1925), and *Aytré qui perd l'habitude* (1926). The early *Le Guerrier appliqué,* a curious war tale inspired by P.'s experiences during World War I, illustrates, through subtle reasonings, the interplay between the realities of a soldier's life and his dreams or reveries, the search for liberation through thought and language.

Complicated and mysterious, all these tales reveal, in the subtle analysis of the subconscious, how at best language merely approximates, or screens, the essence of thought and feeling. P. saw language as a trap, and, in his demand for a means of expression that was more exact and authentic, he rejected the eloquent, the comonplace, and the phrasing that reflects the thinking of acquired social habits.

Ultimately, to achieve his ideal, P. participated in what has been characterized as the "terror" of cubism and surrealism (q.v.), or, as one critic prefers to call it, "irrealism." Hostile toward the rhetorical, he favored the use of a hermetic and audacious vocabulary, one more consistent with the kind used by those who emulated Henry Miller (q.v.) or the Marquis de Sade.

Reveling in paradox and always ready to correct a previous metamorphosis, P. realized that extremes breed new extremes, that the "terror" he had helped to make happen had paralyzed or handicapped the writer's creativity. To remedy this, he later did a *volte-face* in the hope of restoring liberty to the writer and proceeded to demonstrate, in the voluminous essay *Les Fleurs de Tarbes* (1941), how rhetoric could be used effectively.

À demain la poésie (1947), probably P.'s best and clearest work, is a denunciation of those who renounced completely the accepted means of expression and thought to embrace wholeheartedly the dream, automatic writing, and the irrational. While words are dangerous, demonstrably so in P.'s writing, they are undeniably at the root of thought.

Absorbed with problems of language and poetics, into whose meaning and scope he inquired, P. wrote with enigmatic precision, using in his essays and tales a style that is at once, in its associations and affectations, subtle and elegant. Like Mallarmé and Valéry (q.v.), he insisted on an absolute unity of word and meaning, of form and content. Like them, too, he fought relentlessly for the autonomy of literature. An iconoclast, he was an enemy of mediocrity, a friend to innovators, and a guardian of the avant-garde.

FURTHER WORKS: *Entretiens sur des faits divers* (1933); *Clef de la poésie* (1944); *Sept causes célèbres* (1946); *Petit Guide d'un voyage en Suisse* (1947); *De la Paille et du grain* (1948); *Lettre aux directeurs de la résistance* (1952)

BIBLIOGRAPHY: Toesca, M., *J. P., l'écrivain appliqué* (1948); Carmody, F. M., "J. P.'s Imaginative Writings," *Occidental,* Nov.–Dec. 1949, pp. 28–34; Lefebvre, M. J., *J. P., une philosophie et une pratique de l'expression et de la réflexion* (1949); Bousquet, J., *Les Capitales; ou, de Jean Duns Scot à J. P.* (1955); Judrin, R., *La Vocation transparente de J. P.* (1961); Lévy, Y., "J. P.," *Preuves*, No. 153 (1963), pp. 3–21; Elsen, C., "J. P.," *Revue de Paris*, LXXIV (July–Aug., 1966), 152–53; Blanzet, J., *Esquisses Littéraires*, 17 Oct. 1968, p. 3

SIDNEY D. BRAUN

PAUSTOVSKI, Konstantin Georgiyevich

Soviet-Russian novelist, biographer, and dramatist, b. 31 May 1892, Moscow; d. there, 14 July 1968

P., the son of a liberal railway official, attended the University of Kiev. His first story was printed in 1911. P.'s work experiences were varied: he was a streetcar conductor, medical assistant during World War I, factory worker, seaman, newspaper reporter. In the post-Stalin era P. was an advocate of the younger liberal writers who were struggling to be allowed to write and publish more freely.

P.'s early writing—*Minetoza* (1927), *Romantiki* (written between 1916 and 1923; published, 1935), *Blistayushchiye oblaka* (1929)—is dominated by romantic exoticism and the fantastic. His characters, situations, and conflicts seem far from reality, and his works project an artificial, somewhat bookish picture of life that shows his familiarity with non-Russian literatures.

P. the journalist undoubtedly influenced P. the novelist. The magnitude of the communist government's achievement in the U.S.S.R. made an impact on P.'s literary attitude. The themes of some of his best books—*Kara-Bugaz* (1932) and *Kolkhida* (1934)—can be found in his newspaper articles. These novels about the Russian frontier were well-received by the public and the critics. *Kara-Bugaz* was favorably reviewed by Nadezhda Konstantinovna Krupskaya (Lenin's wife), Gorki (q.v.), and S. Marshak.

In these works of the 1930's the romantic antithesis between the individual and society had disappeared, for literature, as P. then saw it, could no longer be divorced from everyday life. The motif of the subjugation of nature runs parallel to that of man's self-transformation. The quest for what is most noble in human nature is basic to P.'s novels of those years.

Though Soviet literary critics feel that P.'s work is often marred by overembellishment

and sentimentality, his keen aptitude for capturing the core of people and situations is undeniable. Not an innovator, P. adopted the form of the traditional novel. Through the descriptions of the Russian countryside that he loved, P. sought to elevate his reader's sense of beauty.

P. also wrote biographies: *Sud'ba Charlya Lonsevilya* (1930), *Isaak Levitan* (1937), *Orest Kiprenski* (1937), *Aleksei Tolstoi* (1939), *Taras Shevchenko* (1941), *Zhizn' Grina* (1939–56). Romantically endeavoring as he does to extract the poetic essence of his subjects and to reveal their unrequited dreams, his idealized portraits are always extremely appealing.

In the eyes of many, P.'s high point of literary achievement is his last work, the unfinished *Povest' o zhizni* ("The Story of a Life," 6 vols., 1947 ff.; I, Childhood and Schooldays, 1964; II, Slow Approach of Thunder, 1965; III, In That Dawn, 1967; IV, Years of Hope, 1969). In this ambitious, beautifully written autobiographical cycle, P. narrated a half-century of prerevolutionary and Soviet life through superbly reported, moving scenes. The special quality of this work comes from the fact that P. was a good and gentle man with unshakable optimism about life.

The publication of these autobiographical volumes in translation brought international acclaim to P., who had hitherto been relatively unknown to Western readers.

FURTHER WORKS: *Morski nabroski* (1926); *Vstrechniye korabli* (1928); *Chernoye more* (1936; The Black Gulf, 1946); *Severnaya povest* (1939); *Poruchnik Lermontov* (1941); *Povest' o lesakh* (1948); *Nash sovremennik: Pushkin* (1949); *Zolotoya rosa* (1955); *Brosok na yug* (1961); *Zolotoi Lin'* (1966); *Nayedine s Osen'fu* (1967); *Sobraniye sochinenii* (1967). **Selected English translation:** *Selected Stories by K. P.* (1967)

BIBLIOGRAPHY: Achkasova, L. S., *Ranneye tvorchestvo K. P. 1916–1932* (1960); Trefilova, G. P., "K. G. P." in *Istoriya russkoi sovyetskoi literatury*, Vol. 3 (1961), pp. 341–62; Bondarev, Yurii, "A Master of Prose," *Soviet Literature*, No. 10 (1962), pp. 166–69; Yglesias, J., "Spirit of Valerian," *Nation*, No. 198 (11 May 1964), pp. 488–90; Bliven, N., "Books," *New Yorker*, No. 40 (2 Jan. 1965), pp. 70–72; Il'in, V. S., *K. P.* (1967); Urman, D., "K. P., Marcel Proust, and the Golden Rose of Memory," *Canadian Slavic Studies*, II (1968), 311–26

OLGA PRJEVALINSKAYA-FERRER

ALAN PATON

ESARE PAVESE

PAVESE, Cesare

Italian novelist and short-story writer, b. 9 Sept. 1908, San Stefano Belbo; d. 27 Aug. 1950, Turin

P. was born in an isolated village of the Piedmontese foothills, where his father (a court official in Turin) owned some property. This circumstance of birth was to leave a special mark on his work, since throughout his life P. was to remain emotionally torn between his identification with his unsophisticated birthplace and his attraction to the world-oriented, avant-garde city of Turin, where he received a humanistic high-school education, and where as a university student he specialized in modern intellectual trends in Italy and abroad.

Although P. hardly traveled at all and was never to visit the United States, he concentrated intensively on North American literature (*La letteratura americana e altri saggi,* 1951) and his first literary publication (1932) was a translation of Melville's *Moby Dick.* His later translations of Joyce, Gertrude Stein, Steinbeck, and Dos Passos (qq.v.) were influential in introducing contemporary English and American works to Italian readers. After teaching for a while, he helped to found the publishing house of Einaudi, at which he was an editor until his death.

This somewhat withdrawn life was interrupted only sporadically by political *engagement.* His first publications offended the fascist regime, and he was forced to spend the year 1935 in *confino* in Calabria. From 1943 to 1945 he lived among the partisans in the Nazi-occupied Piedmontese foothills. Later, like so many Italian intellectuals moved by social problems, he sympathized with communism and contributed to the *Humanità,* but he soon broke away from this sphere. By 1950 his literary reputation was firmly established, especially on the basis of his novel, *La luna e i falò* (1950), so that his suicide came as a general surprise.

The explanation for P.'s inner tragedy is to be sought, not in the facts of his external life, but in his poetry and in his journals. In the same journals P. articulated his poetic theory.

The leitmotif of P.'s work is man's inability to truly communicate. This already formed the core of his first volume of poetry, *Lavorare stanca* (1936), in which the experiences of the young man who exchanges his country hillsides for city streets lead, in P.'s own words, "to

even more tragic loneliness and to the end of youth."

In 1938 and 1939, P. drew upon his experiences during his exile in Calabria to provide variations on the same theme in the novella *Il carcere* (1949).

In the novellas that he wrote after 1939— *Paesi tuoi* (1941); *La spiaggia* (1942); *La bella estate* (1949)—he nevertheless seemed anxious to broaden his picture of reality and to effect, not without a social slant, confrontations between different classes of society. At this time he could be considered an adherent of the *neoverismo* school.

In *Dialoghi con Leucò* (written in 1945 and 1946; published, 1947)—a work in which conversations about the human condition, couched in classical terms but of contemporary relevance, are held betwen mortals and Olympians —P. revealed, however, that what concerned him was more than naturalism (q.v.). Primarily, that is, he was seeking to achieve a grasp of "constitutive, supercorporeal reality," a perception of "inner landscape." His medium was memory, through which he believed he could discover the mythos of earliest experience, of the singular loci of childhood.

In P.'s last works—notably in *La casa in collina, Il carcere,* and in *La luna e i falò*— this is his main objective. His unrhetorical language, classical in its clarity and full of restrained lyricism, often brings him very close to it, even though the composition is sometimes disjointed, and the problem of man's inability to communicate is not really solved.

P.'s novels and short stories are autobiographical only in a very direct sense. The secret arteries of P.'s existence, its predicaments, weaknesses, hopes and metaphysical yearnings, and final desperate decline, with constitutive solitariness as the central theme, are laid bare in his journals (posthumously published in 1952 as *Diario, 1935–1950: Il mestiere di vivere*). The intensity, remorselessness, and precise clear-sightedness of the conversation with himself make this a moving human document and the masterpiece on which P.'s claims to literary immortality rest securely.

See Works for information about translations.

WORKS: *Lavorare stanca* (1936); *Paesi tuoi* (1941; The Harvesters, 1962); *La spiaggia* (1942; The Beach, 1963, in The Beach and A Great Fire); *Feria d'agosto* (1946); *Il compagno* (1947; The Comrade, 1959); *Dialoghi con*

Leucò (1947; Dialogues with Leucò, 1964); *La Bella estate* (1949, in *La bella estate; The Beautiful Summer*, 1955, in The Political Prisoner and The Beautiful Summer); *Tra donne sole* (1949), in *La bella estate;* Among Women Only, 1953); *Il diavolo sulle colline* (1949, in *La bella estate;* The Devil in the Hills, 1954); *Prima che il gallo canti* (1949; contains *La casa in collina* and *Il carcere); La casa in collina* (1949, in *Prima che il gallo canti;* The House on the Hill, 1956); *Il carcere* (1949, in *Prima che il gallo canti;* The Political Prisoner, 1955, in The Political Prisoner and The Beautiful Summer); *La luna e i falò* (1949; The Moon and the Bonfire, 1952); *La letteratura americana e altri saggi* (1951); *Verrà la morte e avrà i tuoi occhi* (1951); *Diario, 1935–1950: Il mestiere di vivere* (1952; The Burning Brand: Diaries, 1935–1950, 1961); *Notte di festa* (1953; The Festival Night, 1964, in The Festival Night, and Other Stories); *Fuoco grande* (1959; A Great Fire, 1963, in The Beach and a Great Fire); *Racconti* (1960); *Lettere 1945–50* (1960); *Romanzi* (2 vols., 1961); *Poesie edite e inedite* (1962); *E quattro lettere a un'amica 1928–29* (1964). **Selected English translation:** *American Literature* (1970)

BIBLIOGRAPHY: Piccioni, L., "Vita e morte di C. P.," *Lettura Leopardiana* (1952); Nostitz, O. von, "Abschied von C. P.," *Wort und Wahrheit,* VIII (1953); Fernandez, D., "C. P., Le bel été," *Nouvelle Nouvelle Revue Française,* VI (1955); Chase, R. H., "C. P. and the American Novel," *SA,* No. 3 (1957), pp. 347–69; Fernandez, D., *Le roman italien et la crise de la conscience moderne* (1958); Ginzburg, N., "In Memoriam: C. P.," *The Atlantic,* CCIII (1959), 75–77; Anon., "A Man and His Novels," *TLS,* 15 Sept. 1961, p. 612; Hösle, J., *C. P.* (1961); Rimanelli, G., "The Conception of Time and Language in the Poetry of C. P.," *IQ,* VIII (1964), 14–34; Baden, H. J., *Literatur und Selbstmord* (1965); Tondo, M., *Itinerario di C. P.* (1965); Biasin, G. P., "The Smile of the Gods," *IQ,* X (1966), 2–32; Hood, S., "A Protestant without God," *Encounter,* XXVI (1966), v, 41–48; Uribe, M., *C. P.* (1966); Guiducci, A., *Il mito P.* (1967); Heiney, D. U., *Three Italian Novelists: Moravia, P., Vittorini* (1968)

OSWALT VON NOSTITZ

Between 1943 and 1945, P. took to the woods as so many thousands of Italians did. On the hills of Nazi-occupied Piedmont, he lived close to those partisan bands around which the best part of the Italian people gathered to fight the foreign occupants and to work for future justice. These proved to be decisive years for P. He felt he had personally discovered that the modern writer, if he is to escape isolation and despair, must align himself with those who are oppressed, and his work must reflect the social struggle. No doubt P.'s convictions were deeply sincere; but they were also peculiarly naïve. Further, the writer's task as he now conceived it was at odds with his lyrical and elegiac temperament. Yet this contradiction is the mainspring of P.'s art.

Paolo Milano, in *New Republic*
(4 May 1953), p. 18

The real unity which is discoverable in P.'s work under its superficial shifts from realism to regionalism, from the political to the archetypal, is his preoccupation with the meanings of America. . . . In rhythm and movement, and in a conviction, an understanding of art that underlie both, P.'s art, profoundly Italian as it is, is rooted in our literature and could not have existed without it. . . . P.'s impulse as an artist was toward a dimension he liked to call "mythic," a dimension he found in Melville and not in Flaubert. It is primarily through the author of *Moby Dick* that P. approaches American literature, and it is through him that he finds in our books an identity of word and thing that goes beyond mere anti-rhetorical immediacy to a special sort of symbolism: not the aristocratic *symbolisme* of the French . . . but a democratic faith that a "colloquy with the masses" might be opened on the level of myth, whose unity underlies the diversity of our acquired cultures. Just as American literature had found a third way between the European poles of naturalism and *symbolisme,* so P. felt we had found an escape from the dilemma of classicizing traditionalism and romantic rebellion, between academicism and futurism. The American artist, P. believed, had discovered how to reject conformism without becoming "a rebel in short pants," how to be at once free and mature.

Leslie Fiedler, in *Kenyon Review*
(Autumn 1954), pp. 539–42

When C. P. died . . . there was a quick moment's revulsion that a man so insistently vibrant with inner life had denied it for himself. . . . But what if "someone had known"? Would this solitary man have been talked round to a tolerance of life, if not of optimism? . . . The fact is that everyone who knew P. and his work "knew." The intense preoccupation with death (*"sei la terra e la morte"*) runs through all his work. . . . The months preceding P.'s death included an emotional experience with a young American woman who epitomized for him the several attempts at a lasting relationship. The writer's chief experiences had ended in bitterness and failure, frequently in self-castigation, inevitably in depression. . . . But can this, if it be accepted as the immediate cause, be then blamed as ultimate cause? Surely not. For his awareness of death as a concomitant of life is in some form present in each of the novels, and in the poems to an obsessive degree. P. was on intimate terms with death from his early stories. Even in his lifelong interest in American letters, he reflected the pull of this lode: it is Melville who, above all, fascinates and moves him.

Frances Keene, introduction to *The Burning Brand: Diaries 1935–1950* (1961), pp. 11–13

[*The Burning Brand: Diaries 1935–1950*] is a document of a strange, harrowing pathos. That it was written without intent to publish is confirmed by internal evidence. The always spontaneous, sometimes cryptic and occasionally valueless entries are those of a note-book. But the notes are by a considerable poet and thinker: he is talking to himself, literally—addressing himself very often in the second person singular. And this dialogue is characteristic of his peculiar mentality, which is of a phenomenal objectivity, a detachment that is almost (although actually not at all) schizophrenic, and of a condition of such tragic isolation that he can write of spending "a whole evening sitting before a mirror to keep myself company."

Philip Mairet, in *New Statesman and Nation* (14 July 1961), p. 59

C. P., who took his life at the peak of his career in 1950, can still be considered today as the most elusively complex Italian writer of his generation. . . . For C. P. introspection was the way of life, it led not to escape through fantasy but to an intensification and "purification" of experience through an anguished search for the truth about himself and the world in which he lived. Intense, paradoxical, tormented by self-destructive fears and doubts, humble in the face of the gifts he knew were his, he poured forth [in his diaries] . . . without trace of self-consciousness, his innermost thoughts on whatever troubled or interested him.

Helene Cantarella, in *The New York Times* (10 Dec. 1961), p. 4

In his native Italy the late C. P. is recognized as one of the country's very best recent novelists. . . . In his diaries P. explores what, in addressing himself, he calls "your own tendency . . . to wallow in your own unhappiness, to touch bottom," thus shedding considerable light on his suicide in 1950. Unquestionably a profoundly melancholy, lonely man. P. was especially bitter during the years when he had to face Fascism in government, neglect in his literary life, and disappointment in love. . . . The "literary" pages of the diaries deserve every conventional compliment. They contain the intelligent observations of a dedi-

cated, thoughtful, extremely learned man of letters. But to read the lines in which P. records his private sorrows is to share the unique experience of his tortuous life, to see his blood staining the printed page.

Henry Popkin, in *Saturday Review* (23 Dec. 1961), p. 23

P.'s work has the dual theme of city and country. The country was a reservoir of recollections, the hills among which he grew up, the mythical age of childhood; the city was a symbol of crowded streets and intellectual development. This theme is like that of Sherwood Anderson, to whom the whole modern world lies in the contrast between country and city, between innocence and empty vanity, between the grandeur of nature and the pettiness of man. In the virile loneliness in which all of his characters are enveloped, P. entered into the world of myth.

Giose Rimanelli, *Perspectives: Recent Literature of Russia, China, Italy, and Spain* (1961), p. 38

The . . . verse of this great novelist shows P.'s gifts—his extraordinary psychological acumen, his close-grained realism, his universal compassion. . . . The early P. prefers the loose line, the poignant human destiny or incident, to tight personal lyricism; in some respects close to E. A. Robinson, his talent runs primarily to ballad and narrative, shot through with nostalgia, which lends an unforgettable aroma to his compositions. . . . Only in the final series of poems . . . written during the poet's last years, do we find the complete translucency and economy of great lyric verse.

Francis Golffing, in *Books Abroad* (Summer 1963), p. 329

For the modern consciousness, the artist (replacing the saint) is the exemplary sufferer. . . . The unity of P.'s diaries is to be found in his reflections on how to use, how to act on, his suffering. . . . Apart from writing, there are two prospects to which P. continually recurs. One is the prospect of suicide, . . . the other is the prospect of romantic love and erotic failure. . . . The two themes are intimately connected, as P. himself experienced. . . . The modern view of love is an extension of the spirit of Christianity. . . . The cult of love in the West is an aspect of the cult of suffering—suffering as the supreme token of seriousness (the paradigm of the Cross). . . . The sensibility we have inherited identifies spirituality and seriousness with turbulence, suffering, passion. . . . The modern contribution to this Christian sensibility has been to discover the making of works of art and the venture of sexual love as the two most exquisite sources of suffering. It is this that we look for in a writer's diary, and which P. provides in disquieting abundance.

Susan Sontag, *Against Interpretation* (1966), pp. 42, 44, 47–8

53

PAYRÓ, Roberto Jorge

Argentinian novelist, short-story writer, and dramatist, b. 19 April 1867, Mercedes; d. 5 April 1928, Buenos Aires

P. participated in the social and political upheaval that transformed Argentina into a modern European-type society. As a newspaperman, publisher, cofounder of literary and political journals, columnist for the well-known dailies *La Prensa* and *La Nación,* active Mason and member of the Socialist and Radical parties, P. worked with the dynamic assurance of a crusader who believed in the legacy of the 18th-c. encyclopaedists.

During P.'s last years he acted as a major catalytic agent in the literary milieu of Buenos Aires, preparing the way for the Boedo group of writers. These writers followed in his tradition of radical partisanship in politics, and preferred naturalism (q.v.) in literature to the elegant aestheticism of the incipient Florida group, which was to be led by Borges, Mallea (qq.v.), and the *Sur* magazine.

P.'s early work was dominated by the influence of Zola (q.v.) and the great Spanish realist Pérez Galdós (q.v.). In his first novel, *Antígona* (1885), as well as in several collections of short stories, P. adapted naturalistic techniques to indicate the social problems of Argentina.

P. was also a playwright. His *Sobre las ruinas* (1904), in which he dramatized the battle between traditional and progressive forces, was well-received by the Buenos Aires theatergoing public. This, however, like his later problem plays, inevitably lost much of its appeal with the passage of time.

P.'s dramas fared better when he utilized historical settings and events, such as he did in *El mar dulce* (1927), in which the discovery of the Río de la Plata by Solís is fictionalized. This is to be expected since the popularity of chronicles that picture the country's past has greatly increased in the present era of cultural self-analysis practiced by the Argentinians.

Another facet of P.'s social and political orientation motivated him to publish accounts of his travels to the then-neglected lands of Patagonia and the northwestern Andean provinces. In *La Australia argentina* (1898) P. achieved a careful balance between the diary and *costumbrista* documentation. Later an extensive journey to the Andean provinces was to result in *En las tierras de Inti* (1909), in which he successfully synthesized regional observations and social criticism.

P.'s most successful writing is to be found in his three picaresque narrative works. In the classic Spanish tradition, his *Casamiento de Laucha* (1906) is structured around an antiheroic protagonist who is the product of social conditions and cultural attitudes that have got to be modified if humanism is to prevail. That novel and *Pago Chico* (1908; reissued as *Cuentos de Pago Chico,* 1965), a collection of picaresque stories, feature the same locale—the Argentinian town and port of Bahía Blanca in which P. was a militant newspaper owner and editor. In these stories P. allowed himself to be more subjective and moralizing than he was in *Casamiento de Laucha.*

In *Divertidas aventuras del nieto de Juan Moreira* (1910), Claudio Herrera, another picaresque anti-hero, is developed as a modern Buscón, a full-fledged scoundrel who embodies the social realities of his day. Astute, predatory, and unscrupulous, he symbolizes the successful politician of Argentina in the 1890's, a prototype of those figures brought to life in the successful novels of a Silvina Bullrich and Martha Lynch today.

FURTHER WORKS: *Scripta* (1887); *Novelas y fantasías* (1888); *Notas de viaje, el paso de Uspallata* (1896); *El triunfo de los otros* (1907); *Crónicas* (1909); *Vivir quiere conmigo* (1923); *Fuego en el rastrojo* (1925); *El capitan Vergara* (1925); *Alegría* (1928); *Nuevos cuentos de Pago Chico* (1929); *Chamijo* (1930); *Teatro completo* (1956). **Selected English translation:** *Tragic Song,* a translation of *Canción Trágica* (play), in *Poet Lore* (n.d.)

BIBLIOGRAPHY: Número de Homenaje, *Nosotros,* XXII (May 1928); Larra, R., *P., el novelista de la democracia* (1938); Anderson-Imbert, E., *Tres novelas de P., con pícaros en tres miras* (1942); García, G., "Pícaros van y vienen," in *La novela argentina, un itinerario* (1952), pp. 101–115; González Lanuza, E., *Genio y figura de R. J. P.* (1965)

H. ERNEST LEWALD

PAZ, Octavio

Mexican poet and essayist, b. 31 March 1914, Mexico City

P.'s formative period was strongly shaped by his presence in Spain during the civil war. As one of the founders and most energetic editors of *Taller* (1938–41), he had a direct influence on emerging writers. In 1943 he received a Guggenheim fellowship for travel and study in the United States. The period of his greatest literary activity coincided with the assumption of several high government posts (particularly his appointments as Mexico's representative to UNESCO and Ambassador to India), which he resigned to protest the Mexican government's handling of student demonstrations before the 1968 Olympic Games.

P.'s impact as a poet preceded his accomplishments in the essay. Public attention came to him for his *Bajo tu clara sombra* (1937), *Entre la piedra y la flor* (1941), and for his editing of *Laurel* (1941), one of the finest anthologies of Spanish and Spanish-American poetry. With *A la orilla del mundo* (1942), P. was recognized as one of the most promising poets in the Hispanic world. *Libertad bajo palabra* (1949; expanded edition, 1960) is praised as the compendium of P.'s talents. In diction that is an unequal mixture of surrealism (q.v.) and traditionally symbolic techniques, P. remains true to the inner necessities of his deeply personal creativity. His gift is to bridge the gap between the personal and the general, between man and society, and by defining his own alienation and anxiety, which is typical of our time, to provide some solace for these widely experienced afflictions.

In *El laberinto de la soledad* (1950; The Labyrinth of Solitude, 1961), P. provided a complex and controversial analysis of the Mexican character. Taking as his point of departure the *pachuco*, the hybrid Mexican-American, P. identifies concealment, the use of a mask, as the most observable feature of the Mexican character. Much "illogical" social behavior is traceable to a profound individual insecurity, which is reflected in a collective identity crisis. The Mexican does not know who he is and is suspicious of others because he is suspicious of himself. In terms that are basically psychological, but that P. extends to history, mythology, and social behavior, the Mexican is revealed as the defensive victim of the social rape in which he was engendered. The historical application of P.'s thesis reveals a Mexico (and, in fact, most of Spanish America) in quest of a national identity: America is not so much a tradition to be carried on as it is a future to be realized. In the book's final chapter on the dialectic of solitude, P. places the problems of individual

integration and social communion in the center of modern existence. *Posdata* (1970) is a critical and autocritical extension and revaluation of the thesis of *El laberinto de la soledad*.

As meritorious as *El laberinto de la soledad*, although not as well known outside Mexico, is *El arco y la lira* (1956), a brilliant analysis of poetry as language, process, and social phenomenon. *Las peras del olmo* (1957) and *Puertas al campo* (1966) contain P.'s literary and art criticism. In his latest works P. continues to blaze new trails in philosophy, history, and the problems of contemporary man. Often referred to as Mexico's dean of letters, P. is qualified both for the breadth of his work and its international prestige to be considered the intellectual heir of the late Alfonso Reyes (q.v.).

FURTHER WORKS: *Raíz de hombre* (1937); *¿Águila o sol?* (1951; ¿Águila o sol?/Eagle or Sun?, 1970); *Semillas para un himno* (1954); *La hija de Rappacini* (1956); *Piedra de sol* (1957; Sun Stone, 1962); *La estación violenta* (1958); *Salamandra* (1962); *Cuadrivio* (1964); *Los signos en rotación* (1965); *Claude Lévi-Strauss, o El nuevo festín de Esopo* (1967); *Blanco* (1967); *Ladera Este* (1969); *Conjunciones y disyunciones* (1969). **Selected English translation:** *Selected Poems* (1963)

BIBLIOGRAPHY: Xirau, R., *Tres poetas de la soledad* (1955); Fein, J. M., "The Mirror as Image and Theme in the Poetry of O. P.," *Symposium*, X (1956), 251–70; Leiva, R., *Imagen de la poesía mexicana contemporánea* (1959), pp. 205–26; Durán, M., "Liberty and Eroticism in the Poetry of O. P.," *BA*, XXXVII (Autumn 1963), 373–77; Rukeyser, M., Foreword to *Selected Poems* (1963), pp. 8–13; Segall, B., "Symbolism in O. P.'s 'Puerta condenada,'" *Hispania*, LIII (May 1970), 212–19

JOHN M. FEIN

P. writes of Mexican masks and what the American remarks as the character of the people of admittedly a single state may be one of them. However the author does not make the connection nor does he admit any but Mexican masks. The tradition of the clown laughing with tears in his eyes, Pagliacci, Andreyev's *He,* is not a picture of the Mexican P. gives us. Instead we get a picture of a sad formalist, indulgent toward homosexuality, regarding woman as a chattel, yet showing the wounds of his love. The Mexican is psychoanalyzed in the light of his Indian heritage, stigmatized with a "servant mentality" and bitterly denounced as a son of the violated. Unlike the European, he is genuinely religious, but we do not learn from P. whether this is good or bad, nor does he say, uncharacteristically, that his own lacerating self-castigation is a purely Mexican trait.

Richard C. Angell, in New Mexico Quarterly,
XXXI (1961–62), iv, p. 372

Since his youth, the poet has lived in the world of the surrealists. This was another very important relationship with his own epoch and a valuable instrument for his poetic language. Later he met and became a friend of some of the principal figures of the surrealist movement, whose meaning he understands deeply. When we add the fact that O. P., a widely learned writer, is familiar with the classics—he can write irreproachable sonnets—we see that he has delved into all trends, especially into all the important trends of his time: surrealism and Marxism, existentialism and sometimes the classics, interest in the Orient, and enthusiasm for national self-consciousness. In the last he goes straight to the substantive, without folkloric frippery or anecdotal adornment. It can be said unhesitatingly that P.'s work, seen as a whole, is a weather-vane to the winds of the present-day literary world.

José Durant, "Octavio Paz, a Mexican Poet-
Diplomat," in Americas (July 1963), p. 33

... Señor P. interprets Mexican history as three major ruptures. Conquest, Independence, Revolution. Abandoned by gods and leaders at the Conquest the Indians were left in fearful spiritual solitude. Catholicism restored them to the supernatural world but, exported in its rusty phase, could not galvanise native religious instincts from the fatalism that exactly suited the Spanish plunderers. The Church became not a pioneer but a refuge.... The rupture from Spain likewise produced no dynamic national myth, republican leaders being largely concerned with consolidating themselves as wealthy legatees. Without the ambitious bourgeoisie Mexican liberalism, another European import, was a sterile geometry, using sonorous words to disguise rhetorical unreality....

The Labyrinth of Solitude's main thesis is that liberalism ignored man's other vital part, that of myth and dream. Examining his countrymen's attitude to work, religion, sexuality, politics, their present economic and political dilemmas, P. sees the Revolution, the first of the major twentieth century revolutions, as a barely conscious attempt to excavate long-buried gifts, Aztec, Spanish, Moorish, mutually involved like a pre-Conquest pyramid superimposed on another. Trying to assimilate the past, to strike a pact with gods, the Revolution, instinctive, brutal, tender, unpredictable, remains an activist equivalent to the fiesta rather than a programme reasoned and thus

academic. The heroes, Zapata, Villa, Carranza, already myths, are sunk as deep in the bloodstream as the tragic Cuauhtemoc and the equivocal Virgin of Guadalupe. The need is to escape pseudo-Mexico and, by returning to origins, build a genuine national self. Simultaneously, Mexico shares with Outside the prosaic need to industrialise, democratise.

The author is a poet and poetry is needed to tackle certain conceptions strictly unprovable: death-wish, revolution as return to the womb, women as "secret and immobile suns." Old myths can create new misunderstandings but, as displayed here, they can also invite the foreigner to consider his own. Where are they, and what? Invigorating or merely humouring the past?

Peter Vansittart, in Spectator (26 May 1967)

... though P. has had a consistent view of poetry and his repertoire of words and images has remained remarkably consistent, too, there has been a change of direction. Early poems tended to be concerned with identity while his more recent works are each intended as an experience, a happening, in which poet and reader attain a sense of unity and completion. The technique, too, has developed from early short-lined, tightly-organised poems, to the long-lined poems of his middle period, and under Eastern influence to the brief, haiku-like poems that he is now writing....

One of P.'s most ambitious poems is "Piedra de sol," written in a circular pattern and having the same number of lines as there were days in the Aztec calendar year. Within this circular container P. sets into play seemingly contradictory aspects of experience which are really one....

Jean Franco, An Introduction to Spanish
American Literature (1969), p. 295

PÉGUY, Charles Pierre

(pseuds. *Charles Pierre Baudouin, Pierre Deloire*), French poet, journalist, and philosopher, b. 7 Jan. 1873, Orléans; d. 5 Sept. 1914, Plessis-l'Évêque

P. came from a provincial family of farmers and craftsmen. In 1885 he received a scholarship to the *lycée* in Orléans, where he distinguished himself by his extraordinary intellectual capacity. Religious doubts led him to atheism, while incidents during the strike at Carmaux turned him into a militant socialist. Having failed the entrance examination for the École Normale Supérieure, he did his military service prematurely.

In October 1893 he received a scholarship to the Collège Sainte-Barbe (Lycée Louis-le-Grand) in Paris, where he was soon the center

ROBERTO PAYRÓ

OCTAVIO PAZ

of the fraternal group *de la cour rose*. With his closest friend, M. Baudouin, he visualized a socialist utopia in *Marcel: premier dialogue de la cité harmonieuse* (1898). In 1894 he passed the entrance examination and entered the École Normale Supérieure with the intention of becoming a professor of philosophy. At this time he was working on his first play, *Jeanne d'Arc* (1987), doing careful research into medieval sources. With a few fellow students, he established a socialist cell in the École Normale Supérieure, having himself joined the Socialist Party.

In December 1895 he unexpectedly took a leave of absence and returned to Orléans, where he learned typesetting, established a "social studies group," and finished his Joan of Arc play. No sooner had he resumed his studies than the controversial Dreyfus Affair diverted him again. Wholeheartedly taking up the cause of the unjustly condemned man, he wrote articles for various socialist papers. In order to devote himself entirely to this new calling, he gave up his chance of a university career and late in 1897 dropped out of the École Normale Supérieure, although he still attended lectures. In 1897 he married the sister of his old friend Baudouin, who had died earlier. A collection taken up by his friends enabled him to have *Jeanne d'Arc* privately printed; it appeared, in an unusual typographical format, in 1897, but attracted almost no attention.

On 5 January 1898, P. opened a socialist press and bookshop near the Sorbonne. His strongly Kantian concept of socialism soon brought him into conflict with the Marxist wing of the party. In 1900 he founded his own journal, the *Cahiers de la Quinzaine* (1900–14), which he edited and published singlehandedly. Through extraordinary effort and sacrifice he managed to keep the magazine going. Its aim was to provide entirely truthful, unbiased information about current political events.

Contributors were not bound to any ideology and represented a wide variety of philosophical positions. Soon the *Cahiers* was also publishing novellas, poems, and essays whose authors included France, Rolland, Bergson (qq.v.), Jean Jaurès, André Suarès, and Georges Sorel. In the course of time P. recruited the entire French intellectual and political elite, and the *Cahiers* became the leading cultural journal of prewar France, although the number of subscribers never reached two thousand.

The *Cahiers* was sharply critical of parliamentary socialism in France. They first fought government-directed anticlericalism. Next they championed the liberation of the oppressed peoples of eastern Europe and protested the abuses of colonialism. P. himself subjected the great exponents of secularism, Taine, Renan, and Durkheim, to devastating criticism. Here he allied himself with Bergson, whose lectures he was still attending, and with Georges Sorel, who was closely connected with the *Cahiers* until 1911. Like Bergson, P. upheld organic life and creative openness in opposition to the then current worship of progress and science, and to intellectualism and the cult of sociology and economics, which, in his eyes, posed a deadly threat to France's existence.

In his *Situations* (1906–07) P. bitterly attacked these forces as the *monde moderne*, evoking against them the spiritual and organic forces of antiquity and Christianity. With *Notre Patrie* (1905) P. began his campaign for a spirit of truthfulness and national awareness. This brought him into contact with nationalist circles (which Barrès and Maurras [qq.v.] were working in), and he became one of the leaders of the "national rebirth." P. already foresaw that the Dreyfusites' pyrrhic victory in accepting a pardon for Captain Dreyfus would be a continually festering sore in French life and would bring the Jews renewed persecution, exile, and even death "by the waysides of the roads to Asia."

Two serious illnesses in 1900 and 1901 had made P. aware of the significance of religion. During the next few years his realization of the bankruptcy of the "modern spirit" led him step by step back to Catholicism. (He was to become a cofounder of the prewar *renouveau catholique*.) St. Louis and St. Joan, Pascal and Corneille, became his models. However, since his wife was still a secularist, P. decided to remain outside the church until he had won her over. In fact, her conversion and the baptism of the children occurred only after his death.

Above all, P. devoted his life to prayer. Friends close to him (*e.g.*, Alain-Fournier [q.v.]) at this time saw in him a "man of God" like Dostoyevski. He sought Catholic Christianity not only within the church but in all its "unsacramental" manifestations. Finding it prefigured in the natural world, he pointed out the mutual penetration of nature and grace. He became the universal advocate of the creatively open, individual man, whose position had become so precarious, over against closed, dead organization. In order to make the sacred fruitful amid the perils of its profane exposure, man must always be hopefully open to God and ready for His coming. P. is thus *the* "poet of incarnation" (J. Onimus).

His recognition that the position of the *Cahiers* in the struggle for social and civil justice was defeated caused P. to keep silence for almost two years. Now he broke free of Kantianism too. Not until 1909, after another serious illness, did he come before the public again with the sensational *À Nos Amis, à nos abonnés,* in which he coined the expression "the defeated generation." Thenceforth P. followed his true calling exclusively—that of the poet.

P. now began to publish poetry, beginning in 1910 with his three *mystères: Le Mystère de la charité de Jeanne d'Arc* (1910; The Mystery of the Charity of Joan of Arc, 1950), which deals with the vocation of public heroism and sainthood; *Le Porche du mystère de la deuxième vertu* (1911), which presents the opening of the human heart to hope; and *Le Mystère des saints innocents* (1912; The Mystery of the Holy Innocents, 1956), in which the mystery of birth as the first tender opening to grace is poetically treated.

After 1910 P. wrote his short "Quatrains," which he intended to combine into a sequence but never published; their sequence still remains doubtful. These are little masterpieces containing his most intimate confessions. They were followed by sonnets and longer poems that P. called *Tapisseries* (1913). Among them are the immediately famous "La Tapisserie de St. Geneviève et de Jeanne d'Arc" (1912) and the "Présentation de la Beauce à Notre Dame de Chartres" (1913).

These *Tapisseries* were the prelude to *Ève* (1913), a work consisting of 1913 alexandrines, which is sheer narrativeless metaphysical reality, with its "climates" interweaving in rich contrast through the seamless, uninterrupted flow of the poetry. The abstract becomes concrete; the concrete becomes spiritually transparent form. By discarding all impressionism and keeping the word rigorously tied to the whole, P. achieves here an unusual simplicity that gives his language the pregnancy and resonance of a *chanson de geste* or of the Bible. Here he breaks with all modern French poetic tradition and opens entirely new horizons to his native tongue, above all great spaciousness and creative freedom. This leads his language (which also has

typically Germanic elements) back—if only unintentionally—toward the ancient epics.

Between 1910 and 1914 P. also published prose works simultaneously with poetry. *Notre Jeunesse* (1910; Temporal and Eternal, 1958), a remarkably freshly recalled final account of the Dreyfus Affair, is at the same time a hymn to his friend Bernard-Lazare, who died young. *Victor-Marie, comte Hugo* (1911) is a meditation on this poet's primeval pagan genius; here P. also fathoms the mystery of the incarnation in its bodily aspect. *L'Argent* (1912) contrasts intellectualism in its economic form (money, organization) with the uncorroded organic life of old France.

Clio (last version, 1914), P.'s prose masterpiece, is a dialogue with History personified about the decay of all earthly things and the impotence and injustice of history—all challenged by the power of grace. This work has the steady luminosity of a life that has already conquered its earthly death. P. looks back at himself as he would look at a man already dead. By projecting examples of judgment (*see* Hugo's *Châtiments*), of death in the bloom of youth (Achilles and Antigone), of the evanescence of even the most splendid youthfulness, P. evolves to the realization that all life depends upon the breakthrough of grace.

A third group of works was written in self-defense against venomous attacks by certain intellectual circles that successfully blocked P.'s election to the French Academy. *Un Nouveau Théologien, M. Fernand Laudet* (1911) denounces one of these opponents and reveals the latent modernism that underlay his proclaimed Catholicism. *Langlois tel qu'on le parle* and *Argent suite* expose the pseudoscientific metaphysics of the Sorbonne.

Finally P. undertook to defend his friend Bergson against the threat of having his works placed on the Roman Catholic Index. In *Note sur M. Bergson et la philosophie bergsonienne* and *Note conjointe sur M. Descartes et la philosophie cartésienne* (both in *Cahiers,* 1914), he attempts to lay bare the deep significance of Bergson's philosophy in shedding light upon such concepts as hope, freedom, grace, etc. The second *Note* was never finished—P. was killed in action in the first few days of World War I.

His death made him a "hero" (Barrès) and a "legendary figure" (L. Gillet) in the eyes of France. Important young writers such as Bernanos and Graham Greene (qq.v.) were strongly influenced by him. Rolland called him "the most forceful genius in European literature." Indeed, his uniqueness still makes it impossible to assign him to any intellectual category. He is a "whole world" (Jean and Jerome Tharaud) unto himself, and cannot be adequately accounted for simply by tracing his development.

FURTHER WORKS: *De la Cité socialiste* (1897); *Œuvres complètes* (15 vols., 1916–34); *La Route de Chartres* (1946); *La République* (1946); *Du Rôle de la volonté dans la croyance* (1947); *Œuvres poétiques complètes* (1948); *Notes politiques et sociales* (1956); *Œuvres en prose* (1956); *Correspondance A. Gide–C. P., 1905–1912* (1958). **Selected English translations:** *Basic Verities* (1943); *Men and Saints* (1944); *God Speaks* (1945)

BIBLIOGRAPHY: Suarès, A., *P.* (1915; Péguy, M., *La Vocation de C. P.* (2 vols., 1925–26); Tharaud, J., and J., *Notre Cher P.* (2 vols., 1926); Mounier, E., Péguy, M., and Izard, G., *La Pensée de C. P.* (1931); Péguy, P., *Pour connaître la Pensée de P.* (1941); Halévy, D., *C. P. et les Cahiers de la Quinzaine* (1941); Rousseaux, A., *Le Prophète P.* (3 vols., 1942–45); Rolland, R., *C. P.* (2 vols., 1944); Gillet, L., *Claudel, P.* (1946); Guyon, B., *L'Art de P.* (1948); Bibliothèque Nationale, *C. P. et les Cahiers de la Quinzaine* (1950); Johannet, R., *Vie et les Cahiers de la Quinzaine* (1950); Reclus, M., *Le P. que j'ai connu* (1951); Martin, A., *P. et Alain-Fournier* (1954); Comiti, P., *Le Dieu de P.* (1955); Druy, A., *P.* (1957); Barbier, J., *Le Vocabulaire, la syntaxe et le style des poèmes réguliers de C. P.* (1957); Fraigneux, M., *Littérature héroïque* (1958); Delaporte, J., *Connaissance de P.* (2 vols., 2nd ed., 1959); Isaac, J., *Expérience de ma vie: P.* (1959); Perche, L., *C. P.* (1959); Guyon, B., *P.* (1960); Nelson, R. J., *P.* (1960); Onimus, J., *P.* (1960); Cattaui, G., *P., témoin du temporel chrétien* (1964); Vadé, Y., *P. et le monde moderne* (1964); Villiers, M., *C. P.: A Study in Integrity* (1965); Quoniam, T., *P.* (1966); P. International Colloquium 1964: *Actes du Colloque International d'Orléans* (1967); Adereth, M., *Commitment in Modern French Literature* (1967); Schmitt, H., *P.: The Decline of an Idealist* (1967)

REINHARD LAUTH

Literature as such never interested him. All he ever wrote came to him as a spontaneous creation. Once he had surrendered to the call of the voice within himself, he could not stop, and we had his endless litanies, hymns, soliloquies and prayers. Words went marching in battle array at his command like so many waves in the World War offensives. P. plowed slowly and painstakingly in the field of words and sentences. He wove patiently and obstinately what he called his tapestries, and there could be seen hanging on the walls the archaic figures of Saint Genevieve, Saint Joan of Arc, and Our Lady of Chartres whom he worshipped as a medieval pilgrim.

Régis Michaud, *Modern Thought and Literature in France* (1934), p. 25

The idealism he championed, the sporting, free action in the constant presence of the eternal good, P. called mysticism. The enemy was politics, lust for power; politics and its offspring, the exploitative, unfaithful, all-prostituting modern world. P. attacked its representatives with unremitting vehemence.... Romain Rolland and Henri Bergson were among his masters, and Bergson's philosophy thrilled him and made him lifelong a fervent Bergsonite. This was not fortuitous. P. was immensely sanguine by nature: in all his despairs and disillusionments constantly in touch with some ground of happy expectations; convinced that what he desired was obtainable.

Paul Rosenfeld, in *Nation* (20 Feb. 1943), p. 276

It is perhaps significant that the three most eminent Catholic writers of modern France, Léon Bloy, P. and Claudel are the least amenable to any selective process. Each of their works is long, and of one piece, incapable of being cut into smaller parts. Their work is one of persistence and explanation, composed in a period when their faith had to be carefully and laboriously defended.... The temporal and the eternal and their commingling— that is the temporal in the eternal—is the problem which pervades most of the long works of P.... Every line recommences the debate on eternity.

Wallace Fowlie, *Poetry* (April 1945), pp. 43, 45

P. was a great man—perhaps a very great man —but he was not a good writer. In fact, he could not write; he *talked* in print. His talk is often very good, even when he talks in verse, which he does for amazingly long periods.... His great fault is repetition. He will not only say the same things, but repeats the same words over and over again, as though he were a teacher addressing a class of half-deaf children. Nevertheless he often hits. His intellectual honesty is amazing, his power of expression is sometimes of the highest order.

Denis Saurat, *Modern French Literature* (1946), p. 93

PEKKANEN, Toivo Rikhard

Finnish novelist, short-story writer, and dramatist, b. 10 Sept. 1902, Kotka; d. 24 May 1957, Copenhagen

The son of a factory worker, P. had to start working at the age of twelve, when his father died. After elementary school, he received vocational training and became a skilled worker. He first published short stories in newspapers and magazines. After his first novel, *Tehtaan varjossa* (1932), which gained him recognition (it has been translated into Danish, Swedish, and French), he supported himself by his writing. In 1955 he was elected to the Finnish Academy.

The novel *Tehtaan varjossa,* which is largely autobiographical, describes a young worker who reads and studies, hoping one day to become a writer. For this reason he feels rejected by his friends, one of whom repeatedly summarizes him as a badly shaped brick that cannot be fitted in any kind of building. Statements like this occur often in P.'s writings. One of his characters states that one cannot read books and be a good mechanic. Another one says that working-class girls should never go to the movies or read books, for knowing what middle-class life can be like will make their own lives hell. This was written during the Great Depression, which affected Finland in the way it did the rest of the world.

P. is at his best as a novelist, and the greatest of P.'s novels are those about his hometown Kotka, an industrial center and a harbor that grew rapidly on the shore of the Gulf of Finland at the end of the 19th c. *Isänmaan ranta* (1937) describes a strike and its moderate leader, who is pushed aside by a younger and more radical man. It was followed by *Ne menneet vuodet* (1940), in which some of the characters from *Isänmaan* reappear, but it lacks some of the strength and concentration of the first novel. (Both were rewritten by P. and published in one volume under the title *Jumalan myllyt* in 1946.)

The trilogy made up of *Aamuhämärä* (1948), *Toverukset* (1948), and *Voittajat ja voitetut* (1952) is about the settling and building of Kotka. Here P. mingles historical and fictitious events and characters. They have been admired for their carefully planned structure and for the art with which their different aspects—"the historical, the social, and the individual," according to one Finnish critic—are balanced.

One characteristic of P.'s writing is the presence of unreal or symbolic elements in his works, especially in his plays. According to P., theater should aim at creating an illusion rather than be naturalistic. He was perhaps not fully aware of the turning away from realism and naturalism that was taking place in the European theater. He approved of the critical description that interpreted his play *Demoni* (1939) as a cubistic work. The three characters in it, he said, showed three different aspects of one person, as a cubistic painting shows several sides of an object not seen simultaneously in reality. At times, the symbolic elements in P.'s plays seem to be not quite relevant, but they are meaningful when they dominate the action, as they do in *Demoni* or *Täyttyneiden toiveiden maa* (published as a novel in 1951). In *Täyttyneiden toiveiden maa,* P. describes the founding of a utopian community by outcasts of society and its failure. The short stories in *Mies ja punapartaiset herrat* (1950) are also structured around fantastic motifs, and the presence in them of humorous and satiric elements makes them atypical of P.

P., who took his calling to write very seriously, avoided informality and wrote first in an overly correct, rather stiff and awkward manner. A Finnish essayist titled an article on him "The Stonecutter at His Work." In his later works, however, P.'s style became more natural and flexible.

P.'s sympathies clearly lay with the working class, and in his memoirs, *Lapsuuteni* (1953), he describes how hard he had to struggle to suppress the feelings of hate and bitterness that welled up in him when he thought of his early life. There is, however, no direct political or social message in his works, unless it is a plea for moderation. The working class, he said, must acquire more knowledge and maturity in order to be able to seize its share of the political power, but he was aware of the fact that such ideas tended to exclude him from the working class.

P., much admired and idealized by young writers of the 1920's because of his working-class background, remained close to his origins throughout his life. He wrote widely on other subjects, however, and is not to be summarized as a working-class writer.

FURTHER WORKS: *Rautaiset kädet* (1927); *Satama ja meri* (1929); *Tientekijät* (1930); *Kuolemattomet* (1931); *Sisarukset* (1933); *Kauppiaiden lapset* (1934); *Ihmisten kevät* (1935);

Takaisin Austraaliaan (1936); *Rakkaus ja raha* (1937); *Ukkosen tuomio* (1937); *Levottomuus* (1938); *Maantie meillä ja muualla* (1939); *Musta hurmio* (1939); *Raja merellä* (1941); *Vihollislentäjä* (1941); *Ajan kasvot* (1942); *Tie Eedeniin* (1942); *Hämärtyvä horisontti* (1944); *Elämän ja kuoleman pidot* (1945); *Nuorin veli* (1946); *Valikoima novelleja ja otteita romaaneista* (1954); *Lähtö matkalle* (1955); *Totuuden ja kirkkauden tiellä* (1957); *Teokset* (vols. I–VII, 1957–58); *T. P. ajatuksia* (1962)

BIBLIOGRAPHY: Österling, A., *Inledning till T. P.: I fabrikens skugga* (1938); Sarajas, A., "P., Siippainen, Viita, Linna: Försök till perspektiv," *Ord och Bild*, LXV (1956), 139–51; Anhava, T., "Kotkan eepos," in *Parnasso* (1957), pp. 149–57; Viljanen, L., "T. P. suomalainen yhteiskunta," in *Lyyrillinen minä* (1959); Vuotila, L., *Kirjailija ja omatunto. P., Linna, Siippainen ja Viita eettisinä kirjailijoina* (1967)

JAAKKO A. AHOKAS

PELIN, Elin
See Elin Pelin

PELLICER, Carlos
Mexican poet, b. 4 Nov. 1899, Villahermosa, Tabasco

P. was educated in Mexico City at the Escuela Nacional Preparatoria. It was there that he met the young poets who were later to collaborate on the magazine *Contemporáneos* (1928–38). The "contemporáneos" group, to which P. belonged, became one of the most influential of the postmodernist groups.

P. continued his studies in Bogotá, to which the government of President Carranza sent him as a representative of the Mexican student federation. From 1926 to 1929, P. studied and traveled in Europe and the Near East.

After P.'s return to Mexico, he devoted himself to teaching literature and history in secondary schools. In recognition of his literary accomplishments, P. was elected to the Academia Mexicana de la Lengua in 1953, and in 1964 he was awarded Mexico's National Prize for Literature by President López Mateos.

In over forty years of literary production P. has published more than a dozen volumes of poetry, beginning with *Colores en el mar y otros poemas* (1921) and culminating with his collected works, *Material poético 1918/1961* (1962).

P.'s first poems remind us of Chocano's (q.v.) *Alma America* (1906), because he, like Chocano, sings of the American landscape. P. is primarily a visual poet, and in his principal poems the images are tropical. Sunlight, forest, jungle, sea, rivers, ruins, and vast expanses of sky suggest the landscape of his native province. In his verses, the tropics, with which P. identifies himself, "sob, shout, clamor, glitter, like a total human being" (R. Leiva, 1959). Hidden within the brilliant imagery are subtleties of thought and depths of feeling that reveal the poet's originality. P.'s poetry is an affirmation of all that life has to offer, and he rejoices in God's creation.

P. has also written many poems dedicated to other countries, which reflect his farflung travels, as well as religious poems. Of all the poets his country has produced, P. has been the most loyal to the past, present, and future of Mexico and, in a larger sense, to that of Latin America.

FURTHER WORKS: *Piedra de sacrificios* (1924); *Seis, y siete poemas* (1924); *Hora y veinte* (1927); *Camino* (1929); *5 poemas* (1931); *Esquemas para una oda tropical* (1933); *Estrofas del mar marino* (1934); *Hora de junio* (1937); *Ara virginum* (1940); *Recinto y otras imágenes* (1941); *Exágonos* (1942); *Discurso por las flores* (1946); *Subordinaciones* (1948); *Sonetos* (1950); *Práctica de vuelo* (1956); *Con palabras y fuego* (1962); *Teotihuacán y trece de agosto* (1965); *Leonardo Nierman* (1968)

BIBLIOGRAPHY: Monguió, L., "Poetas postmodernistas mexicanos," *RHM*, XII (1946), iii-iv, 239–66; Bodet, J. T., *Tiempo de Arena* (1955), pp. 78–80; Puga, M., "El escritor y su tiempo: C. P.," *Universidad de México*, X (1956), vi, 16–19; Dauster, F., "Aspectos del paisaje en la poesía de C. P.," *Estaciones*, IV (1959), xvi, 387–95; Leiva, R., "C. P.," in *Imagen de la poesía mexicana contemporánea* (1959), pp. 91–108; Ruis, L., "El material poético (1918–61) de C. P.," *Cuadernos Americanos*, XXI (1962), 239–70; Carballo, E., *Diecinueve protagonistas de la literatura mexicana del siglo XX* (1965), pp. 189–200; Monsivas, C., *La poesía mexicana del siglo XX* (1966), pp. 362–401; Gamboa, R., "La poesía de C. P.," *DA*, XXVIII (1967), 2681A; Schlak, C., "The Poetry of C. P.," *DA*, XXVIII (1967), 2263A

SONJA KARSEN

PENZOLDT, Ernst

German writer and sculptor, b. 14 June 1892, Erlangen; d. 27 Jan. 1955, Munich

P. attended the art academies of Weimar and Kassel and lived until his death in München-Schwabing. Working as both sculptor and poet, one talent stimulated the other. In this way he hoped to achieve a twofold realization of "life, beauty, love, friendship, nature, and creation." As important as any element in P.'s basic attitude to life were the kindness and humanity behind everything he created.

P.'s literary work includes novels, novellas, dramas, and essays. He was a master of the *causerie,* revealing himself in this genre as a *homo ludens* who combined wit with warmhearted charm. The *causerie* satisfied his instinct for the concrete. His style is precise and airy, elegant without being superficial, graceful without insipid preciosity.

P. expressed his sense of irony (q.v.) and humor through puns. *Die Powenzbande* (1930), his most famous novel, shows his lighthearted mastery of this art. This novel goes beyond satire; it is rooted in humor, "that last, most distant, highest intellectual sphere of humanity" (T. Haecker).

As a humanist P. paid a good deal of attention to the problem of life and death. He sought to explore the human condition and found his formula for life in the title—*Süße Bitternis* ("sweet bitterness"; 1948)—he gave to his collected short stories.

As Kästner (q.v.) said, P. was "a youth, an individual, and—as if that were not enough—a human being imbued with respect for tradition. Humanism is the aesthetic pole of his world, Christianity the ethical one."

FURTHER WORKS: *Der Gefährte* (1922); *Idyllen* (1923); *Der Schatten Amphion* (1924); *Tommaso Cavalieri* (1925); *Der Zwerg* (1927; reissued as *Die Leute aus der Mohrenapotheke,* 1938); *Der arme Chatterton* (1928); *Etienne und Luise* (1929; as drama, 1930); *Die portugalesische Schlacht* (1930; as drama, 1931); *Karl Chlodwig Sand bezw. Der Knabe Karl* (1931); *So war Herr Brummel* (1933); *Kleiner Erdenwurm* (1934); *Idolino* (1935); *Der dankbare Patient* (1937); *Zwölf Gedichte* (1937); *Korporal Mombour* (1941); *Episteln* (1942); *Die Reise ins Bücherland* (1942); *Die verlorenen Schuhe* (1946); *Tröstung* (1946); *Zugänge* (1947); *Der Kartoffelroman* (1948); *Der Diogenes von Paris* (1948; based on the drama *Die verlorenen Schuhe*); *Gesammelte Schriften*

(4 vols., 1949); *Der gläserne Storch* (1950); *Squirrel* (1954; as drama, 1955); *Die Liebende* (1958); *Prosa eines Liebenden* (1962)

BIBLIOGRAPHY: Heimeran, E., *Leben und Werk von E. P.,* ed. by U. Lentz-Penzoldt (1962); Gump, M., "E. P.: Ein Humanist unserer Zeit," *GQ,* XXXIX (1965), 42–45

* * *

PERETZ, Yitskhok Leybush

Yiddish short-story writer, poet, and dramatist, b. 18 May 1852, Zamość, Poland; d. 3 April 1915, Warsaw

Educated in the traditional eastern-European Jewish way, P. soon acquainted himself with modern Russian, Polish, and German literature. In his youth he began to experiment with poetry, prose, and drama in Hebrew and Polish as well as in Yiddish. In the 1870's he published several Hebrew poems and stories in various periodicals while successfully practicing law in Zamość. At thirty-six P. published his first Yiddish work, the ballad *Monish* in Sholem Aleichem's (q.v.) *Yidishe folksbibliotek* (1888). Shortly thereafter he settled in Warsaw, where he was employed by the Jewish Community Organization.

In the course of the next twenty-five years P. produced a large number of stories, poems, and dramas that were published in various literary periodicals. P. was himself involved in the publication of several literary journals, including *Yidishe Bibliotek* (1891, 1895, 1904), *Yontef bletlekh* (1894–95), and *Yidishe Vokhnshrift* (1909), in which many of his works first saw print.

A leading figure in Jewish cultural life in Warsaw, P. became the inspiration and the early mentor of important younger Yiddish writers such as Schalom Asch, I. J. Singer, Opatoshu and Pinski (qq.v.). He played an important part in the 1908 Yiddish Language Conference in Czernowitz.

Together with Mendele Moykher Sforim and Sholem Aleichem, P. is regarded as a founder of modern Yiddish literature. While his approach is highly intellectual, the content of his work derives from three main sources: Jewish folk tales, Hassidic life and lore, and the social conditions of eastern-European Jewry. P.'s focus is primarily upon moral issues, and while his tales are frequently peopled with angels, demons, and wonder-working rabbis, the overwhelming emphasis is upon the centrality of the problem of man's relationship to man.

FURTHER WORKS: *Schriftn* (7 vols., 1901); *Schriftn* (1903); *Die goldene Kette* (1907); *In Polish auf der Keit* (1909); *Ale verk* (18 vols., 1910–13); *Mayn zikhroynes* (1914; My Memoirs, 1964); *Die Verk* (13 vols., 1920); *Oisgevelte Verke* (2 vols., 1951); *Derzeilungen* (1952). **Selected English translations:** *Stories and Pictures* (1906); *Bontche the Silent and Other Stories* (1927); *The Three Canopies* (1948); *As Once We Were* (1951); *In This World and the Next* (1958); *Stories from Peretz,* (ed. Sol Diptyzin, 1964); *Three Gifts and Other Stories* (1964)

BIBLIOGRAPHY: Roback, A. A., *I. L. P.—Psychologist of Literature'* (1935); Meisel, N., *I. L. P., zayn lebn un shafn* (1945); Samuel, M., *Prince of the Ghetto* (1948); Schweid, M., *Treyst mayn folk, dos lebn fun I. L. P.* (1955)
ELI KATZ

PÉREZ DE AYALA, Ramón
Spanish poet, novelist, and essayist, b. 9 Aug. 1880, Oviedo; d. 5 Aug. 1962, Madrid

P. de A.'s nature was a many-sided one in which great sensitivity and cool quietness both existed. Only in the course of his life were these two elements brought into harmony. His historical and political clear-sightedness carried him beyond the "generation of '98." He is to be credited with self-knowledge, an epic view of life, the capacity for sociological observation, and an awareness of the tradition of his native Asturias. Asturian writers and liberal politicians certainly stimulated his thinking and manner of expression as well as aided him in achieving the sobriety of the acute, often satirical criticism so typical of him.

P. de A. shared Ortega y Gasset's (q.v.) universal viewpoint and interest in France, Germany, Italy, and the Anglo-Saxon world. While Asturian life also attracted him, he was always interested in the border at which the local and the universal merged.

P. de A. attended Carrión de los Condes and Gijón, a Jesuit school. He was introduced to Spanish liberalism at the University of Oviedo, where he also came under the influence of Clarín (pseud. of Leopoldo Alas y Ureña, 1852–1901). He finished his studies in London and developed in these years the close tie to England that influenced his whole life.

After his return to Spain, P. de A. published his first poems in *La paz del sendero* (1904). These are poems about the land. He later wrote on sea and river themes. His first novel, *Tinieblas en las cambres,* was published in 1907.

P. de A. was in touch with major writers of the time. Like Ortega y Gasset, he contributed to journals dedicated to the reform of Spanish life. In 1931 the Spanish Republic appointed him ambassador to London. He resigned this position shortly after the outbreak of the Spanish Civil War and went to live in Argentina.

The novel *A.M.D.G.* (i.e., *Ad majorem Dei gloriam,* 1910) is a highly critical and satirical account of life in the Jesuit boarding school P. de A. attended. *Troteras y danzaderas* (1913), another novel, depicts, through realistic satire, the social, political, and intellectual society in a capital city. In his famous novel about doubt and faith, *Belarmino y Apolonio* (1921), P. de A. becomes a good-humored observer of life as well as a satiricist.

Luna de miel, luna de hiel (1924) and *Los trabajos de Urbano y Simona* (1924), the latter rich in themes from erotic Greek pastorals and from Calderón's (1600–81) works, expound a theory of eroticism very similar to that put forth by the scientist-writer Gregorio Marañón y Posadillo (1887–1960) in his critique of Don Juanism. It is no accident that the essays in *Las máscaras* (2 vols., 1917–19) and the novel *Tigre Juan* (1926; Tiger Juan, 1933)—one of his best works—deal with the Don Juan syndrome. Here P. de A. refutes an illusion that menaces life in order to clear the way to a truer reality, a new world of the Eros.

Although P. de A.'s dramatic and art criticism is not always relevant to his subject, it is always lively and witty and offers a creative synthesis of impressions. His language boldly combines various traditional elements and holds the reader's attention by its virtuosity.

FURTHER WORKS: *La pata de la raposa* (1912; The Fox's Paw, 1924); *El sendero innumerable* (1916); *Prometeo* (1916; Prometheus, 1920); *Luz de Domingo* (1916); *Bajo el signo de Artemisa* (1916); *La caída de los limones* (1916); *Herman, encadenada* (1917); *Política y toros* (1918); *El sendero andante* (1921); *Obras completas* (19 vols., 1923–30); *El ombligo del mundo* (1924); *El curandero de su honra* (1926); *Poesías completas* (1942); *Principios y finales de las novela* (1958); *Obras selectas* (1958); *Amistades y recuerdos* (1961); *Fábulas y ciudades* (1961). **Selected English**

translation: *Selections from P. de A.* (ed. by N. B. Adams and S. A. Stoudemire; 1934)

BIBLIOGRAPHY: Agustin, F., *R. P. de A., su vida y sus obras* (1927); Adams, N. B., and Stoudemire, S. A., introduction to *Selections from P. de A.* (1934); Curtius, E. R., "R. P. de A.," *Kritische Essays zur europäischen Literatur* (2nd ed., 1950); McCall, M.-B. M., "An Analysis of R. P. de A.'s Novels as a Plea for Freedom," *DA,* XX (1960), 3747; Urrutia, N., *R. P. de A.* (1960); Dobrian, W. A., "The Novelistic Art of R. P. de A.," *DA,* XXI (1961), 1563–64

FRITZ SCHALK

PÉREZ GALDÓS, Benito

Spanish novelist, historian, and dramatist, b. 10 May 1843, Las Palmas, Canary Islands; d. 4 Jan. 1920, Madrid

P. G., who came to typify Spanish liberalism, derived from the Basque traditionalists. From 1862 on he lived in Madrid, traveling frequently in Europe. In 1907 he became a member of the government. In his solitary old age he was blind.

P. G. is to be credited with renewing the Spanish novel, with freeing it from romantic vagueness and imitation of French models, and leading it back to the tradition of Spanish realism. In addition, because of the overwhelming scope of his work and range of themes, for which he drew both from current events and from a wealth of national history still fresh in living memory, he was also the "standard-bearer" (Salaverría) around whom his contemporaries rallied in great numbers. This liberal, pro-republic statesman was admired for his unaffected style and for his skill in bringing his ideas to life on the stage. He was influenced by the pedagogue Giner de los Ríos (1839–1915), among others.

P. G.'s first novels, written after a period of journalism, were a stimulus to some of his eminent contemporaries. On the other hand, he had no connection with the "Generation of '98," which was more interested in analysis and definite programs than in reportage and fiction.

Spanish history from Trafalgar to the restoration of the monarchy in 1875 was the subject of the forty-six volumes of his *Episodios Nacionales* (1873–1912), which ranged from *Trafalgar* (1873; Eng., 1884) to *Cánovas* (1912). The first series appeared between 1873 and 1875, the second, in the 1875–79 period. The steadily increasing success of this fictionalized history led him to write three more series between 1898 and 1912. Altogether, these works account for almost half of his life's work.

P. G. wrote thirty-two *novelas contemporáneas* (42 vols., 1868 ff.), which dealt with contemporary themes. Among them are: *Doña Perfecta* (1876; Eng., 1896); *Gloria* (1877; Eng., 1882), which treats of a collapsing marriage between a Spanish woman and a Jew; *La familia de León Roch* (1878; Eng., 1888); *Fortunata y Jacinta* (1886–87); *Miau* (1888); *Torquemada en la hoguera* (4 vols.; 1889–95); *Realidad* (1890); *Ángel Guerra* (1891–92); *Nazarín* (1895); *Misericordia* (1897; Compassion, 1962); *La razón de la sinrazón* (1905). In these novels, which, influenced by French naturalism (q.v.), uphold a thesis, P. G. gives freer rein to his inventiveness.

Some of P. G.'s twenty-four plays, written after 1892, are adaptations of his novels—*e.g.,* *Realidad, La loca de la casa,* and *Doña Perfecta.* The performance of *Electra* (1901) ended in a triumphal march and the fall of the conservative government. P. G. stressed the shortcomings of Spanish Catholicism, underlined the dangers of religious fanaticism, and sometimes seems to be anticlerical on principle. It can fairly be said though that in his plays P. G. was often carried away by rhetoric.

P. G. also published fifteen volumes of travel-writing and memoirs (see sampling in volume VI of *Obras completas,* 6 vols., 1940).

Although it was later charged that P. G. saw history "in an anecdotal and familiar form" (Valbuena) and that his prose was "frequently trivial" (J. Marías), he was hailed by Madariaga (q.v.) as "one of the greatest literary creators of the white race" and by Pérez de Ayala (q.v.) as "the greatest Spaniard of our time."

P. G. is still admired for the titanic creativity with which he attempted to portray the 19th c. from the viewpoint of the bourgeois middle class in a gigantic unified block of novels, and for the way he, like Balzac (1799–1850), peopled his work with a host of lifelike characters.

BIBLIOGRAPHY: Alas, L., *Estudio crítico y biográfico de G.* (1912); Cejador y Franca, J., *B. P.* (1918); Gómez de Baquero, E., *Unamuno y G.* (1920); Ortega y Munilla, J., *Los viejos maestros: G.* (1920); Scatori, S., *La idea religiosa en la obra de P. G.* (1927); Walton, L., *B. P.* (1927); Arroyo, C., *G.* (1930); Sánchez Trincado, J. L., *G.* (1934); Sáinz de Robles, F. C. *"Introducción, Biografía, Bibliografía,"* in *B. P. G.: Obras completas* (1940); Casalduero, J., *Vida y obra de G.* (2nd ed., 1951); Schraibman, J., "Dreams in the Novels of G.," *DA,* XX (1959), 1795; MacDonald, M. B., "The Influence of Émile Zola in the Novels of B. P. G.," *DA,* XX (1960), 2294; Gullon, R., *G. novelista moderno* (1960)

ANTON DIETERICH

PERSE SAINT-JOHN

See Saint-John Perse

PERSIAN LITERATURE

In the literature of Persia poetry has occupied a special place. Each poetic genre served as a vehicle for a certain kind of content. The *rubáiyát* gave philosopher-poets such as Omar Khayyám (d. ca. 1123) an opportunity to express gems of wisdom; the *gazal* was appropriate for the expression of romantic, mystical, and literary moods; the *qasideh,* for praise and flattery; the *masnawi,* for fables and historical events. The *tasnif,* most popular with the villagers, was the equivalent of the ballad.

POETRY

In the late 19th c., when the need for political change became imperative, poetry, even though it continued to play its historic role, found its form and content challenged by a change in thought and taste. Poetry since 1890 can be divided into four fairly distinct periods.

1891–1926

The poetry of this period, dominated by revolutionary attitudes, was marked by a simplicity of expression. It concerned itself with such contemporary themes as justice, Iranian progress, world peace, women's rights, and improved conditions for industrial workers and peasants. *Engagement* was the creed of the rebelling poets. The woman poet Parvin-i-d'tisami, for example, wrote about the suffering of the poor.

Boldly voicing their demands for social change, many poets used or invented simple forms of verse to communicate these ideas to the common people and made a valiant effort to avoid the stereotyped expressions so prevalent in traditional verse forms. Iraj Mirza Jalalu'l Mamalik was one of those who ex-pressed his rebellion by means of simple diction and colloquial idioms in his poetry.

Mohammad Reza Ishqi was among those who initiated simpler kinds of verse forms. Ishqi's opera *Rastakhiz* has many of the characters of Ferdowsi's (941–1019) *Shahname,* but these characters speak about modern social ideas and call for independence from foreign domination. Ishqi's favorite subject was the working class.

Mirza Abu'l Qasim Arif (d. 1933) used the *tasnif* as a vehicle for criticizing government leaders, the aristocracy, and foreign infiltration.

Abu'l Quasim Lahuti (1887–1957), the most skillful practitioner of social realism, frequently resorted to familiar fables to convey his ideas.

The poet Pur-i-Davud was among the traditional poets of this period. While generally supporting the constitution of 1906, he retained earlier verse patterns and extolled ancient Persian heritage. Pur-i-Davud's strong sense of nationalism motivated his thought and poetry; he wrote in pure Persian to avoid the contamination of Arabic-derived words.

Socially embattled poets steered public opinion in other ways by editing newspapers and establishing literary societies and journals. Bahar (1886–1951) was the outstanding example. On several occasions the government stopped the publication of *Now Bahar,* but each time Bahar managed to start it up again. In 1916 and 1917 he also founded a literary group, Danish-kada, which enabled young poets to gather and discuss their work. Even though he largely adhered to traditional forms, Bahar, who was probably the major figure in the school of conservative realism, dealt with contemporary events and ideas. In a poem written in 1914 he attacked the privileged groups in Iran and demanded that they receive their just deserts.

The Reign of Reza Shah (1926–41)

During this period the press lost its vitality. Poets were deprived of freedom of expression. They turned to scholarship, as did Bahar, or fled to Russia, as did Lahuti and others. Those less fortunate, such as Ishqi and Farukhi Yazdi, were assassinated. Emphasizing traditional heroic verse, poets turned to the past. Poets such as Ferdowsi, the greatest epic poet of Persia, were glorified.

1945–53

The modern poetry movement was quiescent

until the end of World War II, when it reestablished itself with increased vigor. Bahar, once again carrying the banner for conservative realism, declared that the objectives of poetry could only be attained "if one writes for the sake of the people, in the interest of the people, according to the demands of the people, and in the language of the people."

Confronted by the same problems as those faced by the poets of the 1891–1926 period, the postwar poet wrote out of a context of native social realism, communism, or conservative realism. They wrote about issues of justice in Iran, the problem of individual security, the need for a government of law and order, and the interference Iran suffered from foreign powers. The nationalization of oil deposits in the late 1940's was a clarion call to many poets. Prime Minister Mohammad Mossadegh's national democratic movement raised the hopes of the *engagé* poets.

During this period the younger poets (those born in the late 1920's) began to write in blank verse and stressed thought and meaning over traditional forms. Older poets viewed this trend cautiously, but by 1969 it has become more widely accepted.

1953 to Present

The fall of Mossadegh (1953) brought the curtailment of free speech. The younger poets, who spurned the traditional explanations of life, death, destiny, human emotions, and man's relatedness to the universe, now found no outlet for expression. Among the most prominent younger poets of the 1960's are Nadirpur, Farokh Zad, Mushiri, Bamdad, Shamlu, and Kianush.

Nadirpur angrily condemns his generation for its passivity and accuses his contemporaries of being children. The gifted Bamdad discusses the existential problem of his generation—a generation searching and anxious, a generation that, though weeping of grief, does not know who it is or why it has to suffer so much. In search of identity, the woman poet Farokh Zad seeks to find meaning for her existence. Kianush, trying to picture the social situation, finds that ruler and ruled, prisoner and keeper, guilty and innocent are all melancholic. The guard and the criminal walk hand in hand.

Confronted by profound social problems, Iran's younger poets clearly perceive their own plight and that of their country, but they see no solution in sight. Increased freedom of expression in Iran would enable poets at least to formulate the problems of Iran.

PROSE

Traditionally Persian prose was a vehicle for disseminating historical, philosophical, and scientific knowledge rather than a medium for imaginative writing. Often such learning was embodied in autobiographies. The novel and short story were rarely written. From the 16th c. to the 18th c. the ambiguous, flowery prose style reflected the formalized society of which the writers were a part.

At the beginning of the 19th c. the increase of cultural relations with Europe and social mobility created an audience for prose. This interest was strengthened by the political movements that later culminated in the constitution of 1906.

The forerunners of the modern prose writers, however, recognized the clumsiness of the existing prose style and genres. This their first efforts were directed toward introducing into Iran a simpler and more viable prose. By way of travel books and journalism, translations of such European writers as Molière and Dumas, novels and plays, these early prose writers tried to mold prose into a medium more appropriate to the needs of the 20th c. than traditional Persian prose was. Out of this, Persian prose evolved in three directions: conservative realism, social realism, and social individualism.

The most important writers involved with conservative realism are M. Hejazi, Jamal-zadeh, and Ali Dashti. Mohammad Hejazi wrote his first novel, *Homa,* in 1929, and later published *Parichir* (1930), *Andishe* (1940), and *Ayene* (1954). In all his novels Hejazi deals with the social events of urban life as experienced by middle-class people. Homa, the heroine of Hejazi's first novel, is the author's portrait of the ideal modern girl. She knows the rules of conduct and modestly behaves in a way acceptable to a conservatively liberal group. In contrast, Parichir, in the novel of that title who comes from the same class, rebels against traditional values.

Jamal-zadeh was the first to develop the modern Persian short story. His first book, *Yaki Bud, Yaki Nabud,* was written and published in Berlin in 1920. The first of the six stories, "Farsi Shekar Ast," presents the situation in which the Western-educated individual uses European/American words in his everyday speech, the clergy uses Arabic, and the average Iranian is lost between the two.

More than any other modern writer Ali Dashti desires to give a picture of modern Persian women. His characters are usually upper-class, Western-oriented, wealthy, and attractive. He presents his women, who are frequently the products of two cultures, as wanting social equality without being willing to accept social responsibility.

Sa'aid Nafisi is to be thought of as a link between conservative realism and social realism. He was one of the first to write modern Persian prose and has contributed to the cultural milieu by his translations from the French. Among his works are *Mah-e-Nakhshab, Setaregan-e-Siya, Farangis,* and *Nime Ra Behisht.*

Among the most important of the social realists are Bozorg 'A Lavi, Jalal-Al Ahmad, 'Tatimadzade, and Sadiq Chubak. Bozorg 'A Lavi (b. 1903), was influenced by Freud and created his characters in terms of Freudian psychology. Among his works are *Varaq Parehaye Zendan,* in which he describes his years in prison during the 1930's. In the collection is a superb essay, addressed to his wife, that expresses his emotions just after he received news of his release. He also translated Chekhov (q.v.).

Jalal-Al Ahmad sympathetically describes characters from the devoutly religious lower class and tries to reveal their ways of thinking. Among his early books is *Ziyarat,* which describes the adventures of a young man on a pilgrimage. In the recent *Tat Neshin Mai e Boluk e Zahra,* Jalal-Al Ahmad deals with the life situations of two groups of peasants.

'Tatimadzade pictures different aspects of life and criticizes social conditions. The theme of *Zivar* is that money, regardless of the way in which it is acquired, has become in Iran the criterion of social prestige.

Sadiq Chubak's book *Khayme Shab bazi* contains eleven sections, each of which is a picture of daily life. Like a painter, Sadiq Chubak selects his subjects well and portrays them with considerable skill.

This skill also characterizes the writing of Okhovat, whose story *Sib-e-Sorkh* is told very simply. It expresses the genuine emotional experiences of a maidservant, who is tired of the insults and the way she is treated by her master.

Sadiq Hidayat (1902–1951), perhaps the greatest short-story writer of modern Persian literature, was a diversified and ideologically independent author. Humanism and nationalism inspired him to investigate and describe various social groups, though his kind heart led him to be especially interested in the lower classes. He developed his characters with mastery, revealing their mode of life with perceptive depth.

Among the younger novelists, M. A. Afgani received much acclaim for his novel *Showhar e Ahu Khanum* (1962).

Since the beginning of the 20th c. drama, like the film, has been produced in Iran with varying degrees of success, but in the absence of a free social climate, the potentials of these forms cannot be realized.

BIBLIOGRAPHY: Browne, E. G., *The Press and Poetry of Modern Persia* (1914); Ishaque, M., *Modern Persian Poetry* (1943); Rahman, R., *Post-revolution Persian Verse* (1955); U.S.S.R. Academy of Science, *Sovremenii Iran* (1957); Ehlers, L., *Persische Märchen und Schwänke* (1961); Arasteh, R., *Education and Social Awakening in Iran* (1962); Gelpke, R., *Die iranische Prosaliteratur im 20. Jahrhundert* (1962)

REZA ARASTEH

PESSANHA, Camilo

Portuguese poet, b. 7 Sept. 1867, Coimbra; d. 1926, Macao

The illegitimate son of a law student and a working-class girl, P. studied law in Coimbra. After 1894 he lived most of his life in Macao, working as a teacher. He seems to have been an opium user.

P., who is Portugal's most mature symbolist poet (*see* symbolism), was influenced by the French symbolists Mallarmé and Verlaine and by Walt Whitman. His poems reflect his searching, analytic intellect, his highly sensitized morbidity, his exquisite eroticism, and his unusual verbal artistry. P.'s laments of exile, transitoriness, death emanate from his deep feelings of sad pessimism and fatalism. In his lifetime, though most of his work appeared in periodicals, he did publish one book, *Clépsidra* (1920), which is a collection of this highly charged poetry.

P. wrote essays on Chinese literature and culture (*China,* 1944) and translated Chinese poetry.

FURTHER WORK: *Poesia e prosa,* ed. B. Vidigal (1963)

67

BIBLIOGRAPHY: Miguel, A. D., *C. P.* (1956); De Lemos, E., *C. P.* (1956); Vidigal, B., ed., introduction to P.'s *Poesia e prosa* (1963); Rossi, G., *Geschichte der portugiesischen Literatur* (1964); Sayers, R., "Portuguese Poetry," *Journal of the American Portuguese Cultural Society*, I (1967), iii, 1–14; Simões, J., *C. P.* (1967)

* * * *

PESSOA, Fernando António Nogueira

Portuguese poet and critic (writing in Portuguese and English), b. 13 June 1888, Lisbon; d. there, 30 Nov. 1935

After P.'s father's death in 1893, his mother married the Portuguese consul in Durban, South Africa, where P. lived from 1896 to 1905. He graduated from junior college in South Africa, winning the Queen Victoria Prize for English Composition, and went to Lisbon in 1905 to attend the university. The early British education that P. received was far different from the French culture then pervasive in Portuguese literature and made an everlasting impression on his views and his handling of language. Moreover, through his work he was to exert an anglicizing influence on subsequent poetic diction in Portugal and Brazil. Soon after 1905 he gave up his studies, using his knowledge of English to get employment as a business correspondent. For the rest of his life he lived alone in Lisbon, avoiding social life and the literary world.

At his debut in 1912—which was as a literary critic—he praised the *saudōdismo* movement (*see* Portuguese literature) in such extravagant terms that his articles provoked nationwide polemics. From that year on he proceeded uninterruptedly to comment on politics and literature by means of paradoxical and mystifying articles and pamphlets. He helped to launch the avantgarde movement in Portuguese literature and, through the reviews *Orpheu* (1915) and *Portugal Futurista* (1917), was its leading figure along with Sá-Carneiro (q.v.) and Jose de Almada-Negreiros (1893–1970).

But it is as a poet that P. has won eminence in modern world literature. He wrote poetry under his own name as well as under at least three other names. As Fernando Pessoa, he wrote poems that are marked by their startling innovations of language, though he used traditional stanza and metrical patterns. Alvaro de Campos was the bold modernist, tragically minded, whose forte was for dour and majestic

diction in free verse. Alberto Caeiro was the straightforward empiricist, a sensualist, whose free verse seems indifferent to technique. Ricardo Reis was the classicist, whose Horatian odes surpass the ambitions of most 18th-c. writers. These names were "heteronyms," as P. said of them, not pen names. Each persona had a distinct philosophy of life, wrote at a certain linguistic level, and worked in a distinctive style and form. P. even wrote literary discussions among them. He prepared their horoscopes to fit their lives and personalities—or he may have shaped a personality according to a horoscope. (Like other Western postsymbolist poets he had esoteric tendencies that show in his work.)

What is most impressive is that each of these "heteronyms" (and when he wrote poetry under his own name he was as much of a heteronym as when he "was" somebody else) is a great poet in his own right.

The bulk of P.'s work was published in literary magazines, especially in his own *Athena* (1924–25). Editors did not begin to compile his work until 1942, and the wealth of his scattered or unpublished writings has still to be rescued, in spite of his having been recognized as a master in 1927.

In P.'s lifetime, he published little in book form. His English poems were collected in books: *35 Sonnets* (1917), *Antinous* (1918), *English Poems I–II* (1921), *English Poems III* (1921). Most of them were too "metaphysical" for the time and hence very much in advance of the change of taste that was to occur in English poetry. In addition, he published *Mensagem* (1934), a sequence of emblematic poems in Portuguese on the history of Portugal. Though a minor work it is still controversial today as it can be interpreted as "nationalist" and used to present P. as an apologist for the authoritarian regime that had come into power in 1926, which he was not.

P. is admirable for his terrifying lucidity, his language virtuosity, and his inventive imagery. His deeply felt intellectualism was in the best Portuguese tradition of Luís Vaz de Camões (1524?–80) and Antero de Quental (1842–93). (One of his best-known lines states, "What in me feels is now thinking.") Today, P.'s poetry is still original and audacious. No one in Western literature has been more successful than he in realizing the modern dream of creating an antiromantic "objective correlative." All this qualifies him as one of the greatest poets in Portuguese, and as such he is admired in Portugal and Brazil. Translations of his

NIS PETERSEN

FERNANDO PESSOA

poems in Spanish, French, English, German, and other languages have been appearing since the 1940's, thus opening the way for P. to be recognized as one of the most important and original masters of modern poetry.

FURTHER WORKS: *Poemas de F. P.* (1942); *Poemas de Álvaro de Campos* (1944); *Poemas de Alberto Caeiro* (1946); *Poemas de Ricardo Reis* (1946); *Páginas de doutrina estética* (ed. J. de Sena; 1946); *Poemas dramáticos I* (1952); *Poesias inéditas: 1930–35* (1955); *Poesias inéditas: 1919–30* (1956); *F. P.: Antología* (ed. O. Paz; 1962)

BIBLIOGRAPHY: Prado Coelho, J. do, *Unidade e diversidade em F. P.* (1949); Simões, J. G., *Vida e obra de F. P.* (2 vols., 1951); Monteiro, A. C., *Estudos sobre a poesia de F. P.* (1958); Nemésio, J., *A. obra poética de F. P.* (1958); Sena, Jorge de, *Da poesia portuguesa* (1959); Sena, Jorge de, *O poeta é um fingidor* (1960)

JORGE DE SENA

PETERSEN, Nis

Danish novelist and poet, b. 22 Jan. 1897, Vamdrup; d. 9 March 1943, Laven

P., who was the son of a tanner, was orphaned at an early age. He was then brought up in Herning by his devout Pietistic grandmother. After serving five years (1913–18) as an apprentice pharmacist in Naskov, he abandoned this endeavor to work as a journalist in Holbäk. By 1920 the instability of his character asserted itself, and he gave himself up to erratic, penniless wanderings throughout Europe.

P.'s poetry, which he started to publish in 1926, was of high quality from the beginning. His major poems, most of which are dramatic monologues, are unusual for their original imagery and lyrical quality. Though he tenaciously expressed his repudiation of established religion, P.'s poetry reflects a religiosity that was inherent to P.

In 1931 P. won worldwide success with his novel *Sandalmagernes gade* (The Street of the Sandalmakers, 1932). In this re-creation of the Rome of Marcus Aurelius, he gives a gripping description of the slow but certain victory of Christianity. By his use of slang and startling anachronisms he shocks the reader into seeing historical events as actual happenings that were being enacted by real people.

Spildt mælk (1934; Spilt Milk: A Story of

Ireland, 1935), an equally successful novel, is concerned with the Irish rebellion of 1921–22 as seen from a pro-British point of view, which reflected P.'s personal bias.

P. reached the height of his achievement in his superb novellas. His intimate knowledge of the way of life of the down and out is revealed in a number of these.

Able to handle a variety of subjects, gifted with narrative skill, possessing a masterly style, P. was not invariably successful in maintaining a uniform level of excellence. In a fantasy-like, evocative, and free-ranging style he presents, often in a tragicomic way, episodes of human conflict as well as romanticized pictures of vagabond life, battle scenes, and desert landscapes. All his writing was pervaded by the emotional state that dominated him—that of being tortured and consumed by an irrational, chronic, self-punitive guilt.

As an existential writer, P. was a major influence on the post–World War II Danish poets.

FURTHER WORKS: *En drift vers* (1933); *Til en dronning* (1935); *Engle blaeser paa trompet* (1937); *Stykgods* (1940); *Dagtyve* (1941); *Digte* (1942); *Muleposen* (1942); *Stynede popler* (1943); *Aftenbønnen* (1947); *Brændende Europa* (1947); *Da seeren tav* (1947); *Lad os leve i nuet* (1948); *Samlede digte* (1949); *For tromme og kastagnet* (1951)

BIBLIOGRAPHY: Brix, H., *N. P.* (1947); Petersen, A. N., *Mod Haeld* (1948); Frederiksen, E., *Ung dansk Litteratur* (1952); Andersen, J., *N. P.* (1958); Kristensen, S. Möller, *Moderne dansk Litteratur* (1958)

* * * *

PETRESCU, Camil

Romanian novelist, b. 22 April 1894, Bucharest; d. there, 14 May 1957

P. studied literature and philosophy at the University of Bucharest and was later a high-school teacher, an influential journalist, critic, and polemicist, a director of the Bucharest National Theater (1939), and a member of the Romanian Academy.

In spite of recurrent personal differences, P. was throughout the 1930's and early 1940's close to Eugen Lovinescu's (1881–1943) intellectual circle, which made a stand for an art independent of political influences, one that was modern, urban, and Western-oriented. Somewhat amateurish essays on Bergsonian and

69

phenomenological philosophy, as well as critical essays, particularly *Teze şi antiteze* (1936), are evidence of his adherence to such ideas.

P. was firmly committed to an analytical rationalism, the very mechanism of which, he believed, was productive of aesthetic satisfaction. This is equally reflected in the tough idealism of his poems, *Versuri* (1923), and in the theme underlying his principal dramatic works—*Suflete tari* (1925; Those Poor Stout Hearts, 1960), *Danton* (1931), *Act veneţian* (1931), *Mioara* (1931)—the incompatibility of a power-hungry intellect with the surrounding world.

P.'s significance rests on his novels. *Ultima noapte de dragoste, întâia noapte de război* (1930) probes the consciousness of the World War I generation. With subtlety and precision, parallels are drawn between individual and social psychology on the one hand, between personal, erotic suffering and failure and the cruel experience of war on the other. Even more important is *Patul lui Procust* (2 vols., 1933) in which the series of events leading to the breakdown in erotic and social communication of a lucid and sensitive intellectual is presented from the viewpoint of a number of differing characters.

While these novels are marked by the opposition between the individual and society, *Un om între oameni* (3 vols., 1953–57; A Man amongst Men, 1958) is devoted to a 19th-c. Romanian revolutionary intellectual who emerges from his solitude. Though marred by a sedulous projection of abstract sociological patterns, this novel is distinguished for its finely worked-out historical imagery and seems to offer the outline of a solution of how action can be efficacious to the intellectual's predicament.

P.'s main strength lies in his ability to describe the psychological dimensions of conflict in Romania's increasingly urbanized social structures. His substantial influence upon subsequent prose writers was due in part to his clean factual style and innovative techniques.

FURTHER WORKS: *Jocul ielelor* (1916); *Mitică Popescu* (1923); *Transcendentalia* (1932); *E. Lovinescu sub zodia seninătăţii imperturbabile* (1936); *Modalitatea estetică a teatrului* (1937); *Husserl* (1938); *Teatru* (3 vols., 1946–47); *Turnul de fildeş* (1948); *Bălcescu* (1949); *Nuvele* (1953, 1956); *Versuri* (1957); *Caragiale în vremea lui* (1957); *Teatru* (2 vols., 1957–58)

BIBLIOGRAPHY: Călinescu, G., *Istoria literaturii române* (1943); Călin, V., "One of the many," *Romanian Review,* II (1954), 107–19; Tertullian, N., "P.'s Plays," *Romanian Review,* II (1959), 138–44; Elvin, B., *P.* (1962); Phillipide, A., "The Spirit and Tradition of Modern Romanian Literature," *Romanian Review,* XXI (1967), ii, 5–10

VIRGIL NEMOIANU

PETRESCU, Cezar

Romanian novelist, b. 1 Dec. 1892, Hodora-Cotnari; d. 8 March 1961, Bucharest

P. studied law at the Iaşi University and soon became a noted journalist. In 1921 he founded *Gîndirea*, the most articulate Romanian journal of literary traditionalism, which was later to become an organ of right-wing ideology. In 1936 he was briefly the Secretary General of the Board of Education. After World War II, P. made remarkable translations from Russian and French realistic novels. He was a member of the Romanian Academy.

In many novels and volumes of short stories, P. attempted a fresco of contemporary Romanian society in the manner of Balzac (1799–1850). His most prominent work is *Intunecare* (1927; Gathering Clouds, 3 vols., 1957), which tells the quest of a sensitive and idealist young man for absolute values and purity among the harrowing experiences of war, politics, and love. A restless wanderer through Romanian society he goes down, after repeated failures, to ultimate defeat and suicide. *Calea Victoriei* (1928) renders a lifelike though pessimistic image of the bustle of Bucharest society.

A somewhat bittersweet quality pervades the novels dealing with the decay of patriarchal rural structures under the onslaughts of industrial civilization: *Comoara regelui Dromihet* (1931) and *Aurul negru* (1933). Less characteristic are P.'s books for children, fantastic novels (not without a streak of morbidity), and his novel trilogy devoted to the life of the greatest Romanian writer Mihai Eminescu (1850–89): *Luceafărul, Nirvana,* and *Carmen seculare* (1935–36).

Hugely successful in his lifetime, P.'s stature has diminished in the last decade. Some of this is deserved as his work often slides into commercialized sentimentality and (after the war) biased political simplification. One cannot deny, however, P.'s genuine capacity for epic invention and for providing varied details.

FURTHER WORKS: *Scrisorile unui răzeş*

(1921); *Drumul cu plopi* (1924); *Cheia visurilor* (1925); *Omul din vis* (1926); *Omul care şi-a găsit umbra* (1928); *Carnet de vară* (1928); *Simfonia fantastică* (1929); *La paradis general* (1930); *Aranca, ştima lacurilor* (1930); *Baletul mecanic* (1931); *Flori de ghiaţă* (1931); *Oraş patriarhal* (1932); *Plecat fără adresă* (1932); *Fram, ursul polar* (1932); *Apostol* (1933–57); *Duminica orbului* (1934); *Carlton* (1942); *Pămînt şi cer* (1943); *Ochii strigoiului* (1943); *Adăpostul Sobolia* (1945); *Războiul lui Ion Săracu* (1946); *Doctorul Negrea* (1948); *Două inimi sincere* (1951); *Nepoţii gornistului* (1952); *Despre scris şi scriitori* (1953); *Vino şi vezi* (1954); *Oameni de ieri, oameni de azi, oameni de mîine* (1955); *Insemnări de călător. Reflecţii de scriitor* (1958)

BIBLIOGRAPHY: Constantinescu, P., *Scrieri alese* (1957); Gafiţa, M., Introduction to *Gathering Clouds* (1957); Stancu, H., *C. P.* (1958)

VIRGIL NEMOIANU

PEYREFITTE, Roger

French novelist, b. 17 Aug. 1907, Castres, Tarn

P. received a classical education in Roman Catholic schools and later studied at the École des Sciences Politiques. He was attached to the French embassy in Athens from 1933 to 1939, left the post in 1940, and returned in 1943 for only a few months. The reasons for his departure are still not clear. P. remained strongly attracted to the classical Mediterranean world, which he had learned to love during his years in Athens.

P.'s first novel, *Les Amitiés particulières* (1944; Special Friendships, 1950), won the Théophraste-Renaudot prize. It remains his best book because of its sensitive treatment of adolescent fervor and homosexuality in the closed world of a boys' Catholic school. P. maintains a constantly elegant style as he analyzes the psychological and sexual tensions caused by the emotional demands of the young hero, Georges de Sarre, on a younger schoolmate, who eventually takes his own life.

Les Ambassades (1951; Diplomatic Diversions, 1953) and *La Fin des ambassades* (1953; Diplomatic Conclusions, 1954) are based on P.'s experience in Athens and continue the story of Georges de Sarre. They caused a scandal because of their satire of the diplomatic corps (under all forms of government) and the impli-

cation that the circumstances under which their autobiographical hero was forced to leave the diplomatic service paralleled those behind P.'s own departure.

These two "documentary novels" and *Les Clés de Saint-Pierre* (1955; The Keys of St. Peter, 1957), a satire on the Vatican, were very successful, but it seemed to many critics that P. was endangering his talent by excessive sensationalism—a tendency which he was to continue in *Les Juifs* (1965; The Jews, 1967).

The best passages of his novels reveal, however, considerable erudition and analytic skill, and all of P.'s books contain striking passages that show him to be an interesting observer of society and morality.

FURTHER WORKS: *Mademoiselle de Murville* (1947); *Le Prince des neiges* (1947); *L'Oracle* (1948); *Les Amours singulières* (1949); *La Mort d'une mère* (1950); *Du Vésuve à l'Etna* (1952; South from Naples, 1954); *Jeunes proies* (1956); *Les Chevaliers de Malte* (1957; Knights of Malta, 1959); *L'Exilé de Capri* (1959; The Exile of Capri, 1961); *Le Spectateur nocturne* (1960); *Les Fils de la lumière* (1961); *La Nature du prince* (1963; The Prince's Person, 1964); *Notre Amour* (1967); *Les Américains* (1968)

BIBLIOGRAPHY: Garnier, C., *L'Homme et ses personnages* (1955); Bourdet, D., *Pris sur le vif* (1957); Brodin, P., *Présences contemporaines* (1957)

CHARLES G. HILL

PHILIPPINE LITERATURE

For twenty years before the outbreak of the Revolution of 1896, Filipinos who favored civil reform and freedom without independence published novels and newspapers in Spanish and directed them hopefully to liberals in Madrid and Barcelona. Among them were the essays of Marcelo H. del Pilar and Lopez Jaena, whose grace and fury had few Philippine precedents, and the panoramic, accusatory novels of Jose Rizal—*Noli Me Tangere* (1887) and *El Filibusterismo* (1891)—which cast shadows of excellence far into the 20th c. Yet, with the end of the Spanish-American War in 1898, virtually all Spanish literary as well as political influence ceased.

There are critics who speak of the first half of the 20th c. as the "golden age" of Philippine literature in Spanish. Aside, however, from Claro Recto's poems, *Bajo los cocoteros* (1911), and his play, *Solo entre las sombras* (1917); Antonio Abad's prize-winning novel, *El Campeón* (1939); and occasional speeches left by Recto and President Manuel Quezon; little that is comparable to the end-of-century flowering can be discovered.

Less biased historians record, instead, a prolonged cultural pause before English-language mass education, which replaced Spanish-language education of the elite could produce its own literature and before literature in the vernacular could emerge.

The beginning of commonwealth status in 1935, with anticipation of full independence after ten years, gave special urgency to the search for national identity. Although this was also the year for the founding of the Institute of National Language, which established Tagalog, Filipinos were finding (at least temporarily) in imported, rather than native idioms and literary traditions, the same creative challenge that Spanish once provided them with.

To assert some measure of continuity between otherwise alienated generations, the works of Nick Joaquin have attempted to recover the moral and religious orientation that constitute the most enduring aspect of the Spanish heritage. Aside from several imitations of late-medieval saintly legends and random essays such as "La Naval de Manila," his concern has been less with recreating the past than with its modern vestiges.

Joaquin's "Three Generations" (a short story in *Prose and Poems,* 1952), reveals irrevocable family resemblances—a rigorous Spanish sense of kinship—even in the midst of recurrent revolt against family pieties. Other Joaquin stories, such as "The Summer Solstice," find in Filipinos counterparts of Spanish ambivalences: primitivist sensuousness and Christian asceticism.

Joaquin's 1952 omnibus volume contains his only play, *Portrait of the Artist as Filipino,* in which the descendants of the declining Don Lorenzo finally confirm his inborn integrity by demonstrating their own. Despite impoverishment, they refuse to sell the masterpiece that he painted for them. The painting depicts Anchises being borne by his son Aeneas like a household god from burning Troy. The faces of son and father are identical. Joaquin is suggesting here that the Filipino has got to take the burden of history on his back.

Aeneas, however, was not only deliverer of the past but founder of the future. In Joaquin's novel, *The Woman Who Had Two Navels* (1961), he grants qualified respect to the ex-*revolucionario,* Monson, who hides in Hong Kong exile because he is afraid to face the stresses of postwar independence. Although Joaquin has been accused of romantic nostalgia, since 1946 his view of history has become progressively less static.

The Spanish past is viewed with an equally discriminating eye in *The Peninsulars* (1964), Linda Ty-Casper's novel of the confusion of loyalties that made possible the British occupation of Manila in the mid-18th c. Each figure of colonial authority, even those with the highest concern for the ruled, has some flaw of motive, some high personal ambition that maims his magistracy. The *indios* (as Spaniards called the natives) are also torn between national loyalties and self-interest.

Only the dying governor general and the *indio* priest Licaros achieve a sufficient understanding of the need for mutual dependence: on one level, love; on another, the social contract. Such a novel represents an increasingly selective salvaging by the Philippine writer of his various usable pasts.

The epic impulse, the concern with rendering history as meaningful fable, has shaped the writings of poets such as Ricaredo Demetillo and Alejandrino Hufana. *Barter in Panay* (1961) is the first third of Demetillo's verse adaptation of portions of the Visayan folk epic, *Maragtas.* (This folk epic was recorded on bamboo bark by ten *datu* groups that, in 1212, fled from tyranny.) In his book Demetillo explains the peaceful arrangement between Datu Puti and the pygmy Negrito inhabitants of Panay Island and begins to explore the lust of Guronggurong for Datu Sumakwel's young wife.

Less restricted historically, Hufana's early volume, *Sickle Season* (1959), presents Geron Munar, Malayan wanderer and cultural hero. In *Poro Point: An Anthology of Lives* (1961), Munar is replaced by personae from Hufana's own tribal family, all Ilocanos who, as the most migratory of Filipinos, epitomize both their countrymen's unity and diversity.

The Philippine dream of a national identity— of a homogeneity, age-old and everlasting—is evident in each such adaptation from ethnohistory. Yet, despite the urgency of that dream, it is usually treated critically.

Even Bienvenido Santos, for example, who has been accused of being a sentimentalist, subjects the viability of the dream to tests of the most severe sort. The Philippine expatriates in his story-collection, *You Lovely People* (1956), caught in the United States by World War II, long passionately to return to their kinfolk. In the aftermath of war, however, many discover their homeland changed and their loved ones not inviolate. Disillusioned, some of the characters retreat into exile once more.

Similarly, in his second collection, *Brother, My Brother* (1960), and his novel *Villa Magdalena* (1965), Santos is still involved with the imagery of rejection and return. However far ambition takes his characters from the ancestral home that once seemed to deprive them of personal fulfillment, that home remains the place of least loneliness. Similarly no satisfactory sense of self is to be found outside one's native community.

Although all major Philippine writers may be said to be searching for those constants that define their identity as a people, many have avoided the historical/epic modes and have confined themselves to the fundamentally agrarian aspects continuous in their culture. Their fiction maintains a slowness of pace and cautious simplicity appropriate to the traditional sacred, seasonal mysteries as well as to the patient, modern searchings.

Typically, Manuel Arguilla's rural stories, in *How My Brother Leon Brought Home a Wife* (1940), undercut folk romanticism with the realism of social protest as he presents the causes of the Sakdal uprisings among tenant farmers during the 1930's.

Similarly, N. V. M. Gonzalez's tales of the frontier country, the burned-over *kaingin* ricelands (*Seven Hills Away*, 1947; *Children of the Ash-covered Loam*, 1954; *A Season of Grace*, 1956), reveal both the hardships and enduring self-possession of his tradition-centered pioneers. In his collection, *Look, Stranger, on This Island Now* (1963), the *kainginero* enjoys a loneliness with consolations as compared with the peasant who has migrated to the metropolis. In *The Bamboo Dancers* (1959), the restricted life of the *kainginero* is far more meaningful than that of the sophisticated *ilustrado*, who is a homeless international wanderer.

The *provinciano*'s life is a trial, even in Carlos Bulosan's humorous tales, collected in *The Laughter of My Father* (1941), which were intended as a satiric indictment of sharecropping penury. At the same time, Bulosan expresses his admiration for the good humor, the love, and the other humane virtues that survive the peasant's near-penal conditions.

This same capacity to endure marks each of the four major war novels: Stevan Javellana's *Without Seeing the Dawn* (1947), Juan Laya's *This Barangay* (1950), and Edilberto Tiempo's *Watch in the Night* (1953) and *More Than Conquerors* (1964). Appropriately enough, all of them are stories of small-scale, rural, guerrilla action supported by a kind of primitive "community."

When this close identifying with a group is sacrificed by the ambitious *provinciano* migrant to the city, he suffers from the anonymity of mass living without his poverty's lessening measurably. Only occasionally is adequate human warmth rediscovered among slum-dwellers. This does occur in the stories of Estrella Alfon (*Magnificence*, 1960), of Andres Cristobal Cruz and Pacifico Aprieto (*Tondo by Two*, 1961), and of D. Paulo Dizon (*Twilight of a Poet*, 1962). It similarly occurs in Alberto Florentino's *The World Is an Apple and Other Prize Plays* (1959).

Far less sympathy is directed toward other urban classes. The pretensions of the *nouveau riche* are steadily satirized in Gilda Cordero-Fernando's collection, *The Butcher, the Baker, the Candlestick Maker* (1962), and in Wilfrido Guerrero's three volumes of plays (1947, 1952, 1962). Inherent in movement from rural *barrio* to suburbia is the risk of loss of character.

The consequences of social mobility unaccompanied by maturing morality are more savagely exposed in the novels of Kerima Polotan-Tuvera (*e.g., The Hand of the Enemy*, 1962) and of F. Sionil Jose (*e.g., The Pretenders*, 1962). In both instances, the mountaineer or uprooted rural peasant is corrupted by industrialism and the new self-seeking elite, just as the agrarian revolts at the turn of the century allegedly were betrayed by the *ilustrados*, first to the Spaniards and later to the Americans.

Such works, like Rizal's novels before them, constitute assessments of agrarian values during decades of challenging cultural transition. They will always be of historical value regardless of what other Philippine literatures emerge in the vernaculars.

Though Jose Garcia Villa's five volumes of poetry—from *Many Voices* (1939) through *Selected Poems and New* (1958)—have been criticized for sacrificing national circumstance to disembodied Blakean encounters between God and the luminous poet, they are relevant to the Philippine experience. Villa's dependence on devices of negation and rejection and the nearly solipsistic alienation of the protagonist both parallel the national passion for self-determination and the overcompensatory self-enlargement of a people reduced to colonial status for centuries.

As for inventiveness and the emotions of a dynamic individual in revolt, the Filipino-language counterpart of Villa is A. G. Abadilla (*Piniling Mga Tula,* 1965).

Sometimes as antagonist, sometimes as complement, Abadilla's name is juxtaposed with the socialistically inclined Amado V. Hernandez, former labor leader and later outstanding writer in the vernacular. With his prize plays (*Muntinlupa,* 1958, and *Magkabilang Mukha ng Isang Bagol,* 1961), his poems (*Isang Dipang Langit,* 1961), and his novel (*Mga Ibong Mandaragit,* 1965), Hernandez revived the polemical tradition of the 19th c. and recapitulated the social protest articulated in Lope K. Santos's earlier novel, *Banaag at Sikat* (1906).

Together with Andres Cristobal Cruz (*Sa Tundo, May Langit Din,* 1961), Abadilla and Hernandez, by avoiding the sentimentality and floridity of vernacular conventions, have made Filipino equal to English as an instrument for self-discovery.

BIBLIOGRAPHY: Agcaoili, T. D., ed., *Philippine Writing* (1953); special Philippine issue, *Literary Review* (Summer 1960); Casper, L., ed., *Modern Philippine Short Stories* (1962); Maramba, A. D., ed., *Philippine Contemporary Literature* (1962); Bernad, S. J., Miguel, *Bamboo and the Greenwood Tree* (1963); special Philippine issue, *Beloit Poetry Journal* (Summer 1964); Del Castillo, T., and Buenaventura, Jr., S. M., *Philippine Literature* (1964); special Philippine issue, *Literature East and West* (March 1965); San Juan, Jr., E., "Social Consciousness and Revolt in Modern Philippine Poetry," *BA* (Fall 1965); Casper, L., *New Writing from the Philippines: An Anthology and a Critique* (1966)

LEONARD CASPER

PILLECIJN, Filip de

Belgian novelist and essayist (writing in Flemish), b. 25 March 1891, Hamme; d. 7 Aug. 1962, Ghent

P. started his career as a teacher, biographer, and essayist. Early creative work, *Pieter Fardé* (1926) and *Blauwbaard* (1931), still relied on historical or legendary sources, but in the novellas *Monsieur Hawarden* (1935), *Schadu-*

wen (1937), and *De Aanwezigheid* (1938) P. established himself as a superb prose stylist who gained fame for his evocation of mood and landscape, and for his delicate anatomy of the psychology of eroticism.

In his novellas and the novels *Hans van Malmédy* (1935), *De Soldaat Johan* (1939), and *Jan Tervaert* (1947), P. set a new level for Flemish prose and influenced a generation of writers with his delicate but masculine romanticism. These are works of a poetic sensibility dealing with a *fin-de-siècle* melancholy that found its only solace in the peaceful perpetuity of nature. The autumnal mood and an oneiric imagination found its arcadian perfection in the latter novel *De Veerman en de Jonkvrouw* (1950)—practically a romantic fairy tale.

Experiences of violence, social unrest, and misery during two world wars embittered P., and social considerations replaced his earlier romanticism. The negative ramifications of man as a social and political animal are portrayed in the story "De Boodschap" (1946), the novella *Rochus* (1951), and the novels *Mensen achter de Dijk* (1949), *Vaandrig Antoon Serjacobs* (1951), and *Aanvaard het Leven* (1956). In these last two novels, P. responds to life's pain with the resigned acceptance of an idealist purified by suffering.

Beginning with *De Rit* (1927), the majority of P.'s heroes are soldiers. In conflict with conventional society and subjected to bureaucratic injustice, these outsiders—of a type that has come to dominate 20th-c. fiction—pay dearly (either by imprisonment or death) for their impotent rebellion.

Only women provide solace and hope in this inhospitable and threatening world. However, though physical passion is celebrated, P. insists on man's inability to establish a lasting and authentic relationship. Nature gradually emerges as mankind's only lasting joy. The farmer, in an otherwise anticlerical *œuvre,* assumes the stature of a priest in P.'s telluric devotion.

P. perfected an economical prose style that is suggestive rather than explicit, lyrical rather than realistic; its melodic serenity strikes a fascinating balance between virility and refinement.

P.'s preference for historical settings—used exclusively to provide objectivity and a sense of timelessness—recalls German masters of shorter fiction such as Conrad Ferdinand Meyer (1825–98), Gottfried Keller (1819–90), and Adalbert Stifter (1805–65), with whom he shares stylistic similarities and a preoccupation with the majesty of nature. The romantic and lyric side of P.'s work recalls the melancholy novels of Eugène Fromentin (1820–76) and Alain-Fournier (q.v.). His unsentimental devotion to nature, a characteristic shared with so many Flemish and Dutch writers, is of special interest in an age newly concerned with ecology.

FURTHER WORKS: *Onder den Hiel* (1920); *Dona Mirabella* (1952); *Het Boek van de Man Job* (1956); *Verzameld Werk* (4 vols., 1959–60); *Elizabeth* (1961)

BIBLIOGRAPHY: Ranke, B., *P.* (1941); Wilderode, A., *P.* (1960); Vlierden, B. F., *De romankunst van P.* (1961)

E. M. BEEKMAN

PILNYAK, Boris

(pseud. of *Boris Andreyevich Vogau*), Soviet-Russian novelist and short-story writer, b. 12 Sept. 1894, Mozhaisk; d. 1938

P. was the son of a veterinarian of Volga-German origin. Before the Russian Revolution, his writing had earned him a modest literary reputation. His early short stories are set in rural areas and evoke the primitive, biological aspects of life in a somewhat lyrical style reminiscent of Chekhov, Bunin (qq.v.), and Ivan Turgenev (1818–83). Throughout his career he continued to write short stories on cultural and psychological themes.

Fame came to P. with his second novel, *Golyi god* (1922, The Naked Year, 1927), whose setting is the civil war years of 1919. The first writer to depict the revolution in narratives, P. eulogized it (in his novels of the early 1920's) as a resurgence of the Russian peasant culture that existed before the reign of Peter the Great, one unadulterated by debilitating Western traits. He further associated the revolution with the vital force of life itself. P. was, like Belyi and Remizov (qq.v.), a 20th-c. Slavophile and portrayed Europe as moribund.

In the late 1920's, P. began to incur the displeasure of the Soviet authorities for his undoctrinaire view of the revolution. This was first provoked by his "Povest' o nepogashennoi lune" (1926; The Tale of the Unextinguished Moon, 1967), whose circumstances resembled those existing at the death of the Soviet-Russian army commander General Frunze (1885–1925).

After this, the publication in Berlin of P.'s novel *Krasnoye derevo* (1929) resulted in his expulsion from the Union of Soviet Writers.

This work was rewritten and incorporated in a five-year-plan novel, *Volga vpadayet v Kaspiiskoye more* (1930; The Volga Falls to the Caspian Sea, 1931), which concerns the construction of a vast dam. But this attempt to rehabilitate himself was not very successful. In his narratives of the 1930's, including "Sozrevaniye plodov" (1936), he attempted to present a corrected view of the regime, but his message remained ambiguous.

In these unconventional, episodic novels, P. used liberally such literary conventions as the frame story, the flashback, enigmatic narrative transitions, lyrical digressions, leitmotifs, symbols, insertions of extraneous material, dialect renderings, and typographical and other peculiarities. This complex style, which is called Pilnyakism, derives its musical traits and symbolism from Belyi and other aspects from Nikolai Gogol (1809–1852) and Remizov. After the 1920's P.'s style became more subdued. In certain morbid psychological characterization P. resembles Fiodor Dostoyevski (1821–81). Though P. defended the spontaneous and primitive, he was actually a bookish and derivative writer.

In addition to his fiction, P. published travel journals of his trips to Japan and China (1927; later rewritten as *Kamni i korni*, 1934) and a description of his experiences in the United States (*Okei: Amerikanski roman*, 1933).

In 1937 he was arrested and convicted of "fascist" activities. It is believed that he died in 1938, but it is not generally known what fate he met after his arrest.

FURTHER WORKS: *Tzelaya zhizn* (1915); *Bylye rasskazy* (1919); *Ivan-da-Maria* (1922); *Petersburgskiye rasskazy* (1922); *Mat machekha* (1922); *Tretya stolitzya* (1923); *Povesti o chernom khlebe* (1923); *Tisyache let* (1923); *Lesnaya dacha* (1923); *Starii syr* (1923); *Zavolochye* (1924); *Mashiny i volki* (1924); *Chartopolokh* (1925); *Rossiya v polete* (1926); *Mat syrazemlya* (1926); *Yaponskovo solntza* (1927); *Kitaiskaya povest* (1927); *Rasplesnutoye vremya* (1927); *Kitaiski dnevnik* (1927); *Sobraniye sochinenii* (6 vols., 1929–30); *Izbrannyye rasskazy* (1935); *Rozhdeniye cheloveka* (1935). **Selected English translations:** *Tales of the Wilderness* (1925); *Ivan Moscow* (1935); *The Tale of the Unextinguished Moon, and Other Stories* (1967); *Mother Earth, and Other Stories* (1968)

BIBLIOGRAPHY: Voronski, A., "B. P.," *Krasnaya Nov'*, No. 4 (1922), pp. 252–69;

Trotzki, L., "B. P.," in *Literatura i revolyutziya* (1923), pp. 55–65; Tynyanov, I., "Literaturnoye sevodnya," *Russki Sovremennik*, I (1924), 291–306; Voronski, A., "Na perevale," *Krasnaya Nov'*, No. 6 (1926), pp. 312–22; Shklovski, V., "O. P.," in *Pyat' chelovek znakomykh* (1927), pp. 69–92; Alexandrova, V., "B. P.," in *A History of Soviet Literature* (1963), pp. 135–49; Bristol, E., "B. P.," *SEER*, XLI (1963), 494–512; Kuzmich, L., "Language and Stylistic Characters of B. P.'s Novel *The Naked Year*," *DA*, XXVIII (1967), 29231A

EVELYN BRISTOL

PINGET, Robert

French novelist and dramatist, b. 19 July 1919, Geneva, Switzerland

P. received a law degree in Switzerland before his interest in art led him to become a painter and an art teacher. In 1946, having made Paris his permanent residence, he turned to prose writing in an attempt to adapt the free expression of poetry to the novel form.

P. was first attracted by the verbal acrobatics of the surrealists (*see* surrealism) and by the unbridled imagination of the French poet Jacob (q.v.), who excelled in the spontaneous expression of his own sensibilities. The impetuous style and the burlesque ingenuity of Jacob's flights into fantasy led P. to write esoteric tales such as *Graal Flibuste* (1956) and *Clope au dossier* (1961).

As early as 1957 P. also became attuned to the despairing quality of Beckett's (q.v.) nihilistic philosophy when he translated into French Beckett's drama *All That Fall* (1957; *Tous ceux qui tombent*). P. himself conveyed the same feeling for the emptiness and absurdity of the modern world, as expressed by the inanity of the spoken word, in his first radio scripts such as *La Manivelle* (1960)—adapted by Beckett as *The Old Tune* (1963, 1967).

Between 1951 and 1968, P. published short stories, plays, dialogues, and radio scripts, which have been produced in France and Germany, as well as fourteen novels. His works have been published in translation in thirteen different countries.

L'Inquisitoire (1962; The Inquisitory, 1966) was awarded the Grand Prix de la Critique in 1963. In this lengthy novel, the experience of the past, the endless unfolding of lost time, is conveyed through a deluge of words. An aged, deaf, broken man utters bits of broken sentences. The mumbled recollections of his rambling monologue continue on without a single semicolon or period. What begins to emerge is not only the underlying insecurity of an anguished humanity, but, even more, the elusive, often irrational quality of reality itself. "I only know bits and pieces, I don't know the truth, never shall, and we'll die not knowing."

Thus, the baroque, fablelike, at times dreamlike, fantasies of P.'s early books have taken on, in later years, bizarre and pessimistic undertones. The same almost poignant cries of echovoices appear again in his short novel *Quelqu'un* (1965), which won the Prix Femina. Here again we find the well-known setting of P.'s geography of the imaginary. Again the discourse meanders, and there is no coherent narrative. This is because, for P., literature is exclusively language, exclusively free, "gratuitous" verbal communication. That is why he is not interested in telling a story or in developing a plot. He is concerned only with the transcription of the spoken word.

P.'s stylistic experiments have linked him to the *nouveau roman* school of France, along with Nathalie Sarraute, Robbe-Grillet (qq.v.), and Claude Simon (q.v.). But his originality lies in the fact that—unlike these avant-garde French novelists who perceive visually and try to render minutely, as objectively as possible, a world of things—P. listens acutely and patiently. Painstakingly, he tries to distinguish between the textures of the many dialogues that he discerns within himself. He then translates, at great length, page after page, the way a human being externalizes his sensibility.

Thus, in *Le Libera* (1968), rejecting the old-fashioned stereotyped meaning of words and clichés, and their sclerosed syntax, P. searches for his own method of communication. He attempts what seems an impossible task—to pinpoint the ever-changing aspect of a mobile language.

The preface of *Le Libera* almost constitutes a manifesto. In it, P. defines each one of his novels as a separate quest for a particular mood, more precisely, a distinct tone of voice. He is seeking a certain inflection or a separate modulation, selected among the many original vibrations that constitute P.'s own ways of expressing himself, each and all of them being representative of his true complex sensitivity. The right intonation for a particular novel, which he discerns within himself, is poured forth onto the page spontaneously at first. Then comes the painful labor of filtering, the conscientious effort of composing.

FILIP DE PILLECIJN

ROBERT PINGET

GUIDO PIOVENE

Thus, the very process becomes a literary vein, a style; and the style in turn determines, automatically, the intrigue. The story could have been something else; the authenticity of the speech is what constitutes, for P., his own true creation.

FURTHER WORKS: *Entre Fantoine et Agapa* (1951); *Mahu ou le matériau* (1952; Mahu, or the Material, 1967); *Le Renard et la boussole* (1955); *Baga* (1958; Eng., 1967); *Le Fiston* (1959); *Monsieur Levert* (1961); *Lettre morte* (1959; No Answer, 1961); *Ici ou ailleurs* (includes *Ici ou ailleurs, Architruc,* and *L'Hypothèse;* 1961); *Autour de Mortin* (1965)

BIBLIOGRAPHY: Micha, R., "Une Forme ouverte du langage," *TM*, No. 201 (Feb. 1963), 1484–90; Bjustrom, C.-G., "De Chaminadour à Sirancy-la-Louve," *Crit*, No. 190 (March 1963), 195–202; "P. Adapted by Beckett," in *The Times*, 24 Nov. 1964, pp. 84–85; Robbe-Grillet, A., *For a New Novel* (1966), pp. 127–32; Perros, C., "P. ou le matériau," *Crit*, No. 225 (Feb. 1966), 150–54; Steisel, M.-G., "P.'s Method in *l'Inquisitoire*," *BA* (Summer 1966), pp. 267–71; Steisel, M.-G., "Paroles de R. P.," *PSMLA Bulletin*, XLV (1966), 35–38; Duvert, T., "La Parole et la fiction," *Crit*, No. 252 (1968), 443–61

MARIE-GEORGETTE STEISEL

PINSKI, David

Yiddish dramatist, novelist, and short-story writer, b. 5 April 1872, Mohilev, Ukraine; d. 11 Aug. 1959, Haifa, Israel

After P.'s family moved to Moscow in 1885, he came under secular influences, began to write in Russian as well as Yiddish, and joined the Zionist movement. In 1891, on his way to Vienna to study, he stopped in Warsaw to show his Yiddish stories to Peretz (q.v.). Encouraged, he returned to Warsaw in 1892 and served as assistant editor of Peretz's anthology, *Yomtov Bletter*. By now an active socialist, he was writing highly praised stories about the poor and the oppressed. In 1896 he went to Berlin for further study, and came under the influence of modern European writers, especially Ibsen (q.v.).

In New York City. to which he had migrated in 1899, he edited Yiddish labor periodicals, took an active part in the Labor-Zionist movement, and began to write plays and stories. He early became a leader among Yiddish writers

in the United States and was the first president of the Jewish P. E. N. club. In 1949 he went to live on Mount Carmel in Haifa and continued his literary and political activity until his death a decade later.

In fiction P. was at his best in the short story. His three novels—*Dos hoiz fun Noah Edon* (1913; The Generations of Noah Edon, 1931); *Arnold Levenburg* (1920, Eng., 1928); and *Ven vegan tzugehen sikh* (1950)—are burdened with theses that weaken their quality.

P.'s first drama, *Isaak Sheftel* (1899), stressed the woes of the oppressed worker. *Yenkel der shmit* (1906) was a strong family drama and had a popular run on the Yiddish stage. In other plays, from *Di familie Tzvi* (1904) to *Shabsi Tzvi un Soreh* (1952), he handled the themes of Jewish nationalism, Jewish persecution, and Jewish messianism. His most successful play, *Der oitzer* (1906), was widely acknowledged as one of the best comedies of the time and was produced in several languages.

FURTHER WORKS: *Drames* (8 vols., 1918–20); *Hemelekh Dovid un seine veiber* (1923; King David and His Wives, 1923); *Aleksander un Diogenes* (1930); *Beruriah un andere dertzeylungen* (1946); *Fier tragedies* (1949); *Drei drames* (1952). **Selected English translations:** *Three Plays* (1918); *Temptations: A Book of Short Stories* (1919); *Ten Plays* (1920)

BIBLIOGRAPHY: Roback, A. A., *The Story of Yiddish Literature* (1940); Minkoff, N. B., "D. P.," *Di Goldene Keyt*, No. 12 (1952); Liessen, A., *Zikhroines un bilder* (1954); Goldberg, A., *Unsere dramaturgen* (1961); Mayzel, N., *Tzurikbliken un perspectiven* (1962); Madison, C. A., *Yiddish Literature: Its Scope and Major Writers* (1968)

CHARLES A. MADISON

PINTER, Harold

English dramatist, b. 10 Oct. 1930, London

The son of a tailor, P. was born in London's East End. He briefly attended the Royal Academy of Dramatic Art and in 1949 he joined a repertory company and spent the next ten years as an actor. During this time he wrote poetry (his *Poems* of this period were published in 1968), short prose pieces (some of which were the basis for later revue sketches), and an unfinished novel, *The Dwarfs*. His first play, *The Room* (1957), was produced at the University of Bristol.

While less subtle and more melodramatic than his later work, *The Room* presents the basic P. situation: a room, two people, and an undefined fear of the world outside the door. The action within such a situation stems from an absurd world in which motive is unclear, logic inoperable, and nothing certain. Thus in *The Room* an old woman, Rose, is established in the tenuous security of her room until a mysterious blind Negro makes his way into it with a "message" from her father. Her husband returns and beats the Negro to death, whereupon Rose goes blind.

Out of these puzzling and bizarre elements P. creates a powerful poetic image capable of evoking fear and nameless dread. The mood is intensified by the contrast with realistic dialogue that skillfully captures the inane repetitiveness and essential noncommunication of conversation. The elements of farce and low comedy dialogue that operate on the surface of the tensions that permeate the play led to P.'s early work being punningly labeled "comedies of menace."

Immediately after this debut P. wrote *The Dumb Waiter* (1960), *The Birthday Party* (performed, 1958; published, 1959), a number of radio and television plays, and some revue sketches.

The Caretaker (1960) established P.'s reputation as a major figure in modern British theater. Its setting is a junk-filled room to which Aston, a young former mental patient, brings Davies, a self-important and opportunistic old bum. The action consists of interchanges between Aston, Davies, and Aston's brother, Mick, who owns the house. Out of jealousy or innate nastiness, Mick teases and torments Davies and then pretends to befriend him. To oblige Mick, the old man turns against the simple Aston, venting his spleen upon him until the latter demands that he leave. Davies then confidently appeals to Mick, who cruelly dismisses him.

P. has been highly praised for his use of language, for his accurate reproduction of the patterns and rhythms of colloquial English, for his awareness of and his ability to mimic the ways in which language is conventionally used as a barrier to communication. His dialogue does not convey information directly, but is used as one of many surface elements in the construction of a total, highly evocative image that cannot be reduced to any single message or abstract concept. In *The Caretaker*, for example, Mick's merciless badgering of Davies creates an atmosphere of insecurity that awakes resonances of man's general insecurity in an unknown and threatening universe.

Because of their suggestive quality, the plays have been variously interpreted. To some critics, P. depicts modern man's reduction to inanity and nonentity by sinister and oppressive social structure that inexorably crushes the rebellious. Thus in *The Dumb Waiter*, when Gus, the gunman, begins to question the System he becomes a victim instead of an executioner. Stanley, the down-at-heels expianist in *The Birthday Party*, is systematically terrorized by Goldberg and McCann, representatives of a vague organization that some critics have interpreted to be the Judaeo-Christian tradition.

Other critics see P.'s nightmare-like evocations of nameless guilt in contexts involving possessive, infantilizing women as dramatizations of the Freudian Oedipal situation. Related interpretations see in P.'s plays the middle-class family in its sheltering and destructive manifestations. The situation is most explicit in *The Homecoming* (1965), one of P.'s most powerful full-length works.

P. has also shown considerable skill in adapting novels by other writers for the screen. He prepared the script for the 1963 film version of *The Caretaker*, which was released in the United States as *The Guest*.

Though P.'s dramatic world sometimes seems narrow and lacking in compassion, there is no doubt that he has been able to create a compelling vision of modern man's insecurity, isolation, fear, and jockeying for power.

FURTHER WORKS: *A Slight Ache, and Other Plays* (1961); *The Collection and The Lover* (1963); *Tea Party, and Other Plays* (1967); *Mac* (1968); *Landscape* (1969); *Silence* (1969)

BIBLIOGRAPHY: Dukore, B., "The Theatre of H. P.," *TDR*, VI (March 1962), iii, 43–54; Boulton, J. T., "H. P.: *The Caretaker*," *MD*, VI (Sept. 1963), ii, 131–40; Morris, K., "*The Homecoming*," *TDR*, XI (Winter 1966), ii, 185–91; Schechner, R., "Puzzling P.," *TDR*, XI (Winter 1966), ii, 176–84; Amend, V. E., "H. P.," *MD*, X (Sept. 1967), ii, 165–74; Hinchliffe, A. P., *H. P.* (1967); Kerr, W., *H. P.* (1967); Storch, R. F., "H. P.'s Happy Families," *MR*, Autumn 1967, pp. 703–12; Hayman, R., *H. P.* (1968); Gordon, L., *Stratagems to Uncover Nakedness: The Dramas of H. P.* (1969)

DOROTHY TUCK MCFARLAND

PIONTEK, Heinz

German poet essayist, short-story writer, radio dramatist, and novelist, b. 15 Nov. 1925, Kreuzburg, Upper Silesia

After serving in World War II, P. briefly studied German philology and then held a variety of jobs. He lived for some years at Dillingen, a village on the Danube, later moving to Munich. P. began his writing career primarily as a nature poet. His early poems, showing the influence of Trakl (q.v.), are dominated by his interest in the visual. In 1960, P. translated the poems of John Keats (1795–1821) into German.

Concerned with time, the passage of it and man's position in it, P. attempts to protect man through art from "the limitlessness" of nature, the world, life. His method, which is marked by sharp sensory perception, is to present his flow of observations by means of a series of scenes. Though he approaches language with freedom, he is nevertheless always concerned with presenting precise formulations of his thought. This ability to communicate abstract ideas by means of realistic language makes for unusual tension in P.'s work. An intensely lyrical poet, his free, image-filled unrhymed verse reached a high point with *Klartext* (1966).

From poetry P. has gone on to write short stories, radio dramas, and critical essays. In 1967 he published his first novel, *Die mittleren Jahre*. He brings to the writing of prose the methods he has developed in his poetry.

P.'s voice is among the most audible of the postwar generation in West Germany.

FURTHER WORKS: *Die Furt* (1952); *Die Rauchfahne* (1953); *Licht über der Küste* (radio script, 1954); *Vor Augen* (1955); *Wassermarken* (1957); *Buchstab-Zauberstab* (1959); *Weißer Panther* (radio script, 1962); *Mit einer Kranichfeder* (1962); *Fremde in Sodom* (radio script, 1962); *Damals in den Weinbergen* (radio script, 1962); *Rote Pfeile* (radio script, 1962); *Kastanien aus dem Feuer* (1963); *Die Zwischenlandung* (1963); *Vor Robinsons Insel* (radio script, 1963); *Windrichtungen* (1963); *Hinweise* (1966); *Liebeserklärungen in Prosa* (1969)

BIBLIOGRAPHY: Forster, L., "German Lyric Poetry since Gottfried Benn," *Forum for Modern Language Studies,* II (1966), 291–304; Glenn, J., "Approaching the Contemporary German Lyric: A Selected Annotated Bibliography," *MLJ,* LI (1967), 480–92; Kunisch, H., *Die deutsche Gegenwartsdichtung: Kräfte und Formen* (1968)

* * * *

PIOVENE, Guido

Italian novelist, journalist, and essayist, b. 27 July 1907, Vicenza

P. was educated in private schools and at the University of Milan, where he earned a degree in philosophy. In 1927 he embarked on a freelance career in journalism; by 1935 he was a correspondent for *Il Corriere della Sera.* He traveled extensively through Europe and the United States. Since 1952 he has been associated with *La Stampa* of Turin.

P.'s fiction is characterized by an intense preoccupation with the psychic forces that motivate and shape human behavior. His characters evidence a variety of abnormal traits that ultimately lead to mental derangement, crime, and self-destruction. Since P.'s novels are often in the form of retrospective, first-person narratives, action and events are filtered through a process of lucid rationalization that minimizes external elements while illuminating the moral and spiritual fiber of his characters.

The basic features of P.'s work can be traced to his first novel, *La Gazzetta Nera* (written, 1939; published, 1943). The protagonist, a social misfit estranged from his wife, is hired by an eccentric British philanthropist opposed to capital punishment to compile case histories of homicides as proof that criminal instincts are equally distributed among all human types. Consequently, the work consists of five separate novellas whose respective protagonists, motivated by a congenital aversion toward their mode of existence, seek liberation through a criminal act.

Lettere di una novizia (1941; Confession of a Novice, 1950), the most successful of P.'s novels, portrays the inner struggle of a young novice, unsure of her vocation, who in a desperate attempt to escape a cloistered life is driven to murder. The novel's epistolary form is effectively used to explore the subjective manner in which truth and reality are adroitly distorted to achieve selfish aims. Each character moves in a climate of moral ambiguity, and such contrasting elements as sincerity and duplicity are intellectually diagnosed until they almost seem one. The artistic interest of the work rests, however, on the portrayal of the rebellious and impulsive heroine, a pathetic figure striving for self-assertion and understanding.

Set against the desolate background of World War II, *Pietà contro pietà* (1946) is a *roman à thèse* imbued with philosophical considerations that reflect P.'s pessimistic view of human existence. In it he develops, to an exhausting length, a simple story line—a young woman's amorous relationship with three men. The result is a demonstration of how genuine compassion can be egoistically abused until it degenerates into hypocrisy and deception.

Le Furie (1963) marks an increased tendency toward narrative action and characterization as well as an effort to explore various planes of reality. In it haunting visions of the past are drawn from the impressionable years of adolescence. Thus a gallery of human portraits is juxtaposed to individual experiences during the fascist period. An unusual element of this work is the symbolic treatment of the Furies as evil forces present in disparate forms and varying degrees in human consciousness.

In 1970 *Le Stelle Fredde,* a philosophically ambiguous novel in which the protagonist abandons his urban life and goes off to live in an inherited country house, won the Premio Strega.

P.'s distinguished career in journalism is represented by several works of reportage: *De America* (1953), widely praised as a penetrating study of the United States; *Viaggio in Italia* (1958), a subjective account of Italian life; and *Madame la France* (1967), a collection of articles dealing with the social and political conditions in France in the aftermath of World War II.

Although P. has been linked to 18th-c. French novelists, he is an original writer deeply concerned with the spiritual and moral problems of our time. He brings to contemporary Italian literature a highly personal narrative form rich in psychological insights and intellectual acumen.

FURTHER WORKS: *La vedova allegra* (1931); *I falsi redentori* (1949); *Lo scrittore tra la tirannide e la libertà* (1952); *Processo dell'-Islam alla civiltà occidentale* (1957); *La coda di paglia* (1962); *La gente che perdé Ierusalemme* (1967)

BIBLIOGRAPHY: Travi, E., "I tentativi di P.," *Vita e Pensiero,* March 1948; Petroni, G., "L'inquieto P.," *La Fiera Letteraria,* 13 Nov. 1949; Guiducci, A., "Motivi morali dell'opera di G. P.," *Il Pensiero Critico,* 1953, pp. 78–84; Grisi, G., "P. tra fantasia e realtà," *La Fiera Letteraria,* 4 Feb. 1962; Catalano, G., P. (1967); Kanduth, E., *Wesenszüge der modernen italienischen Erzählliteratur: Gehalte und Gestaltung bei Buzzati, P. und Moravia* (1968)
                    AUGUSTUS PALLOTTA

PIRANDELLO, Luigi

Italian playwright, novelist, and short-story writer, b. 28 June 1867, Agrigento, Sicily; d. 10 Dec. 1936, Rome

One of the major 20th-c. playwrights, P.'s international reputation was established in 1922 when *Sei personaggi in cerca d'autore* (1921; Six Characters in Search of an Author, 1922) was performed in London and New York, and *Il piacere dell'onestà* (1918; The Pleasure of Honesty, 1923) in Paris. The following year P. made the first of a series of tours that took him in the course of time to all leading European theatrical centers, to the United States and South America. He was awarded the Nobel Prize in 1934 for "his bold and brilliant renovation of the drama and the stage."

P.'s Sicilian background, his study of Romance philology first at the University of Rome and then at Bonn, the serious financial reverses in his father's sulfur business that forced him for almost thirty years to sacrifice much of his writing time to teaching duties in a girls' normal school, his wife's mental illness, the anguished years of World War I when his son was a prisoner of war—these are some of the biographical facts that in various ways influenced his writing. But though P. is a highly subjective writer in whose work it is almost impossible to distinguish between the way he himself experienced the world and the manner in which his fictional characters do, his writing is not autobiographical in the ordinary sense of the word.

His perception of the human condition fixed itself early in a number of "living images" in which man's stature is diminished from free agent to helpless object, in which he is afflicted with the mechanical automatism of the puppet, or—as it is put in the essay *Arte e coscienza d'oggi* (1893)—in which he is shown as a mad King Lear "armed with a broomstick, and jumping in front of you in all his tragic comicality." In his important essay on humor (*L'umorismo,* 1908), the indispensable companion piece to his creative works, P. formulated his poetics, which rests on the distinction between the *perception* and the *feeling* of the incongruous, whereby a strong impulse to compassion or pity is injected into the concept of the comic.

Although there is evidence for P.'s sporadic

interest in the theater prior to 1916 (at sixteen he wrote *Barbaro*, a since-lost five-act tragedy), it was only about that time and initially under the influence of Sicilian dialect theater that he resolutely turned to the stage. His novels and short stories had already brought him a measure of recognition; his considerable poetic production, on the other hand—his first collection was *Mal giocondo* (1889) and his last, *Fuori di chiave* (1912)—achieved no particular success.

Of the seven novels, the first, *L'esclusa* (1901; The Outcast, 1925), is thematically significant for its unconventional treatment of adultery, a favorite 19th-c. subject, and historically important for its subtle undermining of the naturalistic assumptions on which it appears to be based. In *Il fu Mattia Pascal* (1904; The Late Mattia Pascal, 1923), with its mixture of pathos, grotesque humor, gaiety, and philosophical reflection, P. created his first major character, the typical "stranger in life" inextricably caught up in the contradictions of existence.

The action of *I vecchi e i giovani* (1908; The Old and the Young, 1928) takes place in 1892–94, a period corresponding to P.'s return from Germany and his encounter with the "bankruptcy" of the new regime of united Italy. This novel and such stories as "Scialle nero" (1900; "The Black Shawl," 1959), "Il fumo" (1901; "Fumes," 1959), "Lontano" (1901), "Difesa del Meola" (1909), and "Ciàula scopre la luna" (1912) are essential reading for an understanding of the role played by P.'s Sicilian background in the formation of his basic views. *Si gira* (1915; Shoot!, 1926), later retitled *I quaderni di Serafino Gubbio operatore*, is without doubt P.'s most original novel insofar as form is concerned. In its use of the device of the plot-within-a-plot it foreshadows the later dramatic works employing the "play-within-a-play" device, and in its weaving back and forth to recapture moments of the past suddenly essential to the plot it creates the kaleidoscopic effect of life unstructured by any unifying concept. The novel's subject is amazingly modern: it attacks the "machine that mechanizes life" and alienates man from his fellow men, and the treatment has lost none of its freshness.

Uno, nessuno e centomila (1926; One, None and a Hundred Thousand, 1933) is the most fragmentary of P.'s novels: its short, discontinuous chapters are the structural counterpart to its protagonist's discovery of the plurality and relativity of the personality. This discovery leads to Vitangelo Moscarda's personal liberation from the inauthentic forms imposed on him by his social role. The novel contains some of P.'s most powerful pages on pantheistic reconciliation with the All.

P.'s earliest plays were one-acters reflecting distinct tendencies in the contemporary drama: *L'epilogo* (1898; The Vise, 1928), later published as *La morsa*, and *Il dovere del medico* (1912; The Doctor's Duty, 1928) are classifiable as *fin-de-siècle* bourgeois problem plays; *Lumíe di Sicilia* (1911; Sicilian Limes, 1928) and *La giara* (1917; The Jar, 1928) belong to the regional theater and exist in dialect versions as well as in Italian; *All'uscita* (1916; At the Gate, 1928) is a "profane mystery" in which symbolism predominates. In *Pensaci, Giacomino!* (1916; Better Think Twice about It, 1955), *Il berretto a sonagli* (1917; Cap and Bells, 1957), and *Liolà* (1917; Liolà, 1952), Sicilian motifs are combined with such basic Pirandellian themes as the triumph of the irrational, the destruction of the individual's self-constructed mask, and the conflict between appearance and reality.

But P.'s first play of fundamental importance is *Così è (se vi pare)* (1917; Right You Are If You Think So, 1923), a parable that uses a provincial bureaucratic milieu as a setting in which to demonstrate the relativity of truth. In this play P. pleads for each man's right to his "phantom"—that private illusion he creates for himself and by which he lives "in perfect harmony, pacified." *Il piacere dell'onestà*, *Il gioco delle parti* (1918; The Rules of the Game, 1959), and *Tutto per bene* (1920) continue the trend of disassociation between the realistic foundations of P.'s art—reflected in the elements of the plot of the story being told—and its "philosophical" superstructure—the "particular sense of life" that gives the stories universal value (cf. Preface to the 1925 edition of *Sei personaggi in cerca d'autore*; Eng. trans., 1952).

P.'s recognized masterpiece is *Enrico IV* (1922; Henry IV, 1923). Here alienation reaches the dimensions of madness: actual madness at first, and feigned madness later, as the only possible solution (short of suicide) by which the nameless protagonist can protect his "phantom" from the corrupt, egotistical, foolish, and vicious world around him. In the play—often designated as a tragicomedy, though not by P. himself—the tremendous and unequivocal pressure of life "on stage," which is one of the distinguishing features of P.'s dramaturgy, is given its fullest tragic impact. *Vestire gli ignudi* (1922; Naked, 1924), whose protagonist *is* driven to suicide, is in many ways a companion piece to *Enrico IV*. Its middle-class setting, however, and a few stock characters from the comic repertoire account for its different tone.

In the trilogy of the theater-within-the-theater, *Sei personaggi in cerca d'autore, Ciascuno a suo modo* (1924; Each in His Own Way, 1924), and *Questa sera si recita a soggetto* (1930; Tonight We Improvise, 1932), the focus of attention shifts from the existential anguish of the protagonist to the anguish of the character in search of being (cf. the short story "La tragedia di un personaggio," 1911; A Character in Distress, 1938). What these plays actually deal with is the problem of artistic creation. For while ostensibly they are concerned with the interaction of character, actor, and spectators in the creating of the illusion of life on the stage—and as such they could be read as little more than amusing though brilliant theatrical experiments—within the broader framework of P.'s thought they must be seen as evidence that for P. the theater itself was only a concretization of the concept of artistic form. This point of view is stated with uncommon force in the Preface to *Sei personaggi in cerca d'autore*.

A second group of three plays, *La nuova colonia* (1928; The New Colony, 1958), *Lazzaro* (1929; Lazarus, 1959), and *I giganti della montagna* (1937; The Mountain Giants, 1958), described by P. as "myths," mark the final stage of his development. In them the frame of reference is no longer the individual whose experience is universalized, but society itself. The last play, though left unfinished at P.'s death, belongs with his masterpieces. In the figure of the magician Cotrone, who lives with his refugees from the real world in an abandoned villa that he has turned into the realm of phantasy, P. created the last projection of himself as the self-effacing artist completely tensed in the perception of the abundant life swirling about him.

P.'s 233 short stories were written between 1884 and 1936 and touch upon all the themes treated in the novels and plays: many of them were dramatized by him. They are an integral part of his work, rated by some critics even higher than his plays. Indeed they belong in any international collection devoted to the genre.

FURTHER WORKS: The standard edition of P.'s works is the so-called *edizione definitiva*, published by Mondadori in Milan. It consists of six volumes: *Novelle per un anno* (2 vols., 1956–57), *Tutti i romanzi* (1957), *Maschere nude* (2 vols., 1958), and *Saggi, poesie, scritti varii* (1960). The last volume includes an extensive bibliography, also covering P. in translation. The major original publications that have not been mentioned in the text are listed below in chronological order.

Pasqua di Gea (1891); *Amori senza amore* (1894); *Elegie renane* (1895); *Il turno* (1902; The Merry-Go-Round of Love, 1964); *Le beffe della vita e della morte* (1902); *Quand' ero matto* (1902); *Bianche e nere* (1904); *Erma bifronte* (1906); *Arte e scienza* (1908); *La vita nuda* (1908); *Su marito* (1911); *Terzetti* (1912); *Le due maschere* (1914); *La trappola* (1915); *Erba del nostro orto* (1915); *E domani, lunedì?* . . . (1917); *L'innesto; La ragione degli altri* (4 vols., 1917); *Un cavallo nella luna* (1918); *Il carnevale dei morti* (1919); *Tu ridi* (1919); *Berecche e la guerra* (1919); *Come prima, meglio di prima* (1921); *La signora Morli una e due* (1922); *La vita che ti diedi* (1924; The Life I Gave You, 1959); *Ciascuno a suo modo* (1924; Each in His Own Way, 1923); *La sagra del Signore della nave; L'altro figlio; La giara* (1925); *L'imbecille; Lumie di Sicilia; Cecè; La patente* (1926); *Diana e la Tuda* (1927; Diana and Tuda, 1950); *L'amica delle mogli* (1927; The Wives' Friend, 1949); *O di uno o di nessuno* (1929); *Come tu mi vuoi* (1930; As You Desire Me, 1931); *Trovarsi* (1930; To Find Oneself, 1943); *Quando si è qualcuno* (1933; When Someone Is Somebody, 1958); *Non si sa come* (1935; No One Knows How, 1949); *Sogno* (1937); *Sgombero* (1951; The Rest Is Silence, 1958). **Selected English translations:** *Three Plays of P.* (1922); *Each in His Own Way, and Two Other Plays* (1923); *One-Act Plays* (1928); *A Horse in the Moon: Twelve Short Stories* (1932); *Better Think Twice About It!, and Twelve Other Stories* (1933–34); *The Naked Truth, and Eleven Other Stories* (1934); *The Medals, and Other Stories* (1938, Eng., A Character in Distress, 1938); *Four Tales* (1939); *Naked Masks* (1952); *Short Stories* (1959); *Henry IV; All for the Best; Right You Are (If You Think So)* (1960); *To Clothe the Naked, and Two Other Plays* (1962); *The Merry-Go-Round of Love, and Selected Stories* (1964); *Short Stories* (1965)

BIBLIOGRAPHY: Tilgher, A., *Studi sul*

LUIGI PIRANDELLO

HENRIK PONTOPPIDAN

teatro contemporaneo (1922); Starkie, W., *L. P.* (1926); Nardelli, F. V., *L'uomo segreto* (1932); Vittorini, D., *The Drama of L. P.* (1935); MacClintock, L., *The Age of P.* (1951); Ferrante, L., *P.* (1958); Bishop, T., *P. and the French Theatre* (1960); Whitfield, J. H., *A Short History of Italian Literature* (1960), pp. 278–88; Leone De Castris, A., *Storia di P.* (1962); Giudice, G., *L. P.* (1963); Poggioli, R., "P. in Retrospect," in *The Spirit of the Letter* (1965), pp. 146–70; Bentley, E., "Il Tragico Imperatore," *TDR*, XXXI (1966), 60–75; Büdel, O., *P.* (1966); Cambon, G., ed., *P.: A Collection of Critical Essays* (1967); Ragusa, O., *L. P.* (1968)

OLGA RAGUSA

All modern philosophy is based on a profound intuition of the dualism which exists between Life which is absolute spontaneity, creative activity, and the forms which tend to restrict and enclose Life. The Life Force, like an inexorable tide, dashes up against those forms created by man; it breaks down barriers which impede its triumphal progress. It is from this point of view that we must start off to criticise P. With him it ceases to be an abstract philosophical theory and becomes dramatic —dramatic because it appeals to him with such intensity and assumes such moral semblance that it causes him to suffer. To him the struggle between the Life Force and the masks with which men try to cover it becomes the material for tragic drama.

Walter Starkie, *Luigi Pirandello* (1937), pp. 43–4

The most fertile property of P.'s dramaturgy is his use of the stage itself. By so boldly accepting it for what it is, he freed it from the demand which modern realism had made of it, that it be a literal copy of scenes offstage, and also from the exorbitant Wagnerian demand, that it be an absolutely obedient instrument of hypnosis in the power of the artist. Thus he brought to light once more the wonderful property which the stage *does* have: of defining the primitive and subtle medium of the dramatic art. "After P."—to take him symbolically rather than chronologically—the way was open for Yeats and Lorca, Cocteau and Eliot. The search could start once more for a modern poetry of the theater, and even perhaps for an Idea of the Theater comparable to that of the Greeks yet tenable in the modern world.

Francis Fergusson in *Partisan Review* (June 1949), p. 603

Italian decadentism is a complex phenomenon. Resulting . . . from the breakdown of scientific determinism on the one hand and the accepted ethical and artistic categories on the other. . . . If there is no reason, there is no plan, no consistency in life or personality, we have no control over

ourselves or our destiny and men are creatures of Chance.

Intellectual and pseudointellectual circles in Italy were infected with this black pessimism and the great feat of L. P. is to have put it into dramatic form, to have translated it into human emotional situations, to have shown what happens to an average, fairly intelligent person when ethical and philosophical props are pulled from under him and he is left floating in a sea of doubt; turning introspectively inward he rends not only himself but those with whom he comes in contact. The resultant suffering is the subject matter of the theatre of P.

Lander MacClintock, *The Age of Pirandello* (1951), p. 175

P. carries on an attack against our animal faith and seems determined to persuade us not merely that we cannot make value judgements, not merely that we cannot distinguish appearance from reality, but that the whole concept of reality as opposed to appearance is inadmissible.

Moreover and in the process, the "I" itself, the thing which perceives appearances and becomes the victim of illusions, disintegrates—if, at least, one means by the "I" any continuous, persisting, relatively stable thing. Every "I" is not merely all the things which at various times it seems to itself to be or all the things which at various times it seems to various people to be. It is also all the different things which at different times it has been. There are the "I's" of yesterday, today, and tomorrow, as well as what every observer has taken each of them to be.

Joseph Wood Krutch, "Modernism," *Modern Drama* (1953), p. 82

Pirandellian man is isolated not only from his fellows, but also from himself at other times. Farther than this, isolation cannot go. This is a "nihilistic vision," and no mistake.

Perhaps it would nowadays be called an existentialist vision: life is absurd; it fills us with dread and anguish; yet, without knowing why, . . . we fight back, . . . and because all living, all life, is improvisation, we improvise some values. Their Form will last until Living destroys them and we have to improvise some more.

P.'s plays grew from his own torment, . . . but through his genius they came to speak for all the tormented, potentially *to* all the tormented—that is, to all men.

Eric Bentley, *In Search of Theater* (1953), pp. 313–4

PLIEVIER, Theodor
German novelist and short-story writer, b. 12 Feb. 1892, Berlin; d. 12 March 1955, Avegno, Switzerland

After a hard childhood, P. left home at

seventeen and tramped through a good part of Europe. After working intermittently as a cattle driver, interpreter, cook, bartender, fisherman, goldpanner, and mineworker, he joined the German navy in 1914. In 1918 he took part in the sailors' revolt at Wilhelmshaven.

P. was entirely self-educated. He himself considered his most important formative experience (apart from the direct effects of his adventurous life) to have been the reading of the Old Testament, of medieval mystics, of Laotsu and Nietzsche (q.v.), and of Ibsen, Gorki, Lev Tolstoi (qq.v.), Heine, and Dostoyevski.

Immediately after World War I, P. became a publisher of political pamphlets, but soon gave this up to devote himself to his writing. In 1933, with the advent of Hitler, he emigrated to Paris; in 1934, to Moscow. Believing his bitter exile at an end, he returned to Berlin in 1945 with the Soviet-Russian army, but only two years later he left the Soviet Zone in protest against the regime, moving to Wallhausen on Lake Constance and later to Avegno.

In 1930 P. published a collection of early short stories, *Zwölf Mann und ein Kapitän* (1930), and a play, *Haifische* (1930), about sea voyages and exotic shores.

P.'s major work was *Des Kaisers Kulis* (1929; as a play, 1932; The Kaiser's Coolies, 1932), a novel about the German imperial navy. Expressing the violent resentment and hatred felt by many in the exploited classes, it protests not just the seamen's plight but the universal condition of the poor.

This is P.'s constant basic theme from *Der Kaiser ging, die Generäle blieben* (1932; The Kaiser Goes, The Generals Remain, 1933), through the sea and adventure stories of *Im letzten Winkel der Erde* (1946; The World's Last Corner, 1951) and *Haifische* (published as a novel in 1945).

P. is hammering at the same anvil in the World War II trilogy: *Stalingrad* (1945; Eng., 1948), *Moskau* (1952; Moscow, 1953), and *Berlin* (1954; Eng., 1956). These novels break away from the bonds of traditional plot development and become epic treatments of mass destiny, in which isolated humanity unceasingly wrestles with organized inhumanity.

P. was almost exclusively a narrative writer. Except for some unimportant expressionist (*see* expressionism) experiments written during his pamphlet-publishing years, he is to be considered a typical representative of the style of *neue Sachlichkeit* (new factualism). His fiction, based either on genuine personal experience or on exact documentary data, is actually very close to reportage, and his explosive style often assaults the reader.

By his matter-of-fact descriptions of oppression, whether it was exerted by those who had power in Kaiser Wilhelm's regime, in capitalist societies, in the Nazi reign, or in the Soviet system, P. assumed the role of spokesman for all the downtrodden and degraded.

FURTHER WORKS: *Der 10. November 1918* (1933); *Das große Abenteuer* (1935); *Die Seeschlacht am Skagerrak* (1935); *Im Wald von Compiègne* (1939); *Das Tor der Welt* (1940); *Der Igel* (1942); *Eine deutsche Novelle* (1947); *Das gefrorene Herz* (1948); *Der Seefahrer Wenzel und die Töchter der Casa Isluga* (1951); *Meine Hunde und Ich* (1957; With My Dogs in Russia, 1961)

BIBLIOGRAPHY: Waidson, H. M., *The Modern German Novel* (1959); Wilde, H., *T. P.: Nullpunkt der Freiheit* (1965); Sevin, D. H., "Individuum und Staat: Das Bild des Soldaten in Ps. Romantrilogie," *DA*, XXIX (1968), 273A

JOSEF STRELKA

PLISNIER, Charles

Belgian poet and novelist (writing in French), b. 13 Dec. 1896, Ghlin-les-Mons; d. 17 July 1952, Brussels

Becoming politically involved when he was still a young man, P. worked on leftist periodicals and newspapers in Brussels while he was studying law.

After helping to found the Belgian Communist Party in 1919, P. established the weekly paper *Le Communisme*, was an activist in party uprisings in Bulgaria, Rumania, Czechoslovakia, and Germany, and expressed his enthusiasm for communism in his early writings. This phase of his life ended abruptly when an eye-opening trip to Moscow in 1927 overwhelmed him with bitter disillusionment. The parting of the ways was made official by his expulsion from the party—for being a Trotzkyite—in 1928. After this, in reverse of a common 20th-c. pattern, he became an ardent Roman Catholic, though he was keenly interested in the findings of psychoanalysis.

Feeling himself to be a spokesman of a generation disappointed by World War I and in rebellion against society's traditional structure and values, P. expressed this stance in strong, thoughtful poetry.

In his penetrating, realistic, psychoanalytically oriented novels, P. sharply criticized inter-war society. Using *la vie en famille* of the industrial upper bourgoisie as a reflection of society's ills, he exposed the emotionally deprived lives of his characters and attacked their hypocrisy, their apathy, and their mediocrity in *Mariages* (1936; Nothing to Chance, 1938), *Meurtres* (1939–41), and *Mères* (1946–49). In *Mères* he focused on Christian motherhood.

FURTHER WORKS: *Voix entendues* (1913); *L'Enfant qui fut déçu* (1913); *La Guerre des hommes* (1920); *Ève aux sept visages* (1921); *Élégies sans les anges* (1922); *Brûler vif* (1923); *Prière aux mains coupées* (1931); *Fertilité du désert* (1933); *Déluge* (1933); *L'Enfant aux stigmates* (1934); *Odes pour retrouver les hommes* (1935); *Périple* (1936); *Faux passeports* (1937; Memoirs of a Secret Revolutionary, 1938); *Sel de la terre* (1937); *Testament* (1939); *Ave genetrix* (1943); *La Matriochka* (1943); *Une Voix d'or* (1944); *Figures détruites* (1945); *Heureux ceux qui rêvent* (1948); *Beauté des laides* (1951; Sabine, 1954); *Folies douces* (1952); *L'Homme et les hommes* (1953); *Le Roman: Papiers d'un romancier* (1955)

BIBLIOGRAPHY: Bay, P., *C. P.* (1952); Bodart, R., *C. P.* (1959); Van Nuffel, R., "C. P.," in *Poètes et polémistes* (1961), pp. 93–122; Bertin, C., ed., *C. P.: Les meilleures pages* (1964); Noulet, E., *Alphabet Critique* (1965), pp. 214–19

* * * *

PLOMER, William

South African poet, novelist, short-story writer, and librettist, b. 10 Dec. 1903, Pietersburg, Northern Transvaal

P., the son of English parents living in South Africa, was educated in both England and South Africa. Because of an eye ailment he did not attend a university. In his youth he worked on a farm beneath the Stormberg and at a trading station in Zululand. He was one of the three cofounders (with Roy Campbell [q.v.] and Laurens van der Post [b. 1906]) of *Voorslag* (1926), a magazine of brief duration but great significance in South African literary history. After leaving South Africa, P. lived from 1926 to 1929 in Japan. In 1929 he settled in England, where he has lived for the most part ever since.

From the age of twenty-three P. has been publishing short-story collections: *I Speak of Africa* (1927), *Paper Houses* (1929), *The Child*

of *Queen Victoria* (1933), *Curious Relations* (1945), and *Four Countries* (1949). The South African stories, emerging frequently from personal experiences, often reveal strong emotional involvement. The Japanese stories reflect the views of a visitor, one who is most interested in the differences between East and West. The stories about Greece, which reveal P. as a perceptive vacationer, usually draw upon history or literature. The stories which are set in France and England possess the greatest detachment. An exceptionally fine short story from P.'s middle years is "The Night before the War" (in *Four Countries*), which pictures a phase of London life during the last hours before World War II.

P.'s five novels record modern man's quest for some kind of certainty. In Africa, the protagonist Turbott Wolfe, weak and confused, pathetic in his desire for answers, is tireless in his search (*Turbott Wolfe*, 1925). Nigel Edge tries to find understanding in an England, which, though supposedly his own, is alien (*The Invaders*, 1934). Nigel is perceptive enough not to reject the object of his quest when he finds part of it, though others around him display less awareness. Through Toby d'Arfey, P. asks meaningful questions about Europe and England in the interwar period (*Museum Pieces*, 1952).

Making every effort to give answers, P. has showed increasing awareness of the difficulty of doing so. He has made it his task to create fiction that presents what exists.

Poetry is the form of writing P. has been most faithful to. First he wrote of Africa. Then, from 1926 to 1956, his poetry ceased to speak of Africa with any frequency. In these years he wrote verse that was, unlike his South African poetry, often light, witty, at times quite playful. A visit to the Transvaal in 1956, however, evoked new, sober poems about his homeland. P.'s most recent book of poems (*Taste and Remember*, 1966) contains compositions as fine as anything he has created.

As a librettist, in collaboration with the well-known English composer and conductor Benjamin Britten, P. has done some interesting work. He has earned recognition as a biographer (*Ali the Lion*, 1936) and autobiographer (*Double Lives*, 1943; At Home, 1958).

P. is one of the most versatile of modern authors. Even in his youth he was able to impart to his writing the characteristic of effortlessness, which actually is the result of a subtle technique.

In his short stories and novels P. evinces an unusual tenderness. This quality, marked by a subtle reserve, occurs most frequently in the poems from the middle of his career onward.

FURTHER WORKS: *Notes for Poems* (1927); *The Family Tree* (1929); *Sado* (1931; Am., They Never Come Back, 1931); *The Fivefold Screen* (1932); *The Case Is Altered* (1932); *Cecil Rhodes* (1933); *Visiting the Caves* (1936); *Selected Poems* (1940); *The Dorking Thigh, and Other Satires* (1945); *Gloriana* (1953); *A Shot in the Park* (1955); *Borderline Ballads* (1955); *Collected Poems* (1960); *Curlew River* (1965); *The Burning Fiery Furnace* (1966); *The Prodigal Son* (1968)

BIBLIOGRAPHY: Miller, G. M., and Sergeant, H., *A Critical Survey of South African Poetry in English* (1957); McLeod, A. L., ed., *The Commonwealth Pen* (1961); Van der Post, L., Introduction to *Turbott Wolfe* (1965); Doyle, J. R., Jr., *W. P.* (1969)

JOHN ROBERT DOYLE, JR.

POLGAR, Alfred

Austrian journalist, theater critic, essayist and satirist, b. 17 Oct. 1875, Vienna; d. 24 April 1955, Zurich

P. began his career as a journalist and critic in Vienna and moved to Berlin in 1927, where he wrote for the *Weltbühne* and the *Berliner Tageblatt*. In 1933 he returned to Vienna, but after the anschluss fled to France in 1938, and from there in 1940 via Spain to New York. He returned to Europe in 1949, after which he made his home for the most part in Zurich. In 1951 he was awarded the Prize of the City of Vienna for Journalism ("Publizistik").

Der Quell des Übels (1908) is a light comedy satirizing the vanity of writers and women. *Goethe im Examen* (1908), a one-act burlesque written in collaboration with Egon Friedell (1878–1938), has the title character failing a school examination on the facts of his own life. *Ja und Nein* (4 vols., 1926–27) is a collection of P.'s theater reviews. *Hinterland* (1929), which P. called his "war book," contains the short stories he wrote from 1916 to 1923.

P. was influenced by the prose miniatures of Altenberg (q.v.), whose literary remains he edited (1925). He became in turn the acknowledged stylistic model of Joseph Roth (q.v.). P.'s significance inheres in his role of moralist in the tradition of such famous French forerunners as La Rochefoucauld (1613–80) and La Bruyère

(1645–96). Like them, he was a trenchant critic of human manners and foibles. Typical of P.'s penchant for unmasking high-flown deceit is his rewording of the inscription on the tomb of the unknown soldier in Paris from "Mort pour la patrie" ("He died for his country"), to "Mort par la patrie" ("He was killed by his country").

P. is especially credited for his feuilletons (q.v.)—brief sketches of cultural and social criticism—which continue to have lasting interest. Distinguished by their acute observation, these witty essays, models of aphoristic brevity and conciseness, earned P. the title "master of the short form."

FURTHER WORKS: *Der Petroleumkönig oder Donauzauber* (with Egon Friedell; 1908); *Bewegung ist alles* (1909); *Brahm's Ibsen* (1910); *Soldatenleben im Frieden* (with Egon Friedell; 1910); *Der Freimann* (with Egon Friedell; 1910); *Talmas Tod* (with Armin Friedmann; 1910); *Hiob* (1912); *Kleine Zeit* (1919); *Pallenberg* (1921); *Gestern und Heute* (1922); *An den Rand geschrieben* (1926); *Orchester von oben* (1926); *Ich bin Zeuge* (1928); *Schwarz auf Weiß* (1928); *Stücke und Spieler* (1929); *Noch allerlei Theater* (1929); *Bei dieser Gelegenheit* (1930); *Die Defraudanten* (1931); *Ansichten* (1933); *In der Zwischenzeit* (1934); *Der Sekundenzeiger* (1937); *Handbuch des Kritikers* (1938); *Geschichten ohne Moral* (1943); *Im Vorübergehen* (1947); *Anderseits* (1948); *Begegnungen im Zwielicht* (1951); *Standpunkte* (1953); *Im Lauf der Zeit* (1954); *Fensterplatz* (1959)

BIBLIOGRAPHY: Lestiboudois, H., "A. P., Meister der kleinen Form," *Literarische Miniaturen* (1948); Torberg, F., "A. P.," *Der Monat*, No. 66 (1954); Luft, F., "A. P.," *Der Monat*, No. 81 (1955); Viertel, B., "Über A. P.," in *Deutsche Literaturkritik im 20. Jahrhundert*, ed. H. Mayer (1965); Reich-Ranicki, M., "A. P.'s sanfte Gewalt," *Die Zeit*, No. 24 (1968)

DAVID BRONSEN

POLISH LITERATURE

I. Pre-1945

The history of Polish literature is cyclical, with clearly distinguishable periods of vigor and decline. The golden ages are, broadly, the 16th c., and the period extending from the end of the 18th c. and beginning of the 19th c.

Around 1900 the major cultural centers were Warsaw and Cracow. Up to about 1900 the memory of the tragic anti-Russian revolt of 1863 pervaded all spheres of intellectual life. Deprived of all hope of independence by the crushing of the revolt, Poles concentrated on immediate problems in economics and public education.

Literature after 1863 was expected to contribute to the common welfare: it was to stimulate national awareness and point the way to the future. The most widely read foreign authors were Auguste Comte (1798–1857), Hippolyte Taine (1828–93), John Stuart Mill (1806–1873), and Charles Darwin (1809–1882). During this positivist period the intellectual ambience gradually became more radical, and the ground was prepared for new political movements.

The positivist tendencies were detrimental to poetry but favorable to prose. The liberal, humanitarian Bolesław Prus (pseud.: Aleksander Głowacki; 1845–1912) wrote *Lalka* (1890), one of the best Polish novels. In this he tells the story of a merchant and self-made man in contemporary Warsaw. Prus's special contribution lies in his skillful handling of detail and social background and in his humor. Other important works of his are *Placówka* (1886), *Emancypantki* (1894), and *Faraon* (1897). Among the typical representatives of social literature were Eliza Orzeszkowa (1841–1910), Aleksander Świętochowski (1849–1938), and Adam Szymánski (1852–1916).

Interest in history and politics is traditional in Polish literature. A representative politically conservative author, as opposed to those in the leftist-liberal bloc, is Henryk Sienkiewicz (q.v.). After subscribing to positivist ideology in his early works, he turned to history and tried to create a kind of saga about feudalist, aristocratic Poland (the "Szlachta"). He won popularity with his trilogy on the 17th-c. period of Cossack and Swedish wars—*Ogniem i mieczem* (1884); *Potop* (1886); and *Pan Wołodyjowski* (1887).

Sienkiewicz is an undeniable master of the historical novel of adventure. His international fame, however, he owed to *Quo Vadis* (1896), which is much weaker than his major works. He was angrily denounced by the leftist-liberal critics, as was the fiction writer Józéf Weyssenhoff (1860–1932), another programmatic conservative.

Literary life was most vigorous in the part of Poland that belonged to Russia—pardoxically so, since censorship there was particularly strict. But glaring social contrasts, rapid industrialization, and the policy of russification acted as a yeast among the workers and the intelligentsia in this region. At the beginning of the 20th c. those who cherished the hope of regaining independence fastened upon socialism. The upheaval of 1905 caused particularly violent reactions in the Polish territory. The writer whose work reflected the gamut of the inner conflicts of the radical intelligentsia most faithfully was Żeromski (q.v.).

1. 1900–1918

The pre-1914 period in Poland was marked by stability and rapid changes in the economic structure. One group of writers—to which, for instance, the dramatist Gabryela Zapolska (1860–1921) belonged—produced devastating social criticism in the tradition of naturalism (q.v.). Others, such as Władysław Orkan (pseud. of Franciszek Szmaciarz-Smreczyński; 1876–1930), a writer of peasant novels, aimed at accurate, objective description. Already there were attempts to use complicated psychological analysis, as in the novels of Berent (q.v.), who was fascinated by symptoms of decadence among artists and the wealthy middle class. Rittner (q.v.), who came from Galicia, was an exponent of psychologically realistic drama. One widely read Nobel Prize winner (1924) was Reymont (q.v.), who liked to describe in his novels and novellas the lives of the little people.

A number of authors who participated in the social revolutionary movement recorded its problems, victories, and defeats in their works. This is very true of Andrej Strug (pseud. of Tadeusz Gałecki; 1873–1937), whose novels are epic songs of praise for the fighters against tzarism, for those whom the Russians imprisoned, hanged, or exiled to Siberia.

Stanisław Brzozowski (1878–1911), the leading critic of this period, was also a socialist. A highly educated man, he was able in his short life to stir up basic philosophical and political discussion, in which he advocated his own interpretation of Marxism. (This devotion did not, however, prevent him from being influenced by the writings of the 19th-c. English convert Cardinal Newman to draw closer to Roman Catholicism.) His novel *Płomienie* (1907) on the Russian nihilists analyzes the moral problems of revolutionary activity that the French writer Malraux (q.v.) was to deal with a few decades later.

About 1900, writers had begun to protest fiercely against the principle that art be subordinated to social tasks. The supporters of *l'art pour l'art,* who maintained lively contact with bohemian circles in Paris and Berlin, demanded complete sovereignty for the artist and the right to express the workings of a totally unrestricted imagination. Cracow became the headquarters of this movement. Its leading pioneer was Przybyszewski (q.v.), who had spent many years abroad and had hitherto been writing in German.

The Young Poland (*Młoda Polska*) movement had an important effect on literature, too, and contributed to the revival of poetry. It brought about a reassessment of values. It also brought about the translation into Polish of foreign poets, especially Charles Baudelaire (1821–67), Samuel Taylor Coleridge (1772–1834), and Arthur Rimbaud (1854–91). The most distinguished translator of foreign poetry was Zenon Przesmycki (pseud.: Miriam; 1861–1944).

Poets previously committed to realism now had a free hand. Wyspiański (q.v.), a poet and painter, taking Greek and Polish romantic drama as his point of departure, created bold scenic visions, which led to the rebirth of the "monumental theater" in Poland.

Although the Young Poland movement, through its cult of inspiration and intuition, encouraged shallowness in language, it nonetheless produced talented poets. Kasprowicz (q.v.), son of a peasant from near Posen, deserves first mention. His background determined the character of his work, which expressed the world of peasant Catholicism. Leopold Staff (1878–1957), a poet who had achieved serenity and reconciliation with the world, and Kazimierz Tetmajer (1865–1940) also belonged to this group. On account of their decorative, lyrical style, the prose writers Żeromski and Reymont are also regarded as related to the Young Poland movement.

2. 1918–1929

In 1918 Poland was re-created as an independent state. This date also marks the initiating of a new literary epoch. The most vigorous new talents were found in poetry. Eager to break from the past, the group of young poets around the journal *Skamander* discovered a poetic theme in modern city life. They wanted "to look at spring, not Poland." Their works molded the public and attracted it by their dynamic élan and a satirical attitude toward accepted authority. At the same time their handling of language assured these poets of an enthusiastic reception from the critics.

Among the members of this group were: Tuwim (q.v.), who gave Polish poetry a sensuous magic it had not known for a hundred years; Kazimierz Wierzyński (q.v.), who extolled youthful *joi de vivre* and sport; Antoni Słonimski (b. 1895), a poetic ironist; and Jan Lechoń (1899–1965), who wrote variations on the classical themes of love and death. The group also included two writers who did not come out of Poland proper and whose language preserved the atmosphere of their native regions: Iwaszkiewicz (q.v.), from the Ukraine, and Kazimiera Iłłakowiczówna (b. 1892), from Lithuania. Other members of this group were Marie Pawlikowska-Jasnorzewska (1894–1945), who succeeded in expressing philosophy in an almost Japanese filigree form, and Stanisław Baliński (b. 1899), who depicted scenes from his travels in Asia.

The evolution of this group illustrates the changes in the literary and political atmosphere of Poland. After the victorious war with Russia, democracy seemed to promise a stable social system and to provide a solution to all problems. Great advances in administration, welfare legislation, and housing produced an ambience characterized by optimism.

3. 1930–1939

About 1930, however, the Great Depression hit Poland severely. Joseph Pilsudski (1867–1935), the ex-socialist who virtually ruled Poland from 1926–35, was not to fulfill the hopes placed in him. Furthermore, he died just at the time the National Socialist party was becoming a force. Nationalistic and anti-Semitic rightists gained visibly in importance. Literary circles saw these developments as a portent of imminent catastrophe. Hence the tone of the *Skamander* poets became more and more tragic.

In poetry, differences between individual groups and schools were becoming blurred. Futurism (q.v.) had sprung up in Poland before World War I. There was also much discussion about pure form under the Parisian influence of cubism. The poet Tytus Czyżewski (1885–1945) succeeded in treating folklore themes from an extremely avant-garde position.

In the work of Bolesław Leśmian (pseud. of Bolesław Lesman; 1878–1937), the stream-of-consciousness technique is merged with a fairy-tale atmosphere. Wittlin (q.v.) writes as a humanitarian and a humanist. Broniewski (q.v.) wrote proletarian poetry derived from the tradition of the romantic socialism of 1905.

In prose fiction Kaden-Bandrowski (q.v.) used a method that may be called "psychologism" mixed with brutal realism. In a certain sense, Dąbrowska (q.v.) continues 19th-c. positivism.

Women novelists are strikingly numerous. Among them are: Zofia Nałkowska (1884–1954); Ewa Szelburg-Zarembina (b. 1899); Helena Boguszewska (b. 1886); Anna Kowalska; Pola Gojawiczyńska (b. 1896); Maria Kuncewiczówa (b. 1899); Zofia Kossak-Szczucka (b. 1890); and Hanna Malewska (b. 1911). They wrote frequently on historical themes, especially medieval ones.

World War I was the subject of the prose of Ferdynand Goetel (1890–1960). One much-discussed novel was *Kordjan i cham* (1932) by Leon Kruczkowski (1900–1962). The fiction of Michał Rusinek (b. 1904) and Gustaw Morcinek (b. 1891) has socially critical implications. Zbigniew Uniłowski, who died young, left a sketch of the working-class quarter of Warsaw in his autobiographical novel *Dwadzieścia lat życia* (1937).

Because of avant-garde directors, such as Leon Schiller, and stage designers, such as Drabik and Draszewski, the currently extraordinarily favorable opportunities for the theater were exploited to the full. Several theaters were supported by municipal authorities and trade unions, and the majority received government subsidies. The new repertory was provided by Jerzy Szaniawski (b. 1887), Rostworowski (q.v.), Włodzimierz Perzyński (1877–1930), Antoni Słonimski, Bruno Winawer (1883–1943), and Antoni Cwojdziński, among others. The most-performed foreign dramatist was Shaw (q.v.), some of whose plays had received their world premieres in Poland.

Translators of foreign literature, especially Tadeusz Żeleński (1874–1941), made a meaningful contribution. Edward Porębowicz, the translator of Dante, concentrated on Romance languages, while Parandowski (q.v.) sought especially to make Greek literary works accessible to his countrymen.

About 1930 awareness of the degeneration of values in Western civilization intensified in Poland. This recognition became most movingly verbalized in Stanisław Witkiewicz (1885–1939), philosopher, theoretician of pure form, and writer of avant-garde plays and science fiction.

The generation that made its literary debut about 1930 attacked the *Skamander* group, accusing it of deliberate antiintellectualism, "vitalism," and overemphasis in poetry on the lyrical. This group, which was arbitrarily called avant-garde, included many writers who reached full maturity only after the invasion of Poland in 1939.

Among them were: Julian Przyboś (1901–70); Ważyk (q.v.); J. Czechowicz (1903–39); and C. Miłosz (q.v.). They had in common an intellectual ardor, which led them to write not only poetry but prose in all its diverse forms—essays, journalism, novels, literary criticism. The poets Jastrun and Gałczyński (qq.v.) were close to this so-called avant-garde group. The religious lyric poetry of Jerzy Liebert (1904–1931) and the work of Władysław Sebyła (1902–1941), cut short by his early death, also deserve attention.

Prose after 1930 began to show the tendencies that later became known in world literature as existentialist. Bruno Schulz (1892–1942) shared with Kafka (q.v.) the same psychological problems and the same Austro-Hungarian background. The novels of Gombrowicz (q.v.), who was at first attacked and ridiculed but later recognized as a genuine talent, expose man's immaturity, often in grotesque, fantastic form. Adolf Rudnicki (b. 1912) attracted attention as a prose writer and perfected his technique after the war. Other writers of this period were Teodor Parnicki (b. 1908), who wrote novels about the decline of the classical world, Tadeusz Breza (1905–1970), Jerzy Andrzejewski (q.v.), and Czesław Straszewicz (1911–63).

4. 1939–1945

Polish literature suffered irreparable loss from the tragic deaths of many gifted writers in World War II. Its development was of course curtailed by the prohibition (lasting five long years) against publishing books in the occupied territory. Clandestine presses and printing houses were active in Warsaw, however, though they existed under the constant threat of discovery by the gestapo. A whole *pléiade* of twenty-year-old poets emerged—almost all of whom were killed fighting in the resistance.

II. 1945–1960

The postwar development of Polish literature can be divided into four literary phases, each of which was determined by the political situation.

Phase One extended from the end of World War II to December 1949. Attempts to resume prewar trends or to take Soviet literature as a model were accompanied by heated controversies on the value of realism.

Phase Two, extending from December 1949 to 1956, is marked by the acceptance of socialist realism (q.v.) as the exclusive literary purpose. Although monotonous party-line writing set the tone for the era, a whole series of remarkable works, most of which were retrospective in nature and avoided any actual commitment, nevertheless appeared.

Phase Three, which is most interesting of all, though short-lived, began in 1956 with the collapse of the official doctrine of style. The characteristic features of this phase were skepticism about the communist way of life, rebellion against official interference with creative work, and a turning toward models free of ideological regimentation. The point at which Phase Three came to an end cannot be exactly determined. The fading out of Phase Three, which occurred between 1957 and 1958, was characterized by the beginning of a gradual tightening of curbs that since 1956 had been fairly lax.

Phase Four, which began around 1958, was marked by the facts that substantive criticism was falling silent and interest in contemporary or political subjects was lessening.

(1) PHASE ONE

Because of the bitter hardships suffered by the Poles during the war and Nazi occupation, protest against the injustice that the Poles had been subjected to became one of the central themes of all postwar literature. These sufferings may have increased the readiness of Polish writers to support the new communist regime willingly, at least in the first years after World War II ended. Jastrun (q.v.) was the first to support it in poetry. His prewar poems, full of disquiet and pessimism, seemed to express his forebodings of catastrophe. What he then experienced during the war years, which he expressed in the volume of poems *Godzina strzeżona* (1944), led him to the conviction that writing should be a chronicle of truth and a

service to man (*Rzecz ludzka,* 1947) rather than an aesthetic activity pursued in a vacuum. Several of the older poets, however, such as Przyboś, who remained undeviatingly true to his avant-garde principles, continued in the prewar tradition.

The postwar period produced a considerable number of remarkable talents, among whom were Tadeusz Kubiak, Anna Kamieńska, Jerzy Ficowski, Witold Wirpsza (b. 1918), and Wiktor Woroszylski (b. 1927), who used forms much like those used by Mayakovski (q.v.). Różewicz (q.v.) should especially be singled out for introducing an individual note into postwar poetry with his frequently proselike diction.

In prose, writers preferred to handle the occupation theme in the shorter genres. Andrzejewski's (q.v.) short stories (*Noc,* 1946), were dominated, as was his entire work, by interest in the conflict of conscience. Zofia Nałkowska also handled the same theme in her short stories, though in a strongly documentary manner (*Medaliony,* 1946). Adolf Rudnicki gave a moving account of the martyrdom of Polish Jews in many of his short stories. The concentration-camp stories of Tadeusz Borowski (1922–51) may well be among the most outspoken of the writing on this painful subject.

Ksawery Pruszyński (1907–1950) describes in his short stories the struggle of the Poles who were working with the allies during the war. *Trębacz z Samarkandy* (1946) in particular demonstrates Pruszyński's great narrative talent. Dygat (q.v.), Artur Sandauer, and Brandys (q.v.), who have stressed the narrative element, have been seeking to come to terms with the past in an intellectual way.

In the postwar period writers began to think about another theme, causally related to the occupation theme. What enabled the Nazis to conquer Poland in 1939? In the novel *Wrzesień* (1952), Jerzy Putrament (b. 1910) answers this question by indicting prewar Polish society. Tadeusz Breza's novels *Mury Jerycha* and *Niebo* (1946–50) dissect with great artistry, skillful psychological intuition, and a slightly ironical and satirical touch the prewar intellectual and social ambience that may have contributed to the conquest.

Żukrowski (q.v.) pursued other aims in his short stories collected in *Z kraju milczenia* (1946), which evoked heated controversy. His novel *Dni klęski* (1952) placed the emphasis on what happened to the individual soldier and civilian during the war.

The political changes of the postwar period and the communist regime's struggle to establish absolute authority against opposition groups, factions, and internal resistance provided additional subjects for fiction writers. The most impressive handling of this topic is unquestionably in Andrzejewski's novel *Popiół i diament* (1948). As Andrzejewski sees it, a serious injustice is committed when the guilt for a war precipitated by political fanaticism is placed upon a whole generation betrayed by history, regardless of the individual's degree of participation.

(2) PHASE TWO

With the postulation of socialist realism at the Stettin writers' conference in December 1949, Polish writers were directed to concentrate on matters of the day and to produce propaganda for increased production, factory discipline, and the so-called building up of socialism. A number of writers, especially the younger ones, were prepared to do this, but many of these revealed little artistic talent. Moreover, it became obvious that they were sometimes impeded by a total lack of familiarity with the milieu. Aleksander Ścibor-Rylski's novel *Węgiel* (1950) about coal mining is, however, a successful example of writing intended to stimulate production.

In addition, the older, more experienced writers began to revert to less topical subjects. The drama *Niemcy* (1949), by playwright Leon Kruczkowski, explores the factors that enabled the Nazis to possess themselves of unlimited power and finds them in the passivity of the German intelligentsia and the middle class. Julian Stryjkowski's novel *Bieg do Fregalà* (1952), which also has a foreign setting, deals with the struggle of the Italian proletariat.

In 1952 one of the most remarkable prose works written in the spirit of socialist realism appeared—the novel *Pamiątka z Celulozy,* by Igor Newerly (pseud. of Abramow; b. 1903). This is the story of a Polish laborer who gradually becomes a part of the socialist revolutionary movement. Newerly, who also wrote *Chłopiec z Salskich Stepów* (1948), is seemingly formally indebeted to the Polish positivist novelists. *Pamiatka z Celulozy* also has something in common with the highly esteemed documentary memoirs, *Stare i Nowe* (1948), of Lucjan Rudnicki (b. 1882).

The novels of Andrzej Braun (b. 1923)— *Lewanty* (1953) and *Piekło wybrukowane*

(1956)—provoked charged debate and conflicting criticisms. This was also true of *Obywatele* (1955) by Brandys. Refusing to expend their talents on the past, both of these writers sought to scrutinize the plain reality of the present with all its conflicts.

The poetry of this period maintained far more artistic independence than the prose. This can be seen in the postwar poetry of Gałczyński (q.v.), such as *Niobe* (1953). Even the originally more submissive poets were beginning to experience a steadily rising feeling of disappointment at being required to relinquish their individuality and to do routine compulsory work. Some of those who had at first been inclined to submit to the communist regime bitterly abandoned this mode and returned to approaches they found more rewarding. It was this swing that motivated Jastrun to write his *Poemat o mowie polskiej* (1952), one of his most mature achievements, which, in succinct, graphic diction, traces the development of the Polish language through several epochs and through its handling by the major poets.

Similarly other older poets tried to disengage themselves. Tuwim (q.v.), for example, devoted himself, after returning from exile, mainly to studies in Old Polish literature and to translations. Antoni Słonimski, too, who returned to Poland in 1951, concentrated, in the 1950's, on organizational activities and journalism, while advocating throughout the emancipation of art from official stylistic regulations as vigorously as seemed feasible.

Although historical and biographical novels existed in all literary phases of postwar Poland, the political currents of the time produced, in Phase Two, an especial interest in this genre. One of the most gifted biographers was Jastrun, who wrote studies of Mickiewicz (1949), J. Kochanowski (*Poeta i dworzanin,* 1954), and Słowacki (*Spotkanie z Salomeą,* 1951). Others were: Paweł Hertz, who wrote *Portret Słowackiego* (1949); Anna Kowalska, who wrote a novel about the Polish humanist Frycz-Modrzewski (*Wójt wolborski,* 1954–56); and Jerzy Broskiewicz (b. 1922), who wrote a popular novel about Chopin (*Kształt miłości,* 1950–51).

In the 1950's, Catholic writers were revealing decided liking for classical antiquity —which Parandowski (q.v.) had been working with since the 1930's—or for the matter of history in general. In addition to Z. Kossak-Szczucka, an older writer, the writers working in the historical-novel genre were: Jan Dobraczyński (b. 1910); T. Parnicki (b. 1908); Hanna Malewska (b. 1911); Władysław Jan Grabski (b. 1901); and Eugeniusz Paukszta. Perhaps the most gifted of this group was Antoni Gołubiew (b. 1907), whose novel *Bolesław Chrobry* (4 vols., 1947 f.) recounts, in language that is sometimes difficult to read because of the deliberate use of archaisms, the penetration of Christian ideas among the Slavic peoples in the 11th c. Jan Wiktor (b. 1890), whose earlier works were chiefly concerned with Polish peasant life, reaches back to the past in several of his novels. Tadeusz Lopalewski should be singled out for his *Kroniki polskie* (4 vols., 1952–56), a chronicle of the years 1863 to 1866.

Tadeusz Hołuj (b. 1907) treated historical subjects from a Marxist vantagepoint (*Próba ognia*, 1949; *Królestwo bez ziemi*, 1953). The short-story writer Stanisław Wygodzki (b. 1907), whose works—*e.g., Opowiadania buchaltera* (1951), *Jelonek i syn* (1951), and *Pusty plac* (1955)—have been termed "artistico-factographic" by the critics, focused on themes drawn from the Polish proletariat's years of struggle.

The inquiry into literary evolution during the 1950's conducted by the journal *Nowa Kultura* precipitated polemical discussion over the "Poemat dla dorosłych" of Ważyk (q.v.). Reaction against aesthetic regimentation was reflected, naturally, first in poetry. Writers of the previous generations, such as Ważyk and Jastrun (*Gorący popiół*, 1956) and Wiktor Woroszylski (*Z rozmów*, 1955), openly expressed their skepticism toward the existing social order. Simultaneously, talented poets making their debut in 1956—such as Miron Białoszewski (b. 1922; *Obroty rzeczy*), Jerzy Harasymowicz (b. 1933; *Cuda*), Zbigniew Herbert (b. 1924; *Struna światła*), and Stanisław Grochowiak (b. 1934; *Ballads rycerska*)—were interested in experimenting with form in poetry.

(3) PHASE THREE

The collapse of the doctrine of socialist realism in 1956 produced a number of remarkable prose writings. A group of prose writers emerged that was repeatedly compared—though not very appropriately—with the "angry young men" of English literature. The spokesman for this group was Hłasko (q.v.), who was influenced by Hemingway (q.v.). Hłasko's short stories (*Pierwszy dzień tygodnia,*

1956) voice most strongly the protest against the injustice being inflicted on the Polish nation. (Hłaskos temperament brought him to a tragic end: in 1969, after seeking asylum in West Germany, he committed suicide.) The young Marek Nowakowski, who followed Hłasko's example in *Ten stary złodziej* (1958), focused especially on the desperate situation of Polish youth.

These expressions of rebellion were paralleled by a better-founded criticism of the intellectual ambience. This begins to appear as early as 1955 in the short stories of Maria Dąbrowska (q.v.; *Gwiazda zaranna*), who had maintained a long silence after World War II, and in Andrzejewski's short stories *Złoty bis* (1955). Andrzejewski's "Ciemności kryją ziemię" (1957) is of enormous moral and artistic importance. Using a historical theme, it presents the moral conflict experienced by the individual whenever he finds himself in confrontation with an intellectual movement the power of which turns out to rest on terror and oppression.

Brandys was unwilling to take such an unequivocal position, although his *Obrona Grenady* (1956) did initiate an attack on cultural dictators. In the following year, however, in his novel *Matka Królów* (1957), which describes the misfortunes of a Polish working-class family, Brandys seemed more inclined to compromise with the system than to criticize it.

The strongest expressions of social criticism occurred in the dramatic works. The witty comedy *Święto Winkelrida* by Andrzejewski, written during the Nazi occupation, lost none of its meaningful point when it was produced in 1956. The Catholic dramatist Roman Brandstaetter (b. 1906), author of *Kroniki Asyżu* (1957), criticized the times in *Milczenie* (1956). Jerzy Zawieyski (q.v.), another Catholic dramatist, wrote moral and philosophical plays (*e.g., Dramaty*, 1957) that used biblical or classical backgrounds as a vehicle for social criticism. In his play *Imiona władzy* (1957), set in three different periods, Jerzy Broszkiewicz attempts to illustrate—perhaps too overtly—the way man has struggled to grasp power through all his known days.

A more subtle treatment, achieved through dialectical reversals remotely reminiscent of the German expressionist Kaiser's (q.v.) "thought play" *Drama aus der Sphäre der Gendarmen*, is *Policja* (1958) by Sławomir Mrożek (b. 1930).

Mrożek was one of the most interesting of those who were writing what the critics named "cross-eyed literature," a genre drawing heavily on the grotesque (q.v.), that developed after 1957. Under the influence of writers such as Gombrowicz (q.v.), however, this Kafka-derived grotesque took on a realistic-satirical vein. Mrożek used this grotesque-modified approach in his play *Męczeństwo Piotra Ohey'a* (1959) and in his short stories *Słoń* (1958) and *Wesele w Atomicach* (1959). The grotesque element in the stories of Stanisław Zieliński, another practitioner of "cross-eyed literature," is closer to the fantastic; these stories too are threaded with social criticism.

Kafka, Faulkner, and Camus (qq.v.) were much admired by the many talented prose writers who were first published in 1956. These were: Monika Kotowska, Magda Leja, Aleksander Minkowski, Eugeniusz Kabatc, S. Grochowiak, and Władisław Terlecki.

Another occurrence during Phase Three was the blooming of the essay and of literary criticism. Two of the most important works are M. Dąbrowska's *Myśli o sprawach i ludziach* (1956) and Adolf Rudnicki's *Niebiskie kartki* (1957).

Along with the most active and consistently Marxist critic Stefan Żołkiewski (b. 1911), the most productive of the older critics were Andrzej Stawar, Kazimiera Wyka (b. 1910), and Jan Kott (b. 1914), who since 1949 has shown a preference for other work, and the especially able Artur Sandauer. Primarily, they are interested in the meaning of socialist realism and the significance of Western literature for Polish literature. Younger critics, such as Jan Błonski, Andrzej Kijowski, and Ludwik Flaszen, also emerged.

(4) PHASE FOUR

The most striking thing about literary development after 1958 was the decline in overt criticism. Although the advocates of deeper political commitment grew more numerous, there was not exactly a return to old conventions but a tendency to shift themes into historical or foreign settings. The tone of skepticism was still most clearly heard in poetry. The "angry young men" fell silent, went away, or toed the official line, while the exponents of "cross-eyed literature" veered increasingly in the realistic-satirical direction and abandoned the confrontation of totalitarianism with the daimonic.

HEINRICH KUNSTMANN

Polish Literature in the 1960's

In 1898, Stanisław Przybyszewski (q.v.), the first Polish writer (perhaps with the exception of Henryk Sienkiewicz, q.v.) to influence literature in western Europe and in the Scandinavian countries, published a manifesto directed both as an incentive to his countrymen and as fair warning to the world that Polish literature was on its way to breaking out of nationalism and to henceforth joining the ranks of world literature. He wrote in *Życie* (15 October 1898): "I have no program because art has none. It is the right of everyone to cram any sort of artistic program into the intention of the artist himself; no one can forbid anyone from reading things into the works an author never dreamed of; but it is difficult to force art into some sort of program. ... We need air, we need to tear down the Chinese walls of provincialism concerning art, be they of Galicia or of Greater Poland, if our literature is to stand on the high ground of general European literature."

Unfortunately Przybyszewski's great design went astray somewhere between the lack of enthusiasm among his peers to displace Polonism with some form of sophistication and World War I. Although talent was not lacking during this period (1900–1939), the Polish writers never succeeded in gaining the recognition that was granted to their no more talented contemporaries from France, England, Germany, and the United States.

It is difficult to say what was lacking in the group during Przybyszewski's day. Certainly in *Życie* (Life) and *Chimera* Przybyszewski and his equally talented contemporary, Zenon Przesmycki had easy access to journals in which they could disseminate their philosophy and theories concerning art and literature and publish the creative works of Polish writers. In poets such as Jan Kasprowicz, Stanisław Wyspiański (qq.v.), Kazimierz Przerwa Tetmajer, and Bolesław Leśmian, and novelists such as Stefan Żeromski and Władysław Reymont (qq.v.), they were fortunate, indeed, to be surrounded with artists possessed of enormous talent. Perhaps the language barrier can account for the fact that little international recognition was bestowed on these writers. Perhaps the reason is simply that no great critic appeared who could focus the attention of the world on the accomplishments of the Polish school of writers.

It could be argued that the group's greatest asset was Jan Kott. Perhaps even more than Jerzy Grotowski (b. 1933), founder and director of the Laboratory Theater, Kott has influenced modern staging more than any other one critic. The English director Peter Brooks's production of *King Lear* was inspired by Kott's essays on Shakespeare, which were published individually in *Dialog* (selected translations were published as *Shakespeare Our Contemporary,* 1964). Even today in 1970 directors and critics throughout the world refer to a certain type of staging (especially those in which classics are updated and made more contemporary) as productions "à la Kott." It seems likely that his new book, *A Fool against the Establishment: A Study of the Heroes in Greek Tragedy,* will create another sensation among scholars and personnel in the theater.

It was not until the late 1950's and early 1960's that the Polish school of writers managed to make an impression on world literature. And the main reason for their gaining attention was not merely talent—a commodity in abundance, especially in the 1930's. The truth was that the Polish writers in the late 1950's and early 1960's made up a "School," a group that of necessity must consist of talented artists (poets, dramatists, novelists, and painters, designers, composers, etc.), critics of international stature, an organ (journal or some sort of record of performance), and, above all, like Przybyszewski himself, a guiding spirit.

Thus, in the late 1950's, when the right factors were present, the Polish school of the absurd was inaugurated. Made up mostly of poet-playwrights, translators, and critics gathered around the monthly *Dialog* (first published in May 1956), the group, under the brilliant guidance of Adam Tarn, set out with a policy similar to Przybyszewski's; that is, "the dissemination of cultural materials" not only within Poland but the world as well.

What Tarn and his group accomplished can be regarded as a phenomenon in the history of contemporary *belles lettres* in eastern Europe. One important objective of the Polish school of writers was to establish contact with their counterparts throughout the world. With a young staff of critics and editors (Halina Anderska, Kazimierz Korcelli, Jerzy Pomianowski, Konstanty Puzyna, and Jerzy

Koenig), Tarn set out to get together the best body of talent that Poland could offer. With the publication of an abridged version of Beckett's (q.v.) *Waiting for Godot* (May 1956) the theater of the absurd was officially inaugurated in Poland. During the next twelve years (the length of Tarn's reign) *Dialog* published almost two hundred foreign plays in Polish translation and almost twice that number of contemporary Polish dramas.

Perhaps the best known of these dramatists are Sławomir Mrożek, Tadeusz Różewicz (q.v.), Zbigniew Herbert, Tymoteusz Karpowicz (b. 1921), S. Grochowiak (b. 1934), and Leszek Kołakowski (b. 1927). An unusual aspect about all these dramatists is that they are primarily recognized for their achievement in other genres, either as poets (Herbert, Różewicz, Karpowicz, and Grochowiak), satirists and prose stylists (Mrożek, Kołakowski, and Różewicz), or, in the case of Kołakowski, as a philosopher. But it is as dramatists that they reached the attention of artists and critics outside of Poland.

Influenced by Beckett and Ionesco (qq.v.), these writers nonetheless made original contributions of their own. Although like their contemporaries in Europe and elsewhere they were concerned with the breakdown of language and the dehumanization of culture, they were also preoccupied with problems peculiar to eastern Europe.

Mrożek in *Tango* (1964; Eng., 1965) dramatized the abortive attempt of his hero (Arthur), who strives to establish order based on the cultural patterns of the past. He is killed by the very force (Edward) that he has been using to effect the change. Karpowicz in *Dziwny pasażer* (1964; The Strange Passenger, in *Drama and Theatre,* 1969) has his hero (Passenger) search for his "lost half," which somehow disappeared during World War II. Passenger's search ends in a graveyard, and the precious package he has been trying to deliver for almost thirty years (a direct order) turns out to be Madeira wine. Różewicz in *Kartoteka* (1960; The Card Index, 1969) and *Wyszedł z domu* (1964; Gone Out, 1969) also dramatizes man's search for self and for some sort of alternative to today's cultural chaos.

Together with Grochowiak and Jerzy Broszkiewicz, these *Dialog* writers have contributed more than a hundred plays to the contemporary Polish theater. Certainly not all of these works will survive the scrutiny that time inflicts on all works of art. But several dozen have already become permanent items in theater repertories all over the world, with the possible exception of the United States. European audiences find these new voices quite relevant to their times. Mrożek's stabs at the ubiquitous hand of unseen powers, Różewicz's tragic games with "life-death," and Karpowicz's attempts at solving unsolvable riddles are recognizable and identifiable problems in Berlin, Vienna, and Paris. But in New York these themes seem alien and incomprehensible.

Besides publishing unknown contemporary writers and nurturing young talent, Tarn and his group also revived writers whose genius was either earlier never recognized or for political reasons not acknowledged. Two of these were Witold Gombrowicz (q.v.) and Stanislaw Ignacy Witkiewicz (also called Witkacy). In the American universities, Gombrowicz and Witkacy are becoming recognized.

Gombrowicz's three plays—*Ślub* (1953; The Marriage, 1969), *Iwona, księżniczka Burgunda* (1958; Yvonne, the Princess of Burgundy, 1967), and *Operetka* (1968)—have been produced even in the United States. A precursor of the absurd, Gombrowicz is probably better known for his novels—*Ferdydurke* (1938; Eng., 1961), *Pornografia* (1960; Eng., 1966), and *Kosmos* (1965; Cosmos, 1967)—than he is for his plays and diaries (*Dziennik 1953–56*, 1957). But his influence on Mrożek, Różewicz, Herbert, and Karpowicz and on the "beat" generation of South America (he lived in Argentina after 1939) has been immense.

The only other Polish writer who deserves greater credit for innovation and originality than Gombrowicz, and who belongs among the great panoply of writers of the theater of the absurd (Beckett, Ionesco, and Jarry, qq.v.), is Witkacy.

Dramatist, novelist, critic, and painter, Witkacy was one of the last of the 20th-c. geniuses who excelled in everything he attempted. His thirty-odd extant plays (most published posthumously in 1962) are the core of the Polish theater of the absurd and contribute to the central body of the worldwide theater of the absurd. Unfortunately, with the absurd now moribund, Witkacy will have to wait for a second revival in order to be fairly acquitted and rightfully honored as one of the great dramatists (and novelists) of the 20th c.

The *Dialog*-centered group gained considerable stature in the mid-1960's and flourished

until the shameful irrational purge of intellectuals and Jews in 1968–69. Expatriation was the fate of Adam Tarn, who now teaches in Canada. In fact, with Tarn in Canada, Kott in the United States, and Kołakowski in England, the driving forces behind the Polish school of the absurd now cease to exist in Poland. It remains to be seen whether the current editorial board of *Dialog* (publication still continues) can regain the eminent position it once had.

But Poland has made other contributions to world literature since gaining back her statehood (the partition of the country had lasted for almost 150 years) after World War I. Strangely enough, great talent in Poland is often discovered and acknowledged late in the writer's career or sometimes posthumously. This has been true of Gombrowicz, Witkacy, and, earlier, of the great poet Cyprian Norwid (1821–83), who died a pauper's death in Paris and was only discovered in the early years of this century. His influence among young Polish poets is still quite immense.

This pattern of belated recognition still awaits a number of Polish writers. Certainly Jerzy Andrzejewski (q.v.) deserves better treatment at the hands of critics for his brilliant short stories—especially, "Złoty lis" (1955; "The Gold Fox," in *The Modern Polish Mind*, 1962) —and his novels *Bramy raju* (1960; Gates of Paradise, 1962) and *Ciemności kryją ziemię* (1957; The Inquisitors, 1960). Bruno Schulz has always been on the verge of being "discovered" but has not yet emerged from the limbo occupied by writers only talked about but never read. His *Sklepy cynamonowe* (1934; Am., The Street of Crocodiles, 1963; Eng., Cinnamon Shops, 1963) can stand on its own as an inventive modern parable, haunted by ghosts from the writer's psychic and cultural vision. Maria Dąbrowska (q.v.), always mentioned when the Nobel Prize for Literature was being discussed, never succeeded in attaining the recognition that her novel *Noce i dnie* (4 vols., 1932–34) should have gained for her.

Also deserving of rescue is Leon Kruczkowski, who, probably more than any writer of talent in eastern Europe, possessed a social conscience even before it was fashionable to admit having one. His novel *Kordjan i cham* (1932) was one of the first modern novels in which Marxist ideology is suggested as a resolution to a nation's social problems. His plays, *Pierwszy dzień wolności* (1959, in *Dialog*) and *Śmierć gubernatora* (1961, in *Dialog*), deal with the problems of individual freedom and man's relationship to the state. In many ways Kruczkowski was Poland's most articulate spokesman for issues being raised all over the world today.

As for the young group of writers that has been published in *Dialog* during the past ten years, it is difficult to make a valid evaluation concerning their works. Most of these writers are in their early thirties and hopefully have their most productive years ahead of them. The most promising of them are: Miron Białoszewski (b. 1922), Tadeusz Konwicki (b. 1926), Jarosław Marek Rymkiewicz (b. 1934), Ireneusz Iredyński (b. 1936), and Grochowiak.

E. J. CZERWINSKI

BIBLIOGRAPHY: Estreicher, K. and S., eds., *Bibliografia Polska* (33 vols., 1870–1939); Dyboski, R., *Modern Polish Literature* (1924); *Literatura polska od początku do wojny światowej* (4 vols.; 2nd ed., 1929–31); Feldman, W., *Współczesna literatura polska* (8th ed., 1930); Giusti, W., *Aspetti della poesia polacca contemporanea* (1931); Czachowski, K., *Obraz współczesnei literatury polskiej 1884–1933* (3 vols., 1934–36); Grabowski, T., *Historja literatury polskiej* (1936); Lednicki, W., *Life and Culture of Poland as Reflected in Polish Literature* (1944); Wyka, K., *Zarys współczesnej literatura polska* (1951); Krejčí, K., *Dějiny polské literatury* (1953); Kridl, M., *A Survey of Polish Literature and Culture* (1956); Maver, G., ed., *Letteratura polacca* (1958); "Writing in Poland," *TLS*, 18 July 1958, p. 412; "Polish Periodicals of Today," *TLS*, 12 Sept. 1958, p. 518; Heyst, A., "Poland's Contemporary Literature," *DubR*, CCXXXIII (1959), 171–78; Matuszewski, R., *Portraits d'écrivains polonais contemporains* (1959); Przyboś, J., *Linia i ˙gwar* (1959); Sandauer, A., *Bez taryfy ulgowej* (1959); Stawar, A., *O Gałczyńskim* (1959); Szczawiej, J., *Owoc dobrego i złego* (1959); "Polish Literature in Exile," *Wiseman Review*, CCXXXV (1961), 177–81; Kunstmann, H., *Die moderne polnische Literatur 1918–1960* (1962); Gillon, A., *Introduction to Modern Polish Literature* (1964); Czerwinski, E. J., "*Dialog*: The Polish Theater of the Absurd," Dissertation, The University of Wisconsin, 1965; Gömöri, G., *Polish and Hungarian Poetry 1945–1956* (1966); Maciuszko, J., *The Polish Short Story in English: A Guide and Critical Bibliography* (1968); Miłosz, C., *The History of Polish Literature* (1969)

PONGE, Francis

French poet, b. 27 March 1899, Montpellier

P. is the poet of things. Perhaps his main poetic dedication can be summarized in his title *Le Parti pris des choses* (1942). "Prejudiced in favor of things," he tries to exclude from his poems man and his falsifying emotions. He describes the orange, the mimosa, the oyster, the snail, or the pebble in verse or prose that deliberately holds no appeal to the ear, for his main concern is the unsentimental purity of things. In his eyes familiar, seductive rhythm would trick the mind into seeing nonexistent continuity and logic. His goal is "the assassination of poetry by its subject matter." His approach, which might be called an attempt at a phenomenology of the world through the poem, has been followed by French exponents of the *nouveau roman* such as Robbe-Grillet (q.v.).

It is language, not man, that confronts the "nature-given thing" (for P. rules out the world of technology). He speaks of "the things challenging language." Not interested in accurately describing what the eye sees, he strives to endow the seen with adequate, true life.

Central then to P.'s poetry is a frantic compulsion (symbolized by the title *La Rage de l'expression,* 1952) to find the words that will pinpoint precisely, and at the same time make recognizable, the natural objects perceived by eye or hand. In this, the immobile and the invariable in the world of things interests P. far more than the mobile—he prefers the rock to the river. For him, whatever possesses hard form seems in itself more likely to possess artistic value.

In keeping with his glorification of things, P. confers on them a twofold value. First, they provide a solution to all of man's problems because in their realm all causality falls away, and in the contemplation of them comes security—even serenity. At the same time the thing is something to be emulated because it exists in accordance with its intrinsic principles. Thus P. becomes a moralist, suggesting that man can derive a lesson from the minute description of things. In his multilevel verbal architecture and the conciseness of his formulations, P. can be considered a descendant of the classicists, such as La Fontaine (1621–95).

FURTHER WORKS: *Douze Petits Écrits* (1926); *Dix Cours sur la méthode* (1946); *L'Oeillet, la guêpe, le mimosa* (1946); *Le Carnet du bois de pins* (1947); *La Crevette dans tous ses états* (1948); *La Liasse* (with bibliography;

1948); *Proèmes* (1949); *Le Peintre à l'étude* (1949); *Braque* (1950); *L'Araignée* (1952); *Le Grand Recueil* (1961); *Pour un malherbe* (1965); *Œuvres* (1967); *Le Savon* (1967); *Nouveau Recueil* (1967)

BIBLIOGRAPHY: Douthat, B., "F. P.'s Untenable Goat," *YFS*, No. 21 (1958), pp. 172–81; Douthat, B., "Le parti pris des *Choses*," *FS*, XIII (1959), 39–51; Denat, A., "F. P. and the New Problem of the Epos," *University of Queensland Papers*, I (1963), vi, 35–41; Walther, E., *F. P.* (1965); Willard, N. M., "A Poetry of Things: Williams, Rilke, P.," *CL*, XVII (1965), 311–24; Temmer, M., "F. P.: A Dissenting View of His Poetry," *MLQ*, XXIX (1968), 207–21

GEORGES SCHLOCKER

PONTOPPIDAN, Henrik

Danish novelist and short-story writer, b. 24 July 1857, Fredericia, Jutland; d. 21 Aug. 1943, Charlottenlund, Sjaelland

P., born into a fine old family of theologians and scholars, soon revolted against his Christian heritage. Though he had originally wanted to study engineering, he became a writer at the age of twenty-two. He joined the freethinking movement that got its name from that of Brandes (q.v.) and took as his models Ibsen and Strindberg (qq.v.), whom he considered naturalists (*see* naturalism). His main interest, however, was the life of country people.

In 1881 he married a peasant girl, from whom he was divorced ten years later. In 1892 he remarried. He traveled frequently throughout Denmark, in pursuit of data for his realistic, critical account of his country's social life. In 1917 he and Gjellerup (q.v.) were jointly awarded the Nobel Prize for Literature. Although by then already outdistanced artistically by younger writers, he still retained great authority as an artist and a critic of his people.

Three major works stand out from a total of some fifty volumes. *Det forjaettede Land* (3 vols., 1891–95; The Promised Land, 1896) describes religious activity in rural Sjaelland and the failure of an idealistic young pastor confronted with the "joyous Christianity" introduced into the Danish church by the theologian and poet Grundtvig and the "somber Christianity" of the tightly organized, Pietistic missionary religion of the Danish Church.

In *Lykke-Per* (8 parts, 1894–1904) P. closely analyzes most of the social and cultural groups (except for labor groups) that existed in Denmark between 1870 and 1890. The course of Lykke-Per's life takes him from his father's parsonage in a provincial town in Jutland into Copenhagen intellectual circles (an account of the Jews of Denmark is an important feature here) and back to Jutland. Lykke-Per, without ever having understood life, lives and dies in solitude on the dreary sandy coast of northernmost Jutland.

De Dødes Rige (5 vols., 1912–16), P.'s third major work, is deeply pessimistic. Describing cultural and political life in Denmark from about 1900 to 1910, it focuses on the aftermath of the successful democratic movement, which in P.'s opinion was accompanied by a collapse of true cultural values. Here P. is particularly critical of the Dane's lack of religious conviction.

P.'s short stories and memoirs are also significant.

FURTHER WORKS: *Staekkede vinger* (1881); *Landsbybilleder* (1883); *Sandinge menighed* (1883); *Ung elskov* (1885); *Mimoser* (1886); *Fra hytterne* (1887); *Isbjørnen* (1887); *Spøgelser* (1888; The Apothecary's Daughters, 1890); *Krøniker* (1890); *Natur* (1890); *Minder* (1893); *Nattevagt* (1894); *Ørneflugt* (1894); *Den gamle Adam* (1894); *Højsang* (1896); *Kirkeskuden* (1897); *Naar vildgaessene traekker forbi* (1897); *Det ideale hjem* (1900); *Lille Rødhaette* (1900); *De vilde fugle* (1902); *Borgmester Hoeck og hans hustru* (1905); *Asgaardsrejen* (1906); *Hans Kvast og Melusine* (1907); *Det store spøgelse* (1907); *Den kongelige gaest* (1908); *Et kaerlighedseventyr* (1918); *Noveller og skitser* (1922–30); *Romaner og fortaellinger* (1924–26); *Mands himmerig* (1927); *Drengeaar* (1933); *Hamskifte* (1936); *Arv og gaeld* (1938); *Familjeliv* (1940)

BIBLIOGRAPHY: Andersen, V., *H. P.* (1917); Thomsen, E., *H. P.* (1944); Woel, C. N., *H. P.* (1945); Ahnlund, K., *H. P.* (1956); Ekman, E., "H. P. as a Critic of Modern Danish Society," *SS*, XXIX (1957), 170–83; Jolivet, A., *Les Romans de H. P.* (1960)

EMIL FREDERIKSEN

PORTER, Katherine Anne

American short-story writer and novelist, b. 15 May 1890, Indian Creek, Texas

A descendant of Daniel Boone, Katherine Anne P. grew up in Texas and Louisiana. In both the United States and Europe, she earned her living for many years as a journalist, editor, and movie scenario writer.

At the heart of Katherine Anne P.'s work are the psychology of human emotions and the conflict between good and evil. Her first published collection of stories was *Flowering Judas, and Other Stories* (1930; rev. ed., 1935). "Flowering Judas" is a haunting tale that touches on this conflict of good and evil. The heroine, Laura, both intellectual and religious, is faced with the insurmountable compromise of bridging the gap between lofty ideals and a colder, more pragmatic reality.

From her earliest work through *Ship of Fools* (1962), Katherine Anne P.'s fiction has conveyed a sense of man's inability to survive the mysterious outside forces that corrupt him. Her stories evoke this feeling by presenting the human situations that bring out man's strange behavior such as in "Noon Wine" (1937). The confusion and unreality that confront the hero, Mr. Thompson, suggest the hostile but inexplicable agencies that play on mankind.

These agencies, however, are sometimes extrapersonal. This view can be seen in "Pale Horse, Pale Rider," from the collection *Pale Horse, Pale Rider* (1939). Perhaps her most moving and finely wrought story, this describes human beings caught up in the inevitable destruction of war. The impersonal menace of war is dramatized adroitly through precision of language and symbolic structure.

Katherine Anne P.'s stories are marked by their tightness of form and their intricately woven images and details. They are rich in implication and brutal in their impact upon the reader. The last lines of "Pale Horse, Pale Rider" point out the masterful irony: "No more war, no more plague. . . . Now there would be time for everything."

The Leaning Tower, and Other Stories (1944) is the final volume of Katherine Anne P.'s stories to date. The first six stories in this volume deal with the childhood of Miranda, who is the protagonist of "Pale Horse, Pale Rider." The Miranda stories are perhaps based on the childhood memories of the author. "The Leaning Tower" deals with an American in Nazi Germany in 1933.

Ship of Fools, Katherine Anne P.'s first novel, was written over a twenty-year period. Many of her earlier themes are present in this longer form. The idea that creative vitality in man is often snuffed out by blind, hostile forces is an important theme. The action takes place aboard a ship sailing from Vera Cruz to Bremerhaven

on the eve of World War II. The recurring problem of evil is brought into sharper focus, for political as well as individual evil is considered. When each character is viewed as a microcosm, the implication of an evil world is apparent. Besides her fiction, Katherine Anne P. has published two collections of essays. *The Days Before* (1952) and *The Collected Essays and Occasional Writings of Katherine Anne Porter* (1970). These essays were written over a period of years and offer an interesting self-portrait of the writer as well as a clear understanding of her belief of the writer's function.

Katherine Anne P.'s position in American fiction is a curious but notable one. She has written relatively little, but she enjoys an extremely high reputation. The measure of her success, except for *Ship of Fools,* a best-selling novel, has been largely critical.

FURTHER WORKS: *Outline of Mexican Popular Arts and Crafts* (1922); *Hacienda* (1934); *The Old Order* (1934); *Collected Stories* (1965)

BIBLIOGRAPHY: Wilson, E., *Classics and Commercials* (1950); Mooney, H. J., *The Fiction and Criticism of K. A. P.* (1957; rev. ed., 1962); West, R. B., *K. A. P.* (1963)

THOMAS F. STALEY

PORTUGUESE LITERATURE

Portuguese literature is characterized by the predominance of poetry and that it lacks close ties with other European literature. Fiction and drama, despite many beginnings—some of which were absorbed or evolved from Spain—never developed a tradition comparable to that of lyric poetry. Of all the European intellectual movements only romanticism had any effect in Portugal. This acceptance occurred because its fundamental mood and its recognition of national individuality were congenial to the Portuguese. In its best works Portuguese literature expresses the specifically Portuguese. As a result it is little read outside Portugal.

The uneasiness gathering in Portugal at the turn of the c. and in the next few decades—a time of restlessness and insecurity—brought about an atmosphere in which the desire for social change and renewal was born. The same uneasiness acted upon the literature, which was equally in need of a new departure. The self-consciousness without which change could not be effected evolved, through inclination and under the pressure of actual conditions, into a nationalistic withdrawal. It was this choice that led Pessoa (q.v.), a fiercely inexorable critic, to speak of the provincial character of Portuguese writing. He did not even except José Maria de Eça de Queiroz (1845–1900), whose important fiction to a large extent determined the character and prestige of Portuguese literature at the end of the 19th c.

In his endeavor to overcome this provincialism, Castro (q.v.) leaned upon the spirit and principles of symbolism (q.v.) and of Mallarmé's circle, but he is by no means merely a follower of the French symbolists. His achievement and influence entitle him to special recognition as a symbolist and a western-European poet. In this sphere he was unequalled in Portuguese literature, even by those of his contemporaries who surpassed him as a poet.

António Nobre (1867–1900), another contemporary symbolist, published in 1892 a volume of poems with the characteristic title *Só* ("lonely"). These poems express beautifully a completely introspective *Weltschmerz* and nostalgia.

Similarly, the ethereal lyricism of the poems of Pessanha (q.v.) expressed pure alienation. Yet their influence has persisted precisely because Pessanha's projection of the psychic state of eating one's heart out in alienation and brooding loneliness seemed genuinely and essentially Portuguese.

Pascoaes (q.v.) named this specifically Portuguese mentality and attitude *säudosismo*. (The word *saudade* in Portuguese means yearning.) He established *säudosismo* as the proclaimed creed for a school of Portuguese poetry aware of its specialness, and as a program for regeneration that the recognition of such specialness would enable one to aspire to. Pascoaes's own poetry is pervaded by this mode of thought and feeling, which he attempted to substantiate through cultural and religious philosophy and to heighten into prophetic visions. The context of his poetry was never, as a matter of fact, especially profound, but it did contribute to the opening up of the Portuguese natural and spiritual landscape.

The poetry of Afonso Lopes Vieira (1878–1946) was inspired by Pascoaes. Other poets who concerned themselves with their native landscape and the Portuguese identity were: Afonso Duarte (1886–1958; *Obra poética*, 1956); Mário Beirão (b. 1891; *Novas estrêlas*, 1940); Sardinha (q.v.); and Manuel da Silva

Gaio (1860–1939). Their aims were most impressively realized by A. Correia de Oliveira (b. 1879) in his now popular, now rhapsodical, now intensely pathetic poems.

By contrast, Sá-Carneiro (q.v.) and Pessoa claimed they were rejecting native tradition in favor of international futurism (q.v.). Actually, both of them derived from Nobre and Pessanha, and for all their sensational, belligerent vehemence, their richest poems, so far as content goes, are also quite traditional. In poetic attitude then, Sá-Carneiro and Pessoa are, in their own way, representative of the Portuguese mentality. Nevertheless, they were innovators. Their contribution seems to be in the direction of loosening and dissolving the tenets of form, but actually they achieved a spiritualizing of it.

Younger poets emulate the credo of Sá-Carneiro and Pessoa. Vitorino Nemésio (b. 1901), J. Régio (q.v.), and Miguel Torga (b. 1907) eschewed rigorous forms, especially in their early works, and prefer free rhythms, though Régio did write some masterful sonnets. Carlos Queiroz (1907–49), in his *anti-soneto*, militated against one of the most popular of the traditional forms. Many poets, including Queiroz, worked for inner consistency, precision of poetic expression, and formal simplicity. Queiroz and Nemésio in fact wrote in straightforward, song-like verse.

This simplicity was also the outstanding characteristic of the *Canções* of Antonio Boto (1902–59), although he is not in the mainstream of Portuguese poetry.

Among the most recent poets who espoused the nature mysticism and lyricism of *säudosismo* were: Sophia de Mello Breyner Andresen (b. 1919); Natércia Freire (b. 1920); Raúl de Carvalho (b. 1920); Ruy Cinatti (b. 1915); the surrealists (*see* surrealism) Mário Cesariny de Vasconcelos (b. 1923), Alexandre O'Neill (b. 1924), and António M. Lisboa (1928–53); António Gedeão (b. 1906); and João Apolinário (b. 1924) and David Mourão-Ferreira (b. 1927), who are the successors of Sá-Carneiro and Pessoa.

The predominance of lyric poetry in contemporary Portuguese literature and its high prestige are indications of Portuguese conservatism. Drama is much less important. The dramas of Castro and Pessoa are highly poetic. Those of Torga are, for the most part, ballad-like. Régio wrote mystery plays. None of these works were successful on the stage. The plays of Dantas (q.v.) and Carlos Selvagem (b. 1890) were relatively effective theatrically, as were the often caustic social comedies of Ramada Curto (1886–1961) and the folk plays of Alfredo Cortès (1880–1946).

Fiction in the 20th c. began in the shadow of the great society novels of Eça de Queiroz and his emulator Carlos Malheiro Dias (1875–1941). In the hands of Antero de Figueiredo (1866–1953), who usually wrote about historical and religious subjects, prose fiction became lyrical. Manuel António Ribeiro (1879–1942) wrote religious-social novels. Brandão (q.v.) wrote rhapsodically about the life of the poor, the oppressed, and the degraded. His emotion-packed, intense, often episodic descriptions re-create the life of the Portuguese people. In his handling of the background he draws close to regionalism.

Regionalism was introduced by Aquilino Ribeiro (q.v.) in his early works. Many writers believed that regionalism could be the means by which new life could be brought to fiction because they could thereby use the themes and idioms of their surroundings. Ferreira de Castro (q.v.) and, more recently, Redol (q.v.) developed the regional social novel; Nemésio evolved the regional psychological novel.

The chief representatives of the psychological —and especially the introspective—novel are Régio and Fernando Namora (b. 1919). João Gaspar Simões (b. 1903) also attempted this genre, but later devoted himself to the light novel. By 1960 the leading exponent of the light novel was Joaquim Paço d'Arcos (b. 1908).

Aquilino Ribeiro, Nemésio, Régio, and José Rodrigues Miguéis (b. 1901), as well as Fonseca (q.v.), have achieved eminence in their handling of the novella. As a novelist Torga goes his own way, notable for his formal brevity and concise style. In the late 1950's Augustina Bessa Luís aroused attention with large-scale novels obviously influenced by Proust and Woolf (qq.v.).

In the 1950's Sardinha (q.v.), the intellectual leader of the integralists, and António Sérgio de Sousa (1883–1969), the representative of intellectual liberalism, were devoting themselves to writing essays on politico-cultural subjects and the history of ideas.

By 1960 the leading literary critics were Fidelino de Figueiredo (1889–1968), who writes from the point of view of historicism and positivism, and Nemésio and Simões, who evaluate by means of aesthetic criteria. (Simões is also interested in the psychological approach.)

Despite writers' complaints about the lack of official responsiveness, there is considerable interest in literature in present-day Portugal.

To a great extent literary life is reflected in the periodicals.

The publication of the group around Pascoaes was A Águia. Sá-Carneiro and Pessoa proclaimed and carried out their futurist program in Orpheu. The periodical of the integralists was the Nação Portuguesa. The reformist republicans, including Brandão, Aquilino Ribeiro, and Sérgio de Sousa, promulgated their position in the Seara Nova. The modernist Presença, published by Simões, Régio, and A. Madeira, was committed to the same objectives as Orpheu. It was succeeded by the more moderate and better balanced Revista de Portugal, which was under the direction of Nemésio.

Though the fact of the establishing of such a number of journals and the formation, splintering, and dissolution of literary groups might be interpreted as indicating that Portuguese writers are involved in intense ideological conflicts, this is not so. In general, the omnipresent Portuguese antipathy to crucial problems (which the writers even avoid formulating) is not conducive to such controversy.

The spiritual and philosophical content of literary works is therefore small. (This cannot, it is true, be said of Pessoa's works, but it is not the content that makes his writing effective.) In the religious and social writing in which such substantive thought does exist, it is confessional, nonproblematic, and lacking in tension. Certainly this is the main reason contemporary Portuguese literature has thus far not exerted much influence. The vigorous attempts on the part of some writers to become familiar with foreign writing and to adopt foreign themes and techniques have not been rewarding. Current social, political, and spiritual trauma also evoke slight response in Portuguese literature. The intellectual and spiritual reality it reflects is at heart unfragmented. Therein lie its limitations—and also its charm.

BIBLIOGRAPHY: Cidade, H., Tendências do lirismo contemporâneo (2nd ed., 1939); Régio, J., Pequena história da moderna poesia portuguesa (1942); Ramos, F., Eugénio de Castro e a Nova Poesia (1943); Pessoa, F., A Nova poesia portuguesa (1944); Ameal, J., Panorama de la littérature portugaise contemporaine (1948); Le Gentil, G., La littérature portugaise (2 vols., 1951); Rossi, G. C., Storia della letteratura portoghese (1953); Dicionário das literaturas portuguesa, galega e brasileira (1958 ff.); A. C. L., ed., Antologia da moderna *poesia portuguesa* (1958); Andrade, J. P. de, ed., *Os melhores contos portugueses* (1958); Conceição Nobre, M. da, *Antologia de poesias angolanas* (1958); Kayser, W., *Die Vortragsreise* (1958); Macedo, C. de, *Poesia no Portugal contemporâneo* (1958); Sicna, J. de, ed., *Líricas portuguesas* (3rd series, 1958); *Antologia da novíssima poesia portuguesa* (1959); Rebelo, L. F., ed., *Teatro português do romantismo aos nossos dias* (1959 ff.); Simões, J. G., *História da poesia portuguêsa das origens aos nossos dias* (3rd vol., 1959); Moser, G., "Portuguese Literature in Recent Years," *MLJ*, XLIV (1960), 245–54; Parker, J. W., *Three Twentieth Century Portuguese Poets* (1960); Moser, G. M., "Portuguese Writers of This Century," *Hispania*, L (1966), 947–54

ALBIN EDUARD BEAU

POUND, Ezra Loomis
American poet and critic, b. 30 Oct. 1885, Hailey, Idaho

One of the most controversial figures of his generation, P. is known for his translations and the *Cantos* (1919–68)—which are generally regarded as his masterpiece—and for his unorthodox economic and social theories. Always concerned with innovation, as well as with what he believed to be vital in tradition, P. both helped to inaugurate new movements, such as imagism, and constantly sought to develop recognition for young and promising writers, *e.g.*, Hilda Doolittle, Eliot, Frost, Joyce, and Hemingway (qq.v.).

Involved in London literary life from 1908 to 1920, P. exerted his influence on the burgeoning American scene by serving as foreign editor of Harriet Monroe's *Poetry* (1912–18) and Margaret Anderson's *The Little Review* (1917–19). International in taste, and particularly interested in current artistic developments in France, P. moved to Paris in 1920. He later settled in Italy, where he remained for much of his life.

P.'s interest in economics became pronounced in the 1930's, although it had been apparent throughout the preceding decade. Strongly influenced by C. H. Douglas's (1879–1952) theory of social credit, P. wrote tracts on the evils of the conventional system of banking, and attacked the use of money as a medium of exchange (*Social Credit: An Impact*, 1935, and others). His anti-Semitism is at least partly traceable to his belief that Jews, prominent in international finance, were participants in the so-called conspiracy of usurers to whom P. attributed responsibility for the erosion of values.

Believing that under fascism sound reforms were possible, P. chose to see Mussolini as a sincere man of action with a clear perception of social problems (*Jefferson and/or Mussolini*, 1935). During World War II he defended fascism on Radio Rome. For this P. was imprisoned in the Disciplinary Training Center at Pisa by army authorities after the American occupation of Italy and was later returned to the United States to stand trial for treason. He was subsequently judged insane and committed to St. Elizabeths Hospital in Washington, D. C., where he remained for twelve years (1946–58). After his release, an action long called for by many fellow writers, P. returned to Europe.

Metrical experimentation and refinement is one of the chief features of P.'s work. His early poetry is rich in adaptations of Latin, Greek, Provençal, Italian, and Chinese poetic forms. This work can be found in *Personae* (1909; revised eds., 1926 and 1949) and other volumes. But further, P. was concerned with the role of art in a hostile and morally deteriorated world (*Hugh Selwyn Mauberley*, 1920). Developing a vision of experience that was partly Confucian in inspiration, P. asserted the values of "sincerity" and "rectitude" to counter what he believed was the destruction of culture by the acquisitive (*Guide to Culture*, 1938, and earlier writings). In the realm of language such destruction was marked by abstractionism and obfuscation; only by a general renovation or rectification (*ch'ing ming*) could language be made to communicate directly. From the beginning P. had called for a poetry that was hard, clear, and vivid.

Influenced by the Orientalist Ernest Fenollosa (1853–1908), he eventually devised the "ideogrammic method," an attempt to capture in English the precision of the Chinese character, which, being graphic, supposedly resisted overabstraction. This method lies behind the mosaic structure of the *Cantos*, which is composed of fragments (ideographs) from mythology, history, and autobiography.

Running to more than a hundred sections and still not complete, the *Cantos* are both a record of P.'s intellectual and aesthetic life and his view of the meaning of history. Theoretically unified by P.'s vision of human life as an interplay between the forces of good (authentic culture, ethical and artistic integrity) and those of corruption (economic exploitation, "usury"), the poem presents revelatory moments, events, quotations, and portraits that are intended to rectify what P. takes to be the habitual misconceptions of his readers. Odysseus, Confucius, the Cid, Sigismundo Malatesta, John Adams, Thomas Jefferson, Martin Van Buren, among others, emerge as heroes because of their ideals, strength of character, or exercise of *directio voluntatis* (a Dantean idea interpreted as the ability to act upon ideas). Ancient Egypt, Greece, Provence, Renaissance and modern Italy, ancient China, colonial and modern America are the major civilizations from which P. presents a wealth of detail, always in fragmented or ideogrammic forms, and therefore with frequent obscurity, on personal and public events of economic, political, and cultural import.

The sequence known as the *Pisan Cantos* (74–84), P.'s response to his imprisonment, is regarded as one of the most impressive sections of the work. It won for P., despite his uncertain legal status, the controversial Bollingen Prize for Poetry for 1948. Since 1919, when the earliest of the *Cantos* were first published in book form, P. has been publishing drafts and revisions of the *Cantos*. In 1965 cantos 1 to 95 were revised and collected (*Cantos*); in 1959, cantos 96 to 109 (*Thrones: 96–109 de los cantares*) were published; in 1968 the most recent installment, cantos 110–16 (*Drafts and Fragments of Cantos CX–CXVI*) appeared.

During his confinement P. completed the arduous task of translating the entire *Shih Ching,* the ancient Chinese collection of folk songs and narratives singled out for praise by Confucius and tirelessly annotated by neo-Confucian scholars. P. sought to render the original in such a way as to make it aesthetically and emotionally effective for a modern audience. His intricate and varied verse forms and his frequent lyricism, in general, are among his highest achievements; on the other hand, he often lapsed into prolixity and banality. The collection was published in 1954 as *The Confucian Odes: The Classic Anthology Defined by Confucius.*

P. has had a great effect on many of the more recent avant-garde writers, who have been influenced by his poetics and admire his craftsmanship.

FURTHER WORKS: *A Lume Spento* (1908); *A Quinzaine for This Yule* (1908); *Exultations* (1909); *Provenca* (1910); *The Spirit of Romance* (1910); *Canzoni* (trans.; 1911); *Ripostes* (1912); *The Sonnets and Ballate of Guido Cavalcanti* (trans.; 1912); *Canzoni & Ripostes* (1913); *Personae & Exultations* (1913); *Cathay* (trans.; 1915); *Lustra* (1916); *Gaudier-Brzeska* (with Ernest Fenollosa; 1916); *Certain Noble Plays of Japan* (with Ernest Fenollosa; trans.; 1916); *"Noh," or, Accomplishment, A Study of the Classical Stage of Japan* (1916); *Lustra, with Earlier Poems* (1917); *Dialogues of Fontenelle* (trans.; 1917); *A Study of French Modern Poets* (1918); *Pavannes and Divagations* (1918); *Quia Pauper Amavi* (1919); *Umbra* (1920); *Instigations* (1921); *Poems, 1918–1921* (1921); *The Natural Philosophy of Love* (trans. of Remy de Gourmont; 1922); *Indiscretions* (1923); *Antheil and the Treatise on Harmony* (1924); *Selected Poems* (ed. T. S. Eliot; 1928); *Ta Hio* (trans.; 1928); *Imaginary Letters* (1930); *How to Read* (1931); *Prolegomena I* (1932); *ABC of Economics* (1933); *ABC of Reading* (1934); *Homage to Sextus Propertius* (trans.; 1934); *Make It New* (1934); *Polite Essays* (1937); *The Unwobbling Pivot and The Great Digest* (trans. of Confucius; 1947); *If This Be Treason* (1948); *Selected Poems* (1949); *Money Pamphlets* (1950–52); *Patrie Mia* (1950); *The Letters of E. P.* (1950); *The Confucian Analects* (trans.; 1951); *The Translations of E. P.* (1953); *The Literary Essays of E. P.* (1954); *The Women of Trachis* (trans. of Sophocles; 1956); *Impact* (1960); *Love Poems of Ancient Egypt* (with Noel Stock; trans.; 1962); *Cavalcanti Poems* (trans.; 1966); *P./Joyce* (1967)

BIBLIOGRAPHY: Kenner, H., *The Poetry of E. P.* (1951); Watts, H., *E. P. and The Cantos* (1952); Espey, J., *E. P.'s Mauberley: A Study in Composition* (1955); Edwards, J. H., and Vasse, W., *Annotated Index to The Cantos of E. P.* (1957); Emery, C. M., *Ideas into Action: A Study of P.'s Cantos* (1958); Fraser, G. S., *E. P.* (1960); de Nagy, N. C., *The Poetry of E. P.: The Pre-Imagist Stage* (1960); Norman, C., *E. P.* (1960); Dekker G., *The Cantos of E. P.: A Critical Study* (1963); Dembo, L. S., *The Confucian Odes of E. P.: A Critical Appraisal* (1963); Gallup, D., *A Bibliography of E. P.* (1963); Davie, D., *E. P., Poet as Sculptor* (1964); Stock, N., *Poet in Exile, E. P.* (1964); Goodwin, K. L., *The Influence of E. P.* (1966); de Nagy, N. C., *E. P.'s Poetics and Literary Tradition: The Critical Decade* (1966); Bauman, W., *The Rose in the Steel Dust: An Examination of The Cantos of E. P.* (1967); Jackson, T. H.,

EZRA POUND

HENRI POURRAT

The Early Poetry of E. P. (1969); Ruthven, K. K., *A Guide to E. P.'s Personae (1926)* (1969); Schneidau, H. N., *E. P.: The Image and the Real* (1969); Witemeyer, H., *The Poetry of E. P.: Forms and Renewal, 1908–1920* (1969); Yip, W., *E. P.'s Cathay* (1969)

L. S. DEMBO

Given a mind that is not averse to labouring, provided that a kernel lies beneath the hard shells, you can reach the purpose of these poems. They contain the subconscious matter deposited by years of reading and observation in one man's mind, and in their residence in this subconscious state they have blended into the man's mental and emotional prejudices and undergone a metamorphosis, in which they become his visualization and interpretation of past men's events. Legendary heroes, kings, dukes, queens, soldiers, slaves, they live again as this man would have them live, and speak words that are partly his and partly their own, in the manner of ubermarionettes. Their fragmentary and often tangled existence—quick appearances and vanishings—is a distinctive feature of the subconscious state that enclosed them before they were extracted from the poet.

Maxwell Bodenheim, in *Dial* (Jan. 1922), p. 91

Some would say the facing in many directions of a quadriga drawn by centaurs, that we meet in the Cantos, puts strain on bipedal understanding; there is love of risk; but the experienced grafting of literature upon music is very remarkable—the resonance of color, allusions, tongues, sounding each through the other as in symphonic instrumentation. Even if one understood nothing, one would enjoy the musicianly manipulation. . . . Mr. P., in the prose that he writes, has formulated his own commentary upon the Cantos. They are as an armorial coat of attitudes of things that have happened in books and in life; they are not a shield but a coat worn by a man, as in the days when heraldry was beginning.

Marianne Moore, in *Poetry* (Oct. 1931), pp. 48–50

The cantos are a sort of *Golden Ass*. There is a likeness, but there is no parallel beyond the mere historical one: both books are the production of worlds without convictions and given over to a hard secular program. Here the similarity ends. For Mr. P. is a powerful reactionary, a faithful mind devoted to those ages when the myths were not merely pretty, but true. And there is a cloud of melancholy irony hanging over the cantos. He is persuaded that the myths are only beautiful, and he drops them after a glimpse, but he is not reconciled to this aestheticism: he ironically puts the myths against the ugly specimens of modern life that have defeated them. . . . He understands

poetry and how to write it. This is enough for one man to know. And the thirty cantos are enough to occupy a loving and ceaseless study—say a canto a year for thirty years, all thirty to be read every few weeks just for tone.

Allen Tate, in *Nation* (10 June 1931), pp. 633–34

The opinion has been voiced that P.'s eventual reputation will rest upon his criticism and not upon his poetry. (I have been paid the same compliment myself.) I disagree. It is on his total work for literature that he must be judged: on his poetry, *and* his criticism, *and* his influence on men and on events at a turning point in literature. In any case, his criticism takes its significance from the fact that it is the writing of a poet about poetry: it must be read in the light of his own poetry, as well as of poetry by other men whom he championed. . . . P.'s great contribution to the work of other poets (if they choose to accept what he offers) is his insistence upon the immensity of the amount of *conscious* labor to be performed by the poet. . . . He . . . provides an example of devotion to "the art of poetry" which I can only parallel in our time by the example of Valéry.

T. S. Eliot, in *Poetry* (Sept. 1946), pp. 331–38

P. was one of the most opinionated and unselfish men who ever lived, and he made friends and enemies everywhere by the simple exercise of the classic American constitutional right of free speech. His speech was free to outrageous license. He was completely reckless about making enemies. His so-called anti-Semitism was, hardly anyone has noted, only equaled by his anti-Christianism. It is true he hated most in the Catholic faith the elements of Judaism. It comes down squarely to anti-monotheism. . . . P. felt himself to be in the direct line of Mediterranean civilization, rooted in Greece. . . . He was a lover of the sublime, and a seeker after perfection, a true poet, of the kind born in a hair shirt—a God-sent disturber of the peace in the arts, the one department of human life where peace is fatal.

Katherine Anne Porter, in *The New York Times* (29 Oct. 1950), p. 4

P. should be credited with having weighed the perils of the method he elected. It pays the reader the supreme compliment of supposing that he is seriously interested: interested, among other things, in learning how to deploy his curiosity without being a dilettante. . . . His utility enters its second phase when disparate materials acquire, if only by way of his personality, a unity of tone which makes them accessible to one another. . . . In his third phase of utility . . . the poet instigates curiosity: how many people in the last thirty years have read the *Odyssey* on account of Joyce, or Donne at the encouragement of Mr. Eliot, or Dante and Confucius thanks to P.? . . . And he would consider that he was performing his maximum service for the fourth kind of reader, the one with the patience to learn and observe, within the poem, how exactly everything fits together and what exactly, page by page and canto by canto, the fitting together enunciates.

Hugh Kenner, in *Poetry* (July 1957), pp. 240–1

This claim for P.—that he recovered for English verse something lost to it since Campion or at least since Waller—may get more general agreement than any other. And [Charles] Olson is surely right to point to this achievement as rooted in something altogether more basic and less conspicuous than, for instance, the luxurious orchestration of the choruses in *Women of Trachis*. It is something that has to do with the reconstituting of the verse-line as the poetic unit, slowing down the surge from one line into the next in such a way that smaller components within the line (down to the very syllables) can recover weight and value. When P. is writing at his best we seem to have perceptions succeeding one another at unusual speed at the same time as the syllables succeed one another unusually slowly. But succession, in any case, is what is involved—succession, sequaciousness.

Donald Davie, in *E.P.: Poet as Sculptor* (1964), p. 246

POURRAT, Henri

French novelist, b. 7 May 1887, Ambert, Puy-de-Dôme; d. there, 17 July 1959

P.'s father was an East Indian who had converted to Roman Catholicism; his mother was a French farmwoman. After attending school in Ambert and a *lycée* in Paris, P. studied agriculture. Partially because of illness he spent most of his life in the quiet town in which he was born, writing exquisitely of the Auvergne that he loved.

Unlike other regional novelists who interested themselves in the interaction of man and nature, P.'s *devoir* was to chronicle lovingly the manifestations of a mythical—but Catholic—Earth Mother. By means of this lyrical exalting of natural phenomena his peasants and shepherds take on epiclike dimensions, though the beliefs and mores honored by the Auvergne inhabitants are presented with scrupulous fidelity.

In 1931, P. won the Prix du Roman de l'Académie Française for *Les Vaillances, farces et gentillesses de Gaspard des Montagnes* (4 vols., 1922–31), a beautifully written novel about Auvergne during the Napoleonic reign. P.'s special visual sense is to be seen in the following quotation: "The fields were bathing

in a sea of summer. Thick stands of clover everywhere, among the lotus trees, between the warm flagstones around the ruins. Just clover but in vast woolly waves, pale rose and bygone here but yonder fresh of hue like a luscious strawberry, turning crimson, garnet, poppy red."

FURTHER WORKS: *Sur la Colline ronde* (1912); *Les Montagnards* (1919); *Le mauvais garçon* (1926); *Ceux d'Auvergne* (1929); *Le Meneur de loupes* (1930); *Les Sorciers du Canton* (1933); *Le Secret des compagnons* (1937); *L'Homme à la bèche* (1939–41); *Vent de mars* (1941); *Sully* (1942); *Le Chemin des chèvres* (1947); *Le Trésor des contes* (10 vols., 1948–59; A Treasury of French Tales); *Le Chasseur de la nuit* (1951); *Le Temps qu'il fait* (1960)

BIBLIOGRAPHY: Tenant, J., *Notre voisin H. P.* (1937); Bal, W., *La comparison* (1958); Roger, G., *Maîtres du roman du terroir* (1959); Timmer, M., "H. P.'s *Trésor des Contes*," *FR*, XXXVIII (1963), 42–51; Genevoix, M., ed., *Gaspard des Montagnes* (1967)

* * * *

POURTALÈS, Guy de

Swiss novelist and biographer (writing in French), b. 4 Aug. 1881, Geneva; d. 12 June 1941, Lausanne

In 1937, P. was awarded the Prix du Roman de l'Académie Française for his novel *La Pêche miraculeuse* (Shadows around the Lake, 1938). Here, as in many of his other narratives, P., who was born into an aristocratic family, presented the emotional and intellectual life of the patricians who lived in Geneva at the beginning of the 20th c. His characters, like P., who lived for many years in France, were more European than Swiss in their attitudes, and this orientation posed emotional difficulties for them.

P. is also to be credited with unusual biographies of great musicians—*Chopin* (1927; Polonaise, 1927), *Wagner* (1932; Eng., 1932), *Berlioz et l'Europe romantique* (1939), and *La Vie de Franz Liszt* (1925; Franz Liszt, 1926).

In both the biographies and novels P. evidences a remarkable ability to present a subtle, profound, complex picture of man—his soul and his mind—and a lively intellectual climate.

FURTHER WORKS: *Marins d'eau douce* (1919); *Louis II de Bavière ou Hamlet roi*

(1928; Ludwig II of Bavaria, 1929); *Nietzsche en Italie* (1929); *Les Contes du milieu du monde* (1941); *Saints de pierre* (1941)

BIBLIOGRAPHY: On *Franz Liszt*—Hill, B., in *SR of Lit*, II (1926), 835; Ramsay, J., in *Books* (*New York Herald Tribune*), 20 June 1926; On *Shadows around the Lake*—Howard, B., in *New Statesman and Nation*, XII (1938), 916; Kazin, A., in *New York Times*, 23 Oct. 1938, p. 6

* * * *

POWELL, Anthony
English novelist, b. 21 Dec. 1905, London

The son of a British army officer, P. took a degree in history from Oxford in 1926. He then joined the London publishing house of Duckworth. At this time he discovered the novels of Firbank (q.v.), whose handling of dialogue and group party scenes was to influence his own work.

In 1936 P. left publishing and worked as a film writer, a step that had important consequences to his novelistic technique. Although he had always conceived of literary character and incident in visual terms, his work with the moving camera led him to resolve the problem of point of view by means of the device of the narrator-character, reminiscent of Conrad (q.v.), which he first used consistently in *What's Become of Waring?* (1939). Between 1939 and 1945 he served as an officer in the British army.

Afternoon Men (1931) was the first of P.'s five pre-World War II novels. In them all, he combines social satire with psychological characterization, and tends to reveal his world in a succession of memorable group scenes. That world is usually the one of upper-middle-class London society, and a recurrent comic pattern is the interplay of confidence man and *candide* figure. The confidence man, unimpeded by moral scruples, usually gets the last laugh, but occasionally the tables are turned, as in *From a View to a Death* (1933).

After World War II, P. embarked on an ambitious and demanding project—a twelve-volume narrative, to be made up of four "movements," that he called "A Dance to the Music of Time." In it he set himself the task of presenting a panoramic view of fashionable English social life from the start of World War I to the aftermath of World War II. The first six volumes are: *A Question of Upbringing*

(1951), *A Buyer's Market* (1952), *The Acceptance World* (1955), *At Lady Molly's* (1957), *Casanova's Chinese Restaurant* (1960), and *The Kindly Ones* (1962).

In this narrative P. traces the lives of four young men, who grow from adolescence to maturity between the two wars. One of them, the narrator Jenkins, provides the entire series with unity, for the reader sees all that is happening through his eyes, as through the lens of a moving camera. The earlier pattern of confidence man–*candide* figure is present, but the characterization is more complex. In fact, Widmerpool, probably P.'s most memorable comic creation, graduates from *candide* figure to confidence man.

In the third "movement" P. transposes his characters to a military setting, which is established from his own wartime experience: Jenkins here has become a British army officer. By 1969 P. has brought his varied characters up through the end of World War II. The World War II novels are: *The Valley of Bones* (1964), *The Soldier's Art* (1966), and *The Military Philosophers* (1969).

P. is now working on the fourth and last "movement," which will take place in postwar England.

The theme throughout this narrative is (and will surely continue to be) the disintegration of traditional English social values under the double onslaught of materialism and irrationality, public and private. The agent of social change is the "man of will," an industrialist or politician, who easily triumphs over the "man of imagination," usually an artist. Although the dimensions of the work are Proustian, the satiric perspective is more comparable to that of P.'s contemporary, Waugh (q.v.).

"A Dance to the Music of Time" is among the major achievements in postwar English fiction.

FURTHER WORKS: *Venusberg* (1932); *Agents and Patients* (1936); *John Aubrey and His Friends* (1948)

BIBLIOGRAPHY: Hall, J., *The Tragic Comedians* (1963); Quesenbery, W. D., "A. P.: The Anatomy of Decay," *Crit*, VII (1964), 5–26; McCall, R. G., "A. P.'s Gallery," *CE*, No. 27 (1964), 227–32; Radner, S., "P.'s Early Novels: A Study in Point of View," *Renascence*, XVI (1964), 194–200

SANFORD RADNER

POWYS, John Cowper

English novelist, essayist, poet, and critic, b. 8 Oct. 1872, Shirley, Derbyshire; d. 17 June 1963, Merionethshire, Wales

P. was the oldest son of a literarily prolific family. Seven children of the Reverend C. F. and Mary Cowper Johnson P. have published books, and an eighth was a book illustrator. Two brothers achieved substantial fame: Theodore Francis (q.v.) and Llewelyn (1884–1939; writer of *Love and Death, Ebony and Ivory*). Of Welsh descent, the Powyses have been in England since 1500; the mother's Johnson blood line traces, collaterally, to William Cowper (1731–1800) and John Donne (1572–1631).

P. grew up in vicarages in Dorset and Somerset, attended Sherborne School, took his degree at Corpus Christi College, Cambridge, and became a lecturer on literature. He toured England for various university-extension series, then "transferred these recitative performances, which were more like those of an actor than a lecturer, to the new world [where I spent] thirty years of my life in American railways." Turning to fulltime writing in 1929, P. lived five years in rural "upstate" New York before moving "home" to Wales.

Of his seven books of poetry, P. named *Lucifer* (1956, written in 1905) "the only poem I feel [tempted] to pray that posterity may read." P.'s nonfiction smacks of the podium. *Visions and Revisions* (1915) exhorts a general audience to read, to enjoy, to share his strong literary enthusiasms. Books such as *The Meaning of Culture* (1929) and *The Art of Happiness* (1935) counsel the same audience. But "[my] fiction is worth much more than my lay-sermons" in conveying "my vision."

The novels center on two convictions: "The deepest thing in life is the soul's individual struggle to reach an exultant peace in relation to . . . cosmic forces." And "below all the great systems of philosophic thought [and] mystical redemption stir these ultimate personal reactions to the terrible urge of sex." In "this irrational multiverse" P.'s "imaginative sensuality" is a prime tool—together with his introspective reaching for the "memories we inherit . . . from the world's remote Past."

On the palimpsest of 20th-c. England in *A Glastonbury Romance* (1932) are the marks of those who sought the mystery of the Holy Grail—Merlin, the Druids, the Fisher Kings, and, indeed, "men older than the worship of gods." The novel's "heroine is the Grail," P. says, and the search is for "the copulation-cry of Yes and No," the "Self-Birth of Psyche."

Wolf Solent (1929), too, is of contemporary Somerset-Dorset, where Wolf teaches grammar-school history, and edits ancient pornography; where he loves "androgynous" Christie and marries "voluptuous" Gerda. The novel's essence "is the necessity for opposites," P. writes.

"Fair needs foul" is a truth shared by "Zany Jack," a common self-label in the *Autobiography* (1934) and in P.'s uniquely revealing letters. He calls the *Autobiography* "a sort of Faustian Pilgrimage of the Soul" containing "No Women at all." Henry Miller (q.v.) names it "the most magnificent of all autobiographies."

The later novels turn backward—to the 15th c. in *Owen Glendower* (1941) and to 499 A.D. in *Porius* (1951)—then move to the future in the cosmic fantasies written when P. was in his eighties. In the last, *All or Nothing* (1960), an Arch-Druid escorts earthlings to the stars, but the unfathomable—the Grail mystery—yet abides.

The questings of P. are gargantuan—in humor and in scope. Friedrich Nietzsche (1844–1900) and Carl Jung (1875–1961) are influences, but so are Homer and Rabelais. Unlike the many seekers who suffer constricting *angst* between the contraries, P. learned expansive acceptance and enjoyment—aided always by nature's objects along the way, the fungi as well as flowers. It seems certain that the dedicated P. cult will prevail, and that he has, in J. B. Priestley's (q.v.) phrase, "not talent but genius."

FURTHER WORKS: *Odes, and Other Poems* (1896); *Poems* (1899); *The War and Culture* (1914; Eng., *The Menace of German Culture*, 1915); *Wood and Stone* (1915); *Confessions of Two Brothers* (with Llewelyn Powys; 1916); *Wolf's Bane: Rhymes* (1916); *One Hundred Best Books* (1916); *Rodmoor* (1916); *Suspended Judgments* (1916); *Mandragora* (1917); *The Complex Vision* (1920); *Samphire* (1922); *Psychoanalysis and Morality* (1923); *The Art of Happiness* (1923; different from same title in 1935); *The Religion of a Sceptic* (1925); *Ducdame* (1925); *The Secret of Self Development* (1926); *The Art of Forgetting the Unpleasant* (1928); *The Owl, the Duck, and—Miss Rowe! Miss Rowe!* (1930); *Debate: Is Modern Marriage a Failure?* (with Bertrand Russell; 1930); *In Defence of Sensuality* (1930); *Dorothy M. Richardson* (1931); *A Philosophy of*

Solitude (1933); *Weymouth Sands* (1934; Eng., *Jobber Skald*, 1935); *Maiden Castle* (1936); *Morwyn* (1937); *The Pleasures of Literature* (1938; Eng., *The Enjoyment of Literature*, 1938); *Mortal Strife* (1942); *The Art of Growing Old* (1944); *Pair Dadeni; or, The Cauldron of Rebirth* (1946); *Dostoievsky* (1947); *Obstinate Cymric: Essays 1935–1947* (1947); *Rabelais* (1948); *The Inmates* (1952); *In Spite Of* (1953); *Atlantis* (1954); *The Brazen Head* (1956); *Up and Out* (includes *The Mountains of the Moon*; 1957); *Letters of J. C. P. to Louis Wilkinson 1935–1956* (1958); *Homer and the Aether* (1959); *Poems: A Selection* (1964)

BIBLIOGRAPHY: Marlow, L., *Welsh Ambassadors* (1936); Jeffares, A. N., ed., Special P. issue, *A Review of Literature*, IV (January 1963); Knight, G. W., *The Saturnian Quest* (1964); Langridge, D., *J. C. P.* (1966); Collins, H. P., *J. C. P.* (1967); Hopkins, K. *The P. Brothers* (1967); Colgate University Press, *The P. Newsletter* (founded 1970)

R. L. BLACKMORE

POWYS, Theodore Francis

English novelist, b. 20 Dec. 1875, Shirley, Derbyshire; d. 27 Nov. 1953, Sturminster Newton

The art of P. is economical, severe, highly organized. The material of his work is local and provincial. Perhaps he is a fabulist rather than a novelist. Yet his best work enshrines a personal vision of man's estate that is religious in its intensity, and cathartic by reason of its emotional purity and ironic compassion.

P. has lived most of his life in a Dorset village. The seclusion was a deliberate choice. Before he published any stories or novels, the *Soliloquies of a Hermit* (1916) suggested his vocation. The two dominant forces in his creative work have been the Bible—in point of style and sensibility, not doctrine—and John Bunyan. Among the great English novelists, his admiration for Jane Austen has lent something to the precision and austerity of his narrative style, and the achievement of Hardy (q.v.) first gave the form of imaginative fiction to the grave, compassionate irony of rural pessimism.

His three most important novels are *Mr. Tasker's Gods* (1925), *Mr. Weston's Good Wine* (1927), and *Unclay* (1931).

Fables (1929) and several other volumes of

short stories appeared between 1920 and 1935. Some of these belong among P.'s most personal and enduring writings. From these volumes another three collections of stories have been published—*Captain Patch* (1935), *Bottle's Path* (1946), and *God's Eyes A-twinkle* (1947).

P. is, in the exact sense, a provincial novelist. But if his stage is narrow and his actors of few and limited types, the vision of life they convey is personal and deep. The life of the Dorset villagers is made to refract a singular awe in face of the mystery of life, a singular response to the vitality of all created being. It refracts also a piercing yet compassionate mockery of the harsh conditions of human livelihood. The experience of love and the conception of death are the pivots of his imaginative world.

P.'s importance lies both in the profound level at which he treats of these and in the assurance and control with which he handles the media of fable and allegory. He and Bunyan are the only distinguished allegorists in English fiction. *Mr. Weston's Good Wine* is his masterpiece: "One of the great things in English literature" (F. R. Leavis, in *Scrutiny*). It can be set beside *Pilgrim's Progress*, its evident forebear. In addition, Mr. Leavis refers to *Fables* as "also a classic" and (in *D. H. Lawrence: Novelist*) names P. as one of the four great masters in English of the shorter forms of significant prose fiction.

FURTHER WORKS: *An Interpretation of Genesis* (1908); *Black Bryony* (1923); *The Left Leg* (1923); *Mark Only* (1924); *Hester Dominy* (1924); *Abraham Men* (1925); *Mockery Gap* (1925); *Innocent Birds* (1926); *Feed My Swine* (1926); *A Strong Girl and the Bride* (1926); *A Stubborn Tree* (1926); *What Lack I Yet?* (1926); *The Rival Pastors* (1926); *The Dew Pond* (1928); *The House with the Echo* (1928); *Christ in the Cupboard* (1930); *The Key of the Field* (1930); *Uncle Dottery* (1930); *Uriah on the Hill* (1930); *The White Paternoster* (1930); *Kindness in a Corner* (1930); *The Only Penitent* (1931); *When Thou Wast Naked* (1931); *The Tithe Barn and the Dove and the Eagle* (1932); *The Two Thieves* (1932); *Coat Green, or The Better Gift* (1937); *Rosie Plum* (1966)

BIBLIOGRAPHY: Hunter, W., *The Novels and Stories of T. F. P.* (1930); Ward, R. H., *The P. Brothers* (1935); Mason, H. A., "American and English Earth," *Scrutiny*, IV (1935–36) 74–79; Coombes, H., *T. F. P.* (1959);

Hopkins, K., *The P. Brothers: A Biographical Appreciation* (1967); Riley, P., *A Bibliography of P.* (1967)

DOUGLAS BROWN

PRADO CALVO, Pedro

Chilean novelist, b. 8 Oct. 1886, Santiago de Chile; d. 1 March 1952, Viña del Mar

Under the influence of the ideas of Lev Tolstoi (q.v.), P. and a group of friends founded the Tolstoyan colony Los Diez in 1915. P. also founded the journal *Revista Moderna*. His works very skillfully depict the life of Chilean *campesinos* and the landscape of the Valle Central.

Alsino (1920), his masterwork and one of the best novels of Spanish-American modernism, synthesizes spirituality and realism. Here P. tells the story of a child who learns to fly and, having incurred the hostility of man and nature, meets death.

P.'s language is of extraordinary lyrical beauty. His novel technique though simple utilizes symbolism very subtly.

FURTHER WORKS: *Flores de cardo* (1908); *La casa abandonada* (1912); *La reina de Rapa Nui* (1914); *Los pájaros errantes* (1915); *Un juez rural* (1924); *Andróvar* (1925); *Camino de las horas* (1934); *Sonetos* (1935); *Otoño en las dunas* (1940); *Esta bella cuidad envenenada* (1945); *No más que una rosa* (1946); *Viejos poemas inéditos* (1949); *Las estancias del amor* (1949)

BIBLIOGRAPHY: Arragiada Angier, J., and Goldsack, H., *P. C.* (1952); Díaz Arrieta, H., *Los cuatros grandes de la literatura chilena durante el siglo XX: . . . P.* (1963); Benge, F., "Bergson y P.," *Cuadernos Americanos,* CXLVII (1966), 116–23; Kelly, J., "The Sentiment of Nature in the Prose Works of P.," *DA,* XVIII (1968), 3187A; Peterson, G., "The Narrative Art of P.," *DA,* XVIII (1968), 1444A–45A

FERNANDO ALEGRÍA

PRATOLINI, Vasco

Italian novelist, short-story writer, and essayist, b. 19 Oct. 1913, Florence

Of working-class origin, P. had little formal education. At twelve he was apprenticed to a printer, but in his twenties his always precarious health broke down, and from 1935 to 1937 he was in a sanatorium. It was there that he first began to write.

During the early 1930's P. had fervently believed in the equalitarian and progressive character of Mussolini's regime. However, the fascist government's support of General Franco in 1936, its alliance with Nazi Germany, the promulgation of anti-Semitic "racial laws" in 1938, and personal difficulties with fascist censors provoked a crisis of conscience that led him in 1943 to embrace communism. Like Vittorini, Pavese (qq.v.), Carlo Bernari (b. 1909), and other writers of the so-called "fascist generation," he participated in the antifascist resistance movement, of which the vanguard was seen, with considerable justification, as the Italian Communist Party.

Personal experience had made him closely identify with the working class, whose fortunes and struggles are sympathetically reflected even in the stories and poems he wrote as a young fascist. His first novel, *Il Quartiere* (1944; The Naked Streets, 1952), is the story of a group of impoverished Florentine adolescents growing up during the mid-1930's. Much of the action centers around the process through which the characters become aware of their responsibilities toward each other and toward the larger social community to which they belong.

Cronache di poveri amanti (1947; A Tale of Poor Lovers, 1949), one of P.'s most popular novels, is simultaneously an intimate chronicle of the lives of oppressed but remarkably resilient Florentine proletarians and an account of the triumph of fascism during the years 1925 and 1926. In spite of his antifascist feelings, S. shows considerable objectivity in this tale of suffering and political conflict. It is rightly considered one of the finest achievements of postwar "neorealist" Italian fiction.

After the novellas *Un eroe del nostro tempo* (1949; A Hero of Our Time, 1951) and *Le ragazze di San Frediano* (1952; The Girls of San Frediano, 1954), P. set to work on *Una storia italiana* (1955–66), an historical trilogy that would describe various aspects of Italian life from 1875 to 1945.

Influenced by Honoré de Balzac (1799–1850), Zola, Dreiser, Martin du Gard, and Sholokhov (qq.v.), P. wanted to reconstruct the past by creating characters who would embody the predominant attitudes of the time and—above all—the social class to which they belonged. *Metello* (1955; Metello, 1968) covers what P. has called "the authentic and obscure heroism" of the Italian working-class movement "at its revolutionary dawn." The repudiation of anarchism in favor of socialism by Metello Salani, a construction worker, is meant to typify the choice made in the 1870's and 1880's by broad sectors of the Italian proletariat. *Lo scialo* (1960) focuses primarily on the lower middle class, a segment of society, P. noted, that by "its conformism, its cowardice, and its inextinguishable devotion to the strong" paved the way for fascism. *Allegoria e derisione* (1966), the concluding volume of the trilogy, deals with the fascist generation itself, highlighting the moral preoccupations of Florentine intellectuals from the heyday of fascism in the 1930's to its defeat in World War II.

In his work P. has moved from personal reminiscence, to chronicle, and finally to social realism within a carefully reconstructed historical framework. His aim has been to combine some of the traditional features of naturalistic fiction (*see* naturalism) with an examination of the more narrowly personal and psychological determinants of human behavior.

P.'s achievements in fiction have made him prominent among contemporary European novelists who have treated the crucial conflicts and problems of our time.

FURTHER WORKS: *Il tappeto verde* (1941); *Via de' Magazzini* (1942); *Le amiche* (1943); *Cronaca familiare* (1947; Two Brothers, 1962); *Mestiere da vagabondo* (1947); *Il mio cuore a Ponte Milvio* (1954); *Diario sentimentale* (1956); *La costanza della ragione* (1963; Bruno Santini, 1964)

BIBLIOGRAPHY: Slonim, M. ed., *Modern Italian Short Stories* (1954), p. 231; Asor Rosa, A., *V. P.* (1958); Pacifici, S., *A Guide to Contemporary Italian Literature* (1962), pp. 57–86; Heiney, D., *America in Modern Italian Literature* (1964), pp. 80–81; Rosengarten, F., *V. P.: The Development of a Social Novelist* (1965); Pacifici, S., ed., *From Verismo to Experimentalism* (1969), pp. 221–24

FRANK ROSENGARTEN

PRERADOVIĆ, Paula von

Austrian poet and novelist, b. 12 Oct. 1887, Vienna; d. there, 25 May 1951

Paula von P. was a descendant of Austro-Croatian officers and a granddaughter of the Croatian poet Petar von Preradović (1818–72). She spent her youth in Pola, went to Vienna in 1914, and in 1916 married Ernst Molden

(1886–1953), publisher of the influential Vienna daily *Neue Freie Presse*. Both suffered at the hands of the Nazi oppressors during the occupation of Austria because of their participation in the resistance movement. Paula von P. wrote the text of the post-World War I Austrian national anthem.

For a long time Paula von P.'s poetry was pervaded by yearning for the southern land of her childhood (*Südlicher Sommer*, 1929; *Dalmatinische Sonette*, 1933). But in time the majestic mountains of her adopted country won her affection (*Lob Gottes im Gebirge*, 1936). From around that time her poetry grew increasingly religious. Originally light and folk-song-like, it became, though it never lost its melodious quality, more austere.

Her epic masterpiece is *Pave und Pero* (1940), a novel set in pre-1848 Austria. It is based on original correspondence about her grandfather's first marriage and its unhappy ending. Her *Königslegende* (1950), in which the Croatian King Slavac overcomes misfortune through renunciation, is also beautiful in its clarity.

FURTHER WORKS: *Ritter, Tod und Teufel* (1946); *Verlorene Heimat* (1951); *Die Versuchung des Columba* (1951); *Gesammelte Gedichte* (3 vols., 1951–53); *Schicksalsland* (1952)

BIBLIOGRAPHY: Henz, R., "P. v. P.," *Wort in der Zeit*, IV (1958), i; Csokor, F. T., "P. v. P.," *Neue österreichische Biographie*, XIV (1960), 194–97; Vogelsang, H., "P. v. P.: Die Dichterin der Ehrfurcht, der Demut und des Glaubens," *Österreich in Geschichte und Literatur*, X (1965), 198–206

ERWIN CHVOJKA

PREVELAKIS, Pandelis G.

Greek poet, novelist, dramatist, and art historian, b. 18 Feb. 1909, Rethymno, Crete

In his early teens P. lost both his parents and was brought up by an unlettered woman (Aunt Rousaki of *O Ílios tou Thanátou*), who initiated him into the beauty and the values of Cretan culture. In 1925 he moved to Athens and studied philology at the University of Athens. He then continued his studies at the University of Paris. He received his doctorate from the University of Thessalonike in 1935. From 1937 to 1941 he was director of fine arts at the Greek Ministry of Education, and since 1939 he has been professor of art history at the Higher School of Fine Arts in Athens.

He has traveled extensively throughout Europe, has received several literary awards, and in 1960 he was decorated by the king.

In 1926 he began a close lifelong friendship and intellectual exchange with his fellow Cretan Kazantzakis (q.v.), twenty-three years his elder. P.'s book *O piitís ke to píima tis Odisías* (1958; Nikos Kazantzakis and His Odyssey, 1961) is perhaps the most perceptive existing study of the man and his work. At the same time, it is a study-in-contrast of Kazantzakis's yielding to conflicting beliefs and ideas and P.'s own decision to stay faithful to his Cretan tradition and culture. This decision stands as the solid foundation of his work.

In P.'s first creative period—the lyrical—he published three books of verse: *Stratiótis* (1928), *I yimní píisi* (1939), and *I pió yimní píisi* (1941). Their Apollonian poetry contains the germ of his creative and ideological creed. The lover who speaks is the poet recognizing his own world and destiny. Nature is his great resource; its laws and beauty, with their fortifying value, will be his armature and solace against the onrushes of estrangement and alienation. Creation of beauty is the only way to conquer time and death.

The beginning of P.'s second period—the epic period—was initiated by *To Hronikó miás politías* (1938; Chronique d'une Cité, 1960), an affectionately and nostalgically drawn picture of his native Rethymno as he knew it in his early days. He tells its history, its society, its harmonious and purposeful life, and reveals it as an approximation of an idealistic, almost Platonic *politía*. He called *To Hronikó* a *mithistoría*, implying the mixture in it of myth and history. The historical facts are chosen by the creative mind to be set in an imaginative and meaningful pattern that reveals general truths. The book was highly popular in Greece during the days of its Nazi occupation, and has been translated into several European languages.

P.'s third period, the tragic one, is represented by his three tragedies: *Ieró sfayó* (1952; The Last Tournament, 1969), *Lázaros* (1954), and *Ta héria tou zontanoú theoú* (1958). In them P. handles the tragic choice and fate of the free individual and his need to conquer death. Juliano Medici, after gaining wisdom and freedom through the love of Simonetta, decides finally for death at the hands of his opponents, as the punishment for his *hybris*. Lazarus, returning to life to preach Christ as he knew him through his experience, meets death at the hands of the establishment. Michael, inspired from Fiodor Dostoyevski (1821–81), after long escaping human justice for his crimes, finally succumbs to the voice of his emerging conscience.

P.'s most recent work is the prose trilogy *I dromí tis dimiouryías* (1959–66; I., *O Ílios tou thanátou* [The Sun of Death, 1964]; II., *I kefalí tis Medoúsas: ena étos mathitías ston eóna*; III., *O ártos ton angélon: peripétia stin Itháki*). It is P.'s own imaginative, spiritual autobiography written in the first person. Its three stages consist of his upbringing in Crete and immersion in his native culture, then his self-exile and exposure to the turmoil of ideas of our modern times, and finally his attempt to return to his Ithaca. But Ithaca is not there any more. The modern individual has no other way than to find that Ithaca within himself by solving all contraries through the act of creation.

Ideologically, intellectually, and artistically, P. is perhaps the most consequential living figure in present-day Greek literature. He is highly respected and widely popular for having always stood for the permanent human values, especially those of his Cretan tradition. His faultless, "virginal" style makes the rough Cretan folk idiom he uses flexible enough to satisfy the most exacting requirements for literary expression. His plays, always successful in Greece, have led his critics to call him the "first genuine playwright of modern Greece." His widely translated novels have caused much enthusiasm abroad.

FURTHER WORKS: *Domenikós Theotokópoulos* (1930); *Dokímio yenikís isagoyís stin istoría tis téhnis* (1934); *O thánatos tou Medikoú* (1939); *Theotokópoulos: Ta Viografiká* (1942); *Pandérmi Kríti* (1945); *O Kritikós* (1948–50; I., *To Déntro*; II., *Próte Levteriá*; III., *I Politía*); *To Eféstio* (1963); *Tetrakósia grámata tou Kazantzáki* (1965)

BIBLIOGRAPHY: Panayotópoulos, I. M., in *Ta prósopa ke ta kímena*, Vols. I and II (1943), pp. 71–81, 208–11; Sahínis, A., in *Anazítisis* (1945), pp. 119–20; Sahínis, A., in *To istorikó mithistórima* (1957), pp. 160–66; Chamson, A., "P. et la Crete," *Mercure de France*, April 1959, pp. 577–88; Laourdas, B., "Introduction to P. P.," *Odyssey Review*, June 1962, pp. 148–55; Coavoux, P., "Reflexions sur *La Chronique d'une Cite*," *Balkan Studies*, IX (1968), ii, 429–50; Manousákis, G., *I Kríti sto logotehnikó érgo tou P.* (1968)

ANDONIS MANGANARIS DECAVALLES

PRÉVERT, Jacques

French poet and film writer, b. 4 Feb. 1900, Neuilly-sur-Seine

P. began writing under the influence of surrealism (q.v.), but soon broke away from its formulas to establish his own style. In his sober yet moving descriptions he communicates the immediacy of man experiencing everyday life. A radical anarchist, who is acutely critical of society and passionately opposed to authority and coercion, P. remains aloof from politics of any kind.

When *Paroles* (1946) appeared, it was an immediate popular success.

Though P.'s poems are usually a mating of laughter and tears, a few of his poems are indeed tragic. His humor, which is both subtle and ferocious, is at all times put at the service of serious social and human ideals. His endeavor to use laughter to combat many social and political evils, as well as the absurd and degrading frailties man is heir to in such abundance, may well stem from a desire to free himself of anguish.

Though P. scrupulously abides by the literal meaning of words, he makes those words bear a meticulous responsibility. In these days when vagueness is rampant this is an especially admirable quality. Like Morgenstern (q.v.), he is alert to the absurdity of pompous language, and his merciless precision effectively underscores the insincerity of much that is uttered at solemn occasions.

P. exploded conventional word patterns and juggles with neologisms. He ridicules once and forever meaningless clichés, but he also proves that old adages still have significance for mankind by his ability to bring out their fresh meaning. Many of his poems contain gruesome images; P. is obviously haunted by bloodshed. P.'s images—used concretely, not symbolically—are frequently of animals (he shows a marked preference for donkeys and giraffes), birds of all kinds, flowers, and even fruit.

Though P. sometimes seems to be playing around with mere words loosely strung together, he is actually working in dead earnest to get his message across—a message of warmth and love of life, of delight in people and things, of faith in eventual progress. P.'s famous dunce shakes his head to say "no," but his heart says "yes," and "despite the teacher's threats . . . he draws on the board the face of happiness."

P. also wrote scripts for movies that were widely acclaimed, the most notable being *Les Visiteurs du soir* (1942), *Les Enfants du Paradis* (1944), and *Les Portes de la nuit* (1946).

FURTHER WORKS: *C'est à Saint-Paul-de-Vence* (1945); *Le Cheval de Troie* (1946); *Histoires* (1946); *L'Ange garde-chiourme* (1946); *Contes* (1947); *Le Petit Lion* (1947); *Tentative de description d'un dîner de têtes à Paris-France* (1947); *Spectacle* (1951); *Vignette pour les vignerons* (1951); *Le Grand Bal du printemps* (1952); *Lettres des îles Baladar* (1952); *La Pluie et le beau temps* (1955); *Fatras* (1966); *Arbres* (with Georges Ribemont-Dessaignes; 1967). **Selected English translation:** *Selections from Paroles* (1958)

BIBLIOGRAPHY: Quéval, J., *J. P.* (1955); Weber, W., *Figuren und Fahrten* (1956); Bieber, K., "J. P. ou ce que parler veut dire," *Le Français dans le Monde,* Jan.–Feb. 1968

KONRAD BIEBER

PRÉVOST, Marcel

(pseud. of *Eugène Marcel*), French novelist, b. 1 May 1862, Paris; d. 8 April 1941, Vianne

After the success of his first novel, *Le Scorpion* (1887), P. gave up his career in engineering. In 1894 he published *Les Demi-vierges* (The Demi-Virgins, 1895), in which he described a type of contemporary young girl. The expression *demi-vierge* became known throughout the world. P.'s many novels center around women characters, though his interest in city girls of easy virtue was replaced by interest in women of the bourgeoisie, as in *Les Vierges fortes* (1900) and *Les Anges gardiens* (1913; Guardian Angels, 1913).

In addition to these novels, which were widely translated, P. wrote the fictitious *Lettres à Françoise* (1902–1924) as "professional advice on the spiritual welfare of the feminine conscience among the middle class" (Thibaud).

P. wrote as a moralist with an antinaturalistic bias in order to refute the reputation French love stories had earned of being salacious, but his world is artificial. Actually he was more a psychologist than he was a novelist.

FURTHER WORKS: *Chonchette* (1888); *Mademoiselle Jauffre* (1889); *Cousine Laura* (1890); *Confessions d'un amant* (1891); *Lettres des femmes* (1892–97; Letters of Women, 1897); *L'Automne d'une femme* (1893); *Le Moulin de Nazareth* (1894); *Le Jardin secret* (1897); *Léa* (1900); *L'Heureux Ménage*

(1901); *Le Pas relevé: nouvelles* (1902); *La Princesse d'Erminge* (1905); *Monsieur et Madame Moloch* (1906); *Frédérique* (1908); *L'Adjutant Benoît* (1916; Benoît Castain, 1916); *Mon Cher Tommy* (1920); *Les Don Juanes* (1922; Eng., 1924); *Sa Maîtresse et moi* (1925; His Mistress and I, 1927); *L'Homme vierge* (1929; Restless Sands, 1931); *Voici ton maître* (1930; Her Master, 1931); *Marie-des-Angoisses* (1932); *Fébronie* (1933); *Clarisse et sa fille* (1935); *La Mort des ormeaux* (1938). **Selected English translation:** *Simply Women* (1910)

BIBLIOGRAPHY: Bertaud, J., *M. P.* (1904); Murciaux, C., "La Bibliothèque de M. P.," *La Table Ronde*, No. 69 (Sept. 1953), pp. 166–69; Bordeaux, H., "Centenaire de M. P.," *Revue de Paris*, LXIX (1962), x, 157–58

* * *

PREŽIHOV, Voranc

(pseud. of *Lovro Kuhar*), Slovene writer, b. 10 Aug. 1893, Kotle; d. 18 Feb. 1950, Maribor

P. emigrated in 1930 and lived in Vienna, Paris, Prague, Norway, and Rumania. In 1939 he returned to Yugoslavia. He spent the war years 1942 to 1945 in prison and in the Sachsenhausen and Mauthausen concentration camps.

P.'s novels and short stories show marked epic talent, understanding of the life and attitudes of the peasants of Carinthia, deep humanity, and socially revolutionary tendencies. His novellas established a new major genre for Slovene prose.

Doberdob (1940) is a war novel about a World War I unit stationed on the Isonzo River. The unit is made up of men of various nationalities from the Austrian-Hungarian empire.

After 1935 P. led Slovene literature back toward the humanistic realism that became a dominating trend.

FURTHER WORKS: *U tujini* (1909); *Povesti* (1925); *Boj na požiralniku* (1935); *Pripovedke* (1939); *Požganica* (1939); *Samorastniki* (1940); *Jamnica* (1941); *Naši mejniki* (1946); *Borba na tujih tleh* (1946); *Od Kotelj do belih vod* (1946); *Solzice* (1949); *Kanjuh iz zagate* (1952)

BIBLIOGRAPHY: Matl, J., "Wien und die Literatur- und Kunsterneuerung der südslavischen Moderne," *Die Welt der Slaven*, IX (1964), 376–91; Glusič, H., *Lirika, epika, dramatika* (1966); Petré, F., "Probleme der slowenischen Erzählkunst," *Die Welt der Slaven*, XII (1967), 337–52; Vukadinović, A., *Srečko Kosovel-P.* (1967)

FRAN PETRÈ

PRIESTLEY, John Boynton

English novelist, dramatist, and essayist, b. 13 Sept. 1894, Bradford, Yorkshire

Son of a schoolmaster, P. served in the British army during World War I. After the end of the war he attended Cambridge, where he studied English literature, modern history, and political science. Already publishing, he was able to finance a good deal of this schooling by selling articles to London and provincial newspapers. In 1922 he went to London, where he soon established himself as a critic, essayist, and novelist. During World War II, P. won a huge popular listening audience with his trenchant, down-to-earth radio broadcasts.

In 1929, *The Good Companions*, a novel about the joys and sorrows of the members of a repertory company in the north of England, appeared and was enormously popular in both Great Britain and America. In 1930 P. published the almost equally successful *Angel Pavement*, whose characters worked in a small business firm in London.

These were followed by other novels: *They Walk in the City* (1936), *The Doomesday Men* (1938), *Let the People Sing* (1939), and *Festival at Farbridge* (1951).

These novels—long, often sentimental, packed with living characters—testify to P.'s astounding power of observation, to his narrative gifts, and to his craftsmanship. Surely it can be said that he has maintained the great tradition of the English picaresque novel with distinction.

P. also won recognition with his works that combine autobiographical matter with astute, left-of-center social criticism, such as *English Journey* (1934), *Midnight on the Desert* (1937), and *Rain upon Godshill* (1939).

P. began his career as a playwright in 1932 with *Dangerous Corner*, which has subsequently been performed all over the world. Its success encouraged P. to organize a company, for which he wrote plays of a consistently high dramatic standard. Among them were the comedies *Laburnum Grove* (1933) and *When We Are Married* (1938).

P. also wrote serious "metaphysical" dramas —*Time and the Conways* (1937), *I Have Been Here Before* (1938), and *Johnson over Jordan* (1939)—in which the theories of time contained

JACQUES PRÉVERT

JOHN PRIESTLEY

MARCEL PROUST

in J. W. Dunne's (1875–1949) *Experiment with Time* (1927) and *The Serial Universe* (1934) are very strongly present.

P. has perhaps identified himself more successfully than any other novelist in the first half of the 20th c. with the thoughts and feelings of the ordinary Englishman, a being whose character he outlines with vigor and good humor.

FURTHER WORKS: *The Chapman of Rhymes* (1918); *Brief Diversions, Being Tales, Travesties and Epigrams* (1922); *Papers from Lilliput* (1922); *I for One* (1923); *Figures in Modern Literature* (1924); *The English Comic Characters* (1925); *George Meredith* (1926); *Talking* (1926); *The English Novel* (1927); *Open House* (1927); *Adam in Moonshine* (1927); *Benighted* (1927; Am. ed., *The Old Dark House*); *Thomas Love Peacock* (1927); *Apes and Angels* (1928); *Too Many People* (1928); *Farthing Hall* (with Hugh Walpole; 1929); *English Humour* (1929); *The Balconinny* (1929); *The Town Major of Miraucourt* (1930); *The Works of J. B. P.* (1931); *Faraway* (1932); *Self-Elected Essays* (1932); *I'll Tell You Everything, A Frolic* (1933); *Albert Goes Through* (1933); *Wonder Hero* (1933); *The Roundabout* (1933); *Eden End* (1934); *Four-in-Hand* (1934); *Cornelius* (1935); *Duet in Floodlight* (1935); *Spring Tide* (with George Billam; 1936); *Bees on the Boat Deck* (1936); *People at Sea* (1937); *Mystery at Greenfingers* (1938); *Postscripts* (1940); *Out of the People* (1941); *Daylight on Saturday* (1943); *They Came to a City* (1944); *Three Men in New Suits* (1945); *How Are They at Home* (1945); *The Secret Dream: An Essay on Britain, America, and Russia* (1946); *Bright Day* (1946); *Russian Journey* (1946); *An Inspector Calls* (1947); *Jenny Villers* (1947); *The Long Mirror* (1947); *The Linden Tree* (1947); *The Plays of J. B. P.* (3 vols., 1948); *The Golden Fleece* (1948); *The High Toby: A Play for the Toy Theatre* (1948); *Ever Since Paradise* (1949); *Home Is Tomorrow* (1949); *Delight* (1949); *Bright Shadow* (1950); *Going Up* (1950); *Summer Day's Dream* (1950); *The P. Companion: A Selection* (1951); *Private Rooms* (1953); *Mother's Day* (1953); *The Other Place* (1953); *Try It Again* (1953); *A Glass of Bitter* (1954); *Low Notes on a High Level* (1954); *The Magicians* (1954); *Treasure on Pelican* (1954); *Journey Down a Rainbow* (with Jacquetta Hawkes; 1955); *The Scandalous Affair of Mr. Kettle and Mrs. Moon* (1956); *The Writer in a Changing Society* (1956); *The*

Art of the Dramatist (1957); *Thoughts in the Wilderness* (1957); *Topside, or The Future of England* (1958); *The Glass Cage* (1958); *The Story of Theatre* (1959); *William Hazlitt* (1960); *Literature and Western Man* (1960); *Saturn over the Water* (1961); *Charles Dickens* (1961); *The Thirty-First of June: A Tale of True Love, Enterprise, and Progress in the Arthurian and Ad-Atomic Ages* (1961); *The Shapes of Sleep* (1962); *Margin Released* (1962); *Sir Michael and Sir George: A Comedy of the New Elizabethans* (1964); *Man and Time* (1964); *Lost Empires* (1965); *The Moment and Other Pieces* (1966); *It's an Old Country* (1967); *Essays of Five Decades* (1968); *The Prince of Pleasure and His Regency* (1969)

BIBLIOGRAPHY: Brown, J., *P.* (1957); Hughes, D., *J. B. P., An Informal Study of His Work* (1958); West, A., *The Mountain in the Sunlight* (1959); Evans, G., *P., the Dramatist* (1964); Fuchs, K., "J. B. P.," *Die Neueren Sprachen*, XV (1966), 221–26

CHRISTOPHER KENT

PRISHVIN, Mikhail Mikhailovich

Soviet-Russian novelist and short-story writer, b. 4 Feb. 1873, Khrushchevo, Orel; d. 17 Jan. 1954, Moscow

From spending his childhood and youth in the country, P. developed a lifelong interest in nature and animals. He graduated from Leipzig University as an agronomist. After the Russian Revolution, P. became associated with the literary group Pereval.

P.'s first book, *V krayu nepugannykh ptitz* (1907), was based on his observations of nature in northern Russia. And it is as a nature writer that he has won recognition. Prose poems, short stories, and sketches make up the following books: *Kalendar' prirody* (1925; The Lake and the Woods, or Nature's Calendar, 1952); *Rodniki Berendeya* (1926); *Okhotnich'i byli* (1926); *Zhen'-shen'; koren' zhizni* (1932; Jen Shing, the Root of Life, 1936); *Lesnaya kapel'* (1943); *Kladovaya solntza* (1945; Treasure Trove of the Sun, 1952). He also wrote an autobiography, *Kashcheyeva Tzep* (1923–36).

P.'s work, permeated with optimism and acceptance of life, is in the tradition of Turgenev (1818–83) and Konstantin Aksakov (1817–60). Enjoying great popularity, he was regarded as an unrivaled master of the sketch and a superb stylist.

BIBLIOGRAPHY: Smirnov, N. G., *P.* (1953); Timrot, A., *P. v Moskovskom kraye* (1963); Dementyev, A. G., ed., *Istoriya russkoi sovetskoi literatury,* (Vol. 2, 1930–41; 2nd ed., 1967)

GEORGE LUCKYJ

PRITCHETT, Victor Sawdon

English critic, novelist, and journalist, b. 16 Dec. 1900, Ipswich

The oldest of four children of an often bankrupt merchant, P. left Alleyn Grammar School, Dulwich, at fifteen to become an apprentice in the leather trade. By then he had been fascinated by Dickens's *Oliver Twist* and Ruskin's *Modern Painters,* and he had been well-exposed to the Christian Science dogma held by his father. Between 1920 and 1927 he lived on the continent and worked as a journalist. In a period in which the difficult or scholarly often dominates literature, P. brings to his fiction and travel and critical writings alike a common-sense and nonacademic viewpoint, a gift for metaphor, and the raconteur's skill for recording impression by the telling, sometimes grotesque, detail. His first book, *Marching Spain,* an account of a walking trip from Badajoz to Leon, was published in 1928. Since then he has divided his time between writing, editing *The New Statesman,* broadcasting, filmwriting, and teaching.

From *Marching Spain* to his memoir, *A Cab at the Door* (1968), the essential of P.'s craft has been the presentation of significant impressions as experienced by an intuitive observer. The style apparent in *Marching Spain* ("At Waterloo my green train boiled in and a score of porters rose out of that white lake of asphalt like a flight of ducks. . . .") grew more controlled and attentive to incident as well as nature description as P. matured. It remains, however, a prose in which the generalization that is the end product of acute impression is founded on often-striking metaphors.

A similar method is the hallmark of his short stories, probably P.'s most significant literary achievement. He is at his best when he is disclosing with ironic affection the ineffectual economic and social pretensions of characters from the lower middle class and the irrational and self-righteous attitudes of members of a religious sect. Central figures in his stories appear in terms of a few dominating characteristics; their acts confirm the generalizations one might make about them, though the insight may

well appear as the result of unpredictable behavior or an unexpected twist of plot, as in "The Landlord." P. rarely employs the devices of "difficult" modern fiction, such as disordered chronology, stream of consciousness, or a narrative point of view detached from an explicitly rendered fictional situation. Instead he creates discrete episodes, presented as ordinary experience, with salient attributes of character revealed by a selection of detail and restrained hyperbole that faintly echo Dickens.

Many stories are in fact drawn from personal experience, for scenes from the stories "Aunt Gertrude," "It May Never Happen," "The Saint," and "The Sailor," for example, are described as childhood memories in *A Cab at the Door. The Collected Stories* (1956) contains all the fiction from the collections *You Make Your Own Life* (1938), *It May Never Happen, and Other Stories* (1945), and *The Sailor, Sense of Humour, and Other Stories* (1956), itself a selection of past work, but nothing from P.'s first collection, *The Spanish Virgin* (1930).

P.'s novels, too, rely on themes and characters closely drawn from experience. His first novel, *Clare Drummer* (1929) was followed by four others, of which *Dead Man Leading* (1937) and *Mr. Beluncle* (1951) have attracted most attention. *Dead Man Leading,* closer to a metaphysical novel than P.'s usual practice, reworks the prototypical search for self and father in the setting of a river journey. In *Mr. Beluncle* P. returns to his more familiar ground and delineates the character of a fantasizing, domineering, and egotistical middle-aged man whose business founders while he dreams of Divine Mind and Boards of Directors. (The parallel with the account of P.'s father in *A Cab at the Door* is marked.)

Whether in the short story or novel, one persistent portrait that emerges in P.'s work is of the person whose self-concern and fantasies are so pervasive that he sees external reality largely in terms of his own projections. In such a world genuine understanding is rarely articulate. It is either swept away altogether in fantasies and everyday habit or, much more rarely, it is the raw and unspoken sentence of persons joined in a struggle for self-preservation.

P.'s criticism, for which he is widely known to readers of British and American literary reviews, is most accessible in three collections: *In My Good Books* (1942), *Books in General* (1953), and *The Living Novel and Later Appreciations* (1967). The title of the last volume suggests his approach: he seeks to appreciate, to reveal why the book he discusses has a claim on his attention, and in so doing he devotes himself more to evaluation than to interpretation, more to description and to recording the impression elicited than to conceptual analysis. To this enterprise he brings the eye of a writer as well as a reader. He is most incisive on the English novel of the 18th and 19th c.'s and least perceptive about the very experimental moderns.

FURTHER WORKS: *Shirley Sanz* (1932; Am., Elopement into Exile, 1932); *Nothing Like Leather* (1935); *This England* (1937); *The Living Novel* (1946; rev. enlgd., 1964); *Why Do I Write?* (with Elizabeth Bowen and Graham Greene, 1948); *The Spanish Temper* (1954); *When My Girl Comes Home* (1961); *London Perceived* (1962); *The Key to My Heart* (1963); *Foreign Faces* (1964; Am., The Offensive Traveler; 1964); *New York Proclaimed* (1965); *The Working Novelist* (1965); *Shakespeare: The Comprehensive Soul* (with others, 1965); *Dublin: A Portrait* (1967)

BIBLIOGRAPHY: Hayes, R., "The Private Necessity," *Commonweal*, LVIII (11 Sept. 1953), 564–66; De Mauny, E., "The Art of V. S. P.," *TLS*, 6 Aug. 1954; Scott-James, R. A., "The Five Mr. Pritchetts," *New Republic*, CXXXV (20 Aug. 1956), 17–18; Bailey, A., "Puritan's Eye," *Commonweal*, LXIV (14 Sept. 1956), 593–95; Fiedler, L., "Class War in British Literature," in *On Contemporary Literature*, ed. by Richard Kostelanetz (1964), pp. 67–69, 78; Graver, L., "Growing Up as Pritchett," *New Republic*, CLVIII (11 May 1968), 36–37

CYRENA N. PONDROM

PROUST, Marcel
French novelist, b. 10 July 1871, Auteuil; d. 18 Nov. 1922, Paris

P.'s father, Adrien, was a professor of medicine, and his mother came from a prosperous Alsatian family. At the age of nine P. suffered his first attack of asthma. His education at the *lycée* and later at the university was interrupted by his periodic ill-health, and he gained none of the prizes there to which his intellectual superiority should otherwise have entitled him. He lived the life of a semi-retired invalid for the greater part of his life.

In 1896 he published his first literary work, a collection of miscellaneous pieces of prose and poetry entitled *Les Plaisirs et les jours* (in *Pleasures and Days, and Other Writings*, 1959). In spite of the enthusiastic introduction written by France (q.v.), who called the young P. a cross between Bernardin de Saint-Pierre and Petronius Arbiter, it did not enjoy any great success with the public. Between 1896 and 1900 P. worked on a novel that was not to be published until 1952 under the title *Jean Santeuil* (Eng., 1956). Actually, this was the first version of his masterpiece, *À la Recherche du temps perdu* (7 vols., 1913–27; Remembrance of Things Past, 1922–32). In the early years of the new c., P. was engaged in translating some works of John Ruskin (1819–1900) into French and in contributing society notes and sketches to the newspaper *Figaro*. In 1903 his father died and two years later, his mother. P. was completely prostrated by grief for a while and entered a sanitarium for the treatment of nervous diseases.

In 1908, P. began to work seriously on *À la Recherche du temps perdu*. This behemoth of modern prose, which is more than four thousand pages in length, was published as follows: I., *Du Côté de chez Swann* (1913; Swann's Way, 1922); II., *À L'Ombre des jeunes filles en fleurs* (1919; Within a Budding Grove, 1924); III., *Le Côté de Guermantes* (1920; Guermantes Way, 1925); IV., *Sodome et Gomorrhe* (1921; Cities of the Plain, 1927); V., *La Prisonnière* (1924; The Captive, 1929); VI., *Albertine disparue* (1925; The Sweet Cheat Gone, 1948); VII., *Le Temps retrouvé* (1927; Time Regained, 1941).

When *Du Côté de chez Swann* was published P. again had the satisfaction of having his work recognized by a few connoisseurs, but it was largely ignored by the public. In 1914 World War I broke out, and plans for the publication of the subsequent volumes had to be postponed. P. was rejected for military service—he was both too old and ill. Instead, he retired to the cork-lined chamber that he had had especially constructed because of his asthma and busied himself with the revision of his novel. It was in the process of revision that it grew to such enormous bulk. In 1919, after the publication of *À l'Ombre des jeunes filles en fleurs*, P., through the astute management of Daudet (q.v.), was awarded the Prix Goncourt, his first important public recognition in France.

From 1919 until his death P. became increasingly celebrated as a writer. At one bound he had entered the class of Gide, Mann, and Joyce

115

(qq.v.). The publication of the whole of *À la Recherche du temps perdu* was not completed until five years after P.'s death. Commentaries on various aspects of the work multiplied, and there were also biographies dealing with the strange life of the writer. Today it seems safe to say that no writer of the first half of the 20th c. has been more extensively analyzed than P.

In spite of its inordinate length, the basic plan of *À la Recherche du temps perdu* is the essence of simplicity. It begins with a recollection of early childhood, a recollection that has been prompted by a sense impression. The narrator of the story, by means of the taste of a *madeleine* dipped in tea, the same as that which he experienced many years before in his Aunt Léonie's house in the country, is enabled with quite startling suddenness to "recapture" a whole segment of the past that he thought had completely vanished from his memory. The secret of revivifying a long-vanished period of time is thus gained. The common element of past and present lies in certain sense impressions. The proper impression is the key with which the past may be unlocked. What follows this initial episode of the novel is a series of memories in chronological order that slowly reconstruct the various periods of the narrator's life.

We are introduced to P.'s childhood experiences in the provincial town of Combray, where the family spent its vacations. Then follows the story of the love affair of Swann, who owns one of the neighboring estates in Combray, Charles Swann is the son of a wealthy stockbroker, and in the scheme of the novel as a whole represents the way of life of the upper *bourgeoisie* whose claim to distinction is based upon their bank accounts rather than upon any inherited titles. But Swann, though middle class in his origins, has succeeded in penetrating the most exclusive, aristocratic circles in the Faubourg Saint-Germain. He has done so by virtue of his wit and aesthetic sensitivity, and he is the model of a whole series of Proustian characters, including the narrator himself, who surmount their social origins and become part of a world that was closed to them at birth.

It is through Swann that we are introduced to the members of the Verdurin circle, which forms the background of Swann's love affair with Odette. This is a circle of artists and savants which is centered around Madame Verdurin, a wealthy bourgeoise (one of P.'s most redoubtable character creations), and her husband, both of whom fancy themselves as patrons of the arts and sciences. The Verdurin clique exists, strictly speaking, on the periphery of fashionable society, the genuine members of which sometimes condescend to enter the Verdurin drawing room for the purpose of meeting an artistic celebrity who may have strayed there.

After the episode of the tragic love affair of Swann and Odette, P.'s main narrative resumes with the adventures of the narrator, who is now presented as an adolescent in Paris, a young man in the city being initiated into the mysteries of love and of the social world. He learns the distinctions of the various bourgeois and aristocratic salons and is able, apparently thanks to his innate charm, to penetrate, as Swann before him had done, into the increasingly rarefied atmosphere of the Faubourg Saint-Germain. His social conquests lead him from the drawing room of the Duchesse de Guermantes to that of the Prince and the Princesse de Guermantes, who stand at the very apex of Parisian high society.

The protagonist's progress in society is enlivened by a number of discoveries that he makes there. One discovery, while the Dreyfus Case is taking place, is that people in general are hardly capable of apprehending the pure and unadulterated truth, and that much of an individual's opinion on socially important matters comes from the opinions embraced by the circle which he belongs to. Qualities of independence and clear thinking are almost entirely lacking to proponents on either side of any political question. The decision of the individual is made up in equal parts of servility and prejudice. Man, as he is revealed in P.'s pages, is what he was for Aristotle—a gregarious animal, one who takes the cue for his particular ideas from the herd he happens to be foraging with. It is only a very rare person who is capable of being guided by an idea of abstract justice, or who is capable of feeling any real compassion for the sufferings of a fellow man.

An even more soul-shaking discovery of P.'s protagonist occurs when he recognizes the important social role played by the world of what he calls "Sodom and Gomorrah"—that is to say, by homosexuality, Lesbianism, sadism, and various other kinds of sexual perversion. The key to this aspect of reality is supplied by one of P.'s most successful character creations, Baron de Charlus, who is generally supposed to have been inspired by P.'s eccentric and gifted friend, the poet and nobleman Robert de Montesquiou. Though Montesquiou's memory survives today partly by virtue of his own verses and partly by the fact that he served as the original of characters in novels by Huysmans and D'Annunzio (qq.v.), his most secure claim to immortality will probably be based upon his friendship with P. and the supposition that he is the model of the character of Charlus.

Charlus reveals to P.'s protagonist how fatally widespread sexual depravity is in the society of which they are a part. This new knowledge not only alters the social view of the protagonist but warps his most precious personal relationships. He discovers evidence of perversion in the person who has been the closest to his heart, the girl Albertine Simonet. The latter volumes of *À la Recherche du temps perdu* are given over to the most painstakingly clinical examination of the consequences of jealousy that the painful knowledge of his sweetheart's corruption inflicts upon the neurasthenic protagonist.

P.'s novel closes as it began—on the theme of memory and its connection with artistic creation. The protagonist is conscious of time slipping through his fingers and of his inability to do anything to hold it back. He has been unable thus far to fulfill his early ambition to become an artist. The past, as he contemplates it, is one vast expanse of waste and loss. And then, just as the eleventh hour strikes, there is an unlooked-for reprieve for him.

While attending a party one day at the house of the new Princesse de Guermantes (who is none other than the bourgeois upstart Madame Verdurin, whom the Prince de Guermantes, fallen upon lean days, has married for her money), the hero is reminded by a number of sense impressions of the various episodes of his own past. They have upon him the effect of the taste of the *madeleine* dipped in tea, which had been described at the beginning of the story. In what almost amounts to a mystical illumination, P.'s hero realizes that he has found his artistic vocation at last. His vocation is to consist of nothing other than recreating in literature the world of his experience that has long since disappeared from time and space.

The exact classification of P.'s colossal literary work presents a serious critical problem. P. himself said concerning his work that it was designed to be simultaneously "a novel, an autobiography, and the history of a period in the form of memoirs." What this statement seems to indicate is that the form in *sui generis* and, strictly speaking, has no real parallel in

what the world had called a "novel" before P.'s time.

It is also true, however, that in spite of its vast extent and the diversity of materials of which it is composed, *À la Recherche du temps perdu* does give the reader a very powerful impression of essential unity and of being at all times strictly under the control of the writer. The patterns of its plot are highly intricate, but they are never confused. P. was fond of speaking of the "architectural labors" that went into writing this book, and the planned construction that this phrase implies is certainly a distinguishing feature of the completed work. Through his arduous labors, he hoped to create a kind of "literary cathedral," an equivalent of those beautiful Gothic structures that he, as well as John Ruskin, so much admired. His form, like that of all builders at their best, gives to the beholder a feeling of vital spontaneity at the same time that it communicates an assurance of the most disciplined self-control.

In addition to his architectonic abilities, P. is supremely gifted as a creator of character. Swann, Charlus, the Duchesse de Guermantes, the Marquis de Saint Loup, Legrandin, Cottard, Bloch, Bergotte, Rachel, Morel—all these and others are so vividly and unforgettably projected into the consciousness of the reader that he can remember their foibles and idiosyncrasies as he can those of few other characters in the modern novel.

Finally, P. has what can only be described as a wonderful prose style, one that is somewhat unusual in French literature. It has little in common with the classic lucidity and directness that distinguish the style of Voltaire, for example. Instead, it is full of voluminous folds and draperies and ornateness. It can be, by turns, silky, serpentine, and exquisitely subtle. P.'s typical sentence tends to be very long and drawn out, leaving a trail of interlocking subordinate clauses behind it. On occasion a sentence may stretch to several pages in length, and this aspect of P.'s work has unfortunately sometimes proved to be a stumbling block to prospective readers. But at its best this style serves him in descriptions of nature as fresh and unfading as those of Rousseau. And it should also be pointed out that he can vary his lengthy sentences with short, sharp pithy aphorisms that in their conciseness recall the work of the best French moralists—La Rochefoucauld, Vauvenargues, and Chamfort. All in all, P. has succeeded in producing what is not only one of the most striking and admired literary creations of the 20th c. but also one that seems destined to be one of the most durable.

FURTHER WORKS: *Portraits de peintres* (1896); *Pastiches et mélanges* (1919); *Œuvres complètes* (16 vols., 1919–37); *Chroniques* (1927); *Morceaux choisis* (1928); *Œuvres complètes* (18 vols., 1929–35); *Lettres et conversations* (1930); *Correspondance au générale* (6 vols., 1930–36); *Le Voyageur voilé* (1947; The Veiled Wanderer, 1949); *À un Ami: Correspondance inédite, 1903–22* (1948; Letters to a Friend, 1949); *Lettres à Gide* (1949); *Correspondance avec sa mère* (1953). **Selected English translations:** *Aphorisms and Epigrams from Remembrance of Things Past* (1934); *Letters of M. P.* (1950); *On Art and Literature, 1896–1919* (1960)

BIBLIOGRAPHY: March, H., *The Two Worlds of M. P.* (1948); Mauriac, F., *P.'s Way* (1950); Hindus, M., *The Proustian Vision* (1954); Auchincloss, L., "P.'s Picture of Society," *PR*, XXVII (1959), 690–707; Hindus, M., *A Reader's Guide to M. P.* (1961); Girard, R., *P.: A Collection of Critical Essays* (1962); Moss, H., *The Magic Lantern of M. P.* (1962); Shattuck, R., *P.'s Binoculars* (1963); Painter, G. D., *M. P.: A Biography* (2 vols., 1964, 1965); Beckett, S., *P.* (1965); Bersani, L., *M. P.* (1965); Brée, G., *The World of M. P.* (1966); Graham, V. E., *The Imagery of P.* (1966); King, A., *P.* (1968)

MILTON HINDUS

. . . I was, by chance, one of the first (1913!) to read *Du côté de chez Swann* and thus also one of the first to admire M. P., which was the natural, immediate consequence of that reading. Recently, on the occasion of his death, André Gide reminded me that I have my place among the earliest admirers of this great writer—and now you can imagine how, with the same attitude, I kept pace with one volume after another, and how strongly the death of this great man has affected me. It is still quite impossible to foretell all that has been opened up to us and to posterity by these books, so packed are they with riches and discovery, and the most singular thing is the already so matter-of-course, and in its way tacit, use of the superlatively bold and often the utterly unprecedented. Anybody else would have dared to use lines of communication of this sort between one event and another only as auxiliary lines—but in P. they immediately become charged at once with ornamental beauty, and they retain, in their graphic

quality too, authenticity and permanence. When with an intuitive stroke, he audaciously makes the most extraordinary connection, he seems again only to be following the existing veins in a polished block of marble, and here we are astonished once more by the consummate tact of his interpretation, which never clings, which effortlessly lets go of what it just now seemed to be holding on to, and which nevertheless, with almost unsurpassable exactitude, admits the purely unforeseeable and makes room for it everywhere.

Rainer Maria Rilke, Letter to Prince Alexander Hohenlohe (23 Dec. 1922)

It is significant that the majority of his images are botanical. He assimilates the human to the vegetal. He is conscious of humanity as flora, never as fauna. (There are no black cats and faithful hounds in P.) . . . This preoccupation accompanies very naturally his complete indifference to moral values and human justices. Flower and plant have no conscious will. They are shameless, exposing their genitals. And so in a sense are P.'s men and women, whose will is blind and hard, but never self-conscious, never abolished in the pure perception of a pure subject. They are victims of their volition, active with grotesque predetermined activity, within the narrow limits of an impure world. But shameless.

Samuel Beckett, *Proust* (1931), pp. 68–69

The world that P. describes excludes everything connected with production. The attitude of the snob, which sets the tone of this world, is, purely and simply systematic, organized, tenacious observation of existence from the standpoint of the out-and-out consumer. Concealed in his work is a ruthless, penetrating critique of contemporary society.

Walter Benjamin, *Zum gegenwärtigen gesellschaftlichen Standort des französischen Schriftstellers*, in *Zeitschrift für Sozialforschung* (1935), p. 68 f.

The beauty of P.'s masterpiece is that while it hits off with such exquisite malice all the fine shades of middle-class snobbishness and upper-class arrogance, and discloses with such subtle sympathy all the humorous refinements of old-family-retainers, its *real theme,* its inmost essence, has to do with the most evasive element in our secret personal life, namely with those obscure feelings of delicious ecstasy which are as hard to arrest or analyse in their swift passage as it is hard to explain why such small, slight, trivial, and casual chances are the cause of their rising up out of the depths.

These rare individual ecstasies are to P.—or at least to that prophetic soul in P. embodied in his hero—precisely what the same experiences were to Wordsworth, that is to say, authentic "intimations of immortality"; and it is impossible to think of any great novel that proves this daring proposition, and this very definite proposition, so effectively as P. does. Neither Goethe in *Wilhelm Meister* nor Romain Rolland in *Jean Christophe* conveys to us such a clear-cut unmistakable "message" as to the nature of the human soul and its relation to the Eternal as P. does in *À la Recherche du temps perdu*.

John Cowper Powys, *Enjoyment of Literature* (1938), pp. 481–82

Also finished the *Jeunes filles en fleurs* (which I find I had never read in full) with a vague mixture of admiration and irritation. Although some sentences (in some places very numerous) are intolerably badly written, P. always says exactly what he wants to say. And it is because he is so good at this that he delights in doing it. So much subtlety is, sometimes, completely superfluous; he is just yielding to a compulsive urge to analyze. But often this analysis leads him to extraordinary finds. And then I read him with delight. I even like the way the point of his scalpel attacks everything that presents itself to his mind, to his memory— everything and anything. Let the chips fall where they may. The main thing here is not so much the result of the analysis as the method.

André Gide, *Journal 1889–1939* (1948), p. 132

The mystery of things surrounds us and conceals a treasure unknown to us that nevertheless belongs to us. Any one of the unknown encounters that await us may precipitate a reaction that illuminates a region of the forgotten and restores to us an emotion long vanished from our life. . . .

The two spheres of being that we are accustomed to distinguish and oppose as art and life are made fluid and unified. Art has lost something of its isolation, life something of its reality. Both converge in higher reality of the soul. Here resides that characteristic impression of spiritualization that we get from P.'s work, a spiritualization that produces, not a diminution of being, but the feeling of a more intensive grasp of reality—and which does so through a kind of relativization. . . .

His mode of seeing is by its very nature more differentiated than ours. The iridescent color spectrum of his world is not the result of painstaking experimenting. It is his mind's innate mode of perception—a mind that registers reality more sharply than we do.

Ernst Robert Curtius, *Französischer Geist im zwanzigsten Jahrhundert* (1952), pp. 290, 294, 336

P. is perhaps the last great historian of the loves, the society, the intelligence, the diplomacy, the literature and the art of the Heartbreak House of capitalist culture.

Edmund Wilson, *Axel's Castle* (1953), p. 190

His despair is fundamental. It is not a theory in him, but an assumption, so that the wreckage of his creation evolves as naturally as the music of the spheres. Consider his insistence on illness. Disease and death await every individual but it is only when we are ill ourselves, or are nursing a friend or passing through a hospital ward that we realize this vividly. . . .

The cumulative effect (and this is an important point) is not macabre. He was too great an artist to indulge in the facile jiggle of a Dance of Death. They are living beings, not masked skeletons or physiological transparencies who climb the height of La Raspelière or talk against the music of Vinteuil. But they are doomed more obviously than ourselves to decay. Avoiding tragic horror, which perhaps he mistrusted, and pity, which he could seldom supply, he has achieved a new view of the impermanence of the human race. . . . Despair underlies all his views of personal relationships. . . .

The worst of them is our inability to love or be loved. . . .

Thus P.'s general theory of human intercourse is that the fonder we are of people the less we understand them—the theory of the complete pessimist.

E. M. Forster, *Abinger Harvest* (1953), p. 116 ff.

Within their passions they [P.'s characters] do nothing: they are passive, they undergo events without acting upon them. We see Swann, for example, accepting the different mistresses whom chance provides him with without showing any kind of reaction. He is absolutely inert and passive, because all of P.'s characters are. It is impossible to find a single one who has true passion, who is animated by a feeling of energy and who clashes with other compensating energies.

His [P.'s] work is entirely lacking in drama. We are merely witnessing a contrived decomposition. The spectacle of decomposition is interesting up to a point, but I must confess that for me it does not go very far. . . . I read him with a great deal of repugnance.

Paul Claudel, *Mémoires improvisés* (1954), p. 321 f.

Most novels that deal with society take on some of the meretricious gaudiness that it is their avowed purpose to deplore. Their authors become guilty of the snobbishness and triviality of which they accuse their characters. . . . P. comes closest to escaping the contamination of his subject matter because he does not set society apart from the rest of mankind. To him the differences between class and class are superficial. Snobbishness reigns on all levels, so why does it matter which level one selects to study? Why not, indeed, pick the highest level, particularly if one's own snobbishness is thus gratified? Society in P. parades before us, having to represent not a segment of mankind, but something closer to mankind itself. It is the very boldness of P.'s assumption that his universe is *the* universe, like the boldness of his assumption that all love is jealousy and all men homosexuals, that gives to his distorted picture a certain universal validity. It is his faith that a sufficiently careful study of each part will reveal the whole, that the analysis of a dinner party can be as illuminating as an analysis of a war. It is his glory that he very nearly convinces us.

Louis Auchincloss, in *Partisan Review*
(Fall 1960), p. 701

PROVENÇAL LITERATURE

Outside of France the term Provençal is generally used in reference to the Romance languages used by the people of southern France, but in France the word Occitan is preferred. (In French usage the term Provençal is used only for the area that lies principally in the Basses-Alpes and Bouches-du-Rhône.) To the Occitan language belong the Limousin, Languedoc, Gascon, and Provençal (in the restricted sense) dialects. Between the 16th c. and the 19th c. few literary works were written in these dialects, though the Occitan can boast of a body of fine poetry in the Middle Ages.

Then in 1825 Jacques Jasmin (1798–1864) published his *Papillotes,* which contained some poems in the Gascon language. In three additional volumes of these *Papillotes,* he made still greater use of his native dialect.

In 1845 Joseph Roumanille (1818–91), who was teaching, and Frédéric Mistral (1830–1914) met at a school in Avignon. Almost a decade later, in 1854, at Font-Ségugne, near Avignon, Roumanille, Mistral, Theodore Aubanel (1829–86), and four others formed the famous Félibrige, which formulated a program for restoring the dignity of the Occitan dialects and advocated an almost mystical coordination of writers, scholars, and propagandists.

Aubanel, a young printer of Avignon, wrote love poetry and a play, *Lou pan dou peccat,* which has not been surpassed in Occitan drama. Roumanille wrote fine prose.

The significant achievement, however, in modern Occitan literature is the work of the great pastoral epic poet Frédéric Mistral, joint winner of the Nobel Prize for Literature in 1904.

Mistral's French-Academy prize-winning masterpiece *Mirèio* (1859), a pastoral epic about the unhappy love of a poor peasant's son for a rich peasant's daughter, was hailed enthusiastically by the French poet Lamartine (1790–1869) and translated widely in Europe. The

basis of all his works are the national characteristics, the way of life, the landscape, and the traditions of his beloved Occitane. Though Mistral wrote in the Provençal dialect, he translated many of his works into French.

After 1851 Mistral became the leader of the Occitanien renascence movement. He developed a regional ideology that emphasized the spiritual and cultural independence of Mediterranean France and hoped to effect the reawakening of the Occitan language and literature, and a Mediterranean classicism that was linked to the literature of antiquity. Up to the turn of the century he even advocated administrative autonomy.

After 1890 the authority of the Félibrige was challenged. A politically minded group, including Maurras (q.v.), withdrew in 1892. Nevertheless, the influence of Mistral continued to dominate for many years.

Marius André (1875–1927), whose major work was *La Glòri d'Esclarmonde,* achieved admirable prosodic variety. Miqueu Camelat (b. 1871) published in 1898 his *Belina* in Gascon. Joan-Sebastià Pons (1886–1962), a native of Roussillon who spoke Catalan, wrote *Conversa, Amor de Pardal* (an idyll in one act), *Canta-Perdiu,* and *L'Aire i la Fulla.* Other poets who followed closely after Mistral are Folco de Baroncelli-Javon (1869–1943), Joseph d'Arbaud (1874–1950), Marius Jouveau (1879–1949), Jean-Baptiste Chèze (1870–1935), and Paul-Louis Grenier (1879–1954).

Among those who broke away from the inspiration of Mistral was Antonin Perbosc (1861–1943) of Montauban. In 1898, in his journal *Montsegur,* he announced the need for realism. His first important work was *Lo Gòt Occitan* (1903). Perhaps his most popular contribution has been his *Fabliaux* (2 vols., 1936), though his major work was *Libre dels Ausèls* (1924, 1930). A fine nature poet and a careful folklorist, he enlarged the scope of Occitan lyric verse, novel, drama, and tale. His work has exerted a strong influence on the writers of the Occitane.

In 1921 Suli-Andrieu Peyres (1890–1961) launched his journal *Marsyas.* It attracted and even helped to develop the young poets who sought to find purely personal and lyric expression. Among these are Pierre Millet (b. 1913), Marcel Bonnet (b. 1922), Charles Galtier (b. 1913), Emile Nonnel (b. 1915), Georges Reboul (b. 1901), and Max-Philippe Delavouet (b. 1920). *Marsyas* ceased publication in 1962.

Of special importance was the founding at

Toulouse of the Institut d'Estudis Occitans, which publishes the journal *Oc.* In 1950, under the auspices of *Oc,* Renat Nelli (b. 1906) and Ismaël Girard, a Gascon, established the series known as Messatges. Primarily, the series was organized for the publication of new Occitan poetry, though some of the older masterpieces were reprinted in it. The Institut also initiated La Seria d'Obres Mestres, which would concentrate on masterpieces of the past, and the Prosa series, in which plays and novels were to be published.

Among the modern Occitanien poets are André Pic (1910–58), Renat Nelli, Max Roqueta, Robert Lafont, Léon Cordes, Joan Mouzat, Denis Saurat, Ives Roqueta, Suzana Vincens, Paul-Auguste Arène, Enric Espieux, and Peire Larga.

Especially noteworthy among the most recent dramas are *La farço dis escut* (1956) of Claude Brueys, *La fiho de l'oste* (1953) of L'Abbé Henry George, *L'Anouncio* (1957) of Jan Vianè, *La font de Bonas-Gràcias* (1955) of Léon Cordes, and *La Loba* (1959) of Robert Lafont. Lafont's historical drama deals with the troubadour Peire Vidal.

A representative Occitan novel is Peire Pessamess's *Nhòcas e bachòcas* (1957), a story of youth in revolt. In 1961 André Berry published an *Anthologie de la poésie occitane.*

It may be said that present-day Occitan literature, except for the predictable tendency toward regionalism, is concerned with the basic themes of modern western European literature.

BIBLIOGRAPHY: Camproux, C., *Histoire de la littérature occitane* (1953); Berthaud, P., and Lesaffre, J., *Bibliographie occitane 1943–1956* (1958); Del Monte, A., *Storia della letteratura provenzale moderna* (1958); Jan, E. van, *Neuprovenzal: Literaturgeschichte 1850–1950* (1959); Roche, A. V., *Provençal Regionalism* (1954); Kirsch, F. P., *Studien zur languedokischen und gaskognishen Literatur der Gegenwart* (1965); Casella, M., *Saggi di letteratura provenzale e catalana* (1966); Vascardi, A., *Le litterature d'oc e d'oil* (1967)

URBAN T. HOLMES

PRZYBYSZEWSKI, Stanisław

Polish novelist and dramatist (writing in German and Polish), b. 7 May 1868, Łojew; d. 21 Nov. 1927, Jaronty

P.'s sensational career began in the 1890's in Berlin, where he lived among bohemian modernist artists and became a friend of Strindberg (q.v.). Revolting temperamentally against positivism and naturalism (q.v.), P. turned to a highly individual, passionately accented, and sensually overintense mysticism. His rhapsodic prose works of this period (which has been called his "satanic" one) in some ways anticipate concepts of psychoanalysis and depth psychology. They deal with unusual psychological types and with the ambivalence of eroticism, which in P.'s eyes stems from hatred, not love, between the sexes. His fight against convention and everything revered by the bourgeoisie assured him of the boundless admiration of the dissident, contentious younger generation.

After his manifesto, *Confiteor* (1898), P. became editor of the Cracow journal *Życie,* the organ of the *Młoda Polska* group of Polish writers. He thus became the spokesman of Polish modernism in literature and very quickly attained great popularity in Poland (he was already well-known in Germany).

Overestimated and turned into a legendary figure by his own generation, P. was repudiated and discarded by the next one. By the time of his death, he had sunk into obscurity and poverty. Ironically, however, P.'s last work, his autobiography *Moi współcześni* (1926–30), still has something to communicate, whereas the turn-of-the-century works that once aroused so much enthusiasm and discussion—such as *Totenmesse* (1893; Polish, *Requiem aeternam,* 1901); *Vigilien* (1894; Polish, *Z cyklu Wigilii,* 1899); *Synowie ziemi* (3 vols., 1904)—are now more interesting as documents of cultural history than as works of literature.

FURTHER WORKS: *Zur Psychologie des Individuums* (2 vols., 1892); *Essays* (1892–1906); *De Profundis* (1895); *Unterwegs* (1895); *Auf den Wegen des Seele* (1896); *Im Malstrom* (1896); *Satans Kinder* (1897); *Homo sapiens* (3 vols., 1898); *Über Bord* (1898); *In diesem Erdental der Tränen* (1900); *Androgyne* (1900); *Nod morzem* (1900); *W godzinie cudu* (1902); *Synagoga szatana* (1902); *Z gleby kujawskiej* (1902); *Poezye prozą* (1902); *Taniec miłości i śmierci* (2 vols., 1902; contains Matka, Dla szczęścia, Zlote runo, Gosce); *Śnieg* (1903); *Slyby* (1906); *Odwieczna baśń* (1906); *Dzień sądu* (1909); *Zmierzch* (1911); *Mocny czlowiek* (3 vols., 1912 ff.); *Popiel* (1912); *Wyzwolcnic* (1913); *Briefe* (1937, ed. by S. Helsztynski)

BIBLIOGRAPHY: Herman, H. *Un sataniste polonais, S. P.* (1939); Helsztynski, S., *P.* (1958)

OSKAR JAN TAUSCHINSKI

PSICHARI, Ernest

French novelist, b. 17 Sept. 1883, Paris; d. 22 Aug. 1914, Rossignol, Belgium

The son of Yanis Psiharis (q.v.), the Greek novelist and linguist, and the grandson of Ernest Renan (1832–92), the eminent philosopher and historian, P., ever conscious of his illustrious family and of his rich intellectual heritage, studied in the best schools in Paris, developing at a precocious age an intense love for literature. His first verses were literary imitations of symbolist (*see* symbolism) poetry. After a few years of emotional confusion, P. found in the military a salubrious discipline and an occupation.

Army life continued to enlighten his spirit and to direct him in the search for a higher order. In Africa, first in the Congo and then in Mauritania, P. made his contribution to his country's colonization and warfare. *L'Appel des armes* (1913) is a thesis novel, reflecting the reawakened sense of nationalism that was influencing many young Frenchmen before World War I.

P.'s conversion to Roman Catholicism took place during the years 1911 and 1912. He was guided by his closest friend, the Catholic writer Jacques Maritain (b. 1882), who had joined the Roman Catholic Church in 1906. Both P. and Maritain came under the influence of Péguy (q.v.), who was a central figure in the religious revival in France during the early 1900's.

P.'s most famous book, *Le Voyage du centurion* (1916), was written during the last winter of his life. It is the story of his conversion, written in the third person. In addition to the autobiographical element, P. is concerned in this book with the roles of nature and solitude in the African setting, the justification of the army and the church in the traditional past of France, and, finally, the theme that in the latter part of the volume dominates all the others—the religious experience operating in the desert. This ultimate message of P. brought to his country a freshness of vision and a renewed vigor in the ancient faith.

FURTHER WORKS: *Terres de soleil et de sommeil* (1908); *Les Voix qui crient dans le*

désert (1920); *Lettres du centurion* (1933); *Œuvres complètes* (3 vols., 1948)

BIBLIOGRAPHY: Péguy, C., *Victor-Marie, Comte Hugo* (1910); Goichon, A. M., *E. P.* (1921); Maritain, J., "Antimoderne," *Revue des Jeunes* (1922); Psichari, H., *E. P. Mon Frère* (1933); Massis, H., *Notre ami P.* (1936); Fowlie, W., *E. P.* (1939); Daniel-Rops, H., *P.* (1942); Duhamel, G., "P.: The Life and Death of a Centurion," *Renascence,* XII (1959), 174–81; Pluchon, P., "'La politique dans l'œuvre de P.,'" *Révue Générale Belge,* LXVII (1964), 54–61

WALLACE FOWLIE

PSIHÁRIS, Yánis

(Also known as *Jean Psichari*), Greek novelist and philologist (writing in Greek and French), b. 3 May 1857, Odessa; d. 30 Nov. 1929, Paris

P. spent his early childhood in Constantinople. At the age of eleven he was sent to school in France, where he was to live the rest of his life. In 1882 he married Naomi Renan, daughter of the philologist and historian Ernest Renan (1823–92). He was divorced from her in 1912. Their son Ernest Psichari (q.v.) also became a writer. After 1884 P. taught philology and modern Greek literature in Paris.

P.'s major achievement was his contribution to the linguistic revolution of Greece, in which demotic Greek succeeded in becoming designated as the official language of modern Greece (*see* Greek literature). The publication in 1888 of P.'s novel *To taxídi mou* aroused such fervent feeling because it was written in demotic Greek that a lingering, half-fought dispute was metamorphosed into an earnest battle. P. was the author of philological studies in French, some of them on demotic Greek, and of a massive Greek grammar.

In the field of belles-lettres P. was primarily interested in the novel, though he also wrote short stories, poetry, and plays. The most salient point of P.'s style was his use of coarse, earthy language. The literary quality of P.'s work, creditable as it often is, suffered from his involvement in the linguistic revolution. He did, however, realize his ambition—that of aiding the development of modern Greek prose and a modern Greek prose tradition.

FURTHER WORKS: *To óniro tou Yaníri* (1897); *Ya to Romaiikó théatro* (1901); *Róda ke míla* (6 vols., 1902–1909); *Zoí ke agápi sti monaxiá* (1904); *Ta dyó adélfia* (1910); *Agní* (1913); *Le Crime du poète* (1913); *Ta dyó triantáfila tou hárou* (1914); *Salomé et la décollation de Saint Jean-Baptiste* (1921); *La Chèvre chez Homère, chez les Attiques et chez les Grecs modernes* (1921); *Ernest Renan* (1925); *Un Pays qui ne veut pas de sa langue* (1928)

BIBLIOGRAPHY: Kambánis, A., *Istoría tis neo-Elinikís logotehnías* (1948); Dimáras, C. T., *Istoría tis neo-Elinikís logotehnías* (2 vols., 1949); Flóres, K., *Y. P.* (1951); Stávrou, T., P., *Pallis, Vlastós, Eftaliótis* (1956); Dimáras, C. T., et al., *La Grèce Moderne et sa littérature* (1966)

* * * *

PSYCHOLOGY AND LITERATURE

Literature and psychology have come to recognize in the 20th c. that they stand upon common ground. Both are concerned with human motivations and behavior and with man's capacity to create myths and use symbols. In this process both have become involved in the study of the subjective side of man. With the incorporation of psychoanalysis—that is, the study of the unconscious from the symbols it projects—into psychology, literature has found itself calling increasingly upon the knowledge derived from Sigmund Freud's (1856–1939) explorations of the psyche at the turn of the century. Any examination of literature and psychology must concern itself alike with the direct fertilization of imaginative writing by psychoanalysis and the use that literary criticism and biography have made of psychological and psychoanalytical tools.

Man's observation of his inner self and his emotions is as old as Aristotle. But it was not until the romantic movement that creative artists showed a deeper awareness of the existence of an unconscious dream-making faculty in the poet. Jean Jacques Rousseau (1712–78), in seeking to recover and examine his early experience; Johann Wolfgang von Goethe (1749–1832), in his belief that fiction must occupy itself with the inner thoughts of man; William Blake (1757–1827), with his personal mythology and his symbolic sense;

Samuel Taylor Coleridge (1772–1834), in perceiving man's involuntary "flights of lawless speculation"—that is, daydream as well as nightdream—and his "modes of inmost being" —all these writers found themselves by this process engaged in psychological exploration.

German romantic critics, such as Friedrich Schlegel (1772–1829) or Jean Paul (1763–1825), in searching for the laws of man's nature that result in the writing of poetry, were pursuing, on a critical level, similar ends. Honoré de Balzac (1799–1850), in his introduction to the *Comédie Humaine* (1st series, 1842), recognized that there existed "phenomena of brain and nerves that prove the existence of an undiscovered world of psychology," and in America, Nathaniel Hawthorne (1804–1864) spoke of the "topsy-turvy commonwealth of sleep." Hawthorne expressed the belief that modern psychology would reduce the dream worlds to a system "instead of rejecting them as altogether fabulous." During the 19th c. the works of Strindberg, Ibsen, Henry James (qq.v.), and Fiodor Dostoyevski showed a profound awareness of unconscious motivation in human beings akin to the insights of Coleridge, while the symbolist movement in France, with its insistence on impressionism and intuition, and its attachment to sensory experience anticipated observations of modern psychology.

But it was not until 1900, with the publication of Freud's *The Interpretation of Dreams,* that students of literature began to recognize the relation between the poet's dreamwork and his actual creativity. In subsequent years Freud's writings on certain nonliterary problems served to illuminate such questions as wit and its relation to the unconscious, the concept of wish-fulfillment, the problems of neurosis, and the associative character of symbols—all of which were applicable to literary study. Even more important for literary criticism and biography were his actual writings on the nature of art and the artist (collected in 1924 under the title *Psychoanalytische Studien an Werken der Dichtung und Kunst*). These included his psychoanalytic study of a minor novel by Wilhelm Jensen (1837–1911), *Gradiva,* his essay on Leonardo da Vinci, with its profound observations on biographical speculation and the relation of a biographer to his subject, and his study "Dostoyevski and Parricide."

Freud held that art represents an attempt to gratify certain wishes in the artist, and that the audience finds similar gratification in what the artist has created, thus extending our understanding of what Aristotle had explained as catharsis. Freud conceived of art as "an intermediate territory between the wish-denying reality and the wish-fulfilling world of fantasy." He held that the content of an artist's work, like the manifest content of a dream, may reveal the unconscious wishes of the creator. He recognized always, however, that psychoanalysis cannot explain the nature of the artistic talent, and that there were mysteries of the creative intelligence and imagination that psychoanalysis could at best only speculate on without hope of scientific answer.

As early as 1910 Wilhelm Stekel (1868–1940) in *Dichtung und Neurose* began the application of Freud's ideas to the study of artistic creativity. In the ensuing years a whole library of books was written concerning the specific relations between literature and psychoanalysis. Notable exponents of "applied psychoanalysis" have been Carl Jung (1875–1961), Otto Rank (1884–1929), Ernest Jones (1879–1958), Oskar Pfister (1873–1956), Ernst Kris (1900–1957), Franz Alexander (b. 1891), and Erich Fromm (b. 1900), while in the camp of literature are to be found such diverse figures as Graves, Edmund Wilson (qq.v.), Lionel Trilling (b. 1905), Maud Bodkin (b. 1875), Louis Cazamian (1877–1965), Charles Baudoin (b. 1883), and others.

The explorations by Jung, who broke with Freud over the libido theory as early as 1912, have had a particular appeal to critics. Jung attached primary importance to symbols. In his study of myths, his search for parallels between primordial images and the fantasy material derived from his patients, he touched on some of the wellsprings of the poetic experience. Jung believed that the experience of an individual's ancestors, embodied in mythical themes, are transmitted in the unconscious. He saw these primordial images as archetypes, common to whole epochs of society. Thus Jung arrived at his concept of the "collective unconscious." Rejecting Freud's emphasis on the instincts, Jung insisted that not only does man seek the gratification of his appetites, but that from the beginning of his history he has required a religion and philosophy of existence.

Of particular interest to poets and critics was Jung's concept of the *persona,* the self-image presented to the world. He believed this to be an image distinct from the real self, which resides in the "uniqueness of the combination of collective psychological elements." From the foregoing it can be seen that Jung's appeal to

those concerned with literary creativity would reside in his taking into account the strange and the bizarre in man, the sum of his mystical experience, which he believed the instinct theorists sought to explain away.

Parallel to the early Freudian explorations of the inner consciousness of man in this century, we find analogous explorations undertaken, wholly on the ground of literature, by the so-called stream of consciousness or interior monologue writers—certain novelists in various countries who tried to tell their stories "from the inside" by lodging the reader within the consciousness of the character. The reader was thus made a direct participant in the mental and sensory experience of the fictitious personality. This represented, in the novel, an extraordinary revolution in narrative technique: time becomes "psychological," vertical instead of horizontal, since the reader experiences the thoughts of the character at the very moment the character is undergoing the experience, that is, in present time—a situation not unlike the experience of the spectator at the cinema.

The material, moreover, is presented without order or chronology, as in the conventional novel. Instead the data is given in the disordered state in which it comes into consciousness through the operation of sensory stimuli, memory, and association. The result, in terms of narration, was the removal of the omniscient author from the actual work. The reader is required to deduce the story and the characters from the mental and emotional data provided without the author seeming directly to assist in the progress of the story.

The novel of subjectivity was influenced in part by the writings of Bergson (q.v.), especially from his exploration of human time (as distinct from mechanical time) and the processes of memory. In the United States, William James's (1842–1910) *Principles of Psychology* (1890) had offered certain illuminating pages on the psychology of thought. It was he who first employed the metaphor "stream of consciousness."

While these philosophical and psychological observations and theories were being advanced, the French and German symbolists, stimulated by the use of thematic material in the Wagnerian operas, had attempted to use language associatively and evocatively in order to give verbal representation of what might be termed the thematic material of the consciousness, including the operation of the senses. This resulted in many literary attempts to capture momentary experience and to frame and preserve these moments in language.

The difference between stream of consciousness or interior monologue and the soliloquies of the classic dramas was that the conventional monologue was wholly intellectual and given in a logical and ordered sequence, whereas the symbolists and their successors sought to convey the actual "flow" of consciousness, and to create the illusion of thought and the impingement of external stimuli upon the inner man—in its unsorted condition: the flotsam and jetsam as it might be found in the "stream" of subjective life.

The earliest attempt to tell a story wholly "from within" is now regarded to have been made by Édouard Dujardin (1861–1949) in his 1888 experiment *Les Lauriers sont coupés*, a work that he said was derived from Richard Wagner's (1813–1883) use of the leitmotiv in his music. So, in thought, he explained, themes occur and recur, and these can be set down in a language designed to capture the innermost thoughts, those which he believed to be closest to the unconscious. Henry James, in his seminal essay on the art of fiction (1884), had echoed the ideas of Goethe and urged upon novelists the re-creation of the "atmosphere of the mind." In this he pointed the way to his own novels written just after the turn of the century, in which he foreshadowed the modern novel of subjectivity by his unremitting efforts to maintain a "point of view" and an "angle of vision"—committing the reader to an interior view of experience and the solipsistic universe of the individual character. He did not, however, actually seek to re-create the illusion of a flow of thought or of a consciousness upon which perceptual experience is impinging.

In England, on the eve of World War I, Dorothy Richardson (q.v.) began the writing of a long subjective novel that she entitled *Pilgrimage*. She completed it in twelve parts, each of which was published separately between 1915 and 1938, and then brought out the entire work in four volumes. A thirteenth part was published posthumously in 1967. In this long novel the reader, if he can translate himself into the mind of the protagonist, is posted wholly in the consciousness of a woman named Miriam Henderson, whose pilgrimage, mental and emotional, takes her from her adolescence to her middle years. Dorothy Richardson's effort, less searching and imaginative, yet of unfailing realism, paralleled that of Proust (q.v.) in France. His novel, however, was not so much

stream of consciousness or interior monologue as a continual probing of memory and association and their relation to human time, carried out by a first-person narrator.

The fountainhead of the subjective movement in fiction was Joyce (q.v.), whose *A Portrait of the Artist as a Young Man* (1916) projected the developing mind and consciousness of the artist on five distinct levels: sensation, emotion, physical passion, religious passion, and, finally, intellectual awareness. Told with a remarkable symbolic use of language, this novel represented a turning point in modern English fiction.

It was followed by *Ulysses* (1922), which showed Joyce's complete verbal mastery by which he conveyed a series of streams of consciousness of certain individuals in Dublin during a single day. At the same time he used the Odyssey myth to represent modern man's voyage and adventures during the one day in the one city. *Ulysses* had a profound influence upon such writers as Virginia Woolf and Faulkner (qq.v.) during the late 1920's.

Joyce's final work, *Finnegans Wake* (1939), stemmed from the Jungian hypothesis of racial memory and the "collective unconscious." It is an attempt to suggest the cyclical nature of history, building upon the postulates of Giambattista Vico (1668–1744), and the role of myth and symbol as an ever-recurring and repetitive phenomenon in human life. *Finnegans Wake* is the only work of fiction—and it might be argued whether it can actually be called a novel—in the whole of literature whose four principal characters—H. C. Earwicker (Here Comes Everybody), his wife, and his two children—are asleep from beginning to end. Around their sleeping figures is the swirl of all time and of all history; the Liffey river at their doorstep is in reality all rivers, and they are also Adam and Eve and Cain and Abel, the eternal family. In this way Joyce produced a book that is a kind of composite of all myths and that portion of eternity in which thinking man, historically aware, functions. By that token the book is poem-epic-drama-novel rolled into one, like its characters and the mythic time-stuff of its texture.

While the novel of the "inner vision" achieved its particular technical development at the hands of Joyce, analogous experiments had been carried out in other literatures. In Vienna, Schnitzler (q.v.) had experimented with a modified interior monologue, and his *Fraülein Else* (1924), both in its technique and the substance of the story, unravels a psychotic episode through the inner vision of the person who suffers it. Döblin (q.v.), in *Berlin Alexanderplatz* (1929), was the chief exponent in Germany of the Joycean *experimenta;* and imitators have been legion during the succeeding decades.

This "inward-turning" in literature, in its first phase, must be recognized as having occurred largely without the benefit of the discoveries of psychoanalysis. It paralleled, rather than derived from, the Freudian development and influence. But there came a moment after World War I when literature and psychology increasingly erased the boundaries between them and psychoanalysis began directly to fertilize imaginative writing.

Thus Italo Svevo's (q.v.) *La coscienza di Zeno* (1923), written in Trieste (Svevo was a personal friend of Joyce), is an account of a psychoanalysis undergone by the protagonist. There are signs in Faulkner's novels of direct exposure to certain psychological ideas. In *Light in August* (1932) we have what might be considered a textbook account of the protagonist's "conditioning"—the way in which Joe Christmas, whipped every hour on the hour because he would not learn his catechism, learns instead how to adapt himself to cruelty but not to kindness. During the 1920's one of the most successful plays produced in New York was *Strange Interlude* in which the characters, through continued soliloquizing, reveal to us their inner thoughts. Eugene O'Neill (q.v.) followed this with a distinctly Freudian play, *Mourning Becomes Electra* (1931), applying primitive psychoanalytic theories to a New England version of Sophoclean tragedy. It showed also, as much of O'Neill's work did, exposure to the psychological plays of the pre-Freudian dramatist Strindberg.

More directly, the work of Thomas Mann (q.v.) derived much from Freud. Mann acknowledged his debt in an essay, *Freud und die Zukunft* (1936), in which he discussed certain of the ideas and themes used by him in the Joseph novels that stemmed from the psychoanalytic movement. But where Mann used Freud as illumination of the romantic self-discovery of man, Kafka (q.v.) found in him the means of constructing eerie writings that contain some of the macabre qualities of an Edgar Allan Poe (1809–1849) and the grotesqueries of a Nikolai Vasilyevich Gogol (1809–1852). Kafka hit upon the idea of treating subjective material as if it were wholly objective: his narratives of dream-states are told as if the dream had actually occurred in reality.

The result is the creation of an often terrible sense of day-nightmare, rendered acutely vivid by the matter-of-fact method of narration.

It would be a comprehensive undertaking to chronicle the full history of the impact of the psychoanalytic movement upon contemporary literature. Few writers of any eminence have escaped being exposed directly or indirectly to certain of its ideas. A number of writers have actually been analyzed; a majority, however, have imbibed psychoanalytic ideas from reading the leading theorists and from the numerous commentaries and popularizations that have accumulated around psychoanalysis.

Psychoanalysis has contributed important aids to three facets of literary study: to criticism itself; to the study of the creative process in literature; and to the writing of biography. In addition, it is helping to illuminate a tangential literary problem that belongs essentially to the field of aesthetics: the relation of the reader to the work.

I. *Psychology within the Work*

Two notable approaches exist in literary criticism, and both are used a great deal today in the exegesis of a given text: (1) the study of psychological elements within the work itself, without relating these in any way to the origin or history of the work; (2) the study of possible myth and archetypal patterns in the work.

(1) A large part of Ernest Jones's essay *Hamlet and Oedipus* (1949) consists of an examination of the motivation and behavior of the characters in Shakespeare's play, a close scrutiny of all of Hamlet's soliloquies for evidence of what they disclose about his inner life, a study of his attitudes toward the significant persons in his family setting—his mother and stepfather—and in general an attempt to speculate more closely than ever before, in the light of psychoanalysis, on what in other times was discussed as the classic question of Hamlet's sanity. Jones sees no madness in Hamlet's behavior, but studies the ambiguities within Hamlet's constituted personality in the light of Freud's hypothesis of the Oedipus complex. Building upon a hint from Freud, Jones presumes that Hamlet's tergiversation springs from his parricidal fantasies. Since, in his unconscious, he has wished to obliterate his father (as the Oedipus complex posits), he identifies himself (again unconsciously) with Claudius, his uncle, who has actually murdered Hamlet's father and married his mother. Claudius, there-

126

fore, is, in his fantasy, the prototype of Hamlet, and represents for him the embodiment of his own unconscious guilt over fantasied incest and obliteration of the father. But to kill Claudius, Jones argues, would thus be for Hamlet the equivalent of killing himself, and for this reason Hamlet hesitates. His conflict does not permit him to act.

(2) Perhaps the most important critic to consider the Jungian theory of myth and archetype has been Maud Bodkin of England, and her book *Archetypal Patterns in Poetry* (1934) has had a profound influence. Her hypothesis is that archetypal patterns or images are "present within the experience communicated through poetry, and may be discovered there by reflective analysis." She likens these patterns to the culture patterns studied by anthropologists. The patterns, she observes, may be "described as organizations of emotional tendencies, determined partly through the distinctive experience of the race or community within whose history the theme has arisen." Among the archetypes or patterns she studies are the "Paradise-Hades, or Rebirth" archetype; or the archetypes of devil, hero, god; or the various forms that the image of woman has taken in folklore and literature.

While Maud Bodkin took her point of departure from Jung, she has also derived from James Frazer's (1854–1941) *The Golden Bough* (1890–1915) and various classical studies in mythology. Her work illuminates the relation between many myths and poetry as well as seeks to show a relation between patterns of religion and "poetic faith." The criticism of her work, and of those who have followed her, has been that in the search of underlying myths and archetypes within a given literary work, the study of the individual qualities of that work is obscured in favor of universal patterns. The critical observation and exegesis become so general, it is argued, as to be virtually without meaning, since it is applicable to so many other works as well. The individual writer, in such a process, is submerged by the critic in his race and in endless time.

A striking adaptation of Jungian thought to criticism is to be found in Northrop Frye's (b. 1912) *Anatomy of Criticism* (1957). The central and longest essay in the book is "Archetypal Criticism: Theory of Myths," while the essay "Theory of Symbols" contains within it a discussion of symbols as archetypes. The entire book is permeated by Jungian thought, and Frye develops a concept of a collective literary imagination akin to the "collective unconscious." Frye speaks of literature as "a complication of a relatively restricted and simple group of formulas" going back to primitive times, and argues that these formulas are repeated in the greatest classics. From this it follows, he believes, that criticism can, by the examination of archetypes of the literary imagination, attempt to be scientific.

Directing his attention to universal symbols rather than archetypal forms, a French physicist-philosopher, Gaston Bachelard, in recent years produced a series of studies on what he calls *l'imagination matérielle*—the thematic use made by poets and novelists of air, water, fire, earth. These also, to a degree, take their inspiration from Jungian thought. They constitute a valuable contribution to the literature of dream symbolism as manifested in works of the imagination. Bachelard's *La Psychanalyse du feu* (1937) was followed by *L'Eau et les rêves* (1942), *L'Air et les songes* (1943), and *La Terre et les rêveries du repos* (1948).

II. *The Creative Process*

Much literary scholarship in the pre-Freudian period was devoted to tracking down the sources, both biographical and literary, of a given work. A vast literature exists in which the books read by certain writers and the events of their lives have been explored to demonstrate how these influenced the works created. Since the advent of psychoanalysis, criticism has turned from such often primitive attempts at penetration of the artistic consciousness to a more systematic study of the imaginative process, that is, the nature of the artist's fantasies and the underlying patterns these take in his work, whether poetry, drama, or prose.

It is now increasingly recognized that most creative writers do not live in a library; and that if they are bookish men, the books they read serve as stimulus to their imaginative faculty—that it is this faculty and not the food it feeds upon that is all-important. If literary sources are discovered today, and the methods of psychoanalysis are applied to them, the scholar seeks to determine how these sources melted together in the creative consciousness to produce the new work of art. The psychoanalytic approach searches out why a given writer attaches himself to certain sources rather than to others. The study of the creative process inevitably involves looking into biographical material, but it also involves certain larger questions that have preoccupied many literary critics as well as psychoanalytical theorists.

Thus, certain literary critics have pointed out that when psychoanalysts study literary works and their creators, they almost inevitably come up with a description of the neurotic character of the artist. The psychoanalyst as literary critic tends to make the work of art seem the product of certain infantilisms lingering in the artist's consciousness. There exists, for instance, a study of Robert Louis Stevenson (1850–94) that describes the "feeding problems" of his infancy. From this the writer tries to prove Stevenson's attachment to his mother and his subsequent difficulties in relating to women, as well as the possible psychogenic origin of his tuberculosis and the extraordinary "orality" from which he suffered. The study reaches the conclusion that Stevenson wrote stories reflecting the imagination of an arrested adolescent.

But all this, it can be argued, tends to reduce an analysis of Stevenson to a diagnosis more suited for the clinic than for literary criticism. The diagnosis may be completely accurate in terms of psychoanalysis, but, in terms of the study of a literary personality, it is wholly reductive in character. The emphasis would seem to be misplaced from the mystery and beauty of creation—from such remarkable fantasies as *Dr. Jekyll and Mr. Hyde* (1886) and *Treasure Island* (1883)—to matters wholly clinical.

It is this type of study Lionel Trilling makes allusion to in the notable essay "Art and Neurosis," in which he reaches the conclusion that the artist, "whatever elements of neurosis he has in common with his fellow-mortals," is nevertheless healthy "by any conceivable definition of health," in that he is given the power to plan, to work, and to bring his work to a conclusion.

Applied to the study of the creative process in literature, psychoanalysis can best be employed in showing precisely, as Charles Lamb (1775–1834) put it in an essay on the sanity of genius, that "the true poet dreams being awake. He is not possessed by his subject but has dominion over it. . . ." (The psychoanalytic critic might be inclined to modify this to the statement that the artist though usually possessed by his subject is capable of gaining possession over it.) While the revelation of the unconscious processes in art has largely interested the psychoanalysts who have used "applied psychoanalysis" to diagnose the personality of the artist, most literary critics and biographers who have used it have been concerned with the actual fabric of the artist's dreamwork, the means by which his verbal imagination gives form and structure to his materials.

The development of ego psychology (Ernst Kris, Heinz Hartmann [1894–1970]) has enabled literary students to recognize that a given poem or story may contain within it unconscious autobiographical material not only originating in childhood, as Freud often showed, but related to other stages of maturation. These ideas have been developed by Erik Erikson (b. 1902) in his studies of developmental stages and "crises of identity" in given lives, although he has focused on religious and political figures (Luther, Gandhi, Hitler) rather than literary figures. Erikson's ideas have had a marked influence in recent years on some literary biographers.

III. *Biography*

The tendencies discussed above (under the heading of "creative process") enter inevitably into the writing of literary biographies. There have been biographies of writers by professional psychoanalysts, such as Marie Bonaparte's (1882–1962) *Life and Works of Edgar Allan Poe* or Phyllis Greenacre's (b. 1894) *Swift and Carroll*, which are more clinical than literary, preoccupied as they are with deducing the workings of the subject's unconscious from his writings and the biographical evidence. Literary biographers have tended, when using psychoanalytical theories, to concern themselves with the gaining of certain insights capable of being assimilated within their own, rather than the psychoanalytic, discipline. Thus the biographer may learn from a slip of the pen in a manuscript or letter much about the subject under study. But where the psychoanalytically trained writer would use the slip as a guide to the unconscious, the literary biographer would be inclined to apply the revelation of this particular slip to verifiable facts to which this particular bit of data leads him.

The use of psychoanalytic concepts can enable the biographer to escape from the web of his subject's rationalizations; and it can help to explain his subject's predilection for certain subjects in preference to others. The psychologically oriented biographer also can note the small and seemingly insignificant detail, which in the past would have been discarded, and use it to illuminate personality.

Above all, such a biographer differs from his predecessors by grasping the contradictions and ambiguities within the subject, where the old-time biographer sought to efface contradiction and to make his figure more consistent—that is, less ambivalent—than people really are. Betty Miller's *Robert Browning* (1952) or my own *Henry James* (4 vols., 1953–69) exemplify the use of psychoanalytical tools so employed as to submerge the clinical aspect and diagnostic and to keep in the forefront the living personality in terms of common reference to the reader—that reader who has had no initiation into the complexities of psychoanalysis.

A unique example of psychoanalytical biography—unique because its subject is the founder of psychoanalysis and because it was written by his coworker—is Ernest Jones's *Life and Work of Sigmund Freud* (3 vols., 1953–57). This is remarkable both as biography and as a lucid explanation of Freud's inner life and its relation to the genesis and history of the psychoanalytic movement. But it suffers, in part, from being written in the language of the profession and within systems of psychoanalytical therapy.

A notable early venture into psychoanalytic biography of great breadth and imaginative scope was the series of portraits that Stefan Zweig (q.v.) projected as *Die Baumeister der Welt: Versuch einer Typologie des Geistes* (1935). Zweig grouped the types he chose in four volumes: "master builders," such as Balzac, Charles Dickens (1812–70), Dostoyevski; the demoniacal genius represented by Friedrich Hölderlin (1770–1843), Heinrich von Kleist (1777–1811), and Nietzsche (q.v.)—figures exalted to creation but driven to self-destruction; "adepts at self-portraiture," Casanova (1725–98), Stendhal (1783–1842), and Lev Tolstoi (q.v.), and finally mental healers such as Franz Mesmer (1734–1815), Mary Baker Eddy (1821–1910), and Freud. These analyses are not always successful and are outdated in terms of psychoanalytic thinking of recent years; but the literary gift possessed by Zweig gives the portraits vividness, and they will be read as pioneering attempts to bring to biography the illumination of psychoanalysis.

IV. *The Reader and the Work*

Here psychology and criticism come together on ground that belongs to the study of aesthetics. The question of reader and work goes back to the beginnings of literature. Even in Homer we may discern the devices by which the poet sought to keep his listeners attentive and engaged. In modern times we can find in Proust a close and analytical discussion of how a reader becomes subjectively involved in the novel he is reading and his process of identification with certain characters and scenes in the story.

In his ghostly tale *The Turn of the Screw* (1898), Henry James deliberately created certain ambiguities which, he explained, were so many blanks the reader's imagination would fill in. Each reader thus brings to the story's ambiguities his own particular and private data. In clinical psychology valuable experiments have been carried out from which the literary critic may derive considerable guidance: these involve the using of unstructured material, such as the ink blots of the Rorschach test, and the use of highly structured materials, such as works of art, in order to study the effect of their stimulus upon the viewer—as related to the viewer's specific needs and his character structure.

Notable in this area have been the works of I. A. Richards (b. 1893) as well as of the school of semanticists, disciples of Alfred Korzybski (1879–1950). Richards, in collaboration with C. K. Ogden (1889–1957), published as early as 1923 *The Meaning of Meaning,* a study of language designed to link criticism more closely to verbal meaning. In *The Principles of Literary Criticism* (1924) and *Science and Poetry* (1926) Richards developed certain ideas that have had a profound effect on contemporary criticism in the Anglo-American world. He focused his search upon the nature and value of poetry, investigating what occurs within a poem and the way in which a reader may be affected by it.

Richards's approach was perforce on the ground of psychology, and his method was descriptive. He believed that readers can be trained to read properly and, when trained, can then appreciate works otherwise generally incommunicable or "difficult." This line of reasoning, pursued by other critics, has led to widespread insistence, particularly in America, upon the importance of explication of text as the primary function of the critical act.

In general it may be said that while there is a great—and ever-growing—awareness of the illumination offered by psychoanalysis in studying human behavior and the mental processes, the relations between this discipline and the disciplines of literary study are still blurred and uncharted. There is a natural resistance among men of letters and the academies to "psychologizing," a strong feeling that human perception into the psyche, already so profound in the works of the master writers, requires no further aid, especially of scientifically oriented psychological exploration. It is further argued that the divergences among the psychoanalytic schools in themselves are sufficiently contradictory to call for great caution—and may render ambiguous and highly arbitrary the uses to which a given theory is put in literature.

The fixed and rigid manner in which the Freudians have used symbols has been much criticized because most students of literature know that while symbols are often universal, they have particular associative meanings for every individual. Otto Rank's theory of anxiety as resultant of the birth trauma offers little to literary study, and the inferiority complex school of Alfred Adler (1870–1937) has much more to do with therapeutic problems than with offering any particular ground of interest for the literary scholar.

The Jungians have supplied, as indicated above, much material for literary study because of their orientation toward religion and mysticism. Of great significance, in the view of some, has been the American school of Harry Stack Sullivan (1892–1949) which sees the individual as a product of interpersonal relations and argues that the pattern of a child's early—and not specifically sexual—relationships with significant figures plays a major role in the individual's personality formation. Because the novel deals in great measure with interpersonal relations, this school has much to offer to the literary student.

Also valuable have been some of the approaches of Karen Horney (1885–1952) and Erich Fromm, who draw upon sociological and anthropological thought in formulating their theories. They emphasize the immediate—and the cultural—problems in the life of an individual, rather than the biological, instinctual emphasis of Freud.

There is little doubt that much of the literary use of psychoanalysis has been to date rather crude and primitive, tending to simplify material highly complex and to make stereotypes of creative personality. It has tended to imitate psychoanalytic use of literary material rather than adapting psychoanalytic insights and methods to literary usage.

The cross-fertilization of the disciplines has been inevitably richest in the case of those writers who have a thorough grounding in both disciplines—and largely in the fields of criticism and biography. There is little evidence today that imaginative writers, relying upon their own observation and feeling, have been able to integrate in a satisfactory fashion the theoretical concepts of psychoanalysis. Where this has been done, the results have been mechanical, save in the special uses put by creative writers not so much to the psychoanalytic process itself as to certain broad insights.

The number of literary critics and biographers thoroughly familiar with psychoanalysis is slight; and the result is that only a few works, among the many published, can be said to have anything more than an ephemeral and most often a superficial value. The literary scholar who "gets up" his psychoanalytic knowledge from books will have highly theoretical concepts and perhaps an intellectual grasp of the psychoanalytic tool, but he is not likely to understand sufficiently well—as Freud warned—the role of the unconscious and in particular its relation to that of the emotions. The difference might be described as analogous to the difference between the novels of a writer such as Gide (q.v.), which are all intelligence and rationality, and the work of Proust, which is all association and emotion.

One distinct advantage that those critics and biographers who have firsthand experience of the psychoanalytic process enjoy is that they are less likely to project ideas and fantasies from their own psyche into the work or the life they are writing. In this respect they have a similar training in self-observation that the psychoanalyst himself has to have in order to deal objectively with his patients.

Psychology has already shown that in literature it can find many fertile examples of the creative imagination that illustrate the psychology of thought and the workings of the unconscious. Literature, on its side, is still absorbing and learning to use the psychological tool and in particular the concepts of pscyhoanalysis. The problem for literature has been in part one of terminology, the technical terms of psychoanalysis being ill-adapted to the needs of literary criticism. The most successful users of psychoanalysis in the study of literature have been those biographers and critics who have found ways of "translating" the specialized terms into the more familiar materials of their own discipline.

The basic factors that must be considered

in defining the relationship between literature and psychology may be stated as follows:

(1) Literary psychology is concerned with man's mythmaking and symbol-creating imagination and his unremitting effort to find the language and form to express these myths.

(2) Literary psychology is the study of the structure and content of a literary work, the imagination that has given it form and pattern, the fantasy that it embodies, the modes of human behavior it describes—a study of all this in the light of what we know of the unconscious and the integrative functions of the personality.

(3) The integrity of the literary work as a creative outcome of a personality must be recognized as distinct from the biography of the personality, although both may be studied in pursuit of "creative process."

(4) Therapeutic systems used in psychiatry and the psychoanalytic methods of treatment are largely irrelevant in literary psychology.

What may be expected in the future will be a further clarification of the respective roles of the two disciplines and a better definition of the uses to which psychoanalysis may be put in literature. As the very word analysis suggests, it will be most useful on the critical-analytic level. And it will quite likely have its greatest usefulness in the continued study of the creative process and therefore in the writing of biography, that is, in that part of literary study that relates the work to the man and treats the work as a part of the creating mind that put it forth into the world.

(See also Drama, Interior Monologue, Literary Aesthetics, Literary Criticism, Novel, Society and Literature, and Symbolism.)

BIBLIOGRAPHY: Stekel, W., Dichtung und Neurose (1909); Rank, O., Das Inzest-Motiv in Dichtung und Sage (1912); Cazamian, L., Études de psychologie littéraire (1913); Mordell, A., The Erotic Motive in Literature (1919); Badouin, C., Psychoanalysis and Aesthetics (1924); Sack, F. L., Die Psychoanalyse im modernen englischen Roman (1930); Prescott, F. C., The Poetic Mind (1932); Praz, M., The Romantic Agony (1933); Rank, O., Art and the Artist (1933); Muschg, M., Psychoanalyse und Literaturwissenschaft (1935); Suttie, I. D., The Origins of Love and Hate (1935); Wilson, E., The Wound and the Bow (1947); Basler, R. P., Sex, Symbolism and Psychology (1948); Campbell, J., The Hero with the Thousand Faces (1949); Auden, W. H., The Enchafèd Flood (1951); Kris, E., Psychoanalytic Explorations in Art (1952); Edel, L., The Psychological Novel (1955); Trilling, L., Freud and the Crisis of Our Culture (1955); Frye, N., Anatomy of Criticism (1957); Hoffmann, F. J., Freudianism and the Literary Mind (2nd ed., 1957); Neumann, E., Art and the Creative Unconscious (1959); Kiell, N., Psychoanalysis, Psychology and Literature (1963); Weisman, P., Creativity in the Theatre (1965); Holland, N., Psychoanalysis and Shakespeare (1966); Crews, F. C., "Literature and Psychology," in Relations of Literary Study (1967), pp. 73–87; Edel, L., "Literature and Biography," in Relations of Literary Study (1967), pp. 57–72; Frye, N., "Literature and Myth," in Relations of Literary Study (1967), pp. 27–55; Edel, L., "Psychoanalysis and the 'Creative' Arts," in Modern Psychoanalysis (1968)

LEON EDEL

PUJMANOVÁ, Marie

Czech novelist, essayist, and poet, b. 8 June 1893, Prague; d. there, 19 May 1958

Marie P.'s literary career began under the auspices of the literary critic Šalda (q.v.), in whose magazines her first reviews, essays, and short stories originally appeared. Her first work of fiction, Pod křídly (1917), an autobiographical account of an upper-middle-class childhood in Prague, is exquisitely light and poetic.

In her early works Marie P. expresses a profound dissatisfaction with the economic inequalities, the social anachronisms, and the hypocrisy of Czech society in the 1920's. Her collection of expressionistic tales, Povídky z městského sadu (1920), deals with moral and social problems. Pacientka doktora Hegla (1931), her first full-length novel, is notable for its protest against the prejudices of the time about woman's role in society.

Marie P.'s most ambitious work is a trilogy, in which the first two volumes present a panoramic view of Czech society from the 1920's to the end of World War II. All that is happening is seen from the point of view of a political radical. Lidé na křižovatce (Vol. I, 1937) focuses on two classes in prewar Prague society—the left-wing intellectuals, and the workers with their emerging socialist and communist sympathies. ("The Journey to Prague," an excerpt from Lidé na křižovatce, appears in Hundred Towers: a Czechoslovak Anthology of Creative Writing, 1945, ed. by F. C. Weiskopf.) Hra s ohněm (Vol. II, 1948), which

131

is based on the Reichstag fire trial (especially insofar as the actions of J. Dimitrov are concerned), describes the anti-fascist activity of Czechoslovakia. These two novels established Marie P. as a gifted writer of the contemporary social novel.

Marie P. analyzed the Czech society of the first half of the 20th c. with considerable accuracy and psychological insight. She is to be credited with a sense of finely balanced composition, a talent for taut plotting, and skillful characterization and dialogue. In her handling of the interior monologue (q.v.), she experimented with the vocabulary and the speech rhythms of popular language.

In the 1950's Marie P. came to prominence as a committed communist writer, propagating the doctrine of socialist realism that she willingly practiced. The result was that the third volume of her trilogy, *Život proti smrti* (1952), is a curious compound of naive tendentiousness and starkly modern realism. Even her sympathetic critics balk at the lapses into didacticism and the frequent failures of taste and artistic tact that appear in her writings of the 1950's.

As a poet, Marie P. never achieved significant success. Her first verse was evoked by the events of World War II and its Munich prologue. Here, images from her personal life and the political sphere are intermixed to express protest against the fascist regime. Her postwar poetry consists mainly of propaganda verse, the best of which is the long narrative poem *Pani Curieová* (1957).

FURTHER WORKS: *Pohled do nové země* (1932); *Božena Benešová* (1935); *Zpěvník* (1939); *Předtucha* (1942); *Rafael a Satelit* (1944); *Radost i žal* (1945); *Slovanský zápisník* (1947); *Verše mateřské* (1949); *Vyznání lásky* (1949); *Svítání* (1949); *Milióny holubiček* (1950); *Čínský úsměv* (1954); *Praha* (1954); *Stavbačka* (1954); *Sestra Alena* (1958); *Modré Vánoce* (1958); *Zpěv o Praze, ten nikdy nedozní* (1959); *Vyznání a úvahy* (1959)

BIBLIOGRAPHY: Blahynka, M., *P.* (1961); Rechcigl, M., ed., *The Czechoslovak Contribution to World Culture* (1964)

HELENA KOSEK

PYNCHON, Thomas

American novelist and short-story writer, b. 8 May 1937, Glen Cove, New York

P. published his first short story while a student at Cornell University. After graduation in 1958, he did a stint in the navy. His place as a talented American novelist was established by the publication of *V.*, which won the William Faulkner prize for the best first novel in 1963. A second novel, *The Crying of Lot 49*, appeared in 1966. P., who has traveled widely throughout the United States and Mexico, now lives in seclusion in California.

V. hardly has any plot in the usual sense of the term, although both novels can be said to be about plots, searches, and quests. Three strands of narrative are interwoven to form a pattern that implies unrelatedness and disorder. The first strand develops the attempt of the Englishman Herbert Stencil to discover the meaning of the mysterious V. in his father's life. The more clues he collects the more inconclusive his evidence becomes, and he is reduced to pondering not upon who but upon what V. is, without ever finding out for certain.

The second strand amplifies the possibilities of V. with an encyclopedic machinery of mock-history and mock-geography, ridiculing not only Stencil's quest but the overelaborateness of the novel itself. V. could be anything from a Victoria Wren who is involved in political plots in Egypt in 1898, to Veronica Manganese in Malta in 1919, to Vera Meroving in South Africa in 1922, to a priest in Malta during World War II where she/he dies as a person. Her v-ness somehow persists in such places as Valetta, Venezuela, Vesuvius, Vheissu, and in the various v-signs that keep punctuating the characters' lives.

The third level, the only wholly and significantly contemporary one, presents Benny Profane and his "whole sick crew"—schlemiels and human yoyos of New York City whose movements are random and repetitive to the extent that they have almost become things instead of beings. The inanimateness of man is P.'s chief metaphor for the inability to love. Benny can communicate better with SHOCK and SHROUD, two robots, than with Rachel Owlglass, who wants to be his friend.

Placed in the indistinguishable suburbs of a maniacal California, *The Crying of Lot 49* deals with Mrs. Oedipa Maas's suspicion of the existence of a secret postal organization called the Tristero system. It is claimed that this system had been originally set up in 1577 in Europe in revolt against the "Thurn and Taxis" mail delivery and was supposedly reactivated in the United States by an organization named W.A.S.T.E. As the executor of a former lover's estate, Oedipa has to supervise the auctioning (the "crying") of a lot of stamps that may provide the final proof of the existence of W.A.S.T.E. The reader is never told what Oedipa discovers. He is left to decide for himself whether the encoded messages will yield intelligible meaning or whether they are bizarre and fantastic products of a confused mind.

The Crying of Lot 49 is an essentially more pessimistic book than *V.* For Oedipa, the truth may be revealed at last, but the horror of that revelation will injure whatever is left of her life, which has become progressively stripped of love in the course of her search. Meaning does lie behind the pattern of events, but man is too weak to bear it in its full implication. It may be that comprehension must be accompanied by the destruction of the person.

In *V.*, personal life is seen as a fragmentary sequence of unconnected episodes, history as an intricate web of plots, a gigantic game played against forever unknowable partners according to unknown rules. In *The Crying of Lot 49*, a less ambitious novel, whatever action takes place is filtered through the consciousness of only one protagonist, Oedipa.

The handful of stories that were written before the publication of *V.* were very well received and frequently anthologized. They already contain some of the basic elements of P.'s two novels. The references to Joseph Conrad (q.v.) in "Mortality and Mercy in Vienna" (1959) mainly allude to the "heart of darkness" (the title of a famous novella by Conrad), which is adopted by P. as one of the central images of man's situation in the world today. The recurring descriptions of drunken parties at strange houses among people that make impossible and yet urgent demands on the protagonist point toward man's loss of direction, his loss of the ability to make sense out of the events of the present, personal as well as political. He is alone amidst a multitude of confusing phenomena that are radiating contradictory but seemingly obligatory commands and messages.

Another basic P. theme is that the coming of the apocalypse is known as imminent and inevitable. This knowledge creates strange patterns of behavior, making misfits of those men who are either the most vulnerable to these events or to their own intuition of them. Pig Bodine, the sailor, a character in *V.*, has already appeared in "Low-lands" (1960). He leads an array of other unhappy nonconformists in their act of going underground to escape from what they can neither bear nor understand. In this story, P.'s stylist technique first becomes evident: he literalizes the metaphoric and metaphorizes the actual and literal. Pig and "that weird crew" go to live in tunnels under the city dump. In this strange underground world, created by a secret society for the purpose of preparing for "the revolution," Pig and his friends feel more at home, more human than in the known world above.

P., who has been grouped with black humorist Kurt Vonnegut (b. 1922) and writers of the neopicaresque such as Joseph Heller (b. 1923) and Bellow (q.v.), writes in the vein that combines the satiric with the apocalyptic mode. His books reveal a desperate, Kafkaesque vision, transmitted through his extraordinarily versatile style that thrives on caricature to the point of the complete loss of an identifiable narrator.

BIBLIOGRAPHY: Feldman, I., "Keeping Cool," *Commentary*, XXXVI (1963), 258–60; Hausdorff, D., "T. P.'s Multiple Absurdities," *Contemporary Literature*, VII (1966), 258–69; Poirier, R., "Embattled Underground," *New York Times Book Review*, 1 May 1966, p. 5; Sklar, R., "The New Novel, USA: T. P.," *The Nation*, 25 Sept. 1967, pp. 277–80; Young, J. D., "The Enigma Variations of T. P.," *Crit*, X (1967), 69–77; Hunt, J. W., "Comic Escape and Anti-Vision: The Novels of Joseph Heller and T. P.," in *Adversity and Grace: Studies in Recent American Literature*, ed. N. A. Scott (1968), pp. 87–112; McNamara, E., "The Absurd Style in Contemporary American Literature," *Humanities Association Bulletin*, XIX (1968), 44–49; Poirier, R., "The Politics of Self-Parody," *PR*, XXXV (1968), 339–53

BRIGITTE SCHEER-SCHAEZLER

Q

QUASIMODO, Salvatore

Italian poet and essayist, b. 20 Aug. 1901, Modica; d. 14 June 1968, Naples

Q., the son of a stationmaster, studied to become an engineer but was unable to complete his training because of financial difficulties. He did, however, manage to teach himself Greek and Latin—two languages he was later to translate from extensively. In the mid-1930's and throughout World War II he lived in Milan. From 1940 until his death in 1968 he was lecturer in Italian literature at the Giuseppe Verdi Conservatory of Music in Milan. In 1959 he was awarded the Nobel Prize for Literature.

The poems in Q.'s major work, *Ed è subito sera* (1942), which are dedicated to communicating what Sicily, particularly the coastal region around Syracuse, meant to him both scenically and historically—become a dithyramb to the landscape and the sea. This area is extolled in obscurely associative imagery that recalls Montale's (q.v.) evocation of the Ligurian coast in "Ossi di seppia." In *Ed è subito sera* echoes can be heard plainly of the "Laudi," in which D'Annunzio (q.v.) glorified Italy's beauties and historic achievements. Here, however, D'Annunzio's programmatic, political bias is replaced by a Sicilian literary regionalism that had already made its appearance in prose fiction in the novellas of Pirandello and Verga (qq.v.).

Q. combined this regionalism with the poetic theories of Ungaretti (q.v.) and of French symbolism (q.v.). In symbolistic theory he found especially useful the principle of word magic, a "poetry of the sovereign word," which he

used for countering D'Annunzio's "lexical" use of words.

Q.'s work is a revealing illustration of how modern poetry deals with its classical heritage. For him, as for Rilke, Cocteau (qq.v.), and Mallarmé, the ideal of "magic" poetry is personified in the figure of the magician-poet Orpheus. Moreover, being a Sicilian, Q. seems to have possessed an almost atavistic kinship with Greek antiquity. This found expression in the Hellenic mood of many of his poems and in his numerous translations from classical writers (*e.g., Lirici greci,* 1940).

After World War I, Q., Ungaretti, and Montale were the outstanding figures in Italian poetry. Q. and Montale were the primary exponents of the group within the "hermeticist" movement (*see* Italian literature) that was interested in writing regional landscape poetry.

In the poetry published after World War II—*Giorno dopo giorno* (1947), *La vita non è sogno* (1949), *Il falso e vero verde* (1956), *La terra impareggiabile* (1958; The Incomparable Earth, 1958)—Q. tried to assimilate into the magical style a simpler, more human, more communicative diction, which recalls that of Brecht and Neruda (qq.v.). In his "Discorso sulla poesia" (published originally in 1956 as an appendix to *Il falso e vero verde*) Q. spoke of this as *poesia sociale*.

FURTHER WORKS: *Acque e terre* (1930); *Oboe sommerso* (1932); *Odore di Eucalyptus* (1933); *Erato e Apollion* (1936); *Poesie* (1938); *Con il piede straniero sopra il cuore* (1946); *Il poeta e il politico* (1960; The Poet and the Politician, and Other Essays, 1964); *Scritti sul teatro* (1961); *Tutte le poesie* (1961); *Dare e avere* (1966; in To Give and to Have, and

Other Poems, 1969); *Un anno di Q.* (1968). **Selected English translations:** *Selected Writings of S. Q.* (1910); *Selected Poems* (1965); *To Give and to Have, and Other Poems* (1969)

BIBLIOGRAPHY: Tedesco, N., *S. Q.* (1959); Lazzara, E., *Introduzione alla lettura di Q.* (1963); McCormick, C. A., "Q. and After," in *Proceedings of the Ninth Congress of the Australasian Universities' Language and Literature Association,* Adams, M., ed. (1964), pp. 85–86; Salvetti, G., *S. Q.* (1965); Amici, G., *S. Q.* (1966); Pento, B., *Lettura di Q.* (1966); Mazzamuto, P., *S. Q.* (1967)

HERBERT FRENZEL

Considered at first as the most typical and extreme representative of *poesia ermetica,* Q. has steadfastly progressed toward a clearer statement, a more lucid style, a chaster feeling.... The man has purified and the poet renewed himself through the trial of war, invasion and defeat. Almost all ... [his later] poems evoke, with classical restraint but with moving sincerity, the tragedy of destruction, hatred and bloodshed. The poet complains that it is impossible to sing "with the stranger's foot upon one's heart," yet he sings: he sings "day by day," not the tragic pageant of history, but the chronicle of life under the pressure of world shattering events. And while he sings, it seems to us that we see new flowers growing again on the soil of an Italy eternally ancient and eternally young.

Renato Poggioli, in Italica (March 1948),
pp. 55–6

S. Q. certainly has an important place in the contemporary Italian Pleiad, even if some of his recent work seems disappointing; and, to be sure, careful reservations on his ultimate validity as a poet, at least in his post-war phase, have come from some critical quarters. His relative position in the hierarchy culminating in Ungaretti and Montale is still a matter of debate; yet when Spagnoletti resents the "literary" quality of his diction (De Robertis would say "Parnassian"), it has to be added in all fairness that this is also a plausible part of his Southern heritage—the rich feeling for words as intrinsic melody.... In Q.'s case we should consider the additional factor of Sicily's insular mentality—not as an excuse, but as a characterization. Likewise, his translation of the Greek lyrical poets before the last war was somehow a return to the Mothers—to the deepest available layer of his culture.

Glauco Cambon, in IQ (Fall 1959), pp. 16–17

I arrived in Rome for a short visit on an unfortunate day. The Nobel Prize had just been awarded to the Sicilian poet S. Q. and this seemed to turn literary circles upside down.... If I had played guessing games and had set down the first twelve likely Italians, my list would not necessarily have included Q.... Even if the list were confined to Italian poets—excluding novelists and other writers —the mystery remains unsolved. In Italy for years there have been three poets whom nearly everybody considers more highly than Q. They are Giuseppe Ungaretti ... Eugenio Montale ... and ... Umberto Saba.

Bernard Wall, in Twentieth Century
(Dec. 1959), p. 486

Q. soon found a style of his own through which he could sing, with both passion and detachment, his loneliness and anguish.... His gradual maturing coincided with his particularly fortunate "encounter" with the Greek lyrical poets, and with his "discovery" of his native soil.... A poet of the highest integrity, supremely conscious of our condition, Q. has never despaired. Not an optimist in any sense of the word, he has an indestructible faith in the written word. He has sought, with words, and with all the intellectual resources at his disposal, to illuminate for himself and for us the meaning of life and man's condition in the universe.

Sergio Pacifici, in SatR (7 Nov. 1959), pp. 20, 42

He has dared, to a degree unusual in this tradition-ridden society, to employ his limpid, sensitive, classical idiom to confront "social" themes: the anguish of contemporary man, and to affirm a new humanism.... What worries ... objective critics is whether Q.'s more recent work has not lost force and beauty precisely to the degree that he has committed himself to a too narrowly conceived "engagement." The earlier work ... is the poignant lyricism of a humanist who has drunk deeply of Greek and Latin springs, and, in the blaze of Mediterranean light, projects a luminous grief-stricken image of modern man.... [His] translations, especially from Greek and Latin, are fresh limpid re-creations, not transcriptions, and, in the judgement of many, represent Q.'s highest achievement.

Sidney Alexander, in Reporter
(10 Dec. 1959), p. 38

Q. goes more easily into English than many other poets, for two reasons. First, he relies for much of his effect on his strikingly concrete and vivid imagery, which gives its own message just because it is so firmly conceived. His keen, observing eye is always at work. Secondly, he avoids rhyme and uses a regular rhythm in his verse which is akin to much that we use ourselves.... [There is] an unusual charge of emotion which Q. puts into his restrained and almost classical verse.... His latest poems show how he can face a situation in all its reality and in all his passionate response to it. For this he was indeed well trained by his "Hermetic" period, when, under the influence of Giuseppe

Ungaretti, he made every word do its full task and pruned his poetry of anything that smacked of padding or rhetoric.... What counts for us with Q. is that he combines this self-control with powerful emotions drawn from the agony of the modern world and the special tribulations of Italy. More than any living European poet he speaks for the whole of Europe, and is not afraid of attempting themes of profound and common concern.

C. M. Bowra, in The New York Times
(3 July 1960), p. 4

While a number of the earlier poems may have seemed derivative, with echoes of D'Annunzio and Pascoli and certain attitudes of despair reminiscent of Ungaretti or Montale, it was also evident that Q. had fused these elements in the alchemy of a personal style. The sensual music of his verse was not audible in any of his contemporaries, who were perhaps wary of the facile musicality of too much Italian poetry. Compared to the harsher line of Montale, for instance, the lush cadences of many of Q.'s earlier poems make him sound less "contemporary." To find the equal of his rich melody one must go as far back as Tasso.... In Q.'s poems of the Thirties one finds phrases whose music, while more subdued, is hardly less striking.... But despite his musicality, Q. shared with Ungaretti a sparse phrase reduced to the bare essentials of discourse, yet rich in suggestive power. Like Montale, his poems encompassed a vast and changing landscape over which moved the elemental forces of winds, tides and rivers, and he filled it with the sound of nature and with things that stand as mute witnesses to the solitude of man. And like his contemporaries, but more than they, he discovered in this world stripped of illusion the presence of mystic signs.

Louis R. Rossi, in ChiR (Spring 1960), p. 4

The poetry of S. Q.... hermetic in its earliest phases and given to what the critic Anceschi called "a metaphysic of aridity," did something of an about-face during the bitter experiences of the Second World War. The German occupation of northern Italy in particular did much to shock Q. out of his poetic seclusion: in grief and protest he began to write poetry of wider appeal, its avowed purpose to rifare l'uomo, to "remake man," a task for which many of Q.'s critics considered his literary talents inadequate.... But few would question the grace of phrasing and rhythm ... and the vividness and power of the imagery in such a poem as "Dalla rocca di Bergamo alta." ... Like many of Q.'s poems, this one is addressed to an impersonal "you." Perhaps for the same reason that the other poems were: the device breaks the circle of the poet's loneliness and establishes communication with someone, if only an ideal reader.

Wallace Fowlie, in The Poem Itself, ed. by
Stanley Burnshaw (1960), p. 326

QUEIROZ, Rachel de
Brazilian novelist, dramatist, and journalist, b. 17 Nov. 1910, Fortaleza

Rachel de Q. started her literary career in 1927 as a journalist in her native city. In 1930 she made a sensational debut as a novelist with O Quinze, which was received with enthusiastic critical acclaim throughout Brazil. The fact of her youth contributed to this success, but more important was the fact that the novel was one of the first, after A Bagaceira (Sugar Mill, 1928) by José Américo de Almeida, to introduce to Brazil a new social-minded literature of the 1930's. Though the periodical droughts in northeastern Brazil had been the theme of a few earlier novels, the literary school initiated with the books of Américo de Almeida and Rachel de Q. substituted social and even socialist intentions and preoccupations for the traditional sentimental approach to that tragedy. The novel's title refers to the year of 1915, in which one of the most catastrophic droughts occurred. All these circumstances explain the immense interest awakened by O Quinze, which was awarded the Graça Aranha Foundation literary prize in 1931.

In 1932, Rachel de Q.'s second novel João Miguel was a tentative effort toward a proletarian novel. Its hero is in fact an antihero, the common man of northeast Brazil. In terms of Rachel de Q.'s development as a novelist, it marks a transition from the social to the psychological approach.

Indeed, after a five-year period of silence, Rachel de Q. published Caminho de pedras (1937), which was followed by As três Marias (1939; The Three Marias, 1963). Both are clearly individualist in accent and purpose. With the exception of O Galo de Ouro (not yet published in book form), which appeared in installments in 1950 in a Rio de Janeiro publication, Rachel de Q. has stopped writing narratives.

In the 1940's Rachel de Q. began to write columns for several newspapers and particularly for the periodical O Cruzeiro. Her crônicas gained widespread popularity in Brazil and assured her reputation as one of Brazil's outstanding writers. Many of those crônicas were subsequently collected into books (e.g., 100 crônicas escolhidas, 1958, 1969).

In the 1950's she became interested in the theater, writing her first play, Lampião, in 1953, about the life and deeds of the famous rural outlaw nicknamed Lampião. It was well

SALVATORE QUASIMODO

HORACIO QUIROGA

received in Rio de Janeiro and São Paulo, where it was awarded the Saci Prize as the year's best play. Five years later, her new play, *A Beata Maria do Egito* (1958), was awarded two other prizes.

In addition, Rachel de Q. is a highly respected translator, having brought out in Portuguese works by Dostoyevski, Jane Austen, John Galsworthy (q.v.), and Emily Brontë.

What can be said about Rachel de Q. without hesitation is that she is to be credited with writing a Portuguese that is highly expressive and that she handles masterfully colloquial Portuguese. In 1957 she was awarded the Brazilian Academy of Letters prize for her total work.

FURTHER WORKS: *Três Romances* (1948); *A Donzela e a Moura Torta* (1948); *Quatro Romances* (1960); *O Brasileiro Perplexo* (1964); *O Caçador de Tatu* (1967); *O Menino Mágico* (1969)

BIBLIOGRAPHY: Ellison, F. P., *Brazil's New Novel: Four Northeastern Writers* (1954)

WILSON MARTINS

QUENEAU, Raymond

French novelist and poet, b. 21 Feb. 1903, Le Havre

As a young writer, Q. was attracted to surrealism (q.v.) and participated actively in the movement between 1924 and 1929. He has been a reader for Gallimard for many years and is the principal editor of their encyclopedias and histories of literature published in the Pléiade series.

Q.'s first novel, and perhaps his best, was *Le Chiendent* (1933; The Bark Tree, 1968). It was one of the first books, through its use of slangy spoken language, to reveal a crisis in the language of the novel. Q., who was at that time still close to surrealism, seems to have reenacted the surrealist rebellion here, insisting that the real subject of his work is language itself, language which is being endlessly created.

Pierrot mon ami (1942; Pierrot, 1950), whose hero moves about an amusement park in a manner reminiscent of Charlie Chaplin, is also a clever exercise in words, a detective story in which one can never be sure a crime has been committed.

The experimental quality of his writing is also apparent in his poems, which are often

built on plays on words and the repetition of key terms, as in *Les Ziaux* (1943).

Loin de Rueil (1944; The Skin of Dreams, 1948), is very much admired by a literary elite. It consists of a long fantasy in which the protagonist Jacques l'Aumône, as he watches a cowboy film, carries on a self-identification with each sequence. The character at times appears to be the novelist, and even the novel itself. *Loin de Rueil* is an intriguing example of a half-poetic, half-mad vision of the world.

Q. continued his experiments with language in *Exercices de style* (1947; Exercises in Style, 1959), where he presented ninety-nine different versions of the same totally insignificant anecdote. Although his *Zazie dans le métro* (1959; Zazie, 1960) was an immediate popular success, some critics feel that it may not be as lasting as the earlier novels. His handling of Zazie, a sort of French Lolita, is perhaps too deliberately farcical and salacious.

In his efforts to rejuvenate the form of the novel and to develop a new means of literary communication, Q. has utilized the traditional literary devices—often in parody form—and added to them the vocabulary and tempo of the spoken language. His objective is not to provide an exact transcription of contemporary life and society, but to create a new vision of it, based on the language he has forged.

This view of language shows Q.'s close affiliation with surrealism; yet he was also a prophet of existentialism (q.v.) in his creation of a sense of the absurd, of the hopelessness and ridiculousness of the contemporary world.

Q. has not reached the vast public of Sartre and Camus (qq.v.), but he has influenced, by reason of his virtuosity and vision, other writers, including Henry Miller and Boris Vian (qq.v.). Among modern French writers, he comes closest to Joyce (q.v.) in the breadth of his learning and in his determination to forge a new kind of structure for the novel through his use of language.

FURTHER WORKS: *Gueule de Pierre* (1934); *Les Derniers Jours* (1936); *Odile* (1937); *Chêne et Chien* (1937); *Les Enfants du limon* (1938); *Un Rude Hiver* (1939; A Hard Winter, 1948); *Les Temps mêlés* (1941); *Bucoliques* (1947); *L'Instant fatal* (1948); *Petite suite* (1948); *Saint Glinglin* (1948); *Petite cosmogonie portative* (1950); *Bâtons, chiffres et lettres* (1950); *Le Dimanche de la vie* (1952); *Le Chien à la mandoline* (1958); *Sonnets* (1958); *Cent mille milliards de poèmes* (1961); *Entretiens avec Georges Charbonnier* (1962); *Bords* (1963); *Les Fleurs bleues* (1965; Am., Blue Flowers, 1967; Eng., Between Blue and Blue, 1967); *Une Histoire modèle* (1966); *Courir les rues* (1967); *Battre la campagne* (1968); *Texticules* (1968); *Le Vol d'Icare* (1968); *Fendre les Flots* (1969)

BIBLIOGRAPHY: Quéval, J., *Q.* (1960); Bourdet, D., "R. Q.," *Revue de Paris,* LXXI (1964), 140–45; Guicharnaud, J., *R. Q.* (1965); Van Treese, G., "Glossaire pour servir à la lecture des romans de R. Q.," *DA,* XXV (1965), 7280; Mercier, V., "R. Q.: The First New Novelist?," *L'Ésprit Créateur,* VII (1967), 102–12; Roy, C., "R. Q.," *NRF,* 16 Sept. 1968, pp. 299–302

CHARLES G. HILL

QUIROGA, Horacio

Uruguayan short-story writer and novelist, b. 31 Dec. 1878, Salto; d. 19 Feb. 1937, Buenos Aires

In 1903 Q. traveled in the area around Misiones in northern Argentina. The impact of this tropical virgin forest on the banks of the Rio Paraná, with its animal life and dense vegetation, was reflected in *Cuentos de amor, de locura y muerte* (1918)—which contains the story "La gallina degollada"—and in several other short-story collections.

Q. later lived alternately in this area and in Buenos Aires, where he became a professor. His life, which was filled with tragedy and unhealthy imaginings, was ended by his own hand.

The themes of Q.'s first book, *Los arrecifes de coral* (1901), show the influence of Edgar Allan Poe (1809–1849) and revealed an early interest in the morbid and the supernatural. In *El crimen del otro* (1904)—a collection of short stories—the influence of *modernismo* becomes apparent. The *Historia de un amor turbio* (1908), a novella, reveals his interest in psychological problems. In the following years he wrote short stories that were dominated by their background—the tropical landscape.

Q.'s last book, *El más allá* (1934), reveals that he was even then haunted by thoughts about death, madness, suicide, and survival after death.

FURTHER WORKS: *Los perseguidos* (1905); *Cuentos de la selva, para los niños* (1918; South American Jungle Tales, 1959); *Las sacrificadas* (1920); *Anaconda* (1921); *Pasado amor* (1929); *Cuentos* (7 vols., 1937)

BIBLIOGRAPHY: Delgado, J. M., *H. Q.* (1939); Etcheverry, J. E., *H. Q.* (1957); Estrada, E. M., *Q.* (1957); Coons, D., "H. Q.—the Master Storyteller," *DA,* XXV (1965), 2978–79; Rodríguez Monegal, E., "Una historia perversa," *Mundo Nuevo,* VIII (1967), 57–60

GUSTAVO CORREA

R

RADAUSKAS, Henrikas

Lithuanian poet, b. 23 April 1910, Cracow, Poland; d. 27 Aug. 1970, Washington, D.C.

R. studied literature in Kaunas. Later he worked as a radio announcer and as an editor on the Commission on Book Publishing of the Lithuanian Ministry of Education. R. left Lithuania in 1944 to escape Soviet occupation. In 1949 he came to the United States and is now with the Library of Congress.

R. stands aloof from the main movements in Lithuanian literature because his purposes in art do not permit him to submit to a literary fashion or ideological trend. For him, genuine poetic achievement is always the result of a single individual's encounter with the infinite promise of language, an encounter which must not be restricted by any given theory of art.

R.'s poetry acquires form and substance by means of his effort to project the interplay between life and death, the absolute entities, in terms of concrete but relative manifestations, such as colors, shapes, and movements as well as ideas and emotions. Thus death is presented in an image that possesses the attributes of living things in the poem "Sunday." In this cozy genre painting of a room "dead for twenty years," an imitation of life is reflected upon the mirror of death.

Conversely, the violent exuberance of life is at times expressed in sets of metaphors and symbols signifying death. In one of R.'s poems, for instance, the birth of Venus is shown as a catastrophe—it is a seastorm that engulfs the villages of fishermen and ruins the fruits of their gardens.

Ultimately, the depiction of life and death in terms of each other leads R. to construct

a series of metaphorical transfigurations in concrete reality, which, when systematically developed, result in structures of the mind embodying aesthetic relationships. It is these that appear to have established in themselves a third absolute reality—that of art as such.

R. draws upon wide-ranging sources for the elements of his poetry. He sometimes uses motifs from classical mythology. The needs of his poetic imagination are especially well served by those myths in which the act of dying lasts eternally in a frozen infinity, which is what happens when one is turned to stone without losing consciousness. This appears in his poem "The Land of Lotus-Eaters," in which old men must lie dying forever because in this land, akin to Paradise, time does not exist.

Other poems are based upon descriptions of landscapes. There again, the verbal structures—contrapuntal arrangements of colors and transformations of physical shapes in direct response to the patterns of sound and of rhythm that follow the hidden lines of emotion—matter much more than any direct representations of nature.

Sometimes R. devises situations that appear to be surrealistic or grotesque because the thrust of his metaphors tears up the fabric of reality, producing new forms, comprehensible only in terms of their own logic. Yet, even his most "explosive" poems fully reveal themselves only to the reader who is sensitive to their subtle nuances and delicate shadings. And what is most important is that the reader listen closely to the tragic human voice that speaks across R.'s turbulent and kaleidoscopic rearrangements of reality.

Some of R.'s bold metaphorical constructions are reminiscent of those in the poetry of

139

Pasternak (q.v.). This is especially so when R. uses metaphors as bridges to forcefully connect two entirely separate semantic categories. At other times one hears the echoes of western-European modernistic and experimental poetry. Generally, however, R. is very much an authentic individual voice, a lonely alchemist who combines and recombines the elements of life and death in a search for the substance of art.

FURTHER WORKS: *Fontanas* (1935); *Strėlė danguje* (1950); *Žiemos daina* (1955); *Žaibai ir vėjai* (1964); *Eilėraščiai* (1965). **Selected English translations:** selections in *The Green Oak: Selected Lithuanian Poetry* (ed. A. Landsbergis and C. Mills; 1962) and in articles listed in Bibliography

BIBLIOGRAPHY: Ivask, I., "The Contemporary Lithuanian Poet H. R.," *Lituanus*, No. 3 (1959); Šilbajoris, R., "H. R.: Timeless Modernist," *BA*, Winter 1969

RIMVYDAS ŠILBAJORIS

RADIGUET, Raymond
French novelist, b. 18 June 1903, Saint-Maur; d. 12 Dec. 1923, Paris

R.'s first literary efforts were poems (published posthumously in *Les Joues en feu*, 1925) that bear some analogy to the early poems of Cocteau (q.v.). They might be placed midway between the productions of the cubists and the fauves. R. first excelled in a form of wit that French literary tradition has always esteemed. His poems belong in the tradition of Jacob and Apollinaire (qq.v.), which banished the mysteriousness of symbolism (q.v.) in order to rediscover the more direct spiritual quality of objects.

As a young boy—R. was only twenty at his death—he went to Paris frequently. Cocteau, who befriended him and believed in his writing talent, was the first to realize the originality with which R. was investing old formulas. Because Saint-Maur was on the Marne River, R. was often called "le miracle de la Marne" by the poets and painters of Montparnasse and Montmartre.

Both R.'s novels—*Le Diable au corps* (1923; The Devil in the Flesh, 1932) and *Le Bal du comte d'Orgel* (1924; The Count's Ball, 1929)—present the new *mal du siècle* that erupted during the years following World War I. *Le Diable au corps,* the story of a boy's poignant, tender love affair with a young married woman, focuses on the sense of limitless freedom felt by the young, and *Le Bal* analyzes the sense of bewilderment that resulted from this very freedom. *Le Bal du comte d'Orgel* is reminiscent of the 17th-c. *Princesse de Clèves* by Madame de La Fayette. R. did not conceal from his friends his intention of using Madame de La Fayette's famous classical novel as a model.

The theme of love in R. is at all times comparable to the high moral conception of love in the tragedies of Racine or in the novel of Madame de La Fayette. Nevertheless, the approach of Cocteau, who saw love never as a moral problem but rather as a curiosity and a willfulness to explore, is also reflected in R.'s novels.

FURTHER WORKS: *Devoirs de vacances* (1921); *Les Pélicans* (1921); *Règles du jeu* (ed. J. Cocteau; 1957); *Œuvres complètes* (1959)

BIBLIOGRAPHY: Magny, C.-E., *Histoire du Roman Français depuis 1918* (1950), pp. 106–27; Fowlie, W., "R. R.," *SR*, Summer 1953; Turnell, M., "The Novels of R. R.," *The Commonweal*, 15 July 1955; Goesh, K. J., "R. R. and the *roman d'analyse*," *Journal of the Australasian Universities' Language and Literature Association*, No. 4 (May 1956), pp. 1–10; Woodcock, G., "The Living Dead: R. R.," *London Magazine*, VII (May 1960), 60–69; Wyndham, F., "The Lost Heroes: R. R.," *Sunday Times Magazine*, 29 Jan. 1967, p. 28

WALLACE FOWLIE

RAINIS, Jānis
(pseud. of *Jānis Pliekšāns*), Latvian poet, dramatist, translator, b. 11 Sept. 1865, Rubene County, Upper Zemgale; d. 12 Sept. 1929, Majori (near Riga)

The son of a well-to-do estate overseer, R. was brought up in the country. After attending the gymnasium in Riga, he obtained a law degree from the University of Saint Petersburg. In 1891 he became editor of the influential political newspaper *Dienas Lapa,* and a staunch champion of the "new current" group, which the first Latvian democrats and socialists rallied around in the 1890's. In 1897 R. was arrested as dangerous to imperial Russia and exiled for six years, during which he finished translating Goethe's *Faust* and wrote poetry.

As one of the central figures in the 1905 revolution (which in Latvia developed into a

JĀNIS RAINIS

GRACILIANO RAMOS

nationalist movement), he had to flee from Latvia. Like many other eastern Europeans of the age, R. and his wife Aspazija (pseud. of Elza Rozenberga, 1868–1943, a well-known Latvian poet and a feminist leader) emigrated to Switzerland. During fourteen years of exile R. wrote his major literary works and became the ideologist of an autonomous Latvian state, envisioning it as neither a slave to the East nor a servant to the West. In 1920 R. returned to the newly proclaimed independent Republic of Latvia, where he held prominent positions in the government (including that of Minister of Education) and in the Social Democratic party. He was instrumental in founding the Riga Art Theater in 1920, and directed the Latvian National Theater from 1921 to 1925.

R.'s translations gave great literary works their footing in Latvia and proved that the Latvian language was a vehicle by which unusual emotional and intellectual experiences could be communicated.

The publication of R.'s *Tālas noskaņas zilā vakarā* (1903) and *Vētras sēja* (1905) heralded a new age in Latvian poetry and established R.'s preeminence as a lyric poet. In these poems R. revealed his fine poetic technique, form, and diction. He liked to use an abbreviated sonnet form consisting of nine lines in iambic pentameter (the "Rainis stanza"). Because they were unrivaled in Latvia for their passionate and rebellious protest against oppression, R.'s poems evoked an unusual response.

In the next three volumes—*Jaunais spēks* (1906), *Klusā grāmata* (officially banned in 1909; republished in 1910 as *Vēja nestas lapas*), and *Tie, kas neaizmirst* (1911)—R.'s objective was to strengthen the national spirit of his compatriots who took part in the abortive 1905 revolution.

Into his most intellectual poetry collection *Gals un sākums* (1912) R. projected the spiritual and social crisis of his own individuality and that of his nation, which in turn was indicative of the underlying restlessness of a whole civilization. One solution, suggests R., is the acceptance of perpetual change/flexibility—a theme which often appeared in his dramas.

R. greeted Latvia's attainment of independence in 1918 with two memorable volumes, *Sveika, brīvā Latvija!* (1919) and *Daugava* (1919).

Though most of R.'s fifteen excellent dramas (all but two written in blank verse) espoused national causes (they drew heavily on Latvian history and particularly folklore), R. was equally interested in appealing to universal human emotions.

R.'s *Uguns un nakts* (1907), one of the most esteemed works in Latvian literature, is based on the ancient legend about the epic hero Lāčplēsis (bearslayer) and his struggle with the Black Knight. Actually, its theme is freedom.

Perhaps R.'s most original drama is *Spēlēju, dancoju* (1919), a poetic drama full of fairies and demons, witches and hobgoblins. It is characterized by somber mysticism and numerous elusive symbols and allegories.

Jāzeps un viņa brāļi (1919; The Sons of Jacob, 1924) is usually considered R.'s greatest drama because of the emotional-psychological handling of its characters. Based on the biblical episode of Jacob and his sons, it expresses the irreconcilable conflict between the individual and society that R. was so aware of.

Since the Soviet takeover of the Baltic countries in 1940, R. has been elevated to a supranational level. Most Soviet critics are willing to accord deserved praise to certain parts of his work for their progressive spirit, but they have largely overlooked his more poetic qualities. Moreover, those of R.'s works that contradict the official view have been either completely suppressed (*e.g. Rīgas ragana*, 1928; *Daugava; Sveika, brīvā Latvija!*) or tampered with and distorted.

R.'s place is unquestionable as the greatest Latvian poet, and perhaps the greatest Latvian writer. He was also the key figure in Latvian literary and intellectual history during the 1900–1930 period. Brilliant and strongly individualistic, R. was independent of any specific literary school. Spiritually and aesthetically he is the best example in modern Latvian letters of the organic relationship between talent shaped by tradition and talent creating tradition.

FURTHER WORKS: *Mazie dunduri* (1888); *Apdziedāšanās dziesmas 3. Vispārīgiem latvju dziesmu svētkiem* (1889); *Pusideālists* (1904); *Ģirts Vilks* (1905); *Ave, sol!* (1910); *Zelta zirgs* (1910); *Indulis un Ārija* (1911); *Kopoti raksti* (2 vols., 1912–14); *Pūt, vējiņi!* (1913); *Sbornik latyšskoj literatury* (1916); *Addio bella* (1920); *Čūsku vārdi* (1920); *Uz mājām* (1920); *Zelta sietiņš* (1920); *Kopoti raksti* (5 vols., 1920–23); *Krauklītis* (1920); *Iļja Muromietis* (1922); *Sudrabota gaisma* (1922); *Mušu ķēniņš* (1923); *Puķu lodziņš* (1924); *Vasaras princīši un princītes* (1924); *Lellīte Lolīte* (1924); *Jaunā strāva* (1925); *Novelas* (1925); *Putniņš uz zara* (1925); *Mēness meitiņa* (1925); *Dzīve un darbi* (11 vols., 1925–31); *Mīla stiprāka par nāvi* (1927); *Saulīte slimnīcā* (1928); *Suns un kaķe* (1928); *Kastaņola* (1928); *Sirds devējs* (1935); *Dvēseles dziemas* (1935); *Rakstu izlase* (ed. P. Dauge; 4 vols., 1935–37); *Izbrannyje sočinenija* (ed. P. Dauge; 1935); *Lielās līnijas* (1936); *Aizas ziedi* (1937); *Rainis un Aspazija dzīvē un mākslā: Sarakstīšanas* (2 vols., 1937); *Mūza mājās* (1940); *Kalnā kāpējs* (1940); *Izbrannoje* (1940); *Kopoti raksti* (14 vols., 1947–51); *Rinktinè* (1952); *Vibrani tvori* (1952); *Raksti* (ed. K. Dziļleja; 17 vols., 1952–65); *Izbrannyje proizvedenija* (1953); *Vybranae* (1956); *Valitud teosed* (2 vols., 1965); *Lirika* (1965); *Tixaja kniga* (1965). **Selected English translations:** selections in *Tricolour Sun* (ed. W. K. Matthews; 1936) and *A Century of Latvian Poetry* (ed. W. K. Matthews; 1957)

BIBLIOGRAPHY: Birkerts, A., *R. dzīvē un darbā* (1930); Andrups, J. and V. Kalve, *Latvian Literature: Essays* (1954); Cielēns, F., *R. un Aspazija* (1955); Rudzītis, J., *R. ritmi: Formas studija* (1958); *Literatūras mantojums: Tautas dzejnieks J. R.* (2 vols., 1957–61); Ziedonis, A., *The Religious Philosophy of J. R.* (1969); *R. un Aspazijas Gadagrāmata* (4 vols., 1966–69)

ROLF EKMANIS

RAMOS, Graciliano

Brazilian novelist and short-story writer, b. 27 Dec. 1892, Quebrângulos, Alagoas; d. 20 March 1953, Rio de Janeiro

R., who worked as a journalist as well as at other occupations, was subjected to government harshness for his communist affiliation. In 1952 he traveled to Czechoslovakia and Soviet Russia and published his impressions in *Viagem* (1954).

R. worked to reproduce objectively the local scene. Although he may appear to the casual reader to be a strong believer in determinism, he is actually a passionate seeker after a better world. His characters are frequently types who represent ideas or are representative of the social groups who live in the interior in northeast Brazil. Molded by their merciless surroundings, they are driven by their needs to act out their tragic existences, losing hope when they are inevitably trapped by life. R. believed that a favorable outcome would occur if the environment were to change but felt that change

was unattainable so long as capitalist society mandated that all men be reduced to animals, clawing against each other for survival.

R.'s fiction is admired by contemporary Brazilian novelists and short-story writers for its psychological analysis, for its impressive use of interior monologue (q.v.), free association, symbolism (q.v.), leitmotivs, and for its careful structure. These elements are at their best in the novels *São Bernardo* (1934), *Angústia* (1936; Anguish, 1945), and *Vidas sêcas* (1938; Barren Lives, 1965), and in such short stories as "Um ladrão," "Dois dedos," and "Ciumes."

In line with his insistence on authentic Brazilian themes, R.'s language is equally "national" in its over-all effect. However much it may give the impression of everyday speech, with its directness, characteristic flow, and friendly tone, it is nevertheless a finely polished literary medium marked by classical clarity.

Following *Vidas sêcas,* which is probably his greatest achievement, R. devoted himself largely to short stories and to memoirs.

FURTHER WORKS: *Caetés* (1933); *A terra dos meninos pelados* (1937); *Histórias de Alixandre* (1944); *Infância* (1945); *Histórias incompletas* (1946); *Insônia* (1947); *Obras* (10 vols., 1947); *Memórias do cárcere* (4 vols., 1953); *Contos e novelas* (1957); *Historias agrestes* (1960); *Alexandre e outros heróis* (1962); *Viventes de Alagoas* (1962); *Linhas tortas* (1962)

BIBLIOGRAPHY: Grieco, A., *Gente nova do Brasil* (1935); Montenegro, O., *O romance brasileiro* (1936); Carpeaux, O. M., *Origens e fins* (1943); Grieco, A., *Homenagem a G. R.* (1943); Pereira, A., *Interpretações* (1944); Gonçalves, F., "G. R. e o romance," introduction to R.'s *Caetés* (1947); Ellison, F. P., *Brazil's New Novel: Four Modern Masters* (1954); Bruno, H., *Estudos de literatura brasileira* (1957); Aguiar Filho, A., *Modernos ficcionistas brasileiros* (1958); Táti, M., *Estudos e notas críticas* (1958); Cavalcanti, V., *Jornal literário: Crônicas* (1960)

CLAUDE L. HULET

RAMUZ, Charles-Ferdinand

Swiss poet and novelist (writing in French), b. 24 Sept. 1878, Cully-sur-Lausanne; d. 23 May 1947, Lausanne

R., who came from peasant stock, grew up near Lausanne and studied in Paris for several years. In 1914 he returned to his native Vaud.

From 1930 until his death he lived in self-imposed isolation near Pully.

R., who does not seem to have been swayed strongly by particular literary influences, showed his interest in simple, regional subjects at the very beginning of his writing career. Among his early works are the book of poems *Le Petit Village* (1903) and the novel *Aline* (1905), which in their concentration on simple rustic themes already reveal his determination to limit his range and to achieve a personal style. In his *Jean-Luc persécuté* (1909) he depicted the mountain peasants of Valais.

The writing of *Aimé Pache, peintre vaudois* (1911), a semiautobiographical novel about the growing up of a painter, may have released him psychologically from his attachment to Paris.

In *Raison d'être*, the manifesto of the "cahiers vaudois" movement, R. justified the new direction his writing was taking. Henceforth he was to devote himself to seeking a more profound understanding of the essence of Vaud. By observing the art of Cézanne he learned that the artist can express universal truths by focusing on the concrete.

World War I confirmed R.'s belief that to find a principle by which life can be seen as a whole one must turn to what is basic and elemental. In the following years R. wrote about the winegrowers of Vaud, about the peasants in the mountains of Valais, and about the fishermen and villagers across the Rhone in Savoy. These sometimes-epic, sometimes-lyrical novels reveal that R., a visionary mystic, had the eye of a painter and the ear of a poet.

In *Passage du poète* (1923) R. defines a poet as anyone who performs his work with love and masterly skill. Thus the quiet, confident hand-movements of a basketmaker mystically lead to the emergence of a new psychic dimension in the inhabitants of the winegrowing village in which he has established himself—a dimension that allows the hard toil of the vineyard workers to take on a more meaningful significance.

In *La Grande Peur dans la montagne* (1926; Terror on the Mountains, 1967) R. deals with his vision of the daimonic abysses in the Swiss character. When an epidemic of hoof-and-mouth disease breaks out among the livestock in a high Alpine pasture, the mounting, almost mystical horror of the herdsmen is pitted against the villagers' fear that the disease may spread down to their animals. Against this dark background runs a gentle love story.

Le Garçon savoyard (1936) tells the tragic story of a country boy, a *drôle de garçon*, whose passionate idealization of a girl acrobat drives him to murder. Ultimately he seeks death in order to escape from "society."

A major literary figure in La Romandie (French-speaking western Switzerland), R. paved the way for the peasant-oriented writings of Giono, Pourrat, and Bosco (qq.v.). His ability to make a region vivid to his readers enabled him to give La Romandie—and the Vaud canton in particular—an identity in literature more carefully formulated than hitherto.

R. can therefore be fairly categorized as a regional novelist, but for the quality of his literary achievement he merits a place in the mainstream of literature in the French language.

FURTHER WORKS: *Les Circonstances de la vie* (1907); *Nouvelles et morceaux* (1910); *La Vie de Samuel Bélet* (1913); *Le Règne de l'esprit malin* (1914); *La Guerre dans le Haut-Pays* (1915); *La Guérison des maladies* (1917); *Le Grand Printemps* (1917); *Les Signes parmi nous* (1919); *Histoire du soldat* (1920); *Chant de notre Rhône* (1920); *Salutation paysanne* (1921); *Terre du ciel* (1921); *Présence de la mort* (1922; The Triumph of Death, 1946); *La Séparation des races* (1922); *L'Amour du monde* (1925); *La Beauté sur la terre* (1927; Beauty on Earth, 1929); *Farinet ou la fausse monnaie* (1932); *Adam et Eve* (1932); *Taille de l'homme* (1933); *Une Main* (1933); *Derborence* (1934; When the Mountain Fell, 1947); *Questions* (1935); *Besoin de grandeur* (1937); *Si le Soleil ne revenait pas* (1937); *Paris, Notes d'un Vaudois* (1938); *Découverte du monde* (1940); *La Guerre aux papiers* (1942); *Pays de Vaud* (1943); *Vues sur le Valais* (1943); *Journal, 1896–1942* (1943); *Nouvelles* (1944); *Les Servants* (1946); *Histoires* (1946); *Journal, 1942–1947* (1949); *Souvenirs sur Igor Stravinsky* (1952); *Lettres 1900–1918* (1956); *Lettres 1919–1947* (1959); *Œuvres complètes* (23 vols., 1940 ff.). **Selected English translation:** *What Is Man?* (1948)

BIBLIOGRAPHY: Zermatten, M., *Connaissance de R.* (1947; rev. ed., 1964); Tissot, A., *C. F. R.* (1948); Guisan, G., *R.* (1958); Steinmann, J., *Littérature d'hier et d'aujourd'hui* (1963); Parsons, C. R., *Vision plastique de C. F. R.* (1964); Guers-Villate, Y., *R.* (1966); Special R. issue, *Europe,* Nos. 459–60 (1967); Guisan, G., *C. F. R., ses amis et son temps* (Vol. I, 1967; Vols. II–IV, 1968)

WERNER GÜNTHER

RANSOM, John Crowe

American poet, critic, teacher, and editor, b. 30 April 1880, Pulaski, Tennessee

R., the son of a Methodist missionary and a schoolteacher, attended Vanderbilt University (Nashville) and Oxford as a Rhodes scholar. In 1914 he began to teach English and literature at Vanderbilt. After serving in France in World War I, R. returned to Vanderbilt.

In 1919 an undistinguished volume, *Poems about God,* was published at the recommendation of Frost (q.v.).

Soon after, R. joined a group of teachers, students, and townsmen who gathered regularly to talk about poetry and to read their own verse. Out of this group emerged *The Fugitive* (1922–25), a little magazine that is said to have initiated the Southern renascence in poetry. The contributors, who came to be known as the "fugitives," included R., Allen Tate, Robert Penn Warren (qq.v.), and Donald Davidson (b. 1893).

R. wrote the body of his poetry between about 1916 and 1928, publishing *Chills and Fever* in 1924 and *Two Gentlemen in Bonds* in 1927. Most of the poems in *Selected Poems* (1945; revised ed., 1963) and in *Poems and Essays* (1955) appeared originally in these two volumes.

R.'s finely wrought poetry achieves ironic effects through subtle combinations of incongruous strains of diction: he freely mixes Latin elegance and Saxon simplicity, the pedantic and the commonplace, the archaic and the colloquial. He seems both involved in and remote from his personae, who most often are failures in a world that has lost its capacity to act as a stabilizing agent. R.'s most frequent theme is decay, whether it be of belief, of the order of society, or of the individual life.

In 1925, as a result of the ridicule the South accrued because of the Scopes trial (which revolved around the teaching of evolution in the schools), R. became a defender of the agrarian traditions of the South. Although the "agrarians" had different aims from those of the "fugitives," R, Tate, Robert Penn Warren, and Davidson were active in both groups.

The "agrarian" defense of the South and the attack upon encroaching industrialism culminated in the intellectually important but practically ineffective book of essays *I'll Take My Stand* (1930), for which R. wrote the "Statement of Principles" and the lead essay.

In *God without Thunder* (1930) R. ascribes the decline of religion and poetry to the influence of science and its abstractionism.

In the early 1930's R. turned his attention to poetics. As a theorist and editor, he was a major influence in the "new criticism" (*see* literary criticism), which focused upon the aesthetic as opposed to the philological, biographical, and historical aspects of the poem.

The new criticism revolutionized the teaching of poetry in college classrooms.

In 1937 R. went to teach at Kenyon College (Ohio), where he founded and edited the important *Kenyon Review.* Through his editing, his numerous essays, and his books *The World's Body* (1938) and *The New Criticism* (1941), R. is a voice to be reckoned with in the academic debates over the nature and value of poetry.

FURTHER WORKS: *Armageddon* (1923); *Grace after Meat* (1924)

BIBLIOGRAPHY: Warren, R. P., "J. C. R.: A Study in Irony," *VQR,* XI (1935), 93–112; Bradbury, J. M., *The Fugitives* (1958); Cowan, L., *The Fugitive Group* (1959); Purdy, R. R., ed., *Fugitives' Reunion* (1959); Knight, K. F., *The Poetry of J. C. R.* (1964); Stewart, J. L., *The Burden of Time: The Fugitives and Agrarians* (1965)

KARL F. KNIGHT

READ, Herbert Edward

English poet, critic, and essayist, b. 4 Dec. 1893, Kirbymoorside, Yorkshire; d. 12 June 1968, Malden

R. was educated at the University of Leeds. After his three years at the front in World War I, which caused him to become a pacifist, he published his first major volume of poems, *Naked Warriors* (1919). From 1922 to 1931 he was Assistant Keeper of the Victoria and Albert Museum in London. Later he taught at the University of Edinburgh (1931–33) and at Harvard (1953–54), and served as a director of the Routledge and Kegan Paul publishing house.

R.'s literary reputation is founded chiefly on his philosophy of art and on his poetry. R. was originally swayed by the antiromantic and antihumanistic doctrines of T. E. Hulme (1883–1917)—whose *Speculations* he edited in 1924—and attracted to a "classical" theory of art, for which he was indebted to Eliot (q.v.). Later R. was influenced by the surrealists (*see* surrealism) and by the psychoanalytic ideas of Freud and Jung.

After the early 1930's R. emphasized in his literary criticism the unconscious sources of poetry and the universality of its reference, though he never abandoned his initial insistence on the primacy of reason. Inclined politically toward an anarchism hostile to the conformities demanded by modern society with its technological bias, R. celebrated in his poetry a pantheistic organicism reminiscent of William Wordsworth (1770–1850).

His most significant works include *Reason and Romanticism* (1926), *Form in Modern Poetry* (1932), *The Innocent Eye* (1933), *The Green Child, a Romance* (1935), *Collected Essays in Literary Criticism* (1938), *The Grass Roots of Art* (1946), and *Collected Poems, 1919–1946* (1946).

FURTHER WORKS: *Songs of Chaos* (1915); *Eclogues: A Book of Poems* (1919); *Mutations of the Phoenix* (1923); *English Pottery* (with Bernard Rackham; 1924); *In Retreat* (1925); *English Stained Glass* (1926); *Collected Poems, 1913–25* (1926); *English Prose Style* (1928); *Phases of English Poetry* (1928); *The Sense of Glory* (1929); *Wordsworth: The Clark Lectures, 1929–1930* (1930); *Julien Benda and the New Humanism* (1930); *Ambush* (1930); *The Meaning of Art* (1931); *Art Now: An Introduction to the Theory of Modern Painting and Sculpture* (1933); *The End of a War* (1933); *Art and Industry: The Principles of Industrial Design* (1934); *Poems, 1914–34* (1935); *In Defence of Shelley* (1936); *Art and Society* (1937); *Poetry and Anarchism* (1938); *Annals of Innocence and Experience* (1940); *Thirty-five Poems* (1940); *The Politics of the Unpolitical* (1943); *Education Through Art* (1943); *World within a War* (1944); *The Education of Free Men* (1944); *A Coat of Many Colours* (1945); *Education for Peace* (1949); *Coleridge as Critic* (1949); *Contemporary British Art* (1951); *Byron* (1951); *The Philosophy of Modern Art* (1952); *Collected Poems* (1953); *The True Voice of Feeling* (1953); *Anarchy and Order* (1954); *Icon and Idea* (1955); *Moon's Farm and Poems Mostly Elegiac* (1955); *The Art of Sculpture* (1956); *The Tenth Muse* (1957); *A Concise History of Modern Painting* (1959); *Kandinsky* (1959); *The Form of Things Unknown* (1960); *The Parliament of Women* (1960); *Aristotle's Mother* (1960); *Truth Is More Sacred* (1961); *A Letter to a Young Painter* (1962); *The Contrary Experience* (1963); *Selected Writings* (1963); *The Origins of Form in Art* (1965); *Henry Moore: A Study of His Life and Work* (1965); *Poetry and Experience* (1966)

BIBLIOGRAPHY: Treece, H., ed., *H. R., an Introduction to His Work by Various Hands* (1944); Berry, F., *H. R.* (1953); Wasson, R., "The Green Child: H. R.'s Ironic Fantasy," *PMLA*, LXXVII (1962), 645–51

GROVER SMITH

REBREANU, Liviu

Romanian novelist, b. 27 Nov. 1885, Târlisina; d. 1 Sept. 1944, Bucharest

R. studied in Vienna and Budapest. Later he was a theater director in Bucharest. When Romania was occupied by the Soviet army in the last year of World War II, R. took his own life.

R. started his literary career in 1916 with the short-story collection *Golanii*. His novel *Ion* (1920; Eng., 1967) is a landmark in contemporary Romanian literature. It describes the typical Romanian peasant, with his almost animal passion for the soil, his deep-rooted instincts, his fantasies, his fears, and his cruelty. On occasion the description in R.'s works of the unconscious and the instinctive drives becomes so dominant that the result is more a monograph on a psychopathic personality than a literary narrative (e.g. *Pădurea Spânzuraţilor*, 1922; The Forest of the Hanged, 1967).

Another admirable feature of R.'s work is his treatment of the crowd when it gathers in the villages. *Răscoala* (1932; The Uprising, 1965), which contains felicitous examples of this handling, gives a true-to-life account of the Romanian peasant revolt of 1907 and its excesses. Eugen Lovinescu (1881–1943) said of *Răscoala* that it was "the work of the greatest epic writer in our literature."

FURTHER WORKS: *Frământări* (1912); *Mărturisire* (1919); *Calvarul* (1919); *Răfuiala* (1919); *Cadrilul* (1919); *Iţic Ştrul dezertor* (1921); *Norocul* (1921); *Catastrofa* (1921); *Nuvele* (1921); *Plicul* (1923); *Adam şi Eva* (1925); *Ciuleandra* (1925); *Apostolii* (1926); *Crăişorul* (1929); *Jar* (1934); *Gorila* (1938); *Amândoi* (1940); *Opere alese* (4 vols., 1958 ff.)

BIBLIOGRAPHY: Giambruno, A., *R.* (1937); Câlinescu, G., *R.* (1939); Dima, Al., "Zur zeitgenössischen rumänischen Literaturkritik und Literaturgeschichte," *Beiträge zur Roman-*

ischen Philologie, III, 1 (1964), 80–87; Special R. issue, *Gazeta Literară,* XII (2 Dec. 1965)

VIRGIL IERUNCA

RÉGIO, José

(pseud. of *José Maria dos Reis Pereira*), Portuguese poet, dramatist, novelist, and essayist, b. 17 Sept. 1901, Vila do Conde, near Pôrto; d. there, 22 Dec. 1969

While studying Romance philology in Coimbra to prepare himself for a teaching career, R. published, at his own expense, his first book of poetry, *Poemas de Deus e do diabo* (1925). Two years later, in 1927, he and his two friends, João Gaspar Simões and Branquinho da Fonseca (b. 1905), founded the literary magazine called *Presença,* which marks the beginning of the second period of modernism in Portuguese poetry. After leaving Coimbra he dedicated himself to teaching and writing, first in Pôrto and then in Portalegre.

Thematically, technically, and stylistically R.'s works form an integrated whole and don't lend themselves to a genre-by-genre study. "Everyone else had a father and a mother," he says in "Cantico negro," "but I was born of the love that exists between God and the Devil." His *fado* (fate) or what he calls preexperience has made R. highly sensitive to this moral duality. His protagonists constantly struggle between madness and sanity, good and evil, perversity and purity. This duality forms part of their vital existence, and when one side triumphs over the other they cease to exist. In *O príncipe com orelhas de burro* (1942), for example, Leonel conquers evil, becomes perfect and purified—symbolized by the loss of the flappy ears—and then ceases to exist. A similar process takes place in the play *Benilde, ou A Virgem Mãe* (1947). Too innocent and pure, the protagonist cannot live in the real world.

R. implements these moral conflicts and heightens their dramatic intensity by playing free with chance and reality. Both the Prince's ears and Benilde's pregnancy, the symbol of their conflict, stem from some sort of contract with the Devil, or with God, or both.

Time in R.'s works moves at a leisurely, day-by-day pace; people grow up, fall in love, get married, have children, and die. The simplicity of the patterns established enables R. effortlessly to capture the timelessness behind a specific moment in the big house, the little

village, and the little, half-forgotten country called Portugal.

R. injects a note of lyrical *costumbrismo* into all his works, especially the *A casa velha* (3 vols.) series, which includes *Uma gota de sangue* (1945), *As raízes do futuro* (1947); *Os avisos do destino* (1953). This he does with a delicacy and restraint that would please Willa Cather (q.v.) and teach his fellow countryman José Maria Eça de Queiroz (1846–1900) how to capture the reality of the five senses without itemizing or photographing it.

R.'s characters, like those in the novels of the Spaniard Juan Valera (1824–1905), are the important inhabitants of the small village—those who live in or belong to "the big house." Like Valera, R. feels he has been more successful in depicting women than men. Letícia in *O príncipe com orelhas de burro,* Benilde in *Benilde, ou A Virgem Mãe,* and Rosa in *A Rosa brava* belong to the literary tradition of the heroine of Gustave Flaubert's (1821–80) classic short story, "Un Coeur simple."

Many aspects of R.'s style, his long flowing, even Cervantine sentences—in *O príncipe com orelhas de burro* he appropriately follows Miguel de Cervantes's (1547–1616) tradition of explaining all the interesting things scheduled to happen in this *true* history—his images, his use of language, all belong to past centuries. His didacticism, his constant preoccupation with moral questions, and his concern over the real values and virtues of Portuguese literature also tend to place his works in an older literary tradition.

R.'s contribution to literature rests on his study of man—quite often grotesque in his abnormality—and his relation to himself. Though he focuses on the young man or woman from a small village, like so many other writers of our century he achieves universality by capturing the essence of his native land and its people.

FURTHER WORKS: *Biografia* (1929); *Jôgo da cabra cega* (1934); *As encruzilhadas de Deus* (1936); *Críticos e criticados* (1936); *Antonio Botto e o amor* (1938); *Essay* (1938); *Em tôrno da expressão artística* (1940); *Fado* (1941); *Jacob e o Anjo* (1941); *Pequena história da moderna poesia portuguêsa* (1941); *Davam grandes paseios aos domigos* (1941); *Mas Deus é grande* (1945); *História de mulheres* (1946); *El-Rei Sebastião* (1949); *A chaga do lado* (1954); *A Salvação do Mundo* (1954); *Três peças em um ato* (1957); *Mário, ou Eu próprio—o outro* (1957); *O filho do homem* (1961); *As monstruosidades vulgares* (n.d.); *Há mais mundos* (n.d.); *Vidas são vidas* (n.d.)

BIBLIOGRAPHY: Lopes, O., *J. R.* (1956); Lisboa, E., *J. R.* (1957); Rossi, C. G., *Geschichte der portugiesischen Literatur* (1964); Teixeira, A., "Sobre o teatro religioso de J. R.," *Espiral*, Nos. 6 and 7 (1965), pp. 123–25; Torres, A. P., *Romance* (1967)

LEO L. BARROW

RÉGNIER, Henri François Joseph de

French poet, short-story writer, and novelist, b. 28 Oct. 1864, Honfleur; d. 23 May 1936, Paris

Cultivated, distinguished, not without vanity and aristocratic pride (he came from a family of minor nobility), R. knew writers such as Stéphane Mallarmé (1842–98), Paul Verlaine (1844–96), and Gide (q.v.). He became a well-known figure in Paris literary salons of the time, particularly after his marriage to a daughter of the most famous of later parnassian poets, José-Maria de Herédia (1842-1905). He was elected to the French Academy in 1911.

R.'s early poetry—*Les Lendemains* (1885), *Apaisement* (1886), *Sites* (1887)—in traditional versification, was largely descriptive and picturesque in the sumptuous style of the parnassians. From 1890 onward, under symbolist (*see* symbolism) influence, he moved over to poetry in free verse, with greater emphasis on musicality and the use of more obscure, less plastic images to express vague states of mind often impregnated with unspecified lassitude and melancholy.

R.'s later poetry is a more direct expression of personal emotion and returns to the use of traditional versification and fixed forms such as the sonnet. In this verse—*Aréthuse* (1895), *La Sandale ailée* (1906), *Le Miroir des heures* (1910)—R. turned for models to earlier poets such as Ronsard (1524–85) and André Chénier (1762–94), to whom he dedicated *Les Médailles d'argile* (1900), and made frequent use of classical allusions to express a mixture of resigned stoicism and refined epicureanism sensitive to the beauty of nature, particularly in its pastoral aspects, and of woman, with an undercurrent of gentle *taedium vitae* and disillusionment.

These later collections contain a good deal of descriptive poetry, neoclassical in content and sober and concise in expression. An excellent example of such descriptive poetry is *La Cité des eaux* (1902), a collection devoted to the vanished splendors of Versailles.

R. also wrote a great deal of prose. Starting with the rather precious and fantastic short stories in *Contes à soi-même* (1893), he moved on with *La Double Maîtresse* (1900) to full-length novels, including some historical novels, set in France or Italy, from his favorite period of the 17th and 18th c.'s. A great admirer of *Les Liaisons dangereuses* of Choderlos de Laclos (1741–1803), in his novels R. frequently assumes a libertine and voluptuous tone. His style is carefully wrought and often elaborate.

R. frequently traveled to the Mediterranean (a source of much of his poetry and prose), particularly to Venice, which he adored for its decaying splendor and for the elegant refinement and delicate, tolerant corruption of its past.

R.'s many literary and travel articles were periodically collected and published: *Figures et caractères* (1901), *Portraits et souvenirs* (1913). He greatly admired the pessimistic 18th-c. French moralist Chamfort (1741–94), and his own maxims and epigrams in *Donc* (1927) show a similar disillusionment with human nature (particularly feminine human nature) expressed with polished concision.

R.'s attempts to deal with modern events, such as World War I, led to embarrassingly trite patriotic poetry. His charm lies in his eclectic use of various poetic veins (parnassian, symbolist, romantic, and neoclassic) to produce an individual amalgam that is musical, melancholy, and gently sensual. He appeals to those who are attracted by conventional poetic forms used with care to express a personal nostalgia for the past, a poignant sense of the evanescence of pleasure expressed with reticent elegance rather than rough vigor.

FURTHER WORKS: *Episodes* (1888); *Poèmes anciens et romanesques* (1890); *Tel qu'en songe* (1892); *Le Bosquet de Psyché* (1894); *Le Trèfle noir* (1895); *Aréthuse* (1895); *Les Jeux rustiques et divins* (1897); *La Canne de jaspe* (1897); *Le Trèfle blanc* (1899); *Les Amants singuliers* (1901); *Le Bon Plaisir* (1902); *Le Mariage de minuit* (1903); *Les Vacances d'un jeune homme sage* (1904); *Les Rencontres de M. Bréot* (1904); *Le Passé vivant* (1905); *Esquisses vénitiennes* (1906); *Sujets et paysages* (1906); *La Peur de l'amour* (1907); *Trois Contes à soi-même* (1907);

147

Les Scrupules de Sganarelle (1908); *Couleur du temps* (1909); *La Courte Vie de Balthazar Aldramin* (1909); *La Flambée* (1909); *L'Amphisbène* (1912); *Contes de France et d'Italie* (1912); *Images vénitiennes* (1912); *Pour Les Mois d'hiver* (1912); *Venise: L'Encrier rouge* (1912); *Le Plateau de laque* (1913); *Modes et manières d'aujourd'hui* (1914); *Romaine Mirinault* (1914); *L'Illusion héroïque de Tito Bassi* (1916); *Odelettes* (1917); *M. d'Amercœur* (1918); *1914–1916 Poésies* (1918); *Histoires incertaines* (1920); *La Pécheresse* (1920); *Le Trèfle rouge, ou Les Amants singuliers* (1920); *Vestigia Flammae* (1921); *Les Scrupules de Miss Simpson* (1921); *Marceline, ou La Punition fantastique* (1921); *Le Médaillier* (1924); *Scènes mythologiques, suivies de petites fables modernes* (1924); *Le Divertissement provincial* (1925); *Les Trois Fils de Mme de Chasans* (1925); *Les Bonheurs perdus* (1925); *Contes pour chacun de vous* (1926); *L'Entrevue* (1926); *L'Escapade* (1926); *Le Veuvage de Schéhérazade* (1926); *Contes vénitiens* (1928); *Flamma tenax* (1928); *L'Altana, ou La Vie vénitienne* (1928); *Lui, ou Les Femmes et l'amour* (1929); *Nos rencontres* (1931); *Escales en Méditerranée* (1931); *Souvenirs sur V. de l'Isle Adam, J. Laforgue, Mallarmé* (1931); *Airs pour l'écho* (1933); *De Mon Temps* (1933); *Lettres diverses et curieuses écrites par plusieurs à l'un d'entre eux* (1933); *Moi, elle et lui* (1935); *Madame Récamier* (1936)

BIBLIOGRAPHY: Bertin, H., *H. de R.* (1910); Lowell, A., *Six French Poets* (1915); Parmée, D., *Classicisme et neo-classicisme dans l'œuvre poétique d'H. de R.* (1939); Jaloux, E., *Souvenirs sur H. de R.* (1941); Maurin, M., "H. de R. et le roman," *MdF*, Jan. 1965; Buenzod, E., *H. de R.* (1966)

DOUGLAS PARMÉE

RÉGNIER, Paule

French novelist, poet, and dramatist, b. 19 June 1890, Fontainebleau; d. 6 Dec. 1950, Paris

After a few poems, several unperformed plays, and the somewhat sentimental diary *Octave* (1913), Paule R. published her first successful novel, *La Vivante Paix* (1924). Dealing with the tragic disintegration of a psychologically complex, unhappy woman, it foreshadows the personally experienced religious conflicts Paule R. was to face in *L'Abbaye*

d'Evolayne (1934; The Abbey of Evolayne, 1935) and her later novels.

In *L'Abbaye d'Evolayne* the action, the background of which is the mystery of divine law, unfathomable to man, centers upon a clergyman accidentally responsible for the death of his wife, who loses her life because of an irreconcilable conflict between love of God and human love and through an attitude toward sacrifice that most people would consider abnormal. *Tentation* (1941), which presents the foundering marriage of a religious writer, again deals with the pitiable state that the protagonist is thrown into because he cannot resolve the conflicting pulls of the will of God.

Paule R.'s diary, *Journal* (1953), reveals the tragedy of her own deeply overshadowed life.

Wearied from striving toward God and the church and preoccupied with pain and death, Paule R. succumbed to the loneliness and despair she was so vulnerable to and took her own life.

FURTHER WORKS: *Les Filets dans la mer* (1948); *Fêtes et nuages* (1956); *Lettres* (1956)

BIBLIOGRAPHY: Ariès, P., et al., *Cinquante ans de pensée catholique française* (1955); Henrey, K. H., "The Priest in the French Novel," *Church Quarterly Review*, CLXV (1964), 82–88

* * *

REISEN, Abraham

Yiddish poet and short-story writer, b. 2 April 1875, Kaidanov (near Minsk); d. 30 March 1953, New York City

A precocious son of poor parents, R. was already tutoring at fourteen and publishing poetry at sixteen. After serving four years in the army (1896–1900), he went to Warsaw, where he made friends with other Yiddish writers. In 1902, R. published *Zaitlieder,* a small book of verse. At the outbreak of World War I in 1914 he settled in New York and became a regular contributor to the Yiddish daily papers.

R.'s characteristic themes are unrelenting poverty, unrequited love, and acute loneliness, all of which are treated with a simple clarity and a depth of feeling and thought.

R.'s poetry is distinguished for its conscious artlessness, and a number of his verses, set to music, have taken on the nature of the folk-song. His quiet reflections, pensive yearning, and feeling of vulnerability are expressed in his

ALEKSEI REMIZOV

spontaneous and pure lyrics. It is because of these qualities that he is the most well-loved Yiddish poet.

R. the gentle humorist appears more often in his fine short stories. In these poignant stories R. treats poverty with exceptional fidelity and pensiveness and without moral overtones. Emphasizing not the happening but how the individual responds to it, R. succeeds in showing convincingly how men and women are intimidated by poverty into becoming humble, docile, dispirited creatures. Unreciprocated love is treated with irony, sympathy, and mild amusement.

R.'s American stories are marked by an artistic falling off. R. felt that the American Jew was paying a high price for the material comforts he was enjoying, but R. was not able to convert his new insights into poems and stories of the quality he had written in Europe.

Some of R.'s best prose is to be found in his three volumes of reminiscences.

FURTHER WORKS: *Gezamelte Lieder* (1908); *Mentchen un Welten* (1908); *Geshtalten* (1908); *Alle Werk* (12 vols., 1912); *Ertzeylungen* (1913); *Alle Werk* (14 vols., 1928); *Epizoden fun mein Leben* (3 vols., 1929–35). **Selected English translation:** *A Game* (1919)

BIBLIOGRAPHY: Rogoff, H., *Nine Yiddish Writers* (1931); Niger, S., Shatsky, J., and others, eds., *Lexicon fun der Neier Yiddisher Literatur* (1956–68); Madison, C. A., *Yiddish Literature: Its Scope and Major Writers* (1968)

CHARLES A. MADISON

REISSIG, Julio Herrera y
See Herrera y Reissig, Julio

REMARQUE, Erich Maria
(pseud. of *Erich Paul Remark*), German novelist, b. 22 June 1898, Osnabrück; d. 25 Sept. 1970, Locarno, Switzerland

R. was wounded in action several times during World War I. Then, in the early 1920's, he tried his hand at a number of occupations before he settled down to writing. In 1931 he moved to Switzerland. In 1933, after the advent of Hitler, R.'s books were burned in Germany and he was stripped of German citizenship. In 1939 he went to New York, becoming a United States citizen in 1947.

Im Westen nichts Neues (1929; All Quiet on the Western Front, 1929), the archetype of the antiwar novel and the most celebrated book of its time, is a realistic documentary, presented by means of a series of episodes of R.'s experience in World War I. It tells of a generation whose ranks were made up of war casualties (though the injuries incurred had not been inflicted by shells) that still managed to retain its faith in such values as self-sacrifice and comradeship.

Der Weg zurück (1931; The Road Back, 1931), which is about a soldier returning from the front, is less effective as a novel. R. went from this, however, to achieve new methods of technique and a richer range of themes in *Drei Kameraden* (1938; first published in English in 1937 as Three Comrades). In this tragic love story the lasting quality of war comradeship, unvoiced and unbreakable, counterbalances the rootlessness of postwar life.

In the 1940's R. turned to the experience of World War II refugees. *Liebe deinen Nächsten* (1941; Flotsam, 1941) and *Arc de Triomphe* (1946; Arch of Triumph, 1946) describe the perennially uprooted status of the politically persecuted, whose right to live is endangered as much by indifference as by authoritarian terrorism. In these novels, as in the concentration-camp novel *Der Funke Leben* (1952; Spark of Life, 1953), R. focuses on the human bonds linking those who are victims of the same fate and the formidable quality of those who possess the will to live.

Zeit zu leben und Zeit zu sterben (1954; A Time to Live and a Time to Die, 1954) reveals, through the experiences of a soldier on leave from the front, the portents of the imminent collapse of Nazism.

R. continues to write novels, but, despite his warmth and humanity, his books of recent years—such as *Der Himmel kennt keine Günstlinge* (1961; Heaven Has No Favorites, 1964), a novel about automobile racing—are of small literary merit.

In R.'s ability to achieve immediacy by means of creating realistic characters and situations lies his strength as a novelist. His famous books, which do not pretend to be intellectually illuminating or to provide fundamental explanations, are fine examples of the honest documentary novel.

FURTHER WORKS: *Die letzte Station* (1956); *Der schwarze Obelisk* (1956; The Black Obelisk, 1957); *Die Nacht von Lissabon* (1964; The Night in Lisbon, 1965)

BIBLIOGRAPHY: Pfeiler, W. K., *War and the German Mind* (1941), pp. 140–44; Van Gelder, R., "Writers and Writing," *NY,* 6 Nov. 1943, pp. 26–38

FRIEDRICH WILHELM WOLLENBERG

REMIZOV, Aleksei Mikhailovich

Russian novelist, short-story writer, poet, and dramatist, b. 24 June 1877, Moscow; d. 28 Nov. 1957, Paris

Born into a pious merchant family, R. was given a rigidly Orthodox education. His youth was steeped in an atmosphere of dogma, traditions, and legends surrounding the church, and this spiritual orientation was reinforced by pilgrimages to numerous monasteries. Impoverished after the death of R.'s father, the family lived in a working-class neighborhood, where R. gained firsthand knowledge of the slum life that was to be reflected in some of his early novels.

After an early commercial training, R. studied natural science and history at the University of Moscow. There he became involved in student political activities, and following a socialist demonstration in 1897 he was imprisoned for several months and then expelled to the northern provinces. During five years of exile, he voraciously read the novels and stories of Fiodor Dostoyevski (1821–81), Nikolai Gogol (1809–1852), and Nikolai Leskov (1831–95). He was also deeply attracted to the French symbolists (*see* symbolism) and even translated some of Maeterlinck's (q.v.) poems.

His term of exile over, R. settled in St. Petersburg and was for a time the business manager of *Voprossy Zhizni.* Among R.'s friends during this period were Rozanov, Gorki, and Blok (qq.v.). In 1921 R. was given permission to go abroad for reasons of health, and after two years in Berlin he settled permanently in Paris.

R.'s first publication was a long poem entitled "Epitalami" (1902), after which his works began appearing frequently in symbolist journals, in spite of the fact that they were of a highly personal literary orientation. His early realistic novels were set in the remote provinces that were the scene of his exile or in the city slums he had known as a youth. The influence of Dostoyevski is clear in novels such as *Prud* (1907), *Chasy* (1908; The Clock, 1924), *Pyataya yazva* (1912; The Fifth Pestilence, 1927), and *Stratilatov* (1922), in which R. ex-

presses his repulsion toward a world dominated by the forces of demonic evil. In these works R. shows a strong preference for the grotesque and for direct and brutal scenes that were considered shocking in their day. *Krestovye siostry* (1910), like Gorki's earlier *The Lower Depths* (1902), uses the inhabitants of a single tenement house as a microcosm of man's suffering and humiliation.

In his language and narrative style R. drew heavily on Leskov, further developing the *skaz* —a first-person account in which the author's personality and point of view are cloaked in a narrator who allows him to make full use of the resources of popular language. Like Gogol, R. distorts conventional relationships by focusing on apparently "senseless" details, emphasizing dreamlike elements.

History, folklore, religious legends, and Greco-Byzantine tradition also played a strong part in R.'s literary production beginning with *Limonar* (1907). His love for children and his predilection for fantasy led to fairy tales such as "Tzarevna Mymra" (1908) and "Petushok" (1911), which many critics rank among his best work. Elements of fantasy and free association also play an important part in some of R.'s later works such as *Plyashushchii demon* (1949) and *Podstrizhennymi glazami* (1951), in which his imagination finds a point of departure in memories and in words themselves. Dreams and their distortions dominate much of R.'s writing, and in *Epopeya* (1927) even the Russian Revolution is presented in a series of dreamlike episodes.

R. took no part in politics after his return from tzarist exile, but his books were antagonistic to the spirit of the revolution, which he saw as inevitable but tragic. *Slovo o pogibeli zemli russkoi* (1917) pinpointed westernization as the cause of Russia's woes. Works such as *Mara* (1917) and *Shumy goroda* (1921) paint a somewhat lyrical picture of St. Petersburg about the time of the revolution. Of a similarly poetic nature is *V pole blakitnom* (1922; On a Field of Azure, 1946), a novel dealing with a provincial girl's childhood and education.

During his time in St. Petersburg, R. facetiously founded "The Great and Free Order of the Apes," to which many important writers belonged. *Akhru* (1922—literally "the language of the apes"—one of the first books he wrote after leaving the Soviet Union, therefore had a special significance to those he left behind. It is a fragmentary series of literary portraits.

Worthy of special mention are R.'s stylized

folk dramas such as *Besovskoye deistvo* (1919) and *Tragediya ob Iyude* (1919). During the revolutionary period soldiers of the Red Army often performed his *Tzar' Maksimilian* (1919).

One of the most versatile writers in the 20th c., R. is nevertheless little known in his native land—where his works are not available— or abroad, except for France, where he found one of his most vigorous champions in Arland (q.v.). Translations of his work have been few because of a difficult prose style in which he assiduously avoided "corruptions" introduced into Russian by way of Latin and modern European languages. His influence, however, continued in the Soviet Union through Leonov, Pilnyak, Zamyatin (qq.v.), and those who came after them.

FURTHER WORKS: *Posolon* (1907); *Morshchinka* (1907); *Chto est tabak* (1908); *Chortov log* (1908); *Rasskazy* (1910); *Podorozhiye* (1913); *Dokuka i balagurye* (1914); *Vesenneye porosh'ye* (1915); *Za sviatuyu Rus* (1915); *Ukrepa* (1916); *Sredi muria* (1917); *Nikoliny pritchi* (1917); *Nikola Milostivyi* (1918); *Russkiye zhenshchiny* (1918); *Strannitza* (1918); *O sudbe ognennoi; Snezhok* (1918); *Sibirski pryanik* (1919); *Elektron* (1919); *Zavetnye skazy* (1920); *Tzar Dodon* (1921); *Tibetskiye skazki* (1921); *Ognenniaya Rossiya* (1921); *Skazki obezyany tzarya Asyki* (1922); *E. Tibetski skaz* (1922); *Chakkhchys-Taasu* (1922); *Lalazar* (1922); *Rossiya v pismenakh* (1922); *Krashenye ryla* (1922); *Travamurava* (1922); *Plyas Irodiady* (1922); *Koriavka* (1922); *Bezpriyutnaya* (1922); *Gore-Zlochastnoye* (1922); *Rusaliya* (1922); *Kukkha* (1923); *Skazki russkovo naroda* (1923); *Zvenigorod oklikannyi* (1924); *Zga* (1925); *Vzvikhrennaya Rus* (1927); *Po karnizam* (1929); *Tri serpa* (2 vols., 1929–30); *Obraz Nikoly Chudotvortza* (1931); *Zvezda nadzvezdnaya* (1932); *Golubinaya kniga* (1946); *Povest o dvukh zveryakh* (1950); *Besnovatye* (1951); *Melyuzina* (1952); *V rozovom bleske* (1952); *Myshkina dudochka* (1953); *Ogon' veshchei* (1954); *Martyn Zadeka* (1954); *Tristan i Isolda: Bova Korolevich* (1957)

BIBLIOGRAPHY: Ivanov-Razumnik, R., *Tvorchestvo i kritika* (1922); Gorbov, A., "Mertvaya krasota i zhivucheye bezobraziye," *Krasnaya nov*, No. 7 (1926); Mirsky, D. *Contemporary Russian Literature* (1926); Poggioli, R., *Pietre di paragone* (1939); Lo Gatto, E., *Storia della letteratura russa contemporanea* (1958); Kodryanskaya, N., *A. R.* (1960); Holthusen, J., *Twentieth-Century Russian Literature* (1971); Jünger, H., *The Literatures of the Soviet Peoples* (1971)

* * * *

RENARD, Jules

(pseud.: *Drauer*), French novelist, short-story writer, and diarist, b. 22 Feb. 1864, Châlons-sur-Mayenne; d. 22 May 1910, Paris

After growing up in the country, R. continued, through his years as a student, a commercial clerk, and a "naturalized" Parisian, to feel a close affinity with peasant life and with nature and animals. During his years in Paris, which were significant for his artistic development, he helped to launch (1889) the *Mercure de France*. Before returning to the provinces he had become a socialist.

The last decade of R.'s short life was dominated by (1) literature and (2) his duties as mayor of Chitry-les-Mines. This office, which he assumed in 1904, had a quasi-religious significance for R. This dual "vocation" (in the Roman Catholic sense of the word) is expressed in the *Journal inédit* (1926; Eng., 1964), which reveals so much about R.'s personality and work.

R.'s major work is *Poil de carotte* (1894; Eng., 1965), a fine novel about a painfully unhappy child. Some unusually frank scenes in this novel, especially those in which the child's bitter hostility toward his mother is revealed, show the exceptional candor that was later to appear in R.'s self-portrait in the *Journal inédit*. With the dramatization of *Poil de carotte* in 1900, R. was recognized as one of the major playwrights of the naturalistic theater.

R. is equally realistic in the *Histoires naturelles* (1896; Natural History, 1960), which is made up of stories about animals, plants, and people that are told with the detachment of a natural scientist. About his objectives, R. had this to say: "Buffon described the animals for the delight of man, but I want to please the animals."

R. continued the tradition of the naturalist fiction initiated by Guy de Maupassant (1850–93). With his description of Norman peasant life he made an important contribution to contemporary regional literature.

FURTHER WORKS: *Paris assiégé* (1871); *Histoire de l'Algérie, racontée aux petits enfants* (1884); *Les Roses* (1886); *Crime de village* (1888); *Sourires pincés* (1890); *L'Écornifleur*

(1892); *Coquecigrues* (1893); *La Lanterne sourde* (1893); *Le Coureur de filles* (1894); *Le Vigneron dans sa vigne* (1894); *La Maîtresse* (1896); *Le Plaisir de rompre* (1898); *Bucolique* (1898); *Le Pain de ménage* (1899); *Huit jours à la campagne* (1906); *Les Philippe, précédé de Patrie!* (1907); *Nos Frères farouches* (1908); *Ragotte* (1908); *La Bigote* (1909); *Les Cloportes* (1919); *Œuvres complètes* (17 vols., 1925–27); *Correspondance de J. R.* (1928); *Journal et correspondance* (5 vols., 1933); *Monsieur Vernet* (1933); *J. R. par lui même* (2 vols., 1956); *Journal 1887–1910* (1960)

BIBLIOGRAPHY: Guichard, L., *L'œuvre et l'âme de J. R.* (1936); Nardin, P., *La langue et le style de J. R.* (1942); Bloch-Michel, J., "J. R. ou la comédie bourgeoise," *Preuves*, No. 107 (1960), pp. 74–77; Mignon, M., "J. R. auteur dramatique," *Table Ronde*, No. 156 (1960), pp. 92–103

BRIGITTE KAHR

REVERDY, Pierre

French poet, b. 13 Sept. 1889, Narbonne; d. 21 June 1960, Solesmes

In 1917 R. became chief editor of the literary journal *Nord-Sud,* which published contributions by Apollinaire, Jacob, and Aragon (qq.v.). After his return to the Roman Catholic Church in 1926, R. lived in seclusion near the Benedictine monastery at Solesmes.

R.'s poetry is concrete, anti-intellectual, and mystical. It attempts to create "the sublime simplicity of true reality" rather than the world of outward appearances. To achieve this, he uses contrasting metaphors and listings and handles reality as a relative, as something which is determined according to who sees it at which moment (perspectivism).

R.'s *Poèmes en prose* (1915) are sketches of human suffering, many of which end with a moralistic twist. The themes of *La Lucarne ovale* (1916) are war and human consciousness. *Les Jockeys camouflés* (1918) contains apocalyptic visions.

Rimbaud's challenge "to embrace stark reality" may be considered the point of departure of R.'s poetry. Like Apollinaire and Cendrars (qq.v.), R. is also a precursor of surrealism (q.v.). R.'s work has had a significant though somewhat indirect influence on recent French lyric poetry.

FURTHER WORKS: *Quelques poèmes* (1916);

Les Ardoises du toit (1918); *La Guitare endormie* (1919); *Self-defense* (1919); *Cœur de chêne* (1921); *Les Épaves du ciel* (1924); *Écumes de la mer* (1925); *Grande nature* (1925); *La Peau de l'homme* (1926); *Le Gant de crin* (1927); *Sources du vent* (1929); *Flaques de verre* (1929); *Ferraille* (1937); *Plupart du temps* (1945); *Le Livre de mon bord* (1948); *Main d'œuvre 1913–1949* (1950); *En vrac* (1956). **Selected English translation:** *P. R., Selected Poems* (1968)

BIBLIOGRAPHY: Rousselot, J., and Manoll, M., *P. R.* (1951); Stojković, E., *L'œuvre poétique de R.* (1951); Bajarlía, J., *La polémica R.-Huidobro* (1964); Brunner, P., *P. R.* (1966); Guiney, M., *La poésie de P. R.* (1966); Rizzuto, A., "The Style and Themes of P. R.'s *Les ardoises du toit,*" *DA*, XXVII (1967), 3878A–79A; Greene, R., *The Poetic Theory of P. R.* (1967)

MARK TEMMER

REXROTH, Kenneth

American poet, critic, and playwright, b. 22 Dec. 1905, South Bend, Indiana

An Autobiographical Novel (1966), focusing on R.'s precocious youth in Chicago, is a brilliant introduction to his intellectual power, his uncompromising revolt against the "Social Lie," and the visionary communion with nature that is the core of his personality. Some of his early experiments in literary cubism, collected in *The Art of Worldly Wisdom* (1949), have endured as contributions to The Revolution of the Word, in which he participated along with Gertrude Stein and Joyce (qq.v.).

R.'s first long philosophical revery, *The Homestead Called Damascus,* was written in his youth but was not published until 1963. His more direct and polemical poems, written during the 1930's and collected in *In What Hour* (1940), confront the total crisis of that decade. His second long philosophical poem, *The Phoenix and the Tortoise* (1944), expresses his anarcho-pacifist ethic of total responsibility, toughened by the terror of World War II.

Some of R.'s most intense lyrics of love and visionary transcendence may be found in *The Signature of All Things* (1950). These themes find dramatic realization in *Beyond the Mountains* (1951), a tragic tetralogy based on classical subjects and first performed by the Living Theater. In *The Dragon and the*

Unicorn (1952), R. explores love and philosophical dilemmas in his travels through decadent postwar Europe.

R. emerged in the 1950's as the mentor of the San Francisco poetry renaissance and the Beat Generation, though he repudiated excesses of the movement. His most famous "Beat" poem is the prophetic "Thou Shalt Not Kill," a memorial to Dylan Thomas (q.v.) in the collection *In Defense of the Earth* (1956). His denunciation of the antipersonal forces of destruction in modern society—militarism, industrialism, capitalism, collectivization—continues in several collections of essays such as *Bird in the Bush* (1959), *Assays* (1961), and *The Alternative Society* (1970). In these works he also seeks renewal in visionary communion and face-to-face community.

R. has long been admired as a translator by many who resist his radical ideas. His translations from Japanese, Chinese, French, Spanish, Greek, and Latin show that his humanism is not merely intellectual, but that his fine sensibility has been shaped by many traditions. Primitive shamanism, classical wisdom, Judeo-Christian prophecy, modern science and philosophy, Chinese and Japanese Buddhism—all have been assimilated into his personal vision. In R.'s most recent long poem, *The Heart's Garden the Garden's Heart* (1967), written in Japan, he conveys the Zen Buddhist experience of *satori*—"Listening / Deep in his mind to music / Lost far off in space and time."

FURTHER WORKS: *Fourteen Poems of O. V. Lubicz-Milosz* (trans., 1952); *A Bestiary for My Daughters Mary and Katherine* (1955); *Poems from the Greek and Latin* (1955); *One Hundred French Poems* (1955); *One Hundred Poems from the Japanese* (1955); *One Hundred Poems from the Chinese* (1956); *Thirty Spanish Poems of Love and Exile* (1956); *Poems from the Greek Anthology* (1962); *Natural Numbers* (1963); *The Collected Shorter Poems* (1967); *Collected Longer Poems* (1968); *The Classics Revisited* (1968); *Pierre Reverdy: Selected Poems* (trans., 1970); *Love and the Turning Year: One Hundred More Poems from the Chinese* (1970)

BIBLIOGRAPHY: Stepanchev, S., *American Poetry since 1945: A Critical Survey* (1965); Hartzell, J., and Zumwinkle, R., eds., *K. R.: A Checklist of His Published Writings* (with Foreword by L. C. Powell, 1967)

MORGAN GIBSON

REYES, Alfonso

Mexican poet, short-story writer, and essayist, b. 17 May 1889, Monterrey; d. 27 Dec. 1959, Mexico City

R. began his literary career in 1906 by writing poems under the influence of the parnassians. Goethe (whom he wrote about), the Spanish poet Góngora (1561–1627), and Mallarmé (1842–98) all contributed to his artistic development. In 1910 R., along with Pedro Henríquez Ureña, Antonio Caso (1883–1946), José Vasconcelos (1881–1959), and others, began to pave the way for a literary renascence in Mexico. In 1913 he obtained his law degree. Until 1939 he was a diplomat, living first in France and Spain and later in Brazil and Argentina. He founded the Colegio Nacional de México.

R.'s first book, *Cuestiones estéticas* (1911), established him as a master of style. R.'s *Visión de Anáhuac* (1917), which Valéry Larbaud called "truly national poetry," recreates the world of the Indians at the time of the arrival of the Conquistadores. In the drama *Ifigenia cruel* (1924) R. presents the mythological Iphigenia from a 20th-c. viewpoint.

The bulk of R.'s work consists of short stories (*El plano oblicuo*, 1920), chronicles (*Las vísperas de España*, 1937), and numerous critical studies and essays (*e.g.*, *La experiencia literaria*, 1942; *El deslinde*, 1944).

R. is generally credited with having made a major contribution to the intellectual life of 20th-c. Mexico.

FURTHER WORKS: *Simpatías y diferencias* (1921–26); *Huellas* (1922); *Noche de Mayo* (1924); *Pausa* (1926); *Fuga de Navidad* (1929); *El testimonio de Juan Peña* (1930); *La saeta* (1931); *En el ventanillo de Toledo* (1931); *Horas de Burgos* (1932); *Algunos poemas* (1941); *La casa del grillo* (1945); *Cortesía* (1948); *Obras completas* (13 vols., 1955–61). Selected English translation: *Mexico in a Nutshell, and Other Essays* (1964)

BIBLIOGRAPHY: Campaña, A., *Catálogo de índices de los libros de A. R.* (1955); Hispanic Institute of New York, ed., *Essays on A. R.* (1957); Olguín, M., *A. R.* (1958); Robb, J. W., *A. R.* (1958); Aponte, B., "The Spanish Friendships of A. R.," *DA*, XXV (1964), 467–68; Koldewyn, P., "A. R. as a Critic of Peninsular Spanish Literature," *LA*, XXVI (1965), 1648–49; Hernandez, D., "A. R. as a Literary Critic,"

DA, XXVII (1966), 775A–76A; Aponte, B., "The Dialogue between A. R. and Spain," *Symposium*, XXII (1968), 5–15

ALÍ CHUMACERO

REYLES, Carlos

Uruguayan novelist, b. 30 Oct. 1868, Montevideo, Uruguay; d. there, 24 July 1938

Born into a wealthy family of Irish descent (O'Reilly), R. belonged to Uruguay's landed aristocracy. After studying at the Colegio Hispano-Uruguayo, he came into a substantial inheritance that permitted him to travel to Europe in 1886 and to live for a while in Spain.

R.'s first novel, *Por la vida* (1888), which contains a good deal of autobiographical data, attacks the social and economic class to which he belonged.

The publication of the masterpiece *Bebá* (1894) secured for R. his position as one of the great writers of the *mester de gauchería* (the rural novel of Latin America). Conceived in the tradition of French naturalism (q.v.), its blatant determinism evoked a storm of protest both in Uruguay and Argentina.

La raza de Caín (1900), whose action takes place in an urban setting, is another venture in determinism. In it R. attempts to examine the psychological defects of his weak characters, all of whom are destined to meet failure at the hands of stronger adversaries.

In *El terruño* (1916), another masterpiece of *mester de gauchería*, R. continued to develop his characters from a deterministic point of view. This is the story of the headstrong confrontation between two brothers that ends in the destruction of both. The novel also contains a subplot in which the regeneration of an impractical idealist is traced.

R.'s best-known work is perhaps *El embrujo de Sevilla* (1922; Castanets, 1929), in which he uses a distinct *modernista* style to convey the heady atmosphere of Andalusia and to evoke the Spanish soul as it is revealed in the popular ballad, dance, and the traditional bullfight. This novel represents R.'s greatest success both from the standpoint of popular international acclaim and from that of technical mastery. Here the sometimes crude realism and the naturalistic determinism of previous novels gives way to blending of impressionistic scenes of fire, color, and passion.

R.'s last novel, *El gaucho Florido* (1932), contains a precisely observed rendering of rural mores in the style of *Béba*. This tale of violent love and death is marred by its excessive use of melodramatic situations.

All of R.'s novels are based on previously published short stories. This technique enabled R. to develop carefully the psychological and sociological aspects of a tale after he had crystallized the plot.

In the minds of a number of critics R. is considered the outstanding Uruguayan novelist of his generation.

FURTHER WORKS: *Primitivo* (1896); *Las Academias* (3 vols., 1896–98); *El extraño* (1897); *El sueño de la rapiña* (1898); *El ideal nuevo* (1903); *La muerte del cisne* (1911); *Diálogos olímpicos* (1924); *El nuevo sentido de la narración gauchesca* (1930); *Ego sum* (1939); *A batallas de amor . . . campos de pluma* (1939)

BIBLIOGRAPHY: Zum Felde, A., *Proceso intelectual del Uruguay*, II (1930); Torres-Rioseco, A., *Grandes Novelistas de la América Hispana* (1941); Lerna Acevedo de Blixen, J., *R.* (1943); Benedetti, M., *La literatura uruguaya del 900* (1950); Menafra, L. A., *C. R.* (1957); Gates, E. J., "Popular Speech, 'Gitanismos,' and Bullfighting Terms in *El embrujo de Sevilla*," *Hispania*, XLV (1961), 422–27; Guillot, M., *La conversación de C. R.* (1966)

HARLEY D. OBERHELMAN

REYMONT, Władysław Stanisław

Polish novelist, b. 2 May 1867, Kobiele Wielkie; d. 5 Dec. 1925, Warsaw

R., who came from peasant stock, was self-educated. At various times he was an actor with a road company, a lay brother in the famous monastery at Częstochowa, and a railway official. R. won the Nobel Prize for Literature in 1924.

One of R.'s major works is *Ziemia obiecana* (1899; The Promised Land, 1927), a novel that recalls Zola's (q.v.) descriptions of the urban community. Here R. presents a grim picture of the unruly expansion of the industrial town of Lodz, which is subject to no check but the debasing struggle for money, with its speculations and other concomitants.

The novel *Chłopi* (1904–1909; The Peasants, 1924–25) is usually rated as R.'s finest work. This peasant epic and chronicle of village life narrates the happenings that occur in a period of a year. This work is divided into four

ALFONSO REYES

CARLOS REYLES

volumes: autumn, winter, spring, and summer. Work in the fields, weddings, christenings, funerals, and Sunday services in the village church are recurring motifs in this saga of eroticism, avarice, and other human passions. The work, written almost entirely in peasant dialect, was translated into many languages.

R.'s later works are of little literary merit. His short stories and novels—*Spotkanie* (1897), *Komediantka* (1896; The Comedienne, 1920)— are written in a naturalistic, factual style. Gradually R. adopted the technique of short, swiftly sketched scenes and a style that was impressionistic, almost pointillistic. Throughout R.'s work one feels his struggle to maintain control over his profuse observations. This prodigality of impressions also dominates *Ziemia obiecana*. The unfortunate result is that R.'s writing is marred by the overuse of embellishing adjectives and other kinds of excessive verbosity.

The literary evaluation of R. is far from consistent. Nevertheless, his ability to capture vividly the aspects of life that aroused his imagination earns for him in the eyes of many the right to be considered one of the major writers of Poland.

FURTHER WORKS: *Pielgrzymka do Jasnej Góry* (1895); *Fermenty* (2 vols., 1897); *Sprawiedliwie* (1899; Justice, 1925); *Lili* (1899); *W jesienną noc* (1900); *Prezed świtem* (1902); *Komurasaki* (1903); *Z pamiętnika* (1903); *Na krawędzi* (1907); *Burza* (1908); *Marzyciel* (1910); *Z ziemi chełmskiej* (1910); *Wampir* (1911); *Rok 1794* (3 vols., 1913–18); *Insurekcja* (1919); *Za frontem* (1919); *Osądzona* (1923); *Legenda* (1924); *Bunt* (1924); *Krosnowa i świat* (1928); *Pisma* (36 vols., 1930–32)

BIBLIOGRAPHY: Schoell, F. L., *Les paysans de L. R.* (1925); Krzyżanowski, J., *W. R.* (1937); Burdecki, L., *W. R.* (1953); Heltberg, K., "W. R.," in *Fremmede digtere i det 20. århundrede,* Kristensen, S., ed. (1967), Vol. I, 369–79

* * *

RHODESIAN LITERATURE

In Rhodesia (formerly Southern Rhodesia) the white inhabitants have produced a fair amount of imaginative writing in English. From the Negro population, only two English-language writers have emerged thus far. There is the renowned poet Dennis Brutus, who was born (1924) in Salisbury but has spent most of his life in the Republic of South Africa. And more recently, there is Stanlake SamKange (b. 1924), who now lives in the United States, where he wrote his historical novel, *On Trial for My Country* (1967).

The Bantu peoples of Rhodesia fall into two main groups: 3,500,000 Shonas and 600,000 Ndebele. Like all preliterate societies, both these groups have a vast legacy of oral lore that deserves more attention than it has as yet received. Contrary to what happened in the Xhosa, Sotho, and Zula languages, the Shonas and the Ndebele did not begin to write belles-lettres in their own languages until quite recently.

The Rhodesia Literature Bureau, modeled after similar institutions set up at earlier dates in Northern Nigeria (1944) and in East Africa (1948), was officially established in 1954.

Since 1957 the bureau has assisted some eighteen Shona and seven Ndebele writers and arranged for the publication of their works in cooperation with British, South African, or Rhodesian publishing firms.

Like Kenneth Bepswa (b. 1927; Shona) and David Ndoda (b. 1925; Ndebele), most of these Rhodesian-Bantu writers are schoolteachers. Others, such as Patrick Chakaipa (b. 1932; Shona) and Emmanuel F. Ribeiro (b. 1935; Shona), are Roman Catholic priests. Solomon M. Mutswairo (b. 1924; Shona) and P. S. Mahlangu (b. 1923; Ndebele) are the only two university graduates (from Fort Hare, South Africa).

It is significant that both Mutswairo and Mahlangu should have turned to an imaginative reassessment of the Rhodesian pre-Christian past and of its values. But the outlook of most Rhodesian-Bantu writers, as it appears in their published works, is determined by their adherence to Christianity, considerably strengthened, one may presume, by the present racial and political conditions in the country. The white man, who plays such a prominent part in Rhodesian experience, is conspicuously absent from Rhodesian-Bantu fiction and poetry. The tribal past is usually presented as a time of superstition and continuous warfare. The theme of love and marriage is consistently handled in terms of Christian ethics. The objects of criticism are usually those members of the *évolué* class, teachers and ministers, who lapse into traditional beliefs and customs.

Little vernacular poetry has been printed in book form. In the late 1960's, however, multilingual, biracial little magazines that provide opportunity for publication of vernacular poetry, such as *Two Tone* and *Rhodesian Poetry,* have been published.

BIBLIOGRAPHY: Krog, E. W., ed., *African Literature in Rhodesia* (1966)

ALBERT S. GÉRARD

RIBA BRACÓNS, Carles

Spanish poet and critic (writing in Catalan), b. 23 Sept. 1893, Barcelona; d. there, 12 Aug. 1959

R. studied law, humanities, and linguistics in Barcelona and Madrid. His translations of Plutarch, the *Odyssey,* the complete tragedies of Aeschylus and Sophocles, and of many modern authors, including Hölderlin (1770–1843), indicate that he was a committed humanist. After the Spanish Civil War R. went to France; he returned to Barcelona in 1942.

Though R.'s poetry continues in the tradition of Carner (q.v.), his work reveals a greater capacity for emotion and reflection and an attention to exact form. His collection *Estances* (I, 1919; II, 1930) contains what may well be the most important poems in the Catalan language. Here, in a constant self-communion from which the world is never absent, R. holds quiet dialogues with his conscience, his soul, his joy or remorse, and with life and death. His poetry has been called intellectual and hermetic, but it does in fact possess a strongly humane and passionate tension.

Human emotional impulses clamor urgently for expression in the beautiful *Elegies de Bierville* (1942), which stems partly from R.'s years of exile.

These were followed by *Del joc i del foc* (1947), a collection of verse written in the *tanka* form—the classic Japanese poetic form of thirty-one syllables. Here are lyrics that were R.'s response to a single thing, a single thought.

The sonnets in *Salvatge cor* (1952) show the excellence of form found in all R.'s earlier work—and an even greater readiness and ability to communicate the clarity of thought and depth of emotion also found in them. In *Esbós de tres oratoris* (1957), which revolves around freely adapted traditional Christian themes (the three Magi, Lazarus raised from the dead, the prodigal son), R. presents movingly the experiences he incurred in his search for God.

FURTHER WORKS: *Escolis i altres articles* (1921); *Els Marges* (1927); *Tres suites* (1937); *Per comprendre* (1937); *Obra poética* (1956); *Obres completes* (2 vols., 1967). **Selected English translation:** *Poems* (1964)

BIBLIOGRAPHY: Ferraté, J., *C. R. avui* (1955); Crusat, P., "C. R. y sus obras completas," *Insula,* XXI (1966), 11; Foster, V., "Examples of *La bella dormida* in Catalan Literature," *RomN,* VIII (1966), 22–28; Prefatory materials to *Obres completes,* ed. J.-L. Marfany (2 vols., 1967)

GONZALO SOBEJANO

RIBEIRO, Aquilino

Portuguese novelist, short-story writer, and essayist, b. 13 Sept. 1885, Carregal (near Sernancelhe); d. 27 Sept. 1963, Lisbon

R. studied philosophy in Lisbon, and then, after being exiled for political reasons, in Paris. After his return to Portugal he was a schoolteacher and later a librarian and curator at the national library in Lisbon.

In 1913, R. published his first book, *Jardim das tormentas,* a collection of short stories. After this he developed the originality of language and narrative technique that characterized his peasant novel *Terras do Demo* (1917) and in *A via sinuosa* (1919), a novel about youth. He wrote of rural life in his native Beira-Alta, with its dour characters and simple, often primitive living conditions. By these novels R. initiated the regional-literature genre in Portuguese literature.

R.'s talent reached its peak in *Estrada de Santiago* (1922), a lively, picaresque first-person account of the adventures of a muleteer. After *Andam faunos pelos bosques* (1926), a novel about a country priest, he turned to other themes.

Maria Benigna (1931) is a disillusioned novel of city society told from the point of view of the main characters, in letters and diaries. *A aventura maravilhosa de D. Sebastião* (1936) is an imaginative treatment of 16th-c. historical material. *Lápides partidas* (1943) is a sequel to the earlier *A via sinuosa,* but is set in Lisbon.

Biographies, historical portraits, essays in literary history, and folklore studies demonstrate the wide range of R.'s vigorous literary interests, which he weighed and analyzed in the polemical *Abóboras no telhado* (1955).

FURTHER WORKS: *Filhas de Babilónia* (1920); *Romance da raposa* (1924); *O homem que matou o diabo* (1930); *A batalha sem fim* (1932); *As três mulheres de Samsão* (1932); *É a guerra* (1934); *Quando ao gavião cai a pena* (1935); *S. Banaboião, anacoreta e mártir* (1937); *Anastácio da Cunha, o lente penitenciado* (1938); *Monica* (1938; Eng., 1961); *Por obra e graça* (1940); *O servo de Deus e a casa roubada* (1941); *Os avós dos nossos avós* (1942); *Volfrâmio* (1943); *O arcanjo negro* (1946); *Caminhos errados* (1947); *Cinco réis de gente* (1948); *Uma luz ao longe* (1948); *Camões, Camilo, Eça e alguns mais* (1949); *Luis de Camões* (1950); *Portugueses das sete partidas* (1950); *Geografia sentimental: história, paisagem, folclore* (1951); *Príncipes de Portugal* (1952); *Humildade gloriosa* (1953); *Arcas encoiradas* (1953); *Quando os lobes huivam* (1954; When the Wolves Howl, 1963); *Obras* (1958)

BIBLIOGRAPHY: Branco Chaves, C., *A. R.* (1938); Mendes, M., *A. R.* (1960); Namora, F., *A. R.* (1963); Moser, G., "A. R.," *Hispania,* XLVII (1964), 339–42; Lopes, O., "O mundo pícaro de A. R.," *Vértice,* XXV (1965), 885–96; Moser, G., "Portuguese Writers of This Century," *Hispania,* L (1967), 947–54

ALBIN EDUARD BEAU

RICE, Elmer

(pseud. of *Elmer Leopold Reizenstein*), American playwright, novelist, and essayist, b. 28 Sept. 1892, New York City; d. 8 May 1967, Southampton, England

Supporting himself by clerical work, R. attended New York Law School and graduated in 1912. When he was admitted to the bar in New York the following year, he was studying drama at Columbia University and writing a one-act comedy, *The Passing of Chow-Chow* (pub., 1935), for a competition there. Though his preference for the theater was quickly confirmed, he remained passionately concerned with the relationship between law and justice.

A "utopian socialist," R. was steadfastly opposed to all forms of authoritarianism. During World War II, as a member of the American Civil Liberties Union, R. vigorously fought for the rights of interned Japanese-Americans, and in the decade that followed he was active in the fight against the blacklisting and antiliberalism that characterized the McCarthy era.

R.'s legal training served as the background for the first of his plays to be produced on Broadway, *On Trial* (prod., 1914; pub., 1919). A critical and popular success, it was the first American play to employ the flashback technique developed by the movies.

In the following years R. was involved with several noncommercial theatrical groups, but in 1923 he was represented on Broadway by *The Adding Machine* (pub., 1923). A highly stylized drama of modern "machine man"— whose protagonist, appropriately enough, is Mr. Zero—the play has retained much of its validity over the years and may ultimately be remembered as R.'s best. Though it makes use of many of the techniques of German expressionist drama (*see* expressionism), R. disclaimed any previous detailed knowledge of these overseas developments.

The high point of R.'s popular success was reached with the Pulitzer Prize drama *Street Scene* (1929), which he called his "most experimental play." In it he presented events during a single day in the lives of the inhabitants of a New York tenement. The careful patterning of fluctuating, disparate elements is given theatrical unity by the constant of the house itself. A musical adaptation of the play was written in 1947 by Kurt Weill on a libretto by R. and lyrics by Hughes (q.v.).

More conventional in form were *Left Bank* (1931), a glimpse into the dissatisfactions of American expatriates in France, and *Counsellor-at-Law* (1931), the drama of a lawyer's fight against efforts to disbar him. An advanced "panoramic" technique was used in *We, the People* (1933) in an attempt to convey a total picture of contemporary life as Dos Passos (q.v.) was doing in his novels. R.'s dissatisfaction with the economic and political trends of the 1930's are expressed in a story whose multifarious strands converge on the central theme of a nation betrayed by self-seeking in high places. Unfortunately, however, in this time of economic depression the people to whom, and for whom, the play spoke most directly had no money for entertainment, and the production folded after six turbulent weeks.

Entertainment, however, was never R.'s purpose in the theater. "I have always been, and still am," he said in 1934, "interested in the drama as an art form, a social force, and a medium for the expression of ideas." That same year he acquired the David Belasco Theatre and attempted to establish a permanent repertory group. Among the plays he presented there during the company's brief life were *Judgement Day* (1934), a drama

157

based on the burning of the Reichstag by the Nazis, and *Between Two Worlds* (prod., 1934; pub., 1935), in which he contrasted the political ideologies of the United States and the Soviet Union. Both plays were more enthusiastically received abroad than at home, where they were considered exaggerated and propagandistic.

Blasting the critics in the satire *Not for Children* (pub., 1935; prod. as "Life Is Real," 1937), R. announced his retirement from the theater, but soon decided to become the New York Regional Director of the WPA Federal Theater Project. His consistent refusal to compromise cut short his tenure (1935–36). In 1937 he joined with Maxwell Anderson, Sherwood (qq.v.), S. N. Behrman (b. 1893), and Sidney Howard (1891–1939) in forming the famous Playwrights' Company, which disbanded in 1950.

Among R.'s better-known later plays were *American Landscape* (prod., 1938; pub., 1939), which dealt with radical intolerance and the conflict between labor and capital; *Two on an Island* (1940), a romantic comedy; *Flight to the West* (prod., 1940; pub., 1941), an indictment of Nazism; and *Dream Girl* (prod., 1945; pub., 1946), a comedy about an over-imaginative girl, which starred his actress wife, Betty Field. Several new plays were produced during the 1950's, but all were relatively unsuccessful, even though they showed continued advances in combining experimental techniques with dramatic realism.

R.'s nondramatic writings include the novels *Voyage to Purilia* (1930), *Imperial City* (1937), and *The Show Must Go On* (1949), as well as two collections of essays—*Supreme Freedom* (1949) and *Living Theatre* (1959)—and an autobiography, *Minority Report* (1963).

A bold and innovative writer, R. was not always successful in his execution of dramatic themes, but he held fast to his ideal of theater as "an instrument of enlightenment." He was important in making American theater audiences receptive to a wide range of ideas and techniques.

FURTHER WORKS: *The Iron Cross* (prod., 1917); *The Home of the Free* (prod., 1917–18; pub., 1934); *Find the Woman* (prod., ca. 1918); *For the Defense* (prod., 1919); *Wake Up, Jonathan* (with Hatcher Hughes; prod., 1920; pub., 1928); *It Is the Law* (prod., 1922); *Close Harmony, or the Lady Next Door* (with Dorothy Parker; prod., 1924; pub., 1929); *Cock Robin* (with Philip Barry; prod., 1928; pub., 1929); *The*

Subway (1929); *See Naples and Die* (prod., 1929; pub., 1930); *Black Sheep* (prod., 1932; pub., 1938); *House in Blind Alley* (pub., 1932); *A New Life* (prod., 1943; pub., 1944); *The Grand Tour* (prod., 1951; pub., 1952); *The Winner* (1954); *Cue for Passion* (prod., 1958; pub., 1959); *Love among the Ruins* (1963)

BIBLIOGRAPHY: Levin, M., "E. R.," *Theatre Arts Monthly*, Jan. 1932, pp. 54–63; Collins, R. L., "The Playwright and the Press: E. R. and His Critics," *Theatre Annual: 1948–1949*, VII (1949), 35–58; Hogan, R., *The Independence of E. R.* (1965)

VERGENE F. LEVERENZ

RICHARDSON, Dorothy Miller

English novelist, b. 17 May 1873, Abingdon, Oxfordshire; d. 17 June 1957, Beckenham, Kent

From the point of view of Miriam Henderson, the protagonist of *Pilgrimage* (collected in 4 vols., 1938; expanded ed., 1967), Dorothy R. gives in detail the biographical data of her own first thirty years—her personal associations, her experiences, her development. This narrative is made up of the following novels: *Pointed Roofs* (1915), *Backwater* (1916), *Honeycomb* (1917), *The Tunnel* (1919), *Interim* (1919), *Deadlock* (1921), *Revolving Lights* (1923), *The Trap* (1925), *Oberland* (1927), *Dawn's Left Hand* (1931), *Clear Horizon* (1935), *Dimple Hill* (1938), and *March Moonlight* (1967).

In the lengthy *Pilgrimage*, Dorothy R. attempts to represent the whole effect of every experience on Miriam's sensibility. The narrative, whose most important action is set in London, provides, at one level, descriptions of Miriam's jobs, of her membership in an avant-garde intellectual group, of her friendships with the prototypes of Amy and H. G. Wells (q.v.), and other *engagé* people, of her conflict between individualism and her intellectual commitments, of her love affairs, of her association and later disillusionment with the Fabians ("Lycurgans") and other groups, of her interest in the Quakers (about whom Dorothy R. wrote three books), of her turning to writing, of the fortunes of her three sisters. It ends in 1915 with the meeting of Miriam with the artist Mr. Noble (Dorothy R. married Alan Odle, an artist, in 1917).

Unified by themes as well as by a central consciousness, *Pilgrimage* traces a threefold spiritual quest for self-realization and for "an available identity" as an "indestructible individuality," a timeless and universal self or "being"; as an intellectual, modern English woman, reacting to experience or "becoming"; as an immortal soul, seeking and finding the light of God and immortality. The quest for identity as an artist is largely implicit.

In her conception and technique, Dorothy R. was influenced by John Bunyan, Charlotte Brontë, Dostoyevski, Conrad (q.v.), and James (q.v.). In the formulation of her ideas she was indebted to Ralph Waldo Emerson, Evelyn Underhill, the Quaker Rufus Jones, and J. M. E. McTaggart.

Varied qualities distinguish Dorothy R.'s achievement. In her day the techniques by which she represented Miriam "eagerly watching her thoughts" were original. Light images recur throughout *Pilgrimage* as thematic motifs; imagistic impressionism and stream-of-consciousness free association of ideas decrease in frequency as the narrative proceeds; and interior monologue (q.v.), discursive analysis of self and others, and meditation on ideas increase to reflect Miriam's developing maturity. Blocks of objective time provide a framework for free-flowing subjective time. Some intensely painful episodes are presented only in reminiscence.

A pioneer in psychological fiction, Dorothy R.'s importance in literary history has been overshadowed by that of such successors as Virginia Woolf (q.v.). Dorothy R.'s achievement is that she provided a cultural history of her times through the medium of a selective feminine consciousness, born in the 19th c. but reborn as a "new woman" in the 20th. The reader will profit from immersion in an intense, free-ranging, sensitive, intelligent feminine personality.

FURTHER WORKS: *The Quakers Past and Present* (1914); *Gleanings from the Works of George Fox* (1914); *John Austen and the Inseparables* (1930)

BIBLIOGRAPHY: Powys, J. C., *D. M. R.* (1931); Beach, J., "Imagism: D. R.," in *The Twentieth Century Novel* (1932); Edel, L., *The Modern Psychological Novel, 1900–1950* (1955); Edel, L., "D. M. R., 1882–1957," *MFS*, IV (1958), 165–68; Blake, C., *D. R.* (1960); Glikin, G., "D. M. R.: The Personal Pilgrimage," *PMLA*, LXXVIII (1963), 586–600; Gilkin, G., "Checklist of the Writings of D. M. R." (pp. 1–11) and "D. M. R.: An Annotated Bibliography of Writings about Her" (pp. 12– 35), *English Literature in Transition*, VIII (1965); Gregory, H., *D. R.: An Adventure in Self-Discovery* (1967)

ELIZABETH M. KERR

RICHARDSON, Henry Handel

(pseud. of *Ethel Florence Lindesay Richardson Robertson*), Australian novelist, b. 3 Jan. 1870, Melbourne; d. 20 March 1946, Sussex, England

Mrs. R. lived outside of Australia after 1887. After studying music in Leipzig for three years, she began her writing career with articles on music and Scandinavian authors. In 1896 she translated J. P. Jacobsen's (1847–85) *Niels Lyhne* (Siren Voices) and Bjørnstjerne Bjørnson's (1832–1910) *Fiskerjenten* (The Fisher Lass). From *Niels Lyhne* Mrs. R. formulated her lifetime fiction-writing objective: she would adhere to a "romanticism imbued with the scientific spirit and essentially based on realism."

All of Mrs. R.'s works (except her last book) are ultimately founded on some aspect of her personal life. *Maurice Guest* (1908), set in the bohemian music world of Leipzig in the 1890's, pictures love as a destructive passion and suggests that success in art and love depends on a Nietzschean genius for transcending the ordinary. An apprenticeship work, it shows the combined influences of Jacobsen, Flaubert, Turgenev, Dostoyevski, Lev Tolstoi (q.v.), D'Annunzio (q.v.), and Nietzsche (q.v.).

The Getting of Wisdom (1910) is the story of Mrs. R.'s adolescent years at the Presbyterian Ladies' College in Melbourne in the 1880's. With realism and comic irony, she traces a girl's growth to worldly wisdom through struggles with the problems of truth, sin, sex, and art. The work shows the influence of Bjørnson, Charlotte Brontë, and Nietzsche.

Mrs. R. reached artistic independence with *The Fortunes of Richard Mahony* (revised complete ed., 1930), a cycle of three biographical novels: *Australia Felix* (1917), *The Way Home* (1925), and *Ultima Thule* (1929). *Ultima Thule* is widely regarded as her best work. An interpretive, naturalistic rendering of Mrs. R.'s father's life, this trilogy is the history of a hypersensitive Anglo-Irish physician, a social and psychological misfit in Australia and, indeed, in the whole world itself. The tension between established colonials and English immigrants from the 1850's through the 1870's forms the background of this narrative. The protagonist's unsuccessful battle with his environment and himself, in which he is mentally and physically destroyed, has the inevitability, irony, and existence of fate as an all-powerful agency of Greek tragedy.

The End of a Childhood (1934) is a collection of short stories, the longest of which centers on Mahony's young son. Eight of its sketches depicting young girls are written in the same vein as *The Getting of Wisdom.*

In *The Young Cosima* (1939), a heavily documented but unsuccessful biographical novel, Mrs. R. returns to the questions of *Maurice Guest*—the nature of genius and the motives of a woman who flouts convention. Here disastrous love is presented as it affected the famous triangle of Richard Wagner, Cosima Liszt von Bülow, and Hans von Bülow.

Despite faults of style and limitations of imagination in all of her fiction, Mrs. R. is a superior Australian novelist in the English-European tradition.

FURTHER WORKS: *Two Studies* (1931); *Myself When Young* (1948)

BIBLIOGRAPHY: Richardson, H. H., "Some Notes on My Books," *VQR,* XVI (1940), 334–47; Robertson, J. G., "The Art of H. H. R.," in R.'s *Myself When Young* (1948); Palmer, N., *H. H. R.: A Study* (1950); Gibson, L. J., *H. H. R. and Some of Her Sources* (1954); Haynes, M. S., "H. H. R.," *BB,* XXI (1955), 130–5; Hope, A. D., "H. H. R.'s *Maurice Guest,*" *Meanjin,* XIV (1955), 186–99; Buckley, V., *H. H. R.* (1962); Triebel, L. A., "The Young Cosima," *Australian Letters,* V (1962), 53–7; Wilkes, G. A., ed., Special H. H. R. issue, *Southerly* (1963); Barnes, J., "Australian Fiction to 1920," and Kramer, L., "H. H. R.," in *The Literature of Australia,* ed. G. Dutton (1964)

VERNA D. WITTROCK

RIDDER, Alfons de
See Elsschot, Willem

RILKE, Rainer Maria
German poet, b. 4 Dec. 1875, Prague; d. 29 Dec. 1926, Valmont (near Montreux), Switzerland

R. was the son of a railway official who for medical reasons had had to resign from his

military career without obtaining the commission he coveted. His mother came from a family of manufacturers and government servants, who had for a time enjoyed a certain degree of wealth. According to a family tradition—to which R. himself attached great importance—the Prague Rilkes were descended from the oldest Carinthian nobility, but this legendary noble lineage proved to be inauthentic. The Prague Rilkes, in fact, came from an old Sudeten-German peasant family.

R. was raised in a bourgeois milieu—he himself called it petit-bourgeois—and was indoctrinated within this milieu with a conventional Catholic piety and a rigid German-nationalist contempt for the Czechs. This was the background of the man. Yet in his life he suggested that he was of noble birth and had always moved exclusively in aristocratic circles; he seemed to feel more at home in any country of continental Europe, even in Slavic Russia or Latin France, than in the German-speaking lands; he seemed never to have heard of or to have encountered, even in earliest childhood, any "God relationship" other than the one that "needs no mediator" and in which God is "a great, never fully acquired conviction," which all his life "challenged him productively . . . in his private genius for invention."

These attitudes on the part of the "real" R.—nonbourgeois, supradenominational, and supranational—were not developed as an outgrowth of his background, as it might first appear. On the contrary it represents a radical break with that irreproachably bourgeois, German-Catholic background. It is the result of his "most refractorily, most defiantly getting off the track."

But as R. came in time to like himself less and less in the role of the flaming rebel or the law-unto-himself, he managed to interpret his adult temperament as a pious reaching back beyond his accidental and unauthentic lineage toward his real, more ancient origins—those that can be felt only intuitively, "in the blood." Thus at the age of twenty-five R. had created for himself a second nativity (or, to use the expression of Novalis, a "synthetic childhood") to which he clung to the last and at whose service he placed his ingenious, shrewd, and thoroughly sophisticated mind.

This early evasion of the actual circumstances of his background is not only the most important development R. underwent but also provides the indispensable condition for all his later developments. Although the permanently

RAINER MARIA RILKE

immature alter ego that R. created for himself proved serviceable enough for most purposes of art and for many purposes of real life, it retained for R. himself a slight but indelible touch of the unreal—of the spurious even. If it were not for this secret lack of confidence in his own cause, which shows itself in his attraction to figures such as the adventurer, the charlatan, and the imposter, R. would be less important as a poet, less moving as a man.

The first phase in the major self-transformation of the youthful R. took place during his years at military school (1886–91). There, "after long and anxious struggles," the hitherto indulged boy, who was neither physically nor mentally equipped for rough institutional life, renounced his "vigorous Catholic childish godliness" and "freed himself from it, in order to be more—and more disconsolately—alone." This experience at about the age of fourteen, seemed at first to be nothing but a loss. But later, between 1892 and 1895—when R., who was no longer attending military school, was being privately tutored for the *Abitur* and was developing an exuberant, though sometimes somewhat immature, gift for poetry—he began to regard his loss of faith more positively, to see it as a liberation.

Though his attitude toward the Czechs in 1893 was still the negative one of German nationalism, he was by 1896 in active contact with the Czech literary circles of Prague and was constantly proclaiming his great sympathy for the Czech independence movement. This was declaimed in *Larenopfer* (1895), his first important volume of poetry.

In September 1896 R. succeeded in breaking away from Prague and his family. At first he continued his never-to-be-completed university studies in Munich. There, in May 1897, he met Lou Andreas-Salomé (1861–1937), who had grown up in Russia and for a time had been the friend of Nietzsche (q.v.). At her instigation he changed his baptismal name of René to Rainer. Under her influence he became passionately interested in Russia and became sure—on the basis of intuitive evidence—that through his veins pulsed Slavic (but not Czech) blood.

Tuscany and Russia, which R. visited in 1898 and 1899, and the major contemporary philosophical directions, such as those initiated by Nietzsche and Jens Peter Jacobsen (1847–85) and represented by Lou Andreas-Salomé, produced impressions that were essential to R.'s evolving anti-Christian cult of life and of "this-worldliness," which R. continued to modify until his death but never rejected. His "this-worldly" religiosity, however, takes on a quasi-mystical, transcendental hue from the genius of the spirituality that feeds it, from the existential fear on which it is based and the fruitless effort to overcome this fear, and from the conviction, one that pervaded his mind in constantly changing images, that the world was to be redeemed by art and by art alone.

In a slow transition, without any radical break with his previously somewhat facile, rhyme-loving, lyrical style, the mood poet of *Traumgekrönt* (1896), *Advent* (1897), and *Mir zur Feier* (1899) became the "praying" poet of the three phases (1899—1901—1903) of the *Stundenbuch* (Poems from the Book of Hours, 1941). In a letter of January 1910 R. commented on this first, broadly conceived expression of his volatile worship of immanence and art—which were richly studded with traditional Christian images and concepts, especially with those of the Russian Orthodox church—yet plainly claimed that "God has no use for the Christians." In this letter R. called prayer an outpouring of our suddenly kindled being, an endless reaching without a goal, in which God "is created."

The *Stundenbuch,* in both form and language, marks the end of R.'s first, youthful phase. By 1900, as a result of his encounter with the "unyielding style" of George (q.v.), he was already dissatisfied with the work of this phase, imputing to all his work thus far a lack of definition—what he was later to speak of as "a lyrical superficiality and a facile . . . approximation."

R. now wanted to express pure mood through "images" (*i.e.,* symbols). Therefore, the inherently strong feeling for the visual arts that was such a fundamental element in his mentality gradually gained the upper hand over the boundless subjectivity stimulated by his Russian experiences. This led him, in 1900, to join the Worpswede artists' colony. In 1901 he married Clara Westhoff, a sculptor in the colony who had been a pupil of Rodin.

R.'s Worpswede years (1900–1902), which are essentially a transitional period, are important in terms of his development rather than in terms of actual achievement. In the characteristic poetic work of this period, the first version of the *Buch der Bilder* (1902), his visually conceived poems still fall short of his goal of plastic monumentality. His marriage was even less successful: despite the birth of a daughter, Ruth, in December 1901, the emotional and financial difficulties led to the dissolution in the fall of 1902 of the R. household, which was never to be reestablished.

The importance of the Worpswede phase lies in the fact that it prepared R. for the decisive shift that began in 1902 with R.'s first visit to Paris. R. went to Paris to meet and to write a book about Rodin, whom he had long been interested in. Only in Paris under Rodin's influence did R. succeed in what he had attempted in Worpswede without any real success: in disciplining his art to achieve something objective, plastic, and precise. Although the first poem of this new type, the "Panther," was written in the winter of 1902–1903, three years were to elapse before R. made this new, rigorous, Rodin-oriented technique entirely his own—years of important visits to Rome, Denmark, and Switzerland, years in which R.'s early period was brought to an end with the completion and publication of the *Stundenbuch* (1905) and the second edition of the *Buch der Bilder* (1906).

In his last years R. sometimes spoke misleadingly of his "move" to Paris in the autumn of 1902. Actually Paris did not become his home until September 1905, when he returned there, after more than two years' absence, to be first Rodin's guest, then his unofficial secretary at Meudon. After barely eight months this domestic arrangement came to a stormy end when the unpredictable Rodin turned R. out, *"comme un domestique voleur,"* on a trivial charge. Then, in May 1906, the great Paris period in R.'s work really began. By the winter of 1909–1910 he had finished the *Neue Gedichte* (1907–1908; New Poems, 1964) and his most substantial prose work, *Die Aufzeichnungen des Malte Laurids Brigge* (1910; The Notebooks of Malte Laurids Brigge, 1949). In two loosely chronological cycles the *Neue Gedichte* evoke representative phenomena and figures from mankind's great cultural achievements (the Bible, classical antiquity, the Middle Ages, the Renaissance, the rococo, etc.) and from nature (plants and animals) as well as individual destinies from modern times. These poems have been regarded—on the whole unjustly—as purely objective and "not felt" and have therefore been neglected. Actually, just as much of the inward, the mood-filled, and the mystical is discernible in these *Dinggedichte* ("thing poems") as in R.'s earlier and later poetry. The difference is that in the *Neue Gedichte* these qualities are projected in clearly outlined symbols and are disciplined by a rigorous use of language that strives constantly for objectivity. At that time R., almost like a painter, had set himself to working "from the model." At first, of course, he was emulating Rodin; later, above all others, Cézanne. R.'s own explanation of the relationship between factuality and spirituality in the *Neue Gedichte* was that precisely in the act of looking "things [seem to] happen inside us that have been waiting longingly not to be noticed." The inner happening is envisioned "under the spell of a thing that was alien before this minute and becomes alien again the next moment."

The charge of insufficient spirituality, so often leveled unjustifiably against R.'s *Neue Gedichte,* could never be brought against the other great work of his Paris period, *Die Aufzeichnungen des Malte Laurids Brigge.* While this work is extremely close in language and in its symbolic vision to the *Neue Gedichte,* the spirituality that floods from its depths inundates the sharp contours of the outer world. These notes, begun in Rome in 1904 and written for the most part in Paris between 1908 and 1909, deal with the ecstasies and afflictions of a physically and mentally hypersensitive young man. Malte Laurids Brigge is an imaginary young Danish poet of noble birth, who faces perdition in Paris partly through the sight of the misery in the city but more, in some unspecified way, through himself. R. said the character of Brigge was created "partly out of his own perils." Brigge undergoes on the most diverse levels all man's borderline experiences, notably excessively violent physical disgust, acute loneliness, the threat of madness, and generalized *Angst. Malte* and the *Neue Gedichte* are also linked in that in both works the comforting, affirming attitude pointing to something beyond empirical reality is less in evidence than it is in R.'s earlier and later writing, and that the gloomy, the disintegrating, the negative, indeed the weirdly ludicrous, seem to predominate and to prevail. This is probably one major reason why these two works have received less recognition than anything else R. wrote. R. himself often said that the negation and despair in *Malte* were meant only in a paradoxical sense, that this book was to be read "as it were, against the current," and that it was basically not about one man's perdition as much as it was about "a strangely dark ascension into a neglected and remote part of Heaven." This ambiguity also emerges very strongly from those singular statements on love,

162

which is to be purged of "everything transitive," that accumulate toward the end of *Malte*. This is especially noticeable in R.'s revising of the parable of the prodigal son into "the legend of the man who did not want to be loved." This links up with the idea that God is "just a direction of love, not an object of love" and that therefore there is no danger of "being loved by Him in return." Is this just the stammering of an already half-deranged man facing perdition? Or is it something R. himself is professing as the deepest truth? The answer is obvious, for Brigge's strange words represent a formulation, however grossly exaggerated, of a concept of love and God that constantly recurs, in various guises, throughout R.'s poetry and letters from the very beginning, but is articulated with special intensity in the years between 1907 and 1915.

The completion of *Malte* in the winter of 1909–1910 brought R.'s Paris period to its inward end. He continued to make his home there until July 1914, but of the four and a half years remaining before the outbreak of World War I he spent less than one and a half years in Paris, to which he had taken a dislike.

R. now underwent a particularly difficult crisis, and the many long journeys of this period, notably to North Africa (1910–11) and Spain (1912–13), indicate that he was in flight from himself. The crux of this crisis was a feeling, one by no means new that had now become particularly tormenting, of an irreconcilable conflict betwen the demands of life and art. Often he doubted art's very right to exist, since it "cannot heal any wounds." He believed his health to be seriously threatened. He even considered undergoing psychoanalytical treatment, but did not go through with this because of his "piety." He became more and more involved in reckless, short-lived, bitter-ending love affairs. Among his worst sufferings was the loss of his creative powers for two years—he feared that he would never write poetry again.

The crisis of these years (1910–14) was also to a great extent a philosophical one, though here, as in every phase of his development, R. was less concerned with ultimate, purely philosophical questions, or with human existence itself, than with two more limited matters that were constantly on his mind—the overcoming of Christianity (he spoke, about 1912, of his "almost rabid anti-Christianity") and the loathing he felt for modern technology.

At this time R. became receptive for the first time to the great German poetic tradition. He also sought to broaden his perceptive and creative range, hitherto dominated by the visual arts, by drawing closer to music and its laws. Then, early in 1912 at Duino Castle in Istria, out of this complex of pain and confusion, of philosophical striving and aesthetic stimuli, he was moved to write two poems, whose form, tone, language structure, and predominantly dactylic rhythm can be traced back unmistakably (though perhaps remotely) to the prototypes of the great classicizing elegies as written by Klopstock, Hölderlin, and Goethe ("Euphrosyne").

Between 1912, when he began to write *Duineser Elegien* (1923; Duinese Elegies, 1930) at Duino Castle, and February 1922, when he completed it at the château of Muzot in Switzerland, lay many events: the visit to Spain in the winter of 1912–13, which has often been mistaken for the definitive turning point in R.'s life; World War I, which caught R. in Germany, where he was forced to remain (for the most part in Munich) until its end; R.'s extraordinary susceptibility to the general patriotic fervor of the early days of the war, which he expressed in the "Fünf Gesänge"; the negative, detached attitude R. maintained toward the war after this time; R.'s brief service in the Austrian army and later in its propaganda service (December 1915–June 1916); many distressing love affairs, notably with Magda von Hattingberg, Lulu Albert-Lasard, Claire Studer, and "Merline" Klossowska; his long search for the propitious setting that would enable him to resume the *Elegien;* the important interludes at Soglio, Locarno, and Berg am Irchel Castle; and finally, in the summer of 1921, his discovery of the old tower at Muzot, in Valais.

Until November 1915, despite his predominant mood of despair, R. had always had productive periods, and he had already written about half of the *Duineser Elegien*. But the blow inflicted on his spirit by his induction into the army and by the bleakness of the war years in general just about totally crippled his creative powers for almost four years. Even in the more favorable living conditions of Switzerland they revived only very slowly. The fear that he might have to publish the *Elegien*— which he himself believed to be his most important work—in fragmentary form tormented him beyond measure.

The ten *Duineser Elegien* form a complex of laments of the utmost diversity, which are introduced by a kind of overture (the First Elegy). They lament not only the particular privations and afflictions of the artist but also more universal human predicaments and problems—especially those arising from love, death, and existence in time. R. conceives these problems, to be sure, in a peculiarly aloof and distorted way that is hardly to be called humane.

Yet from this tangle of laments and questions emerges one single problem, one which, as it were, represents and displaces all others, as if its solution would either automatically solve the others (particularly the problem of death) or reveal them as no longer important. This one problem, which in the *Elegien* supersedes all others, is the ineluctable dwindling of the former share of feeling in the shaping of the outer, visible world, a consequence of modern technology with its mass-produced goods and its exploitation of nature. The solution to this problem—and thus to the whole existential predicament—is found in a message of magic inwardness. All beautiful things in the human and natural world that are threatened by mechanization, even—by a peculiar leap—the earth as such, which has fallen victim to transitoriness, are to be taken into man's inwardness to bring them to safety in a mysterious invisible kingdom. The poet who so redeems the beautiful visible things by taking them into his spirit also redeems himself in the process.

Thus the *Duineser Elegien*, like virtually all of R.'s work, is concerned primarily with the special problem of the poet's fate, while the applicability, if any, to man in general remains doubtful. The non-Christian angel, who, as the mythical counterpart of the poet, gives this almost inconceivable theme heroic and monumental contours and a solid dramatic structure, represents, among other things, that absolute subjectivity of feeling for which R. struggled throughout his life. (Being "solipsism," it was denied to him, as to anybody subject to human limitations.)

The climactic resolution of the Duino dissonances that occurs in the Seventh and Ninth Elegies, written in 1922 at Muzot, in no way hinges, as has commonly been supposed, upon a new experience R. underwent at this later stage. It was, in fact, always part of the original Duino vision, as various letters and other writings from the year 1912 show. It was not that R. had had to wait for ten years to find a solution to a problem that he was incapable of solving in those years. It was, rather, that he had to wait for the unflagging, continuous inspiration that would enable him to formulate

the abstraction evolved long ago with the necessary sensuousness and malleability of language. R.'s whole concern was to finish the *Elegien* as if no hiatus, no world war, had intervened, or rather as if there had been no change since January 1912 either in himself or in the world. And that, in his own opinion, was precisely what he succeeded in doing in February 1922.

This does not mean, of course, that R. had really not changed at all during that long interval, but simply that a remarkable process in his unconscious had allowed him to go back, for just long enough to complete the *Elegien,* to an almost forgotten earlier spiritual and mental state. Had R. undergone any radical, irrevocable change in the course of these ten years it would hardly have been possible for him, in February 1922, to have thus reached back and bridged the past decade. (Similarly, it is not possible to establish that R. at any time in his evolution experienced any such definitive change.) Yet it is also true that all he went through in those years, especially his depressing war experiences and the now inescapable fact that he was growing older, had in many ways made him, in both outlook and emotional reactions, a different man: more acquiescent, more serene, closer to reality, calmer, more human.

During February 1922, immediately before and after the completion of the *Duineser Elegien,* this generally less "steeply ascending" attitude found its poetic expression in the two parts of the completely novel *Sonette an Orpheus* (1923; Sonnets to Orpheus, 1936). Their effortless rhythm, rhyme, form, use of language, and inner presence are as characteristic of all the poetry of R.'s last phase (1920–26), including the poems in French, as the density of the *Duineser Elegien* is characteristic of his penultimate phase (1912–15). R. himself, who always regarded the unhoped-for completion of the *Elegien* as the greatest miracle of his life, first conceived the *Sonette* as merely "a little cluster of works welling up at the same time" which "complemented" the *Elegien*. Both cycles are concerned with a vision of existence from the aspect of artistic creativity in which the poet, in redeeming the world, is himself redeemed. But the remarkable contrast between the angel of the *Elegien* and the Orpheus of the *Sonette*—a relationship something like that between Narcissus and Saint Francis—is enough to show that these two works can be meaningfully connected, if at all, only by positing their polarity. The language, form, and spirit of the *Elegien* and their related poems from the years 1912 to 1915 can be regarded as the systole balancing the diastole of the *Sonette* and their related poems from the years 1920 to 1926.

Although the *Sonette*, which seems more "human" than the *Elegien*, goes beyond the latter in many respects, this does not indicate any drastic philosophical change in R., least of all a return to Christianity, from which, as he said himself in November 1925, he "drew away more and more passionately." R.'s religious testament is the letter to a young worker, written during the time of the *Sonette*, and the last poems of the *Elegien*. Here he attacks everything Christian even more violently than before, offering instead the positive message of the "unavowed joy of sex." "Why do we not belong to God from this point, too?" he asks. This again is something that R. had proclaimed throughout his life in various formulations but had never developed.

In the last years, after the great "storm of creativity" of February 1922, R. turned more and more noticeably toward the French spirit. This is demonstrated in his absolutely unqualified admiration for Valéry (q.v.) and in the fact that after 1923 he himself wrote chiefly in French and became actively interested in building up his reputation in French literary circles, especially during a six months' visit to Paris in 1925.

During these years he revealed a readiness to rejoice in existence, even to enjoy it, though he was more and more handicapped in this by increasingly grave physical conditions. Fearful of mental derangement, he begged, "even implored," his friends "to shield him from any priestly assistance" if this befell him. R. died of leukemia and was buried in the graveyard of the village church at Raron, in Valais.

FURTHER WORKS: *Wegwarten* (1896); *Jetzt und in der Stunde unseres Absterbens* (1896); *Christus, Visionen* (1896–98; Visions of a Christ, 1967); *Im Frühfrost* (1897); *Ohne Gegenwart* (1898); *Am Leben hin* (1898); *Zwei Prager Geschichten* (1899); *Vom lieben Gott und Anderes* (1900; republished as *Geschichten vom lieben Gott*, 1904; Stories of God, 1963); *Die Letzten* (1902); *Das tägliche Leben* (1902); *Worpswede* (1903); *Auguste Rodin* (1903); *Die Weise von Liebe und Tod des Cornets Christoph Rilke* (1906; Lay of the Love and Death of Cornet Christopher Rilke, 1959); *Requiem* (1909); *Die frühen Gedichte* (1909);

Das Marienleben (1913; The Life of the Virgin Mary, 1947); *Die weiße Fürstin* (1920); *Vergers suivi des Quatrains Valaisans* (1926); *Les Fenêtres* (1927); *Les Roses* (1927); *Gesammelte Werke* (6 vols., 1927); *Erzählungen und Skizzen aus der Frühzeit* (1928); *Briefe an A. Rodin* (1928); *Verse und Prosa aus dem Nachlaß* (1929); *Briefe an einen jungen Dichter* (1929; Letters to a Young Poet, 1954); *Briefe an eine junge Frau* (1930); *Über Gott, zwei Briefe* (1933); *Späte Gedichte* (1934); *Briefe an seinen Verleger* (1934); *Gesammelte Briefe* (6 vols., 1936–39); *Tagebücher aus der Frühzeit* (1942); *Gedichte in französischer Sprache* (1949); *Nachlaß, vier Teile* (1950); *Briefe* (2 vols., 1950); *Die Briefe an Gräfin Sizzo 1921–26* (1950); *Aus dem Nachlaß des Grafen C. W. Ein Gedichtkreis* (1950; From the Reminiscences of Count C. W., 1952); *Briefwechsel mit Marie v. Thurn und Taxis* (1951; The Letters of R. M. R. and Princess Marie v. Thurn und Taxis, 1958); *R. M. R. und L. Andreas-Salomé* (1952); *A. Gide: Correspondance 1909–26* (1952); *Briefe an Frau Gudi Nölke* (1953; Letters to Frau Gudi Nölke, 1955); *Gedichte, 1909–26* (1953); *Briefwechsel in Gedichten mit Erika Mitterer* (1954; Correspondence in Verse with Erika Mitterer, 1953); *R. M. R. an Benvenuta* (1954; Letters to Benvenuta, 1954); *R. M. R. et Merline: Correspondance 1920–26* (1954); *R. M. R. und K. Kippenberg* (1954); *R. M. R. et A. Gide/E. Verhaeren: Correspondance inédite* (1955); *Lettres Milanaises, 1921–26* (1956); *R. M. R. und Inga Junghanss: Briefwechsel* (1959); *Ewald Tragy* (1959; Eng., 1959); *Briefe an Sidonie Nádherny von Borutin* (1969). **Selected English translations:** Poems by R. M. R. (1918; enlarged ed., 1943); The Journal of My Other Self (1930); Requiem, and Other Poems (1935); Translations from the Poetry of R. M. R. (1938); Wartime Letters of R. M. R., 1914–21 (1940); Fifty Selected Poems (bilingual ed., 1940); Primal Sound, and Other Prose Pieces (1943); Letters (2 vols., 1945–48); Thirty-one Poems by R. M. R. (1946); Selected Letters of R. M. R., 1902–26 (1946); Five Prose Pieces (1947); R. M. R.: His Last Friendship (1952); Selected Works (1954 ff.); Poems 1906–26 (1957); Selected Works: Prose and Poetry (2 vols., 1960); The Book of Hours (includes Of the Monastic Life, Of Pilgrimage, and Of Poverty and Death, 1961)

BIBLIOGRAPHY: Mason, E. C., *R.'s Apotheosis* (1938); Mason, E. C., *Lebenshaltung und Symbolik bei R. M. R.* (1939); Butler, E. M.,

R. M. R. (1939); Kunisch, H., *R. M. R.* (1944); Kunisch, H., *R. M. R. und die Dinge* (1946); Holthusen, H. E., *Der späte R.* (1949); Kassner, R., *Umgang der Jahre* (1949); Hamburger, K., *R. M. R.* (1950); Demetz, P., *René Rs. Prager Jahre* (1953); Buddeberg, E., *R. M. R.* (1953); Mason, E. C., *R. und Goethe* (1958); Wood, F., *R. M. R., The Ring of Forms* (1958); Fürst, W., *Phases of R.* (1958); Mason, E. C., *R., Europe and the English-speaking World* (1961); Shaw, P., *R., Valéry and Yeats: The Domain of Self* (1964); Mandel, S., *R. M. R.: The Poetic Instinct* (1965); Puknat, E. M., and S. B., "American Literary Encounters with R.," *Monatshefte,* LX (1968), 245–56; Saas, C., "Rs. Expressionismus," *DA,* XXVIII (1968), 3683A

EUDO C. MASON

R.'s purpose might be regarded as an attempt to harmonise and combine two different kinds of poetry. On the one hand, it demanded the fullness which comes from living in the imagination, from yielding to every impression, and in this it recalls the Romantics with their eager quest of sensations and their belief in the unique nature of the poet's calling. On the other hand, it recalls Mallarmé's conception of the ideal poem as something absolute in itself and free from anything that might be called the private tastes of its maker. . . . Like Valéry, R. found in the creative joy of poetry something marvellous and unique. But unlike Valéry, he exalted this to a special and central place, interpreted life through it and thought that it alone gave importance to anything. For him poetry was not one activity among others but a fundamental power. Song was the root of his being, the means of his mystical excitements, the basis of his philosophy.

C. M. Bowra, *The Heritage of Symbolism* (1943), pp. 60, 96

The Romantics tried to think of it [death] as a state of existence. By the 1840's, this had become an obsession, and had degenerated into curiosity. By the later nineteenth century, and up to our own time, it had resulted in a clearly apparent "Death Wish," as the only solution to the problem—since the solution must come in sensual terms. It was left to the necrophilous Germany, to R. in fact, to provide the best solution short of actually dying. That is why there had to be a "Poet of Death" in the twentieth century; and why R. is the most important poet since Goethe and Wordsworth. . . .

Sidney Keyes, *The Collected Poems* (1947), p. xix f.

R. . . . appears here as the patron-saint of the loneliness of modern man; not as an advocate of a spurious retreat into otherwordliness, but as the authentic opposite of the mass-mind and of the civilisation of machines and ideologies; as a poet who, though his words are separated by an immense gulf from what today passes for "public opinion" and from the ways of thinking common in our world, remains inseparably linked with this world as the prophet and interpreter of its other, its secret nature.

Hans Egon Holthusen, *Rainer Maria Rilke* (1952), p. 7

Both Nietzsche and R., experiencing life as wholly immanent, . . . stake it on the supreme 'Wagnis,' the daring experiment: man himself must become the redeemer of existence. This is the ultimate consequence of the Will to Power, or of humanism thought out and felt to its radical conclusion by the *anima naturaliter religiosa.* Nietzsche replaces the mystery of the Incarnation by the Superman, the Will to Power incarnate; and R. by the angelic vision of a world disembodied in human inwardness. . . . Theirs is a *religio intransitiva.*

Erich Heller, *The Disinherited Mind* (1952), pp. 134, 136

The self-renunciation which any relationship of friendship or love between living people demands was foreign to his nature and inclinations. . . .

It was not small-heartedness or lack of generosity, not willfully preconceived opinions about life or art, that drove our poet to such growing loneliness and isolation; it was fear for the vulnerable, threatened core of his own existence. . . .

And so this man, standing entirely on his own, to whom all support seemed more dubious than his own defenselessness, moved from loneliness to ever deeper loneliness, to the extreme point at which an ever-wakeful horror henceforth prevented him from desiring either the life of man or that of the gods, and even permitted him to desire that of the animals and plants only insofar as it seemed to him a transition on the way back to the dark element that, underneath the threshold of all that is formed and all that forms, of all that is born and all that gives birth, promises peace and refuge. For him this was the road to freedom.

R. A. Schröder, *Die Aufsätze und Reden* (1952), vol. i, p. 928 ff.

What nobody has sung better perhaps than he, is solitude. That of children and that of lovers. Perhaps he was primarily the poet of solitude.

R.'s god was not on any altar, but the great naves, vaulted by twilight, felt his great breath pass through them, and the rose windows kindled their most beautiful red and their deepest blue at his light. His god was immensity. His god was not faith but presence.

Antonina Vallentin, "Rainer Maria Rilke," in *Les Temps Modernes* (1953), p. 390 ff.

There are very few prose works by great poets which are at once as exacting and exciting to read as this slender notebook [*Malte Laurids Brigge*] of R.'s. Though its form is roughly that of a novel, and though it purports to be the diary of a Danish poet living in Paris. it is anything but fiction in the accepted sense of the word; it is an extended prose poem which borrows the tonalities of prose in order to weave, with deceptive precision and coolness, a poetic reality. I can think of few little books so densely packed with the matter of poetic observation, few books where every line counts so heavily. Moreover, the nature of the poetry in it is so unwaveringly accurate in its vision and so coolly, surgically presented to the reader that one hesitates to use the word at all. . . . No, this is something very different—the tracing of a fugitive reality which lies underneath those deluding appearances we call Time, History, and Memory. . . . Our poet does not take up attitudes, does not allow the temperature of his language to rise to the consciously "poetic" in the bad sense of the phrase. On the contrary he places himself before his inner vision and quietly fills his notebook with accurate transcriptions of what he sees. . . . This almost scientific detachment gives the poetry a unique kind of resonance. It evokes the past without nostalgia, it creates the present without regret or disdain, it peers into the curvature of the future without fear.

Lawrence Durrell, in *GL&L* (1962–63), p. 138

The similarity between R.'s Narcissus and Valéry's consists in the fact that both not only see their image and long for it, but that this seeing broadens and becomes a knowledge of being. Both of them see themselves first in nature; to both the mystic union with nature is denied. Both think of the possibility of finding themselves in the beloved other one, and both learn that they are deceived in this attempt. Both must return to their own Selves, and both realize that to see one's own Self means to look death in the face. And both are overpowered by this knowledge; both "see themselves" and die.

The difference between the two Narcissus-images consists in the way they are expressed. Valéry's Racine-like verses make the complex problem of Narcissus transparent. . . . R.'s Narcissus-poems are more difficult to interpret because the spiritual problems remain embedded in the lyrical emotional substance and, in a way, refuse to become completely transparent. Some expressions which he has anticipated in poetical intuition and which attain their final meaning only in R.'s late poems, can be understood . . . only by referring to the late works.

Maja Goth, in *WSCL* (1966), p. 19

. . . The *Duino Elegies* and the *Sonnets to Orpheus* constitute in their entirety one coherent poetic statement. . . . The *Sonnets* that flowed from R.'s pen almost as a piece of automatic writing during a few January days in 1922 provided the catalyst that brought the *Elegies* to completion within a very short time. . . .

As their title implies, the *Elegies* are written in a minor key. They sound a note of heartbreak, of infinite anxiety, anguish, doubt, and fear, although strains of ecstatic jubilation frequently interrupt the throb of the despairing heart. The *Sonnets* are written in a major key, sounding a theme of praise that brooks no qualification. They proclaim a pan-ecstatic view of life. In the explicit language of the *Sonnets,* even lament is nothing but a muted form of praise. Praise of existence is a total musical statement as it were, requiring the minor themes of wailing and lament for its development. . . .

Hermann J. Weigand, *PMLA* (1967), p. 3

RISSE, Heinz

German novelist, short-story writer, essayist, b. 30 March 1898, Düsseldorf

After military service in World War I, R. studied economics and philosophy in Marburg, Frankfurt, and Heidelberg. Since 1922 he has worked with economics in several capacities, finally becoming a public accountant in Solingen.

The work of R., who did not begin to publish until 1948, is characterized by the transformation of traditionally religious concerns into the language of the modern existential situation. In the anecdotal quality of his prose, with its emphasis upon individual "cases," R. has found a highly effective means of conveying the fragmentary nature of contemporary life. His singular preoccupation with what human reason can only term errors of justice and undeserved suffering provides the thematic complex of all his works.

This is especially true of the novels *Wenn die Erde bebt* (1950; The Earthquake, 1953) and *So frei von Schuld* (1951), the most characteristic and sustained of his longer works. The central figure in *So frei von Schuld* is sentenced to twelve years in prison for a murder he did not commit. As he continues to fail to find a rational explanation for such injustice he begins to come to terms with the ambiguity of innocence. What kind of world is it, R. asks in which a miscarriage of justice can be the means whereby man comes at last to be convinced of his guilt?

The recognition of God's inscrutability and of the necessity for each man to comprehend his complicity in his destiny leads to the central theme of the *Gottesurteil* ("divine judgment"). The short story of that name (from the collection *Buchhalter Gottes*, 1958) may well be the most concise expression of R.'s thought. The acceptance of complicity in one's guilt makes one's ability to comprehend the charge and the punishment irrelevant.

Because man is unable to respond appropriately to a seemingly capricious divinity, he is subject to suffering and finally to madness. The existence of "madmen," humorless and uncompromising, is important in R.'s fiction. The intensely lonely existence of these "privileged" persons is spoken of in *Dann kam der Tag* (1953), in *Einer zuviel* (1957), and in many of the shorter works (*e.g.,* "Verkehrsunfall," from *Buchhalter Gottes;* "Die Insel der Seligen," from *Fort geht's wie auf Samt,* 1962) as well as in *Wenn die Erde bebt* and *So frei von Schuld.* It is these "madmen" alone who are able to escape from the total uncertainty of this world into an illusion-free inner reality, one in which one can with integrity submit to the only important concerns of life: pain, justice, and death.

Particularly striking is the long anecdote at the end of *Einer zuviel* about two slightly crazy old soldiers who live and die "on the edge of the desert." The image of a barren, forbidding wilderness as proper to those who have put themselves beyond the problems of daily life is of great significance in R.'s preeminently philosophical fiction. Only by positively evaluating this "desert" can one understand the passionate search for "paradise" by which so many of R.'s protagonists are consumed.

FURTHER WORKS: *Die Flucht hinter das Gitter* (1948); *Irrfahrer* (1948); *Das letzte Kapitel der Welt* (1949); *Fledermäuse* (1951); *Schlangen in Genf* (1951); *Die Fackel des Prometheus* (1952); *Belohne dich selbst* (1953); *Verrat an Gott* (radio script, 1953); *Die Grille* (1953); *Simson und die kleinen Leute* (1954); *Sören der Lump* (1955); *Fördert die Kultur!* (1955); *Große Fahrt und falsches Spiel* (1956); *Die vollkommene Maschine* (radio series, 1956); *Gestein der Weisen* (1957); *Paul Cézanne und Gottfried Benn* (1958); *Die Schiffsschaukel* (1960); *Ringelreihen oder die Apologie des Verbleibs im Zimmer* (1963); *Feiner Unfug auf Staatskosten* (1963)

BIBLIOGRAPHY: Horst, K. A., "Vor dem

letzten Kapitel," *Merkur,* XLVIII (1952); Uhlig, H., "Die Gefangenen Gottes: Zum Werk von H. R.," *Der Monat,* No. 45 (June 1952)

EDWARD BAUER

RITTNER, Tadeusz

Polish dramatist and novelist (writing in German and Polish), b. 31 May 1873, Lwow; d. 20 June 1921, Bad Gastein, Austria

R. was the son of a minister in the government of Austria, who had been a professor of canon law. After studying at the excellent Theresianum in Vienna, R. attended the university and received a degree in law. He became a high-rank official at the Ministry of Education in Vienna.

The characters in R.'s melancholy, pessimistic, erotic plays inhabit a world that lies between dream-fantasy and reality. Nevertheless R.'s observation is acute and even his most subtle psychological studies remain concrete.

Many of R.'s plays, once internationally famous and now undeservedly forgotten, were first performed at the Vienna Burgtheater. They include: *W małym domku* (1904; German, *Das kleine Heim,* 1908); *Don Juan* (1909; German *Unterwegs,* 1909); his dramatic masterpiece, *Der dumme Jakob* (1910; Polish, *Głupi Jakub,* 1910); and *Wölfe in der Nacht* (1914; Polish, *Wilki w nocy,* 1916).

R.'s most significant works of fiction are: *Geister in der Stadt* (1921; Polish, *Duchy w mieście,* 1921), a novel of fantasy; *Die Brücke* (1920; Polish, *Most,* 1923), a psychological novel; and *Zimmer des Wartens* (1918; Polish *Drzwi zamknięte,* 1922), the still-fascinating autobiographical novel dealing with R.'s youth.

FURTHER WORKS: *Lulu, Dora* (1894); *Drei Frühlingstage* (1900); *Sąsiadka* (1902); *Maszyna* (1904); *Przebudzenie* (1905); *Nowele* (1907); *Lato* (1912); *Ich kenne Sie* (1912); *Der Mann aus dem Souffleurkasten* (1912); *Kinder der Erde* (1912); *Powrót* (1915); *Ogród młodości* (1917); *Tragedja Eumenesa* (1920); *Między nocą i brzaskiem* (1921); *Feinde der Reichen* (1921); *Spotkanie* (1928); *Dziela* (8 vols., 1930 ff.)

BIBLIOGRAPHY: Herman, M., *Histoire de la littérature polonaise* (1963); Kaszyński, S., "Polnisch-österreichische Theaterbeziehungen," *Maske und Kothurn,* XII (1966), 236–46; Żabicki, Z., "Glossy do R.," *Dialog* (*Warsaw*), XII (1967), viii, 85–94

OSKAR JAN TAUSCHINSKI

RIVERA, José Eustasio

Colombian poet and novelist, b. 19 Feb. 1889, Neiva; d. 1 Dec. 1928, New York City

After finishing teachers college, R. went on to the National University and received a law degree in 1917. Most of his life was subsequently spent in political service to his country. Diplomatic missions took him to Peru and Mexico. While a member of Congress, R. participated in two important investigations. In 1925, he was chairman of a committee sent to study problems relating to Colombia's oil lands. More importantly, he had earlier been sent to the swamp-infested jungle region in the southeast as a member of a government commission whose purpose it was to investigate a boundary dispute between Colombia and Venezuela. It was while on this expedition that he became familiar with the geography of the region as well as the socioeconomic problems connected with the exploited rubber gatherers. Extensive notes that he took at that time were later used as a basis for his great regional novel, *La vorágine* (1924; The Vortex, 1935).

R.'s literary works consist of one volume of poetry, *Tierra de promisión* (1921), in addition to the above-mentioned novel. In this volume of sonnets, R. paints word pictures of the tropical Colombian landscape. There are echoes of Rubén Darío (q.v.) and other modernists in the rhythms and especially the parnassian plasticity. But perhaps the most salient effect produced by R., especially through the poetic device of personification, is that of a pantheistic relationship between the poet and nature.

It is, however, for *La vorágine* that R. is best known. The sprawling, episodic narrative, with interpolated stories and primitive folk elements, follows for the most part Arturo Cova's quest for the woman Alicia. Yet the story itself seems mere pretext. The central purpose, aside from an exposé of the cruelly inhuman treatment of the rubber workers, is the epic portrayal of the struggle to the death between man and an overwhelming and devouring nature. R.'s descriptions are unsurpassed in vividness and power as he creates a tension between the awe-inspiring surface beauty of the jungle on the one hand, and its pulsating, destructive force on the other; horrible, terrifying, all-consuming.

BIBLIOGRAPHY: Neale-Silva, E., "The Factual Bases of *La vorágine*," *PMLA*, LIV (1939), 316–31; Spell, J. R., "J. E. R.," in *Contemporary Spanish-American Fiction* (1944); Neale-Silva, E., *Estudios sobre J. E. R.* (1951); Olivera, O., "El romanticismo de J. E. R.," *RI*, XVII (1952); Valente, J. A., "La naturaleza y el hombre en *La vorágine* de J. E. R.," *CHA* (1955); Neale-Silva, E., *Horizonte humano: Vida de J. E. R.* (1960)

ROBERT SCOTT

RIVIÈRE, Jacques

French critic, novelist, and editor, b. 15 July 1886, Bordeaux; d. 14 Feb. 1925, Paris

At the *lycée* R. met Alain-Fournier (q.v.), whose sister he later married. They shared a strong admiration for symbolism (q.v.) and for Jammes, Verhaeren, and Maeterlinck (qq.v.). Their correspondence is well worth reading (*Correspondance, 1905–14, avec Alain-Fournier*, 4 vols., 1926–27; Mirror of an Epoch, The Correspondence of J. R. and Alain-Fournier, 1953).

Though R. had in his youth rejected the church he had been brought up in, he longed for religious security. Through his relationship with the Roman Catholic Claudel (q.v.; *Correspondance, 1902–14, avec Claudel*, 1926), he converted to Catholicism in 1913. Nevertheless, he never resolved his religious conflict, continuing throughout his lifetime to fluctuate between orthodoxy and disbelief. This doubt is voiced frequently in his correspondence with Gide and Proust (qq.v.).

From 1914 to 1918, R. was a German prisoner of war. During those years he wrote *À La Trace de Dieu* (pub., 1925). This quasi-letter to intellectuals, in which extracts from R.'s diary appear alongside theological reflections, was prepared in part as an antidote to the intellectualism from which he suffered all his life.

L'Allemand (1918) reflects R.'s experiences as a prisoner of war. His personal observations of the Germans are accurate and basically fair, but his analysis of the German character is somewhat biased. He was barely kinder to his own countrymen, whom he bluntly criticizes in *Le Français*.

R.'s major achievement was his original, sensitive, and influential writing on the arts, especially as revealed in his *Études* (1912). They reveal his sympathetic understanding of writers, painters, and musicians.

In 1925, R.'s "De la foi" appeared in the *Nouvelle Revue Française*. An autobiography and an apologia, this shows R. to be, above all, an erudite student of literature, though his reactions to the *Zeitgeist* are those of an artist rather than a thinker.

As co-founder and editor of the *Nouvelle Revue Française* (1919–25) and a leading critic, R. was in a position to work on behalf of young writers, and handled this responsibility in an admirable way. He played a decisive part in effecting the acceptance of Proust as a writer of major status and was one of the first to recognize Claudel's merit. Similarly, he is to be credited with intelligently disseminating Freudian theory in France (*Freud et Proust*, 1927).

R. deserves to survive in literary history for the substantial salutary influence he exerted on his generation. He won the respect of many of the ambivalent young intellectuals who were floundering in the 1920's and 1930's because of his decisive stand on contemporary problems and the fact that he did not deny his own doubts and vacillations as well as for his morality, devotion to sincerity, and sensitivity to spiritual conflicts.

R. attracted some of his disciples because he "always chose the middle way between two extremes: between Claudel and Gide, France and Germany, Classicism and Romanticism" (Martin Turnell).

FURTHER WORKS: *Aimée* (1922); *Lettres: J. R. et Antonin Artaud* (1923); *Carnet de guerre* (1929); *Rimbaud* (1930); *Moralisme et littérature* (1932); *Florence* (1935); *Nouvelles Études* (1947). **Selected English translation:** *The Ideal Reader: Selected Essays* (1960)

BIBLIOGRAPHY: Mauriac, F., *Le Tourment de J. R.* (1926); Gide, A., *J. R.* (1931); Jans, A., *La pensée de J. R.* (1938); Boc, C., *J. R.* (1940); Turnell, M., *J. R.* (1953); Cook, B., *J. R.* (1958); Naughton, H. T., "The Realism of J. R.," *MLQ*, XXV (1964), 171–80; Naughton, H. T., *J. R.: The Development of a Man and a Creed* (1966)

KONRAD BIEBER

ROBBE-GRILLET, Alain

French novelist, critic, scenarist, film director, b. 18 Aug. 1922, Brest

R.'s studies for a degree in agronomy, an interest since childhood, were interrupted by World War II, during which he was deported to work in a German tank factory. After the war he obtained his degree and was briefly employed as a government agronomist. His first known publication is a survey of the condition of French cattle. Later R. became overseer on a Martinique banana plantation, but following a tropical illness he decided on a literary career and returned to France. In connection with a miscellany of activities— varying from communist-sponsored youth trips to writers' congresses, film-making assignments, and lecture tours—R. has traveled widely throughout Europe and visited the United States and North Africa.

In 1953, setting aside his first attempt at a novel, the still-unpublished *Un Régicide*, R. wrote *Les Gommes* (1953; The Erasers, 1964), contributed his first critical pieces to *Critique,* and began his association with Jérôme Lindon's press, Les Éditions de Minuit, for which he still acts as literary director.

R. is probably the chief exponent of the *nouveau roman,* a term that loosely categorizes the work of such writers as Nathalie Sarraute, Butor, Beckett, Pinget, and Marguerite Duras (qq.v.). Among the most active and vocal of this group, he published a number of literary manifestoes on the novel. These were later collected in *Pour un Nouveau Roman* (1963; Towards a New Novel, 1966).

Over the years, R. has become increasingly preoccupied with often psychopathological subject matters and with an attempt to reinvigorate the novel as an art form by developing original techniques of style and structure. In his work the eye of the narrator is essentially a "camera's eye," registering without emotion the objects in its field of vision. It is structure that provides the key to meaning in R.'s novels and films.

In *Les Gommes* R. integrates such diverse symbols of destiny as the Oedipus legend and Tarot cards into a plot involving a detective's attempt to solve a presumed murder. When the detective himself ends by killing the assumed victim—who may be his father—the parallel with the classical legend is complete.

Already apparent in this novel is R.'s "objectal" style: a precise, neutral description of *things*. This emphasis gave rise to the term *chosisme,* which is still favored by those critics who prefer to see R.'s novels as devoid of meaning.

Le Voyeur (1955; The Voyeur, 1958) won the Prix des Critiques and so brought R. to the attention of the general public. It is an elliptical story of a sadistic schizophrenic who builds hallucinatory alibis in an attempt to blot from memory his murder of a young girl. Here R.'s characteristic "false scenes"—imaginary or hypothetical events—are used more frequently than in *Les Gommes*. Chronology is distorted and subjectivity is objectified by embodying psychic obsessions in series of objects that act as objective correlatives of emotional states. The whole is presented without the usual textual "clues" to such passages, thus enlisting the reader's own creative collaboration.

The narrative mode of *La Jalousie* (1957; Jealousy, 1959) carries R.'s subjective viewpoint still further. The "narrator," a jealous husband, watches his wife and her putative lover, searching for signs of infidelity. Though the protagonist is an absent first-person—or *je-néant*—who never uses "I" or other terms of self-reference, all his mental activity is objectified in terms of his visual or sensorial experiences. It is up to the reader to "create" the emotional content that is implicit but never described.

The exteriorization of his characters' mental images is further pursued in R's film, *L'Année dernière à Marienbad* (1961; Last Year at Marienbad, script published in 1962), wherein the mental seduction of a woman is presented in a mixture of images from the past and the present. Real and imaginary scenes are not distinguishable, and the soundtrack provides a counterpoint of monologues and dialogues often out of phase with the images on the screen. Similar techniques are used in *L'Immortelle*, which concerns a European in Istanbul who vainly seeks to establish the identity of a young woman who has given herself to him.

A similarly exotic locale is the scene of the novel *La Maison de Rendez-vous* (1965; Eng., 1966), which focuses on Hong Kong's streets, hotels, bars, and houses of assignation. Using the humor of semiparody, R. constructs an "impossible" story of espionage, drug traffic, prostitution, and murder. The end result seems designed to outdo James Bond, but what redeems these unlikely materials is a masterly control of both technique and style.

The collection of short texts entitled *Instantanés* (1962; Snapshots, 1969) provides miniature studies of techniques and themes used by R. in his novels: minute panoramic descriptions ("The Dressmaker's Dummy"), image reversals ("Three Reflected Visions"), temporal dead ends ("The Way Back"), narrational ambiguity ("Scene"), serial urban patterns ("In the Corridors of the Metro"), Breton landscapes and seascapes ("The Shore"), and

decadent eroticism reminiscent of paintings by Gustave Moreau ("The Secret Room").

R.'s universe increasingly becomes an imaginary domain subject only to the laws of its own invention. In it time is often "bent" without regard for "logical" explanation, and the end goal emerges as the creation of a wholly self-contained fiction.

FURTHER WORK: *Dans le labyrinthe* (1959; In the Labyrinth, 1959)

BIBLIOGRAPHY: Bernal, O., *A. R.-G.: Un Roman de l'absence* (1964); Stoltzfus, B. F., *A. R.-G. and the New French Novel* (1964); Morrissette, B., *Les Romans de R.-G.* (2nd ed., 1965); Morrissette, B., *A. R.-G.* (1965)

BRUCE MORRISSETTE

ROBERTS, Elizabeth Madox

American novelist, b. 30 Oct. 1886, Perrysville, Kentucky; d. 13 March 1941, Orlando, Florida

Elizabeth R.'s writing career began with the publication of a book of poems—*In the Great Steep's Garden* (1915).

Elizabeth R. achieved an international reputation with *The Time of Man* (1926), which recounts the struggles of Ellen Chesser, a Kentucky poor white, to achieve self-definition and peace for herself and her family on the land.

My Heart and My Flesh (1927) charts the decline of a Kentucky aristocrat, Theodosia Bell. Having lost everything, she is on the brink of starvation and psychosis when the will to live finally asserts itself. The novel anticipates Faulknerian themes and situations in its analysis of Theodosia's disordered mind, in its honest presentation of aristocratic decline, and in its symbolic depiction of moral decay.

The Great Meadow (1930), Elizabeth R.'s best-known book, traces Diony Hall's physical and spiritual journey to the pioneer Kentucky wilderness and her adjustments to life there.

In *A Buried Treasure* (1931) the rich life of the Kentucky dwellers is set against the background of nature and a legendary past. *He Sent Forth a Raven* (1935) is a symbolic parable that celebrates contrasting kinds of spiritual strength: outward defiance in Stoner Drake and inner self-assurance in Jocelle Drake, his granddaughter. The folk idyl, *Black Is My True Love's Hair* (1938), has as its theme the contrast between life-destroying and life-renewing sexual passion.

In style of discouragement, ill-health, and her relatively late beginning in fiction, Elizabeth R. accomplished much in her fifteen years of novel-writing. She helped to establish in America the novel of sensibility as practiced by such innovative novelists as Virginia Woolf (q.v.). A conscious stylist, she utilized the vivid image and the rhythms of the spoken language to secure her most brilliant effects.

In her explorations into the psyche, Elizabeth R. was able to achieve expansion of consciousness in a character while maintaining an overall firmness of structure. Elizabeth R. achieved a fusion of realism and of evocative poetic symbolism in her work. In this respect, as in other ways, she anticipated the novels of Woolf, Faulkner, and Eudora Welty (qq.v.).

FURTHER WORKS: *Under the Tree* (1922); *Jingling in the Wind* (1928); *The Haunted Mirror* (1932); *Song in the Meadow* (1940); *Not by Strange Gods* (1941)

BIBLIOGRAPHY: Adams, J. D., *The Shape of Books to Come* (1934); Wagenknecht, E., *Cavalcade of the American Novel* (1952); Campbell, H. M., and Foster, R. E., *E. M. R.: American Novelist* (1956); Rovit, E. H., *Herald to Chaos: The Novels of E. M. R.* (1960); McDowell, F. P. W., *E. M. R.* (1963)

FREDERICK P. W. MCDOWELL

ROBINSON, Edwin Arlington

American poet, b. 22 Dec. 1869, Head Tide, Maine; d. 6 April 1935, New York City

Born into an old New England family, R. grew up in Gardiner, Maine, and attended Harvard for two years. After 1897 he lived in New York City, where he wrote poetry and lived from hand to mouth, and succumbed to alcoholism. Then Theodore Roosevelt, who admired his poems, secured him a Treasury job, a sinecure R. held from 1905 to 1909.

In 1896 R. financed a printing of his first volume of poems, *The Torrent and the Night Before*. R. first won acclaim for *The Town down the River* (1910), and his reputation was established with the publication of *The Man against the Sky* (1916). He did not, however, become financially successful until the publication of *Tristram* (1927).

The contribution of R.'s New England background is pervasive and general, rather than specific. The influence of Robert Browning (1812–89) is to be seen in such dramatic

monologues as "The Clinging Vine" and "Ben Jonson Entertains a Man from Stratford." To a lesser extent that of Kipling (q.v.) is to be seen in R.'s explicitness, and that of W. M. Praed (1802–1839) in such poems as "Old King Cole."

Actually, however, R. was a solitary writer, whose self-involvement isolated him from influences and from his contemporaries. The decline in his reputation in recent years may be related to this isolation. His influence on succeeding writers has been negligible.

R.'s dwindling readership is perhaps best explained by the fact that the fashion for long poems has passed. His long psychological narratives based on Arthurian legend (*Merlin,* 1917; *Lancelot,* 1920; *Tristram,* 1927) contain undeniable passages of power, but they are too pointlessly diffuse and too elaborately plotted for modern taste. Of the three, plot and character probably come off best in *Lancelot.* All of R.'s long narrative poems suffer from redundancy, involution of plot, heavy allegorizing, and excessive philosophizing. Of these, *Captain Craig* (1902) is perhaps the best of the group.

The thinness of texture and attenuation of affect that defeat much of R.'s voluminous work are not apparent, however, in his best poems—short lyrics such as "Luke Havergal," "Richard Cory," "Miniver Cheevy," and "Mr. Flood's Party." Here the diction is concentrated with irony. The precision of rhythm increases the pathos of these people, who are, like R. himself, studies in isolation. To the list of these fine short poems are to be added "The Poor Relation," "The Wandering Jew," and "Eros Turannos"—all of which are remarkable for their stark power.

The vision of the agnostic R. is indeed a tragic one. An almost humorless man, he pursued his own way with a single-minded earnestness that was more remarkable for its integrity than for its intensity. It is likely that he will continue to be known for a dozen or two short lyric or dramatic poems in which his particular gifts for directness, irony, and a bleak pathos find economical and powerful expression.

FURTHER WORKS: *The Children of the Night* (1897); *Van Zorn* (1914); *The Porcupine* (1915); *The Three Taverns* (1920); *Avon's Harvest* (1921); *Collected Poems* (1921); *Roman Bartholow* (1923); *The Man Who Died Twice* (1924); *Dionysus in Doubt* (1925); *Sonnets 1889–1927* (1928); *Cavender's House* (1929);

Collected Poems (1929); *The Glory of the Nightingales* (1930); *Selected Poems* (1931); *Matthias at the Door* (1931); *Nicodemus* (1932); *Talifer* (1933); *Amaranth* (1934); *King Jasper* (1935); *Collected Poems* (1937); *Selected Letters* (1940); *Letters of E. A. R. to Howard George Schmitt* (1943); *Untriangulated Stars* (1947); *Tilbury Town* (1953); *Selected Early Poems and Letters* (1960); *Selected Poems* (1965); *Letters to Edith Brown* (1968)

BIBLIOGRAPHY: Van Doren, M., *E. A. R.* (1927); Hagedorn, H., *E. A. R.: A Biography* (1938); Kaplan, E., *Philosophy in the Poetry of E. A. R.* (1940); Winters, Y., *E. A. R.* (1946); Neff, E., *E. A. R.* (1948); Fussell, E. S., *E. A. R.: The Literary Background of a Traditional Poet* (1954); Coxe, L. O., *E. A. R.* (1962); Anderson, W. L., *E. A. R.: A Critical Introduction* (1967); Richards, L. E., *E. A. R.* (1967); Robinson, W. R., *E. A. R.: A Poetry of the Act* (1967); Franchere, H., *E. A. R.* (1968)

CHARLES BURKHART

ROBINSON, Lennox

Irish dramatist, b. 4 Oct. 1886, Douglas, Cork; d. 14 Oct. 1958, Dublin

Son of a Protestant clergyman, R. was educated privately and attended Bandon Grammar School. The Abbey Theatre Company performances of plays by Yeats (q.v.) and Lady Augusta Gregory (1852–1932) converted him to Irish nationalism. Through practically all of his adult life, from 1909 to his death, he devoted much of his time to the Abbey Theatre, working as manager for nine years and as director after 1923.

R.'s first play, *The Clancy Name* (1908), was a peasant tragedy. Though its grim realism was in contrast to the poetic, imaginative drama his Irish contemporaries were writing, the play was produced by the directors of the Abbey Theatre.

After turning away from peasant themes, R. wrote light satiric comedies about middle-class life in small country towns, which are remarkable for their brilliant technique, shrewd observation, and sure touch. R. won success with *The White-Headed Boy* (1916), "one of the finest pieces of natural human comedy in the Irish National Theatre" (Ernest Boyd).

In later plays, such as *The Big House* (1926) and *Killycreggs in Twilight* (1939), he described the decline of the wealthy landowners and the Unionist Party in revolutionary Ireland.

FURTHER WORKS: *The Cross-Roads* (1910); *Harvest* (1910); *Two Plays* (1911); *Patriots* (1912); *The Dreamers* (1915); *A Young Man from the South* (1917); *Dark Days* (1918); *The Lost Leader* (1918); *Eight Short Stories* (1920); *Crabbed Youth and Age* (1924); *The Round Table* (1924); *The White Blackbird, Portrait* (1926); *Plays* (1928); *Give a Dog—* (1928); *Ever the Twain* (1930); *The Far-Off Hills* (1931); *Bryan Cooper* (1931); *Is Life Worth Living?* (1933); *More Plays* (includes *All's Over, Then?* and *Church Street;* 1935); *Three Homes* (with Tom Robinson and Nora Dorman; 1938); *Curtain Up* (1942); *Towards an Appreciation of the Theatre* (1945); *Pictures in a Theatre: A Conversation Piece* (1947); *The Lucky Finger* (1948); *Palette and Plough* (1948); *Ireland's Abbey Theatre, 1899–1951* (1951); *Drama at Irish* (1953); *Never the Time and the Place* (1953); *I Sometimes Think* (1956)

BIBLIOGRAPHY: O'Neill, M., *L. R.* (1964); Everson, I., "Young L. R. and the Abbey Theatre's First American Tour," *MD*, IX (1966), 74–89; Ellis-Fermor, U., *The Irish Dramatic Movement* (1967); Hogan, R., *After the Irish Renaissance: A Critical History of Irish Drama since "The Plough and the Stars"* (1967)

AUSTIN CLARKE

ROBLÈS, Emmanuel

French novelist, playwright, and journalist, b. 4 May 1914, Oran

The posthumous son of a Spanish mason, R. was raised by his mother and grandmother. After attending the École Normale in Algiers on a scholarship, he studied meteorology, languages, and journalism, later traveling in Europe, the Far East, and South America as a reporter and an interpreter. His friendship with Camus (q.v.) prompted R.'s first literary efforts.

During World War II, R. was a war correspondent, later settling briefly in Paris before returning to his beloved Algiers, where he founded and edited the review *Forge*. During the Algerian War, R. and Camus made a vain attempt to arrange a civilian truce. A personal tragedy forced R. to leave Africa and return to Paris where since 1957 he has been an editor at Le Seuil—a leading French publisher—and has been instrumental in introducing French readers to such "Mediterranean" writers as Dib (q.v.) and José Luis de Villalonga (b. 1920).

R.'s literary production to date can be

divided by thematic emphasis into three periods: rebellion and social protest (1938–44); war and the impact of war (1944–64); and introspection and poetic escape (1964 to the present).

L'Action (1938), R.'s first novel, is a terse and poignant account of a doomed attempt to organize a strike against inhuman employers. In the subsequent *Vallée du paradis* (1941), R. analyzes the unsuccessful dream of desperate people to emigrate to Argentina. In both these initial works personal efforts at rebellion are thwarted by trivial circumstances. In R.'s third novel, *Travail d'homme* (1943; The Angry Mountain, 1948), the hero undergoes a real initiation into the brotherhood of man by overcoming personal hatred and joining a team of dam workers who sacrifice their lives to save a village from flood danger.

The searing experience of World War II forced a change in emphasis in R.'s writing. Between 1944 and 1961 he wrote five novels, three plays, and several volumes of short stories dealing in a variety of ways with man's behavior under the duress of war. Tortured by conflicting psychological demands, consumed by a Mediterranean reverence for life and beauty, the Roblesian protagonist seeks his escape from the inferno of war in the "otherness" of love. In a world gone mad, man finds a temporary solace in conjugal love or in the tender understanding of a mistress.

In both *Les Hauteurs de la ville* (1948) and *Le Vésuve* (1961) intimate companionship is a prerequisite to happiness. R.'s anguished awareness of life's futility gives way to a determined faith in the love and self-sacrifice that make life possible. *Montserrat* (1948; Eng., 1950), one of the most powerful dramas of the contemporary stage, ends with the assertion that "what must be saved at any price is hope."

R.'s most recent works of fiction, *La Remontée du fleuve* (1964), *La Croisière* (1968), and *L'Ombre et la rive* (1970), transmit reality through the mirror of poetic imagination and memory, skillfully employing symbols to integrate various levels of significance. The modulations of a reverie replace the razor-sharp descriptions of encounters with violence and death. This new manner seems to indicate withdrawal from a life of action to a life of contemplation.

R.'s dynamic style, his ability to communicate the urgency of human problems, and his skill in recharging our emotions by exposing them to the impact of beauty and love, would seem to guarantee him a permanent place in world literature.

FURTHER WORKS: *Nuits sur le monde* (1944); *Garcia Lorca* (1950); *La Mort en face* (1951); *Cela s'appelle l'aurore* (1952; Dawn on Our Darkness, 1954); *La Vérité est morte* (1952); *Fédérica* (1954; Flowers for Manuela, 1958); *Les Couteaux* (1958; Knives, 1958); *L'Horloge, Porfirio* (1958); *L'Homme d'avril* (1959); *Plaidoyer pour un rebelle* (1965)

BIBLIOGRAPHY: Special R. issue, *Simoun*, No. 30 (Dec. 1959); Joyaux, G., "E. R.," *Kentucky Foreign Language Quarterly* (1964); Special R. issue, *Livres de France,* Feb. 1965; Rousselot, J., "E. R. et le monde réel," *Les Lettres Françaises,* May 1965; Depierries, J. L., *Entretiens avec E. R.* (1967); Chavardes, M., "E. R.," in *Littérature de notre temps* (1968); Landi, F., *E. R., ou Les raisons de vivre* (1969)

ANNE-MARIE DE MORET HAMBURG

RODE, Helge

Danish poet, dramatist, and essayist, b. 16 Oct. 1870, Copenhagen; d. there, 23 March 1937

R., who was born into a respectable middle-class Danish family, lost his father early and was brought up in Oslo, Norway.

R. earned his first success as a lyric poet with *Hvide blomster* (1892), which was followed by *Digte* (1896). These are the first poems in Danish literature that anticipated in form the modernist movement in poetry. They were inspired by Nietzsche's (q.v.) *Zarathustra* and by a religious, pantheistic emotion that awakened in R. in the Valdres Mountains of Norway. In them R. seeks to merge themes from everyday life with dithyrambic expressions of his awareness of eternity and acceptance of life.

In the 1890's R. wrote a series of poetic dramas. Of them only *Kongesønner* (1896), a tragedy set in ancient Greece, is of significant literary merit. Later, under the influence of Ibsen (q.v.), R. wrote realistic plays. Among them are *Grev Bonde og hans hus* (1912), which is about Lev Tolstoi's (q.v.) last years and death, and *Det store forlis* (1917), a drama of World War I.

In the essays he published after 1912, R. criticized the tradition of freethinking intellectualism and glorification of natural science that Brandes (q.v.) had exalted. R. defended

HELGE RODE

MAURICE ROELANTS

religious experience in opposition to the secular *Weltanschauung*, although he was not an orthodox Christian.

FURTHER WORKS: *Digte, gamle og nye* (1907); *Morbus Tellermann* (1907); *Ariel* (1914); *Krig og ånd* (1917); *En mand gik ned fra Jerusalem* (1920); *Moderen* (1921); *Den stille have* (1922); *Regenerationen i vort åndsliv* (1923); *Pladsen med de grønne træer* (1924); *Det store ja* (1926); *Det sjælelige gennembrud* (1928); *Den vilde rose* (1931); *Udvalgte digte* (1945)

BIBLIOGRAPHY: Hansen, H. J., *Dramatikeren H. R.* (1948); Durand, F., *Histoire de la littérature danoise* (1967)

EMIL FREDERIKSEN

RODÓ, José Enrique

Uruguayan essayist and critic, b. 15 July 1872, Montevideo; d. 1 May 1917, Palermo, Sicily

R. became famous at the age of twenty-nine for his work *Ariel* (1900), which came to be regarded as a gospel of Latin-American culture. With Darío (q.v.) he was a leader of the modernist movement. His special contribution to this was an element of mellow meditation and a devotion to the problems of Latin America. In this way he led to fulfillment the artistic insurrection that Darío had initiated.

In content R.'s work is related to that of his contemporaries in Spain—the "Generation of '98." The formative forces in his intellectual development, however, were French thinkers of the second half of the 19th c., such as Renan, Taine, and Guyau. In his makeup this European-type philosophical idealism merged with the intellectual traditions of Latin America.

In 1895 R. became one of the founders of the *Revista Nacional de Literatura y Ciencias Sociales*. In the pages of this periodical he won distinction for his commentary on contemporary Spanish and Latin-American writers and for his reevaluation of the literary past of the Rio de la Plata countries. Later his interest in literary criticism receded as he began to study Latin-American life and to write philosophical essays.

Ariel, a purported lecture that the teacher Prospero gives to his pupils, is an appeal to Latin-American youth to abandon the path of utilitarian democracy—exemplified by the United States—and to work for a democracy

that would be structured around spiritual and ideal values.

R.'s last projected work, which he called "Geórgicas morales," was to consist of a series of essays in harmonious sequence on such topics as the protean nature of the soul and its metamorphoses, on vocation and will, on grief and its creative powers, on the art of criticism, and on the dualism of personality. A preliminary selection was published under the title *Los Motivos de Proteo* (1908). After R.'s death ungrouped drafts intended for the "Geórgicas morales" were published in the collection *Los últimos motivos de Proteo* (1932).

FURTHER WORKS: *La vida nueva* (1897); *La novela nueva* (1897); *El que vendrá* (1897); *Rubén Darío* (1899); *El mirador de Próspero* (1913); *Cinco ensayos* (1915); *El camino de Paros* (1917); *Epistolario* (1921); *Nuevos motivos de Proteo* (1927); *Obras completas* (1956)

BIBLIOGRAPHY: Ureña Henriquez, M., *R. y Rubén Darío* (1919); Scarone, A., *Bibliografía de J. E. R.* (1930); Pereda, C., *R.'s Main Sources* (1948); Monegal, E. R., *J. E. R. en el Novecientos* (1950); Albarrán Puente, G., *J. E. R.* (1953); Scroggins, D. C., "*Motivos de Proteo* by J. E. R.: A Stylistic Study," *DA,* XXVII (1967), 2161A

EMIR RODRIGUEZ MONEGAL

ROELANTS, Maurice

Belgian novelist and short-story writer (writing in Flemish), b. 19 Dec. 1895, Ghent; d. 1966, Brussels

In 1922, R., an elementary-school teacher, became chief editor of the Catholic weekly *De Spectator*. In 1922 he established, together with Richard Minne (b. 1391), Karel Leroux (b. 1895), and Raymond Herreman (b. 1896), the influential literary journal *'t Fonteintje* (1922–24), whose purpose was to keep alive the tradition of individual self-expression. In 1932 R. started, with his Flemish colleagues Gijsen, Walschap (qq.v.), and Herreman, and with the northern Netherlands authors Menno ter Braak (1902–1940) and Edgar du Perron (1899–1940), the literary monthly *Forum*. Frowning upon nationalism, these writers aimed to be true Europeans.

In 1922 R. accepted the post of literary adviser in the Department of Education. Soon after he became curator of the historic castle of Gaasbeek near Brussels, which once housed the Count of Egmont and his family.

R. is the father of the psychological novel in Flanders, in the tradition of Stendhal (1783–1842) and Gustave Flaubert (1821–80). In his novels R. pictures the life and thought of members of the Flemish middle class. He concentrated on the emotions experienced in close relationships—among members of a family, among friends, or between lovers.

In *Het leven dat wij droomden* (1931), R. analyzes the responses of a young woman, Maria Danneels, who, wanting to devote herself to her medical studies in order to help her father in his medical work, has banished from her mind all thoughts of love and marriage. But, against her will, she falls seriously in love with the fiancé of her friend Irene. R. acutely analyzes Maria's painful conflicts between love and duty and loyalty. The resolution of the novel, that Maria will become Richard's wife, is convincing.

In *Alles komt terecht* (1937) R. relates the same events twice, first as they are seen by Hélène's hypochondriac husband and second as seen by his and Hélène's optimistic and rather lighthearted friend Willem.

R.'s best work is the title story of the short-story collection *De Jazzspeler* (1928; The Jazz-player, 1947), in which a middle-aged well-to-do husband tries to suppress his longing for the more adventurous life led by young bachelors.

R.'s basic concern is the struggle for happiness, which, for him, is the most important aim in life. Happiness, according to R., can be obtained by knowing oneself, by positive belief and practical action. He was also a disciple of Pascal (1623–62), believing that "Knowing oneself brings man to God." These attitudes are expressed in R.'s autobiographical novel *Gebed om een goed einde* (1944), in which the narrator prays God not to let him die through lack of courage as his mother and his grandfather had done, for they had simply given up the belief in human happiness.

R. is one of the major writers in modern Flemish literature. He is to be credited for his contribution to the revival in Flemish literature through the psychological novel and through his stimulating work on *'t Fonteintje* and *Forum*. R.'s greatest merit, however, is his warm feeling for human life, which is expressed in a simple, almost classic style.

FURTHER WORKS: *Eros* (1915); *De driedubbele verrassing* (1917); *De kom der*

loutering (1918); *Komen en gaan* (1927); *De twee helden* (1928); *Van de vele mogelijkheden om gelukkig te zijn* (1929); *Het verzaken* (1930); *Schrijvers, wat is er van den mensch* (1942–57); *De weduwe Becker* (1943); *Drie romanellipsen* (1943); *Gun goede wijn een rans* (1947); *Pygmalion* (1947); *Lof der liefde* (1949); *Vuur en dauw* (1965)

BIBLIOGRAPHY: Closset, F., *M. R.* (1946); van der Ween, A., *M. R.* (1960); Hermanowski, G., *Die Stimme des schwarzen Löwen* (1961), pp. 61–67; Hermanowski, G., *Die moderne flämische Literatur* (1963), pp. 34–49; Kemp, B., *De Vlaamse letteren tussen gisteren en morgen* (1963), pp. 110–11; Mallinson, V., *Modern Belgian Literature* (1966), pp. 97–98; Lissens, R. F., *De Vlaamse letterkunde van 1780 tot heden* (4th ed., 1967), pp. 185–86, 192–93; Hermanowski, G., *Säulen der modernen flämischen Prosa* (1969), pp. 3–15, 78–81

JUDICA I. H. MENDELS

ROETHKE, Theodore

American poet, b. 5 May 1908, Saginaw, Michigan; d. 1 Aug. 1963, Seattle, Washington

R. was the son of a florist who owned one of the largest greenhouses in the country. He graduated from the University of Michigan and did graduate work at Harvard. From 1931 until his death he taught English at the University of Washington (1947–63) and other colleges. His adult life was marked by a recurrent manic-depressive disorder that affected his poems, though not to their detriment.

Auden's (q.v.) comment on R.'s first book, *Open House* (1941), throws light on the emotional source of nearly all R.'s work: "Many people . . . feel physically soiled and humiliated by life . . . but both to remember and to transform the humiliation into something beautiful, as Mr. R. does, is rare."

More specifically, this sense of soilure and humiliation is a combined fear of and loathing for his own body, sexuality, parental figures, loneliness, the growth of the body's "dull decrepitude," and death. These feelings impelled him toward an otherworldliness, a longing for another life that he associated with images of movement-in-place (such as a dance or a swaying plant) and with light. They also account for his many expressions of empathy with various forms of life and even with inanimate objects. But despite his inclinations toward such "mystical" thought, R. found submission to belief in divine creation and personal immortality difficult and frequently impossible.

Whereas *Open House* registers the cry of pain of sentient being, *The Lost Son, and Other Poems* (1948) probes for the sources of pain and offers glimpses of joy. In his poems of the 1950's, R. merely reworks with greater professionalism his earlier achievements. His gropings solidify into preachments concerning reincarnation and Bergsonian spiritual evolution. But his last book, *The Far Field* (1964), reaches a new height. Here, beautifully handled landscape imagery is used to evoke particular states of mind and relationships between these states. In these poems, what the critic Philip Rahv (b. 1908) calls "the cult of experience" is given new and startling expression.

Throughout his career R. experimented with various traditional line forms and stanzas and with short- and long-line free verse. His most pervasive device is the end-stopped line, often used for epigrams that are less than effective. He effortlessly avoided the iambic foot and was a master at varying the pace of his lines.

After a strictly metered and rhymed first book, R. wrote a series of highly successful free-verse pieces called "The Greenhouse Poems." He then proceeded to work on a narrative sequence, of which he said, "Rhythmically, it's the spring and rush of the child I'm after." He identified the "ancestors" of these and of the poems of the 1950's as: "German and English folk literature, particularly Mother Goose; Elizabethan and Jacobean drama, especially the songs and rants; the Bible; Blake and Traherne; Dürer." In *The Far Field*, where Whitman is the presiding spirit, the accents lighten and the end-stopping subsides. This book marks the peak of R.'s achievement.

R. combines the best of the "cooked" or university poets, their sense of a usable past, and the best of the "raw" poets, their sense of a usable and concrete present. Though not a major poet, R. has left about a dozen pieces whose loss would seriously diminish American poetry of the 20th c.

FURTHER WORKS: *Praise to the End!* (1951); *The Waking: Poems 1933–1953* (1953); *Words for the Wind* (1958); *I Am! Says the Lamb* (1961); *Party at the Zoo* (1963); *Sequence, Sometimes Metaphysical* (1964); *On the Poet and His Craft: Selected Prose* of T. R. (ed. Ralph J. Mills, Jr.; 1965); *The Collected Poems of T. R.* (1966); *Selected Letters* (1968)

BIBLIOGRAPHY: Burke, K., "The Vegetal Radicalism of T. R.," *SoR* (1950), pp. 68–108; Southworth, J. G., "The Poetry of T. R.," *CE*, XXI (March 1960), 326–38; Mills, Jr., R. J., *T. R.* (Minnesota Pamphlets, 1963); Ostroff, A., ed., *The Modern Poet as Artist and Critic* (1964), pp. 189–219; Staples, H. B., "Rose in the Sea-Wind: A Reading of T. R.'s 'North American Sequence,'" *AL*, XXXVI (May 1964), 189–203; Kunitz, S., "R.: Poet of Transformations," *New Republic*, 23 Jan. 1965, pp. 23–29; Stein, A., ed., *T. R.: Essays on the Poetry* (1965); Malkoff, K., *T. R.* (1966); Seager, A., *The Glass House: The Life of T. R.* (1968)

GEORGE WOLFF

ROJAS, Manuel

Chilean novelist and short-story writer, b. 8 Jan. 1896, Buenos Aires

R. left school at the age of fourteen, after which he worked at a variety of jobs—grape-picker, construction laborer on the Trans-Andean Railroad, stevedore on the Valparaiso docks, linotype operator, prompter with itinerant acting groups, and journalist. Although he was active as an Anarchist during his youth, he later repudiated such activities and as a writer has never espoused political causes. In 1957 he received the Premio Nacional de Literatura.

R. began his literary career in 1926 with the publication of *Hombres del Sur*, a book of short stories. In them he portrays rugged outdoor types and emphasizes dramatic, fast-paced action and regional settings, especially the Andes mountains. Some of the characters R. drew from personal acquaintance.

Two subsequent volumes, *El delincuente* (1929) and *Travesía* (1934), contain stories that reveal a more mature writer who depicts lonely, alienated men in a bewildering urban environment. Slower in their movement, with a minimum of action, these stories convey subtle changes in mood and mental states that the characters undergo. Examples of this latter type of story are "El vaso de leche," "El mendigo," and "El delincuente."

In his first novel, *Lanchas en la bahía* (1932), R. exploits his personal experiences as a stevedore in Valparaiso. With visual and auditory imagery, he paints an impressionistic picture of the port city, evoking the wharves and the city at night as well as the atmosphere of a low-class brothel. At the same time, the novel is an exploration of character, that of an adolescent in the ambivalent stage between boyhood and manhood. While the pain of adolescence is certainly present, R. prefers, through irony, to stress the humorous aspects of his young protagonist's dilemma.

Hijo de ladrón (1951; Born Guilty, 1955) is without a doubt R.'s greatest achievement. In this novel, he raises his autobiographical character, Aniceto Hevia, to the level of a universal symbol of man and his existence in a broken world. Condemned to his past because of his father, a thief, Aniceto is a young man in search of his authentic self, of at least a modicum of freedom in his relationship with the world and with others. Inherent in the novel's structure is the mythical pattern of man's fall from innocence into the discovery of a broken world and the quest for salvation that naturally follows. It is R.'s purpose to show that man can attain a degree of freedom from the past and for the future and that salvation from the wounds inflicted by the world can be healed to a great extent by the solidarity of human brotherhood.

Two later novels, *Mejor que el vino* (1958) and *Sombras contra el muro* (1963), complete R.'s trilogy on Aniceto Hevia. The former explores the psychophysiological maze of Aniceto's sexual relationships; the latter in a kaleidoscopic burlesque depicts his Anarchist activities. Although both are good novels, neither approaches *Hijo de ladrón* in artistry or depth.

In general, R.'s work, while almost entirely autobiographical, is of high artistic quality. A master of ironic understatement, quiet humor, and a prose style that evokes the spoken word, R.'s novels and stories exude life and authentic, human experience.

FURTHER WORKS: *Tonada del transeunte* (1927); *La ciudad de los césares* (1936); *De la poesía a la revolución* (1938); *Imágenes de infancia* (n.d.); *Punta de rieles* (1960); *El árbol siempre verde* (1960); *Obras completas* (1961); *Pasé por México un día* (1964)

BIBLIOGRAPHY: Cannizzo, M., "M. R., Chilean Novelist and Author," *Hispania*, XLI (1958), 200–201; González Vera, J. S., *Algunos* (1959); Goic, C., "Hijo de ladrón: libertad y lágrimas," *Atenea*, No. 389 (1960), pp. 103–13; Silva Castro, R., "M. R., novelista," *Cuadernos Hispanoamericanos*, XLIV (1960), 5–19; Alegría, F., *Fronteras del realismo* (1962); Licht-

blau, M. L., "Ironic Devices in M. R.'s *Hijo de ladrón*," *Symposium*, XIX (1965)

ROBERT SCOTT

ROLAND HOLST, Adriaan

Dutch poet and essayist, b. 23 May 1888, Amsterdam

The son of a stockbroker, and the nephew of the painter Richard Roland Holst and the Christian-socialist poet and activist, Henriëtte Roland Holst-van der Schalk (q.v.), R. H. was a student at Oxford from 1908 to 1911. There he thoroughly familiarized himself with the poetry of the English romantics, especially Percy Bysshe Shelley (1792–1822), and was attracted to the poets of the Irish revival, in particular to Yeats (q.v.).

R. H. was an associate editor of *De Gids,* the magazine of the literary establishment, from 1920 to 1934. After World War II, he spent several months in South Africa as an unofficial literary envoy. In 1959 he was awarded the prestigious Netherlandic Literature Prize.

R. H.'s first volume of poems, *Verzen* (1911), reveals a nostalgic dreamer who in a highly stylized poetical idiom expresses his inner feelings. Winds, waves, islands are the symbols of his isolation. He sets himself apart from mankind much as a true believer sets himself apart from those who do not have the faith.

R. H. was fond of symbolism drawn from the Trojan War. He saw Helen's smile as the doom of Troy, celebrating the power of beauty. This idea is perhaps best expressed in his greatest poetic achievement, *Een winter aan zee* (1937), a series of more than sixty poems.

Among his poetic accomplishments are translations of Shakespeare's *King Lear* (1914) and *Richard III* (1929) and a brilliant rendering of Yeats's *Countess Cathleen* (1941). The best of R. H.'s prose writings is *Deirdre en de zonen van Usnach* (1916), a doom-shadowed account of the Celtic legend that shows the influence of Yeats. He was instrumental in establishing the reputation of the poet J. H. Leopold (1865–1925) with his article "Over den dichter Leopold" (1926). In "Shelley, een afscheid" (1928) he repudiated his former idol.

Though R. H.'s verse is sometimes obscure, sometimes deliberately so, it is always melodious and reveals a vision of the springtime of human existence before what he saw as the corruption of civilization.

ADRIAAN ROLAND HOLST

HENRIËTTE ROLAND HOLST-
VAN DER SCHALK

FURTHER WORKS: *De belijdenis van de stilte* (1913); *Voorbij de wegen* (1920); *De wilde kim* (1925); *De afspraak* (1925); *Het elysisch verlangen* (1928); *De vagebond* (1931); *Tussen vuur en maan* (1932); *De pooltocht der verbeelding* (1936); *Voortekens* (1936); *Uit zelfbehoud* (1938); *Onderweg* (1940); *Eigen achtergronden* (1945); *In memoriam Herman Gorter* (1946); *Sirenische kunst* (1946); *De twee planeten* (1947); *Tegen de wereld* (1947); *In ballingschap* (1947); *Verzamelde werken* (4 vols., 1948–49); *Van erts tot arend* (1948); *Swordplay, Wordplay* (with S. Vestdijk; 1950); *Woest en moe* (1951); *Bezielde dorpen* (1957); *In gevaar* (1958); *Omtrent de grens* (1960); *Het experiment* (1960); *Onder koude wolken* (1962); *Onderhuids* (1963); *Uitersten* (1967)

BIBLIOGRAPHY: Sötemann, A., *A. R. H. en de mythe van Ierland* (1950); Stenfert Kroese, W. H., *De mythe van A. R. H.* (1951); *De Gids*, May 1958; *Maatstaf*, May 1958; Elemans, J., *A. R. H.* (1962); *Maatstaf*, May 1963, special R. H. issue

FRANCIS BULHOF

ROLAND HOLST-VAN DER SCHALK, Henriëtte

Dutch poet, dramatist, essayist, and biographer, b. 24 Dec. 1869, Noordwijk; d. 21 Nov. 1952, Amsterdam

Henriëtte R. came from a wealthy, middle-class, liberal Protestant background. Soon after her marriage to the painter R. N. Roland Holst in 1896, she embraced doctrinaire Marxism. By 1927, however, she had coalesced her beliefs into an ethical, religious socialism.

Henriëtte R.'s first published work was the *Sonnetten en verzen in terzinen geschreven* (1895), which was in the spirit of Spinoza. Her political convictions were reflected in *De nieuwe geboort* (1902) and *Opwaartsche wegen* (1907). The sorrowful poetry that she wrote in *De vrouw in het woud* (1912) stemmed from her conflict between her adherence to orthodox communist dogma and her warm love for people.

Christian submissiveness and love are the themes of *Verworvenheden* (1927) and *Tusschen tijd en eeuwigheid* (1934).

FURTHER WORKS: *Kapitaal en arbeid in Nederland* (1902); *Generalstreik und Sozialdemokratie* (1906); *De opstandelingen* (1910); *Thomas Moore* (1912); *J. J. Rousseau* (1912);

Het feest der gedachtenis (1915); *Verzonken grenzen* (1918); *De helden de schare* (1920); *Het offer* (1921); *De kinderen* (1922); *Tusschen twee werelden* (1923); *Arbeid* (1923); *Heldensage* (1927); *Vernieuwingen* (1929); *Tolstoj* (1930); *Kinderen van dezen tijd* (1930); *Wij willen niet* (1931); *Gustaaf Landauer* (1931); *Guido Gezelle* (1931); *De moeder* (1932); *De roep der stad* (1933); *Der vrouwen weg* (1933); *Herman Gorter* (1933); *Rosa Luxemburg* (1935); *Gedroomd gebeuren* (1937); *Uit de diepte* (1946); *R. Rolland* (1946); *Van de shaduw naar het licht* (1946); *In de webbe der tijden* (1947); *Ghandi* (1947); *Wordingen* (1949); *Het vuur brandde voort* (1949); *Romankunst als levensschool* (1950); *Bloemlezing* (1951)

BIBLIOGRAPHY: Kaas-Albarda, M., *Inleiding tot de poëzie van H. R.* (1935); Proost, K. F., *H. R.* (1937); Verhoeven, B., *De zielegang van H. R.* (1939); Van Praag, J., *H. R.* (1946); Riethof, H., "H. R.," *Gids*, CXXXI (1967), v, 334–43

KAREL REIJNDERS

ROLLAND, Romain

French novelist, dramatist, musicologist, and biographer, b. 29 Jan. 1866, Clamecy; d. 30 Dec. 1944, Vézelay

R. came from a Burgundian Protestant family that in 1880 moved to Paris, where he attended the Lycée Louis-le-Grand and later the École Normale Supérieure. While studying for his degree in history, R. passionately read Nietzsche and Lev Tolstoi (qq.v.), both of whom were to have an important influence on his work. In addition, R. formed a lasting and influential friendship with André Suarès (1868–1948), the future social historian, the two young men being drawn together by their common interest in music.

In 1889, R. went to Rome to continue his studies at the École Française d'Archéologie and to work on his thesis, *L'Histoire de l'opéra en Europe avant Lulli et Scarlatti* (1895). The rich souvenirs of Renaissance civilization were a revelation to R. During this time he formed another of those lasting relationships that were to play so important a part in his life. While in Rome he met Malwida von Meysenbug (1816–1903), a friend of both Nietzsche and Richard Wagner (1813–83) and an intimate of Italian literary and cultural circles.

It was under Mme. von Meysenbug's influence that on his return to Paris R. became a champion of Wagnerian music and was drawn to the German composer-poet's concept of a drama based on elementary national themes. However, no doubt it was through Suarès that R. was first introduced to Maurice Pottecher's (1867–1960) ideas on a "people's theater." The result was a series of plays in which R. tried to appeal to the masses with dramas that attempted to combine art and social commentary. His two cycles of plays on French history— *Tragédies de la foi* (pub. 1913) and *Le Théâtre de la révolution* (pub. 1903)—very often pointed up contemporary parallels in their presentation of the conflict between social organization and individual liberty. This was probably particularly true of *Les Loups* (1898; The Wolves, 1937), which indirectly reflected the bitter controversy raging in France over the infamous Dreyfus affair in which an innocent Jewish army officer was indicted for treason in order to protect high army circles against the scandal of corruption.

At about this time R. recorded in his diary his determination never to belong to any organized group or political party and his conviction that the intellectual's primary responsibility was toward truth. In 1903, R. was made a professor of music history at the Sorbonne and published the first of his biographies of great men, *Vie de Beethoven* (1903; Beethoven, 1917). Over the course of years he was to add to the series with *Vie de Michel-Ange* (1905; revised 1906; Michelangelo, 1921), *Haendel* (1910; Handel, 1916), *Vie de Tolstoi* (1911; Tolstoy, 1911), *Mahatma Gandhi* (1923; Eng., 1924), and *La Vie de Vivekananda et l'évangile universel* (1930; The Life of Vivekananda and the Universal Gospel, 1960).

Thanks to R.'s friendship with Péguy (q.v.), 1904 saw the beginning of the serial publication of *Jean-Christophe* (1904–1912; Eng., 1910–13) in the Catholic poet's famous *Cahiers de la Quinzaine*. In this major work, an impressive *roman-fleuve* with a protagonist whose temperament and genius recall Beethoven, R. tried to reconcile the German and the French mentalities, and to point up the necessity of these complementary contributions to Western civilization. A developmental novel constructed on the Goethean model, the book traces its musician-hero's restless attempt to establish a psychological "home" after he is hounded from Germany to exile in France, where until he meets young Olivier Jeannin he is depressed and misled by superficial, frivolous qualities

in French art. *Jean-Christophe* established R.'s international reputation.

World War I began while R. was in Switzerland finishing *Colas Breugnon* (1918; Eng., 1919), a lively tale of 17th-c. Burgundy. He protested this outbreak of fratricidal madness, and electing to remain in exile he wrote a series of articles, published as *Au-dessus de la mêlée* (1915; Above the Battlefield, 1916). in which he inveighed against both camps. Spitteler, Stefan Zweig, and Hesse (qq.v.) rallied to his support, but the book angered both the French and the Germans. Nevertheless, it was largely responsible for R.'s being awarded the Nobel Prize for Literature in 1915. In his *Journal des années de guerre, 1914–19* (1952) and *Aux Peuples assassinés* (1918), R. further elaborated his denunciation of the national and economic corruption, which he saw as the real reasons for war.

R. greeted the Bolshevik Revolution in Russia with hope and enthusiasm, and though toward the end of his life he was to confide in Hesse his disappointment in the U.S.S.R., as late as 1935 he violently attacked Gide (q.v.) for the latter's sharp criticism of the Soviet regime after both writers had returned from a trip to Moscow. *Le Voyage intérieur* (1942; Voyage Within, 1947) shows that R.'s conception of Marxism was later influenced by his attraction to Eastern mysticism.

After publishing the novels *Pierre et Luce* (1920; Pierre and Luce, 1922) and *Clérambault* (1920; Eng., 1921), R. set to work on his second great *roman-fleuve*, *L'Âme enchantée* (1925–33; The Soul Enchanted, 1925–34), an account of a woman's struggle to realize her spiritual possibilities.

When World War II broke out, R. abandoned his pacifist stand. During the years of the German occupation he devoted his energies to a two-volume *Péguy* (1944) in which he honored his friend, who had been killed during World War I at the Battle of the Marne, as a man of "inflexible moral conscience."

As a man and a writer, R. was torn between his belief in the need for revolution and his abhorrence of violence. His major works are moving evidence of his disappointed humanitarian aspirations. They paved the way for the cyclical novels of Martin du Gard and Romains (qq.v.).

FURTHER WORKS: *Empédocle* (1891); *Saint-Louis* (1897); *Aërt* (1898); *Le Triomphe de la raison* (1899); *Quatorze Juillet*

(1902; The Fourteenth of July, 1918); *Le Théâtre du peuple* (1903, The People's Theater, 1918); *Le Temps viendra* (1903); *Musiciens d'autrefois* (1908; Some Musicians of Former Days, 1915); *Musiciens d'aujourd'hui* (1908; Musicians of Today, 1922); *Danton* (1909; Eng., 1918); *Liluli* (1919; Eng., 1920); *Voyage Musical au pays du passé* (1921; A Musical Tour through the Land of the Past, 1922); *La Marquise de Montespan* (1923; Eng., 1927); *Choix des lettres à Malvida von Meysenbug* (1923; Letters of R. R. and Malvida von Meysenbug, 1890–91); *Le Jeu de l'amour et de la mort* (1925; The Game of Love and Death, 1926); *Pâques fleuries* (1926; Palm Sunday, 1928); *Goethe et Beethoven* (1927; Goethe and Beethoven, 1931); *Les Leonides* (1928, Eng., 1929; *Œuvres* (1931 ff.); *Quinze Ans de combat* (1935; I Will Not Rest, 1937); *Compagnons de route* (1936); *Par la Revolution, la paix* (1936); *Robespierre* (1939); *Le Seuil* (1946); *De Jean-Christophe à Colas Breugnon: Journal 1912 á 1913* (1947); *Souvenirs de jeunesse* (1947); *Lettres de R. R. à un combattant de la résistance* (1947); *Correspondance entre L. Gillet et R. R.* (1948); *Richard Strauss et R. R.: correspondance* (1951; R. R. and Richard Strauss, 1968); *Lettres de R. R. à Marianne Czeke* (1951; Letters of R. R. to Marianne Czeke, 1966); *Le Cloître de la rue d'Ulm: Journal à l'École Normale 1886–89* (1952); *Printemps R. Lettres à sa mère, 1889–90* (1954); *Correspondance R. R. et Lugné-Poë, 1894–1901* (1955; Correspondence between R. R. and Lugné-Poë, 1957); *Une Amitié Française, correspondance entre Charles Péguy et R. R.* (1955); *Mémoires et fragments du journal* (1956); *Choix de lettres de R. R. à S. B. Guerrini-Gonzaga* (1959); *Inde: Journal de 1915–1943* (1960); *Histoire d'une amitié, R. R. et Alphonse de Châteaubriand* (1962). **Selected English translations:** *Prophets of the New India* (1930); *The Living Thoughts of R. R.* (1939); *Essays on Music* (1948)

BIBLIOGRAPHY: Jouve, P. J., *R. R. vivant 1914–1919* (1920); Bonnerot, J., *R. R.: sa vie, son œuvre* (1921); Zweig, S. *R. R.* (1926); Starr, W. T., *A Critical Bibliography of the Published Writings of R. R.* (1950); Starr, W. T., *R. R. and a World at War* (1956); Cheval, R., *R. R. et la guerre* (1963); Karczewska, Markiewicz Z., *R. R.* (1964); Special R. issue, *Europe*, Nos. 439–40 (1965); Myers, R., ed., *Richard Strauss and R. R.*

(1968); Sices, D., *Music and the Musician in Jean-Christophe: The Harmony of Contrasts* (1968)

* * * *

RØLVAAG, Ole Edvaart

(pseud. of *Paal Mørck*), Norwegian-American novelist, b. 22 April 1876, Dönna, Norway; d. 5 Nov. 1931, Northfield, Minnesota

R. emigrated to America at the age of twenty. He attended St. Olaf College (Northfield) but returned to the University of Oslo for graduate work. From 1906 to 1931 he was professor of Norwegian at St. Olaf, where he was honored for his lectures on Ibsen (q.v.) Though he wrote his novels in Norwegian, he translated them into English himself.

The best of R.'s novels is the well-known *Giants in the Earth* (1925; first published in Norwegian as *I de dage* and *Riket grundlægges*, 1924–25). Through the use of a mixed point of view and a modified stream-of-consciousness technique, R. ably demonstrates the varying results of the frontier upon the Norwegians. Per Hansa and Beret are case studies in frontier personality; their psychological natures cause them to react in startlingly opposite ways to the stimuli of the prairie and its challenge, and, ironically, their fates are in inverse proportion to their attitudes. Per, stubborn, strong, resourceful, and optimistic, dies in a blinding blizzard; Beret, only partially recovered from her recurrent insanity, ascends to a plateau of serenity—the malignant prairie can no longer harm her.

Giants in the Earth is the first part of a trilogy. The following two novels—*Peder seier* (1928; Peter Victorious, 1929) and *Den signede dag* (1931; Their Fathers' God, 1931)—do not measure up to the powerful *Giants in the Earth*.

In this trilogy R. portrays vividly and realistically the problems faced by the Norwegian immigrants in subduing the Dakota prairies, and by their children in adapting themselves to their new culture. This saga of empire-building in a strange land is told in a powerfully poetic style that heightens the drama of the pioneers' struggle against an impersonal nature.

Although he has been unjustly neglected in recent years, R. remains the most perceptive spokesman for the Scandinavian immigrants in America.

FURTHER WORKS: *To tvillinger, et billede fra idag* (1920; Pure Gold, 1930; republished as *Rent guld,* 1932); *Længselens baat* (1921; Boat of Longing, 1933)

BIBLIOGRAPHY: Jorgenson, T., and Solum, N. O., *O. E. R.* (1939); Boewe, C. "R.'s America: An Immigrant Novelist's Views," *WHR,* XI (1957), 3–12; Steensma, R. C., "R. and Turner's Frontier Thesis," *NDQ,* XXVII (1959), 100–4

ROBERT C. STEENSMA

ROMAINS, Jules

(pseud. of *Louis Farigoule*), French novelist, dramatist, poet, and essayist, b. 26 Aug. 1885, Saint-Julien-Chapteuil

As an adolescent, R. attended a Paris *lycée* and afterward went to the École Normale where he later taught. He frequented the literary cafés and, through his friendship with Gide (q.v.), met many of the young symbolist (*see* symbolism) writers. But though his first poems were published in the symbolist review *La Plume,* R.'s basic orientation was scientific, sociological, and political. The major influences on him were philosopher Henri Bergson (1859–1941) and sociologist Émile Durkheim (1858–1917), a reflection of whose theories on group psychology can be seen even in the poems of R.'s first book, *L'Âme des hommes* (1904), which immediately attracted critical attention.

By 1905, R. had already published several articles in which he began to develop his theory of unanimism, according to which the psychology of a group—whether it be formed of immediate friends and neighbors, the inhabitants of a city, or those drawn together by a common belief—transcends, energizes, and orientates the individual. This theory is at the heart of his novella *Le Bourg régénéré* (1906) —the story of a small city given new pride and direction by a shared belief—and it is developed at length in *La Vie unanime* (1908), a long poem basic to the understanding of all R.'s future writing. Both these works were written while R. was somewhat vaguely associated with the Groupe de l'Abbaye (*see* French literature), whose guiding spirit was Duhamel (q.v.).

Unanimism found further literary development in R.'s first play, *L'Armée dans la ville* (1911), a verse drama about the conflict between two "groups"—the vanquished inhabitants and the military occupiers of a town— and in the novel *Mort de quelqu'un* (1911; The Death of a Nobody, 1914), in which the death of an insignificant apartment-house dweller gives the other tenants in the building a new sense of community. *Les Copains* (1913; The Boys in the Back Room, 1937) is a witty and joyous expression of the workings of unanimism in a student community.

Initially R. had conceived of unanimism as a basically benevolent force, but the shocking experience of the effects of group dynamism in World War I led him to consider its dangers and abuses. After another verse drama, *Cromedeyre-le-Vieil* 1920), a modern retelling of the rape of the Sabine women, set in a tradition-oriented small town, R. wrote a series of sparkling comedies in which unanimism is shown in the service of unscrupulous, though attractive, frauds. In 1920, R. had published a satirical novel, *Donogoo-Tonka, ou Les Miracles de la science,* in which the error of an absent-minded geographer, Monsieur Le Trouhadec, is turned into a reality when people flock to a marvelous but nonexistent city he describes. Employing the same protagonist, R. continued his unanimistic adventures in the comedies *Monsieur Le Trouhadec saisi par la débauche* (1923) and *Le Mariage de Le Trouhadec* (1925). Later, the novel itself was dramatized as *Donogoo-Tonka* (1930; Donogoo, 1961). R.'s best-known play is *Knock, ou Le Triomphe de la médecine* (1923; Dr. Knock, 1925), in which a unanimistic doctor imposes a "religion" of hypochondria on the healthy inhabitants of a provincial city.

R.'s major work is *Les Hommes de bonne volonté* (1932–46; Men of Good Will, 14 vols., 1934–46), twenty-seven novels forming a vast fresco of French society between 6 October 1908 and 7 October 1933. These novels show the interrelation of various individuals and social groups. Though the series has no central protagonist—this function being unanimistically fulfilled by the interaction of all the characters as they create the entity known as France—the friends Jallez and Jeraphanion are generally assumed to be autobiographical reflections of R. himself.

R.'s optimistic hope that the efforts of men of good will would prevail was frustrated by the rise of Hitler in Germany and by the subsequent events that led to World War II. Renouncing his efforts to build the city of the future, Jallez determines to seek a "miraculously spared" corner in which he will be shel-

ROMAIN ROLLAND

JULES ROMAINS

tered from "the fire raging around." When France fell, R. sought refuge in the United States. The disappointment of his hopes for humanity is reflected in the decadence and incest of *Le Fils de Jerphanion* (1956).

Though R.'s comedies continue to hold the stage—especially *Knock* and the adaptation of Ben Jonson's (1573–1637) *Volpone* on which he collaborated with Stefan Zweig (q.v.)— recent critics have tended to downgrade the impressive *roman-fleuve* that R. had intended to be his major work. It nevertheless remains a fascinating and often brilliant chronicle of French society during the first half of this century.

FURTHER WORKS: *L'Âme des hommes* (1904); *À La Foule qui est ici* (1909); *Premier Livre de prière* (1909); *Un Être en marche* (1910); *Manuel de Déification* (1910); *Puissances de Paris* (1911); *Odes et prières* (1913); *Sur les Quais de la Villette* (1914; second edition, *Le Vin blanc de la Villette*, 1923); *Europe* (1916); *Les Quatre Saisons* (1917); *Le Voyage des amants* (2 vols., 1920); *Amour couleur de Paris* (1921); *La Vision extra-rétinienne* (1921; Eyeless Sight, 1924); *Psyché* (3 vols., 1922–29; The Body's Raptures, 1967); *Théâtre* (7 vols., 1923); *Petit Traité de versification* (1923); *Lucienne* (1923; Eng., 1925); *Ode Génoise* (1925); *Le Dictateur* (1926); *Jean Le Maufranc* (1927); revised edition, *Jean Musse, ou L'École de l'hypocrisie*, 1930); *La Vérité en bouteilles* (1928); *Chants de dix années* (1928); *Pièces en un acte* (1930); *Problème d'aujourd'hui* (1931); *Le Roi masqué* (1932); *Problèmes européens* (1933); *Le Couple France-Allemagne* (1934); *Zola et son example* (1935); *Sept Mystères du destin de l'Europe* (1940; Seven Mysteries of Europe, 1941); *Stefan Zweig* (1941); *Une Vue des choses* (1941); *Grâce encore pour la terre* (1941); *Salsette découvre l'Amerique* (1942; Salsette Discovers America, 1942); *Actualité de Victor Hugo* (1944); *Bertrand de Ganges* (1944); *L'An mil* (1947); *Le Problème numero un* (1947); *Le Moulin et l'hospice* (1949); *Violation de frontières* (1951); *Hommes, medicines, machines* (1954); *Examen de conscience des français* (1954; A Frenchman Examines His Conscience, 1955); *Passagers de cette planète, où allons-nous?* (1955); *Une Femme singulière* (1957; The Adventuress, 1960); *Le Besoin de voir clair* (1957); *Maisons* (1957); *Souvenirs et confidences d'un écrivain: Autobiographie* (1958); *Situation de la terre* (1958; As It Is on

Earth, 1962); *Mémoires de Mme Chauverel* (1959); *Un Grand Honnête Homme* (1961); *Pour Raison garder* (1961); *Lettre ouverte contre une vaste conspiration* (1966; Open Letter against a Vast Conspiracy, 1967)

BIBLIOGRAPHY: Israel, M., *J. R.* (1931); Cuisenier, A., *J. R. et l'unanimisme* (1935); Blanchard, P., *J. R.* (1945); Cuisenier, A., *L'Art de J. R.* (1948); Berry, M., *J. R.* (1953); Norrish, P., *Drama of the Group: A Study of Unanimism in the Plays of J. R.* (1958); Widdem, W., *Weltbejahung und Weltflucht im Werke J. Rs.* (1960); Wilson, C., "Sartre's Graveyard of Chimeras: *La Nausée* and *Mort de quelqu'un*," FR, XXXVIII (1965), 744–53

* * * *

ROMANIAN LITERATURE

The "father" of Romanian literature is generally said to be Mihail Eminescu (1850–89). He is often referred to as Romania's Shakespeare, the poet of his country's national consciousness, the reigning bard at the time of his country's emancipation from centuries of Turkish rule. There were men who wrote in Romanian before Eminescu, but the language of 19th-c. polite society was French. Even after Eminescu's establishment of Romanian as a literary language, the influence of French culture remained substantial. Tristan Tzara (q.v.), the founder of dadaism (q.v.), and Ilarie Voronca (1903–1945), for example, wrote in French. But the Tzaras and the Voroncas were the rearguard of the xenophiles.

Eminescu made Romanian literature, and in particular Romanian poetry, not only accessible to all his fellow countrymen but a literature in its own right. Whatever the purely literary merits of his work (and its universality is debatable if only because the Romanian experience at that time was unique), Eminescu wrote well not only in Romanian but also about things Romanian. He was as far removed from the literary salons of Paris, Vienna, and Berlin (though his debt to German romanticism is considerable) as was the Moldavian peasant; and the Moldavian peasant, like the patriotic Romanian intellectual, responded gratefully. Every Romanian writer acknowledges his debt to Eminescu, and criticism of his work is always thought to be mildly sacrilegious. In 1930, a selection of his poems appeared in English translation (*Poems*) with a foreword by George Bernard Shaw (q.v.), and another volume of selected English translations, *Poems* (1971), is soon to be published.

But it was left to Tudor Arghezi (q.v.) to refine the language of Romanian literature, and in particular Romanian poetry, and to give it both a Romanian and a universal quality. Arghezi's lifetime spanned virtually the whole history to date of what we think of as Romanian literature. He was poet, critic, novelist, pamphleteer, journalist, and philosopher. He lived through a period of alien monarchy, through fascism and socialism, and made his comments on them all. His death came as a great shock to the millions who read his works (a book of his poems was published six weeks before his death, and sold out in three days) because he had become something apparently indestructible.

Arghezi's first major contribution to Romanian literature was to define the Romanian personality. This personality is complex, as is to be expected in a country at the crossroads of both eastern- and western-European civilizations. The Romans settled in Dacia and gave the country as a whole its name and language, a language that is still the oldest daughter of Latin. Enriched with Slavonic and Turkish, and to a lesser extent Magyar and Greek words, Romanian has been described by Professor Elwin Kuhn of the University of Marburg as "having the greatest neologistic capacity of any Romance language in Europe." Perhaps this strength is responsible for the survival of the Romanian language and a Christian culture, throughout many centuries of Turkish Muslim occupation.

Arghezi was fascinated by this survival. Eminescu had identified himself with the national aspirations of his fellow countrymen, yet he had virtually ignored the metropolis, drawing his imagery from the sensory perceptions of the peasants in the fields, in the Carpathian Mountains, by the Black Sea, and along the Danube. Arghezi was no less patriotic, but his horizons were wider and his blood a little cooler. He saw that there were two opposing, often conflicting, traits in the character of the Romanian. One, he said, was the swiftness to act and react, which made talk of a struggle for independence meaningful. The other was the patient, almost stoical, acceptance of fate. Both traits are equally Romanian, and are the stuff of Romanian literature of all genres.

Arghezi's second major contribution to the development of a Romanian literature was his insistence that his fellow writers avoid the temptation to work outside the mainstream of European culture. On his travels to Germany, Switzerland, and France he came into contact with literature and literati of all sorts, and on his return before World War I urged the necessity of a "personal translation program" for every writer. A great deal of translation (especially from the German and the French) had been done during the 19th c. Arghezi established it as a tradition in the 20th. Today Romania probably has more professional writers with a good knowledge of foreign languages and literatures than any other country in the world.

The first decade of the 20th c. was a busy time not only for the so-called Arghezi generation, but also for committed poets. Octavian Goga (q.v.) and Emil Isac (1889–1955) were both Transylvanians, born in a part of Romania under Austro-Hungarian domination, and involved in their teens in the local struggle for independence. Goga, a future prime minister, had already been imprisoned twice by 1914 and remained a fervent nationalist all his life. Contact between the literate minority and the illiterate or semiliterate majority was, in fact, virtually limited to that made by politically active young poets.

After World War I, and the incorporation of Transylvania into Romania, there was intense activity, led by Lucian Blaga (q.v.) and war poets such as Vasile Voiculescu (q.v.), aimed at bringing the new, greater Romania into contact with the arts. Blaga and his friends thought that the answer lay in a vigorous national theater that would be a natural home for poetry and drama and an inspiration to writers of both. Blaga's belief is still held by many, and the links between the genres are strong.

Zaharia Stancu (b. 1902), poet and novelist, was for many years director of the National Theater in Bucharest. (*See* his *A Gamble with Death,* 1969, and *Gypsies,* 1971.) Marin Preda (b. 1922), one of the foremost critics, has also written plays. Dumitriu Radu Popescu (b. 1933), one of the most gifted Transylvanian novelists, has adapted many of his books into scenarios. Horia Lovinescu (b. 1914) is director of the Nottara Theater, a playwright, and founder of the Romanian PEN Center. Aurel Baranga (b. 1913), a doctor turned playwright, has written many plays "explicating" problems concerning his contemporaries.

Other writers in the 1920's and 1930's, politically committed to the left, believed that a direct approach must be made to the working class to convince it of its "revolutionary responsibilities," and that an appreciation of the arts should be integrated into a general program of social education. There was something of the puritan as well as of the Marxist about the manifestos attacking corruption in private and public life in the interwar years. Still other writers saw in the general decadence of life in Europe an occasion for a retreat from the cultivation of all the 'isms, even a retreat from literature itself. Ion Barbu (1895–1961) found satisfaction in science, becoming a mathematician of European stature.

Some sort of unity was restored to Romanian writers during the later years of the drift toward fascism. Antipathy to the new regime became so wholehearted that when Romania became involved in World War II on the side of Germany, the concentration camp at Tirgu Jiu became a place of mass internment for poets, novelists, dramatists, and other intellectuals. Life at Tirgu Jiu tended to produce a general identification with the left, and after 1948 contact with the West became difficult. Contacts—cultural, economic, and political— with the Soviet Union were much easier, and there was for a time an imbalance about the ideas coming into literary Romania.

In the 1960's, however, the intellectuals became more responsive to a variety of ideas. Poets such as Nichita Stănescu (b. 1933; *Eleven Elegies,* 1971), who is *sui generis,* and the urbane Geo Dumitrescu (b. 1920) and Marin Sorescu (b. 1936) are well in the mainstream of world literature. The novel in Romania has tended to remain Romanian in inspiration, even among the very young. Ştefan Bănulescu (b. 1929) and Fanus Neagu (b. 1935) draw their inspiration from peasant life, as often as does Stancu, and as did Eminescu himself. This is not to say that the universal, however, is not visible in the particular.

BIBLIOGRAPHY: Iorga, N., *Istoria literaturii românesti contemporana* (2 vols., 1934); Lovinescu, E., *Istoria literaturii române contemporana* (5 vols., 1937); Munteano, B., *Modern Rumanian Literature* (1939); Călinescu, G., *Istoria literaturii române* (1944); UNESCO Translations Program, *Anthology of Contemporary Romanian Poetry* (1969)

ROY MACGREGOR-HASTIE

RØRDAM, Valdemar

Danish poet, b. 23 Sept. 1872, Dalby, Zealand; d. 14 July 1946, Svendborg, Fünen

R. came from an old Danish family of scholars and churchmen but broke with Christianity in his youth.

Until 1942, R. enjoyed great popularity and respect among the Danish people. But in that year the seventy-year-old poet, whose unfortunate ambivalence had become obvious during the Nazi occupation of Denmark, glorified Hitler's attack on Russia. Though not prosecuted after the defeat of the Nazis in 1945, R. died in lonely obscurity.

R.'s first publication was a book of conventional poems *Sol og Sky* (1895). Among his works are: *Bjovulf* (1899), a narrative poem about an episode in the Nordic legendary past (the Old English *Beowulf* tells the same story); *Dansk tunge* (1901), the poems of which express national emotions; *Gudrun Dyre* (1902), a widely read verse epic that deals with erotic themes; *Den gamle kaptajn* (3 vols., 1906–1907), which is made up of lyrical and epic descriptions of the war of 1864 (in which a defeated Denmark was forced to sacrifice a substantial amount of its territory to a conquering Germany); and *Jens Hvas til Ulvborg* (2 vols., 1922–23), which treats Danish commercial ties with the Far East.

In Danish poetry R.'s melodiousness, his handling of meter, and his sensitivity to the poetic possibilities of the Danish language have not been surpassed.

FURTHER WORKS: *Tre strenge* (1897); *Paa høiskoles* (1898); *Karen Kjeldsen* (1900); *Karneval* (1903); *Kaerlighedsdigte* (1903); *Ved midsommertid* (1904); *Stumme strænge* (1906); *Under aben himmel* (1908); *Grønlandsfærd* (1909); *Luft og land* (1910); *Strid og strengeleg* (1912); *De sorte nætter* (1913); *Kampen mod Bål* (1914); *Krigen og duerne* (1915); *Den gamle præstegaard* (1916); *De dernede* (1917); *Købstad-Idyller* (1918); *Udvalgte digte fra 20 år* (2 vols., 1918); *Regnbuen* (1919); *Afrodites boldspil* (1920); *Over det indiske have* (1920); *Nordisk hilsen* (1921); *Sangen om Danmark* (1923); *Fugleviser* (1924); *Blomstervers* (1925); *Kongeofret* (1927); *Jeg gik mig over sø og land* (1930); *Huset ved volden* (1932); *Udendørs* (1933); *Alderoms fæstning* (1938); *Holeby* (1940); *Danmark i tusind år* (1940); *Halv-student* (1942); *Kursus ind og ud* (1943)

BIBLIOGRAPHY: Thomsen, E., "V. R.," in

Festskrift til Vilhelm Andersen (1934); Svendsen, H. M., and W., *Geschichte der dänischen Literatur* (1964); Thrane, F., "Profetisk fejlsyn: V. R.'s *'Berengarias Fletning,'*" in *Infaldsvinkler,* ed. O. Friis (1964)

EMIL FREDERIKSEN

ROSTAND, Edmond

French dramatist and poet, b. 1 April 1868, Marseilles; d. 2 Dec. 1918, Paris

R. came from a Provençal family; his father was a member of the Marseilles Academy. After attending the École Thedenat and the *lycée* he studied literature, history, and philosophy at the Collège Stanislas in Paris. Under the direction of his teacher René Doumic, R. developed through the study of the works of Victor Hugo, Alfred de Musset, and Shakespeare. In 1884 R. published his first poetry in the journal *Mireille.* In the controversial Dreyfus Affair that rocked France in the 1890's, R., along with Zola and France (qq.v.), supported Captain Dreyfus, the Jewish officer atached to the general staff who was unjustly convicted of treason. In 1901 R. was elected to the Académie Française. Sarah Bernhardt was the outstanding interpreter of his works.

Cyrano de Bergerac (1897; Eng., 1898), which made R. world-famous, was a result of the Midi spirit as influenced by a centuries-old dramatic tradition. It revitalized the verse drama as created by Victor Hugo. The theme of love in conflict with friendship—as well as R.'s dialogue, vocabulary, and backgrounds—derive from standard romantic subjects and settings.

In the patriotic drama *L'Aiglon* (1900; The Eaglet, 1921), the Duc de Reichstadt, Napoleon I's son, is endowed with Hamlet's characteristics. In the dramatic satire *Chantecler* (1910; Chanticleer, 1921) R.'s protagonists are creatures of the barnyard and forest. His plays ended at the time the reign of vaudeville comedy.

FURTHER WORKS: *Le Gant rouge* (1888); *Les Musardises* (1890); *Les Romanesques* (1894; Romantics, 1921); *La Princesse lointaine* (1895; The Far Princess, 1935); *La Samaritaine* (1897; The Woman of Samaria, 1921); *La Dernière Nuit de Don Juan* (1921; The Last Night of Don Juan, 1930); *Théâtre* (6 vols., 1921–29); *Le Vol de la Marseillaise* (1922); *Le Cantique de l'aile* (1922); *Œuvres Complètes*

(1926). **Selected English translation:** *Plays of E. R.* (1921)

BIBLIOGRAPHY: Gérard, R., *E. R.* (1935); De Gorsse, P., *E. R.* (1951); Kilker, J. A., "Cyrano Without R.: An Appraisal," *Canadian Modern Language Review,* XXI (1965), iii, 21–25; Lutgen, O., *De père en fils: Edmond et Jean R.* (1965); Rostand, J., "E. R.," *Nouvelles Littéraires,* 11 April 1968, pp. 1, 13

BRIGITTE KAHR

ROSTWOROWSKI, Karol Hubert

Polish dramatist, b. 3 Nov. 1877, Rybna; d. 4 Feb. 1938, Cracow

R. belonged to an aristocratic Roman Catholic family. He studied agriculture in Halle and music and philosophy in Leipzig and Berlin. From 1914 until his death R. played an active part in the public life of Cracow.

In the early 1900's many intellectuals in Poland, in reaction against the realistic, bourgeois theater, were militating for the revival of the kind of drama that Leon Schiller, the leading Polish stage director between 1900 and 1950, called "monumental theater"—a blending of the elements of Polish romantic theater and Greek drama. R., like Wyspiánski (q.v.), played an important role in this struggle to revive the drama of great conflicts.

In *Judasz z Kariothu* (1913) R.'s main theme is man's relationship to God. It is similarly the theme of many other works of the militantly Catholic R.

R.'s major work is a cycle of three short tragedies (*Niespodzianka,* 1928; *Przeprowadzka,* 1930; *U mety,* 1932) on the problem of guilt and atonement, as experienced by Polish peasants.

Recognizing the social reality of his times, R. endeavored to illustrate it through the personality and action of a contemporary or historical personality and by focusing on the psychological and sociological factors that were acting upon that character. Because of R.'s excellent sense of theater, his skill at characterization, and his dynamic mass scenes, his plays were dramatically effective.

FURTHER WORKS: *Tandety* (1901); *Pod góre* (1910); *Via crucis* (1911); *Echo* (1911); *Zeglarze* (1912); *Kajus Cezar Kaligula* (1917); *Miłosierdzie* (1920); *Straszne dziece* (1922); *Zmartwychwstanie* (1923); *Antychryst* (1925); *Czerwony marsz* (1930); *Zygzaki* (1932)

BIBLIOGRAPHY: Borowy, W., "Fifteen Years of Polish Literature," *Slavonic Review,* XII (1933–34), 670–90; Czachowski, K., "R.-Polish Tragic Dramatist," *Slavonic Review,* XVII (1938–39), 677–88

* * * *

ROTH, Henry

American novelist and short-story writer, b. 8 Feb. 1906, Tismenitz, Austria-Hungary

R. is known almost exclusively for his one novel, the largely autobiographical *Call It Sleep.* In 1956, at its second publication, influential critics were applying to it such unequivocal superlatives as: "astonishing, sheer virtuosity; no one has ever distilled such poetry and wit from the counterpoint between maimed English and the subtle Yiddish of the immigrant" (Leslie Fiedler); "a wonderful novel, the deepest and the most authentic, and certainly the most unforgettable example of this subject" (Alfred Kazin); "the most distinguished single proletarian novel" (Walter Rideout). In view of the relative indifference that greeted the novel at its appearance in 1934, this was ironic.

Call It Sleep covers approximately seven years in the life of David Schearl, a haunted, inordinately sensitive little boy who is endlessly in search of a talisman. Accompanied by his overprotective mother, the tender and faithless Genya, David arrives at Ellis Island at nearly age two in 1907. There he receives an icy welcome from his tormented father, Albert (a parricide, as we learn), who suspects that the boy is not his. Three years follow in a Brownsville (Brooklyn) tenement, where David is instructed in sex play, much to his disgust, by a neighbor's crippled child, and where Genya probably commits adultery with a boarder (an act of which David remains vaguely conscious throughout the book). David also comes to associate the darkness of the rat-infested tenement cellar with sex and evil.

Four more years in a teeming Lower East Side slum plunge David, who is now attending Reb Yidel Pankower's Hebrew school, into a desperate search for God. Here David is befriended by the Polish-American boy, Leo Dugovka. In exchange for a rosary, David procures Esther, stepdaughter of Genya's sister Bertha, for Leo. After reading a passage from Isaiah (6:6–7), he comes to associate the radiance of the rooftops with purification and ultimate salvation. Finally, against a dense background of highly suggestive barroom chatter and an anarchist's political harangue, David's striving for purification and the light that symbolizes it for him induce him to poke a milk ladle into the third rail of a streetcar track and lead to his near-electrocution at about age nine in 1914.

But *Call It Sleep* is much more than just another naturalistic wallow in the sights, sounds, and smells of lower Manhattan in the first decades of the century. Certain elemental themes transfigure the *personae* and elevate the *peripeteiai* so that the novel attains to the dignity of high tragedy. Among the major themes are: The Stranger (in the guise of immigrant), The Changeling (David himself), Oedipus (David as lover of his mother, Albert as murderer of his father), and The Quest (here for mystical certitude).

Other minor themes are: an elaborate symbolism of dark as Evil and light as Good; the problem of identity—of being a Jew and simultaneously of being an individual whose being transcends Jewishness; and a kind of existential anguish that comes from the victim's helplessness in the face of adversity. From this it may be seen that *Call It Sleep,* in 1934, adumbrates many of the archetypal fictional preoccupations of post-World War II American, and indeed world, literature.

R. published little (only three charming short stories, all in more or less the same vein) from 1939 to 1956. In 1959 and 1960, at the invitation of *Commentary* magazine, he wrote two parables: "At Times in Flight" is about a horse who breaks a leg during a race and must be shot; "The Dun Dakotas" seems to herald his liberation from the contradiction between political commitment and creative perception.

There also exists a lengthy manuscript— tentatively entitled "Portrait of the Artist as an Old Fiasco"—that contains rambling speculations, poems, a play, a novel, and many short stories.

BIBLIOGRAPHY: "Brief Review," *New Masses,* XIV (12 Feb. 1935), 27; Fiedler, L., and Kazin, A., "The Most Undeservedly Neglected Books of the Past 25 Years" (symposium), *The American Scholar,* XXV (Autumn 1956), 478, 486; Rideout, W. B., *The Radical Novel in the United States* (1956), pp. 185–90; Fiedler, L., "H. R.'s Neglected Masterpiece," *Commentary,* XXX (Aug. 1960), 102–7; Ribalow, H. U., "H. R. and His Novel *Call It*

Sleep," *WSCL,* III (Fall 1962), 5–14; Knowles, A. S., Jr., "The Fiction of H. R.," *MFS,* XI, 4 (Winter 1965–66), 393–404

GERALD KAMBER

ROTH, Joseph

Austrian novelist and short-story writer, b. 2 Sept. 1894, Schwabendorf bei Brody, East Galicia; d. 27 May 1939, Paris

R. studied German philology and literature for a few semesters at the University of Vienna, volunteered for service in World War I, and was taken prisoner by the Russians. Turning to journalism in 1918, he worked, from 1923 on, on the *Frankfurter Zeitung.* After 1931 he devoted himself to writing novels.

Leaving Germany for good even before the advent of Hitler in 1933, R. lived for the most part in Paris, where he became the figure his fellow refugees could rally around and the polemical spokesman of the Hapsburg legitimist movement against Hitler (whom R. in one of his essays characterized as a leviathan). His early death (he died from alcoholism in a charity hospital) may in a sense not have been unwelcome because of his mounting despair at the grim unfolding of World War II—a despair masked by his kindness and helpfulness toward those in trouble.

R.'s early works—namely *Die Rebellion* (1924), *Die Flucht ohne Ende* (1927; Flight without End, 1930), *Zipper und sein Vater* (1927), and *Rechts und Links* (1929)—should be evaluated primarily as the results of observation rather than as literature. His literary models at that time were Flaubert, Stendhal, Lev Tolstoi (q.v.), and Gogol. Later he was to be influenced by Schnitzler and Hofmannsthal (qq.v.). R. felt the world had fallen on unpropitious days, and criticism of the times became his main theme. He wrote of the revolt of a simple-hearted victim of the war against the government machine; of the displacement of ex-soldiers condemned to be men without a country; of the enmity between the old generation yearning for bygone days of security and the younger, insecure one; of the senselessness of political decision-making.

R.'s reaching toward religion was first revealed in *Hiob* (1930; Job, 1931), his "novel of a simple man." This is the story of an eastern European Jewish teacher, Mendel Singer, who quarrels with God because of the afflictions that pursue him all the way to New York until he finally recognizes the meaning of the trials he has been subjected to.

Radetzkymarsch (1932; Radetzky March, 1933)—R.'s masterpiece—although sharply critical in some ways, is a pensive, affectionate memoir of Austria-Hungary under the Hapsburg monarchy. The life stories of the Trotta family of officers and government officials, three generations of which have served the Emperor Franz Josef, form the framework for a broadly conceived yet precisely drawn picture of the old Austria of the period between 1859 and 1914. A sequel to this book, *Die Kapuzinergruft* (1938), takes the lives of another branch of the Trotta family from 1914 up to the period of Hitler's annexation of Austria.

Geschichte der 1002. Nacht (1938), a novel pervaded by the imminence of doom, is an account of the gradual but inevitable downfall of an aristocratic officer in the imperial cavalry. It reveals the sharpness of R.'s persistently critical and ironical attitude toward Austria, which coexisted with a very understanding, warmhearted yet never overindulgent, love for his country and its way of life.

The mood of R.'s last book, *Die Legende vom heiligen Trinker* (1939; The Legend of the Holy Drinker, 1943), had been adumbrated in an earlier work, *Tarabas: Ein Gast auf dieser Erde* (1934; Tarabas: A Guest on Earth, 1934), which is about a Russian officer who has become a repentant vagabond by the end of his life. In *Die Legende vom heiligen Trinker,* R., humbly reaching out toward a Christian, if not a Roman Catholic, philosophy of life, writes of the virtues of confession, penance, and renunciation of the world.

Generally, R.'s fiction is dominated by the plight of that Austrian generation that was deeply injured psychologically (and often materially) by the partition of the Austro-Hungarian empire in 1918. R.'s work mirrors the disaffection of that generation with the godless Europe of the postwar years, and the way that generation sought to cope with it by heaping devastating criticism on the new order or by retreating permanently into a melancholy yearning for the bygone days that now seemed so desirable.

FURTHER WORKS: *Hotel Savoy* (1923); *April* (1925); *Der blinde Spiegel* (1925); *Juden auf Wanderschaft* (1926); *Das Spinnennetz* (1928); *Panoptikum* (1930); *Der Antichrist* (1934); *Studien* (1934); *Die hundert Tage* (1936);

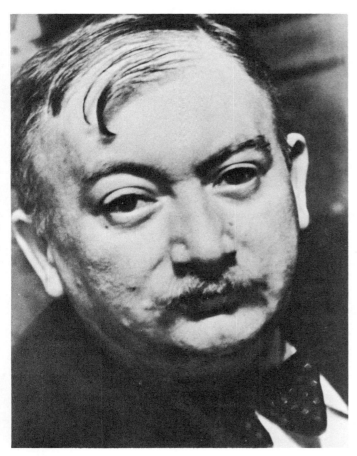

JOSEPH ROTH

PHILIP MILTON ROTH

Beichte eines Mörders (1936); *Das falsche Gewicht* (1937); *Der Leviathan* (1940); *Werke* (13 vols., 1956); *Romane, Erzählungen, Aufsätze* (1964); *Der stumme Prophet* (1966)

BIBLIOGRAPHY: Linden, H., *J. R. Leben und Werk* (1949); Kesten, H., *Meine Freunde* (1953); Cusatelli, G., "Realismo di R.," *Palatina*, IX (1965), xxx, 55–70; Bronsen, D., "Das literarische Bild der Auflösung im *Radetzkymarsch*," *Jahrbuch der Grillparzer Gesellschaft*, IV (1966), 130–43; Trommler, F., *Roman und Wirklichkeit* (1966); Rosenfeld, S., "Die Magie des Namens in J. Rs. *Beichte eines Mörders*," *GQ*, XL (1967), 351–62; Ziolkowski, T., *Dimensions of the Modern Novel* (1969), p. 273

ERNST ALKER

ROTH, Philip Milton

American novelist, short-story writer, and essayist, b. 19 March 1933, Newark, New Jersey

R. comes from an American Jewish background, which he often exploits with comic, sometimes grotesque, sometimes poignant effect. Like a number of other contemporary American Jewish writers—*e.g.*, Malamud, Bellow, Mailer (qq.v.), Herbert Gold (b. 1924)—he is not, however, concerned with Jewishness for its own sake. Instead, he is concerned with the insight it offers into the mystery of individuality and the struggle to achieve identity in contemporary America.

R. is dedicated to creating individuals who are determined to discover some way of acting meaningfully within American society, however absurd it be. Nevertheless, almost to a man (and woman), they are utter failures at achieving anything but destructive ways of acting.

Indeed, it is a misnomer to call any of R.'s protagonists "heroes." Unlike true heroes, they cannot face the evil they find within and without.

Neil Klugman, the hero of "Goodbye, Columbus" (in *Goodbye, Columbus, and Five Short Stories*, 1959), is so repelled by the phony values his sweetheart's family tries to impose on him that he rejects the possibility of a warm human relationship—the first he has found—and accepts instead isolation and despair.

Gabe Wallach, the protagonist of R.'s first novel, *Letting Go* (1961), cannot reconcile the ambivalence he suffers toward those whose lives have crossed with his. He cannot use the past to build on, nor can he reject it. He cannot give himself deeply to anyone, nor can he achieve complete indifference. Driven from one extreme to the other, he is unable to effect a higher reconciliation and remains a self-conscious, ineffectual human being, wreaking havoc everywhere he goes.

Nor does Lucy Nelson of *When She Was Good* (1966), the only female protagonist in R.'s novels, succeed any better. Ironically, it is her obsession with the values of American society that cut her off from creative involvement in that society. Incapable of accepting others as they are, committed to remaking them in her image of what people should be, she seems ridiculous, pathetic, almost crazed. In a moving scene, the defeated, pregnant Lucy meets her death in a snowstorm.

By contrast, Alexander Portnoy, the protagonist of R.'s latest novel, *Portnoy's Complaint* (1969), is a throwback to some of R.'s earlier nonheroes. Like Neil Klugman, Portnoy is unable to love. But even more than Gabe Wallach, he suffers the extreme pathos of unreconciled self-love and self-hate. His grotesque debaucheries, although ostensibly attempts to reject the unbearable restrictiveness symbolized by his Jewish mother and his Jewish upbringing, are at least as much techniques of self-castigation and self-punishment as of self-righteousness. His contempt of the world is at heart a deep, pain-filled contempt of himself.

R. has given us, as the critic Alfred Kazin said, "a deepened sense of the painful decisions on which life rests," and he has created a clear vision of "the bruised and angry and unassimilated self—the Jew as individual, not the individual as Jew—beneath the canopy of Jewishness." Though his characters retreat from life, R. shows us the desperation of their struggles to avoid such a retreat, and even implies the possibility of an affirmative view of life.

BIBLIOGRAPHY: Kazin, A., "Tough-minded Mr. R.," *Contemporaries* (1962); Deer, I. and H., "P. R. and the Crisis in American Fiction," *Minnesota Review*, No. 4 (1966); Leer, N., "Escape and Confrontation in the Short Stories of P. R.," *Christian Scholar*, XLIX (1966); Meeter, G., *Bernard Malamud and P. R.: A Critical Essay* (1968)

IRVING DEER

ROZANOV, Vasilii

Russian autobiographical writer, philosopher, and critic, b. 20 April 1856, Vetluga; d. 23 Jan. 1919, Sergiyev Posad

The son of a minor civil servant who left his family poverty-stricken, R. grew up in a household torn by tensions over money and the fact that his mother had taken a lover. He nevertheless managed to complete his studies and was appointed to a teaching post in a provincial school.

R.'s passionate admiration for Fiodor Dostoyevski (1821–81) led him to make the acquaintance of Apollinaria Suslova, the great novelist's former mistress and "diabolic muse." They were married and for six years lived together in a neurotic and tormented relationship. R.'s wife refused to divorce him when she left, and after much soul-searching R. entered into a bigamous but blissful marriage with the widow of a church deacon.

O ponimanii (1886), a voluminous polemic against the University of Moscow, was R.'s first book, and though unsuccessful it was instrumental in attracting the attention of the influential conservative critic Nikolai Strakhov, who rescued R. from his hated life in the provinces and obtained a government post for him in St. Petersburg. After 1899 R. was associated with the rightist journal *Novoye vremya*, and his financial situation allowed him to travel occasionally in Italy, France, and Germany. The suppression of that publication by the bolsheviks in 1918 once more thrust R. into a life of poverty. Though he had often attacked the church in his earlier writings, during the final months of his life R. took refuge in the Troitski Monastery near Moscow.

R.'s first major work was the critical essay *Legenda o velikom inkvizitore* (1890), in which he examined the importance of the figure of the Grand Inquisitor in Dostoyevski's *The Brothers Karamazov* and related it to a general view of the novelist's philosophy. The essay is also important for its evaluation of Nikolai Gogol (1809–1852) in relation to what R. saw as new trends in Russian literature.

In the following years R. wrote a series of important works in which he examined the philosophical and human basis for religion, relating it to culture in general, literature in particular, and—with particular emphasis—to the nature of man's sexual drives. *Krasota v prirode i yevo smysl* (1894) outlined his approach to cultural history; the two-volume

Semeinyi vopros v Rossii (1903) examined the problems of Russian family life and raged against contemporary divorce laws; *Okolo tzerkovnykh sten* (1906), *Russkaya tzerkov'* (1906), *Tiomnyi lik* (1911), and *Lyudi lunnovo sveta* (1913) investigated the link between religion and sex and vigorously rejected the ascetic tendency of Christianity.

R. favored the earthier views of pre-Christian religions and was drawn to the Old Testament, but he turned against contemporary Judaism with murderous ferocity. During the notorious Beilis ritual murder case with which the tzarist government attempted to distract the traditionally anti-Semitic Russian people from the basic causes of their woes, R. spewed out his hatred of Jews in *Obonyatel'noye i osyazatel'noye otnosheniye yevreyev k krovi* (1914)—literally "the olfactory and tactile behavior of Jews in relation to blood"—and *Yevropa i yevreyi* (1914).

The 1905 Revolution temporarily aroused R.'s enthusiasm, and in *Kogda nachalstvo ushlo* (1909) he praised the new spirit it brought, but he was profoundly antagonistic to the Revolution of 1917. His final work, *Apokalipsis nashevo vremeni* (1918), once more focuses on the antihumanistic nature of Christianity and examines the causes that led to its revolutionary rejection in Russia.

In addition to his criticism, R.'s greatest claim to literary importance rests on the fragmentary and intimately autobiographical *Uyedinionnoye* (1912; Solitaria, 1924) and the two volumes of "fallen leaves"—*Opavshiye listya* (1913; Fallen Leaves, Bundle One, 1929) and *Opavshiye listya: Korob vtoroi* (1915)—in which he candidly and beautifully conveyed intimate details of his thoughts, dreams and the happy life he found with his "friend" after his wife's desertion.

A highly controversial figure, R.'s brilliant insights into the sexual and antirational nature of man anticipated much that currently dominates world literature. In addition, though many of his books are now forgotten, the moving "prose poems" of his autobiographical writings have earned him a permanent place in Russian literature.

FURTHER WORKS: *Mesto khristianstva v istorii* (1890); *Sumerki prosveshchenia* (1893); *Religia i kultura* (1899); *Literaturnye ocherki* (1899); *Priroda i istoria* (1900); *V mire neyasnovo i nereshennovo* (1901); *Italanskiye vpechatleniya* (1909); *Literaturnye izgnanniki*

(1913); *Sredi khudozhnikov* (1914); *Apokalipsicheskaya sekta* (*Klysty i skopt̩zy*) (1914); *Voina 1914 goda i russkoye vozrozhdeniye* (1915); *Iz vostochnykh motivov* (1916–17)

BIBLIOGRAPHY: Griftsov, B., "R.," in *Tri myslitelya* (1911); Gollerbakh, E., *V. V. R.* (1922); Mirsky, D. S., *Contemporary Russian Literature* (1926); Kurdyumov, G., *O. R.* (1929); Spasovski, M., *R. v. posledniye gody svoyei zhizni* (1935); Poggioli, R., *R.* (1962); Holthusen, J., *Twentieth-Century Russian Literature* (1971)

* * * *

RÓŻEWICZ, Tadeusz

Polish poet, dramatist, and short-story writer, b. 9 Oct. 1921, Radomsko

Born into a middle-class family, R. had to interrupt his studies because of the outbreak of World War II. Later he took an active part in the underground movement against the Nazis. After the war he enrolled at the Jagiellonian University in Cracow to study art history. While at the university he began his literary career. In 1955, 1962, and 1966 he was awarded the State Prizes in Poland; in 1966, the Jurzykowski Foundation Prize in the United States.

The impact of the war was clearly visible in his early collections of poems *Niepokój* (1947) and *Czerwona rękawiczka* (1948), in which R. expressed in his own poetic idiom the anxieties and obsessions created in him by the war experiences. The poems come close to an objective prose account since R. had abandoned such traditional forms as regular meter, rhymes, or stanzas. Saturated with juxtaposed images these poems are distinctive by R.'s skill in maintaining an emotional tension under the surface of seemingly detached narration. Widely imitated, R. thus established a new trend in postwar Polish poetry.

After a brief period of succumbing to the dictates of socialist realism, which was imposed most stringently in Poland in 1949–55 (*Pięć poematów*, 1950; *Czas który idzie*, 1951), R. was able to return to his own way of searching for answers to the philosophical and moral dilemmas created by the postwar chaos. The resulting poems are collected in *Poemat otwarty* (1955), *Rozmowa z księciem* (1960), and *Regio* (1969). To the fore came his imaginative power and lyricism. He further developed his poetic art by defying the traditional patterns of versification. His poems, often described as "antipoetic," were stripped of metaphors, but became metaphoric in a new way. His style became rigid, cool, yet charged with concealed intense lyricism. English translations of a representative selection of the work published in 1947–68 appear in *Faces of Anxiety* (1969).

R. turned to drama in 1960 with the grotesque *Kartoteka* (The Card Index, 1969). This was followed by: *Grupa Laokoona* (1961); *Świadkowie albo nasza mała stabilizacja* (1962); *Akt przerwany* (1964; The Interrupted Act, 1969); *Śmieszny staruszek* (1964); *Wyszedł z domu* (1964; Gone Out, 1969); and *Spaghetti i miecz* (1964). (The Card Index, The Interrupted Act, and Gone Out were published together in one volume.) Closely related to the avant-garde theater of the 1920's and to the modern theater of the absurd, R.'s dramas are grotesque and tragic. In them he explores the human condition of modern man while satirizing the peculiarities of socialist society in contemporary Poland. Thus R. has become a dramatist of universal appeal and a diligent social critic.

The short stories collected in *Przerwany egzamin* (1960) and *Wycieczka do muzeum* (1966) often deal with R.'s reminiscences of the war and their connection with the postwar generation, which is incapable of understanding those horrors that shaped the author's world. That past, so heavy with cruel memories, recurs as an ever-present motif in R.'s poetry, dramas, and narratives.

R. is one of the most original writers in modern Polish literature. His philosophical themes combined with his artistic vision and his individual style have gained him international recognition. In Poland he is considered an innovator of literary forms and a courageous spokesman for an unrestricted freedom of expression.

FURTHER WORKS: *W łyżce wody* (1949); *Wiersze i obrazy* (1952); *Wybór wierszy* (1953); *Kartki z Węgier* (1953); *Równina* (1954); *Srebrny kłos* (1955); *Uśmiechy* (1955); *Opadły liście z drzew* (1955); *Poezje zebrane* (1957); *Formy* (1958); *Zielona róża* (1961); *Głos Anonima* (1961); *Nic w płaszczu Prospera* (1962); *Twarz* (1964); *Utwory dramatyczne* (1966); *Poezje wybrane* (1967); *Wiersze i poematy* (1967); *Twarz trzecia* (1968); *Opowiadania wybrane* (1968); *Wybór poezji* (1969); *Wiersze* (1969). **Selected English translations:** selections in *The Broken Mirror* (ed.

P. Mayewski; 1958); *The Modern Polish Mind* (ed. M. Kuncewicz; 1962); *Introduction to Modern Polish Literature* (eds. A. Gillon and L. Krzyzanowski; 1964); *Polish Writing Today* (ed. C. Wieniawska; 1967)

BIBLIOGRAPHY: Leach, C., "Remarks on the Poetry of T. R.," *PolR*, XII (1967), 105–26; Lourie, R., "A Contest for T. R.," *PolR*, XII (1967), 97–104; Czerwinski, E. J., "T. R. and the Jester-Priest Metaphor," *SEEJ*, XIII (1969), 217–28; Milosz, C., *The History of Polish Literature* (1969), pp. 462–70

JERZY R. KRZYŻANOWSKI

RUIZ, Antonio Machado y
See Machado y Ruiz, Antonio

RUIZ, Manuel Machado y
See Machado y Ruiz, Manuel

RUSSELL, George William
(pseud.: *A. E.*), Irish poet, essayist, and dramatist, b. 10 April 1867, Lurgan, County Armagh; d. 17 July 1935, Bournemouth, England

The three major figures in the Irish literary revival were Yeats, Synge (qq.v.), and R. R.'s personal influence, both on his contemporaries and on the younger generation, was enormous. Though he lies outside the mainstream of the movement, he is nevertheless an important integral part of it, stressing the ideals and spiritual aspirations that helped to create it. His early friendship with Yeats was an important factor in the latter's development.

The biographical data about R.'s early years is somewhat hazy. R.'s parents moved to Dublin when R. was ten years old. Between 1879 and 1890 he spent some of his time at the Dublin Art School, where Yeats was a fellow student. In 1890 he went to work for a Dublin dry goods firm.

After 1887 he seems to have devoted much of his time to the Hermetic Society and, later, to the Dublin lodge of the Theosophical Society. For some years he lived with other members of the society, and his connection with official theosophy was severed only after Madame Blavatsky's death. It was theosophy and Eastern religious thought that provided him with his first literary subjects.

Later, after becoming editor (1905) of *The Irish Homestead,* the journal of the agricultural cooperative movement, R.'s interests widened. In the years ahead he was to continue to write poetry and to paint pictures, in addition to working as an editor and an organizer. He was also to work for Irish home rule and to help found the Abbey Theatre (1904).

In 1910 he became editor of the newly founded Dublin literary weekly *The Irish Statesman,* which he made a forum for writers of all schools and which became the focal point of literature in Ireland. R. contributed freely to it himself, and it probably helped to stimulate a revival of his poetic faculty, for his later poetry, *e.g., Voices of the Stones* (1925), was superior to the poetry of his earlier years.

By 1910 R. was a literary figure in Dublin, and the portrait that George Moore (q.v.) draws of him in *Hail and Farewell* (1911–14) is excellent. The publication of *The Candle of Vision* (1918), which came in the wake of Moore's book, brought him to the notice of a wider public. The mystic was becoming the philosopher and political sage, respected on both sides of the Atlantic for the balanced integrity of his outlook. In 1920 he published *The Interpreters,* in which various political systems are discussed with a Platonic detachment.

In 1932 R. published *Song and Its Fountains,* in which he discussed the nature of inspiration. This was followed by *The Avatars* (1933), which R. described as "a futurist fantasy," and in which he gave a fictional setting to many of the hopes and aspirations of his youth.

In 1933, after the death of his wife, R. gave up his modest Dublin home, where so many young poets and celebrities from all over the world had assembled at one time or another, and went to live in London.

His versatility both as writer and painter should not blind us to R.'s essential and steadfast unity as a man. He is emphatically the achieved mystic and sage. As Ernest Boyd said, "The mysticism of A. E. is entirely different from the symbolism which has given Yeats the reputation of being a mystic. That which is purely decorative in the poetry of the latter is, in A. E., the expression of fundamental truths."

In fact one might say that the words with which R. prefaced his first book of verse, *Homeward: Songs by the Way* (1894), could be taken as the text of all his literary labors: "I know I am a spirit and that I went forth in old time from the self-ancestral to labours yet unaccomplished; but filled over and again with homesickness I made these homeward songs by the way."

FURTHER WORKS: *The Earth Breath, and Other Poems* (1897); *The Future of Ireland and the Awakening of the Fires* (1897); *Ideals in Ireland: Priest or Hero?* (1897); *Literary Ideals in Ireland—Nationality and Cosmopolitanism in Literature* (1899); *An Artist of Gaelic Ireland* (1902); *The Divine Vision, and Other Poems* (1903); *The Nuts of Knowledge* (1903); *Controversy in Ireland* (1904); *The Mask of Apollo* (1904); *By Still Waters* (1906); *Some Irish Essays* (1906); *Deirdre* (1907); *The Hero in Man* (1909); *The Renewal of Youth* (1911); *Cooperation and Nationality* (1912); *Collected Poems* (1913); *Gods of War* (1915); *Imaginations and Reveries* (1915); *The National Being* (1916); *Thoughts on Irish Polity* (1917); *Michael* (1919); *Open Letter to the Irish People* (1922); *Midsummer Eve* (1928); *Dark Weeping* (1929); *Enchantment* (1930); *Vale* (1931); *The House of the Titans, and Other Poems* (1934); *Selected Poems* (1935); *Some Passages from the Letters of A. E. to W. B. Yeats* (1936); *The Living Torch* (ed. M. Gibbon; 1937); *A. E.'s Letters to Minanlabain* (1957); *Letters from A. E.* (ed. Alan Denson; 1961)

BIBLIOGRAPHY: Magee, W. K., *A Memoir of A. E.* (1937); Denson, A., *Printed Writings by . . . A. E., A Bibliography* (1961); Boyd, E., *Appreciations and Depreciations: Irish Literary Studies* (1968); Denson, A., *G. W. R. (A. E.) 1867–1935: A Centennial Assessment* (1968)

MONK GIBBON

RUSSIAN LITERATURE

BEFORE 1917

In 1890, Konstantin Leontiyev (1831–91), a remarkable Russian thinker who has more than once been described as a Russian Nietzsche (q.v.) and also—with less justice—as a precursor of fascism, wrote an interesting and stimulating essay on the art of Lev Tolstoi (q.v.), in which he proclaimed the dominant realist school in Russian literature "quite unbearable in some respects." One of its greatest defects he saw in its concentration on minute, "superfluous" details, whether external or psychological. He said that, by way of natural reaction, one could prefer to it practically anything that differed from it. "Byron's *Childe*

Harold and Zhukovski's *Undine*, the Lives of Saints and Voltaire's philosophical novels, Tyutchev's ethereal poetry and Barbier's fierce revolutionary iambs, Victor Hugo and Goethe, Corneille and Calderón, George Sand's novels and monk Parfeni's *Legends of the Holy Land*, Horace's *Odes*, and *Manon Lescaut*, Sophocles's tragedies and the childlike epic songs of the modern Greeks."

The beginnings of the Russian school Leontiyev saw in Nikolai Gogol (1809–1852), while in Lev Tolstoi it had, according to him, reached its point of saturation. It was Lev Tolstoi himself who, said Leontiyev, with the instinct of a genius, turned away from it and adopted a new manner, bare and simple, in his stories for the people. Though Leontiyev, who was himself a novelist, can hardly be regarded as a forerunner of any specific trends in modern Russian literature (and, in view of his "reactionary" philosophy, his influence, during his lifetime, was limited to a narrow circle of admirers), he voiced in that essay a reaction against realism that was soon to become widespread. What is more, underlying his general outlook, his religion, his politics, his historical-philosophical ideas, was a deeply rooted aestheticism that was to be an important factor in shaping the destinies of modern Russian literature. His aristocratic individualism (see his bitingly satirical *The Average European as the Means and End of Universal Progress*) was also a sign of the times. There is no doubt that in his essay on Lev Tolstoi he gave a pointed diagnosis of the malaise then affecting Russian literature, which but a decade earlier had completed the great and brilliant cycle of the realistic psychological novel—the period that came to an end with the deaths of Fiodor Dostoyevski (1821–81) and Ivan Turgenev (1818–83) and the voluntary (albeit partial and temporary) withdrawal of Lev Tolstoi from art (1879–80).

In 1893, two years after the publication of Leontiyev's essay, the general crisis in Russian literature was analyzed in greater detail, and in the light of incipient modernism, by Dimitri Sergeyevich Merezhkovski (1864–1941) in his essay *On The Causes of Decline and the New Trends in Russian Literature* (1893). Merezhkovski was another harbinger of the revolt that was soon to seize hold of a large section of Russian intelligentsia. It was a revolt against the traditional values of the intelligentsia as they had become crystallized in the 1860's and the 1870's—against its positivism, against its tendency to subordinate art to social utility and duty toward the people. It was a revolt in the name of individualism, of aestheticism, of religious and philosophical idealism.

Speaking of those trends that first manifested themselves in the 1890's, D. S. Mirsky, in his *Contemporary Russian Literature* (1926), says: "Aestheticism substituted beauty for duty, and individualism emancipated the individual from all social obligations. The two tendencies, which went hand in hand, proved a great civilizing force and changed the whole face of Russian civilization between 1900 and 1910, bringing about the great renascence of Russian art and poetry, which marked that decade." The aesthetic revival of the 1890's contributed to the enrichment and greater complexity of Russian culture.

What was the background of that renascence and what were its sources? The last decade of the 19th c. in Russia—that "iron, truly cruel century," in the words of the poet Blok (q.v.) —is often thought of as a period of darkest reaction, of stagnation, of *bezvremenyye* (an untranslatable Russian word, particularly associated with the futility and frustration that permeate Chekhov's [q.v.] stories and plays). But this is only one side of the picture. It was also a period of political, social, and artistic fermentation. It saw the birth of an organized social-democratic party in Russia, and it also saw the pitched battles between the Marxists —whose principal spokesmen in the legal press and at the crowded meetings of the Imperial Free Economic Society were Peter Struve and Mikhail Tugan-Baranovski—and the *narodniki* (populists), over whom presided the venerable longbearded Nikolai Mikhailovski, the noted sociologist and editor of *Russkoye Bogatstvo*. In the late 1890's occurred also the first defections from the Marxist camp into the camp of neo-Kantian idealism of men such as Frank, Berdyayev (qq.v.), Struve, and Mikhail Afanasyevich Bulgakov (1891–1940), all of whom were to later play a prominent part in the Russian religious-philosophical revival.

A significant landmark in this movement was the publication of a collection of essays entitled *Problems of Idealism* (1902), to which all the above-named contributed. A direct sequel to it was *Vekhi* (1909), in which seven authors— Struve, Frank, Berdyayev, Bulgakov, Mikhail Osipovich Gerzhenzon (1869–1925), Izgoyev, and Kistyakovski—joined forces in a frontal attack on the Russian intelligentsia and its

Weltanschauung, its positivism and materialism, as well as—in the light of the revolution of 1905 and its political lessons—its revolutionary maximalism. To the "nihilistic moralism" of the traditional intelligentsia, Frank opposed the ideal of "religious humanism," while Bulgakov, who was already a practicing Russian Orthodox Catholic believer, contrasted the Christian saintly ideal with the ideal of revolutionary heroism.

A great role in the *fin-de-siècle* thought was played by Vladimir Sergeyevich Solovyev (1853–1900), who combined the religious-mystical approach (with eschatological overtones) with political liberalism, and to whom the Russian religious-philosophical revival owed a great debt. An important stage in the rapprochement between the intelligentsia and the Church were the religious-philosophical meetings organized by Merezhkovski and Zinaida Nikolayevna Gippius (1869–1945) in the early years of the century. For a short time they had their mouthpiece in the review *Novyi Put'*, on which some of the symbolist poets (*see* symbolism) collaborated.

In the same period fall the pioneering efforts of Rozanov (q.v.), Akim Volinski (pseud. of Akim Flekser; 1863–1926), Sergei Andreyevski (1847–1919), Vladimir Sergeyevich Solovyev (1853–1900), and others to reappraise anew the past heritage of Russian literature and to revise the labels that the dominant 19th-c. social-utilitarian criticism had affixed to many a writer. Rozanov's studies of Gogol and Dostoyevski; Volinski's books on Dostoyevski and Nikolai Leskov (1831–95) and his bold denunciation of such idols of the 19th-c. intelligentsia as Vissarion Grigoryevich Belinski (1811–48), Nikolai Gavrilovich Chernishevski (1828–89), and Dmitri Ivanovich Pisarev (1840–68), together with the emphasis laid on such an unfashionable literary critic as Apollon Aleksandrovich Grigoriyev (1822–64); Andreyevski's "rediscovery" of Yevgenii Abramovich Baratinski (1800–1844); Solovyev's famous article on Fiodor Ivanovich Tyutchev (1803–1873) (whom the popular critic Skabichevski had dismissed as an insignificant eclectic)—all these were important stages in the unfreezing of the Russian mind.

In art, a reaction against the pedestrian realism of the dominant *peredvizhniki* school and the programmatic, illustrative tendencies went hand in hand with the heightened interest in the modern movements in western European art—in pre-Raphaelitism in England and in impressionism in France. In the 1890's this desire to renovate Russian art and to bring it abreast to Western movements found its vehicle in the excellent magazine *Mir Iskusstva,* founded in 1898 by Sergei Diaghilev of the future Russian Ballet fame. Around Diaghilev were grouped some of the most talented younger painters—Aleksandr Benois, Konstantin Somov, Eugene Lanceray, and others—who later formed the *Mir Iskusstva* group and did much to revolutionize Russian art and art criticism. Along with its propaganda of new western European art, *Mir Iskusstva* was instrumental in reappraising the past legacy of Russian art, in helping to "discover" the little-known world of the Russian ikon (here the names of Igor Grabar and, later, Pavel Muratov stand out especially) and in reassessing the art of the 18th c. (the chief credit goes here to Diaghilev himself and to Aleksandr Benois who, besides being an artist, was a first-rate art historian and art critic). *Mir Iskusstva,* though primarily interested in visual arts, stood also in the vanguard of modern literature and could boast of the collaboration of such writers as Rozanov, Merezhkovski, and Lev Shestov (1866–1938). Among other things it serialized Merezhkovski's *Tolstoi i Dostoyevski* (1901).

The close alliance between literature and visual arts became a hallmark of Russian avant-garde periodicals, such as *Vesi* (1904–1909), *Zolotoye Runo* (1906–1919), and *Apollon* (1909–1916). It is also characteristic of all these periodicals, which represented the *fine fleur* of Russian civilization, that they followed closely all the latest trends and movements in Western art and at the same time helped, in various ways, to propagandize Russian art, old and modern, in western Europe. Russian interest in modern European art, which was at its highest in the period preceding World War I, found its expression also in the acquisitions of private collectors. Thus the Shchukin collection in Moscow (later known as the Moscow Museum of Western Art) became famous for its early Picassos and Matisses, as well as excellent specimens of the post-impressionists.

In the drama and the theater new paths were also sought in the 1890's. Founded in 1898, the Moscow Art Theater of Stanislavski and Vladimir Ivanovich Nemirovich-Danchenko (1858–1943) initiated the same year a series of Chekhov productions with his *Chaika* (1896; The Seagull, 1921), which but three years earlier had been a complete fiasco on the traditional stage. Chekhov, who in his dramatic

innovations was to some extent influenced by Ibsen and Maeterlinck (qq.v.), became in turn an important factor of influence outside Russia, especially in Anglo-Saxon countries. And so did some of the principles that underlay the theatrical work of Stanislavski and Nemirovich-Danchenko. For its part, the Moscow Art Theater introduced to the Russian public such modern playwrights as Ibsen, Hamsun, Gerhart Hauptmann, and Maeterlinck (qq.v.). Chekhov's "atmospherical" plays, produced by the Moscow Art Theater in the slice-of-life-realism manner, were the last word in the "detheatralization" and "deconventionalization" of the theater, and they produced a natural reaction both in dramatic literature and in the theater.

On different levels and at different removes from them stood: Andreyev's (q.v.) symbolical-romantic melodramas; Gorki's (q.v.) attempts —as in *Na dne* (1902; Down and Out; 1903)— to infuse a social meaning and a breath of optimism into the Chekhovian drama; Sologub's (q.v.) and Zinaida Gippius's endeavors to combine realism and symbolism (q.v.); Blok's masterly exercises in lyrical drama—*Balaganshchik* (1906) and *Neznakomka* (1906), with their superb romantic irony—and in verse tragedy (*Roza i krest,* 1913); V. I. Ivanov's (q.v.) imitations of ancient Greek tragedies; and Nikolai Yevreinov's (1879–1953) *Samoye glavnoye,* underlying which was an idea that was diametrically opposed to Chekhov's "deconventionalization" of the theater—that of the "theatralization of life." All these, as well as the establishment of the Old Theater in Leningrad (an attempt to revive Spanish and other old drama), can be regarded as endeavors to lead the Russian theater out of the Chekhovian impasse.

A similar reaction to Stanislavski's ultra-realistic methods is to be seen in the innovations introduced into the theater by Vsevolod Meyerhold (1874–1942) and Aleksandr Tairov (1885–1950) both of whom proceeded along the principle of the primacy of the producer not only over the actors (this had already been realized in the Stanislavski theater) but also over the author. It is interesting to note that Meyerhold, who began his career under Stanislavski, left the Moscow Art Theater as a protest against its realism and in the first theater of his own treated Chekhov's plays as symbolic. Stanislavski himself experimented at one point along nonrealistic lines when he secured the assistance of Gordon Craig for his Shakespearean productions. Further experiments in the theater were made during the first years after the revolution when the theater became especially popular in Russia.

In poetry the period before World War I was dominated by symbolism. Just as French symbolism was a reaction against parnassianism and naturalism (q.v.), so its Russian namesake was a reaction against civic-minded realism. An anticipation of it will be found in Merezhkovski's book of poems, which is significantly entitled *Simvoly* (1892; "symbols"). In his already-mentioned 1893 essay Merezhkovski touched on the French symbolists. Somewhat earlier they were the subject of an article by Zinaida Vengerova in one of the oldest Russian monthlies, *Vestnik Yevropy*. But the beginnings of Russian symbolism as a literary school should be dated from 1894–95, when Bryusov (q.v.) and his friend, A. Lang (pseudonym: Miropolski), published three slender volumes under the title *Russian Symbolists*. They contained original poetry and prose and translations from Stéphane Mallarmé (1842–98), Maeterlinck, Arthur Rimbaud (1854–91), and Paul Verlaine (1844–96). There was nothing in these plaquettes of intrinsic value (the only author to make subsequently a name for himself was Bryusov, who contributed to all three volumes, both over his own signature and under various pen names). But their appearance was symptomatic.

The definitions of symbolism and of its purpose, which Bryusov gave in the first two issues, were derived directly from Mallarmé. ("The object of symbolism is to hypnotize as it were the reader by a series of juxtaposed images, to evoke in him a certain mood"; "The purpose of poetry is not 'objective description', but 'suggestion' "; "The poet conveys a series of images ... [which are] to be looked upon as signposts along an invisible road, open to the imagination of the reader. Therefore symbolism can be called ... 'poetry of allusions' "). Primacy of intuition over logic, refusal to accept the reality that is but a distortion of the true though inaccessible world—these fundamental tenets were accepted by the Russian symbolists. The mission of the poet was seen in the revelation, beyond the world of senses, of the world of superreality. "De realibus ad realiora," as V. V. Ivanov (q.v.), one of the principal later theoreticians of symbolism, was to phrase it.

Similar definitions of symbolism and its purpose were given by other poets of the period. Balmont (q.v.) said that while the realists were bound to concrete reality beyond which they saw nothing, the symbolists were severed from it and saw in it only their dream—"they look at life out of a window." Balmont also developed his philosophy of the moment, "momentalism": "Moments are always unique. I live too quick a life, and I know no one who loves moments so much as I do ... I give myself to the moment," he wrote in a preface to one of his most characteristic volumes of verse *Goryashchiye zdaniya* (1899; Burning Edifices, 1904). Zinaida Gippius, who sought her inspiration in Baratynski and Tyutchev rather than in French symbolists, compared poetry to prayers. Belyi (q.v.), another leading theoretician of symbolism, wrote: "All art is symbolic—present, past and future. What is then the significance of contemporary symbolism? What new thing did it give us?—Nothing. The school of symbolism merely reduces to a unity the declarations of artists and poets to the effect that the meaning of beauty is the artistic image and not in the emotion that the image arouses in us; and certainly not in the rational interpretation of that image. A symbol is irreducible either to emotions or to discursive concepts; it is what it is."

Ridiculed and scorned on their first appearance, the symbolists, by the middle of the first decade of the 20th c. won wide respect and recognition. They had at their disposal several periodicals and publishing houses (Scorpio, Musagetes, and others), as well as access to some of the general literary reviews, such as *Russkaya Mysl* one of the oldest and most respectable. The years 1900–1912 can be rightly described as the second golden age of Russian poetry (the first being the Zhukovski-Pushkin period at the beginning of the 19th c.). If of French symbolism it has been said that "Du point de vue technique ... le symbolisme a tenté et réussi l'affranchissement du vers français—sous toutes ses formes" (Lalou), with regard to Russian symbolism one should speak not so much of the "liberation" of the Russian verse as of the simultaneous restoration of the pristine standards (of the Pushkinian era) and complete renovation. The complexity and richness of the poetic world of symbolism defy a brief analysis. Balmont, Sologub, V. I. Ivanov, Zinaida Gippius, Annenski (q.v.)—whose full stature as a poet was revealed only after his death and who, of all the symbolists, was the closest to some of their French masters—

Baltrusaitis (q.v.), Blok, and Belyi represented different facets of symbolism. Not all of them were equally indebted to their French masters. This debt was particularly great in the case of Bryusov and Annenski, both of whom translated Verlaine, Rimbaud and Mallarmé (Annenski also translated Jules Laforgue [1860–87], while Bryusov came under a strong influence of Verhaeren [q.v.]). It was less so in the case of Sologub, although he also translated Verlaine and other French poets. Balmont was more eclectic, his favorite poets being Edgar Allan Poe (1809–1849) and Percy Bysshe Shelley (1792–1822), whom he translated. (Poe and Charles Baudelaire [1821–67], just as Nietzsche's *Geburt der Tragödie* and Arthur Schopenhauer's [1788–1860] ideas on music, meant a great deal to all the symbolists. Baudelaire's *Correspondances,* with its "forest of symbols" and its idea of synaesthesia, was a kind of credo for them). Of Zinaida Gippius it has already been said that her masters were the Russian poets Tyutchev and Baratinski (whom Bryusov and other symbolists also regarded as their forerunners, as symbolists *avant la lettre*). As for Blok and Belyi they owed much more to another symbolist *avant la lettre* (even though he headed the chorous of those who derided and parodied *Russian Symbolists* on their appearance)—to Vladimir Solovyev and his mystical philosophy. Blok had also affinities with Vasili Andreyevich Zhukovski (1783–1852), Mikhail Yuryevich Lermontov (1814–41), and Afanasii Afanasyevich Fet (1820–92), while both he and Belyi, at one stage of their poetic work, were very much inspired by Nikolai Alekseyevich Nekrasov's (1821–78) civic poetry.

Generally speaking, Russian symbolism became divided into what can be seen as two main currents in Russian symbolism: the purely aesthetic, represented by Bryusov and Balmont, which depended more on foreign sources and was concerned above all with formal, technical innovations, and the metaphysical or religious, represented by Blok, Belyi, and V. I. Ivanov, and to some extent Zinaida Gippius (Sologub occupied a place apart), which was rather of native lineage. This metaphysical current in symbolism aspired to be something more than a literary school. Its exponents, Belyi and V. I. Ivanov especially (Blok was not very much of a theoretician), spoke of "new consciousness," of "mythmaking," of the "theurgical" significance of poetry. The inner crisis in symbolism became clear when, in 1910, Blok and Ivanov on the one hand, and Bryusov on the other, engaged in a controversy in *Apollon.* For Blok himself, symbolism at this point was a past stage and he was soon to desert it. Its aloofness from life, its absorption in mystical profundities, began to horrify him. "Back to the soul, not only to 'man,' but to the 'whole man' —with spirit, soul, and body, with the everydayness—three times so" and "What we want is reality, there is nothing more terrifying in the world than mysticism"—this is what he wrote in 1911 and 1912. Ivanov also began to speak of *realistic* symbolism, though what he meant was not quite the same thing. Belyi alone remained true to the tenets of symbolism, regarding Blok as a traitor to the common cause. At the same time the fortress of symbolism was attacked from outside. In 1910, one of the peripheral symbolist poets, Kuzmin (q.v.), published in *Apollon* (a review of art and literature, founded in 1909 and edited by Sergei Makovski in close collaboration with Annenski) an article entitled "Beautiful Clarity." It was a call to come down to earth from the nebulous metaphysical heights.

A year later, two younger poets, Nikolai Gumilev (q.v.) and Sergei Mitrofanovich Gorodetzki (1884–1917), launched a new movement to which they gave the name of "acmeism." Gumilev, who was a disciple of Bryusov and the French parnassians, became its theoretician and *maître d'école.* To the symbolists' emphasis on the hidden, associative, musical elements in poetry ("*De la musique avant toute chose*"), the acmeists opposed the elements of sense and logic in the art of words. To Ivanov's and Belyi's tendency to view the poet as a prophet, a mythmaker, or to stress his passive, mediumistic nature, Gumilev proposed the conception of the poet as a craftsman, and the literary organization founded by him and his consorts was accordingly named "Poets' Guild." As preached and practiced by Gumilev, acmeism bore some resemblance to the movement launched within French symbolism by Jean Moréas (1856–1910). Although the movement as a whole had some neoclassical characteristics, it lacked real unity. Its best-known adherents, Anna Akhmatova and Mandelstamm (qq.v.), who contributed greatly to the further enrichment of Russian poetry in the years preceding the revolution and immediately after it, were poets with sharply defined individualities who could hardly be described as Gumilev's followers. Certain aspects of acmeism, which represented a reaction against symbolism—its lucidity, manliness, zest for life —had a great influence on some of the post-revolutionary poets.

Another movement that arose in opposition to symbolism but was also largely its own off-spring was futurism (q.v.). It was a movement parallel to, but in many ways different from, the Italian futurism of Filippo Tommaso Marinetti (1876–1944). Its very beginnings in Russia go back to 1909.

In 1912 its exponents published a provocative manifesto entitled "Poshochina obshchestvennomu vkusu" ("A slap in the face of public taste"), in which they declared war on all the art of the past. By 1912 it was repre-sented by a number of small groups and coteries, known under such names as ego-futurists, cubo-futurists, centrifuga, the mezzanine of poetry, etc. Of these, the cubo-futurists came to play the most important role. As the name implies, they were connected with the cubist movement in painting. *Du Cubisme* (1912) of Albert Gleizes and Jean Metzenger became one of their bedside books. Some of their experiments with words and verse have led some students of futurism to speak of their "verse cubism," although the analogy is rather arbitrary.

The cubo-futurists, whose center was in Moscow (as opposed to the ego-futurists of Leningrad, led by Igor Severyanin, 1887–1941), had for their leaders two poets who were also painters—David Burlyuk (b. 1882) and Vladimir Mayakovski (q.v.). The former made his home, after the revolution, in New York and became better known as a painter, though he continued to write Russian poetry and preach futurism. The latter became the acknowledged leader of Russian avant-garde poetry. Connected with them was Khlebnikov (q.v.), the Russian Rimbaud. The futurists proclaimed the absolute autonomy of art, its complete independence from life. In one of their early publications they declared that, apart from its starting point, which is to be seen in the creative impulse, poetry has no relation with the world, is not coordinated with it.

They saw their mission in "unshackling" the word, in freeing it from the subservience to meaning, and thus arriving at "direct percep-tion." Their slogan was "the word per se" or "self-valuable word." They visualized, and attempted to practice, a new, universal, "trans-sense" language (*zaum'*). Fundamentally, this attitude had much in common with that of the

symbolists, among whom Andrei Belyi espe-cially had freely indulged in word-coining. The influence of Mallarmé is equally obvious. Burlyuk spoke of both the Russian and the French symbolists, as well as the *poétes maudits,* as the masters of the futurist poets, naming Baudelaire, Rimbaud, Tristan Corbière (1845–75), and Laforgue. But the futurists went far beyond their predecessors. This is how they themselves formulated the difference between them and the symbolists: "Symbolism, in the main, tried, both theoreti-cally and practically, to deepen the inner mean-ing of the word, admiring its aroma: the word mattered not *per se,* but because it contained the symbol, the world, the essence, the soul of things or the mystical other world . . .

"Today's poets are approaching the word from another side. The shape of words, their appearance, their sounds matter more than the meaning. The secret of lyrical poetry is in the magic of word organization. . . . If the word represents acoustic or graphic material, then it can be magnified or split, or one can invent afresh a trans-sense language. Hence the intoxication with the element of words, the cult of form" (*Moskovskiye mastera,* 1916).

In the experimental works of the Burlyuk brothers (David and Vladimir) and of Aleksei Krutchonykh (b. 1886), the bounds of intelligi-bility were overstepped. Burlyuk continued to write in what he called "upside-down" words in his New York period. Khlebnikov, whom the futurists came to regard as their "slovozhdy" or "verbal leader" (actually, the Russian word is a contamination of the words *slovo*-word and *vozhd'*-leaders), also produced his share of trans-sense poetry, but unlike that of his fellow futurists it had a firm linguistic substratum and showed a keen sense of the Russian language. Nor does it by any means exhaust his poetic output.

Mayakovski, who after the revolution was to become the leader of futurism, never indulged in the extremes of "wordmaking," contenting himself with all sorts of "shifts" in the language —phonetic, morphological, semantic, rhythmic. His principal innovations were in the realm of versification, where he tended to substitute tonic verse for the traditional syllabo-tonic pattern, introduced by Vasili Kirilovich Tredyakovski (1703–1769) and Mikhail Vasilyevich Lomonosov (1711–65) and canon-ized and perfected in 19th-c. Russian poetry. In these prosodic innovations his direct masters were Blok and Belyi, but he adopted more revolutionary procedures. Characteristic for Mayakovski was also the "depoetization" of the vocabulary and imagery, in which some Soviet students of Mayakovski (Fedorov, Chardzhiev, Mechenko) see the influence of Rimbaud, Corbière, Laforgue, Verhaeren, and Walt Whitman (1819–92). But whereas western European futurism (and especially that of Marinetti) had a distinctly urbanistic flavor, this cannot be said of Russian futurism as a whole. Two of its leading representatives, Khlebnikov and Vasili Vasilyevich Kamenski (1884–1961), had a strong antiurban bias. In Khlebnikov there were elements of utopian romanticism, and he had very strong anti-Western and pro-Asian leanings. In Mayakovski's poetry, however, urbanistic motifs were very prominent, but his urbanism was more of a social than a technological character and even before 1917 had a distinctly revolutionary orientation. For Mayakovski the art of the future, of which all the futurists spoke, was closely interrelated with the imminent social revolution, and his postrevolutionary development was in many ways quite logical.

Another poet who began before the revolution as a futurist but who belongs essentially to the postrevolutionary period was Boris Pasternak (q.v.).

While in poetry, symbolism, throughout the first decade of the century, held undivided and unchallenged sway, in prose fiction it shared the floor with realism. The older generation of the realists was represented by Lev Tolstoi, Chekhov, and Vladimir Korolenko (1853–1921). Tolstoi stood more or less outside current literature, but enjoyed a great moral prestige and to many people personified the collective conscience of the nation. Chekhov's last years were devoted almost entirely to playwriting. Korolenko engaged mainly in journalism but produced during this period what may be his best work—*Istoriya moyevo Sovremenika* (4 vols., 1906–1922).

The younger writers were grouped around Gorki and his publishing house Znaniye. Gorki himself had begun as a revolutionary romanticist with strong Nietzschean leanings, but with time was tending more and more toward social-oriented realism. Those who gravitated toward him—Bunin, Andreyev, Kuprin (qq.v.), Ivan Shmeliyov (1875–1950)—were writers of very different dispositions though certain common characteristics make it possible to class them together as realists. Their predilec-

tion for the short story as a medium reflected the influence of Chekhov. In Andreyev, however, certain affinities with the "modernists" were also apparent—in the symbolist overtones of some of his plays and stories and in his interest in erotic themes. These latter became generally prominent in literature after the revolution of 1905, when sexual licence became rampant among the Russian intelligentsia. A literary reflection of it was the enormous success of *Sanin* (1907; Eng., 1917), the pornographic novel of Mikhail Artzybashev (q.v.), who was later described as "a curious and, on the whole, regrettable episode in the history of Russian literature" (Mirsky). Andreyev and Artzybashev reflected also the mood of nihilistic pessimism that was fairly widespread at the time in Russian society and led to numerous suicides. Eroticism and pessimism characterized also much of the prose fiction of Sologub, but here they were presented with superb and subtle stylistic mastery.

Generally speaking, the prose fiction of the symbolist writers (Sologub, Belyi, Bryusov, Zinaida Gippius) was, to one degree or another, related to their poetry and reflected the same concern with problems of style and form. Belyi's and Sologub's novels certainly belong to the most memorable prose works of this period. Belyi's, moreover, were very influential, both structurally and thematically, in molding some of the younger postrevolutionary writers. Several prose writers who made their appearance during this decade were influenced by the symbolists and have been described as neorealists. They include Remizov, Aleksei Tolstoi (qq.v.), and Sergei Nikolayevich Sergeyev-Tzenski (1875–1958). Remizov, alongside with Belyi, was to influence considerably the postrevolutionary developments in Russian prose.

In literary criticism the prevalent social-utilitarian approach gave way to subjectively colored impressionist (Aichenwald, Kornei Chukovski [1882–1969], partly Annenski) or philosophical (Rozanov, Shestov) criticism. There was also, however, a genuine interest in problems of style, especially poetic style, and this was reflected in the valuable studies of Belyi and Bryusov and, toward the very end of the period being discussed, in the work of young adherents of formalism.

AFTER 1917

The Bolshevik Revolution of October 1917 and the final victory of the communists in the

199

ensuing civil war, accompanied by the exodus of thousands of people, among whom the intelligentsia was represented by a large percentage, resulted in a bifurcation of Russian literature. After 1920 it is possible to speak of two branches of Russian literature—the literature at home and the one in exile. Whereas in the first three or four years there was a certain amount of osmosis between them (with Berlin as the geographical meeting point), ultimately their divergence grew and became irrevocable. This was largely due to the fact that literature at home was becoming more and more involved in the general totalitarian setup, and its fortunes more and more dependent on politics.

The first three years of the revolution were dominated by poetry (this was largely due to purely external reasons, such as shortage of paper and of publishing facilities in general). While it is true that several major poets of the prerevolutionary period did emigrate—Balmont, V. I. Ivanov, Khodasevich, Tzvetayeva, Georgii V. Ivanov, Adamovich (qq.v.), Zinaida Nikolayevna Gippius (1869–1945)—most of them, however, after 1920, they are not only balanced but outweighed by those who remained—Blok, Belyi, Sologub, Bryusev, Gumilev, Anna Akhmatova, Mandelstamm, Mayakovski, Yesenin, Pasternak (qq.v.).

Of these, not only Mayakovski and Yesenin, who belonged to the younger generation and avant-garde movement, but also Blok and Belyi, the two pillars of erstwhile religious symbolism, sided with the revolution. They welcomed it as a beneficent spiritual cataclysm. Blok's poem *Dvenatzat* (1918; The Twelve, 1920) was the most significant individual poetic work of those years. But he died an utterly disillusioned man. Of the other poets of the symbolist generation, Bryusov alone embraced communism wholeheartedly—at least externally. Gumilev was one of the early victims of the Red terror, and Sologub, Anna Akhmatova, and Mandelstamm came to be treated virtually as inside *émigrés*. Mayakovski and Yesenin led the two avant-garde movements (futurism and imaginism), which identified themselves with the revolution, and tried to establish a literary monopoly. Both poets, though very different, had undoubted appeal to wide audiences and enjoyed a great success. But in the mid-1920's the Communist Party had to open its guns on "Yeseninism," which was identified with the widely spread "decadent" and "demobilizing" moods. Somewhat later, and not long before his spectacular suicide, Mayakovski also came under fire from

party pundits. But, later, his reputation as "the most talented poet of the revolution" was officially sanctioned by Stalin. Such poets as Tikhonov, Pasternak, Mandelstamm, Selvinski, Klyuyev, Klychkov, and Zabolotzki (qq.v.) added spice and variety to the literary scene in the first postrevolutionary decade. Experiment and innovation were very much the order of the day, and several of these poets went through a stage in which they were under the influence of Khlebnikov (q.v.), who was held in great esteem during this period.

Experimenting characterized also the Soviet theater of this early period (Mayakovski's *Misteriya-buff* [1918] and the experiments in stagecraft of Meyerhold [1874–1942], Aleksandr Tairov [1885–1950], Yevgenii Vakhtangov [1883–1922], and their disciples). In the drama there was an influence of German expressionists. Variety and vitality marked also the prose fiction of that first decade.

After the revolution the short story at first predominated over the novel, and the approach was decidedly and deliberately a-psychological, often lyrical-emotional, with the revolution and the civil war, and the situations and problems arising from them, as practically the sole subjects. Here, too, there was a great deal of experimenting with forms and techniques. The predominant influences were those of Belyi (the broken, multiplanar narrative, the musically constructed prose, with recurrent leitmotifs) and Remizov (q.v.; the *skaz* or imitation of individual spoken intonation). The typical writers of this period were Pilnyak, Babel, Vsevolod T. Ivanov (qq.v.), and Nikolai Nikitin (b. 1895). Some of the younger writers, members of the Serapion Brotherhood in Leningrad—Lev Natanovich Lunc (1901–1924) and Kaverin (q.v.)—toyed with the idea of "renovating" Russian literature, which seemed to them too "static" and "plotless," and which they wanted to invigorate by injecting into it doses of Edgar Allan Poe (1809–1849) and E. T. A. Hoffmann (1776–1822), of Robert Louis Stevenson (1850–94), and even Dumas père (1802–1870). Some of these younger writers went to school with Zamyatin (q.v.), whose narrative art had affinities with surrealism (q.v.).

An important role was played during this period by the so-called formalists in literary criticism—Viktor Shklovski (b. 1893), Yurii Tynyanov (1894–1943), Boris Eichenbaum (1886–1959)—who had evolved their theories in close contact with the futurist poets of the prerevolutionary period and now passed on to the younger writers their interest in problems of literary structure. These formalist critics (of whom Tynyanov himself wrote interesting prose fiction) and their close allies among the more academic scholars (Tomashevski, Zhirmunski) clashed with the exponents of Marxism and were later hounded out of existence or made to renounce their errors. But in the early 1920's even Marxist literary criticism—which stemmed in Russia from Plekhanov (1857–1918), one of the pioneers of Russian Marxism —was not yet reduced to a uniform pattern and displayed enough varieties of approach to make the critical controversies sufficiently lively and stimulating.

Though left-wing currents in various European literatures, which as a rule were in sympathy with the revolution in Russia, Soviet literature kept in touch with modern trends in the West. Western literature was freely translated and discussed. One of the most popular contemporary foreign writers in the earliest period was Pierre Hamp (b. 1876), nearly all of whose work was translated into Russian. Later, Dos Passos (q.v.) attracted the attention of several young Soviet writers by his combination of revolutionary sentiments with novel literary techniques. Joyce (q.v.) was little known in Russia until the early 1930's, when some of his work was translated. At that time he was hailed by some communist writers as a painter of the putrescent bourgeois world and a great literary rebel. But in 1934, at the First Congress of Soviet Writers, he was branded as a rotten decadent, and Soviet writers were discouraged from imitating him or even taking an interest in him.

The year 1924 marked the beginning of the revival of the novel as a literary form. Leonov's (q.v.) *Barsuki* (1924–25; The Badgers, 1947), Fedin's (q.v.) *Goroda i gody* (1924; Cities and Years, 1960), and Gladkov's (q.v.) *Tzement* (1924; Cement, 1929) were followed by numerous other novels. In some of these early Soviet novels traditional elements were blended with new techniques and devices borrowed from Belyi or Western modernists. One of the most interesting works of this fruitful decade of Soviet literature was Olesha's (q.v.) *Zavist'* (1927; Envy, 1947). The young writer was hailed by the critics as a rising star. His subsequent fate serves as a good illustration of the difficulties experienced in Soviet Russia by a nonconforming writer. Continuing to show his obsession with the theme of *Envy* (which was,

in a way, an anticipation of Koestler's [q.v.] theme of the Yogi and the Commissar), Olesha drew upon himself the fire of orthodox communists who denounced his "bourgeois individualism," his preoccupation with himself, his inability to portray the life of the working class. He was bluntly told to "reeducate" himself. He tried his best but had to confess his failure and spoke pathetically of himself as a writer of "unwanted" and "untimely" themes. In one of his plays he probably had himself in mind when he had one of his characters quote Hamlet's rebuff to Guildenstern: "Call me what instrument you will, though you can fret me, you cannot play upon me." By 1939 Olesha drifted out of literature and he did not reappear until 1956, when it was suddenly decided to reissue his selected works, including *Envy*.

Symbolically enough, 1927 saw also the appearance of another short novel, Fadeyev's (q.v.) *Razgrom* (1927; The Nineteen, 1929), which was to be of much more decisive importance for the subsequent evolution of Soviet literature. It marked a return to psychological realism. Its dependence on Lev Tolstoi was immediately noted by Soviet critics. Coming from an orthodox communist writer, one of the leaders of the Association of Proletarian Writers, it was a symptomatic prefiguration of the back-to-realism movement, which some communist writers were to oppose to the followers of Belyi, Pilnyak, and Zamyatin. As yet there was no talk of socialist realism (q.v.)—though the expression "proletarian realism" was occasionally used—and the demand was for realism *tout court,* for the portrayal of the unadorned, "living" man. One of the major early achievements in this line was Sholokhov's (q.v.) *Tikhii Don* (1928–40; The Silent Don, 1942), which, of all the individual Soviet novels, enjoyed the greatest success both in the U.S.S.R. and abroad.

The late 1920's were also rich in works of satirical intent—stories by Zoshchenko (q.v.), novels by Ilya Ilf (1897–1937) and Yevgenii Petrov (1903–1942), stories and plays by Mikhail Afanasyevich Bulgakov (1891–1940), Katayev (q.v.), and others—behind which was a long and respectable tradition in Russian literature. Under the regime of control exercised by the Communist Party over literature the scope of satirical writing was restricted, and the only truly, political satire written in the 1920's—Zamyatin's novel *My* (1920; We, 1925), which anticipated Huxley's (q.v.) *Brave*

New World and Orwell's (q.v.) *1984*—was banned by Soviet censorship. (The principle of this control was set down in the famous 1925 resolution of the Central Committee of the Communist Party, which granted certain liberties to noncommunist writers, the so-called fellow travelers, but took the party interference in literary matters for granted.)

The period of relative freedom in Soviet literature, which had produced this variety and florescence, came to an end in 1929, when it was decided to harness literature and all other arts to the government's five-year plan of industrialization. Very little of lasting value was produced during the next three years, as most writers proceeded to turn their attention to "production" (*proizvodstvennye*) novels and plays, to sketches of documentary or propaganda interest, or to such vast collective enterprises, sponsored by Gorki (q.v.), as the volume on the construction of the White Sea Canal, a History of Factories and Plants, and a History of the Civil War. Among the few exceptions was Kaverin's anachronistic little novel, *Khudozhnik neizvesten* (1931).

The outstanding event in the literary world during this period was the suicide of Mayakovski, who, five years earlier, had addressed a poetic reprimand to Yesenin for his voluntary exit from life.

An end was put to the five-year-plan period in literature in 1932, when the Central Committee of the Communist Party disbanded the RAPP (Russian Association of Proletarian Writers), blaming it, as well as other "fictional" literary bodies, for the stagnation in literature, and proposed to set up in their place a single homogeneous Union of Soviet Writers. Thus the division of Soviet writers into communists and fellow travelers was obliterated. It is usually said that the instrumental behind-the-scenes factor in this literary "revolution" was Gorki, whose prestige gave him a growingly important position in Soviet letters after his return to the U.S.S.R. in 1929. The 1932 measure had a twofold significance. It was designed to restore some freedom and security to noncommunist writers, to free them from the tutelage of RAPP, and, incidentally, to raise the general standard of literature.

This end was undoubtedly achieved, and it was this "progressive" aspect of the 1932 act that at first made a great impression both at home and abroad. But in the long run it became increasingly clear that the reverse side of the event was of greater and more lasting

importance. The literary reform of 1932 set Soviet literature on the path of total subjection to the party. The setting up of the Union of Soviet Writers and the imposition of "homogeneity" to prevent factional squabbles made it possible for the Communist Party to control and channelize literature much more effectively and thoroughly. Membership in the union implied adherence to the political program of the Communist Party. Those who did not join the union or were refused membership were *eo ipso* positioned outside the pale. Moreover, by joining the union the writer subscribed to socialist realism (q.v.)—this was the only method permitted to Soviet artists, and there was a clause to this effect in the statutes of the union. True, the formula seemed to be vague and controversial, capable of many various interpretations. Gorki practically equated it with revolutionary romanticism, but this view failed to meet with general acceptance. A clue to the real meaning of socialist realism was supplied by Andrei Zhdanov (1896–1948) who was the government's spokesman at the First Congress of Soviet Writers in 1934. Zhdanov spoke of "Bolshevik tendentiousness" as the duty of all Soviet writers.

Later, Lenin's formula of "party-minded literature" (*partiinaya literatura*) was recalled, and subsequent developments made it clear that in reality socialist realism, when shorn of all its verbal ambiguities, amounted to strict compliance with the current party line. The latter, however, was subject to change. Thus, in the period between the first writers' congress and the outbreak of the war with Nazi Germany, socialist realism implied a persistent, systematic campaign against all and any "formalistic" experiments, against anything that smacked of "modernism" or "decadence," a campaign that affected not only literature but also all other fields of art, including music (in fact, one of the first major antiformalist pronouncements was an attack, in 1935, on Shostakovich's opera *The Lady Macbeth of the Mtzensk District*). It also meant: a preoccupation with the enemies of the Soviet Union at home and abroad, thus resulting in a crop of novels, stories, and plays "exposing" fascist and Trotskyite agents; a new attitude to the family, a revival of Victorianism; a revision of the historical approach, implying a glorification of Russia's past achievements, especially her military victories, and bringing in its wake a number of historical novels and plays that contrasted sharply with those of the earlier period, revolutionary in content. The party line, as it was expressed in literature through adherence to socialist realism, included also a growingly abject deification of Stalin, "the Great Leader and Teacher" and the all-round genius.

Among the more interesting and characteristic works of the pre-World War II period of socialist realism are: Sholokhov's *Podnyataya tzelina* (1932; Seeds of Tomorrow, 1935); Leonov's *Doroga na Okean* (1934; Road to the Ocean, 1944); Nikolai Yevgenyevich Virta's (b. 1906) *Odinochestvo* (1935); Aleksandr Malyshkin's (1892–1938) *Lyudi iz zacholustya* (1937); Yurii German's (1910–67) *Nashi znakomye* (1936); and Aleksei Tolstoi's great historical novel, *Piotr Pervyi* (1929–45; Peter the First, 1959). An example of a novel that arose out of Stalin's having been made the object of a cult is *Khleb* (1937; Bread, 1938), also by Aleksei Tolstoi, which later (in 1956) was openly downgraded as opportunistic and unworthy of its author. Throughout this period Soviet critics were on the lookout for ideological blunders, and those writers who could not live up to the demand for bolshevik tendentiousness or muster enough patriotic fervor to produce the "right" kind of historical fiction were gradually ceasing to appear in print or even being hounded out of literature.

The effect of socialist realism was particularly deadly on poetry. Boris Pasternak, regarded by many as the best Soviet poet of the period, did not publish a single volume of poetry between 1933 and 1943. Instead he concentrated on translations. A number of poets disappeared from literature, either not to return at all (Mandelstamm, Klyuyev, Klychkov, Boris Kornilov, Pavel Vasilyev) or to reappear much later, tamed and hardly recognizable (Zabolotzki).

When the U.S.S.R. entered World War II in 1941 its literature was virtually mobilized as part of the country's general war effort. Often, of course, the response to the government's appeal to patriotic feelings was sincere and spontaneous. Most of the writers then active in literature contributed to a vast body of wartime literature. There were even a few who effected an unexpected comeback, as, for instance, Anna Akhmatova, who had not published any original poetry since the early 1920's, and Pasternak. Both now came out with new volumes of poems, some of which were prompted by the war. In addition to war poetry, of which there was plenty, of very uneven quality,

the bulk of wartime literature consisted of war reportage and patriotic propaganda. Many leading writers served as war correspondents with frontline troops or the Black Sea and White Sea fleets, or else contributing impassioned newspaper articles to newspapers—*e.g.,* Aleksei Tolstoi and Ehrenburg (q.v.). It is usual to speak of a partial relaxation of party controls over literature during the war. Perhaps it would be more correct to say that, being aware of the limited appeal of purely communist slogans, the party, in the interests of national unity, withdrew for a time into the background and allowed writers to play on the national-patriotic strings of their readers' hearts.

This national-patriotic strain is clearly felt in such wartime plays as Simonov's (q.v.) *Russkie lyudi* (1942; The Russians, 1943) and Leonov's *Nashestviye* (1942) and *Lionushka,* in Simonov's novel *Dni i nochi* (1944; Days and Nights, 1945), and in much of Simonov's war poetry. (Very conspicuous is this poignant patriotic note in "You Remember, Alyosha, the Roads round Smolensk"—the well-known poem addressed to his fellow poet Aleksei Surkov.) The playing down of the role of the Communist Party is to be seen in Fadeyev's novel *Molodaya gvardiya* (1946; The Young Guard, 1959), which depicts the underground activities of young Soviet people in German-occupied territory. Published originally in 1945, this novel had to be considerably revised, for the author was accused of having minimized the role of the party in those days and those circumstances. It took Fadeyev four years to adapt the novel to this demand from above, and the revised version appeared in 1951.

On the whole there was little of lasting artistic value in wartime literature while its documentary value was often marred by a tendency toward patriotic stylization and the inevitable *suppressio veri.* Some works do succeed in conveying something of the epic grandeur of the events, but they are usually devoid of human, psychological interest inasmuch as on this level they tend to avoid conflicts, to simplify, to speak in the tone of yea-saying optimism. Leonov's war plays, which do succeed in creating a genuine dramatic conflict, are among the exceptions. Had literature been free from the necessity to keep an eye on the party and on the demands of socialist realism, it probably would have produced more effective war works. It is significant that the much-advertised novel by Sholokhov, *Oni srazhalis' za Rodinu*, only a few installments of which have appeared, was never completed.

Almost as soon as the war was over, the party hastened to tighten, with a vengeance, its control over literature. The resolution passed by the Central Committee on 14 August 1946 inaugurated a new period that became associated with the name of Andrei Zhdanov, who was entrusted with the task of supervising all cultural life. It can be said without exaggeration that in this period Soviet literature reached its low-water mark. Renewed attacks on "bourgeois formalism" were launched, and a number of writers were accused of servility to the West, denounced as "rootless cosmopolitans," and purged out of literature or forced to confess and recant their "sins." It was in the fields of literary scholarship and literary and dramatic criticism that this anti-West witch hunt wrought particular havoc. At the same time novels and plays were written to order to denounce Anglo-American "imperialists" and "warmongers" or to "prove" Russia's superiority in every field of human endeavor. Annual literary prizes bearing the name of Stalin were awarded for obviously mediocre works, while much of the best in earlier Soviet literature was repudiated and banned.

All this was to be openly and generally admitted ten years later when, after the debunking of Stalin at the 20th Congress of the Communist Party, all the mistakes and failures in literature were ascribed to the "cult of the individual" (*kul't lichnosti*).

At the end of 1956 a leading Soviet literary periodical published three very revealing articles. One, by S. Stut, discussed the "blank spots" on the map of Soviet literature as a serious literary-historical problem. Many of those blank spots were said to be a result "of the devastations wrought in literature by the cult of the individual and its consequences." Writers were mentioned who were "physically torn out of the ranks of literature"—Babel, Yasienski, Koltzov—others who were posthumously subjected to ideological persecution— Bagritzki (q.v.), Ilf, and Petrov. Critics and literary scholars were accused of distorting all yardsticks and criteria: "As a living reproach to Soviet criticism there stand on our shelves volumes of articles about Stalin laureates in which such novels as *Zemliya Kuznetzkaya*

[by Voloshin] and *Molodaya gvardiya* [by Fadeyev] were appraised with equal enthusiasm. Four young scholars devoted their dissertations to the work of S. Babayevski. Four people were awarded degrees for studying the work of Mikhail Bubennov [b. 1909]" (*Novyi Mir,* 1956, No. 9).

The second article, by none other than Konstantin Simonov, asserted that without a careful analysis of the way in which the cult of the individual had affected literature, "it is impossible to write a truthful history of literature nor is true literary criticism thinkable." Simonov saw the chief trouble not so much in the "direct, immoderate . . . glorification of Stalin" (of which he admitted himself guilty) as in the fact that there were even more works in which no such glorifying passages occurred but in which the portrayal of life was untrue or half-true. "We cannot say that our literature spoke downright lies about our postwar life, but often it said only one half of the truth— and half-truth is an enemy of art" (*Novyi Mir,* 1956, No. 12).

The third article by one of the lesser-known Soviet critics and literary scholars, A. Mechenko, insisted on the necessity of a historical approach to Soviet literature—something, he said, that had never been attempted—and suggested a complete revaluation of its past (*Novyi Mir,* 1956, No. 12).

These breast-beatings, together with some other phenomena in Soviet literature between 1953 and 1956 (such as, for example, the complete swing of the pendulum regarding the attitude to the West and its literature, and the consequent rehabilitation of the majority of "rootless cosmopolitans"), created that atmosphere of "thaw," which was foreshadowed in Ehrenburg's short novel under that title, published soon after the death of Stalin. The Soviet literary scene in 1956 showed signs of bewilderment and disorientation as far as the older, established writers were concerned, but at the same time of a definite loosening of ideological pressure, which led to the appearance of several works imbued with critical spirit and free from the tailored-to-order optimism. As examples one may name Victor Nekrasov's (b. 1911) *V rodnom gorode* (1955) and Vladimir Dudintzev's (b. 1918) *Ne Khlebom yedinym* (1956; Not by Bread Alone, 1957). But, unlike what happened in Poland, no criticism of the fundamental tenets of socialist realism was as yet tolerated, and the impression remained that literature was still a handmaiden of politics and that the easing of pressure was part of the current party line.

LITERATURE IN EXILE

As a result of the bolshevik revolution there sprang up, side by side with Soviet literature inside Russia, Russian literature in exile. Among those who chose to emigrate after the civil war was over in 1920 was a large percentage of writers, artists, scholars, and journalists. In the early 1920's they were joined by other voluntary expatriates as well as by a large group of writers, scholars, and journalists who were deported abroad (in 1922) on orders of the Soviet government. This unprecedented and unique action not only helped to swell the ranks of the *émigrés* numerically but also greatly strengthened the quality of their membership, for among the new deportees were such outstanding philosophers as Nikolai Berdyayev, Semion Frank, Father Sergei Bulgakov, Nikolai Losski, Ivan Ilyin, Lev Karsavin, and Fiodor Stepun, as well as several well-known writers, journalists, and scholars. By 1924 Russian literature outside Russia could boast of an impressive list of names, which numbered both prose writers—Bunin, Remizov, Kuprin, Aleksei Tolstoi (qq.v.), Dmitrii Sergeyevich Merezhkovski (1864–1941), Ivan Sergeivich Shmelyov (1875–1950), Boris Konstantinovich Zaitzev (b. 1881), Nadezhda Teffi (1876–1957), Ilya Surguchov, and others —and poets—Balmont, Vyatcheslav Ivanov, Khodasevich, Adamovich, Tzvetayeva, G. V. Ivanov (qq.v.), Zinaida Gippius (1869–1945), and others—who represented a variety of literary schools and currents. From the early 1920's the *émigrés* had published, in addition to many newspapers (daily and weekly) and various short-lived publications, two firmly established literary reviews, which in the course of their existence published some first-class fiction and verse: *Sovremennye Zapiski* in Paris (1921–40) and *Volya Rossii* in Prague (1922–32). The following periodicals of shorter duration should also be mentioned: *Russkaya Mysl'* (Sofia-Prague-Berlin-Paris), *Zveno* (Paris), *Chisla* (Paris), *Novyi Grad* (Paris), *Russkiye Zapiski* (Paris). While at first, for a number of reasons, the principal center of *émigré* cultural activity was Berlin, by 1925 it shifted to Paris, with important subsidiary centers in Prague, Belgrade, and the Far East, not to speak of the Russian cultural activities in Poland and the Baltic countries, in which there was a considerable Russian minority. Several older writers—Bunin, Remizov, Merezhkovski, Shmeliov, Zaitzev—produced in exile some of their most important work. Among the poets, Khodasevich, Tzvetayeva, G. V. Ivanov, and Zinaida Gippius wrote some excellent poetry. Two writers made in exile their names and acquired international reputations—Mark Aldanov and Vladimir Nabokov (qq.v.). The latter, who became an *émigré* at the age of twenty, came to be almost unanimously recognized as the most original and brilliant product of *émigré* literature. There were also several talented young poets, born around the turn of the century, who as writers were formed in exile (Antonin Ladinski, Vladimir Smolenski, Anna Prismanova, Dovid Knut—to name but a few). Naturally enough, younger writers, especially in France, fell under the influence of Western writers—Proust, Joyce, Kafka, Apollinaire (qq.v.). The influence of Soviet literature was much less noticeable, with the exception of some poets in Prague who looked up to Pasternak (q.v.). Like their fellow writers in Russia, *émigré* writers were up against extra-literary handicaps, though of a different nature. They were free from tutelage and external dictation, but they had to contend with very real material hardships, the absence of an adequate outlet for their books (when they could have them printed), and the necessity of relying on some source of livelihood outside literature (for many of the younger ones it meant manual labor), not to mention the limitations imposed on all expatriates by the severance from the native soil. This last handicap was particularly keenly felt by some of the older, established writers; the younger bore up with it more easily. Under the circumstances one must marvel at the quantity and quality of the *émigré* literary output. When all is said and done, some of the works of Bunin, Aldanov, Remizov, Nabokov (qq.v.), Zaitzev, Shmeliov, and a few others will remain as a more permanent acquisition to Russian literature than the great majority of novels and stories published inside the U.S.S.R. The same is true of much *émigré* poetry. Even more unquestionable is the superiority of *émigré* literature over Soviet literature in the field of literary criticism and essays. Here *émigré* writers were free from the deadening influence of "uniformed" thought. It is enough to mention the names of Khodasevich, Fedotov, Viedlé, Bem, Stepun, and Adamovich. The same is true of memoir literature, some of which is valuable not only as documents but also as works of art (*e.g.*, Stepun's *Byvsheye i nesbyvsheyesya,* some of Tzvetayeva's literary recollections).

Within the younger generation of *émigré* writers the process of their literary "denationalization" was more or less inevitable. The most striking example is Nabokov, who, with nine novels, two collections of stories, two plays, and some poetry—all in Russian—to his credit, became, after 1940, to all intents and purposes, an American writer. Those who were still younger often became writers without ever becoming part of Russian literature—the best-known illustrations are Henri Troyat and Romain Gary (qq.v.) in France.

The ranks of *émigré* literature, depleted by the end of World War II by the natural process of death, were again increased by new expatriates from the Soviet Union, known as displaced persons. There were no outstanding established writers among them, but a few talented poets (Ivan Yelagin, Dmitrii Klenovski, Nikolai Morshen, and Vladimir Markov, the latter more interesting as a critic and essayist) soon attracted attention. As for the prose writers it was perhaps inevitable that they should bring with them some Soviet influences and at the same time display a certain lack of sophistication and culture. In their preoccupation with social-political problems they differ from the much more individualistically inclined young writers of the old emigration who were bent on their personal, moral, philosophical, and religious quests. There was, after the war, an activizing of *émigré* literary life, particularly in the United States and in Germany. The *émigrés* had again several literary periodicals: *Novyi Zhurnal* (New York, founded 1942), *Grani* (Frankfurt on the Main, 1946), *Vozrozhdeniye* (Paris, 1948), and *Opyty* (New York, 1953). Of these, *Novyi Zhurnal* tried to keep up the tradition of *Sovremennyye Zapiski*; *Grani* was the principal mouthpiece of the new *émigrés*; and *Opyty* bore a somewhat aloof and highbrow look of a "little review." More than two dozen volumes of verse published in Paris between 1950 and 1956 by Rifma (under the general editorship of Sergei Makovski) testify to the vitality of *émigré* poetry.

But the prospects of survival for *émigré* literature were far from bright. The young generation of the new *émigrés* was facing the same danger of denationalization (if anything a more rapid one inasmuch as so many of them

found themselves in the United States), and the general cultural level of the emigration, with the dying out of its older members and the growing absorption of many of the intermediate generation into the cultural life of their adopted countries, showed distinct signs of declining. It had to be proud of its past achievements rather than hopeful of its future unless and until the two branches of Russian literature are to meet again.

GLEB STRUVE

SOVIET LITERATURE IN THE 1960's

Events in Soviet literature and politics of the 1960's reinforce the Soviet writer's growing inclination to define his role in Soviet life with respect to present-day politics. Official policy on literature has vacillated between liberalization and tightening of bureaucratic controls. Soviet writers themselves tend to choose either the liberal position, out of which some outstanding work has been done, or the conservative position, which has led to mediocrity and restraint of artistic talent. The struggle between these two positions is revealed most clearly by two major events: the "liberalization" that is supposed to have occurred during the "false thaw" of winter 1962, and the 1966 public trial of the two Soviet writers Andrei Sinyavski (pseudonym Abram Tertz) and Yulii Daniel for publication of anti-Soviet literature abroad.

The pressure of politics is noticeable especially in the literary works of the poets Yevtushenko and Voznesenski, the prose writers Sinyavski, Kazakov, Aksinov, and Solzhenitzyn, and in the literary memoirs of Ehrenburg and Paustovski (qq.v.).

In November 1962, Khrushchev himself was instrumental in the publication of Solzhenitzyn's (q.v.) novel *Odin den' Ivana Denisovicha* (One Day in the Life of Ivan Denisovich, 1963), which became famous in America. Derived from Solzhenitzyn's experience during the late 1940's and early 1950's, the novel describes an inmate's life in a prison camp. It indicates that Stalinism was not just a matter of Stalin's personal aberration but was a pervasive, corrupt system, affecting all modes of social behavior. Khrushchev's approval seemed to sanction a liberalization of the arts in Soviet Russia. Liberal writers began to publish works directed against the legacy of Stalin. But Khrushchev, who had underestimated the intransigent power of conservative elements in the bureaucracy, was forced to halt this direction in December 1962.

Nevertheless, the "liberalization" had been partially successful in that it prompted the development among the more independent writers of a spirit of opposition to bureaucratic controls. This spirit is evidenced in an active literary underground, the members of which circulate their writings in manuscript form in the U.S.S.R. and publish works abroad.

In 1966, Andrei Sinyavski (b. 1924) and Yulii Daniel (b. 1925) were publicly tried for anti-Soviet activities. Sinyavski, the more accomplished of the two writers, had published novels, stories, and essays abroad. Sinyavski and Daniel were sentenced to five years of hard labor, a verdict that was publicly protested by a large segment of the Soviet literary intelligentsia. Their trial brought to the surface once again the underlying tensions between the conservative bureaucracy and the liberal intelligentsia.

With notable exceptions the lasting achievements of Soviet literature in the 1960's have been in the field of poetry. The deaths of the two remaining poets of the silver age—Pasternak and Anna Akhmatova (qq.v.)—signaled the transfer of the poetic tradition to such young poets as Yevtushenko, Voznesenski, Okudzhava, and Brodski.

Yevgeni Yevtushenko (q.v.) in particular has gained recognition for his political poetry and declamatory style, which is much like that of Mayakovski (q.v.). Yevtushenko is known for: "Nasledniki Stalina" (1962; The Heirs of Stalin, in *The Poetry of Yevgeny Yevtushenko: 1953–1965*, 1965), in which he attacks those of Stalin's bureaucrats who were still holding office in the Soviet Union; "Baby Yar" (1961; Babii Yar, in *Poems*, 1966), which links World War II Nazi atrocities to present-day Soviet anti-Semitism; the political allegory " 'Da' i 'net' " (1965; Yes and No, in *Poems*, 1966); his *Avtobiografiya* (1963; Precocious Autobiography, 1963).

As a poet Yevtushenko shows little innovation on the modern and highly accomplished techniques of Mayakovski and Pasternak and reveals an occasional lack of sensitivity for language and even, at times, for social reality.

Andrei Voznesenski (q.v.), on the other hand, has made substantial innovations by fusing intimate lyrical poetry and civic, declamatory poetry. The best examples of this are the short poems of the collection *Antimiry* (1964; Anti-worlds, 1966) and the long narrative poem "Oza" (in *Akhillesovo serdtze*, 1966). "Oza"

deals with the theme of advancing scientific and technological organization and its effect on man's most personal relationships.

Among the less famous poets, two figures stand out: Bulat Okudzhava and Iosif Brodski. Okudzhava (b. 1924) is known for his outspoken treatment of the problems of Soviet youth. His poems, although often diffuse and unconventional in form, are chanted to the accompaniment of a guitar. Oftentimes they are betrayed because sense is sacrificed to melodic effect.

Brodski (b. 1940), on the other hand, displays unusual precision in the use of the poetic word. His style presents a skillful interweaving of sound and sense, as in the long poem "Bol'shaya elegiya: Dzhonu Donnu" (1963; Elegy for John Donne, *Russian Review*, XXIV, 341–53). In this, Brodski invokes in rhythms and sounds the anguish of Donne's personal life and professional work. Brodski, known also as a translator of poetry, was tried and convicted of "parasitism" in 1964. He was found guilty of allowing himself to be supported by his parents while he was working on his writing. His punishment was not severe, and he is again publishing translations in official publications and his own works in the underground publications.

The area of prose, subject to more rigid bureaucratic controls because of its wider circulation and broader popularity, has failed to produce a corpus of major literature in the 1960's.

Sinyavski's novel *Lyubimov* (1964; The Makepeace Experiment, 1965) is a political allegory that portrays the subversion of all humanistic ideals by means of the concentration of power in totalitarian hands. Far from exemplifying Sinyavski's views on the value of the fantastic in literature, as his *Fantasticheskiye povesti* (1961; Fantastic Stories, 1963) does, *Lyubimov* seems to indicate that fantasy is of value only as political allegory.

On the surface, the short-story writer Yurii Kazakov (b. 1927) avoids all political implication in his haunting stories of those unfitted for life, the rejected, and the alienated. Like Chekhov (q.v.), Kazakov presents the forces of social life by means of writing about the everyday. His stories show individuals awash in a fast-changing world, who have somehow been left behind by that change but are yet conscious of the irretrievably lost possibilities that would once have enabled them to rejoin that world.

Such stories as "Po doroge" (1961; Going to Town, in *Going to Town, and Other Stories*,

1964) and "Otshchepenetz" (1962; Silly-Billy, in *Going to Town, and Other Stories*) reveal a mastery of expository style equal to that of Chekhov or Paustovski in its deft descriptions of nature and its verbal economy.

The young novelist Vasilii Aksionov (b. 1932) takes up a contemporary social problem, that of the quest of Soviet youth, in his short novel *Zvezdnyi bilet* (1961; A Ticket to the Stars, 1963). Aksionov brings new life to Russian literary language through abundant use of street jargon in this novel that examines the queries of Soviet youth as it is faced with an increasingly regimented society. In this novel Aksionov criticizes Soviet society for its pervasive concern with function to the exclusion of all concern with values. Failing, however, to assert the values that it calls for, he ends the novel in a sentimental acknowledgment of the need for progress.

Perhaps the only new writer in the 1960's of major significance is Aleksandr Solzhenitzyn (q.v.), whose novels *One Day in the Life of Ivan Denisovich* and *Dlya pol'zy dela* (1962; For the Good of the Cause, 1964) testify readily to his ability. His major triumph has been the publication abroad of *V kruge pervom* (1968; The First Circle, 1968) and *Rakovyi korpus* (1968; The Cancer Ward, 1968), both of which did not pass Soviet censorship.

Solzhenitzyn presents characters who, supremely aware of their actual unfreedom, make a valid individual response to the ideal of freedom. This theme, so central to the great writers of 19th-c. Russia, is forcefully pursued in *One Day in the Life of Ivan Denisovich* and *The First Circle*. Through a terse style, sometimes marked by the use of vulgarity and obscenity, Solzhenitzyn develops vivid and highly individual character portrayals that are unlike any in Soviet literature since the stories of Babel (q.v.) in the 1920's.

In 1967 Solzhenitzyn called for the abolition of censorship in the Soviet Union in an open letter, which was published in *The New York Times* (5 June 1967). His outspoken appeals for liberalization of artistic expression in the Soviet Union resulted in his expulsion from the Union of Soviet Writers in 1969.

This event, taken together with the theme of freedom in Solzhenitzyn's works, serves to point up the interdependence of art and politics in the present-day Soviet Union.

ELLIOTT D. MOSSMAN

BIBLIOGRAPHY: Belyi, A., *Simvolizm; kniga statei* (1910); Bryusov, V., *Dalekiye i blizkiye* (1912); Chuzeville, J., *Anthologie de poetès russes contemporains* (1914); Ehrenburg, I., *Portrety russkykh poetov* (1922); Tartakower, S., ed., *Das russische Revolutionsgedicht* (1923); Eliasberg, A., and Guenther, J. v., *Rußland in dichterischen Dokumenten* (1924); Gorlov, N., *Futurizm i revolutziya* (1924); Olkienizkaia-Naldi, *Antologia dei poeti russi del XX secolo* (1924); Yeshov, I., and Shamurin, E., *Russkaya poesiya XX veka. Antologiya* (1925); Mirsky, D. S., *Contemporary Russian Literature (1881–1925)* (1926); Engelhardt, B., *Formal'nii metod v istorii literatury* (1927); Goriély, B., *La nouvelle poésie en U.R.S.S.* (1928); Arseniev, N. v., *Die russische Literatur der Neuzeit und Gegenwart in ihren geistigen Zusammenhängen* (1929); Brodskii, N., *Literaturnye manifesty: ot simvolizma k Oktyabryu* (1929); Pozner, V., *Panorama de la littérature russe contemporaine* (1929); Adamovich, G., and Kantor, M., *Yakor': Antologiya zarubezhnoi poezii* (1930); Gourfinkle, N., *Le théâtre russe contemporain* (1931); Reavey, G., and Slonim, M., *Soviet Literature: An Anthology* (1933); Bukharin, N., *Poeziya poetika i poeticheskoye tvorchestvo v SSSR* (1934); Eastman, M., *Artists in Uniform* (1934); Goriély, B., *Les Poètes dans la révolution russe* (1934); Markov, P., *The Soviet Theatre* (1934); Medvedev, P., *Formalizm i formalisty* (1934); Radek, K., *Sovremennaya mirovaya literatura i zadachi proletarskovo iskusstva* (1934); Selivanovskii, A., *Ocherki po istorii russkoi poezii* (1936); Poggioli, R., *Politica letteraria sovietica* (1938); Bowra, C. M., *Book of Russian Verse* (1943); Gyseghem, A. van, *Theatre in Soviet Russia* (1943); Kaun, A., *Soviet Poets and Poetry* (1943); Thorgevsky, I., *De Gorki à nos jours: la nouvelle littérature russe* (1945); Jirásek, J., *Přehledné dějiny ruské literatury,* Vols. II–IV (1946); Reavey, G., *Soviet Literature To-Day* (1946); Goriély, B., *Science des lettres soviétiques* (1947); Rais, E., and Robert, J., *Anthologie de la poésie russe* (1947); Bowra, C. M., *A Second Book of Russian Verse* (1948); David, J., *Anthologie de la poésie russe,* Vol. II (1948); Lavrin, J., *From Pushkin to Mayakovsky* (1948); Pertzov, V., et al., *Russkaya sovetskaya poeziya (1917–1947)* (1948); Bowra, C. M., *The Creative Experiment* (1949); Poggioli, R., *Il fiore del verso russo* (1949); Wilczkowski, C., *Écrivains soviétiques* (1949); Yarmolinsky, A., *A Treasury of Russian Verse* (1949); Struve, G., *Soviet Russian Literature: 1917–1950* (3rd ed.,

1951); Markov, V., *Prigiushennye golosa* (1952); Stender-Petersen, A., *Den russiske literarhistorie* (3 vols., 1952); Brown, E. J., *The Proletarian Episode in Russian Literature 1928–1932* (1953); Ivask, J., *Na Zapade: Antologiya russkoi zarubezhnoi poezii* (1953); Ripellino, A. M., *Poesia russa del Novecento* (1954); Erlich, V., *Russian Formalism: History–Doctrine* (1955); Yevreinov, N., *Istoriya russkovo teatra* (1955); Harkins, W. E., ed., *Dictionary of Russian Literature* (1956); Struve, G., *Russkaya literatura v izgnanii* (1956); Rühle, J., *Das gefesselte Theater* (1957); Lettenbauer, W., *Kleine russische Literaturgeschichte* (2nd ed., 1958); Lo Gatto, E., *Storia della letteratura russa* (2nd ed., 1958); Mathewson, R. W., *The Positive Hero in Russian Literature* (1958); Shabinski, V., *Prosvety* (1958); Simmons, E. J., Russian Fiction and Soviet Ideology (1958); Eng-Liedmeier, A. M. van der, *Soviet Literary Characters: An Investigation into the Portrayal of Soviet Men in Russian Prose* (1959); Reavey, G., *14 Great Short Stories by Soviet Authors* (1959); Ehrhard, M., *Die russische Literatur* (1960); Gibian, G., *Interval of Freedom: Soviet Literature during the Thaw 1954–1957* (1960); Guenther, J. v., ed., *Heiligunheiliges Rußland: Meistererzählungen* (1960); Guenther, J. v., ed., *Neue russische Lyrik* (1960); Guerney, B., *An Anthology of Russian Literature in the Soviet Period from Gorki to Pasternak* (1960); Poggioli, R., *The Poets of Russia 1890–1930* (1960); Rühle, J., *Literatur und Revolution* (1960); Rühle, J., ed., *Der Prozeß beginnt: Neue russische Erzähler* (1960); Yarmolinsky, A., *Literature under Communism* (1960); Gibian, G., "New Trends in the Novel: Kazakov, Nagibin, Voronin," *Survey*, No. 36 (1961), pp. 49–55; Jelagin, J., *Kunst und Künstler im Sowjetstaat* (1961); Hingley, R., "Soviet Literary Attitudes," *Survey*, No. 40 (1962), pp. 42–48; Ermolaev, H. *Soviet Literary Theories, 1917–1934* (1963); Forgues, P., "The Young Poets," *Survey*, No. 46 (1963), pp. 31–52; Alexandrova, V., *A History of Soviet Russian Literature: 1917–1964* (1964); Brown, E. J., *Russian Literature since the Revolution* (1964); Erlich, V., "Post-Stalin Trends in Russian Literature," *SlavR*, XXIII (1964), 405–40; Gibian, G., "Themes in Recent Soviet Literature," *SlavR*, XXIII (1964), 420–31; Hayward, M., and Crowley, E. L., eds., *Soviet Literature in the Sixties* (1964); Reeve, F. D., "The Work of Russian Poetry Today," *KR*, XXVI (1964), 533–53; Slonim, M., *Soviet Russian Literature: Writers and Problems* (1964); Davie, D., ed., *Russian Literature and Modern English Fiction: A Collection of Critical Essays* (1965); Dunham, V. S., "Poems about Poems: Notes on Recent Poetry," *SlavR*, XXIV (1965), 57–76; Johnson, P., and Labedz, L., eds., *Khrushchev and the Arts: The Politics of Soviet Culture, 1962–1964* (1965); Lindstrom, T., *A Concise History of Russian Literature* (1966); Medish, V., "The Soviet Literary Scene," *Russian Review*, XXV (1966), 150–59; Blair, K., *A Review of Soviet Literature* (1967); Gibian, G., *Soviet Russian Literature in English: A Checklist Bibliography* (1967); Gasiorowska, X., *Women in Soviet Fiction 1917–1964* (1968)

RUYRA I OMS, Joaquim

Spanish short-story writer and poet (writing in Catalan), b. 27 Sept. 1858, Gerona; d. 15 May 1939, Barcelona

R. lived for many years in the village of Blanes, managing his estates and devoting himself to literary work. Most of his later work indicates his commitment to realism and naturalism (q.v.). His fiction has been compared to that of Alphonse Daudet (1841–97) and Selma Lagerlöf (q.v.). Good will and brotherly love that stems from a Catholicism in the spirit of Saint Francis is to be seen throughout his work.

R. is more significant as a storyteller than as a poet, although the realism of the poetry in *El país del pler* (1906) is remarkable. His short stories have the character of 19th-c. genre paintings. Far from merely romanticizing his native landscape (Ampurdàn and the Costa Brava), however, these stories are exceptional because of their impressionistic description and subtle nuances of style.

In "Les senyoretes del mar" a Shakespearean fairyland mood dominates the realistic narrative element. "El primer ilustre d'amor" is a poetic description of first love. *Jacobé* (1902) deals with the theme of madness. "La fineta," which tells of an attempted rape, combines mythical and psychological elements. "La fi del món a Girona" is in the tradition of Edgar Allan Poe's (1809–1849) short stories.

R. is not to be categorized as a realist. M. de Montoliu wrote of R. that he "achieved an equilibrium between two complementary elements: reality and fantasy, objectivity and perceptivity."

FURTHER WORKS: *Marines i boscatjes* (1903); *La parada* (1919); *Pinia de rosa* (1920); *El malcontent* (1924); *La bona nova* (1927); *La cobla* (1931); *Entre flames* (1931); *Obres completes* (1949)

BIBLIOGRAPHY: Capdevila, J. M., "La obra de J. R.," *Hora de España,* XXI (Sept. 1938), 73–82; *La littérature Catalane,* special issue of *Europe,* No. 464 (1967)

GONZALO SOBEJANO

RWANDA LITERATURE

The Republic of Rwanda is one of the smallest, although one of the most densely populated, of the new African states. Thanks to intensive research by Belgian and Rwanda scholars, it is also the one whose traditional literature is best known. Until political independence led to the abolition of monarchy and the instauration of majority rule, Rwanda society was rigidly stratified: the agriculturists (Hutu), who made up the bulk of the population, were the subjects of an ethnically distinct aristocracy of pastors and warriors (Tutsi), who had elaborated a political-religious system of sacral monarchy. Rwanda literature reflects the organization and the preoccupations of Rwanda society.

Like all preliterate societies, Rwanda produced in prose folk tales, genealogies, and gnomic lore in abundance. It also developed prose chronicles that provide semilegendary accounts of the noble families. In them the origins of the Tutsis are traced back to a culture hero who introduced the techniques of hunting, iron smelting, and cow milking, and beyond that to the birth of the ruling dynasties from the incestuous union of a mythical brother and sister descended from heaven.

But the more important and valued part of oral literature was composed of three sharply distinct poetic genres: dynastic poetry, war poetry, and pastoral poetry.

Dynastic poetry—composed, memorized, and recited by certain privileged families—was devoted to the celebration of the high deeds of the ruling dynasties. It consists of long poems that seem to have originated in the 18th c. from the grouping and elaboration of previously existing shorter praise poems.

War poetry was composed by the warrior. Tradition decreed that each warrior chant boast songs and praise poems of his own making to whet his emotion before and during battles and to perpetuate his prowess.

Rwanda pastoral poetry has nothing bucolic about it. The cow is a sacred animal. One of the dynastic poems says that "God created kings primarily so that cows could multiply." The third purpose of poetry, therefore, is to sing the praise of cattle. The poets celebrate not only the strength and beauty and fecundity of cows but also such unexpected qualities as their courage and their cunning.

The traditional poetry of Rwanda is of special interest because it preserved in a remarkably pure state, well into the colonial period, features of oral art that used to be characteristic of a number of similar societies in the Great Lakes region, such as the kingdoms of Burundi, Nunyoro, Buganda, and Akole.

The impact of Western civilization has so far produced only one notable writer in Rwanda: Alexis Kagame (b. 1912), a Roman Catholic priest. Apart from a number of scholarly studies, both in the vernacular and in French, on the oral art of his country and on the philosophy, history, and political organization of its people, Kagame's most ambitious work is *Umulirimbyi wa Nyiliibiremwa,* a vast epic poem of Christian inspiration. Composed in traditional style, it tells the story of man from the creation down to the recent Vatican II council. Kagame himself has translated the first two volumes into French under the titles of *La Divine pastorale* (1952) and *La Naissance de l'univers* (1956).

ALBERT S. GÉRARD

S

SABA, Umberto

(pseud. of *Umberto Poli*), Italian poet, b. 9 March 1883, Trieste; d. 25 Aug. 1957, Gorizia

S.'s mother was Jewish, and his father deserted her before the boy's birth. Largely self-educated, at twenty S. enlisted for several years in an infantry regiment. When Trieste was returned to Italy after World War I, S. established the antiquarian book shop that was to occupy him off and on for the rest of his life. During World War II, because of Italian racial laws, S. went to Paris, but he later returned to live secretly in Rome and Florence. After the liberation, he resettled in Trieste. In the last decade of his life he was awarded several literary prizes and honors, including the coveted Viarreggio prize (1946).

More than any other 20th-c. poet, S. succeeds in achieving the tone as well as the edge and subtlety of modern poetry without discarding conventional forms and meters. His language is for the most part conventional, even in poems where the pulse of modernity beats most strongly. But unlike Ungaretti, Quasimodo, or Montale (qq.v.), S. is an extremely uneven poet and his reputation is based on a comparatively small portion of his total output. S.'s artistic maturity is the result of gradual development and experimentation rather than something that is inborn and present almost from the very outset.

Literary influences and poetic theories play an insignificant role in S.'s mature poetry, which may account for the simplicity and naturalness of his style. His early poetry, however, is full of echoes of Giacomo Leopardi (1798–1837) and displays the worst weaknesses of derivative verse. In addition, his choice of themes often

betrayed him into sentimentality, and because his style is perilously close to the rhythms of prose, he did not always avoid the pitfall of writing versified prose.

However, in *Casa e campagna* (1909–1910), S. achieved a masterly ease and naturalness, and a happy union between prose and poetic cadences. *Trieste e una donna* (1910–12)—his most original volume of verse—is the supreme illustration of what Montale calls "pure feeling, comparable to music." The lyric poems in it show a poetic and linguistic maturity guided by a stricter architectonic compactness. Topographical realism combined with an impressive degree of lyric intensity gives the verse its hard and crystalline timbre. These poems also evidence a more complex synthesis between S.'s own life and feelings and his attitude to Trieste.

In *Autobiografia* (1924), too, there is a striking consistency of lyric tone in dealing with what Robert Browning (1812–89) called "incidents in the development of the soul." Other volumes of lesser poetic depth or originality followed—*I prigioni* (1924), *Fanciulle* (1925), *Cuor morituro* (1925–30) and *Preludio e fughe* (1928–29).

In *Parole* (1933–34) and *Ultime cose* (1935–43) S. sounds an altogether new note. Verbal diffuseness gives way to a quintessential laconism without leading to the sort of obscurity associated with hermetic poetry. Concentration and economy both at the verbal level and at the level of the organization of thought and feeling are complemented by an inner moral ripening.

Poetic images and terms of moral and psychological reference change significantly and point up both the underlying symbolism of the familiar and the poet's awareness of things previously ignored. Painful and joyous youthful memories revive and show him the present in a new light and himself in a different perspective. *Mediterranee* (1946) contains two of S.'s best-known poems: "Ebbri canti" and "Ulisse." However, *Uccelli* (1948) and *Quasi un racconto* (1951), S.'s last two volumes, register a notable decline in poetic powers.

S.'s contribution to 20th-c. Italian poetry is undoubtedly both substantial and original. Like Ungaretti and Gozzano (q.v.), he helped emancipate the language of poetry from both Giosuè Carducci's (1835–1907) academic pastoralism and D'Annunzio's (q.v.) rhetoric. For a long time, the very originality and revolutionary character of his innovations prevented recognition of him as a major poet.

FURTHER WORKS: *Coi miei occhi* (1912); *Poesie* (1919); *Figure e canti* (1920); *La serena disperazione* (1920); *Cose leggere e vaganti* (1920); *L'amorosa spina* (1921); *Il Canzoniere 1900–1921* (1921); *Preludio e canzonette* (1923); *Figure e canti* (1928); *Ammonizioni ed al tre poesie* (1933); *Il Canzoniere 1900–1945* (1945); *Storia e cronistoria del 'Canzoniere'* (1948); *Scorciatoie e raccontini* (1956); *Epigrafe: Ultime prose* (1959); *Il piccolo Berto* (1961); *Prose* (1964)

BIBLIOGRAPHY: Bacchelli, R., "Su un libro di versi d'un Giovane Triestino," *Voce,* Dec. 1912; Ferrata, G., *La fiera letteraria,* 29 July 1928; Montale, E., Special S. issue, *Solaria,* III (1928), v; Debenedetti, G., *Saggi critici* (1929); Gargiulo, A., *Letteratura italiana del Novecento* (1940); Borlenghi, A., *Poesia,* VII (1947); De Robertis, G., *Scrittori italiani del Novecento* (1947); Flora, F., *Saggi di poetica moderna* (1949); Luzi, M., *Letteratura e arte contemporanea,* No. 10 (1951); Pasolini, P. P., *Passione e ideologia* (1960); Solmi, S., *Scrittori negli anni* (1963); Bergin, T. G., "S. and His Canzoniere," *BA,* XLII (1968), 503–8; Singh, G., "The Poetry of U. S.," *Italian Studies,* XXIII (1968)

G. SINGH

SABBE, Maurits

Belgian novelist and critic (writing in Flemish), b. 9 Feb. 1873, Bruges; d. 12 Feb. 1938, Antwerp

S.'s father, Julius, a well-known advocate of Flanders's liberation from French domination and clerical fanaticism, had a great influence on his son's ideas and philosophy. Young S. studied Dutch, Flemish, and German literatures at the University of Ghent from 1891 to 1896. In 1896 he received his Ph.D., writing a dissertation on the Dutch mystic poet and etcher Jan Luyken (1649–1712).

From 1898 to 1919 S. taught in Belgian colleges. In 1919 he was appointed a curator of the printers' museum in Antwerp, a position he held until his death. During those years S. was a professor at the Antwerp drama school, where he modernized the methods of acting. This function inspired him to write several plays, the best known of which is *Caritate* (1913). Its sentimental mysticism is reminiscent of Claudel (q.v.). In 1923 S. became a professor at the University of Brussels.

Like his father, S. belonged to the progressive fighters for Flemish rights. Against particularism, he was among those who believed in the desirability of a close cooperation with northern Belgium. Nevertheless, this concern is expressed in only a few of his works.

S., who was independent of the literary movements of his time, mixed elements of romanticism and of realism in his work. He was the first Flemish author to use the everyday dialect of the people in his novels.

S.'s best-known novel is *Een Mei van vroomheid* (1900). Against the background of medieval Bruges, S. pictures the timid love of the young organist Free for his pious neighbor, Bethjie, whose only wish is to become a nun. S.'s kind humor and his love for folk traditions appears most clearly in *De filosoof van 't Sashuis* (1907). *De nood der Bariseeles* (1912), S.'s best novel, glorifies the eternal feminine. Here he pictures with sharp psychological awareness the characters of two brothers, one selfish and strong, the other dreamy and weak, who are both lonely until a young girl, hardly more than a child, opens their eyes to the beauty and goodness in life. *Het Kwartet der Jacobijnen* (1920) is the only novel in which S. expresses his social ideas, advocating better living conditions for workmen and urging the people to develop their own Flemish culture.

S.'s books were in his time popular and well-received. He has excelled in describing past life in the old city of Bruges with great love and artistry. It may be that his claim to lasting value lies in his expression of his insights into cultural history.

FURTHER WORKS: *Historische plekjes in*

Vlaanderen (1891); *Aan 't Minnewater* (1898); *Pinksternacht* (1902); *Het proza in de Vlaamsche letterkunde* (1905); *Het leven en de werken van Michiel de Swaen* (1905); *Fanny's sonnet* (1910); *Mozaiek* (1912); *Bietje* (1913); *Vlaanderen door de eeuwen heen* (1913); *De tooneelles* (1914); *Het kleintje* (1915); *In 't gedrang* (1915); *Vrouwenhart* (1917); *Dierkennis en diersage by Vondel* (1917); *'t Pastoorken van Schaerdijcke* (1919); *Kiliaen* (1920); *Wat oud-Vlaanderen zong* (1920); *Vondel's Herbarium* (1920); *Christoffel Plantin* (1921); *Uit het Plantijnsche huis* (1923); *Vlaamsche menschen* (1923); *Handschriften en vroegdrukken* (1923); *Redevoeringen en studies* (1924); *Uit het Plantijnsche Huis* (1924); *Het Museum Plantin* (1926); *Antwerpsche Drukkerije* (1926); *The Moretus and Their Work* (1926); *La Vie des livres à Anvers aux XVIᵉ et XVIIᵉ et XVIIIᵉ siècles* (1926); *Rubens en zijn leven* (1927); *De Moretussen en hun kring* (1928); *Letterkundige verscheidenheden* (1928); *Pluk den dag* (1928); *Peter Heyns en de Nimphen uit de Lauerboom* (1929); *Brabant in het verweer* (1933); *De Plantijnsche werkstede* (1935); *Peilingen* (1935); *De meesters van den gulden Passer* (1937); *l'Œuvre de Christophe Plantin et de ses successeurs* (1938); *Vondel en Zuid-Nederland* (1939); *Uit den Taalstrijd in Zuid-Nederland tusschen 1815–1830* (1939)

BIBLIOGRAPHY: Monteyne, L., *De "S.'s"* (n.d.); Roemans, R., *M. S.* (n.d.); Stuiveling, G., *Steekproeven* (1950), pp. 141–60; Lissens, R. F., *De Vlaamse letterkunde van 1780 tot heden* (1967), pp. 133–34

JUDICA I. H. MENDELS

SÁ-CARNEIRO, Mario de

Portuguese poet and short-story writer, b. 19 May 1890, Lisbon; d. 24 April 1916, Paris

As an associate editor of the journal *Orpheu*, S. was particularly close to Pessoa (q.v.). Most of S.'s poetry was written when he lived in Paris.

In the volume of novellas *Princípio* (1912) and the artistically more valuable novella *A Confissão de Lúcio* (1914) he revealed himself to be obsessed by thoughts of madness and suicide (which he committed at the age of twenty-six), and by the fantasies of an uninhibited sexuality. These works show that S. was influenced by Wilde (q.v.) and that Wilde's

aestheticism and amorality were even intensified in S.

The artistic charm of the volumes of poetry *Dispersão* (1914) and *Indícios de Oiro* (1937) derives from their synesthesia and bold imagery.

Neither their extreme subjectivism nor their obscurity of meaning detracted from the impact of S.'s symbolistic (*see* symbolism) poetry and fiction. This influence is most obvious among the *Presença* group, which declared its allegiance to him as a founder of modern Portuguese literature.

FURTHER WORKS: *Amizade* (with T. Cabreira, Jr.; 1912); *Céu em fogo* (1915); *Poesias completas* (1946); *Cartas a F. Pessoa* (2 vols., 1958 ff.)

BIBLIOGRAPHY: Woll, D., *Wirklichkeit und Idealität in der Lyrik M. de S.* (1958); Galhoz, M., *M. de S.* (1963); Post, H., "M. de S.: Premier poète surréaliste portugais," *Neophilologus*, XLIX (1965), 301–306; Lopes, M. "Pessoa e S.," *Colóquio*, XLVIII (1968), 56–58

ALBIN EDUARD BEAU

SACHS, Nelly

German poet, b. 10 Dec. 1891, Berlin; d. 18 May 1970, Stockholm

Born into an assimilated Jewish family, Nelly S. grew up in upper-middle-class comfort and security. She studied music and briefly considered becoming a dancer. At about seventeen she began writing conventional poetry that was resolutely in opposition to the expressionist modes (*see* expressionism) popular in Berlin at that time. In later years, she declined to include these early poems in her collected work.

When the Nazis came to power in 1933, Nelly S.'s comfortable and cultured world began to disintegrate. For the next seven years she lived in fear and seclusion, immersing herself in a study of German and Hebrew mysticism. As a child, Nelly S. had been so moved by reading *Gösta Berling* that she entered into a correspondence with its author, Selma Lagerlöf (q.v.), from which a friendship developed. In 1940 Selma Lagerlöf prevailed upon Prince Eugene of Sweden to intercede on Nelly S.'s behalf, and the poet and her mother fled from war-torn Germany to resettle in Stockholm. She soon began to earn a limited income by translating Swedish poetry into German.

From the precarious safety of Stockholm,

Nelly S. watched in anguish as the Nazi war machine inexorably rolled over Europe. The intensity of this experience enabled her to find her own personal voice as a poet. Now fifty, she began writing as a means of "mute outcry" against terror and evil, as the only way left to free herself of anguish. An exile whose only possession was the language of the land that had rejected her, she wrote with no thought or hope of publishing.

After the war, however, a small volume of her poems, *In den Wohnungen des Todes* (1946), appeared in East Berlin. It was followed in 1949 by the publication of *Sternverdunkelung* in Amsterdam.

During the war years, Nelly S. had also written a series of plays that she described as "scenic poetry" (*szenische Dichtungen*). These have the simplicity and directness of medieval miracle plays. *Abraham in Salz*—written in 1942 but not published until 1962—is an attempt at total theater. In it Nelly S. employed pantomime, dance, music, dialogue, and a chorus to express in dramatic form man's longing for a God.

It was *Eli: Ein Mysterienspiel vom Leiden Israels* (1951; Eli, 1962) that was instrumental in bringing Nelly S.'s work to the attention of a wider public. Set in a Polish village that conveys the atmosphere of a Chagall painting, this "scenic poem" recounts the death of an eighty-year-old shepherd at the hands of a Nazi soldier. The play was originally printed by Nelly S.'s Swedish friends in a private edition of 200 copies, some of which found their way to West Germany, where it was produced over the radio. Its success was such that it was eventually given a stage production (1962) and used by the Swedish composer Moses Pergament as the libretto for an opera.

The publication in West Germany of *Flucht und Verwandlung* (1959) firmly established Nelly S.'s reputation as a poet, and she received several prestigious German literary prizes. Nevertheless, she was still relatively unknown internationally when in 1966 she and Agnon (q.v.) were made the joint recipients of the Nobel Prize for Literature.

In establishing her own approach to poetry, Nelly S. drew upon the German mystic Jakob Böhme (1575–1624), Martin Luther's (1483–1546) translation of the Bible, the following language of Hölderlin (1770–1843), Novalis (1772–1801), and Rilke (q.v.), and the mystic traditions of the cabala and Chassidic literature. Echoes of Old Testament prophetic language

pervade the hard masculinity of the modern, metaphorical language of her verse, which Spender (q.v.) described as "apocalyptic hymns rather than 'modern poetry.'"

In this hymnal language, she was able to speak of the unbearable. Persecution, concentration camps, flight, and homelessness are her themes. Ecstatic yet precise, her poetry transcends the fate of European Jews and identifies their suffering, aspirations, and rejection with the destiny of all mankind. Acknowledging the role of evil in the world, she nevertheless speaks not of God's wrath or punishment, but about man's longing for peace. Past, present, and future merge in her work, which focuses on the continuing drama of death and redemption.

In Nelly S.'s later work allusions to historical events gradually receded; her writing became more abstract, but there was no change in her underlying attitude toward the mysteries of life and death. On being informed that she had won the Nobel Prize for Literature she said: "Agnon represents the State of Israel. I represent the tragedy of the Jewish people."

FURTHER WORKS: *Legenden und Erzählungen* (1921); *Und niemand weiß weiter* (1957); *Der magische Tänzer* (1959); *Fahrt ins Staublose: Die Gedichte der N. S.* (1961); *Nachtwache* (1962); *Zeichen im Sand: Szenische Dichtungen* (1963); *Glühende Rätsel* (1964); *Späte Gedichte* (1966); *Die Suchende* (1966). **Selected English translations:** *O the Chimneys* (1967); *The Seeker, and Other Poems* (1970)

BIBLIOGRAPHY: Berendsohn, W., et al., eds., *N. S. zu Ehren* (1966); Schwebell, G. C., "N. S.," *SatR*, 10 Dec. 1966; Bianquis, G., "L'an dernier, N. S. recevait le prix Nobel," *Revue de Paris*, LXXIV (1967), 104–08; Spender, S., "Catastrophe and Redemption," *New York Times Book Review*, 8 Oct. 1967; Kunisch, H., *Die deutsche Gegenwartsdichtung* (1968)

GERTRUDE C. SCHWEBELL

SACKVILLE-WEST, Victoria Mary

English poet and novelist, b. 9 March 1892, Knole; d. 2 June 1962, Sissinghurst

Victoria S. was born in Knole castle, the seat of the Sackville family from the time that Queen Elizabeth I gave Knole to her cousin, Lord Treasurer Thomas Sackville, She was

G. W. RUSSELL (pseud.: A.E.)

NELLY SACHS

educated at home, and Knole and its traditions exerted a major influence on her life. In 1913 she married diplomat Harold Nicolson (1886–1968) and they traveled extensively during his years in the Foreign Office. In London she was a member of the Bloomsbury group, an informal group of literary and artistic friends including Virginia Woolf, Lytton Strachey, E. M. Forster (qq.v.), and others. She was a close friend of Virginia Woolf and is said to have been the model for the character of Orlando in Virginia Woolf's novel of that name.

Victoria S. first gained literary recognition for her long poem *The Land* (1926), which won the Hawthorndon Prize and was praised as one of the most beautiful bucolics in English literature. She deeply loved England's rural civilization, and in *The Land* celebrates the "mild, continuous epic of the soil," and those yeomen, shepherds, and simple craftsmen who live in organic relation to it. Her poetry is traditional in form, reminiscent of the work of the English nature poets of the age of romanticism. *Solitude* (1938) is a long poem of philosophical and personal musings written in measured, melodious verse. Her long poem *The Garden* (1946) won the Heinemann Prize.

Victoria S. drew on her own background for the setting of *The Edwardians* (1930), the story of a young aristocrat who, while enjoying the privileges of his position, is nonetheless tempted to rebel and be free of the tradition he finds confining. Written in lucid and vigorous prose, *The Edwardians* is remarkable for its vivid depiction of a class and an era. Though meticulously delineating the hypocrisy and foolishness of her aristocratic characters, Victoria S. seems still vulnerable to their charm, and her satire, though brilliant, is tender. *All Passion Spent* (1931) resembles *The Edwardians* in its description of the conflict between the heroine's secret desire to be an artist and the 19th-c. tradition that decreed her role as a self-effacing wife. In both these novels, however, the thematic conflict between tradition and modernity is tangential, and the significance of the work consists in its vivid re-creation of setting and characters.

A prolific writer, Victoria S. is the author of fifteen novels, as well as biographies, travel books, and a number of books on gardening. She has written about her own family and its background in *Knole and the Sackvilles* (1922), a history of the lords of Knole since the 16th c., and *Pepita* (1937), a biography of her colorful grandmother, a Spanish dancer.

Though Victoria S.'s novels are more widely known, her poetry may prove to be more enduring; there is a depth of feeling and perception in the best of her poems, a quality at once stately and moving, that is rare in her fiction. Nevertheless, her prose is of consistently high quality, supple, clear, and craftsmanlike. Viewed as one of Britain's promising young writers in the 1920's, she is now regarded for her personality and influence as much as for her writing.

FURTHER WORKS: *Poems of East and West* (1917); *Heritage* (1918); *The Dragon in Shallow Waters* (1920); *Orchard and Vineyard* (1921); *The Heir and Other Stories* (1922); *Challenge* (1923); *Grey Wethers* (1923); *Seducers in Ecuador* (1924); *Passenger to Teheran* (1926); *Aphra Behn* (1928); *Twelve Days* (1928); *Andrew Marvell* (1929); *King's Daughter* (1930); *Sissinghurst* (1931); *Family History* (1932); *Thirty Clocks Strike the Hour, and Other Stories* (1932); *Collected Poems* (1933); *The Dark Island* (1934); *St. Joan of Arc* (1936); *Some Flowers* (1937); *Country Notes* (1939); *Country Notes in Wartime* (1940); *English Country Houses* (1941); *Selected Poems* (1941); *Grand Canyon* (1942); *The Eagle and the Dove* (1944); *The Women's Land Army* (1944); *The Devil at Westease* (1947); *Nursery Rhymes* (1947); *In Your Garden* (1951); *The Easter Party* (1953); *In Your Garden Again* (1953); *More for Your Garden* (1955); *A Joy of Gardening* (1958); *Even More for Your Garden* (1959); *Daughter of France* (1959); *Faces: Profiles of Dogs* (1961); *No Signposts in the Sea* (1961)

BIBLIOGRAPHY: Overton, G., "The Lady of a Tradition: V. S.," *Bookman*, LVII (June 1923), 411–17; On *Collected Poems*—Benet, W. R., *SatR*, 24 March 1934, p. 580; Warren, R. P., "Set in a Silver Sea," *Poetry*, Sept 1935, pp. 346–49; Irwin, W. R., "Permanence and Change in *The Edwardians* and *Tale Told by an Idiot*," *MFS*, May 1956, pp. 63–67; On *No Signposts in the Sea*—Morris, A., *New York Times Book Review*, 16 April 1961, p. 4

DOROTHY TUCK MCFARLAND

SADOVEANU, Mihail

Romanian novelist and short-story writer, b. 5 Nov. 1880, Pașcani, Moldavia

S., the son of a lawyer, was originally a magazine editor and theater director, then for a time a politician.

He is one of the most important storytellers in Romanian literature. Though his first work, *Povestiri* (1904), a volume of short stories, deals with primitive characters in the grip of alcohol, crime, and superstition, he never lapsed into the exaggerations of naturalism (q.v.). Instead, by means of poetic realism, he allowed his characters to emerge. The world he presents in these short stories centers around the mill and the tavern, which provide the backdrop for his peasant characters. His major short-story collection is *Crâşma lui Moş-Precu* (1905), in which he writes movingly of elemental people and the stunted passions and infinite sadness of their existence, actions, and dreams.

In novels and short stories written between 1906 and 1908, S. draws a similar portrait of slightly more sophisticated small-town society, with its bourgeois dramas, marital scandals, and narrow-minded attitudes.

Venea o moară pe Siret (1925) tells of the decline of a boyar family, although the strength of this novel lies not in its characterization but in the description of nature.

S.'s characters, especially those in *Hanul Ancuţei* (1928), are happy in their deep attachment to their native soil.

Baltagul (1930; Eng., The Mud-Hut Dwellers, 1964; Am., The Hatchet, 1965), an epic of peasant mentality, is the story of a woman's avenging of her husband, in which life and death are closely intertwined. The plot is enacted against nature that becomes destiny.

In the 1930's S. wrote chiefly grandiose historical novels and novels about legendary subjects.

When (after Romania had become part of the communist bloc in 1945) socialist realism was required by the party leaders, S. disavowed his past and recast his work, discarding tradition, awareness of history, and God. His novel *Mitrea Cocor* (1949) is characteristic of this period.

FURTHER WORKS: *Dureri înăbuşite* (1904); *Soimii* (1904); *Povestiri din răsboi* (1905); *Amintirile căprarului Gheorghiţă* (1906); *Floare Ofilită* (1906); *Mormântul unui copil* (1906); *La noi în Viişoara* (1907); *Vremuri de bejenie* (1907); *O istorie de demult* (1908); *Insemnările lui Neculaie Manea* (1908); *Duduia Margareta* (1908); *Oameni şi locuri* (1908); *Apa morţilor* (1911); *Bordeienii* (1912); *Neamul Şoimăreştilor* (1915); *Cocostârcul albastru*

(1921); *Dumbrava minunată* (1922); *Ţara de dincolo de negură* (1926); *Împărăţia apelor* (1928); *Demonul tinereţii* (1928); *Zodia Cancerului* (1929); *Măria Sa, puiul pădurii* (1931); *Nunta Domniţei Ruxanda* (1932); *Uvar* (1932); *Creanga de aur* (1933); *Nopţile de Sânziene* (1934); *Viaţa lui Ştefan cel Mare* (1934); *Fraţii Jderi* (3 vols., 1935); *Cazul Eugeniţei Costea* (1936); *Ochiu de urs* (1939); *Divanul persian* (1940); *Vechime* (1940); *Ostrovul lupilor* (1941); *Povestile lui Bradu-Strâmb* (1943); *Anii de ucenicie* (1944); *Mitrea Cocor* (1951); *Nicoară Potcoavă* (1952); *Opere* (18 vols., 1954–59). **Selected English translations:** *Tales of War* (1962); *Evening Tales* (1969)

BIBLIOGRAPHY: Special S. issue, *Gazeta Literária*, XIII (28 Oct. 1965); Philippide, A., "The Spirit and Tradition of Modern Romanian Literature," *Romanian Review*, XXI (1967), ii, 5–10; Oprişan, I., "I. M. S.—Schiţa Biografică," *Revista de Istorie şi Teorie Literară*, XVI (1967), 235–59

VIRGIL IERUNCA

SAGARRA I DE CASTELLARNAU, Josep Maria de

Catalan poet, dramatist, essayist, and novelist, b. 5 May 1894, Barcelona; d. there, 27 Sept. 1961

S. published his first poems in Catalan when he was twelve. Although he got a law degree in 1914, an intellectually enlightening trip to Italy and his friendship with Joan Maragall i Gorina (1860–1911), Joan Alcover i Maspons (q.v.), Miguel Costa i Llobera (1854–1922), and Ignasi Iglesias (1871–1928) led to his pursuing a literary vocation.

Prior to the Spanish Civil War (1936–39) S. wrote articles for many journals, especially for *La Publicitat* and *Las Noticias*. In 1936, after becoming editor of the weekly *Mirador* of Barcelona, he emigrated to France when the Spanish Civil War broke out. His trip to Polynesia in 1937 inspired his *Entre l'equador i els tròpics*, which is the first Catalan poetic reaction to the South Sea Islands. S. returned to Barcelona in 1940 and continued writing until his death. His memoirs were published in 1955.

The theme of *El mal caçador* (1916), a candid, descriptive poem, is the glorification of the Montseny mountains. Spontaneous realism, inspired rural imagery, and an effective direct style are its prominent qualities. This poem reveals the true essence of S., expressing both his sensitiveness toward the Catalan landscape and his sense of universal values.

El Compte Arnau (1928), a narrative poem, is a free elaboration of the most popular of the Catalan legends, the story of Count Arnau, a passionate, cruel libertine. S.'s originality lies in making the legendary Arnau come alive and in focusing on the story's human elements rather than on the theological or metaphysical ones.

Marçal Prior (1926) is a symbolistic, violent, and fanciful play. Until the protagonist's redemption and return to his wife, S. presents a Goethean concept of life and death and a Faustian notion of the universe and man. Although uneven, this drama reveals, especially in its expert blending of the real and the fantastic, S.'s attainment of dramatic maturity.

La filla del Carmesí (1929) is a subtle, symbolical, psychological study of Carmesina and her neglectful husband. The culmination of the play approaches the "pure soul" concept developed earlier by Angel Guimerà (1849–1924). The suspense is skillfully planned and the denouement is in keeping with S.'s technique of the logical happy ending.

L'hostal de la Glòria (1931), a prize-winning drama, is one of S.'s most balanced plays. The heroine, who is painstakingly characterized, incarnates the virtues of Catalan women in her industry, her capacity to endure suffering silently, and her ability to forgive. Suspense and gaiety, a picturesque atmosphere, facility of expression, and colorful dialogue make this play a landmark in Catalan neoromantic theater.

A successful translator and adapter, S. cast into Catalan all of Shakespeare and the *Divine Comedy* of Dante, poems by Alfred Lord Tennyson (1809–1892), Giacomo Leopardi (1798–1837), and Michelangelo, and plays by Molière (1622–73), Carlo Goldoni (1707–1793), Nicolai Gogol (1809–1852), Pirandello, and Pagnol (qq.v.).

S.'s longest poems are essentially theatrical in plot and character. His best poetry, written in his youth, is sensuous and musical and shows the influence of Leopardi and Maragall i Gorina. S. enriched Catalan poetry by drawing upon popular sources and by presenting the qualities and savour of the Catalan people. S.'s dramas, most of which are in verse, reveal a modernist base and lean toward sentimentality. His four novels—*Paulina Buxareu* (1919),

All i salobre (1929), *Café, copa i puro* (1930), *Vida privada* (1932)—which deal chiefly with satirized social miseries, fall within the boundaries of a naturalist realism.

S. was one of the most accomplished writers of his generation, winning all the prewar literary prizes of Catalonia. A prolific writer of prose and verse, he was a master of dialogue and description and a subtle psychologist.

FURTHER WORKS: *Primer llibre de poemes* (1914); *Rondalla d'esparvers* (1918); *Dijous Sant* (1918); *Joan Enric* (1918); *Poemes i cançons* (1920); *L'estudiant i la pubilla* (1920); *El jardinet de l'amor* (1921); *Cançons de taverna i d'oblit* (1922); *Els ocells amics* (1922); *El matrimoni secret* (1922); *El foc de les ginesteres* (1923); *Les veus de la terra* (1923); *Cançó d'una nit d'estiu* (1923); *Cançons de rem i de vela* (1924); *La careta* (1924); *La fidelitat* (1924); *La follia del desig* (1925); *Cançons de carrer* (1925); *Cançó de totes les hores* (1925); *La màscara* (1925); *L'assassinat de la senyora Abril* (1927); *La Llúcia i la Ramoneta* (1928); *Les llàgrimes d'Angelina* (1928); *Judit* (1929); *Poema de Nadal* (1930); *El cas del senyor Palau* (1930); *La corona d'espines* (1930); *La perla negra* (1930); *La priora del Roser* (1931); *L'alegria de Cervera* (1932); *Desitjada* (1932); *El cafè de la Marina* (1933); *L'estrella dels miracles* (1933); *La rosa de cristall* (1933); *La plaça de Sant Joan* (1934); *La Rambla de les floristes* (1935); *Reina* (1935); *Roser florit* (1936); *La cançó de la filla del marxant* (1936); *Àncores i estrelles* (1936); *Ruta blava* (1937); *Poema de Montserrat* (1945); *El prestigi dels morts* (1946); *La fortuna de Silvia* (1947); *Ocells i llops* (1948); *La Galatea* (1948); *Obres completes: Teatre* (1948 ff.); *L'hereu i la forastera* (1949); *Els comediants* (1950); *L'amor viu a dispesa* (1952); *L'alcova vermella* (1952); *La ferida lluminosa* (1954); *El pobre d'esperit i els altres* (1954); *La paraula de foc* (1955); *Sopar a casa* (1959); *Obres completes: Poesia* (1962)

BIBLIOGRAPHY: Carbonell, J., "L'obra dramàtica de J. M. de S.," in *Obres completes: teatre*, Vol. IV (1948); Triadú, J., Introduction to Sagarra, in *Anthology of Catalan Lyric Poetry*, (ed. J. Gili (1953); Espinàs, J. M., "J. M. de S. como valor total," *Ínsula*, No. 95 (1953); Ruiz i Calonja, J., *Història de la literatura catalana* (1954); Saltor, O., "El poeta J. M. de S.," in *Obres completes: poesia* (1962); Espinàs, J. M., *J. M. de S.* (1962)

ALBERT M. FORCADAS

SAINT-EXUPÉRY, Antoine de

French novelist, short-story writer, and journalist, b. 29 June 1900, Lyon; d. 31 July 1944, near Corsica

S. came from an old Limousin family; his mother belonged to the landed aristocracy of Provence. His father having died in 1904, S. was brought up by his mother, together with his four brothers and sisters, and spent a happy childhood in country houses in southern France. Between 1909 and 1917 he attended Roman Catholic schools in Le Mans, Villefranche-sur-Saône, and Fribourg.

In 1921 a stint in the military took S. first to North Africa, then to an air force unit at Le Bourget. Although he was in the business world from 1924 to 1925, his passion for flying never left him. After flying a French-African mail route, he became the manager (1927–28) of the Cap Juby airfield in the African desert. He returned to France in 1928 and the following year published his novel *Courrier sud* (1929; Southern Mail, 1933). In 1929 he became director of the Argentina airmail service. There in Buenos Aires he rejoined his friend Henri Guillaumet as well as other fliers he had previously worked with. During this period he wrote his second novel, *Vol de nuit* (1931; Night Flight, 1932).

Restless, troubled years followed, during which S. tried his hand at various occupations. In 1932 he was a test pilot; in 1934, advertising director of Air France. He went to Moscow in 1935 as correspondent for *Paris Soir;* in 1937, he covered the Spanish Civil War. While convalescing after a crash, he worked a series of articles into the book *Terre des hommes* (1939; Wind, Sand and Stars, 1939), which won the Grand Prix du Roman de l'Académie Française.

When World War II broke out in 1939, S. became an air force officer. In November 1940, after the fall of France, he came to the United States, where he published *Pilote de guerre* (1942; Flight to Arras, 1942), the fairy tale *Le Petit Prince* (1943; The Little Prince, 1943), and *Lettre à un otage* (1944; first published in the United States as Letter to a Hostage, 1943). During that period of exile he also worked on his major, posthumously published work, *Citadelle* (1948; Wisdom of the Sands, 1950).

After the Allied landing in North Africa S. succeeded, in April 1943, in rejoining his squadron in what was then the Free French army. A year later he failed to return from a recon-

naissance flight over the western Mediterranean.

For S., writing's *raison d'être* was to provide a "distillation" of something actively experienced. His work is therefore to a great extent autobiographical. *Courrier sud,* a novelistic account of his early years as a pilot is interwoven with a love story that incorporates the painful experiences he suffered in a love relationship. *Vol de nuit* deals with adventures in Argentina in pioneering and testing night-flying techniques.

By *Terre des hommes* the novel form has been discarded once and for all. This book contains reflections and descriptions dealing with flying, with S.'s attitudes toward technology and nature, with personal exploits and those of his fellow pilots, and with human relationships. The point of departure is always concrete experience. For example, *Pilote de guerre* is an account of a hopeless reconnaissance flight in May 1940, after France had already been defeated. Interspersed through the book are youthful memories culminating in critical observations on contemporary culture.

Le Petit Prince expresses the unhappiness of S.'s exile in the U.S.A. It gently caricatures the outward forms of civilization but also expresses personal experiences in symbols. *Lettre à un otage* is addressed to S.'s friend Léon Werth, a Jew then living under the German occupation. Finally, *Citadelle*—for all its Oriental background and lofty, sometimes biblical language—contains in the images, prayers, and meditations uttered by its legendary desert ruler a critique of present times and references to a new order.

Together with the *Carnets* (1953), notebooks of spontaneously jotted down reflections, and a series of articles (particularly his reports from Russia and Spain), S.'s correspondence, especially *Lettre au général X* (1948), is of special value in understanding the man and his work.

From the outset S. was successful in graphically communicating both direct, sensuous impressions and his intellectual searchings. Throughout his work one can trace that hard-to-achieve synthesis of active living and contemplation by which S. managed to make fruitful the tensions that threaten to sunder contemporary man, imperiled as he is by the "daemonism of technology." S.'s development is to be found in the gradual maturing of his meditativeness. He was by nature a moralist filled with genuine love of mankind, but for a long time he was content with quite hazy

ANTOINE DE SAINT-EXUPÉRY

SAINT-JOHN PERSE

formulations. Only with *Pilote de guerre*—for the *Carnets* are still agnostic—does this mysticism give way to a more precise humanism, now unmistakably oriented toward God. Yet God remains the Unapproachable, offering no sign by which He may be recognized.

S. belonged to no literary school. His relationship with Gide (q.v.), who smoothed the way for him in his early days, was somewhat superficial. His acquaintanceship with Drieu La Rochelle, Breton (qq.v.), and others had equally little influence on his work. Parallels, however, do exist. He has less affinity with Montherlant (q.v.), with whom he shared, at most, certain aristocratic traits, than with Malraux (q.v.), who arrived at his contemplative humanism by closely related paths. In a certain sense, S., even more strikingly than Malraux, continues the line of great French moralists. But he was no skeptic; he was closer to Pascal than to Montaigne. In his last works it becomes clear that in his own way he continues the intellectual revolution against Cartesian thinking, rationalism, and determinism that started to ferment in France at the turn of the century. Thus Bergson (q.v.) and Maurice Blondel (1861–1949), who combined pragmatic thinking with a doctrinaire Roman Catholic philosophy, seem to have provided the impetus for meditations in *Citadelle*.

Stylistically, however, S. is entirely individual. The lyrical tone and the characteristic rhythm that mark his prose cannot be attributed to any literary models.

FURTHER WORKS: *L'Aviateur* (1926); *Œuvres complètes* (1950); *Lettres de jeunesse, 1923–31* (1953); *Œuvres* (1953); *Lettres à sa mère* (1955); *Un sens à la vie* (1956; A Sense of Life, 1966); *Lettres aux américains* (1960). **Selected English translation:** *Airman's Odyssey* (1943; includes Wind, Sand and Stars, Night Flight, Flight to Arras)

BIBLIOGRAPHY: Anet, D., *S.* (1946); Werth, L., *La vie de S.* (1948); Gide, A., *A. de S.* (1951); Rumbold, R., and Stewart, M., *The Winged Life* (1953); Estang, L., ed., *S. par lui-même* (1956); Galantière, L., *S.* (1960); Albérès, R.-M., et al., *S.* (1963); Cordo, A., "God, Man and the Wind: S., Symbolist," *DA*, XXVI (1965), 1643; Ball, B., "S. and 'le culte du passé,' " *Brigham Young University Studies*, VIII (1968), 444–48

OSWALT VON NOSTITZ

SAINT-JOHN PERSE

(pseud. of *Alexis Saint-Léger Léger*), French poet and diplomat, b. 31 May 1887, Guadeloupe, French West Indies

Financial reverses forced S. P.'s long-established, aristocratic family to leave Guadeloupe in 1899 and resettle in France. His childhood impressions were deep, however, and S. P.'s poetry was to combine an awareness of his New World origins and the perspective of French culture.

Though S. P. matriculated in law at the University of Bordeaux, he also studied the classics, geology, and medicine. During his university years he met many of the men who were to dominate French culture during the first half of this century, particularly the group surrounding the *Nouvelle Revue Française*: Gide, Alain-Fournier, Rivière (qq.v.), etc. At this time he published his first book, *Éloges* (1911; Éloges, and Other Poems, 1944), a collection of brilliant prose lyrics recalling his childhood in the Caribbean tropics. It appeared under the name "Saintléger Léger."

In 1914 S. P. entered the French Foreign Service, and two years later he was sent to Asia, where he remained for five years. During the 1920's S. P. was the protégé of Foreign Minister Aristide Briand (1862–1932), and in 1932 he was appointed secretary general of the French Foreign Office. An outspoken enemy of German expansionism, S. P. was dismissed in 1940 by France's Vichy government. He went to Washington, D.C., where he still maintains his permanent residence.

During his Asian tour of duty S. P. wrote the poem that established him as one of the great 20th-c. poets: *Anabase* (1924; Anabasis, 1930). Feeling that he could not be publicly effective as both a diplomat and a poet, he initially forbade publication of the work, but was eventually prevailed upon by Gide and others to publish *Anabase* under his henceforth famous pseudonym. The real identity of S. P. was a well-kept secret from 1924 to 1940.

Anabase is a powerful, sweeping, and difficult epic-style poem. S. P. has described it as a poem of personal and public solitude in the midst of action. Characterized by brilliant imagery and a sense of the vast spaces of inner Asia, *Anabase* evokes man's conquering and questioning spirit as well as his aloneness. From its initial publication it has exerted wide influence. The English translation is by T. S. Eliot (q.v.).

After 1940 S. P. devoted himself entirely to poetry. *Exil* (1942; Exile, and Other Poems, 1949) expresses his somber yet tough response to the disasters shaking a war-torn civilization. It combines a clearly audible private voice with a grand epic vision.

In a tone of triumphant renewal, *Vents* (1946; Winds, 1953) begins the last and greatest phase of S. P.'s poetic career. Over a hundred pages long, *Vents* is a vast prophetic utterance of a specifically anti-*Wasteland* ethic. The winds of the title represent the forces of history and man's spirit; the poem itself ranges symbolically over the real and imagined frontiers of North America, and seeks out a message of courage, expectation, danger, action, and hope for Western civilization.

But S. P.'s masterpiece was yet to come: *Amers* (1957; Seamarks, 1958), the work that had most to do with his winning the Nobel Prize for Literature in 1960. Even larger in its physical and poetic dimensions than *Vents,* it has as its object nothing less than the exaltation of the drama of the human condition. Its master metaphor is a ceremonial march of mankind around the sea, that great symbol of the self-renewing dynamism of life. The climax of *Amers* is a long dialogue between Man and Woman that seeks the central mystery of existence in human love. It has been called the greatest love poem in the French language.

In the text of the poem, S. P. calls *Amers* his last and definitive work. He has, however, continued to write, though on a much more modest scale.

Perhaps no other poet in the West has written from such a major and significant experience of public responsibility as has S. P. Full of the fruits of this experience, his poetry offers a vast, inclusive, and grand view of man in an epic style and magnificent imagery entirely commensurate with its vision.

FURTHER WORKS: *Briand* (1943; Eng., 1942); *Quatre Poèmes* (1944); *Chronique* (1959; Chronicle, 1961); *Discours d'acceptation du Prix Nobel de littérature* (1960; On Poetry, 1961); *Œuvre poétique* (2 vols., 1960); *Oiseaux* (1962; Birds, 1966); *Dante* (1965; Two Addresses: "On Poetry" and "Dante," 1966)

BIBLIOGRAPHY: Poggioli, R., "The Poetry of S.-J. P.," *YFS,* No. 2 (1948), pp. 5–33; Tate, A., "Mysterious P.," *Cahiers de la Pléiade,* No. 10 (1950), pp. 144–50; Watts, H., "*Anabase:* The Endless Film," *UTQ,* XIX (1950), 224–34; Charpier, J., "S.-J. P. and the Fertile Woman," *YFS,* No. 11 (1953), pp. 101–5; Caillois, R., *Poétique de S.-J. P.* (1955); Guicharnaud, J. "Vowels of the Sea: *Amers,*" *YFS,* No. 21 (1958), pp. 72–82; Charpier, J., *S.-J. P.* (1962); Nelson, C., "S.-J. P. and T. S. Eliot," *WHR,* XVII (1962), 163–71; Paulhan, J., ed., *Honneur à S.-J. P.* (1965); Knodel, A., *S.-J. P., a Study of His Poetry* (1966)

CONNY NELSON

The poetry of P., with its presentness of time, its odor of eternity, its vast image of life like a landscape without trees, is a poetry written not out of action but against it or behind it.... I believe the poetry of P., which has been a powerful influence in the minds of many men who could not remember what it was that so deeply moved them but only that they were moved as a man might be moved by a fragrance he could not remember—that this poetry, like all true poetry, will take its place outside literature and all doctrine, in the desert sunlight where the stone survives.

Archibald MacLeish, Introduction to *Éloges* (1944), pp. 11, 14

In this magnificent poem ("Rains") which is at once a kind of litany, or litany of litanies, and an allegorical history of mankind, a history in terms of metaphor, the poet drives his tandem of methods with complete mastery. The *whole meaning,* the history of man in terms of rain, or the interpretation of him in terms of rain—rain as the fertilizer, rain as the purifier, even as the principle itself of life and change—gives a majestic centripetal design to the poem, and a tremendous sense of controlled richness, but it is also of such a nature...as to make the utmost possible use of incidental, but directed, improvisation.... It isn't *about,* it becomes and is, our sad rich dreadful glorious disastrous foul and beautiful history.

Conrad Aiken, in *New Republic* (16 April 1945), pp. 512–4

P. has taken his place beside the four or five major poets of modern France: Baudelaire, Mallarmé, Rimbaud, Valéry, Claudel. Like theirs, his work defies any facile nomenclature of romantic or classical.... The official attitude of the symbolists was aloofness. The official attitude of the surrealists was aggressiveness. S-J. P. represents a more traditional, more central attitude of the poet. The precise word is difficult to choose, because on the whole this attitude is seldom felt today, but it would be perhaps solemnity or sacredness. It would be a word powerful enough to contain and harmonize the contradictions of man's fate as it appears to us within the limits of time and space.

Wallace Fowlie, in *Poetry* (Sept. 1953), pp. 347, 350

Movement, progress, action. S-J. P.'s crowds and heroes, worthy of praise or blame, belong to the epic poems to the extent that they are never at rest. Each one devotes himself to an act of conquest by means of physically taking possession or through knowledge. These men do not represent static moods; they change, consume, and travel through the world, they come and go; if they stop, it is to praise their acts or to express their demands. They might be said to be a positive sign. They exercise powers.

Jacques Guicharnaud, in *YFS* (Spring-Summer 1958), p. 75

One of the first characteristics of his world is the complete absence of proper names. Landscapes are vividly described but no indication is given of where they are situated. As befits a modern world in which historical knowledge has made all past present, the events which occur in S-J. P.'s poems could be taking place in any historical epoch. Its inhabitants have neither names nor genealogies; they have functions.

There is suffering and death in this world, but not tragedy. What the poet celebrates, that is to say, is not the refusal of the noble individual to live at any price, but the inexhaustible power of life to renew itself and triumph over every disaster, natural or human. What he looks for and tries to express in every one of his poems is the sacredness of being.

W. H. Auden, in *The New York Times* (27 July 1958), p. 1

P.'s poetry should be read as an exercise in spiritual intrepidity. His poems offer a man no shelter from the night and bad weather; they are themselves an encampment under the open sky. No roots here: wings. His theme is singular and plural: time, the times. History minus any characters, because the only real character in history is a nameless and faceless being, half flesh and half dream: the man all we other men are and aren't.... P.'s theme is time, our very substance. The poetry of time, which buries and banishes us. Insofar as we are men, we are a metaphor of time. A migrant image.

Octavio Paz, in *Nation* (17 June 1961), pp. 522–3

SAINT-POL-ROUX

(pseud. of *Paul Pierre Roux*), French poet and dramatist, b. 15 Jan. 1861, Saint-Henry (near Marseilles); d. 18 Oct. 1940, Brest

S.'s early works show his indebtedness to symbolism (q.v.). In his poetry (*Lazare*, 1886; *Le Bouc émissaire*, 1889) and poetic dramas (*L'Âme noire du prieur blanc*, 1893; *Les Personnages de l' individu*, 1894! *La Dame à*

la faulx, 1899) he sought to evoke inner, ideal reality, the representation of which he called "ideo-realism." The poet's role in this is that of a godlike creator of a world. From 1898 until his death in Brittany, S. remained aloof from all organized literary activity, clinging throughout his life to this "symbolistic super-image."

S.'s significance in modern poetry was recognized by the surrealists, notably by Breton (q.v.), who, in a widely noticed article in *Les Nouvelles Littéraires* in 1925, acclaimed S. as a precursor of surrealism (q.v.). He is entitled to this position because at the end of the 19th c. he had anticipated the cryptic metaphor of the 20th c. in his exuberant imagery that violently links divergent, incompatible ideas. Because his torrential stream of images is always determined by traditional humanist value concepts, it, especially in *Les reposoirs de la procession* (1893), avoids any tendency toward the absurd.

In 1901, in *La Rose et les épines du chemin*, S. proclaimed the liberating—though for him not yet form-shattering—power of the image. Ten years later the image was to be hailed as the driving force of poetry by the imagist school of Pound (q.v.).

FURTHER WORKS: *Épilogue des saisons humaines* (1893); *Anciennetés* (1903); *De la Colombe au corbeau par le paon* (1904); *Les Féeries intérieures* (1907); *La Mort du berger* (1938); *La Supplique du Christ* (1939); *Bretagne est univers* (1941); *L'Ancienne à la coiffe innombrable* (1946)

BIBLIOGRAPHY: Briant, T., *S.* (1961); Steinmetz, J.-L., "*S.*, ou les dangers de l'écriture," *Annales de Bretagne*, LXXIII (1966), 463–82; Edwards, J., "Une mystification littéraire de *S.*," *Revue des Sciences Humaines*, CXXVIII (1967), 633–43

GEORGES SCHLOCKER

SALACROU, Armand

French dramatist, b. 9 Aug. 1899, Rouen

S., the son of a pharmacist, grew up in Le Havre and attended the *lycée* there. As a boy, he was rebellious against religious and political institutions, and after first studying medicine in Paris, he worked for the communist newspaper *L'Humanité*. S. was involved for a time with both the Communist Party and the surrealist movement (*see* surrealism).

In 1949 S. was elected to the Goncourt Academy.

S.'s first plays were not successful, but he was encouraged to continue writing for theater by the directors Lugné-Poe and Dullin. The most interesting of these early plays is *Le Pont de l'Europe* (1927), where S. raises the philosophical problem of choice: a man, by choosing one thing or belief, excludes all the rest, but if he does not choose, he denies the very conditions of existence and action.

Atlas-Hôtel, produced by Dullin in 1931 (pub. in 1937), was the first of a long series of successes. Two plays in particular were not only highly successful, but also revealed metaphysical considerations that set them apart from ordinary comedies.

The first of these, *L'Inconnue d'Arras,* was directed by Lugné-Poe in 1935 (pub. in 1936). Ulysse, the principal character, shoots himself at the beginning of the play because of his wife's infidelity. Using the cinematic technique of the flashback, S. allows Ulysse, between his pistol shot and his death, to relive his life. At the core of these scenes is a barely remembered encounter with an unknown woman for whom he felt a deep sense of pity. The memory stirs an awareness of life's possibilities. Ulysse regrets his suicide decision—but the bullet is already on its way.

The second important play is *La Terre est ronde* (1938; The World Is Round, 1967), produced by Dullin at l'Atelier. The hero is the Florentine reformer Savonarola. With Nazi Germany casting its shadow over Europe, the first audiences interpreted the play as a commentary on fascism and tyranny. But the real meaning is undoubtedly deeper, involving the universal struggle between the flesh and the spirit, between the relative and the absolute. It develops one of S.'s principal preoccupations: the impotence of God to overcome the evil which pervades the history of mankind.

S.'s best play since World War II, *Les Nuits de la colère,* was produced by Barrault in 1946 (pub. in 1947). It deals with the moral dilemma posed by armed French resistance to the German occupation and was often compared with Sartre's *Morts sans sépulture.*

S. is exclusively a man of the theater, and his plays are extremely well constructed. His earlier plays were so deeply pessimistic that they are now considered by many to foreshadow the philosophical approach of Sartre and Camus (qq.v.). S.'s entire work is a meditation on human fate, especially the problem of evil and the suffering of innocent people. He is unable to integrate belief in the existence of God and the fact of a universe dominated by injustice.

FURTHER WORKS: *Le Casseur d'assiettes* (1922); *Tour à terre* (1925); *Patchouli* (1930); *Les Frénétiques* (1934); *Une Femme libre* (1934); *Un Homme comme les autres* (1936); *Histoire de rire* (1939; When the Music Stops, 1967); *La Marguerite* (1944; Marguerite, 1967); *Les Fiancés du Havre* (1945); *Les Soldats et la sorcière* (1945); *L'Archipel Lenoir* (1947); *Poof* (1950); *Pourquoi pas moi?* (1950); *Dieu le savait!* (1950); *Sens interdit* (1953); *Les Invités du Bon Dieu* (1953); *Le Miroir* (1956); *Une Femme trop honnête* (1956); *Les Idées de la nuit* (1960); *Boulevard Durand* (1961); *Comme les chardons* (1964); *Impromptu délibéré* (1966); *La Rue noire* (1967)

BIBLIOGRAPHY: Van den Esch, J., *A. S.* (1947); Radine, S., *Anouilh, Lenormand, S.* (1951); Mignon, P.-L., *S.* (1960); Silenieks, J., "Themes and Dramatic Forms in the Plays of A. S.," *DA,* XXIV (1964), 3343–44; Lusseyran, J., "La malédiction de la solitude chez Anouilh et S.," *FR,* XXXIX (1965), 418–25; Silenieks, J., "Circularity of Plot in S.'s Plays," *Symposium,* XX (1966), 56–62

CHARLES G. HILL

ŠALDA, František Xaver

Czech critic, essayist, poet, novelist, and dramatist, b. 22 Dec. 1867, Liberec, Bohemia; d. 4 April 1937, Prague

Š. studied law in Prague but was after 1892 a frequent contributor to literary journals and the standard Czech Encyclopedia. Š.'s first collection of essays was called, characteristically, *Boje o Zítřek* (1905), which means "battles for tomorrow." For a time (1901–1910) he edited *Volné směry,* the main Czech art magazine. In 1916 Š. became a *docent,* and in 1919 Professor of Western Literatures, at the Charles University in Prague. In 1928 he founded a monthly review, *Šaldův zápisník* ("Šalda's Notebook"), which he wrote from cover to cover until his death.

Š. completely reformed Czech criticism, which up to then had been provincial or professorial. His first important article, "Synthetism v novém umění" (1892), was an account of symbolist (*see* symbolism) aesthetics and poetics drawn mainly from French sources. This and many other essays soon put Š. into the forefront of the new generation of the 1890's, which rejected the parnassian or folklore literature of the 19th c. and exalted a new group of poets, the symbolists such as Březina (q.v.) and Antonín Sova (1864–1928) or realists such as Machar (q.v.).

With the years, Š. outgrew his original symbolist creed, which had been somewhat incongruously combined with an interest in "scientific" criticism, particularly that of Émile Hennequin (1859–88). Š. developed a clearly articulated, fiercely defended view of literature that allowed him to judge the whole Czech literary past and present. Besides this, Š. made frequent excursions into foreign literatures, particularly French and German.

The collection *Duše a dílo* (1913) contains essays on the problem of romanticism from Rousseau to the early Flaubert; it centers on the Czech romantic poet K. H. Mácha (1810–36). Later Š. wrote pamphlets on Shakespeare (1916), on Dante (1921), and a short book on Rimbaud (1930). But his main work was devoted to commentary on the Czech literary scene.

After World War I, Š. became a fervent defender of the avant-garde movements, such as proletarian poetry and poetism, though he always avoided an ideological commitment, rejecting both Marxism and Roman Catholicism. In literary theory Š., late in life, claimed to be a "structuralist," *i.e.*, he defended the unity of form and content, suspicious of both didacticism and naturalism (q.v.). He rejected both impressionistic and dogmatic criticism and cultivated an art of characterization and portraiture that might remind one of Sainte-Beuve (1804–1869) in its breadth and evocative power, if Š. had not been so deeply engaged in the polemics of the time. With all his wide historical knowledge he remained a militant critic: praising, exhorting, chastising, never shirking the main duty of the critic of judging, and judging from the center of his personality which, he felt, guarantees a final justice and the only objectivity man can reach.

Especially since the founding of his own journals, Š. moved more and more into a general criticism of civilization. He became a great public figure comparable only with Thomas G. Masaryk. His last essays, often phrased with poetic power or polemical harshness, examine almost every topic of the times: literature as well as art, religion, and politics. But the fervor of a commitment to great poetry as a source of insight and as a preservative of the belief in the reality and value of the individual always remained central.

Compared to Š.'s work in criticism, his many attempts at writing fiction (*e.g.*, a two-volume novel, *Loutky i dělníci boži,* 1917), plays (*e.g., Tažení proti smrti,* 1926), and lyrical poetry (*e.g., Strom bolesti,* 1920) are considered comparatively unsuccessful.

Š. was not only the greatest Czech critic. Wide-ranging, open to all the winds of doctrine from the West, with a passionate personal core, he also became the conscience of his nation between the wars.

FURTHER WORKS: *Moderní literatura česká* (1909); *Život ironický a jiné povídky* (1912); *Umění a náboženství* (1914); *In memoriam R. Svobodové* (1920); *Zástupové* (1921); *Dítě* (1923); *Antonín Sova* (1924); *Juvenilie* (1925); *Pokušení Pascalovo* (1928); *O nejmladší poesii české* (1928); *Krásná literatura česká v prvním desetiletí republiky* (1930); *Mladé zápasy* (1934); *Dřevoryty staré i nové* (1935); *Časové a nadčasové* (1936); *Mácha snivec i buřič* (1936); *Studie literárně historické a kritické* (1937); *Kritické glossy k nové poesii české* (1939); *Tajemství zraku* (1940); *Medailony* (1941); *Soubor díla* (22 vols., 1948–63). **Selected English translations:** "The Death of Count Christopher des Loges," in *Selected Czech Tales* (ed. by M. Busch and O. Pick; 1925); "Poetry, Immortality, and Eternity," in *Hundred Towers: a Czechoslovak Anthology of Creative Writing* (ed. by W. C. Weiskopf; 1945)

BIBLIOGRAPHY: Novák, A., "F. X. Š. jako kritik," in *Zvony domova* (1916); Malý, R. I., and Pujman, F., eds., *F. X. Š. k padesátinám* (1918); Hora, J., ed., *F. X. Š. k 22. prosinci 1932* (1932); Fischer, O., *Š. češství* (1937); Goetz, F., *F. X. Š.* (1937); Mukařovský, J., "F. X. Š.," *Slovo a slovesnost*, III (1937); Lifka, B., ed., *Na pamět F. X. Š.* (1939); Svoboda, L., *Studie o F. X. Š.* (1947); Wellek, R., "Š.," in *Columbia Dictionary of Modern European Literature,* ed. Horatio Smith (1947); Pistorius, J., *Bibliographie díla F. X. Š.* (1948); Wellek, R., "Modern Czech Literary Criticism and Literary Scholarship," *HSS,* II (1954), and in *Essays on Czech Literature* (1963); Vodička, F., ed., *F. X. Š. 1867, 1937, 1967* (1968)

RENÉ WELLEK

SALINAS, Pedro

Spanish poet and essayist, b. 27 Nov. 1892, Madrid; d. 4 Dec. 1951, Boston, Massachusetts

In his youth S. was a lecturer in Spanish at the Sorbonne. As professor of Spanish literature at the University of Seville (1918) and as a professor at Cambridge (1922–23) he was extremely active as a lecturer, critic, and supporter of cultural projects. As a poet, he held a leading position among the representatives of his generation, which included Jorge Guillén, Alberti, and García Lorca (qq.v.). After 1936, at the eruption of the Spanish Civil War S. lived in the United States and was a professor at Johns Hopkins University.

S.'s first poems—*Presagios* (1923), *Seguro azar* (1929), and *Fábula y signo* (1931)—are strongly original despite their indications that S. was somewhat influenced by Jiménez (q.v.) and despite certain parallels with Guillén. No aspect of life is rejected as a subject; every aspect calls forth a lyrical reaction and a sympathetic response.

These early books already announce that love is to be S.'s central theme; it assumes the dominant role in the great poem *La voz a ti debida* (1933) and in *Razón de amor* (1936). Into the tradition of the love lyrics of Garcilaso de la Vega (1503–1536) and Gustavo Bécquer (1836–70), S. introduces new approaches. In his handling of the experience of love, S. shows an inclination toward reasonableness, a tendency to analyze closely emotional states, and a striving to express all that is most intimate and most unutterable. All things are related to woman, toward whom the poet constantly turns as to a completely concrete yet at the same time indeterminate, invisible being—an indispensable, very close "thou."

S.'s poetry, like that of Guillén, is closer to thought than to visual fantasy. He usually uses traditional forms but nearly always dispenses with rhyme. The "inner conceptism" characteristic of S. emerges even more clearly in the poems written after 1936 that are collected in *El contemplado* (1946) and *Todo más claro* (1949).

In his last years S. devoted himself principally to literary criticism and the theater. He also wrote the science fiction novel *La bomba increíble* (1950), which expresses his hope that spontaneity and feeling may rescue man from the perils of technology.

FURTHER WORKS: *Amor en vilo* (1931); *Error de cálculo* (1938); *Poesía junta* (1942); *Aprecio defensa del lenguaje* (1944); *Jorge Manrique o Tradición y Originalidad* (1947); *La poesía de Rubén Darío* (1948); *Literatura Española* (1949); *El desnudo impecable y otras narraciones* (1951); *Teatro: La cabeza de Medusa. La estrato esfera. La isla del Tesoro* (1952); *Confianza* (1954); *Poesías completas* (1955); *Teatro completo* (1957); *Poesías, teatro y narraciones completas* (1961); *La responsabilidad del escritor* (1961); *Ensayos de literatura Hispánica* (1967). **Selected English translations:** *Lost Angel, and Other Poems* (1938); *Truth of Two, and Other Poems* (1940); *Zero* (1947); *Sea of San Juan* (1950)

BIBLIOGRAPHY: Baader, H., *P. S.* (1956); Darmangeat, P., *P. S.* (1956); Dehennin, E., *P. S.* (1957); Feal Deibe, C., *La Poésia de P. S.* (1965); Marichal, J., "P. S.: la voz a la confidencia debida," *Revista de Occidente*, IX (1965), 154–70; Palley, J., *La luz no usada* (1966); Baeza Betancourt, F., *La amada más distante* (1967)

GONZALO SOBEJANO

SALINGER, Jerome David

American novelist and short-story writer, b. 1 Jan. 1916, New York City

S. grew up in the city of his birth. Although he attended three colleges, he has no degree. He has been writing since the age of fifteen, publishing his first short story when he was twenty-one.

S.'s first major work, *The Catcher in the Rye* (1951), is the testament of a whole generation in search of new values. Its adolescent hero, Holden Caulfield, expresses a quixotic rebellion against the sham and corruption of the world. Set in New York and written in a neopicaresque manner, the novel also creates a piquant and unique language of stammering youth. Alternately breezy in its comedy and poignant, the novel still implies a deep awareness of spiritual collapse.

In *Nine Stories* (1953) S. reveals that he is a master of the short story form. Love and squalor are contrasted with one another in daily life; irony is constantly modified by whimsy. S.'s series of novellas—*Franny and Zooey* (1961) and *Raise High the Roof Beam, Carpenters, and Seymour—An Introduction* (1963)—spin out, in hilarious and discursive fashion, the myth of the gifted Glass family.

224

The intense spiritual concerns of that family, which also manage to reflect the manners and motives of middle-class society, affirm a sacramental view of life. The view, which owes as much to primitive Christianity as to Zen and Buddhist thought, required that S. reconceive the art of fiction and discover new forms for silence or speech.

S. was one of the most controversial authors of the postwar era, and was certainly one of the most influential among college youth from the mid-1950's to the mid-1960's. Ironically his own personal reticence, his insistence on privacy in an age of exposure, contributed to the cult that grew around his work. The cult extols the virtues of childlike innocence and spiritual love at the expense of the more robust demands of life.

S.'s critics find his interest in childhood and adolescence limited, and his religious view exclusive. In his evolution from a satirical toward a religious writer, S. shows that his main concern is a kind of love that reaches out to mystical experience but usually falls back to redeem the vulgarity of the world below.

BIBLIOGRAPHY: Grunwald, H., ed., *S.* (1962); McCarthy, M., "J. D. S.'s Closed Circuit," *Harper's Magazine,* Oct. 1962; Special S. issue, *WSCL,* III (1962), i; Rees, R. "The S. Situation," in *Contemporary American Novelists,* ed. H. T. Moore (1964), pp. 95–105; Miller, J., *J. D. S.* (1965); Special S. issue, *MFS,* XIII (1966), iii; Schultz, M., "Epilogue to *Seymour: An Introduction:* S. and the Crisis of Consciousness," *Studies in Short Fiction,* V (1968), 128–38

IHAB HASSAN

SALMON, André

French poet, novelist, journalist, and art critic, b. 4 Oct. 1881, Paris; d. 12 March 1969, Sanary

Though S.'s interest in painting and painters was fostered by his father, an engraver, and his grandfather, a painter of animal life, he did not find an outlet for his talents until one of his earliest teachers, parnassian poet Gaston de Raismes, encouraged him to write verse and began taking him to Francois Coppée's (1842–1908) "Thursdays."

S. had visited Russia as a child, and he returned to work there as a clerk in the French Embassy in Moscow. Later he drew upon his knowledge of Russian language and history in

writing three of his most effective works: *Prikaz* (1919), an apocalyptic poem about the Russian Revolution; *Natchalo* (1922), a four-act drama, written in collaboration with René Saunier; and *Orgie à Saint-Petersbourg* (1925), a candid, voluptuous novel depicting a dissolute and depraved society.

Between 1890 and 1910 S. frequented the haunts of the Paris literati, where he met Mac Orlan and Cendrars (qq.v.), who would read the first drafts of their poems to one another, Apollinaire (q.v.), who introduced him to Pablo Picasso, and Jacob (q.v.), whom he later considered to have been his soul brother. He was also a familiar figure in the Closerie des Lilas circle that included T. S. Eliot, Hemingway, and Gertrude Stein (qq.v.).

In 1902, S. joined Apollinaire and Jacob in launching a short-lived poetry review, *Festin d'Esope.* During this period he supported himself by law reporting for *Le Matin* and *Le Petit Parisien* and contributed to various French and Belgian reviews.

In 1903 S. began publishing poetry in *La Plume.* His first book of verse, *Poèmes* (1905) —which included one of his finest poems, "Les Clés ardentes"—was published by Fort (q.v.).

Until he wrote his epic poem *L'Âge de l'humanité* (1920), S.'s prose and poetry marked him as a *fantaisiste.* Though his subjects were often Baudelairian in their bitterness, they were never morbid or macabre, and his pure lyricism recalled Paul Verlaine (1844–96).

Marked by a passion for life expressed in a delicate, image-rich style, S.'s most mature poetry is found in *Créances* (1926) and *Carreaux* (1928). In these volumes of poems S.'s sensitive reflections on the turbulent events of his day show an intellectual vigor that stamps him as independent of any school.

S.'s creativity is fully carried over into his novels, one of the best of which, *La Négresse du Sacré Coeur* (1920), he adapted for the stage, using the pen name Septime Fébur. The last novel he wrote, *Monocle à deux coups* (1969), displays the same burlesque imagination, delicate sensitivity, and a spicy naturalism—just a shade removed from the vulgar— that characterized the works of his youth.

A vigorous and creative art critic, S.'s study of the birth of cubism, *L'Art vivant* (1920), and his writings about individual painters— *Othon Friesz* (1920), *Derain* (1923), and *La Vie passionnée de Modigliani* (1957; *Modigliani, A Memoir,* 1961)—would by themselves have established his reputation at home and abroad. Three volumes of memoirs, *Souvenirs sans fin* (1945–61), deal with both painters and writers S. had known from 1903 to 1940.

In 1958 S. was awarded Le Grand Prix de la Société des Poètes, and in 1964, at the age of eighty-three, he was awarded the Grand Prix de Poésie de l'Académie Française.

FURTHER WORKS: *Féeries* (1907); *Monstres choisis* (1918); *Moeurs de la famille Poivre* (1918); *Bob et Bobette en ménage* (1919); *Ventes d'amour* (1920); *Peindre* (1920); *L'Entrepreneur d'illuminations* (1921); *C'est une belle fille!* (1921); *Propos d'atelier* (1921); *Le Manuscrit trouvé dans un chapeau* (1924); *Métamorphoses de la harpe et de la harpiste* (1926); *Tout l'or du monde* (1927); *Archives du club des onze* (1928); *Donat vainqueur* (1928); *Histoire d'un crime* (1929); *Caporal Valentine* (1932); *L'Année poétique* (1933); *Troubles en Chine* (1935); *Saint André* (1936); *Le Jour et la nuit* (1937); *L'Eventail de Marie Laurencin* (1937); *Odeur de poésie* (1944); *L'Air de la Butte* (1945); *Montparnasse* (1950); *Les Étoiles dans l'encrier* (1952)

BIBLIOGRAPHY: La Vaissière, R. de, *Anthologie poétique du XXe siècle* (1923); Lalou, R., *Histoire de la littérature française contemporaine* (1940); Nadeau, M., *Histoire du surréalisme* (1945); Emié, L., *Dialogue avec Max Jacob* (1954); Berger, P., *S.* (1956)

ARTHUR SIMON

SÁNCHEZ FERLOSIO, Rafael
Spanish novelist, b. 4 Dec. 1927, Rome

S. F. was urged toward literature by his father, Rafael Sánchez Mazas, a lawyer who was himself a writer. However, after publishing several books that are unusual in contemporary Spanish writing, S. F. shifted his creative interests to linguistic and scientific studies.

Industrias y andanzas de Alfanhuí (1951) is a highly inventive picaresque work in which reality and fantasy are interwoven. Its episodical short stories relate the extraordinary adventures of young Alfanhuí, a contemporary Lazarillo de Tormes who travels throughout Castile engaging in strange tasks and serving unusual masters. Somewhat of a dreamer, Alfanhuí lives in an atmosphere of magic reminiscent of Oriental tales, Lewis Carroll's (1832–98) *Alice in Wonderland,* and the sur-

realistic stories of Supervielle (q.v.). S. F.'s rich, sober Castilian adds a rural flavor to a highly sophisticated framework.

El Jarama (1956; The One Day of the Week, 1962) won the Premio Nadal, the first book in the history of that literary award to do so by the jurors' acclamation. An extraordinarily perceptive *tranche de vie,* its objective technique opened a new path for the contemporary Spanish novel. Though its realism is photographic in precision, by focusing on details S. F. achieves a poetic intensity that verges on the superrealistic.

Dwarfed against a landscape that is continually changing as the day wanes, a group of urban clerks spend a lazy summer Sunday picnicking on the banks of the Jarama River. Our knowledge of them is confined to the present, and as we watch their interaction we participate in the grayness of lives drained of individuality and introspection. S. F.'s achievement is to make them psychologically interesting without resorting to sharp contrasts or speeding up the slow tempo of the narration.

Alfanhuí y otros cuentos (1961) includes the previously published adventures of Alfanhuí plus two short stories written in 1956. Although artistically interesting additions, these stories lack the verve of the first tales.

BIBLIOGRAPHY: Castellet, J. M., "Notas para una iniciación a la lectura del *Jarama,*" *Papeles de Son Armadans,* I (1956), ii, 205–17; Pérez Minik, D., *Novelistas españoles de los siglos XIX y XX* (1957), pp. 343–46; Sáinz de Robles, F. C., *La novela española en el siglo XX* (1957), pp. 257–58; Alborg, J. L., *Hora actual de la novela española,* Vol. I (1958), pp. 305–20; Nora, E. G. de, *La novela española contemporánea,* Vol. II (1962), pp. 299–305; Torrente Ballester, G., *Panorama de la literatura española contemporánea* (1965), p. 528

ALBERT M. FORCADAS

SANDBURG, Carl
American poet and biographer, b. 6 Jan. 1878, Galesburg, Illinois; d. 22 July 1967, Flat Rock, North Carolina

One of the important American poets of the 20th c., S. is also notable as a historian and biographer of Abraham Lincoln. In addition he was for a half century a familiar figure on the lecture and concert stage, reciting his own poetry and singing many of the American folk songs that he collected in *The American Songbag* (1927).

S., the son of a Swedish railroad worker, attended Galesburg schools but also worked in his youth as a dishwasher, milk-wagon driver, and harvest laborer. He served in the Spanish-American War (1898), then attended Lombard College in his home town. Subsequently he became an organizer for the Socialist party and a Chicago newspaperman; for many years he was associated with the Chicago *Daily News*.

S.'s earliest verse was published by a private press in Galesburg under the title *In Reckless Ecstasy* (1904). In 1914 he contributed his famous tribute to Chicago to Harriet Monroe's *Poetry* magazine, and two years later published his first important volume of poetry, *Chicago Poems*. Subsequent books of verse include *Cornhuskers* (1918), *Smoke and Steel* (1920), and *Slabs of the Sunburnt West* (1922). *The People, Yes* (1936) is an extraordinary compilation of popular beliefs, folk idiom, anecdotes, proverbs and original verse. The first collected edition of his poetry, *Complete Poems*, appeared in 1950. *The Sandburg Range* (1957) includes additional verse.

Early in life S. fixed his attention on Lincoln and began to accumulate material for his biography. In 1926 he published *Abraham Lincoln: The Prairie Years*. The four volumes that chronicled the presidential period, *Abraham Lincoln: The War Years*, appeared in 1939.

But neither poetry nor biography exhausted S.'s enormous vitality. His interest in children's tales resulted in *Rootabaga Stories* (1922). At the age of sixty-five he began a long panoramic novel, which, entitled *Remembrance Rock*, appeared in 1948. His autobiographical account of life in Galesburg, *Always the Young Strangers*, was published in 1952.

A Pulitzer prizewinner in both poetry and history, S. is notable for verse that is virile, rough, and yet sensuously appealing. T. K. Whipple once spoke of it as having "much power ill controlled." In his early poetry, in which he expressed a strong sympathy with the proletariat, S. did not hesitate to be colloquial and slangy, while, following Walt Whitman (1819–92), he used long lines with a strong rhythm but no regular meter.

S.'s prose, which to the historian Allan Nevins was marked by a "rich promiscuity," is both eloquent and flexible. In his autobiography he captured some of the charm and color of life on the Illinois prairies. His long devotion to Lincoln enabled him to profile his protagonist against the age and to reveal in vigorous narrative how Lincoln rose superior to the frustrations and antagonisms of America's most critical ordeal. S.'s optimism and faith in the people made him unusual during a period when sanguine confidence in the United States and its destiny was not common among American writers.

FURTHER WORKS: *The Chicago Race Riots* (1919); *Rootabaga Pigeons* (1923); *Selected Poems* (1926); *Good Morning, America* (1928); *Steichen the Photographer* (1929); *Potato Face* (1930); *Mary Lincoln, Wife and Widow* (1932); *Bronze Wood* (1941); *Storm over the Land* (1942); *Home Front Memo* (1943); *The Photographs of Abraham Lincoln* (with Frederick Hill Meserve; 1944); *Lincoln Collector* (1949); *Abraham Lincoln* (condensed and revised; 1954); *Harvest Poems, 1910–1960* (1960); *Six New Poems and a Parable* (1961); *Honey and Salt* (1963); *Letters* (1968)

BIBLIOGRAPHY: Hansen, H., *Midwest Portraits* (1923); Whipple, T. K., *Spokesmen* (1928); Detzer, K., *C. S.* (1941); Flanagan, J. T., and Dunlap, L. W., *The S. Range: An Exhibit of Materials from C. S.'s Library* (1958); Golden, H., *C. S.* (1962); Crowder, R., *C. S.* (1964); Durnell, H., *The America of C. S.* (1965); MacLeish, A., "A Memorial Tribute to C. S.," *Massachusetts Review*, IX (1968), 41–44

JOHN T. FLANAGAN

The free rhythms of Mr. C. S. are a fine achievement in poetry. No one who reads *Chicago Poems* with rhythm particularly in mind can fail to recognize how much beauty he attains in this regard. But the more arresting aspect of Mr. S.'s achievement is, for myself, the so-called imagistic aspect. . . . At first these poems may seem too innocent of self-interpretation to mean anything, too impressionistic to compel the name of beauty—to give that completion which has no shadow and knows no end beyond itself. But such exquisite realization of the scenes that give Mr. S. the mood of beauty is in itself a creation of the beautiful.

Francis Hackett, *Horizons* (1918),
pp. 304–5, 309

There must be some powerful principle of life in the man, that he can make one feel so much. There must be some rocky strength, some magnetic iron in him, that compels, despite coatings of muck and dust, and draws iron to iron. For S. is an almost rudimentary artist. His successful effects are almost sparks of fire out of a chaos, sudden tongues of flame that leap out of smoking matter and subside as suddenly again. He appears to be as nearly unconscious as an artist can be and still remain a creator; it is well-nigh in spite of his technique that he manages to communicate.

Paul Rosenfeld, in *Bookman* (July 1921), p. 393

Buried deep within the He man, the hairy, meat eating S. there is another S., a sensitive, naïve, hesitating C. S., a S. that hears the voice of the wind over the roofs of houses at night, a S. that wanders often alone through grim city streets on winter nights, a S. that knows and understands the voiceless cry in the heart of the farm girl of the plains when she comes to the kitchen door and sees for the first time the beauty of prairie country.

The poetry of John Guts doesn't excite me much. Hairy, raw meat eating He men are not exceptional in Chicago and the middle west.

As for the other S., the naïve, hesitant, sensitive S.—among all the poets of America he is my poet.

Sherwood Anderson, in *Bookman* (Dec. 1921), p. 361

S., for all his strength, is not without his weakness.... In giving way to a program of mysticism, S. gives the unconscious an absolutely free hand; he lets it dictate its unfettered—and, one might almost add, its unlettered—fantasies. There are times, more frequent than one might wish, when he completely fails to guide the current of his thought; it directs or misdirects him so that he follows blindly what, too often, is merely a blind alley.... But though the meaning is not always clear, there is no mistaking the emotion. It is implicit in every line; a concentrated exaltation, rich in its sweeping affirmations, rich in suggestive details.

Louis Untermeyer, *American Poetry since 1900* (1923), pp. 86–7

C. S., unlike Masters and Lindsay, has a genuine talent for language; with a hard-boiled vocabulary and reputation, he offers what is perhaps the most attractive surface of any of the men of the group. But, when we come to read him in quantity, we are disappointed to find him less interesting than we had hoped; his ideas seem rather obvious, his emotions rather meager.

Edmund Wilson, "The All-Star Literary Vaudeville" (1926), *The Shores of Light* (1952), p. 239

C. S. petered out as a poet ten years ago. I imagine he wanted it that way. His poems themselves said what they had to say, piling it up, then just went out like a light. He had no answers, he didn't seek any. Without any attempt at the solace which the limitations of art (as with a Baudelaire) might bring the formlessness of his literary figures was the very formlessness of the materials with which he worked. That was his truth. That was

what he wanted truthfully to make plain, that was his compulsion. That form he could accept but at a terrible cost: failure deliberately invited, a gradual inevitable slackening off to ultimate defeat.

William Carlos Williams, in *Poetry* (Sept. 1951), p. 346

In all his poetry a single effort was represented —that of refounding his derived romanticism, its vision and imaginative ecstasy upon the common realities of a labor and populist experience. This latter remained for him a fixed element, one he would not place in perspective and seemingly could not alter.... Consequently, the only mobile or adaptable part of his work lay in its other half— the essentially rhetorical and willful exercise of fancy to embellish and stage impressively his obdurate poetic matter. Like the other mid-westerners, S. was a poet of subject. Where his subject was itself arresting, moving, and satisfying, his poem likewise could achieve these qualities.

Bernard Duffey, *The Chicago Renaissance in American Letters* (1954), pp. 216–7

Everybody loved C. S. in our town. Nobody knows where he went.... Compare "I Am the People, The Mob" with *The People, Yes*. It's enough to make you weep. In the early poem you see so clearly behind the abstraction the stark individuals of the other poems in *Chicago Poems*. Behind the second *People* is only mush.... It is a terrible pity, but after about 1925 there is nothing of value. Since most of the prose comes after that, S. the historian, novelist, autobiographer, writer of children's stories simply does not exist for literature. I suppose the last thing was the *Songbag*.

Kenneth Rexroth, in *Nation* (22 Feb. 1958), pp. 171–2

SANDEMOSE, Aksel

Danish-Norwegian novelist and essayist, b. 19 March 1899, Nyköbing; d. 5 Aug. 1965, Copenhagen

S. grew up in Jante in Denmark, left school at fourteen and went to sea, attended a seminary one year, and worked intermittently as a farmhand, office clerk, teacher, and journalist. His voyages took him to Canada, Newfoundland, and the West Indies. *Klabavtermanden* (1927) and *Ross Dane* (1928) established him as a successful author and won him a pension.

To satisfy a long-cherished dream of living in the land of his mother's ancestry, however, and encouraged by the enthusiastic reviews by the prominent novelist and critic Sigurd Hoel (1890–1960), in Oslo's *Arbeiderbladet*, S. moved to Norway in 1929. Soon after he started to write in Norwegian, and all his work after

CARL SANDBURG

AKSEL SANDEMOSE

1931 appeared in Norwegian. He remained there until 1941 when his involvement in the resistance movement forced him to escape to Sweden. At his return he settled his family on a farm, Kjørkelvik, near Risør. From 1951 to 1955 he published Årstidende, a quarterly magazine made up exclusively of his own writings. In 1952, in recognition of his merit as a literary artist, the Norwegian government awarded him a lifelong pension.

Four novels—En sjømann går iland (1931), En flyktning krysser sit spor (1933; A Fugitive Crosses His Tracks, 1936), Der stod en benk i haven (1937), and Brudulje (1938)—all concern Espen Arnakke's striking out against the tyrannical conformity of his childhood surroundings. An impulsive seventeen-year-old sailor, rebellious to the point of murdering a rival, becomes an anxiety-ridden runaway in search of explanations for his own irrational act. Espen is the fictionalization of the youthful S., and Espen's growing up reflects S.'s life in Jante, where he absorbed crushing and demoralizing commandments that he suffered from for the rest of his life. This Arnakke quartet, however, is not a mere tabulation of indictments against small towns, conventional mores, or the disciplined life. It is a bill of rights for all men to dream dreams, test values, and live in terms of their own problems.

Philip Houm said that Det gångna är en dröm (Swedish, 1944; Norwegian, Det svundne er en drøm, 1946) is "a hundred percent S.," the finest account offered of 9 April 1940 (the day of the German invasion of Norway), and a genuine testimony to the indomitable fiber of the Norwegian people.

Varulven (1958; The Werewolf, 1966) is the poignant story of the struggle of two men and a woman against the same Jante intolerances, symbolized by the werewolf. The three stand up heroically to the inhibitions bred by their past and to the judgments of their fellow men, but in the end they are indeed battle-scarred. Whether they are also vindicated is left to the reader's determination.

In both style and substance one can detect the influence of Sigmund Freud (1856–1939) and see flashes of similarity to writers such as Sinclair Lewis, Faulkner, Hemingway, Strindberg, Joyce, and D. H. Lawrence (qq.v.). Nevertheless, S.'s views and methods are highly individualistic and his approach interestingly original. In his psychological probing he has been compared to an archeologist scrutinizing artifacts laid bare by excavation and trying to fit the shards together into a once operative whole.

In spite of loosely constructed plots and philosophical digressions, S.'s exciting narrative and vividly introspective characterization create suspense, stimulate speculation, and invite fresh insights. Purposeful obscurity adds mystery. S.'s language is at once rich and poetic, bold and explicit.

S. ranks among the most articulate enemies of sophistry, prudery, and parochialism in our 20th-c. adjustment-oriented society and among the most ardent advocates of self-examination and environmental analysis as man's only means of liberation and fulfillment. Love and hate, trust and jealousy, joy and anguish—all persistently recurring motives—are often exposed as paired opposites of the same passion, commonly generated by feelings of inferiority and struggles for autonomy. S. never loses sight of the clash between mind and spirit, the individual and the group, reason and emotion. The inevitable question—whether any point of resolution exists at which these contenders can meet on equal terms—remains unanswered.

FURTHER WORKS: Fortaellinger fra Labrador (1923); Storme ved jaevndøgn (1924); Ungdomssynd (1924); Maend fra Atlanten (1924); Vi pynter oss med horn (1936; Horns for Our Adornment, 1938); Sandemose forteller (1937); Fortellinger fra andre tider (1940); Tjaerehandleren (1945); Alice Atkinson og hennes elskere (1949); En palmegrønn øy (1950); Reisen til Kjørkelvik (1954); Mureneø rundt Jeriko (1960); Felicias bryllup (1961); Mytteriet pa barken Zuidersee (1963); Dans, dans, Roselill (1965)

BIBLIOGRAPHY: On A Fugitive Crosses His Tracks—Kronenberger, L., New York Times Book Review, 12 July 1936, Jarrett, O., SatR, XIV (18 July 1936), and Guterman, N., The New Republic, LXXXVIII (26 Aug. 1936); On Horns for Our Adornment—Kronenberger, L., New York Times Book Review, 25 Sept. 1938; Houm, P., "A. S.," in Norsk litteraturhistorie, eds. P. Bull et al. Vol. VI (1955), pp. 420–38; Naess, H., Introduction to The Werewolf (1966), pp. 7–14

AMANDA LANGEMO

SANSOM, William

English novelist, short-story writer, and essayist, b. 18 Jan. 1912, London

After various clerical positions, S. served as

a fireman during World War II, an experience that provided the basis for the title story of his first book, *Fireman Flower* (1944). This fable of a man striving to reach the core of a fire while capricious assistants, an old schoolmaster and distracting colleagues impede him is clearly influenced by Kafka (q.v.), as are most of the other stories in the collection. A Kafkaesque atmosphere also pervades S.'s novella *The Equilibriad* (1948), which focuses on a young man whose sense of imbalance is so strong that it literally causes him to slide over surfaces. These works abound in grotesque human behavior, and though they create a convincing world of dreamlike unpredictability, they are excessively weighted by symbols and metaphysical pronouncements.

In his first novel, *The Body* (1949), S. shifts from a vision of universal irrationality to the insane perspective of the narrator, whose all-consuming (and erroneous) suspicions of his wife's infidelity result in tragedy. Coincidence plays a part in the novel's complications, but this study of paranoia is effectively claustrophobic.

S.'s extensive travel writings influenced his next novels and stories. *The Passionate North* (1950), by combining a series of romantic encounters with exotic settings, provides agreeable, if undemanding, reading. The same is true of *The Face of Innocence* (1951), which by combining descriptions of a vacation locale with speculations on the evils of an unwise marriage resembles the "entertainments" of Graham Greene (q.v.).

S.'s novel *A Bed of Roses* (1954), a study of the arbitrary cruelty of a girl's lover, is an unsuccessful departure from the predominantly comic tone of his writing during this period. More typical is *The Loving Eye* (1956), a novel of a young man's growing infatuation with a girl he first sees at a garden window. After a series of misunderstandings and a murder investigation, the two are married. Of S.'s later works, only *Goodbye* (1966) explores a serious subject, that of a man who reacts to his wife's threat to leave him by planning murder and suicide; however, the novel's frequently facetious tone jars with its subject matter.

S.'s short stories are on the whole more effective than his novels. His stress on locale and daily routine, as opposed to the inner qualities and motives of his characters, seems best suited to brief studies. *A Contest of Ladies* (1956) is probably his best collection, and the title story the best in it. Its account of the

impingement of a group of beauty contestants upon a middle-aged bachelor maintains the right mood of cheerful disbelief throughout.

Though he shifted direction after his first works of short fiction, S. has shown remarkable skill in developing a vein of successful light fiction.

FURTHER WORKS: *South: Aspects and Images from Corsica, Italy, and Southern France* (1948); *Something Terrible, Something Lovely* (1948); *A Touch of the Sun* (1952); *It Was Really Charlie's Castle* (1953); *Pleasures Strange and Simple* (1953); *Lord Love Us* (1954); *Among the Dahlias* (1957); *The Icicle and the Sun* (1958); *Collected Short Stories* (1960); *Blue Skies, Brown Studies* (1960); *The Last Hours of Sandra Lee* (1961); *Stories* (1963); *Away to It All* (1964); *The Ulcerated Milkman* (1966); *Grand Tour Today* (1968); *Christmas* (1968)

BIBLIOGRAPHY: Tindall, W. Y., *Forces in Modern British Literature* (1946); Mason, R., in *Modern British Writing*, ed. D. V. Baker (1947), pp. 284–85; Rosenfeld, I., *PR*, Sept. 1949, pp. 950–51; Bowen, E., *New York Times Book Review*, 18 June 1961, p. 1

RICHARD PEARSE

SANTAYANA, George

American philosopher, novelist, and poet, b. 16 Dec. 1863, Madrid; d. 27 Sept. 1952, Rome

S., who was born into an old aristocratic Spanish family, spent his early years in Castile and came to Boston in 1872. He studied philosophy at Harvard and in Berlin. In 1889 he became an instructor in philosophy at Harvard. From 1912 on he was a private scholar and visiting professor in Spain, England, France, and Italy. From 1929 on he lived in a Roman Catholic nursing home in Rome.

S.'s position in literature was always that of a mediator between opposites. As a poet, he was a philosopher; as a philosopher, a poet. In his thinking, materialistic, pragmatic, and hedonistic elements exist side by side with aesthetic and mystical ones. Without ever considering himself a poet "in the magical sense," he began and ended his literary career with poetry, which is classical in form, often rhetorical in vocabulary, and academic in its strongly predominating reflectiveness.

In 1896 S. published *The Sense of Beauty*,

a psychology of aesthetic responsiveness inspired by Schopenhauer (1788–1860). With *The Life of Reason* (5 vols., 1905–1906; new ed., 1954), a "comprehensive history of the human imagination," which evaluates the development of modern civilization according to the classical criterion of rational harmony, S. established philosophical naturalism in America.

Several volumes of essays—S.'s favorite genre was the cultural-historical essay—bridge the transition to his European, "postrational" phase, which was introduced by *Scepticism and Animal Faith* (1923) and brought to culmination in his systematic masterpiece *Realms of Being* (I, *The Realm of Essence*, 1927; II, *The Realm of Matter*, 1930; III, *The Realm of Truth*, 1938; IV, *The Realm of Spirit*, 1940). In these works a dynamic, Aristotelian "realm of matter" stands opposed to a static, Platonic "realm of essence." The "realm of spirit" is both the human mirror of the process of nature and the gateway to ascension into the disillusioned, contemplative "spiritual life."

S.'s novel *The Last Puritan* (1936), the action of which takes place among the wealthy aristocracy and the educational institutions of New England, tells the story of the highly gifted but puritanically inhibited Oliver Alden. Technically, S. relies on a wide range of psychological close-ups and unrealistically structured conversations, liberally sprinkled with unexpected, often aphoristically formulated aperçus.

S.'s pious skepticism toward religions, in which he sees myths of human aspirations, expresses itself in *The Idea of Christ in the Gospels* (1946). The essays in *Dominations and Powers* (1951) contain his aristocratic critique of democracy.

My Host the World (1953), the third and last volume of S.'s autobiography, *Persons and Places* (1944–53), was published posthumously. (The previous volumes are *The Background of My Life*, 1944, and *The Middle Span*, 1945.) In these S.'s understanding of the psychology of men and nations achieves its most perfect expression in a melodious style.

FURTHER WORKS: *Sonnets, and Other Verses* (1894; enlarged ed., 1896); *Lucifer* (1899; revised ed., 1924); *Interpretations of Poetry and Religion* (1900); *A Hermit of Carmel* (1901); *Three Philosophical Poets* (1910); *Winds of Doctrine* (1913); *Egotism in German Philosophy* (1916; revised ed., 1940); *Character and Opinion in the United States* (1920); *Little Essays* (1920); *Soliloquies in England* (1922); *Poems* (1923); *Dialogues in Limbo* (1926; enlarged ed., 1948); *Platonism and the Spiritual Life* (1927); *The Genteel Tradition at Bay* (1931); *Some Turns of Thought in Modern Philosophy* (1933); *Obiter Scripta* (1936); *The Philosophy of S.* (1936); *Works* (1936–40); *The Poet's Testament: Poems and Two Plays* (1953); *Letters* (1955); *Essays in Literary Criticism* (1956); *The Idler and His Works, and Other Essays* (1957); *G. S.'s America* (1967); *The Genteel Tradition* (1967); *Selected Critical Writings* (1968)

BIBLIOGRAPHY: Howgate, G. W., *G. S.* (1938); Seidler, I., *Das philosophische System Ss.* (1953); Ames, V., "S. at One Hundred," *JAAC*, XXII (1964), 243–47; Young, D., "A Skeptical Music: Stevens and S.," *Criticism*, VII (1965), 263–83; Arnett, W. E., *G. S.* (1968); Henfrey, N., Introduction to *Selected Critical Writings of G. S.* (1968); Wilson, D., Preface to *The Genteel Tradition: Nine Essays by G. S.* (1968)

INGO SEIDLER

SARKIA, Kaarlo Teodor

(Surname originally *Sulin*), Finnish poet, b. 11 May 1902, Kiikka; d. 16 Nov. 1945, Sysmä

The illegitimate son of a country servant girl, S. was left an orphan at fourteen. With financial assistance, he was able to finish high school and study at Turku University, where he came under the influence of V. A. Koskenniemi (1885–1962), a poet and professor of literature; however, S. soon abandoned his studies for poetry. His first two collections, *Kahlittu* (1929) and *Velka elämälle* (1931), passed almost unnoticed, and it was his translation of Arthur Rimbaud's (1854–91) *Le Bateau ivre* that made him famous. The latter work and other translations from French and Italian poets appeared in the anthology *Ranskan kirjallisuuden kultainen kirja* (1934).

Afflicted with tuberculosis, S. never had a steady job and led an irregular though rather quiet life. His next collection, *Unen kaivo* (1936), was a great success. In 1937 his publisher gave him financial help so that he could spend several months in Switzerland and in Italy. *Kohtalon vaaka* (1943), S.'s final collection of poems, was not as well received as the former ones. As his health was failing again,

S. went to Sweden for treatment, but he soon returned to die in Finland.

S.'s works are entirely traditional in form and feeling, as was almost all Finnish poetry in his time. His facility with rhyme, rhythm, and sound effects led one critic to say that meaning was sometimes of secondary importance in S.'s poems, and his pyrotechnical displays of dubious artistic value were mildly parodied by younger poets. S. was not, however, an ivory-towered aesthete who despised the common herd. The formal elaboration of his poems does not extend to vocabulary and syntax, and the feelings expressed in them are simple and human.

In spite of his difficult childhood, he wrote a warm poem to his mother's memory. His poems about childhood and children are set in everyday Finnish surroundings and are generally happy, although they also contain intimations of something fateful and frightening. For example, in a poem much admired for its rhythm and sound effects, a child listening to the humming of his mother's spinning wheel drowses and dreams of fairylands, but suddenly he sees the wheel as a gigantic, threatening spider.

"Dream" and "sleep"—for which there is but one word in Finnish—often appear in S.'s poems. In one work, the poet has sunk to the bottom of a well and lies dreaming—yet awake —unable to rise to the surface again. The painful ecstasy produced by this experience of unreal beauty expresses S.'s conviction that beauty is not to be found in this world.

Nevertheless, it was toward the world that S. resolutely turned in his last collection. In a time of official patriotism, his protest against war alienated some critics and readers, although it had no more specific target than the spirit of evil—which he typically enough called Ugliness—that was driving men and nations to madness. His love of man, he proclaimed, made him want to mingle with the crowds, even if it meant, he added with a hint of humour, that he would be pushed and squeezed among them. After all, he noted, it was his brothers who did the pushing and squeezing.

FURTHER WORK: *Runot* (1944). **Selected English translations:** *Voices from Finland* (ed. E. Tompuri; 1947); *The Stone God and Other Poems* (eds. L. Vuosal and S. Stone; 1953); *Singing Finland* (ed. K. V. Ollilainen; 1956)

BIBLIOGRAPHY: Koskimies, R., "Ett finskt diktaröde," *Finsk Tidskrift,* No. 146 (1949), pp. 88–100; Anttila, A., "S. runojen musiikill-isesta rakenteesta," in *Parnasso* (1952), pp. 89–95; Hormia, O., "Unen kaivon rytmejä," in *Parnasso* (1952), pp. 115–20; Marjanen, K., "K. S. runouden kehitysviivoja," in *K. S.: Runot* (7th ed., 1959); Viljanen, L., "K. S. lapsuuden runoilijana," in *Lyyrillinen minä* (1959)

JAAKKO A. AHOKAS

SAROYAN, William

American novelist, short-story writer, and dramatist, b. 31 Aug. 1908, Fresno, California

S. was the son of an Armenian-American small vineyard owner who had previously been a Presbyterian minister. As a result of his father's early death, S. was forced to spend his early years in an orphanage in Alameda. When he was seven he returned with his mother to Fresno, where he went only as far as the ninth grade. After leaving school he took one job after another in rapid succession until becoming the local manager of the Postal Telegraph office in San Francisco. (He was later to create one of his most endearing characters, Homer Macauley in *The Human Comedy,* from this experience.) The *Overland Monthly* published a few of his short articles, and then, in 1933, the *Hairenik,* an Armenian magazine, published his first short story written under the pseudonym of Sirak Goryan.

S.'s appearance on the literary scene came suddenly and spectacularly in 1934 with the publication of *The Daring Young Man on the Flying Trapeze,* short stories of freshness and ebullience that caught the fancy of a depression-ridden nation. "Try to be alive, you will be dead soon enough" was the incontrovertible advice of its breezy preface. The bold image of the title soon became an epithet for the brash young author himself as his stories began to appear in increasing number in such prominent periodicals as *Harper's, The Atlantic Monthly,* and *The Yale Review* and were collected in book form almost annually.

Though temperamentally disinclined to rewrite, S. nevertheless worked hard to develop a style that at its best was lean, swift, and vigorous. *My Name Is Aram* (1940), a story-cycle that represents his finest achievement in short fiction, proved that he had acquired the ability to make his work look spontaneous and easy, like the performance of a trapeze artist.

GEORGE SANTAYANA

NATHALIE SARRAUTE

KAARLO TEODOR SARKIA

At the center of S.'s writing is his own personality and his remembered past among the Armenian-Americans of Fresno and San Francisco. His stories contain many vignettes of old-world figures whose personal eccentricities reflect their serious-comic struggle to maintain an integrity of personality amid the impersonal, competitive society of their adopted land. For them alienation is an inevitable condition of life. The profound spiritual uprootedness of the foreign-born American is S.'s finest theme.

This theme and the Fresno setting are the focus of S.'s first successful Broadway play, *My Heart's in the Highlands* (1939), in which he adapted the parable of the loaves and fishes to make a memorable comment on the brotherhood of man. *The Time of Your Life* (1939), for which he refused to accept the Pulitzer Prize, is a mood piece that spoofs the myth of the West while making the timely points that power dehumanizes and that the traditional ideals of America are indispensable to a nation facing the growing menace of fascism.

S.'s plays, like his fiction, were outside the main conventions of modern literature. Deriving from that most indigenous of American art forms, the vaudeville, they were conceived not in terms of character or action, but of incident. To S. the stage was a symbolic place, and he wanted no imaginary fourth wall to separate his actors from the audience. His reluctance to write about evil in the human heart severely limited the possibilities of conflict in his plays, which must in the final analysis be judged on the basis of their lyricism. At their best they present both a poetry of suffering and heartwarming vagaries of fancy that are rare in the American theater.

The Human Comedy (1943), the first of S.'s novels, again presents the world of Fresno, though this time thinly disguised in name. It was enormously popular during World War II, for it pointed to a national unity of purpose and offered a humanizing view of the struggle: one must hate not the enemy but that quality in the enemy that should be controlled.

S. worked as determinedly in the medium of the novel as he had in the short story. The culmination of this phase of his career came with *The Laughing Matter* (1953), which represents his most sustained effort in the tragic mode. Though well-constructed in plot, setting, and dialogue, it nevertheless demonstrates that S. was never at his best with tragic themes nor with the longer genres. In fiction as in drama,

he has been most effective in the art of situation, of character seen instantaneously.

Though he has read widely and has learned much from other writers, S. has always been independent. His approach to art has been strongly influenced by popular music, the western tall-tale, and the movies. Back of his achievement must be seen the age-old storytelling habits of Asia Minor with its respect for oral traditions and the ancient fable.

FURTHER WORKS: *Inhale and Exhale* (1936); *Three Times Three* (1936); *Little Children* (1937); *Love, Here Is My Hat, and Other Short Romances* (1938); *The Trouble with Tigers* (1938); *Peace, It's Wonderful* (1939); *Three Plays* (1940); *Three Plays* (1941); *Saroyan's Fables* (1941); *Razzle-Dazzle* (1942); *Get Away Old Man* (1944); *Dear Baby* (1944); *The Adventures of Wesley Jackson* (1946); *Jim Dandy: Fat Man in a Famine* (1947); *The Saroyan Special* (1948); *Don't Go Away Mad, and Other Plays* (1949); *Twin Adventures* (1950); *The Assyrian, and Other Stories* (1950); *Rock Wagram* (1951); *Tracy's Tiger* (1951); *The Bicycle Rider in Beverly Hills* (1952); *The Whole Voyald, and Other Stories* (1956); *Mama I Love You* (1956); *Papa You're Crazy* (1957); *The Cave Dwellers* (1958); *W. S. Reader* (1958); *Here Comes/There Goes/You Know Who* (1961); *Boys and Girls Together* (1963); *Not Dying* (1963); *One Day in the Afternoon of the World* (1964); *After Thirty Years: The Daring Young Man on the Flying Trapeze* (1964); *Short Drive, Sweet Chariot* (1966); *Look at Us; Let's See; Here We Are; Look Hard, Speak Soft* (1967); *I Used to Believe I Had Forever, Now I'm Not So Sure* (1968); *Letters from 74 rue Taibout* (1969); *Making Money, and 19 Other Very Short Plays* (1969)

BIBLIOGRAPHY: Kherdian, D., *A Bibliography of W. S.* (1965); Floan, H. R., *W. S.* (1966); Angoff, C., *The Tone of the Twenties and Other Essays* (1967), pp. 203–08

                                HOWARD R. FLOAN

SARRAUTE, Nathalie
French novelist, b. 18 July 1902, Ivanovo-Vosnesensk, Russia

Since she came to France at the age of three, French was the first language that Nathalie S. learned, but Russian and English were also spoken in her home. At the Sorbonne, she took *licenses* in English and in law. In the early

1920's Nathalie S. spent a year at Oxford and another at the University of Berlin studying literature. Until 1939 she practiced law.

Tropismes (1938; Tropisms, 1964), her first book, was begun in 1932. In it her distinctive mode of psychological fiction is already apparent as she offers a series of detailed studies of middle-class behavior. Tropisms, she has explained, are "the things which are not said and the movements which cross the consciousness very rapidly, and which are the basis of most of our life and of our relations with others—everything that happens within us which is not spoken by the interior monologue and which is transmitted by sensations."

When Nathalie S. returned to writing after the rigors of raising a family during World War II, she examined the problems of contemporary fiction in a series of essays collected as *L'Ère de Soupçon* (1956; An Age of Suspicion, 1964). Widely misunderstood, these essays affirm her admiration for the psychological novel; her own novels are built on psychological nuance and what she calls "subconversation," or unspoken thoughts that exist at the threshold of verbalization.

Portrait d'un inconnu (1947; The Portrait of a Man Unknown, 1958), called an "antinovel" by Sartre (q.v.) in his preface, deals with a father and daughter relationship that recalls Honoré de Balzac's (1799–1850) *Eugénie Grandet*. The daughter's request for money becomes a climactic incident in a suffocating world. Though father and daughter fling murderous taunts at each other, violence eventually fades into habitual gesture and mechanical phrase; the novel's narrator remains haunted by the "unknown" father and daughter. "If one described avarice...as Balzac did, it would appear simple, primitive, even infantile," Nathalie S. noted in an interview. "One can no longer describe everything. ...One can't convey the entire human being and everything he includes...what happens within a miser bears no relation to what one thinks of as avarice."

The protagonist of *Martereau* (1953; Eng., 1958) is similarly unknown and unknowable to the narrator. Plain, solid, a man with business experience, Martereau buys a villa for the narrator's uncle, delivers no receipt for the money, and moves into the villa. The narrator imagines or hears monologues and subconversations that reveal Martereau's dishonesty. Finally, however, Martereau sends the receipt, leaves the villa to its owners, and

expresses himself in bourgeois platitudes; Martereau as a thief may exist only in the narrator's imagination.

In Nathalie S.'s next two novels—*Le Planétarium* (1959; The Planetarium, 1962) and *Les Fruits d'or* (1963; Golden Fruits, 1965)—the narrator has been eliminated. Centered in the Paris literary world, both novels consist of dialogues and subconversations. In the first, Nathalie S. offers a study of "literary astronomy" in which satellites are seen to revolve about a woman novelist who figures as the sun. *Les Fruits d'or*, like Gide's (q.v.) *Les Faux-monnayeurs*, is a novel about a novel. Through conversations and subconversations we follow from its first publication to its virtual disappearance from the literary scene the fate of a book called *Les Fruits d'or*.

More and more adroitly in each work, Nathalie S. delineates unspoken thoughts grounded in platitude and insecurity but revealing a hidden truth. In her own words, "What is a work of art if not a break through appearances toward an unknown reality?"

FURTHER WORK: *Entre la Vie et la mort* (1968; Between Life and Death, 1969)

BIBLIOGRAPHY: Cohn, R., "N. S.'s Subconsciousversations" *MLN*, LXXVIII, 261–70; Matthews, J. H., "N. S.: An Approach to the Novel," *MFS*, VI, 337–45; Roudiez, L. S., "A Glance at the Vocabulary of N. S.," *YFS*, No. 27, pp. 90–98; Weightman, J. G., "N. S.," *Encounter*, XXII (June 1964), vi, 36–43

RUBY COHN

SARTRE, Jean-Paul

French philosopher, dramatist, novelist, and essayist, b. 21 June 1905, Paris

The greatest influence on S.'s boyhood was his Alsatian grandfather, Charles Schweitzer (an uncle of Albert Schweitzer), with whom S. and his mother lived in Paris after his father's early death. When S.'s mother remarried in 1916, the family moved to La Rochelle. S. later studied at the *lycées* Henri IV and Louis-le-Grand in Paris and obtained the "agrégation de philosophie" at the École Normale Supérieure, where in 1929 he met Simone de Beauvoir (q.v.), with whom he formed an enduring liaison.

After teaching philosophy in Le Havre from 1931 to 1933, the following year S. studied the writings of the German philosophers Edmund

Husserl (1859–1938) and Martin Heidegger (b. 1889) in Berlin. From 1934 to 1939, S. taught at Le Havre, Laon, and Neuilly. He was taken prisoner by the Germans in June 1940 and liberated in 1941. After teaching in Paris until 1945, he founded the magazine *Les Temps Modernes* and gave up teaching entirely.

By that time, S.'s "existentialist" philosophy had won world-wide acclaim, especially among the young (*see* existentialism). Active in the Resistance during the German occupation, S. has since then been "committed to his time," as he said in a manifesto for *Les Temps Modernes,* taking strong stands against the French policies in Indo-China and Algeria, the Russian invasions of Hungary in 1956 and of Czechoslovakia in 1968, and the American involvement in Vietnam. He was awarded, but refused, the Nobel Prize for Literature in 1964.

S.'s largely autobiographical first novel, *La Nausée* (1938; Am., Nausea, 1949; Eng., Diary of Antoine Roquentin, 1949), shows the influence of Husserl's phenomenology and Heidegger's existential philosophy. It describes Roquentin's growing awareness of the purposelessness of the physical world and of his own existence, his discovery of the obscene overabundance of the world around him. Roquentin's perception of his own gratuitousness and solitude merely induces several experiences of psychological nausea, and he is unable to use this revelation effectively.

The stories in *Le Mur* (1939; The Wall, and Other Stories, 1948) are studies in "bad faith," or inauthenticity, of people unwilling to recognize that the absurdity of life imposes on them complete responsibility for what they do and what they become. All the characters take refuge in some value outside of their own consciousness.

In his first play, *Les Mouches* (1942; The Flies, 1947), S. was able to discuss the values of resistance under the very noses of the German occupiers by selecting ancient Argos as the scene of his dramatic action. Here S.'s emphasis is on commitment and responsibility to others as well as to oneself. After the murder of Agamemnon, the people of Argos are visited by a plague of flies—S.'s version of the Eumenides—a symbol of their guilty torments over their complicity in the king's death. Freely taking upon himself responsibility for avenging his father, Orestes murders Aegisthus and Clytemnestra, thus liberating the people of the city from the burden of guilt that has kept them in submission to both Jupiter and the usurpers

of Agamemnon's throne. Electra, after urging her brother to this double murder, shrinks from sharing responsibility for the deed and remains within the protection of Jupiter's temple. Orestes leaves, pursued by the flies, that now abandon Argos.

The most influential literary figure in post-Liberation France, S. offered in his second play, *Huis-Clos* (1944; No Exit, 1947), a powerfully concentrated dramatization of the tenets of existentialism. Choosing an imaginatively conceived contemporary notion of Hell as his setting, he analyzed the bad faith of a trio—a collaborationist, a lesbian, and a nymphomaniac—who after their deaths are forced to "live" their inauthenticity throughout eternity. Confined to a small, ugly room beyond which they fear to venture, they attempt to justify their behavior on earth while they tensely await the demonic torturers. Gradually they come to realize that each, through his unwillingness or inability to satisfy the expectations of the others, has been assigned to torture his companions by his presence. "Hell is other people," we are told.

S.'s next play, *Morts sans sépulture* (1946; Am., The Victors, 1949; Eng., Men without Shadows, 1949), explored the existential situation of a group of resistance fighters captured and tortured by the collaborationist *miliciens*. *La Putain respectueuse* (1946; Am., The Respectful Prostitute, 1949; Eng., The Respectable Prostitute, 1949) is a dramatic cartoon exploring racial tensions in the American South. Molested by a white man of good family, Lizzy is prevailed upon by an adroit manipulation of her "respectful" adherence to the pieties and patriotism of a society from which she herself is excluded to identify an innocent Negro as her attacker.

S.'s earlier ontological study *L'Être et le néant* (1943; Being and Nothingness, 1956) had presented the philosophical basis for these literary works. "Being" is the objective world of things (being-in-itself), which exists independently of human consciousness. The discovery of this undifferentiated matter produced Roquentin's "nausea." But consciousness must be consciousness of its distinction from things (being-for-itself) and consciousness of something to the exclusion of all else. This "else" becomes S.'s "nothingness" in relation to our consciousness.

In other words, man must detach himself from things to give them meaning. The fact that neither the objective world nor human existence has any meaning in itself is the freedom given everyone to "become," since he "is" nothing. Only one who chooses to assume the responsibility of acting in a particular situation, like Orestes, makes effective use of his freedom. Most people prefer to "be" what someone else (like the others in *Huis-Clos*) has chosen for them and are therefore merely "things."

This is the meaning of the famous phrase "existence precedes essence" from *L'Existentialisme est un humanisme* (1946; Existentialism, 1947); *i.e.,* that man "exists" first, then must make an authentic, "free" choice, "en situation," thereby defining himself by *his* act.

S. explored these ideas in a still-uncompleted tetralogy of novels entitled *Les Chemins de la liberté. L'Age de raison* (1945; The Age of Reason, 1947) describes the paralysis of French intellectuals in the 1930's, as Mathieu Delarue, a young philosophy professor, is unable to assume his responsibility either to his pregnant mistress or to the Spanish Loyalists, whose cause he supports.

In *Le Sursis* (1945; The Reprieve, 1947), S. focuses on the appeasement pact negotiated with Hitler in September 1938 by the leaders of England and France. The action, which covers less than a week, moves without transition—often in the middle of a sentence—among several groups of characters in various parts of the world. The close integration of the private concerns of the protagonists with the public concerns of world leaders points to collective responsibility for the pact.

In *La Mort dans l'âme* (1949; Am., Troubled Sleep, 1951; Eng., Iron in the Soul, 1950), Mathieu finally redeems all his weaknesses and frees himself from the past by making the positive gesture of firing on the advancing German troops in 1940 just before he is killed by them. S.'s plans for a final volume to be entitled *La Dernière Chance* seem to have been abandoned.

In *Baudelaire* (1947; Eng., 1950), an essay in existential psychoanalysis, S. attempts to show that the poet—Charles Baudelaire (1821–67)—despite his creative genius, chose to accept the definition of himself imposed by the world around him. S.'s own view of the relationship between the writer, his work, and society is outlined in *Qu'est-ce que la littérature?* (1947; What is Literature? 1949). (It was later included in *Situations II* (1948), the second volume of a continuing series of literary and philosophical essays.) For S., literature must be

totally concerned with the problems of the writer's own time, and writing is a form of commitment in the practical world.

Les Mains sales (1948; Dirty Hands, 1949) stresses the practical necessity for commitment even though the choice is ambiguous. Hoederer, a communist leader, chooses in this play to "dirty" his hands in political action despite his disagreement on some points with his party's policies. Hugo, the young bourgeois intellectual, is unwilling, on the other hand, to make a commitment that may compromise the "principles" of the party he has adopted.

In *Le Diable et le bon Dieu* (1951; Am., The Devil and the Good Lord, 1960; Eng., Lucifer and the Lord, 1953), a drama set in Reformation Germany, the problem of commitment reaches an impasse. Though Goetz, a man of action, finds that it is impossible to do either absolute evil or absolute good, he is finally persuaded to take practical action in the peasants' revolt. However, Heinrich, a man of the Church, is unable to choose either the Church, which has abandoned the poor, or the poor, who have abandoned the Church.

S.'s last important play is *Les Séquestrés d'Altona* (1960; Am., The Condemned of Altona, 1961; Eng., Loser Wins, 1961), in which Franz, unable to find "law" in his father or in the postwar society of Germany, retreats into madness rather than assume the responsibility for his war crimes. But S. is really concerned here with the ambiguous problem of guilt for French atrocities in Algeria, which was his primary preoccupation in the late 1950's, and with the more general problem of the individual's entanglements with history and collective political policy.

The difficulty of effective independent action had been anticipated by S.'s own abortive attempt to form a noncommunist leftist political party in 1948. It led to his collaboration with the French Communist Party in hopes of helping the working classes. After Camus (q.v.) published *L'Homme révolté* (1951), S. broke with him because he saw the book as an attack on his own growing tendency to act with reference only to the immediate historical context.

This evolution of S.'s thought is also evident in his long essay *Saint-Genet, comédien et martyr* (1952; Saint Genet, 1963), a brilliant analysis of Genet's (q.v.) novels and plays. S. sees Genet as conditioned by society to be a criminal, totally accepting this conditioning to evil and making himself a poet within

JEAN-PAUL SARTRE

the limits of the framework established. S. does not condemn Genet, as he had Baudelaire, but rather praises him for taking "certain routes which were not initially given."

The limitation of freedom is one aspect of *Critique de la raison dialectique, 1: Théorie des ensembles pratiques* (1960; Am., Search for a Method, 1963; Eng., Problems of Method, 1964), in which man is seen as at least partially conditioned by societal and historical factors. By combining this view with the somewhat contradictory insights in *L'Être et le néant,* he attempts to forge a new collective human ethic based on the interaction of existentialist and Marxist philosophies.

In his autobiography *Les Mots* (1964; The Words, 1964), S. satirizes the conscious and unconscious bad faith of his own childhood and affirms that his previous desire, as a bourgeois intellectual, to achieve salvation through his writing has been at least partially replaced by his current involvement with social and political concerns.

In 1966, S. published in *Les Temps Modernes* a long study on Gustave Flaubert (1821–80), a writer whose conception of literature and view of society were almost the opposite of his own. S. uses the huge amount of material available on Flaubert to show the encounter between the development of the person (the *"lived* experience") and the development of history—in other words, Flaubert's ironic reaction to the bourgeois world within which he operated.

This study is a practical application and further development of the interaction of individual and collective values presented in the first part of *Critique de la raison dialectique.* Some critics consider it a transition to the still-unpublished second volume of the *critique,* which will presumably place even greater emphasis on the historical conditioning —or "totalization"—of individual action. In this sense, it has a function similar to the study on Genet in the evolution of S.'s philosophy from its phenomenological beginnings through an emphasis on total individual responsibility to his present preoccupation with collective realities.

Through the variety and pertinence of his literary and philosophic writings, S. is probably the single most important figure in mid-20th-c. French literature. He captured the French sense of despair during the German occupation, yet insisted on man's freedom to go beyond despair in creative action.

The active conscience of an entire generation, S. has played a leading role in the political, social, and intellectual life of his country and the world, supporting many writers and taking vigorous stands on a variety of causes. His early phenomenology has influenced the later so-called new novels, and his remarkable lucidity has allowed his philosophical position to evolve to meet the changing demands of the contemporary world as he sees it.

FURTHER WORKS: *La Transcendance de l'égo: Esquisse d'une description phénoménologique* (1936; The Transcendence of the Ego, 1957); *L'Imagination: étude critique* (1936; Imagination: A Psychological Critique, 1962); *Esquisse d'une théorie des émotions* (1939; Am., Outline of a Theory of the Emotions, 1948; Eng., Sketch of a Theory of the Emotions, 1962); *L'Imaginaire: Psychologie phénoménologique de l'imagination* (1940; The Psychology of Imagination, 1949); *Réflexions sur la question juive* (1946; Am., Anti-Semite and Jew, 1948; Eng., Portrait of the Anti-Semite, 1948); *Les Jeux sont faits* (1947; The Chips Are Down, 1951); *Situations I* (1947; Literary and Philosophical Essays, 1955); *Théâtre* (1947); *L'Engrenage* (1948; In the Mesh, 1954); *Visages* (1948); *Entretiens sur la politique* (1949); *Situations III* (1949; Literary and Philosophical Essays, 1955); *L'Affaire Henri Martin: Commentaire* (1953); *Kean, ou Désordre et génie* (1954; Kean, or Disorder and Genius, 1954); *Nekrassov* (1956; Nekrassov, 1956); *Voyage à Cuba* (1960; Sartre on Cuba, 1961); *Théâtre* (1962); *Situations IV: Littérature et peinture* (1964; Situations, 1965); *Situations V: Colonialisme et néo-colonialisme* (1964); *Situations VI: Problèmes du marxisme 1* (1964; The Communists and Peace, 1968); *Les Troyennes* (1965); *Œuvres romanesques* (5 vols., 1965); *Situations VII: Problèmes du marxisme 2* (1965; The Ghost of Stalin, 1968); *Que peut la littérature* (1965); *Le Génocide* (1967; On Genocide, 1968); *Les Communistes ont peur de la révolution* (1969)

BIBLIOGRAPHY: Campbell, R., *S., ou une littérature philosophique* (1945); Jeanson, F., *Le problème moral et la pensée de S.* (1947); Murdoch, I., *S., Romantic Rationalist* (1953); Champigny, R., *Stages on S.'s Way, 1938–1952* (1959); Thody, P., *J.-P. S: A Literary and Political Study* (1960); Albérès, R.-M., *J.-P. S., Philosopher without Faith* (1961); Jameson, F., *S.: The Origins of a Style* (1961); Salvan, J. L., *To Be and Not To Be: An Analysis of*

J.-P. S.'s Ontology (1962); Desan, W., The Marxism of J.-P. S. (1965); Fell, J. P., Emotion in the Thought of S. (1965); Manser, A. R., S.: A Philosophic Study (1966); Barnes, H., An Existentialist Ethics (1967); Stern, A. S.: His Philosophy and Existential Psychoanalysis (1967); Prince, G. J., Métaphysique et technique dans l'œuvre romanesque de S. (1968); Sheridan, J. R., Jr., S., The Radical Conservative (1969)

CHARLES G. HILL

Any worthwhile thought implies that it will be surpassed, and one cannot go beyond the thought without at least partially refusing to accept it. But not to accept is not necessarily to refute. There are degrees of refusal, from simply insisting on preserving one's own freedom of judgment to wishing to combat one thought with another. S. gives us a means of understanding human reality which is fully satisfying. One can't deny that this method opens up dangerous perspectives; the moral undertaking which everyone is called upon to engage in on his own responsibility is—as Plato suggested —a "fine risk." And it is doubtless impossible to run such a risk without committing others, to some degree, to the consequences of an adventure which cannot remain strictly personal.

Francis Jeanson, Le Problème moral et la pensée de S. (1947), p. 293

[S.] is a thinker who stands full in the way of three post-Hegelian movements of thought: the Marxist, the existentialist and the phenomenological. He has felt the impact of each and has brought to each his own modifications. He uses the analytical tools of the Marxists and shares their urgent passion for action, but without accepting a theological view of the Dialectic. He remains at heart a liberal social democrat. He takes from Kierkegaard the picture of a man as a lonely anguished being in an ambiguous world, but he rejects the hidden Kierkegaardian God. He uses the methods and terminology of Husserl but lacks Husserl's dogmatism and his Platonic aspirations. In philosophy his attempts to define "human reality" take the form of extensive and subtle descriptions. These descriptions imply and depend upon a picture of "consciousness" wherein a Husserlian and Hegelian vocabulary combines with psychological insights suggested by Freud.

Iris Murdoch, S., Romantic Rationalist (1953), p. vii

In his insistence that man must always be responsible for what he becomes, and that he can never legitimately claim to be better than his acts, S. is laying the foundation for an extremely healthy approach to personal morality. He does away

with all alibis and excuses and makes each person look his own failures straight in the eye. His arguments depend, it is true, on an assertion that free will exists rather than on a convincing refutation of the arguments for determinism, but like all "libertarian" approaches it is a very healthy one. The nihilism which it fails to transcend is perhaps the inevitable darker side of a theory which also does away with all fixed values and shows man his complete and terrifying freedom. The challenge to try to go beyond this nihilism is in itself perhaps the most stimulating part of S.'s moral philosophy.

Philip Thody, J.-P. S. (1960), p. 236

Because S. does not describe any situation from an absolute perspective, he rejects the concept of the omniscient novelist and adopts in all his novels the characters' points of view, which are "in situation," relative, changing. And in presenting his universe from various vantage points, he moves constantly from the exterior to the interior, from the objective to the subjective, thus emphasizing the alienation of the self inherent in the consciousness and instability of that universe. In order not to vitiate the duration and therefore the freedom of his characters, he does not cut off their conversations but presents them in their babbling and revealing entirety. S. substitutes for the traditional causal relationships aesthetic ones based on fictional combinations, in order to emphasize the contingency of events and to preserve the essential freedom of the characters.

Gerald Joseph Prince, Métaphysique et technique dans l'œuvre romanesque de S. (1968), pp. [137]–138

SAUSER-HALL, Frédérick
See Cendrars, Blaise

SAYERS, Dorothy
English poet, novelist, essayist, and translator, b. 13 June 1893, Oxford; d. 17 Dec. 1957, Witham, Essex

Dorothy S. studied French literature at Oxford University. Her first published work was a book of poems (Opus I, 1916).

In 1923 she began to publish the detective novels centered on her aristocratic amateur detective, Lord Peter Wimsey. In the early novels Lord Peter was developed as what the British call a "silly ass" character, in the tradition of Wodehouse (q.v.), but he was later developed both artistically and seriously until he became a romantic and intellectual hero. The settings are ingenious and accurate. The best of them are: *Murder Must Advertise* (1933), whose action takes place in a big advertising firm; *The Nine Tailors* (1934), which resolves an intricate problem of campanology in East Anglia; and, above all, *Gaudy Night* (1935), a mystery of true excellence, which is set in an imaginary Oxford college for women, as well as one of the best novels ever written about Oxford.

Dorothy S. turned at this point to the consideration of a subject of great interest to her—theology from the Anglican viewpoint. She may here be approximately linked with Eliot, C. S. Lewis (qq.v.), and Charles Williams (q.v.), whose writings on Dante she often referred to; but she herself disclaimed any connection with a "school" of Anglican writers and denied being influenced by others.

Dorothy S.'s first venture in the area of religious drama were her plays for the Festival at Canterbury (*e.g., The Zeal of Thy House,* 1937). Her most famous and popular work of this kind was undoubtedly the series of plays for radio (performed many times on the BBC) on the life of Jesus Christ, called *The Man Born to Be King: Play Cycle on the Life of Christ* (1941). With a distinguished cast speaking the colloquial dialogue these plays presented a moving and graphic version of the New Testament story.

Dorothy S. also wrote essays on theological themes. Her most notable example of this kind is her book *The Mind of the Maker* (1941), which is a well-written and ably argued examination of the creative activity of the artist in terms of divine creation.

In the last decade of her life Dorothy S. devoted herself to the study of Dante. She published a book of critical papers, *Introductory Papers on Dante* (1954), which earned mixed but stimulating reviews; translations in *terza rima* of the *Inferno* and the *Purgatorio*; and *Further Papers on Dante* (1957).

FURTHER WORKS: *Whose Body?* (1923); *Clouds of Witness* (1926); *Unnatural Death* (1927); *The Unpleasantness at the Bellona Club* (1928); *Lord Peter Views the Body* (1928); *The Documents in the Case* (1930); *Strong Poison* (1930); *The Five Red Herrings* (1931); *Have His Carcase* (1932); *Hangman's Holiday* (1933); *Busman's Honeymoon* (1936); *In the Teeth of the Evidence* (1939); *The Devil to Pay* (1939); *Love All* (1940); *Begin Here* (1940); *Even the Parrot: Exemplary Conversations of Enlightened Children* (1944); *Unpopular*

Opinions (1946). *The Just Vengeance* (1946); *Creed or Chaos?* (1947); *The Lost Tools of Learning* (1948); *Where Do We Go from Here?* (1948); *The Emperor Constantine* (1957); *The Poetry of Search and the Poetry of Statement* (1963)

BIBLIOGRAPHY: Zimmermann, L., *Das religiöse Schrifttum D. S.* (1948); Wölcken, F., *Der literarische Mord* (1953); *TLS*, 13 Sept. 1963, p. 690; Burleson, J., "A Study of the Novels of D. L. S.," *DA*, XXVI (1965), 2204
MARYVONNE BUTCHER

SCHALLÜCK, Paul

German novelist and television and radio writer, b. 17 June 1922, Warendorf, Westphalia

The son of a Russian mother and a German father, S. originally intended to become a Catholic missionary, but the experience of captivity during World War II caused him to alter his plans. After the war he studied widely in the humanities. Joining the writers known as Gruppe 47, he started writing radio and television plays, essays, and novels.

S.'s reputation was established with his first novel, *Wenn man aufhören könnte zu lügen* (1951), which deals with the problems of postwar youth, torn between cynical hedonism and the need to establish new values. In subsequent novels S. experimented with narratives projected against kaleidoscopic backgrounds of a society in transition. *Ankunft null Uhr zwölf* (1953) makes use of flashbacks, dialogue, and stream-of-consciousness techniques to create a simultaneous portrait of several members of a family. *Die unsichtbare Pforte* (1954) is a far more tightly knit account of the Kafkaesque intricacies of a drug addict's cure.

Engelbert Reinecke (1959)—significantly subtitled "the forgotten guilt"—forcefully depicts the efforts of a young teacher, who returned to his home town after the war, to come to terms with his unassimilated past by exploring the motives of his guilty or indifferent colleagues who remained at home. A volume of short stories, *Lakrizza* (1966; Eng., 1969), shows S.'s mastery of this medium in satirical yet warmhearted sketches that give evidence of a keen sense of humor.

Don Quichotte in Köln (Part I, 1968) is S.'s most ambitious work to date. In it he breaks with traditional straight narrative and interweaves his text with dramatic and lyrical episodes. The result is an unorthodox, psychologically and intellectually stimulating tale of a sensitive and confused modern knight-errant on his quest for truth. Bigotry and mindless success-hunting are the main targets of S.'s biting humor.

In 1966, S. edited a special issue of *Dokumente* (Eng., 1970) devoted to German letters, arts, and theater. An incisive essayist, he is an articulate spokesman for Franco-German understanding. One of the few postwar German writers to be invited to Israel, S. has insisted in his writings on the necessity for reconciliation between Jews and Germany.

S.'s novels have shown his contemporaries as a generation, marked by the death and destruction of the war, that is struggling to understand the present so that it can successfully shape the future. He insists that his countrymen must come to terms with the unresolved (*unbewältigte*) past of the Nazi era and this theme was probably most successfully presented in *Engelbert Reinecke*.

FURTHER WORKS: *Gericht über Kain* (radio play, 1949); *Vom Dynamit zum Friedenspreis* (radio play, 1952); *Armer schwarzer Teufel* (radio play, 1953); *Angst vor dem Happy End?* (radio play, 1953); *Unsichtbar* (radio play, 1954); *Keiner ist verloren* (radio play, 1955); *Das wildgewordene Saxophon* (radio play, 1955); *Schleuder und Harfe* (radio play, 1955); *Weiße Fahnen im April* (1955); *Q 3 und die Hohe Straße* (1956); *Köln—alte, heilige und schöne Dinge* (radio play, 1956); *Der Türmer von Sankt Lamberti* (radio play, 1956); *William Faulkner* (television script, 1957); *Ich und Du, Martin Buber* (television script, 1957); *Der Schmerz und die Schönheit, Albert Camus* (television script, 1960); *Sie nahmen ihn nicht auf* (radio play, 1960); *Großer Baum der Sprache, St. John Perse* (television script, 1960); *Nächtliche Gespräche* (radio dialogue, 1961); *Hand und Name* (Israel travelogue, 1962); *Harlekin hinter Gittern* (radio play, 1962); *Zum Beispiel* (1962); *Prager Etüden* (television script, 1962); *Wie werde ich ein Snob?* (radio play, 1963); *Rückkehr der Götter* (radio play, 1964); *Sehnsucht, mein geliebtes Kind* (radio play, 1964); *Der grüne Daumen, Peter Suhrkamp* (television script, 1965); *Kölner Exodus* (radio play, 1965); *Provinz in der Großstadt* (radio play, 1965); *Jesse Thoor* (radio play, 1965); *Porträt V. O. Stomps* (television script, 1966); *Abschied von Bremen* (1965); *Die Hand* (1966); *Nachts im Kloster* (1966); *Auf eigenen*

Füßen (1966); *Viola Gregg Liuzzo* (radio play, 1966), *Franz Oppenhoff* (radio play, 1966); *Helmut Hübner* (radio play, 1966); *Krum Hörn* (radio play, 1967); *Orden* (1967); *Heimat, Satire und Pferdeäpfel* (1967); *Gesichter* (literary collages, 1968); *Pipo oder Panik in Planstelle O* (radio play, 1968); *Rund um den Ochsenkopf* (television play, 1968); *81 Jahre im Innern der Erde* (radio play, 1969); *Karlsbader Ponys* (1968); *. . . .bis daß der Tod euch scheidet* (satire, 1970); *Der Mann aus Casablanca* (television play, 1970); *Beim Metzger* (television play, 1970); *Unter Ausschluß der Öffentlichkeit* (television play, 1970); *Bekenntnisse eines Nestbeschmutzers* (1970)

BIBLIOGRAPHY: Uhlig, H., "Ein junger deutscher Erzähler," *Der Monat*, 1955; Lennartz, F., in *Deutsche Dichter und Schriftsteller unserer Zeit* (1959); Glaser, F., in *Wege der Literatur* (1963); Görtz, W., in *Schriftsteller der Gegenwart* (1963); Rehn, J., in *Das neue Bestiarium der deutschen Literatur* (1963); Erné, N., in *Handbuch der deutschen Gegenwartsliteratur* (1965); Kosch, W., in *Deutsches Literatur-Lexikon* (1965); Cluytmans, J., *P. S.*, Dissertation, Ghent, 1967; Krohn, P. C., in *Lexikon deutschsprachiger Schriftsteller* (1967); Rübenach, L., *P. S.*, Dissertation, Rostock, 1968

KONRAD BIEBER

SCHAPER, Edzard Hellmuth

German novelist, b. 30 Sept. 1908, Ostrowo, Poland (formerly Germany)

S. studied music, tried his hand at acting, and at nineteen published his first novel, *Der letzte Gast* (1927). After working as a gardener and then as a sailor on an Arctic fishing smack, in 1930 he settled in Reval, Estonia, as a correspondent for the United Press. His thorough knowledge of Baltic civilization was to be reflected in many of his books.

When the Russians invaded Estonia in 1940, S. was condemned to death, *in absentia,* by both the communists and the Nazis. He had fled to Finland, escaping to Sweden in 1944 as the Soviet army advanced into Finland. After the war he resettled in Brieg, in the German-speaking part of Switzerland.

S. was raised as a Protestant, but during his youth he was attracted to Russian Orthodoxy. His later studies of its teachings gave him an insight into the Slavic soul equaled by no previous non-Russian writer. At forty-three he converted to Catholicism, and his intimate knowledge of the three main branches of Christianity—the determining influence in his life—is reflected in his novels and novellas.

S.'s ten years in Reval were a crucial factor in his ability to depict the Estonian peasantry caught in the conflict between East and West and fighting to maintain a national identity under the successive domination by powerful nations. His novel *Die sterbende Kirche* (1935) is set near the Russian border during the time between the two world wars. In this work, whose vigorous characterizations won it considerable recognition, a small Estonian Orthodox congregation is shown in a life-and-death struggle with communism. *Der Henker* (1940) is the story of a German-Baltic nobleman, a czarist officer, who is torn between duty and his conscience when the Estonian peasants rise against Russian oppression in 1905–1906. In *Der Gouverneur* (1954), the "governor" is a Swede who tries in vain to keep Estonia, then a Swedish dominion, from being taken over by Russia at the beginning of the 18th c. In this complex political tug of war the governor attempts to maintain a balance between law and mercy, love and guilt.

S.'s later novels are set during the Thirty Years' War, the Napoleonic wars, in the period of Finland's heroic struggle against Russia, and the time of the clash between the German and Soviet armies. However, the problems he examines focus on essentially timeless conflicts of conscience in the battle for religious or political freedom. In *Hinter den Linien* (1952), a Western spy encounters primitive Christianity in a Russian concentration camp in north Finland.

More recent novellas such as *Unschuld der Sünde* (1957) and *Geisterbahn* (1959) deal with contemporary problems and show an increase in subtlety over his earlier work.

S. has also written radio plays—*Der Gefangene der Botschaft* (1965), *Das Feuer Christi* (1965), and *Wagnis der Gegenwart* (1966)—and published translations of Lagerkvist, Sillanpää, Gunnarsson, Munk (qq.v.), Sally Salminen (b. 1906), and others.

FURTHER WORKS: *Die Bekenntnisse des Försters Patrick Doyle* (1928); *Erde über dem Meer* (1934); *Die Insel Tütarsaar* (1934); *Die Arche, die Schiffbruch erlitt* (1935); *Das Leben Jesu* (1936); *Das Lied der Väter* (1937); *Der große, offenbare Tag* (1949); *Der letzte Advent* (1949); *Die Freiheit des Gefangenen* (1950); *Die Macht der Ohnmächtigen* (1951); *Stern über der Grenze* (1951; Star over the Frontier, 1961); *Der Mensch in der Zelle* (1951); *Finnisches Tagebuch* (1951); *Norwegische Reise* (1951); *Vom Sinn des Alters* (1952); *Untergang und Verwandlung* (1952); *Der Mantel der Barmherzigkeit* (1953); *Um die neunte Stunde* (1953); *Bürger in Zeit und Ewigkeit* (1956); *Erkundungen in Gestern und Morgen* (1956); *Die letzte Welt* (1956); *Attentat auf den Mächtigen* (1957); *Die Eidgenossen des Sommers* (1958); *Das Tier* (1958; The Dancing Bear, 1961); *Der Held: Weg und Wahn Karls XII* (1958); *Der vierte König* (1961); *Macht der Freiheit* (1961); *Die Söhne Hiobs* (1962); *Unser Vater Malchus* (1962); *Dragonergeschichte* (1962); *Aufruhr der Gerechten* (1963); *Gesammelte Erzählungen* (1966); *Schattengericht* (1967); *Die Heimat der Verbannten* (1968)

BIBLIOGRAPHY: On *Die Freiheit des Gefangenen*—Aichinger, I., *Welt und Wort* (1950); On *Der Mensch in der Zelle*—Großrieder, H., *Welt und Wort* (1953); Krömler, H., "E. S.s Christliches Werk," *Schweizer Rundschau* (1954); Uhlig, H., "E. S.," in *Christliche Dichter der Gegenwart*, eds. H. Freedmann and O. Mann (1957); On *Der vierte König*—Beckmann, H., *NDH* (1962); Krolow, K., "E. S.: Gesammelte Erzählungen," *Merkur* (1966); On *Die Heimat der Verbannten*—Baldus, A., *Welt und Wort* (1969)

GERTRUDE C. SCHWEBELL

SCHEHADÉ, Georges

Lebanese poet and dramatist (writing in French), b. 2 Nov. 1910, Alexandria, Egypt

S. comes from a French-speaking Lebanese family residing in Beirut, and neither his ethnic origins nor extended contacts with other cultures have diverted his literary orientations, which remain basically French.

Though S.'s early poetic works attracted little attention from either the critics or the general public, they were acclaimed by a small but determined group of enthusiasts. It was only with his plays that S. reached a wider audience and established himself in the forefront of the modern poetic theater. However, the switch in genres brought little change to the inner landscape of S.'s work.

S. is a verbal magician who adroitly exploits the evocative powers of words by employing startlingly kaleidoscopic images drawn from the realm of the familiar. His poetry lures the reader into an enchanted land in which men converse with animals, and ambulant trees talk. But S. often sounds a dissonant note with comic ironies, ambiguities, and eccentricities. This land of beauty and happiness also nurtures the desire for escape and adventure. Absence and voyage, imagined and real, therefore become characteristic themes of S.'s work.

S.'s first play, *Monsieur Bob'le* (1951), was coldly received by the critics. Few found the allusive language, the loosely constructed plot, and the absence of psychologically well-delineated characters to their liking. Monsieur Bob'le is a kind of prophet and sage whose personality has an illuminating and purifying effect on the inhabitants of his village. Although loved and admired, for financial reasons he decides to leave. He returns to die in misery and defeat, but his gentle influence has transformed all who have come into contact with him.

The inherent pacifism and antimilitarism of *Histoire de Vasco* (1957; Vasco, 1964), first produced during the French-Algerian War, aroused partisan passions. Vasco, a gentle barber, is tricked into accepting a dangerous mission in a seemingly comic opera war. As the play unfolds, the initial farcical situation assumes tragic and universal dimensions. Incapable of recognizing evil and malevolence in his fellow man, the simple-hearted hero is betrayed by his own naïveté.

Les Violettes (1960) is a satirical fantasy on modern intellectuals and scientists. Behind the light anecdotal story, set in a respectable, middle-class boardinghouse that is later turned into an atomic power plant, lurks S.'s nightmarish vision of the effects of modern technocracy.

With *Le Voyage* (1961) and *L'Émigré de Brisbane* (1965), subjects of immediate social and political import give way to a meditation on the interplay between presence and absence. *Le Voyage* deals with an imagined adventure and its effect on a dreamer who longs for faraway places and sea voyages. In *L'Émigré de Brisbane* the presence of a mysterious dead man precipitates a bitterly ironic tragedy in an Italian village.

Though the admixture of paradox and parody, farce and grotesqueness, varies, the poetic character of S.'s plays remains constant. He continuously enchants the spectator by his facility in bringing out subtle tonal harmonies, in evoking lyrical moods through sensitive imagery and symbolism, and in the use of metaphors that have an undefinable, unspoiled quality.

FURTHER WORKS: *Étincelles* (1928); *Poésies* (1938); *Rodogune Sinne* (1947); *Poésies II* (1948); *Poésies III* (1949); *L'Écolier Sultan* (1950); *Si Tu rencontres un ramier* (1951); *Les Poésies* (1952); *La Soirée des proverbes* (1954); *L'Habit fait le prince* (1958)

BIBLIOGRAPHY: Special S. issues, *Cahiers de la Compagnie Renaud-Barrault*, No. 4 (1954), No. 17 (1957), and N. 34 (1961); Pronko, L., "Poetry and Purity: The Theater of G. S.," *FR*, XXXI (1958), 378–86; Knapp, B., "G. S.: 'He who dreams diffuses into air. . . ,'" *YFS*, XXIX (1962), 108–15; Richard, J.-P., *Onze Études sur la poésie moderne* (1964); Silenieks, J., "G. S.: The Transfiguration of a Poetic Theater," *MD*, X (Sept. 1967), 151–60

JURIS SILENIEKS

SCHENDEL, Arthur van

Dutch novelist, b. 5 March 1874, Batavia; d. 11 Sept. 1946, Amsterdam

For several years S. was a teacher in England and the Netherlands; after 1920 he lived for the most part in Italy.

S.'s orientation shifted from neoromanticism, to somber realism, and finally to skepticism. However, in one guise or another he always remained a romantic, and as such he generally described not objective reality but an imagined reality that seemed sometimes to be longed for and sometimes to be dreaded.

Initially, S. wrote romantic love stories, such as *Een zwerver verliefd* (1904) and its sequel *Een zwerver verdwaald* (1907), which were often set in the Middle Ages. After he settled in Italy, he began employing Italian cities and the Renaissance as a background in novels that included *Der liefde bloesems* (1921), *Rose Angélique* (1922), and *Angiolino en de lente* (1923).

A second period in S.'s creative life began with a series of far more realistic works that were tied to the society and daily life of 19th-c. Holland. The first of these novels was *Het fregatschip Johanna Maria* (1930; The Johanna Maria, 1935), the story of a Dutch seaman's tenacious and fatal loyalty to his ship. Afterward, S. went on to write a series of large-scale novels about the 19th-c. Calvinist Dutch bourgeoisie: *De waterman* (1933; The Waterman, 1963), *Een Hollandsch drama* (1935; The

House in Haarlem, 1940), *De rijke man* (1936), and *De grauwe vogels* (1937; Grey Birds, 1939).

In 1938, S.'s writing turned in an entirely new direction with *De wereld een dansfeest*, a fantasy in which dance motifs are used to convey the attractive and repellent aspects of love. This playful work was followed shortly before his death by the more staid *Het oude huis* (1946). All the works of this final period are pervaded by what one critic has called "the awareness of the inscrutability of man and life."

FURTHER WORKS: *Drogon* (1896); *De schoone jacht* (1908); *Shakespeare* (1910); *De berg van droomen* (1913); *De Mensch van Nazareth* (1916); *Verhalen* (1917); *Pandorra* (1919); *Tristan en Isolde* (1920); *Blanke gestalten* (1923); *Oude italiaansche steden* (1924); *Verdichtsel van zomerdagen* (1925); *Verlaine* (1927); *Merona, een edelman* (1927); *Fratilamur* (1928); *Florentijnsche verhalen* (1929); *Een eiland in de Zuidzee* (1931); *Jan Compagnie* (1932); *Bijbelsche verhalen* (1932); *Herinneringen van een dommen jongen* (1934); *Nachtgedaanten* (1938); *De Zomerreis* (1938); *Le Dessin de Lombardie* (1938); *De zeven tuinen* (1939); *Anders en eender* (1939); *Mijnheer Oberon en mevrouw* (1940); *De menschenhater* (1941); *De fat, de nimf en de nuf* (1941); *De wedergeboorte van Bedelman* (1942); *Een spel der Natur* (1942); *Sparsa* (1944); *De Nederlanden* (1945); *Menschen en honden* (1947); *Voorbijgaande schaduwen* (1948); *Een zindelijke wereld* (1950); *De pleiziervaart* (1951)

BIBLIOGRAPHY: Pulinckx, R., *A. v. S.* (1944); s'Gravesande, G. H., *A. v. S.* (1949); Stuiveling, G., *Steekproeven* (1950); Eijk, H., *Mededelingsvormen bij A. v. S.* (1965); Flaxman, S., "Nationalism and Cosmopolitanism in Modern Dutch Literature," in *Proceedings of the IVth Congress of the International Comparative Literature Association*, ed. F. Jost, Vol. I (1966), 511–19

KAREL REIJNDERS

SCHICKELE, René

German-French novelist, poet, and dramatist (major writings in German), b. 4 Aug. 1883, Obernai, Alsace; d. 31 Jan. 1940, Vence, France

Born of an Alsatian father and a French mother, S. published his first volume of poetry, *Sommernächte* (1901) when he was only eighteen. In 1902 he founded the polemical

journal *Der Sturmer,* nine issues of which appeared with contributions by Ernst Stadler (1883–1914), Flake, Arp (qq.v.), and others. The main objective of this journal and its contributors was to Europeanize German culture by an infusion of Gallic spirit. S. afterward founded the journals *Der Merker* (1903) and *Das neue Magazin* before going to Paris as a journalist.

In Paris S. wrote the lyrical, erotic novel *Meine Freundin Lo* (1911). *Der Fremde* (1909) —the counterpart of Barrès's (q.v.). *Les Déracinés*—is a developmental novel about a pre-World War I Alsatian broken by the conflict in his family background. In *Benkal der Frauentröster* (1914), S. recounted the remarkable adventures of an intellectual Don Quixote in his relations to women, love, art, and freedom. The play *Hans im Schnakenloch* (1916) depicts the dual cultural allegiance and tragic situation of the Alsatians. In another play, *Am Glockenturm* (1920), S. satirizes impostors and espionage during the war.

For all its artistic independence, S.'s poetry —*Weiß und Rot* (1910), *Die Leibwache* (1914), *Mein Herz, mein Land* (1915)—reveals the influence of Arthur Rimbaud (1854–91), Paul Verlaine (1844–96), and Péguy (q.v.).

In 1920 S. moved to Badenweiler, though without committing himself to Germany. The novel *Sinfonie für Jazz* (1925) mirrors the greed of the postwar period; its hero, however, is granted the grace of spiritual renewal. *Die Witwe Bosca* (1933), set in Provence, expresses the poetry of the landscape. The basic themes underlying S.'s life and work—love of country and the land, and a belief in peace— are summed up in *Das Erbe am Rhein*, a realistic trilogy that includes *Maria Capponi* (1925; Eng., 1928), *Blick auf die Vogesen* (1927; Heart of Alsace, 1929), and *Der Wolf in der Hürde* (1931).

S. wrote his last book, *Le Retour* (1938), in French while in the south of France. In 1939, he translated it into German as *Heimkehr*. Here he once again mournfully expressed the tragedy of his destiny as an Alsatian poet torn between two cultures.

FURTHER WORKS: *Pan* (1902); *Mon Repos* (1905); *Der Ritt ins Leben* (1906); *Das Glück* (1910); *Schreie auf dem Boulevard* (1913); *Trimpopp und Manasse* (1914); *Aïssé* (1915); *Der 9. November* (1919); *Die Genfer Reise* (1919); *Die Mädchen* (1920); *Wir wollen nicht sterben* (1922); *Die neuen Kerle* (1924);

Die Grenze (1932); *Himmlische Landschaft* (1933); *Liebe und Ärgernis des D. H. Lawrence* (1934); *Die Flaschenpost* (1937); *Werke* (3 vols., 1960 ff.)

BIBLIOGRAPHY: Kesten, H., *Meine Freunde* (1953); Bieber, K., "R. S.: A Hyphen Between France and Germany," *Jadavpur Journal of Comparative Literature,* II (1962), 7–15

R. SCHNEIDER

SCHNITZLER, Arthur

Austrian novelist, dramatist, short-story writer, and essayist, b. 15 May 1862, Vienna; d. there, 21 Oct. 1931

S., the son of an eminent laryngologist, studied medicine and practiced in Vienna for a number of years. He became interested in psychoanalysis, which Vienna, the home of Sigmund Freud (1856–1939), was the center of. S. gave up medicine to devote himself exclusively to literature. He was influenced by a literary school that became famous about the turn of the century as the "Vienna modernists"; it included Bahr, Altenberg, Beer-Hofmann, and Hofmannsthal (qq.v.).

S. spent his whole life in Vienna; his plays and prose works repeatedly deal with decadent, upper bourgeois society in that city, though he was less interested in social than in psychological problems. S. reached the peak of his fame in the years immediately before World War I, when his plays were performed throughout the German-speaking world and translated into many languages.

In 1893 S. wrote *Anatol* (Anatol: A Sequence of Dialogues, 1911), a series of seven (later eight) little dialogue scenes, for which Hofmannsthal wrote a prologue under the pseudonym Loris. This early work about the love affairs of a spoiled, irresponsible, melancholy young man revealed S.'s talent for evoking subtly shaded moods and for treating delicate themes with charm and elegance. Sentimentality and irony, seriousness and frivolity, are closely intermingled.

Anatol was followed by several socially critical plays—*Das Märchen* (1894); *Freiwild* (1898; Free Game, 1913); *Das Vermächtnis* (1899; The Legacy, in *Poet Lore,* July/Aug. 1911)—in which S., knowing the limitations of the psyche and its subconscious workings, doubted himself that his postulations could be realized.

Liebelei (1896; Light-O'-Love, 1912), S.'s first big success, is about a romance between a trusting young girl and a well-born young man who takes the relationship lightly. He is killed in a duel about another woman he is also involved with. Here S. achieved an unsophisticated, even popular tone; the characterization is simple and true to life.

In the novella *Sterben* (1895) S. utilizes his knowledge as a doctor and a psychologist to describe the progressive physical and psychic disintegration of a dying man, his changes of mood, and his growing fear of death and eagerness for life. The awareness of the transience of human existence and the inevitability of death—an ending that made life senseless—appears in almost all S.'s works and basically determines the action. But S. carried this theme, which is well established in the tradition of Austrian literature, even further: for him none of man's external and internal states could be lasting.

Another of S.'s characteristic themes, the merging of truth and falsehood, appearance and reality, is presented in a particularly striking way in the one-act play "Der grüne Kakadu" (1899; The Green Cockatoo, in *The Green Cockatoo, and Other Plays,* 1913). On the eve of the French Revolution members of the degenerate aristocracy hire unemployed actors to improvise the mood of revolution.

S. soon began to draw steadily closer to a system of relative ethics, which receives its clearest expression in the play *Der Schleier der Beatrice* (1901). Here he paid homage to the yearning for beauty and to the "Renaissanceism" that Jacob Burckhardt (1818–97), Nietzsche (q.v.), and Conrad Ferdinand Meyer (1825–98) had made fashionable.

A tendency frequently to be found in S.'s other works is the attempt of his characters—which is always doomed to failure—to escape from the dismal reality of their existence into imaginary fantasies and self-deception, into art, into the detachment of a bystander, into concentrating upon the immediate moment, and even into suicide.

S. came to romantic themes by way of depth psychology. While he liked to claim he was a rationalist natural scientist, he wrote occult and spiritualist novellas—*Die Hirtenflöte* (1911; The Shepherd's Pipe, in *The Shepherd's Pipe, and Other Stories,* 1922); *Der Mörder* (1911; The Murderer, in *The Shepherd's Pipe, and Other Stories,* 1922), etc.—and even made use of romantic irony ("Zum großen Wurstel,"

DOROTHY SAYERS

ARTHUR SCHNITZLER

1905). Skeptical of all metaphysics and of the idea of free will and constantly emphasizing the rigorous determined causality that governs life, he nevertheless regarded fate as an unacceptable fact.

Yet S. was constantly attracted by subjects that provided scope for his masterly psychological talent for analyzing the internal mental states of his characters. This is seen in the novellas *Frau Bertha Garlan* (1901; Bertha Garlan, 1913) and *Frau Beate und ihr Sohn* (1913; Beatrice, 1926).

Leutnant Gustl (1901; None but the Brave, 1926), in which the technique of interior monologue (q.v.) is used, is the story of what goes on in the mind of a young officer who feels that he is compelled to shoot himself on the following day because he has been dishonored. (This and *Der blinde Geronimo und sein Bruder* [1900; Blind Geronimo and His Brother, in *Viennese Idylls*, 1931] represent S.'s major novellas—a genre for which he had an affinity, as he had for the one-act play.) The novel *Der Weg ins Freie* (1908; The Road to the Open, 1923) is also in essence a novella; it describes the death of the love between an artist and a bourgeois girl. In this book S. for the first time dealt with the problem of anti-Semitism, which was later to become the central theme of his play *Professor Bernhardi* (1912; The Anti-Semites: Professor Bernhardi, 1920).

The play *Der einsame Weg* (1904; The Lonely Way, 1904) shows S.'s subtle talent for creating mood and his mastery of delicate overtones. In conveying circumstances such as advancing age, loneliness, or the error of isolating oneself in life, he likes to suggest rather than make statements. This play also marked his break with relative ethics. In lieu of this he postulated the challenge: "More backbone, less intellect!" By "backbone" S. meant one's determination to prove oneself, by not passively accepting fate. While he remained a skeptic to his dying day, he was now convinced that one must actively persevere in actual life and do one's duty by one's fellowmen.

Among the plays S. wrote before the outbreak of World War I, two should be singled out—*Zwischenspiel* (1906; Intermezzo, in *The Lonely Way*, 1915) and *Das weite Land* (1911; The Vast Domain, in *Poet Lore*, Sept. 1923)—in which he again describes bourgeois society in prewar Vienna.

In 1910 his historical drama *Der junge Medardus* was performed—a tragicomedy

about the struggle of a young, irresolute Austrian rebel against Napoleon, in which the protagonist's plans keep miscarrying and he finally becomes an almost ludicrous figure.

World War I, which brought the collapse of the Austro-Hungarian monarchy and its society, made S. even more pessimistic. The element of mood receded, while the element of fact became more important. The frivolous irresponsibility of his early period completely disappeared. The language, too, became sharper and lost its charm and musicality. The later work is characterized by harsher criticism of aestheticism, by the demand for a sense of responsibility and self-conquest, and by a deeper skepticism so far as the potentialities of human character are concerned. S. did not succeed in freeing himself from his tragic sense of life.

In the late novellas *Doktor Gräsler, Badearzt* (1917; Dr. Graesler, 1923), *Casanovas Heimfahrt* (1918; Casanova's Homecoming, 1921), and *Fräulein Else* (1924; Eng., 1925), and in the novel *Therese: Chronik eines Frauenlebens* (1928; Theresa: The Chronicle of a Woman's Life, 1928), social problems become more important, although psychological questions are still paramount. In the dramas of this period S. was concerned with the ambiguities of language—*Komödie der Worte* (1915, includes "Stunde des Erkennens," "Große Szene," and "Das Bacchusfest"; The Hour of Recognition, The Big Scene, and The Festival of Bacchus, in *Comedies of Words, and Other Plays*, 1917); *Fink und Fliederbusch* (1917). In the verse play *Der Gang zum Weiher* (1926) he tried to come to grips with philosophical and political questions. *Komödie der Verführung* (1924) and *Im Spiel der Sommerlüfte* (1930) are predominantly psychological dramas that express S.'s nostalgia for the bygone prewar period that he had criticized so sharply yet had loved, too.

In his theoretical writings *Buch der Sprüche und Bedenken* (1927) and *Der Geist im Wort und der Geist in der Tat* (1927; The Mind in Words and Actions, 1971), S. tried to produce a philosophical justification for his world view.

FURTHER WORKS: *Die Frau des Weisen* (1898); *Der grüne Kakadu* (1899; includes "Der grüne Kakadu," "Paracelsus," and "Die Gefährtin"); *Reigen* (1900; Hands Around, 1920); *Lebendige Stunden* (1902); *Die griechische Tänzerin* (1905); *Marionetten: Drei Einakter* (1906); *Der Ruf des Lebens* (1906);

Dämmerseelen (1907); *Der tapfere Kassian: Singspiel in einem Aufzug* (1909); *Komtesse Mizzi, oder Der Familientag* (1909; Countess Mizzie, 1907); *Der tapfere Cassian: Puppenspiel in einem Akt* (1910; Gallant Cassian, 1914); *Der Schleier der Pierrette* (1910); *Masken und Wunder* (1912); *Die Theaterstücke* (5 vols., 1912–22); *Erzählende Schriften* (6 vols., 1912–28); *Die griechische Tänzerin, und andere Novellen* (1914); *Die Schwestern, oder Casanova in Spa* (1919); *Die dreifache Warnung* (1924); *Die Frau des Richters* (1925); *Traumnovelle* (1926; Rhapsody: A Dream Novel, 1927); *Spiel im Morgengrauen* (1927; Daybreak, 1927); *Flucht in die Finsternis* (1931; Flight into Darkness, 1931); *Traum und Schicksal: Sieben Novellen* (1931); *Die kleine Komödie: Frühe Novellen* (1932); *Abenteurernovelle* (1937); *Flucht in die Finsternis, und andere Erzählungen* (1939); *Über Krieg und Frieden* (1939; Notes on War and Peace, 1971); *Ausgewählte Erzählungen* (1950); *Der Briefwechsel A. S.—Otto Brahm* (1953); *Meisterdramen* (1955); *Georg Brandes und A. S.: Ein Briefwechsel* (1956); *Egon Friedell: Briefe* (1959); *Große Szene* (1959); *Die erzählenden Schriften* (2 vols., 1961); *Die dramatischen Werke* (2 vols., 1962); *Hugo von Hofmannsthal—A. S. Briefwechsel* (1964); *Erzählungen* (1965); *Spiel in Morgengrauen, und acht andere Erzählungen* (1965); *Jugend in Wien: Eine Autobiographie* (1968). **Selected English translations:** *The Green Cockatoo, and Other Plays* (1913; includes "The Green Cockatoo," "The Mate," and "Paracelsus"); *Living Hours* (1913; includes "Living Hours," "The Lady with the Dagger," "Last Masks," and "Literature"); *Viennese Idylls* (1913; includes "Flowers," "The Sage's Wife," "Blind Geronimo and His Brother," "Andreas Thameyer's Last Letter," "The Farewell," and "The Dead Are Silent"); *The Lonely Way* (1915; includes "The Lonely Way," "Intermezzo," and "Countess Mizzie, or the Family Reunion"); *Anatol* (1917; includes "Anatol," "Living Hours," "The Lady with the Dagger," "Last Masks," "Literature," and "The Green Cockatoo"); *Comedies of Words, and Other Plays* (1917; includes "The Hour of Recognition," "The Big Scene," "The Festival of Bacchus," "Literature," and "His Helpmate"); *The Shepherd's Pipe, and Other Stories* (1922; includes "The Shepherd's Pipe," "The Murderer," and "The Blind Geronimo and His Brother"); *Beatrice, and Other Stories* (1926; includes "Beatrice," "Flowers," "A Farewell,"

"The Wife of the Wise Man," "The Hour of Fame," and "The Dead Are Silent"); *Little Novels* (1929); *Viennese Novelettes* (1931), *Reigen, The Affairs of Anatol, and Other Plays* (1933)

BIBLIOGRAPHY: Reik, T., *S. als Psycholog* (1913); Liptzin, S., *A. S.* (1932); Lantin, L., *Traum und Wirklichkeit in der Prosadichtung A. Ss.* (1958); *Journal of the International A. S. Association* (founded 1962); Reichert, H. W., and Salinger, H., eds., *Studies in A. S.: A Centennial Commemorative Volume* (1963); Baumann, G., *A. S.* (1965); Allen, R., *An Annotated A. S. Bibliography* (1966); Von Nardroff, E., "Aspects of Symbolism in the Works of A. S.," *DA*, XXVII (1966), 1842A; Weiss, R., "The Psychoses in the Works of A. S.," *GQ*, XLI (1968), 377–400

REINHARD MÜLLER-FREIENFELS

It cannot be denied that S. in his writings reveals a philosophy that is above all else that of the determinist. What his characters are and what they do depends fundamentally upon what has preceded and under what conditions they exist. Natural instincts and pathological tendencies, converging at times with fatal external influences, deprive them almost entirely of any freedom of the will. The erotic element, . . . is the predominant force in the majority of his characters. In cases, as, for instance, in the characters of *Reigen*, it has resulted in the inevitable and has reduced human beings to derelicts. . . . But very few of S.'s characters are irredeemably perverted through their natural instincts alone. This Austrian dramatist, who is primarily occupied with the moral and emotional nature of man, has not excluded accident and chance from the chain of cause and effect. . . . At such times we perceive what a weak and ineffectual thing the human will apparently is. And from S.'s revelations of the inner conflicts in man, when nature contends with reason, we see how easily man's will-power is dethroned. . . .

. . . Man is at best the creature of destiny, and rarely is it permitted him to shape his own lot in life. . . .

Selma Koehler, in *Journal of English and Germanic Philology* (1923), pp. 409–10

Reading these works today we soon realize that S. is rooted in the period before the first World War. With this period his world collapsed. But once the distance is sufficiently great—and that is now the case—it proves that an entire epoch took on form in S.'s work. . . . In S.'s day it was the custom to drape the inner void and bankruptcy with sumptuous, borrowed costumes. This habit had almost become a kind of style. S. stripped off the trappings at the outset, tore off the masks and wiped the rouge off people's cheeks. What was left was in truth not much: a little instinct and a good deal of fear—avowed or otherwise—a little bit of love or rather flirtation, that is; playing with love, a wisecrack or two followed by devastating vapidity and emptiness.

K. W. Maurer, in *GL&L* (1948–49), p. 215

Anatol is a good example of S.'s early light touch in treating the problem [of self-absorption]. This sequence of witty, gay and coquettishly wistful dialogues on the illusion of love is not a "major" work, but it is perfect of its kind, excellent reading and very amusing on the stage even now, in spite of the somewhat artificial flavour of the nineties in their Viennese version. The underlying theme is that sort of self-absorption which destroys the capacity of loving while heightening the taste for pleasure, but the surface is all frothy talk about "love." The talkers are the weak, impulsive, introspective and charming hero, the poet Anatol, and his skeptical, sharply observant friend Max. Anatol is in love with himself, particularly with his weaknesses and sensitive susceptibilities and forever falling in love with still another woman; his passion never lasts, he never tries to know the human being in his beloved, but every time he hopes that the new "she" might still his unrest.

TLS (15 June 1951), p. 366

... The basic picture which is crystallizing out of the mass of S. criticism, and which is finding its place in literary histories, shows an exquisite Viennese decadent tirelessly delineating the frivolous amours of effete Anatols and anonymous *süsse Mädel*. It is not a flattering picture, with its implications of immorality, of superficiality, and above all of monotony....

If a more objective evaluation of S. is to prevail, it must begin with a recognition that the "erotic" rubric is utterly inadequate. The concept of pure eroticism fails to account for a great part of the author's range of interest and even within that part where eroticism is in the foreground results in a dangerous oversimplification. There are, of course, valid criticisms to be made. It is true, for example, that the longer plays lose in unity through a tendency to break up into a series of *Einakter*; there are certainly highs and lows of the emotional range beyond the reach of S.'s relaxed, objective tone; there is justice in the observation that works like *Spiel im Morgengrauen* and *Der Gang zum Weiher* suffer from a plethora of themes in a small compass; S. is admittedly not the man for those who, in literature, seek inspiration, or answers to the eternal questions....

What can, in a phrase, be justly said of S.'s themes is that he is a student, a brilliant and devoted student, of the human soul. He wrote of many things, but only as those things clarify,

symbolize, or in some way lay bare the functioning of personality. ... What we do find are shrewd revelations of the infinite complexity of the human mind and heart ...

Frederick J. Beharriell, in *Monatshefte* (1951), pp. 301, 310

What S. has given creative form in *Liebelei*— and over and over again in his works—is not the foregrounds, deceptively genuine and unforgettable as they are, but the ultimate things of human existence: sweet painful love and the bitterness of having to die; the longing to hold firmly to something, to someone, although one, even before the first step is taken, knows perfectly well that nothing has permanence, least of all happiness; the realization how fruitless is our attempt to help the one we love, to lighten his burden, fruitless even when the attempt comes from one's purest, deepest heart. The brief shining forth of happiness, the deep sadness of the knowledge of how transitory everything is, how darkly the shadow has already spread its wings: all this transpires in S.'s work *sotto voce*, without pathos, without grand gestures, in the simplest conversational tone. This clever and controlled speech melody was probably what deceived his contemporaries, made them overlook the depths which are hidden behind the urbane lightness and elegance of S.'s speech cadence.

Oskar Seidlin, in *GQ* (1962), pp. 250–51

Frank Wedekind called *Leutnant Gustl* S.'s best work. *Leutnant Gustl* is a monologue, something halfway between a novella and a play. It is a voiceless recitation within the hero's mind. He is under pressure either to commit suicide or to resign from the service because of some accidental bad luck. He is saved by a new and most unlikely occurrence. But one cannot always count on such luck since at a certain point in life Fortune tires of every cheerful, thoroughly spoiled Lieutenant Gustl. His still young creator already understood this. Only occasionally are we saved. Because we grow old, danger remains and increases. Old age is in itself a misfortune; it is precisely this that S. perceived.

Heinrich Mann in *Deutsche Literaturkritik im 20. Jahrhundert* (1965), pp. 771–72

His virile knowledge of people and the world, the charm of the problems he poses, the graceful purity and elevation of his style; his assured cultural taste, which has protected him throughout his life from every blunder, every failure; his fine and strong intelligence; the lively episodes, the fictionally polished mood of his plays, the well-bred and striking form of his fiction, along with an amiable good will, the opposite of any misanthropic rigidity; and, best of all, the personal charm that emerges from everything he has created: all this has made the time I have passed with his works, in the theater or at home in my easy chair, hours of esthetic refuge, of the most undoubted pleasure, of a happily enhanced feeling for life.

Thomas Mann

At his service are all the tools that artisanship places in the hands of an experienced and very reflective artist to enable him to master even substance that is apparently unmalleable and to elicit from the subject its inner riches. None of them does he use with greater and more charming virtuosity than irony. The more boldly he applies it, the more he forces his material and his motives into a corner with it, all the broader, paradoxically, his intellectual horizon seems to be. Thus I would say that, next to the *Liebelei*, a work of an entirely unique kind, several of his *small* works of art—tales and plays—emerge, through the magic of irony, as his greatest.

Hugo von Hofmannsthal

SCHNURRE, Wolfdietrich

German novelist, short-story writer, and poet, b. 22 Aug. 1920, Frankfurt on the Main

S., the son of a librarian, grew up in Berlin. After spending more than six years in the army of the Third Reich during World War II, S. returned to West Berlin in 1946 as a confirmed pacifist. He is one of the cofounders of Gruppe 47 (*see* German literature).

From 1946 to 1949 S. confined himself to writing film and theater criticism. In 1950 he began to try his hand at other genres, and in the past twenty years he has written novels, short stories, poetry, autobiographical sketches, radio and television dramas, and animal fables. He sometimes illustrates his writings.

In both his poetry—*Kassiber* (1956), *Abendländler* (1957), and *Formel und Beschwörung* (1964)—and the story collections—*Die Rohrdommel ruft jeden Tag* (1950) and *Man sollte dagegen sein* (1960)—S. is trying to come to terms with a nightmarish and still unreconciled past. He succeeds in these volumes in writing matter-of-fact language, in firmly keeping diction and syntax simple, without injury to his imagery, rhythm, and poetic conception. In response to both style and content, the reader becomes genuinely involved in these works.

S.'s protest against man's inhumanity to man and beast alike in the midst of a heartless and unfeeling world recalls "die Trägheit des Herzens" (the sluggishness of the heart), a leitmotif in the novels of Jakob Wassermann (q.v.). In *Eine Rechnung, die nicht aufgeht*

(1958; An Account That Does Not Balance, 1961), the world is presented as distorted, as comic, as grotesque. Symbolically, S. questions the indiscriminate use of authority.

Some of his writings of the 1950's bear little resemblance to his iconoclastic period of harsh criticism and of moral outrage. One such work —which seems to allow S. to escape from the everyday miseries—is the collection of animal fables *Sternstaub und Sänfte: Die Aufzeichnungen des Pudels Ali* (1953), noteworthy for their delightfully relaxed tone. Another such work is the "novel" *Als Vaters Bart noch rot war* (1958), in which S. proves himself a skillful satirist who exhibits German society with all its failings as it existed between 1945 and 1947.

S. used the parable form in the imaginative, kaleidoscopic phantasy *Das Los unserer Stadt: Eine Chronik* (1959). Here he offers his reader a compellingly lively canvas, one that is macabre, nightmarish, and surrealistic. By means of this starkly distorted, grotesque view, S. is symbolically making statements of profound significance.

S. is untiring in his efforts to reveal the disfigured face of man who is enmeshed and trapped by a malevolent fate. Bizarre in their mood, many of his short stories are in conception and meaning highly relevant to modern man.

As his works indicate, S. is an innovator who delights in doing the unexpected and the unusual. He surprises with the variety and unpredictable form of his writing and impresses with his originality and his poetic insights, which are conveyed economically, and even in the form of epigrams. A hard-hitting and masterful stylist, he has written poetry and prose that express both the seriousness of the biblical parable and the lightheartedness of his inimitable and irreverent sense of humor.

S., who has won several important literary awards, is generally recognized as one of the most gifted of the postwar German writers.

FURTHER WORKS: *Rettung des deutschen Films* (1950); *Kalünz ist eine kleine Insel* (1952); *Stimmen über dem Fluß* (1953); *Das Haus am See* (1954); *Nächtliche Begegnung* (1954); *Canaima* (1954); *Die Reise zur Babuschka* (1955); *Kranichzug* (1955); *Die Blumen des Herrn Albin: Aus dem Tagebuch eines Sanftmütigen* (1955); *Spreezimmer möbliert* (1955); *Eine gut befestigte Stadt* (1956); *Krähenkolonie* (1957); *Eine Chance für*

Humbsch (1957); *Alle Vöglein alle* (1957); *Liebe, böse Welt* (1957); *Protest im Parterre* (1957); *Ein Fall für Herrn Schmidt* (1957; revised, 1962); *Steppenkopp* (1958); *Barfußgeschöpfe* (1958); *Anaximanders Ende* (1958); *Das Efeublatt* (1958); *Der Fleck an der Wand* (1958); *Jenö war mein Freund* (1960); *Das Schwein, das zurückkam* (1960); *Nur ein kurzer Aufenthalt* (1961); *Die Mauer des 13. August* (1962); *Berlin—Eine Stadt wird geteilt: Ein Dokument* (1962); *Funke im Reisig* (1963); *Ohne Einsatz kein Spiel* (1964); *Schreibtisch unter freiem Himmel* (1964); *Die Erzählungen* (1966); *Eine schöne Bescherung* (1967); *Die Zwengel* (1967); *Was ich für mein Leben gern tue* (1967); *Der Rapport des Verschonten* (1968). **Selected English translations:** Selections in *Modern German Stories* (ed. H. M. Waidson; 1961); *Modern German Poetry 1910–1960* (eds. M. Hamburger, and C. Middleton; 1963); and *Twentieth-Century German Verse* (ed. P. Bridgwater; 1963)

BIBLIOGRAPHY: Lennartz, F., *Deutsche Dichter und Schriftsteller unserer Zeit* (1959), pp. 690–92; Horst, K. A., *Kritischer Führer durch die deutsche Literatur der Gegenwart* (1962), pp. 162–63; Soergel, A., and Hohoff, C., *Dichtung und Dichter der Zeit: Vom Naturalismus bis zur Gegenwart*, Vol. II (1963), pp. 826–27; Nusser, P., "W. S.'s Short Stories," *Studies in Short Fiction*, III (1966), 215–24; Reich-Ranicki, M., Afterword to *Die Erzählungen* (1966); Mayer, H., *Zur deutschen Literatur der Zeit* (1967), pp. 304, 320–22; Welzig, W., *Der deutsche Roman im 20. Jahrhundert* (1967), p. 310; Otten, A., "W. S. 'Was ich für mein Leben gern tue,'" *BA*, XLII (1968), 270

HENRY REGENSTEINER

SCHWARTZ, Delmore

American poet, short-story writer, and critic, b. 8 Dec. 1913, Brooklyn; d. 11 July 1966, New York City

S. grew up in Brooklyn. He studied philosophy at the universities of Wisconsin, New York, and Harvard. From 1940 to 1947 he taught English at Harvard. He served on the editorial board of *Partisan Review* (1943–55), was poetry editor of *The New Republic* (1955–57), and was *Kenyon Review* Fellow in 1957. S. was a visiting lecturer at various American universities and received awards from *Poetry* magazine and from the National Institute of Arts and Letters.

S.'s first major book was *In Dreams Begin Responsibilities* (1938), named after the title short story. It contains, as well, a modern adaptation of Shakespeare's *Coriolanus*; lyric poems, among which are "The Heavy Bear Who Goes with Me" and "In the Naked Bed, in Plato's Cave"; and a rather feeble drama, "Dr. Bergen's Belief."

S.'s long autobiographical poem, *Genesis, Book I* (1943), confirmed his earlier poetic promise. *Vaudeville for a Princess, and Other Poems* (1950) was a collection of prose sketches and lyrics, with emphasis on the sonnet form.

S. received the Bollingen Poetry Prize and the Shelley Memorial Award for *Summer Knowledge: New and Selected Poems, 1938–1958*. The new poems represent a noticeable change from the somberness of his earlier poetry, much of which is included in this volume.

S. also published two volumes of stories: *The World Is a Wedding* (1948) and *Successful Love, and Other Stories* (1961). The first title has been praised for its depiction of middle-class Jewish life during the 1930's.

S.'s criticism, appearing chiefly in periodicals, has ranged widely, with essays on Eliot, Marianne Moore, and Lardner (qq.v.). He has also translated Rimbaud's *A Season in Hell* (1940).

S.'s verse is extremely allusive. He was much influenced by Eliot and Joyce (qq.v.), Plato and Shakespeare. His favorite theme is what he calls "the wound of consciousness." This involves at least three factors: the ego, a sense of guilt and alienation operating within a consciousness of his Jewish background, and a troubled awareness of the vastness and weight of history and time. In his concern for self-identity he emphasizes the role of the poet in the modern world.

FURTHER WORK: *Shenandoah* (1941)

BIBLIOGRAPHY: Strickhausen, H., "Extensions in Language," *Poetry*, XCV (Feb. 1960), 300–03; Rosenthal, M. L., *The Modern Poets: A Critical Introduction* (1960); Flint, R. W., "The Stories of D. S.," *Commentary*, XXXIII, (April 1962), 336–39; Deutsch, R., "Poetry and Belief in D. S.," *SR*, LXXIV (1966), 915–24

B. BERNARD COHEN

SCIASCIA, Leonardo
Italian novelist, dramatist, and essayist, b. 8 Jan. 1921, Racalmuto, Agrigento

Luigi Barzini says of S. that he "has one advantage many Italian writers envy him for. He is Sicilian."

For almost ten years, S. was an elementary-school teacher in his native town. He was, therefore, directly exposed to the problems of his pupils and their families—sulphur and salt miners, farmers—who were victims of centuries of poverty. During those years S. wrote a book of fables, *Favole della dittatura* (1950), and a volume of poems, *La Sicilia, il suo cuore* (1952), that form a significant prelude to his later works. In the Aesopian fables, S.'s historical approach is evident in his allusions to the wretched conditions of life under the fascist dictatorship. In the poems S. deals with the children of the poor at school or in the fields, and he offers arresting glimpses of the landscape of the Sicilian interior.

It was only with *Cronache scholastiche* (1955), a long essay based on his teaching experiences, that S. became known to the general Italian public. S. sent the manuscript to novelist and editor Italo Calvino (b. 1923), who recommended it for publication in the journal *Nuovi Argomenti*. Because of the essay's success, S. was asked to write an entire book about his birthplace. The result was *Le parrocchie di Regalpetra* (1956; Salt in the Wound, 1969). These narrative essays, as well as the essay *Pirandello e la Sicilia* (1961), are of paramount importance in understanding S.'s artistic world and the major themes he developed in later books.

Sicily, where for centuries injustice and crime, poverty and plague, oppression and abuse, have been the people's lot, is S.'s constant theme and preoccupation. With the sun-baked Sicilian landscape as a background, S. portrays the victims and the oppressors of the past, as in *Morte dell'inquisitore* (1964; The Death of the Inquisitor, 1969; included in the collection Salt in the Wound), and of the present, as in *Il giorno della civetta* (1961; Mafia Vendetta, 1964). S.'s narratives are always based on facts, even when, as in *A ciascuno il suo* (1966; A Man's Blessing, 1968), they take the form of a detective story.

S.'s primary model is the Alessandro Manzoni (1785–1873) of *The Column of Infamy*. Sifting the complex and varied history of his Sicilians—victims of man and nature—he searches in the wounds of the past for a cure to present evils. Because he is able to universalize both the oppressors and the victims, giving them an importance that transcends the particular, it is possible for him to render a portrait of man appropriate to all times, all societies. Though his books are an implicit condemnation of the Italian upper class, they all carry a message of redemption. In the very last words of *Morte dell'inquisitore*, S. points out that he has written Fra Diego's story because he "was a man, who held aloft the dignity of man."

Some critics have called S. an "Enlightenment writer," and they consider his works "philosophical stories." S. himself notes that as a child he was given the works of Denis Diderot (1713–84) before he had even read *Pinocchio*. "I believe in human reason, and in the liberty and justice it engenders."

S. describes himself as "a very impure writer," because his stories are always intertwined with criticism, and "a pamphleteer," because there is no work in which he does not denounce some form of injustice. As a writer and a Sicilian he believes that "a slash of the pen . . . like a slash of the sword, is enough to right a wrong or rout injustice and exploitation."

S.'s style, modeled on the writers of *La Ronda* (see Italian literature), is precise and vivid, condensed, yet rich and colorful, particularly in the use of dialect words and idioms. Certainly one of the major contemporary Italian writers, like other Sicilian writers such as Luigi Capuana (1839–1915), Verga, Pirandello, and Lampedusa (qq.v.), S. has portrayed the people of his "exasperated and tragic Eden" in such a way that men everywhere can identify with their search for selfhood and dignity.

FURTHER WORKS: *Pirandello e il pirandellismo* (1953); *Gli zii di Sicilia* (1958); *Il consiglio d'Egitto* (1963; The Council of Egypt, 1966); *L'onorevole* (1965); *Feste religiose in Sicilia* (1965); *Recitazione della controversia liparitana dedicata ad A. D.* (1970)

BIBLIOGRAPHY: Addamo, S., *Vittorini e la narrativa siciliana contemporanea* (1962); Biasin, G.-P., "The Sicily of Verga and S.," *IQ*, IX (1965), xxxiv–xxxv, 3–22; Mauro, W., *Cultura e società nella narrativa meridionale* (1965); West, A., "Games That Are Played for Keeps," *NY*, 19 March 1966, pp. 206–08; Salinari, C., *Preludio e fine del realismo in Italia* (1967); Piroué, G., "Guide pour la Sicile,"

La Quinzaine littéraire, 1–15 May 1967, p. 11; Fernandez, D., "S. et la Sicile," *La Quinzaine littéraire,* 15–31 May 1967, pp. 13–14;; Renard, P., "S. ou le refus du mythe," *Le Monde,* No. 5 (8 Nov. 1967); Barzini, L., "Dangerous Acquaintances," *The New York Review* (9 Oct. 1969), 36–44

M. RICCIARDELLI

SCOTTISH LITERATURE

If 20th-c. Scottish literature is to be thought of as the creation of any writer who declares his nationality Scots, one must then consider works in Gaelic and English as well as in the Scots dialects. The dominant feature of Scottish literature in the 20th c. has been the Scottish renaissance, a post-World War I movement born of reaction. Its commanding spirit was MacDiarmid (q.v.).

In the late 19th c. Scottish writers were concentrating on Kailyard treacle, parochial satire, bothie humor, and whaup-and-heather romance. This approach was also to be used in the 20th c. in such poems as "Hamewith" by Charles Murray (1864–1941), and it appears in "Shy Geordie" by Helen Cruickshank (b. 1886). It continued through Barrie (q.v.) and, with an increasing skill, in the works of J. Logie Robertson (b. 1846), R. B. Cunninghame Graham (1852–1936), John Buchan (1875–1940), and Albert Mackie (b. 1904).

Early objection to the concentration on the tender and the homespun is evident in the grimness of the novel *Weir of Hermiston* by Robert Louis Stevenson (1850–94). It is also manifest in the comments on Robert M'Queen in Stevenson's essay "Some Portraits by Raeburn" and in the precise language of his poems, such as "Epistle to Charles Baxter" ("The hale toon glintin', stane an' stane,/Wi' cauld an' weet"). Later and stronger reaction came with George Douglas Brown (1869–1902) and his novel *The House with the Green Shutters,* an uncompromising study of Scottish brutality and decadence. Even later, reaction continued to appear with the translations of German ballads by Sir Alexander Gray (b. 1882) and with the lyricism and graceful simplicity of Violet Jacob (1863–1946) and the superior poetry of Marion Angus (1866–1946).

On a longer scale, the sense of national identity that Scotland developed during World War I hastened the rejection of Kailyard tradition and quickened the first impulses of the Scottish renaissance. The war years heightened proletarian revolt against industrialism, and weakened the conviction that in order to deal with the most basic human problems a Scotsman must use English.

MacDiarmid, seeking a personal base from which to move forward in the 1920's, grandly conceived of a national regeneration, which was to begin with literature. MacDiarmid's tough, masculine poem "A Drunk Man Looks at the Thistle" (1926) and his anthologies of current Scottish poetry encouraged others to treat serious and modern themes in an eclectic Scots that revived both dictionary usages and borrowed dialect idioms. Further experiments of this "mad, persuasive Gael" came in the 1930's and thereafter, to be set forth in his issues of the magazine *Voice of Scotland.*

Once again, others were won over to the theme of revolt against accepted things and to the medium—synthetic Scots. Thus we have such poetry as the "lemanrie" *Under the Eildon Tree* (1948) by Sydney Goodsir Smith (q.v.), "Letter to Hugh MacDiarmid" by Douglas Young (b. 1913), "Embro to the Ploy," by Robert Garioch (b. 1909), "The Tryst" by Soutar (q.v.), "Orpheus," by Tom Scott (b. 1918), and *The Book of Scottish Nursery Rhymes* (1964) coedited by Nora and William Montgomerie.

Further impetus for the Scottish renaissance came from the criticism of David Daiches (b. 1912) and the journalism of Mackie. Also of help was the founding of the Saltire Society (1936) and the launching of its quarterly, the *Saltire Review* (1954), for the preservation, encouragement, and development of Scottish art, literature, and music. Poets like Sydney Goodsir Smith remained constant to the ideal of a synthetic Scots fashioned from the language of 16-c. "makars" (poets) and from local dialects with modern jargon. MacDiarmid, however, went on to champion Gaelic in his search for the true spirit of Scotland.

Gaelic writers, of course, had already been utilizing the qualities for which Gaelic is known: for a richness of sound from rhyme, assonance, and alliteration, a traditional intricacy of syllabic meter, and a sharp clarity. The finest modern examples of these qualities may be found in the poems, *Dàin do Eimhir* by Somhairle Maclean (b. 1911) and *Fuaran Sléibh* by George Campbell Hay (b. 1915). Even when writing in English, as in "The Kerry Shore" or "The Old Fisherman" from *Wind on Loch Fyne* (1948), Hay's voice is that of the

Gael. A similar voice speaks in some of the English poetry of MacCaig (q.v.) and Joseph Macleod (b. 1903). Most recently, Fionn MacColla (b. 1900), Derick Thomson (b. 1921), and Iain Crichton Smith (b. 1928) have contributed to the Gaelic revival.

From the start, the Scottish renaissance was countered by many disparate influences. Public apathy was manifested by the failure of both the *Saltire Review* (1960) and the *New Saltire Review* (1964); the *New Scottish Dictionary* was also poorly received. English became the principal language in the schools, and the publishing market and most literary circles were centered in London. In addition, the purely regional concerns of much Scottish literature confronted a formidable challenge in the attitudes of many young writers, whose experiences included World War II and the subsequent threat of nuclear destruction, as well as such contemporary phenomena as the bomb, space exploration, and the rebellion of the young.

MacDiarmid could not have had a more formidable opponent than Muir (q.v.), the first great metaphysical poet of Scotland, the finest critical intelligence, and the chief advocate of Anglo-Scot intent. In his lectures *Scott and Scotland* (1936), Muir repudiated the renaissance. He argued that a writer in Scots lacked an organic community, a major literary tradition, a unified diction, and a livelihood; he must therefore accept English as his medium and absorb English tradition. The measure of Muir's own accomplishment in poetry (*The Labyrinth,* 1949; and *One Foot in Eden,* 1956), as much as his critical persuasion, influenced others. MacCaig in *The Sinai Sort* (1957) and W. S. Graham in *The Nightfishing* (1955) gave further proof that good poetry could be written in English by Scotsmen, and such writers as Lewis Spence (1874–1955) became increasingly impatient with the renaissance.

One of the latest to leave the movement was Maurice Lindsay (b. 1918), who had lent the renaissance a strong hand in his periodical *Poetry Scotland* (1944–49) and his anthology *Modern Scottish Poetry* (1946). Lindsay prefaced his latest volume of poetry, *Snow Warning, and Other Poems* (1962), with an assertion that English must be the dominant language of Scottish literature. He cited the influence of television, which through its wide dissemination of English-language programs has drastically reduced opportunities for use of the Scots tongue. The latter, Lindsay noted,

has become little more than a local dialect and has scarcely been used at all in any literary work of significance for the contemporary reader. Lindsay therefore chose English for all of his new poems.

Much of the disenchantment with the Scottish renaissance undoubtedly arose from an inherent confusion in the principles first enunciated by MacDiarmid at the beginning of the movement. Throughout his career, moreover, he continued to recognize the linguistic dilemma confronting Scots poets, as shown in his own work: "I write now in English and now in Scots/To the despair of friends who plead/For consistency" ("The Caledonian Antisyzygy"). His early cry "Back to Dunbar" became "Back to ancient Gaelic heritage."

Later MacDiarmid seemed to favor a movement toward Marxism in a world literature enriched by Joyce (q.v.; "In Memoriam James Joyce"). Throughout his varied careers, however, he never lost his genius for superlative lyricism ("The Eemis Stane," "Water Music," "The Bonnie Broukit Bairn"), although each of his latest major poems seemed more erudite, scientific, polemical, free, and abstract than the last. This genius became clearer with such volumes as *A Lap of Honour* (1967), a volume of poetry to honor MacDiarmid's seventy-fifth birthday, and *The Uncanny Scot* (1968), a selection of prose pieces by this "most important poet now alive in Great Britain."

Scots writers in the second half of the 20th c. responded restlessly to supranational modes or quietly persisted in fashioning individual expression. Their work in general was marked by an increasing refusal to accept attitudes and dogmas of older poets. Such a refusal, however, was usually expressed in English rather than in, for example, the Lallans of Tom Scott, who suggested the need of laws "To gar auld bards sit back and tak their ease/Afore our 'gratitude' for whit they're duin/Is swallowed up in ae gret stifled yawn." This discontent with the use of the Scots tongues extended to the compilation of anthologies. Thus in 1954 an anti-Lallans group led by W. Price Turner, editor of *The Poet* (1952–57), published *Eleven Scottish Poets,* a volume that, dedicated to Muir, included only works in English. In 1959 MacCaig's anthology of modern Scottish poetry, *Honour'd Shade,* printed poems by twenty-seven contributors. Two-thirds of the seventy-eight pieces were in English. Protesting the views of the nationalistic "Rose Street" establishment (MacCaig, Iain Crichton Smith,

MacDiarmid, and others) propounded in this book, seven "non-Abbotsford" poets recorded their poems on tape as *Dishonour'd Shade* (1960). In this way the younger poets Ian Hamilton Finlay, Tom Buchan, Turner, and Tom Wright presented their new ideas. Finlay later joined Jessie McGuffie in founding the Wild Hawthorn Press to print such poetic broadsheets as *Poor, Old, Tired Horse,* an attack on MacDiarmid.

The elder poet's caustic reply to his adversaries is *The Ugly Birds without Wings* (1962). The critic W. A. S. Keir replied just as severely to authors of three of the "scruffy little pamphlets." He found Finlay's *The Dancers Inherit the Party* "eccentric doodles in the margin of a misdirected talent." He called *My Friend Tree* by Lorine Niedecker "tiny neo-surrealistic scrawls" and characterized the *Occasional Pieces* of Harry Wordon as "still gazing at the rear end of a vulture." None of MacDiarmid's opponents won the last *New Saltire Review* Poetry Prize in 1963; instead, it was shared by David Craig (b. 1932), Alastair Mackie (b. 1937), and Robert Fulton (b. 1935) for three poems, all in English.

The spirit of the Scottish renaissance extended beyond poetry, even though it did not develop anything like a common prose idiom. Not a single Scottish playhouse existed in the early 1930's, and in 1939 only the Perth Repertory functioned as a fully professional, native enterprise. Vital advances occurred, however, in the 1940's: first in the establishment of the Glasgow Unity Theatre, and then in the Glasgow Citizen's Theatre (1943) and the College of Drama (1950), with a bilingual system of training. The last two were incomparable legacies from Bridie (q.v.). The International Arts Festival established in Edinburgh in 1948 offered new opportunities to Scots playwrights and actors, as did the opening of The Gateway in 1950 and the Traverse Theatre in 1963. Among the relatively small number of plays by Scots dramatists the most notable are *Campbell of Kilmohr* by John Ferguson and *The Ancient Fire* by Neil M. Gunn (b. 1891).

Bridie's reputation was made in London with some forty-two plays directed primarily toward an English audience and including *Gog and Magog, The Anatomist,* and *Tobias and the Angel,* rather than with such late moralities as *The Queen's Comedy* and *The Baikie Charivari,* produced in Glasgow. John Brandane (1869–1947), also a playwright, is remembered for *The Glen Is Mine,* depicting conflict in Highland life. Gordon Bottomley (1874–1948), a native Yorkshireman inspired by the Scottish past, published two volumes of plays, *Lyric* (1932) and *Choric* (1939), of which "Gruach" is perhaps the most representative. *Jamie the Saxt* by Robert MacLellan (b. 1907) and *The Lass wi' the Muckle Mou'* by Alexander Reid contribute light-hearted Scottish comedy written in Doric, a rustic dialect of England. Promising material has appeared in the experimental work of such writers as Robert Kemp (b. 1908) and Alexander Scott. Eric Linklater (b. 1899) occasionally turns to sharply pointed satiric comedy (*The Mortimer Touch*), and Sydney Goodsir Smith to verse tragedy (*The Wallace*), after writing comedy in *Colickie Meg.*

Three Scottish-born novelists have gained wide popular favor in London for their works: Mackenzie (q.v.) with *Whisky Galore* and *Carnival*; John Buchan with *Witch Wood* and *The Thirty-Nine Steps*; Linklater with *White-Maa's Saga* and *Juan in America.* Life in West Scotland has been treated in the fiction of such writers as J. MacDougall Hay, known for his *Gillespie* (1914), and Alexander McArthur, Dot Allan, John Cockburn, and George Blake, all having written in the 1930's about Glasgow. Among the leading novelists who have made West Scotland their theme are Neil Munro (1864–1930), Gunn, Lewis Grassic Gibbon (b. 1900), and MacColla. Munro, a "Stevenson of the Highlands," dwells on the need of the Highlands for modern ways in *The New Road* and on the years of the Great Depression in *The Clydesiders.* Gunn writes searchingly and beautifully of the crofting and fishing communities in Caithness and Sutherland. His *Sun Circle, Butcher's Broom,* and *Highland River* may represent the peak of modern Scottish fiction. He is seconded in his concern for the Gael by MacColla, who, in *The Albannach* (1932), angrily protests the wastage of men and land in the Highlands.

Certainly the most impressive extended work is Gibbon's trilogy *A Scots Quair* (*Sunset Song,* 1932; *Cloud Howe,* 1933; and *Grey Granite,* 1934). His theme that nothing endures but the land is stated dramatically through the life of Chris Guthrie, a crofter's daughter. Gibbon's Scots language, used for narrative as well as dialogue, has been cited by critics as the most promising attempt yet made toward creation of a modern Scots prose. Another remarkable work of fiction is Sydney Goodsir Smith's

Carotid Cornucopius in the revised and enlarged edition of 1964. A complex wordplay about Edinburgh's modern "roarin' Willies," it has been greeted by MacDiarmid as "the very quintessence of Scottishness." Less ardent patriots may prefer the truths of Scottishness in the diaries of Soutar or the autobiographies of John Buchan, Mackenzie, Linklater, and, above all, Muir.

Today the literature of Scotland can be described neither as a "cultural ruin" (Ian Hamnett) nor as the rich harvest forecast by Gunn in the 1930's. Since 1966 the University of Edinburgh Press has been publishing an impressive annual anthology entitled *Scottish Poetry*. In 1969, Southside, a new Scottish imprint, has been introduced with a first publication, *Fifteen Poems and A Play,* by Sydney Goodsir Smith. One sees, however, no single unified movement, but rather a general agreement that Scottish writers choose to write about "anything that comes up their backs" and in whatever manner inspires them. The famous Scottish historian William Robertson (1721–93) anticipated that, as a result of Scotland's union with the British Empire, English would eventually dominate almost to the exclusion of Scots. This has all but come to pass. Yet, as Thomas Henderson observed, "Vernaculars are always dying . . . but they have a knack of continually evading the official, definite announcement of their passing." Scots still possesses an amazing tenacity and capacity, witnessed by Sydney Goodsir Smith's poem "The Secret Isle," Garioch's excellent epic *The Muir,* or Tom Scott's impressive volume *The Ship, and Ither Poems* (1962). Outside the vernacular, MacCaig is moving rapidly from early "apocalypticism" to the stature of a Muir or MacDiarmid; he may perhaps become the finest Scottish poet in two hundred years. His latest volumes—*A Common Grace* (1960), *A Round of Applause* (1962), and *Measures* (1965)—present beautifully structured pieces, full of dramatic phrases, brilliant details, and intense feeling for nature, with rich imagery from everyday experience of Edinburgh and the western Highlands.

New and old novelists continue to be drawn to Scottish materials. Clifford Hanley (*Dancing in the Streets,* 1958) offers a "great jolly dollop of the old nostalgia" in his story about Glasgow tenements and back courts. Alexander Trocchi weaves diarylike recollections of his Glasgow boyhood into *Cain's Book* (1963). Meanwhile, Linklater explores the possibilities of alternate passages of irregular verse and prose in *Roll of Honour* (1961) and succumbs to the memorable heroism of Bonnie Prince Charlie in *The Prince and the Heather* (1965).

BIBLIOGRAPHY: Davidson, J., *Fleet Street* (1909); Thomson, D. C., ed., *Scotland in Quest of Her Youth* (1932); Graham, R. B. C., *Rodeo* (1936); Gray, A., *Selected Poems* (1948); Soutar, W., *Collected Poems* (1948); Smith, S. G., *A Scots Anthology* (1949); Angus, M., *Selected Poems* (1950); Young, D. C., ed., *Scottish Verse* (1952); Magnusson, M., ed., *Saltire Review* (1954–61); Muir, E., *An Autobiography* (1954); Soutar, W., *Diaries of A Dying Man* (1954); Kinsley, F., ed., *Scottish Poetry* (1955); Reid, A., *Two Scots Plays* (1958); Wittig, K., *The Scottish Tradition in Literature* (1958); Muir, E., ed., *New Poets* (1959); Muir, E., *Collected Poems* (1960); Smith, S. G., *The Wallace* (1960); Scott, A., ed., *New Saltire Review* (1961–64); Duval, K. D., and Smith, S. G., eds., *Hugh MacDiarmid* (1962); MacDiarmid, H., *Collected Poems* (1962); Mackenzie, C., *My Life and Times* (1963); Scott, T., *The Ship* (1963); Finlay, I. H., *The Sea-Bed, and Other Stories* (1964); Luyben, H. L., *James Bridie* (1965)

ROBERT D. THORNTON

SEFERIS, George

(pseud. of *Yórgos Seferiádis*), Greek poet and essayist, b. 29 Feb. 1900, Smyrna

The son of a diplomat and professor of international law at the University of Athens, S. moved with his family to Athens in 1914. He studied law in Athens and later in Paris. His diplomatic career began in 1931 when he was appointed to the staff of the Greek Consulate in London, at which he stayed until 1934. He was press officer to the Ministry of Press and Information in Athens in 1941 when Greece fell to the Nazis. He thereupon accompanied the Greek government into exile. From 1944 until 1962, he held many important diplomatic posts in the Middle East and England, the last of which was the ambassadorship to Great Britain. S. was awarded the Nobel Prize for Literature in 1963.

In 1931, when the tradition of the lofty poetry of Palamás and Sikilianós (qq.v.) had worn thin, S.'s first book of poetry, *Strofí,* opened new dimensions for Greek poetry. Working in the symbolist (*see* symbolism) vein, especially in the direction indicated by

Stéphane Mallarmé (1842–98) and Valéry (q.v.), S. was writing what have been called the "best Greek specimens of *poésie pure.*" His verse is characterized by simplicity, directness, and exquisite music lyricism.

In the poem *I Stérna* (1932), S. wrote about the ravages of time, human suffering, the role of memory, and destiny, themes that S. keeps returning to throughout his life. The "we" of the poem, like that of the chorus in ancient Greek tragedy, speaks for the individual as well as for Greek humanity. The "cistern" (Greek, *stérna*), S.'s first important symbol, stands for consciousness as it accumulates the experience of losses, personal and historical. The simple natural beauty of Greece is haunted by the ghosts of unfulfilled dreams and longings.

The year 1935 was significant in modern Greek letters for the establishment of *Ta néa grámata*, the magazine that fostered new departures in Greek poetry; the appearance of Andréas Embiríkos's (b. 1901) *Ipsikáminos*, the first important Greek collection of surrealist (*see* surrealism) verse; and the publication of S.'s *Mithistórima* (Eng., 1960). This collection is marked by a colloquial yet often cryptic language and an intensification of simplicity and directness, which stems from his sensitive assimilation of the techniques of Cavafy (q.v.) and of Eliot (q.v.), many of whose poems he translated into Greek (some are collected in *I írimi hóra ke ála É piímata*, 1963), including *Murder in the Cathedral* and *The Waste Land.* (The translation of the latter has been very influential in Greece.)

In a series of fifteen dramatic monologues, the voice of modern Greek consciousness speaks. A contemplative, murmuring voice, it is deeply aware of the past as well as the present, and all ages of Greece live as one in a haunting interplay. In superb images, S. weaves together the ingredients of life in Greece —the sea and ships, the islands, the barren soil, the mountains, the whimsical winds, the ancient ruins. He explores movingly the historical and human truths that lie behind the picturesque appearances. The dead, still important to the living, send insistent messages that are no solution to our problems, no solace to our despair but yet reveal patterns of experience that are very much like our own. S. could not have selected a persona more appropriate than Odysseus the wanderer, the most expressive figure of the Greek temperament and reality.

It is with him and his companions that S. identifies himself. Fatality rules. As the odyssey continues, the expected miracle never arrives. We are left with the impression of the broken oars that prevented the mariners from reaching the islands of the blessed.

S.'s *Yimnopediá* (1936) and *Tetráthio Yimnasmáton* (1940) contain some of his earlier experiments, as well as the poems he was writing in the late 1930's. In several dramatic monologues S. created the persona of Stratís Thalasinós (the sea traveler), who reflects S.'s actual experience in terms of the myth of the Odyssean wanderer.

Stratís the sea traveler was the persona S. spoke through in the three poetic journals: *Imerolóyo katastrómatos A'* (1940; Log Book I, 1960), *Imerolóyo katastrómatos B'* (1944; Log Book II, 1960), and *Imerolóyo katastrómatos C'* (1955; Log Book III, 1960).

Imerolóyo katastrómatos A', written when S. was consul in Albania from 1936 to 1938, is full of the premonitions evoked by the darkening world situation. This collection contains S.'s masterful "O Vasiliás tis Asínes." In this S. poses the problems of time and of human vanity by means of a haunting dialogue between the past and the poet.

Imerolóyo katastrómatos B' (1944), written during S.'s World War II years in Africa, is inspired by the loneliness of being in exile and the longing to return home.

The subject of *Imerolóyo katastrómatos C'* (1955) is Cyprus and the nature of its deeply rooted Greekness.

Much different and more integrated than the *Imerolóyo* poems is *Kíhli* (1947; The Thrush, 1960), a poem in three movements. S.'s most metaphysical poem, it seems to project by means of the myth and metaphor the destiny of the human soul. The *Thrush,* a ship sunk during the war off the shores of Poros Island, becomes symbolic of the black ship that carried Odysseus to Hades. On his way down to Hades, Odysseus becomes Oedipus at Kolonos. Subsequently the spirit that rises to light again is that of Antigone, symbol of self-integration.

S.'s superb prose style and his critical perception are best revealed in *Dokimés* (1944; On the Greek Style, 1966). This is a book of essays on poetry, T. S. Eliot, Andréas Kalvos (1792–1869), and the Greek chronicler General Makriyánis.

S. is the great renovator of modern Greek poetry in our time. Gifted with an unfailing

255

feeling for the language, thoroughly versed in the Greek tradition, endowed with a deep historical sense, and highly sensitive to the problems of our century, he brought Greek verse to a new flowering.

FURTHER WORKS: *Tris méres sta monastíria tís Kapathokías* (1953); *Delphí* (1961); *Discours de Stockholm* (1963); *Piímata* (1964); *Tria krifá piímata* (1960); *Déka éxi Haikus* (1969); *I glósa stin píisi mas* (n.d.). **Selected English translations:** *The King of Asine, and Other Poems* (1948); *Poems* (1960); Selections in *Six Poets of Modern Greece* (1960); *On the Greek Style* (1966); *Collected Poems* (1967)

BIBLIOGRAPHY: Stanford, W. B., *The Ulysses Theme* (1954), pp. 176–78; Keeley, E., "T. S. Eliot and the Poetry of G. S.," *Comparative Literature*, Summer 1956, pp. 214–26; Keeley, E., "G. S. and Stratis the Mariner," *Accent*, Summer 1956, pp. 153–57; Sherrard, P., "G. S.," in *The Marble Threshing Floor* (1956), pp. 185–231; Karandónis, A., *O piitís Yórgos Seféris* (1957); Savidis, G. P., ed., *Ya ton Seféri* (1961); Friar, K., "G. S.: The Greek Poet Who Won the Nobel Prize," *Saturday Review*, 30 Nov. 1963, pp. 16–20; Arnákis, G. G., "The Tragedy of Man in the Poetry of G. S.," *The Texas Quarterly*, Spring 1964, pp. 55–67; Keeley, E., "S.'s Elpenor: A Man of No Fortune," *The Kenyon Review*, Summer 1966, pp. 378–90; Decavalles, A., "Greekness and Exile," *Spirit*, Sept. 1968, pp. 111–15

ANDONIS MANGANARIS DECAVALLES

In his poetry the Greek Nobel Prize winner G. S. is subtle, indirect, evocative, illusive, and allusive. But in his prose he is simple, direct, precise and logical, cutting through verbiage and tributary temptation to unfold with a disarming humility those fundamental truths, which shibboleths of generations tend to distort and hide.
Kimon Friar, in *The New York Times Book Review* (19 Nov. 1963), p. 19

The man who has caught the spirit of eternity which is everywhere in Greece and who has embedded it in his poems is George Seferiádhis, whose pen name is S. I know his work only from translation, but even if I had never read his poetry I would say this is the man who is destined to transmit the flame. S. is more Asiatic than any of the Greeks I met; he is from Smyrna originally but has lived abroad for many years. . . . He is the arbiter and reconciler of conflicting schools of thought and ways of life. He asks innumerable questions in a polyglot language; he is interested in all forms of cultural expression and seeks to abstract and assimilate what is genuine and fecundating in all epochs. He is passionate about his own country, his own people, not in a hidebound, chauvinistic way but as a result of patient discovery following upon years of absence abroad. This passion for one's country is a special peculiarity of the intellectual Greek who has lived abroad. In other peoples I have found it distasteful, but in the Greek I find it justifiable, and not only justifiable, but thrilling, inspiring.
Henry Miller, "George Seferiádhis," in *Greek Heritage* (Spring 1964), p. 104

One might say that this apocalyptic volume ["Mithistorima"], which officially marks the arrival of "modern poetry" in Greece, is a consequence —in a way—of the psychology that goes with the diplomatic profession. As a diplomat, S. could have no fixed abode, no still center in his outward life —although Greece always remained at the heart of his inner life and spiritual adventures, firm and unwavering. He moved from country to country, according to the requirements of his profession. . . . But it is a typical feature of S.'s poetry that he was never swayed by any "cosmopolitan" element, even though he lived in so many different countries. What concerned him was to find deep and eloquent symbols to help him express his innermost feeling: the anguish born from a nightmare vision of life coupled with death, doomed to waste away and perish. This vision is given vivid form in the brief images, so essentially Greek, which make up the general landscape of "Mithistorima": dry rocks, naked islands, old disused harbors, broken oars, old shipwrecks washed ashore, a few scattered pine-trees, deserted shores and low-backed mountains, an occasional oleander or a plane-tree; the scarcity of water, the yearning for coolness; dried-up wells, mutilated statues, ancient stones, solitary hovels thickly whitewashed under a sun that seems to empty the eye-sockets and strip faces down to the bone. This world appears for the first time in our poetry; in "Mithistorima," it is transposed into a dream which assumes the fascination of a nightmare. We do not want to look, yet our eyes remain fixed upon it. This is so because the nightmare is deeply and essentially poetic; because it is expressed in terms of the purity of line, the solidity, the density and simplicity which one finds in Greek stone-work and ancient art (for we have here a neo-Hellenic classicism); because it opens up a deeper perspective for a fresh appraisal, both more accurate and more human, of Greek history (which is, in fact, the history of every civilization); and finally because it is a voice that rises from the ruins and despair of our age.

"Mithistorima" is a new "Waste Land." But it has no connection with Eliot's London. Its invisible prototype is to be found in S.'s consciousness where Asia Minor, together with Smyrna and the

Hellenism of Homer, lies buried forever. As for the tangible prototype, we can see it in the pure, classical Greek landscape, as utterly humanized as ancient Greek art itself. It is a landscape which has registered a long and glorious history of civilization, so human that only a landscape such as this could give birth to it, and make possible, for instance, the miracle of ancient Attic tragedy. A distant echo of this world has managed to reach us through one of the purest poetical voices of our times: through S.'s "Mithistorima," and through all the other volumes that came to widen, transform, and enrich this vision....

Andréas Karandónis, "George Seferis," in
Greek Heritage (Spring 1964), p. 97

SELVINSKI, Ilya Lvovich

Russian poet and dramatist, b. 24 Oct. 1899, Simferopol, Crimea; d. 21 March 1968, Moscow

Son of a merchant, S. worked at many jobs —stevedore, actor, wrestling teacher, etc.—in his youth. He published his first poetry in 1915. After attending the University of Moscow (1921–23), he became the leading poet of the Constructivists, until the group broke up in 1930. During World War II he was a lieutenant colonel in the army and wrote propaganda verses; S. was decorated for his war service.

S.'s first book of verse, *Rekordy* (1926), is the closest to the doctrine of constructivism. In the late 1920's S.'s major works were: —*Ulyalayevshchina* (1927), a civil war novel in verse; *Zapiski poeta* (1928), a semiautobiographical work; *Pushtorg* (1929), a poem about the fur trade; and *Komandarm 2* (1929), a verse play about the civil war. All of them treat the theme of a romantic intellectual struggling with the revolution and with postrevolutionary problems.

After having been sharply criticized, S. stopped experimenting and wrote several historical plays in verse, more conventional in style and essentially reflecting party views on history, such as *Rytzar' Ioann* (1939), *Babek* (1940), and *Rossiya* (1941–54). He has also written one novel, *Arktika* (1957), in which prose alternates with verse.

S.'s poetry of the 1920's is still of interest because of its clever imitation of speech and song, its unusual rhymes, and colorful naturalistic descriptions.

FURTHER WORKS: *Pao-Pao* (1933); *Lirika* (1937); *Orla na plechshe nosyashchi* (1940); *Livonskaya voina* (1944); *Lirika i drama* (1947); *Tragedii* (1952); *Chitaya Fausta* (1952); *Bolshoi Kirie* (1954); *Izbrannyye proizvedeniya* (2 vols., 1960); *O yunost moya* (1966)

BIBLIOGRAPHY: Lezhnev, A., "I. S.," in *Sovremenniki* (1927), pp. 72–94; Gelfand, M., "Peredelka mechtatelya," *Pechat i revolyutziya*, No. 10 (1929), pp. 41–63, and No. 11 (1929), pp. 32–57; Reznik, O., "Dramaturgiya I. S.," *Oktyabr'*, XLIV (1967), ii, 197–209; Maguire, R., *Red Virgin Soil: Soviet Literature in the 1920's* (1968)

VLADIMIR MARKOV

SENDER, Ramón José

Spanish novelist and critic, b. 3 Feb. 1902, Chalamera de Cinca (near Alcolea de Cinca, Huesca)

The son of small farmowners, S. was educated in Saragossa and Madrid. He early became involved in radical politics and was briefly imprisoned during the Primo de Rivera dictatorship (1925–30). During the civil war he served as an officer with the Loyalist forces, escaping to France late in 1938. In March 1939 he emigrated to Mexico and entered the United States on a Guggenheim fellowship in 1942. S. became an American citizen in 1946, and from 1947 until 1963 he taught Spanish literature at the University of New Mexico. He is at present a writer-in-residence at the University of Southern California.

In 1930, while on the editorial staff of *El Sol* in Madrid, S. published his first novel, *Imán* (Am., Pro Patria, 1935; Eng., Earmarked for Hell, 1934). This was based on his experiences in Morocco during a tour of compulsory military service from 1922 to 1925. It was an immediate success and was widely translated abroad.

Before the outbreak of the Spanish Civil War, S. published six other novels, of which perhaps the best known is *Mr. Witt en el cantón* (1935; Mr. Witt among the Rebels, 1937), an historical novel describing a republican uprising in 1873. The book was awarded Spain's highest literary award, the Premio Nacional de Literatura.

S.'s most partisan book is *Contraataque* (1938; Am., Counterattack in Spain, 1937; Eng., The War in Spain, 1937), a personal narrative based on his experiences during the civil war.

257

In general, S.'s literary evolution reveals a gradual shift from a realistic, revolutionary, and direct portrayal of moral and sociopolitical problems in his preexile period to a poetic, symbolic, and philosophical treatment. His most ambitiously philosophical novel, *La esfera* (1947; The Sphere, 1949), was, however, a critical failure because its excessively long didactic-lyrical passages were felt to have been insufficiently integrated with the book's narrative elements.

Crónica del alba (1942; Chronicle of Dawn, 1944), *Hipogrifo violento* (1963), and *La quinta Julieta* (1967) make up a trilogy that is often considered S.'s spiritual autobiography. In these works he returns in time to rediscover and examine the sources of his idealism, an idealism that impelled him and others to fight for human justice in Spain. (This trilogy appeared in American translation as *Before Noon* in 1957).

S.'s fiction is characterized by a deep concern for the fate of man in society as well as man's relation to the cosmos. These two themes are most effectively given fictional treatment in *El lugar del hombre* (1939; A Man's Place, 1940) and *El rey y la reina* (1949; The King and the Queen, 1948). S.'s best work is noteworthy for its superb fusion of poetic-philosophical with realistic-narrative elements, and for the intensely lyrical sense that suffuses novels such as *Epitalamio del Prieto Trinidad* (1942; Dark Wedding, 1943), *El lugar del hombre,* and *El rey y la reina.*

FURTHER WORKS: *El problema religioso en México* (1928); *El verbo se hizo sexo* (1931); *O.P.* (1931); *Siete domingos rojos* (1932; Seven Red Sundays, 1936); *Viaje a la aldea del crimen* (1934); *La noche de las cien cabezas* (1934); *El secreto* (1935); *Proverbio de la muerte* (1939); *Viento en la Moncloa* (1940); *Mexicayotl* (1940); *El verdugo afable* (1952; The Affable Hangman, 1954); *Mosén Millán* (1953; Requiem for a Spanish Peasant, 1960); *Ariadna* (1955); *Bizancio* (1956); *Los cinco libros de Ariadna* (1957); *Los laureles de Anselmo* (1958); *Las imágenes migratorias* (1960); *La llave* (1960); *Examen de ingenios, los noventayochos* (1961); *Novelas ejemplares de Cíbola* (1961; Tales of Cibola, 1964); *La tesis de Nancy* (1962); *La luna de los perros* (1962); *Carolus Rex* (1963); *La aventura equinoccial de Lope de Aguirre* (1964); *Jubileo en el Zócalo* (1964); *Valle-Inclán y la dificultad de la tragedia* (1965); *Cabrerizas altas* (1966);

Las gallinas de Cervantes y otras narraciones parabólicas (1967); *Las criaturas saturnianas* (1968); *Poesías y memorias bisiestas* (1969)

BIBLIOGRAPHY: Penn, D., "R. J. S.," *Hispania,* XXXIV (1951), 79–84; King, C. L., "S.'s 'Spherical' Philosophy," *PMLA,* LXIX (1954), 993–99; Rivas, J., *El escritor y su senda; Estudio crítico-literario sobre R. J. S.* (1967); Carrasquer, F., *'Imán' y la novela historica de R. J. S.* (1968); King, C. L., "Surrealism in Two Novels by S.," *Hispania,* LI (1968), 244–52

CHARLES L. KING

SENGHOR, Léopold Sédar

Senegalese poet, philosopher, and statesman (writing in French), b. 6 Oct. 1906, Joal

Black Africa's most famous and respected poet, S., the son of a prosperous trader from a minority tribe, was born and raised in a small Senegalese coastal town. After primary training in a Catholic mission there and secondary education in Dakar, he studied in Paris from 1931 to 1935, and was the first black African to obtain his *agrégation*. While teaching and writing in Paris in the 1930's, he developed close ties with black West Indian intellectuals, especially with Césaire (q.v.). Together these two poets evolved the concept of *négritude* (*see* Neo-African literature), of which S. is today the most important spokesman.

Shortly after the outbreak of World War II, S. joined the French army. He was captured during the fall of France and remained a prisoner of war until 1942. After the war he became active in West African politics. In the 1950's he represented Senegal in the French National Assembly and also founded the Bloc Populaire Sénégalais. The champion of African socialism and of a united French West Africa, he was the architect of the short-lived Mali Federation in 1959. Since 1960 he has served as President of the Republic of Senegal.

S.'s first volume of poetry, *Chants d'ombre,* appeared in 1945. The poems, many of which were written in Paris in the 1930's, reflect his sense of physical exile and cultural alienation. By invoking masks, ancestors, and protecting spirits, the poet attempts to recover both his African identity and the richness and innocence of Africa itself. S.'s experiences as a prisoner of war inspired *Hosties noires* (1948), which speaks of the Christ-like suffering of the black troops. Many of the poems combine a

GEORGE SEFERIS

RAMÓN SENDER

LÉOPOLD SENGHOR

tone of deep mourning with a note of nationalistic affirmation in which the poet sees the struggle and suffering of Africans bringing about the "bright dawn of a new day."

After the charming love poems in *Chants pour Naëtt* (1949), S. published *Éthiopiques* in 1956. In contrast to the Naëtt poems, which are personal in tone and subject, the major poems in *Éthiopiques* are declamatory, public statements concerning Africa and *négritude*. The famous poem "New York" shows S.'s concept of *négritude* to be one of association and synthesis. "Let black blood flow into your blood," he enjoins the great city. *Nocturnes* (1961), his last published volume, contains probing comments on the nature of poetry and the poetic process. Always a poet very much in the French tradition, S. shows an affinity not only with Césaire but also with Claudel and Saint-John Perse (qq.v.). The influence of Walt Whitman is also strong.

S. defines *négritude* as "the sum total of Africa's cultural values." For him these values include not only Africa's past greatness and such social virtues as brotherhood and egalitarianism, but also a unique African process of acquiring knowledge. This emotional and intuitive process, which S. calls the "reasoning embrace," penetrates to the reality that underlies the world. Sartre (q.v.) and others have noted in this an affinity with European surrealism (q.v.). For S. these values are "a yeast that can leaven the whole world."

It is important to note that *négritude* has become for S. part of a larger world view. Influenced deeply by the philosophy of Pierre Teilhard de Chardin (1881–1955), he sees *négritude* not only as the basis of the black African's claim to cultural equality but also as his vital contribution to *la civilisation de l'universel*—the world culture and community toward which society is evolving.

FURTHER WORKS: *Nation et voie africaine du socialisme* (1961); *Liberté I: Négritude et humanisme* (1964); *On African Socialism* (1965). **Selected English translation:** *S.: Prose and Poetry* (ed. J. Reed and C. Wake; 1965)

BIBLIOGRAPHY: Sartre, J., "Orphée Noir," preface to *Anthologie de la nouvelle poésie nègre et malgache,* ed. L. S. Senghor (1948); Guibert, A., *L. S. S.* (1961); Jahn, J., *Muntu* (1961); Crowder, M., *S., a Study in French Assimilation Policy* (1962); Moore, G., *Seven African Writers* (1962); Beier, U., *Introduction to African Literature* (1967), pp. 59–109; Wauthier, C., *The Literature and Thought of Modern Africa* (1967)

THOMAS R. KNIPP

SEPULVEDA, Manuel Rojas y
See Rojas, Manuel

SERNA, Ramón Gómez de la
See Gómez de la Serna, Ramón

SHAPIRO, Karl Jay
American poet and critic, b. 10 Nov. 1913, Baltimore, Maryland

S. was interested in poetry from the time he was in high school. In 1935 he published, privately, his first collection, called *Poems*. In 1941, New Directions published a number of his poems in *Five Young American Poets*. In the same year he was drafted into the army; while he was overseas he continued to write.

Person, Place and Thing appeared in 1942, *V-Letter and Other Poems* in 1944, and *Essay on Rime* in 1945. These volumes attracted widespread notice—*V-Letter and Other Poems* won the Pulitzer Prize in 1945—and when S. returned to civilian life he found himself established as a poet. He was Consultant in Poetry to the Library of Congress in 1946 and 1947, editor of *Poetry* magazine from 1950 to 1956, and, later, editor of *Prairie Schooner*. He has been teaching at universities since 1946 and is now at the University of California at Davis.

S.'s poetry is the poetry of his personal experience, of daily life; it is unencumbered by any consistent world view. His concern with the concrete is reflected in the word "Noun," which was the title of his section in *Five Young American Poets* and in the title of *Person, Place and Thing*. Humorous, ironical, warm, occasionally lyrical, sometimes serious and strong, his poetry is marked by sharpness of perception and imagery. It embodies his critical belief that a poet sees with always new vision what others have forgotten how to see.

S.'s early critical stance, expressed in flexible blank verse in his *Essay on Rime,* was an original but measured and moderate critique of the confusion in modern poetry. In *Beyond Criticism* (1953; reprinted as *A Primer for Poets*) he further analyzes that confusion, which he attributes to the dominance of various ideological systems in modern poetry, and suggests as a remedy a view that regards poetry as purely personal knowledge, springing from the personal experience of the poet and not subject to any preexisting belief or system. *In Defense of Ignorance* (1960) launched a full-scale attack on the literary establishment. The poetry and criticism produced in the decade between 1915 and 1925, especially that written by Pound, Eliot, Yeats (qq.v.), and their followers, was accused by him of being hostile to modern life, tradition-oriented, intellectual, antiscientific, and destructive to authentic poetry and its enjoyment. Against this dictatorship of "modernism" S. would restore to the reader, rather than the critic, the prerogatives of judgment.

As a critic and essayist S. has become increasingly individualistic in style, writing in sharp, colloquial prose that tends to be aphoristic in statement and pungent in observation. Though he disclaims adherence to any system and relies on the truth of personal feeling, he is clearly a romanticist and antitraditionalist who deals with the modern degeneration of values by acclaiming that degeneration is liberating. The subjectivity of his poetry is at once its strength and its weakness.

FURTHER WORKS: *The Place of Love* (1942); *English Prosody and Modern Poetry* (1947); *Trial of a Poet* (1947); *Bibliography of Modern Prosody* (1948); *Poems, 1940–53* (1953); *Poems of a Jew* (1958); *Start with the Sun: Studies in Cosmic Poetry* (with James E. Miller, Jr., and Bernice Slote; 1960); *The Bourgeois Poet* (1964); *Selected Poems* (1968); *To Abolish Children* (1968); *White-Haired Lover* (1968)

BIBLIOGRAPHY: Kohler, D., "K. S.: Poet in Uniform," *English Journal*, Feb. 1946, pp. 63–68; Glicksberg, C. I., "K. S. and the Personal Accent," *Prairie Schooner*, XXII (1948), 44–52; Southworth, J. G., "The Poetry of K. S.," *English Journal*, March 1962, pp. 159–66; Rubin, L. D., Jr., "The Search for Lost Innocence: K. S.'s *The Bourgeois Poet*," *The Hollins Critic*, Dec. 1964, pp. 1–16

DOROTHY TUCK MCFARLAND

SHAW, George Bernard

English dramatist, novelist, and critic, b. 26 July 1856, Dublin; d. 2 Nov. 1950, Ayot St. Lawrence, Hertfordshire

S. came of genteel Irish Protestant stock, but his father was a drunkard. His mother migrated to London in 1876, where she supported herself by teaching music. S., who had proceeded from uncongenial schools to an uncongenial job in a real estate agent's office, followed his mother to London. For a short time he worked for a telephone company. Then, supported by his mother, he wrote five unsuccessful novels before he drifted into journalism, becoming successively a book reviewer, an art critic, a music critic (1888–94), and finally the drama critic of *The Saturday Review* (1895–96). In 1898 he married Charlotte Payne Townshend, a wealthy Irish Fabian, later one of the founders of the London School of Economics.

This phase of S.'s career is best represented by *The Quintessence of Ibsenism* (1891), *The Perfect Wagnerite* (1898), and the magnificent dramatic criticism, *Our Theatres in the Nineties* (1932), in which he campaigned brilliantly for the new drama of ideas. The same campaign was also waged in his long correspondence with Ellen Terry, whom he admired as an actress, though he deplored the plays in which she appeared. S.'s later correspondence with the actress Mrs. Patrick Campbell is also of great interest.

In 1882 S. was converted to socialism after hearing Henry George speak and after reading the first volume of Marx's *Kapital*. (S. was always to consider himself a Marxist, though he was often at odds with the orthodox theoreticians.) He became a friend and warm admirer of William Morris (1834–96), who was then in his political phase.

In 1885 S. joined the Fabian Society, which, under his guidance and that of socialist intellectuals Beatrice (1858–1943) and Sidney Webb (1859–1947), was to have a profound influence on the political opinions of two generations and to be the midwife of the Labour Party.

During this period S. edited a volume of *Fabian Essays* (1889), served for many years as an effective political speaker, and gained some practical experience of local government.

S.'s most substantial contributions to political theory are *The Intelligent Woman's Guide to Socialism and Capitalism* (1928), the prefaces to *The Apple Cart* (1929) and *On the Rocks* (1933), and the more irresponsible treatise *Everybody's Political What's What* (1944). S.'s basic tenet was equality of income. In his later years (partly as a result of the Ramsay MacDonald government) he became skeptical of parliamentary government and of universal suffrage, and he flirted with the idea of dictatorship, though he always defended the sacred right of criticism.

Apart from socialist writers, S. was mainly influenced by Percy Bysshe Shelley (1792–1822), Charles Dickens (1811–70), and Samuel Butler (1835–1902). From Shelley he derived his vegetarianism; from Shelley and Dickens, his passion for reforming the world; and from Butler, his views on evolution and his skeptical attitude toward the society of his day.

With the exception of *Arms and the Man* (1894), S.'s first plays were performed only before coterie audiences. Published in *Plays Pleasant and Unpleasant* (1898), along with entertaining polemical prefaces, they were better known to readers than to theater audiences. It was not until the famous season at the Court Theatre (1904–1907), directed by Harley Granville Barker, that S.'s plays became popular on the stage. This popularity soon spread to Germany and the United States.

Generally misunderstood when they were first performed, S.'s plays were particularly popular in provincial repertory theaters, especially at Birmingham, where *Back to Methuselah* (1921) was first performed, and at the Malvern Festival, for which he wrote several new plays between 1929 and the outbreak of World War II, when his reputation, if not the quality of his work, was at its height.

S.'s first play, *Widowers' Houses*, was begun in collaboration with William Archer in 1885, but in its completed form it is entirely Shavian. It is concerned with the problem of slum property, and it was designed to show that many respectable people derive their incomes from this source. The theme is dramatically developed with realistic characters, a powerful second act, and an effective surprise in the third.

Mrs. Warren's Profession (1893) is a searching study of the economic causes of prostitution, and because of its theme it was originally banned. Mrs. Warren is brilliantly depicted, and the scene in which she defends her conduct to her daughter is one of the most dramatic in S.'s works. But the play is partially spoiled by unconvincing love scenes and faulty characterization.

S.'s first real success was *Arms and the Man*, one of his "pleasant" plays. In it he brilliantly satirizes romantic ideas of war and of love, contrasting the professional Swiss soldier, Bluntschli, who carries chocolate instead of bullets, and the would-be professional, Sergius.

The dialogue is sparkling, plot and characterization are first-rate, and the play is in its minor way a masterpiece.

Candida (1895) is regarded by many of S.'s critics as one of his best plays, but it has not worn well. In it S. wanted to contrast the apparent weakness and actual strength of the poet, Eugene, with the apparent strength and actual weakness of the socialist parson, Morell. But the poet is flowery and unconvincing, and Candida is idealized and more irritating than S. intended.

You Never Can Tell (1897), another popular play, is a good-natured satire on the way progressive ideas soon become out of date. Mrs. Clandon, a woman of advanced ideas in her youth, returns to England after a long absence to find herself shocked by the new socialist ideas. The action is gay and farcical, and two of the minor characters, the waiter and his barrister son, are S.'s happiest inventions.

The Devil's Disciple (1894) is a kind of burlesque melodrama in which a profligate sacrifices himself to save the life of a clergyman, and the clergyman becomes a military leader of the American colonists—both men denying their apparent faiths. The opening of the play is slow, but the scenes in which General Burgoyne appears are delightful.

Caesar and Cleopatra (1899) was S.'s first attempt to depict a superman. The construction of the play is loose and episodic, but it is full of incident, and Caesar is allowed to deliver some noble speeches on the immorality of revenge.

Man and Superman (1903), published with preface and appendices, consists of two plays in one. The main play presents the pursuit of the revolutionist Tanner by Ann, a woman—who in fact stands for "Everywoman"—unscrupulously determined to entrap the best available father for her child. Woven into this action, is another play, *Don Juan in Hell*. In a dream sequence, the Spanish profligate debates with the devil on the contrast between the sentimentalists who seek happiness and the realists who seek to understand reality (there is a similar contrast between the poet Octavius and Tanner in the main play), and on the need for man to control his own evolution. The scene in hell contains some of S.'s most eloquent prose and his most profound arguments.

The main play, based on a characteristic paradox in the relations between the sexes, is probably S.'s most satisfactory comedy, though Ramsden and Octavius are mere caricatures. Ann and Tanner are superbly realized, and both plot and dialogue are consistently masterly.

Major Barbara (1905) deals with "the crime of poverty" and the need for the idealist, whether Fabian or Christian, to face the problem of power. Undershaft, the armaments manufacturer, acts as a Nietzschean Mephistopheles who succeeds in shaking Barbara's faith and in persuading Professor Cusins (a semiportrait of Gilbert Murray, the translator of Euripides) to join his firm. The meaning of the play lies in an implied synthesis of Barbara's Christianity, Cusins's Fabianism, and Undershaft's gospel of power.

The Doctor's Dilemma (1906) is partly an amusing satire on the pretensions of medical science and partly a discussion of human values. Is it better to save a good artist who is a scoundrel, or to save a second-rate but honest doctor? S. calls it a tragedy, though the total effect is comic. Dubedat is a more successful portrait of an artist than S. elsewhere achieved, but most of the doctors are deliberate caricatures.

Androcles and the Lion (1912) has a long and superficial critique of Christianity in its preface. The play itself, about the persecution of the early Christians, is short and mainly farcical. The heroine, Lavinia, is a very Shavian Christian, and Ferrovius—like the parson in *The Devil's Disciple*—discovers that he is really a worshiper of Mars.

Pygmalion (1913) is a lighthearted play about a flower girl who is trained to speak like a duchess, the moral being the absurdity of the class system. Doolittle, the flower girl's father, is one of S.'s most delightful characters.

Heartbreak House (1917), which is the work of S. in a Chekhovian mood, is a compelling symbolic picture of the impact of World War I on the British ruling class. The leading character, Captain Shotover, eloquently prophesies doom; the capitalist and the burglar are killed in an air raid, and a rectory is destroyed. S. implies that the war will be the deathblow of capitalism and that the church will have to reform its doctrines.

Back to Methuselah was regarded by S. as his masterpiece and shows the influence on him of Bergson (q.v.). The first scene (in the garden of Eden) and the last speech of Lilith (in Part 5) are very beautiful, but in between are wastes of boredom. The theme of the play, that men can live for hundreds of years if they so desire, links up with the creative evolution of *Man and Superman*; but S. does not convince us that longevity would make us wiser.

Saint Joan (1923), on the other hand, is a masterpiece and S.'s one successful tragedy, only slightly flawed by farcical touches in the epilogue and elsewhere. The canonization of Joan was the occasion of the play, but S. attempts to show that her judges were sincere and humane men, not the villains of legend. The tragedy arises from an irreconcilable conflict.

The plays of S.'s final period betray evidences of a decline, though almost all of them contain brilliant scenes. *The Apple Cart* exposed what S. regarded as the weaknesses of parliamentary democracy and the failure of a labor government in a capitalist state. *Too True to Be Good* (1931) is an allegorical play on the state of the world, the Invalid representing the sick world, the Clergyman symbolizing the loss of faith, and Sweetie the revolution with regard to sex. The play is full of eloquent speeches, and it is lightened by some pleasant farce.

S. himself misled the critics by claiming early in his career that he was a propagandist who used the stage as a platform. He was nearer the truth when he said in his old age that his masters were not his naturalistic predecessors—or even Ibsen—but Shakespeare, Mozart, and Wagner. His plays are quite unnaturalistic in style, and even if (as Eliot [q.v.] says) the poet in S. was stillborn, his method was that of the poetic dramatist.

Nor is it true that S.'s characters are mere mouthpieces for his ideas. The meaning of all his best plays emerges from a conflict of opinion, and this emergent meaning is by no means identical with the views of the Fabian propagandist who wrote the prefaces.

S.'s work is very uneven, and he spoiled some of it by playing the fool. But his best plays are the finest examples in English of the comedy of ideas; and his prose style, though to Yeats (q.v.) it was as irritatingly efficient as a sewing machine, was a wonderful instrument of persuasion. He makes his ideas—which are never so profound as he imagines—so lucid that though we may reject them, we are helped in the process to discover our own thoughts. The best-known English dramatist since Shakespeare, S. was an influential propagan-

GEORGE BERNARD SHAW

ROBERT SHERWOOD

dist for socialism, a debunker of manifold illusions, and a superb prose stylist—eloquent, witty, and lucid.

FURTHER WORKS: *Cashel Byron's Profession* (1885–86); *An Unsocial Socialist* (1887); *The Fabian Society, What It Has Done and How It Has Done It* (1892); *The Philanderer* (1893); *The Impossibilities of Anarchism* (1893); *The Man of Destiny* (1898); *Three Plays for Puritans* (1900); *Fabianism and the Empire* (1900); *Love among the Artists* (1900); *Captain Brassbound's Conversion* (1901); *The Admirable Bashville* (1903); *Fabianism and the Fiscal Question* (1904); *The Common Sense of Municipal Trading* (1904); *Passion, Poison, Petrification* (1905); *The Irrational Knot* (1905); *Dramatic Opinions and Essays* (2 vols., 1906); *John Bull's Other Island* (1907); *How He Lied to Her Husband* (1907); *The Sanity of Art* (1908); *Press Cuttings* (1909); *The Shewing-up of Blanco Posnet* (1909); *Getting Married* (1909); *Misalliance* (1910); *The Dark Lady of the Sonnets* (1910); *Socialism and Superior Brains* (1910); *Fanny's First Play* (1911); *Great Catherine* (1913); *The Music-Cure* (1914); *Common Sense about the War* (1914); *Overruled* (1915); *O'Flaherty, V. C.* (1915); *Lord Augustus Does His Bit* (1917); *Annajanska, the Bolshevik Empress* (1919); *Peace Conference Hints* (1919); *The Fascinating Foundling* (1926); *The Glimpse of Reality* (1927); *Do We Agree?* (1929); *Immaturity* (1930); *What I Really Wrote about the War* (1931); *Ellen Terry and B. S.: A Correspondence* (ed. C. St. John; 1931); *Complete Works* (1931–50); *Essays in Fabian Socialism* (1932); *Pen Portraits and Reviews* (1932); *The Adventures of the Black Girl in Her Search for God* (1932); *Doctors' Delusions, Crude Criminology and Sham Education* (1932); *Music in London, 1890–94* (1932); *Major Critical Essays* (1932); *A Village Wooing* (1933); *Short Stories, Scraps and Shavings* (1934); *The Millionairess* (1935); *The Simpleton of the Unexpected Isles* (1935); *The Six of Calais* (1936); *London Music in 1888–89* (1937); *Prefaces* (1938); *In Good King Charles's Golden Days* (1939); *Geneva: A Fancied Page of History* (1939); *S. Gives Himself Away* (1939); *Cymbeline Refinished* (1946); *The Crime of Imprisonment* (1946); *Buoyant Billions* (1947); *Sixteen Self Sketches* (1949); *S. on Vivisection* (ed. G. H. Bowker; 1949); *Shakes versus Shav.* (1950; *The Complete Plays* (1950); *Farfetched Fables* (1950);

B. S. and Mrs. Patrick Campbell: Their Correspondence (ed. A. Dent; 1952); *Selected Prose* (ed. D. Russell; 1953); *Advice to a Young Critic* (1955); *The Illusions of Socialism* (1956); *My Dear Dorothea* (1956); *B. S.'s Letters to Granville Barker* (ed. C. B. Purdom; 1956); *S. on Theatre* (ed. E. J. West; 1958); *An Unfinished Novel* (ed. S. Weintraub; 1958); *How to Become a Musical Critic* (ed. D. H. Lawrence; 1960; *S. on Shakespeare* (ed. E. Wilson; 1961); *To a Young Actress: Letters to Molly Tompkins* (ed. P. Tompkins; 1961); *Platform and Pulpit* (ed. D. H. Lawrence; 1962); *Complete Plays with Prefaces* (1962); *The Matter with Ireland* (ed. D. H. Lawrence and D. H. Greene; 1962); *Religious Speeches* (ed. W. S. Smith; 1963); *The Rationalization of Russia* (ed. H. M. Geduld; 1964); *The Complete Plays* (1965); *Collected Letters, 1874–1897* (ed. D. H. Lawrence; 1965); *The Complete Prefaces* (1965); *Selected Non-Dramatic Writings* (ed. D. H. Lawrence; 1965); *Selected One-Act Plays* (2 vols., 1965); *S.'s Ready-Reckoner* (ed. N. H. Leigh Taylor; 1966)

BIBLIOGRAPHY: Chesterton, G. K., *G. B. S.* (1909); Bab, J., *B. S.* (1909, 1926); Palmer, J. L., *S.* (1915); Harris, F., *B. S.* (1931); Wilson, E., *The Triple Thinkers* (1938); Strauss, E., *B. S., Art and Socialism* (1942); Winsten, S., ed., *G. B. S. 90* (1946); Bentley, E., *G. B. S.* (1950); Ward, A. C., *B. S.* (1951); Mander, R., and Mitchenson, J., *Theatrical Companion to S.* (1954); Weintraub, S., *Private S. and Public S.* (1962); *The Shavian,* journal published since 1963; Watson, B., *A Shavian Guide to the Intelligent Woman* (1964); Smith, J. P., *The Unrepentant Pilgrim* (1965); Fromm, H., *B. S. and the Theater in the Nineties* (1967)

KENNETH MUIR

Mrs. Warren is a powerful and stimulating, even an ennobling, piece of work—a great failure, if you like, but also a failure with elements of greatness in it. It is decried as unpleasant by those who cannot bear to be told publicly about things which in private they can discuss, and even tolerate, without a qualm. Such people are the majority. For me, I confess, a play with an unpleasant subject, written sincerely and fearlessly by a man who has a keenly active brain and a keenly active interest in the life around him, is much less unpleasant than that milk-and-water romance (brewed of skimmed milk and stale water) which is the fare commonly provided for me in the theatre. It seems to me not only less unpleasant, but also less unwholesome. I am thankful for it.

Gratitude, however, does not benumb my other faculties. With all due deference to Mr. Archer, "Not a masterpiece, no! with all reservations, not a masterpiece" is my cry. The play is in Mr. S.'s earlier manner—his 'prentice manner. It was written in the period when he had not yet found the proper form for expressing himself in drama. He has found that form now. He has come through experiment to the loose form of *Caesar and Cleopatra,* of *The Devil's Disciple*—that large and variegated form wherein there is elbow-room for all his irresponsible complexities. In *Mrs. Warren* he was still making tentative steps along the strait and narrow way of Ibsen. To exhaust a theme in four single acts requires tremendous artistic concentration. When the acts are split up loosely in scenes the author may divagate with impunity. But in four single acts there is no room for anything that is not strictly to the point. Any irrelevancy offends us. And irrelevancy is of the essence of Mr. S.'s genius.

Max Beerbohm, in *The Saturday Review of Literature* (1 Feb. 1902), pp. 139–40

An intelligent critic of G. B. S.'s *Man and Superman*—without doubt the author's most notable and mature book—entitled his article "The New St. Bernard." There was a certain felicity in this emphasis of the resemblance between S.'s attitude and that of the great saint with whom he is so closely connected. The famous Christian ascetics of mediaeval times, and very notably St. Bernard, delighted to disrobe beauty of its garment of illusion; with cold hands and ironical smile they undertook the task of analysing its skin-deep fascination, and presented, for the salutary contemplation of those affected by the lust of the eyes, the vision of what seemed to them the real Woman, deprived of her skin. In the same spirit S.—developing certain utterances in Nietzsche's *Zarathustra*—has sought to analyse the fascination of women as an illusion of which the reality is the future mother's search of a husband for her child; and hell for S. is a place where people talk about beauty and the ideal.

While, however, it may be admitted that there is a very real affinity between S.'s point of view in this matter and that of the old ascetics—who, it may be remarked, were often men of keen analytic intelligence and a passionately ironic view of life —it seems doubtful whether on the whole he is most accurately classified among the saints. It is probable that he is more fittingly placed among the prophets, an allied but still distinct species. The prophet, as we may study him in his numerous manifestations during several thousand years, is usually something of an artist and something of a scientist, but he is altogether a moralist. He fore-

sees the future, it is true—and so far the vulgar definition of the prophet is correct—but he does not necessarily foresee it accurately.

Havelock Ellis, *From Marlowe to Shaw* (1904), p. 291

The announcement that B. S., moralist, Fabianite, vegetarian, playwright, critic, Wagnerite, Ibsenite, jester to the cosmos, and the most serious man on the planet, had written a play on the subject of Don Juan did not surprise his admirers. As Nietzsche philosophized with a hammer, so G.B.S. hammers popular myths. If you have read his *Caesar and Cleopatra* you will know what I mean. This witty, sarcastic piece is the most daring he has attempted. Some years ago I described the S. literary pedigree as—W. S. Gilbert out of Ibsen. His plays are full of modern-odds-and-ends, and in form are anything from the Robertsonian comedy to the Gilbertian extravaganza. They may be called physical force, an intellectual *comédie rosse*—for his people are mostly a blackguard crew of lively marionettes all talking pure Shaw-ese. Mr. S. has invented a new individual in literature who for want of a better name could be called the *Super-Cad;* he is Nietzsche's Superman turned "bounder" —and sometimes the sex is feminine.

James Huneker, *Iconoclasts* (1908), p. 234

English people have been disconcerted by S.'s ability to view them from the outside, as it were. They should remember that he is merely exercising the privilege of the expatriate. Denationalised Irishmen are all capable of similarly disinterested criticism, and do not refrain from it, even in Ireland, where their position imposes obligations of caution. S. has no such obligations, and is, therefore, in a position to say more freely and more generally, what the others have whispered or felt, at least in some particular connection....

S. is never more faithful to Irish Protestant tradition than when he exhibits scepticism towards the virtues of England, without, however, turning definitely against her. He is sufficiently aloof to be critical, but his instincts draw him so inevitably to the English people that he cannot be really inimical. In short, he is that perfect type of *sans patrie* which the anglicisation of Ireland has produced; men who cannot understand their own compatriots, and must necessarily take refuge among a people with whom they are condemned to be aliens.

Many critics of B. S., struggling with the postulate that he is a puritan, have pointed out flaws in the theory. The contradictions can be resolved by reference to his Protestantism. Irish Protestantism differs considerably from English puritanism, although their lines coincide at certain points. The former has the advantage of presenting an undivided religious front, whereas the latter, by the exclusion of the Anglican Church, loses its homogeneity. S. himself has explained this solidarity of

Episcopalian and Dissenter in Ireland, which enabled him to be educated at a Methodist College, where the minority of pupils belonged to that sect. Social and political circumstances make cohesion possible amongst Irish Protestants. The negative virtue of being non-Catholic dispenses with those dogmatic *nuances* which render intercourse between Anglican and Nonconformist a different problem in England. S. had the typical school life of his class, and justly boasts that, in consequence, his is the true Protestantism.

Ernest A. Boyd, *Appreciations and Depreciations* (1917), pp. 111–13

... Mr. S. brags and boasts and lays claim to an omniscience that would scandalize most deities, but no one who has the ability to distinguish between sincerity and mere capering is in the least deceived by his platform conceit. He is one of the very few men in the world who can brag in public without being offensive to his auditors. He can even insult his audience without hurting its feelings. There is a quality of geniality and kindliness in his most violent and denunciatory utterance that reconciles all but the completely fat-headed to a patient submission to his chastisement; and his most perverse statements are so swiftly followed by things profoundly true and sincerely said that those who listen to him are less conscious of his platform tricks than are those who merely read newspaper reports of his speeches.

St. John G. Ervine, *Some Impressions of My Elders* (1922), p. 190

I get the keenest pleasure watching S. squirm through a tattooed subject. He confesses he couldn't write words Joyce uses: "My prudish hand would refuse to form the letters; and I can find no interest in his infantile clinical incontinences, or in the flatulations which he thinks worth mentioning. But if they were worth mentioning I should not object to mentioning them, though, as you see, I should dress up his popular locutions in a little Latinity. For all we know, they may be peppered freely over the pages of the lady novelists of ten years hence; and Frank Harris's autobiography may be on all the bookstalls."

You will observe that he can find no interest in these matters, yet he appears to have read them all and remembers them pretty well; which would seem to belie his lack of interest in them. When I find no interest in a thing I simply drop it and forget it, but S. is made of sterner stuff. Like reformers and censors and smut-hounds generally, he wallows in what he likes to call dirt, not from pleasure, but as duty. This completely contradicts his simile that pornographic novels are like offering a hungry man a description of dinner, and that, even if the description was very lifelike, it could not satisfy his hunger. All I can reply is that these descriptions seem to have satisfied S.'s hunger, for

he seems to have read them all and gone without his dinner.

Frank Harris, *On Bernard Shaw* (1931), p. 230

One feels, indeed, that S. was always at his happiest when he left his own period and lived for a while with the people of another age; that although *Heartbreak House, John Bull's Other Island* and *The Doctor's Dilemma* may be revived as "period pieces" quite as often as *The School for Scandal, She Stoops to Conquer* and *The Importance of Being Earnest*, yet the most natural, most convincing, most imaginative, least self-conscious of his works are *Caesar and Cleopatra, Androcles and the Lion,* and *Saint Joan.* These will live as long as there is an English stage devoted to anything better than the sort of play from which he redeemed it.... Most of his characters do not get far enough away from himself to attain a life of their own, and the really vital ones, the religious and self-conscious types, come straight from their creator. But in the three plays just mentioned the subsidiary characters catch some of the radiance spread by the protagonists and the strings of the puppet-master are fainter. S. must have felt where his real weakness lay as a dramatist of contemporary life; for he confessed that he had always been a sojourner on this planet rather than a native of it; that his kingdom was not of this world; that he was at home only in the realm of his imagination, and at ease only with the mighty dead: with Bunyan, with Blake and with Shelley; with Beethoven, Bach and Mozart.

Hesketh Pearson, *Bernard Shaw* (1942), p. 394

It is worth noting, I think, that in his fight for the recovery of right values, in a social order which had become so mentally and morally defective under its veneer of Christianity, S. (though much more a Christian in principle than most of us) was entirely secular in his method of attack on the social conscience; and it was not until he wrote his preface to *Androcles and the Lion* that he openly championed Christianity against the charge that it had become a proved failure, and declared that it had not failed because it had never yet been tried, and that it was about time that it *was* tried. It was a case of the Humanist once again (as has happened before) coming to the rescue of Christian realism from the cold formalism of other-wordliness.

Laurence Housman, in *G. B. S. 90,* ed. by Stephen Winsten (1946), p. 49

If S.'s plays are in the first place the meeting-ground of vitality and artificial system and in the second of male and female they are in the third place an arena for the problem of human ideals and their relation to practice. His characters may be ranged on a scale of mind, ideas, aspirations, beliefs and on a scale of action, practicality, effectiveness. At one extreme there are men of mind who make as little contact with the world of action as possible. Such are most of S.'s artists. At the other extreme are men of action who lack all speculative interests and ideal impulses. Such are S.'s professional men: soldiers, politicians, doctors. At a little distance from the one extreme are the men of mind who are interested in this world even if they can do nothing about it. Such, in their different ways, are Tanner, Cusins, Keegan, Shotover, and Magnus. At a little distance from the other extreme are certain practical men with a deep intellectual interest in the meaning of action. Such are the businessmen Undershaft and Tarleton, the soldiers Napoleon and Caesar.

The conversations which all these men, of mind or of action, have with each other have, perhaps, more nervous energy, a more galvanic rhythm, than any other disquisitory passages in all S. For they are all pushing, probing towards the solution of the problem of morals in action. They are all part of the search for the philosopher-king. Keegan talks with the politician Broadbent, Shotover with the businessman Mangan, Magnus with his cabinet. Most strikingly, perhaps, Undershaft talks with his Professor Cusins. They are agreed that there is no hope until the millionaires are professors of Greek and the professors of Greek are millionaires.

Eric Bentley, Bernard Shaw
(1947), pp. 158–59

S. postulates a universe containing or consisting of two factors, life and matter. Admittedly, he sometimes speaks of life as creating matter as when, by willing to use our arms in a certain way, we bring into existence a roll of muscle, but the general rule is that matter is, as it were, there to begin with. Thus, matter is spoken of as life's "enemy." "I brought life into the whirlpool of force, and compelled my enemy, Matter, to obey a living soul," says Lilith at the end of *Back to Methuselah*. Regarding matter in the light of an enemy, life seeks to dominate and subdue it. Partly to this end, partly because of its innate drive to self-expression, life enters into and animates matter. The result of this animation of matter by life is a living organism. A living organism, then, derives from and bears witness to the presence of both the fundamental constituents of which the universe is composed; it is life expressed in matter. S. suggests rather than explicitly states that life cannot evolve or develop *unless* it enters into matter to create organisms; these are, in fact, the indispensable instruments wherewith it promotes its own development.

C. E. M. Joad, Shaw (1949), p. 178

In the plays of the first decade especially, [a] cheerful determination to tame the wild men and to draw the fangs of revolution seems particularly striking. Nietzsche's doctrine of the superman— which might seem to others to foreshadow a blond beast, amoral and ruthless—tends to become no more than a rather extravagant method of recom-

mending self-help and improvement. *The Revolutionist's Handbook,* supposed to have been written by the rebellious John Tanner, hero of *Man and Superman,* begins by breathing fire and then carefully explains that in democratic England there is all the revolution necessary every time the voters have recourse to the ballot box. In the same book a shocking section ridiculing sexual morality and especially the sentimental word "purity" ends by demonstrating that, since the number of men and women in England is approximately equal, monogamy is the only sensible system. In that same play even Strindberg's battle of the sexes, described by Tanner in the first scene as a remorseless struggle where the only question is which party shall destroy the other, turns out to be but a sort of sham battle in the course of which the Life Force makes the hero and heroine temporarily irrational in order that it may benevolently trick them into sacrificing what they believe to be their desires in favor of their deepest impulse—which is to try to create better offspring.

Joseph Wood Krutch, Modernism in Modern
Drama (1953), p. 51

But because he was an iconoclast, this does not mean, as many people imagine, that all his work will "date" itself into obscurity. I suspect that all the "dating" that can happen has already happened. His best pieces, those comedies unique in style and spirit, have the vitality that defies time and all social changes. Their character, their appeal, may be different—for notice how early plays like *Arms and the Man* and *You Never Can Tell,* once thought to be grimly shocking, now seem to bubble and sparkle with wit and delicious nonsense—but they will be alive. And existing still behind the work will be the memory and the legend of the man, half saint and half clown, preposterous in his long Jaegar outfit and assorted fads, glorious in his long stride towards some kingdom worthy of the spirit —the wittiest of all pilgrims, humming an air by Mozart.

J. B. Priestley, Thoughts in the Wilderness
(1957), p. 187

SHAW, Irwin

American playwright, short-story writer, and novelist, b. 27 Feb. 1913, New York City

After graduation from Brooklyn College in 1934, S. spent the next two years writing radio serial dramatizations of famous comic strips such as Dick Tracy and The Gumps. Following *Bury the Dead* (1936), the first of his plays to be produced commercially, he left radio and began writing film scripts for Hollywood. Since 1963 he has lived in Switzerland.

Bury the Dead—an antiwar drama in which

soldiers killed in battle refuse to be buried—and the equally successful *The Gentle People* (1939) immediately established S.'s reputation as a playwright. These early plays and the short stories that began to appear in *The New Yorker* magazine in the late 1930's successfully captured the *Zeitgeist* of Depression America.

S.'s first novel, *The Young Lions* (1948), a commercially successful story about World War II, was marred by sentimentality and structural deficiency. In *The Troubled Air* (1951) S. capitalized on a contemporary and controversial issue, the privately sponsored blacklisting of suspected communists and fellow travelers in the entertainment world. *Lucy Crown* (1956), the story of a married woman whose infidelity wrecks her life and the lives of her husband and son, is perhaps the most disappointing book S. has written. The plight of a still competent artist who may be past his creative prime is the focus of *Two Weeks in Another Town* (1960). *Voices of a Summer Day* (1965), the story of a middle-aged American's failure to adapt to an ever changing suburbia with which he can no longer identify, is repetitive and frequently marred by a self-imitative style. However, in *Love on a Dark Street* (1965), the author's own choice of his best short stories from 1954 to 1964, S.'s narrative expertise is still evident.

While S.'s short stories never approach the polemical intensity of the fiction of Dos Passos and Steinbeck (qq.v.), they do have powerful sociological overtones that give them an immediacy not always found in his novels. Now essentially a novelist rather than a short-story writer, S.'s talent is still best suited to descriptions of mood and atmosphere. When he expands this talent and writes a novel, he is frequently forced to rely on cliché and contrivance. Most of S.'s novels, however, are redeemed by conscientious craftsmanship and the excellence of individual scenes and episodes where the hand of the experienced writer of shorter fiction is still visible.

FURTHER WORKS: *Sailor off the Bremen* (1939); *Welcome to the City* (1942); *Sons and Soldiers* (1944); *Act of Faith* (1946); *The Assassin* (1946); *Mixed Company* (1950); *Tip on a Dead Jockey* (1957); *Children from the Fair* (1963); *Rich Man, Poor Man* (1970)

BIBLIOGRAPHY: Aldridge, J. W., *After the Lost Generation* (1951); Evans, B., "I. S.," *CE*, XIII (Nov. 1951), 71–77; Fiedler, L. A., "I. S.: Adultery, the Last Politics," *Commentary*, XXII (July 1956), 71–74; Startt, W., "I. S.: An Extended Talent," *The Midwest Quarterly*, II (Summer 1961), 325–38; Alpert, H., "The Joys of Uncertainty," *SatR* (29 Dec. 1962), p. 27

WILLIAM STARTT

SHEN Yen-ping

(pseuds.: *Mao Tun, Hsüan Chu,* etc.), Chinese novelist and short-story writer, b. 1896, Tung-hsiang, Chekiang Province

S. came from a small-town, middle-class family and was educated in the big cities. After graduation from the junior division of the National Peking University, he worked in the editorial office of the Commercial Press, one of the large publishing companies in Shanghai. In 1921 he became editor of the company's *Hsiao-shuo yüeh-pao* ("Fiction Monthly"). He was also one of the founding members (1920) of the Literary Research Association (*see* Chinese Literature). With the support of the Association members, the *Hsiao-shuo yüeh-pao* soon became a leading literary periodical of the time (1921–32), and in it were published many important works of modern Chinese fiction, including those of S. himself.

A prolific writer, S. wrote more than ten novels, of which the most popular are the trilogy *Shih* ("The Eclipse," 1930), which includes *Huan-mieh* ("Disillusion"), *Tung-yao* ("Vacillation"), and *Chui-ch'iu* ("Pursuit"); *Hung* ("Rainbow," 1930); and *Tzu-yeh* (1933; Midnight, 1957). He also published several story collections that include such well-known tales as "Ch'un-ts'an" (Spring Silkworms, 1956) and "Lin-chia p'u-tzu" ("The Shop of the Lin Family").

During the Sino-Japanese War (1937–45), S. joined the exodus of Chinese intellectuals to the southwest interior. His important works in this period were the novels *Fu-shih* ("Corrosion," 1941), *Shuang-yeh hung szu erh-yüeh hua* ("Frosted Leaves as Red as Flowers in February," 1943), and the play *Ch'ing-ming ch'ien-hou* ("Before and After the Spring Festival," 1945).

S. shared the modern Chinese writers' interest in politics, which was often inseparable from literature. Although he was not a member of the Communist party at that time, he had pronounced leftist tendencies and associated with authors who were articulate in their denunciation of the Kuomintang government. After the founding of the People's Republic of China in 1949, he rose high in the literary hierarchy of the new regime and was elected chairman of the All-China Federation of Literary Workers (later called the Chinese Writers Union). For sixteen years (1949–65) he was minister of culture in the Communist government. Beginning in 1951, he also served as editor of "Chinese Literature," the official literary organ of Communist China. Since 1967, however, his name has disappeared from the masthead.

A faithful chronicler of his time, S. records in a realistic manner the men and events of modern Chinese society, focusing on its ugliness and evils and on class distinctions that separate the rich from the poor. He analyzes with meticulous care the disruptive social and political forces that plunged the country into chaos during the most critical years prior to the socialist revolution that ushered in the communist regime. In recent years, he has done little creative writing beyond revising and reissuing his earlier works in ten volumes that have been published under his pseudonym as *Mao Tun wen-chi* (1958–61; "Mao Tun's Collected Works"). His fate since the recent "cultural revolution" is unknown.

Selected English translations: *Spring Silkworms, and Other Stories* (1956); *Three Seasons, and Other Stories* (n.d.)

BIBLIOGRAPHY: Monsterleet, J., *Sommets de la littérature chinoise contemporaine* (1953); Ting Yi, *A Short History of Modern Chinese Literature* (1959); Hsia, C. T., *A History of Modern Chinese Fiction, 1917–1957* (1961); Liu Wu-chi, "Book the Ninth—The Modern Period," in *A History of Chinese Literature,* ed. Herbert A. Giles (supplemented ed., 1967)

WU-CHI LIU

SHERWOOD, Robert Emmet

American dramatist, b. 4 April 1896, New Rochelle, New York; d. 14 Nov. 1955, New York City

S.'s life and literary career closely reflect the intellectual currents of his generation. He left Harvard early in his college career to serve with the Canadian Expeditionary Forces in France. He returned to America at a time when intellectuals, disillusioned by World War I, were exhibiting a detached and amused cynicism. From 1920 to 1928, S. edited *Life*, the humor magazine.

Turning to the theater, he achieved immediate success with *The Road to Rome* (1927), a sophisticated and witty pacifist play about Hannibal and his march on Rome. In *Waterloo Bridge* (1929) he decried war somewhat more seriously, but most of his early plays are witty comedies that deride traditional values.

By the mid-1930's, however, many intellectuals began to find cynical detachment untenable and empty. In *The Petrified Forest* (1935) and *Idiot's Delight* (1936, Pulitzer Prize), S.'s cynical, materialistic heroes come to the serious discovery that serving others, even self-sacrifice, is what gives life meaning and dignity. *Abe Lincoln in Illinois* (1938; Pulitzer Prize, 1939) and *There Shall Be No Night* (1940; Pulitzer Prize, 1941) present their protagonists (Lincoln in *Abe Lincoln in Illinois,* and a Finnish Nobel-Prize-winning doctor and his American wife in *There Shall Be No Night*) discovering that detachment is pointlessly selfish and heroically offering their lives for the benefit of others.

During World War II S. was prominent as the intellectual involved in contemporary life —he worked for the U. S. Office of War Information and wrote at least parts of Roosevelt's speeches. From such experience came material for his Pulitzer Prize biography *Roosevelt and Hopkins* (1949). His Academy-Award-winning script for the film *The Best Years of Our Lives* (1946) also presented a group of men who had given heavily of themselves in support of the America cause.

S.'s last theatrical success, *Miss Liberty* (1949), a musical comedy written with Moss Hart and Irving Berlin, at least shows S.'s sensitivity to one more intellectual current—the American tendency to consider musical comedy a serious dramatic genre.

FURTHER WORKS: *The Love Nest* (1927); *The Queen's Husband* (1928); *This is New York* (1930); *Reunion in Vienna* (1931); *The Virtuous Knight* (1931); *Revelation* (1941); *The Rugged Path* (1945); *Small War on Murray Hill* (1957)

BIBLIOGRAPHY: Shuman, R., *R. E. S.* (1964); Brown, J. M., *The World of R. E. S.: Mirror to His Times* (1965)

JAMES T. NARDIN

SHOLEM ALEICHEM
See Aleichem, Sholem

SHOLOKHOV, Mikhail Aleksandrovich

Soviet-Russian novelist and short-story writer, b. 24 May 1905, Kruzhilan (Vyeshenskaya)

S. grew up in a small village in the Don River region. He attended school only until 1918 and two years later joined a military detachment engaged in fighting the antirevolutionary bands that were plundering the Don districts. After the civil war S. was active in the literacy drives and in local musical and drama ensembles, as a musician, playwright, and actor.

In 1922 S. went to Moscow to continue his education. There he supported himself as a laborer and studied informally under the writers Ossip Brik (b. 1888) and Viktor Shklovski (b. 1893). His first story, "Ispytaniye," appeared in 1922. In 1924 S. returned to the Don region to marry a young schoolteacher and make his home in an area whose beauty and way of life have always been a source of inspiration for him.

S.'s short stories now began appearing regularly in the Moscow press and in 1925 *Donskiye rasskazy* (The Tales of the Don, 1962) was published with a preface by the Cossack writer A. S. Serafimovich (1863–1949). This was followed by a second collection, *Lazorevaya step'* (1925; The Azure Steppe, included in *The Tales of the Don,* 1962). Both books depict the Don Cossacks during the civil war.

After 1925 S. attempted the longer narratives that were to become his medium. He began a novel whose working title was *Donshchina,* but after completing about a hundred pages he realized that this story of the Cossacks' part in the revolution required wider scope. He therefore started to work on the epic *Tikhii Don* (1928–40; The Silent Don, 1942: I, And Quiet Flows the Don, 1934; II, The Don Flows Home to the Sea, 1941). Millions of copies of the first volume were sold on publication, and the twenty-three-year-old author became famous throughout Russia overnight. By 1941 his reputation was worldwide.

Tikhii Don is a powerful and authentic work that offers a panoramic view of life and events in the Don Cossack territory during 1912–22. In his central character, Gregory Melekhov, S.

embodies the uneasiness of the Russian peasantry and the Cossacks, who were puzzled and disoriented by the social revolution underway. Historical necessity presides over the structure of the novel. In recounting his protagonist's tragic search for truth amidst the agonizing perplexities of the period, S. offers in the relationship between Gregory and Aksinia one of the most stirring and beautiful love stories in Russian literature.

S. focuses on the traits and behavior that define the essence of a psychological moment, singling out the subtle changes that occur within the mind. Mingling the epic and the lyric he makes free use of humorous incidents, moving descriptions of nature, and echoes of Russian folklore. Because of this, his socialist realism (q.v.) is strongly tied to the great Russian tradition of critical realism, to the classics—mainly Nikolai Gogol (1809–1852) and Lev Tolstoi (q.v.)—and to Gorki (q.v.) among the Soviet writers.

In 1930, S. interrupted his work on Part III of *Tikhii Don* and began a new epic novel designed to dramatize the collectivization program that was part of the first five-year plan. *Podnyataya tzelina* (2 vols., 1932, 1955–59; I, Am., Seeds of Tomorrow [1935], Eng., The Virgin Soil Upturned [1935]; II, Harvest on the Don [1961]) draws a broad picture of these difficult transition years in the Don region. Though it focuses on the hardships, self-sacrifice, and heroism involved, S. adds touches of humor and tenderness. The book was awarded the Lenin Prize in 1960.

At one time, S. wrote to Stalin protesting various injustices against Cossack farmers. Aware of the dangers that such an act exposed him to, S. secretly left the Don region before the NKVD could arrest him. Nevertheless, he succeeded in having the cases of deported *kolkhoz* workers reviewed and many of the decrees were reversed. His involvement in public affairs explains his years of literary silence and the delays in publishing parts of *Tikhii Don* and *Podnyataya tzelina.*

Oni srazhalis' za rodinu (1943–44, 1949, 1954; They Fought for Their Country, 1943–44; expanded translation, 1959) is an as yet unfinished novel. Taken with his two other major works, it constitutes the last part of S.'s vast trilogy on thirty crucial years in the history of Russia—the revolution, the collectivization, and World War II—as reflected through the prism of the Cossack world. The novel starts with the Russian retreat in the

Don area during World War II. It is designed to culminate with the battle of Stalingrad and the defeat of the Nazis.

Among S.'s better postwar stories is "Sud'ba cheloveka" (1957; The Fate of a Man, 1957), an account of one man's spiritual resistance to the horrors and destruction of war.

S. has written many essays, articles, and speeches on current topics of national and international importance. They have always been genuinely inspired by the thinking behind his declaration at the Second Congress of Soviet Wrtiers in 1954: "Each of us writes according to the dictates of his heart, but our hearts belong to the party and to our people, whom we serve with our art." In 1966 this principle moved S. to denounce (in his speech at the XXIII Congress of the Communist Party) Soviet writers who present a critical view of the U.S.S.R. in manuscripts smuggled abroad.

S.'s art goes beyond the limitations of regionalism and achieves a universal significance. His ability to combine historical synthesis with psychological analysis has won him international stature and brought his best writing recognition as contemporary classics. In 1965, when S. was awarded the Nobel Prize, "the artistic power and integrity" of Tikhii Don was cited by the Nobel Prize Committee as itself being of sufficient merit to have won the prize for its author.

FURTHER WORKS: Nakhalionok (1925); Nauka nenavisti (1942; The Science of Hatred, 1943); Sobraniye sochinenii (8 vols., 1956 ff.); Sobraniye sochinenii (9 vols., 1965 ff.); Pervenetz velikikh stroik (n.d.). Selected English translation: One Man's Destiny, and Other Stories, Articles, and Speeches. 1923–1963 (1967)

BIBLIOGRAPHY: Grinberg, J., "M. S.," International Literature, July 1945; Ozerov, V., "Foremost Man in Soviet Literature," Soviet Literature, Nov. 1949; Muchnic, H., "S. and Tolstoy," The Russian Review, XVI (April 1957); Kokta, M., Publitzistika M. S. (1960); Ermolaev, H., "S. Thirty Years After," Survey, No. 36 (April-June 1961); Sofronov, A., "The Priceless Manuscript of And Quiet Flows the Don," Soviet Literature, Nov. 1961; Carlisle, O., Voices in the Snow (1962); Maslin, N., Roman S. (1963); Britikov, A. F., Masterstvo M. S. (1964); Tsai-Hui, "The Renegade Features of S.," Chinese Literature, No. 7 (1966); Stewart, D. H., M. S.: A Critical Intro-duction (1967); Prijma, K., "Cherez kostry Chan Kai-Shi i Mao Tze-Dung," Ogoniok, April 1969

OLGA PRJEVALINSKAYA-FERRER

[In Virgin Soil Upturned, S.] attacks the all-important subject of the collectivization of the village. On the whole, in the plots, in some of the characters, and in the general atmosphere, this novel, because of the subject matter, is necessarily reminiscent of Panferov's Brusski, Zamoyski's Lapti, and other novels of this kind. But S.'s book is much less obtrusive propaganda and much more artistic than these other works. This is due partly to the author's unmistakable genius, partly to the fact that the work of collectivization is farther advanced now, and the writer can see it better at this stage than could his predecessors, and partly, no doubt, to the development of self-criticism in Soviet Russia in general. Be this as it may, it is both instructive and esthetically inspiring to read this grandiose portrayal of Soviet village life, the clash of social forces, the truthful delineation of characters, in whom the good and the bad mix as they do in life, whether they are communists, kulaks, or occupy any other position in the struggle.

Sophie R. A. Court, in BA (Autumn 1933), pp. 431–32

Mr. S.'s novel [And Quiet Flows the Don] has no unity of time or place; we follow the Don Cossacks from their village to the front, from the front to Petrograd, and the small recurring sections of natural description (the Don in spring, summer, autumn, winter) is too mechanical a device really to impose on the story a sense of unity. It is a weakness that the incidents we could least happily dispense with ... touch only in their beginning and their end the fortunes of the Cossack villagers who are Mr. S.'s main theme. There is no obvious reason why this novel should begin or end where it does. There is no lack of economy in the treatment of each incident, but the incidents themselves are too numerous.

Graham Greene, in Spectator (6 April 1934), p. 551

Of the Russian authors I have read, S. is almost the only one with a highly developed sense of locality.... But besides his sense of locality, he also has a sense of people that is somewhat commoner in Russian fiction, though rare enough in the literature of any country. He writes about them as if he had always known and loved them and wanted the outside world to understand just why they acted as they did. They are of course his own people, the community or nation of the Don Cossacks, and another writer might have a hard time making them seem plausible. They are peasants tied to the soil, and yet until the end of the civil wars they were soldiers wandering over the face of the earth. They are miserly with their wheat but prodigal with their money and their lives; they are heavy drinkers, brawlers, wife beaters and, on occasion, brutalized killers, yet they are full of simple kindliness; they are honest citizens descended from outlaws and ready in any period of disorder to resume the life of their ancestors.... Another writer might have insisted on combing ... their hair and wiping the blood from their hands before admitting them to his hygienic fiction.

Apparently "The Silent Don" is the greatest of all the novels that have been written about the Russian revolution; and I say "apparently" for the one reason that it is hard to tell just how good the book may be in the original. Stephen Garry's translation is by no means the worst that I have read during the past few years; at least he has a feeling for English prose. But to judge from sections of the novel that appeared in International Literature, it is far from being complete, and it is full of meaningless expressions and misunderstandings of the Russian text. Not for a single page does it let you forget that it is being translated from a very foreign language.

Malcolm Cowley, in New Republic
(18 Aug. 1941), pp. 225–26

S.'s novels answer one of the basic requirements of the real epic, that the personal destiny of each character, each participant in the course of events, be interwoven with the destiny of the people and hinge directly on it. The fate of S.'s heroes coincides and forms a single whole with the historical subject.

The role of labour is preeminent in S.'s books, as in the life of the people.

In *And Quiet Flows the Don,* we nearly always see the Cossacks at their tasks. All kinds of farm work are described—ploughing, haymaking, fishing, tending livestock, felling timber.

Together with his songs and thoughts, his labour is the Cossack's boon companion all his life. How the Cossacks love their soil, how they pine for their villages, ploughs and ox teams when they are away at war!

Labour as S. describes it, is full of that moral inspiration, poetry, struggle, that are possible only in the creation of a new world. It is the key to the character of the man who is building that world, his intelligence, his passions, his temperament, his inmost self.

The creative task S. set himself in *Virgin Soil Upturned* was a very novel and difficult one. The usual love story of the old novel, with its intrigues and surprises, is missing here. In fact, there are practically no women in the novel, except for the minor characters Lushka Nagulnova and Marina Poyarkova. Neither has it the highly dramatic historical sweep of *And Quiet Flows the Don.* The *Virgin Soil Upturned* reproduces not a whole

decade bursting with events and battles, but a few months of 1930. But that was the period of collectivization—words that speak volumes. The content, theme, interest of this novel lie in the rise of a new, Communist attitude towards labour. How much action, how many thrilling events take place in little Gremyachensky village!

I. Lezhnev, in Soviet Literature
(Aug. 1948), p. 122

[S.] made sweeping statements about the West such as, "All Western literature is effeminate." And it was useless to argue or to invoke writers like Hemingway or the younger generation of American novelists, because he wasn't that interested. But about Russia and Russians he was perceptive and lyrical. It was no affectation; he loved them with an open and irrepressible love. I have seldom encountered a more earthy yet haunting feeling for Russia. S.'s world as a writer and as a man is not intellectual; neither is it spiritual, although it is poetic. No one in Russia in his generation has caught so well the nostalgia of fleeting time. S.'s realm is that of the sentiments and, even more, that of the elusive sensuous perception. The finite nature of the moment as he describes it causes a certain melancholy to pervade his writings. His conversation was full of concrete touches, tangy and yet tender. Through Remizov, I had heard spoken Russian raised to the level of an art. Remizov had a special sense for words and for syntax. But then, he was a medievalist, a man of immense culture and his conversation was often elliptic and even archaic. S.'s was as effective in an entirely different way: free-flowing and yet exact and sharp. Its expressiveness captivated me and I regret my inability to convey it.

Olga Andreyev Carlisle, Voices in the Snow
(1962), pp. 46–47

Approximately 10 million peasants were victims of calculated starvation during the years of forced collectivization. It is unknown how many perished in concentration camps. But the main goal, the consolidation of Party rule, was achieved.

It was this process of liquidating a Russian village that M. S. powerfully and truthfully described in *Seeds of Tomorrow.* No other Soviet novel contains an account as candid as S.'s. Paradoxical as it may seem, the explanation lies in the fact that S. had been dedicated to the Party heart and soul all his life and was a true believer in Communism, just like the people who crucified Russia, and he could therefore allow himself to depict reality much more truthfully than those who did not share his belief. He described reality honestly because he believed that in spite of all sacrifices the imposed collectivization would benefit Russia in the long run. And we ought to be grateful to him for his candor. For any reader who does *not believe* in Communism, this novel will always provide a key to understanding the evil which dictatorships, be

271

they Communist or Fascist, bring to the world—
a total, final evil: death of the soul and then of the
body.

Mihajlo Mihajlov, *Russian Themes*
(1968), pp. 194–95

SIENKIEWICZ, Henryk

Polish novelist, short-story writer, essayist,
and journalist, b. 6 May 1846, Wola Okrzejska;
d. 5 Nov. 1916, Vevey, Switzerland

The son of an impoverished noble family,
S. was educated in Warsaw and in 1871 graduated from the Szkoła Głowna University. Subsequently, he was a reporter and columnist,
coowner of the biweekly *Niwa* (1872–82), and
then editor of the newspaper *Słowo* (1882–87).

After travels in North America (1876–78)
and Africa (1890–91), S. published his famous
travel reports, *Listy z podróży* (1876–78;
Portrait of America: Letters, 1959) and *Listy z
Afryki* (1891–92).

S.'s literary activity and involvement in the
cause of Polish freedom and national survival
made him a major figure in his native land.
World War I found him in Switzerland, where
he became active in organizing relief for Polish
war victims and promoting the cause of Polish
independence.

S.'s literary works, aside from his newspaper
columns, travel reports and somewhat less
successful plays, fall into two categories: psychological and social novels or short stories,
and historical novels. From a modern vantage
point, his psychological novels, such as *Bez
dogmatu* (1889–90; Without Dogma, 1893) and
Rodzina Połanieckich (1893–94; Children of
the Soil, 1895), suffer from a simplistic and at
times sentimental treatment. But S.'s numerous short stories are masterpieces of composition in which he depicts: the hardship and
misery of the peasant life in *Szkice węglem*
(1880; Charcoal Sketches, 1897) and *Janko
Muzykant* (1800; Am., Yanko the Musician,
1893; Eng., A Country Artist, 1899); the tragic
fate of the poor emigrant in *Za chlebem* (1880;
Am., For Bread, 1898; Eng., Her Tragic Fate,
1899); the nostalgic life of a refugee in
Latarnik (1881; The Light-House Keeper,
1893); the fight for national survival in *Z
pamiętnika poznańskiego nauczyciela* (1879;
Paul, 1884).

It is as a writer of historical fiction that S.
excels. Though his scholarship has at times
been questioned, his ability to captivate the
reader is undisputed. Colorful plots, vivid nar-

rative, broad canvases of battle scenes, and
an idealistic realism are combined with a
superb craftsmanship and unexpected touches
of humor that make these novels perennial
favorites. The Polish historical novels were
written "to strengthen the spirit" of the Poles,
subjected at that time to both Russian and
Prussian chauvinistic policies. His famous
trilogy—*Ogniem i mieczem* (1883–84; With
Fire and Sword, 1890); *Potop* (1884–86; The
Deluge, 1891); and *Pan Wołodyjowski* (1887–
88; Pan Michael, 1893)—deals with Poland's
struggle for national survival in the 17th c.
These novels contain the immortal Falstaff-
ian character Pan Zagloba. *Krzyżacy* (1897–
1900; Am., The Knights of the Cross, 1900;
Eng., The Teutonic Knights, 1943) describes
events in early 15th-c. Poland; it was decisive
in his winning the Nobel Prize for Literature
in 1905.

S.'s works depicting the early Christian era
show a profound knowledge of Roman culture
and a deep understanding of the life of early
Christian converts. These insights illuminate
the short story "Pójdźmy za Nim" (1893; Am.,
Let Us Follow Him, 1897; Eng., Anthea, 1899)
and his most popular novel, *Quo Vadis* (1895–
96; Eng., 1896), which describes the dying
pagan Roman world with something close to
perfection.

S.'s works have been translated into forty-
two languages and have established him as a
master storyteller in both Polish and world
literature.

FURTHER WORKS: *Na marne* (1872; In
Vain, 1899); *Humoreski z teki Worszyłły*
(1872); *Stary sługa* (1875; The Old Servant,
1897); *Sielanka: Obrazek leśny* (1875;
Sielanka: A Forest Picture, 1898); *Hania*
(1876; Eng., 1897); *Selim Mirża* (1877);
Komedja pomyłek (1878; Comedy of Errors,
1893); *Przez stepy* (1879; Lillian Morris, 1893);
Orso (1879; Am., 1899; Eng., A Circus
Hercules, 1899); *Z pamiętnika korepetytora*
(1879); *W krainie złota* (1880–81); *Czyja
wina?* (1880; Whose Fault?, 1899); *Jamioł*
(1880; Yamyol, 1893); *Niewola tatarska* (1880;
Tatar Captivity, 1897); *Na jedną kartę* (1880;
On a Single Card, 1898); *Czy ci najmilszy?*
(1880; Is He the Dearest One?, 1904);
Wspomnienie z Maripozy (1882; Memories of
Mariposa, 1959); *Z puszczy Białowieskiej*
(1882); *Bartek Zwycięzca* (1882; Bartek the
Victor, 1893); *Sachem* (1883; Eng., 1893);
Legenda żeglarska (1884; A Legend of the Sea,

1904); *Ta trzecia* (1888; That Third Woman, 1897); *Sabałowa bajka* (1889); *Walka byków* (1889; The Bull-Fight, 1893); *Wyrok Zeusa* (1890; The Decision of Zeus, 1898); *Lux in tenebris lucet* (1891; Light in the Darkness, 1959); *U źródła* (1892; At the Source, 1897); *Organista z Ponikły* (1893; The Organist of Ponikla, 1897); *Bądź błogoslawiona* (1893; Am., Be Thou Blessed, 1897; Eng., Be Blessed, 1899); *Z wrażen włoskich* (1893); *Sen* (1893); *Żurawie* (1896; The Cranes, 1904); *Na jasnym brzegu* (1897; Am., On the Bright Shore, 1897; Eng., In Monte Carlo, 1899); *Muszę odpocząć* (1897); *Na Olimpie* (1900; The Judgement of Peter and Paul on Olympus, 1899); *Zagłoba swatem* (1900); *Kordecki* (1903); *Na polu chwały* (1903–1905; Am., On the Field of Glory, 1906; Eng., The Field of Glory, 1906); *Dwie łąki* (1904; Life and Death: A Hindu Legend, 1904); *Diokles* (1906); *Sąd Ozyrysa* (1908); *Wiry* (1909–1910; The Whirlpools, 1910); *W pustyni i puszczy* (1910–11; Am., In Desert and Wilderness, 1912; Eng., Through the Desert, 1912); *Legiony* (1913–14)

BIBLIOGRAPHY: Gardner, M. M., *The Patriot Novelist of Poland, H. S.* (1926); Birkenmajer, J., "H. S.," *Thought*, XIV (1939), pp. 579–93; Lednicki, W., *H. S., 1846–1916* (1948); Lednicki, W., *H. S., A Retrospective Synthesis* (1960); Coleman, A. P., *Wanderers Twain, Modjeska and S.: A View from California* (1964); Giergielewicz, M., *H. S.* (1968)

                                 MARK LIWSZYC

SIKILIANÓS, Angelos

Greek poet and playwright, b. 28 Mar. 1884, Leukas; d. 19 June 1951, Athens

S. studied law at the University of Athens, but left after two years and traveled for a time in Egypt, western Europe and the United States. With his first wife, an American, he established at Delphi a successful arts festival at which classical Greek plays were performed in the restored ancient amphitheater before international audiences (1926–32). To expound his "Delphic" views he planned to found an "international university" dedicated to peace, the cultivation of the various arts, and the projection of a dogma-free religious view of life; however, the outbreak of World War II put a definitive end to this project.

S.'s first important work, *Alafroískiotos* (1909), immediately established his reputation as a poet whose powerful lyrics rivaled those of Palamás (q.v.). Essentially a spiritual autobiography, it already shows him a visionary by the manner in which he relates nature and objective events to his own highly subjective world. In his lyrics, S. identifies with the boundless creative powers of nature, which he sees as Orphically renewed and transformed. He was inspired by an ideal vision that encompassed all Hellenic civilization from classical to contemporary Greece.

Drawing on mythology, religion, and history, S.'s poetry establishes symbols for the creative forces working toward a synthesis that alone can bring beauty and harmony to mankind. In his Orphic poem, *I Ierá Odós* (1935; The Sacred Road, 1960), the poet yearns for a personal synthesis that will enable him to unite within himself the seemingly disparate world around him.

In his later verses S. showed a marked ability to control a lyric impatience that often marred his early poetry. S.'s attempts at verse dramas were unsuccessful because he showed an insufficient command of dramatic structure, but the plays are admired for their beautiful lyrics.

One of the leading Greek poets of the 20th c., S. forcefully related the Hellenistic tradition to the contemporary world.

FURTHER WORKS: *Próloyi sti zoí* (4 vols., 1915–17); *Mitír tou Theoú* (1917); *To Pásha ton Elínon* (1918); *Delfikós lógos* (1927); *Sinídisi tis prosopikís dimiouryías* (1943); *Antídoron* (1943); *O Dédalos stin Kríti* (1943); *Sívila* (1944); *O Hristós sti Rómi* (1946); *Lirikós Víos* (3 vols., 1946–47); *O thánatos tou Diyení* (1947); *Thiméli* (2 vols., 1950). **Selected English translation:** *Akritan Songs* (1944)

BIBLIOGRAPHY: Xidís, T., *I thriskeftiki voúlisi tou S.* (1932); Katsímbalis, G., *Vivliografía A. S.* (1946); Sherrard, P. S., *The Marble Threshing Floor: A Study in Modern Greek Poetry* (1956); Dimáras, C. T., "The Work of A. S.," *Charioteer*, I (1960), i, 65–69; Avyéris, M., *A. S.* (1966); Laourdas, B., "Ideas and Ideals in Contemporary Greek Culture," *Balkan Studies*, IX (1968), 155–66

                                 * * * *

SILLANPÄÄ, Frans Eemil

Finnish novelist, short-story writer, and poet, b. 16 Sept. 1888, Hämeenkyrö; d. 3 June 1964, Helsinki

S. was the son of a day laborer in the province of Satakunta. His medical studies at the University of Helsinki led him to take a biological, monistic view of the world. At the same time he was influenced by foreign writers, especially Hamsun and Maeterlinck (qq.v.)

In 1939 he received the Nobel Prize.

S.'s first novel, *Elämä ja Aurinko* (1916), describes a summer love affair between two young people. In it nature plays a central role.

The civil war that broke out in Finland after it attained independence in 1918 is the subject of S.'s first major work, *Hurskas kurjuus* (1919; Meek Heritage, 1940). Of this Edzard Schaper (q.v..) said: It is "a novel about the overcoming of a human destiny. [The] utterly gray, monotonous, misshapen, unaware life [of a cottager] is seen in the great context of his nation's history and the even greater one of his universal human frame of reference."

The tautly constructed novella *Hiltu ja Ragnar* (1923) marked the climax of a period of Maeterlinckian mysticism and compassionate naturalism.

In 1931, S. achieved international success with his broad-scale family novel of human destinies *Nuorena nukkunut* (Am., The Maid Silja, 1931; Eng., Fallen Asleep While Young, 1939).

The elective affinity between two people is the theme of the peasant novel *Miehen tie* (1932); the way the problem is posed recalls D. H. Lawrence (q.v.).

The most appealing testimony of S.'s musical gift for words appears in *Ihmiset suviyössä* (1934; People in the Summer Night, 1966).

S.'s prose is rooted in the rural background from which he draws his subject matter. His characters—peasants, cottagers, farmhands, milkmaids—are passive and instinctual; they are slow, rough, unappealing people who bear their fates stoically. S. expressed their innermost feelings coolly and undramatically. But in his inspired moments, he wrote movingly and lyrically of these people he was so sensitive to. S. saw life and suffering in terms of the common biological relationship of all living creatures. His originality stems from the mixture of rural spontaneity, that does not shirk from realistic expressions, and an awareness of emotions, by means of which he endows reality with a dimension of rapture. S. is generally recognized as one of the outstanding writers of the 20th c.

FURTHER WORKS: *Ihmislapsia elämän saatossa* (1917); *Rakas isänmaani* (1920); *Enkelten suojatit* (1923); *Maan tasalta* (1924); *Töllinmäki* (1925); *Rippi* (1928); *Kiitos hetkistaä, Herra . . .* (1929); *Kootut teokset* (12 vols., 1932–48); *Virran pohjalta* (1933); *Viidestoista* (1936); *Elokuu* (1941); *Ihmiselon ihanuus ja kurjuus* (1945); *Erään elämän satoa* (1947); *Poika eli elämänsä* (1953); *Päiviä korkeimmillaan* (1957); *Novellit* (1961)

BIBLIOGRAPHY: Koskimies, F., *F. E. S.* (1948); Laurila, A., *F. E. S.* (1958); Gumérus, E., "La Letteratura findlandese contemporanea," *Nuova Antologia,* No. 500 (1967), pp. 499–512; Laitinen, K., *Suomen kirjallisuus 1917–1967* (1967)

LAURI VILJANEN

SILONE, Ignazio

(pseud. of *Secondo Tranquilli*), Italian novelist, essayist, and dramatist, b. 1 May 1900, Pescina dei Marsi

S. came from a family of small landowners. He was educated in the seminary at Pescina and the gymnasium at Reggio Calabria. At seventeen, he joined the Socialist Youth League in Rome; four years later, at the Socialist Congress in Livorno, he became one of the founders of the Italian Communist Party.

During the 1920's S. served as editor of *Il Lavoratore* and *L'Avanguardia.* The party also sent him on several missions abroad: Spain (1923), France (1924), and Moscow (1927). After the fascists passed the "exceptional laws" (1926), S. coordinated all communist underground activities in Italy.

In 1931, ill health and political pressure forced him into exile to Switzerland. During this period many of his works were first published abroad in foreign translation. Conflict with the communist leadership resulted in his expulsion from the party one year later. S. did not return to active politics until 1941, when he was appointed secretary of the foreign headquarters of the Italian Socialist Party.

After his return to Italy in 1944, S. continued to devote himself to the politics and literature of his country. But as his presidency of the International Committee on Cultural Freedom and his founding, with Nicola Chiaromonte, of the review *Tempo Presente* indicate, S.'s thinking has a pronounced ecumenical cast.

Other details of S.'s life can be found in his

MIKHAIL SHOLOKHOV

FRANS SILLANPÄÄ

IGNAZIO SILONE

essays, *Uscita di sicurezza* (1965; Emergency Exit, 1968). They document the harrowing conversion of the young S. to revolutionary socialism and his even more painful acceptance of the "Christian certainties" after his political disillusionment.

Yet S.'s type of Christianity does not constitute a profession of faith. "It is rather a trust," he explains in "A Choice of Companions," "that we are free and responsible beings, that each man has an absolute need to open his heart to another man's realities, and that it is possible for souls to communicate with each other."

These words describe the dream of a medieval anarchist who rejects the temptations of power for the politics of charity. It is the dream of all the Abruzzese saints and proletarian heroes (*cafoni*) S. writes about. Their paradigm is Pieter of Murrone, who, as Celestino V., abdicated from the papacy because he considered religious faith incompatible with any established system of government (*L'avventura d' un povero Christiano*, 1968).

How power invades and corrupts the remotest corners of space and spirit in modern times is narrated in *Fontamara* (Eng., 1930; It., 1947; revised, 1958). The *cafoni* of an isolated mountain village in the Abruzzi rise up against the fascists only to be brutally suppressed.

In *Pane e Vino* (1937; Bread and Wine, 1937; revised as *Vino e Pane*, 1955), S. continues his exploration of the psychology of revolt. The hunted socialist Pietro Spina dwells hidden among the tenant farmers and rural poor disguised as a priest. His work has mixed results and his life remains ambiguous. Only when he takes upon himself the blood-guilt of a near deaf-mute day laborer at the climax of *Il seme sotto la neve* (The Seed beneath the Snow, 1942; It., 1952; revised, 1961), does Spina attain to meaning and clarity.

The necessity for a free and ordered society does not cease with a change of regime. The heroes of *Una manciata di more* (1952; A Handful of Blackberries, 1953) and *Il segreto di Luca* (1956; The Secret of Luca, 1958) are still outlaw saints, sacrificial scapegoats, and martyrs to honor and integrity. Lazzaro and Luca are literally the living conscience of the people. Their Christ-like, lunatic, and gratuitous charity collides head on with the world of planned compromise.

No matter how deep the revolutionist's commitment, however, he cannot solve all the problems that confront the radical personality when he finds himself suddenly without an organization. On the contrary, the person caught in this tragic dilemma must pay for his freedom—frequently with his life. Still, S. totally rejects the solution of nihilism, which he defines as "the prevalent tendency to identify history with the conquerors."

In spite of his integrity as man and artist, S. has had many detractors. They accuse him of political naiveté, ethical inadequacy, and literary dilettantism. S.'s own life and witness easily refute the former two charges.

As to the latter charge, S. himself has admitted that on occasion he was prone to exaggeration, sarcasm, and melodrama. For that reason he revised *Fontamara, Pane e Vino*, and *Il seme sotto la neve*. The revisions resulted in a sharper focus on the inner life of the characters and produced a greater sense of irony (wine in *Vino e pane* indeed plays a larger role than bread).

But in returning again and again to the same works—like a painter who spends a lifetime portraying the same landscape—S. does not seek greater technical sophistication. By striving for an ever more faithful rendition of the popular mind in which lie the true roots of human discourse, he wants to reach the "absent majority" that is ordinarily little concerned with literary matters.

This also explains why S. does not treat literature as an icon and refuge from the world. For him it is strictly a contingent, imperfect expression of social, political, and mental forces. Nevertheless, his poetic appraisal of experience and the poetic account of it are full of a clarifying artistic passion. In this way, S. has been able to dramatize man's conflict with history and challenge the claims of totalitarianism. This makes him perhaps the most representative author of his generation.

FURTHER WORKS: *Der Faschismus* (1934); *Mr. Aristotle* (1935); *Mazzini* (1939); *Ed egli si nascose* (1944; And He Hid Himself, 1945); *La volpe e le camelie* (1960; The Fox and the Camellias, 1961); *La scuola dei dittatori* (The School for Dictators, 1938; It., 1962)

BIBLIOGRAPHY: Scott, N., "I. S., Novelist of the Revolutionary Sensibility," in *Rehearsals of Discomposure* (1952); Lewis, R. W. B., "I. S.: The Politics of Charity," in *The Picaresque Saint* (1956); Howe, I., "Malraux, S., Koestler: The Twentieth Century," in *Politics and the Novel* (1957); Krieger, M., "Satanism,

Sainthood, and the Revolution," in *The Tragic Vision* (1960); Heiney, D., "S.: Emigration as the Opiate of the People," in *America in Modern Italian Literature* (1964); Mueller, W. R., "The Theme of the Remnant," in *The Prophetic Voice in Modern Fiction* (1966); Brown, R. M., "I. S. and the Pseudonym of God," in *The Shapeless God* (1968); Camus, A., "On I. S.'s *Bread and Wine*," in *Lyrical and Critical Essays* (1968)

FRANZ K. SCHNEIDER

He is a standing menace to Caesar, this sad-eyed little editor who has become the whole of Italian literature to thousands beyond the Fascist garrisons, a walking arsenal of the world's contempt for the brass Molochs, and one of the most honest democrats alive. An exile, ... he has refused to fight Fascism on the level of its own culture, and has so purified his own philosophy of society that he finds himself alone amidst the factions who are only too eager to claim his warm humanism for their own. There is a modern tragedy in that, and an immemorial lesson. S. has moved up slowly to a point where nothing the liberal and radical enemies of Fascism may offer will satisfy him. He personifies the profound disillusionment that has come with the disintegration of the nineteenth-century philosophies of hope, and he has dismissed the twentieth-century answers one by one.

Alfred Kazin, in *New York Herald Tribune*
(25 Dec. 1938), p. 2

As [S.] has stated, ... Christianity is a heritage for the revolutionist to draw upon. But as S.'s development as an imaginative artist indicates, Christianity is not so much an ethical heritage for him as a living tradition, the symbolism and literal meaning of which are becoming the basic sources of his work. This, I am sure, must present a difficulty to all his old admirers. The world from which S. comes as a radical, and whose conscience he now represents more clearly and more personally than any other living writer, insists, as a matter of its own tradition and its own inner necessity, upon a natural morality, and conceives its struggle as neither sacred nor secular but entirely self-sustaining, a drama in which man is the sufficient character. And yet S.'s examination of natural morality and the questions he has put to the revolutionary conscience, asking it precisely how far it has come and how far it is going, remain the most searching that any man has posed in our time.

Isaac Rosenfeld, in *Nation*
(22 June 1946), p. 760

A riddle that baffles foreigners [is] the failure of S. to become popular in Italy.... S., despite the

prestige that he personally merits and enjoys, is not a great writer in Italian. His books do not come alive in our language; they necessitate laborious deciphering. And this difficulty arises not from any technical inadequacies of his style, but because he lacks expressive power.

Elena Craveri Croce, in *New Republic*
(10 May 1948), p. 24

S.'s desire to locate the ethic of an unspoiled primitive Christianity in the insulted and injured of our time is an act of intellectual desperation. Abstractly, it is hard to defend. He himself must surely know this better than anyone else, for nowhere in his work is his desire presented in the language of fanaticism or even self-assurance. There shines through all of his writing a tone of modesty, the tone of a man who knows it is his fate to expend himself so thoroughly on a question that the very idea of an answer fades into inconsequence.

For S. the socialist and S. the novelist, the only miracle of Christianity is Christ, a man whose sufferings have burdened humanity with an *intolerable* example.... His whole effort, after *Fontamara,* has been to reduce—perhaps the verb should be, to exalt—Christ to the level of a secular participant, a fellow sufferer and thereby a sustaining example, in the misery of our time.... He has tried to bring to life an image of the lonely and forsaken Christ, so as to reclaim the moral possibility of socialism, though not of socialism alone.

Irving Howe, in *New Republic*
(22 Sept. 1958), p. 18

[Like] *The Grapes of Wrath* ... *Fontamara* is also a legend of families dispossessed from the soil, but one that belongs to a different tradition. What the novel suggests—or rather what it suggested in the original version—is the group of medieval fables that deal with peasants and the Devil. The peasants are always preposterously stupid and ignorant, but shrewd in their own fashion. The Devil is full of artifice, and sometimes he is helped by a priest, but he is sure to be defeated in the end. *Fontamara* couldn't have that happy ending because it was written in 1930 ... however, there was the hint of the apocalypse to come.... Among those few lasting novels of a revolutionary era, *Fontamara* is the only one to have been revised after the Second World War.... We still have the sense of hearing a medieval legend, rough-hewn and angular, reduced to its essential outlines as if by generations of storytellers in the village marketplace, but it is no longer a *fabliau* about peasants and the Devil. Instead it becomes a golden legend about Christ reborn, tempted in the wilderness, and crucified in Jerusalem—or is Berardo rather John Baptist, who prophesies the coming of the Solitary Stranger? ... Losing some of its humor, the new version gains in somber intensity, being stripped of everything inessential so as to reveal the permanent themes of poverty, brotherly love, and sacrifice.

Malcolm Cowley, Foreword to *Fontamara* (1960), pp. v–viii

Fontamara does not, of course, surprise the reader as it did in the thirties. Few people today lend much faith to the worn legend of the Italian South as a land of music, sunshine, heady wines, and sensual passions. Yet, despite the three decades that have elapsed since its original publication, *Fontamara* (Bitter Fountain) has lost little of its power and none of its relevance. Indeed, in its new slightly revised form, it is less the sociopolitical document it was, and more a profoundly human story about people and their immense capacity for suffering.

Sergio Pacifici, *A Guide to Contemporary Italian Literature* (1962), p. 122

S. . . . is preoccupied by the will to shape a just and harmonious social order. This preoccupation dates from the time S., in 1925, joined the Communist Party. . . . Adopting communism in an act he has described as a "conversion, a complete dedication," he sought to advance its cause as the best means to accomplish his lifelong ideal: the establishment of a humane community to replace the inhumane aristocratic one. When that god failed . . . he left the Party.

This shift of politics . . . is an act typical both of S.'s life and of his art. Despite a general diminution of faith in the idea of Utopia, S. has remained steadfast in commitment to a single belief: men possess resources of moral energy which society can either channel or divert. This energy is constant; it cannot be depleted. Forestalled here, it is diverted there, ever quick to adopt diverse means in order to achieve its ends.

Each of S.'s heroes . . . exhibits this kind of constancy and this kind of resourcefulness. . . . Under whatever stress, however isolated, they choose to resist, they remain intransigent.

William Wasserstrom, *The Modern Short Novel* (1965), p. 293

SIMENON, Georges

French novelist, b. 13 Feb. 1903, Liège, Belgium

Forced by his father's ill health to abandon his studies before he was sixteen, S. became a reporter and humorous columnist for the *Gazette de Liège*. He published his first novel when he was seventeen. In December 1922 he went to Paris to build a career as a fiction writer. He began by putting himself through an apprenticeship that lasted almost ten years, in which he published more than one thousand short stories and more than 180 popular

novels, under almost two dozen different pen names. It was a useful as well as extraordinarily productive apprenticeship. S. emerged from it with an almost total mastery of the style and of the narrative technique required to fulfill his objectives in fiction.

As a result the first book he published under his own name, *Pietr-le-Letton* (1930; The Strange Case of Peter the Lett, 1933), is plainly of a piece with his most mature work. The style is beautifully spare and undecorated, and the narrative moves quickly and surely, dealing only with essential matters.

In 1931 S. published eight books. Like *Pietr-le-Letton*, all were *romans policiers* about Inspector Maigret of the Paris police. They launched what must be one of the most widely read series of books in the world. Maigret books have been published in thirty-one countries, translated into eighteen different languages, and dramatized repeatedly in European films and television. By 1970, there were eighty titles in the Maigret series.

Though S. has described his Maigret books as sketches, comparable to the sort of thing a painter might do for pleasure or as a preliminary study, they continue to delight ordinary readers and to win the respect of writers who are seriously engaged with the craft of fiction.

In 1932 S. published his first mature work outside the genre of the *roman policier*, *Le Passager du "Polarlys"* (The Mystery of the "Polarlys," 1942). Since then S. has published more than 110 serious novels. Though they demand more of both writer and reader than the Maigret books do, these novels have been, almost from the beginning, as well received internationally as the Maigret books.

By the mid-1930's writers as disparate as Henry Miller and Hemingway (qq.v.) were reading S.'s novels with respectful care, and Gide (q.v.) was making copious notes in the margins of his copies. In Europe, S. is now commonly, if not generally, recognized as a significant modern writer. In England, such recognition has been somewhat slower in coming. But in America, critics have scarcely begun to read his books, let alone to recognize the quality of his achievement.

Amid such a profusion of books one cannot make many generalizations that are both simple and valid. However, with the single exception of *Pedigree* (1948; Eng., 1962), a long, naturalistic, and highly autobiographical novel that is thoroughly uncharacteristic of S., all of his books are short. Almost all involve acts of violence—though in *Les Anneaux du Bicêtre* (1963; Am., The Bells of Bicêtre, 1963; Eng., The Patient) the "violence" is a severe heart attack—because they are usually concerned with people who are driven to their limits. Though they are set in many different countries and tell of characters in all walks of life, they all, without exception, compel the reader to join the writer in recognizing that the other man is like himself, even when the other man is a pervert and a murderer, as he is in *La Neige était sale* (1948; Am., The Snow Was Black, 1950; Eng., The Stain on the Snow).

It has been customary to speak of S. as a tragic writer. Certainly there is a great deal of grim suffering in the world of such books as *L'Homme qui regardait passer les trains* (1938; The Man Who Watched the Trains Go By, 1942), *Le Petit homme d'Arkhangelsk* (1956; The Little Man from Archangel, 1957), and *La Chambre bleue* (1964; The Blue Room, 1965).

Yet *Le Petit saint* (1965; The Little Saint, 1966) strikes a very different note, for its artist-hero is, as S. himself has commented, "a perfectly serene character in immediate contact with nature and life." S. considers the book a breakthrough, coming as it does at the end of twenty years of trying to externalize the optimism, the *joie de vivre* that lies at the base of his vision. But glimpses at least of that joy and serenity can be found in such earlier works as *Trois chambres à Manhattan* (1946; Three Beds in Manhattan, 1964), *Les Mémoires de Maigret* (1950; Maigret's Memoirs, 1963), and *Le Président* (1958; The Premier, 1961). Thus, in a perceptive, enthusiastic essay written in 1961 Henry Miller saluted S. as "a happy man."

FURTHER WORKS: *Les Gens d'en face* (1933; The Window over the Way, 1951); *Touriste de bananes* (1938; Banana Tourist, 1946); *Les Sœurs Lacroix* (1938; Poisoned Relations, 1950); *La Vérité sur Bébé Donge* (1942; The Trial of Bébé Donge, 1952); *Le Fond de la bouteille* (1949; The Bottom of the Bottle, 1954); *L'Enterrement de Monsieur Bouvet* (1950; Inquest on Bouvet, 1958); *Les Frères Rico* (1952; The Brothers Rico, 1954); *Les Complices* (1955; The Accomplices, 1966); *En Cas de malheur* (1956; In Case of Emergency, 1960); *Strip-Tease* (1958; Striptease, 1959); *Dimanche* (1959; Sunday, 1960); *Le*

Train (1961; The Train, 1964); *Le Confessionnal* (1966; The Confessional, 1967); *La Mort d'Auguste* (1966; The Old Man Dies, 1968); *Le Chat* (1967; The Cat, 1968); *La Prison* (1968; The Prison, 1969). (The above is a selected list of S.'s novels; the Maigret books are not included.)

BIBLIOGRAPHY: Narcejac, T., *Le Cas S.* (1950); Parinaud, A., *Connaissance de G. S.* (1957); de Fallois, B., *S.* (1961); Stéphane, R., *Le Dossier S.* (1961); Raymond, J., *S. in Court* (1968)

EDWARD L. GALLIGAN

SIMON, Claude
French novelist, b. 10 Oct. 1913, Tananarive, Madagascar

Like Nathalie Sarraute (q.v.), S. is older than the other "new novelists" and has been an adult witness to events such as the Spanish Civil War and World War II. Born in the colonies and raised partly in the Pyrénées Orientales, where his father was a winegrower, he has retained a certain solitary independence and has been undistracted by theorizing and the frequentation of a literary milieu.

Originally a painter, S. has continued to be "visual," treating words as though they were pigment and creating landscapes in which the human figure is drowned in the larger phenomenon. The titles of S.'s works indicate his need for a starting point in objects and sites: *Le Vent* (1957; The Wind, 1959), *L'Herbe* (1958; The Grass, 1960), *Le Palace* (1962; The Palace, 1963), *La Route des Flandres* (1960; The Flanders Road, 1961). Only recently have they become more abstract and mythical as his style has become more mannered, his vision more blurred: *Histoire* (1967; Histoire, 1968), *La Bataille de Pharsale* (1969).

Not a central ambiguity suggestive of solipsism, but a personal archeology directs his composition, offering a configuration of objects and souvenirs perceived before a baroque background tapestry picturing a public square swept by the wind of corruption and time, or a desolate battlefield on which corpses and memories decompose. Like the hero of *Le Vent*, S. seems to carry a camera like a fetish around his neck; like the heroine of *L'Herbe*, he seems to absorb the vegetation itself. The center of S.'s imagination is not in language or ideas but in an affectionate, sensory acquaint-

CLAUDE SIMON

KONSTANTIN SIMONOV

ance with the elements and the most common objects of existence.

Whatever the subject or the particular framework—a detective story, a death in the family, the rememoration of a revolution or a battle, the evocation of a certain atmosphere in a particular place—the drama that unfolds is in the telling more than in the specifics of what is related. We are always midway between chaos and a rage for order, submerged in a fluid environment of birth or putrefaction that is constantly coagulating in fixed *tableaux vivants* and then, kaleidoscope-like, reshifting and sliding into new patterns. As an epigraph for *L'Herbe,* S. quotes Pasternak (q.v.): "Nobody makes history, nobody sees it happen, any more than one can see the grass growing."

In an attempt to give a sense of depersonalized, implacable and invisible movement, S. writes in a style resembling various effects of photography—grainy enlargements, blurred, jerky or slow-motion sequences, zooming close-ups, superimpositions, fadeout or run-on transitions, scratchy newsreel surfaces. These techniques suggest, by their very context, the ravages of time, the atomistic disintegration of all material things, and the limited perspective derived from even an accumulation of points of view. Long sentences, lacking capitalization or punctuation, interspersed with parentheses, appositions, comparisons; waves of adjectives, conjunctions, approximations, suppositions, hypotheses and denials; the series of present participles—these are devices that help us identify with the confusion of emerging perceptions.

Though S. has obviously followed the development of French masters—Gustave Flaubert (1821–80), Proust, Malraux, Sartre (qq.v.)—an Anglo-Saxon influence has prevailed as well—Conrad, Joyce, and most of all Faulkner (qq.v.), whose techniques and themes S. has assimilated to such an extent that his own novels seem a sort of literary metempsychosis.

Rather than a role of action, the S. hero seeks, in objects or memories, a visionary mode. Though it does not allow him to dominate history and the narrative, any more than S. or his reader dominates them, in opening himself to the entire amalgam of sounds, smells, and sights, he expands, breaks down, and disappears into a larger experience. His aim, like S.'s, as implied by the subtitle of *Le Vent* —"the reconstitution of a baroque altarpiece" —is a form of spiritual contemplation;

reverence, not for some traditionally sacred subject, but for the anonymous inevitability of the life process.

FURTHER WORKS: *Le Tricheur* (1945); *La Corde raide* (1947); *Gulliver* (1952); *Le Sacre du printemps* (1954); *Femmes* (text accompanying works of Miró, 1966)

BIBLIOGRAPHY: Guicharnaud, J., "Remembrances of Things Passing: C. S.," *YFS*, No. 24 (1959), pp. 101–8; Ricardou, J., "Un Ordre dans le débacle," *Critique*, XVI (1960), 1011–24; Merleau-Ponty, M., "Cinq notes sur C. S.," *Médiations*, No. 4 (1961), pp. 5–10; Deguy, M., "C. S. et la représentation," *Critique*, XVIII (1962), 1009–32; Simon, J. K., "Perceptions and Metaphor in the New Novel: Robbe-Grillet, C. S., Butor," *Tri-Quarterly*, No. 4 (1965), pp. 153–82; Mercier, V., "C. S.: Order and Disorder," *Shenandoah*, XVII (1966), iv, 79–92

JOHN K. SIMON

SIMONOV, Konstantin Mikhailovich

Soviet-Russian novelist, poet, dramatist, and journalist, b. 28 Nov. 1915, Petrograd

While employed as a lathe operator, S. attended a Moscow night school for workers. He subsequently graduated from the Gorki Literary Institute (1938). During World War II he was a war correspondent for the newspaper *Krasnaya Zvezda*. These experiences were to provide the material for much of his later writing.

From 1946 to 1956, S. held numerous high party positions and was a deputy to the Supreme Soviet. He edited *Literaturnaya Gazeta* from 1950 to 1953, and *Novyi Mir* from 1954 to 1957 and is the recipient of numerous state awards, including four Stalin Prizes.

In the West, S. is generally associated with his popular wartime poem "Ty pomnish, Aliosha, dorogi Smolenshchiny" (1941; You Remember, Aliosha, in *Soviet Literature*, XII, 1956) and his best-selling novel about the siege of Stalingrad, *Dni i nochi* (1944; Days and Nights, 1945). The poem reflects the wartime sufferings of the Russians and stresses a patriotic return to and defense of the soil. An underlying popular wartime theme is the personal discovery of the "true," quasi-mystical Russia in the rural village.

Dni i nochi, S.'s most widely discussed work, is a detailed portrayal of the common man's defense of his invaded homeland, and it is generally conceded to be one of the best Soviet novels on World War II. Against a background of bombings, raids, confusion, hope and despair, S. tells of the romantic encounter between a Red Army captain and a woman in the medical corps. Though the novel's treatment of love has been attacked as "joyless," even hostile critics, after enumerating its literary flaws, concede that the book offers a realistic and impressive panorama of wartime Stalingrad.

The "loose patriotic exultation" of the war years gave way in 1946 to a drab literary period characterized by a much stricter interpretation of socialist realism (q.v.). S. seems to have gone along with this. But after Stalin's death, at the Second Congress of Soviet Writers in 1954 S. joined the ranks of the dissidents and called for a broadened concept of socialist realism.

In August 1954, S. was appointed to replace Aleksandr Tvardovski (b. 1910) as editor of the magazine *Novyi Mir,* which had been found "in error." His editorship coincided with the most exciting period in Soviet literature since the 1920's, and his efforts during this time greatly contribute to his importance as a central figure in postwar Soviet literature.

For the first time since 1930, opposing views were expressed at a party congress, and exiled writers were again published. The height of the post-Stalinist "thaw" (*see* Russian literature) was reached in 1956, and in the same year that saw the Polish and Hungarian revolutions S. published Vladimir Dudintzev's (b. 1918) novel *Not by Bread Alone,* which was considered a shocking attack on the bureaucratic system. When in August 1957 Krushchev attacked "revisionists on the literary front," S. was removed from his editorship of *Novyi Mir* and Tvardovski reinstated.

Critical appraisals of S.'s attitude at the time vary; S. is alternately seen as publishing Dudintzev, attacking Dudintzev, and steering a conciliatory course between Dudintzev and his attackers. In addition, S.'s comments on Solzhenitsyn's (q.v.) exposé of Soviet concentration camps in *One Day in the Life of Ivan Denisovich* (1962) are variously interpreted as praise and "nauseatingly hypocritical" attacks.

In a like manner, S.'s works have been attacked as both pro- and anti-Western potboilers, and as either "heroic romantic works of faith" or trivial melodramas cranked out according to bureaucratic directives.

S.'s convictions would seem to coincide with the ideals of the Soviet dream and with a loose interpretation of the literary guidelines of socialist realism. However, the doctrinaire solutions that presumably stem from a personal faith in communism inevitably lead him as an artist into a conflict with a bureaucracy that does not trust even the faithful in their personal search for the most powerful vehicle for expressing the common ideal.

Whatever his true convictions, S. has a tremendous mass appeal that cannot be ignored. An evaluation of him as a writer inevitably forces us to examine the problem of Western taste in the critical appraisal not only of his works but also of the basic concepts of Soviet literature.

In a recent autobiographical sketch, S. concludes: "In my view, poetry must always call people to courage, to resolution never to retreat in the face of obstacles, in the face of threats, or when faced with the necessity of giving one's life for a just cause. Without this, poetry is worthy of its name neither in days of war, nor in days of peace."

FURTHER WORKS: *Pavel Chiornyi* (1938); *Ledovoye poboishche* (1938); *Suvorov* (1939); *Dorozhnyye stikhi* (1939); *Istoriya odnoi lyubvi* (1940); *Paren' iz nashevo goroda* (1941); *Ot Chernovo do Barentzova morya* (1941–45); *Russkiye lyudi* (1942; The Russians, 1944); *Pod kashtanami Pragi* (1945); *Russki vopros* (1946; The Russian Question, 1947); *Druz'ya i vragi* (1948); *Chuzhaya ten'* (1949); *Srazhayushchiisya Kitai* (1950); *Tovarishchi po oruzhiyu* (1952); *Sochineniya* (1952); *Stikhi 1954 goda* (1954); *Dym otechestva* (1956); *Norvezhski dnevnik* (1956); *Zhivyye i miortvyye* (1959; The Living and the Dead, 1962)

BIBLIOGRAPHY: Lazarev, L., *Dramaturgiya K. S.* (1952); Gibian, G., *Interval of Freedom* (1960); Alexandrova, V., *A History of Soviet Literature* (1963); Brown, E., *Russian Literature Since the Revolution* (1963); Hayward, M., and Crowley, E., *Soviet Literature in the Sixties* (1964); Vishnevskaya, I. L., *K. S. Ocherk tvorchestva* (1966); Slonim, M., *Soviet Russian Literature* (1967)

RICHARD L. DAUENHAUER

SINCLAIR, May

English novelist, critic, and poet, b. 24 Aug. 1863, Rock Ferry, Cheshire; d. 14 Nov. 1946, Bierton, Buckinghamshire

The daughter of a Liverpool shipowner,

May S. was the only girl in a family with five boys. Tutored and self-taught, she spent one year at the Cheltenham Ladies College (1881–82).

Her first ambition was to be a poet. Under the pseudonym of Julian Sinclair she published *Nakiketas, and Other Poems* (1886). She was never completely to abandon verse, and in later years she wrote *The Dark Night* (1924), a novel in free verse.

With *Audrey Craven* (1897) she launched a series of dramatic novels of psychological discovery, and was one of the first to employ the "stream of consciousness" technique. *The Divine Fire* (1904), a romance about a storeworking poet, a county lady, and a gentleman critic, established her reputation. Her most self-revealing novel is *Mary Olivier: A Life* (1919); the story of a woman's life-long struggle against familial restraints and hereditary weaknesses. *Arnold Waterlow: A Life* (1924) is the story of a similar struggle by a man.

May S. described marriage with complete honesty in *Mr. and Mrs. Nevill Tyson* (1898), *The Judgment of Eve* (1907), and *The Helpmate* (1907). She described family life in *The Three Sisters* (1914), *The Tree of Heaven* (1917), *Anne Severn and the Fieldings* (1922), *The Rector of Wyck* (1925), and *The Allinghams* (1927).

As a writer, she focused attention on unconscious motivation, on the tragedy of the unfreed self, on the belief that the happiness of the body is an essential to the joy of the spirit, and on the infinite capacity of human beings to be unselfish through love and to be selfish from want of love. In many of her novels she investigated the complex conscious life of the creative writer and the relationships between his social chances and his creative writing. *The Creators* (1910) and *Far End* (1926) contain excellent characterizations of writers.

May S. was active in the women's suffrage movement and contributed generously of her time and talent. She opposed intolerance in either sex, and was unhappy over the terror tactics of unfeminine feminists.

Serious as are her psychological probings and discoveries, May S. had a very rich sense of the humorous and the comic, and she could relax in an ironic mood that enabled her to create a wide range of entertaining effects. Her scenes in dialogue are masterful and her narrative skill in relating episodes in close sequences of soundly-motivated chain reactions is of a high order.

FURTHER WORKS: *Essays in Verse* (1892); *Two Sides of a Question* (1901); *Kitty Tailleur* (1908); *The Flaw in the Crystal* (1912); *The Three Brontës* (1912); *The Return of the Prodigal* (1914); *Journal of Impressions in Belgium* (1915); *Tasker Jevons* (1916); *A Defence of Idealism* (1917); *Mr. Waddington of Wyck* (1921); *The New Idealism* (1922); *Uncanny Stories* (1923); *A Cure of Souls* (1924); *Tales Told by Simpson* (1930); *The Intercessor, and Other Stories* (1931)

BIBLIOGRAPHY: Chevalley, A., *The Modern English Novel* (1925); Elwin, M., *Old Gods Falling* (1939); Wagenknecht, E., *A Cavalcade of the English Novel* (1943); Boll, T. E. M., "M. S. and the Medico-Psychological Clinic of London," *Proceedings of the American Philosophical Society*, CVI (1962), 310–26; Allen, W., *The Modern Novel in Britain and in the United States* (1964), pp. 15–16

THEOPHILUS E. M. BOLL

SINCLAIR, Upton

American novelist, journalist, essayist, and playwright, b. 20 Sept. 1878, Baltimore, Maryland; d. 25 Nov. 1968, Bound Brook, New Jersey

The son of a liquor salesman who was overly fond of his own wares, S. belonged to a financially unsuccessful branch of the wealthy Sinclair family. His boyhood was strongly influenced by the long shadow of his prominent relatives and by his father's drinking habits—a factor that made him into a lifelong, fanatical teetotaler and led him, in *The Cup of Fury* (1956), to denounce the debilitating effect of alcohol on such writers as Stephen Crane (1871–1900), Jack London (1876–1916), and Dylan Thomas (q.v.).

An omnivorous reader, though a haphazard student, after the family moved to New York, S. was accepted at the College of the City of New York when he was only fourteen, supporting himself then and during four years of graduate studies at Columbia University by writing adventure stories for the pulp magazines. His real education, he was to say, came from his reading of the Biblical prophets, John Milton (1608–1674), and Percy Bysshe Shelley (1792–1822), whom he saw as crusaders against social injustice, prophets of rebellion.

Following his first marriage in 1900, S. decided to devote himself to serious fiction and for the next six years lived in soul-draining poverty while he published five novels that brought him a total of $1000. The best of these is *Manassas* (1904), an ideological tale of a southerner who joins the crusade against slavery, which Jack London called the best Civil War novel he had read to date. S.'s writing attracted the attention of socialist editors, and the pages of their journals were open to him. The story of these early years is fictionalized in *Love's Pilgrimage* (1911), published the year of his divorce.

When the Chicago stockyard workers struck in 1904, the magazine *The Appeal to Reason* offered S. $500 for a novel about the situation. S. went to Chicago and lived among the workers for seven weeks before returning to his New Jersey home to write *The Jungle* (1906). Serialized in the socialist periodical, the novel attracted immediate attention. Nevertheless, five publishers refused to bring it out in book form unless it were expurgated. With the help of Jack London and others, S. had gathered money to publish it at his own expense, but it was at this point accepted by Doubleday, Page and Co.

An intense and indignant story of a Lithuanian immigrant family's heartbreaking struggle to survive as stockyard workers, the novel brought S. immediate fame and wealth. However, what attracted the public's attention was not the story of human exploitation but the unrelentingly realistic descriptions of the poisonous conditions under which meat was packed and shipped. Voter clamor forced the passage of the Pure Food and Drug Act (1906), though little was done to ameliorate the lot of the workers themselves.

S. plowed the profits from *The Jungle* into Helicon Hall, a utopian experiment in community living that harked back to the traditions of Brook Farm. Established in Englewood, New Jersey, the community attracted as permanent residents young writers such as Sinclair Lewis (q.v.), and drew distinguished visitors such as philosophers John Dewey (1859–1952) and William James (1842–1910). However, encouraged by salaciously moralistic stories in the popular press, the public soon came to look upon the community as a local scandal, and Helicon Hall burned to the ground under mysterious circumstances in 1907.

S. was among the first to conceive of a mobile theater to bring revolutionary issues directly to the people. In 1912 he published his *Plays of Protest*, and though he returned to dramatic form from time to time, he was never to have much success in this genre. His best-known plays are *Singing Jailbirds* (1924) and *The Enemy Had It Too* (1950), a scientific fantasy of the atomic age.

S. continued his efforts as a socialist propagandist and on several occasions ran for public office in New Jersey and California, where he settled for many years after 1915. In 1917, however, he temporarily broke with the socialists because of their opposition to this country's entry into World War I.

The Profits of Religion (1918) was the first of S.'s famous "pamphlets" on the influence of capitalism on American life. *The Brass Check* (1919) employs S.'s own experiences as a newspaperman as the basis for a muckraking exposure of the press. In *The Goose-Step* (1923) and *The Goslings* (1924) S. focused on the defects of our educational system, while in *Mammonart* (1925) and *Money Writers* (1927) he concentrated on the relationship between capitalism and the arts.

It was, however, in his novelistic investigations into aspects of the American industrial scene that S. achieved major success with works such as *King Coal* (1917), which described conditions in the Colorado coal mines; *Oil!* (1927), an independent operator's struggle against the oil monopoly during the Harding era; and *Little Steel* (1938), which employs the background of the steel strikes of the 1930's. *Boston* (1928) turned from the industrial scene to a flagrant example of legalized injustice: the Sacco-Vanzetti case.

In 1934 S. unsuccessfully ran as Democratic candidate for governor of California. His campaign platform, EPIC (End Poverty in California), was probably the first of the now current acronymic antipoverty programs. Though it aroused the Depression electorate's enthusiasm, S.'s financial resources were no match for the bitter campaign mounted against him by the business community.

World's End (1940) introduced Lanny Budd, S.'s picaresque, ubiquitous hero who was to be his spokesman for a Marxist interpretation of world history beginning with the causes of World War I. Lanny goes everywhere, knows everyone, is privy to secrets that make neither the newspapers nor the history books, and is generous with his advice to world leaders. The series was to end with the tenth volume, *O Shepherd Speak!* (1949), which described the end of World War II, but the growing menace of Soviet power caused S. to bring his hyperenergetic hero back for a final bow in *The Return of Lanny Budd* (1953).

S. had been an early but brief convert to communism, and this period of his life is best represented by the novel *Jimmie Higgins* (1919). However, though a lifelong revolutionary and iconoclast, S.'s vigorous indignation of man's exploitation of man remained within the American idealistic tradition and ill-accorded with antilibertarian Soviet dogmatism.

Critics have condemned S.'s often superficial characterizations and naiveté, but the fact remains that his best novels are stimulating and cathartic experiences that have enthralled millions of readers both here and abroad. G. B. Shaw (q.v.) has noted that in the future when people want to know what our era was like they will have to turn to S.'s novels to bring it alive.

FURTHER WORKS: *Springtime and Harvest* (1901; also published as *King Midas*, 1901); *The Journal of Arthur Stirling* (1903); *Prince Hagen* (1903); *A Captain of Industry* (1906); *What Life Means to Me* (1906); *The Industrial Republic* (1907); *The Overman* (1907); *The Metropolis* (1908); *The Moneychangers* (1908); *Good Health and How We Won It* (with Michael Williams; 1909); *Prince Hagen* (1909); *Samuel the Seeker* (1910); *The Fasting Cure* (1911); *Damaged Goods* (1913); *Sylvia* (1913); *Sylvia's Marriage* (1914); *100% The Story of a Patriot* (1920); *Mind and Body* (1921); *They Call Me Carpenter* (1922); *Love and Society* (1922); *Hell* (1923); *The Millennium* (1924); *The Pot Boiler* (1924); *The Naturewoman* (1924); *My Life and Diet* (1924); *What's the Use of Books* (1926); *The Spokesman's Secretary* (1926); *Mountain City* (1930); *Mental Radio* (1930); *What Is Socialism and Culture?* (1931); *Roman Holiday* (1931); *The Wet Parade* (1931); *American Outpost* (1932); *I, Governor of California and How I Ended Poverty* (1933); *An Upton Sinclair Anthology* (1934); *The EPIC Plan for California* (1934); *The Book of Love* (1934); *I, Candidate for Governor: and How I Got Licked* (1935); *Depression Island* (1935); *Co-op* (1936); *Our Lady* (1938); *Terror in Russia?* (with Eugene Lyons; 1938); *Marie Antoinette* (1939); *Between Two Worlds* (1941); *Dragon's Teeth* (1942); *Wide Is the Gate* (1943); *Presidential Agent* (1944); *Dragon Harvest* (1945); *A World to Win* (1946); *Presidential Mission* (1947); *One Clear Call* (1948); *A Giant's Strength* (1948); *Another Pamela* (1950); *A Personal Jesus* (1952); *What Didymus Did* (1954; Am. edition, *It Happened to Didymus*, 1958); *My Lifetime in Letters* (1960); *Affectionately, Eve* (1961); *Autobiography of U. S.* (1962)

BIBLIOGRAPHY: Dell, F., *U. S.* (1927); Kazin, A., *On Native Grounds* (1942); Gaer, J., ed., *U. S.: Bibliography and Biographical Data* (1969)

* * * *

The fierce and humorless intensity of U. S.'s youthful masterpiece *The Jungle* has here (in *Oil!*) given place to a maturer kind of writing, with a surprising new tolerance in it for the weaknesses of human nature, and a new curiosity which fills it with the manifold richness of the American scene on every social plane. It restores U. S. to us as a novelist, and it constitutes one of the great achievements in the contemporary discovery of America in our fiction.

Floyd Dell, in *New York Herald Tribune* (12 June 1927), p. 7

Mr. S. is a major figure—and I make the statement ungrudgingly. He is a thoroughly American personality. A fluent—a fatally fluent—writer with an unconquerable desire to preach and teach, he has a heart honorably moved by human suffering. ...His insight into society is sometimes shrewd, and his prophecies are occasionally correct. Above all, his courage is...the courage of American individualism, which has nothing to do with the socialism of Mr. S.'s dream.

But when Mr. S. explicitly or implicitly demands that one's sympathy for his courage be translated into one's admiration for him as a literary artist, one can only deny the confusing plea.

Howard Mumford Jones, in *Atlantic Monthly* (Aug. 1946), p. 151

The secret of U. S. nobody yet knows—except to the degree that he still represents a flourishing of those provincial rebels, free-thinkers, and eccentrics who in the 1900's, from Robert Ingersoll to Veblen, marked the climax of our earlier agrarian and mercantile society. But what is the secret of the Lanny Budd series? ... Mr. S.'s familiar villains are here, to be sure, including the international bankers, the Fascists, and the military. Yet there is very little sense of evil in this entire chronicle of modern corruption and decay. Even Hitler has sense enough to listen to Lanny Budd.... This central view of life, which corresponds to our own earlier dreams of national destiny and to the Europeans' wildest fancy, seems to me the main element in the success of the Lanny Budd novels.

Maxwell Geismar, in *SatR* (28 Aug. 1948), p. 13

SINGER, Isaac Bashevis

American novelist, short-story writer, and essayist, b. 14 July 1904, Radzymin, Poland

S. was born into a family of rabbis—both his father and grandfather were Hassidic rabbis—and received a traditional Jewish education in the seminary. However, he was interested in secular literature, and inspired by his older brother, Israel Joshua Singer (q.v.), he began to love such worldly writers as Nikolei Gogol (1809–1852), Edgar Allan Poe (1809–1852), Fiodor Dostoyevski (1821–81), and E. T. A. Hoffmann (1776–1822).

S. and his brother fled Poland in 1935. Although he first considered going to Palestine, he settled in the United States that same year. Since then he has worked for the *Jewish Daily Forward* (a Yiddish newspaper in New York), in which many of his books were published in serial form.

In a magazine interview S. stated that he did not feel himself to be "part of the Yiddish tradition." The statement is partly true. Although he writes in Yiddish, he supervises all of the English translations of his works so closely that he occasionally lists himself as cotranslator. He is, in this important respect, an American writer and has appropriately been made a member of the National Institute of Arts and Letters.

S.'s works can usefully be discussed in terms of genre. Although he has written lengthy historical novels—*The Family Moskat* (1950, reissued 1965), *The Manor* (1967) and *The Estate* (1969)—he is not as impressive in this genre as in the short story. These three novels —the last two are part of a projected trilogy— attempt to weave together the fates of Polish Jews from 1863 (the date at the beginning of *The Manor*) to the 1939 bombing of Warsaw. In these works S. gives us a broad, realistic canvas that illuminates the destruction of old Jewish values in the wake of fascism, secularism, and scientific progress. "Conservative," the novels show that in combating the *shtetl* the world wins hollow victories. The Jew becomes an exile—at times even from his own heritage—but he nevertheless retains a loyalty to some sense of "community." The last words of *The Family Moskat* are: "Death is the messiah. That's the real truth." But S. does not completely accept such nihilism; he writes with longing for another, truer messianic hope.

S. is more impressive in his "closed" novels —*Satan in Goray* (1955), *The Magician of Lublin* (1960), and *The Slave* (1962). In these the emphasis is upon the tightrope of faith that the Jew must walk; in the absence of orthodoxy—although religion remains a central concern—he fashions existential beliefs. The novels employ the recurring themes of balance, madness, and bondage. Because the right "objective correlative" is found for each theme, though tight and constrained, these novels are curiously "expansive" parables.

Satan in Goray takes place in the 1600's after a pogrom lays waste Goray, a small town in Poland. Rechele, the "mad" heroine, is tortured by various visions. Her plight is never psychologically clear, but it becomes an overpowering symbol of a now possibly perverted lust for messianic rebirth. Her condition is universalized—is she the town and/or the Jews? —because S. believes that if we abandon traditional rituals, we are prone to fall off the tightrope of faith and mistake Satan for the Messiah.

The Magician of Lublin gives us Yasha, who pursues a hectic career as escape-artist, lover (of a Gentile), thief, and ascetic. His adventures lead to his eventual realization that his own "magic" is not enough, and he returns to the beliefs of his ancestors. We see him finally in a cell removed from the outside world that he once captivated.

The Slave is also set in the 1600's. Its protagonist is Jacob, another transplanted hero—all of S.'s heroes tend to be exiles and perhaps mirror his departure from Poland—who lives surrounded by Gentiles. Though their "slave," Jacob falls in love with Wanda—later she is named Sarah—who becomes his "Jewish" wife. She dies in childbirth and their son, Benjamin, survives. Eventually we see Jacob returning after twenty years of wandering to be buried alongside his wife. Though the love story is deeply moving, the book is essentially another ironic parable about the Jew's inescapable commitments to his faith.

S. has published four collections of short stories, *Gimpel the Fool* (1957), *The Spinoza of Market Street* (1961), *Short Friday* (1964), and *The Seance* (1968). Although the stories vary in quality, the most powerful ones— "Gimpel the Fool," "The Gentleman from Cracow," "Blood," "The Spinoza of Market Street," "The Slaughterer"—are as haunting as any written during this century. They tend to describe Orthodox rituals and old-world settings in a peculiarly modern manner. They take nothing for granted. They refuse to settle for convenient psychological assurances and motivations because they are after a somewhat mysterious, lasting "game." They present the designs that rule (or are ruled by?) us. They are bravely hesitant. It is possible to dismiss S.'s demons—who sometimes narrate stories—as merely fanciful or hallucinatory, but such a misreading neglects the author's intent. The demons *may* (or may not) exist—as do the ghosts of James (q.v.).

The compelling importance of these stories results from the fact that S. usually concentrates upon (1) a specific, controlling image (as in "Blood"); (2) an intense, obsessive hero or heroine; (3) a stylized plot; and (4) a combination of pity and irony. The resulting mixture of realism and fantasy, psychology and faith, upsets our usual separations and categorizations.

S.'s reputation has grown slowly but steadily since the publication of "Gimpel the Fool" in 1953 (translated by Bellow [q.v.]—a cultural event future critics will have to note). He is now read by the general public, and in 1966 Edmund Wilson (q.v.) proposed that S. be given the Nobel Prize for Literature.

FURTHER WORKS: *In My Father's Court* (1966); *Zlateh the Goat, and Other Stories* (1966); *The Fearsome Inn* (1967); *Mazel and Schlimazl, or the Milk of a Lioness* (1967); *A Friend of Kafka, and Other Stories* (1970)

BIBLIOGRAPHY: Buchen, I., *I. B. S. and the Eternal Past* (1968); Allentuck, M. ed., *The Achievement of I. B. S.* (1969); Malin, I. ed., *Critical Views of I. B. S.* (1969)

IRVING MALIN

[S.] set out challengingly. He wished to present us [in *Satan in Goray*] with the entire Shabbati-Zevi epoch, the complete drama of a people on the bridge between faith and superstition, going from deepest despair to highest ecstasy—and back. He wished to show us the appearance in Goray, a secluded and half-destroyed Polish town, of the mixture between despair and hope, falsehood and truth, asceticism and eroticism, licentiousness and ecstasy, loneliness and joy.... He depicts its atmosphere in the 17th century—but not the Shabbati-Zevi tragedy. Indeed, he made a comedy out of the great folk tragedy. Perhaps this coincides with historic reality. Perhaps it was really as petty and comical as it is in *Satan in Goray*.... But if the author is unable to rise upward, what is his accomplishment? Sober we can be by ourselves. No talent is needed to destroy illusions, and certainly no imagination. In his historical novel [S.] demon-

strates both talent and imagination, but he does not use them to elevate the reader, but on the contrary, to show that there is no hope of wings.... Characteristic of the novel is the tone of mockery, as if to say: "See how things which seem wonderful, mysterious, and tragic are in reality common, childish, if not foolish."

S. Niger, "Singer's Soten fun Goray," in Tzuk
(Dec. 1933), pp. 735, 737

The Family Moskat ... deals with the evolution, the rise, and the final disintegration of a wealthy and prolific Jewish clan in Warsaw.... *The Family Moskat* is much rather anthropology than history. What it lacks in continuity and analysis it makes up in variety and color of cultural and folkloristic detail. The manners and morals of the quickly risen rich, the widening gap between old and young, the face, ways and vocabulary of the ghetto street, the running debate between modernists and traditionalists, Zionists and socialists, cosmopolites and provincials, and the infinite and self-winding quibbles of the Hasidim and Orthodox—these spectacles crowd a vivid review, almost a circus, of Jewish mores. But whereas history can meet fiction on the common ground of story, anthropology and sociology cannot of themselves supply a forward-driving impulse. In *The Family Moskat,* the conveniences and necessities of plot and character are so often sacrificed by the author to the temptations of still another detail, and yet another dab, that the novel is finally jerked out of alignment with its own meaning and objective

Solomon F. Bloom, in Commentary
(Feb. 1951), p. 200

S. has many virtues, a wiry, inescapable style, an intensely personal, inimitable vision, a Machiavellian wit, but above all else it is the bracing, revivifying character of his insight that makes him important.... Perhaps it is that, so far out along that road which we really, all fooling aside, know we each must travel, his people remain so unkillable, and their comradeship in humanity so inextinguishable, that makes him important.

Kenneth Rexroth, in Commentary
(Nov. 1958), p. 460

The mystical inquiries and the meditations on the works of God and the ways of man are so adroitly interwoven through the operatic plot of [*The Slave*] that the reader is never conscious of a change of pace or tone: one is never admonished to stop a leap in mid-air to ponder a philosophical proposition although the protagonist ceaselessly ponders and proposes.... In the hands of another writer, lacking Mr. S.'s genius at spinning a yarn, this story of torture and forbidden love, of dishonor among thieves, of cruel separations and amazing reunions, of coincidences with arms as long as a gorilla's, would be preposterous. But he is a spell-binder as clever as Scheherazade; he arrests the reader at once, transports him to a far place and a far, improbable time and does not let him go until the end.... The proof of I. B. S.'s remarkable gifts as a storyteller is that he can keep the attention and sympathy of his reader through a fiction that is a combination movie scenario and hagiography. It is an admirable performance.

Jean Stafford, in New Republic
(18 June 1962), pp. 21, 22

Mr. S., regardless of language, is one of the best writers of fiction now in America.... At present we have many short-story writers in this country, but few tellers of tales. This distinction is cardinal in understanding Mr. S.'s unusual qualities. Because his work is rooted in a people, he is a superior kind of folk artist who brings narrative to the original meaning a story had: a tale passed on by word of mouth from one person to another. His style—spare, energetic, and lyrical—has the rhythm of spoken language. Moreover, his people, whatever their troubles, are not alienated from their community (though this community was cut off from the larger society around them); nor are they estranged from a deep religious view that gives meaning to life. These are formidable advantages for a writer, however remote from the places and times he deals with may seem.

William Barrett, in Atlantic Monthly
(Jan. 1965), p. 129

SINGER, Israel Joshua

Yiddish novelist and short-story writer, b. 30 Nov. 1893, Belgoray, Poland; d. 10 Feb. 1944, New York City

Son of a pious rabbi in Poland, S. studied for the rabbinate until he was seventeen. By that time he had secretly read books by modern Western writers. Deciding against a religious career, he left his father's home; he worked in Warsaw as a laborer and studied during the evenings. He became idealistically enthusiastic over the Russian Revolution and, in 1917, went to live in Kiev. There he became a member of a local group of Jewish writers. He began to publish short stories written in Yiddish. At this time he was earning his living as a proofreader on a Yiddish newspaper.

By 1921 S. was disillusioned with communism. He returned to Warsaw, where he published a collection of short stories, *Perl un Andere Dertzeylungen* (1922; Pearl, 1923). It was very favorably received. The book reached Abraham Cahan, editor of the Yiddish newspaper, the New York *Forverts*. He was so impressed with the stories that he engaged S. as a regular contributor, making him a corre-

spondent for the *Forverts* in Poland. In this capacity, S. visited the Soviet Union in 1926. He was both repelled and depressed by what he saw, which he reported in a book, *Nei-Russland* (1928). He was attacked for this by his socialist-minded colleagues. He had been active in Warsaw literary circles; he now stopped writing fiction because of his political disagreement with his pro-Russian colleagues.

In 1931 Cahan persuaded S. to resume writing fiction. He held out the promise of publication in his newspaper in America, which was an important guarantee to a writer whose mother tongue was Yiddish, a very small minority language with relatively few publishing outlets for fiction. In 1932 the *Forverts* serialized S.'s novel *Yoshe Kalb* (The Sinner, 1933), as did a Warsaw Yiddish-language newspaper, the Warsaw *Heint*. The novel traces the decline of Hasidism in a richly structured plot. The writing is simple, direct, full of insight into a world little known outside the Yiddish literary tradition. A successful play adaptation was presented in New York in 1932.

In 1934, S. emigrated to New York. His next novel, *Di Brieder Ashkenazi* (1936; The Brothers Ashkenazi, 1936), was a major literary achievement. It is a novel of Tolstoyan proportions dealing with the entire epoch of Polish-Jewish industrial development and its effect on life in Poland. It tells of the industry of the Jews in building up a center of commerce, as with textiles, only to see the German and Polish politicians in World War I seize the Jewish-owned factories in the end. It is generally regarded as one of the finest novels in Yiddish literature.

Khaver Nakhman (1938; East of Eden, 1939) is a poignant story of Polish-Jewish disillusionment with communism. Acutely pained by reports of Nazi brutality, S. wrote the deeply moving *Di Mishpokhe Karnovsky* (1943; The Family Carnowsky, 1969), dramatizing the plight of the Jews in Germany during the 1930's. The publication of the American translation caused little enthusiasm for a Singer revival, despite the fact that his younger brother, Isaac Bashevis Singer (q.v.), had become a widely recognized Yiddish writer in the United States. Together, the two brothers represent a peak of fiction writing in the dwindling tradition of Yiddish literature, which suffered an all but death-dealing blow when Yiddish culture was destroyed in Europe during World War II.

All his adult life, S. was inclined to restlessness and pessimism. Depressed by the holocaust in Europe and the horrors of the death camps, S. was planning to make his home in Israel (then Palestine) when he suffered a heart attack that proved fatal.

FURTHER WORKS: *Shtoll un Eizen* (1927); *Freeling* (1937); *Fun a Velt Vos Is Nishto Mer* (1946). **Selected English translation:** *The River Breaks Up* (1938)

BIBLIOGRAPHY: Niger, S., *Di Tzukunft* (May 1924); Roback, A. A., *The Story of Yiddish Literature* (1940); Mayzel, N., *Forgeyer un Mittzeyler* (1946); Rivkin, B., *Unsere Prozayiker* (1951); *Lexicon fun der Neier Yiddisher Literatur* (vol. 3, 1960); Madison, C. A., *Yiddish Literature: Its Scope and Major Writers* (1968)

CHARLES A. MADISON

SITWELL, Edith

English poet, essayist, biographer, b. 7 Sept. 1887, Scarborough, Yorkshire; d. 9 Dec. 1964, London

The daughter of Sir George Sitwell and Lady Ida Sitwell, Edith S. and her brothers Sir Osbert and Sacheverell were reared in a tradition of wealth, leisure, and culture. Educated privately, she spent much of her childhood at Renshaw Hall, the family seat in Derbyshire. At an early age she announced her intention to become "a genius."

With her brothers Edith S. was instrumental in the publication from 1916 to 1921 of *Wheels*, an aggressive answer to Sir Edward Marsh's *Georgian Poetry*. The three Sitwells startled the literary world in the 1920's by reading their own eclectic poetry, supporting modern art, and attacking current reviewers and others whom they considered philistines. Edith S.'s views, her striking appearance, and her unusual manner of dress won her the reputation as something of an eccentric.

Edith S.'s early poems, exemplified by "The Sleeping Beauty" (1924) and the witty series written for recitation with William Walton's musical suite *Façade* (1922), show what was to be her lifelong concern: pure aesthetic values in poetry. Her work has been compared to baroque art for its precision in welding disparate and remote allusions into a polished contemporary idiom.

That Edith S. was preoccupied with technical devices is shown in the introduction to her *Collected Poems* (1957), where she remarks that the poems of *Façade* "are abstract poems —that is, they are patterns in sound." Characteristic of her craft is the use of synaesthesia. For example, about "Said King Pompey" she wrote: "It is built around a scheme of *R*'s, which in this case produces a faint fluttering sound, like dust fluttering from the ground, or the beat of a dying heart." She also favored highly personal images. Queried on her use of the term "Martha-colored," she explained that a childhood governess named Martha wore a dress of the color indicated in the poem.

The finely attuned rhythms of her verse have been attributed to her skill as a musician and to her study of the French symbolists (*see* symbolism). At times despairing of the contemporary world, Edith S. reached into the past for allusions and models, drawing from such sources as classical mythology, the *commedia dell'arte*, and medieval poetry. But, perhaps more than any other period, the Augustan Age seems to have appealed to her. Her critical study *Alexander Pope* (1930) was an effort to rescue the 18th-c. poet from Victorian disesteem.

Edith S.'s early poetry was sometimes characterized as fanciful, brittle, and artificial. Even today it is not as widely appreciated as it deserves to be. During World War II, however, Edith S. gained a wider public and produced what many consider her finest poems, particularly those expressions of anger at human cruelty contained in *Street Songs* (1942), *Green Song* (1944), and *Song of the Cold* (1945). Tempering her anguish at the human condition is a faith in God and in the holiness of nature. This religious emphasis was to become stronger in her later work, *e.g.*, *Gardeners and Astronomers* (1953) and *The Outcasts* (1962). In 1955 Edith S. was received into the Roman Catholic Church.

Although her poems are rarely autobiographical, in such themes as the transience of youth and the fear of old age and death a deeply personal emotion is evident. Poetic technique remains in the forefront of her mind, although later works show less personal imagery, more sweeping rhythms, and a surer cadence. Edith S.'s technical mastery, her recurrent imagery, and her tendency to retain different versions of a single poem in collected editions create a consistency throughout the body of her poetry. Yeats (q.v.), in attempting to cull certain of her poems for inclusion in an anthology, complained that selecting a few was like cutting pieces from a tapestry.

As early as 1933 Edith S. was awarded the medal of the Royal Society of London, and in 1954 she was made a Dame Grand Cross of the Order of the British Empire.

FURTHER WORKS: *The Mother* (1915); *Twentieth Century Harlequinade* (with Osbert S.; 1916); *Clowns' Houses* (1918); *The Wooden Pegasus* (1920); *Bucolic Comedies* (1923); *Poor Young People* (with Osbert S. and Sacheverell S.; 1925); *Troy Park* (1925); *Poetry and Criticism* (1925); *E. S.: Poems* (1926); *Elegy in Dead Fashion* (1926); *Rustic Elegies* (1927); *Five Poems* (1928); *Popular Song* (1928); *Gold Coast Customs* (1929); *Collected Poems* (1930); *Jane Barston: 1719–1746* (1931); *Bath* (1932); *The English Eccentrics* (1933); *Five Variations on a Theme* (1933); *Aspects of Modern Poetry* (1934); *Victoria of England* (1934); *Selected Poems* (1936); *I Live under a Black Sun* (1937); *Trio* (with Osbert S. and Sacheverell S.; 1938); *Poems New and Old* (1940); *English Women* (1942); *A Poet's Notebook* (1943); *Fanfare for Elizabeth* (1946); *The Shadow of Cain* (1947); *A Notebook on William Shakespeare* (1948); *The Canticle of the Rose: Selected Poems 1920–1947* (1949); *Poor Men's Music* (1950); *Façade, and Other Poems* (1950); *Selected Poems* (1952); *A Book of Flowers* (1952); *The Pocket Poems: E. S.* (1960); *The Queens and the Hive* (1962); *Taken Care Of: An Autobiography* (1965); *Selected Poems* (1965); *Selected Letters 1919–1964* (eds. J. Lehmann, and D. Parker; 1970)

BIBLIOGRAPHY: Sitwell, O., *Left Hand, Right Hand* (1944), and *The Scarlet Tree* (1946); Bowra, C. M., *E. S.* (1947); Sitwell, O., *Great Morning* (1947), and *Laughter in the Next Room* (1948); Villa, J. G., ed., *Celebrations for E. S.* (1948); Sitwell, O., *Noble Essences* (1950); Lehmann, J., *E. S.* (1952); McKenna, J. P., "The Early Poetry of E. S.," *DA,* XXIV (1964), 3752; Salter, E., *The Last Years of a Rebel: A Memoir of E. S.* (1967); Brophy, J., *E. S.: The Symbolist Order* (1968); Lehmann, J., *A Nest of Tigers* (1968)

VERGENE F. LEVERENZ

Whatever may ultimately be said of the permanent value of their work, few will deny that, while they [the Sitwells] were fighting for new values, they did pull down the Gates of Gaza, perfectly willing to break their own heads along with those of the Philistines.... in some sort they have won

now, the gates are down, and the Philistines are at their oldest and most dangerous trick of attempting to persuade themselves (and the Sitwells) that they were on the side of the rebels all the time, and, indeed, that there was never any rebellion at all. ...The Sitwells have not done more than prove that they have a vision, and they have not yet imposed it on their own minds. They are all young, and are all developing.... As a family and as individuals they have invented a new idiom, but if they do not now adapt it to express a new truth it will become a dead invention in their own hands.

SR (26 March 1927), p. 474

Her book [*The English Eccentrics*] is a friendly excursion rather than a guide, and fuller of acknowledgements than of references. The lesson to be drawn from it—if so heavy a draught as a lesson be required—is that eccentricity ranks as a national asset, and that so long as it is respected there is some hope that our country will not go mad as a whole.... Those of us who assume (perhaps wrongly) that we are sane, can learn from her pages the lesson most necessary for a sane man; the need of a tolerance which is touched by pity but untouched by contempt.

E. M. Forster, in *Spectator*
(19 May 1933), p. 716

Miss S....has done her pioneering, and we are now able to regard her work, not as controversy, but as poetry. The fact remains that she was one of the writers who bridged the gap between the sterile years of the early war and the post-war years of excited experiment; that she helped to keep the interest in poetry alive when it was near extinction.... Her view of life remains in essence that of a child, a sensitive child seeing everything in terms of its own private world.... Miss S. has retained a child's imagination while acquiring an adult's power of voluptuous expression.... She has not merely recreated, she has created a world. ...In her verse the discords which torment her as a person suffer metamorphosis; they become poetry. And so for once we really are confronted with the romantic poetry of escape.

Dilys Powell, *Descent from Parnassus*
(1934), pp. xiii, 127–34

One cannot think of her in any other age or country. She has transformed with her metrical virtuosity traditional metres reborn not to be read but spoken, exaggerating metaphors into mythology, carrying them from poem to poem, compelling us to go backward to some first usage for the birth of the myth.

W. B. Yeats, Preface to *Oxford Book of Modern Verse* (1936), p. xviii

In spite of Swinburnian and symbolist characteristics, it is clear from her latest poems that Miss S.'s place in English literature is with the

ISAAC BASHEVIS SINGER

OSBERT, SACHEVERELL, AND EDITH SITWELL

religious poets of the seventeenth century. Again and again the audacity of her sensuous images reminds us of Crashaw; she has Traherne's rapture at created things, and Vaughan's sense of eternity. ...Miss S. is essentially a religious poet; that is to say, she has experienced imaginatively, not merely intellectually, the evil and misery of the world and has overcome that experience by conviction—the full, imaginative conviction—that all creation is under the Divine Love.

Kenneth Clark, in *Celebration for Edith Sitwell*, ed. by J. G. Villa (1948), p. 66

It has been firmly maintained by her critics that *Façade* derives its chief interest from the technical acrobatics of the work.... Yet this does not constitute the poetic totality of *Façade*. These poems are not merely impressionistic exercises in poetic technique. Had they been so, not even William Walton's scintillating musical accompaniment could have enhanced their literary value.... The dazzling virtuosity and concentrated brevity of the music provides a pungent, allusive commentary, and is a perfect embellishment of Dame Edith's incisive wit and parody.

Geoffrey Singleton, *Edith Sitwell: The Hymn to Life* (1960), p. 48

SITWELL, Osbert

English poet, short-story writer, essayist, and novelist, b. 6 Dec. 1892, London; d. 4 May 1969, Montagnana, Italy

The brother of Edith and Sacheverell S. (qq.v.), S. was raised at the family's ancestral home in Renishaw, Derbyshire, where he was "educated during...holidays from Eton." During World War I he served in the trenches with the Grenadier Guards, and one of his earliest poems, "Babel," written in 1916, describes a young soldier's despair and sense of futility.

Along with his brother and sister, S. began in 1916 to edit *Wheels,* an annual poetry anthology whose chief contributors were the S.'s themselves. *Argonaut and Juggernaut* (1919), his first important collection of poems, was a wittily unconventional attack on the "profiteers, scamps, fools, and the selfishly sentimental" who had flourished in the wartime atmosphere. In that same year S. and critic Herbert Read (1893–1968) became co-editors of *Arts and Letters,* a quarterly whose offices served as a meeting place for authors such as Bennett, Huxley, and Virginia Woolf (qq.v.).

Triple Fugue (1924), S.'s first collection of short stories, consists of six studies of the complexity of human behavior and satirizes many of the political and social tendencies that he saw as a threat to individuality. Two years later S. published a satirical novel, *Before the Bombardment* (1926), which he described as "the foundation of my reputation." It wittily zeros in on pre-World War I life in Scarborough before that city was pointlessly shelled by German cruisers in 1914.

Over the years the "Three Sitwells" enlivened English literary life and, in S.'s words, "conducted...a series of skirmishes and hand-to-hand battles against the Philistine." *England Reclaimed* (1927) contained dexterous and precise portraits in poetry of English rural types. The book's title was eventually used for a series of similar collections whose second and third volumes were *Wrack at Tidesend* (1952) and *On the Continent* (1958).

No doubt S.'s major achievement is the five-volume autobiography that takes its overall title from the first volume, *Left Hand, Right Hand!* (1944). In it he magnificently recaptures the world of his youth and leaves a series of vivid portraits of eccentric types whose appearance in a novel might challenge the reader's credulity. The subsequent volumes—*The Scarlet Tree* (1946), *Great Morning!* (1947), *Laughter in the Next Room* (1948), and *Noble Essences* (1950)—proved that S.'s brilliant prose style and his novelistic ability to capture the details of character and the atmosphere of special times and places were particularly suited to the memoir form. The work has claimed a permanent place in the literature of 20th-c. England.

FURTHER WORKS: *Twentieth-Century Harlequinade* (with Edith S.; 1916); *The Winstonburg Line, Three Satires* (1919); *At the House of Mrs. Kinfoot* (1921); *Who Killed Cock-Robin?* (1921); *Discursions on Travel, Art and Life* (1925); *Poor Young People* (with Edith and Sacheverell S.; 1925); *Winter the Huntsman* (1927); *All at Sea* (with Sacheverell S.; 1927); *The People's Album of London Statues* (1928); *The Man Who Lost Himself* (1929); *Miss Mew* (1929); *Dumb Animal* (1930); *The Collected Satires and Poems of O. S.* (1931); *Three-Quarter Length Portrait of Michael Arlen* (1931); *Three-Quarter Length Portrait of the Viscountess Wimbourne* (1931); *Dickens* (1932); *Winters of Content* (1932); *Miracle on Sinai* (1933); *Brighton* (1935); *Penny Foolish* (1935); *Mrs. Kimber* (1937);

Those Were the Days (1938); *Trio* (with Edith and Sacheverell S.; 1938); *Escape with Me!* (1939); *Open the Door* (1941); *A Place of One's Own* (1941); *Gentle Caesar* (1943); *Selected Poems Old and New* (1943); *Sing High! Sing Low!* (1944); *A Letter to My Son* (1944); *The True Story of Dick Whittington* (1946); *Alive—Alive Oh!* (1947); *The Novels of George Meredith* (1947); *Four Songs of the Italian Earth* (1948); *Demos the Emperor* (1949); *Death of a God* (1949); *England Reclaimed, and Other Poems* (1949); *Collected Stories* (1953); *The Four Continents* (1954); *Fee Fi Fo Fum!* (1959); *A Place of One's Own* (1961; short stories); *Tales My Father Taught Me* (1962); *Pound Wise* (1963)

BIBLIOGRAPHY: Mégroz, R. L., *The Three S.'s* (1927); Mégroz, R. L., *Five Novelists of Today* (1933); Bullough, G., *The Trend of Modern Poetry* (1934); Fulford, R., *O. S.* (1951); Filfoot, R., *A Bibliography of Edith, Osbert and Sacheverell S.* (1963)

* * * *

SITWELL, Sacheverell

English poet and art critic, b. 15 Nov. 1897, Scarborough

Though S. received a formal education at Eton and Oxford, he, like his sister and brother, Edith and Osbert S. (qq.v.), considers himself "mainly self-educated." In 1916 the three S.'s invaded the world of letters with *Wheels*, an annual anthology of contemporary poetry that served as a showcase for their own work.

The more classically minded of the trio, S. was often compared to the Elizabethans, but his early work also clearly shows the futurist influence (*see* futurism) of the Italian poet Filippo Tommaso Marinetti (1876–1944) and of classical Chinese poetry. *The Hundred and One Harlequins* (1922) profits from the disciplines of painting and music; and in what Arnold Bennett (q.v.) called a "damnably difficult" style, S. attempts to make us hear sounds and see colors. Critics tend to agree, however, that in spite of its occasional brilliance S.'s poetry suffers from structural weakness and often seems like little more than improvisation.

S.'s major achievement has been a remarkable series of poetically insightful books on baroque art: *Southern Baroque Art* (1924), *German Baroque Art* (1927), *Spanish Baroque*

Art (1931), and *German Baroque Sculpture* (1938). In addition, his *Conversation Pieces* (1936) is generally credited with having stimulated critical interest in the English painters Hogarth, Gainsborough, Constable, and Turner. *The Gothick North* (1929–30) is a study of medieval life and art.

A perennial traveler, S. has written several books in which with alert enthusiasm and relaxed scholarship he records "the splendors and miseries of the world and the glory of being alive." The best of these are *Roumanian Journey* (1938), *Spain* (1950), and *Arabesque and Honeycomb* (1957), impressions of the Near East.

Like his brother Osbert, S. has recorded the aristocratic and somewhat eccentric world of his youth. The rich and rhythmic prose of *All Summer in a Day: An Autobiographical Fantasia* (1926) imaginatively conjures up the spirit of a vanished age in a work that bears evidences of the influence of Yeats and Joyce (qq.v.).

FURTHER WORKS: *The People's Palace* (1918); *Dr. Donne and Gargantua, First Canto* (1921); *Dr. Donne and Gargantua, Canto the Second* (1923); *The Parrot* (1923); *The Thirteenth Caesar* (1924); *Poor Young People* (with Edith and Osbert S.; 1925); *Exalt the Eglantine* (1926); *Dr. Donne and Gargantua, Canto the Third* (1926); *The Cyder Feast* (1927); *A Book of Towers . . . of Southern Europe* (1928); *S. S.: Selected Poems* (1928); *Two Poems, Ten Songs* (1929); *Dr. Donne and Gargantua, The First Six Cantos* (1930); *Beckford and Beckfordism* (1930); *Far from My Home* (1931); *Mozart* (1932); *Canons of Giant Art* (1933); *Liszt* (1934); *Touching the Orient* (1934); *A Background for Domenico Scarlatti 1685–1757* (1935); *Dance of the Quick and the Dead* (1936); *Collected Poems* (1936); *Narrative Pictures* (1937); *La Vie Parisienne: A Tribute to Jacque Offenbach* (1937); *Edinburgh* (with F. Bamford; 1938); *Trio* (with Edith and Osbert S.; 1938); *Mauretania* (1940); *Poltergeists* (1940); *Sacred and Profane Love* (1940); *Valse des Fleurs* (1941); *Primitive Scenes and Festivals* (1942); *The Homing of the Winds* (1942); *Splendours and Miseries* (1943); *British Architects and Craftsmen* (1945); *The Hunters and the Hunted* (1947); *Selected Poems* (1948); *Morning, Noon and Night in London* (1948); *Theatrical Figures in Porcelain* (1949); *Cupid and Jacaranda* (1952); *Truffle Hunt with S. S.* (1953); *Selected Works*

(1953); *Portugal and Madeira* (1954); *Selected Works* (1955); *Denmark* (1956); *Malta* (1958); *Journey to the Ends of Time* (1959); *Bridge of the Brocade Sash* (1959); *Golden Wall and Mirador* (1961); *The Red Chapels of Banteai Srei* (1962)

BIBLIOGRAPHY: Mégroz, R. L., *The Three S.'s* (1927); Filfoot, R., *A Bibliography of Edith, Osbert and S. S.* (1963); Smith, J., "Shall These Bones Live?," *Poetry Review*, LVIII (1967), 75–120, 121–29

* * * *

SKALBE, Kārlis

Latvian poet and fairy-tale writer, b. 7 Nov. 1879, Vecpiebalga, Latvia; d. 15 April 1945, Stockholm

Even in his youthful works—the collections of poetry *Cietumnieka sapņi* (1902) and *Kad ābeles zied* (1904)—S. protested against social injustice and oppression. In the modern fairy tale "Kā es braucu Ziemeļmeitas lūkoties" (1904), he castigated the lack of social development. It was the first of many achievements in this genre.

As an active participant in the 1905 revolution against Russian autocracy and the German landed gentry, S. went into exile to Switzerland and, later, to Norway. Upon his return, he was jailed for eighteen months for repeatedly voicing a demand for an independent Latvia. Out of the tragic experiences of these years grew the collections of verse *Zemes dūmos* (1906), *Veļu laikā* (1907), and *Emigranta dziesmas* (1909).

At the end of his life, S. had to leave his country again, after having lived through the Soviet and German occupations and suffered under their censorship. In the fall of 1944, he crossed the Baltic Sea in a fisherman's boat to the shores of Sweden.

The abortive revolution of 1905 brought heavy censorship in its wake, which in turn precipitated a preoccupation with personal themes in Latvian literature. Symbolism (q.v.) acted as a catalyst and started Latvian poetry on the road to modernism. S. benefited from symbolism, but grew toward greater simplicity and poetic concentration akin to that of the Latvian folksong. Without ever directly imitating its form, S. achieved a similar concreteness of images and economy of poetic means.

During World War I, S. joined the Latvian fusiliers on the Riga front as a war correspon-

dent and began his poetic daily notes (*Mazās piezīmes*, 1917–20), which he continued after the war. By means of them he exerted considerable influence on Latvian cultural and political life.

The collection of poems *Daugavas viļņi* (1918) expresses the feelings animating the Latvian nation during the achievement of its hard-won independence. The collection takes its title and *leitmotiv* from Latvia's largest river, Daugava, echoing the river's waves in its original rhythms.

The verse collections *Sirds un saule* (1911), *Sapņi un teikas* (1912), *Zāles dvaša* (1931), and *Klusuma meldijas* (1941) show the growth of S.'s poetic vision toward a marked individuality. Gravitating to ethical values, his poetry is suffused with peace and serenity.

In his fairy tales, S. made use of motifs from Latvian folk tales as well as of those from the folk tales of other countries. They are informed by the same ethical principles as Latvian folklore, where good triumphs over evil. S. was devoted to small things and humble people. The tiny, unnoticed flower in the shadows of the forest is greeted by God. The title of his first collection of fairy tales, *Pazemīgās dvēseles* (1911), which means "humble souls," is characteristic of his world.

In the later collections, *Ziemas pasakas* (1912), *Pasaka par vecāko dēlu* (1924), *Manu bērnības dienu mēnesis* (1926), *Muļķa laime* (1933), and *Gaŗā pupa* (1933), he achieved a concreteness and vividness of images unsurpassed in Latvian. His tales resemble those of Hans Christian Andersen in their form and degree of literary excellence, though S. placed more emphasis on ethical values and the expressiveness of each single sentence. Like Andersen, he often digressed in his openings out of the sheer joy of storytelling.

One of the most outstanding Latvian poets, S.'s poetry is characterized by great subtlety and conciseness. In his works he expressed a strong belief in humanitarian ideals and took a stand against authoritarian power. His own life was marked by repeated clashes with foreign political power.

The thematic range of S.'s poetry and fairy tales is not a wide one; his writings remain within the limits of personified, spiritualized nature and the world of the peasant with its inherent values. Yet he was able to capture fine shades of emotion in simple words. The specific ethos of the Latvian nation may well have found its characteristic expression in his works.

FURTHER WORKS: *Sarkangalvīte un citas pasakas* (1913); *Pēclaikā* (1923); *Kopoti raksti* (5 vols., 1922–23); *Kaķīša dzirnaviņas* (1952); *Kopoti raksti* (5 vols., 1952–55)

BIBLIOGRAPHY: Baumanis, A., *Latvian Poetry* (1946); Andrups J., and Kalve, V., *Latvian Literature* (1954); Matthews, W. K., *A Century of Latvian Poetry* (1958)

JĀNIS ANDRUPS

SLOVAK LITERATURE

At present the Slovaks, who live in east central Czechoslovakia, number just over four million, less than one-third of the total population of Czechoslovakia. The small province of Slovakia, settled in the 6th and 7th c.'s, was a part of the Austro-Hungarian Empire until 1918. At the end of World War I, when that empire was dissolved, the adjacent Czech (Bohemia and Moravia) and Slovak provinces were united to form the new republic of Czechoslovakia.

The literary history of the Slovaks is closely connected with that of the Czechs (*see* Czechoslovakian literature), both because of the extremely close similarities between the Czech and the Slovak languages, and because of the common political history. From the 15th c., Czech was used, along with Latin, as the literary language of the Slovaks. The best-known of all Slovak poets, Ján Kollár (1793–1852), wrote in Czech. Pavel Jozef Šafárik (1795–1861), the leading Slovak philologist and ethnographer, wrote his works in Czech and German. But in the 1840's Slovak began to be used as a literary language, and it subsequently became the dominant literary medium of the Slovakians.

Throughout the 19th c. and until the end of World War I, Slovak literature was primarily an instrument in the struggle for national survival against an ever increasing dynastic oppression. The first concern of the Slovak writers was with fighting for the right of the people to use the Slovak language in schools and in public life and with helping to develop Slovak national consciousness.

The literary scene in the 1880's and 1890's was dominated by Svetozár Hurban Vajanský (1847–1916), a journalist and literary critic, the writer of romantic poetry, and the author of several novels in which the influence of Russian realists, especially the novelist Ivan Turgenev (1818–83), was quite discernible. Like Kollár and other earlier pan-slavists he believed in Russia as a liberator of all the oppressed Slavic peoples. He had little respect for the countries of Western Europe, "degenerate France" in particular, and he rejected even democracy and modern philosophy and art, which he felt might threaten the assistance for Slovakia that he expected from the czarist regime. Vajanský's influence was strongest during the 1890's, and most of his works were published before the end of the century.

Some younger intellectuals, dissatisfied with the conservative ideas and political passivity of Vajanský and his followers, and seeking a closer cooperation with the Czechs, founded the monthly *Hlas* ("The Voice") in 1898. In literature the so-called *hlasisti* rejected romanticism and sought to promote realism, stressing at the same time the social function of literature. A similar but expanded literary program was advocated in the journal *Sborník slovenskej mládeže* ("Almanac of Slovak Youth"), established in 1909, and in the periodical *Prúdy* ("Trends"), published from 1909 to 1914.

Both romanticism and realism appear in the poetry of Hviezdoslav (q.v.), but the short stories and novels of Kukučín (q.v.) are dominated by realistic elements.

Among Vajanský's followers Terézia Vansová (1857–1942), the editor of *Dennica* ("The Morning Star"), the first Slovak ladies' journal, and the author of romantic and sentimental stories from the life of country teachers and clergy, asserted herself with some success. Another woman writer whose work parallels that of Vajanský was Elena Maróthy-Šoltésová (1855–1939), known for her novel *Proti prúdu* (1894; "Against the Stream") and for her valuable books of reminiscence.

The realistic methods introduced by Kukučín were used by Jozef Gregor-Tajovský (1874–1940), who, like his mentor, dealt in his stories with the life of Slovak villagers; he was also an accomplished playwright. Themes taken from village life also appear in the works of Timrava (pseudonym of Božena Slančíková, 1867–1951). In her almost naturalistic stories (*see* naturalism) she often used the colloquial language of her peasant protagonists. Another writer who dealt with naturalistic elements was Jégé (pseudonym of Ladislav Nádaši, 1866–1940). His best-known novel, *Adam Šangala* (1923), is set during the counter-Reformation. Jégé also published several comedies satirizing the petty doings of small-town people. The short stories and novels of Kristína Royová (1867–1937), imbued with moral and religious preoccupations, were avidly read at home and widely translated abroad, although many of them lack artistic value.

The most popular Slovak playwright of the period before World War I was Ferko Urbánek (1859–1934), author of some fifty plays, all of them patriotic and educational, but generally shallow and excessively sentimental.

The generation of intellectuals grouped around the journals *Sborník slovenskej mládeže* and *Prúdy* produced a literary school influenced by symbolism (q.v.) and known as the Slovak Moderna. The most representative members of this school are the poet Botto (q.v.), writing under the pseudonym Ivan Krasko; the poet and novelist Jesenský (q.v.); and Martin Rázus (1888–1937), the author of fiery and tendentious patriotic, social and political verse. Some of his better-known collections are the World War I *Z tichých i búrnych chvíl* (1919; "From Times Quiet and Stormy"), *Hoj, zem drahá* (1919; "Oh, My Beloved Land"), and *Cestou* (1935; "On the Road").

In the 1920's Rázus turned to prose and published several novels, notably the four-volume *Svety* (1929; "The Worlds"), which portrayed the contemporary countryside and political milieu. Another representative of the Slovak Moderna was Vladimír Roy (1885–1935), the author of melancholy and dreamy verse, and an accomplished translator of English, French, and German poetry.

After the establishment of the republic of Czechoslovakia in 1918, Hungarian was immediately discarded and Slovak became the official language in Slovakia. A number of high schools and a university were established; hundreds of public libraries, two state theaters, and several publishing houses were founded; many new newspapers and magazines as well as literary journals began publication; and the size of the reading public increased greatly. This spectacular cultural expansion created most favorable conditions for the development of literature, and in the 1920's and 1930's every major literary movement of the time was represented among the increasingly numerous Slovak writers.

Several of the older writers whose reputation had been established prior to 1918, such as Kukučín, Jégé, Jesenský, and Rázus, continued publishing after the liberation.

In the postwar years a new group of writers who completed their spiritual formation just before the war emerged. The prose writers of this "middle" generation included Jozef Cíger-Hronský (1896–1960), the author of several books for children and of such important novels as *Jozef Mak, Pisár Gráč* (1933; "The Scribe Gráč") and *Andreas Bur Majster* (1947; "Master Andreas Bur"), written in lyrical prose. Hronský fled Slovakia at the end of World War II and died in exile in Argentina.

Another member of this group was the prose writer Tido J. Gašpar (b. 1893), sometimes called "the Slovak D'Annunzio," in allusion to the Italian poet D'Annunzio (q.v.). The third most important member of this group, poet and literary critic Štefan Krčméry (1892–1955), became known for his work as secretary of Matica slovenská, the principal Slovak cultural organization. Among Krčméry's most notable works is *Stopať desiat rokov slovenskej literatúry* (1943; "One Hundred and Fifty Years of Slovak Literature").

The most important poets of the 1920's and the 1930's were Ján Smrek (pseudonym of Ján Čietek, b. 1899) and Emil Boleslav Lukáč (b. 1900), both active also as editors of literary magazines. Smrek wrote patriotic verse and love poems notable for their vitality and optimism. His many volumes include *Cválajúce dni* (1925; "The Galloping Days"), *Básnik a žena* (1934; "The Poet and Woman"), and *Obraz sveta* (1958; "The Image of the World"). Lukáč's symbolic, meditative, and patriotic verse, which is rather sad and pessimistic in tone, appears in *Spoved* (1922; "The Confession"), *Dunaj a Seina* (1925; "The Danube and the Seine"), *Spev vlkov* (1929; "The Singing of the Wolves"), and *Dies irae*.

During this period several younger writers attempted to express attitudes derived from their Roman Catholic faith, as in the works of Andrej Žarnov (pseudonym of František Šubík, b. 1903), who published his patriotic and meditative poems in *Stráž pri Morave* (1925; "The Sentinel on the Moravian Border"), *Hlas krvi* (1932; "The Voice of the Blood"), *Štít* (1940; "The Shield"), and *Mŕtvy* (1941; "The Dead Boy"). Noted for his translations of Polish and classical Greek works, Žarnov went into exile in the United States.

Milo Urban (b. 1904), another writer influenced by Catholicism, is the author of the trilogy *Živý bič* (1927; "The Living Scourge"), *Hmly na úsvite* (1930; "The Fog at Dawn"), and *V osídlach* (1940; "In the Trap"). In *Živý bič,* one of the most significant and widely read Slovak novels of the interwar period, Urban dramatically portrays the life of a Slovak village during World War I; the other two works describe the countryside in the 1920's and 1930's.

In the early 1920's a group of young Marxist intellectuals became associated with the periodical *DAV,* which was published from 1924 to 1937. The title was an acrostic derived from the first names of Daniel Okáli, Andrej Sirácky, and Vladimír Clementis, the founders of the journal. Shortly after the establishment of *DAV,* however, these writers abandoned literature, devoting themselves instead to politics and social problems. The most prominent members of the *davisti* were the poet Ladislav ("Laco") Novomeský (b. 1904) and the Czechborn novelist Peter Jilemnický (1901–1949).

Novomeský, who is generally regarded as second only to Kollár and Hviezdoslav among Slovak poets, worked as editor of several communist newspapers and after 1945 held high offices in the Slovak legislature and administration. In the 1950's he served a long prison term as a "bourgeois nationalist," but was eventually rehabilitated and permitted to resume the publication of his works. Influenced by such Czech poets as Nezval (q.v.) and later by the Russians Mayakovski and Esenin (qq.v.), he published his largely proletarian, but occasionally lyric and meditative, poems in *Neděľa* (1927; "The Sunday"), *Otvorené okná* (1935; "The Open Windows"), *Svätý za dedinou* (1939; "The Saint behind the Village"), *Pašovanou ceruskou* ("Written with a Smuggled Pencil"), and other collections. In the 1960's, after his release from prison, he published the collections *Vila Tereza* ("The Mansion Tereza") and *Do mesta 30 minút* ("30 Minutes to the City"), which include reminiscences of his youth, descriptions of the social conditions in Czechoslovakia during the period between the two world wars, and evaluations of the literary avant-garde.

The schoolteacher Peter Jilemnický (1901–1949) is the author of the best-selling novels *Víťazný pád* (1929; "Victorious Downfall") and *Pole neorané* (1932; "The Untilled Field"), both dealing with "the misery and beauty of Kysúca," the impoverished region in northeast Slovakia. In *Kompas v nás* (1937; "The Compass in Us"), probably his best book, he shows the effect of external events on man's sense of himself, and in *Kronika* (1951; "The Chronicle") he recounts the 1944 uprising against the Germans and their Slovak collaborators. A long visit to the Soviet Union in the late 1920's provided material for the study *Dva roky v krajine Sovietov* ("Two Years in the Land of the Soviets") and the novel *Zuniaci krok* (1930; "The Resounding Step").

Other young writers, uniting around the journal *Mladé Slovensko* ("Young Slovakia"), attempted to bring new themes and methods into Slovak literature, often in a boldly experimental fashion. Among the most gifted were Gejza Vámoš (1901–1956), whose novels *Atomy Boha* ("The Atoms of God") and *Odlomená haluz* ("The Broken-off Branch") criticized bourgeois society and its petty views, and Ivan Horváth (1904–1960), author of the novella collections *Človek na ulici* ("The Man in the Street") and *Vízum do Evropy* ("A Visa for Europe").

The leading Slovak playwright of the period between the wars was Ivan Stodola (b. 1888), whose realistic plays satirize the shortcomings and vices of individuals as well as of society. Some of Stodola's more successful plays are *Jožko Púčik a jeho kariéra* (1931; "Jožko Púčik and His Career"), a satire "on the wrongly understood humanism"; *Posledná symfónia* ("The Last Symphony"); and *Kráľ Svätopluk* (1931; "King Svätopluk").

No significant Slovak literature was produced during World War II. The temporary dismemberment of Czechoslovakia under German occupation and the brief establishment of the German-dominated state of Slovakia, though proclaimed as a recognition of Slovak nationalism, actually resulted in a period of stagnation for Slovak literature. Most writers, to be sure, continued publishing but on the whole produced only the mediocre works that the political climate encouraged.

During the first three years after World War II, Czechoslovakia was ruled by a coalition government, and both the Czech and the Slovak literatures displayed a certain freedom, as indicated by a saying of the time: "Everything is allowed except the criticism of the Russians." The most interesting poets were Rudolf Fábry (b. 1915), Pavol Bunčák (b. 1915), Ján Rak (b. 1915), and Vladimír Reisel (b. 1919), all strikingly influenced by surrealism (q.v.).

The first book of the Slovak *nadrealisti,* Fábry's *Uťaté ruky* ("The Severed Hands"), had been published as early as 1935, and his *Vodné hodiny, piesočné hodiny* ("The Water Clock, the Hour Glass") soon followed in 1938. But the movement did not develop fully until after 1945 —following a period of wartime opposition to the Nazi Slovak regime—with the publication of another book by Fábry, *Ja je niekto iný* (1946; "I Is Somebody Else"). Other works that helped to foster the movement include: Bunčák's *Neusínaj, zažni slnko* ("Don't Fall Asleep, Turn on the Sun"), *S tebou a sám* ("With You and Alone"), and *Zomierat zakázané* ("It's Prohibited to Die"), all of which also include some nonsurrealist writing; and Rak's *Je vypredané* ("It's Sold Out"), *Nezanechajte nádeje* ("Don't Abandon Hope"), *V údolí slnka* ("In the Valley of the Sun"), and *Vietor krvi* ("The Wind of the Blood").

The theoretician of surrealism was Vladimír Reisel, a writer of great poetic imagination who published literary essays and several volumes of poems, including *Vidím všetky dni a noci* (1939; "I See All the Days and Nights"), *Neskutočné mesto* (1943; "The Unreal City"), and *Zrkadlo a za zrkadlom* (1946; "The Mirror and Behind the Mirror").

The only notable prose work of this period, among a number of undistinguished war novels, was the four-volume novel *Babylon* (1946) by Margita Figuli (b. 1909), whose work suggested similarities between the human condition in ancient times and in contemporary society.

When the communist party assumed power in Czechoslovakia in 1948 it imposed a systematic control on Slovak literature, despite such factors as the traditional independence of Slovak writers, the predominance of Catholicism, and the Western orientation of the country. The control and indoctrination were exercised by the ideological section of the party through the Ministry of Information and the Association of Slovak Writers, which, although theoretically an organization based on voluntary membership, actually exercised a total monopoly on literary activity through its control of all opportunities for publication.

Most Slovak writers subsequently conformed to the political requirements imposed by communism, which basically meant adopting the technique of socialist realism (q.v.) and using literature primarily as a means of promoting political objectives. Literary themes approved by the government included accounts of resistance against the German occupation and in particular the 1944 uprising; the collectivization of agriculture and the growth of heavy industry; the struggle of the police and

border troops against Western infiltrators; the army life; and peace campaigns.

Despite such restrictions, however, the literary community, as during the Hungarian oppression prior to 1918, was in the political vanguard, constituting the most democratic and liberal element in Slovak public life. It was this literary community, along with Czech intellectuals, that fostered the brief period of cultural, economic, and political liberalization that occurred in Czechoslovakia in 1968.

The subsequent Soviet-led invasion of the country had, besides political and economic consequences, a devastating effect on Slovak literature and cultural life in general. New pressures were applied to publishing houses, books, and the press, this time under the supervision of Soviet "advisers." Among the first to be suppressed was *Kultúrny život* ("The Cultural Life"), the influential weekly magazine of the Writers' Association.

Important contemporary Slovak poets include Ján Kostra (b. 1910), author of the collection of love poems *Ave Eva* and the socialist-realist *Za ten máj* ("For the Socialist May") and *Javorový list* ("The Maple Leaf"). Another important poet is Pavol Horov (b. 1914), who, after writing the socialist *Moje poludnie* ("My Noon") and *Slnce nad nami* ("The Sun above Us"), published lyric and meditative poems in *Vysoké letné nebo* ("The High Summer Sky") and *Balada o snu* ("Ballad on a Dream").

Other poets worth mentioning are Andrej Plávka (b. 1907), who also published short stories and a novel; Štefan Žáry (b. 1918); Ctibor Štítnický (b. 1922); Vojtech Mihálik (b. 1926), who at present serves as president of the Writers' Association; and Milan Lajčiak (b. 1926).

Better-known prose writers are František Hečko (1905–1960), author of the best-selling novels *Červené víno* ("The Red Wine") and *Drevená dedina* ("The Wooden Village"); Dominik Tatarka (b. 1913), noted for his wartime novel *Farská republika* ("The Priests' Republic"); Katarína Lazarová (b. 1914); and Vladimír Mináč (b. 1922).

In drama the works by Štefan Králik (b. 1909), Peter Karvaš (b. 1920), and the Czech-born Ladislav Mňačko (b. 1919) were received with considerable attention.

Mňačko, a lifelong communist and reporter of several party newspapers, holds a particular place in contemporary Slovak literature. His war novel *Smrť sa volá Engelchen* (1959;

"Death Is Called Engelchen") was translated into a dozen languages. Perhaps the first Slovak author to describe the mistakes of the party and the brutality of the communist regime, he was widely acclaimed for his works on these issues, *Oneskorené reportáže* ("Belated Reports") and *Ako chutí moc* (1967; "The Taste of Power"). After the suppression following the Soviet invasion, Mňačko, like several other intellectuals, fled to the West.

Literary history and criticism have been produced in Slovakia by several first-rate scholars, including Andrej Mráz (1904–1964), Milan Pišút (b. 1908), Alexander Matuška (b. 1910), and Karol Rosenbaum (b. 1920). Their studies have appeared in the journals *Slovenské pohľady* ("The Slovak Views"), *Slovenská literatúra* ("Slovak Literature"), *Romboid,* and *Slovenské divadlo* ("The Slovak Theater").

BIBLIOGRAPHY: Mráz, A., *Die Literatur der Slowaken* (1943); Matuška, A., *Pre a proti* (1956; "For and Against"); *Dejiny slovenskej literatúry* (6 vols., 1958 ff.; "A History of Slovak Literature"); *The Linden Tree: An Anthology of Czech and Slovak Literature, 1890–1960* (1962); Števček, P., *Nová slovenská literatura* (1964; "The New Slovak Literature"); *Československá kniha v zahraničí 1961–1965* (1966; "The Czechoslovak Book Abroad"); Matuška, A., *Človek v slove* (1967; "Man in the Word"); *Literárny almanach Slováka v Amerike* (1967; "Literary Almanac of the Slovak in America"); Meriggi, B., *Le letterature ceca e slovacca* (1968); Mráz, A., *Mezi prúdmi,* Vols. I and II (1969; "Among the Tendencies")

RUDOLF STURM

SMITH, Sydney Goodsir
Scottish poet, b. 1915, Wellington, New Zealand

S. first went to Scotland during English school holidays only after he was seventeen. He studied medicine at Edinburgh University and history at Oxford, settling permanently in Edinburgh in 1942, where he now writes on cultural subjects regularly for *The Scotsman.*

S.'s poetry has from first to last been written in Scots, a language S. had to learn on his own because his Scottish family in New Zealand did not speak it.

In an early volume of poetry, *The Wanderer, and Other Poems* (1943), S. introduces his

abiding interests and methods: leftist revolutionary heroism; Scottish nationalism; freedom and erotic love; the old traditional prosody of Scotland and the ballads; folk-art songs like those of Robert Burns (1759–96); and the skillful use of very short, rhymed lines. The main influence here and later was MacDiarmid (q.v.), in whose Scottish renaissance movement S. is, after MacDiarmid and perhaps Soutar (q.v.), the most consistently excellent poet writing in Scots.

Unlike MacDiarmid, S. never abandoned the Scots language. He experimented from the beginning with free verse, irregular-ode forms, and near rhymes. But like MacDiarmid, S. has reconciled his fierce nationalism with a wide contemporary European awareness, as seen, for example, in his many translations of French, Czech, Polish, and Russian poetry. After *The Deevil's Waltz* (1946), there are relatively few political poems.

In *Under the Eildon Tree* (1948), S.'s best book, twenty-four related elegies tell the story of a love affair with characteristically Scottish transitions of tone and mood. S.'s love lyrics are intense in their controlled desperation, like Mark Alexander Boyd's late 16th-c. sonnets, which appear to have influenced S. greatly.

Most recently, S.'s separately published poems are of two kinds: (1) long, rambling, reflective, pub-crawling poems about Edinburgh; (2) free-verse poems with more imagery than before, but fractured and discontinuous (*e.g.,* "Sea Poem" and "Serpent of Old Nile" in *Agenda,* 1968). S. seems deeply troubled by modern life. It may be because of this that he has not found a way to express his genius fully.

S. has published an undescribable prose work *Carotid Cornucopius* (4 fits, 1947; 8 fits, 1962). On a Scots base but with invariable Joyce-like punning neologisms and portmanteau words, it relates—with great humor and wit— the bawdy, bibulous adventures and speeches of the title character, the Caird of the Cannongate. S. described the book as "a fantastic Rabelaisian-cum-Joycean extravaganza." MacDiarmid said that it was "alive as a hilarious old tinker—a fine reeking haggis of a book."

FURTHER WORKS: *Skail Wind* (1941); *Selected Poems* (1947); *A Short Introduction to Scottish Literature* (1951); *So Late into the Night* (1952); *Fifty Lyrics 1944–48* (1952); *Cokkils* (1953); *A Collection of Poems* (1954); *Orpheus and Eurydice* (1955); *Omens* (1955);

The Merrie Life and Dowie Death of Colickie Meg, the Carlin Wife of Ben Nevis (1956); *Figs and Thistles* (1959); *The Vision of the Prodigal Son* (1960); *The Wallace* (1960)

BIBLIOGRAPHY: McCaig, N., "The Poetry of S.," *Saltire Review*, No. 1, (1954), pp. 14–19; Kitchin, G., "The Modern Makars," in *Scottish Poetry*, ed. J. Kinsley (1955), pp. 266–68; Scott, T., "Some Poets of the Scottish Renaissance," *Poetry*, LXXXVIII (1956), 43–47; MacKie, A., "Just S.," *Lines Review*, No. 16 (1960), pp. 22–24; MacDiarmid, H., *S. G. S.* (pamphlet, 1963); Crawford, T., "The Poetry of S.," *Studies in Scottish Literature*, VII (1969), 40–59; *Akros*, IV (May 1969), x—Garioch, R., "Under the Eildon Tree," pp. 41–47, MacDiarmid, H., "A Redeeming Feature," pp. 17–20, and Scott, A., "The Art of Devilment," pp. 21–28

JOHN C. WESTON

SNOW, Charles Percy

English novelist, b. 15 Oct. 1905, Leicester

The son of a clerk in a shoe factory, S. has achieved remarkable success in both science and literature. Rising in science through prizes and scholarships, he was a Cambridge fellow for twenty years. After personnel work for the wartime government, he became a Commissioner of Civil Service as well as a member of the board of directors of Britain's largest power utility. In 1950, S. married novelist Pamela Hansford Johnson (b. 1912), with whom he wrote several plays, all published in 1951.

After venturing into literature with a detective story (*Death under Sail,* 1932) and scientific fantasy (*New Lives for Old,* 1933), S. published *The Search* (1934), in which a scientist is shown maneuvering for financial support and prestige. At the novel's end, the protagonist abandons science because his interest in subjective human muddle has become stronger than his quest for scientific knowledge. This book forecasts the grand design of "Strangers and Brothers," a sequence of novels—begun in 1940—relating the career of their narrator, Lewis Eliot, a lawyer, teacher, and administrator whose social experiences roughly follow the author's. Unity is given the series through recurring situations, often involving the same characters, and by the narrator's constant return to the same themes in different books. As a slum boy who has made his way by intelligence and nerve into the rooms where decisions are made, Eliot is keenly aware of the pursuit of power in our society. But as a complex being who in his personal relationships has experienced, sometimes willed, failure even more than success, his interest finally is in those gifted misfits who serve and contribute, but who do not succeed as the world goes. As a thoughtful man who has spent much of his own time on committees, Eliot is a master at conveying the personal conflicts and loyalties that flicker and surge through such groups.

Though each novel is designed to stand as a separate work, the series has been created as a total experience. *Time of Hope* (1949) gives Eliot an adolescence rather like that depicted by D. H. Lawrence (q.v.) in *Sons and Lovers.* He is shown resenting and pitying his parents, resolved to use his brain and will to escape genteel poverty in a Midland town. Turned to the law by the town's iconoclast, George Passant (one of the recurring major figures of the series), young Eliot goes to London to study law. However, his career suffers setbacks through illness and marriage to unstable Sheila Knight. In *Homecomings* (1956) Sheila commits suicide; during the war Eliot remarries, fathers a son, and seemingly reaches a personal haven.

The other novels in the series all find Eliot involved—sometimes intimately, sometimes as an observer—in more public events centered on the university, the laboratory, and government bureaus. *Strangers and Brothers* (1940; the first of the series) relates the downfall of Eliot's mentor, Passant, whose fierce honesty and intelligence are unfortunately coupled with adolescent sensuality and small-town crankiness. *The Conscience of the Rich* (1958)—one of the most sensitively written of the group— deals with a conflict in an upper-middle-class Jewish family between Eliot's friend Charles March and the latter's tyrannical father, Sir Leonard. *The New Men* (1954) focuses on the part British scientists played in developing the A-bomb during World War II, dwelling on the temptations to power the project brought the hitherto secluded scientists.

Three of the novels form a special subgroup dealing with the fellows of a Cambridge college over a twenty-year period. In *The Light and the Dark* (1947), Eliot and several friends seek a college appointment for Roy Calvert, a brilliant but erratic young linguist. The first of the novels to be widely acclaimed, *The Masters* (1951) depicts the coalitions and fallings-out of this intimate group of scholars as they politic—in the best and worse senses of the word—in order to choose a new leader. In *The Affair* (1960) the same group seventeen years later deals with a complex case of injustice: a novice scientist is accused of faking an experiment, and his radical politics and sullen impertinence lead his elders to suspect the worst and judge the man, not the deed.

Corridors of Power (1964) concerns a defense minister's abortive attempt to lead England out of the nuclear arms race. In *The Sleep of Reason* (1968) Eliot and his brother Martin return to their home town to see their old friend Passant through the ordeal of the scandalous trial of his niece, who with a lesbian companion has perpetrated a sadistic child murder—an atrocity similar to the real-life 1966 Moor murders in England.

S.'s articles and lectures on science and government have sometimes caused vigorous controversy. In *The Two Cultures and the Scientific Revolution* (1959) S. argued for a better understanding of science and scientists and for the wider application of technical knowledge to social problems.

Science and Government (1961) surveys the harmful influence exerted on British war policy by F. A. Lindemann (Lord Cherwell) and argues that scientists should be brought into the government of technological societies, but that they should be subjected there to the same critical scrutiny and control as politicians. *Variety of Men* (1967) offers slight impressionistic sketches of men prominent in recent science, letters, and politics.

Often carelessly categorized as a Bennett or a Galsworthy (qq.v.) of the welfare state, S. is, despite the placid quality of his narrrative, a thoroughly modern novelist, who in his own way is as much aware of the darkly ambiguous nature of man as Thomas Mann and Joyce (qq.v.) were in theirs. His great theme is not the quest for power, but how a few men resist its temptations through the application of conscience in order to avoid deceiving themselves and others. This creation of a tenuous yet profound moral wisdom in a too often immoral society could be called S.'s distinctive contribution to the modern novel.

Unlike many contemporary fictional heroes, S.'s public men do not abandon society out of frustration, but continuously return to its dilemmas. They remain aware of the selfish passions not only within the group but also within themselves. Perhaps no other writer of

our day has brought so much social fact into his novels, while at the same time neither ignoring nor sentimentalizing the complex character of individual man as attested to by modern philosophy and psychology.

FURTHER WORKS: *Magnanimity* (1962); *Last Things* (1970)

BIBLIOGRAPHY: Cooper, W., *C. P. S.* (1959); Millgate, R., "Structure and Style in the Novels of C. P. S.," *Review of English Literature,* Nos. 1 and 2 (Jan. 1960), pp. 34–41; Stanford, D., "C. P. S.: The Novelist as Fox," *Meanjin,* XIX (1960), iii, 236–51; Greacen, R., *The World of C. P. S.* (1962); Stanford, R., "The Achievement of C. P. S.," *WHR,* XVI (Winter 1962), i, 43–52; Karl, F. R., *C. P. S.: The Politics of Conscience* (1963); Davis, R. G., *C. P. S.* (1965); Thale, J., *C. P. S.: The Man and His Work* (1965)

RANEY STANFORD

SOCIALIST REALISM

The two articles that follow represent interpretations of (1) a Western-oriented critic and (2) the prominent Soviet writer Aleksandr Fadayev (q.v.), which reflects the official Soviet position on this term.

The theory of literature common to the socialist-communist countries. It has been the standard and obligatory doctrine in these countries since it was proclaimed by Maksim Gorki (q.v.) and adopted by the First Congress of Soviet Writers in 1934. Socialist realism has replaced "critical realism," the socially conscious literary theory of the 19th c., in Russian literature, since criticism is no longer allowed to seriously attack existing conditions under the new social system.

The official definition of the Congress was vague enough to permit a multiplicity of interpretations and changing commentaries right down to the present time. "Socialist realism as the fundamental method of socialist literature and literary criticism demands from the artist a correct historically concrete representation of reality in its revolutionary development," that is, reality as it changes is to be viewed in terms of communist theory. (A second sentence imposing the task of ideological education on socialist realism was eliminated in 1954.)

The essential requirements were: (1) Faithfulness to life (reality) and simplification to the point of deliberate banality in the interest of greater effectiveness; hence the avoidance of experiments, individualism, religious mysticism, sexual themes, and especially every sort of formalism. (2) Representation of the social struggle as a struggle for progress and proving that social ideas in every selected and historical period were in agreement with communist theory, that is, deliberate tendentiousness and limitation in choice of subject. (3) Adherence to social optimism and hope in a better future. (4) The positive hero and the representation of the so-called typical, by which is meant not what is characteristic of reality, but what is worth emulating—the idealized manifestation, the manifestation as it ought to be in the sense of Marxism-Leninism, even if it is atypical.

The dangers of socialist realism, in part recognized by its practitioners, lie in schematism, monotony of writing due to exclusion of all other literary currents and techniques, lack of conflict in the drama, the stereotyped black-and-white portrayals, tendency to ideological sentimentality and journalistic superficiality, photographic reproduction of reality.

According to Gottfried Benn (q.v.), "This Russian theory of art asserts no more and no less than that everything that goes on in our minds, in Western man—that is, our crises, tragedies, dissensions, our irritations and pleasures—are pure capitalist decadent phenomena, capitalist snares."

From *Sachwörterbuch der Literatur*,
Gero von Wilpert, Stuttgart:
Alfred Kröner Verlag, 1969

The outline of the rules for the Union of Soviet Writers published in *Pravda* is not the usual drafting of rules for a literary organization but the most important programmatic document in all Soviet literature.

During the years of proletarian dictatorship Soviet literature took shape and evolved ideologically into the world's most progressive literature. The new principles of artistic creation found their main expression in socialist realism, the "fundamental method of Soviet literature and literary criticism."

The method of socialist realism is neither a dogma nor a collection of legal edicts that limits the development of the artistic creation or the variety of artistic forms and hampers the search for literary tenets. On the contrary, socialist realism is the only expression of the new socialist relationships and revolutionary philosophy. It takes as its point of departure the unprecedented upsurging of the creative drive, the unprecedented expansion of themes, the development of the most varied forms, genres, styles, and literary techniques.

The basic demand of socialist realism is that of the "correct, historically concrete representation of reality in its revolutionary development," that is, a representation that performs the service of "ideologically molding and educating the working masses in the spirit of socialism."

These features of socialist realism, which should become more prominent in growing Soviet literature, are fundamental in distinguishing that literature not merely from the literature of the contemporary bourgeoisie but also from all previous aristocratic-bourgeois literature. The class-conditioned, limited point of view of even the best and most progressive writers of the past kept them from expressing plainly and clearly the truth about reality. Their world view did not permit them to see reality in its revolutionary development. Only socialist realism is capable of achieving the representation of reality's historical process because it is armed with a revolutionary viewpoint and is enriched by the experience of the establishment of socialism in our country. It can show how tomorrow is born within the womb of today. Socialist realism does not exclude revolutionary romanticism. On the contrary, it presupposes and confirms it as a necessary attribute of socialist literary creation.

The more completely and profoundly Soviet literature assimilates these qualities of socialist realism—that is, the correct, historically concrete representation of reality in its revolutionary development—the more effectively it will fulfill the task of ideologically molding and educating the working masses in the spirit of socialism.

The statute correctly states that socialist realism emerged as the product of the critical appropriating of the literary heritage of the past, on the one hand, and out of the study of the experience of the victorious establishment of socialism and the growth of socialist culture on the other hand.

Soviet literature did not spring into existence full-blown. It has paid and continues to pay attention to everything that is progressive and best in works written by artists of the past. Now, when literary youth is moving forward in an ever-widening front into the ranks of

Soviet writers—a youth maturing in our socialist construction sites, factories, *kolkhozes* and *sovkhozes*—the task of the critical appropriating of the literary heritage must be more strongly emphasized. The experience of the literature of the past must be refracted through the prisms of socialist experience and revolutionary ideology before it enters contemporary socialist literature.

We need a great art, one that unites a profound intellectual content with high artistic form. Naturally, there is no reason to insist that the writer master the philosophy of Marxism as a condition of his creativity. But it can be unconditionally demanded that the writer raise himself to the level of contemporary culture. Marxism-Leninism is the most consistent expression of contemporary culture. The writer should master the philosophy of Marxism-Leninism because it embodies the greatest wisdom of humanity; it alone offers the true understanding of the laws of social development, an understanding of psychology and ideology.

A knowledge of the philosophy of Marxism-Leninism increases immeasurably the ideological power of literary creation. However, an artistic product can be worthwhile and convincing only if it achieves concrete, palpable embodiment of its idea, if intelligence and will, good and evil, love and hate, courage and cowardice, honesty and hypocrisy, are embodied in living and full-blooded figures, if content finds its appropriately clear form.

Engels wrote in his well-known letter to Minna Kautsky that he was in no sense an opponent of *Tendenz* literature (writing with a social and/or political bias) as such. Both the father of tragedy, Aeschylus, and the father of comedy, Aristophanes, as well as Dante and Cervantes were writers of *Tendenz* works . . . the modern Russian and Norwegian writers, authors of superb novels, were in general and particular, *tendenziö* writers. However, he believed the polemical viewpoint had to spring from the plot and situation without being explicitly referred to. . . .

The idea of socialism should not be attached externally and artificially to the work, but should appear as its very essence, embodied in its characters. The cause of socialism should become the personal cause of the writer. To rejoice and suffer, love and hate, in common with the working class—this and only this endows the socialist work of art with deep authenticity and emotional completeness and increases the force of its artistic impact on the reader. The great idealistic dialectician Hegel hit the mark when he pointed out the nature of the power radiated by literary characters. He wrote that the literary work is created so that through it the reader can find pleasure in meditation. It exists so the public can find in it what it desires, an object that represents its true beliefs, that contains ideas and gives it the opportunity of feeling itself in harmony with the represented figures and objects.

We need a great, all-embracing art. That Shakespeare, Goethe, Balzac, Pushkin, Swift, Dante, Lev Tolstoi (q.v.), and, in our time, Maksim Gorki (q.v.), tower so high above the average level of literature is because their art was an art of great abstracting. The science of our epoch has taken upon itself as never before in history the task of synthesis. In our country the task of scientific synthesis grows out of the very nature of socialist relationships. The policy of our party appears as the greatest and most complete synthesis. Everything, most decidedly everything that occurs in the fields of the economy, politics, culture, ideology, science, and technology—all this is subject to a single, guiding will and placed in the service of victorious socialism.

Art, too, in the epoch of socialism, faces synthesis as its most important task. The works of our writers still often suffer from a poverty of abstracting. This leads either to a worthless accumulation of facts, details, observations or to arbitrarily imposing on the reader a work without inner logic. In this way the writer tries to "compensate" as it were for his artistic weaknesses.

"The writer," Gorki wrote, "must master the ability to condense. The art of literary creation, the art of shaping characters and types requires ideas, speculations, inventions. When a writer describes an individual shopkeeper, official, or worker whom he knows, he provides a more or less successful photograph of the particular person, but it is a photograph deprived of socioeducational significance, which hardly contributes to the extension and deepening of our knowledge of mankind and life. But if the writer knows how to abstract the specially characteristic class features, habits, tendencies, gestures, views, speech mannerisms, etc. and condenses them in the form of *a* shopkeeper, official, worker, then with this technique the writer creates a type that is art."

The writer can attain this goal only if he

diligently studies our reality, penetrates the material, and becomes thoroughly familiar with it. Then the truth of our reality will pervade all the artist's feelings and become one with his personality. Artistic haste will accomplish nothing in this situation. What is needed is organic fusion with the reality of triumphant socialism. Socialist realism requires the uniting of artistic creativity with the great whole. Intellectualism and the primitive compiling of isolated facts are equally alien to it.

Our reality is great and rich. Our present will be followed by a still more beautiful and mighty future. This future is no chimera but a scientifically grounded, practically proved potentiality that even now is coming into existence. Soviet literature is obligated to show this future to millions of workers in living forms in order to strengthen their will and energy in the struggle for the triumph of socialism in the entire world. These are the basic conditions of socialist realism as they are formulated in the statute of the Union of Soviet Writers.

ALEKSANDR FADAYEV

SOCIETY AND LITERATURE

Literature in this century has been concerned above all with a renewed attempt to answer the question "what is man?" in terms that are usually Freudian and often verge on the solipsistic. Yet because of its heritage it cannot escape entirely from considering man as a social being even when it turns away with some violence from the goals and assumptions of a preceding age. Whereas the writers of the Romantic generation of the early 19th c., engaged in much the same kind of inquiry, were inclined to see man as essence, not existence, as abstraction, not concrete, mutable entity, and thus were able to remove him from his social milieu or to present it also in general and abstract terms, writers of our day are more empirical than philosophical and feel that some filiations with external reality must be given the persona. It may be said, in short, that the prevailingly realistic mode of the last part of the 19th c. acted as a bridge between these two major explorations of the human psyche, that we have come back to the romantic quest better equipped in knowledge and with a sense of the importance of the social matrix that did not exist before.

The general scientism of the latter part of the 19th c., positivistic in temper, inductive and experimental in method, had for a time an overwhelming influence on literary endeavors. It was not merely that writers sought to explore society in all its manifestations, but they became convinced that they were servants of truth, that their "experiments" à la Zola (q.v.) had the same fundamental utility as the laboratory findings of a Pasteur. They were disenchanted with the invented personalities which appeared in the works of their predecessors, they had doubts about the possibility of reliable access to the mind, and they were intoxicated by the broad vistas of external social depiction which suddenly opened up before them. Thus they gave primacy to that which they could observe in the world around them, often in the process adopting a kind of epiphenomenalism by which they reduced mental states to ineffective shadows accompanying the material causal process. Though the impulsion of this literary scientism showed a decided slackening by the turn of the c. (particularly in Europe; the United States and other provincial areas were at least a generation behind), it has never disappeared. It has continued to produce works in the traditional social framework of the realist-naturalists and has at the same time helped to shape the literature called psychological, giving it a social reference and density which the Romantics were not equipped to bring to it.

To many writers after the turn of the c. these inherited social preoccupations were an albatross around the neck, something that they felt they must throw off at any cost if they were to develop in their proper bent. They sought to repudiate Zola and all his pomps, in the fashion of Proust (q.v.) at the end of *Le Temps retrouvé*, asserting in concert with Dostoyevski, though with a different emphasis, that they practiced a "higher realism," that truth was not to be found on the surface of things. In particular they repudiated the basic realistic assumption that truth was objective, inherent in the data of perception, accessible to all on nearly equal terms. Influenced by the new psychology and the new physics, they shifted their emphasis from the perceived object to the perceiving mind and made their capital of the myriad possibilities, the myriad patterns of individual perception. Society as a thing in itself, mapable and analyzable, capable of dissection like a corpse upon a table, was dissolved into multiple fluctuating perceptions, to a very real extent into a country of the mind, or of many minds.

Yet quietly the inherited realistic conceptions continued to exert their pull, to topple the exuberant antisocial hyperbole of the surrealists, for example, to provide a constant reminder that the new object of literary cultism, psychological man, was also social man. Zola's reputation, which had been the barometer of the fortunes of the naturalist doctrine and had subsided to insignificance with the dominance of the poetic, the symbolic, and psychological way of writing, began to rise again after World War I. There was guarded admission that the realists had a point in their insistence on society as a subject for literature. A populist school arose in France, a neorealist group in Portugal; and after World War II a group of practicing realists emerged in Italy. Meanwhile, in Russia writers found it advisable to conform to the dictates of socialist realism (q.v.). Even if it is doubtful that realism as a doctrine will ever hold sway again, it is evident that in the 20th c. it exerts a steady influence on literature and acts as a brake on writing which would remove man from his habitat.

To be sure, the authentic voice of poetry in our age is ruminative, self-probing, self-revelatory. Always teetering on the precipice of the uniquely private system of reference, it does attempt to draw away from the public world of social data or it filters them through the sieve of association to the point where they lose objective importance. But not entirely. A Rilke, a García Lorca, above all a Yeats, an Auden, or a Pound (qq.v.) will suddenly reveal the grounding of the private experience in the public condition or event. A William Carlos Williams (q.v.) will write a long poem, *Paterson*, one of the major themes of which is "Outside outside myself there is a world," which has the power to inform thoughts concretely. In another way, too, poets find that they cannot ignore society, as the young Russians attest in their increasingly open attack on rigid and restrictive social attitudes. And, of course, the poetry which has sprung from two world wars must, even in its anguished rejection of war, still incorporate the distant rumble of the guns.

With this partial qualification made for poetry, we must recognize that 20th-c. literature cannot avoid placing man in his setting, that it adopts a practical Thomism in accepting the fact that at least most of what exists in the mind must previously have existed outside it, and that it accepts for better or worse that social forms are dominant in the shaping of a human being. However, writers today are much less interested in the representative, average man than were their predecessors. They are not epiphenomenalists either, but phenomenalists. What man makes of the world via perception is more important than what it may be in itself, if indeed it is anything in itself. In other words, there is a shift away from the realist view that man is essentially subject to his environment and a kind of fixture in it to the view that social data are merely the raw material to be fed into the hopper of the mind from which will issue, not something rich and strange, in the spirit of the Romantics, but something rich and substantial in its contribution to an understanding of the human condition.

From this standpoint it is no accident that the quest story, the *Bildungsroman*, should have become a major genre of the age. It is, naturally, most frequently a *Bildungsroman* of the mind: what a man learns *from* his inescapable involvement in society, not what he learns *about* society, is the important thing. To a considerable extent what a man must learn is that there are no solutions to social problems, which he can only endure; therefore he must come to know himself, for only in that way can he live with the unresolved and the paradoxical, anesthetizing himself to the goring horns of the dilemma of his life. Since value systems are no longer achieved by putting a coin in the appropriately designated slot of tradition, the hero of the quest has to make them up as he goes, not out of whole cloth, but in full awareness of the patchwork nature of the society in which he lives.

This is to put the most optimistic tone to the process. It is what is achieved by Robert Jordan in Hemingway's (q.v.) *For Whom the Bell Tolls*, by Jack Burden in Warren's (q.v.) *All the King's Men*, perhaps by Lewis Elliott in the novels of Snow (q.v.). The provenance of titles is significant: such an unbeleaguered achievement of insight is less frequent outside the Anglo-American literary tradition. Beyond this zone of partial comfort we confront the noman's-land of existentialism (q.v.), a pessimistic obverse of statements like the above, exhorting men to make the best of what is, by common agreement, the worst. Since the time of Kierkegaard religious existentialism has had a growing influence in the West, but on the whole it is its secular counterpart which manifests itself in contemporary literature. It is significant that the novels of Kafka (q.v.), which seem to yield most by a religious and/or Freudian reading, are seized upon by the common reader as reflecting the dilemma of the social man. Even without the metaphor of arrest and trial, which is certainly an invitation to such a reading, readers would no doubt seize upon a central concept that reflects the capricious and impersonal working of institutions, since their own existential predicament is not highfalutin' or abstract, but is seen most clearly in terms of their daily life in society, subject as they are to being parts of the machine and to decisions by the supermachine.

This is one of the major points where the literature of self-analysis is thrown back into the broad stream of literature about society. Existentialist thought does not allow man to withdraw from society, since that is impossible, in order to loaf and invite his soul. And the reason this is impossible is the same reason which has caused the popularity of this doctrine—a galling awareness of the adverse conditions of life. Sartre (q.v.) has bridged the two kinds of literature effectively in his categorical imperative "Choose thyself," which has its foundation both in a sense of the social barriers to authentic being and in psychological fracture or incapacity. The Sartrean protagonist is physically hemmed in on every side by institutions and social attitudes which function less absurdly than ineluctably. His act of choosing, his attempt at authenticity, must be made in full awareness of his act's being a wager in which the cards are stacked against him.

Finally, in this spectrum of the possibilities of self-knowledge open to the social man, we go beyond existentialism to the existential monster, whose being is less an act of knowing than a sly revenge on the tyrannical forces which mutilate him. His act is to choose a grotesque, perverted, and ultimately (by repetition) banal self in the manner of Beckett, Genet, and Henry Miller (qq.v.). This is less a choice of self than a retreat into the porcupine ball of an authorially contrived *Ur*-self, a recoil into a fetal id position from which to make an ultimate, despairing, defensive self-assertion. To the reader who is not hypnotized by doctrine, such postures in time come to seem frenetically inauthentic, though their purpose of arousing nausea toward current social values by means of a shower of ordure is clear enough.

These existentialist and subexistentialist attitudes are frequently referred to under the general rubric of "alienation," the contemporary idiom for *Angst* or even *Weltschmerz*. Though alienation is frequently offered as a kind of absolute, it is a relative term, for it necessitates a referent, that from which man is alienated. He may, to be sure, be alienated from himself or, in traditional religious terms, from God; but the usual form in our literature is the man alienated from society. This common adolescent phenomenon becomes alarming when it is prolonged into maturity, when it becomes the gestalt of middle age. Partly it is a delayed reaction to disillusionment over the promises of rationalism and optimism; partly it is the result of shock from the lurid events of the 20th c., though the most vocal exponents of alienation have usually suffered those shocks only at second hand. In its basis it is born merely of frustration, of a sense of inadequacy in a world which is too mechanical and too complex to regard the individual. There has been a good deal of rushing about during the 20th c. for a formula, a doctrine, which would provide the basis for a manageable and predictable society, which would set up values both immutable and man-directed. The failure of these frenetic quests has merely compounded the sense of alienation from which they arise.

It is to be concluded that even that body of writing which is not by definition social, which is in revolt against the conceptions and the literary practices of the 19th c., must be seen to be conditioned by society and societal problems. Beyond it lies that body of literature which is a direct continuation of the social representation dominant in the earlier period, which takes for granted the primacy of social subjects for literature and seeks to present man's condition in those terms. Certain important modifications of view are to be noted, however. Most important is a sense of society as process rather than fixed tableau, as becoming rather than being, as dynamic rather than static. This is an inevitable result of close observation of modern life. It is a condition which was only vaguely discernible when Zola wrote the Rougon-Macquart, although he did capitalize on it in *Germinal*.

This change in turn entails important modifications of the sense of causality which underlies society. A strict materialistic determinism no longer suffices, except in that intellectual climate where it is a basic article of faith; in its place there is both a reliance on interaction and an allowance for the random event, intolerable as the latter concept is to any tightly rational system. Brilliant as Thomas Mann's (q.v.) *Der Zauberberg* is in its analysis of the process of breakdown and resynthesis of social forms, it does in a way rest on a simplified and old-fashioned base in the symmetry and inevitability of social patterns which it hypothesizes. It states that when a social complex (institutions and values) ceases to meet human needs adequately, it is undermined by the pull of those elements which are lacking and is moved to a position which incorporates them. As Mann conceived of it, the formal elements of the bourgeois culture of western Europe tend ultimately to squeeze out life-giving content. The individual and his society out of inner necessity move toward the latter and eventually create a new complex where needs for order and vital being are in balance. By this argument Germany became the land of the middle, the geographical and cultural locus of the new synthesis which would harmonize East and West. Satisfying as this structure is as hypothesis, the failure of actuality to conform to it may derive from the restrictive causal pattern on which it rests.

The third shift away from traditional conceptions has already been dealt with. The individual human being has been raised to a level of greater importance than they accorded him. Men do not exist in society merely as objects for the steamroller of impersonal social force to run over and crush. Rather they exist in the midst of exterior social forces as dynamic beings, fighting back significantly if not efficaciously instead of inertly allowing themselves to be destroyed. It is a David-against-Goliath struggle, with David losing—or at least not winning; but man as hero has been reinstated to a degree, even though the naïve and shocked idealist may speak of him as antihero. This is the importance of Joyce's (q.v.) Leopold Bloom. In its social dimension *Ulysses* is an unsparing demonstration of the inertia of Dublin life at the turn of the c. The background figures have been ground down to immobile stumps. A promising creative personality, Stephen Dedalus, is frustrated by the social attitudes which rule over him from the past (though some of the blame for his failure is shown to lie within him). But the Everyman of the novel, Leopold Bloom, who is crushed many times a day, whose creative capacities are abortive, nonetheless bounces back, carries on a running fight with his society, refusing to be crushed, looking hopefully to the future, insisting that man is more than a speck of dust

in interstellar space or more than a black dot in a white space at the bottom of a page.

For purposes of convenience we may designate two types of social depiction in the literature of our time. These are social chronicle and social parable, the primary distinction between them being the degree of literalness of representation which they offer.

Social Chronicle

It is in this area that the direct inheritance from 19th-c. realism makes itself most strongly felt. The powerful examples of Zola, Tolstoi, Pérez Galdós (qq.v.), even of Balzac and Stendhal, are undeniably present to the 20th-c. writer even when he feels he must repudiate them as being *vieux jeu*. With a few exceptions the social chronicles of today do not have the compelling power or novelty of their prototypes, but they still flourish as a conventional (and prolix) way of fiction. Such works are responsive to a compulsion to tell what life is like in a given time and place, not least in those areas without a previous literary history where current inventory seems of immediate importance. There is continuous evidence of this compulsion from unexpected places. In response to an outcry raised against the play, *A Touch of Brightness,* for its depiction of the red-light district of Bombay, the author, Partap Sherma, defended himself by saying: "But if I am wrong to write about them, then so were Ibsen [q.v.] and Zola when they wrote about the less attractive aspects of nineteenth-century Europe." This desire to set down the truth is no doubt closely allied to a rising social and political consciousness in developing areas, which wishes to set the record of social conditions straight so that something can be done about them, proving once more that since Zola social action and social depiction have been linked together in the popular mind.

On a more sophisticated level the 20th c. has provided a host of panoramic novels on a large scale. There come to mind the social chronicles of modern Brazil, Cela's (q.v.) *La colmena,* set in modern Madrid, or Dos Passos's (q.v.) *USA.* The most notable example is Romains's (q.v.) *Les Hommes de bonne volonté,* which in twenty-seven volumes attempts to give an overview of French and European life from 1908 to 1933, playing down, though not ignoring, salient historical events in the interest of giving the "feel" of the period. The novel is straight empiricism, raising the question as to what were the major causal forces in the development of the period, but containing an inherent irony in that the men of good will whom the work traces are found to be helpless against the downhill rush of events which culminates in Hitler's rise to power in 1933. There are certain to be more works like this, for the genre is capable of infinite variation. Potentially what Romains did for Paris and France can be done for Belgrade and Bombay, for Johannesburg and Jakarta, and moreover can be reattempted for random time-spans for generations to come. Such chronicles adhere to the slice-of-life, average-man convention. They make capital, not of exciting events, but of what life is like in its mediocre, unheroic continuity and repetition. They do, however, depend on a sense of historical process, first exhibited by Tolstoi in *War and Peace.* They depend also on an acute awareness of social change: the attempt to seize on the significant pattern of an era would make no sense in a society of fixed social values and observances.

A limited derivative from this broad genre is the depiction of institutions in the specific sense of the term. The relationship is much like that of the individual Zola novel to the total sweep of the Rougon-Macquart, though usually without the continuing matrix of the *roman fleuve.* Here the emphasis is often informational: what it is like to make one's living in steel foundry or coal mine, as stevedore or laboratory technician; what the interplay of forces, human and material, is in factory, department store, hospital, or university, not to mention big government. Such works no doubt serve a useful function in a world of compartmentalized experience, where it is rarely possible for a single individual to have close experience of more than three or four institutional worlds. From one standpoint this kind of writing was the forte of Sinclair Lewis (q.v.), with the obvious added dimension of satire; it was the avowed program of Pierre Hamp (b. 1876); it was the domain of Albert Halper, as on a different level it has been that of Snow. It is a genre which is factually revealing of transient data but which with predictable regularity bogs down in those data, which are by the nature of vocational and institutional process highly transitory and as a result incapable of much illumination. An exception of some importance is Winifred Holtby's (1898-1935) novel, *South Riding,* which shows the working of local government in Yorkshire. This form

becomes more sophisticated when it provides a background for psychological growth, as in Meyer Levin's (b. 1905) *Citizens,* where the events of a strike are no more important than the protagonists' response to them.

The essence of the kind of chronicle just described is the humdrum, nonexceptional train of life which it depicts. What the 20th c. has provided in plenty is the exceptional social event, the public catastrophe, jarring to moral conviction and literary convention alike. To such events writers of the last fifty years have been drawn with inescapable fascination. This has been the era of the war novel, not war seen as an arena for private heroism or despair, but war in its broad social sweep, as impersonal machine that mows down men and nations and engulfs social landmarks. The protagonist may be multiple and faceless. Whoever he is, what happens to him is less poignant in itself than in the insistent sense of general suffering and waste which the account provides. Emphasis in this genre has varied over the years: Barbusse's (q.v.) pioneer work *Le Feu* is more personal and lyrical than Romains's *Verdun.* Remarque's (q.v.) *Im Westen nichts Neues* is narrower in focus than Arnold Zweig's (q.v.) tetralogy, of which *Der Streit um den Sergeanten Grischa* is removed from the scene of active fighting and seeks to show the general demoralization produced by the military machine of the necessary safeguards of civilian life. James Jones's (q.v.) *The Thin Red Line* and Plievier's (q.v.) *Stalingrad, Moscow,* and *Berlin* are masterpieces of the impersonal ballet of military action. Whereas the works emanating from experience of World War I had a tendency to outrage and anger, this is less true of those about World War II. Certainly such writing is not complacent about war, but it seems to imply that a full and honest account is more compelling than any amount of special pleading.

Not only has this c. been a time of war, but it has been an age of revolution, of revolutions which have produced vast social changes at dramatic cost. These have inevitably cried out for chronicles, if only in justification of the triumphant regime. Sholokhov (q.v.), Nobel laureate in 1965, received that prize primarily for his *Tichii Don,* completed in the 1930's, which portrayed world war, revolution, and civil war from the vantage point of the Don Cossacks. Something of the same effort was made by Aleksei Tolstoi (q.v.) in *The Years Between* and by Fedin (q.v.) in *Goroda i gody,* though the latter is notable in that it does not adhere to the Tolstoi saga of war and peace but attempts by a mosaic of symbolic actions to convey the dislocating effects of a social convulsion. Recently in Germany, Böll and Grass (qq.v.) have used this type of symbolic structure for an analysis of the descent of Germany into the abyss under the Nazi regime, a path which had earlier been marked out by Thomas Mann in *Doktor Faustus*. Doderer (q.v.) charted crucial events of breakdown in Austria in his leisurely novel *Die Dämonen*. For the civil war in Spain there is the sweeping chronicle composed by Gironella (q.v.), of which two volumes, *Los cipreses creen en Dios* and *Un millón de muertos*, deal with the war.

The development of Gironella's three-part chronicle (1951–1966) is especially interesting in that it begins with a narrow circle of personal experience in separatist Catalonia and then gradually widens to take in the whole of Spain as the avalanche of disaster spreads. For Italy under the domination of Mussolini there were the works of Ignazio Silone (q.v.), written in exile, especially his *Fontamara* and *Pane e vino*. It is significant that since the fall of the regime the author has rewritten the former in less reportorial terms, in tacit recognition of the limitations of the strictly chronicle account.

There have also been accounts of more special situations during these seven decades of misery and loss. The ravages of anti-Semitism in prewar Europe, the calculated effort at extermination of the Jewish people, the painful building of a new Jerusalem have been documented *in extenso*. Of equal scope is the literature arising from the great economic depression of the 1920's and 1930's. Fallada's (q.v.) *Kleiner Mann—was nun?*, a novel dealing with the plight of the white-collar class in Berlin, is a well-known example. Works of this sort written in the United States and England have tended to become special pleading, an attempt to advocate basic, even revolutionary reforms in the economic system by recounting the plight of people living under that system. This particular outburst was preceded in the United States at the turn of the c. by an unusual phenomenon, the muckraking movement, by which a group of magazine writers and writers of fiction concerted together to delve into the various ways in which malefactors of great wealth acquired their riches and abused their privileges to the danger of the fundamental institutions of the country. This was the first instance of reporter turned man of letters, though it soon fizzled off into sensationalism.

Because of this widespread effort at chronicling the events of the time it is easy to see that virtually no aspect of the history of this c., in Europe and America at least, has been left untouched. The popular success of this kind of writing has led to an extension retrospectively into the social history of the past, particularly in industrial countries where the ravages of the recent changes provided dramatic materials. American writers have also tried retrospectively to recreate the experience of life on the frontier and to treat the Civil War in fictional terms as social phenomenon. Historical fiction of documentary nature is less prevalent on the continent, though Giuseppe di Lampedusa's (q.v.) *Il gattopardo* is an important exception.

A new genre of considerable importance which is very largely the product of this c. is reportage. This need not be social in subject matter, for it often is a form of biography, but in practice it is usually an account of a social situation. It differs from the traditional parliamentary report or sociological treatise in that it is directed at a mass audience and seeks to involve readers in a way that straight analysis cannot do. In part this genre is made possible by the rapidity of communication of our era—while there cannot always be a Pliny on hand when Vesuvius erupts, a reporter can reach the center of catastrophe in hours by jet while the lava is still flowing. In part this development depends on the reading public with a taste for fact which newspapers and news services have created by their world-wide networks of reporters, though it must be observed that reportage demands a skill and objectivity not always available to the reporter on the spot. Such writing embraces both the great general human catastrophes—fire, flood, famine, drought, and earthquake—but it can also be evoked by much more particular events, provided they have a broad human (that is, social) relevance. What it depends on for effect is an eye for significant detail and a disposition to let the facts speak for themselves. The classic instance is John Hersey's (b. 1914) *Hiroshima*. More recently in the United States a somewhat exaggerated furore has been caused by Capote's (q.v.) *In Cold Blood*, which he has called a "nonfiction novel." While the label is more arresting than meaningful, it does attest to a tendency of modern fiction to rely on and move toward the actual in its depictions. What is more important about the Capote book is that it is squarely astride the two major interests of contemporary writing: it attempts to make sense of the aberrant personalities that committed a horrible and senseless crime, and it attempts to see that crime, not as an isolated and sensational event, but in a social perspective.

Social Parable

Frost (q.v.), in the midst of the spate of Depression writing in the United States, made an important distinction between the literature of griefs and the literature of grievances: the former, he said, dealt with the constants of the human condition; the latter was concerned with limited and transitory situations, and though it produced detailed and often poignant pictures of suffering, they were of too local and passionate a nature. This distinction has some relevance in drawing a line between social chronicle and social parable. To avoid the limiting effects of overminute documentation many writers have turned their backs on social history and have sought out another path, that which will lead to illumination of social situations without dulling them with detail. Here the literary work aims at a general, not a specific, statement; the attachment to specific setting or situation is less fully delineated, such elements being purged of the local and being raised to the universal. Sometimes to its loss, it aims to avoid the emotional involvement which comes from the situation seen too near at hand. Immediacy of experience does have its dangers in literature, as can be seen by the passion aroused after three decades by any literary treatment of the Spanish Civil War. It is this kind of partisan readership which the social parable tries to avoid. It provides imaginative constructions which are tantalizingly similar to real historical situations but are not facsimiles of them. With a much more immediate social reference than most great works of the past, such writing nonetheless is engaged in the same process as that which made of the Seven against Thebes more than a local conflict or raised the failure of Richard II to a parable on kingship.

A popular form, and one close to chronicle, is the historical reconstruction which emphasizes its parallel to a contemporary situation at the cost of historical exactness. Werfel's (q.v.) *Die vierzig Tage des Musa Dagh*, ostensibly treating an episode of Turkish oppression of the Armenian minority during World War I,

is more important as an analogue to the treatment accorded the Jews in Germany under Hitler. Such a device is both necessary and effective under an authoritarian regime: witness the impact of Anouilh's (q.v.) *Antigone* in Paris during the German occupation. It is one that is used with a more general reference by Camus (q.v.) in *Caligula* and Dürrenmatt (q.v.) in *Romulus der Große*. So widespread are the biographical and historical studies in semifictional guise of the decline of the Roman Empire and the fragmented society of the Middle Ages that they seem to reflect a preoccupation with the fate of contemporary society.

Still another variation is the pseudohistory of future events, a forward projection of outcomes inherent in current social tendencies. Sinclair Lewis's (q.v.) *It Can't Happen Here* is a well-known instance; Orwell's (q.v.) *Nineteen Eighty-Four* is another. This form is rather transparent in its polemic purpose, but is effective up to a point. Sometimes called the inverted utopia, it is a natural vehicle in a pessimistic age, when social disaster seems more likely than the achievement of an ideal state. It is to be observed, moreover, that this c. has not been prolific of true utopias, the last impressive blueprint of an ideal future being Wells's (q.v.) *A Modern Utopia,* published in 1905, though B. F. Skinner's (b. 1904) *Walden Two*, some four decades later, offers a challenging and controversial formula for the "behavioral engineering" necessary as a precondition to the establishment of a utopia.

An important subgenre, almost entirely of this c., is the science fiction story, which, when it goes beyond mere adventure, readily takes on the mantle of social parable. Habitable stars millions of light years away from Terra have an uncanny likeness to our planet and provide a ready environment in which to re-enact Terran errors or to make a fresh start on new principles in an effort to avoid those errors. Such stories, which manipulate time as well as space, sometimes pick a critical juncture in the operation of historical causality and project forward on the road not taken. More important than the utopian overtones of this genre is the general reflection it provides of social anxieties in the contemporary world. A somewhat monotonous preoccupation is the danger of annihilation by atomic bombs and the necessity of saving a remnant of humanity for a new start somewhere out in space. Another anxiety is the pressure of population; a third is the

307

general tyranny of an automated society. Both these last conditions are seen as forcing man out into space in order to re-establish the old simple, homo-centered way of life.

Interesting and voluminous as science fiction is, it cannot thus far be considered of major literary importance, but it does provide a useful oblique reflection of the temper and attitudes of the Age of Anxiety. Of more enduring value is the strict social parable, which provides a fictive microcosm as a mirror to the real world. The plays of Brecht (q.v.) often fall into this category, though with an obvious doctrinal slant. Golding's (q.v.) *The Lord of the Flies* is an unusually powerful parable of the havoc wrought by original sin, that is, human imperfection, in attempts at social harmony. Of utmost relevance are the works of Faulkner (q.v.), which at one and the same time are a syncopated social history of a specific region and a parable for human endeavor generally, thus generalizing from the fall of the Old South to the fall of man. Similar, though more limited in scope, is Camus's *La Peste,* which takes a very local situation in Oran as a springboard for broad implications about the human condition. In both these cases the place is real, the events are largely imaginary, and the human responses are both realistic and archetypal. By its very extent Faulkner's work is the more elaborate parable, but the significant thing is that fictive works of this kind are always massively rooted in actuality, or rather by pervasive reference they summon up that actuality to buttress the imaginary action.

Beyond social chronicle and social parable there has continued to exist the traditional area of social satire, running a gamut from comedy of manners to bitter social polemic. Though literature in this c. has made no significant innovations in this realm, it is notable for the wide range of subject which it treats. In every country there are incongruities of statement and behavior which provide ready targets. Mossbacks and angry young men, bureaucrats and starry-eyed idealists, do-gooders and do-nothings, men in gray-flannel suits and *stilyagi* have been ticked off in virtually every language. No situation is too poignant or too ominous to escape the flick of satire or the rough and tumble of burlesque. If we cannot neutralize the bomb, we can learn to live with it, as many a thriller devoted to atomic crisis has shown. The prospect for the newly established African states is dark indeed, but this has not prevented Georges Conchon (b. 1925) from

making sport of their viability in *The Savage State* by means of a plot that resembles a Marx Brothers script. Ephemeral as most of these works are, they provide indication of a healthy skepticism and of the readiness of literature to make use of social subjects, all social subjects, in this c.

It is easy to forget in a period of relatively free expression that there is another aspect to the relation of literature and society: to what extent does society exert a formal pressure on literature, determining what paths it shall venture upon, what paths it shall avoid? Certainly in terms of positive encouragement there is little evidence of influence. The academies, where they exist, seem to have no power except, perhaps, to excite rebellion against convention, as if that were ever necessary, and it is doubtful that the great literary prizes do more than bring to notice works of varying degrees of merit. Similarly the educational establishment, in those countries where contemporary literature is taught, may help to provide a reading public but is ineffectual in determining what writers shall provide for that public. Even in the United States, where the university is increasingly a patron of the arts, there is no discernible influence on the course of literature from that source except for the ephemeral faddism which is as indigenous to the classroom as to the Left Bank café.

There is, to be sure, the negative power of censorship which attempts to coerce thought and art into approved channels. Psychological literature most commonly comes up against censorship concerned with faith and morals, social literature with that involving political and economic doctrine; but in practice the two types of censorship are not that easily separable. Political authority, finding a book dangerous on doctrinal grounds, may prefer to ban it on moral grounds; thus we have frequently seen books labeled "decadent" and "obscene" when the real charge against them was political and economic heterodoxy. Each of the authoritarian regimes during this c. has implemented a severe censorship as a matter of course. Such restrictions continue in communist countries; in Spain, where Cela was obliged to publish *La colmena* initially in Argentina; in Ireland, where certain authors are still banned, though *Ulysses* is now freely circulated; and most recently in South Africa because of that country's obdurate race policy. Such curbs certainly prevent publication within the country, but they are not successful in preventing a manuscript's being smuggled out or the published copy's being smuggled in. Neither do they prevent clandestine circulation of illicit foreign books. Nonetheless such coercion can be said to have a considerable effect either in drying up literary activity altogether or in forcing it into approved channels. It has taken nearly fifty years for Russian writers to rebel against the restrictions of "socialist realism," and that battle is by no means won.

Fortunately such a coercive situation is exceptional—for the time being—and the relationship of literature to society in the 20th c. is for the most part one of free use of the materials which social life provides. The very terms of reference of contemporary life, the rapidity of communication by which readers become aware of events in the social environment, the provision of a way of thinking about society by the social sciences, and indeed a general disposition to seek out the lines of causality in the data of experience—all these forces have caused the literature of this c. to shun for the most part isolation in a dream world of the imagination and to make greater use of the data of social experience than has ever been the case before.

BIBLIOGRAPHY: Trotsky, L., *Literature and Revolution* (1925); Guérard, A., *Literature and Society* (1935); Plekhanov, G., *Art and Society* (1936); Fox, R., *The Novel and the People* (1937); Read, H., *Art and Society* (1937); Agosti, H. P., *Defensa del realismo* (1945); Sartre, J.-P., *Existentialism and Humanism* (1947); Ortega y Gasset, J., *The Dehumanization of Art* and *Notes on the Novel* (1948); Camus, A., *The Myth of Sisyphus* (1955); Sartre, J.-P., "Présentation des temps modernes," in *Situations*, II (1948), 7–30; Escarpit, R., *Sociologie de la littérature* (1960); Bo, C., "Letteratura e società," *Opere*, Vol. I (1964), pp. 347–69

GEORGE J. BECKER

SÖDERGRAN, Edith

Finnish poet (writing in Swedish), b. 4 April 1892, Leningrad; d. 24 June 1923, Raivola

The daughter of Finno-Swedish parents, Edith S. was educated at the Hauptschule zu Sankt Petri in the former Russian capital. Most of her Heinesque schoolgirl verse was written in German, which was also the language spoken at the Davos sanatorium, in which she was a patient (1911–14). On the eve

of the war, Edith S. and her mother settled permanently in the family's summer home at Raivola on the Carelian isthmus, among a population partly Finnish, partly Russian. She therefore never lived in a community where Swedish, her home tongue, was substantially represented.

In her isolation Edith S. entertained dreams of taking Finland's literary world by storm. She made several short visits to Helsingfors in 1915 and 1916, where she showed her manuscripts to the poet Arvid Mörne (1876–1946), and the critic Gunner Castrén (b. 1878). An unhappy love affair seems to have been the direct inspiration of much of the poetry in her first collection, *Dikter* (1916). She was influenced by the German expressionists Else Lasker-Schüler (1869–1945) and Mombert (q.v.) and the exoticist Dauthendey (q.v.), as well as Walt Whitman (1819–92), Maeterlinck (q.v.), and the Russians Balmont (q.v.) and Igor Severyanin (1887–1942).

Save for two figures from the first half of the 19th c.—C. J. L. Almqvist (1793–1866), with his quasi-naive *Songes,* and J. L. Runeberg (1804–1877), with his epigrammatic lyrics— Swedish literature interested her very little— a blessing in disguise, if one considers the extreme conservatism of Swedish and Finno-Swedish prosody at the time.

The critical reception of *Dikter* ranged from puzzled admiration to ridicule. A final clumsy attempt by Edith S. in the autumn of 1917 to enter the literary circles of Helsingfors ended in flight to Raivola. The October Revolution wiped out the family's Russian savings; poverty was added to illness and loneliness.

The events of Finland's Civil War (January-May 1918) put Edith S. into a state of febrile and sometimes morbid excitement, during which she wrote a new lyric collection, *Septemberlyran* (1918). It gave rise to a journalistic debate that cast doubts—first in jest and then in earnest—upon her sanity. However Hagar Olsson's (b. 1893) enthusiastic review in *Dagens Press* led to a close friendship between the two women. A standardbearer of "modernism," Edith S.'s newly found "sister" encouraged her in the composition of the aggressively Nietzschean and anti-Christian verse of *Rosenaltaret* (1919), the sheaf of aphorisms, *Brokiga iakttagelser* (1919); and the cosmic-prophetic poems of *Framtidens skugga* (1920).

A religious crisis, prompted by readings in Rudolf Steiner (1861–1925) and scripture, caused Edith S. to divide her remaining strength between anthroposophy and poetry. Nonetheless, she selflessly pursued a scheme for the publication of "Finland's new Swedish literature" in German translation. Through Hagar Olsson, she had become familiar with the work of one of its representatives, R. R. Eklund (1895–1946), and had met and begun a correspondence with Elmer Diktonius (1896–1961). In the short-lived bilingual magazine, *Ultra* (Finnish and Swedish, 1922), one of whose editors was Hagar Olsson, Edith S. saw the whole "modernist" parnassus—including Björling and Enckell (qq.v.)—briefly assembled: she had been their pioneer. In an act of gratitude, Diktonius assembled and issued her uncollected poems (from 1915 until the last month of her illness) as *Landet som icke är* (1925).

After Edith S.'s death, Raivola became a place of pilgrimage for lyricists from Finland and Sweden. She was revered by younger contemporaries with styles of their own—for example, Ekelöf (q.v.)—and imitated by weaker talents. Her example was of central importance in liberating Scandinavian verse from the confines of rhyme, regular rhythm, and traditional imagery.

The work of Edith S. is unmistakable in its intensity and its almost gauche frankness. Small wonder, therefore, that such poems in *Dikter* as "Vierge moderne" ("I am not a woman. I am a neuter") and "God" ("God is a couch, on which we lie outstretched in the cosmos") immediately gave rise to parody. Her tormented eroticism (variously heterosexual, homosexual, narcissistic), her persistent attempts to achieve a union with nature, and her equally obstinate passion for beauty are all facets of her honest (and defenseless) personality. Her simple directness, coupled with a rare and genuine *furor poeticus,* wins its greatest triumphs, however, when Edith S. is overwhelmed by forces outside herself, as in the hymnic poetry of *Septemberlyran* and the concluding poems of the posthumous collection.

FURTHER WORKS: *Min lyra* (1929); *Dikter* (1940); *Samlade dikter* (1949); *Ediths brev: Brev från E. S. till Hagar Olsson* (1955); *E. S.'s dikter 1907–1909* (ed. O. Enckell, 1961; I., *Inledning och kommentar*; II., *Texten).* **Selected English translation:** selections in *Seven Swedish Poets* (ed. F. Fleisher; 1963)

BIBLIOGRAPHY: Enckell, O., *Esteticism och nietzscheanism i E. S.'s lyrik* (1949); Tide-ström, G., *E. S.* (1949); Holmqvist, B., *Modern finlandssvensk litteratur* (1951); Warburton, T., *Finlandssvensk litteratur 1898–1948* (1951); Schoolfield, G. C., "E. S.'s 'Wallensteinprofil,' " in *Scandinavian Studies: Essays Presented to Henry Goddard Leach* (1965); Ekelöf, G., "E. S.," in *Svenska Akadamiens Handlingar* (1967); Laitinen, K., *Suomen kirjallisuus 1917–1967* (1967)

G. C. SCHOOLFIELD

SOLDATI, Mario

Italian novelist, film director, and journalist, b. 17 Nov. 1906, Turin

S. first studied with the Jesuits and then took a doctorate in literature and philosophy at the University of Turin in 1927. During his student days he came into contact with those young writers associated with Piero Gobetti's (1901–1926) *Rivoluzione Liberale,* a periodical that was eventually closed down by the fascists. S. first attracted critical attention with a *catalogue raisonné* of 19th-c. Italian painters. After studying at the Istituto Superiore di Storia dell'Arte in Rome, in 1929 he was granted a two-year fellowship by Columbia University. The experiences of this period are recorded in *America, primo amore* (1935), literary snapshots of the United States, with special emphasis on New York, during the 1930's.

On his return to Italy, S. initiated a long association with the movie industry that was by the 1940's to make him Italy's most active film director. Many of his films were based on works by Antonio Fogazzaro (1842–1911), Honoré de Balzac (1799–1850), Pirandello, Moravia, and Graham Greene (qq.v.). Though he complained in *Storie di Spettri* (1962) that he never had the opportunity to do a film entirely of his own creation, his predilection for literary sources would seem to come from an attraction toward complex psychological situations akin to those he analyzed in his own fiction. Employing the pseudonym Franco Pallavera, S. expounded his ideas about the cinema in *24 ore in uno studio cinematografico* (1935).

Beginning with *Pilato* (1924), an unpublished three-act play that was awarded a prize by the Catholic Youth Federation in Turin, S. has from time to time written for the stage: *La prova decisiva* (1955) and the libretto for Nino Rota's *Scuola di guida* (1959 Spoleto Festival). His poems were published under the collective title *Canzonette e viaggio televisivo* (1962).

EDITH SÖDERGRAN

ALEKSANDR SOLZHENITZYN

S.'s major literary contribution is as a novelist and short-story writer. In *Salmace* (1929) and in his later collections—*La messa dei villeggianti* (1959) and *I racconti del maresciallo* (1968)—he captured critical attention with short stories that reveal the basic human condition beneath rapidly sketched situations and persons. *La verità sul caso Motta* (1941), a novella, achieves surprising effects by grafting a surrealistic narrative onto a detective story.

Of S.'s novels, *Il vero Silvestri* (1957; The Real Silvestri, 1961) has the most interesting structure in that it reveals the psychological complexity of the protagonist by means of a tenacious debate between the narrator and one of the main characters. However, in S.'s longer novels the charm derived from the emblematic compactness of the short stories is often diluted in a subtle analysis that renders the characters elusive. In *Le lettere da Capri* (1954; The Capri Letters, 1956) character development suffers from the multitude of autobiographical incidents employed.

Perhaps S.'s most successfully structured novel is *La busta arancione* (1966; The Orange Envelope, 1969), whose protagonist is caught between two diversely emblematic women (in this instance his mother and Meris) and finally breaks through to the maturity of profound human experience. The psychological portrait drawn is one that has attracted S. strongly and that appears in various guises throughout his work. As in *Le lettere de Capri* his protagonists are driven by a need "to understand all the part of reality which we usually refute, a desire to be like others, a need for normality."

S. has also shown unusual talent as a journalist. His account in *Fuga in Italia* (1947) of the plight of Italian soldiers in 1943 and his report in *Fuori* (1968) of his travels in Russia, Greece, and Africa make fascinating reading.

Though strongly influenced by the many stylistic experiments of the early part of the 20th c., S. traces his roots as a writer back to post-romantic bourgeois and mystic literature, the heritage of which becomes in his own works a restless search for ambiguous seductions.

FURTHER WORKS: *L'amico Gesuita* (1943); *A cena col commendatore* (1950; Dinner with the Commendatore, 1953); *L'accalappiacani* (1953); *La confessione* (1955; The Confession); *I racconti* (1957); *Le due città* (1964); *L'attore* (1970)

BIBLIOGRAPHY: Bassani, G., "Nota su S.," *Paragone*, II (1951); Colombo, S., "M. S.," *Cinema*, No. 78 (1952); Cecchi, E., *Di giorno in giorno* (1954), pp. 395–400; Ravegnani, G., *Uomini visti*, Vol. II (1955), pp. 282–87; De Tommaso, P., "M. S.," *Belfagor*, XIV (1959); Bolzoni, F., "M. S.," *Centrofilm*, No. 20 (1961); Grisi, F., *Incontri in libreria* (1961), pp. 393–410; De Robertis, G., *Altro Novecento* (1962), pp. 359–65; Seroni, A., *Esperimenti critici sul Novecento letterario* (1967), pp. 44–47

GIOVANNI SINICROPI

SOLOGUB, Fiodor

(pseud. of *Fiodor Kuzmich Teternikov*), Russian poet, short-story writer, and novelist, b. 17 Feb. 1863, Leningrad; d. there, 5 Dec. 1927

After his father, a tailor, had died, S.'s mother became a domestic servant. S. was educated at the expense of her employers. In 1882 he graduated from Teachers' Institute in Leningrad. For the next twenty years S. devoted himself to a pedagogic career, first as a schoolmaster in small provincial towns, which served as a somber background for some of his novels, and later in Leningrad, ending up as inspector of elementary schools. From 1907 on he devoted himself exclusively to literature.

S. had been writing long before that, his first stories appearing in *Severnyi Vestnik*, the first Russian journal to open its pages to modernist writers. S.'s first book of stories, *Teni*, was published in 1894; his first novel, *Tyazhelyye sny*, and first book of poems, *Stikhi*, in 1896. S. was regarded by contemporaries as a typical *fin-de-siècle* decadent, but is now usually included among the symbolists (*see* symbolism). He was a prolific writer, and when an edition of his collected works was undertaken in 1913, it constituted twenty volumes.

During World War I, S. wrote some patriotic stories (*Sochtennyye dni*) and poems.

After the Russian Revolution S. published several slender volumes of exquisite poetry. Being out of sympathy with the bolshevik regime, he requested permission in 1921 to go abroad for reasons of health. This was refused. Soon after that, S.'s wife, Anastasia Chebotarevskaya, a well-known translator, committed suicide by throwing herself into the Neva. Her body was not recovered until many months later, and all that time S. refused to believe

311

that she was dead. When her death was established, he withdrew into himself and died a lonely, broken man.

Only a few of S.'s poems were published in Soviet periodicals between 1922 and his death, but some of his best work was reissued in 1933 and 1939. Much of his postrevolutionary poetry remains unpublished.

Unlike Balmont or Blok (qq.v.), S. was equally proficient in prose and verse. His unanimously recognized prose masterpiece, begun in 1892, is the novel *Melki bes* (1907; The Petty Demon, 1962). Translated into most European languages, it has been described by the Russian critic D. S. Mirsky as "the most perfect Russian novel since the death of Dostoyevski." Its principal character, Peredonov, a provincial schoolmaster like S. himself, has given rise in Russia to the word *peredonovshchina*. An embodiment of petty, joyless, and vulgar evil, he has been likened to Karamazov senior, but he has more kinship with Mikhail Y. Saltykov-Shchedrin's (1826–89) "little Judas" Golovliov. The background and the majority of minor characters are painted in terms of grotesque realism. The realistically described provincial town, with its suffocating atmosphere, is really a microcosm of evil. Parallel to the main Peredonov story runs the innocently erotic love story of two young people. This corresponds to S.'s essentially dualistic, Manichean view of life as an evil from which one must seek escape and solace in beautiful dreams or in death or in both.

Death is S.'s true muse. Many of his stories, especially his stories about children, end with suicides. One of the best volumes is *Zhalo smerti* (1904). In his poetry death appears as the great comforter and rescuer. The sun, on the other hand, as the life-generating source, becomes a symbol of evil and is often identified with a cruel dragon (S.'s most characteristic book of poems is *Plamennyi krug,* 1908).

Of S.'s other novels the most interesting is *Tvorimaya legenda* (3 vols., 1908–1912; The Created Legend, 1916), which is also a blend of topical realism and fantasy. In it there are elements that smack of necrophilia, and its hero is a satanic superman. As a whole it is, together with some of S.'s poetry reflecting the cruel ugliness of life, a good example of his weird and perverse imagination.

As a short-story writer S. has few equals as a stylist: his prose has been described by

Mirsky as "limpid, clear, balanced, poetical, but with a keen sense of measure." The same is true of the best of his poetry, especially that which presents the vision of his ideal world, his land of dreams. Unlike most other decadents and symbolists, he scorned external embellishments; his rhymes are classically simple, his meters monotonous but exquisite, his vocabulary, in Mirsky's words, "almost as small as Racine's."

S. wrote plays, some of which are symbolical, in the manner of Maeterlinck (q.v.), while others are realistic. He also wrote some political fables "rich in verbal effects . . . and reminiscent of the grotesque manner of Leskov" (Mirsky).

S. translated, as well, Verlaine, Rimbaud, Voltaire, and Kleist.

FURTHER WORKS: *Pobeda smerti* (1908; The Triumph of Death, 1916); *Politicheskiya skazochki* (1908); *Kniga ocharovanii* (1908); *Sobraniye sochinenii* (20 vols., 1913–14); *Lyubov nad bezdnami* (1914); *Voina* (1915); *Yaryi god* (1916); *Alyi mak* (1917); *Fimiamy* (1921); *Nebo goluboye* (1921); *Odna lyubov* (1921); *Sobornyi blagovest* (1921); *Zaklinatelnitza zmei* (1921); *Charodeinaya chasha* (1922); *Kostior dorozhnyi* (1922); *Baryshnya Liza* (1923); *Veliki blagovest* (1923). **Selected English translations:** *The Old House, and Other Tales* (1915); *The Sweet-scented Name, and Other Fairy Tales, Fables, and Other Stories* (1915); *Little Tales* (1917)

BIBLIOGRAPHY: Chebotarevskaya, A., *F. S.* (1911); Lundberg, E., "Lirika F. S.," in *Russkaya Mysl,* Vol. IV (1912); Gornfield, A., "Tiomnyi put'," in *Boyevyye otkliki na mirnyye temy* (1924); Grabher, C., "F. S.," in *Russia,* Vol. IV (1925); Gippius, Z., in *Zhivyye litza,* Vol. II (1925); Gobetti, P., "S.," in *Il paradosso dello spirito russo* (1926); Mirsky, D. S., *Contemporary Russian Literature* (1926); Chulkov, G., *Gody stranstvii* (1930); Khodasevich, V., "F. S.," in *Nekropol'* (1939); Struve, G., "Tri sud'by," *Novyi zhurnal,* Nos. 16 and 17 (1947); Poggioli, R., *Il fiore del verso russo* (1949); Ivanov, G., *Petersburgskiye zimy* (1952); Reeve, F. D., *MFS,* III (1957); Holthusen, J., *F. S.s Romantrilogie* (1960); Poggioli, R., *The Poets of Russia: 1890–1930* (1960); Simmons, E. J., Introduction to *The Petty Demon* (1962)

GLEB STRUVE

SOLOUKHIN, Vladimir Alekseyevich

Soviet-Russian poet, novelist, short-story writer, and journalist, b. 14 June 1924, Alepino

The son of a peasant, S. grew up on a kolkhoz in the Vladimir province. He graduated from Vladimir Technical College in 1942, served four years in the army, and then entered the famous Gorki Literary Institute. From 1951 to 1957 he worked as correspondent and feature writer for *Ogoniok* and for several years was on the editorial board of *Literaturnaya Gazeta*.

Basically a lyricist and romantic, S. perceives reality very personally, primarily trusting and expressing his emotional response to events and surroundings. His imagination tends to lead him back toward his roots, to his youthful experiences in rural, primitive Russia —the inspiration and theme of much of his poetry and prose.

Vladimirskiye proselki (1957; A Walk in Rural Russia, 1967), a travel diary; *Kaplya rosy* (1960), an autobiographical sketch on his native village; and *Mat'-machekha* (1964), a novel about his student years in Moscow, reveal his fascination with his past and with nature and humanity in an untamed, unsophisticated environment. In these books he attempts as an artist to come to terms with a world in rapid transition from an untechnical and pastoral society steeped in time-honored traditions and rituals to a modern civilization characterized by bureaucratization, dehumanized efficiency, and aesthetic sterility.

S.'s sympathies are clearly with the byways of bygone days, with the mores and values of peasant life, its hardships and joys. He lingers lovingly over the memory of dewdrops, fishing excursions, berrypicking, the taste of various herbs, haymaking, or eccentric peasant characters discovered during pilgrimages through his native district. Avoiding intellectual generalizations and abstractions, he focuses on particulars, searching in his poems for a fresh expression of uniquely felt personal experiences. He attempts new forms, frequently eliminating rhymes, rejecting strict rhythmic patterns and conventional meters. Because of this, his poems often read like heightened prose in which emotive effects are achieved by the repetition of words or groups of words. They are dependent for their essential unity on the ever-present lyrical, impassioned voice of the author.

S. has shown an inclination to search out not only his own past but also the roots of

Russian national and cultural life. *Pis'ma iz Russkovo Muzeya* (1966) focuses on the official indifference to the icons and old frescoes that he found buried in the Leningrad Russian Museum.

In the Soviet ideological context, S.'s emphasis on the individual and on moral and emotional growth divorced from organizational influences strike an unusual note. His quasi-religious attitude toward all things natural recalls Esenin (q.v.). In addition, his stress on the primacy of emotion—however fleeting or unshared—and his belief in the unpredictability and subconsciousness of the creative process are manifestations noteworthy of his deeply rooted, almost mystical irrationalism. In modifying established literary forms and in reactivating Slavophile ideas on cultural values, S. has made a significant but controversial contribution to contemporary Soviet literature.

FURTHER WORKS: *Dozhd' v stepi* (1953); *Za sin'-moryami* (1956); *Zolotoye dno* (1956); *Ruch'i na asfal'te* (1958); *Zhuravlikha* (1959); *Veter stranstvii* (1960); *Otkrytki iz V'etnama* (1961); *Chernyi omut* (1961); *Kak vypit' solntze* (1961); *Imeyushchii v rukakh tzvety* (1962); *Liricheskiye povesti: Rasskazy* (1964); *Zhit' na zemle* (1965); *S liricheskikh pozitzii* (1965); *Rabota* (1966); *Sorok zvonkikh kapelei: Osenniye list'ya* (1968)

BIBLIOGRAPHY: Starikova, Y. V., *Poeziya prozy* (1962), pp. 152–78; Esmein, I., "Le premier roman de V. S.: *Le tussilage*," *TR*, No. 226 (1966), pp. 137–39; Holthusen, J., *Russische Gegenwartsliteratur II, 1941–1967* (1968), pp. 116–20

WOLFGANG HIRSCHBERG

SOLZHENITZYN, Aleksandr Isayevich

Soviet-Russian novelist and short-story writer, b. 11 Dec. 1918, Rostov on the Don

Born into a family of intellectuals, S. took his degree in mathematics from the University of Rostov on the Don and took correspondence courses in literature at the University of Moscow. He was an artillery captain in World War II. In 1945 he was arrested on a political charge and sentenced to eight years in forced-labor camps to be followed by exile. In 1957, S. was rehabilitated and allowed to return from exile. He settled in Riazan, where he worked as a mathematics teacher.

In November 1969, S. was expelled from the

Writers' Union. His editor, Aleksandr Tvardovskii, was forced to resign from *Novyi Mir* in 1970.

S.'s first novel, *Odin den' Ivana Denisovicha* (1962; One Day in the Life of Ivan Denisovich, 1963), created a sensation in Russia and abroad. For the first time the Central Committee had allowed the publication of a book about Stalin's forced labor camps.

The protagonist, Ivan Denisovich Shukhov, a simple peasant, an innocent victim of Stalin's espionage mania, was sentenced to eight years at hard labor. A good, meek man, he endures his sufferings without complaining. Survival being the only goal, he cannot afford the luxury of reflecting on his predicament or rebelling against it. His life is dragged down to a level where happiness means getting an extra bowl of mush and some tobacco or *not* being put in the "cooler."

The story easily yields to an attempt to use it as source material for sociopolitical information, and thus makes it possible to overlook its place in Russian literature. S., ignoring the precepts of socialist realism (q.v.), wrote here about the perennial theme of the suffering of the innocent, the virtue of meekness, and the struggle between good and evil.

The same themes are treated in S.'s short story "Matrionin dvor" (1963; Matryona's House, 1963). Although this story has remained little known in the West, it is one of the most significant contemporary Russian short stories. A woman about sixty years old, abandoned by her husband, having seen her six children die, incapacitated from time to time by attacks of a strange disease, living in utter poverty, Matriona is the embodiment of innocent suffering. Loneliness and suffering, however, have not marred her soul. Without curiosity, envy, or greed, she knows no bitterness, and her whole being radiates peace and joy. The story ends with Matriona's death when her body is crushed by an engine backing into a sledge.

A major work, the novel *V kruge pervom* (1968; The First Circle, 1968), has not been published in the Soviet Union. Dante's conception of the First Circle of Hell inspired the title. The setting of the novel takes the reader to the special prison, the Mavrino Institute for Scientific Research near Moscow. The prisoners, all professional scientists, live and work under physical conditions that are much better than those in the forced labor camps. The mathematician Nerzhin, the protagonist,

has refused to work on perfecting the design of a telephone instrument, ordered by Stalin, that would encode and visibly record individual speech traits. Knowing that their punishment will be immediate transport back to labor camps, "the lower circles of Hell," Nerzhin and others refuse to use their technical training for devising systems by which thousands more can be arrested, interrogated, and imprisoned.

In brief, concise yet spontaneous scenes, each character—from Stalin down to Spiridon, the blind, old prison janitor—comes to life. Limiting the action to four days, S. reveals the terror that one man inspired in millions and the slow, agonizing process whereby many, now possessionless and without hope of ever living in the "outside world" again, free themselves from fear. These are the few who can now act according to their personal ideals, having learned from each other how to maintain dignity even in bitterly humiliating circumstances.

Rakovyi korpus (1968; The Cancer Ward, 1968), like *V kruge pervom*, has not been published in the Soviet Union. Based on S.'s own experience with cancer and Russian medical treatment while in exile, it describes movingly the plight of the protagonist, Oleg Kostoglotov, who knows that the treatment he is undergoing will destroy his sexual capacity. S. draws Kostoglotov as a rough, sometimes almost crude, political exile who is determined to control what is left of his life—even to control his tender love for the compassionate woman doctor Vera Gangart. Through Kostoglotov, S. also tells of the cautious hope triggered by the astounding news of the complete changeover in the Soviet Supreme Court in 1955.

The highly diverse characters in *Rakovyi korpus* are brought together in a provincial hospital in Soviet Central Asia. Stalinist communists and exiles alike share a terrible, humbling bond. Patients, doctors, and hospital employees are forced to reexamine the meaning of life under the higher authority of cancer. Some find old, buried values reawakened as, for example, the communist librarian Shulubin, who in a very moving scene describes for Kostoglotov his dream of a socialistic state in which all decisions would be based on their moral validity and the goal would be the highest achievement of man—love.

With S., Russian literature returns to its classical concern about the basic aspects of the human situation. Few contemporary writers are his equal when it comes to creating real people who find within themselves the resources that enable them to resist degradation. S.'s artistic vision is as far removed from the shallow, false concept of socialist realism as it is from the Western predilection for morbid negativism or romanticized physiology.

In 1970 S. won the Nobel Prize for Literature. The citation said he was chosen "for the ethical force with which he has pursued the indispensable traditions of Russian literature."

FURTHER WORKS: *Sluchai na stantzii Krechetovka* (1963; An Incident at Krechetovka Station, 1963); *Dlya pol'zy dela* (1963; For the Good of the Cause, 1964); *Etyudy i krokhotnyye rasskazy* (1966); *The Love-Girl and the Innocent* (1970)

BIBLIOGRAPHY: Gul', R., "A. S. Sotzrealizm i shkola Remizova," *Novyi zhurnal*, No. 71 (1963); Koehler, L., "A. S. and Russian Literary Tradition," *Russian Review*, No. 2 (1967); Rossbacher, P., "S.'s 'Matrena's Home,'" *Études Slaves et Est Européennes*, XII (1967), v; Friedberg, M., "The Other Soviet Literature," *Midstream*, XV (1969), v; Koehler, L., "Eternal Themes in S.'s *Cancer Ward*," *Russian Review*, No. 1 (1969); "A. V. Belinkov's Defense of Solzhenitsyn's *The Cancer Ward* at a Special Meeting of the Writers' Union, 17 Nov. 1966," *Russian Review*, No. 4 (1969)

PETER ROSSBACHER

One Day in the Life of Ivan Denisovich is not a document in the sense of being a memoir, nor is it notes or reminiscences of the author's personal experiences, although only such personal experiences could lend this story its sense of genuine authenticity. This is a work of art and it is by virtue of the artistic interpretation of this material from life that it is a witness of special value, a document of an art which up to now had seemed to have few possibilities.

The reader will not find in A. S.'s story an all-encompassing portrayal of that historic period which is particularly marked by the bitter memory of the year 1937. The content of *One Day* is naturally limited in time and place of action and the horizons of the main hero of the story. But in the writing of A. S., who here enters the literary scene for the first time, one day in the life of the camp prisoner, Ivan Denisovich Shukhov, develops into a picture which gives extraordinary vitality and fidelity to the truthfulness of its human characters. Herein above all lies the uncommon power of the work to impress. The reader can visualize for him-

self many of the people depicted here in the tragic role of camp inmates in other situations—at the front or at postwar construction sites. They are the same people who by the will of circumstance have been put to severe physical and moral tests under special and extreme conditions.

In this story there is no deliberate concentration of terrible facts of the cruelty and arbitrariness that were the result of the violation of Soviet legality. The author chose instead to portray only one of the most ordinary of days in the life at camp from reveille to retreat. Nevertheless this "ordinary" day cannot but arouse in the heart of the reader a bitter feeling of pain for the fate of the people who, from the pages of this story, rise up before us so alive and so near. Yet the unquestionable victory of the artist lies in the fact that the bitterness and the pain have nothing in common with a feeling of hopeless depression. On the contrary, the impression left by this work is so extraordinary in its unvarnished and difficult truth that it somehow frees the soul of the burden of things unsaid that needed to be said and at the same time it strengthens one's manly and lofty feelings.

This is a grim story—still another example of the fact that there are no areas or facts of reality that can be excluded from the sphere of the Soviet artist in our days or that are beyond truthful portrayal. Everything depends on the capabilities of the artist himself.

Aleksandr Tvardovskii, in *Novyi mir* (Nov. 1962), pp. 8–9

[*One Day in the Life of Ivan Denisovich* is] not just a new book, a good book, a great book. Anyway, these adjectives have been dulled for us by soap ads and by political slogans. This book is as important as Dostoevsky's first book. It not only marks the emergence of an unknown and major literary craftsman but it also revives and reshapes the language and culture to which it belongs. S.'s great trick, like Dostoevsky's before him, is that he identifies the motions of awareness so accurately that they take on, in a world in which awareness is death (what else is a political prisoner but a man incarcerated for too much reliance on his own awareness?), all the meaning of symbolic acts. The smallest gesture in the compound—Shukhov's standing patiently in front of Caesar, hoping for a drag—is equally the profoundest affirmation of human value and human dignity. In this book, an "average" man in inhuman surroundings is studied to the depths. His story is presented as the catalogue of his motivations as he proceeds through the physical and moral odyssey of one day in his life. And "all" he wanted was to get to the end, to get home, to be himself. The brilliance of the book is that he does become himself, though he has none of the tools which for thousands of years we have said a man must have. This book tells us how great a thing a man's life is.

F. D. Reeve, in *KR* (Spring 1963), p. 357

As a medical novel, "The Cancer Ward" offers a fair and quite interesting picture of medicine as practiced in a Central Asian city in 1955. The author himself was cast up in Tashkent, sick with cancer, at about the same period, after spending eight years in prisons and camps. Still in exile—he was not "rehabilitated" until 1957—he entered a hospital where his cancer, never clearly diagnosed as malignant, was arrested. As S. is the ultimate realist writer, whose life story is indistinguishable from his fiction, it can be assumed that the cancer ward he describes is much as he observed it.

In spite of S.'s clinical preoccupations, the reader must strain hard to read this novel as a book about cancer. What are we to make of this question posed by the author: "A man sprouts a tumor and dies—how then can a country live that has sprouted camps and exile?" Again and again S. is compelled to return, perhaps despite himself, to his great theme. Who are his cancer-ridden patients? Exiles, an ex-prisoner, a concentration-camp guard, and a secret-police bureaucrat whose denunciations have sent dozens of people to prison. As "One Day" stands for the agony of all Russia under Stalin, so "The Cancer Ward" irresistibly conveys an image of the immediate post-Stalin period when both victims and executioners were confined, all equally mutilated, in the cancer ward of the nation.

Patricia Blake, in *The New York Times Book Review* (27 Oct. 1968), p. 50

... S.'s lack of self-consciousness about being judged is part of his strange distinction. His choice of willing alienation from the business of life, from any of the projects of life, his commitment to contemplation, this is the only consistency in him, and it shows up just as clearly, though much less powerfully and interestingly, in *The Cancer Ward,* the subject of which my reader can by now predict for himself. What I keep trying not to imply is that S.'s naively simple-minded view of life is valuable just because it is so decidedly his own, but I wonder why it should be so wrong to say that. It's a rare enough thing to meet in anybody past a certain age. And that's the other point: S. isn't, on any page of this novel, sophomoric: he isn't callow, cocksure; he isn't under the illusion that he's bringing you news, he doesn't shout or wave his arms. It's merely that every word he writes is guaranteed by his own experience. One can see that it's his unaggressive but unshakable individualism, together with his lack of interest in politics and his interest in a church-less and dogma-less religious contemplation, that alarmed the Russian censors; and one can understand, too, the American reviews that were also alarmed by these strange qualities and then helplessly took their clue from this sort of thing in the publisher's blurb: "It is a sublime hymn of praise to man, an outpouring of love and pride, a celebration of nobility, courage, selflessness, honor." Let me take my clue from James'

wonderful sentence about Mrs. Capadose in "The Liar": "she had no imagination and only the simpler feelings, but several of these had grown up to full size." If S. were a good novelist he might be a great one; in any case, he is a human being grown up to full size.

Robert Garis, in *HudR* (Spring 1969), p. 154

SOTHO LITERATURE

Southern Sotho is the language of the independent kingdom of Lesotho, a small South African enclave that prior to 1966 had been the British protectorate of Basutoland. Its written literature began early in the 20th c. under the Protestant aegis of the Paris Société des Missions Evangéliques, whose missionaries had set up a printing press at Morija as early as 1841.

Of the half-dozen writers of fiction who emerged between 1906 and 1912, the most gifted was Thomas M. Mofolo (1876–1948). The first Sotho novel was his *Moeti oa bochabela* (1906; The Pilgrim to the East, 1934), which fuses native lore with the influence of John Bunyan's (1628–88) *Pilgrim's Progress,* a Sotho version of which had appeared in 1872. It was soon followed by Everett L. Segoete's (1858–1923) *Monono ke moholi, ke mouane,* the first literary treatment of a henceforth recurrent South African theme: the experiences of a young tribesman who is lured to the industrial city by dreams of pleasure and wealth. Mofolo's masterpiece is *Chaka* (1925; Eng., 1931), the story of the ruthless Zulu conqueror who died in 1828. An impressive tale of hubris and vaulting ambition, it is the first major contribution of modern Africa to world literature.

The interwar period saw a literary decline but was nevertheless the time of D. C. T. Bering's (b. 1900) *Lithothokiso tsa Moshoeshoe le tse-ding* (1931), a collection of traditional oral praise-poetry, and T. M. Mofokeng's *Sek'ona sa joala* (1939), the first Sotho play.

During the 1940's Sotho authors found new outlets for their works. The first of these was the printing press installed in Mazenod in 1932 by the Catholic (French-Canadian) Oblats de Sainte-Marie Immaculée. Of the scores of works published there, many were descriptions of tribal life or dealt with the Jim-goes-to-Jo'burg motif and warned against the dangers and depravity of city life. Some, like Albert Ngheku's (b. 1912) *Lilahloane,* have a militant anti-Protestant and anticommunist character; others, like the short stories of C. R. Moikangoa (1880–1951), make imaginative use of tribal myths.

The literature was further enriched when the large Southern Sotho population of the Republic of South Africa began to produce its own writers. These were more intimately acquainted with life in an urbanized society and they were often better educated than their opposite numbers in Lesotho. The best of these writers was Sophonia M. Mofokeng (1923–57). A promising linguist and folklorist, Mofokeng wrote both essays and short stories (*Leetong*, 1954). However, his best work is *Senkatana* (1952), a drama about a Herculean Sotho hero who destroyed that many-hearted monster that was ravaging his country.

In the post-World War II period the Protestant press of Morija was responsible for launching many new authors. Among these was Bennett M. Khaketla (b. 1913), a promising playwright, poet, and novelist who played a considerable part in the preparation for Lesotho's independence. Khaketla's novel *Meokho ea thabo* (1951) illustrates the modern approach to the recurrent culture-clash motif. In it modernization is no longer synonymous with Christianization, as it was for earlier writers; instead, it takes the form of individual freedom in conflict with the authority of the clan, especially in the sphere of love and marriage.

ALBERT S. GÉRARD

SOUPAULT, Philippe

French poet, novelist, and essayist, b. 2 Aug. 1897, Chaville, Seine et Oise

In 1917, S. met Breton (q.v.) at one of Apollinaire's (q.v.) Tuesday gatherings at the Café de Flore in Paris. Later in this first important year of the dada movement (*see* dadaism), S. and Éluard (q.v.), who would soon call themselves surrealists (*see* surrealism), published their first collections of poems.

The following year, S. and Breton, in company with Aragon (q.v.) and Éluard, formed the nucleus of the first surrealist group in Paris. In 1919, S. contributed to a dadaist anthology, and to the first issues of the surrealist magazine *Littérature*.

In 1921, S. and Breton published the early surrealist novel *Les Champs magnétiques*. The first major text of the movement, this book was also the first example of automatic writing that had the approval of the other surrealists. But today, the vocabulary, which is neither slangy nor esoteric, seems quite conventional.

Until 1927, S. contributed regularly to *La Révolution Surréaliste,* the principal surrealist magazine of the period. By then he had become dissatisfied with the political entanglements of the movement and the growing efforts of Breton to codify surrealist theory. Since 1923, S. had served as the director and one of the editors of *La Revue Européenne*, which was not a surrealist publication, thereby incurring Breton's wrath. S.'s expulsion from the movement was clearly stated in Breton's *Second Manifeste* (1929).

S. later became a journalist and established a radio station in Tunis in 1938. After 1945 he directed the overseas program of the French broadcasting system and later traveled in Europe, Africa, and Asia in behalf of UNESCO.

S.'s first novel, *Le Bon Apôtre* (1923), attracted very little attention, but his second, *Les Frères Durandeau* (1924), was the runner-up for the Prix Goncourt.

S. has written several biographies of poets and artists, but even the best of them, such as *Apollinaire* (1927), *Uccello* (1929), *Lautréamont* (1946), and *Musset* (1957; Eng., 1963), overstress the contemporaneity of their subjects and tend to become quickly outdated.

S.'s best volumes of poetry were published in the early years of surrealism: *Rose des vents* (1920); *Westwego* (1922); and *Georgia* (1926). His *Ode à Londres bombardée* (1944; Ode to a Bombed London, 1944) was inspired by the event itself.

S.'s most successful poems reveal his admiration for Rimbaud (1854–91) and Lautréamont (1847–70), but his writing is more simple than theirs, the emotions he describes more tenuous, more subdued. In its fluidity and transparency, his poetry is closer to Apollinaire's than to surrealism. His poems are often derived from secrets of his inner life, his sense of melancholy, and his childhood experiences.

FURTHER WORKS: *Aquarium* (1917); *Premières chansons* (1920); *L'Invitation au suicide* (1921); *A la dérive* (1923); *Wang-Wang* (1924); *Chansons des buts et des rois* (1925); *Voyage d'Horace Pirouelle* (1925); *Le Bar de l'amour* (1925); *En joue!* (1925); *Le Nègre* (1927); *Henri Rousseau, le douanier* (1927);

William Blake (1928; Eng., 1928); *Les Dernières nuits de Paris* (1928; The Last Nights of Paris, 1929); *Baudelaire* (1931); *Charlot* (1931); *Poésies complètes 1917–1937* (1937); *Souvenirs de James Joyce* (1943); *Eugène Labiche* (1945); *Le Temps des assassins* (1945; Age of Assassins, 1946); *Chansons* (1949); *Essai sur la poésie* (1950); *Helman* (1959); *Profils perdus* (1963); *L'Amitié* (1964); *Le Vrai André Breton* (1966)

BIBLIOGRAPHY: Dupuy, H.-J., *P. S.* (1952); Clancier, G. E., *Panorama critique de Rimbaud au surréalisme* (1953); Bersani, L., *Marcel Proust: The Fictions of Life and of Art* (1965); Matthews, J. H., *An Introduction to Surrealism* (1965); Nadeau, M., *The History of Surrealism* (1965); Sanouillet, M., *Dada à Paris* (1965)

CHARLES G. HILL

SOUTAR, William

Scottish poet and diarist, b. 28 April 1899, Perth; d. there, 15 Oct. 1943

The son of a master cabinetmaker, S. attended the University of Edinburgh and served a stint in the navy. He spent the last thirteen years of his life as a bedridden invalid. He read and wrote voluminously until the day he died and received the visits of all the literary Scots of his day. He kept diaries, literary journals, descriptions and analyses of his dreams, all amounting to more than eighty manuscript volumes (now in the National Library of Scotland), but only a very small fraction of this fine English prose has been published.

Reviewing S.'s *Diaries of a Dying Man* (1954), the *Times Literary Supplement* said of S.: "No poet since Burns has so resembled him in . . . the nature of his gifts." The two poets do share humanity, humor, freedom from orthodoxy, and a colloquial Scots diction; but S., whose life style was the antithesis of that of Robert Burns, responded to Keats's notion of "negative capability" and suppressed poetic displays of his personality. Although his native language was Scots, S. (like Burns) wrote a great deal of embarrassing verse in English. But, after an early romantic period and after coming under the influence of D. H. Lawrence and Wilfred Owen (qq.v.), he wrote some powerfully direct English poems in *A Handful of Earth* (1936), *In the Time of Tyrants* (1939), and *The Expectant Silence* (1944).

The poems in his native language, begun in 1923 under the influence of Hugh MacDiarmid's (q.v.) turn to Scots, are by common consent his best work. Only a very few are longer than two or three dozen lines, most employ the stanza and the manner of the Scots traditional ballad, and generally they succeed more than any other modern poems in Scots, except some few by MacDiarmid, in uniting the rural, colloquial, national literary tradition with a sophisticated European view. He thus departed from sentimental imitators of Burns and contributed to MacDiarmid's Scottish renaissance movement.

S. wrote "bairnrhymes" (humorous tales and descriptions for children, many of them beast fables), riddles, epigrams, lyrics, satires, "whigmaleeries" (views of life and human nature embodied in wry, often grotesque fantasies of eccentric characters, mostly animals), and a type that he called "theme and variation" (his own handling of themes and subjects suggested by particular poems of others).

The principal formal influences on S.'s poems in Scots, besides the ballad, were the Middle Scots poets, Burns, and MacDiarmid. He was particularly interested in Marx, Freud, Jung, and John Middleton Murray (1889–1957). After he lost his early Calvinist faith, he became a socialist, a pacifist, and a Scottish nationalist. His favorite symbol was the unicorn.

Although limited by his refusal to engage in higher and longer flights and his inappropriate overuse of the ballad stanza, S. is perhaps second to MacDiarmid as a 20th-c. writer of poems in Scots.

FURTHER WORKS: *Gleanings by an Undergraduate* (1923); *Conflict* (1931); *Seeds in the Wind* (1933; revised, 1943); *Brief Words* (1935); *Poems in Scots* (1935); *Riddles in Scots* (1937); *The Solitary Way* (1943); *But the Earth Abideth* (1943); *Collected Poems* (ed. Hugh MacDiarmid; 1948); *Poems in Scots and English* (ed. W. R. Aitken; 1961)

BIBLIOGRAPHY: Smith, M., "The Poetry of W. S.," *The Poetry Review*, XXIV (1938), 301–11; MacDiarmid, H., Introduction to *Collected Poems* (1948); On *Diaries of a Dying Man*—Young, D., *Saltire Review*, No. 3 (1954), pp. 83–84; Aitken, W., "W. S., Bibliographical Notes and a Checklist," *The Bibliotheck*, I (1957), ii, 3–14; Scott, A., *Still Life: W. S., 1898–1943* (1958); Montgomerie, W.,

Saltire Review, No. 17 (1958), pp. 78–9; Wittig, K., *The Scottish Tradition in Literature* (1958), pp. 289–92; Scott, A., "W. S.," in *Burns Chronicle for 1959,* pp. 18–25; Buist, A., "*Still Life:* An Appreciation of W. S.," *The Poetry Review,* LII (1961), 89–93; Mackie, A., "Tomb with a View," *Lines Review,* No. 17 (1961), pp. 59–62; Goodwin, K. L., "W. S., Adelaide Crapsey, and Imagism," in *Studies in Scottish Literature,* III (1965), 96–100

JOHN C. WESTON

SOUTH AFRICAN LITERATURE: ENGLISH LANGUAGE

Probably no other African region has been so vigorously analyzed by its own critics and creative writers in the 20th c. as has South Africa. International interest in the literature of the English-speaking writers of this country was first aroused by the work of Paton (q.v.), whose novel *Cry, the Beloved Country* (1948) expressed the principal theme of South African writing in its concern with the violence engendered by racial tension. Earlier fiction was strongly influenced by Olive Schreiner (1862–1920), whose best-known work is *The Story of an African Farm* (1883). This influence is evident in *Jock of the Bushveld* (1907) by Percy Fitzpatrick (1862–1931) and in many other novels, particularly those of the women novelists who have contributed so extensively to South African literature.

Racial affairs and justification of segregation, or apartheid, were important themes in the work of Sarah Gertrude Millin (b. 1889), particularly in such novels as *The Dark River* (1920), *Adam's Rest* (1922), *God's Stepchildren* (1924), *The Herr Witchdoctor* (1941), and *The Wizard Bird* (1962). Plomer (q.v.), in his *Turbott Wolfe* (1926), anticipated the theme of miscegenation and South African social codes with which Paton was to deal in his second novel, *Too Late the Phalarope* (1953). The struggles of the white settlers of South Africa were portrayed by Pauline Smith (1900?–1960) and Herman Charles Bosman (1905–1951) and by Cloete (q.v.) in his novel *The Curve and the Tusk* (1952). Laurens van der Post (b. 1906), who writes in both Afrikaans and English, showed a compassion for nonwhites in his *In a Province* (1934). The first English novel by a black South African was *Mhudi* (1930) by Solomon Plaatje (1878–1932). More recent nonwhite novelists have included Peter Abrahams

(b. 1919), known for his *A Night of Their Own* (1965); other nonwhite writers have generally preferred short fiction for their portrayals of race problems in the urban environment. Similar subjects have appeared in Paton's short fiction, notably in *Debbie, Go Home* (1961), as well as in the stories and novels of several other white writers, including Nadine Gordimer (b. 1932), known for her *A World of Strangers* (1958), and Dan Jacobson (b. 1929), in his *The Evidence of Love* (1960).

Many of the best South African dramas in English have apartheid as their subject, a notable example being Athol Fugard's (b. 1938) *The Blood Knot* (1963), or to a lesser extent his moving *Boesman and Lena.* Similar works include *The Rhythm of Violence* (1964) by Lewis Nkosi (b. 1938). Poets too have expressed their concern over the racial problems of South Africa, particularly since the emergence of the movement pioneered by Francis Carey Slater (1876–1959) and culminating in the work of Campbell (q.v.), who achieved an international reputation. The works of many new poets have appeared in the periodical *New Coin Poetry,* sponsored by Gary Butler (b. 1918).

Many white South African poets have viewed their society almost as though they were strangers in their own land. By contrast several black poets have drawn directly on images of the South African landscape and on elements of vernacular song.

In South African literature in general the English language has served primarily as a vehicle of protest, particularly in such critical journals as *The Purple Renoster* and *English Studies in Africa,* published in Johannesburg, and *Standpunte,* published in Cape Town. These journals continue to deal primarily with the two great themes of South African literature and life: the great fear of racial fraternization and the humane desire for reconciliation among the various races of South Africa.

BIBLIOGRAPHY: Snyman, J. P. L., *A Bibliography of South African Novels in English Published from 1880 to 1930* (1951); Miller, C. M., and Sargeant, H., *A Critical Survey of South African Poetry in English* (1957); Astrinsky, A., *A Bibliography of South African English Novels, 1930–1960* (1965); Jahn, J., *A Bibliography of Neo-African Literature* (1965); Jones, J., *Terranglia: The Case for English as World Literature* (1965); Silbert, R., *Southern*

African Drama in English, 1900–1964 (1965); Abrash, B., *Black African Literature in English since 1952: Works and Criticism* (1967)

ROBERT E. MCDOWELL
and JOSEPH JONES

SOYINKA, Wole

Nigerian dramatist, poet, novelist, essayist, and translator (writing in English), b. 1935, Abeokuta

S. was educated at University College, Ibadan, and the University of Leeds, where he studied English literature. He is currently head of the School of Drama at the University of Ibadan.

One of the most versatile and innovative of African authors, S. is known primarily for his plays, which range from high comedy (*The Lion and the Jewel*, 1963) and burlesque (*The Trials of Brother Jero*, 1963) to fateful tragedy (*The Strong Breed*, 1963; *The Swamp Dwellers*, 1963), biting social and political satire (*A Dance of the Forests*, 1963; *Kongi's Harvest*, 1967), and the theater of the absurd (*The Road*, 1965). His plays reflect the influence of both traditional African and modern European drama, and they invariably contain penetrating social criticism based on a close reading of human nature. S. has been a vital, moving force in the development of contemporary Nigerian theater, often serving as director, producer, and actor in professional stage companies that perform in the Yoruba language as well as in English.

S.'s poetry is equally wide-ranging and morally committed. In his collection *Idanre, and Other Poems* (1967), he proves himself the master of many different poetic moods, some of them inspired by the events that led to the Nigerian civil war. Gloom, depression, and grief are balanced by comic invective, mordant irony, and tender, lyrical reflections on death.

S.'s only novel, *The Interpreters* (1965), is the most complex narrative work yet written by an African. Frequently compared to works by Joyce and Faulkner (qq.v.), it has an intricate, seemingly chaotic structure, a dense and evocative verbal texture, and a throng of tantalizingly emblematic characters. It is a kaleidoscopic view of human life as seen in modern Nigeria and a graphic illustration of S.'s belief that the African artist should function "as the record of the mores and experience of his society and as the voice of vision in his own time."

FURTHER WORKS: *Five Plays* (1965); *Poems from Prison* (1969)

BIBLIOGRAPHY: MacLean, U., "S.'s International Drama," in *Black Orpheus*, No. 15 (1964), pp. 46–51; Jones, E., "W. S.'s *The Interpreters*—Reading Notes," in *African Literature Today*, No. 2 (1969), pp. 42–50; Ricard, A. "Les paradoxes de W. S.," in *Présence Africaine*, No. 72 (1969), pp. 202–11; Ogunba, O., "The Traditional Content of the Plays of W. S.," in *African Literature Today*, No. 4 (1970), pp. 2–18; Moore, G., *W. S.* (1970)

BERNTH LINDFORS

SPANISH-AMERICAN LITERATURE

(see also *Brazilian Literature*)

The Conquistadores transplanted their entire national culture to the regions of the New World that were colonized by Spain. As a result of this process of colonization, the development of Spanish-American literature largely followed that of its Spanish models. Although colonial literature possessed its own distinctive characteristics from the very beginning, the literary differences between Latin-American and Spanish writers were not nearly so great as the ethnic differences between the people of Spain and the indigenous populations of the New World. The fusing of European and Indian civilizations had, indeed, brought about a completely new society, but the natives, having no well-developed written language, were unable to influence the development of literature. Spanish has therefore been the only literary language of Spanish America, even though many words were taken from native languages and some old Spanish expressions were given new meanings.

Early in the 19th c. the Spanish colonies began to attain political independence, forming a number of autonomous republics. Attempts to describe the unique environment of Spanish America, which was notably different from the European milieu, were made successively by neoclassicists, romantics, and realists, leading to the creation of a literature common to the whole continent, with differentiations consisting merely in variations of local color. The difference between Spanish-American literature as a whole and continental Spanish literature lies in this local coloration. Not until about 1885, when the republics had achieved internal security and relative prosperity, did Spanish-American writers begin to free themselves from the influence of Spanish literature. Drawing on such French movements as late romanticism, the school of the parnassians, and symbolism (q.v.), they attempted not to imitate them but to raise their own writing to the levels achieved by European literature. Although their movement, known as *modernismo,* was strongly influenced by European literature, these writers wished primarily to develop their own uniquely American style. By about 1900 a new style had been developed in virtually all literary genres, and the literature of the former colonies was attracting the admiring attention of critics and authors in Spain itself.

The most brilliant representative of the exquisite, highly refined *modernismo* poetry was the Nicaraguan Darío (q.v.), whose poems in *Prosas profanas* (1896) are ecstatic hymns in praise of life. Those in the *Cantos de vida y esperanza* (1905), which are profoundly marked by the terror of death, are equally typical of a movement whose principal concern was aristocratic perfection of form and language. With the publication of *Prosas profanas,* Darío became the leader of a group of contemporary and younger poets known as the second generation of *modernismo.* Among these poets were: the Argentinian Lugones, the Bolivian Jaimes Freyre, the Peruvian Chocano, the Mexican González Martínez, the Uruguayan Herrera y Reissig (qq.v.), the Mexican Amado Nervo (1870–1919), and the Colombian Guillermo Valencia (1873–1943), many of whom also wrote excellent prose.

The contributions to the language of the writers of this group can be observed even in the prose style of the writers influenced by naturalism (q.v.), although the novelists of *modernismo* were not completely successful in combining their majestic, resonant style with the necessities of realistic plot development. The ideal of the superman as developed by Nietzsche (q.v.) is a special element in the *modernismo* of the Venezuelan novelist Díaz Rodríguez (q.v.), but the alienated characters of his novels are usually defeatist pessimists, who end in exile or suicide.

The historical novel offered another form of escape from immediate reality, notably in the work of the Argentinian impressionist novelist Enrique Rodríguez Larreta (1875–1961). The writers of this school openly declared themselves to be outsiders and emotionally troubled decadents. An important representative of the literature of the abnormal was the Uruguayan

novelist Quiroga (q.v.), whose work shows an unusual blending of aestheticism and naturalism. His short stories are usually set against a background of wild, untamed nature, and he displays a quality characteristic of some Latin-American literature in his concern with landscape and wild life and his avoidance of historical and human problems.

Several *modernismo* writers, on the other hand, were concerned with the customs and characteristics of the people of their own locale, occasionally expressing an idealization of the Creoles and Indians. One realist novelist, the Argentinian Payró (q.v.), satirized the practices of Argentinian politics. Reyles (q.v.) wrote powerful descriptions of rural life in his native Uruguay. The short stories of López Albújar (q.v.), marked by a protest against social injustice, reveal a deep understanding of the Indians of Peru. Although the talented Venezuelan Rufino Blanco-Fombona (1874–1944) destroyed the artistic unity of his work by an excess of political passion, his example of the *engagement* of the writer in the political struggles of his time became a characteristic feature of much Spanish-American literature. Another notable example of such involvement may be found in the work of the Mexican writer Azuela (q.v.), whose novels contain powerful descriptions of events in the Mexican revolution of 1910.

There was little activity in the theater life of Latin America during the early years of the 20th c. Buenos Aires was one of the few cities where the works of such authors as Ibsen, Gerhard Hauptmann, Lev Tolstoi (qq.v.), and Bjørnstjerne Bjørnson (1832–1910) were performed and always by European companies. Also in Buenos Aires the Uruguayan dramatist Florencio Sánchez (1875–1910) used the traditional techniques of the realistic theater to depict social conflict between city and countryside, natives and gauchos, and progress and tradition, thus becoming an advocate of a somewhat anarchistic socialism.

In philosophy, positivism, imported from Europe, was the strongest philosophical movement in Latin America until 1900, but soon after the turn of the century its first opponents came forward. In fact, the first signs of the breakdown of positivism appeared in literature rather than in the lectures of philosophy professors. The thinker who most successfully combined idealistic thought and modern principles was the Uruguayan Rodó (q.v.). The *Divulgaciones filológicas* (1934) of Baldomero

321

Sanín Cano (1868–1922) constitute another important humanist work.

The writers of the golden age of *modernismo,* Darío and his circle, continued to publish well into the 20th c., although most of them had little to say after 1910.

The generation that emerged between 1910 and 1920 was stimulated principally by symbolism, and is often called the postmodernist, or transitional, generation. Some of its members, such as Baldomero Fernández Moreno (1886–1950), wrote simple realistic works based on a direct contact with life. Others, among them the Mexican Reyes (q.v.), exhibited their great scholarship and knowledge of classical art forms. The most effusive frankly confessed their attitudes toward life, as in the poems of the Chilean Gabriela Mistral, the Uruguayan Juana de Ibarbourou (qq.v.), the Colombian Miguel Angel Osorio (1883–1942), the Argentinian Alfonsina Storni (1892–1938), the Uruguayan Delmira Agustini (1886–1914), and Domingo Moreno Jiménez (b. 1894). Such novelists as the Argentinian Ezequiel Martínez Estrada (b. 1895) were generally reserved and speculative.

Writers devoted to the depiction of a particular region include the Uruguayan poet Fernán Silva Valdez (b. 1887) and the poets who extolled the life of the Creoles and Indians. Certain authors, conspicuous for their eccentricities or their extravagance, sometimes attached more importance to startling metaphors than to genuine human feeling, or burdened their poems with excessive emotions, as in the works of the Chilean Huidobro, the Peruvian Vallejo (qq.v.), and the Mexican Ramón López Velarde (1888–1921). Although the latter belong chronologically to the transitional school, their literary purposes are those of the next generation, which definitively rejected the program of *modernismo.*

Novels and short stories conforming to the lyrical prose ideals of the Darío period continued to be written by such authors as the Chilean Prado Calvo (q.v.). Even the realistic short stories of this era reflect the solemn, grandiloquent manner that served as a model for virtually every writer of the period, including the Venezuelan Gallegos, the Colombian Rivera, the Argentinian Güiraldes, the Chilean Barrios, the Bolivian Arguedas (qq.v.), the Guatemalan Rafael Arévalo Martínez (b. 1884), the Mexican Martín Luis Guzmán (b. 1890), and the Venezuelan Teresa de la Parra (1891–1936). The realists and naturalists, while

maintaining their own style, steadily improved their technique and broadened their appeal. Most wrote about rural life, although some, especially in Argentina, described urban settings. One of the most successful of these realistic narrative writers was the Argentinian Gálvez (q.v.).

Another very popular genre was the philosophical and literary essay. Important essayists are the Argentinian Bicardo Rojas (1882–1957), Pedro Henriquez Ureña (b. 1884), and José Vasconcelos (b. 1881). Spanish-American writers have always tended to express their thoughts in essays for periodicals rather than in books. The journal *Sur,* published in Buenos Aires by Victoria Ocampo (b. 1900), is particularly notable.

After the symbolist period writers became increasingly aware that literature is essentially a "permanent revolution." This realization was soon turned against symbolism itself. The new writers attacked the symbolists' precious chains of metaphor and broke the thread of meaning linking the individual images; they pushed the irrationality of symbolism to its ultimate conclusions by negating the logical principles of identity and causality and the categories of space and time.

Because of the influence that Europe had always exerted on Spanish-American literature, and because many writers had spent the decisive years of World War I in Europe, many of the *isms* made their appearance in Latin-American literature after 1920. They included expressionism, futurism, dadaism, surrealism (qq.v.), and cubism—all of which expressed reactions to violence, meaninglessness, and disillusionment about prewar ideals.

The writers born between 1895 and 1905 were the actual creators of postwar literature, variously called "avant-garde," "new sensibility," and "*ultraismo.*" The outstanding figure of this generation, both in artistic stature and influence, is the Argentinian poet, essayist, and short-story writer Borges (q.v.), perhaps the most original of all present-day writers in the Spanish language. Two other Argentinian writers, Ricardo Molinari (b. 1898) and Francisco Luis Bernárdez (b. 1900), are also worthy of mention.

Whereas Borges never oversteps the boundaries of the rational or discards logical continuity in his lyrical and meditative poetry, the fervent outbursts of the Chilean Neruda (q.v.), frequently marked by political passion, are obscure and often difficult to understand.

The other major poets of this school, who became prominent after World War I, and who include the Ecuadorian Carrera Andrade (q.v.) and the Colombian Rafael Maya (b. 1898), are much calmer than Neruda.

One of the most interesting and unexpected by-products of avant-garde literature was the black poetry (*see* Neo-African literature) that developed in the Antilles. This movement, too, derived its inspiration from Europe. Ethnological research by Africanists, the cult of African art among Parisian painters, literati, and choreographers, and the creation of black art in the United States, all indicate that African and black subjects and approaches were particularly in vogue during the ultraist period. Also indicative of this interest was the use of themes from gypsy and black folklore by García Lorca (q.v.), after his visit to the Antilles, and by other continental Spanish poets. The existence in Cuba and Puerto Rico, for example, of a genuine indigenous black culture considerably encouraged this movement. In fact, in this case it would be more accurate to speak of self-discovery than of a vogue. The amazing achievements of this school, whose foremost representatives were the Cuban Nicolás Guillén, the Puerto Rican Palés Matos (qq.v.), Ramón Guirao (b. 1908), and Emilio Ballagas (1908–1954), may have resulted partly from their choice of great European models. Eugenio Florit (b. 1903) held aloof from this movement and its African themes.

Some of the outstanding writers of Latin America—notably Pellicer, Torres Bodet, Villaurrutia (qq.v.), and Salvador Novo (b. 1904)—were associated with the Mexican journal *Contemporáneos* (1928–38). At the same time many novels continued to be written in the style of the 1880's, because the French and Russian realists were still popular. The Latin-American novel, however, was beginning to develop somewhat in the way that the European novel had developed in the works of Proust, Kafka, and Joyce (qq.v.), and experiments in various directions can be recognized. Many novelists had no strong ties to the reality they detested. They wished to withdraw to the inmost recesses of the mind, as in the novels of the Cuban writer Carpentier (q.v.) and of Enrique Labrador Ruiz (b. 1902). Many writers of fiction were inspired by existentialism (q.v.), or at least by an anxiety-ridden pondering about man as an isolated individual haunted by guilt and a sense of responsibility, such as may be found in the works of the Danish philosopher Soren Kierkegaard (1813–55). They produced a literature that was neither realistic nor idealistic. Its identifying characteristic was, rather, that it rejected any clear distinction between consciousness and the outside world as in the work of the Argentinian Mallea (q.v.).

Most Latin-American writers, however, were less interested in the existential approach than in a generalized description of their milieu. The individual plays no part in their novels and short stories—or, at most, a part of no particular significance. Much of this literature upholds a fundamentally materialistic and often Marxist interpretation of history. Creole rightists, however, produced a literature of their own, but this was less influential. The greatest influence on the reading public was maintained by the liberal and socialist writers, who were politically oriented but not dogmatically intransigent. They described a world of the masses in which individuals no longer exist.

In technique these writers belong to the realistic or naturalistic schools, although some of them attempted to enliven their style in the way of ultraist metaphors or allegories and "messages for mankind" in the manner of expressionism. These novels of social protest can be classified according to their central theme: the position of the Indian in modern society; the conflict between landowner and laborer or between the cultivator of the land and his hostile natural environment; the extraordinarily rapid transformations in economic systems; contemporary political disasters, such as wars, revolutions, and dictatorships; the infiltration of foreign capital and the exploitation of markets and people, and North-American imperialism; and the agony of urban life and the conflicts between bourgeoisie and proletariat.

The best writers of fiction in Spanish America neither deny reality nor slavishly reproduce it, but attempt instead to discern the poetry inherent in even the most brutal events. Among such writers are the Venezuelan Arturo Uslar Pietri (b. 1906) and the Guatemalan Asturias (q.v.) in his *El señor presidente*. The need to elucidate the situation of Latin America in greater detail sometimes led writers from the novel to the essay. Outstanding essayists are the Venezuelan Mariano Picón Salas (1901–1965), Juan Marinello (b. 1898), and the Colombian Germán Arciniegas (b. 1900).

For political and economic reasons the 1930's and 1940's were not a good time for literature. In addition to economic depression, the spread of fascism, and World War II, Spanish America was divided by struggles for power, civil wars, revolutions, and insurrections. Although such events had always constituted the background of life, the sudden recognition of their significance by the intellectual community made them seem more destructive than ever before.

Drama was produced, as before, by playwrights whose sole concern was financial success, as well as by uncompromising dramatists dedicated entirely to experimental theater. The Mexican Usigli (q.v.) is the major dramatist of this period.

It is more difficult to assess the poetry of this time fairly. Uncritical admiration for surrealistic fragmentation of language led many young writers to use such techniques irresponsibly. The reader could interpret their poetry as he chose, because these writers were no longer attempting to communicate specific poetic visions but were content with evoking a certain vague, scarcely tangible mood. Other poets, however, such as the Uruguayan Sara de Ibáñez (b. 1909), forced their poetic exuberance into rigorous forms. In their works mastery of rhythm, rhyme, meter, and stanza compensates for the obscurity of the images. Others again, such as Martín Adán (b. 1908), brought into the traditional forms of Spanish poetry—sonnet, *décima,* and *romance*—bold metaphors and apparently unconnected enumerations, creating a new word magic that demonstrates their self-confident delight in creativity. In contrast to these writers are poets with metaphysical tendencies, such as Humberto Díaz Casanueva (b. 1905) and, on a higher level, the Mexican Paz (q.v.), as well as poets who undertake aesthetic experiments in a scientific spirit, such as Vicente Gerbasi (b. 1913) and Otto d'Sola (b. 1912). Other poets explored unsuspected relationships between men and things, refusing to make their visions accessible to the reader, as in the poems of the Cuban José Lezama Lima (b. 1910). Finally such poets as Eduardo Carranza (b. 1913) affirmed tradition, writing poetry in praise of their country and of religion.

The novelists attached little importance to plot or to exact descriptions of setting; they preferred to set their material before the reader in its raw state, without embellishing it artistically, so that he might look at it from various points of view, as though he himself were standing attentively in the midst of the reality they depicted. Among these novelists are the

Ecuadorian Icaza, the Peruvian Alegría Bazan (qq.v.), the Ecuadorian Adalberto Ortiz (b. 1914), and the Bolivian Augusto Céspedes, who made his reputation with *Sangre de mestizos* (1936), a chronicle of the Gran Chaco war between Bolivia and Paraguay (1932–35). The influence of the North-American novelists Faulkner and Caldwell (qq.v.) can be seen in the work of the Cuban Lino Novás Calvo (b. 1905).

A new generation began to write as Latin America was reacting in horror to World War II. At first these young writers were emotional, even taking seriously the verbal acrobatics and clowning of the ultraists and surrealists of the period from Borges to Neruda. Although their poetry was as difficult to understand as that of their predecessors, it did contain a new didactic element. Previously poetry had been absurd. These poets sought to show that life itself is absurd. A basically tragic tone pervades this new literature. Precisely because all their ethical values had been destroyed, these young poets were again concerned with moral problems. Surrealism, which the avant-gardists of the 1920's had adopted after recognizing the frivolous nature of dadaism, became the basic technique of the new generation. The young Latin Americans fused surrealism with ideas derived from existentialism, principally those expounded, not by the existentialist thinkers of Spain, but by Sartre (q.v.) and the German philosopher Martin Heidegger (b. 1889).

The young writers wished to create a "poetry of the vision of essences" and to express the "truth of being." Other poets produced the kind of stylized poetry that García Lorca had written a generation earlier in Spain, and a number of writers returned to religious verse and to the forms of the celebrated poetry of the Spanish renaissance and baroque periods. The literature of this generation was characterized by a mingling of aestheticism and social protest, idealism and materialism, the cult of beauty and of ugliness, outbreaks of despair and revolutionary patriotism.

Two constant factors in all of this tremendous stylistic diversity are the deep seriousness inspiring all of these writers and their great respect for form. Among the most important figures are the Peruvian Sebastián Salazar Bondy (1924–65), Cintio Vitier (b. 1921), Ida Gramcko, Eliseo Diego (b. 1920), Juan Rodolfo Wilcock (b. 1919), Alfredo Gardona Peña, and Francisco Matos Paoli (b.

1914). Julio Cortázar (b. 1914) is an imaginative author of short stories, as in *Bestiario* (1951), *Final del juego* (1956), *Las armas secretas* (1959), and *Los premios* (1960). Some of the other promising prose writers are Juan José Arreola (b. 1918); Juan Rulfo, author of *El llano en llamas* (1953) and *Pedro Páramo* (1955); and the realist Augusto Roa Bastos (b. 1917).

ENRIQUE ANDERSON IMBERT

Spanish-American Literature in the 1960's

The gradual coming-of-age of Spanish-American literature, a process characteristic of recent decades, has been significantly accelerated in the last few years. Because of the world revolution in communications media, the great increase in book production in the Spanish-speaking nations, the growing numbers of writers in all genres in Hispanic America and the numerous translations of their works, contemporary Spanish-American writing is much better known than was the literary production of earlier periods not only among the hemisphere countries themselves but also in the United States, Europe, and other world areas.

This gratifying development, however, may not yet mean that Spanish-American literature, regardless of its admittedly great intrinsic value, is widely known enough to be considered one of the major bodies of world literature. For it to attain such status beyond all possible debate, Spanish-American literature, and particularly those of its works that deal with universal issues, values, and situations, must awaken sympathetic understanding among ever larger numbers of readers all over the globe. This will not happen, of course, until more of its greatest books become available in many languages. And such widespread availability, in turn, will occur only after many publishers are convinced that there are indeed sufficient readers for such translations in their countries. This has not been the case until very recent years, when translations have sprouted prolifically in Europe and the United States. Yet it must be noted that Mexico's Octavio Paz (q.v.) was the 1963 winner of the Grand International Poetry Prize, while Chile's poet Pablo Neruda (q.v.) has been a leading contender for the Nobel Prize for Literature, and Guatemala's Miguel Ángel Asturias (q.v.), a noted novelist, received this coveted award in 1967.

Two principal, long-standing, deep and powerful currents are distinguishable in Spanish-American literature: one that is devoted primarily to native themes (rural or urban, regional or national) and is often nationalistic if not chauvinistic; and another, more sophisticated, that is concerned with more universal issues. In the first, objective, dominant nature is often the leitmotif, and in the second, subjective, anguished man. Both currents have produced excellent albeit often radically different works. But in the past ten or twelve years one notes a to-be-welcomed tendency among the best cultivators of each direction to transcend or fuse their sometimes relatively narrow realistic or surrealistic approaches into one that is wider, more universal in nature and more sophisticated in style, language, and psychological character development. Like those in other countries, Spanish-American writers are preoccupied with the problem of an alienated, divided society, solitude, evil, the loss of personal identity, and the decline of traditional values. This salutary new tendency to universalize the national or regional is clearly an important symptom of and a contribution toward the emergence of Spanish-American literature as an increasingly significant body on the cultural horizon of the Western world.

FICTION

Fiction has long been a prolific field in Spanish America, and in the last decade the novel and short story have undergone a veritable boom. Old masters have been sharing the limelight with many emerging writers, and authors in their twenties are becoming more quickly known than ever before.

The general trend has been for the lingering traces of realism-naturalism to give way before a sort of literary *aggiornamento,* as the writers have sought to adapt avant-garde, post-Joycean techniques (dislocation of linear time, shifts in the narrator and his viewpoint, interior monologue, the probing of the psyche) to their subject matter and so to enter rapidly into the mainstream of modern Western literature. Thus one notes in their books the influence of Proust, Kafka, Joyce, Faulkner, and Sartre (qq.v.), often combined with certain common features: an attack on the *form* of the novel, on narrative, and, even more radically, on the structure of language itself, in an attempt by these authors to create their own mode of expression. Thus books are produced whose form

325

is often shaped by their lyric content. Some notion of what this process can mean is evident in the Uruguayan critic Emir Rodríguez Monegal's description of what José Lezama Lima was trying to do in a new Cuban novel (*Paradiso*): "to complete a work of fiction that has the appearance of a novel of manners, which is at the same time a treatise on the paradise of childhood and the hell of sexual perversions; to build the chronicle of the education of a young man from La Habana thirty years ago who becomes, through the metaphysical play of language, the mirror of both the visible and the invisible world" ("The New Latin American Novel," *BA*, XLIV [Winter 1970], 45).

Among older writers of fiction who have published in the 1960's are the Argentinians Jorge Luis Borges (q.v.), with his *Antología personal* (1962) and *Nueva antología personal* (1968), and Eduardo Mallea (q.v.), with *La vida blanca* (1961) and a trilogy, *El resentimiento* (1966). Also well-established is the Cuban Alejo Carpentier (q.v.), author of *El siglo de las luces* (1962). Asturias published in this decade a collection of short stories, *El espejo de Lida Sal* (1967), as well as two novels, *Los ojos de los enterrados* (1961) and *Mulata de tal* (1963).

Slightly younger novelists and short-story writers who have been productive include: Juan Carlos Onetti (Uruguay, b. 1909; *El astillero*, 1961, and *Cuentos completos*, 1967); José Lezama Lima (Cuba, b. 1910; *Paradiso*, 1966); Eduardo Caballero Calderón (Columbia, b. 1910; *El buen salvaje*, 1965), winner of Spain's Nadal Prize; José María Arguedas (Peru, 1911–69; *Todas las sangres*, 1964); Julio Cortázar (Argentina, b. 1914; *Los premios*, 1960, *Rayuela*, 1963, *Todos los fuegos el fuego*, 1966, and *62. Modelo para armar*, 1969); Elena Garro (Mexico, b. 1917; *Los recuerdos del porvenir*, 1963); Juan José Arreola (Mexico, b. 1918; *La feria*, 1963); and Carlos Martínez Moreno (Uruguay, b. 1918; *El paredón*, 1962, and *Con las primeras luces*, 1966).

Still younger are the outstanding, productive authors of fiction born in the 1920's, truly the most numerous and dominant group now writing. These include: Mario Benedetti (Uruguay, b. 1920; *La tregua*, 1960, and *Gracias por el fuego*, 1965); Marco Denevi (Argentina, b. 1922; *Ceremonia secreta*, 1960, and *Un pequeño café*, 1967); H. A. Murena (Argentina, b. 1924; *Los de la promesa*, 1965, and *Las leyes de la noche*, 1968); Beatriz Guido (Argentina, b.

1924; *La mano en la trampa*, 1961, and *El incendio y las vísperas*, 1964); José Donoso (Chile, b. 1925; *Este domingo*, 1965, and *El lugar sin límites*, 1966); Rosario Castellanos (Mexico, b. 1925; *Oficio de tinieblas*, 1962, and *Los convidados de agosto*, 1964); Sergio Galindo (Mexico, b. 1926; *La comparsa*, 1964); Enrique Lafourcade (Chile, b. 1927; *La fiesta del rey Acab*, 1960, *Pronombres personales*, 1967, and *Frecuencia modulada*, 1968); Carlos Fuentes (Mexico, b. 1928; *Aura, La muerte de Artemio Cruz*, 1962, *Cantar de ciegos*, 1964, *Zona sagrada*, 1965, and *Cambio de piel*, 1967); Gabriel García Márquez (Columbia, b. 1928; *El coronel no tiene quien le escriba*, 1961, and *Cien años de soledad*, 1967); and Guillermo Cabrera Infante (Cuba, b. 1929; *Tres tristes tigres*, 1964).

Fiction is also being adeptly cultivated by writers still in their thirties. Among those with established reputations in this youngest group are Tomás Mojarro (Mexico, b. 1932; *Cañón de Juchipila*, 1960 *Bramadero*, 1963, and *Malafortuna*, 1966); Vicente Leñero (Mexico, b. 1933; *Los albañiles*, 1963, *Estudio Q*, 1965, and *El garabato*, 1967); Mario Vargas Llosa (Peru, b. 1936; *La ciudad y los perros*, 1963, *La casa verde*, 1966, *Los cachorros*, 1967, and *Conversaciones en la catedral*, 1969); and Gustavo Sainz (Mexico, b. 1940; *Gazapo*, 1965).

POETRY

The general animation in the literary world, the notable increase in book production, and the proliferation of journals and "little" magazines in Spanish America have all contributed to the further development of poetry, a genre that has always been popular in the Spanish-speaking countries. Many of the older, well-known poets are still writing, and new, younger lyricists are appearing, sometimes momentarily, on the literary scene. The latter are far too numerous for any one observer to keep track of them.

In general, the experimental, surrealistic (*see* surrealism), often hermetic tendencies of many poets over the last two decades seem to be giving way to a widespread struggle among both older and younger generations to express themselves in an ever more pure, more personalized idiom, one divorced from over-blown rhetoric, in order to communicate more directly and simply their deeply felt tensions. Spanish-American poets of every age, in addition to their preoccupation with such eternal themes as life and death, are reacting today to the same stimuli that animate their colleagues in the field of fiction: worldwide feelings of alienation, social injustice, the problem of personal identity, the decline in older traditions, forms, values, etc.

A representative but certainly not exhaustive sampling of significant poets might include the following. One senior Colombian, León de Greiff (b. 1895), published *Obras completas* (1911). Another established Colombian poet, Germán Pardo García (b. 1902), published *30 años de labor poética* (1961) and *El defensor* (1964). The Venezuelan Miguel Otero Silva (b. 1908) is the author of *La mar que es el morir* (1965) and *Casas muertas* (1968). In Mexico, always a country of poets, those active in the 1960's are: Carlos Pellicer (q.v.; *Material poético*, 1962, *Con palabras y fuego*, 1963, and *Teotihuacán, y el 13 de agosto: ruina de Tenochtitlán*, 1965); Elías Nandino (b. 1903; *Nocturna palabra*, 1960); Salvador Novo (b. 1904; *Poesía*, 1961); Octavio Paz (*Libertad bajo palabra*, 1961, *Salamandra*, 1962, *Vindrabam Madurai*, 1965, *Viento entero*, 1966, and *Discos visuales*, 1968); Alí Chumacero (b. 1918; *Páramo de sueños*, 1960, and *Palabras en reposo*, 1965); José Emilio Pacheco (b. 1939; *Los elementos de la noche*, 1963, and *El reposo del fuego*, 1966); Homero Aridjis (b. 1940; *Los ojos desdoblados*, 1960, *La difícil ceremonia*, 1963, *Antes del reino*, 1963, *Mirándola dormir*, 1964, and *Perséfone*, 1967).

Chile has two major poets. Pablo Neruda, a world figure, has published *Navegaciones y regresos* (1960), *Las piedras de Chile* (1961), *Cantos ceremoniales* (1961), *Obras completas* (1962, 1968), and *Plenos poderes* (1962). Nicanor Parra (b. 1914), whose stature is growing rapidly, is the author of *Versos de salón* (1962), *Manifesto* (1963), and *Obra gruesa* (1969).

The black Cuban poet Nicolás Guillén (q.v.) published *Tengo* (1964), and his contemporary Ecuadorian Jorge Carrera Andrade (q.v.), *Angel planetario* (1963). In Argentina, Jorge Luis Borges collected his verse in *Obras poéticas* (1964), while a girl a third of his age, Ana Weyland, gained critical acceptance with *La vida simple: Poemas* (1966), a book of fresh, deeply felt lyrics.

DRAMA

Although the drama has always existed in Spanish America, it is the last genre to develop

significantly. It is currently in a promising state, particularly in the university theaters and in small experimental theater productions in the larger cities. Playwrights show the same fundamental preoccupations as their colleagues in fiction and verse and, in addition, exhibit an exceptionally strong tendency to satirize politics and social mores. As one might expect, influences range all the way from the Greek tragedies to Edward Albee (b. 1928), Beckett, Genet, Miller, Tennessee Williams (qq.v.), the black theater, and the theater of the absurd. As a further indication of progress in the Spanish-American theater, the recent founding of the *Latin American Theater Review* (University of Kansas) in 1968 should be noted.

Mexico and Argentina, by far the largest and most populous Spanish-speaking nations in the New World, also have the largest metropolitan centers and, consequently, the most active dramatists and the largest theatergoing public.

In Mexico, outstanding playwrights include: Salvador Novo, author of *Yocasta, o casi* (1961), *Ha vuelto Ulises* (1962), *Cuauhtémoc* (1962), *In Pipiltzintzin, o La guerra de las gordas* (1963), *El sofá* (1963), and *In ticitézcatl, o El espejo encantado* (1965); Rodolfo Usigli (q.v.), with *Teatro completo* (2 vols., 1963, 1966), *La corona de fuego* (1960), and *Corona de luz* (1965); Wilberto Cantón (b. 1923), who wrote *Tan cerca del cielo* (1961), *Nosotros somos Dios* (1963), *Murió por la patria* (1964); and Jorge Ibargüengoitia (b. 1928), who wrote *El atentado* (1964), *La conspiración vendida* (1965).

Three Argentinians have produced successful plays. Agustín Cuzzani (b. 1924) is to be credited for his *Para que se cumplan las Escrituras* (1965). Osvaldo Dragún (b. 1929) wrote the well-received *Heroica de Buenos Aires* (1966). The achievement of Roberto Cossa (b. 1934) was *Nuestro fin de semana* (1964).

Fine Cuban dramatists are: Manuel Reguera Saumell (b. 1928; *Recuerdos de Tulipa*, 1962); José Triana (b. 1933; *El Parque de la Fraternidad*, 1962, and *La noche de los asesinos*, 1965); and Antón Arrufat (b. 1935; *El vivo al pollo*, 1961, and *El velorio de Pachencho*, 1961).

The Chilean Jorge Díaz (b. 1930), an angry dramatist who is maturing, wrote *Topografía de un desnudo* (1967). The Peruvian Sebastián Salazar Bondy (1924–65) is also denunciatory in *Todo queda en casa* (1961), *Pobre gente de París* (1961), and *El fabricante de deudas*

(1962). Enrique Buenaventura (b. 1925), a Colombian director and dramatist, is author of *En la diestra de Dios Padre* (1960), *La tragedia de Henri Christophe* (1962), and *Réquiem para el Padre Las Casas* (1963).

One notable Puerto Rican playwright is Francisco Arriví (b. 1915), who wrote *El coctel de Don Nadie* (1964). Also deserving of recognition is René Marqués (b. 1919), author of *La casa sin reloj* (1961), *Carnaval adentro, carnaval afuera* (1963), *El apartamiento* (1964), and *Mariana, o El alba* (1964).

ESSAY

The essay, a paramount vehicle for reflective thought from the personal viewpoint, has become an important genre in Spanish America during the present century, although its cultivators are less numerous than authors of verse or fiction. Talented writers, fusing lyricism and didacticism, have probed the Spanish-American character, delving into the essence of the *ser hispanoamericano* (Spanish-American being or existence) and attempting to lay the ideological foundation for a new way of life, one rooted in the Indo-Hispanic cultural history but capable of assimilating the best of the new ideas of Europe and North America. Given the heterogeneous nature of the Spanish-American nations, their individual or inner diversity, and the tendency of syntheses to yield half-truths at best, these essayists are obviously engaged in a very difficult and long-term enterprise. Two of the best of them, Alfonso Reyes (Mexico, q.v.) and Ezequiel Martínez Estrada (Argentina, 1895–1964), have died recently. Publication of Reyes's *Obras completas,* begun in 1955, was virtually complete by the late 1960's.

Martínez Estrada, whose fame was established early with such works as *Radiografía de la pampa* (1933), *Cabeza de Goliat* (1940), and *Muerte y transfiguración de Martín Fierro* (1948), produced in his last years somewhat inferior works: *Cuadrante del pampero* (1956) and *Semejanzas y diferencias entre los países de la América Latina* (1962). Also in the process of publication during the late 1960's were the *Obras completas* of the noted Peruvian Marxist essayist, José Carlos Mariátegui (1895–1930).

The Colombian Germán Arciniegas (b. 1900) published his monumental cultural survey of the Spanish Americas, *El continente de siete colores,* in 1965. In the same year the Argentinian scholar Guillermo de Torre (b. 1900) issued his massive literary-cultural compendium, *Historia de las literaturas de vanguardia.* In 1962 the Venezuelan Mariano Picón Salas (1901–1965) published *Los malos salvajes* (1962). In the late 1960's the Mexican philosopher Leopoldo Zea (b. 1912) wrote several important essays in cultural history: *América Latina y el mundo* (1965), *El pensamiento latinoamericano* (1965), and *El positivismo en México* (1968). Venezuela's Arturo Uslar Pietri (b. 1906) is also preoccupied with the profound meaning of the Spanish-American character in *En busca del Nuevo Mundo* (1969).

But the most prolific essayist of the 1960's has been Octavio Paz, whose analysis of the Mexican character, *El laberinto de la soledad* (1950), established him as one of the foremost living essayists. His poetic talent for striking figures of speech and the wide range of his active mind (literature, philosophy, psychology, society, and politics) are exemplified in such books as *Cuadrivio* (1965), *Puertas al campo* (1966), *Corriente alterna* (1967), *El arco y la lira* (2nd. ed., 1968), and *Posdata* (1969).

LITERARY HISTORY AND CRITICISM

Scholarly production in these fields has continued to increase quantitatively and to improve in quality, and has kept pace in recent years with the general development of Spanish-American literature. Enrique Anderson Imbert's (Argentina, b. 1910) standard *Historia de la literatura hispanoamericana* appeared in its latest, revised edition in 1970. Other recent works of literary history include: *Literatura hispanoamericana* (1962) by Angel Valbuena Briones (Spain, b. 1928); *Esquema generacional de las letras hispanoamericanas* (1963) by José Juan Arrom (Cuba, b. 1910); *Historia de la literatura hispanoamericana* (2 vols., 1965, 1967) by Raimundo Lazo (Cuba, b. 1904); *Outline History of Spanish America* (3rd, rev. ed. 1965), prepared by a group of United States scholars under the general editorship of John E. Englekirk; and *Historia crítica de la literatura hispanoamericana* (1968) by Orlando Gómez-Gil. One massive history of Spanish-American literature is the four-volume multilingual—Spanish, Portuguese, English, French—*Panorama das Literaturas das Américas* (1965), carried out by numerous contributors under the general editorship of Joaquim de Montezuma de Carvalho.

328

Another major work is the eight-volume history projected by Pedro F. de Andrea, of which five volumes had appeared by 1968. Fernando Alegría (Chile, b. 1918) wrote *Historia de la novela hispanoamericana* (1965); Luis Leal (Mexico, b. 1907), *Historia del cuento hispanoamericano* (1966); José Juan Arrom, *Historia del teatro hispanoamericano colonial* (1967); Frank Dauster (United States, b. 1925), *Historia del teatro hispanoamericano, siglos XIX y XX* (1966); and Boyd G. Carter (United States, b. 1908), *Historia de la literatura hispanoamericana a través de sus revistas* (1968).

Literary journals, too, are contributing to a better knowledge of Spanish-American authors among the hemisphere countries themselves (something that did not always happen quickly in former times) and in the non-Spanish-speaking world. There are the longtime journals, among which the most worthy are: *Atenea* (Santiago de Chile), *Cuadernos Americanos* (Mexico), *La Torre* (Puerto Rico), *Revista Hispánica Moderna* (United States), *Revista Iberoamericana* (United States), and *Sur* (Argentina). Recently a number of promising new journals have emerged: *Cuadernos* (Paris-Buenos Aires; title changed to *Mundo Nuevo* in 1966), *La vida literaria* (Mexico), *Número* (Montevideo), and *Zona Franca* (Caracas).

ROBERT G. MEAD, JR.

BIBLIOGRAPHY

I. General

Valle, R. H., *Indice de la poesía centroamericana* (1941); Hespelt, E. H., *An Outline of Spanish American Literature* (1942); Spell, J. R., *Contemporary Spanish-American Fiction* (1944); Henríquez Ureña, P., *Literary Currents in Hispanic America* (1945); Leguizamón, J. A., *Historia de la literatura hispanoamericana* (1945); Vitier, M., *Del ensayo americano* (1945); Somma, L., *Storia della letteratura (hispano-) americana* (1946); Trenti Rocamora, J. L., *El teatro en la América colonial* (1947); Palán y Dulcet, A., *Manual del librero hispanoamericano* (2nd ed., 1948); Saz, del A., *La poesía hispanoamericana* (1948); Torres Rioseco, A., *Grandes novelistas de la América hispana* (2 vols.; 2nd ed., 1949); Trenti Rocamora, J. L., *El repertorio de la dramática colonial hispanoamericana* (1950); Topete, J. M., *A Working* *Bibliography of Latin America Literature* (1952); Sánchez, L. A., *Proceso y contenido de la novela hispanoamericana* (1953); Anderson Imbert, E., *Historia de la literatura hispanoamericana* (1954); Torres Rioseco, A., *Cautiverio: Antología poética 1940-1955* (1955); Abril, X., ed., *Antología de la poesía moderna hispanoamericana* (1956); Alpern, H., and Martel, J., eds., *Teatro hispanoamericano* (1956); Cruz, S. de la, *La novela iberoamericana actual* (1956); García Prada, C., ed., *Poetas modernistas hispanoamericanos* (1956); Onis, F. de, *Anthologie de la poésie ibéro-américaine* (1956); Panero, L., *Antología de la poesía hispanoamericana*, Vol. II (2nd. ed., 1957); Pan American Union, Sección de Letras, eds., *Diccionario de la literatura latinoamericana* (1958); Carter, B. G., *Las revistas literarias de Hispanoamérica: Breve historia y contenido* (1959); Zum-Felde, A., *Indice crítico de la literatura hispanoamericana*, Vol. II (1959); Modern Language Association of America, *Annual Bibliographies* (1960-69); *Handbook of Latin America Studies*, Nos. 23-29 (1961-68); Monegal, E. R., *Narradores de esta América* (1963); Solórzano, C., *El teatro latinoamericano en el siglo XX* (1964); Mallea, E., *Poderío de la novela* (1965); Jones, W. K., *Behind Spanish American Footlights* (1966); Schulman, I., *Génesis del Modernismo* (1966); Corvalán, O., *Modernismo y vanguardia* (1967); Schulman, I. A., et al., *Coloquio sobre la novela hispanoamericana* (1967); Stabb, M. S., *In Quest of Identity: Patterns in the Spanish American Essay of Ideas* (1967); Fuentes, C., *La nueva novela latinoamericana* (1969).

II. Individual Countries

ANTILLES: Loudet, E. *Letras argentinas en las Antillas* (1957); Olivera, O., *Breve historia de literatura antillana* (1957).

ARGENTINA: Aita, A., *La literatura argentina contemporánea: 1900-1930* (1931); González Carvalho, J., *Indice de la poesía argentina contemporánea* (1937); Pinto, J., *Panorama de la literatura argentina contemporánea* (1941); Morales, É., *Literatura argentina* (1944); Giménez Pastor, A., *Historia de la literatura argentina* (2 vols., 1945); Leguizamón, J. A., *Historia de la literatura argentina* (1945); Borges, J. L., and Bioy Casares, A., *Poesía gauchesca* (2 vols., 1955); Costazar, A. Raul, *Indios y gauchos en la literatura argentina*

(1956); Ghiano, J. C., *Testimonio de la novela argentina* (1956); Yunque, A., *Síntesis histórica de la literatura argentina* (1957); *Teatro argentino contemporáneo* (1960); Anderson Imbert, E., *Genio y figura de Sarmiento* (1967).

BOLIVIA: Finot, E., *Historia de la literatura boliviana* (2nd ed., 1955).

CHILE: Azócar, R., *La poesía chilena moderna* (1931); Solar, H. del, *Indice de la poesía chilena contemporánea* (1937); Mann, W., *Chile auf der Schwelle der neuen Zeit* (1938); Cruz, P. N., *Estudios sobre la literatura chilena*, Vols. II and III (1940); Latorre, M., *La literatura chilena* (1941); Lillo, S. A., *La literatura chilena* (2nd ed., 1942); Lefebvre, A., *Poetas chilenos* (1945); Alegría, F., *La poesía chilena* (1954); Dussuel, F., *Historia de la literatura chilena* (1954); Undurraga, A. de, *Atlas de la poesía de Chile, 1900 hasta 1957: Antología integrada por 92 poetas más un prefacio* (1958); Yáñez, J. F., *Antología del cuento chileno moderno* (1958); Fein, J. M., *Modernismo in Chilean Literature: The Second Phase* (1964); Monegal, E. R., *El viajero inmóvil: Introducción a Pablo Neruda* (1966).

COLOMBIA: Ortega, T. J., *Historia de la literatura colombiana* (2nd ed., 1935); Gómez Restrepo, A., *Historia de la literatura colombiana* (4 vols., 1936–45); Caparroso, C. A., *Poesía colombiana* (1942); Arrazola, R., *Antología poética de Colombia* (1943); Maya, R., *Consideraciones críticas sobre la literatura colombiana* (1944); Sanín Cano, B., *Letras colombianas* (1944).

CUBA: Báez, G. P., *Poetas jóvenes cubanos* (1932); Salazar y Roig, S., *Historia de la literatura cubana* (1939); Remos y Rubio, J. J., *Historia de la literatura cubana* (3 vols., 1945); Rivero Muñiz, F., *Bibliografía del teatro cubano* (1957).

DOMINICAN REPUBLIC: Henríquez Ureña, P., *Panorama histórico de la literatura dominicana* (1945); Balaguer y Ricardo, J., *Historia de la literatura dominicana* (1956).

ECUADOR: Rojas, A. F., *La novela ecuatoriana* (1948); Barrera, I. J., *Historia de la literatura ecuatoriana*, Vol. IV (1955); Pareja Díez-Canseco, A., *De la literatura ecuatoriana contemporánea* (1956).

GUATEMALA: Porta Bencos, H., *Parnaso guatemalteco* (1928); Vela, D., *Literatura guatemalteca* (2 vols., 1942–43).

HONDURAS: Castro, J., *Antología de poetas hondureños* (1939).

MEXICO: Gonzales Peña, C., *Historia de la literatura mejicana* (2nd ed., 1940); Maples Arce, M., *Antología de la poesía mexicana moderna* (1940); Altamirano, I. M., *La literatura nacional* (3 vols., 1949); Martínez, J. L., *La emancipación literaria de México* (1955); Monterde, F., and Esquival, A. M., *Teatro mexicano del siglo XX* (3 vols., 1956); Meregalli, F., *Narratori messicani* (1957); *Teatro mexicano contemporáneo* (1959); Phillips, A. W., *Ramón López Velarde* (1962); *Diccionario de Escritores Mexicanos* (1965); Robb, J. W., *El estilo de Alfonso Reyes* (1965); Brushwood, J. S., *Mexico in Its Novel* (1966); Sommers, J., *After the Storm: Landmarks of the Modern Mexican Novel* (1968).

PANAMA: Miró, R., *Indice de la poesía panameña contemporánea* (1941); Tourtellot, M., and Lee, B. G., *Vida y obras de autores panameños* (1943).

PERU: Sánchez, L. A., *La literatura peruana* (3 vols., 1936); Sánchez, L. A., *La literatura del Perú* (1943); Escobar, A., ed., *La narración en el Perú* (1956); *Teatro peruano contemporáneo* (1959).

PUERTO RICO: Saez. A., *El teatro en Puerto Rico* (1950); Valbuena Briones, A., *La poesía puertorriqueña contemporánea* (1952); Rivera de Álvarez, J., *Diccionario de literatura puertorriqueña* (1955); Cabrera, F. M., *Historia de la literatura puertorriqueña* (1956).

URUGUAY: Zum-Felde, A., *La literatura del Uruguay* (1939); García, S. I. *Panorama de la poesía gauchesa y nativista del Uruguay* (1941); Caillava, D. A., *Historia de la literatura gauchesca en el Uruguay* (1945); Borges, J. L., *Aspectos de la literatura gauchesca* (1950); *Teatro uruguayo* (1960).

VENEZUELA: Picón Salas, M., *Formación y proceso de la literatura venezolana* (1940); Venegas Filardo, P., *Novelas y novelistas de Venezuela* (1955); Insausti, R. A., *Caminos y señales: Glosas de emoción a poetas venezolanos* (1956); Medina, J. R., *Examen de la poesía venezolana contemporánea* (1956); Albareda, G. de, and Garfias, F., *Antología de la poesía hispanoamericana: Venezuela* (1958)

SPANISH LITERATURE

Seldom does the turn of a century coincide so closely with a new literary consciousness as in Spain in 1900. The disastrous defeat suffered by Spain in the Spanish-American War of 1898 triggered profound psychological reactions and far-reaching literary reverberations, which were reflected particularly among the diverse personalities of the so-called Generation of '98, who were united by a concern about the "decadence" of the Spain of their day. Led by Unamuno (q.v.), a multi-faceted, controversial, and often self-contradictory thinker, teacher, novelist, dramatist, poet, and essayist, they analyzed national problems in many genres, most notably in the essay. Their attempts to understand the Spanish character were one result of their efforts to bring new areas into the domain of Spanish literature. An introspective self-criticism thus led to some of the most significant literature ever written in Spain, with influences reaching beyond the 1950's, leading some critics to call this era a second Golden Age of Spanish letters.

Spanish writers of the 20th c. usually fall into four chronological divisions, each with certain common characteristics:

(1) The Generation of '98 includes writers born between 1864 and about 1880.

(2) The Generation of 1925 includes those writers born from about 1885 until about 1900. This group is also called the Generation of Ortega, the Generation of 1927, the Generation of the Dictatorship, or the Nietos del '98.

The Generation of 1925, under the intellectual leadership of Ortega y Gasset (q.v.), was more subjective and self-consciously aesthetic than the Generation of '98. It was also less concerned with national problems, and was considerably influenced by European writers who were experimenting with expressionism, futurism, surrealism (cq.v.), and the application of impressionism and psychoanalysis to literature. Ortega y Gasset analyzed these characteristics in his article *La deshumanización del arte* (1925), which many readers misinterpreted as a defense of tendencies he was examining. Several members of the group subsequently deserted their initial non-utilitarian and aristocratic aestheticism to devote themselves to various ideologies.

(3) The Generation of 1936 includes writers born from about 1900 until about 1920. It is also called the Generation of the Republic, although not all of its members were Republicans, or La Generación Escindida.

The factor that unites this group is that their lives and works were so significantly affected by the Spanish Civil War, which raged between 1936 and 1939. The war was bitterly fought between the Republicans (or Loyalists), who were trying to maintain the government established in 1931, and the insurgent Nationalists (or Falangists), under the leadership of General Francisco Franco (b. 1892), who were seeking to establish a totalitarian state. The Nationalists captured Madrid on 28 March 1939, and Franco became chief of state.

The war interrupted significant literary activity for several years and marked postwar writing with political animosity, imposing certain themes and forms from which Spanish literature has yet to free itself. Studies of this era frequently omit writers for ideological reasons, or otherwise overlook the writers who were forced to flee from Franco's Spain.

The Generation of 1936 includes young writers whose first works were published during the days of the Republic, as well as their contemporaries who had published nothing before 1936. Many fought on opposing sides in the Civil War, during which some of them died and others went into exile. This generation was not as inclined toward revolutionary attitudes as its predecessors had been. Its members did not break with the immediate past but admired both the masters of the Generation of '98 and the experiments of the avant-garde. Less extreme than Ortega y Gasset, whose mastery they acknowledged, they were also more eclectic, initiating a trend away from aesthetic principles and toward utilitarian art. The return to realism was carried to extremes after the Civil War.

(4) Many contemporary writers can be grouped in a loose category, called the post-Civil War writers. Each writer tends to identify himself with one of the various literary movements (*tremendismo, objetivismo, social realismo*) or political ideologies. The nebulous distinction between the Generation of 1936 and those called the postwar writers is often based less on age than participation in the Civil War, which had such complex personal and literary consequences to those involved.

The repressive censorship, both monarchical and (in the postwar period) Falangist, has influenced Spanish writing in form and content to an extent it may never be possible to evaluate accurately. This is particularly true of writing during the Franco regime, when moral, religious, and political censorship, officially nonexistent but nonetheless real, obliges the writer to restrict and carefully select his ideas and expression. While the overall trend, especially in the past decade, may be described as a gradual thawing or relaxation, the average writer still finds it dangerous and problematic to attempt to exercise "freedoms" ostensibly granted by the government. Writers choosing to avoid sociopolitical themes, adhering to "pure" art, have at times produced works admirable as creative literature, but have been unkindly treated by younger, "committed" social critics inside Spain, as well as a majority of intellectuals outside the peninsula, in whose numbers Republican sympathizers predominate.

On the other hand, the frequently political postwar literary expressions, when unfavorable to the regime, must usually be deviously expressed or published outside Spain. A majority of younger writers (those who were children during the Civil War, or born since then) are liberal, at times overtly opposed to the regime. Most of Franco's literary spokesmen belong to the older generation, and while there has been considerable productivity by the conservative faction, it is less significant and original in general than that of the opposition, even though this group is not primarily characterized by originality. The contemporary social consciousness and utilitarian concepts of art (and particularly literature), which began in the 1950's, have produced drama, poetry, and fiction of protest, and criticism, reform, and sociological "testimonial." A gray literature whose protagonist is often the mass or stereotyped representative of a class, with few themes and little variety in treatment, "social" writing does not propose to entertain and has not won wide public favor. The subjective, psychological, imaginative, and artistic veins, labeled "evasive" by the *social realistas* (who tend to group neutral or uncommitted writers with mouthpieces of the regime), are directions cultivated by some independent writers. At the present moment, as *realismo social* begins to decline, the uncommitted writers are gaining momentum. The *social realistas,* favorites of liberal intellectuals and critics for the past fifteen years, are showing less vigor, finding fewer publishers. Changing generational goals are visible to varying degrees in the several genres, particularly the more "creative" ones. While some of these new writers may be labeled "evasive" for some time to come, they are not pro-Franco (once the principal meaning of this term), but simply apolitical, or writers who believe that literature has other functions than the social and utilitarian.

332

1. Philosophy, Criticism, and the Essay

After years of relatively obscure philosophical activity, Spain produced two world-famous thinkers, Ortega y Gasset and Unamuno (qq.v.), and many admirable critics, essayists, historians, and theoreticians. Among the most prominent figures of the early 1900's were: the pedagogue and literary theorist Francisco Giner de los Ríos (1839–1915); Santiago Ramón y Cajal (1852–1934), an important essayist on national problems and a winner of the Nobel Prize; the critic, aesthetician, and literary historian Marcelino Menéndez y Pelayo (1856–1912); Manuel Bartolomé Cossío (1858–1935); Juan Maragall (1860–1911); and Azorín (q.v.), the author of highly personal criticism and evocative essays.

Slightly later came the works of the literary historian and critic Menéndez Pidal (1879–1968), a specialist in the literature of the Middle Ages; the political theorist Ramiro de Maeztu (1876–1936); the translator and critic Manuel Azaña (1880–1940); and the renowned art critic and philosopher Eugenio D'Ors (1882–1954). Philosophically, D'Ors is the opposite of Unamuno, and critically, of Ortega y Gasset. Essentially European, a didactic intellectual who exalted classical values, he wrote in many genres, making the *glosa,* or scholarly commentary, particularly his own.

Manuel García Morente (1886–1942), a collaborator in Ortega y Gasset's campaign to introduce significant contemporary European letters and ideas to the Spanish public, was a notable thinker and teacher in his own right.

Other prominent philosophical writers include: Américo Castro (b. 1885), a philologist, historian, linguist, and interpreter of Spanish language, literature, and culture; the politician, essayist, and polemicist Madariaga (q.v.); the novelist and critic Francisco de Cossío (b. 1887); the scientist, historian, sociologist, and interpreter of literature Gregorio Marañón (1888–1970); the aesthetician and historian Antonio Marichalar (b. 1893); the essayist, critic, and translator Ricardo Baeza (1890–1955); the thinker, essayist, and writer of aphorisms and literary doctrine José Bergamín (b. 1894); the critic, essayist, and expert on *tauromaquia* (bullfighting) José Maria de Cossío (b. 1895); the critic, historian, and biographer Melchor Fernández Almagro (1895–1966); the philologist, phoneticist, and critic of poetry Amado Alonso (1896–1952); the art historians and critics J. A. Gaya Nuño and Enrique

Lafuente Ferrari (1898); the theorist of avant-garde movements Ernesto Giménez Caballero (1899); and the political essayist José Antonio Primo de Rivera (1902–1936).

Noteworthy critics are César Barja (1892–1952); Federico Carlos Sainz de Robles (b. 1899); A. Valbuena Prat (b. 1900); Guillermo de Torre (b. 1900); Angel del Río (1900–1968); Bartolomé Mostaza (b. 1907); Ricardo Gullón (b. 1908); and Guillermo Díaz Plaja (b. 1909).

Unamuno and Ortega y Gasset anticipate several aspects of existentialism (q.v.), as in their concern with the inadequacy of reason to explain the enigma of the universe, but Unamuno chooses irrationality (faith) while Ortega y Gasset goes beyond existentialism, attempting to resolve the perennial opposition between reason and "life" (irrationality), creating a dynamic fusion, which he called "vital reason," as described in his *El tema de nuestro tiempo* (1922). For both thinkers, the point of departure is individual human existence, which has no abstract meaning apart from that which man creates.

Unamuno is closer to the Danish philosopher Soren Kierkegaard (1813–55) in that the problem for him is basically religious, comprising a longing for immortality and an anguish at the prospect of death, which he expresses in *El sentimiento trágico de la vida* (1913). As a professor of metaphysics, Ortega y Gasset devoted little attention to the hereafter; his personal involvement is less than Unamuno's, although his concept of *naufragio* ("shipwreck") resembles existential anguish.

Ortega y Gasset and Unamuno avoid the extreme nihilism and hopelessness of some existentialists, concentrating on investing existence with meaning. Unamuno finds meaning in the search itself, in the struggle against eternal mystery (*Mi religión y otros ensayos*, 1910). Ortega y Gasset emphasizes ethical aspects, postulating an imperative of excellence and the preservation of individuality in a mass society (*La rebelión de las masas*, 1930), considering radical solitude and the problematic relation of the individual to the other in his posthumously published *El hombre y la gente* (1957). Ortega y Gasset's concept of history (*Historia como sistema*, 1935) anticipates that of Sartre (q.v.), while his analysis of the lack of effective national leadership, in *España invertebrada* (1921), continues a basic preoccupation of the Generation of '98. Ortega y Gasset's importance as a literary critic and interpreter of other philosophers is likewise considerable.

For the first time since the Middle Ages a philosophical school may be said to exist in Spain. Most of the members of the so-called *escuela de Madrid* have been influenced to some degree by Ortega y Gasset. Perhaps most important is Xavier Zubiri (b. 1898), followed closely by José Luis Aranguren (b. 1909). Aranguren, a professional philosopher especially qualified in theology, represents advanced European Catholic thought. The group includes: José Gaos (b. 1902); the important Catholic thinker and interpreter of Spanish culture Pedro Laín Entralgo (b. 1908); and Julián Marías (b. 1914), a leading interpreter of Ortega y Gasset and the author of other philosophical studies, as well as of penetrating literary criticism. Also important is the teacher and thinker José Ferrater Mora (b. 1909), who has lived outside of Spain for many years.

The work of Ortega y Gasset and Unamuno continues to influence new generations of Spanish intellectuals, and more may be expected from the revival of philosophical thought in the 20th c., particularly in the work of Zubiri and Aranguren.

2. The Theater

The two principal tendencies of 19th-c. drama, the realist (realism and naturalism, q.v.) and the antirealist (neoclassicism, romanticism), continue to exist in varying forms and degrees in the modern Spanish theater. The realist tradition, represented by Pérez Galdós, Benavente y Martínez, Arniches y Barrera, the *costumbristas* (exponents of *costumbrismo*, which is the concern with describing customs of a particular region), the *género chico* (exponents of the short theater piece, often with music, deriving from *costumbrismo*), and Pedro Muñoz Seca, was dominant from 1900 to 1930. The postwar *teatro social*, more successful with critics and intellectuals than with the general public, is a variant of realism-naturalism.

In the antirealistic vein are: José Echegaray y Eizaguirre; the *modernistas*; the cultivators of drama in verse, Marquina and Villaespesa (qq.v.); the lyric theater of the brothers Machado y Ruiz (qq.v.); Jacinto Grau; and aspects of the theater of García Lorca, Casona and Fernando Arrabal. The antirealist tendency, except in the theater of Echegaray and García Lorca, has attracted only a small audience, as has most significant Spanish drama on its first presentation.

José Echegaray y Eizaguirre (1832–1916), a winner of the Nobel Prize in 1904, dominated the last quarter of the 19th c. His dramas, which combined exaggerated romanticism with the presentation of significant ideas, continued to attract the public until well into the 20th c.

Echegaray was followed by Pérez Galdós (q.v.), known as the Spanish Ibsen for his introduction of the drama of ideas in which the individual is shown in conflict with society. Although he is not considered a major dramatist, Pérez Galdós is noted for his use of analytical dialogue and for the psychological content and realistic atmosphere of his plays. Because of his attempt to influence or reform certain aspects of society, the work of Pérez Galdós may be regarded as an antecedent of the *teatro social.*

Benavente y Martínez (q.v.), winner of the Nobel Prize in 1922, represents the antithesis of Echegaray. The action in his dramas is subtle, ironic, and understated, with sly dialogue replacing the cloak-and-sword intrigues. He satirizes the pretentious artificiality of the upper and middle classes, although never so severely as to prevent them from constituting his best audience. Though elegant, malicious, caustic, and clever, he was basically conservative, his criticism nonrevolutionary, and his theater intended primarily for entertainment.

Subordinating theatricality to ideas, and action and character to a mastery of language, Benavente y Martínez inspired a school of imitators, among whom the most important is Gregorio Martínez Sierra (b. 1881). He differs from Benavente y Martínez primarily in his preference for portraying feminine problems and personalities, and in his tendency to sentimentalism.

Arniches y Barrera (q.v.) enjoyed great popularity with the humble people of Madrid, and he presented them as the protagonists of his plays. In the *costumbrista* tradition and independently of Benavente y Martínez's reforms, Arniches y Barrera portrayed the characters, customs, and environment of Madrid, just as the brothers Álvarez Quintero (q.v.) portrayed those of Andalusia. Pedro Muñoz Seca (1881–1931) could be cruel and bitterly sincere in his extravagantly comic farces, exposing the moral bankruptcy of his times.

The experiments of Unamuno, Valle-Inclán,

and Azorín (qq.v.), none of whom was primarily a dramatist, kept Spanish theater in line with the more advanced movements of European literature. Each questioned the nature of reality, attempting to fuse realist and nonrealist currents. Unamuno dealt with the problem of personality, perspectives, and the multiplicity of reality, showing the impossibility of knowing the nature of truth completely. For Unamuno, as for the Italian dramatist Pirandello (q.v.), the identity of character depended on constant creation, leading to a certain amount of metaphysical speculation in his works.

Valle-Inclán attempted to give dramatic representation to the intrinsic values of the essence of Spanish life, which he viewed as a somewhat distorted reflection of European life, particularly as shown in an exaggerated sense of honor, religious fanaticism, and false pride. Believing that this attitude could be conveyed only by systematic deformation, he created the *esperpento,* which has been defined as the presentation of traditional values through a distorting mirror of reality. His work, in its attempt to give a visual representation of the emotion of a situation, showing the internal reality without showing the external appearance, coincides essentially with expressionism (q.v.).

The techniques of another artistic movement, surrealism (q.v.), were first applied to Spanish drama by Azorín, who attempted to use elements of psychoanalysis in his portrayals of dreams and the subconscious (anticipating García Lorca, as did Valle-Inclán in other ways), and in his experiments with time and space.

Jacinto Grau (b. 1887), who wrote most of his works outside of Spain, ignored contemporary reality and produced exquisitely polished plays. His themes are universal and eternal, comprising the great myths and transcendental problems: Don Juan, good and evil, love and death, and human destiny. Grau's lofty, poetic, often archaic language, and his concept of his art as essentially tragic were barriers to popularity. His work, despite excellent literary qualities, is little known and more often read than performed.

García Lorca (q.v.) is regarded as one of the outstanding dramatists of the 20th c. As he drew closer to the advanced views of the Generation of 1925 and developed an increasing interest in expressionistic and surrealistic elements, he turned from a treatment of historical themes to a concern with more universal and timeless ideas. He revived and modernized the chorus of classical tragedy and, by changing from the traditional division by acts to a scheme consisting of several *cuadros*, he gave increased mobility to the action. García Lorca's works, usually placed in rural settings, are characterized by their formal perfection and dramatic intensity. He used lyrical, dynamic dialogue and a variety of symbols and myths, which are strikingly combined with music, dances, and poetry from Andalusian folklore.

In the mature works of García Lorca, characters are primitive, larger than life, and often depersonalized, as in the Mother or the Groom; they may be archetypes or incarnations of such abstract elements as maternal instinct or death. The passions, lyrically or symbolically transformed, are elemental and biological, instinctive, semi- or subconscious, obsessive, and destructive. García Lorca conceived the theater in its totality, writing music, sketching sets, designing scenery, and giving expert attention to the technical aspects of the performance, including costumes, lighting, casting, and direction. He has been called the only Spaniard of the last fifty years who has been fully endowed for the theater. He met his death during the Civil War.

Casona (q.v.), another important innovator, lived, after Franco's victory in the Civil War, in exile in Argentina from 1936 to 1962. Before the Civil War he had cooperated with García Lorca in the program of the Republic for taking the theater to isolated provinces and villages. Both dramatists combined realism with other elements, offered original treatments of eternal themes, and incorporated legend, folklore, and a sense of timelessness in their works. Casona used Asturian customs, songs, children's games, and superstitions, as well as portrayals of witches, devils, and other elements of fantasy and the supernatural. He thus produced a continual interplay of fantasy and reality, mingled with humor and lyricism.

A moralist who dealt repeatedly with the problem of personal happiness, Casona questioned whether it can be found in deceit, escape, or madness, or in an acceptance of reality and responsibility. His mature work, produced in exile, was unknown in Spain until after his return in 1962. Reality always triumphs in his plays, but Casona's work has been classed with the *teatro de evasión* (a pejorative label applied to almost all non-political works), and among contemporary critics favoring *social realismo,* this classifica-

tion has produced an undeserved scorn for a master of theatrical resources.

As is true of the novel and poetry, postwar Spanish drama falls basically into two divisions —the sociopolitical, "committed" theater and the theater with other goals. The goals of the "noncommitted" theater were not necessarily similar or compatible—all dramas that had ends different from those of the "committed" dramas were lumped together because of the lingering belligerence still found just beneath the surface of the Spanish literary scene. The *teatro social* is shown variously as *teatro comprometido, teatro testimonial,* or *teatro de la vida,* while most other works are classed as *teatro de evasión.* "Evasiveness" is the word applied to works wherein the writer is motivated not by his wish to criticize or attempt to change society but by artistic considerations, moral or metaphysical concerns, or the simple desire to entertain. That the categorizing is not simply literary is indicated by the fact that the *teatro social* dramas are usually written by opponents of the present regime and that their works are closely related to their politics.

In the days following the Civil War, the propagandistic *teatro de la victoria* glorified the victors. When the military euphoria faded these dramas gave way to revivals of the classics and of Benavente y Martínez, and contemporary playwrights were subjected to a stricter censorship than that imposed on any other genre. Works with no purpose other than entertainment, or having principally artistic rather than social (political) aims, found easier approval and production. The works usually grouped as *teatro de evasión* include some dramas with admirable artistic qualities, and more intransigent *realismo social* critics have included Casona and even Buero Vallejo in this group. It must be admitted, however, that the most typical *teatro de evasión* is pure meringue, largely conventional and innocuous, typified by the prolific Alfonso Paso (b. 1926), whose popular plays lack artistic stature. Other well-known writers in this group are Luca de Tena (b. 1879); José María Pemán y Pemartín (b. 1898); Edgar Neville (b. 1899); the more talented José López Rubio (b. 1903); Joaquín Calvo Sotelo (b. 1905); and Víctor Ruiz Iriarte (1912). At least one playwright of real talent, Enrique Jardiel Poncela (1901–1952), followed by Miguel Mihura (b. 1906), whose potential talent has not developed fully, anticipated aspects of the theater of the absurd, which subsequently appeared in France and elsewhere.

Among the most significant contemporary Spanish dramatists are Antonio Buero Vallejo, Lauro Olmo (b. 1922), Alfonso Sastre, Ricardo Rodríguez Buded (b. 1930), and Carlos Muñiz (b. 1930). Their works, realistic, critical, and motivated by essential disagreement with prevailing political, social, and economic policy, are limited by government censorship to the "objective" presentation of seemingly non-political situations. (Such plays are performed once in noncommercial theaters, or are being published without performance.) Typical themes of these plays are poverty, inadequate housing or employment, and the demonstration of the ways in which substandard conditions and opportunities rob the individual of his dignity, affect him psychologically, or bring family tragedy. When political problems are treated, the method is indirect, frequently using settings and periods of time far from contemporary Spain.

Antonio Buero Vallejo (b. 1916), who wrote *Historia de una escalera* (1949), is considered the father, but not one of the most extreme proponents, of the *teatro social*. Thoroughly aware of contemporary developments in European theater, he attempted to fuse and adapt them to the Spanish situation.

The other of the two most important postwar Spanish dramatists, Alfonso Sastre (b. 1926), is, like Buero Vallejo, a dramatic theorist, expressing his ideas in numerous articles and lectures, and in several theoretical studies. Although Sastre's work constitutes a moderate revolutionary theater, characterized by necessary and realistic restraint, the performance and even the publication of many of his plays have been prohibited by Franco's censors. Sastre has thus encountered problems similar to those encountered by Buero Vallejo, although Sastre is undoubtedly more of an ideologist. Sastre believes firmly, however, in maintaining the distinction between art and propaganda. Both Buero Vallejo and Sastre, despite the almost total lack of performances of their plays in the past several years, continue to be regarded as the leading postwar theatrical writers in Spain.

The work of Fernando Arrabal (b. 1932), constituting the most notable Spanish contribution to the contemporary theater of the absurd, resembles that of Ionesco and Beckett (qq.v.), and is definitely one of the most interesting of the new dramatic developments. His work has been performed almost entirely outside of Spain, and Arrabal has lived for the last several

years in self-imposed exile in Paris, where he writes in French as a protest against conditions in Spain. Despite his success abroad, his work in his homeland is virtually unknown.

3. Poetry

The two major currents in Spanish poetry after 1900 are the aesthetic and the sociophilosophic. The former is derived from French symbolism (*see* symbolism) and the classic tradition of emphasis on form, a search for ideal beauty, submission to aesthetic formulas, the concept of art as an end in itself, and the flight from everyday reality. The latter is related to romanticism, taking man as its theme and end, emphasizing content, sentiment, and unembellished reality. The overall tendency in the 20th c. is away from aestheticism toward an increasing realism, as exemplified by the evolution of the Generation of 1925.

Certain common characteristics may be found in the works written at the end of the century by such writers as Salvador Rueda (1857–1933), Tomás Morales (1886–1921), Manuel Machado y Ruiz, Díez-Canedo, Jiménez, Valle-Inclán (qq.v.), Emilio Carrère (1880–1947), and in the early works of the Generation of 1925. Despite many differences, these writers are all subjective, depicting not an object but an effect, and seeking musicality, mood, or suggestion rather than exact communication. An art for a small audience, their writing, which is largely abstract, esoteric, enigmatic, and hermetic, is not generally understood.

The mature Antonio Machado y Ruiz, Unamuno (qq.v.), and most postwar poets are relatively objective in that they depict recognizable, sometimes prosaic realities. Their poetry, constituting an art of the masses in which the poet feels a sense of human solidarity, is conceived of as communication, a means to an end, leading to simple, colloquial language, clear meanings, and a certain disdain for "literary" expression.

The influence of *modernismo* in Spain has probably been exaggerated. After all, two of the greatest poets of the century, Unamuno and Antonio Machado y Ruiz, who reacted against it, continue as vital forces more than forty years after the passing of the movement. *Modernismo* affected formal elements, style, and vocabulary. Its themes did not outlive it, while those of Unamuno and Antonio Machado y Ruiz have influenced poetic substance and intent until the present. Unamuno, though not known primarily as a poet, wrote a considerable amount of poetry that is admired by other poets for its intensity. His inspirations are his personal life, the family, national life and history, and religion, which Unamuno rehabilitated as a poetic theme, and which again became important in the poets of the transition from *modernismo* to surrealism (q.v.), and from the Civil War to contemporary social poetry.

Antonio Machado y Ruiz believed firmly in the spoken language as poetic medium and is with Unamuno the most important immediate precursor of the postwar poets. He anticipated García Lorca (q.v.) in the attempt to write a new *romancero,* or collection of legendary tales, and in incorporating elements from popular culture and folklore. His outspoken critical patriotism has likewise inspired much postwar poetry, and his metaphysical preoccupation with time prefigures a preoccupation of contemporary poets. Although all of his poems are collected in only one volume, Antonio Machado y Ruiz is generally regarded as one of the greatest Spanish poets of this or any century, with a magnificently sober and noble expression, a deceptively simple appearance, and a deep, obsessive philosophy of doubt underlying even his "lightest" verses.

Jiménez (q.v.) was extremely sensitive, solitary, of exquisite and cultivated taste. He lived for his art, repeatedly purifying and refining it. The poet of Andalusian landscape, gardens and fountains, delicate melancholy and vague pantheism, he exercised a veritable dictatorship in the years from 1917 to 1930. Although he outlived by some twenty-five years the currents he represented and the school he created, his personal influence should never be underestimated.

A reaction against the superficiality and stylized sentiment of *modernismo* in favor of the irrationality of the subconscious characterized the poets of the Generation of 1925. Among those men were: León Felipe (Camino Galicia, 1884–1968); Basterra (q.v.); José Moreno Villa (1889–1954); Salinas (q.v.); Jorge Guillén (q.v.); Antonio Espina (b. 1894); Diego Cendoya (q.v.); Alonso (q.v.); Juan Chabás (1898–1955); Emilio Prados (b. 1899); Aleixandre (q.v.); Alberti (q.v.); Antonio Oliver (b. 1903); Altolaguirre (q.v.); Cernuda (q.v.); and poet-dramatist García Lorca (q.v.). Attempting to free pure emotion from logical control, they cultivated metaphor extensively and

sought to divorce poetry from logic, in order to lend a sense of mysterious enchantment to their works, which, when further imbued with elements of Freudian psychoanalytic theory, often became difficult to understand. Free association of words, images, and ideas formed an important part of this poetic process, and these poets, without ever reaching the extremes of poetic surrealism that were attained in other parts of Europe, tended strongly enough in that direction to produce several surrealistic volumes, found primarily in the works of Aleixandre, Alberti, and García Lorca. In 1927 these poets revived and rehabilitated the elaborate style derived from the works of the 17th-c. poet Luis de Góngora y Argote (1561–1627). The baroque "angel of darkness" dominated one phase of their development toward increasingly individual and personal modes of expression. Their various phases are epitomized in the work of García Lorca, whose poetry evolved metrically from classic forms to free verse and from the influence of Góngora y Argote and folklore to a cult of the metaphor and surrealism, resulting eventually in his unique tone, which was subjective, pantheistic, mythic, expressionistic (*see* expressionism), and cautiously rebellious.

Alberti, like García Lorca a dramatist and painter, resembles him in using popular elements and Andalusian settings, but differs in temperament, in the greater spontaneity of his early works and the irony of his later work, and in the proletarian elements that characterized much of his verse after 1930. Cernuda and Alonso similarly progress toward the social and humanitarian attitudes of the postwar writers.

Aleixandre, perhaps the greatest Spanish poet of recent years, is essentially romantic in his vital preoccupation with love and death. He made poetry of his most intimate personal experience, from amorous emotion to cosmic thought. Positive and constructive, he used the idea of life as his central motif. His mastery of language has influenced the styles of many younger writers, and he enjoys great popularity and a reputation as the leader of Spanish lyricists.

Although Hernández (q.v.) is considered the poet of the Civil War, most poets of the Generation of 1936 represent a transition between aestheticism and the subsequent sociopolitical themes. Among the leading figures are Carmen Conde (b. 1907), Luis Felipe Vivanco Bergamín (b. 1908), Leopoldo Panero (1909–1962), Luis Rosales (b. 1910), José Luis Cano

(b. 1910), Victoriano Crémer (b. 1910), Gabriel Celaya (pseud. Rafael Múgica, b. 1911), Dionisio Ridruejo (b. 1912), Ildefonso M. Gil (b. 1912), Germán Bleiberg (b. 1915), Blas de Otero (b. 1916), Leopoldo de Luis (b. 1918), José Luis Hidalgo, Rafael Morales (qq.v.), and Vicente Gaos (b. 1919). Less concerned with form and beauty than with human destiny and the economic and religious problems of men, they considered such problems form an individual standpoint, producing the anguished verse of Crémer, Bleiberg, Hidalgo, and Morales, or the more meditative, religious, or philosophic themes of recent books by Gaos and Carlos Bousoño (b. 1923). Younger poets conceive these same problems as collective, within the specific present historical Spanish context. The changing concept of poetry is seen in the dedication of one of Otero's books to the "immense majority," and in Celaya's statement that poetry is not an end in itself, but "an instrument to transform the world." This social protest, dominating the poetry written between 1950 and 1970, reflects the themes of the novel and the theater: social injustice, class problems, and the sufferings and aspirations of men in our time. Numerous poets have followed this fashion to some extent; others have adopted it almost as a religion. Notable in a very large and still evolving group are José Hierro (b. 1922), Eugenio de Nora (b. 1923), José Maria Valverde (b. 1926), Angel Crespo (b. 1926), José Caballero Bonald (b. 1926), José A. Goytisolo (b. 1928), Carlos Barral (b. 1928), José Angel Valente (b. 1929), Jaime Gil de Biedma (b. 1929), Jesús López Pacheco (b. 1930), and Claudio Rodríguez (b. 1934).

These writers characteristically search for the poetic potential in various types of employment, emphasizing the dignity of labor and the beauty of the everyday objects. As in the theater, a more aesthetic countercurrent has also appeared, and the most recent trend seems to be away from the predominantly social poetry; this tendency is best exemplified by such younger poets as Francisco Brines (b. 1934). Because the *poesía social,* despite its altruistic and humanitarian motives, was decidedly opposed to lyricism, it was virtually certain to be of relatively short duration.

4. The Novel

The Spanish novel in the 20th c. has moved through a number of phases, including the early predominance of 19th-c. realism and

naturalism (q.v.); *modernismo*; experiments both individual and of the avant-garde schools (aestheticism, decadence, psychological exploration); a transitional period of humour, and a subsequent return to traditional realism; *tremendismo*; and the present objectivist-"social" groups, with a lesser "evasive" current.

In 1912 Pérez Galdós (q.v.) completed his *Episodios Nacionales,* a series of novels based on the national history of Spain and combining factual and fictional elements. Although much of his popular success occurred before 1900, he continued to have a major influence on subsequent writers during the 20th c., and his later writing has great importance for students of literary theory. Convinced that no real barrier existed between the novel and drama, Pérez Galdós, evoking the classical precedent of the 16th-c. dialogue novel *La Celestina,* adapted some of his novels to the theater, creating a hybrid genre in the form of novels in dialogue without descriptive and narrative elements. Although these works, with their attempt to penetrate deeply into human psychology, are different in intent from the narrative works of the *objetivista* style, the results in both genres are often strikingly similar.

A modified naturalism, combined with a defense of the doctrines of the French novelist Zola (q.v.), was introduced into Spain by Emilia de Pardo Bazán (q.v.). Although she wrote most of her narratives of Galician life before 1900, she continued to be a controversial literary figure throughout the early part of the 20th c. Palacio Valdéz (q.v.), a late exponent of *costumbrismo,* blends good humor and an attempt at psychological analysis with an occasional outmoded romanticism.

A stronger personality is evident in the novels of Blasco-Ibáñez (q.v.), who carried naturalism to Valencian settings for his tales of violence and passion. With relatively little style or culture, he displayed a brilliant imagination, and despite the low esteem of his contemporaries, he is one of the best-known Spanish novelists internationally.

Material resembling that of Blasco-Ibáñez was used by Felipe Trigo (1865–1916), who wrote mostly of sexual problems, attacking the morality of his time. The erotic novel of the period, popular until about 1930, is also represented by such writers as Pedro Mata (1875–1946); the prolific R. López de Haro (b. 1867); A. Insúa (b. 1883), with his mystic, pansexual primitivism; and Antonio de Hoyos (1885–

1940), who offers a sometimes brilliant, malicious chronicle of society.

The *nivolas* of Unamuno (q.v.) were significant experiments that excluded realistic description and environmental detail and concentrated on dialogue, action, and character. In his much-discussed *Niebla* (1914), an analytical and intellectual work that is more ideological than fictional, he questions the relationship of literary character and creator, or mortality and immortality. His *Abel Sánchez* (1917) analyzes the problems of envy, personality, and identity. The questioning of man's destiny, and the examination of the negative possibilities of family life and of the conflict between will and circumstance continue in Unamuno's searching narratives, culminating in the religio-philosophical *San Manuel Bueno, Mártir* (1930). Here the principal virtue of the protagonist is his self-sacrificing struggle to maintain the faith that he himself lacks.

In the four *Sonatas* (1902–1905) of Valle-Inclán (q.v.), a *modernista* perfection of style and a refined, decadent sensuality are combined with human, natural, and cultural elements of great beauty. This initial aestheticism evolved through three novels of the Carlist wars (1908–1910), mingling historical interest with a rather sentimental defense of the monarchical loyalties of Carlism, to *Tirano Banderas* (1926) and *El ruedo ibérico*, which used the stylized deformation and the systematic degradation of reality characteristic of the *esperpento.*

From 1900 until his death in 1956, Pío Baroja y Nessi (q.v.) published almost seventy novels and numerous other works. One of the most important Spanish novelists of the 20th c., he has been considered leftist, anarchist, and revolutionary, but the elements of anarchy and pessimism in his writing, as well as his negative criticism of traditional Spain, were combined with an intense moral skepticism. His views of human egoism and cowardice are therefore so cynical that such a label as "revolutionary" seems inappropriate for his work. His style, criticized as careless, monotonous, and grammatically imperfect, is nevertheless clear, rapid, and precise. Baroja y Nessi conceived the novel as multiform and formless, an indefinable genre in which anything could be attempted. His novels are loosely constructed, with few unified plots and often without even a protagonist or narrative continuity. The unifying factors in his novels are style, environment, rhythm, preference for action, and a rather uniform psychology. His "heroes," though surprisingly real, lack tenacity, will, and psychic depth, and are often frustrated, maladjusted, and impotent. His most popular works are *La busca* (1904), *Mala hierba* (1904), *Aurora roja* (1905), *Paradox, Rey* (1906), *El árbol de la ciencia* (1911), and *El mundo es ansí* (1912).

The experimental novels of Azorín (q.v.) consist almost entirely of description and evocation, lacking action but achieving a sense of movement through variations in descriptive technique. His characters, settings, and time periods, however, often seem to exist without motion. Although Azorín's novels are sentimentally inhibited, with little psychological change and a relative lack of vigor, they are pervaded by a gentle, contemplative melancholy and transparent beauty. The best of his novelistic technique may be found in *Doña Inés* (1925), although some critics believe that *La isla sin aurora* (1944), one of the few examples of surrealism (q.v.) applied to the Spanish novel, is of greater theoretical significance.

Manuel Ciges Aparicio (1873–1936), once much esteemed for his political authenticity, and for his moral and aesthetic qualities, is now largely forgotten, as is López Pinillos (1865–1922), a possible precursor of *tremendismo*. The prolific Ricardo León (1877–1943) was a facile, sentimental defender of throne, church, and tradition. The works of the novelist and poetess Concha Espina (q.v.), although conventional in prose, technique, and ideology, were distinguished by her compassion and sensitivity, especially in her defenses of Spanish womanhood and in *El metal de los muertos* (1920), an undogmatic anticipation of contemporary themes of social problems and conflict. Emilio Moreno Carrere (1881–1947) peculiarly continued *costumbrismo* and the picaresque, exalting misery, prostitution, and the "innocent" vice of the demimonde of Madrid.

The stylistic preoccupations of *modernismo*, as well as Azorín's timelessness and static effects, are combined with the aesthetic concerns of the Generation of 1925 in the work of Miró (q.v.). A much-translated prose master, he displays a love of landscape in his novels, which are characterized by melancholy and sensualism and by exquisite audible, visible, and tangible impressions. Miró's work generally lacks ideas, however, and offers little passion or excitement.

Pérez de Ayala (q.v.) created a literary

scandal with *A.M.D.G.* (1910), a cruel vision of life in a Jesuit school, combining characteristic irony and cynicism with an early enthusiasm for Galdosian realism. Intellectual, didactic, and moralistic, he fused local color with myths, joined analysis and symbol, and excelled in the interpretation of vacillation and insecurity. His *Belarmino y Apolonio* (1921) is an experiment with multiple narrative viewpoints, simultaneous action, and contrapuntal technique. After *Tigre Juan* (1926) and *El curandero de su honra* (1926), this talented innovator inexplicably lapsed into almost complete literary silence.

Eugenio Noel (pseud. of Muñoz; 1885–1936) was anticlerical, antiflamenco, and antitorero, with a flair for the picaresque and the macabre. His contemporary Fernández Flórez (q.v.), much read in Europe, is often neglected by Spanish critics. Usually dismissed as a humorist, he is a complex and original writer who combines naturalism, political satire, and fleeting lyricism with bitter, skeptical, virulent humor and caricature. His most typical and best-known works are *El secreto de Barba Azul* (1923) and *Las siete columnas* (1926).

The leader of avant-garde rebellion in Spain from 1911 to 1936 was Gómez de la Serna (q.v.), who wrote plays, chronicles, criticism, biography, and autobiography (*Automoribundia*, 1948), as well as novels. His special creation is the axiomatic *greguería*, which he defined as humor plus metaphor. His work, which apparently ignores social, moral, and political problems, is fragmentary and chaotic, "reflecting the disorder of the world," but shows exceptional linguistic vitality and was extremely influential. The talent of another innovator, Jarnés (q.v.), was obscured by his literary ambitions. He produced the "dehumanized" narrative of the Generation of 1925, a morbid, voluptuous confusion of formal brilliance, sensual imagery, and metaphors that retard action, obscure character, and make his work difficult to understand. Other aesthetic experiments include: the lyrical, symbolic, and psychological writings of Mario Verdaguer (b. 1893); the dehumanized, fragmentary novel of Antonio Espina (b. 1894); the lyrical narrative of Claudio de la Torre (b. 1898); and the introspective, evocative monologue of Rosa Chacel (b. 1898), a disciple of Ortega y Gasset (q.v.).

Mostly superficial novels of humour, sprinkled with *costumbrismo,* fill the transitional early postwar period, during which Edgar Neville (b. 1899), A. Robles (b. 1897), and

Miguel Villalonga (1899–1947) achieved a limited literary merit. Antonio Botín Polanco (b. 1898) and Samuel Ros (b. 1905) combine the avant-garde and humor. A return to Galdosian realism is seen in the works of B. Soler (b. 1894), blending vigor, pathos, and elemental passion with local color and Catalan country dialect. Similar traditional elements are perceptible in Rafael Sánchez Mazas (b. 1894); Huberto Pérez de la Ossa (b. 1897); Ledesma Miranda (b. 1901); and Zunzunegui y Laredo (q.v.). The latter, probably the foremost exponent of traditional critical realism in the postwar era, wrote voluminous accounts of economic and industrial change in the north (Bilbao), and precisely observed neopicaresque chronicles of Madrid (*La vida como es,* 1954). Despite some bitter humor and caricature, his works are generally valuable historical documents. Other traditional realists are S. J. Arbó (b. 1902); Manuel Halcón (b. 1903), with his novels of rural Andalusia; José Antonio Giménez Arnau (b. 1912); the more talented and original Angel María de Lera (b. 1912), who has moved closer to the socialist realists; and Ignacio Agustí (b. 1913), with his notable trilogy on prewar Barcelona, *La ceniza fue árbol* (1944–45 and 1957).

The exiles were for the most part originally traditional realists, obsessed by the war, as in the much-translated trilogy of Arturo Barea (1897–1958), *La forja de un rebelde* (first Spanish edition, 1951); the novelistic cycle *El laberinto mágico* of Max Aub (b. 1902); *La cabeza del cordero* (1949) of Francisco Ayala (b. 1906); and the narratives of Segundo Serrano Poncela (b. 1912). Most prolific of the exiles was Ramón Sender (q.v.), who combined fiction and reporting in his prewar novels (*Imán,* 1930; *Siete domingos rojos,* 1932), which were motivated by revolutionary combativeness. Autobiographical elements appear in his later work, including memories of childhood (*Crónica del alba,* 1942) and adolescence (*El lugar de un hombre,* 1939), and the obsession with the Civil War (*Contraataque,* 1938; *El rey y la reina,* 1947; and the masterful *Cinco libros de Ariadna,* 1957). Most exiles dwell on their memories of an earlier era in Spain, as in the works of M. Andújar (b. 1913) and in Aub's recreations of Madrid, which are permeated by nostalgia and the problematic return. Ayala progresses to criticism of the new and alien environment in *Muertes de perro* (1958), while Aub transcends purely Spanish problems to confront the tragedy of the Jewish prisoners in concentration camps, as well as other catastrophes of modern life.

The Civil War is also an obsession for novelists inside Spain, where the need to understand it has produced almost four hundred novels, which are often more an expression of conflicting passions or attempts to convince than literature as such. If published in Spain, such novels are usually attempts to justify the Nationalist revolt, although there are some milder efforts to review the years of strife from a nonpartisan (implicitly leftist) perspective. Strongly pro-Republican works, of course, could only appear outside of Spain. In addition to these works dealing primarily with the war there are many others in which the conflict serves as background. Notable among those treating the conflict *per se* is *Madrid de Corte a Checa* (1938) of Agustín de Foxá (1903–1959). Of equal worth, though written from a strongly Nationalist viewpoint, are *La fiel infantería* (1943) and *Plaza del castillo* (1951) by Rafael García Serrano (b. 1917). Other outstanding novels were written by Paulino Masip (b. 1900); Herrera Pétere (b. 1919); Mercedes Fórmica (b. 1916), and Emilio Romero (b. 1917).

Most famous of the works attempting to explain the war from a supposedly objective viewpoint (but with an evident conservative bias) is the ten-year study of prewar Gerona by José María de Gironella (b. 1917) whose *Los cipreses creen en Dios* (1953) is considered superior to its sequel, *Un millón de muertos* (1961), which deals with the conflict proper in a rather journalistic manner. While unable to be as overtly critical of the Nationalists as the writers in exile, notable studies of the Civil War have been written from an opposition stance by Ana María Matute (b. 1926), whose *Las luciérnagas* was prohibited by the censors and published in an expurgated edition as *En esta tierra* (1955). This was a prelude to her magnificent novel dealing with some thirty years before, during and after the conflict, *Los hijos muertos* (1958).

De Nora's *La novela española contemporánea* (1962) lists over two hundred new postwar novelists, providing only a selection among many working writers. The historical novel is represented by Alejandro Núñez Alonso (b. 1908), with a voluminous cycle on the Roman empire during the time of Christ, and by the *Episodios nacionales contemporáneos* of

Ricardo Fernández de la Reguera (b. 1912) and his poetess-wife, Susana March (b. 1918). The picaresque reappears, not only in novels, but in the spirit and environment of travel books, whose authors often make walking pilgrimages through the poorest regions of Spain. Generally realistic, but more artistic or philosophical than the writers of the *objectivista-realista social* school are Elizabeth Mulder (b. 1904), Eulalia Galvarriato (b. 1905), Eusebio García Luengo (b. 1919), Manuel Pombo Angulo (b. 1912), Mercedes Ballesteros (b. 1912), José Suárez Carreño (b. 1914), José Luis Sampedro (b. 1917), Pedro de Lorenzo (b. 1917), and Rosa M. Cajal (b. 1920).

The postwar movement known as *tremendismo,* so called because of the "tremendous" horrified reaction that it was intended to produce, derives partly from naturalism, partly from Baroja y Nessi's thematic and structural influence, and partly from the classic tradition of the picaresque, in the vein of the 17th-c. satirist Francisco Gómez de Quevedo y Villegas (1580–1645). A much imitated work, *La familia de Pascual Duarte* (1942) by Cela (q.v.), typifies the *tremendismo* of environment and events, while *Nada* (1945) by Carmen Laforet (b. 1921) represents a more psychological strain of *tremendismo,* as does her second novel, *La isla y los demonios* (1952). Cela, less often considered a novelist than a caricaturist and stylist or a negative aesthetician of the *esperpento,* is a tireless experimenter with form and technique, a creator of numerous though incomplete characters. *La colmena* (1951), probably his masterpiece, influenced many younger writers in their choice of environment, types, and technique. A similar work, also lacking plot and protagonist, is *La noria* (1952) of Luis Romero (b. 1916). Also somewhat in the *tremendista* vein is José Luis Castillo Puche (b. 1919), an imitator of Hemingway (q.v.).

G. Torrente Ballester (b. 1910), also a critic, is a novelist primarily in the psychological vein, whether analyzing an individual or a provincial town, as in his trilogy *Los gozos y las sombras* (1957–62). Another adherent of psychological experimentation and investigation, Elena Quiroga has utilized a different form and technique in each of her novels to date, steadily maturing and improving. *Algo pasa en la calle* (1954) and *Tristura* (1962) exemplify varying aspects of her best production.

Two of the leading contemporary Spanish novelists, Delibes (q.v.) and Ana María Matute

341

have remained independent of *tremendismo* and *objetivismo,* at least from a technical standpoint, while influenced by the prevailing climate of protest. From thoroughly traditional beginnings, Delibes, novelist of Castilla, has produced veritable masterpieces in *El camino* (1950), *La hoja roja* (1959), and *Las ratas* (1963). He is also important as a recorder of regional dialogue and linguistic peculiarities, especially in such prize-winning works as *Diario de un cazador* (1958). He has recently departed from his initial style to a more subjective, psychological approach in his two latest novels, *Cinco horas con Mario* (1967) and *Parábola del naúfrago* (1970). Perhaps Ana María Matute's most significant effort is her trilogy *Los mercaderes* (*Primera memoria,* 1959; *Los soldados lloran de noche,* 1964; and *La trampa,* 1969), in which she subtly criticizes and exposes bourgeois values and conformity. Ana María Matute is more subjective, more of a stylist than Delibes, and occasionally given to lyric fantasy, as in *Tres y un sueño* (1961), but she has also written a massive and highly honored interpretation of the causes and effects of the Civil War in *Los hijos muertos* (1958). She is also one of the most important cultivators of children's literature in Spain.

Objetivismo, appearing about 1955, follows Robbe-Grillet (q.v.) and the French *nouveau roman,* striving to eliminate all subjective interpretations and evaluations by the author in favor of a reproduction of reality similar to that achieved in motion pictures. The *objetivistas,* who are usually far left politically and vaguely existentialist in philosophy, abstain from psychological probing, describing only external phenomena, as exemplified in *El Jarama* (1956) by Sánchez Ferlosio (q.v.). The objectivity of the school is often merely apparent; most of its members are committed to the social criticism and politico-economic reform that frequently served as goals for the neorealist writers of the *novela social.* Among the more talented, successful, or prolific representatives of these latest tendencies are: the popular, altruistic Dolores Medio (b. ca. 1920); intellectual Ignacio Aldecoa (b. 1925), the best stylist of the generation; F. Candell (b. 1925); A. Ferres (b. 1925); Carmen Martín Gaite (b. 1925); Armando López Salinas (b. 1925); Rafael Azcona (b. 1926); Jesús Fernández Santos (b. 1926); García Hortelano (b. 1928); M. Arce (b. 1928); Alfonso Grosso (b. 1928); Juan Goytisolo (b. 1931), a belligerent ideologist who has shown an increasingly

analytical approach in his extremely difficult novel *Señas de identidad* (1968). Also worthy of mention are D. Sueiro (b. 1931); Ramón Nieto (b. 1934); and Luis Goytisolo Gay (b. 1935).

Resembling the postwar poets and dramatists in their purposes, all of these writers typify the strengths and weaknesses of a large portion of the most recent Spanish literature. Their work is characterized by a progressive humanitarianism and a considerable documentary value, although it is flawed by occasional monotony. Two works of outstanding significance in the evolution of the postwar novel are *Tiempo de silencio* (1962) by Luis Martín Santos (1916–1964), and the previously mentioned *Señas de identidad* of Juan Goytisolo. Both novels are obvious attempts to transcend the pseudo-objective forms, without renouncing many of the inherent critical aims of the writers of the postwar period. Like the *teatro social* and *poesía social,* the *novela social* seems to have given the best that it had to give, and authors in all of these genres appear presently to be exploring new means of expression.

BIBLIOGRAPHY: Madariaga, S. de., *Spain* (1930); Diego, G., *Poesía española: Antología; Contemporáneos* (2nd ed., 1934); Barja, C., *Libros y autores contemporáneos* (1935); González Ruíz, N., *La literatura española, siglo XX* (1943); *Contemporary Spanish Poets* (1945); Laín Entralgo, P., *La generación del '98* (1945); Domenchina, J. J., *Antología de la poesía española contemporánea, 1900–1936* (2nd ed., 1946); Río, A. del, *El concepto contemporáneo de España* (1946); *Diccionario de la literatura española* (1949); García Bacca, J., *Nueve grandes filósofos contemporáneos y sus temas* (1949); Brenan, G., *The Literature of the Spanish People* (1951); Díaz Plaja, G., *Modernismo frente a '98* (1951); Baroja, R., *Gentes del '98* (1952); Chabás, J., *Literatura española contemporánea: 1898–1950* (1952); Sastre, A., *Drama y sociedad* (1956); Castellet, J. M., *La hora del lector* (1957); Cernuda, L., *Estudios sobre poesía española contemporánea* (1957); Pérez Minik, D., *Novelistas españoles de los siglos XIX y XX* (1957); Saínz de Robles, F. C., *La novela española en el siglo XX* (1957); Vivanco, L. F., *Introducción a la poesía española contemporánea* (1957); Alborg, J. L., *Hora actual de la novela española* (2 vols., 1958–62); Alonso, D., *Poetas españoles contemporáneos* (1958); Baquero Goyanes, M., *Problemas de la novela contemporánea* (1958); Cano, J. L., *Antología de la nueva poesía española* (1958); Nora, E. G. de, *La novela española contemporánea* (3 vols., 1958–62); Cardona, R., *Novelistas españoles de hoy* (1959); Cossío J. M. de, *Cincuenta años de poesía española* (1960); Eoff, S. H., *The Modern Spanish Novel* (1961); Zardoya, C., *Poesía española contemporánea* (1961); García Pavón, F., *Teatro social en España* (1962); Baquero Goyanes, M., *Proceso de la novela actual* (1963); Marra López, J. R., *Narrativa española fuera de España, 1939–1961* (1963); Río, A. del, *Historia de la literatura española,* Vol. II (2nd ed., 1963); Sastre, A. *Anatomía del realismo* (1965); Torre, G. de, *Historia de las literaturas de vanguardia* (1965); Castellet, J. M., *Un cuarto de siglo de poesía española* (1967); Valbuena Prat, A., *Historia de la literatura española,* Vol. IV (4th ed., 1968); Zardoya, C., *Poesía española del '98 y del '27* (1968); Schwartz, K., *The Meaning of Existence in Contemporary Hispanic Literature* (1969); Torrente Ballester, G., *Panorama de la literatura española contemporánea* (4th ed., 1969); Torrente Ballester, G., *Teatro español contemporáneo* (2nd ed., 1969)

JANET WINECOFF DÍAZ

SPARK, Muriel Camberg

English novelist, short-story writer, poet, critic, and biographer, b. 1918, Edinburgh

Early in her career Muriel S. worked on a trade magazine for the precious stone industry, was associated with the Poetry Society, and edited *The Poetry Review* (1947–49). Her first volume of poems, *The Fanfarlo and Other Verse,* appeared in 1952. During this time she explored scholarly interests that prefigure her continuing preoccupation with the dilemma of man's inherent duality. Her conception of the "passion of the intellect" served as her critical tool in *Child of Light: A Reassessment of Mary Shelley* (1951) and in *Emily Brontë, Her Life and Works* (with Derek Stanford; 1953). In 1954 she became a Roman Catholic; in 1957 her edition (with Stanford) of the *Letters of John Henry Newman* was published. Since 1957, also the year in which her first novel, *The Comforters,* appeared, Muriel S. has devoted her talents mainly to the writing of fiction. Her reputation has grown steadily, and she has received numerous honors (*e.g.,* Fellow of the Royal Society of Literature, 1963; Officer of the Order of the British Empire, 1967).

Although her early novels were often criticized as being sportive, even frothy, Muriel S.'s wit invited comparison with Ivy Compton-Burnett and Evelyn Waugh (qq.v.). In 1960 a *Times Literary Supplement* reviewer (14 Oct.) pointed out that even when her characters were "improbably sinister," they were also "larger than life and much funnier." She regularly exploits eccentric personalities participating in odd events, but they are artfully arranged on a "collision course" which permits her relentless logic to expose simultaneously the laughable trivialities of behavior and the darker motives of the soul.

Muriel S.'s fiction is consistently notable for its polished surface and brilliant dialogue. Particularly notable for this excellence is *Memento Mori* (1959), a tale of aged persons reminiscing and revealing inadvertently their earlier, "animal" selves (adapted for the stage in 1964).

Even more successful was *The Prime of Miss Jean Brodie* (1961), adapted for the stage in 1966 and made into a motion picture in 1969. The basis of the novel is the relationship over a decade between six favorite pupils, who comprise the "set" and the dominating person who is their unorthodox teacher in a conservative Edinburgh girls' school. Miss Brodie's "educational policy" is typified in her statement: "Safety does not come first. Goodness, Truth, and Beauty come first. Follow me." The novel's wry disclosure of the teacher's betrayal by the pupil she had considered "most dependable" is also a ruthless exposure of a woman's own self-deception.

In *The Public Image* (1968) Muriel S. continues to probe the mysteries of appearance and reality, of identity and self-knowledge, in a taut portrait of a woman who comes to believe the publicity that surrounds her as a famous movie star.

Her moral imagination, operating within the framework of Catholic belief, can at times lend considerable power to Muriel S.'s explorations of the problems of conscience. At her best, the accuracy of thought and word she displays is that of the poet, the wit that of the skeptic.

FURTHER WORKS: *John Masefield* (1953); *Robinson* (1958); *The Go-Away Bird, and Other Stories* (1958); *The Ballad of Peckham Rye* (1960); *The Bachelors* (1960); *Voices at Play* (1961); *Doctors of Philosophy: A Play* (1963); *The Girls of Slender Means* (1963); *The Mandelbaum Gate* (1965); *Collected*

Stories I (1967); *Collected Poems I* (1967); *A Very Fine Clock* (1968)

BIBLIOGRAPHY: Hynes, S., "The Prime of M. S.," *Commonweal,* LXXV (1962), 562–68; Schneider, H., "A Writer in Her Prime: The Fiction of M. S.," *Critique,* V (Fall 1962), 28–45; Stanford, D., *M. S.: A Biographical and Critical Study* (1963); Potter, N., "M. S.: Transformer of the Commonplace," *Renaissance and Modern Studies,* XVII (Spring 1965), 115–20; Wildman, J., in *Nine Essays in Modern Literature,* ed. D. Stanford (1965); Fay, B., "M. S. en sa fleur," *NRF,* XIV (Feb. 1966), 307–15; Grosskurth, P., "The World of M. S.: Spirits or Spooks?" *Tamarack Review,* No. 39 (1966), pp. 62–67; Berthoff, W., "Fortunes of the Novel: M. S. and Iris Murdoch," *Massachusetts Review,* VIII (Summer 1967), 301–32; Greene, G., "A Reading of M. S.," *Thought,* XL (1968), 393–407

VERGENE F. LEVERENZ

SPENDER, Stephen

English poet and critic, b. 28 Feb. 1909, near London

Educated at University College, Oxford, S. came to be associated with other writers then at Oxford—Auden, Day Lewis, and MacNeice (qq.v.). These were linked chiefly by the dominant influence of Auden on subject matter and imagery and by a shared social consciousness in reaction to the antipolitical writers of the 1920's. During his years at Oxford S. traveled much in Germany. His acquaintance with German literature resulted in translations of Schiller's *Mary Stuart,* Rilke's (q.v.) poetry (with J. B. Leishman), and Toller's (q.v.) play *Pastor Hall.*

S.'s first volume of poetry, *Nine Experiments* (1928), was followed by *Twenty Poems* (1930) and *Poems* (1933), which established his reputation. These express his persistent beliefs that the poet must realize in concrete images things of his most personal life that are also significant to the public world, and that the imagination has power to move events. Thus when his lyrics make their strongest plea for individualism, they most embody a profound commitment to social action.

In *The Destructive Element* (1935) S. analyzes the work of James, Eliot, Joyce (qq.v.), and others for their concern with factors threatening civilization. Shortly after the publication of *Forward from Liberalism* (1937) he became a communist, but his writings and talks stressing individual responsibility as opposed to doctrinaire policy kept him in disrepute with English communists. The International Writers' Conference which he attended in Spain in 1937 provided him with material for a story, *Engaged in Writing* (1958), satirizing such conferences as a dissipation of creative energies.

A volume of poems, *The Still Centre* (1939), renews with irregular success his attempt to give private images universal significance. In subject they reveal his continuing search for a faith to live by. Co-editorship of *Horizon* with Cyril Connolly (q.v.) in 1939 ended two years later in disagreement over editorial policy, with S. a strong advocate for encouraging new writers. From this time until the end of the war he was a fireman in the National Fire Service, stationed in London. After the war he traveled widely. *European Witness* (1946), a report on his trip to the British-occupied zone of Germany, analyzes the condition of the German intellectual under Hitler. *Learning Laughter* (1952) is an account of his observations in Israel. In 1953 he joined with Irving Kristol to edit the magazine *Encounter.*

S.'s search for the relationship between private belief and public conduct took him in 1968 to Prague, Berlin, Paris, and New York to speak with the student demonstrators. His report on that journey, *The Year of the Young Rebels* (1969), concludes with an analysis of the changing role of the university as it shapes and is shaped by youthful activists. In 1970, S. continued his long association with universities by accepting a chair in English literature at University College in London.

S. has represented in his writings and activities the self-analysis and quest for certainty characteristic of midcentury thought. He has described himself as an autobiographer restlessly searching for forms in which to express the stages of his development. An autobiography of candid introspection, *World within World* (1951), expresses his view that the only true hope for civilization is the individual's belief that his inner life can affect outward events. This sense of individual responsibility, which underlay S.'s repudiation of communism, accounts in part for his continuing influence, beyond his poetry, in lectures and essays.

FURTHER WORKS: *Vienna* (1934); *The Burning Cactus* (1936); *Trial of a Judge* (1938); *The Backward Son* (1940); *Ruins and*

STEPHEN SPENDER

CARL SPITTELER

Visions (1942); *Life of the Poet* (1942); *Citizens in War and After* (1945); *Poems of Dedication* (1946); *The Edge of Being* (1949); *The Creative Element* (1953) *Collected Poems* (1954); *The Making of a Foem* (1955); *The Struggle of the Modern* (1963); *Selected Poems* (1965)

BIBLIOGRAPHY: MacNeice, L., *Modern Poetry* (1938); Seif, M., "The Influence of T. S. Eliot on Auden and S.," *South Atlantic Quarterly*, LIII (1954), 61–69; "A Poetry of Search," *TLS*, 28 Jan. 1955, p. 56; Jacobs, W. D., "The Moderate Poetical Success of S. S.," *CE*, XVII (1956), 374–78; Maxwell, D. E. S., *Poets of the Thirties* (1969)

MANLY JOHNSON

SPITTELER, Carl

Swiss poet, epic and narrative writer, essayist, dramatist, and critic, b. 24 April 1845, Liestal; d. 24 Dec. 1924, Lucerne

Son of a high state official, S. became a Protestant minister, though he was to become a freethinking atheist early in life. Giving up his parsonage at the age of twenty-two, he spent the years 1871–79 as a tutor and teacher in Russia and Finland. Returning to Switzerland in 1880, he took up a teaching position in Berne and subsequently became an editor of the *Neue Zürcher Zeitung*. An inheritance from his wife's parents gave him financial independence, permitting him to devote himself exclusively to his writing.

S. is known for more than his epics; his melodious and often moving poetry, his masterful naturalistic stories, and his profound literary criticism must not be forgotten. Yet despite his great achievements, the impact of his work has been minimal. Germany hardly took notice of it, and even in Switzerland its reception was cool. The award of the Nobel Prize in 1919 for his *Olympischer Frühling* (1900–1905) made him world-famous, but only briefly.

Prometheus und Epimetheus (1881; Eng., 1931) combines the elements of the epos and the novel. The ancient myth, still in classical guise, is freely transformed into a modern allegory. Prometheus, whose name signifies foresight, is contrasted in his sincere human striving with Epimetheus's retrospective, cautious timidity and eager practicality. S.'s gigantic mythical creation symbolizes the suffering of the great in the shrunken world of the small-minded. S. lets Prometheus, after

tragic suffering, soar aloft to the superhuman, to the realm of the soul, for he alone can comprehend the divine.

A variation of this work is S.'s *Prometheus der Dulder* (1924). The subject matter is that of the earlier epic. One being, however, a work of his youth, the other of his old age, they differ greatly in style.

Olympischer Frühling is a poetic cosmogony filled with fantasy, ideas, and episodes. The gods of antiquity, Christianity, and the Far East blend with religious concepts of our time. A pessimism of cosmic proportions is the sinister background of this highly imaginative allegory. Only rarely (Apollo, Heracles) is inexorable fate conquered. What is human in all its vulnerability is heightened in the life of the gods.

Many of S.'s writings are of a very high order, particularly *Imago* (1906), after which Sigmund Freud (1856–1939) named his psychoanalytical periodical, and the autobiographical *Meine frühesten Erlebnisse* (1914). Today S. is, undeservedly, almost forgotten. His allegorical epics have marked him as a great writer, one completely and deliberately out of tune with his time, an incarnation of his own rejection of his age.

FURTHER WORKS: *Extramundana* (1883); *Der Parlamentär* (1889); *Schmetterlinge* (1889); *Friedli der Kolderi* (1891); *Literarische Gleichnisse* (1892); *Gustav* (1892); *Der Ehrgeizige* (1892); *Balladen* (1896); *Der Gotthard* (1897); *Lachende Wahrheiten* (1898; Laughing Truths, 1927); *Conrad, der Leutnant* (1898); *Glockenlieder* (1906); *Gerold und Hansli, die Mädchenfeinde* (1907; The Little Misogynists, 1923); *Meine Beziehungen zu Nietzsche* (1908); *Rede über Gottfried Keller* (1919); *Briefwechsel mit A. Frey* (1933); *Gesammelte Werke* (11 vols., 1945–58); *Klassiker der Kritik* (1965); *Kritische Schriften* (1965). **Selected English translation:** *Selected Poems* (1928)

BIBLIOGRAPHY: Widmer, M., *Die Götter in S.'s "Olympischem Frühling"* (1963); Baur, P., *Zur Bewertung von S.'s Poesie* (1964); Cicero, V. L., "A Reappraisal of S.'s View of Schopenhauer," *GR*, XXXIX (1964), 37–49; Rommel, O., *S.'s "Olympischer Frühling" und seine epische Form* (1965); Stauffacher, W., "S.," in *Proceedings of the IV Congress of the International Comparative Literature Association*, ed. F. Jost, II (1966), 888–96

* * * *

STAFFORD, Jean
American novelist and short-story writer, b. 1 July 1915, Covina, California

Raised and educated in Colorado, Jean S. spent a year in Germany after college. After returning to the United States she taught in Missouri and wrote for the *Southern Review* in Louisiana. She has lived in almost every geographical region of the United States.

The art of Jean S. is distinguished by a carefully disciplined, flexible style that permits her imagination to draw from widely varied places and persons an essential vision of human aspirations and the incongruous reality that so frequently betrays them. Her first novel, *Boston Adventure* (1944), was immediately a popular and critical success. Her story of the daughter of an impoverished immigrant family who is introduced to Beacon Hill society is humanely compassionate and socially irreverent.

The Mountain Lion (1947), set in Colorado, focuses sharply upon a complex awareness of good and evil, innocence and experience, dawning in the consciences of a brother and sister who are inseparable in childhood and adolescence. In *The Catherine Wheel* (1952) the milieu once again is New England, treated with the elegance of style that has more than once caused Jean S. to be compared to Edith Wharton (q.v.).

The short story has remained Jean S.'s most consistently satisfying medium, providing in its relatively small framework and intense concentration a vehicle peculiarly appropriate to her penetrating yet delicate insights. Since 1944 her stories have appeared in such diverse periodicals as *The New Yorker, Harper's, Atlantic Monthly, Kenyon Review, Partisan Review, Sewanee Review,* and *Mademoiselle.* She received the O. Henry Prize in 1955.

In *The Collected Stories of J. S.* (1969) the range of her short fiction is made particularly apparent by her own arrangement of the stories into geographical groupings. Stories delineating Americans abroad echo experiences of the sort Henry James (q.v.) described, and with something of his sense of "dislocation," as Jean S. herself calls it. Her view of the American scene ranges from decadent proprieties of Boston and its latter-day tea parties to the open freedom and astringent air of the Rocky Mountains. But the overriding impressions are made by the people who animate her scenes; none can be easily or simply described in a word, yet each is indelible in his fictional being.

Her brilliant style coupled with a peculiarly satiric sense of the human scene has brought Jean S. high regard from many discriminating readers.

FURTHER WORKS: *Children Are Bored on Sunday* (1953); *Elephi, the Cat with a High I.Q.* (1962); *Bad Characters* (1964); *A Mother in History* (1966)

BIBLIOGRAPHY: Vickery, O., "The Novels of J. S.," *Crit,* V (Spring-Summer 1962), 14–26; Vickery, O., "J. S. and the Ironic Vision," *South Atlantic Quarterly,* LXI (Autumn 1962), 484–91; Mazzaro, J., "Remembrances of Things Proust," *Shenandoah,* XVI (Summer 1965), 114–17; Greiner, C., "S.'s 'Traveling Through the Dark': A Discussion of Style," *EJ,* LV (1966), 1015–18, 1048; Burns, S., "Counterpoint in J. S.'s *The Mountain Lion,*" *Crit,* IX (1967), ii, 20–32

VERGENE F. LEVERENZ

STEIN, Gertrude
American novelist, poet, dramatist, and critic, b. 31 Feb. 1874, Allegheny, Pennsylvania; d. 27 July 1946, Paris

From very early in her life Gertrude S. was a traveler. Born in Pennsylvania, reared in Vienna and Paris, she spent her youth in the San Francisco Bay area. In 1893 she studied at Radcliffe College under William James and other distinguished scholars. She became interested in experimental psychology, a concern that led, for one thing, to collaboration with Leon Solomons on a study, "Normal Motor Adjustment," published in the *Psychological Review* (Sept. 1896).

Gertrude S. took advance work in brain anatomy in 1897 at Johns Hopkins University. But she gave up her ambition to study medicine. In 1902 she moved to London to begin her European life. In 1903 she moved to France, where she lived until her death.

The forty-three years Gertrude S. spent in Paris and elsewhere in France proved to be an important period for modern American literature. She established herself in an apartment in Paris and soon became the hostess (with her lifelong companion, Alice B. Toklas) of an informal salon of modern writers. Many members of the younger generation of American writers came to her for advice, encouragement, and aid. They included Hemingway, Sherwood Anderson, and Fitzgerald (qq.v.).

Gertrude S. was an especially important influence on Hemingway. Although in later years he dismissed her contribution, there is no doubt that in the years 1921–25 he learned much from her and that some of it became part of his established technique. With the help of her brother Leo, Gertrude S. also encouraged Pablo Picasso (at the beginning of his career) and other new painters.

After having advised about literature and pronounced her theories of "modernism" in her Paris salon, Gertrude S. began another career, that of a lecturer. She made an important statement on modern style called *Composition as Explanation* (1926), given at both Oxford and Cambridge Universities in 1925 and published by the Hogarth Press of Virginia Woolf (q.v.) and her husband, Leonard. In 1934 and 1935, Gertrude S. extensively toured the United States, lecturing along the way to university groups and other audiences. From this experience came *Narration* (1935) and *Lectures in America* (1935). Her frequent preoccupation with style and method made her name prominent in the literary reviews of her time, including Ford's (q.v.) *Transatlantic Review* and Eugene Jolas's *transition*.

Gertrude S.'s value to modern experimental literature is testified to in her very first book, *Three Lives* (1909). A collection of three short novels, it offers portraits of three persons: Melanctha, a Negro girl, and Anna and Lena, German servants. This work is an expression of Gertrude S.'s method, later to be exhaustively analyzed in her critical writings, which strove to represent in the mode and idiom of her subjects their inner quality and meaning. The style is therefore a compromise of traditional narration with internal analysis. The reader is aware of narrative progression, but the primary impression is gained from the analysis of the minds of her subjects. The style takes its character from those minds and, in a way, is tuned to the rhythms of thought and feeling rather than to external acts.

Later Gertrude S. cited *Three Lives* as having anticipated her method, the three principal rules of which were to "begin again and again," to "use everything," and to maintain a "continuous present."

Gertrude S.'s work moved beyond these beginnings and developed its individual experimental style in a variety of ways. *Tender Buttons* (1914), when it succeeds in doing what she apparently wishes it to do, has the effect of arresting an object or a situation; there is much emphasis on sound repetition, on echoes, and on the concrete value of objects.

In *The Making of Americans* (1925), which she wrote in 1906–1908, she tries to present time and history as slow movement from grandfather to grandson: the time span is a long one, and it is filled with familiar sounds, gestures, and mannerisms. It is a very unusual representation of history, but it does succeed in pointing up the basically familial core of most human time.

Gertrude S.'s most persistent genres for communicating her ideas were criticism (in which she offered many nuances of a relatively few ideas) and autobiography (in which she talked about how her ideas came to her and what effects they had upon her contemporaries). Of the latter, the most famous is *The Autobiography of Alice B. Toklas* (1933), a beautifully written and eminently readable book. Ostensibly about Miss Toklas, it served both to explain as well as to publicize Gertrude S. herself as an especially gifted person and to describe her associations with other artists of her time. Critical theory is dispersed throughout, in reports of conversations and in other forms. She is, above all, presented here as the "critic as conversationalist."

In Gertrude S.'s published criticism the remarks are formalized and presented in sequence in the manner of an "experimental lecture" (as so many of her creative pieces seem more like subjects caught in the process of being formed rather than as finished products).

In her view, the major concern in 20th-c. writing is to achieve a representation of the immediate present, the "thing seen in the way that it is seen." Style must therefore conform to the requirements of immediacy: by means of slow progression, with much repetition and turning back to the beginning, introducing only slight nuances of difference as the time proceeds. She suggested that by this means the quality of the present (its specific meaning to the sensibility of a writer living in the present moment) will be recreated. The most representative expressions of her method are to be seen in *Three Lives* and in the play *Four Saints in Three Acts* (1934), for which the music was written by Virgil Thomson.

Gertrude S. also wrote a number of occasional works. *Picasso* (1938) is a brief but precise discussion of modern painting. *Paris France* (1940) is a discussion of expatriation and especially of the role played by France in the history of 20th-c. American literature. *Wars I Have Seen* (1945) and *Brewsie and Willie* (1946) are memoirs of her encounters with American soldiers in World War II and of her own state of semiisolation in the south of France during that war. She was able to communicate with a genuine sense of reality the manners, speech habits, and basic qualities of the American GI.

Gertrude S.'s principal role is that of tutor and example, not writer. While many of her publications have merit of their own, her chief distinction lies in the ways in which she defined new attitudes and perspectives in 20th-c. literature and art. She was affected above all by the newness of modern art, and she tried to define the difference between it and traditional art, hoping throughout either to isolate the present as uniquely valuable or (as in *The Making of Americans*) to eliminate time lines and treat the past as a slow movement into the present.

Hers was a philosophy of consciousness, derived eccentrically from William James, Bergson (q.v.), and (at several removes) from the theorists of cubism and modern art. The method was designed to reveal consciousness independently of conventional descriptions of time and to combine the precision of objects with the almost indiscernible flow of consciousness. In these terms, her work acted as a stimulus to writers who, like Hemingway, wanted to describe their experience in a manner suited to its essential quality.

FURTHER WORKS: *Geography and Plays* (1922); *Lucy Church Amiably* (1930); *How to Write* (1931); *A Long Gay Book* (1932); *Portraits and Prayers* (1934); *The Geographical History of America* (1936); *Everybody's Autobiography* (1937); *The World Is Round* (1939); *Selected Writings* (ed. C. van Vechten; 1946); *Four in America* (1947); *Blood on the Dining Room Floor* (1948); *Last Operas and Plays* (1949); *Things as They Are* (1950); *Mrs Reynolds and Five Earlier Novelettes* (1952); *Bee Time Vine* (1953); *Alphabets and Birthdays* (1957)

BIBLIOGRAPHY: Wilson, E., *Axel's Castle* (1931), pp. 237–56; Sutherland, D., *G. S.: A Biography of Her Work* (1951); Sprigge, E., *G. S.* (1957); Brinnin, J. M., *The Third Rose* (1959); Hoffman, F. J., *G. S.* (1961); Hoffman, M. J., *The Development of Abstractionism in the Writings of G. S.* (1965); Stewart, A., *G. S. and the Present* (1967); Weinstein, N., *G. S. and the Language of the Modern Consciousness* (1970)

FREDERICK J. HOFFMAN

We find . . . that Miss S.'s method is one of subtraction. She has deliberately limited her equipment. . . . Obviously, any literary artist who sets out to begin his work in a primary search for music or rhythm, and attempts to get this at the expense of (the) "inherent property of words," obviously this artist is not going to exploit the full potentialities of his medium. He is getting an art by subtraction; he is violating his *genre*. . . . Miss S. continually utilizes this violation of the *genre*. Theoretically at least, the result has its studio value. . . . By approaching art-work from these exorbitant angles one is suddenly able to rediscover organically those eternal principles of art which are, painful as it may be to admit it, preserved in all the standard textbooks.

Kenneth Burke, in *Dial* (April 1923), pp. 409–10

In her detachment, her asceticism, and her eclecticism, Miss S. can only remind us of another American author who lived in Europe and devoted himself more and more exclusively to the abstract. The principal difference between Henry James (whom Miss S. reads more and more these days) and Gertrude S. is that the former still kept within the human realm by treating moral problems. . . . Moreover, what Miss S. has in common with James she has in common with Poe, Hawthorne, Melville, and several other important and characteristic American writers: an orientation from experience toward the abstract, an orientation that has been so continuous as to constitute a tradition, if not actually *the* American tradition. Of this tradition it is possible to see in Miss S.'s writing not only a development but the pure culmination.

William Troy, in *Nation* (6 Sept. 1933), pp. 274–5

It is true that, as one reads this book [*The Autobiography of Alice B. Toklas*], one is more forcibly struck than ever by Hemingway's debt to Gertrude S. . . . passages . . . suggest that he has been influenced by her conversational as well as by her literary style (I hardly dare suggest that the writing of Miss S. may in turn have been somewhat affected by the conversations of Hemingway's characters). . . .

Edmund Wilson, "Gertrude Stein Old and Young" (1933), *The Shores of Light* (1952)

Her writing is harder than traditional prose, as a foreign tongue is harder than a native tongue; at first glance we catch a word here and there, or a phrase or two, but the over-all meaning must be figured out arduously. Yet a tension is created, a question asked and in Miss S. at her best, dramatic context mounts to a climax and then a conclusion. It's pure creative activity, an exudation of personality, a discharge, and it can't be defined more exactly. The mysterious surge of energy which impels a boy who is idling on a corner to race madly down the street is part and parcel of the same thing. When people call it elementary, they mean elemental.

W. G. Rogers, *When This You See Remember Me* (1948), pp. 69–70

"In writing a word must be for me really an existing thing." Her efforts to get at the roots of existing life, to create fresh life from them, give her words a dark liquid flowingness, like the murmur of blood. She does not strain words or invent them. Many words have retained their original meaning for her, she uses them simply. Good means good and bad means bad—next to the Jews the Americans are the most moralistic people, and Gertrude S. is an American Jew, a combination which by no means lessens the like quality in both. Good and bad are attributes to her, strength and weakness are real things that live inside people, she looks for these things, notes them in their likenesses and differences. She loves the difficult virtues, she is tender toward good people, she has faith in them.

Katherine Anne Porter, *The Days Before* (1952), p. 39

As a scientific demonstration of Gertrude S.'s belief in the final absolutism of human character, *The Making of Americans* carries the weight of its conviction and the conviction of its enormous weight. As a work of literature, it is all but swept bare of the felicities of detail, color and anecdote that beguile the attention in great books as well as minor ones. But Gertrude S. had had enough of the picaresque trappings and sentimental diffusions that recommend novels to the insatiable reader. She wanted to come to essentials—to ideas in action rather than ideas comfortably couched in formulation, and to character as an entity alive rather than character as an identity pinned to the wall like a butterfly. Her conception would test the power of the intellect to usurp the power of the emotions in communicating living experience, yet she was ready to face the challenge. . . . The pages of *The Making of Americans* are as full of rolling and repeated cadences as the Bible, but its more prevalent sound, like that of Oriental ritual, is the music of the continuous present, always going on and always, almost always, but not quite, the same. . . . Gertrude S. had come early to a notion that was to dominate her creative life—the notion that the "continuous present and using everything and beginning again" was the final reality in fact and thus the final reality that words could communicate. Escaping from the conventions of beginning, middle, and ending, she simply laid out a

space—a space of time as big in its proportions as a canvas of Jackson Pollock—and proceeded to make sure that it would be "always filled with moving."

John Malcolm Brinnin, *The Third Rose* (1959), pp. 94–5

In serious literary circles, as distinguished from the large public, Gertrude S.'s real accomplishments were always known. There, her influence was at one time considerable, though it worked in very different ways and degrees on different individuals. It was known that her writing had influenced, in certain respects, Sherwood Anderson and, later, Hemingway. It was supposed that Steinese had found echoes in Don Marquis' *archy and mehitabel* as well as in the difficult poetry of Wallace Stevens, who once wrote "Twenty men crossing a bridge,/ Into a village,/ Are/ Twenty men crossing a bridge/ Into a village." Her insistence on the primacy of phenomena over ideas, of the sheer magnificence of unmediated reality, found a rapturous response in Stevens, a quiet one in Marianne Moore.

F. W. Dupee, in *Commentary* (June 1962), p. 522

Gertrude S. lived in a literary period bubbling with linguistic experimentation. Tzara and Hugo Ball's dadaist poems were being published, as were the first dissociated, cubist poetry of that other rich American abroad, Walter Arensberg. Little magazines including *Broom* and *transition* were printing experimental poems by Laura Riding and Mina Loy that, for the *Saturday Evening Post* reader, were as lunatic as those by Gertrude S. . . . To suppose that Gertrude S.'s work can all be traced back to such intellectual currents is foolish. . . . Testimony from some of those who knew Gertrude S. best—Carl Van Vechten or Thornton Wilder—supports the idea that Gertrude S., although a woman intensely aware of the intellectual life about her, was nonetheless her own woman. With a single-mindedness bordering on preposterous megalomania she stubbornly kept writing according to her most singular program.

Norman Weinstein, *Gertrude Stein and the Literature of the Modern Consciousness* (1970), p. 57

STEINBECK, John

American novelist, short-story writer, playwright, and essayist, b. 27 Feb. 1902, Salinas, California; d. 20 Dec. 1968, New York City

S. grew up in central California in the town of Salinas, the locale of the Long Valley (*The Long Valley,* 1938) of his fiction. The son of a small businessman and a former schoolteacher, he attended Stanford University but took no degree. During and after college he worked at various jobs (including farm work) while writing his first three novels: *Cup of Gold* (1929), an historical novel about the pirate Henry Morgan; *The Pastures of Heaven* (1932), stories of a farm valley near Monterey, California; and *To a God Unknown* (1933); a mystical idyl of 19th-c. rural California. *Tortilla Flat* (1935), a collection of amusing stories of the indolent and antimaterialistic "paisanos" of Monterey, was a critical and financial success that enabled S. to devote himself entirely to writing.

In Dubious Battle (1936), *Of Mice and Men* (1937), and *The Grapes of Wrath* (1939) established S. as a major author. All three novels focus on the problems of California farm labor during the Depression. The first is an objective account of a strike. *Of Mice and Men,* which also achieved success as a play, is a poignantly naturalistic tale of George and Lennie, farm workers whose desire for a place of their own is frustrated by personal and economic circumstances.

S.'s masterpiece, *The Grapes of Wrath,* is a novel of social criticism that fuses myth and symbol with its attack on aspects of American life during the 1930's. The chief characters, the Joads, are a family of Oklahoma farmers whose land is taken over by the bank after the drought makes it impossible for them to keep up mortgage payments. As they move west in search of work and new homes, the "Okies" are victimized by California ranchers. At the time it appeared, the novel focused national attention on the problems of the migratory farm workers in California. It has since taken a place among the classics of 20th-c. American literature.

The *Sea of Cortez* (1941), S.'s next book, is an account of a marine expedition to the Gulf of California, and it reflected S.'s amateur interest in marine biology. *The Moon Is Down* (1942) is an uncharacteristic novel of the Norwegian resistance during the German occupation. However, in *Cannery Row* (1944) S. returned to his beloved Monterey locale in a series of loosely linked stories about Doc and "the boys" on the Monterey waterfront. The latter work, along with *The Pearl* (1947), a parable about a Mexican Indian whose discovery of a fabulous pearl brings him only grief, and *The Wayward Bus* (1947), which creates a microcosm of American society and features a Mexican-American protagonist, Juan Chicoy, whose ways are a challenge to middle-class values, form a novelistic trio that probes the underlying assumptions of American society.

At the end of the 1940's, S. left California for New York, where he lived until his death. He continued to write, but his four novels published after 1950, though popular successes, disappointed the critics. *East of Eden* (1952) is a long and partly autobiographical novel set in the Salinas Valley. S. concerns himself with a modern version of the Cain-and-Abel story that affirms sinful man's ability to choose good over evil. *Sweet Thursday* (1954), which reworks the material of *Cannery Row,* was written as the basis for a musical comedy. *The Short Reign of Pippin IV* (1957) is a satire on French politics. *The Winter of Our Discontent* (1961) returns seriously to S.'s earlier themes: the examination of middle-class morality and the indictment of values based on money. Its locale is Long Island rather than California.

S. was honored during his career with the Pulitzer Prize in 1940 and the Nobel Prize for Literature in 1962.

FURTHER WORKS: *The Blood Is Strong* (1938); *Bombs Away* (1942); *The Red Pony* (1945); *The Portable Steinbeck* (1946); *A Russian Journal* (1948); *Burning Bright* (1950); *Once There Was a War* (1958); *Travels with Charley* (1962); *Short Novels* (1963); *America and Americans* (1966)

BIBLIOGRAPHY: Tedlock, E. W., and C. V. Wicker, eds., *S. and His Critics: A Record of Twenty-five Years* (1957); Lisca, P., *The Wide World of J. S.* (1958); French, W., *J. S.* (1961); Fontenrose, J. E., *J. S.: An Introduction and an Interpretation* (1964)

JAMES WOODRESS

He is primarily a masculine writer.... He has proved himself an original and highly individualistic force. His books provoke the masculine mind because of his fearless grappling with ideas and human passions as well as sacred taboos. The dry rot of gentility has never touched him and neither sex nor a woman's honor nor romantic love looms large as a man's serious problems in his view.

Edmund C. Richards, in *North American Review* (June 1937), p. 409

Handling complex material rather too easily, he has been marked by the popularizing gift—this indigenous American blessing which has, however, in the case of so many literary figures (a William Lyons Phelps, a Woollcott, a Louis Bromfield, as well as S. himself) become a blessing not altogether unmixed. In S.'s work the false starts and turns, the thwarting problems of material and of the artist in the process of penetrating it, which usually mark the effort to portray truth, these are singularly lacking. If S. has reminded us of a Thomas Wolfe rejoicing in the mournful questioning of youth which wants no answers, he has never, like Wolfe, found himself disturbed by the final enigma of existence itself. For S., Wolfe's famous stone is a stone, a leaf a leaf, and the door is sure to be found.

> Maxwell Geismar, *Writers in Crisis*
> (1942), p. 260

We have been right all along in suspecting that there are nearly two S.'s. There is the S. of *Grapes of Wrath,* of *In Dubious Battle,* and of a number of short stories, an angry man whose anger has put a real tension in his work; and there is also the S. who seems at times to be only a distant relative of the first one, the warm-hearted and amused author of *Tortilla Flat, Cannery Row, The Wayward Bus, The Pearl,* capable of short stretches of some really dazzling stuff but, over the length of the book, increasingly soft and often downright mushy. In other words, S. has achieved his success by working within the limitations which are perhaps self-imposed on him by his temperament. They tie him down to an exclusive preference for one type of character, which recurs with surprising consistency throughout his work, and to a maximum of two emotional attitudes, one compounded of some delight and much compassion toward the people he writes about, the other of compassion and wrath.

> W. M. Frohock, *The Novel of Violence in America* (1950), p. 147

If S.'s characters seldom achieve true novelistic reality, it is precisely because they are so little individualized, so little individuals and finally so little human. Their emotions always remain obscure and somewhat opaque, situated, it seems, under the diaphragm or around the solar plexus; it is hard to picture them, even in a distant time, reading a clear consciousness of themselves.... We may say that there is something false and suspicious, at any rate monstrous, in the very innocence of S.'s heroes. ...Because of this very amputation, S.'s universe and the artistic domain in which he can succeed will be perforce very limited.... One cannot help wondering whether there are very great possibilities open to a "novelist of animality," however perfect his art may be and however deep the bond of sympathy between his subject and himself.

> Claude-Edmonde Magny, in *Steinbeck and His Critics,* ed. by F. W. Tedlock and C. V. Wicker (1957), pp. 225–7

As far as the central narrative about the education of the Joads is concerned, *The Grapes of Wrath* is not even truly what I have defined as a social novel. It stresses the achievement of individualism as much as the works of Thomas Wolfe and depicts the necessity of each individual's educating and reforming himself, rather than the causes of a national disaster. If the Joads had not been caught up in the events of a particular time and place that had profoundly affected S. and troubled his public, we might more easily recognize that their story belongs with Shakespeare's *The Tempest* and other masterpieces of the travail and triumph of the human spirit.

> Warren G. French, *The Social Novel at the End of an Era* (1966), p. 44

STEPHANSSON, Stephan Guðmundsson

Icelandic-Canadian poet, b. 3 Oct. 1853, Kirkjuhóll, Skagafjörður; d. 10 Aug. 1927, near Markerville, Alberta

S. came to the United States in 1874, and finally settled on a farm near Markerville in Canada. He had read the sagas and the Eddas as a boy. Otherwise he had no schooling. Yet he was to become one of the greatest poets of Iceland in his day and perhaps the greatest poet in Canada.

S. made his poetical debut with *Úti á víðavangi* (1894) and *Á ferð og flugi* (1900). Then came *Andvökur* (Vols. I–III, 1909–1910; Vols. IV–V, 1923; Vol. VI, 1938), containing the bulk of his poetry. To this were added: *Kolbeinslag* (1914), about a sorcerer who tested his poetic mettle against the Devil; *Heimleiðis* (1917), occasioned by his trip to Iceland as a guest of the nation; and *Vígslóði* (1920), his pacifist answer to the passions aroused by World War I. His prose and letters were printed in *Bréf og ritgerðir* (4 vols., 1938–48) and a final edition of his *Andvökur* (4 vols., 1953–58).

The name of S.'s poetical collection—literally "wakeful nights"—reveals his working hours. S. was anticlerical and anticapitalistic; he was a realist, a pacifist, a great individualist, and an ardent lover of nature. The face of North America, especially western Canada, as well as visions of Iceland, rises from the pages of his poems. His poetry is ornate, intellectual, lyrical, and full of Norse symbolism. A greater poet than either Matthías Jochumsson (1835–1920) or Benediktsson (q.v.), S. was the greatest Icelandic poet of his time.

FURTHER WORK: *Úrvalsljóð* (1945)

BIBLIOGRAPHY: Kirkconnell, W., "Canada's Leading Poet," *UTQ,* V (1936), 263–77; Cawley, F. S., "The Greatest Poet of the Western World: S. G. S.," *SS,* XV (1938–39), 99–109; Nordal, S., Introduction to *Andvökur* (1938)

STEFÁN EINARSSON

STEPHENS, James

Irish poet, novelist, and short-story writer, b. 2 Feb. 1882, Dublin; d. 26 Dec. 1950, London

S. grew up in utter poverty, acquired sparse formal education, but taught himself stenography and obtained a job as typist in a lawyer's office. He later became assistant curator at the Dublin National Gallery.

An ardent nationalist, he was active in Sinn Fein, learned Gaelic, and absorbed the native sagas and folklore. After long being rejected, his writings were discovered by Russell (q.v.), the poet and essayist who wrote under the penname A. E.

S.'s poems show the influence of William Blake (1757–1827) in their simple diction, fluent rhythms, and sense of wonder. *Insurrections* (1909), a vigorous departure from contemporary conventions, contains a gallery of rich and bitter character-sketches depicted in colloquial terms. *The Hill of Vision* (1912) is as powerful, if less caustic, and as questioning in its attitude toward God and Christian morality. *Songs from the Clay* (1915) is notable for vivid imagery and themes from nature.

S.'s best-known novels are *The Crock of Gold* (1912), an allegory of lyric fantasy, philosophic caprice, and social protest, for which he received the Polignac Prize, and *Deirdre* (1923), a sensitive rendition of the tragic love legend, for which he was awarded the Tailltean Medal.

S.'s short stories recall Turgenev's (1818–83) ill-favored, frustrated characters and Strindberg's (q.v.) themes of destructive domestic conflict. In *Here Are Ladies* (1913) the tone is comic, the form casual. In *Etched in Moonlight* (1928) the accent is grim and the form takes on a modern stringency, which also characterizes all of S.'s later poetry. He ceased writing prose for publication after 1924.

FURTHER WORKS: *The Charwoman's Daughter* (1912); *The Demi-Gods* (1914); *The Adventures of Seumas Beg* (1915); *Green Branches* (1916); *The Insurrection in Dublin* (1916); *Reincarnations* (1918); *Irish Fairy Tales* (1920); *In the Land of Youth* (1924); *A Poetry Recital* (1925); *Theme and Variations* (1930); *Strict Joy* (1931); *Kings and the Moon* (1938); *Collected Poems* (1954); *James, Seumas and Jacques* (ed. L. Frankenberg; 1964)

BIBLIOGRAPHY: A. E. [George Russell], *Imaginations and Reveries* (1915), pp. 34–44; Boyd, E. A., *Ireland's Literary Renaissance* (1916), pp. 265–74, 391–94; Colum, P., "J. S. as a Prose Artist," *Dublin Magazine*, XXVI (July–Sept. 1951), 38–46; Frankenberg, L., Introduction to *James, Seumas and Jacques: Unpublished Papers of J. S.* (1964); Pyle, H., *J. S.: His Work and an Account of His Life* (1965); Angoff, C., "Recollections—Elinor Wylie, Thomas Mann, Joseph Hergesheimer, J. S., Logan Clendening," *Literary Review*, X (1967), 169–79

RICHARD CARY

STERNHEIM, Carl

German dramatist, novelist, and essayist, b. 1 April 1878, Leipzig; d. 3 Nov. 1942, Brussels

S. was the son of a banker who also owned a newspaper and wrote theater criticism. His early days were spent in Hanover and Berlin, studying philosophy and literature in several leading German universities. Later he and Franz Blei (1871–1942) founded the journal *Hyperion*. In 1930 S. emigrated to Belgium.

S.'s first plays were romantic tragedies, but after the failure of *Don Juan* (1909) he turned to comedies that sharply satirized German society during the reign of Wilhelm II. He pinpointed its driving force as greed for money and power, deflating the superficial ideals that were mere smokescreens for its vices. As he himself put it, he wanted to show a middle class that "until 1914 has excelled chiefly in terms of its practical success and its bank accounts and that is now not even up to its own pet ideology."

His major comedies were collected in 1922 under the descriptive title *Aus dem bürgerlichen Heldenleben*. The first plays in the series trace the rise of the Maske family through several generations. Love and marriage are shown being dictated by a lust for property in *Die Hose* (1911; A Pair of Drawers, 1927); the older generation is cynically shunted aside in the interests of social climbing in *Der Snob* (1914; A Place in the World, 1927); and the family finally achieves an important place in the industrial power structure in *1913* (1915; Eng., 1939).

Later plays in the series focus on a proletariat determined to move up into middle-class society (*Bürger Schippel*, 1913; Tabula rasa, 1916). In *Die Kassette* (1912) S. presents a struggle for the promised inheritance in the casket that gives the play its title, a saturnalia around the golden calf that ends with the disappointment of all.

Again and again S. shows the fraudulence of high-flown sentiment and idealistic phrases that betray themselves as empty talk or statements of calculated egoism. His often telegraphic style and expressionistically puppet-like protagonists heighten the effect of scenes rich in contrast.

S.'s later plays, beginning with *Die Marquise von Arcis* (1919), are on historical subjects. *Oscar Wilde* (1925) demonstrates his originality and independence by its sympathetic portrayal of a man persecuted and exiled by society.

In prose works such as *Chronik von des zwanzigsten Jahrhunderts Beginn* (2 vols., 1918; revised in 3 vols., 1926–28), S. continues his critical analysis of his time. *Libussa, des Kaisers Leibroß* (1922) is presented as the memoirs of the kaiser's horse.

Strongly influenced by Nietzsche (q.v.), S. expresses in his experimental plays and other writings the need for radical individualism and determined self-preservation in a commercially inspired society bent on eradicating both.

FURTHER WORKS: *Der Heiland* (1898); *Fanale!* (1901); *Judas Ischarioth* (1901); *Ulrich und Brigitte* (1907); *Der Kandidat* (1914); *Busekow* (1914); *Napoleon* (1915); *Das leidende Weib* (1915); *Der Scharmante* (1915); *Der Geizige* (1916); *Schuhlin* (1916); *Die drei Erzählungen* (1916); *Der Stänker* (1916); *Meta* (1916); *Mädchen* (1917); *Perleberg* (1917); *Posinsky* (1917); *Prosa* (1918); *Vier Novellen* (1918); *Ulrike* (1918); *Die deutsche Revolution* (1919); *Europa* (2 vols., 1919); *Berlin, oder Juste milieu* (1920); *Der entfesselte Zeitgenosse* (1920); *Manon Lescaut* (1921); *Tasso, oder Die Kunst des Juste milieu* (1921); *Der Nebbich* (1922); *Der Abenteurer* (1922); *Fairfax* (1922; Eng., 1923); *Gauguin und Van Gogh* (1924); *Das Fossil* (1925); *Lutetia* (1926); *Die Schule von Uznach, oder Neue Sachlichkeit* (1926); *Die Väter, oder Knock Out* (1928); *J. P. Morgan* (1930); *Aut Caesar aut nihil* (1930); *Vorkriegseuropa im Gleichnis meines Lebens* (1936); *Werke* (4 vols., 1947 ff.); *Gesamtwerk* (7 vols., 1963–67)

BIBLIOGRAPHY: Blei, F., *Wedekind, S. und das Theater* (1914–15); Eisenlohr, F., *C. S.* (1926); Beckley, R., "C. S.," in *German Men of Letters,* ed. A. Natan, Vol. II (1963), pp. 133–54; Karasek, H., *S.* (1965); Wendler, W., *C. S.* (1966); Paulsen, W., ed., *Aspekte des Expressionismus* (1968)

* * *

STEVENS, Wallace

American poet, b. 2 Oct. 1879, Reading, Pennsylvania; d. 2 Aug. 1955, Hartford, Connecticut

After attending Harvard University, S. studied law at New York Law School and received his degree in 1903. He practiced law in New York City until 1916, when he moved to Hartford, Connecticut, to begin a lifelong association with the Hartford Accident and Indemnity Company, first as a lawyer and then, in 1934, as a vice-president.

Though he received some recognition in 1914 when he won a prize for four poems in *Poetry* magazine, S. did not emerge as a significant poet until 1923 when, at the age of forty-three, he published his first volume of poems, *Harmonium.* The book was acclaimed as a solid if bizarre achievement. The poems' often startling language, imagery, and metrics seemed fashionably chic in 1923. At the same time their highly conscious comedy of aesthetic perception, and their oddly elegant satire on imperception, seemed to reveal talents more philosophic than modish in nature. "Sunday Morning," with its casual yet elaborate atheism, remains a superior poem. Many anthologists and some critics regard *Harmonium* as S.'s most interesting book.

For the most part, the literary public of depression-plagued America found S.'s peculiar intelligence, subtlety, and elegance politically unacceptable. His aesthetic response was twofold: *Ideas of Order* (1935), his second volume of poetry, contained starker, less bizarre poems that were, however, poetically weaker; the long poem entitled "Owl's Clover" (1936) was an attempt to engage political realities directly—especially Marxist analyses of them—and to translate them into S.'s own complicated poetic categories. But this attempt led to an unsuccessful work whose politics and poetics were strained, rhetorical, and shrill.

In 1937 S. published *The Man with the Blue Guitar,* whose title piece is his most widely read longer poem. Eschewing political debate entirely, S. achieved a work that successfully fused the starkness of his second volume with the bright comedy of the first. The implicit theme of much of S.'s best previous work—*i.e.*, the constant and shifting interactions between reality and the imagination—became the explicit subject matter of "Blue Guitar." Thus, the poem at once summed up the deeper intellectual currents in S.'s past poetry and forecast the increasingly philosophic, self-reflective direction his later poems would take.

In the 1940's, S. published *Parts of a World* (1942) and *Transport to Summer* (1947). As a whole, the former neither advanced nor retarded S.'s art and is thus his *safest* book. The latter is perhaps his finest single volume, if only because its four longer poems are among his greatest: "Esthétique du Mal," "Description without Place," "Credences of Summer," and "Notes toward a Supreme Fiction." In these four poems S.'s mature style is fully realized as a synthesis of philosophy and comedy within which intellectual propositions about poetry, imagination, and reality are asserted in elegant, witty language that can mock, heighten, or further the thought—and occasionally all three at once. Moreover, the poems' structures are as assured as they are airily casual, and their consistent persona of a university lecturer is S.'s masterful invention. The result, especially in "Notes," is a philosophic poetry of complex gaiety and richest feeling.

S.'s last single volume, *The Auroras of Autumn* (1950), is his most varied effort. The mythic intricacy of the long title poem contrasts with the dry, pedantic air of the even longer "An Ordinary Evening in New Haven," while both contrast with the elaborate but clear parable of the short "A Primitive like an Orb"—yet all three are successful. The next year saw S.'s only book in another genre: a collection of essays devoted to his own poetic theory, *The Necessary Angel: Essays on Reality and the Imagination*. Like the poems, the essays are "notes toward" a theory of poetry and not an elaboration of one. They are therefore best read as rational versions of the poems' ideas rather than explanations of them.

Collected Poems (1954) contains most of S.'s previously published poetry—with the important exception of "Owl's Clover"—as well as twenty-five new poems. Two years after S.'s death, his biographer, Samuel French Morse, edited *Opus Posthumous* (1957), which included all previously uncollected poetry and prose, two trivial dramatic efforts, and a selection from S.'s notebooks.

S.'s reputation is certain within the academic world—especially in the United States, where an enormous amount of critical commentary has been produced. Equally assured is S.'s eminence and influence among recent poets. Yet these domains of response have tended to

remain separate, with academic critics seeing S. as a professor of aesthetics who happened to write poems, and poets considering him as an elegantly perceptive comedian and aesthete who now and then dabbled in philosophy. However, some recent writers have begun to sense the inner coherence of S.'s poetry beneath such dualism. Just as S. himself forged his art only late in his life, so a commensurate reputation was slow in coming. Genuine understanding is still on its way.

FURTHER WORK: *Letters of W. S.* (1966)

BIBLIOGRAPHY: Kermode, F., *W. S.* (1960); Bryer, J., and Riddel, J., *A Checklist of S. Criticism* (1962); Borroff, M., ed., *W. S.: A Collection of Critical Essays* (1963); Enck, J., *Images and Judgments* (1964); Riddel, J., *The Clairvoyant Eye* (1965); Doggett, F., *S.'s Poetry of Thought* (1966); Sukenick, R., *W. S.: Musing the Obscure* (1967); Baird, J., *The Dome and the Rock* (1968); Vendler, H. H., *On Extended Wings* (1969); Morse, S. F., *W. S.: Life as Poetry* (1970)

DONALD SHEEHAN

S. is precise among the shyest, most elusive of movements and shadings. He sees distinctly by way of delicacy the undulations of the pigeon sinking downward, the darkening of a calm under waterlights, the variations of the deep-blue tones in dusky landscapes. Quite as regularly as the colors themselves, it is their shades of difference that are registered by him.... Yet this fastidious, aristocratic nature possesses a blunt power of utterance, a concentrated violence, that is almost naturalistic. ... But sensation alone is liberated to new intensity by S.'s forms. Emotion, on the contrary, is curiously constrained by them within a small range of experience and small volume of expression.... S.'s rhythms are chiefly secondary rhythms. Scarcely ever is his attack a direct and simple one. Generally, it is oblique, patronizing and twisted with self-intended mockery.

Paul Rosenfeld, *Men Seen* (1925), pp. 152–5

S. is more than a dandy, a designer, and esthete. Each of these persons is a phase of a central person, each a mask in a masquerade at the heart of which philosophy and tragi-comedy view the world with serenity. If the earth is a tawdry sphere, America a tawdry land, the relation of human to human the most tawdry of all, S. refuses to despair.... Behind the veils there is always a meaning, though the poet employs supersubtlety for veiling the meaning as well. No one hates the obvious more. No one knows better than he that all these things have been felt and thought and known before. One can only improvise on material used over and over again and improvise for oneself alone.

　　　　Alfred Kreymborg, *Our Singing Strength*
　　　　　　　　　　　　　　(1929), pp. 501–2

[S.] gives us, I believe, the most perfect laboratory of hedonism to be found in literature. He is not like those occasional poets of the Renaissance who appear in some measure to be influenced by a pagan philosophy, but who in reality take it up as a literary diversion at the same time that they are beneath the surface immovably Christian. S. is released from all the restraints of Christianity, and is encouraged by all the modern orthodoxy of Romanticism: his hedonism is so fused with Romanticism as to be merely an elegant variation of that somewhat inelegant System of Thoughtlessness. His ideas have remained essentially unchanged for more than a quarter of a century, and on the whole they have been very clearly expressed, so that there is no real occasion to be in doubt as to their nature; and he began as a great poet, so that when we examine the effect of those ideas upon his work, we are examining something of very great importance.

　　　　Yvor Winters, *The Anatomy of Nonsense*
　　　　　　　　　　　　　　(1943), p. 119

The poems of Mr. W. S. have now been collected in a volume, with the title *Harmonium*. Mr. S. is the master of a style: that is the most remarkable thing about him. His gift for combining words is baffling and fantastic but sure: even when you do not know what he is saying, you know that he is saying it well. He derives plainly from several French sources of the last fifty years, but—except for an occasional fleeting phrase—he never really sounds like any of them.

　　　　Edmund Wilson, "Wallace Stevens and e. e.
　　　　cummings," in *The Shores of Light* (1952),
　　　　　　　　　　　　　　　　　　　　　　p. 49

The starting point of S.'s poems is often the aesthetic experience in isolation from all other experiences, as art is isolated from work, and as a museum is special and isolated in any modern American community. And if one limits oneself to the surface of S.'s poetic style, one can characterize S. as the poet of the Sunday: the poet of the holiday, the week-end and the vacation, who sees objects at a distance, as they appear to the tourist or in the art museum. But this is merely the poet's starting point. S. converts aestheticism into contemplation in the full philosophical and virtually religious sense of the word.

　　　　Delmore Schwartz, in *New Republic*
　　　　　　　　　　　　　　(1 Nov. 1954), p. 16

Opulence—it is the quality which most of us, I expect, ascribe before all others to the poetry of W. S.: profusion, exotic abundance, and luxuri-

ance. We carry in our minds an image of poems which teem with rich, strange, somehow forbidden delights, omnifarious and prodigious. . . . S. is Elizabethan in his attitude towards language, highhanded in the extreme. . . . S. is the delighted craftsman whose delight is, in part, the access of gratification which comes upon the exercise of mastery. His pleasure is endless because it is part of his work, past and present; it is transmissable because we too, in reading his poems, share that mastery.

　　　　Hayden Carruth, in *Poetry*
　　　　　　　　　　　　　　(Feb. 1955), pp. 288–92

Technically S. was not, as were many of his contemporaries, an experimentalist. He did not write staid classroom lines that can be regularly scanned, but they lie, for all that, in regular units of 2s and 3s and 4s quite according to custom. There is an intrinsic order which they follow with a satisfying fidelity which makes them indefinably musical, often strongly stressed by S., his signature.

His is not strictly speaking a colloquial diction, but there are especially in his later works no inversions of phrase, "for poetic effect," no deformities of the normal syntax.

　　　　William Carlos Williams, in *Poetry*
　　　　　　　　　　　　　　(Jan. 1956), pp. 235–6

STOESSL, Otto

Austrian novelist, poet, essayist, and dramatist, b. 2 May 1875, Vienna; d. there, 15 Sept. 1936

S. was the son of a physician who made a name for himself by several publications in his special field (pediatrics). His father's early death not only clouded his youth—S. was deeply devoted to his father—but also explains the sadness that pervades his writings. Early in his life his eyes were opened to the futility of human destiny, to the tragedy of wasted, ruined, lost life and happiness. The unburdening of oppressive childhood remembrances—the grievous memory of a beloved father, so early lost, and of an unmotherly mother—is a recurring motif in his writings.

S.'s early literary endeavors and successes— he published his first longer novella *Leile* in 1898—brought him into contact with Peter Altenberg, Karl Kraus (qq.v.), and Adolf Loos, the architect (1870–1933). He contributed to Kraus's periodical *Die Fackel* until 1911, when Kraus proceeded to do all the writing for this publication by himself. In spite of his aspirations to establish himself as a writer, S. continued his studies at the University of Vienna and took his degree as a doctor of law in 1900. However, the insecurity of a writer's existence,

355

more difficult then than today, together with his obligations to his family (he married in 1900) prompted him to enter the service of the Kaiser Ferdinand Nordbahn railroad. This bread-winning employment was to bring him the security enabling him to establish himself as a writer, but the double exertion of energy also made for the doubled consumption of his strength. The problem of such division of an artist's life, in the midst of an uncomprehending, indifferent, even hostile environment, occurs in always new refractions in S.'s writings. After 1919 he was the Burgtheater critic of the *Wiener Zeitung.* He left his position at the Nordbahn (as *Hofrat*) in 1923. In the same year he received the Prize of the City of Vienna awarded then for the first time.

The decade before World War I was the happiest and most productive of S.'s life. In rapid succession a number of works appeared that made him favorably known and brought him the friendships of noteworthy personalities. At first he was drawn to the drama and toward naturalistic social criticism, but he soon turned his attention to the art of narration. His models were the past masters of poetic realism, Gottfried Keller (1819–90), C. F. Meyer (1825–98), and Adalbert Stifter (1805–1868), about whom he wrote superb critical essays, thereby describing that kind of poetic writing most congenial to his own.

"Criticism and self-criticism," wrote Ernst Krenek in the *Wiener Zeitung* (5 May 1935) "guarantee the purity of O. S.'s language, a value whose preservation has become one of Austria's special tasks. Perhaps this is the most important Austrian responsibility in the realm of German culture due to the wretched debasement of the language in Germany in the Third Reich. It is certainly no accident that the most passionate and unyielding defender of the German language, Karl Kraus, is an Austrian. German culture owes him an eternal debt for stimulating Austria's best minds to maintain unflagging vigil over the dignity and purity of the German language."

The Austrian school of the novella is the heir of a great tradition beginning with Franz Grillparzer (1791–1873) and Ferdinand von Saar (1833–1906). S. carried on this tradition in a truly noble way. What gives his novellas their vigor and conviction is, beyond all aesthetic merits, their profound humanity.

S. did not want to be anything but a quiet observer, who, from his window, watched people's lives. His keen but kindly eye pierced the most secret and most ramified passageways of the anthill called human society. But what compelled his greatest compassion were the strangely blurred border areas of this seemingly so solidly built society and the people who lived in an oddly hazy, indescribable twilight. These outsiders of society, who despised bourgeois life yet were caricatures of its members, are his favorites. Unforgettable for everyone who has met them are: Heinrich Frantzel in *Das Haus Erath* (the Frantzels are to Austria what the Buddenbrooks and Forsytes are to Germany and England); or that master of the art of living, Lieutenant Roszkowski in *Sonjas letzter Name;* or that funniest specimen of an ingenious heel, Egon de Alamor, in the magnificent story *Egon und Danitza.* But in addition to buffoons, hypocrites, and adventurers, we meet such wondrously fine women as the patiently suffering Antonia and the angelic Agnes in *Das Haus Erath.*

The end of World War I, the collapse and destruction of the Austrian-Hungarian monarchy, seemed to deprive S. of the main elements of his life and art, but his unbroken creative energy turned this downfall too from a painful experience into a subject of artistic creation. The novel *Das Haus Erath* shows this collapse by means of presenting the fate of three generations of a widely branched out, originally solid and wealthy family; its moral and financial decline represents the degeneration of the middle class generally and so warrants the empire's ruin. *Das Haus Erath,* justly considered S.'s main achievement, was his most successful work. About it Karl Nötzel in the *Kunstwart* (February 1926) wrote: "It would be hard to find in the current crop of novels one that compares with S.'s *Das Haus Erath* in its richness—no word is more apt— of psychological penetration, warmth, brilliance and breadth of ideas, inventive power, beauty and rightness of language. . . . With this writer we live an undreamed-of multidimensional and strangely enchanting existence. We forget ourselves in the process, yet know that we have a right to do so because we return to ourselves richer, more knowing, and inwardly gayer."

In the novel *Sonnenmelodie,* Ludwig Mainone, through whom S. speaks, describes his relation to the collapsed monarchy: "For he loved it, although he suffered from it. One cannot have been born in a country and have wandered through all its regions, have delighted in the sight of them—the plains and the Alps, the powerful river streaming through it, the southern landscape, people with many customs and idioms—and not partake with one's heart of this century-old structure." In the same novel Mainone calls himself a mourner of the Austrian empire, because by its destruction his favorite toy had been smashed.

When, in 1933, the first volume of his collected works (4 vols., 1933–37) appeared, S. titled it *Arcadia*, gathering in it a series of poetic creations almost all of which deal with classical antiquity or are rooted in antiquity. The typical Austrian, a synthesis of German and Mediterranean elements, of antiquity and Christianity, pervades S.'s work. This is particularly apparent in his *Griechisches Tagebuch* (in the above-mentioned volume), which combines Goethe's wide vision with the realism of Grillparzer's notes on a similar journey through Greece. The problems of artistic creation of the novellas had been preoccupying S. They are treated in *Das Erlebnis des Dichters* (which can be freely translated as "The Creative Process of the Literary Artist"), which is one of the most significant articles in the third volume of the collected works.

For the volumes comprising his novellas S. planned a division into *Schöpfer* (Creators) and *Geschöpfe* (Creatures). He did not live to see their publication. Only the volume *Schöpfer* appeared after his death in 1937. With the emigration of his publisher in 1938 this edition of his collected works came to an end.

Behind every poetic creation of S. a spiritual, moral force is operative. To look at it from a merely aesthetic point of view does not do justice to S.'s work. In S.'s own words: "The homeland of all morality is art. It gives direction and uniqueness, it enlivens man's wretched life through its manifold interpretations, it provides variety for the moments of perpetual tension and so lightens the burden on his shoulders."

FURTHER WORKS: *Ware* (1897); *Tote Götter* (1898); *Kinderfrühling* (1904); *Gottfried Keller* (1904); *Conrad Ferdinand Meyer* (1906); *In den Mauern* (1907; republished as *Das Schicksal pocht an die Pforte*, 1956); *Negerkönigs Tochter* (1910); *Allerleirauh* (1911); *Morgenrot* (1912); *Was nützen mir die schönen Schuhe* (1913); *Unterwelt* (1914); *Lebensform und Dichtungsform* (1914); *Basem, der Grobschmied* (1916); *Der Hirt als Gott* (1920); *Irrwege* (1922); *Opfer* (1923); *Adalbert Stifter* (1925); *Johannes Freudensprung* (1926); *Nacht-*

geschichten (1926; republished as *Menschendämmerung*, 1929); *Die Schmiere* (1927); *Antike Motive* (1928); *Griechisches Tagebuch* (1930); *Die wahre Helena* (1931); *Gesammelte Werke* (14 vols., 1933–38); *Nora, die Füchsin* (1934)

BIBLIOGRAPHY: Alker, E., "Zu O. S.s 50. Geburtstag," *Die Literatur*, XXVII (1924–25), p. 61; Bing, S., "O. S., Ein Dichter Österreichs," *Frankfurter Zeitung* (9 July 1925), p. 1; Leszer, J., "O. S.," *Neue Schweizer Rundschau* (1928), pp. 753–58; Lissauer, E., "Ein Gedichtband O. S.s," *Die Literatur*, XXXI (1928–29), p. 17; Nötzel, K., "O. S.," *Kunstwart* (Feb. 1929); Wied, M., "O. S. zum 60. Geburtstag," *Wiener Zeitung* (1 May 1935); Krenek, E., "O. S.," *Wiener Zeitung* (5 May 1935)

FREDERICK UNGAR

STRACHEY, Giles Lytton

English biographer, essayist, and critic, b. 1 March 1880, London; d. 21 Jan. 1932, Inkpen, Berkshire

S. was born into an upper middle-class family. His father was a general in the British army with extensive service in India as a soldier and civil administrator. From an early age S. suffered from poor health, which would afflict him throughout his life. Added to this was intense loneliness, despite a large family, and the oddity of his frail appearance in adolescence. In 1897 he entered Liverpool University College, where he remained for two years; he then matriculated at Trinity College, Cambridge, where he studied until 1905. It was there that he met many of those who, with S., were later to form the nucleus of the Bloomsbury Group: Clive Bell, Leonard Woolf, John Maynard Keynes, and E. M. Forster (q.v.).

Failing to be elected a Fellow of Trinity College, S. became a reviewer in 1907 for the *Spectator* and the *New Quarterly*. In 1910, he began work on a brief account of French literature, which he was commissioned to write for the Home University Library. Published in 1912, *Landmarks in French Literature* reveals S.'s extensive knowledge of the subject in an urbane, graceful style that anticipated the greater works to come. Primarily intended as a guide for students, the work reveals S.'s profound admiration of French literature and of the civilization that nurtured it.

In 1912, S. first conceived of *Eminent*

Victorians, which was to contain biographical studies of a dozen distinguished figures of the previous century. When he completed the work six years later, it was made up of essays on Florence Nightingale, Cardinal Manning, General Charles George Gordon, and Dr. Thomas Arnold. Prefacing the work with his statement of the historian's intention, S. wrote: "It is not his business to be complimentary; it is his business to lay bare the facts of the case, as he understands them."

When *Eminent Victorians* appeared in 1918, it brought S. immediate fame, but it also brought down upon him the wrath of some reviewers and professional historians, for S. had rejected traditional conventions of biography and had injected irony and psychological analysis within a consciously designed dramatic framework. For S., biography was not simply the organization of historical fact designed to reveal the noble qualities of revered figures but an artistic design expressing the personal vision of the biographer. Thus, through S.'s exposure of the less admirable qualities of his subjects, even the title *Eminent Victorians* was clearly ironic.

S.'s next major work, *Queen Victoria* (1921), is decidedly less ironic, less a deliberate attempt to reduce myth to human proportions. Stylistically, the narration has greater maturity; and since S. was dealing with only one major figure, the narration results in an aesthetically satisfying unity. Though *Queen Victoria* has come to be regarded as S.'s classic work, it has had less of an influence on historical writing than has *Eminent Victorians*.

In 1925, while planning to write a collection of essays on famous love affairs, S. decided instead to write a book on Queen Elizabeth and Essex. This time, however, he was to bring greater imaginative qualities to the study. Indeed, *Elizabeth and Essex: A Tragic History* (1928) is a work more of historical drama than of historical research, a presentation of imaginatively conceived truth rather than scholarly fact. In addition there are obvious Freudian (and personal) implications in, for example, the treatment of the mother-son relationship between the Queen and Essex, an idea no doubt derived from S.'s brother, James, who had studied with Freud and, in fact, translated his works. (Freud himself sent S. a letter praising *Elizabeth and Essex,* adding that as a historian, S. was "steeped in the spirit of psychoanalysis.")

A phenomenal popular success in England,

America, and the Continent, *Elizabeth and Essex* did not rival *Queen Victoria* and *Eminent Victorians* in achievement or influence. Many reviewers and professional historians regarded it as a mere trifling with history. Indeed, it has been facetiously called S.'s only work of fiction.

S.'s last work, *Portraits in Miniature, and Other Essays* (1931), consists of a dozen essays on obscure writers, scientists, and scholars whose lives appealed to S.'s sense of the grotesque paradoxes in human nature. His least important book, it nonetheless reveals S.'s gift for graceful, witty portraiture.

Though S.'s reputation declined after his death, his influence in the craft of biographical writing continued to be widely felt. S.'s main contribution to the art of biography was his insistence that truth must be imaginatively and intuitively grasped. The recent revival of interest in S. indicates that, as historian and writer, he not only remains a major force but also an enduringly interesting creative artist.

FURTHER WORKS: *Books and Characters: French and English* (1922); *Pope* (1925); *Characters and Commentaries* (1933); *Virginia Woolf and L. S.: Letters* (1956); *Spectatorial Essays* (1964)

BIBLIOGRAPHY: Dobrée, B., "L. S.," in *Post Victorians,* ed. W. R. Inge (1933); Iyengar, K. R. S., *L. S.: A Critical Study* (1939); Johnstone, J. K., *The Bloomsbury Group* (1954); Sanders, C. R., *L. S.: His Mind and Art* (1957); Kallich, M., *The Psychological Milieu of L. S.* (1961); Holroyd, M., *L. S.: A Critical Biography* (2 vols., 1968)

KARL BECKSON

STRAMM, August
German poet and dramatist, b. 29 July 1874, Münster; d. 1 Sept. 1915, Horodec, Russia

The son of a railroad official, S. studied economics. After receiving a doctorate for his dissertation on international postal rates, he joined the Post Office Department and became an inspector. He was killed in action on the Russian front during World War I.

S.'s poetry had been consistently rejected for publication until in 1913 he met Herwarth Walden (1878–1941?), the editor of the expressionist magazine *Der Sturm.* S. quickly became the leading poet in the group of abstract expressionists (*see* expressionism) who contributed both poetry and art to that publication.

A radical development of the theories of Holz (q.v.) and Filippo Marinetti (1876–1944), S.'s ejaculatory poems are rhythmic structures of a few lines, in which language is reduced to symbolic key words arranged in repetitive and parallel patterns. His principal themes are love as a cosmic experience (*Du*, 1915) and war as the symbol of death (*Tropfblut*, 1919).

The explosive effect of S.'s poetry is the result of a process of word deformation and linguistic alchemy that belongs in the tradition of Stéphane Mallarmé (1842–98) and has similarities with the laboratory theory of Benn (q.v.). It anticipates dadaism (q.v.) and modern *poésie concrète*.

The same stylistic elements are carried over into S.'s plays—the so-called *Schreidramen*. Brief condensations of his philosophy of cosmic love, they are similar to Kokoschka's (q.v.) dramatic experiments and develop the theatrical tradition of Holz and Schlaf (q.v.). *Sancta Susanna* (1914; Poet Lore, 1914) provided the libretto for Paul Hindemith's 1921 opera.

After naturalistic studies and symbolist plays S. turned to works that emphasized abstract pantomimes—*Erwachen* (1915), *Kräfte* (1915), and *Geschehen* (1916)—in which light, sound, and gesture were synthesized. The actor became a structural element within a stage composition, and language was reduced to sound symbols.

FURTHER WORKS: *Rudimentär* (1914); *Die Haidebraut* (1914; The Bride of the Moor, 1914); *Die Unfruchtbaren* (1916); *Die Menschheit* (1916); *Dichtungen in drei Bänden* (1918–19; only first two vols. published); *Dein Lächeln weint* (1956); *Das Werk* (1963)

BIBLIOGRAPHY: Pokowietz, T., "A. S.," in *Expressionismus*, ed. H. Friedmann, and O. Mann (1956), pp. 116–28; Hering, C., "Die Überwindung des gegenständlichen Symbolismus in den Gedichten A. S.," *Monatshefte*, LI (Feb. 1959), 63–74; Huder, W., "A. S.," in *Welt und Wort*, XV (1960); Popper, H., "Reflections on Form in German Poetry," *Trivium*, I (1966), 169–81

CHRISTOPH HERING

STRINDBERG, Johan August

Swedish dramatist, novelist short-story writer, poet, and essayist, b. 22 Jan. 1849, Stockholm; d. there, 14 May 1912

S. was the fourth of the eleven children of a shipping agent of peasant origin; his mother had been a servant in the S. household. In 1850, S.'s father went bankrupt, and this adversely affected the sensitive boy's development. This is where S.'s autobiography *Tjänstekvinnans son* (1886–87; The Son of a Servant, 1913) begins, with its description of the gloomy home atmosphere and the awakening of a willful, talented, but hypochondriac personality. S.'s relations with his father deteriorated after his mother died in 1862 and his father married the maid in 1863. His family's tendency to sectarian piousness left permanent traces in S.'s emotional life, shown first in a reaction of atheistic defiance and later in an unremitting struggle to find a personal relationship to God.

In 1867 S., who at that time possessed only the bare necessities of life, entered the University of Uppsala. After one semester he left the university and became, successively, an elementary-school teacher, a tutor, and an apprentice at the Dramatic Theater in Stockholm. Although he was assigned nothing but walk-on parts, he sensed that the theater was to become the major vehicle for his genius, now clamoring for action and self-expression. His first works were in fact plays: *Fritänkaren* (1870) and *Hermione* (1871).

Returning to Uppsala in 1870 for a few semesters, S. found himself strongly attracted to the liberal movement, to neorationalism (Victor Rydberg [1828–95], Ernest Renan [1823–92]), Darwin's theories, and the neo-Nordic renaissance. He founded the Runa Brotherhood of writers and wrote *I Rom* (1870) and *Den fredlöse* (1871), which were performed at the Stockholm Dramatic Theater. Significant factors in his later development were his periodic sojourns in the Skär Islands near Stockholm—where this restless, much-disappointed man repeatedly sought solace—and an ardent interest in natural science, which led him to think briefly of studying medicine.

In the fall of 1873, S. became a telegraph operator on one of the most remote of the Skär Islands and later an editor on the liberal *Dagens Nyheter*. From 1874 to 1882 he was an assistant in the Royal Library. In 1875 he made the acquaintance of Siri von Essen, the wife of an officer. She left her husband to marry S. (a marriage that lasted from 1877 to 1891), and from 1877 to 1881 she was an actress at the Dramatic Theater.

The 1870's was a period of philosophical and artistic struggle as S. came to grips with

359

Kierkegaard's religious rigorism. His study of the early work of Brandes (q.v.) prepared the way for his turn to realism. S. frequented a world of radical artists and bohemians whose meeting place was Bern's Restaurant. For years he struggled with the final version of his historical drama *Mäster Olof,* producing a prose version in 1872 and one in verse in 1876. This play, first performed in 1878, presents a naturalistic picture, completely contrary to the conventional one, of the Swedish Reformation.

In 1879 S.'s novel *Röda rummet* (The Red Room, 1913) appeared; it proved a major breakthrough. S. had taken Dickens and Twain (q.v.) as models for his remarkably sure satirical style. The result of his library studies was the prose works *Kulturhistoriska studier* (1881), *Svenska folket* (1882), and *Det nya riket* (1882), which are of dubious value. He also wrote short stories on themes from Swedish history in *Svenska öden och äventyr* (4 vols., 1882–91). All these works are critical of contemporary Sweden and drew violent critical fire. They are full of mistrust for the cultural optimism of the period of industrial expansion and reflect the strong influence of the German philosopher Eduard von Hartmann (1842–1906), whose works S. was studying at that time, and Jean Jacques Rousseau (1712–78).

The 1880's were marked by the approaching crisis in S.'s relationship to his country and by the increasing friction in his marriage with Siri von Essen. S.'s years of voluntary exile between 1883 and 1889, when he "turned his back on his country," were years of restlessness. S. and his wife changed domiciles twenty-two times in a journey across Europe that took them through France, Switzerland, and Denmark. The novellas about marriage in the collection *Giftas* (1884), which dealt with problems of female emancipation but also reflected a freethinking attitude toward religion, led to an official charge against S. The case came to trial in Stockholm in 1884, and S. was acquitted amid the jubilation of his compatriots.

S.'s suspicious nature, however, lost him the support of his progressive-minded friends when he attacked female emancipation in a second collection, *Giftas II* (1886). At the same time his hatred of women, who were unable to live up to his personal ideal of madonnalike femininity, became an *idée fixe.* It was the persistent theme of his naturalistic plays *Fadren* (1887; The Father, 1907),

Kamraterna (1888; Comrades, 1919), *Fröken Julie* (1888; Miss Julie, 1913), and *Fordringssägare* (1880; The Creditors, 1910). While technically fascinating, these controversial dramas often seem to border upon the pathological.

The above plays, which received their first performances in Paris, Berlin, and Copenhagen, established S.'s reputation. Nevertheless, S.'s increasing tendency toward self-induced isolation led him to write autobiographical defenses in *Tjänstekvinnans son* and *Le Plaidoyer d'un fou* (The Confessions of a Fool, 1925), the latter written in French between 1887 and 1888 and translated into Swedish in 1914 (*En dåres forsvarstal*) by John Landquist (b. 1881), the philosopher and literary critic. As Karl Jaspers (b. 1883), has pointed out, psychiatry detects typical symptoms of pathological paranoia in these works.

Mention should be made of the *Dikter* (1883)—some of them written earlier—which show the influence of Heinrich Heine (1797–1856); of the Swiss novellas, *Utopier i verkligheten* (1885); of S.'s short stories about the Skär Islands—*Hemsöborna* (1887; The Natives of Hemsö, 1965) and *Skärkarlsliv* (1888)—some of whose themes date back to his happy years in the early 1870's; of the novel *I havsbandet* (1890), in which Nietzsche's (q.v.) influence first becomes apparent.

In 1889, S. returned to Sweden, where he remained until 1892—a nonproductive period. During these years his painful separation from Siri von Essen occurred. He then went to Berlin, where he was the guest of Hansson (q.v.) and was associated with the group of writers that was known as the Black Pig. It included O. E. Hartleben (1864–1905), Dehmel, Przybyszewski, Hamsun (qq.v.), and the painter Edvard Munch (1863–1944). Here he met the young Austrian journalist Frieda Uhl, whom he married in 1893. They went to Austria and, in 1894, to Paris. But psychological disturbances (new paranoid episodes precipitated partly by unsuccessful scientific experiments and failures in the theater) marred their marriage and led to a separation.

A passionate desire for knowledge drove S. to amateur chemical experiments and studies in the fantastic and the occult to which he sacrificed money, time, and his personal happiness. Between 1896 and 1897, these interests culminated in a philosophical crisis, the successive stages of which S. later described with the exactitude of a pathological case his-

GERTRUDE STEIN

JOHAN AUGUST STRINDBERG

tory in *Inferno* (1897; Eng., 1913) and *Legender* (1898; Legends, 1912). He wandered across half of Europe, finally regaining his mental balance during a visit to Lund and a summer (1899) on Furusund Island.

S.'s defiant opposition to malevolent "forces" gave way to deep resignation and a spirit of atonement. Variations on this theme became the central focus of the drama of his artistic maturity, which broke completely new ground formally and had a lasting influence on the drama of expressionism (q.v.) and other modern stylistic movements. Works of this period include: the three-part play *Till Damascus* (1898–1904; To Damascus, 1933–35), in which the past is relived in the present; *Brott och brott* (1899); *Advent* (1899; Eng., 1912); *Påsk* (1901; Easter, 1912); *Dödsdansen* (1901; The Dance of Death, 1912); and *Ett drömspel* (1902; The Dream Play, 1912). S.'s study of the Swedish theosophist Swedenborg (1688–1772) played an important part in his religious development.

After 1899, S. lived in Stockholm. From 1901 to 1904 he was married to the actress Harriet Bosse. Together with August Falck, he founded the Intimate Theater, a little theater for which he wrote his famous and expressive Chamber Plays: *Oväder* (1907; The Thunderstorm, 1913); *Brända tomten* (1907; After the Fire, 1913); *Spöksonaten* (1907; The Spook Sonata, 1916); and *Pelikanen* (1907).

In the last decade of his life, S., despite his shy loneliness, was inexhaustibly creative, critically alert, and ready at any time for sharp polemical attacks on conformity and national arrogance. Among the works of these years were: the long series of important historical plays; the short stories in *Fagervik och Skamsund* (1902); the moving confession *Ensam* (1903); *Sagor* (1903; Tales, 1930); the novel *Götiska rummen* (1904; The Red Room, 1913); the novellas in *Historiska miniatyrer* (1905; Historical Miniatures, 1913); and the novel *Svarta fanor* (1907).

In 1908, S. moved into his last home, which he called the Blue Tower. Now living in deliberate isolation, he defended his ruminations and scientific experiments in one of his most significant works, the aphoristic *En blå bok* (1907–1908; Zones of the Spirit, 1913), and wrote his final confessional drama, *Vid stora landsvägen* (1909; The Great Highway, 1965). In his collection of speeches *Tal till svenska nationen* (1911–12) he attacked Heidenstam (q.v.) and neoromanticism.

On his birthday in 1912 S. was awarded a state subsidy. He died that year of cancer.

FURTHER WORKS: *Än Bogsveigs saga* (1872); *Från Fjärdingen och Svartbäcken* (1877); *Gillets hemlighet* (1880); *Herr Bengts hustru* (1882); *Lycko-Pers resa* (1882; Lucky Pehr, 1912); *Sömngångarnätter på vakna dagar* (1883); *Marodörer* (1886); *Tschandala* (1888); *Paria* (1889; Pariah, 1913); *Bland franska bönder* (1889); *Den starkare* (1889; The Stronger, 1964); *Blomstermålningar och djurstycken* (1890); *Himmelrikets nycklar* (1892; The Keys of Heaven, 1965); *Bandet* (1892); *Författeren* (1892); *Folkungasagan* (1899; The Saga of the Folkungs, 1959); *Gustav Vasa* (1899; Eng., 1916); *Erik XIV* (1899; Eng., 1931); *Gustav Adolf* (1900; Eng., 1957); *Carl XII* (1901; Eng., 1964); *Midsommar* (1901; Midsummertide, 1912); *Engelbrekt* (1901; Eng. 1949); *Kronbruden* (1902; The Bridal Crown, 1916); *Svanevit* (1902; Swanwhite, 1914); *Näktergalen i Wittenberg* (1903); *Kristina* (1903; Queen Christina, 1955); *Gustav III* (1903; Eng. 1955); *Ordalek och småkonst* (1905); *Svenska miniatyrer* (1905); *Hövdingaminnen* (1906); *Taklagsöl* (1906); *Syndabocken* (1906; The Scapegoat, 1967); *Nya svenska öden* (1906); *Sista riddaren* (1908; The Last of the Knights, 1956); *Bjälbo Jarlen* (1908; Earl Birger of Bjalbo, 1956); *Riksföreståndaren* (1908; The Regent, 1956); *Öppna brev till Intima teatern* (1909; Open Letter to the Intimate Theater, 1966); *Fabler* (1909); *Religiös renässans* (1910); *Samlade skrifter* (55 vols., 1912–20); *Samlade otryckta skrifter* (5 vols., 1918–21); *Skrifter* (14 vols., 1946); *S.s ungdoms journalistik* (1946); *Från Fjärden till Blå tornet* (1947); *Brev* (12 vols., 1948 ff.); *Brev till min dotter Kerstin* (1961); *Ur ockulta dagboken* (1963; From an Occult Diary, 1965). **Selected English translations:** *Easter, and Stories from the Swedish of A. S.* (1912); *Three Plays* (1955); *Five Days* (1956); *The Chamber Plays* (1962); *Selected Plays and Prose* (1964); *Seven Plays* (1964); *Eight Expressionistic Plays* (1965)

BIBLIOGRAPHY: McGill, V. L., *A. S.* (1931; 2nd ed., 1965); Campbell, G. A., *S.* (1933); Jaspers, K., *S. und Van Gogh* (1949); Sprigge, E., *The Strange Life of A. S.* (1949); Adamov, A., *S. dramaturge* (1955); Hamsun, K., *Etwas über S.* (1958); Mortenson, B. M., and Downs, B. W., *S.* (1965); Johanneson, E. O., *The Novels of A. S.* (1968)

OTTO OBERHOLZER

A few evenings ago I read the old S.'s "Chamber Plays": they are terrible, terrible: it is ghastly that old men should end like the little twenty-three-year-old Dauphin: *fin de la vie—ne m'en parlez plus*. . . . But there must be forces in Strindberg, the massed forces of a landslide; to call *this* world his own and yet to be, to achieve—this is beyond all understanding. For he doesn't only *speak* of this despair, which is aroused by everything, he makes something out of it, and he does it splendidly—that one has to admit.

Rainer Maria Rilke, *Briefe aus den Jahren 1907–1914* (1934), p. 200

For utterly biased pig-headedness, for wailing and accusations, he is worse than any woman he ever depicted. . . .
Ibsen writes of human destinies—S. of mono-manias. . . .
Ibsen is a creator of characters—S. (speaking purely technically) only a creator of certain aspects.

Alfred Kerr, *Die Welt im Drama* (1954), pp. 250, 264

As a writer, thinker, prophet, and bearer of a new sense of the world, he thrust so far ahead that today he could never seem the least bit passé. Standing outside—and above—schools and trends, he united them all. A naturalist as much as a neo-romantic, he anticipates expressionism, putting in his debt a whole generation that answered to that name, and, besides, he is the first surrealist as well —the first in every sense.

Thomas Mann, *Altes und Neues* (1953), p. 234

With expressionism (which first comes to mind) he shares the monologue, which breaks down an individual into many figures, and he unquestionably influenced expressionism. But there remains his symbolism, which he shared with contemporaries such as Maeterlinck; there is his romantic cynicism reminiscent of Heine—in short: he cannot be definitively classified. Anybody who comes to him with the prejudice of an "ism" will never do him justice. And yet with the exception of Poe there has been no writer since E. T. A. Hoffman capable of so nonchalantly introducing the weird and the symbolic into everyday life, with the result that one moves imperceptibly from dream world into reality and back again, without the writer laying any particular stress on the motivation of such shifts of scene.

Hans Schwarz, *August Strindberg, Werke*, Vol. IX (1959), p. 350

S. was suffering from a recognized, definable process, which took up more than two decades of his life and which we may call schizophrenia, paraphrenia, or paranoia—not that these names make any difference. . . . Thus it cannot be proved that in his religious crisis S. acquired a new sustained attitude or a philosophical structure, whether invariable or evolving. Actually, the constant factor —it was new insofar as it was new to him—is only the sustained schizophrenic mode of experience; and so the least changeable factor is that which this experience immediately contains, together with the most direct interpretations it leads to. Thus what remains more or less constant is, let us say, the contrasting of his world and the beyond, the presence of demons, spirits, directly intervening forces and powers, and also the idea of these powers giving signs, educating, and punishing.

Karl Jaspers, *Strindberg und Van Gogh* (1949), p. 82, p. 90 f.

STYRON, William
American novelist, b. 11 June 1925, Newport News, Virginia

A Southerner who does not limit himself to the subjects or attitudes of Southern fiction, Styron has shown remarkable versatility in his career as a novelist. His varied characters dramatize the dilemmas of the age.

S.'s first novel, *Lie Down in Darkness* (1951), is a powerful and tragic account of a willful Southern girl, Peyton Loftis. The work unravels brilliantly the social and psychological intricacies of family life, focusing on the Oedipal relation of Peyton to her father. The techniques of symbolism, flashback, and stream of consciousness are deftly used; and though the dark rhetoric of the novel owes something to the example of Faulkner (q.v.), its evocation of love and death reveals a sensibility akin to the sensibility of John Donne and Sir Thomas Browne.

The Long March (1952), a novella about the Marine Corps, is a terse parable of rebellion and conformity presented in a realistic manner with subtle, symbolic undertones.

S.'s third work, *Set This House on Fire* (1960), is a crowded and violent novel set in Italy. It portrays the struggle of an American artist to rid himself of the evil tutelage of a friend, and thereby to regain his self-respect as a free man. As an existential work, the novel was more widely acclaimed in France than America; yet its theme is an old American theme: the definition of freedom through responsibility and courage.

S.'s most controversial work, *The Confessions of Nat Turner* (1967), purports to be a "meditation on history." Written from the point of view of Nat Turner himself, leader of one of the earliest slave rebellions in the U.S., the novel develops, in narrative and introspective scenes, the religious, political, and sexual intricacies of that abortive revolt. The novel was sharply criticized by black writers and white critics for its subtle distortions of history and of the black experience.

S.'s brooding imagination, at times almost obsessive, and his dark gift of poetry, are enhanced by his novelistic sense of action, and by his ability to create memorable characters. Critics who find him willful or obscure overlook these qualities. But the depth of his perceptions into contemporary experience may still remain in question.

BIBLIOGRAPHY: *Crit*, Summer 1960; Hassan, I., *Radical Innocence* (1961); Baumbach, J., *The Landscape of Nightmare* (1965); Klein, M., *After Alienation* (1965); *Crit*, Winter 1966; Friedman, M., and Higro, A. J., eds., *Configuration critique de W. S.* (1967); Clarke, J. H., ed., *W. S.'s Nat Turner* (1968)

IHAB HASSAN

SU Man-shu

(also known as *Su Yuan-ying*), Chinese poet, essayist, and novelist, b. 1384, Yokohama, Japan; d. 2 May 1918, Shanghai

S. was the son of Su Chao-ying, a Cantonese merchant in Yokohama, and a Japanese girl. When he was five years old, S. was taken to Chung-shan in the province of southern Kwangtung to live with his father's clan. There he received a traditional Chinese education. At fourteen he went back to Japan to study at a Chinese school in Yokohama and later at Waseda school in Tokyo. He participated in a movement of the Chinese students to overthrow the Manchu government in China.

In 1903 S. went to Shanghai to engage in teaching and newspaper work. In 1904, while on a trip to Kwangtung, he became a Buddhist monk. He spent the remaining fourteen years of his life in writing, teaching, and traveling. He shuttled between Shanghai and Tokyo, visited Thailand, Ceylon, and Java, but never stayed long in any one place. Back in China, he made friends with prominent men of letters, particularly members of a revolutionary literary society known as Nan-shê, and with leaders of the Kuomintang Party, including Sun Yat-sen (1866–1925) and Chiang Kai-shek (b. 1886). In the last years of his life, disillusionment with political events in the country after the 1911 Revolution and failing health made him pessimistic and melancholic.

S. wrote extensively on a variety of topics, ranging from Sanskrit grammar to the flora of the Western hemisphere. He also prepared a Chinese-English dictionary as well as the geographical terms and itinerary charts for the travelogues of two Buddhist pilgrims. He also compiled three anthologies of English translations of Chinese poems and essays. A fine painter, his landscapes were treasured by friends and other contemporaries.

As a poet, S. specialized in the *chüeh-chu*—a four-line poem with five or seven words to the line. His poems, though written in traditional Chinese forms, are delicate, refreshing, and spontaneous. They show the sensitivity of a young poet in love with women and nature, which he describes with consummate skill. Especially original and exquisite are the descriptions that pertain to the rural scenery in Japan: the ice flag atop a thatched store signaling a nearby market; himself with straw sandals and a broken alms bowl, walking across bridges where cherry blossoms bloom. Buddhism adds a new dimension to his poetic mood in the following lines: 'The cherry blossoms that dot everywhere my cassock / Are one-half rouge specks and one-half tear stains."

The best-known of S.'s works, *Tuan-hung ling-yen chi* (1912; The Lone Swan, 1924), is a semiautobiography of Su San-lang, a Chinese youth of Japanese origin. Upon returning to his home in Japan, he meets and falls in love with his Japanese cousin, Shizuko, and is thus torn by a conflict between his affection for her and his Buddhist vow to remain celibate. Both characters are well drawn. Though she is the traditional well-bred, reserved Oriental girl, Shizuko has a vivacity that urges her to action in her expressions of love for San-lang. The latter, a rather passive character, assumes in the end a heroic stature when, casting aside his doubts and timorous desires, he resolutely renounces his mundane affection to roam like a "lone swan" in this floating world. The delineation of delicate and yet poignant emotions, the novelty of a Sino-Japanese love affair, the conflict between love and religion, combined to make the novel an instant success upon its publication.

S.'s other literary works include a collection of miscellaneous writings entitled *Yen-tzu-han sui-pi* (1913, "Random Notes from a Swallow's Mausoleum"). Though written in traditional style, these notes differ from their prototypes in content and substance. Their interest lies in the author's knowledge of Western language and literature, his familiarity with Sanskrit and with India, and his experiences in Japan and southeast Asia.

"A Sino-Japanese genius," S. bridged the cultural gap between China and Japan and contributed to the development of East-West literary relations. His works were immensely popular and his influence was widespread from the 1920's to the 1940's. His melancholic, romantic mood exerted a fascination on the young people of that period. S.'s writing occupies a prominent place in the literature of 20th-c. China.

FURTHER WORKS: *Wen-hsüeh yin-yüan* (1908, "Affinities in Literature"); *Ch'ao-yin* (1911, "Voices of the Tide"); *Han-Ying san-mei chi* (1914, "Esoteric Essences of Chinese-English Poetry"); *S. M. ch'üan-chi* (ed. Liu Ya-tzu; 5 vols., 1928–31, "Collected Works of S. M."); *S. M. ta-shih chi-nien chi* (ed. Wu-chi Liu; 1943, "A Memorial Volume of the Reverend S. M.'s Works")

BIBLIOGRAPHY: McAleavy, H., *S. M., A Sino-Japanese Genius* (1960); Wu-chi Liu, *S. M.* (1970)

WU-CHI LIU

SUPERVIELLE, Jules

French poet, novelist, and dramatist, b. 16 Jan. 1884, Montevideo, Uruguay; d. 17 May 1960, Paris

Son of French parents, bankers at Montevideo, S. was orphaned at the age of eight. He spent a relatively happy childhood in the pampas, often evoked in his poems and fiction. S. was educated in Paris and lived there all his adult life, except for the years during World War II, which were spent in Uruguay.

S.'s fame rests primarily on his poems. Viewed within the framework of contemporary French poetry, his verse is characterized by an unusual intimacy and lightness of touch. As it reaches beyond the self, his search appears devoid of sentimentality, introspection, and dramatization.

S.'s are the eternal themes of lyric poetry: love, solitude, remembrance, death, and nature. Man's anguish, according to S., stems from his deceptive, insufficient knowledge of himself and the universe. The outer and the inner worlds—those of the dead and the living, of dream and reality—belong to one vast

organism where everything yearns for communion. Nevertheless, this resemblance does not enhance our familiarity and tranquility.

Oblivion, above all, haunts the poet. He forgets, but at least he "knows" that he forgets. *Oublieuse Mémoire* (1943) is the significant title of one of S.'s poetry collections. In another, *Les Amis inconnus* (1934), S. reveals his fear of not recognizing the more intimate features of man and the world. This fear explains his desire to bring remoteness within easy reach, to change the cosmic into the intimate: God into a benign or sad man, the sun into a daisy.

S.'s tales and plays have a poetic delicacy of language and imaginative plots that sometimes unfold with deliberate unreality. The heroes and heroines find themselves in bewildering dilemmas because they usually belong to two worlds: that of the present and of the legendary past in his play *La Belle au bois* (1932), that of high seas and of everyday reality in the short stories of *L'Enfant de la haute mer* (1931), and that of biblical tradition and of modern speed in the stories included in *L'Arche de Noé* (1938).

With subtle irony S. exploits these situations, animating characters of old legends, endowing them with their own peculiar poetic sensitivity, innocence, and awe. Thus, in his works we rediscover not only our fear of grasping nothing in a world of erosion and constant metamorphosis, but also our need to marvel and in a sense relive the day of creation.

FURTHER WORKS: *L'Homme de la pampa* (1923); *Le Voleur d'enfants* (1926; Am., The Man Who Stole Children, 1967; Eng., The Colonel's Children, 1945; play, 1949); *Le Survivant* (1928; The Survivor, 1951); *Le Forçat innocent* (1930); *Bolivar* (1935); *La Fable du monde* (1938); *Orphée et autres contes* (1946); *À La Nuit* (1947); *Choix de poèmes* (1947); *Robinson* (1949); *Shéhérazade* (1949); *Premiers pas de l'univers* (1950); *Le Jeune Homme du dimanche et des autres jours* (1955); *L'Escalier* (1956). **Selected English translations:** *Along the Road to Bethlehem* (1933); *The Ox and the Ass at the Manger* (1945); *The Shell and the Ear* (1951); *J. S.: Poems* (1967); *J. S.: Selected Writings* (1967)

BIBLIOGRAPHY: Sénéchal, C., *J. S., poète de l'univers* (1939); Roy, C., *J. S.* (1949); Greene, T., *J. S.* (1958); Blair, D., *J. S., A*

Modern Fabulist (1960); Etiemble, R., *S.* (1960); Hiddleston, J., *L'Univers de J. S.* (1965)

RENÉE RIESE HUBERT

SURREALISM

As defined by its founder and chief exponent, Breton (q.v.), in his first manifesto in 1924, surrealism has two meanings. In one sense, it is a form of psychic automatism intended to liberate the modes of literary and artistic expression from the traditional limits set by reason; in its encyclopedic connotation, it is a philosophical belief that a superior reality can be achieved by human imagination through the free use of those forms of verbal and pictorial associations that tend to break the barrier of the dream.

In the aftermath of World War I surrealism crystallized into doctrine a series of avant-garde movements that had attracted to Paris writers and artists from all parts of Europe to participate in the artistic renewal previously heralded by both romanticism and symbolism (q.v.). In painting, cubism had cleared away many of the conventions of form earlier in the 20th c., and futurism and dadaism (qq.v.) had challenged bourgeois morality and taste in literature and art. Proceeding beyond the revolutionary nihilism of dada, surrealists were joined by erstwhile cubists and dadaists in a concerted effort to evolve a positive credo and an affirmative technique to add depth and breadth to the aesthetic domain.

Breton borrowed the word "surrealist" from the preface of a fragmentary, experimental play, *Les mamelles de Tirésias* (1917), written by Apollinaire (q.v.) shortly before his death. The surrealists hailed Apollinaire as the foremost poet of the new century because as the spokesman of cubism he had tightened the link between art and poetry and had foreseen a superior destiny for the poet who, in the new spirit, would become "more pure, more live, and more learned."

According to the surrealists, "the great modern tradition" had been launched by Charles Baudelaire (1821–67) in the last two lines of his poem "Le Voyage" (1861 ed. of *Les Fleurs du mal*), in which he called upon man to turn the ordinary voyage into an adventure into the abysses of the unknown, whether the journey lead to heaven or to perdition. Because science in the latter part of

the 19th c. had made the metaphysical infinite a less than satisfactory objective for seekers of the absolute, the poet aimed to free the notion of reality from the restrictions of what the logical mind called "reason" and "nature."

Early evidences of the cult of the irrational were apparent in French poets who around 1870 had best expressed the spiritual crisis of the epoch: the hallucinatory writings of Lautréamont (1846–70), *Les Illuminations* of Arthur Rimbaud (1854–91), and Stéphane Mallarmé's (1842–98) *Igitur*, which was later recast as the most esoteric poem of the 19th c., "Un Coup de dés jamais n'abolira le hasard" (1897).

The surrealists also found support in the occultists and oneirocritics among the German romantics such as Achim von Arnim (1781–1831), Novalis (1772–1801), Johann Hölderlin (1770–1843), Jean Paul (1763–1825), and E. T. A. Hoffmann (1776–1822). They defined the poet as any man who was endowed with imagination and had a passion for liberty, who was ready to substitute for the theological beyond the infinite possibilities of the concrete world, *hic et nunc,* in a daring transgression of form and of the rational processes of cause and effect. This was the materio-mystical climate of surrealism.

Among the French writers who at some time during the period 1924–39 assumed the surrealist trademark were: Breton as the head of school, Aragon, Tzara, Artaud, Desnos, Éluard, Michaux, Soupault, Prévert (qq.v.), and Benjamin Péret (1889–1959). Artists of various nationalities became their associates: Salvador Dali, Marcel Ducham, Max Ernst, Alberto Giacometti, Valentine Hugo, René Magritte, Jean Miró, Francis Picabia, Yves Tanguy. Picasso, if never literally a surrealist, was closely affiliated with both Breton and Éluard.

Beginning with *Les Champs magnétiques* (first published in 1919 in the avant-garde journal *Littérature*) co-authored by Breton and Soupault, surrealism maintained itself as a distinct literary movement all through the period between the two world wars. The principal journals were: *Révolution Surréaliste* (1924–30), transformed into *Le Surréalisme au Service de la Révolution* (1930–33); *Minotaure* (1933–38); *Cahiers GLM* (1936–39); *VVV* in New York during World War II, when Breton temporarily exiled himself in America; and the short-lived *Medium* in France (1953–54).

Surrealism had its polemics, metaphysics,

and *art poétique*. Its polemics, given free expression in the periodicals and in Breton's *Second Manifeste* (1930), centered around the disloyalty of certain of the early surrealists and the short-lived political affiliations with that other dream of transforming the world, a dream that had been implied in early forms of communism. The metaphysics is most directly stated in Breton's *Premier Manifeste* (1924)—which had taken him five years to formulate and which marked the official birth of the movement—and his *Nadja* (1928; Eng., 1960) and *Les Vases communicants* (1932), in Aragon's *Le Paysan de Paris* (1926), René Crevel's (1900–1935) *L'Esprit contre la raison* (1927), Éluard's *Les Dessous d'une vie ou la Pyramide humaine* (1926).

These works crystallized in a fusion of poetry and prose the new philosophy of reality. Inspired by Hegel's monistic notion of the universe, they aimed at a synthesis of the spiritual and the material, believing in the continuity of the state of consciousness and the dream, of life and death; they conceived of existence as the composite of two connected urns, a conciliation between apparent contradictions in form and phenomena. Refuting all notions of a spiritual order in nature, they accepted hazard or chance as the manifestation of a "divine disorder." According to Aragon in *Le Paysan de Paris*: "The concrete form of disorder is the outer limit of the mind." If the mind can sufficiently free itself from logic to be receptive to this disorder, then it will have pierced the outer shell of reality and arrived at a more comprehensive notion of the material world.

The *art poétique* is also clearly exposed in Breton's first and second manifestoes as well as in Aragon's *Traité du style* (1928) and Tzara's "Essai sur la situation de la poésie" (published in *Le Surréalisme au Service de la Révolution*, No. 4, 1931). A radical blow was dealt to descriptive writing and at the same time to the abstract imagery and analogy of correspondences of symbolist writing.

Abandoning the imitation of nature to photography, the surrealists attempted to make of art an act of creation rather than of representation. The creative role of language was stressed. The poem became the composite of a series of images that were not dependent on any central subject: "Images think for me," said Éluard.

It was Breton's belief that words brought together by creative intuition could form a dynamic image whose effect would be much more provocative than that of abstract thoughts groping for words to give them a countenance.

In restoring language to a state of effervescence, the surrealist poet investigated the potential meaning captive within words that had become tired and shopworn through abuse. Even more important than the choice of words was the combination of words. Poetic analogy was replaced by the juxtaposition of the farfetched chance encounters of two images.

This concept of the new metaphor had been suggested in the presurrealist era by Reverdy (q.v.) in a statement that was often to be quoted: "The image is purely a creation of the mind. It cannot be produced by comparison but by bringing together two more or less distant realities." Images thus constructed contain a dose of absurdity and an element of surprise that in the opinion of Apollinaire was one of the fundamental resources of the modern mind. The surrealist poet and artist found themselves in a magnetic field where, by the attraction of one image to another, the objects of reality deviated from their traditional roles. The result is an incongruous unit—fashioned out of sensory data but in combinations undecipherable to the outsider—that establishes an intimate link between the subject and the object.

As a young medical student in mental hospitals during World War I, Breton had become acquainted with the works of Freud and Jean-Martin Charcot. Later, with his surrealist colleagues he explored Freudian methods as means of preparing the subconscious mind for creative writing and painting. Among these activities was automatic writing. These "surrealist texts" were not poems. They served to enrich poetic consciousness and break down traditional word associations too deep-set to be avoided by the rational mind.

The surrealists also participated in *séances* designed to promote collective dreaming and the uninhibited interpretation of dreams. Breton noted that the effect of the dream on imagery—the disorientation of objects, the distortion of events, the verbal condensation of the dream—provided a transfiguration of reality worthy of poetic transcription.

Freudian influence also accounted for the surrealists' interest in the mentally deranged. *L'Immaculée Conception* (1930), a collaboration between Breton and Éluard, set out to imitate delirium and to stimulate the various stages of insanity. Breton's novel *Nadja* represented a heroine, mentally disturbed, who makes no distinction between reality and hallucination as she gracefully hides her fern-colored eyes behind the imaginary feather of her hat and sees a blue wind passing through the trees. The surrealists considered that the study of these aberrations served as a gateway to a better comprehension of the total working of the human intellect. Breton put his faith in the unexpected, in psychic spontaneity; logic having so obviously failed, the world might well be transformed, he thought, through the liberation of the irrational forces in man.

Surrealism essentially attempted to capture the state of the *merveilleux,* to express the disordinate in nature as perceived by the irrational qualities of the mind. This is the driving vision of Breton's poetry in collections of verse such as *Clair de terre* (1923), *Le Revolver à cheveux blancs* (1932), Éluard's *Capitale de la douleur* (1926) and *Défense de savoir* (1928), Péret's *Le Grand jeu* (1928), and Tzara's *L'Homme approximatif* (1930).

World War II had the double effect of dissolving the surrealist coterie, already depleted in the 1930's and of disseminating the surrealist style abroad. Aragon and Éluard, who had committed themselves to the resistance and to communist affiliations, reverted to a more directly communicative lyricism that retained much of the surrealist type of imagery while abandoning its ideology.

The transformations in French poetic language gradually encouraged similar mutations in the literary language of other countries. Foreign surrealist magazines included *Surrealismus* in Prague, *Nadrealizam Danas I ovde* in Yugoslavia, *Gaceta de Arte* in Spain, *Konkretion* in Denmark, *L'Echange Surréaliste* in Japan, and *Negro sobre Blanco* in Argentina.

The repercussions were more far-reaching in the realm of the plastic arts, and surrealist exhibits were organized in most countries. Twenty-four nations were represented in the International Surrealist Exposition held in Paris in 1949. The vertiginous freedom of expression unleashed by surrealism eventually affected the form and technique of the novel, and Artaud's *Le Théâtre et son double* (1938) provided the theater of the absurd with many of its techniques.

However, the philosophy of surrealism became more specifically involved with the destiny and presence of Breton, whose later writings—*Fata Morgana* (1940), *Les États généraux* (1943), and *Ode à Charles Fourier* (1947)—identified him more and more with the Hermetic tradition, *i.e.,* with the desire to comprehend the great circuit of creation, to establish a firmer bond between sense perceptions and the power of intellectual metamorphosis. The "convulsive beauty" he discerned in the unpredictability of universal phenomena found confirmation in the scientific doctrines of probability and non-Euclidean geometry. Exceeding its historical moment, surrealism became a style and philosophy attuned to the inventive spirit of 20-c. science. As the antithesis of both the literature of escape and the literature of despair, surrealism expressed a consuming desire to master the human condition.

BIBLIOGRAPHY: Breton, A., *Le Surréalisme et la peinture* (1928); Read, H., *Surrealism* (1936); *Lemaître, G., From Cubism to Surrealism in French Literature* (1941); Nadeau, M., *Histoire du surréalisme* (1945); Balakian, A., *Literary Origins of Surrealism* (1947); Tzara, T., *Le Surréalisme et l'après guerre* (1947); Crastre, V., "Le Drame du surréalisme," *TM,* July 1948; Nadeau, M., *Documents surréalistes* (1948); Raymond, M., *From Baudelaire to Surrealism* (1949); Carrouges, M., *André Breton et les données fondamentales du surréalisme* (1950); Fowlie, W., *Age of Surrealism* (1950); Breton, A., *Entretiens* (1952); Breton, A., *La Clé des champs* (1953); Alquié, F., *Philosophie du surréalisme* (1955); Friedrich, H., *Die Struktur der modernen Lyrik* (1956); Sedlmayr, H., *Die Revolution der modernen Kunst* (1956); Balakian, A., *Surrealism: The Road to the Absolute* (1959); Sauro, A., *Le surréalisme* (1964); Browder, C., *André Breton, Arbiter of Surrealism* (1967)

ANNA BALAKIAN

SVEVO, Italo

(pseud. of *Ettore Schmitz*), Italian novelist and short-story writer, b. 19 Dec. 1861, Trieste; d. 13 Sept. 1928, Motta di Livenza

S. is seen as the first and, virtually, the only psychological novelist in Italian literature. It is no coincidence that James Joyce (q.v.) discovered him; his influence on Joyce has been investigated on a comprehensive scale (Louis Gillet).

Although the Schmitz family came from the Rhineland, S.'s father considered himself an Italian. The families of S.'s mother and grandmother can be traced back to Italian-Jewish origins. As a young man, S. was sent by his father to study at Segnitz near Würzburg to improve his German. While there, he read the German classicists, and also concentrated upon Jean Paul (1763–1825) and Schopenhauer (1788–1860). S. felt at an early age that his calling was to be a poet. His father's financial failures, however, forced him to earn his livelihood at the Trieste branch of the Viennese Union Bank.

In 1892 S. published his first novel, *Una vita* (originally, *Un inetto*; A Life, 1963), which relates the story of a young man from the country who moves to Trieste, becomes employed at a bank, and is defeated by love and life. The book was later compared to Flaubert's *L'Éducation sentimentale*. As an analytical work it fits into none of the literary mainstreams prevailing at that time in Italy. Its ostensible naturalism is a conscious turn toward the stream of thoughts in the mind.

Aside from the vivacious milieu portrayed that exquisitely evokes old Trieste, the subject of this pitilessly accurate description is the interior world of its hero, Alfonso Nitti. This unveiling of a sensitive, complicated soul is somewhat reminiscent of the famous novella *The Poor Fiddler* by Franz Grillparzer (1791–1872). Purists found the language here to be "barbaric" because of its mixture of German and Slav elements. The book was called "nontopical," since it did not take into account the pressing issue of the time, Italian irredentism (referring to the annexation of Trieste).

For the same reason S.'s second novel *Senilità* (1898; As a Man Grows Older, 1932) met with even less success, despite the unprecedented individuality, power and terseness with which love was analyzed. S.'s irony is already evident here.

Discouraged by these literary failures, S. henceforth became a distinguished businessman in Trieste society. In 1904 he met Joyce, with whom he formed a genuine friendship.

S.'s third and final novel, *La Coscienza di Zeno* (Confessions of Zeno, 1930), did not appear until 1923. It was styled in the form of a life confession written by a patient at the instigation of his psychoanalyst.

S., who knew Freud, defined his relationship to Freud as follows: "We novelists are given to tinker with the great philosophers...We

misinterpret them but give them human form nevertheless." *Zeno* is not chronologically ordered; instead, it consists of "experience cycles" that overlap one another in time. ("The past is always new; it changes as life progresses.") S. rejects "beautiful writing" in favor of veracity and preserves the veneer of old Austrian Trieste. Yet, despite E. Montale's (q.v.) enthusiasm for the novel, it too was looked upon by Italians as alien.

Not until Joyce interested Valéry Larbaud in S. was he truly discovered, an event that took place first in France in 1926. After his death appeared the following: *La novella del buon vecchio e della bella fanciulla* (1930; The Nice Old Man and the Pretty Girl, 1930); the significant fragment, *Corto viaggio sentimentale* (1949); and six unfinished prose pieces that continue the saga of Zeno (Further Confessions of Zeno, 1969).

His work is thoroughly independent of all movements, though the Italian neoclassicists take special interest in his work. Its analytical quality is not a "'style" so much as the spontaneous, almost documentary expression of how S. experienced life and how he related to it emotionally.

FURTHER WORKS: *Diario per la fidanzata* (1896); *Vino generoso* (1927); *Una burla riuscita* (1928; The Hoax, 1929); *Carteggio inedito di I. S.—James Joyce*, in *Inventario* (Vol. 1, 1949); *Saggi e pagine sparse* (1954); *Opere* (1954); *Commedie* (1960); *Lettere alla moglie* (1963); *Epistolario* (ed. L. Svevo; 1966). **Selected English translations:** *Short Sentimental Journey, and Other Stories* (1967)

BIBLIOGRAPHY: Sternberg, F., *L'Opera di S.* (1928); Punter, M., *I. S.* (1936); Cambon, G., "Zeno come anti-Faust," *Verri*, VIII (1963), ix, 69–76; Gastaldi, M., *I. S.* (1964); Wais, K., *Der Erzähler I. S.* (1965); Furbank, P. N., *I. S.: The Man and the Writer* (1966); Ellman, R., "Speaking of Books: I. S. and Joyce," *New York Times Book Review*, 21 Jan. 1968, pp. 2, 21; Montale, E., "I. S. in the Centenary of His Birth," *Art and Literature*, XI–XII (1968), 9–31

PIERO RISMONDO

SWAHILI LITERATURE

Swahili is well known as the lingua franca of a large part of eastern Africa; for literary purposes, however, it has not been used outside the area where it originated: Zanzibar and the coast and islands of Kenya and Tanganyika. Until the European conquest, Swahili was written in the Arabic script. The literature in this language, according to popular tradition, began as early as the 12th c., with the works of the legendary warrior-poet, Liongo, whose character, motivations, and deeds recall the Viking skalds of early Scandinavian literature.

The earliest extant Swahili manuscript, the *Ubendi wa Tambuka* (1728), exhibits the main characteristics of most later Swahili writing. An epic poem (*ubendi*) based on an Arabic original, it deals with the beginnings of the growth of Islam.

The first important Swahili writer whose work has been preserved was Saiyid Abdallah bin ali bin Nasir (died ca. 1820), an Arab, whose family originated in Hadhramaut. He has left two fine poems: one, *Takhmis wa Liongo,* is based on native traditions; the other, *al-Inkishafi,* is a devotional piece inspired by the precepts of Mohammedanism.

The 19th c. was the golden age of classical Swahili writing with such authors as Sheikh Muhyi 'l-Din bin Sheikh Kahtan al-Waili (ca. 1790–1870), Saiyid 'Umar bin Amin bin 'Umar bin Amin bin Nasir al-Ahdal (1798–1870), and Saiyid Mansab Abu Bakr bin Abd al-Rahman al-Husseini (ca. 1828–1922). While these poets were bringing the traditional religious epic to a high degree of formal perfection and disseminating other prosodic forms derived from Arabic poetry, others infused new, more realistic trends into Swahili literature: the poems of Muyaka bin Haji al-Ghassaniy (1776–1840) brought lyrical poetry out of the mosque into the marketplace; Abdallah bin Masud bin Salim al-Mazrui (1797–1894) used the *ubendi* techniques for the narration of contemporary events in his *Ubendi wa al-Akida.*

This type of secular epic became very popular as a result of the colonization of Africa by European powers in the last decade of the 19th c. Hemedi bin Abdallah bin Said bin Abdallah bin Masudi al-Buhriy wrote many works in the usual Muslim manner, but he also composed the *Utendi wa vita vya wadachi kutalamaki Mrima* on the German conquest of the Swahili coast in the late 1880's. Abdul Karim bin Jamaliddini wrote the *Utenzi wa vita vya Maji-Maji,* which deals with the native revolt of 1905–1907.

European colonization, the creation of mission schools, and the introduction of the printing press prompted some Swahili writers to resort to the Roman alphabet instead of the Arabic script that had been used previously. One of the earliest works in this form was *Habari za Wakilindi* by Abdallah bin Hemedi bin Ali Liajjemi. A prose chronicle of the semihistorical origins of the Kilindi tribe, it was printed in three parts on a missionary press in 1895, 1904, and 1907. The new medium, however, did not bring any real revolution in style or inspiration, although Matthias E. Mnyampala was to use the traditional epic form for an adaptation of the gospel, the *Utenzi wa Enjili takatifu* (1963).

Shaaban Robert (1909–1962) was the first Swahili author to write in such modern genres as the short story, the political allegory, and the essay. He also produced translations of European works and became especially noted for his novel *Adili na Nduguze* (1952). Despite his use of these new genres, both his poetry and his prose fiction are characterized by the sedate, refined, and dignified style, the somewhat *précieux* taste for rare terms and turns, and above all the strongly edifying and devotional purposes that constituted the classical tradition.

As in Ethiopia, the most significant change in Swahili literature occurred in the late 1950's and early 1960's. In those years a group of young Tanzanian writers composed stories in a racy version of everyday speech, dealing with picturesque lowlife types of the Tanga coastal region.

A substantial amount of classical Swahili writings has been edited and translated under the aegis of the East Africa Swahili Committee.

ALBERT S. GÉRARD

SWEDISH LITERATURE

The development of Swedish literature since about 1880 falls within the mainstreams of world literature. During the 1880's Sören Kierkegaard's (1813–55) philosophy, the social drama of Ibsen (q.v.), and the literary criticism of Brandes (q.v.) helped to bring about the breakthrough of naturalism (q.v.) in Sweden as elsewhere. It worked not merely as a new literary program but primarily as an intellectual and moral revolt against the Christian view of life and the whole social structure founded upon it. All of this found expression in literature that analyzed the major social problems of its time. Its most brilliant representative was Strindberg (q.v.), who launched the movement toward such literature in 1879 with his novel *Röda Rummet* and brought it to its peak with his marital dramas and pre-1890 novels.

Compared with Strindberg's powerful work, that of the other naturalists seems somewhat flat and mediocre. Few of them go beyond a meticulously analytical realism in a negatively critical vein such as that exemplified by Ernst Ahlgren (pseudonym of Victoria Benedictsson, 1850–88). The short stories of Anna Charlotte Leffler (1849–92) about the feminist movement also have a strong social slant. In addition to gloomy novels about psychopaths, Gustaf af Geijerstam (1858–1909) wrote a series of pseudomystical short stories that brought him unmerited popularity, especially abroad. Regionalism was an important factor in the prose of Strindberg, Ahlgren, and Geijerstam; and in the satirical short stories of August Bondeson (1854–1906), a physician. Regionalism was also important to a few poets of this period. The best of these were Albert Ulrik Bååth (1853–1912), who wrote down-to-earth social poetry, and Hansson (q.v.), who, for all his naturalistic technique and satirical tone, was primarily a poet of mood and thus a supporter of the so-called *skånska diktarskolan* (Skåne school of poetry). (Ekelund, q.v., was later to be numbered among the talented members of this group.)

The internationally oriented generation of the 1880's, known as the *åttiotalet*, was as short-lived as it was explosive, and the reaction against it was not long in coming. About 1890 Strindberg turned away from naturalism in an evolution that was to lead him by way of Nietzsche (q.v.) to symbolism and expressionism (qq.v.). He thus became a precursor of the neoromanticism of the *nittiotalet*, the generation of the 1890's which inaugurated a golden age, especially in poetry, and set the tone of literature for the next twenty years. In 1889 Heidenstam (q.v.) in his article "Renässans" made the first critical attack on the principles of the 1880's and quickly found supporters. Among the earliest were Hallström, Selma Lagerlöf (qq.v.), and Gustaf Fröding (1860–1911), all of whom made their literary debuts in 1891. They were to be joined later by other writers, among whom were the dramatist Hedberg (q.v.), the influential critic and literary historian Levertin (q.v.), and the novelist Axel Lundegård (1861–1930), who broke away from naturalism.

Among the *nittiotalister* faith in the positive life forces and in the power of art to edify and ennoble man replaced the gloomy pessimism of the *åttiotalister*. No longer seeing man as a creature conditioned by his heritage and environment, they revered the strong personality. Like their predecessors, they favored regionalism, not tendentiously but in order to explore more deeply nature and the religious and imaginative life of their own people. Heidenstam upheld aestheticism and called attention to the past of Sweden as a source of power for the present. Selma Lagerlöf saw man as driven by irrational forces yet striving for ethical values. Fröding, who, like Selma Lagerlöf, had his roots in the rich tradition of Värmland, a province of southwestern Sweden, was a virtuoso poet of appealing mood lyrics and hallucinatory, visionary poetry. Karlfeldt (q.v.) came to the fore as a popular nature poet.

In addition to these writers, who were primarily poets (among whom three were Nobel Prize winners—Selma Lagerlöf, Heidenstam, and Karlfeldt), several prose writers emerged: Hallström, a master of vivid atmospheric prose; Pelle Molin (1864–96), a painter and writer full of humor and naïve romanticism; the historical novelist Högberg (q.v.), and the popular humorist and regionalist Engström (q.v.).

The younger members of the *nittiotalet* hardly constitute a school. Still strongly linked to the *nittiotalet* by their love of truth and their optimistic belief in progress, they cultivated beauty and atmosphere but not the romantic rhapsodic evasion of reality typical of the *nittiotalister*.

This attitude is most evident in two singular yet closely related *fin-de-siècle* figures, both of whom were extreme individualists, skeptics, and aesthetes, who stand at the turn of the century: Bo Hjalmar Bergman (q.v.) and Hjalmar Söderberg (1869–1941). One of their favorite themes was the sensual, weak-willed big-city *flâneur*. A tone of skeptical resignation also marks the work of Henning Berger (1872–1924), best known for his American sketches and his descriptions of Stockholm. Ekelund, an exclusive aesthete, pursued classical harmony and a heroic idealism in life.

The period from 1910 to 1930 was dominated for the most part by the *tiotalisterna*, the generation of 1910, which, stimulated by the aesthetic individualism of Söderberg and Bergman, prepared the way for neorealism. Unlike their immediate predecessors, they paid considerable attention to social and contemporary problems and were interested in people of widely divergent social classes. The novels of Hjalmar Bergman (q.v.), the first Swedish writer to be deeply influenced by Sigmund Freud (1856–1939), depicted with humor, sarcasm, and objectivity the world of the small-town bourgeoisie. The morose moralist Nordström (1882–1942) explored the psychology of the common man, while the novels and short stories of Gustaf Hellström (1882–1953), Elin Wägner (1882–1949), and Marika Stiernstedt (1875–1954) concentrated on contemporary problems. Meanwhile the essayist and literary historian Fredrik Böök (1883–1961) was violently attacking aestheticism; while another brilliant critic, John Landquist (b. 1881), also well known as a philosopher, successfully fought the determinism of the 1880's by introducing into Sweden the principles of free will formulated by Bergson (q.v.). Among the writers strongly influenced by these principles were Sigfrid Siwertz (b. 1882) and Sven Lidman (1882–1960).

The poetry of this period shows tendencies similar to those of the prose: a turning away from the solemn, pompous style of the *nittiotalister* in favor of simplicity and a realistic range of themes. Here the leading role was played by Österling (q.v.), whose *intimism,* a kind of lyrical humanism, found many followers in the 1920's, among them Karl Asplund (b. 1890), Sten Selander (1891–1957), and Gunnar Mascoll Silfverstolpe (1893–1942), all academicians of an intellectual and cultural bent.

The idyllic optimism of these bourgeois realists, however, was not shared by other writers of the same generation. The latter saw in World War I a collapse of all human and spiritual values, making an optimistic view of culture impossible. Tormented by insecurity, anxiety, and disgust, these writers attempted to discover a profound meaning in existence. This generation expressed itself most tellingly in the profound work of Lagerkvist (q.v.), who was to dominate modern Swedish literature for four decades. A closely related attitude to life marks the original work of Birger Sjöberg (1885–1929) and the verbally austere, world-scorning poetry of Malmberg (q.v.), a sovereign artist whose skillfull use of language recalls George and Hofmannsthal (qq.v.). The subtly ironical religious poetry of Harriet Löwenhjelm (1887–1918) reflects some of the attitudes prevalent at this time.

The quest for metaphysical values led Lagerkvist and some other writers, notably such socially oriented authors as Ivan Oljelund (b. 1892) and Ragnar Jändel (1895–1939), to take a religious turn—sometimes short-lived—usually toward an undogmatic Christianity. The 1920's were even marked by a religious revival in a deeper sense. Here the ecumenical movement of Bishop Nathan Söderblom (1866–1931) and the founding of the Sigtunastiftelsen, a center for religious meditation, by Manfred Björkquist (b. 1884) certainly played important roles. Shortly after 1930 the Oxford Movement, which originated in England as an attempt to restore the religious faith of the Middle Ages, found many adherents among such Swedish intellectuals as Sven Stolpe (b. 1905), Harry Blomberg (1893–1950), Jändel, and for a time Malmberg.

Modernism in poetry reached its peak in the 1920's, still under the direct influence of Lagerkvist. While Ekelund was the first to use free verse, Lagerkvist deserves credit for being the first Swedish writer to recognize and adopt such European literary and artistic techniques as expressionism, dadaism, and futurism (qq.v.), using them to express a sense of the chaos of contemporary life. His example was closely followed by Swedish-language poets in Finland around 1920; there a group of poets including Björling, Enckell (qq.v.), Elmer Diktonius (1896–1961), Kerstin Söderholm (1897–1943), and Henry Parland (1908–1930) were experimenting with avant-garde poetry under the leadership of the extremely talented Edith Södergran (q.v.) and the critic Hagar Olsson (b. 1893).

In Sweden the anthology *Fem unga* (1929) finally brought about the definitive break-through of modernism; the title of the anthology was later applied collectively to its writers, although they never really constituted a school. This anthology gave a hearing to several working-class writers who were committed to a Freudian vitalism and primitivism and whose poetry and prose sought to treat contemporary reality in new experimental forms and in a matter-of-fact style. Their models were D. H. Lawrence, Gide (qq.v.), and the French surrealists (*see* surrealism). The tenets of these young writers—comprising a pagan glorification of life (*livsdyrkan*), a romantic attitude to sex, and an extreme emphasis on the development of new forms—were seen most clearly in the works of Artur Lundkvist (b. 1906), as well as in those of

Boye, Martinson (qq.v.), Gustaf Sandgren (b. 1904), and Josef Kjellgren (1907–1948).

The early years of the 1930's, known as the *trettiotalet,* were marked by extremely lively controversy. The novel series *Fröknarna von Pahlen* (7 vols., 1930–35) by Agnes von Krusenstjerna (q.v.) aroused violent discussion. Stolpe, in his journal *Fronten,* attacked vitalism, sexual romanticism, and the idyllicism of the lyrical humanists, while the principles of the *Fem unga* school were strongly supported by the journals *Clarté* and *Spektrum,* for which Boye, Arnold Ljungdal (b. 1901), Stellan Arvidson (b. 1902), Blomberg, and the surrealist Ekelöf (qq.v.) were the most distinguished spokesmen.

These academic revolutionaries of bourgeois origin prepared the way for the generation that became prominent in the 1930's, notably in the work of an imposing group of *proletärförfattare* (proletarian writers). Novels with a strong working-class orientation were written by Maria Sandel (1870–1927), Gustav Hedenvind-Eriksson (1880–1967), and Martin Koch (1882–1940). During the periods from 1910 to 1930, known successively as the *tiotalet* and the *tjugotalet,* proletarian poetry was represented by Karl-Gustaf Ossianilsson (1875–1970), Jändel, Dan Andersson (1888–1920), Erik Lindorm (1889–1941), and Oljelund, among others. About 1930, as a result of the growing cultural emancipation of the working class brought about primarily by the adult-education movement, a new generation of self-educated writers came of age and dealt, at first hesitantly but then with increasing self-confidence, with their own experiences. Often their work shows a return to naturalism, except that these writers covered Swedish national life more comprehensively than the naturalist writers had done; in addition, they adopted the findings of psychology, and particularly of psychoanalysis.

Almost all of these writers were devout, violently anticlerical Marxists. Like their foreign models, such as Zola, Gorki, and Andersen Nexø (qq.v.), they used much autobiographical or sociological material in their novels and short stories. Among the outstanding members of this group were the *statardiktare,* who described the life of the impoverished farm laborers known as the *statare,* as in the works of Fridegård and Moberg (qq.v.); Moa (Helga Maria) Martinson (1890–1964), who wrote *Mor gifter sig* (1936), *Kyrkbröllop* (1938), *Drottning Grågyllen* (1937), and *Vägen under stjärnorna* (1940);

Eyvind Johnson (q.v.), an intellectual who was responsible for a stylistic renewal; and Rudolf Värnlund (1900–1945), whose novels and plays deal with problems of big-city working-class youth. Closely related to their work is that of the younger proletarian writers who first appeared in *Fem unga,* and the novels of Harald Beijer (1896–1955; *Brita,* 3 vols., 1940–43) and Folke Fridell (b. 1904; *Död mans hand,* 1946), and, after 1940, the novels of Björn-E. Höijer (b. 1907; *Bergfinken,* 1944; *Rosenkransen,* 1953; *Befriaren,* 1956).

A wide gulf separates these *proletärförfattare* from the more tradition-bound group of bourgeois and academically trained writers whose contribution to the novel of the 1930's and subsequent years was no less significant. The tradition of the generation of 1910 was maintained by Hedberg (q.v.), whose masterful psychological insight and merciless sarcasm exposed the foibles of the Stockholm bourgeoisie. Another satirist is Gösta Gustaf-Janson (b. 1902; *Stora famnen,* 1937). On the other hand, Arvid Brenner (pseudonym of Helge Heerberger, b. 1907; *En dag som andra,* 1939; *Så går vi mot paradis,* 1944; *Fixeringsbild,* 1955) is purely a psychologist.

Aspects of the life of the lower and upper middle class are described with subtle psychological insight in the works of Fritz Thorén (1899–1950), Walter Ljungquist (b. 1900), Hans Botwid (b. 1901), Waldemar Hammenhög (b. 1902; *Pettersson & Bendel,* 1931), Hans Hergin (b. 1910), and Per Erik Rundquist (b. 1912), and in those of the women novelists Gertrud Lilja (b. 1887; *Hök och duva,* 1942; *Det hemlösa hjärtat,* 1946), Irja Browallius (b. 1901; *Nagon gång skall det ljusna,* 1941), and Eva Berg (b. 1904; *Ny kvinna,* 1936). Stina Aronson (1892–1956) and Tage Aurell (b. 1895; *Smärre berättelser,* 1946; *Nya berättelser,* 1949) are outstanding novella writers.

The novels of Bengtsson (q.v.), an academician who is also an important essayist, combine great learning with scintillating imagination and a brilliant narrative talent. Arnold Norlind (1883–1929) and G. H. Sigfrid Lindström (1892–1950), authors of profound reflections and aphorisms, deserve special mention, as do Ferlin (q.v.) and humorists Fritiof Nilsson Piraten (b. 1895) and Peder Sjögren (1905–1966). The poetry of the 1930's, insofar as it remains traditional, departs from earlier poetry chiefly in its powerful formal expressiveness, which also characterizes the work of Gullberg, Edfelt (qq.v.), Gabriel Jönsson (b. 1892), Einar

Malm (b. 1900), Karl Ragnar Gierow (b. 1904), and Olof Lagercrantz (b. 1911).

Among the modernists, the experiments of Ekelöf and Lundkvist are of major importance. Their influence—and thus indirectly the influence of French surrealism and, later, of Eliot (q.v.)—strongly affected the generation of the 1940's, the *fyrtiotalister,* especially its two most significant representatives, Lindegren (q.v.) and Karl Vennberg (b. 1910), who expressed the emotional, melancholy view of life characteristic of the "lost generation." A discordant, rebellious attitude linked with an attempt to evoke the subconscious dream-world through surrealistic, associative techniques also marks the poetry of their numerous successors, among whom the most important are probably Harald Forss (b. 1911), Maria Wine (b. 1912), Werner Aspenström (b. 1918), Arne Nyman (b. 1918), Sven Alfons (b. 1918), Ragnar Thoursie (b. 1919), and Bernt Erikson (b. 1921). Toward the end of this decade, Stig Sjödin (b. 1917), Axel Liffner (b. 1919), Stig Carlsson (b. 1920), Lars Gyllensten (b. 1921), a typical transitional figure, and Åke Nordin (b. 1922) also became prominent.

The sense of doom, the feeling of disillusionment and impotence, and the attitude of nihilistic skepticism that characterized much of the writing of this period were expressed in prose even more strongly than in poetry. Such attitudes appear most prominently in the work of Thorsten Jonsson (1910–50), whose models were Hemingway, Faulkner, and Steinbeck (qq.v.); in Peter Nisser (b. 1919; *Den röda mården,* 1954; *Vredens födelse,* 1955), whose popularity soon waned; and in Ahlin (q.v.), Gustaf Rune Eriksson (b. 1918), and Olov Jonason (b. 1919), The search for a striking, sober, down-to-earth style led to new achievements in the novella, notably on the part of Dagerman (q.v.), Aspenström, Lars Göransson (b. 1919), Gösta Oswald (1926–50), and—last but not least—Sivar Arnér (b. 1909), a mystically inclined intellectual. Closely related to their work both in spirit and form is the prose of Mårten Edlund (b. 1913), Gösta Petterson (b. 1919), Bengt Anderberg (b. 1920), and Owe Husáhr (1921–58).

The generation of the 1950's, known as the *femtiotalisterna,* by no means broke with revolutionary modernism, and the influence of Lindegren and Vennberg, now regarded as classics, was as strong as ever. On the other hand, the surprisingly romantic tone that pervades the works of all the young poets of the early 1950's is in marked contrast to the severe sobriety of the *fyrtiotalister.* Shortly after their emergence, however, the members of the generation of the 1950's began to be dominated by the need for metaphysical or religious beliefs. A widespread use of Catholic religious symbols—often without real understanding of their significance—became apparent in the poetry of Ann Margret Dahlquist-Ljungberg (b. 1915), Östen Sjöstrand (b. 1925), Staffan Larsson (b. 1927), and Bo Setterlind (b. 1929). The aim of other young poets such as Ingemar Gustafson (b. 1928), who was influenced by Michaux (q.v.), and Lars Forssell (b. 1928) is the creation of poetry based on purely aesthetic considerations. Other characteristics of the poets of the 1950's are a pronounced intellectualism and a vital interest in the theoretical basis of formal problems, including the "new criticism" (*see* literary criticism). Of the poets who made their debut around 1955 Sandro Key-Åberg (b. 1922), Folke Isakson (b. 1927), Majken Johansson (b. 1930), Åsa Wohlin (b. 1931), and C. Fredrik Reuterswärd (b. 1934) most deserve mention.

In this period prose was less important than poetry. The analytical short stories of Willy Kyrklund (b. 1921), Vilgot Sjöman (b. 1924), and Tomas Tranströmer (b. 1931) are new and refreshing. The most traditional novel technique of Sara Lidman (b. 1923; *Tjärdalen,* 1953; *Hjortronlandet,* 1955; *Regnspiran,* 1958), who has also written plays, and of Per Anders Fogelström (b. 1917; *Sommaren med Monika,* 1951) and Arne Sand (b. 1927) brought them great success. After 1955, however, prose flourished. Its best younger representatives include Sven Fagerberg (b. 1918; *Höknatt,* 1957), Olle Mattson (b. 1921), Knut Nordström (b. 1930), Knut Salomonsson, and the even younger Lennart Engström (b. 1928) and Per Wästberg (b. 1933).

Like other Scandinavian literatures, modern Swedish literature is preponderantly agnostic. Spiritual and religious tendencies, however, have recently become increasingly significant in the works of many writers in Sweden. Specifically Protestant literature rarely rises above the mediocre, except for the novels of Olov Hartman (b. 1906; *Död med förhinder,* 1948; *Såsom i en spegel,* 1953), Tore Zetterholm (b. 1915), and Ulla Isaksson (b. 1916; *Trädet,* 1940; *Kvinnohuset,* 1952). Catholicism, which for decades had been forced into a defensive position, found in the critic Stolpe a champion as talented as he was aggressive. Stolpe, who also wrote several distinctly "Catholic" novels, certainly contributed more than any other writer to the religious trend in the poetry of the *femtiotalister*. Following his example, many intellectuals were converted to Catholicism, among them the Thomist philosopher and critic Lechard Johannesson (b. 1917), the critic Gunnel Vallquist (b. 1918), and the novelists Anna Lenah Elgström (b. 1884) and Birgitta Trotzig (b. 1929).

Drama declined after Strindberg, although dramatically effective plays were written by Lagerkvist, Moberg, Gierow, and Siwertz, and by younger writers including Dagerman, Sara Lidman, Alf Henrikson (b. 1905), Lars-Levi Laestadius (b. 1909), Axel Strindberg (b. 1910), and Elsa Grave (b. 1918).

In literary criticism Sweden has produced a number of outstanding scholars, among whom were Böök, Landquist, Henrik Schück (1855–1947), and Erik Hjalmar Lindér (b. 1906). Criticism and the essay are well represented in such journals as *Bonniers Litterära Magasin, Ord och Bild, Svensk Litteraturtidskrift,* and *Samlaren.*

JORIS TAELS

SWEDISH LITERATURE IN THE 1960'S

In *The Public Dialogue in Sweden* (1964), a penetrating analysis of the social, aesthetic, and moral issues that dominated the Swedish cultural scene in the early 1960's, Lars Gustafsson (b. 1936) isolated "nihilism of values" (*i.e.,* the emotive theory of values) and "liberation" (freer sexual morals, equality, responsibility to developing countries) as the two prevailing intellectual concerns of his contemporaries. After connecting the modern Swedish outlook to a philosophical tradition of logical positivism (or logical empiricism), he traced its literary manifestations through the clear-cut social and religious radicalism of the 1930's, the existentialism (q.v.) of the 1940's, and the secularization (*i.e.,* concern with moral norms in "the vacuum after Christianity") of the 1950's. In literature, this was a double tradition, for besides rebelling against established moral values, the best writers during these decades had also been bold innovators who experimented with new artistic genres and contributed to the development of a new poetics.

Gustafsson saw this intellectual and aesthetic tradition as culminating in the novels of Lars Gyllensten (b. 1921), who had attacked fanati-

cism and intolerance and urged the relativity of values in such remarkable novels as *Senatorn* (1958), *Sokrates död* (1960), and *Kains memoarer* (1963). Although Gustafsson felt that the literature of the 1960's continued—and would perhaps realize—the double tradition he had defined, he did perceive one important change: whereas the most exciting literary experimenters of the 1940's and 1950's had been poets—*e.g.,* Ekelöf (q.v.), Lindegren (1910–68), Tomas Tranströmer (b. 1931)—now they were novelistis—*e.g.,* Sven Fagerberg (b. 1918), P. O. Sundman (b. 1922), Birgitta Trotzig (b. 1929), Knut Nordström (b. 1931), and Gustafsson himself. He traced this "new Swedish novel" back to the theory and practice of Ahlin (q.v.), who regards the novel as a form of communication between the narrator and the reader that can only be realized through the active collaboration of the reader.

Inspired by science and philosophy and by the example of Ahlin—later reinforced by impulses received from the works of Robbe-Grillet and Butor (qq.v.)—the new novelists had abandoned the naturalistic, psychological novel in favor of a narrative form that allowed a "more doubting, more experimental and more open investigation of the conditions of experience." Gustafsson even suggests that this kind of novel had inspired younger poets to free themselves from the lyrical asceticism of earlier poets in favor of a simpler, more reflective style. He ends his essay with a rational defense of Swedish petitions of protest, which show a healthy need "to present our own sense of engagement and our evaluations of what is happening in the world around us."

Although it is still too early to characterize this literary decade with a high degree of precision, one can discern the broad outlines of its development, which have proved to be quite different from the course that Gustafsson foresaw in 1964. The aesthetic issues he defined (and emphasized) did indeed feed into a lively debate about poetry, which swirled for a time around such terms as "open art," "concretism" (language as the "concrete" subject of poetry), and "the new simplicity" (simpler poetic diction, freed from metaphor) and provoked much discussion by important young critics such as Lars Bäckström (b. 1925), Göran Palm (b. 1931), and Gustafsson himself.

By 1968, however, when Gustafsson wrote a short article entitled "Konkretism: in memoriam" in Sweden's leading literary magazine, *Bonniers Litterära Magasin,* world events had sharpened the intellectual issues, so that the two components of the tradition he had defined in 1964 had diverged and were, in fact, pitted against each other. Nihilism of values had become the passionate questioning of the power structure in modern society and of the clichés by which we live. Liberation had become an obsession with social and political questions: war, hunger, the population explosion, and ecology. And both of these had forced aesthetic problems into the background. The novel had moved away from the tradition of Ahlin and Robbe-Grillet toward "facticity," documentation, and reportage. Indeed, Gustafsson even asserted (in another issue of *Bonniers Litterära Magasin* in 1968) that under certain conditions literature can function as a form of research. In other words, instead of sparking a renewal in poetry and drama, the novel itself had undergone many changes as the concept of literature broadened to accommodate subliterary forms such as journals, official documents, eyewitness accounts, and travelogues.

By 1968, the New Left took precedence over "the new simplicity," and relativism was less interesting to young writers than "awareness" —not (as in the 1940's) private awareness of anguish and the limitations of one's own consciousness, but public awareness, the conviction that each Swede is a participant in world problems. Petitions of protest had given way to political activism. "Don't talk, mobilize" is the motto of the literary generation that began the 1970's.

This new activism issues in part from a decade of Swedish writers who protested social and economic injustice, especially in the developing countries. The internationalism of two important writers of the 1950's, Sara Lidman (b. 1923) and Per Wästberg (b. 1933) make their recent work especially relevant to the latest trends in Swedish literature. Wästberg's powerful descriptions of injustice in Rhodesia and South Africa and his astute analysis of African political questions in *Förbjudet område* (1960) and *På svarta listan* (1961) make him a transitional figure between the 1950's and the 1960's. Likewise, Sara Lidman, who was one of the leading representatives of "neoprovincialism" in the 1950's, has turned away from Swedish concerns to consider African problems in such novels as *Jag och min son* (1961) and *Med fem diamanter* (1964).

In this connection one should also mention two other important writers, Jan Myrdal (b. 1927) and Sven Lindqvist (b. 1932). Myrdal gained an international reputation for his anthropological study of a Chinese village, *Rapport från en kinesisk by* (1963). In his autobiography, *Confessions of a Disloyal European* (written and first published in English, 1968), he shows how the confrontation of East and West is reflected in his personal crisis.

Wästberg, Lidman, and Myrdal have used a variety of genres to explore social and political problems: the reflective travelogue, the novel, autobiography, and the objective report. Lindqvist, whose point of departure was the opposition of life and art as a theme in Proust, Musil, and Hesse (qq.v.), seems to subsume all of these genres in his remarkable book, *Myten om Wu Tao-tzu* (1967), a profound meditation not only on the confrontation of East and West but on that of life and art as well. The conflict at the heart of the book—the author's desire to alleviate human suffering as opposed to his wish to escape from life into an aesthetic idyll of his own making—brings him very close to the aesthetic problems of some of the most important new novelists of the decade.

The novel has proved to be the most significant literary form of the 1960's. In addition to Per Olaf Sundman and Lars Gustafsson a number of important new novelists have emerged: Torsten Ekbom (b. 1938), Erik Beckman (b. 1935), Björn Runeborg (b. 1937), P. C. Jersild (b. 1935), Sven Delblanc (b. 1931), and Per Olov Enquist (b. 1934). In early works such as *Jägarna* (1957) and *Undersökning* (1958) Sundman developed an objective style of narration that presents characters solely through their words and actions, without authorial interpretation or commentary. In his later masterpieces, *Expeditionen* (1962) and *Ingenjör Andrées Luftfärd* (1967), he uses this technique not only to describe the dynamics of the antagonisms within small groups of isolated men in quest of some form of heroic action, but also to explore the nature of "heroism" itself.

Lars Gustafsson, a professional philosopher, is more directly concerned with intellectual problems than are most of his contemporaries. His chief interest in a novel like *Bröderna* (1960) is the problem of personal identity and the relations between external reality and the individual personality. Ekbom and Beckman are both interested in the nature of verbal reality. Whereas Ekbom uses a collage technique in order to confront the reader with a series of "language events" and to show how language influences experience, Beckman concentrates more on the actual relation between the real and the verbal. Runeborg and Jersild, on the other hand, tend to concentrate on social problems, especially those confronting the individual in a highly developed welfare state. In *Calvinols resa genom världen* (1965), Jersild abandoned the whimsical unreality of his earlier satires in favor of the kind of fantasy that characterizes most of Delblanc's novels. But in his best works, *Prästkappan* (1963) and *Homunculus* (1965), Delblanc uses fantasy not so much to satirize current political and social abuses as to unmask human ideals and to show that our dream of a freer, more authentic life is impossible.

Enquist has become increasingly important. In his earlier novels, he used fiction to explore different alternatives in life and to reflect the interplay between reason and irrationality, belief and skepticism. These same concerns inform his later masterpieces, *Hess* (1966) and *Legionärerna* (1968), where he abandons fiction in order to reconstruct the complex reality behind, in the one case, a political personality (in *Hess*) and, in the other, the political crisis that arose in Sweden in 1946 when the Swedish government returned 146 Baltic refugees to the Soviet Union (in *Legionärerna*). Enquist's documentary novels probably represent the most vital new tendency in Swedish literature.

The only important new dramas to be produced during this decade were all written by older writers; Werner Aspenström (b. 1918), Sandro Key-Åberg (b. 1922), and Lars Forssell (b. 1928). Though the stage has suffered during this period, that neglected form, the radio play, has attracted the attention of a number of talented writers: Björn-Erik Höijer (b. 1907), Sivar Arnér (b. 1909), Björn Runeborg, and Sven Delblanc. An even more significant development has been the emergence of several young writers who have been inspired by Robbe-Grillet's work with film. The most interesting representatives of the new Swedish *cinéma d'auteur* are Vilgot Sjöman (b. 1924) and Bo Widerberg (b. 1930).

By far the most important modern Swedish poet is Ekelöf, whose work epitomized the poetic aspirations of the lyrical modernists of the 1940's and 1950's. In a sense he may also be said to have adumbrated the more drastic experiments of the 1960's, for the "anti-poetry" of his collection entitled *Strountes* (1955) has inspired the whole new generation of younger poets, as have the works of several important

figures from the 1950's: Lars Forssell, Sandro Key-Åberg, Tomas Tranströmer, and Göran Printz-Påhlson (b. 1931). The most important new poets of this decade are Göran Palm, Sonja Åkesson (b. 1926), Carl Fredrik Reuterswärd (b. 1934), Bengt Emil Johnson (b. 1936), and Björn Håkanson (b. 1937). All of them have been involved in the development of "concrete poetry" and have felt the need for new clarity and immediacy in poetic expression, but none has yet achieved a style that seems destined to replace lyrical modernism.

BARRY JACOBS

SWEDISH-FINNISH LITERATURE

Swedish literature also includes the Swedish-language literature of Finland, or Swedish-Finnish literature, as it is often called, a purely minority literature written chiefly by educated people of bourgeois extraction. In this literature, themes of a specifically patriotic and regional nature are much more common than social ones, and the Swedish *arbetardiktning* (proletarian literature) of the 1930's has no real counterpart. The movements of the 1880's and 1890's, moreover, although highly significant in Sweden, had little impact on Swedish-Finnish literature. The works of Karl August Tavaststjerna (1860–98), the only important Swedish-Finnish writer active immediately before the turn of the century, do indeed have certain characteristics of naturalism; in his later poetry, however, he turned to neoromanticism.

A golden age in Swedish-Finnish literature began with the important novelist, poet, and dramatist Mikael Lybeck (1864–1925), whose works include *Dikter* (1890), the prose works *Tomas Indal* (1911) and *Breven till Cecilia* (1920), and the drama *Ödlan* (1908). Although some of his writing is still close to the 1880's in its ethical emotionalism, Lybeck's fondness for weak-willed figures in his later work points to a closer identification with the *fin-de-siècle* and to the increasing influence of Maeterlinck (q.v.) and Söderberg.

About 1910 *dagdrivarliteratur,* a "literature of the outsider," arose; its best representative was Runar Schildt (1888–1925), but Gustav Alm (pseudonym of Richard Malmberg, 1877–1944) and Ture Janson (1886–1954) also contributed to it. Unlike their Swedish models, they were not merely following a contemporary trend; their melancholic irony stemmed, rather, from a feeling of disillusionment and impotence resulting from the political difficulties encountered by Finland at the turn of the century.

About 1900 the poets were strongly influenced by the *nittiotalister*, but gradually they liberated themselves. Hjalmar Procopé (1868–1927) wrote patriotic and contemplative poetry, Jacob Tegengren (1875–1956) religious nature lyrics. The work of Bertel Gripenberg (1878–1947), too, consists mainly of nature lyrics and patriotic or nationalistic poems, while Emil Zilliacus (1878–1961), an admirer of the French Parnassians, sought to synthesize the Nordic spirit and classicism.

The outstanding poet, novelist, and dramatist of this generation is Arvid Mörne (1876–1946). At first a political radical, then the melancholy singer of the Finnish landscape, Mörne became a militant humanist after 1930, strongly influenced by Lagerkvist and the younger Finnish modernists.

Among the writers who began to publish about 1914 Jarl Robert Hemmer (1893–1944) was the most important. After passing through a romantic phase, he expressed the disillusionment of the war generation and its search for religious certainty; these themes appear both in his poetry (*Över dunklet*, 1919; *Du land*, 1940) and in his novels (*Onni Kokko*, 1920; *En man och hans samvete*, 1931; *Morgongåvan*, 1934; *Skrifter*, 4 vols., 1945 ff.). The poet Ragnar Rudolf Eklund (1895–1946) also deserves mention here.

The greatest lyrical talent since Edith Södergran (q.v.) is Solveig von Schoultz (b. 1907). Eva Wichman (b. 1908) and Ralf Parland (b. 1914) are also notable lyric poets. Regionalism predominates in the prose of Olsson, Tito Colliander (b. 1904), Sally Salminen (b. 1906), and Göran Stenius (b. 1909), a significant Catholic novelist. Other novelists are Harald Hornborg (b. 1890), Ulla Bjerne (1890–1956), Olof Enckel (b. 1900), Håkan Mörne (b. 1900), Anna Bondestam (b. 1907), and Mirjam Tuominen (b. 1913). Such recent literary trends as *fyrtiotalet*, *femtiotalet*, existentialism (q.v.), or the experiments of the 1960's have had no appreciable influence on Swedish-Finnish literature.

JORIS TAELS

BIBLIOGRAPHY: Maury, L., *Panorama de la littérature suédoise contemporaine* (1940); Bredsdorff, E., et al., *An Introduction to Scandinavian Literature* (1951); Brandell, G., *Svensk litteratur 1900–1950* (1958); Wizelius, I., *Swedish Literature: 1956–1960* (1960); Tiger-

stedt, E. N., *Svensk litteraturhistoria* (1963); Gustafsson, L., *The Public Dialogue in Sweden* (1964); Bäckström, L., *Klippbok. Litterärt in i sextitalet* (1965); Bäckström, L., and Palm, G., eds., *Sweden Writes* (1965); Vowles, R. B., "Visions and Revisions: The State of Swedish Letters," *Literary Review*, IX (1965), 165–75; Björck, S., et al., *Litteraturhistoria i fickformat* (1966); Håkanson, B., and Nylén, L., eds., *Nya Linjer* (1966); Lagerlöf, K. E., ed., *Ny Svensk lyrik* (1966); Wizelius, I., ed., *Sweden in the Sixties* (1967); Holmbäck, B., "About Sweden 1900–1963: A Bibliographical Outline," *Sweden Illustrated*, XV (1968), 5–94

SWISS LITERATURE

Switzerland, a land of six million people, has four official languages, each with its own literature. German is spoken in the northeast and central region by about seventy percent of the population. French, which is spoken by about twenty percent, is the language of the western section, which borders on France. This region, called Romandie, includes the cantons Vaud, Geneva, Neuchâtel, and parts of Valais, Fribourg, and Bern. The Italian-speaking population (about nine percent) lives mostly in the southern region, in the canton Ticino and in sections of the southeastern canton Graubünden. In 1938, under the federalist principle of Swiss unity within diversity, Romansh was declared the fourth national language of Switzerland. This language of only about one percent is spoken in the upper Rhine valleys of Graubünden, and a dialectic variant, Ladin, is spoken in the Engadine valley of Graubünden. An interesting dialect literature is written in the Alamannic dialects, spoken in central, northern, and eastern Switzerland.

I. GERMAN LITERATURE

The three major literary figures participating in the cultural and moral formation of the new Swiss Confederation during the 19th c. were Jeremias Gotthelf (1797–1854), noted for his depictions of the conservative Bern farmer in realistic, rural language; Gottfried Keller (1819–90), who, as liberal state secretary of Zurich, observed the civic-minded behavior of the small burgher, whom he re-created ironically in his "Seldwyla" stories; and Conrad Ferdinand Meyer (1825–98), who excelled in Swiss themes and lyricism inspired by the Renaissance.

1. Essays and Literary Criticism

In Basel, during the second part of the 19th c., two Swiss scholars established an international reputation. They were Jakob Burckhardt (1818–97), an authority on the aesthetic and social history of the Renaissance, and Johann Jakob Bachofen (1815–87), a student of the religions and myths of antiquity. Subsequent critics and journalists, benefiting from the political stability and neutrality of Switzerland during two world wars, have maintained an important voice of independent thought in Europe.

Among the 20th-c. historians, Carl Burckhardt (q.v.) wrote biographies of such figures as Charles V and Richelieu. An elegant diplomat in the great cities of Europe, he carried on a literary and artistic correspondence that constitutes a valuable documentation of his own time, as collected in *Erinnerungen an Hugo von Hofmannsthal* (1943). Another cosmopolitan writer is Jean R. de Salis (b. 1901), whose *Weltgeschichte der neuesten Zeit* (3 vols., 1951–60) is an outgrowth of his noted radio lectures, collected as *Weltchronik;* he also wrote masterful biographies of several important political and literary figures. Political-literary relationships are also discussed by Fritz Ernst (1889–1958), author of *Helvetia Mediatrix* (1939); by Hans Zbinden (b. 1893), who investigated democratic governments in *Um Deutschlands Zukunft* (1946) and translated Alexis de Tocqueville (1805–1859) into German; in the essays of Karl Schmid (b. 1907), collected in *Unbehagen im Kleinstaat* (1963); and by Georg Thürer (b. 1908), whose writings, partially in dialect, deal with the democratic institutions of Switzerland, as in *Bundesspiegel* (1964).

Among the leading contemporary critics are Max Rychner (b. 1897), Walter Muschg (1898-1966), Emil Staiger (b. 1908), and Max Wehrli (b. 1909). Notable contributions to European thought and scholarship were made by the extremely influential psychiatrist Carl Gustav Jung (1875–1961), the editor-encyclopedist Gustav Keckeis (b. 1884), and the theologians Karl Barth (1886–1968) and Hans-Urs von Balthasar (b. 1905). Eduard Korrodi (1885–1955), an influential literary critic and essayist,

called in his *Schweizerische Literaturbriefe* (1918) for an expansion of Swiss thought beyond narrow-minded provincialism.

2. Poetry

Carl Spitteler (q.v.) was the first major Swiss poet of the 20th c. Influenced by the aesthetic humanism of Jakob Burckhardt and by the pessimistic thought of Arthur Schopenhauer (1788–1860), he wrote his masterpiece, *Olympischer Frühling* (1900–1905 and 1910), after having published ballads and prose under the pseudonym of Felix Tandem. He received the Nobel Prize for Literature in 1919. In spite of his theological studies he was alienated from Christian thought, creating a world based on Greek mythology, and presenting Apollo and Zeus as antagonists. He created his own mythology, which is partially ancient-classic, partially allegorical-philosophical. He may rightly be called the greatest allegorist of world literature. Although he maintained an international viewpoint in his poetry, Spitteler became involved with Switzerland's political affairs in his dramatic defense of Swiss neutrality, *Unser Schweizer Standpunkt* (1914). This, as he knew in advance, was to result in his boycott by German readers.

The effects of World War I may be seen in the work of Karl Stamm (1890–1919), who wrote his last poems, *Der Aufbruch des Herzens* (1919), in a mood of sadness and mysticism. Poems by the prolific Max Geilinger (1884–1948), written during the 1920's, show the influence of expressionism (q.v.), as in *Der große Rhythmus* (1923). Other poets of this period are Max Pulver (1889–1952) and Konrad Banninger (b. 1890).

Man's religious preoccupations and the influence of the seasons are the major themes in the lyrical collections of the poet Hermann Hiltbrunner (1893–1961). Albin Zollinger (1895–1941) wrote such influential political works as *Sternfrühe, Stille des Herbstes,* and *Haus des Lebens,* all collected in *Gedichte* (1962), in which he used his artist's sense for color and landscape to create images emanating out of the poet's mood. The finely crafted poems in the *Gedichte* (1943, 1967) of Werner Zemp (1906–1959) express a sense of solitude and anticipation of death, drawing much of their inspiration from classical traditions.

Among the poets writing after World War II, those who stand out are: Albert Ehrismann (b. 1908), Paul Adolf Brenner (b. 1910), Urs

Martin Strub (b. 1910), Urs Oberlin (b. 1919), Silja Walter (b. 1919), and Erika Burkhart (b. 1922). The poems in the *Gedichte* (1950) of Silja Walter, a nun of the Benedictine order (Sister Hedwig), show a delicate appreciation for beauty in nature and for the rhythms of dance, and Erika Burkhart's lyricism reveals a lofty sense of motion and space in "Die Weichenden Ufer" from *Gedichte* (1967).

3. Drama

The first two nationally known Swiss dramatists in the early 20th c. were Arnold Ott (1840–1910) and Cäser von Arx (1895–1949), both of whom based their plays on themes from Swiss history. Since 1940 the principal theater of Zurich has received international attention through the premieres of plays by Frisch and Dürrenmatt (qq.v.).

Frisch came to the stage after experimenting with journalism and renouncing a successful career in architecture. He often evokes memories of World War II, as in *Nun singen sie wieder* (1945–46), a requiem for the victims of Nazism. His characters are desperately in search of identity, as in *Santa Cruz* (1944–47). One of his most successful plays is *Biedermann und die Brandstifter* (1958), a stage adaptation of an earlier radio play (1953), which depicts the impotence of the individual in his conflict with an amoral society. Frisch's recent drama, *Andorra* (1961), a failure in the United States, was thought by some critics to be excessively conventional in its treatment of anti-Semitism and collective guilt.

Dürrenmatt defended his stage theories in *Theaterprobleme* (1955). Believing that a comical approach is the only effective means of exposing the hypocrisy and corruption of modern society, he has attempted to shock his audience into an understanding of themselves through exaggeration and a use of the grotesque. *Der Besuch der alten Dame* (1956), staged in the United States in 1958 as *The Visit,* is the tragicomical account of a woman's cunning revenge on the townspeople who once betrayed her. The scientists of *Die Physiker* (1963) seek to escape responsibility for the destructive effects of their discoveries by voluntarily retiring to a madhouse. Dürrenmatt's recent play, *Die Wiedertäufer* (1967), reveals the author's background and interest in theological problems. His radio plays and television drama have recently given him a new audience for his work.

Other authors of radio plays include: Jakob Bührer (b. 1882), who became well-known for *Das Volk der Hirten* (1914) and many witty, satirical comedies; Max Gertsch (b. 1893), known for the biographical radio play *Henry Ford* (1960); Albert Jakob Welti (b. 1894); and Otto Steiger (b. 1909). Also noteworthy are Max Werner Lenz (b. 1887), who wrote comedies for the Zurich cabaret Cornichon; David Wechsler, who coauthored with Richard Schweizer the film *Die Gezeichneten* (1947); Franz Fassbind (b. 1919), composer of musical drama; the actor Herbert Meier (b. 1928), author of puppet plays and television drama; and Brigitte Meng (b. 1932), author of one-act plays.

4. The Novel

In the novel, as in poetry, Spitteler was the first prominent Swiss author of the 20th c. with his influential *Imago* (1906). Other early 20th-c. Swiss novelists found inspiration for their works in scenes of mountain life. Thus Jakob Christoph Heer (1859–1925) evoked the legendary chamois hunters of Graubünden in his *Der König der Bernina* (1900). Ernst Zahn (1867–1952) wrote of the central Gothard area in *Albin Indergand* (1900). And in *Bergführer Melchior* (1929) Johannes Jegerlehner (1871–1937) depicted scenes of the rugged Oberland.

The disillusionments following World War I are best defined by Jakob Bosshart (1862–1924), whose farm background is evident in his stories and in his novel *Ein Rufer in der Wüste* (1921). His works are marked by opposition to industrial materialism and by a concern over the political stagnation of democratic institutions in his time. The compassion of Heinrich Federer (1866–1928), a priest forced by poor health to renounce his parish, is shown especially in *Kaiser und Papst in Dorfe* (1925), which reduces the medieval clashes between temporal and spiritual powers to the rivalries between mayor and pastor in a Swiss town. Sharing Federer's background of Catholic Switzerland are Meinrad Lienert (1865–1933) and Josef Maria Camenzind (b. 1904).

The social changes of the 1920's, resulting from the transition from rural and small-town traditions to rapid industrialization, brought an end to much of the provincialism of Swiss literature, leading to a greater involvement in European affairs. Jakob Schaffner (1875–1944), for example, turned from the Switzerland of his youth to become a supporter of Nazism.

His autobiographical *Johannes* novels (1922–30) reveal resentment as well as nostalgia.

The opposite approach was taken by Robert Walser (q.v.) in such lyrical works as the novel *Jacob von Gunten* (1908, 1950). In recent years, his poetry and prose have enjoyed increasing popularity. International society, as seen in a Swiss resort, forms the subject of *Grand Hôtel Excelsior* (1928), written in a polished, realistic style by Meinrad Inglin (b. 1893). One of Inglin's best and most characteristic novels, *Schweizerspiegel* (1938) reflects his preoccupation with social and cultural changes in the Swiss family structure during World War I.

Expressionistic, psychological, and abstract novels were written by Max Pulver (1889–1952), Otto Wirz (1877–1946), and Albert Steffen (1884–1963); the last was a disciple of Rudolf Steiner (1861–1925), the founder of anthroposophic humanism. Novelists concerned with questions of the social environment of the individual are: Paul Ilg (1875–1956) in *Das Menschlein Matthias* (1913); Felix Moeschlin (b. 1882), known for *Der Amerika-Johann* (1912); and John Knittel (b. 1891), some of whose novels, such as *Via mala* (1934), have been adapted for films.

Noteworthy writers in Zurich include: Arnold Kübler (b. 1890), Jakob Job (b. 1891), A. J. Welti (1894–1965), Traugott Vogel (b. 1894), Kurt Guggenheim (b. 1896), and Edwin Arnet (1901–1962). The influential educator, critic, and novelist Robert Faesi (b. 1883) narrated a history of his native city of Zurich in the trilogy *Die Stadt der Väter* (1941), *Die Stadt der Freiheit* (1944), and *Die Stadt der Friedens* (1952). Among Faesi's stories, "Füsilier Wipf" (1917) has become a Swiss classic on the screen. The city of Basel has an excellent chronicler of its history and art life in the novelist Emanuel Stickelberger (1884–1962). Among his work are his novels about *Holbein* (3 vols., 1942–46).

Well-known women novelists include Maria Waser (1878–1939), Agnes von Segesser (b. 1884), Cecile Lauber (b. 1887), and Mary Lavater-Sloman (b. 1891).

Frisch, in addition to his work in drama, became the major Swiss novelist of the generation writing after World War II. Much of the material for his fiction is developed in the genre known as the *Tagebuch* (diary), as in *Blätter aus dem Brotsack* (1940), in which he describes his experiences with the Swiss military service, or *Tagebuch 1946–1949* (1950), in which he

recounts his artistic and literary development and discusses his acquaintance with Brecht (q.v.) and others. In his novels *Die Schwierigen, oder J'adore ce qui me brûle* (1943) and *Stiller* (1954), he depicts artists in search of identity and shows their attempts to escape from the limitations of their narrow environment. The sense of alienation evoked in these novels is also present in *Homo Faber* (1957), written in the form of a report, and in his recent autobiographical novel *Mein Name sei Gantenbein* (1964). Albert Zollinger's novels *Pfannenstiel* (1940) and *Bohnenblust* (1941) were important influences in Frisch's transformation from architect to writer.

Many young Swiss authors write an unconnected, fragmentary prose, as in the work of Raffael Ganz (b. 1923), Hans Boesch (b. 1926), Otto F. Walter (b. 1928), Max Bollinger (b. 1929), Hugo Loetscher (b. 1929), Jörg Steiner (b. 1930), and Jürg Federspiel (b. 1931). Concerned with the emotional turbulence of a rapidly changing society, these writers call for the involvement of the artist in the affairs of his time.

II. FRENCH LITERATURE

1. The Novel

The major literary figure of 20th-c. Romandie is Ramuz (q.v.). After disappointing contacts with academic life, he retreated to the canton of Vaud on Lake Leman, finding inspiration there for his novels about winegrowers, fishermen, and mountain people. The struggle of these people with nature, and the sense of one's inescapable destiny, form the central themes of Ramuz's novels, as in *Les Signes parmi nous* (1919), *La Grande Peur de la montagne* (1926), and *Aimé Pache, peintre vaudois* (1941); the latter is partly autobiographical. His style is that of a visionary painter; he is a poet writing in prose. His original use of language in *Cahiers vaudois* and his essays have had an extraordinary influence on Romandie literature.

In the tradition of Ramuz is Maurice Zermatten (b. 1910). Other notable Romandie novelists of the 20th c. include Pourtales (q.v.), whose masterpiece, *La Pêche miraculeuse*, portrays the author's aristocratic background and the conflict between his sense of Swiss nationality and his broader European outlook. The love of a citizen of Geneva for his region is revealed in *L'Homme dans le rang* by Robert de Traz (1884–1951). Another inhabitant of Geneva, Jacques Chenevière (b. 1886), is known for his novels depicting feminine psychology, notably *Connais ton Coeur* (1935). Other Romandie novelists worthy of note are Jacques Mercanton (b. 1910) and George Borgeaud (b. 1914). Mercanton, a convert to Catholicism, is preoccupied with psychological and religious conflicts, notably in *Thomas l'incrédule* (1942) and *Christ au désert* (1948). Borgeaud, from Valais and now living in Paris, recalled nostalgic details of a youth spent in Romandie in his novel *Le Préau* (1952). The best-known woman novelist of Romandie is Monique Saint-Hélier (1895–1955). Her work was influenced by her acquaintance with Rilke (q.v.).

2. Essays and Literary Criticism

Most of the literary and publishing activities in Romandie take place in the old university cities: Geneva, Lausanne, Sion, Neuchâtel, Fribourg, and Porrentruy. Scholarship is closely associated with publication in literary magazines and editorial work on books and periodicals. The literary men of Romandie, although closely identified with the cultural heritage of the region, are not parochial. Along with their interest in Romandie, they participate in Swiss and international affairs. Romandie writers feel close to Paris, where many of them live for at least a part of their lives.

A notable example of a European-oriented Romandie writer is Gonzaque de Reynold (b. 1880), who ranks with Ramuz in Romandie's literature. Because of his strong ties to his ancestral home in the hills of Fribourg, he is bound to both the French and German traditions of Swiss culture. His masterpiece, *Cités et pays suisses* (1914–48), is a lyrical evocation of the history of the four Swiss cultures. In many other essays, as in *La Grandeur de la suisse* (1938–40), de Reynold glorifies Swiss federalism, using the Saint Gothard mountains as its symbolic fortress.

In the region of the Lake of Neuchâtel, Denis de Rougemont (b. 1906) participated in intellectual movements concerned with promoting the unity of Europe. His essays range from Swiss and European themes, in *L'Attitude fédéraliste* (1946) and *Vingt-huit Siècles d'Europe* (1961), to American impressions in *Vivre en Amérique* (1947). In America he is well-known for two thought-provoking books: *Love in the Western World* (1940; published originally as *L'Amour et l'occident,* 1939), which deals with the historical paradox between the universal acceptance of marriage and the attraction of the romantic, passionate love that is outside marriage, and *Love Declared* (1963).

Other notable critics from Neuchâtel are Léon Bopp (b. 1896), known for his *Philosophie de l'Art* (1954); Charly Guyot (b. 1898), who wrote *Écrivains de suisse française* (1961); and Albert Béguin (1901–1957), author of *L'Âme romantique et le rêve* (1937).

Romandie can also boast of being the home of the architect Le Corbusier (Charles-Édouard Janneret-Gris, 1887–1965), whose visionary writings *Vers Une Architecture* (1923) and *Manière de penser l'urbanisme* (1947), strongly influenced the social ideas of 20th-c. Europe.

3. Drama and Poetry

In 1908 Rene Morax, founder of the Romand theater, began to stage outdoor drama in Mézières, a village in Vaud with a splendid view of the Lake of Geneva. For his popular theater, Morax restricted himself to legendary and historical themes of local or national history, as in *Davel and Guillaume Tell*. The Fribourg festivals had similar patriotic appeal with *La Gloire qui chante* and *La Cité sur la montagne*, with text by de Reynold and music by Abbé Bovet. *Mystères* with biblical motifs were revived by Fernand Chavannes and Charly Clerc. On the modern stage, Alfred Gehri (b. 1895) attained international success with *Sixième Étage*. Younger playwrights are Pinget (q.v.), who lives in France, and Yves Velan (b. 1925).

Poetry in Romandie has developed slowly; only since 1920 has it been of any significance, and it has not enjoyed an outstanding position in Romandie literature. Nevertheless, in the canton of Vaud three poets have produced good poetry. Pierre-Louis Matthey (b. 1893) translated Shakespeare, Blake, and Keats; his own poetry is influenced by the English romantics, as in *Semaines de passion* (1919) and *Au Jardin du père*, an elegy (1949). Gustave Roud (b. 1897), a mystic influenced by romanticism, wrote poetic prose from his seclusion in a village high above Lake Leman, describing the landscape before him in *Haut-Jorat* (1949). The tragic end of the restless émigré Edmond-

Henri Crisinel (1897–1948) is anticipated in the psalmlike *Le Veilleur* and *Alectone*.

Important poets of a later generation include: Maurice Chappaz (b. 1916), author of *Testament du Haut-Rhône* (1953), and Philippe Jaccottet (b. 1925), whose *Requiem* (1947) recalls the German romantic poetry that he translated into French.

III. ITALIAN LITERATURE

Rhetorical temper, and a preoccupation with a workable synthesis of their Swiss nationality and their Italian linguistic and cultural heritage, have produced, among the inhabitants of Ticino, statesmen, orators, and essayists of national stature. Stefano Franscini (1796–1857), historian, economist, and educator, set the liberal foundations for this development in his *Giornale, Annali,* and *Epistolario.* The major followers of his sociopolitical and humanitarian ideas were Brenno Bertoni (1860–1945), whose prolific writings in essay form have been collected in *Pagine scelte* (1941), and Romeo Manzoni (1847–1919). Conservative attitudes were represented by Giuseppe Motta (1871–1941), the multilingual Swiss president with a truly European outlook, whose three-volume *Testimonia temporum* (1931–41) describes his struggle for world peace and defends the Swiss cultural-linguistic minorities who opposed the irredentists who wished to unite their regions with the fascist powers.

A prominent place among contemporary scholars and essayists is held by Guido Calgari (b. 1905), who occupies the chair of Italian literature at the Zurich Federal School of Technology. His works, such as *Coscienza, breviario patriotico,* express the need for strong cultural links among the Swiss-Italians and the Italians, who are divided by the Saint Gothard mountains. Besides historical, educational, and literary essays, he has written a collection of short stories, *Quando tutto va male* (1933). Other writers influential in education and literature include A. M. Zendralli (b. 1887) in Chur, Reto Roedel (b. 1898) in Saint Gall, Giovanni Laini (b. 1899) in Fribourg, Adolfo Jenni (b. 1911) at the University of Bern, and Giovanni Bonalumo (b. 1920) in Basel.

With Chiesa (q.v.), Tecinese literature attained national importance in Switzerland and recognition in Italy. Chiesa, a teacher, published his first volume of poetry, *Preludio,* in 1897. He wrote *Calliope* (1903–1907), a symbolic trilogy on the evolution of civilization. It was made up of: *La cattedrale,* in which he evoked the Middle Ages; *La reggia,* the Renaissance; and *La città,* the modern period. In his prose, Chiesa becomes deeply involved with nature and man. His best narratives are *Racconti puerili* (1920), *Raconti del mio orto* (1929), *Scoperte nel mio mondo* (1934), and *Recordi dell' età minore* (1948) all rich in local color and autobiographical material.

Religion figures prominently in Chiesa's *Sant' Amarillide* (1938), which is marked, like all of his work, by his continuing effort to improve his craft, a concern expressed by the title of a collection of his poems, *L'artefice malcontento* (1950). In 1957, sixty years after the publication of his first poetry, he revealed his attitudes toward his craft in a series of radio interviews entitled *Colloqui con Francesco Chiesa.*

Angelo Nessi (1873–1932) wrote in a satirical-humoristic mood; his masterpiece is the autobiographical novel *Cip* (1934). The anthologist and critic Giuseppe Zoppi (1896–1952) wrote lyrically about mountain life in his successful *Libro dell'Alpe* (1922). In the work of Piero Bianconi (b. 1899) the fragmentary sketch, written with a strong sense for artistic observation, prevails, as in *Ritagli* (1935) and *Cartoline locarnesi* (1959). Bianconi is also the author of many works on art and folklore. Other Swiss-Italian novelists are: Elena Bonzanigo (b. 1897), known for *Serena Serodine* (1944); Orlando Spreng (1908–1945), author of *La recluta Senzapace*; Piero Scanziani (b. 1908), represented by *Felix*; Carlo Castelli (b. 1909), an author of television and radio plays and of the novel *Gli uomini sono tristi* (1950); and Felice Filippini (b. 1917), who wrote about rural life.

In poetry, Valerio Abbondio (1891–1958) ranged from sensitive descriptions of nature in *Betulle* (1922) to human and transcendental themes in *Cerchi d'argento* (1944). The religious poet Don Felice Menghini (1909–1947) wrote *Parabola* (1943) in his native and isolated Poschiavo.

IV. ROMANSH LITERATURE

Romansh, which is a *lingua rustica* of the Roman Empire, and its dialectic variant Ladin are, like their counterparts in other countries, maintained mainly by societies founded for that purpose and by devotees. It is chiefly spoken in a few areas of the canton Graubünden. Teaching and publishing Romansh literature is centered in Chur, the capital of Graubünden, and the Benedictine Abbey of Mustér. In Chur, Romansh literature has been taught and promulgated by Gion Cahannes (1872–1947), an anthologist and grammarian; Ramun Vieli (1895–1953), editor and lexicographer; Alfons Maissen (b. 1905), essayist, radio commentator, and musicologist; and Gian Caduff (b. 1900) who wrote literary criticism. The monks of Mustér Abbey are active as teachers, historians, editors, and writers. Among them are: Iso Müller (b. 1901), Flurin Maissen (b. 1906), and Ursicin Derungs (b. 1935).

Poetry is the dominant genre of Romansh literature. Flurin Camathias (1871–1946) created *Ils retoromans,* which was inspired by the *Mirèio* of the Provençal poet Frédéric Mistral (1830–1914). Popular poets of humor and satire include Gion Cadieli (1876–1952), author of *Brumbels e Stumbels;* Luis Candinas (b. 1892), known for his *Suolegliadas;* and G. B. Sialm (b. 1897), represented by *Giud Crunamatg.* Aluis Tuor (1873–1939) excelled in nature description. Among poets writing after 1950 are Flurin Darms, Riget Bertogg, Gion Deplazes, Mihel Maissen, Theo Candinas, and Henri Spescha.

The most successful Romansh novelist was Dom Maurus Carnot (1865–1935), author of *Gieri Genatsch,* a novel treating the same theme as Meyer's German novel *Jürg Jenatsch,* but written from a different historical and ideological point of view. The two leading novelists in the region before 1940 were G. M. Nay (1860–1920), a portrayer of mountain life (*La vacca pugniera*), and Gian Fontana (1897–1935), who was deeply involved with the problems of common townspeople (*Il president de Valdei*). Carli Fry (1897–1956), Gugliem Gadola (1902–1964), and Toni Halter (b. 1914) are the best-known short-story writers.

The home of Ladin is the Engadine Valley, a sixty-mile area on the Inn River. Prominent among Ladin writers was Peider Lansel (1863–1943), who wrote essays in defense of the language. Other Ladin poets worthy of note are: Schimun Vonmoos (1868–1940), Gian Gianett Cloetta (1874–1966), Eduard Bezzola (1875–1948), Men Rauch (1888–1958), Jon Guidon (b. 1892), Artur Caflisch (b. 1893), and Andri Peer (b. 1921).

Talented Ladin writers of prose are: Peer, Reto Caratsch (b. 1901), and Cla Biert (b.

1920). Among women writers, Selina Chönz (b. 1911) has attained international recognition for her children's stories, *Uorsin* (1945) and *Flurina* (1957).

Ladin dramatists are experimenting with radio and television plays and cabaret sketches as well as writing for the theater. The leading dramatists are: Jon Semadeni (b. 1910), Gian Belsch (b. 1913), and Tista Murk (b. 1915).

V. SWISS DIALECT LITERATURE

The Alamannic dialects constitute one of the strongest links of national unity because it is the language of a folk literature strongly rooted in the growth of Swiss federalism. During the romantic movement of the 18th and 19th c.'s the folksong was rediscovered, and even such universal scholars as Jakob Burckhardt wrote dialect poetry, as in his *E Hampfeli Lieder* (1853). Early in the 20th c., the dialect of Bern was elevated to literary prominence by three poets and playwrights. Otto von Greyerz (1863–1940), critic and professor of literature, published the influential anthology *Im Röseligarte* (1908) and in 1914 created the *Berner Heimatschutztheater,* for which he wrote dialect comedies. Simon Gfeller (1863–1943) portrayed the language and spirit of cheesemakers and farmers in his rustic stories of Emmenthal, *Em Hag no, Müsterli und Geschichten us em Ämmethal* (1918). The greatest Swiss dialect writer, the patrician Rudolf von Tavel (1866–1934), wrote in the vernacular of the city of Bern, not for amusement, but because he regarded this speech as especially suitable for artistic expression. A strong sense of regional history, Protestant traditions, and a vein of sincere humor permeate his novels, especially *Der Houpme Lombach* (1903), *Unspunne* (1923), and *Meischter und Ritter* (1933).

Other regions also have a pronounced dialect tradition. In the canton Schwyz, the cradle of Swiss democracy, Lienert found fertile ground for his simple, very lyrical songs, collected in *S'schwäbelpfyfli* (1925). In the canton Solothurn, at the foot of the Jura hills, Josef Reinhart (1875–1957) was most successful with his short stories. In the canton Thurgau, Alfred Huggenberger (1867–1960) injected subtle irony into his comedies of farm life, creating a humorous hypochondriac in his play *Dem Bollme sy bös Wuche* (1914). A perfect language for satire is the rapid, witty Basel dialect

—the poet Dominik Müller (pseudonym of Paul Schmitz, 1871–1953), wrote and staged humorously biting plays about the mores of his city's burghers, collected as *Basler Theater* (1922).

With the rise of German Nazism and during the subsequent isolation of Switzerland throughout World War II, dialect literature became synonymous with the moral defense of the country. The spirit of the 1939 National Exposition in Zurich inspired an extensive use of the vernacular in journalism, youth literature, radio, the cabaret, and later in television.

In Switzerland the use of the dialects is an indication of an authentic Swiss quality. Thus dialect literature enjoys popularity and has an excellent future. An example of this is the work of one of the leading Swiss composer-lyricists, Paul Burkhard, whose Christmas play *D'Zäller Wiehnacht* (1960), written in the Zurich dialect, was a great success. Most dialect authors, especially the essayists and novelists, also write in German in order to reach an international audience.

BIBLIOGRAPHY

I. GERMAN: Spitteler, C., *Unser Schweizer Standpunkt* (1915); Korrodi, E., *Schweizerische Literaturbriefe* (1918); Faesi, R., *Anthologia Helvetica* (1921); Faesi, R., *Gestalten und Wandlungen schweizerischer Dichtung* (1922); Korrodi, E., *Schweizerdichtung der Gegenwart* (1924); Nadler, J., *Literaturgeschichte der deutschen Schweiz* (1932); Ermatinger, E., *Dichtung und Geistesleben der deutschen Schweiz* (1933); Moser, J., *Le roman contemporain en Suisse allemande: de C. Spitteler à J. Schaffner* (1934); Staiger, E., "Deutschschweizerisches Schrifttum," in *Deutschschweiz: Sprachverein* (1937); Korrodi, E., *Geisteserbe der Schweiz; Schriften von Albrecht Haller bis zur Gegenwart* (1943); Bohnenblust, G., *Vom Adel des Geistes* (1944); Blöchlinger, M., *La poésie lyrique contemporaine en Suisse allemande* (1947); Friederich, W. P., "Chief Traits in Swiss Literature," in *South Atlantic Quarterly*, XLVII (1948), 173–85; Bettex, A., *Die Literatur der deutschen Schweiz von heute* (1949); Zäch, A., *Die Dichtung der deutschen Schweiz* (1951); Bettex, A., *Spiegelungen der Schweiz in der deutschen Literatur 1870–1950* (1954); Wildi, M., *Lyrik und Erzählkunst in der deutschen Schweiz* (1956); Linder, H. P., *Die schweizerische Gegenwart im modernen Roman der deutschen Schweiz* (1957); "Contemporary Swiss Literature," *German Life, and Letters*, XII (1958–59), 1–45; Wehrli, M., "Gegenwartsdichtung der deutschen Schweiz," in *Deutsche Literatur in unserer Zeit* (1959); Guggenheim, K., *Heimat oder Domizil? Die Stellung des deutschschweizerischen Schriftstellers in der Gegenwart* (1961); *Schweizer Schriftsteller der Gegenwart* (1962); Arx, B. von, "Von Sprache, Literatur, Theater und Film in der deutschen Schweiz," in *Die Schweiz-heute* (1964); Mariacher, B., and Witz., F., eds., *Schweizer Schrifttum der Gegenwart* (1964); Schwengeler, A. H., *Vom Geist und Wesen der Schweizer Dichtung* (1964); Zbinden, H., *Schweizer Literatur in europäischer Sicht* (1964); Christ, R. B., ed., *Schweizer, Dialekte* (1965); Calgari, G., *Die vier Literaturen der Schweiz* (1966); Frisch, M., *Öffentlichkeit als Partner* (1967); Günther, W., *Dichter der neueren Schweiz* (2 vols.; 1963, 1968)

II. FRENCH: Faesi, R., *Anthologia Helvetica* (1921); Kohler, P., *La littérature d'aujourd'hui dans la Suisse romande* (1923); Clerc, C., *Panorama des littératures contemporaines de Suisse* (1938); Ramuz, C. F., *Besoin de grandeur* (1938); de Rougement, D., *Mission ou démission de la Suisse* (1940); Martinet, E., *Portraits d'écrivains romands contemporains* (2 vols., 1944, 1954); de Boccard, E., ed., *Anthologie des poètes de la Suisse romande* (1945); Weber-Perret, M., *Écrivains romands 1900–1950* (1951); Guyot, C., *Écrivains de Suisse Française* (1961); Tougas, G., *Littérature romande et culture française* (1963); Jost, F., "Y a-t-il une littérature suisse?," in *Essais de littérature comparée* (Vol. I, 1964); Mariacher, B., and Witz, F., eds., *Lettres suisses d'aujourd'hui* (1964); Calgari, G., "Französische Schweiz," in *Die vier Literaturen der Schweiz* (1966)

III. ITALIAN: Faesi, R., *Anthologia Helvetica* (1921); Zendralli, A. M., *Quaderni grigioni italiani* (1931 ff.); Zoppi, G., *Nuova Antologia* (1932); Vieli, F. D., "Scrittori del Grigione italiano," in *Scrittori della Svizzera italiana*, ed. G. Zoppi (1936); Zoppi, G., ed., *Scrittori della Svizzera italiana* (2 vols., 1936); Bianconi, P., *Panorama des littératures contemporaines de Suisse* (1938); Zoppi, G., *La Svizzera nella letteratura italiana* (1944); Pedrazzini, B., "Il Ticino nella letteratura tedesca," in *Svizzera*

Italiana (1945); Locarnini, G., *Die literarischen Beziehungen zwischen der italienischen und der deutschen Schweiz* (1948); Calgari, G., *Il libro del Cittadino* (1953); Calgari, G., "La Svizzera italiana, in *Storia delle quattro letterature della Svizzera* (1958); Nessi, A., "Antologia degli scrittori ticinesi," in *Archivio Storico Ticinese* (1960–61); Mariacher, B., and Witz, F., eds., *Lettere elvetiche d'oggi* (1964)

IV. ROMANSH: Bertoni, G., *Letteratura ladina dei Grigioni* (1916); Lansel, P., *La Musa Ladina: Antologia* (1918); Faesi, R., *Anthologia Helvetica* (1921); Carnot, P. M., *Im Lande der Rätoromanen* (1934); Maxfield, E., *Studies in Modern Romansh Poetry in the Engadine* (1938); Piguet, E., "La Suisse rétoromanche," in *Panorama des littératures contemporaines de Suisse* (1938); Bezzola, R. R., *La littérature en Suisse rétoromanche* (1954); Billigmeier, R., and Maissen, A., *Contemporary Romansh Poetry—Poesia Romontscha Contemporana* (bilingual anthology; 1959); *Scriptours svizzers da noss dis* (1962); Mariacher, B., and Witz, F., eds., *Vuschs svizras da nos temp* (1964); Calgari, G., *Rätoromanische Schweiz: Die Vier Literaturen der Schweiz* (1966), pp. 255–332; "Rätoromanisch," *Der Bogen*, No. 47 (n.d.)

AUGUSTIN MAISSEN

SYMBOLISM

Historically, symbolism follows parnassianism as a continuation of the great romantic revolution in French poetry of the 19th c. Its subject matter shows a return to the intimate emotional and aesthetic experience of the individual after the more objective stress of the Parnasse; but symbolism differs from historical French romanticism in its greater subtlety and preoccupation with the inner life and in its general avoidance of sentimentality, rhetoric, narration, direct statement, description, public and political themes, and overt didacticism of any kind. It marks a fusion of the sensibility and imagination, which the romantics had restored to French poetry, with the lucid craftsmanship of the Parnassians, and a turn toward music and *le rêve* for evocative expression. Symbolist poetry is a poetry of indirection, in which objects tend to be suggested rather than named,

or to be used primarily for an evocation of mood. Ideas may be important, but are characteristically presented obliquely through a variety of symbols and must be apprehended largely by intuition and feeling. Symbolist poets use words for their magical suggestiveness—what Rimbaud termed *l'alchimie du verbe* and Baudelaire *une sorcellerie évocatoire*; and one of their essential aims is to arouse response beyond the level of ordinary consciousness, in what was called after Eduard von Hartmann (1842–1906) *l'inconscient*. For the symbolists the power of the Word goes far beyond ordinary denotative verbal limits through suggestive developments in syntax and interrelated images and through what may be termed the "phonetic symbolism" of musicality and connotative sound-relationships. Profoundly evocative poetry of this sort is essentially different from that which had predominated in France since the late Renaissance; and its appearance in French literature entailed a more evident renovation of lyric poetry than would have been possible in England and Germany, many of whose earlier poets had already much in common with the later French symbolists.

Among the more important foreign writers and philosophers influencing or showing affinities with French symbolism may be cited, from the British Isles: George Berkeley (1685–1753), Samuel Taylor Coleridge (1772–1834), Percy Bysshe Shelley (1792–1822), John Keats (1795–1821), Thomas Carlyle (1795–1881), John Ruskin (1819–1900), Dante Gabriel Rossetti (1828–82), William Morris (1834–96), Charles Swinburne (1837–1909), and Walter Pater (1839–94); from Germany: Friedrich von Schiller (1759–1805), Johann Gottlieb Fichte (1762–1842), Friedrich Hegel (1770–1831), Friedrich Hölderlin (1770–1843), Novalis (1772–1801), Friedrich Wilhelm Schelling (1775–1854), E. T. A. Hoffman (1776–1822), Arthur Schopenhauer (1788–1860), and Richard Wagner (1813–83); and from the United States: Ralph Waldo Emerson (1803–1882), Edgar Allan Poe (1809–1849), and Walt Whitman (1819–92). Wagner was especially important, not only for his music but for his insistence upon the ideal relation between music and poetry (". . . the most complete work of the poet must be that which, in its final achievement, would be a perfect music"). But the greatest single influence was exerted by Poe, who came to prefigure an ideal of the poet for several of the great French symbolists. More important than his poems, Poe's theories proclaimed the idea of an absolute Beauty and the importance of the poem "written solely for the poem's sake"; urged in poetry "a certain taint of sadness," the need for images with indefinite sensations, and the "absolute essentiality" and vast importance of music; and represented the poet as a thoroughly conscious artist.

Among native French writers, links have been seen between the symbolists and the mystical and idealistic predecessors of the *Pléiade* in *l'école lyonnaise* (Antoine Héroët [d. 1568], Gilles Corrozet, Maurice Scève, and Louise Labé [1526–66]). Jean Jacques Rousseau (1712–78) and François René de Chateaubriand (1768–1848; "the Enchanter") may be considered precursors of symbolism in their use of musical and affective language. The *tristesse lamartinienne* with its remarkable musicality is a prelude to the more delicate music of Verlaine. In the poetry of Alfred Victor de Vigny (1797–1863), the function of such symbols as the waterfall (in "Le Cor") that establishes the strange ambience for the fall of Roland and the Peers at Roncevaux, and the sound of the weathercock *en deuil* (in "La Mort du loup"), with its premonitory note of mourning, anticipate symbolist techniques. Charles Augustin Sainte-Beuve (1804–1869) is a precursor of French symbolism; and Victor Hugo (1802–1885), in his visionary power and his evocative mingling of image and music, often shows symbolist qualities. But of all the French romantic poets Gérard de Nerval (1808–1855) is nearest to the new poetry, and in the compressed, musical, and difficult sonnets of *Les chimères* (1854) seems to anticipate the art of both Verlaine and Mallarmé.

Charles Baudelaire (1821–67) is the first great symbolist poet of France. It has become apparent that with Baudelaire's *Les Fleurs du mal* (1857) French poetry had assimilated the lessons of English and German romanticism and rejoined the great European lyric tradition from which it had been in great part separated since the Renaissance. With *Les Fleurs du mal,* Baudelaire (in his proclaimed effort to "extraire la *beauté du Mal*") brought to French poetry a renewed sense of the magical power of words and a symbolic, mythical vision of the great modern city and of modern man ("l'héroisme de la vie moderne"). His sonnet "Correspondances" describes man moving through a "forest of symbols" familiarly related to his existence, and proclaims two kinds of interrelated *Correspondences:* (1) those (in the manner of Emanuel Swedenborg [1688–1772]

and the great mystics generally since Plato) between the material world and spiritual realities and (2) those between the different human sense modalities. Baudelaire's memorable depiction of the "delicate monster" Ennui and of the struggle in man between Spleen and the Ideal; his Satanism; his exploiting of the various senses, especially that of smell; his interest in the "artificial paradises" (opium, hashish, wine), in dandyism, in decadence; his development of the prose poem; his theories on *correspondences* and on art and the artist; his translations and adaptations from Poe; and his enthusiasm for Wagner combined with the general prestige of *Les Fleurs du mal* to make Baudelaire the most significant native influence upon the rising symbolist movement in France.

Verlaine, Rimbaud, and Mallarmé, the three great symbolist poets of the later 19th c., all felt Baudelaire's influence. Paul Verlaine (1844–96), one of the most delicate French lyricists, published his first volume of poetry (*Poèmes saturniens*) in 1866. Already in this collection, where Verlaine shows himself still influenced by parnassian theory, such poems as "Chanson d'automne" and "Mon Rêve familier" sound a characteristic note of musical nostalgia in which "the language is vaporized and reabsorbed into the melody" (Michaud). Among Verlaine's significant later volumes are *Fêtes galantes* (1869), *La Bonne Chanson* (1870), *Romances sans paroles* (1874), *Sagesse* (1881), and *Jadis et naguère* (1884). Verlaine's "Art poétique" advocates "music before everything," use of *le vers impair* (verse of an uneven number of syllables: 5,7,9,11 instead of the usual 6,8,10,12), and urges that ideal poetry should be as fugitive and intangible as the scent of mint and thyme on the morning wind—something very like the conception of *poésie pure* championed in the 20th c. by the Abbé Bremond (1865–1933). Aside from his influence on French prosody, Verlaine was influential as a symbol of "decadence." His lyric gifts were personal, and his evocative poems introduced into French literature an intimate impressionism hardly known before his time. Verlaine was not by nature a theorist or a poet of ideas. But he brought music and poetry into a relationship that is in itself a kind of miracle.

Arthur Rimbaud (1854–91), the precocious boy-genius among the symbolists who gave up poetry before he was nineteen, inspired a "myth" that has not yet lost its fascination and that in itself symbolizes a rebellious aspect of the modern creative mind. Rimbaud saw the poet as a *mage,* a *seer,* and wrote that "the poet makes himself a *seer* by a long immense and reasoned *derangement* of all the senses." Rimbaud's "Bateau ivre" (September 1871), composed before his seventeenth birthday, is one of the most memorable poems of the century. Its strange rhythms, hallucinatory descriptions of land and sea, brilliant colors, and alternating violence and calms; its employment of symbols concerned with the beginning of the world (Tohu-Bohu, Behemoth, Leviathan); its powerful mingling of fresh, adolescent sensations with apocalyptic visions; and the ultimate evocation, from what seems at first a chaos of images, of impressive form and meaning combine to make the poem a masterpiece of French symbolism. The sonnet "Voyelles" (1871) is of less importance; but its sensational proclamation that the vowels are colored ("A noir, E blanc, I rouge, U vert, O bleu, voyelles. . . ."), though not original, aroused violent controversy and led to extreme exaggeration in such analogous attempts as René Ghil's (1862–1925) *Traité du verbe* (1885) and P.-N. Roinard's *Cantique des cantiques* (1891). Between 1871 and 1873 Rimbaud wrote a collection of verses and prose poems (*Les Illuminations*) published in 1886, and the autobiographical *Une Saison en enfer* (published by Rimbaud in 1873, but never circulated; reprinted, 1892). Rimbaud's experiments with rhythm in *Les Illuminations* (*e.g.,* in "Mouvement" and "Marine") have led to his being identified by some critics as the inventor of *vers libre* (*see* lyric poetry). His influence has been enormous. Edith Sitwell (q.v.) calls him "the originator of modern prose rhythms" and adds that "Rimbaud is, to modern English verse and to modern English and American prose poems, what Edgar Allan Poe was to Baudelaire and Mallarmé." In the words of Pierre Jean Jouve (q.v.): "With Rimbaud we come to the modern language of poetry."

The last of the great French symbolist poets of the 19th c. is Stéphane Mallarmé (1842–98), the exquisite, hermetic master whose Tuesday evenings in his apartment on the Rue de Rome were attended at one time or another by most of the famous symbolists of the day. Mallarmé's early poems show already the influence of Baudelaire, along with that of Hugo, Théophile Gautier (1811–72), and Théodore de Banville (1823–91). Poems of the second period (*e.g., Hérodiade* and *L'Après-midi d'un faune*) have more characteristic developments of complex suggestion, imagery and verbal music; and

those of the third period become increasingly condensed and remote and culminate in the variously interpreted *Un Coup de dés jamais n'abolira le hasard.* Mallarmé is known as one of the most difficult French poets; and the bitterness of his frustration in not finding words for the ideal is seen in his symbol of the white swan with wings imprisoned in a frozen lake ("Le vierge, le vivace et le bel aujourd'hui. . . ."), and in his unhappy admission to Louis le Cardonnel (1862–1936): "Mon art est une impasse." But Mallarmé was by no means a sterile poet. He saw life differently from those around him, and evolved his own technique of combining symbols with verbal music, typography, and patterned suggestion to *evoke* as nearly as possible his aesthetic and metaphysical ideal. According to Mallarmé, a poem is a mystery whose key must be sought by the reader, and poetry is primarily suggestion: "To name an object is to suppress three-fourths of the delight of the poem which is derived from the pleasure of divining little by little: to *suggest* it, that is the dream." A passage in "Crise de vers" (from *Divagations,* 1897) indicates at once the difficulties and fascination of his method: "Abolished, the claim, aesthetically an error, although it governs masterpieces, of including on the subtle paper of the volume anything more for example than the horror of the forest, or the silent thunder scattered through the leaves: not the intrinsic, dense wood of the trees." Although critics find Hegelian influence in Mallarmé (*e.g.,* in *Igitur,* 1925), ideas in his poems are not meant to be apprehended directly by reason, but indirectly, symbolically, through poetic intuition. "I say: a flower!" he writes, "and, out of the oblivion into which my voice consigns any outline, apart from the known calyxes, there arises musically, the delicate idea itself, the flower absent from all bouquets."

About 1885, the year of Hugo's death, the symbolists became more widely known through such works as Verlaine's *Les Poètes maudits* (1884), Huysmans's (q.v.) *A Rebours* (1884), and the amusing parodies in Gabriel Vicaire's (1848–1900) and Henri Beauclair's *Les Déliquescences d'Adoré Floupette, poète décadent* (1885). This period saw the discovery of two "decadent" poets related to symbolism who introduce a new note of irony into French poetry: Tristan Corbière (1845–75), the author of *Les Amours jaunes* (1875), who was brought to the attention of the public as one of Verlaine's *poètes maudits,* and Jules Laforgue

(1860–87) with *Les Complaintes* (1885) and *L'Imitation de Notre-Dame la Lune* (1886).

Between Baudelaire, Verlaine, Rimbaud, and Mallarmé and the last great symbolist poets (Claudel and Valéry [qq.v.]) French symbolists like Ghil, Stuart Merrill (1863–1915), Vielé Griffin, Moréas (q.v.), Henri de Régnier (q.v.), and Gustave Kahn (1859–1936) seem on the whole less important than their Belgian contemporaries (Georges Rodenbach [1855–98], Verhaeren [q.v.], Maeterlinck [q.v.], Charles Van Lerberghe [1861–1907], and Elskamp [q.v.]). The last years of the century teemed with theoretical discussion in print and in the symbolist cafés of the Latin Quarter (Le François Ier, Le Vachette, Le Panthéon, Le Procope, Le Soleil d'Or). On 8 Sept. 1886, *Le Figaro* published the symbolist manifesto of Moréas. Important periodicals championed the symbolist cause: *La revue wagnérienne* (1885–88), *La Wallonie* (1886–92), *La plume* (1889–1905), *Mercure de France* (founded 1890), *L'Ermitage* (1890–1906), *La revue blanche* (1891–1903); and symbolism became recognized as a movement. But the greatest symbolist poets had already done their work. In 1891, Jules Huret's famous *Enquête sur l'évolution littéraire* indicated the triumph of the symbolists and the fading prestige of naturalism in France.

In the 20th c., Apollinaire (q.v.) echoes at times the music of Verlaine; Claudel, turning to Catholicism under the influence of Rimbaud, brings a liturgical quality to his symbolism; and Valéry, the follower of Mallarmé, in *La Jeune Parque* and *Le Cimetière marin* creates two of the most memorable of symbolist poems. The surrealists discovered Isidore Ducasse (1846–70; "le comte de Lautréamont"), whose *Chants de Maldoror* (1868–69) afford another link between symbolism and the *poème en prose*. French symbolists are important in the background of surrealism (q.v.) itself, as Breton (q.v.) recognized in remarks on Nerval, Baudelaire, Rimbaud, and Mallarmé. Their influence is evident also in contemporary drama and brief fiction and in the novel since Gustave Flaubert (1821–80). (D. Hayman has recently shown the significant influence of Mallarmé on *Finnegans Wake,* and Fiser identifies Proust [q.v.] as the greatest symbolist of all.) Thus the music, the dream, and the poetic symbol of symbolism, like romantic lyricism and imagination in an earlier day, have invaded the most important literary genres of the present century.

Influence of the French symbolists may be traced in many poets from other lands; *e.g.,*

the British Isles: in Arthur Symons (1865–1945), Ernest Dowson (1867–1900), De La Mare (q.v.), Lionel Johnson (1867–1902), Wilde, George Russell, and Yeats (qq.v.); Germany: in George and Rilke (qq.v.); Austria: in Hofmannsthal (q.v.); Russia: in Bryusov, Annensky (qq.v.), Zinaida Gippius (1869–1945), Sologub, Balmont, Blok, Belyi, and Vyacheslav Ivanov (qq.v.); Spain: in Machado y Ruiz, Jiménez, and Jorge Guillén (qq.v.); Portugal: in Eugénio de Castro (q.v.); also, Nicaragua: in Darío (q.v.); Uruguay: in Herrera y Reissig (q.v.); and the United States: in Amy Lowell (1874–1925), Hilda Doolittle, Fletcher, Pound, Eliot, Crane, Cummings, and Stevens (qq.v.).

BIBLIOGRAPHY: Symons, A., *The Symbolist Movement in Literature* (1899); Yeats, W. B., "The Symbolism of Poetry," in *Ideas of Good and Evil* (2nd ed., 1903); Barre, A., *Le Symbolisme: essai historique . . .* (1911); Charpentier, J., *Le Symbolisme* (1927); Taupin, R., *L'Influence du symbolisme français sur la poésie américaine* (*de 1910 à 1920*) (1929); Fiser, E., *Le Symbole littéraire: essai sur la signification du symbole chez Wagner, Baudelaire, Mallarmé, Bergson et Marcel Proust* (1941); Bowra, C. M., *The Heritage of Symbolism* (1943); Johansen, S., *Le Symbolisme: étude sur le style . . .* (1945); Cazamian, L., *Symbolisme et poésie: l'exemple anglais* (1947); Davies, G., "Stéphane Mallarmé: Fifty Years of Research," *FS,* I (1947); Mathews, A. J., *La Wallonie, 1886–1892: The Symbolist Movement in Belgium* (1947); Michaud, G., *La Doctrine symboliste: Documents* (1947); Michaud, G., *Message poétique du symbolisme* (3 vols. 1947); Eliot, T. S., *From Poe to Valéry* (1948); Cornell, K., *The Symbolist Movement* (1951); Maslenikov, O. A., *The Frenzied Poets: Andrey Biely and the Russian Symbolists* (1952); Clancier, G.-E., *De Rimbaud au surréalisme* (1953); Temple, R. Z., *The Critic's Alchemy: A Study of the Introduction of French Symbolism into England* (1953); Austin, L. J., *L'Univers poétique de Baudelaire: symbolisme et symbolique* (1956); Chiari, J., *Symbolism from Poe to Mallarmé: The Growth of a Myth* (1956); Gicovate, B., *Julio Herrera y Reissig and the Symbolists* (1957); Hatzfeld, H., *Trends and Styles in 20th Century French Literature* (1957); Ragusa, O., *Mallarmé in Italy* (1957); Cornell, K., *The Poet-Symbolist Period* (1958); Donchin, G., *The Influence of French Symbolism on Russian Poetry* (1958); Décaudin, M., *La Crise des valeurs symbolistes*

(1960); Block, H. M., *Mallarmé and the Symbolist Drama* (1963); Ellmann, R., and Feidelson, C., "Symbolism," in *The Modern Tradition* (1965), pp. 7–207; Balakian, A., *The Symbolist Movement: A Critical Appraisal* (1967)

ALFRED GARVIN ENGSTROM

SYNGE, John Millington

Irish poet, dramatist, and essayist, b. 16 April 1871, Rathfarnham (near Dublin); d. 24 March 1909, Dublin.

S. was born into a family that had contributed a long line of bishops and archbishops to the Protestant church. At Dublin University he studied Hebrew and Irish, and it was his knowledge of the latter language that perhaps proved crucial to his career, for it enabled him to communicate with the peasants that he has depicted in his plays.

After leaving the university in 1892 S. studied music, visited Germany, and divided his time between Ireland and the Continent. Early in 1896 he was in Florence and Rome. In March 1898, when Yeats (q.v.) found S. in Paris in a students' hostel in the Latin Quarter, he advised him to "Go to the Aran Islands. Live there as if you were one of the people themselves; express a life that has never found expression."

The advice was taken. S. gradually deserted France for Ireland, and in 1902 he gave up his lodging in Paris altogether. Only seven years of life remained to him, but in those years he was to produce the six plays that have given him his claim to immortality. Four of these plays were produced in the Abbey Theatre in Dublin during S.'s lifetime.

In addition to the plays, S. wrote two "notebooks"—*The Aran Islands* (1907) and *In Wicklow and West Kerry* (1908)—and a volume of *Poems and Translations* (1910). The translations, even when from writers like Villon and Petrarch, use the same Anglo-Irish idiom as the plays.

In the last year of his life S. became engaged to Maire O'Neil, who with her sister and fellow actress, Sara Allgood, had helped to build up the fame of the Abbey Theatre. Under the impression that he was convalescing from a throat ailment, S. went to Germany in 1908, but he returned to Dublin when his mother died. He himself died in a nursing home soon afterward.

S.'s greatness lies in his strength, simplicity,

and absolute sureness of touch. His long and apparently unsuccessful apprenticeship to literature in Paris was to bear fruit in the end, once Yeats had given him a theme. Until then —as Yeats tells us—his writing had been highly subjective, giving the effect of a man "looking on his face in a mirror but breathing all the time upon the glass." However, in *The Aran Islands* everything is told objectively. The impression is that of an intensely silent and lonely man viewing life in a spirit of dispassionate detachment. The book's nostalgic simplicity is thought by some critics to owe much to Loti (q.v.).

But if the prose of the notebooks is restrained, that of the plays is ablaze with color and imagination. S. is a realist, but his preface to *The Playboy of the Western World* (1907) makes it plain that he considered realism inadequate. "On the stage one must have reality, and one must have joy; and that is why the intellectual modern drama has failed, and people have grown sick of the false joy of musical comedy.... In a good play every speech should be as fully flavored as nut or apple, and such speeches cannot be written by anyone who works among people who have shut their lips on poetry."

The *Playboy of the Western World* tells of a youth who claims to have killed his father in a brawl. The inhabitants of a small village listen in spellbound admiration as he eloquently narrates "the crime," but they are shocked and angry when he attempts to turn fiction into fact. The play scandalized the Irish, and there were riots in the theater when it was first produced. But its gusto and humor soon triumphed.

"Of the things which nourish the imagination," S. wrote in his preface to *The Tinker's Wedding* (1908), "humor is the most needful and it is dangerous to limit or destroy it." Every phrase has its pungent significance in this play in which a priest agrees to marry the tinker and his doxy for ten shillings and a new can.

In *Deirdre of the Sorrows* (1910) the poetic force of the prose speeches carry one back to Elizabethan times, when poetry and drama were inseparable.

FURTHER WORKS: *In the Shadow of the Glen* (1903); *Riders to the Sea* (1904); *The Well of the Saints* (1905); *Collected Works* (4 vols., 1910); *Plays by J. M. S.* (1932); *Complete Works* (1935); *Plays, Poems, and*

Prose (1935); *Translations* (ed. R. Skelton; 1961); *Collected Works* (5 vols., 1961 ff.); *Poems and Plays* (ed. T. R. Henn; 1963); *The Autobiography of J. M. S., Constructed from the Manuscripts* (ed. A. Price; 1965)

BIBLOGRAPHY: Bourgeois, M., *J. M. S. and the Irish Dramatic Movement* (1913); Yeats, W. B., *J. M. S. and the Ireland of His Time* (1924); Corkery, D., *S. and Anglo-Irish Literature* (1931); Ellis-Fermor, M., *The Irish Dramatic Movement* (2nd ed., 1954); Greene, D. H., and Stephens, E. M., *J. M. S.* (1959); Henn, T. R., Introduction to *Poems and Plays* (1963); Johnston, D., *J. M. S.* (1965); Flood, J., "S.: A Study of His Aesthetic Development," *DA,* XXVIII (1968), 5052A

MONK GIBBON

T

TAGORE, Rabindranath

(pseud. of *Ravīndranátha Thākura*), Indian poet, dramatist, narrative writer, essayist, and philosopher (writing in Bengali and English), b. 6 May 1861, Calcutta; d. 7 Aug. 1941, Santiniketan, Bengal

The tolerant, religious family tradition established by T.'s grandfather, a friend of Ram Mohan Roy (1772–1833), who founded Brahmo-Samaj, the theistic Church for the Worship of God, exerted a formative influence upon the poet. In 1878 T. made his first visit to England to study law. He published his first polemical work in 1881. By 1890, when his father put him in charge of the family estates, he had already made a reputation as a poet with *Sandhyā sangīt* (1881, "Evening Songs") and *Prabhāt sangīt* (1883, "Morning Songs").

Uprooted from his city background of wealth and culture, among the peasants and farmers the young man now came to know poverty, backwardness, and the suffering caused by disease. The posthumously published collection *Towards Universal Man* (1961) contains the basic essays and speeches in which T. proved himself as a social reformer, politician, and pedagogue.

During the next nineteen years T. did so much for agriculture, rural hygiene, cooperatives, and public education that his work became exemplary for the new India, even before Gandhi entered the campaign for independence, in which T. played a decisive role. In 1901 T. founded his school Santiniketan—"asylum of peace"—near Bolpur. In 1918 this became the cultural center Visva-Bharati—"universal voice"—an international university designed as a meeting ground between East and West. Visva-Bharati was taken over by the government after T.'s death.

In his extensive travels throughout Asia, Europe, and America, T. was an open-minded ambassador of goodwill, always ready to learn. In 1905, during the demonstrations against the partition of Bengal, he led mass protest marches through Calcutta and composed patriotic battle hymns. T.'s last years were marred by his disappointment in the West, which seemed to be destroying its culture in internecine struggles for power. This disillusionment led him to resign his English title of knighthood. T. was awarded the Nobel Prize for Literature in 1913.

T. wrote more than a thousand poems, many of which he set to music himself. He soon turned away from the fashionable, erudite, somewhat precious verse of his youth in favor of popular simplicity. These poems, however, cannot be called neoromanticism, as some of them, especially the late ones, are extremely realistic. Besides his love songs, the best of which are contained in *The Gardener* (1913), the heartfelt songs of childhood and motherhood that he wrote for his own children after the early death of his wife deserve special mention. These are collected in *Śiśu* (1903), which T. himself translated into English as *The Crescent Moon* (1913). The religious and contemplative poetry of *Gītanjāli* (1909; Song Offerings, 1912) was the first of T.'s own translations of his work to be published in the United States. Amiya Chakravarty's anthology *A Tagore Reader* (1961) contains late poems on social themes that are almost expressionistic in style.

Most of T.'s numerous plays were written for his students at Santiniketan, and he himself took part in their performance. They were given outdoors, without sets, the audience surrounding the actors, and they were generally interspersed with songs and dances. Often there is no taut dramatic plot in the sense that the European theater knows it; instead, the scenes reflect moods, thoughts, or ideas. T.'s most frequently performed play is *Dākghar* (1912; The Post Office, 1914), which is about a child who longs for freedom in a world that is anxious to keep him under control because he has duties. The child Amal, symbol of the soul, is locked in his sickroom by his timid foster father; all he sees of the world is the people passing by his window, until death brings him freedom. In *Bisarjan* (1891, "Sacrifice") a devout youth is defeated by a hidebound, unyielding priest. Its theme is essentially the conflict between tradition and humanity. In *Sannyasi* (1880; Eng., 1918) the protagonist has to learn that true freedom lies in communion with the world, not in flight from it. *Rakta Karubī* (1924; Red Oleanders, 1925) deals with a modern problem: power, which instead of serving man dehumanizes and enslaves him, before it finally destroys itself and permits liberty to triumph. *Chitrāṅgadā* (1892; Chitra, 1913) deals with love's search for the true self of the beloved. With the exception of *Mālinī* (1895; Eng., 1918) T.'s early dramas are written in blank verse in five acts, like Shakespeare's.

As a narrative writer T. is a master of the short story (*The Hungry Stones*, 1916; *The Supreme Night*, 1919). Better known, however, is his novel *Gharē bahirē* (1916; The Home and the World, 1919), set in the time of the struggle for self-rule. The essay *Sādhanā, the Realization of Life* (1913) is a confession of faith in the Indian holy scriptures.

FURTHER WORKS: *Yurop-pravāsīr patra* (1881); *Chabī o gān* (1884); *Prakṛtir pariśodh* (1884); *Nalinī* (1884); *Kadi o komal* (1886); *Rājarṣi* (1889); *Rājā o rānī* (1889); *Mānaṣī* (1890); *Sonār tari* (1893); *Caitālī* (1896); *Pañcabhūt* (1897); *Kanikā* (1899); *Kathā* (1900); *Kāhinī* (1900); *Kṣaṇikā* (1900); *Kalpanā* (1900); *Naivedya* (1901); *Cokher bāli* (1902; Binodini, 1959); *Smaraṇ* (1903); *Svadesi samāj* (1904); *Naukādubi* (1905); *Kheyā* (1906); *Śāradotsava* (1908); *Śabdatattva* (1909); *Gorā* (1910); *Rājā* (1910; The King of the Dark Chamber, 1914); *Acalāyatan* (1911); *Bharatvarser itihāser bhārā* (1911); *Jīvansmṛti* (1912); *Utsarga* (1914); *Gītāli* (1914); *Gitāmālya*

(1914); *One Hundred Poems of Kabir* (1915); *Phālgunī* (1915; The Cycle of Spring, 1917); *Caturaṅga* (1916; Chaturanga, 1963); *Balākā* (1916; The Flight of Swans, 1956); *Fruit-Gathering* (1916); *Stray Birds* (1916); *Nationalism* (1917); *Personality* (1917); *Palātakā* (1918); *Siśu bholānāth* (1922); *Muktadhārā* (1922); *Vasanta* (1923); *Gṛha-praves* (1925); *Pūrabī* (1925); *Natīr pūjā* (1926); *Mahuyā* (1929); *Śeṣer kavitā* (1929); *Yogayog* (1930); *Religion of Man* (1930); *Vanavāṇī* (1931); *Pariśes* (1932); *Punaśca* (1932); *Caṇḍālikā* (1933); *Tāser deś* (1933); *Dui bon* (1933; Two Sisters, 1945); *Vicitritā* (1933); *Mālañca* (1934); *Cār adhyāy* (1934; Four Chapters, n.d.); *Śeṣ saptak* (1935); *Bīthikā* (1935); *Patraput* (1936); *Śyāmalī* (1936; Eng., 1955); *Citrāṅgadā* (1936); *Khāp-chādā* (1937); *Chadār chabi* (1937); *Chaṇḍālikā* (1938); *Śyāmā* (1938); *Prāntic* (1938); *Señjuti* (1938); *Prakāsinī* (1939); *Ākāś pradīp* (1939); *Banglā bhāsā paricay* (1939); *Navajātak* (1940); *Sānāi* (1940); *Rogaśayyāy* (1940); *Chelebelā* (1940; My Boyhood Days, 1940); *Ārogya* (1940); *Jammadina* (1940); *Galpasalpa* (1941); *Ravindrasahitya* (n.d.). **Selected English translations:** *The Message of India to Japan* (1916); *Caliph for a Day and Kedar* (1916); *Sacrifice, and Other Plays* (1917); *My Reminiscences* (1917); *Mashi, and Other Stories* (1918); *Stories by R. T.* (1918); *Love's Gift and Crossings* (1918); *The Home and the World* (1919); *Sakuntala* (1920); *Glimpses of Bengal: Letters* (1921); *The Fugitive* (1921); *Creative Unity* (1922); *Broken Ties, and Other Stories* (1925); *The Meaning of Art* (1926); *The Golden Boat* (1932); *Collected Poems and Plays* (1936); *Poems* (1942); *Rolland and R. T.: Letters* (1945); *Three Plays* (1950; includes Mukta dhara, Natir Puja, Chandalika); *More Stories* (1951); *Sheaves; Poems and Songs* (1951); *Rabindraracanavali* (1953–58); *A T. Testament* (1954); *The Garden* (1956); *The Herald of Spring* (1957); *Our Universe* (1958); *The Runaway* (1959); *Wings of Death* (1960); *On Art and Aesthetics: Letters and Essays* (1961); *Abanindranath T.* (1961); *Wit and Wisdom of R. T.* (1961); *Letters from Russia* (1961); *Diary of a Westward Voyage* (1962); *The Co-operative Principle* (1963); *Mahatma Gandhi* (1963); *Boundless Sky* (1964); *Abanindranath T.: His Early Work* (1964); *Faith of a Poet* (1964); *Housewarming, and Other Selected Writings* (1965); *A T. Reader* (1966); *One Hundred and One: Poems* (1966); *Moon, for What Do You Wait?* (1967)

RABINDRANATH TAGORE

TANIZAKI JUN'ICHIRŌ

BIBLIOGRAPHY: Thompson, E., *R. T., Poet and Dramatist* (1926); Anon., *The Golden Book of T.: An Homage to R. T. from India and the World* (1931); Sykes, M., *R. T.* (1943); Ghose, S. K., *R. T.* (1961); Kripalani, K., *R. T.* (1961); Shahane, V. A., "R. T.: A Study in Romanticism," *Studies in Romanticism,* III (1963), 53–64; Narasimbaiah, C. D., "Indian Writing in English: An Introduction," *Journal of Commonwealth Literature,* V (1968), 3–15

EMIL ENGELHARDT

TALEV, Dimitur

Bulgarian novelist and short-story writer, b. 14 Sept. 1898, Prilep (Macedonia); d. 20 Oct. 1966, Sofia

Macedonian by birth and upbringing, T. briefly studied medicine in Agram and then philosophy and Slavic literature in Vienna and Sofia. After 1921 he settled in Sofia, and for several years he edited the journals *Makedonija* and *Zora,* in which some of his short stories were first published. In 1960 he received the Dimitroff Prize.

T.'s most significant works were written during the 1950's when Bulgarian literature was most strongly dominated by the Soviet aesthetic theory of socialist realism (q.v.). The efforts of Bulgarian writers were directed toward the nation's past, and T. wrote almost exclusively about the period from the 17th to the late 19th c. In his case, however, the use of historical settings stemmed from a genuine and deep attachment to the turbulent history of the Macedonian people.

Without obviously discarding them, T.'s novels transcend the limitations of official socialist realism. While stressing the traditional moral values of simple country folk and dealing with the problems caused by class differences and man's possessive instincts, he penetrates deeply into the complexity of human nature and becomes an eloquent spokesman for individualism and the creative mind's need for freedom.

The trilogy composed of *Zhelezniyat svetelnik* (1952; The Iron Candlestick, 1964), *Ilinden* (1953), and *Prespanskite kambani* (1954) traces the lives of three generations of a family against the background of the 19th-c. Macedonian wars of liberation. T. shows his protagonists in situations ranging from youth to old age, providing vivid character portraits such as those of the strong-willed Sultana and her childlike husband, Stoyan Glaoushev, in *Zhelezniyat svetelnik.* He is able to reflect the life pattern of the whole region while paying keen attention to significant details, which are unforgettably impressed on the reader's mind. Without ever becoming didactic, this sweepingly epic work uncovers and subtly evaluates the constant tension in man between good and evil.

T.'s other novels also benefit from his intimate knowledge of Macedonian social history and folklore. The early and ambitious three-volume *Usilni godini* (1928–30) deals with the Ilinden revolution. The character of the national Bulgarian hero Samuil, who spent his life fighting Turkish domination of his homeland, dominates the trilogy *Samuil* (1958–60), which focuses on the leader's moral decisions and strength of character.

Sulzite na mama (1925) is a collection of delightful stories and fairy tales for children. T.'s stories and novellas, many of which were first published in Bulgarian journals and dailies, reflect his awareness of the complexity and the intangible problems of human character. By their atmosphere of resignation and wistful speculation about man's ambiguous nature, some of the later stories—such as "Poslednoto puteshestvie" ("The Last Journey," 1968)—are clearly in conflict with the "optimistic objectivity" prescribed by socialist realism. However, in addition to containing forced images and occasionally trite situations, these last works lack the powerful character portrayals and the masterly style of T.'s best novels.

T.'s work opens a door on a society still little known in the West. The power of his novels and stories make them of importance to both the cultural historian and the lay reader.

FURTHER WORKS: *Otkusletzi* (1927–28); *Zlatniyat Klyuch* (1935); *Starata Kushcha* (1938); *Na zavoi* (1940); *Khilendarskiyat monakh* (1962); *Razkazi, Povesti 1927–1962* (1962)

BIBLIOGRAPHY: Picchio, B., *Storia della letteratura bulgara* (1957); Manning, C. A., and Smal-Stocki, R., *History of Modern Bulgarian Literature* (1960); Konstantinov, G., *Moeto pokolenie v Literaturata 1917–1967* (1967); Shishkova, M., "Idei i obrazi v rannite razkazi na D. T.," *Literaturna Misul,* XI (1967), vi

MARKETA GOETZ STANKIEWICZ

TAMMSAARE, A. H.

(pseud. of *Anton Hansen*), Estonian novelist, short-story writer, and dramatist, b. 30 Jan. 1878, Albu; d. 1 March 1940, Tallinn

T. was the son of an independent farmer. While studying law in Tartu, he began to publish stories and to contribute to newspapers. From 1911 to 1913 he lived in the Caucasus because of tuberculosis. After 1918 T. lived in Tallinn and was associated with the Young Estonia movement. He translated from a number of languages, and was influenced by Gogol (1809–1852), Friedrich Hebbel (1813–63), Dostoyevski (1821–81), Hamsun, Conrad, G. B. Shaw, and Oscar Wilde (qq.v.), among others.

T. was soon to find his distinctive manner. Having begun as a rural realist, he turned to writing novellas about emancipated academics. He strikingly reinterpreted the biblical Judith story in his tragedy *Juudit* (1921), which reveals his growing preoccupation with problematic characters.

T.'s principal work, the saga *Tõde ja õigus* (5 vols., 1926–33), broadly and penetratingly depicts three decades of Estonian life, presenting town and country, coarse materialism and mystical idealism, peasant stubbornness and religious longings, revolutionary intellectual broodings and the tragic achievement of maturity. Here, as well as in his later works, especially in the skeptical comedy *Kuningal on külm* (1936) and the grotesque allegory *Põrgupõhja uus Vanapagan* (1939), his paradoxical, questioning streak becomes more dominant.

Dialectic keenness, subtle simplicity of diction, epic vigor, subdued but vibrant emotion, and restless delving into the fundamental problems of the human situation characterize all of T.'s work since *Juudit*.

FURTHER WORKS: *Raha-auk* (1907); *Uurimisel* (1907); *Pikad sammud* (1908); *Noored hinged* (1909); *Üle piiri* (1910); *Vanad ja noored* (1913); *Keelest ja luulest* (1915); *Poiss ja liblik* (1915); *Kärbes* (1917); *Varundid* (1917); *Sõjamõtted* (1919); *Kõrboja peremees* (1922); *Põialpoiss* (1923); *Sic transit* (1924); *Meie rebana* (1932); *Elu ja armastus* (1934); *Ma armastasin sakslast* (1935)

BIBLIOGRAPHY: Sillaots, M., *A. H. T.* (1927); Mihkla, K., *A. H. T. looming* (1938); Siimisker, H., *A. H. T.* (1962); Jänes, H., *Geschichte der estnischen Literatur* (1965); Puhvel, H., *A. H. T. elu ja looming 1878–1922* (1966)

ANTS ORAS

TANIZAKI Jun'ichirō

Japanese novelist, short-story writer, essayist, and dramatist, b. 24 July 1886, Tokyo; d. 30 July 1965, Yūgawara

Born into a declining merchant family in Tokyo, T. was in his formative years while Japan was emerging as a world power. Owing to the family's precarious economic situation, he received schooling only through the charity of friends and relatives and was encouraged by teachers who recognized his talent. After studying law and English language and literature, he entered Tokyo University's Department of National Literature, in 1908, with the intention of becoming a writer. Two years later T. had to leave the university for failure to pay tuition.

In 1910, T. published the best-known of his early stories, "Shisei" (The Tattoo, in *Modern Japanese Literature,* ed. I. Morris, 1962). During the years that followed, he devoted himself to writing. "Who was it," T. wrote in "Itansha no kanashimi" (1917; "The Sorrows of a Heretic"), an autobiographical story, "that created in me the strange propensity to be more deeply concerned not about what is good but rather what is beautiful?"

Following the Great Earthquake of 1923, in a move symbolic of his return in spirit to traditional Japan, T. rejected his native city of Tokyo and retreated to the quieter, old-fashioned world of the Kansai area, around Kyoto and Osaka. This is the setting of *Manji* (1928–30; "Whirlpool"), a novella that foreshadowed the novel *Tade kuu mushi* (1928–29; Some Prefer Nettles, 1955), about a hopeless marriage and a conflict between the old and new ways of life.

T.'s changing attitude in this decade is reflected in his essay "In'ei raisan" (1933–34; excerpts titled In Praise of Shadows, published in the *Japan Quarterly,* 1955), which expresses the view that traditional Japanese art flourished in the shade and that the dazzle of the modern world destroys it. Therefore one must diminish the lights.

At the peak of his creative powers, T. published, in 1939 to 1941, a modern version of the 11th-c. classic *Genji monogatari* (written

1001–1022; The Tale of Genji, 1925–34), the greatest work in Japanese literature.

In *Sasame Yuki* (1943, 1946–48; The Makioka Sisters, 1958), an elegy to a vanished era and his longest novel, an old but declining merchant family clings to the belief that suitably arranged matches preserve one's heritage and social position. Two unmarried sisters display conflicting styles of life. The older girl, Yukiko, emerges as a quiet, traditional woman; the younger, Taeko, scandalously impulsive and modern, indulges in a variety of adventures.

In 1956 T. published *Kagi* (The Key, 1961), a study of adultery and middle-aged depravity set in Kyoto. In this novel husband and wife keep parallel diaries, largely about their sexual experiences, in which they describe a complex web of reality and fantasy.

T.'s last novel, *Fūten rōjin nikki* (1962; The Diary of a Mad Old Man, 1965), presents the satirical portrait of an ill but unruly patriarch, revealing a childish and obdurate sensibility long attuned to art, to the nuances of sexuality, and to the imminence of death.

Nothing that occurred in the world around T. deterred him from his quest for the "eternal woman" of traditional Japan, whom he deified. Concurrently, he wrote with fondness of the past and of the losses suffered in the course of modernization. Translating the conflict between old and new from the world of thought into the realm of feeling, he reduced it to sexual terms. A prolific writer and painstaking craftsman, he desired to entertain, enlighten, and shock his audience. The alarming implications of his art and his skill in revealing disturbing truths to the reading public evoked wide attention. In the opinion of the critic and translator E. Seidensticker, T. was one of the "strongest, most independent, and most admirable persons Japan has produced this last century."

FURTHER WORKS: *Shisei* (1911); *Akuma* (1913; "Satan"); *O'Tsuya-goroshi* (1915; A Springtime Case, 1927); *Kyōfu jidai* (1920; "Age of Fear"); *Mumyō to Aizen* (1924; "Mumyo and Aizen"); *Chijin no ai* (1924–25; "Idiot's Love"); *Ashikari* (1932; English translation in *Ashikari, and The Story of Shunkin*, 1932); *Shunkinshō* (1933; English translation in *Ashikari, and The Story of Shunkin*, 1932); *Seishun monogatari* (1933; "Story of My Youth"); *Bunsho tokuhon* (1934; "A Reader of Essays"); *Shōshō Shigemoto no haha* (1949–50; "The Mother of Captain Shigemoto");

Gendai Nihon bungaku zenshū (vols. 18 and 71, 1953–59; "T. J.'s Selected Works"); *Yume no ukihashi* (1960; The Floating Bridge of Dreams, in *Seven Japanese Tales*, 1963); *T. J. zenshū* (28 vols., 1966–68; "T. J.'s Complete Works"). **Selected English translations:** *Modern Japanese Literature* (ed. D. Keene, 1956; includes excerpts from The Mother of Captain Shigemoto); *Seven Japanese Tales* (ed. H. Hibbett, 1963)

BIBLIOGRAPHY: Keene, D., *Japanese Literature* (1953); Seidensticker, E., *Atlantic Monthly*, Jan. 1955; McClellan, E., *Monumenta Nipponica*, XVI (1960–61); Hyman, S., *New Leader*, XLVI (30 Sept. 1963), xx; Olson, L., *American Universities Field Staff: East Asia*, XI (1964), v; Hashimoto, H., *T. J. no bungaku* (1965; "The Literature of T. J."); Takada, Z., "T. J.," *Gendai Nihon bungaku daijiten* (1965; "Encyclopedia of Modern Japanese Literature"); Seidensticker, E., *Japan Quarterly*, XII (Oct./Dec. 1965); Hibbett, H., *Daedalus* (1966); Saegusa, Y., *T. J. ronkō* (1969; "A Study of T. J.")

LEON M. ZOLBROD

TARDIEU, Jean

French poet and dramatist, b. 1 Nov. 1903, Saint-Germain-de-Joux, Ain

T. lived for a time in Lyon and then in Paris, where he was educated at the Lycée Condorcet and the Sorbonne. For a time he worked for a publisher, and during World War II he was active in the resistance movement. After 1944, he was appointed head of the drama section of Radiodiffusion Télévision Française.

A protean personality, T. has written poetry, drama, children's stories, radio and television scripts, translations, essays, and artistic and musical criticism. His literary career began with the evanescent, suprarational poems collected in *Accents* (1939). One section of *Accents* is T.'s French version of *Der Archipelagus*, by Friedrich Hölderlin (1770–1843). In his early poetry, T. favors extravagant brittleness not unlike Hölderlin's. Later, inspired by his resistance activity, T. wrote verse that pulses with lyrical fever: *Le Témoin invisible* (1943); *Poèmes* (1944); *Le Démon de l'irréalite* (1946); *Les Dieux étouffés* (1946); and two volumes entitled *Jours pétrifiés 1943–1944, 1942–1944* (1947 and 1948). In this same period he also wrote whimsical children's fiction such as *Il était une fois, deux fois, trois fois* (1947).

Unusual in structure and theme, T.'s plays stem mainly from his radio and television work. A majority of them are contained in two volumes: *Théâtre de chambre, I* (1955) and *Théâtre II, Poèmes à jouer* (1960).

An outstanding drama in the first collection is *La Serrure,* a strident two-character vignette that teeters on the edge of voyeurism. A wildly imaginative dramatist, T. probes the enigma of the relationships of language and pure feeling. Strongly influenced by the poets of the 1940's—notably Queneau, Prévert, and Artaud (qq.v.)—T.'s theater and poetry often show hermetic or surrealistic facets. *Les Amants du métro* (1954), probably his best theater piece, is a bittersweet Romeo-Juliet dream play, the action of which takes place in a subway.

In addition to radio and television performances, T.'s plays (which are too abstruse for the boulevard audiences) have been produced in small, experimental theaters.

A penetrating critic of art and music, T. analyzed European aesthetics in *De la Peinture que l'on dit abstraite* (1960), *Hans Hartung* (1962), and *Hollande* (1963).

FURTHER WORKS: *Figures* (1944); *Lapicque* (1945); *Monsieur Monsieur* (1951); *Un mot pour un autre* (1951); *La Première Personne du singulier* (1952); *Une Voix sans personne* (1954); *Théâtre de chambre, I* (1955; includes: *Qui est là?, La Politesse inutile, Le Sacre de la nuit, Le Meuble, Le Guichet, Monsier Moi, Faust et Yorick, La Sonate et les trois messieurs, La Societé Apollon, Oswald et Zénaïde, Ce que parler veut dire, Il y avait Foule au manoir, Eux Seuls le savent; Un Geste pour un autre, Conversation-sinfonietta*); *L'espace et la flûte* (1958); *Théâtre de chambre, II, Poèmes à jouer* (1960; includes: *L'ABC de notre vie, Rythme a trois temps; Une Voix sans personne, Les Temps du verbe, Tonnerre sans orage); Histoires obscures* (1961); *Choix de poèmes, 1924–1954* (1961); *Pages d'écriture* (1967)

BIBLIOGRAPHY: Esslin, M., "The Theatre of J. T.," *The London Magazine,* II (1962), ii, 85–90; Evans, C. H., "The New Dramatists: J. T.," *DramS,* II (1963), iii, 305–21; Noulet, E., *J. T.* (1964); Réda, J., "J. T.," *NRF,* 16 Oct. 1968, pp. 494–501

KENNETH S. WHITE

TATE, Allen

American poet, novelist, biographer, and essayist, b. 19 Nov. 1899, Winchester, Kentucky

Born into an old Southern merchant family of Scotch-Irish and English ancestry, T. graduated from Vanderbilt University in 1922. In 1924 he married novelist Caroline Gordon (b. 1895).

T. edited *The Sewanee Review* from 1944 to 1946. He is currently professor of English at the University of Minnesota, an appointment which he has held since 1951. T. has received many awards and honors including the coveted Bollingen Prize. In 1950 he was converted to Roman Catholicism.

During his second year at Vanderbilt, T. became associated with the group around *The Fugitive.* It was this "little magazine," founded by T.'s English professor Ransom (q.v.), that provided the first serious outlet for T.'s poetry. Nine of the some forty poems he contributed were good enough to survive in his *Poems* (1960), which included the famous "Homily" (1925).

In 1924, T. moved to New York City and worked at free-lance reviewing to support himself. During this period his Southern experience began to take on significance in his work. It led to his best-known poem, "Ode to the Confederate Dead" (1928), a romantic exultation of Southern chivalry, its tradition of excess and faith during the Civil War. His *Mr. Pope, and Other Poems* (1928), combined a tightly disciplined, traditional stanzaic form with modern subject matter.

From 1928 to 1930 T. lived in Paris, where he wrote the moving "Mother and Son" (1928), a description of how even maternal love fails to follow an emotionally threatened man who "withdraws into his private mind." T. is greatly concerned with the uses and influences of the past, but his poem "To the Romantic Traditionalists" (1934–36) was addressed to those who destroy the past by trying to live in it.

While poetry remained his main interest, T. increasingly turned to prose. He published two historical biographies: *Stonewall Jackson* (1928) and *Jefferson Davis* (1929). In 1930, he contributed "Remarks on the Southern Religion," to a collection of twelve essays entitled *I'll Take My Stand,* a tract of the Southern agrarian movement. This essay, like his two biographies, celebrates agrarian resistance to

Northern industrial society, a recurrent theme in T.'s prose and poetry.

T.'s essays and poems appeared frequently in periodicals, and collections of his poetry were published in 1930, 1932, and 1936. The merciless culling out and critical revision that went into T.'s *Selected Poems* (1937) fittingly expressed his credo that the poet's concern is not solely with his own experience but also with that of his readers. This volume, the highpoint of which is his revision of "Ode to the Confederate Dead," established T.'s prominence in American poetry.

In 1938 T. published *The Fathers,* an historical novel of the conflicts within an aristocratic Virginian family at the time of the Civil War. *The Forlorn Demon* (1952), a collection of essays written after his conversion, reflects his use of Catholic doctrine to reorganize his critical and poetic perceptions.

With the publication of T.'s *Collected Essays* (1959) and his revised "Seasons of the Soul" (1960), a sensuous and lyrical poem that relates individual human experience to the life cycle, T.'s stature was further enhanced. Some have termed this last poem one of the most important of the 20th c.

T. is one of the few American authors to insist on both the intellectual and the emotional sides of life. His predilection for words of Greek and Latin origin is a reflection of the "fierce Latinity," which he sees as his chief personal characteristic. His restrained, measured, yet deeply moving verse, and his social and literary criticism have become increasingly regarded as among the best in the American literary tradition.

FURTHER WORKS: *The Golden Mean, and Other Poems* (1923); *Three Poems* (1930); *Robert E. Lee* (1932); *Poems: 1928–1931* (1932); *Reactionary Essays on Poetry and Ideas* (1936); *The Mediterranean, and Other Poems* (1936); *America through the Essay* (1938); *Reason in Madness* (1941); *Sonnets at Christmas* (1941); *The Vigil of Venus* (1943); *The Winter Sea* (1944); *Poems: 1920–1945* (1946); *Poems: 1922–1947* (1948); *On the Limits of Poetry* (1948); *The Hovering Fly, and Other Essays* (1949); *Two Conceits for the Eye* (1950); *The Man of Letters in the Modern World* (1955); *Essays of Four Decades* (1968)

BIBLIOGRAPHY: Schwartz, D., "The Poetry of A. T.," *SoR,* V (1940), 419–38; Burnham, J., "The Unreconstructed A. T.," *PR,* XVI (1949), 198–202; Koch, V., "The Poetry of A. T.," *KR,* XI (1949), 357–78; Cowan, L., *The Fugitive Group* (1959); Kermode, F., "Old Orders Changing," *Encounter,* XV (1962), 72–76; Meiners, R., *The Last Alternatives* (1963); Hemphill, G., *A. T.* (1964); Bishop, F., *A. T.* (1967); Tate, A., "Poetry Modern and Unmodern: A Personal Reflection," *HudR,* XXI (1968), 251–62

STANLEY J. PACION

TAYAMA Katai

Japanese novelist, short-story writer, and essayist, b. 22 Jan. 1872, Tatebayashi; d. 13 May 1930, Tokyo

In the complex arena of modern Japanese literature T. is best remembered, along with Shimazaki Tōson (1872–1943), Tokuda Shūsei (1871–1943), and Masamune Hakuchō (1879–1963), as one of the four pillars of naturalism. In both his criticism and his fiction he played an influential role as a literary innovator. In addition to his book-length works, he wrote more than four hundred short stories, travel sketches, and essays.

The literary career of T. can be divided into three quite distinct periods. The first spans the last decade of the 19th c. and may be termed romantic. The second, following a brief period of transition, lasted from 1906 to 1912 and is characterized by his full commitment to the naturalist movement. The third, which takes us to the end of his life, is one of Buddhistic idealism.

In 1891, with a few short travel sketches to recommend him, T. came to the attention of Ozaki Kōyō (1867–1903) and under his influence became a writer of sentimental love stories and romantic poetry. In a few years he was to collaborate, with such rising figures as Kunikida Doppo (1871–1908) and Yanagida Kunio (1875–1962), on the poetic collection *Jojōshi* (1897; "Lyric Poetry"). The young poets' efforts to present a frank and fresh expression of emotion resulted in T.'s turning his attention to the problem of *gembun-itchi* (the unification of the written and spoken languages). He attempted to free literature from the shackles of classical diction and formulated his future stylistic dictum: "candid description."

Even during this early period T. read contemporary European literature extensively. Such names as Gustave Flaubert (1821–80), Fiodor Dostoyevski (1821–81), Lev Tolstoi, and Zola (qq.v.) appear frequently in his critical writings. His interest even led him to translate several of their works. We learn from his diary, however, that it was Guy de Maupassant (1850–93) who had the most influence on T. and gave him a new perspective on his craft.

During the early years of this century, T. began his shift toward naturalism with several short novels. In *Rokotsu naru Byōsha* (1904; "Candid Description") he condemned contemporary literature as frivolous and perverted by subjectivism, and he called for a new freedom of expression capable of uncovering the hidden secrets of human nature.

The publication of Shimazaki Toson's *Hakai* (1906; "The Broken Commandment") accelerated the trend toward naturalism. In 1906, T. became editor of the newly established journal *Bunshō sekai* ("Literary World") and for the next six years followed an editorial policy in support of the naturalist movement.

T.'s *Futon* (1907; "The Quilt") was followed in rapid succession by his trilogy: *Sei* (1908; "Life"), *Tsuma* (1908–1909; "Wife"), and *En* (1910; "Bondage"). These four works established T. as the nation's most influential spokesman for naturalism. Strongly autobiographical, the novels examined T.'s own emotional life with shocking frankness. Their confessional nature influenced enumerable younger writers who were to develop this technique into the *watakushi-shōsetsu,* or "I-novel," of the next generation.

This autobiographical period also yielded *Inaka kyōshi* (1908; "Country Teacher"), a carefully researched and fastidiously recorded account of the life of a rural teacher; his best-known short story, "Ippeisotsu" (1908; One Soldier, 1956); and a critical work, *Katai Bunwa* (1911; "Katai's Literary Discourses"). In these works the close observation of external phenomena contributes to a vivid description of human psychology.

By 1912, when T. left *Bunshō sekai,* naturalism had run its course in Japan. Thereafter, T.'s writings, while continuing to treat the same basic themes, take an idealistic turn and reflect a strong Buddhist influence. In *Aru sō no kiseki* (1918; "The Priest's Miracle") a Mahayana Buddhist tone of resignation emerges, and in his later critical works a Zen Buddhist note is struck. By 1920, when both he and Tokuda Shūsei were honored with a fiftieth birthday celebration, T. was eulogized as one of the grand old men of modern Japanese literature.

FURTHER WORKS: *Hana no no* (1901;

"Flowers of the Field"); *Júemon no saigo* (1902; "The Fate of Júemon"); *Kami* (1911; "Hair"); *Zansetsu* (1917–18; "Remaining Snow"); *Kawa-zoi no haru* (1919; "Spring along the River"); *Momoyo* (1927; "One Hundred Nights")

BIBLIOGRAPHY: Kokusai Bunka Shinkōkai, *Introduction to Contemporary Japanese Literature* (1939); Bonneau, G., *Histoire de la littérature japanaise contemporaine* (1940); Benl, O., *Flüchtiges Leben: moderne japanische Erzählungen* (1942); Okazaki Y., *Japanese Literature in the Meiji Era* (1955); McKinnon, R. N., *The Heart Is Alone* (1957)

RICHARD L. SPEAR

TECCHI, Bonaventura

Italian novelist and critic, b. 11 Feb. 1896, Bagnoregio; d. 30 March 1968, Rome

T., Italy's most distinguished Germanist, first came in contact with the German world during World War I. While he was a prisoner of war in a camp near Hamburg, he began to read Wilhelm Heinrich Wackenroder (1773–98), the German romantic poet who was to be the subject of his first major critical work, *Wackenroder* (1927). T. lived in Berlin from 1922 to 1923. After serving as director of the Gabinetto Vieusseux, a literary and artistic organization in Florence, T. taught in Czechoslovakia and then at the universities of Padua and Rome. A contributor to many journals and periodicals, T. was also a correspondent for *Corriere della Sera.* He was the first Italian Germanist invited to teach at the Sorbonne.

T. was strongly influenced by the German and Italian romantics. He shares Wackenroder's anguish and anxieties and the tendency of the Italian romantics to turn from the external realities and seek refuge in contemplation. In his work he is particularly concerned with the identification of essential reality and the mysterious interrelation of good and evil.

His first book, *Il nome sulla sabbia* (1924), a collection of stories and autobiographical pieces, contains in embryo the themes that were to intrigue T. throughout his life: man's fundamental solitude and egocentricity and the necessity of acknowledging external reality. It shows T.'s affinity for sensual, restless female protagonists. He also had a very special feeling for plants and animals.

T.'s preoccupation with the problem of evil first manifests itself in *Giovani amici* (1941), in which he attempts by means of character analysis to reconcile the psychological novel and the realistic novel. The protagonists are all essentially static; they do not so much change as become themselves. The major narrative development of this structurally weak novel is the main character's discovery of the presence of evil.

Valentina Velier (1950) combines two elements basic to T.'s narrative works: a northern European locale and a woman driven by pride and by love. More successful structurally than *Giovani amici,* the novel is a study of individual egoism. In spite of some traces of sentimentality, it achieves a coherent resolution.

In his most famous novel, *Gli egoisti* (1959; The Egoists, 1964), T. goes beyond the individual to consider the collective egoism of a social group: the intellectuals. Each of his many characters is shown as being enclosed in his own egocentric universe, insensitive to the feelings and suffering of others. As in most of T.'s novels, moral and didactic considerations take the upper hand, and the novel, though psychologically and intellectually interesting, lacks cohesive narrative tension.

The highest expression of T.'s art is to be found in his many volumes of short stories, travel pieces, prose poems, and autobiographical confessions. One such collection, *L'Isola appassionata* (1945), which is based on the author's experiences as military censor in Sicily during World War II, exquisitely conveys the idyllic aspect of the island and the fundamental sadness of its people. In *Storie di bestie* (1957) and *Storie di alberi e di fiori* (1963), T. expresses his profound affinity for animals, trees, and flowers in a prose that contains moments of genuine lyrical intensity.

As a critic and literary historian, T. published numerous monographs, essays, and reviews. The best measure of both his scholarship and literary judgment is perhaps the volume *Scrittori tedeschi del Novecento* (1941), a collection of critical notes and reviews dealing with a wide range of authors and individual works.

FURTHER WORKS: *Il dramma del Foscolo* (1927); *Il vento tra le case* (1928); *Tre storie d'amore* (1931); *Maestri e amici* (1934); *Wackenroder: scritti di poesia e di estetica* (1934); *Carossa: Adolescenza* (1935); *I Villatàuri* (1935); *La signora Ernestina* (1936); *Amalia* (1937); *Idilli moravi* (1939); *Alverdes: La*

stanza dei fischiatori (1940); *Vigilia di guerra* (1940); *Un'estate in campagna* (1945); *Carossa* (1947); *La presenza del male* (1949); *Sette liriche di Goethe* (1949); *Creature sole* (1950); *Carossa: Aus des Dichters Werken* (1953); *Luna a ponente* (1955); *Le due voci* (1956); *L'Arte di Thomas Mann* (1956); *Teatro tedesco dell'età romantica* (1957); *Romantici tedeschi* (1959); *Scrittori tedeschi moderni* (1959); *Officina segreta* (1959); *Baracca 15 C* (1961); *Le fiabe di E. T. A. Hoffmann* (1962); *Mörike* (1962); *Svevia, terra di poeti* (1964); *Gli onesti* (1965); *Goethe e la fiaba* (1966); *Antica terra* (1967); *Goethe in Italia* (1967); *Il senso degli altri* (1968)

BIBLIOGRAPHY: Pischedda, N., *B. T.* (1948); Grana, G., "B. T.," in *Profili e letture de contemporanei* (1962), pp. 247–76; Cossu, N., "B. T.," in *I Contemporanei* (1963), pp. 1127–61; Orilia, S., *B. T.* (1965)

ZINA TILLONA

TEIRLINCK, Herman

Belgian novelist, playwright, and essayist (writing in Flemish), b. 24 Feb. 1879, Brussels; d. there, 4 Feb. 1967

T. had a long career as a public official. He taught literature and the dramatic arts in the public schools of Brussels and advised three Belgian kings on matters concerning Flemish culture. He was the cofounder and director of what is still one of the most important literary periodicals in Belgium, *Nieuw Vlaams Tijdschrift* (founded in 1946). Among many other awards and prizes, T. received in 1956 the Prize for Dutch Letters established by the combined governments of Holland and Belgium.

T. was the most prolific and protean of 20th-c. Flemish authors. In novels, plays, tales, countless essays, speeches, and introductions, he rallied to the standard of his friend Vermeylen (q.v.): "We want to be Flemings in order to be Europeans." Unlike his compatriots Maeterlinck or Verhaeren (qq.v.), who wrote in French, T. opted for writing in his mother tongue, in spite of the inevitable restrictions of a less well-known language.

After an initial volume of poems, *Verzen* (1900), T. published three regional novels. The stylistic virtuosity that is a hallmark of T.'s work is most evident in his elegant novel *Mijnheer J. B. Serjanszoon, orator didacticus* (1908). In this ironic and baroque portrait of an 18th-c. epicure, T. presents a dilettante whose dazzling verbal mask cannot protect him from loneliness and fear of death. In *Het ivoren aapje* (1909) T. wrote the first Flemish novel to deal exclusively with the metropolis. Reminiscent of Döblin's (q.v.) *Alexanderplatz,* it paints the teeming life of the Belgian capital around 1900.

Other novels followed, but in 1922, T. temporarily stopped writing fiction and turned to the theater. For over a quarter of a century his expressionistic plays and his influence as a theoretician and director dominated the development of the Flemish stage.

T. saw plays not as mirrors of everyday reality but as independent structures of ideas. He boldly discarded threadbare techniques and topics and introduced a concept of total theater in which dance, mime, recorded music, and cinematic effects were utilized to break down the barrier between the spectators and the stage. Examples of plays employing these techniques include: *De vertraagde film* (1922); *Ik dien* (1923); *De man zonder lijf* (1925); *Ave* (1928); and *De ekster op de galg* (1937). T.'s desire to duplicate the union and intimacy of the medieval miracle plays is evident in his scenarios for outdoor theater (1923 and 1925) and an adaptation of the classic *Everyman* (1934). In later years, T. wrote an impressive adaptation of the *Oresteia* (1946).

T. returned to fiction during World War II. *Maria Speermalie* (1940) and *Het gevecht met de engel* (1952) are masterpieces that celebrate the primitive forces of nature. The latter book is a particularly fine presentation of the major themes that occupied T. throughout his life: sexual passion and perversion; the fierce majesty of the female; and the exuberant eternality of nature. In both novels the celebration of the blood and the atavistic mystery of nature reminds one of D. H. Lawrence, Giono, and Hamsun (qq.v.). T. shares Lawrence's interest in pitting decadent civilization against the forces basic to mankind and to nature, though the Lawrentian figures pale beside the ebullient primitives of T.

In his final novel, *Zelfportret of het galgemaal* (1956; The Man in the Mirror, 1963), T. investigated the anatomy of the modern psyche. Its hero, Henri M., is a far more complex Serjanszoon. Aware of his masks, he scrutinizes the various roles he plays. A *roman d'analyse, Zelfportret* makes use of all T.'s stylistic powers, profound psychological insights, and ironic subtlety to describe the dis-

contented winter of a life in which there is no hope of spring.

Though he hedonistically put the imagination ahead of reality, T. succeeded in speaking directly to a large audience in novels and plays that deal with every level of society. His lyric imagination, the tragic dimension of his characters, the dramatic conflict between the sexes and between nature and modern civilization culminate in a positive vision that gives T.'s work a quality that is both of our time and beyond it.

FURTHER WORKS: *Verzen* (1900); *Landelijke historiën* (1901); *De wonderbare wereld* (1902); *Het stille gesternte* (1903); *Het bedrijf van den kwade* (1904); *De doolage* (1905); *Zon* (1906); *De kroonluchter* (1906); *Het avontuurlijk Leven van Lieven Cordaat* (1907); *Johan Doxa* (1917); *De nieuwe Uilenspiegel* (1920); *De wonderlijke mei* (1926); *De lemen torens* (1928); *Griseldis* (1942); *Rolande met de Bles* (1944); *Verzameld Werk* (ed. W. Pée; 8 vols., 1955 ff.); *Taco* (1958)

BIBLIOGRAPHY: *T. Gedenkboek 1879–1929* (1929); *Van en Over T.* (1954); Brachin, P., *L'expressionisme dans le théâtre de T.* (1958); Van der Wal, T., *T.* (1965); Bousset, H., *T.* (1968)

E. M. BEEKMAN

TERZÁKIS, Angelos

Greek short-story writer, novelist, dramatist, and critic, b. 16 Feb. 1907, Nauplion

Born into a wealthy family, T. studied law at the University of Athens, but though he was admitted to the bar in 1929, he gave up law for writing. From 1928 to 1930 he edited the literary magazines *Pnoí* and *Lógos.* Beginning in 1937 T. held various executive posts in the National Theater. During the Greco-Italian war he served in Albania.

Since 1947 T. has regularly contributed articles and dramatic criticism to the Athenian newspaper *To Víma* and other publications. From 1963 to 1967 he edited the cultural review *Epohés.* He has on several occasions been honored by the government.

A leader of the renaissance of the 1930's, T. was instrumental in helping modern Greek literature shake off its ethnic provincialism and achieve a more than local interest by embracing wide-ranging contemporary problems.

O Xehasménos (1925) and *Fthinoporiní* (1927), two early collections of short stories, marked T.'s future themes and subjects: misery, stifling routine, sickly sensibility, passivity and lack of purpose of lower-middle-class life between the two world wars. His first novels —*Desmótes* (1932), *I parakmí ton sklirón* (1933), and *I menexedénia politía* (1937)—are family dramas, psychological studies of weak souls victimized by circumstances and a self-imposed fate.

From the beginning T. showed extraordinary gifts as a narrator and psychological observer. His nakedly realistic prose was soon enriched with symbolistic and lyrical elements without loss of directness. Faultless structure, a lucid style, solidly and sharply delineated characters, depth of observation, and compassion have been his prominent characteristics.

T.'s voluminous *Pringípisa Izambo* (1945) was a surprise to his readers because it plunged into the heroic past, the life of the 13th-c. Morea under its Frankish rulers. This epic historical novel, breathtakingly faithful to the time it revives, subtly illuminated the burning issues of the time in which it was written: the sufferings of Greece during the German occupation. Technically perfect, panoramic in its historical-imaginative conception, this novel is a recognized masterpiece.

Taxídi me ton Éspero (1946) was T.'s contribution to the novel of adolescence, a theme popular with such writers of the 1930's as Kosmás Polítis (b. 1888). It relates a tragic first-love experience and provides a subtle psychological analysis of its young hero, Gláfkos.

Díhos Theó (1951) once more deals with the tragedies of family life. The time is again the troubled years between the two world wars, but T.'s scope and vision are much broader and encompass a wide variety of human types as he focuses on modern political and social ideas, big-city alienation, and the traits of a lost generation.

Mistikí Zoí (1957), which won a First State Award, adapts such modern techniques as stream-of-consciousness writing, the interplay of the conscious and the unconscious, and flashbacks. There is a mystical element in this novel about the search for an elusive truth by two exceptional human beings, a man and a woman, and their ultimate failure to achieve communication and union.

Since 1936 T. has written more than a dozen plays. His historical dramas such as *Aftokrátor Mihaíl* (1936), *O Stávros ke to spathí* (1939) and *Theofanó* (1936) focus on the failure of mediocre leaders in the past to connect their lives

with great events. Most of his other plays are social tragedies and comedies or a mixture reminiscent of his novels.

T. is as yet insufficiently known abroad, but in Greece he has both a large popular readership and a critical reputation as a master of prose fiction and the drama.

FURTHER WORKS: *Gamílio emvatírio* (1937); *Ílotes* (1939); *O Exousiastís* (1942); *Tou érota ke tou thanátou* (1943); *To megálo pehnídi* (1944); *Aprílis* (1945); *Agní* (1949); *Níhta sti Mesóyo* (1957); *Ta lítra tis eftihías* (1959); *Thomás o dípsihos* (1962); *Prosanatolismós ston eóna* (1963); *O Prógonos* (1970)

BIBLIOGRAPHY: Panayotópoulos, I. M., *Ta prósopa ke ta kímena*, Vol. II (1943), pp. 117–36; Sahínis, A., *I pezografía tis katohís* (1948), 44–52; Thrilos, A., "A. T.," *Néa Estía*, XLIX (1 Jan. 1951), 38–42, and (15 Jan. 1951), 107–09; Demáras, C., et al., "A. T.: A Critical Mosaic," *The Charioteer*, No. 4 (1962), pp. 50–54; Proussis, C. M., "The Novels of A. T.," *Daedalus*, XCV (Fall 1966), 1021–45

ANDONIS MANGANARIS DECAVALLES

THARAUD, Jérôme Ernest and Jean Charles

French novelists: Jérôme, b. 18 March 1874, Saint-Junien; d. 29 Jan. 1953, Varengeville-sur-mer. Jean, b. 9 May 1877, Saint-Junien; d. 8 April 1952, Paris

The T. brothers collaborated on their books, taking Maurice Barrès (1862–1923) as their model. Péguy (q.v.) introduced them in his *Cahiers*. They initiated the documentary novel technique in modern French literature, and their subjects were always topical.

In *Dingley, l'illustre écrivain* (1902) the T. brothers dealt with British imperialism—and offered a fictional portrait of Kipling (q.v.). In *La Bataille à Scutari* (1913) they wrote about the Balkan problem. The subject of *Rabat, ou Les Heures marocaines* (1918) and *Marrakech, ou Les Seigneurs de l'Atlas* (1920) is the colonization of North Africa. Their trilogy on East European Jews—*L'Ombre de la croix* (1917), *Un Royaume de Dieu* (1920), and *La Rose de Sâron* (1927)—draws much of its subject matter from a drama by the Polish writer Wyspiánski (q.v.). *Quand Israël est roi* (1920), their account of the Hungarian revolution under Béla Kun, is, however, generally considered anti-Semitic.

The books by the T. brothers were much admired for their vividness, atmosphere, and narrative skill.

FURTHER WORKS: *Le Coltineur débile* (1899); *La Maîtresse servante* (1911); *La Fête arabe* (1912); *La Tragédie de Ravaillac* (1922); *Le Chemin de Damas* (1923); *Une Relève* (1924); *L'An prochain à Jérusalem* (1924); *La Vie et la mort de Déroulède* (1925); *Rendez-vous Espagnols* (1925); *Nôtre cher Péguy* (2 vols., 1926); *Noël des Deux Magots* (1927); *Mes Années chez Barrès* (written by Jérôme alone; 1927); *Petite Histoire des Juifs* (1927; The Chosen People, 1929); *La Randonnée de Samba Diouf* (1928); *La Chronique des frères ennemies* (1929); *Œuvres* (4 vols., 1929 ff.); *Fez, ou Les Bourgeois de l'Islam* (1930); *L'Oiseau d'or* (1931); *La Nuit de Fès* (1932); *Paris Saigon dans l'azur* (1932); *Les Bien-aimées* (1932); *Quand Israël n'est plus roi* (1933); *La Jumante errante* (1933); *Vienne la Rouge* (1934); *Les Cavaliers d'Allah* (1935); *Les Milles et un jours de l'Islam* (4 vols., 1935–50); *Le Passant d'Éthiope* (1936); *Cruelle Espagne* (1938); *Les Contes de la Vierge* (1943); *Vielle Perse et jeune Iran* (1947); *La Double Confidence* (1951)

BIBLIOGRAPHY: Bonnerot, J., *T.* (1927); Halévy, D., *Eloge de J. T.* (1954); Schmidt, J., "Les frères T. et la colonisation en Afrique du Nord," *Revue des Sciences Humaines*, No. 120 (1965), pp. 537–51

BRUNO BERGER

THEOTÓKAS, George

Greek novelist, dramatist, and essayist, b. 27 Aug. 1906, Constantinople; d. 30 Oct. 1966, Athens

Born into a distinguished Chiot family in the old Imperial City of Byzantium, T. was strongly influenced by his father's role as legal counsel to the Orthodox Patriarchate and as friend and advisor of Elefthérios Venizélos (1864–1936), the great Greek prime minister. This background gave T. a perspective on recent Greek history that few of his contemporaries in the "Generation of the Thirties" could match.

T. worked in every genre: the epic novel, the novella, the short story, the drama, the polemical and familiar essay, travel impressions, and even poetry. He was Director of the National Theater twice (1945–46 and 1950–52)

and had an important role, as contributor and advisor, with three of the most significant journals of his time, *Néa Grámata, Anglo-Elinikí Epitheórisi,* and *Epohés.*

Like most Greek writers of the 1930's, T. was marked by the Asia Minor Disaster of 1922. After the catastrophic defeat of the Greek army by the Turks, T. called for a complete reassessment and reorientation of Greek social and literary values. *Eléfthero Pnévma* (1929), a collection of essays—written under the pen name Oréstes Diyenís—was considered the manifesto of his generation. In these essays T. attacks the older schools of writing for their lack of originality and power, ridicules provincialism and dogmatism, and—in a nation that has always valued poetry above prose—demands respect for the novel.

An ideological commitment to the epic novel as a mirror of individual and social tensions marks T.'s most ambitious undertakings: *Argó* (1936; Eng., 1951) and *Asthenís ke Odipóri* (1964). Both are two-volume novels of great narrative interest and psychological penetration; the former is about a group of university students in the 1930's, the latter about young men and women living through the events of World War II and the Decembrist Rising. Although marred by a lack of balance and structure, both novels are among the most interesting produced by the writers of his time.

It is in shorter works like *To Demónion* (1938) and *Leonís* (1940), particularly the latter, that T. succeeds in expressing the personal tensions that the large canvases of his more ambitious novels repressed. A developmental novel, *Leonís,* more than any of T.'s other works, is a personal testament, a "portrait of the artist" and thinker. Considered by most critics to be his masterpiece, this novella reconstructs the lives of Constantinople Greeks before World War I and recounts the exchange of populations. The action is seen from the viewpoint of a boy, whose growth from childhood to maturity is presented against the background of these events.

In his theatrical works, T. attempted to blend the Greek folk tradition with the more developed theatrical tradition of Western Europe. Though not always successful, his "folk comedies" are imbued with a genuine charm.

T.'s value as an essayist is inestimable, not only for his clarity of style and depth of perception, but for his wide range of interests. He was preeminently a social and political man, however, and won enormous public esteem when he warned King Constantine of the dangers inherent to the Greek state in the removal from office of Premier Papandreou in July 1965. Always a democrat, T. in regular articles in the influential liberal newspaper *To Víma* probed issues that the Greek establishment preferred to ignore or misinterpret until it was too late. Because of his political involvement, he was asked to resign from "The Twelve," a powerful literary award committee he had helped form. He continued, however, to comment on complex social and political issues, predicting the repressive dictatorship that inevitably followed two years of political crisis. His death almost certainly saved him from imprisonment.

FURTHER WORKS: *Óres aryías* (1931); *Embrós sto kinonikó próvlima* (1932); *Evripídis Pendozális* (1937); *Andára sto Anápli* (1944); *To pehnídi tis trélas ke tis fronimádas* (1944); *To yefíri tis Ártas* (1944); *Dokímio ya tin Amerikí* (1954); *To Tímima tis lefteriás* (1958); *Sinapándima stin Pendéli* (1958); *Alkiviádis* (1959); *Taxídia stin Mési Anatolí ke ston Áyon Óros* (1961); *Pnevmatikí Poría* (1961); *I Ethnikí Krísi* (1966). **Selected English translations:** *Alkiviádis* (in *Théatro,* 1966); *The Game of Folly Versus Wisdom* (in *Introduction to Modern Greek Literature,* ed. M. Gianos; 1969)

BIBLIOGRAPHY: Panayotópoulos, I. M., *Ta prósopa ke ta kímena* (1943); Karandónis, A., *Pezográfi ke pezografímata tis yeneás tou triánda* (1962); Hatzínis, Y., *Protimísis* (1963); Sahínis, A., *Pezográfi tou keroú mas* (1967)

THOMAS DOULIS

THOMA, Ludwig

German novelist, short-story writer, dramatist, and essayist, b. 21 Jan. 1867, Oberammergau; d. 26 Aug. 1921, Rottach on the Tegernsee

After a childhood in the lodge of his father, a forester, T. lived with relatives in Landstuhl, Munich, and Landshut while he completed his studies. Between 1894 and 1897 he practiced law in Dachau. After meeting Albert Langen, the publisher of the satirical magazine *Simplizissimus,* T. devoted himself to writing. Thereafter he lived in Munich and on his country estate.

As a contributor to *Simplizissimus* under the pseudonym Peter Schlemihl, T. began his lifelong war on philistinism and society under Wilhelm II. In 1906 he was imprisoned for six weeks for his attacks on the "Lex Heinze," under which obscenity in art was censored.

T.'s satire was extremely earthy and direct. He used to refer to himself as "a pothouse politician with ink." Anything Prussian was an immediate target for his ridicule, but his aim was truest when his fire was directed against his native Bavaria. In such cases the charm of the dialect heightened his characterization (*Jozef Filsers Briefwexel,* 2 vols., 1909–1912).

Two especially popular books were the memoirs of his youth, *Lausbubengeschichten* (1905) and *Tante Frieda* (1907). The same satirical precision is found in the comedies *Die Medaille* (1901), *Erster Klasse* (1910), *Lottchens Geburtstag* (1911), *Brautschau* (1916), and *Die kleinen Verwandten* (1916), which clearly derive from the traditional folk play. The comedy *Die Lokalbahn* (1902) and the peasant tragedy *Magdalena* (1912) rank with these, but the comedy *Moral* (1908; Eng., 1916) is weakened by the lack of moral counterforces to the hypocrisy T. describes.

T.'s naturalistic talent for creating a true-to-life atmosphere is most apparent in his narrative writing, for which he took as a model the works of Jeremias Gotthelf (1797–1854), Ludwig Anzengruber (1839–89), and Theodor Fontane (1819–98). Their influence is most evident in the novel *Münchnerinnen* (1923). Another important literary mentor was Wilhelm Raabe (1831–1910), to whom T. devoted a critical study in his *Stadelheimer Tagebuch* (1923).

T. also wrote a series of peasant novels dealing with contemporary social and economic problems. *Andreas Vöst* (1905) deals with the plight of the small farmer bound to his land. Marital problems and family disputes over inheritances are the themes in *Der Wittiber* (1911) and *Der Ruepp* (1922).

FURTHER WORKS: *Agricola* (1897); *Witwen* (1900); *Assessor Karlchen* (1901); *Grobheiten* (1901); *Neue Grobheiten* (1903) *Peter Schlemihl* (1906); *Kleinstadtgeschichten* (1908); *Briefwechsel eines bayerischen Landtags-abgeordneten* (1909); *Das Säuglingsheim* (1913); *Christnacht* (1914); *Der Postsekretär im Himmel* (1914); *Nachbarsleute* (1916); *Heilige Nacht* (1916); *Altaich* (1918); *Erinnerungen* (1919); *Die Jagerloisl* (1922); *Gesammelte Werke* (7 vols., 1922–33); *Ausgewählte Briefe*

(1927); *Briefwechsel mit E. Thöny* (1935); *Unbekannte Werke* (1956); *Ein Leben in Briefen, 1875–1921* (1963); *Gesammelte Werke* (1968)

BIBLIOGRAPHY: Dehnow, F., *L. T.* (1925); Ziersch, W., *L. T.* (1928); Hederer, L., *L. T.* (1941); Heinle, F., *L. T. in Selbstzeugnissen und Bilddokumenten* (1963); Thumser, G., *L. T. und seine Welt* (1966); Lemp, R., ed., *L. T. zum 100. Geburtstag* (1967)

HELMUT GOLL

THOMAS, Dylan

Welsh poet and writer, b. 27 Oct. 1914, Carmarthenshire; d. 9 Nov. 1953, New York City

T., the son of a grammar-school teacher of English, was educated at the local grammar school in Swansea but did not go on to a university. For a short time he was a reporter on a local newspaper, and in this period he had his first poems published.

Soon T. made the almost traditional move to London; in his case to a literary group then centering around Charlotte Street in Bloomsbury. Much of the grotesque comedy as well as the emotional meanings of this move is revealed in his unfinished novel *Adventures in the Skin Trade* (1955), just as much amusing and touching detail of his childhood in Wales may be found in the short stories of *Portrait of the Artist as a Young Dog* (1940). After being rejected for service in World War II, T. worked somewhat intermittently for the British Broadcasting Corporation, the Ministry of Information, and in films.

T. began to write at a time when it was popular for a writer to take a political stand. He set in motion a reaction from political commitment. He himself had no interest in founding movements or in poetic theorizing. Yet his *Eighteen Poems* (1934), *Twenty-Five Poems* (1936), and the few poems in the next volume, *The Map of Love* (1939), did help to initiate a movement calling itself "the new apocalypse."

T.'s poems were received with such extreme enthusiasm in some quarters that a strong counterattack on T. began at once. It can be seen that, whatever the literary politics of the period, these early poems indicated the important qualities that T. would develop: an exceptional verbal ability and a striking intensity of feeling toward certain aspects of experience.

There is some waste, some surrealistic unintelligibility, and some undigested imagery. But there is also undeniable rhythmic, harmonic, and metaphorical skill and a passionate energy, as may be seen from poems such as "The force that through the green fuse...," "Especially when the October wind...," and "A grief ago...."

But it was the volume T. came out with after the long experience of war that most clearly confirmed the strength and the nature of his gifts. For this volume, *Deaths and Entrances* (1946), shows a greater ability to control the pressures of his imagination and an increase in what perhaps can best be called "humanity." He is, it reveals, a poet of very few themes and these the elemental ones: birth, the magical innocence of childhood and the continuing memory of its fairy landscapes, sexual experience, aging, endurance, and death (see "Fern Hill," "Poem in October," "A Winter's Tale," and "A Refusal to Mourn the Death, by Fire, of a Child in London"). He is essentially a poet of celebration rather than of abstraction or critique. He is a rhetorical and ritualistic poet who, where he weakens, can be vague and gesturing, but where he succeeds, has both grandeur and clarity. He fiercely rejoices in his own sense experiences and sings with a tough innocence of the wonder of life's great surge.

T.'s poems gain their peculiar richness of evocation chiefly from the interaction, or dialectic, of images. When a poem was about to be written, T. found himself, he said, *possessed* by an image. This image set up an intense conflict in his mind: "Out of the inevitable conflict of images, I try to recreate that momentary peace which is a poem." In keeping with his themes, his images are usually cosmic and elemental. Where this struggle fails, the poems can be intensely obscure or rather loosely incantatory. Where it succeeds —and the struggle is hard and intellectual, not a succumbing to an emotional hypnosis— they hold together magnificently.

Thereafter, apart from a group of six poems published only in America, *In Country Sleep, and Other Poems* (1951), there were no more volumes of poetry until the *Collected Poems 1934–52* (1953), which sold the unusual number (for poetry) of ten thousand copies. It contains only a half-dozen poems written since *Deaths and Entrances*. T. was certainly finding it harder to write, but the poems he actually wrote show no failing of powers. He wasted

DYLAN THOMAS

THÓRBERGUR THÓRÐARSON

much in his life but, as a poet, he was always dedicated and uncompromising. Thus, one of the new poems is a splendidly moving lament on his father's sad and sick old age: the villanelle, "Do not go gentle into that good night."

Sudden death came to T. in New York while on a lecture tour. The event inspired an unusual outburst of feeling on both sides of the Atlantic, not only among writers but among people who would hardly have noticed the death of any other poet. Conversely, some writers and critics restated the strong attack on T.'s work they had been making throughout the twenty years of his writing.

T. had published less than a hundred poems and only a small number of other works. He had lived what many people regard as a poet's typical bohemian life ("this raging ranter man and boy," Stephen Spender [q.v.] called him on his death), and this life style partly accounted for his public repute. T. was a poet of limited thematic and emotional range. The intensity of his response to his natural themes, and his power to embody them in grand and vivid language, allowed him to write a few perfect poems that should ensure him a place among the poets we remember.

FURTHER WORKS: *The Doctor and the Devils* (film scenario; 1953); *Quite Early One Morning* (1954); *Under Milk Wood* (radio play; 1954); *A Prospect of the Sea, and Other Stories and Prose Writings* (ed. D. Jones; 1955); *The Letters of D. T. to Vernon Watkins* (1957)

BIBLIOGRAPHY: Olson, E., *The Poetry of D. T.* (1954); Rolph, J. A., *D. T., A Bibliography* (1956); Treece, H., *D. T., Dog Among the Fairies* (1956); Fraser, G. S., *D. T.* (1957); Thomas, C., *Leftover Life to Kill* (1957); Fitz-Gibbon, C., *The Life of D. T.* (1965); Moynihan, W. T., *The Craft and Art of D. T.* (1966); Murdy, L. B., *Sound and Sense in D. T.'s Poetry* (1966); Maud, R., ed., *Poets in the Making: The Notebooks of D. T.* (1967); Reddington, A. M., *D. T.: A Journey from Darkness to Light* (1968)

RICHARD HOGGART

THOMAS, Henri
French novelist and poet, b. 7 Dec. 1912, Anglemont

T. grew up in a bleak environment where literature was virtually nonexistent ("*la longue misère incolore de mon enfance*"). After studying in the provinces, he received a scholarship to the Lycée Henri IV in Paris. His decision to reject a career of teaching and not attend the École Normale is described in *La Dernière Année* (1960).

T. traveled widely in the years preceding World War II, often on foot. After the liberation, he was literary secretary of the magazine *Terre des Hommes* and, along with several others, founded the *Revue 84*. Gide (q.v.) was instrumental in finding him work as a translator for the B.B.C., and he remained in London ten years. In 1958, T. went to the United States as professor of French Literature at Brandeis University. Since 1960 he has been a reader in German literature for Éditions Gallimard in Paris.

T.'s first novel, *Le Seau à charbon* (1940), is a moving evocation of adolescence, given larger reference by the counterpoint of older characters who face similar problems. Paul Souvrault, the main character and the closest to T. himself, reappears in *La Vie ensemble* (1945), and in *La Nuit de Londres* (1956), a novel in journal form that begins with a meditation on the crowd and proceeds to record the introspective creation of a mythic underworld out of the streets of London.

Several novels are written as journals in which the hero's self-awareness and insights come largely through the examination that follows events. This intimate alliance between emerging consciousness and the process of writing is one of the most compelling aspects of T.'s work, especially in *Le Promontoire* (1961).

T.'s characters are men whose lives are or have become uncertain, and who find themselves involved in an intense search, both personal and philosophical. This invariably leads to a withdrawal from society, a "desertion" or "disappearance," and sometimes to an almost Oriental sense of oneness with all of existence. There is generally also a "witness," whose attempt to understand the hero's revolt and escape becomes in itself an adventure.

As a poet, T. has often been compared to Paul Verlaine (1844–96). His poems have the haunting simplicity of songs, and, unlike much modern poetry, they register an implicit faith in the ability of language to reflect particular relations between poet and world.

Though he has been awarded three literary prizes—Prix Sainte-Beuve, *La Cible* (1955); Prix Médicis, *John Perkins* (1960); Prix Fémina, *Le Promontoire*—general recognition of T.'s

405

stature has come slowly. The publication of *La Relique* (1969), however, would seem to assure his reputation as a profound observer of man's secret revolt.

FURTHER WORKS: *Travaux d'aveugle* (1941); *Le Précepteur* (1942); *Signe de vie* (1944); *Le Monde absent* (1947); *La Porte à faux* (1948); *Nul Désordre* (1950); *Les Déserteurs* (1951); *Histoire de Pierrot et quelques autres* (1960); *La Chasse aux trésors* (1961); *Sous Le Lien du temps* (1963); *Le Parjure* (1964)

BIBLIOGRAPHY: Berger, Y., *"H. T., ou la tentation de l'impersonnel," NRF,* XV (1960), 1118–29; Brenner, J., et al., *"Portrait de H. T.," Cahiers des Saisons,* XXIII (1960), 269–309; Micha, R., *"L'Œuvre de H. T.," Crit,* XX, (1964), 52–65; Borel, J., *"H. T., poète de la rêverie," NRF,* XIV (1966), 488–97; Frohock, W. M., "After the 'New Novel': H. T.," *SoR,* new series, V (1969), 1055–68

ROGER DAVID HORWITZ

THOMPSON, Francis Joseph

English poet, b. 18 Dec. 1859, Preston; d. 13 Nov. 1907, London

T.'s father, a doctor, and his mother were both Roman Catholic converts. At the age of eleven T. was sent to a seminary at Ushaw. He later studied medicine in Manchester, but gave this up after six years. During this period he read Thomas De Quincey's (1785–1859) *Confessions of an English Opium Eater,* which tragically influenced the course of his whole life and work. In November 1885 he went to London. Impoverished, homeless, and addicted to opium, he lived there pitifully as a messenger boy and street vendor. He sent his first poems to Wilfrid Meynell, editor of the literary magazine *Merry England.* Meynell and his wife Alice later befriended him, helped him financially, and encouraged him to contribute to Catholic journals.

George Wyndham called T.'s *Essay on Shelley* (1909), originally written in 1889 for the Roman Catholic *Dublin Review,* the most important achievement of contemporary English literary criticism. It deals with the relationship of the church to art and combines the biography of the unhappy and misjudged Shelley with a treatise on poetics. At the same time it also reveals T.'s own artistic personality.

T.'s own poems are deeply religious and rich in sensual, bold, unusual images. Their baroque heightening of expression and their unexpected association of objects often recall the 17th-c. English metaphysical poets. T. opposed the romantic glorification of pure nature with the Franciscan glorification of nature redeemed by divine grace. K. W. Kraemer said: "The full immensity of Thompson's significance derives from his great theme of man's return to God out of his insecurity."

T.'s best-known religious poem, "The Hound of Heaven," which was included in his first collection, *Poems* (1893), depicts the inescapable power of God's love in a manner reminiscent of old Christian allegories. T.'s lyrically purest work is "The Daisy, a Song of Youth and Age." *Sister Songs* (1895) and *New Poems* (1897), written while T. was living at the Franciscan monastery at Pantasaph in North Wales, contain children's poems which, while revealing deeper insight, are pervaded by the melancholy of a heartsick man. The "Orient Ode" and "Ode to the Setting Sun" use pagan themes.

Critical judgment of T. varies. Arnold Bennett (q.v.) compared him to Shakespeare. Theodor Haecker, who translated his works into German, ranks him with Dante, Shakespeare, and Goethe. Harold Nicolson (1886–1968), on the other hand, calls him "a good second-class lyric poet."

FURTHER WORKS: *Health and Holiness* (1905); *Eyes of Youth* (1909); *Life of St. Ignatius of Loyola* (1909); *Works* (3 vols., 1913); *Collected Works of F. T.* (1913); *Uncollected Verse* (1917); *Poems* (1937); *Literary Criticisms* (1948)

BIBLIOGRAPHY: Meynell, E., *The Life of F. T.* (6 eds., 1916–31); Meynell, V., *F. T. and Wilfrid Meynell* (1952); Reid, J. C., *F. T.* (1959); Walsh, E., *Strange Harp, Strange Symphony: The Life of F. T.* (1967)

ROLAND HILL

THÓRÐARSON, Thórbergur

(Icelandic: Þórbergur Þórðarson), Icelandic poet, essayist, and biographer, b. 12 March 1889, Breiðabólsstaður

T. was born on a farm in a remote district in southeastern Iceland. A precocious youth, he was deeply influenced by the ambience of his youth and by local beliefs in ghosts and other supernatural forces.

T.'s early years were marked by poverty, and his formal schooling was fragmentary. His desire for learning was gratified in his five-year study (1913–18) of Old Icelandic language and literature at the University of Iceland. This study resulted in his collections of folklore and specimens of dialectical speech (*Gráskinna*, 1928–36), which are a notable contribution in that field. After some years of intermittent teaching in schools in Reykjavík, he devoted himself to literary work.

Politically, T. is a radical leftist. He has assiduously studied Oriental philosophy, theosophy, and spiritualism, and practiced yoga. His internationalism is attested by his championship of Esperanto. On all these subjects he has written extensively. His firm belief in the supernatural goes hand in hand with a rational approach in his writings and a deep-rooted credulousness. His radical views, which he has propagated with great polemical skill, have made him a highly controversial figure.

T.'s first important work, one of his greatest, was *Bréf til Láru* (1924), a collection of highly personal essays. In them T. fearlessly attacked prevailing literary and moral conventions with biting irony and rapier-sharp satire. Kristján Karlsson said that the autobiographical passages "shone with a kind of humor and self-mockery that was to become T.'s unique trademark as an artist." *Bréf til Láru* sparked fierce criticism and wide controversy, to which T. replied with characteristic polemical effectiveness. Important as the book was for its contents, it was still more significant because of its style. With it T. became an innovator of modern Icelandic prose style.

In many respects, however, T.'s richest and most notable work is his autobiography *Íslenzkur aðall* (3 vols., 1938–41; In Search of My Beloved, abridged translation of Vol. I, 1967). The autobiography is a detailed account of T.'s early years, describing both external events and his inner life. His fertile imagination, as well as the romanticism and rationalism that are so integral to his writing, are here much in evidence. Vivid characterization, striking irony, self-examination, brilliant style— all these contribute to the strong appeal of this work that stands alone in the field of Icelandic autobiography.

Among T.'s biographical works the most important is *Æfisaga Árna Þórarinssonar* (6 vols., 1945–50), the memoirs of a country pastor.

With wit and warmth, T. recorded here the old man's wide-ranging reminiscences, which include tall tales, supernatural episodes, and a wide variety of prejudices and superstitions affirmed by the pastor.

T.'s latest major work, *Sálmurinn um blómið* (2 vols., 1954–55), consists of his conversations with a child. It often sparkles with his rich humor and is distinguished for its narrative excellence.

A versatile writer, T. is primarily known as a brilliant essayist and humorist and for his impressive autobiographical and biographical writings. T.'s contribution to the development of a modern Icelandic prose style, as well as his best works, assure him of a lasting place in the history of Icelandic literature.

FURTHER WORKS: *Hálfir skósólar* (1914); *Spaks manns spjarir* (1915); *Ljós úr austri* (1920); *Hvítir hrafnar* (1922); *Alþjóðamál og málleysur* (1933); *Pistilinn skrifaði* (1933); *Rauða hættan* (1935); *Refskák auðvaldsins* (1940); *Ofvitinn* (2 vols., 1940 ff); *Edda* (1941); *Indriði miðill* (1942); *Steinarnir tala* (1956); *Um lönd og lýði* (1957); *Rökkuróperan* (1958); *Ritgerðir, 1924–59* (1960); *Marsinn til Kreml* (1962); *Í Unuhúsi* (1962); *Einar ríki* (1967). **Selected English translation:** "The Brindled Monster" (appeared in *Anthology of Scandinavian Literature,* ed. H. Hallmundsson, 1966)

BIBLIOGRAPHY: Einarsson, S., *History of Icelandic Prose Writers* (1938), pp. 212–19; Einarsson, S., *A History of Icelandic Literature* (1957), pp. 302–04; Einarsson, S., "T. T., Humorist: A Note," *SS,* XXXV (1963), i, 59–63; Hallmundsson, H., Introduction to "The Brindled Monster," in *Anthology of Scandinavian Literature* (1966); Karlsson, K., Introduction to *In Search of My Beloved* (1967)

RICHARD BECK

THURBER, James Grover

American short-story writer, dramatist, and illustrator, b. 8 Dec. 1894, Columbus, Ohio; d. 2 Nov. 1961, New York City

Rejected by the army during World War I because he had lost an eye in a childhood accident, T. spent the war as a code clerk in Washington and then in Paris. After completing his education at Ohio State University, he worked for a while as a reporter in Columbus and then returned to France, where he remained with the Paris edition of the *Chicago Tribune* until 1926.

On his return to the United States, T. began his long association with *The New Yorker* magazine, first as managing editor and then as a writer on the "Talk of the Town" column. Though after 1933 he no longer held a staff position on the magazine, he remained a regular contributor, and he and editor Harold W. Ross are credited with having set the publication's tone of sophisticated fun.

Is Sex Necessary? (1929), T.'s first book, was written in collaboration with E. B. White (b. 1899), and immediately established his reputation as a humorist. It was followed by several other collections of stories and "casual" pieces and then in 1933 by *My Life and Hard Times,* an antic and highly unreliable chronicle of the Thurber family.

T.'s reputation continued to grow with each succeeding collection of short pieces in which he often cleverly combined the techniques of the storyteller and essayist. In addition, his cartoons featuring woeful dogs, somewhat menacing women, and befuddled men were recognized as a personal vision conveyed with wit and superior draftsmanship.

T.'s best-known story is probably "The Secret Life of Walter Mitty," in which a timid and anxious man imagines a series of adventures in which he plays a heroic role until he is sharply recalled to reality by his wife's impatient and penetrating voice. The humor of the story is underlined by the pathetic incongruity between his life and his daydreams.

In 1940, T. collaborated with Elliot Nugent on the Broadway success *The Male Animal,* a comedy about a seemingly ineffectual college professor who makes a stand for academic freedom. Beginning in 1943 with *Many Moons,* T. wrote a series of children's fairy tales, including the delightful *The Thirteen Clocks* (1950). By this time, T. was almost totally blind and unable to illustrate his own stories.

Recognized from the very beginning of his career as a humorist of rare talent, T. is now credited by critics with having provided a subtle and penetrating comment on the agonies and accidents of life.

FURTHER WORKS: *The Owl in the Attic, and Other Perplexities* (1931); *The Seal in the Bedroom and Other Predicaments* (1932); *The Middle-Aged Man on the Flying Trapeze* (1935); *Let Your Mind Alone! and Other More or Less Inspirational Pieces* (1937); *The Last*

Flower (1939); *Fables for Our Time and Famous Poems Illustrated* (1940); *My World— And Welcome to It* (1942); *Men, Women and Dogs* (1943); *The Great Quillow* (1944); *The T. Carnival* (1945); *The White Deer* (1945); *The Beast in Me, and Other Animals* (1948); *The T. Album* (1952); *T. Country* (1953); *T.'s Dogs* (1955); *Further Fables for Our Time* (1956); *The Years with Ross* (1957); *The Wonderful O* (1957); *Alarms and Diversions* (1957); *Lanterns and Lances* (1961); *Credos and Curios* (1963)

BIBLIOGRAPHY: Morsberger, R. E., "The Predicaments and Perplexities of J. T.," Dissertation, State University of Iowa, 1956 (University Microfilms, Ann Arbor, Mich.; No. 17, 476); Brady, C. A., "Our Man in the Moon What T. Saw," *Commonweal,* LXXV (8 Dec. 1961), 274–76; Cowley, M., et al., "Salute to T.," *SatR,* XLIV (25 Nov. 1961), 14–17; Petrullo, H. B., "Satire and Freedom: Sinclair Lewis, Nathanael West, and J. T.," *DA,* XXVIII (1967), 1445A

* * * *

TIKHONOV, Nikolai Semenovich

Soviet-Russian poet, essayist, and translator, b. 3 Dec. 1896, Leningrad

T. was born into a middle-class family. In World War I, he fought in the cavalry, and during the Civil War he was a volunteer in the Red Army. In 1922 T. joined the Serapion Brothers—a group of young writers, including Kaverin (q.v.), who felt that Russian literature was too static and wanted to "renew" it. Later he abandoned his essentially apolitical stance and conformed to official literary policy.

In 1935, T. was a delegate to the antifascist congress held in Paris. During World War II, he was a war correspondent and was decorated for his work. After the war, he became a prominent cultural diplomat and traveled widely, especially in Asia.

T.'s early war experiences inspired many of the poems in the two volumes with which he made his successful debut: *Orda* (1922) and *Braga* (1922). His romantically virile ballads were especially popular.

T.'s poetry during the mid-1920's became increasingly experimental and showed the influence of both Pasternak and Khlebnikov (qq.v.). This experimental period ended after *Poiski geroya* (1927), a book of travel impressions and anticapitalist satire.

A prolific prose writer, T.'s first success in this genre was *Riskovannyi chelovek* (1926), a book of short stories that offered sharp dramatic sketches of the Soviet Orient. From that time on the themes introduced in his prose were also dealt with in his poetry. *Ten druga* (1936), impressions of T.'s European travel, marked a definite rejection of avant-garde techniques. In 1941, T. received the Stalin Prize for his poem "Kirov s nami." His later poetry —dealing with travel, war, and love—shows no important changes in verse texture.

FURTHER WORKS: *David* (1919); *Sami* (1920); *Ballada o sinem pakete* (1922); *Ballada o gvozdyakh* (1922); *Ot morya do morya* (1928); *Kochevniki* (1931); *Yurga* (1931); *Klinki i tachanki* (1932); *Voina* (1932); *Klyatva v tumane* (1933); *Vechnyi tranzit* (1934); *Stikhi o Kakhetii* (1935); *Druzya* (1937); *Rastet, shumit vikhr narodnoi slavy* (1941); *Leningradskiye rasskazy* (1942; Tales of Leningrad, 1942); *Ognennyi god* (1942); *Geroicheskaya zashchita Leningrada* (1943; The Defense of Leningrad, 1943); *Leningradttzy* (1944); *Stikhi o Yugoslavii* (1947); *Gruzinskaya vesna* (1949); *Rasskazy o Pakistane* (1950); *Dva potoka* (1951); *Dagestanskiye liriki* (1961); *Dvoinaya raduga* (1964); *Izbrannyye stikhi* (1939); *Izbrannyye proizvedeniya* (2 vols., 1955); *Sobraniye sochinenii* (5 vols., 1958 ff.); *Izbrannaya lirika* (1964); *Izbrannyye proizvedeniya* (2 vols., 1967)

BIBLIOGRAPHY: Struve, G., *Soviet Russian Literature, 1917–1950* (1951); Slonim, M., *Modern Russian Literature* (1953); Grinberg, I., *Tvorchestvo N. T.* (1958); Shoshin, V., *Gordyi mir* (1966)

VLADIMIR MARKOV

TIME IN LITERATURE

Ever since the historical awakening of man's consciousness, time, to which man is inescapably bound, has confronted him with a deeply disquieting problem. The thinkers of classical antiquity saw temporality as change, in contrast to the duration of cosmic substances— as an imperfection in, if not a transgression (*adikia*) on the part of the mortal being. Escape from it lay in belief in an eternal recurrence of the same, that is, by a cyclical assimilation of that which is earthly, and therefore subject to change, to that which is eternal.

For medieval Christian man temporal change as such was even more radically sinful but more readily redeemable through the incessant activity of divine grace. Man, split into two beings, the one of the body, the other of the spirit, bore two elements within himself: first, the physical state of his "fallenness," or the tendency to disintegrate (*habitudo ad nihili*); second, according to beliefs derived from Aristotle, a spiritual condition of the enduring potential of perfectibility, the striving toward God (*habitudo ad primam causam*). This striving was constantly regenerated and given duration by the Creator's continually effective grace. Insofar as this regeneration occurred, time was abolished; where time did exist, however, it had a goal: it led to God.

Toward the end of the Middle Ages pantheistic mysticism located the divine creative power in the potential capability of the human soul: God was no longer thought to work from without, but from within man. Here began the great twofold process of secularization. Renaissance man proudly felt himself to be the creator of his own destiny. The Protestant, on the contrary, considered himself entirely a victim of his innate original sin because of the withdrawal of permanent divine intervention on earth. ("The earth," Calvin said, "totters on the brink of a deep abyss into which it threatens to fall at any moment.")

In this view, man lives from one moment to the next, because only the incessantly repeated act of faith lifts him each time over this abyss and restores his bond with unfathomable divine grace, which never abandons its elect. Only with this radical separation of divine durability and earthly mutability, effected by the Reformation, did pure temporality emerge as neither flowing nor cyclical continuity, but as a disjointed chain of moments; this belief led to an awareness of the naked moment in its transience and futility, drifting above nothingness and the angst of the creature.

In subsequent centuries these two reactions to newly experienced modes of feeling persisted: on the one hand, the triumph of an incessantly repeated recreation of human existence through a momentary act of thought or will (posited in the Cartesian *cogito*) or through a sequence of sensations (Condillac); on the other hand, a growing terror at the nothingness beneath this existence, precariously continued from thought to thought, from feeling to feeling, and a fear of the uncertainty of the divine decision. The whole baroque period abounded in laments over the frailty of human life. Later, to be sure, as the two originally opposed tendencies moved toward convergence in modern science, rationalistic materialism found consolation in the growing subjugation of nature through technology and in the happiness and civilization this is supposed to bring.

Time, considered in this way, no longer leads to blessedness; in fact, it no longer leads anywhere; it is as such identical with "progress," with continuous improvement in the human condition. The more fervently man pursued this aspiration, however, the more he undermined its promise. The natural sciences and technology, the bearers of progress, established the hegemony of the empirical fact; they promoted unlimited analysis and quantification of the given world; they relativized all values. The proliferation of things and facts saturated human consciousness and destroyed all sense of duration. The crises of the 20th c. did the rest.

The result was a perpetual, unremitting splitting up of man's world view as well as of his psyche, and a splitting up of all sense of continuity in human affairs. The moment expanded without hindrance, and superficially it dominated the arena of life. Its dominance, however, was on the surface because beneath the surface one factor persisted—almost the only one that did so: man's ancient existential fear and his need to hold on to something beyond the moment.

Thus, in 20th-c. literature, the problem of time has become more urgent than ever before. This literary concern with the nature of time was reinforced by new scientific distinctions between subjective, psychological, biological time as opposed to objective, that is, astronomical-chronological time. Such distinctions, however, were first recognized by literature, where several ways of classifying time are shown.

Even in the 18th c. such novelists as Henry Fielding (1707–1754) in *Tom Jones* (1749) had succeeded in differentiating the qualities of time according to the intensity of the characters' experience of particular events. Awareness of an inner, mental time, independent of external clock time, rose to full consciousness and indeed became the real theme in *Tristram Shandy* (1760–67) by Laurence Sterne (1713–68).

From the end of the 19th c., the amplification and expansion of the personal momentary aspect of life proceeded vigorously, producing the epic techniques of interior monologue

(q.v.), stream of consciousness, and free association (*see* novel). The opposition of interior and exterior time found expression in depictions of the manifold contrasts, intersections, and fusions between the various times or in presentations of local and periodic time-islands within general time.

With this fragmentation of the time sense and this dominance of the isolated moment, went a growing uneasiness over the disappearance of duration and personal identity. Men attempted to recapture both of these by escaping from time, by entering more deeply into the inner self, by recollection. The personal life that lay seemingly in the past was discovered actually present in the depths of a living memory. Through the hypothesis of a cyclical movement of time—that is, a homologous recurrence of all happenings—the historical past was to be drawn into the here and now, to be fused with the present. Both these forms of simultaneity abolish time and turn it into something spatial.

At the beginning of the 20th c. the time problem was already felt in all its depth, especially by the Viennese poets. Hofmannsthal (q.v.), for example, was obsessed by the terrifying experience of transience and the paradoxical way it both holds together and breaks up the self:

That everything slides and glides past,
That my own self, unimpeded,
Glided toward me out of a little child,
Uncannily mute and foreign to me, like a dog.

The moment is experienced in its futility, but also in all its generative force and in such fullness that it shatters personal identity. The compulsion to seize and drain to the dregs the limitless moment produces its contrary in a yearning for the security and permanence of human loyalty and steadfastness, as in Hofmannsthal's *Gestern, Der weiße Fächer, Florindo und die Unbekannte, Der Abenteurer und die Sängerin, Christinas Heimreise,* and *Unendliche Zeit.* These works already show a groping toward universal coherence beyond time, toward the "linking of everything earthly" (*Die Frau ohne Schatten*).

In the novel *Der Tod Georgs* (1901) by Beer-Hofmann (q.v.) the psychological time of a whole life, with all its stratifications of dream and experience, unrolls under the experimental impact of one external event lasting only a few hours of one night—the arrival and death of a friend. The external occurrence seen from with-

410

in can no longer be distinguished from the associatively ramified inner event or from emotions, thoughts, and memories; the two are one.

A meditatively controlled, transcending first-person narrative of this type may be called an "interior monologue" in the narrower sense; such epic novelists of the 20th c. as Broch, Proust, and Virginia Woolf (qq.v.) were to develop this technique in their individual ways. Even earlier, in 1887, Edouard Dujardin (1861–1949) had used the "stream of consciousness" technique. Here interior and exterior events not only mingle, as the contemplative mind tries to make sense of them, but they also shift simultaneously with the course of direct actuality. "Narrated time" and "narrator's time" coincide; in fact, the event is not "narrated" at all, but lived out aloud in its raw state, as in *Leutnant Gustl* (1901) and *Fräulein Else* (1924) by Schnitzler (q.v.) and the novels of Dorothy Richardson (q.v.).

Many 20th-c. novelists have used this technique at times. In the free association sometimes used by Joyce and Faulkner (qq.v.), which might be termed "stream of unconsciousness," external events serve merely as material for the flow of ideas and feelings; the moment has been completely drawn into inwardness, constituting only interior time; fundamentally this means nullified time, the lowest level of timelessness. In contrast, Dos Passos (q.v.) in the novels *Manhattan Transfer* (1925) and *The 42nd Parallel* (1930) attempted to depict the various facets of simultaneous happenings in the collective entity of a city.

As a result of the multiple divisions of one time, in both its progression and its depth, the various times were put in relation to one another, and the investigation of these relationships yielded an immensely complex temporality. The nature of time emerged as the seminal problem of a completely secularized generation and became the theme of a whole series of great novels.

Proust in the series of novels titled collectively *A la Recherche du temps perdu* (1913–27) was the instigator of these new literary researches. By dredging up into the present long-buried moments in all their sensual perfection and thus retrieving from the depths of his life-time his lost personal identity, he proved time to be in fact an inward dimension, a dimension of psychological space. The "past" lives on within man himself, in the somatic depths of his memory, as alive today as it has ever been,

jumping or expanding the distances between the years. It moves with the movement of our lives and must be preserved, laboriously linked up with us, every minute: "It made me giddy to see so many years beneath me, and yet within me, as though I were several miles tall."

Proust traced paths that his successors widened and from which they branched out. In *Ulysses* (1922) and *Finnegans Wake* (1939) Joyce used the cycle of a modern day or night to make transparent the mythical and historical cycle of human time, suspending the truly temporal by this circular "simultaneity." Virginia Woolf experimented with the relation of individual times to collective time. In her *Mrs. Dalloway* (1925) the interior monologues or streams of consciousness of individuals are measured by and coordinated with the regular striking of Big Ben, which represents not so much abstract clock time as the city time common to all characters.

In Virginia Woolf's *Orlando* (1928), indeed, the basic law of biogenetics serves as a model: an "ontogenetic," biographical time is visualized simultaneously with a "phylogenetic," historical, ancestral time; migration in time is linked with transmigration of the soul; changing generations are even equated with change of sex. Seconds swell into centuries; years vanish in the flash of a moment, and this equivocality itself oscillates uncertainly in man's feeling. ("Some weeks added a century to his age, others no more than three seconds at most.... Life seemed to him of prodigious length. Yet even so, it went like a flash.") Thus time evaporates into nothing or slips away in the all-embracing, eternity-containing moment. In the fragment *The Sense of the Past* (1917) Henry James (q.v.) attempted something similar, but bogged down in abstraction.

In *Der Zauberberg* (1924) Thomas Mann (q.v.) juxtaposed a whole series of external and internal forms of time—times expanded and contracted in accordance with events and experiences, "degrees of past time," and not only interior time as opposed to clock time but individual circumstantial and local variations of time, the time of the flatlands and the island time of the sanatorium, which, however, is really "no time at all" but "extensionless actuality." Here again, the only escape from this mental coexistence and jumbling of the various times exists in the cyclical eternal recurrence, examples of which are presented by the movement of the ocean and the courses of the planets.

411

In Thomas Mann's *Joseph und seine Brüder* (1933–42) salvation no longer lies only in cyclical recurrence but also in the mythical identity of present-day man with his ancestry. Mann transfers to all mankind Proust's experience of the transformation of personal time into a psychic space dimension: the "dirt" of primeval barbarism lives on in man as the "dirt" of his unconscious. Similarly, the process of sublimation operates in the subconscious. History becomes mythical actuality, and the individual is "mythically protected" in his changes.

Doktor Faustus (1947), one of Mann's most important novels, shows even more clearly than Joyce's *Ulysses* the symbolic function of the stratification of time, because here the strata of time shift in relation to each other and overlap. The later time stratum of Zeitblom, the narrator, who lives through the rise and fall of Nazism in Germany, makes it possible to present a symbolic mutually enlightening insight into the protagonist Adrian Leverkühn and Germany's destiny.

This novel also suggests another quality of time—its intensity, as exemplified in Leverkühn's decision to choose a short survival-time of intense creative activity rather than a merely extensive life-time.

More recently Butor (q.v.) in his novel *L'Emploi du temps* (1956) made extremely sophisticated use of this overlapping of time strata to suggest the meaning of his story, and in very recent epic novels the mingling of times is becoming increasingly common as a means of giving the event simultaneity and deeper, pan-dimensional space, as in the novels *Lie Down in Darkness* (1951) by Styron, *Schlußball* (1958) by Gaiser, *Mutmaßungen über Jakob* (1959) by Uwe Johnson, and *Billard um halbzehn* (1961) by Böll (qq.v.).

For Huxley (q.v.) time is evil pure and simple. His escape is the ancient flight into mystically experienced timelessness. In the same way Elizabeth Langgässer (q.v.) takes refuge in faith. Eliot and Jorge Guillén (qq.v.), however, experience eternity in the moment itself. In Eliot an experience recurs that had struck Hofmannsthal—and later Virginia Woolf—as a revelation: the wordless richness of the sensory image, of physical existence in an object, an animal's movement, the scent of a flower, a human scene. Here the moment, unique and unrepeatable as it is, reaches down into such unfathomable depths that it seems to

contain everything that exists, a point where temporality and eternity intersect.

The poet must keep both time and eternity unified in his feeling: "Not the intense moment/ Isolated with no before and after/But a lifetime burning in every moment." Similarly the poetry of the Spaniard Guillén is an exuberant paean to the *"plenitud inmediata,"* the immediate abundance, to the *"ahora eterno"* and the *"absoluto presente,"* the eternal moment, the absolute present.

BIBLIOGRAPHY: Lewis, W., *Time and Western Man* (1927); Mendilow, A. A., *Time and the Novel* (1952); Meyerhoff, H., *Time in Literature* (1955); Kahler, E., "Die Verinnerung des Erzählens," *Die Neue Rundschau,* LXVIII and LXX (1957, 1959); Poulet, G., *Studies in Human Time* (1957); Freedman, R., *The Lyrical Novel* (1963); Meyer, H., *The Poetics of Quotation in the European Novel* (1968)

ERICH KAHLER

TIMMERMANS, Felix

Belgian novelist and short-story writer (writing in Flemish), b. 5 July 1886, Lier; d. there, 24 Jan. 1947

T., the thirteenth child of a peddler, began to paint and write at an early age. His first book of poetry was *Door de dagen* (1907), In 1905 he had written short stories in collaboration with A. Thiry, which were published in 1912 under the title *Begijnhofsproken*. Both of these early books reveal the melancholy that later, in his gloomy *Schemeringen van den Dood* (1910), had become pessimism and fear of life as he began to doubt his religious convictions.

After a serious illness, however, had effected a radical change, T. wrote *Pallieter* (1916; Eng., 1924). It is a work full of Dionysian joy, an exuberant hymn to life and glorious nature. A colorful mosaic of episodes, it is held together by the unusual character Pallieter, a man who lives each day to the full, in the idyllic setting of the little town of Lier and the Arcadian valley of the Nete. The novel was very successful and made T. famous outside the borders of his own country, particularly in Germany.

T. wrote many novels and short stories after this. Although uneven in quality, they are all marked by a very original narrative style, by the successful suggestion of an intimate atmosphere, by imagination and humor, and by unexpected turns of speech and imagery.

Het Kindeken Jezus in Vlaanderen (1917) is a delicate retelling of the gospel story of the nativity in the style of the primitive Flemish painters. The novels *Anne-Marie* (1921) and *De pastoor uit den bloeyenden wijngaerdt* (1924)—like the short stories in *Het Keerseken in den lanteern* (1924) and the novellas *Driekoningentryptiek* (1923) and *Bij de krabbekoker* (1934)—are both set in the little provincial town of Lier, with its picturesque national types and folklorist peculiarities.

In *Pieter Brueghel* (1928; dramatized by T., and K. Jacobs, 1943) and *De harp van Sint Franciscus* (1932), T., more through intuitive identification than exhaustive psychology, told the stories of two men whom he felt deeply akin to: the one a person who enjoyed life sensuously, the other a mystic.

T.'s gift for poetic narrative is seen at its height in the charming short story "De zeer schone uren van Juffrouw Symforosa, begijntjen," in *Ik zag Cecilia komen* (1938), and in *Minneke Poes* (1942). His novel *Boerenpsalm* (1935) is a realistic counterpart of the poetic *Pallieter,* simple in language but deep in its revelations of experience and human understanding. T. also wrote delicate stories for children (*Vertelsels,* 3 vols., 1942–45; *Anne-Mie en Bruintje,* 1944).

Behind T.'s enthusiasm for life lay a profoundly religious nature, as shown in his last work, the volume of poetry *Adagio* (1947). Here with moving sincerity, though his technique is uneven in quality, he develops variations on the "vanity of vanities" theme.

FURTHER WORKS: *Schemeringen van den dood* (1910); *Boudewijn* (1919); *De vier heemskinderen* (1922); *Uit mijn rommelkas* (1922); *Mijnheer pirroen* (with E. Veterman; 1922); *En waar de ster bleef stille staan* (with E. Veterman; 1924); *Naar waar de appelsienen groeien* (1926); *Leontientje* (with E. Veterman; 1926); *Schoon Lier* (1926); *Het hovenierken Gods* (1927); *Pijp en tobak* (1937); *Het filmspel van Sint Franciscus* (with H. Caspeele; 1938); *Het kindeke Jezus in Vlaanderen* (with K. Jacobs; 1938); *De familie Hernat* (1941); *Adriaan Brouwer* (1948). **Selected English translation:** *The Perfect Joy of St. Francis; Molly Bird* (1956)

BIBLIOGRAPHY: Hatzfeld, A., *F. T.* (1935); Gilliams, *In memoriam F. T.* (1947); Westerlinck, A., *De innerlijke T.* (1957); Ceulaer, J., *F. T.* (1959); Brachin, P., ed., *Anthologie de la prose néerlandaise: Belgique I 1893–1940* (1966)

JORIS TAELS

TOLKIEN, John Ronald Reuel

English scholar and novelist, b. 1 Jan. 1892, Bloemfontein, South Africa

Educated at Exeter College, Oxford, T. served in World War I. He taught at the University of Leeds and Oxford until his retirement in 1959.

Of his many scholarly publications and editions the best-known are *A Middle English Vocabulary* (1922), *Sir Gawain and the Green Knight* (edited in collaboration with E. V. Gordon, 1925), *Chaucer as a Philologist* (1924), and *Beowulf; the Monsters and the Critics* (1937).

To most readers, T. is widely known as the creator of an extensive and elaborate romance epic concerning a struggle for power during the third age of "Middle Earth." The central participants in this final conflict are certain hobbits, "an unobtrusive, but very ancient people," small, somewhat human in form, comfort-loving, modest and peaceable, but in time of need capable of heroic feats.

The story has its inception in *The Hobbit* (1937), in which Bilbo Baggins gains possession of a ring that bestows unimaginable power. This master ring is coveted by the malign forces of Sauron, the dark lord of Mordor, for possession of it will give him control of Middle Earth. It becomes the duty of Bilbo's heir, Frodo, to retain the ring, against the efforts of organized evil, until he can destroy it by throwing it into the cracks of doom in the fire mountain Orodruin.

The trilogy entitled *The Lord of the Rings* (which includes *The Fellowship of the Ring,* 1954; *The Two Towers,* 1954; and *The Return of the King,* 1955) details the completion of the quest and the rescue of Middle Earth from Sauron's threatened tyranny. In their effort the hobbits are assisted by wizards, magicians, elves, dwarves, rangers, ents—very rarely by humans. They are opposed by trolls, orcs, ringwraiths, black riders, and other embodiments of ultimate force and fraud. The tenets of the literary theory on which T. based his trilogy are described in a long discourse "On Fairy Stories," written in 1938 and published in a volume entitled *Essays Presented to Charles Williams* (1947).

T.'s extraliterary purposes, however, are less clearly indicated. He himself denies that the work is an allegory or that he intended "any inner meaning or 'message.' " He concedes that readers may apply the story to their own knowledge, thought, and experience. Accordingly, many readers see in T.'s fiction a projection of a cosmic conflict of good and evil within the framework of a created mythology that has affiliations with traditional mythologies. This interpretation seems all the more plausible because of T.'s personal friendship with Charles Williams and C. S. Lewis (qq.v.), both avowed propagators of the faith *via* fiction, and because of the consistency, if no more, of T.'s formulations, with their Christian orthodoxy in dogma, ethics, psychology, and view of history. All three are writers of what may be called "theological romance."

FURTHER WORKS: *Fairy Stories: A Critical Study* (1946); *Farmer Giles of Ham* (1949); *The Adventures of Tom Bombadil* (1962); *Tree and Leaf* (1964)

BIBLIOGRAPHY: Sale, R., "England's Parnassus: C. S. Lewis, Charles Williams, and J. R. R. T.," *HudR*, XVII (1964), 203–25; Barber, D. E. "The Structure of *The Lord of the Rings*," *DA*, XXVII (1966), 470A; Matthewson, J., "The Hobbit Habit," *Esquire*, LXVI (1966), iii, 130–31, 221–22; "The T. Papers," *Mankato State College Studies*, II (1967); Auden, W. H., "Good and Evil in *The Lord of the Rings*," *CritQ*, X (1968), 138–42; Isaacs, N. D., and Zimbardo, R., *T. and the Critics* (1968)

W. R. IRWIN

TOLLER, Ernst

German dramatist, poet, and narrative writer, b. 1 Dec. 1893, Samotschin (near Bromberg); d. 22 May 1939, New York City

T.'s father, a merchant, died while T. was still a youth. T. attended college briefly, enlisted in the army for World War I, and was injured and discharged. In 1919 he was sentenced to five years' imprisonment for communist agitation. In 1933 he emigrated to the United States. Six years later he committed suicide.

T. was one of the leading representatives of revolutionary, activist expressionistic drama (*see* expressionism), whose basic theme is man's struggle for a more humane social order. Conflicts between ideals and reality became crucial experiences as in the following plays. In *Masse Mensch* (1921; Man and the Masses, 1924), an idealistic bourgeois woman finds that communism betrays true humanity. In *Hoppla, wir leben* (1927; Hoppla! Such Is Life, 1935), a onetime revolutionary, who has risen to high office and prestige, exploits his former comrades.

T. also dramatized the misery and suffering caused by the existing social order and the tragic human destinies that stem from it. He wrote about the British workmen's last-ditch fight against the machine in the early days of the industrial revolution in *Die Maschinenstürmer* (1922; The Machine Wreckers, 1923). He described the fate of a man castrated in World War I in *Der deutsche Hinkemann* (1923; Broken Brow, 1926), and Nazi concentration camps in *Pastor Hall* (1946; Eng., 1939).

T. was more interested in exhortation than in poetry. His early plays are shrill, hard-hitting manifestoes, their language sometimes intellectually taut and honed like that of Georg Kaiser or Carl Sternheim (qq.v.), sometimes luxuriantly rhetorical and poetic. His *Schwalbenbuch* (1924; The Swallow Book, 1936), written in prison, reveals a sensitive lyric poet. The later T. was more interested in inner purification than outward revolution. In these works the pathos of self-overcoming, patient endurance, and self-sacrifice is predominant.

FURTHER WORKS: *Die Wandlung* (1919; Transfiguration, 1935); *Der Tag des Proletariats* (1920); *Requiem den gemordeten Brüdern* (1920); *Gedichte der Gefangenen* (1921); *Der entfesselte Wotan* (1923); *Vormorgen* (1924); *Justiz* (1927); *Bourgeois bleibt Bourgeois* (1929); *Feuer aus den Kesseln* (1930; Draw the Fires, 1935); *Quer durch* (1930; Which World —Which Way?, 1931); *Wunder in Amerika* (1931; Mary Baker Eddy, 1931); *Die blinde Göttin* (1932; Am., Blind Man's Buff, 1938; Eng., The Blind Goddess, 1936); *Eine Jugend in Deutschland* (1933; I Was a German, 1934); *Weltliche Passion* (1934); *Briefe aus dem Gefängnis* (1935; Look Through the Bars, 1937); *Nie wieder Krieg* (1936; No More Peace, 1937); *Ausgewählte Schriften* (1959); *Prosa, Briefe, Dramen, Gedichte* (1961)

BIBLIOGRAPHY: Willibrand, W. A., *E. T.— Product of Two Revolutions* (1941); Willibrand, W. A., *E. T. and His Ideology* (1945);

FELIX TIMMERMANS

ALEKSEI TOLSTOI

Beckley, R., "E. T.," in *German Men of Letters,* ed. A. Natan (Vol. 3, 1964), pp. 85–104; Fishman, S., "E. T. and the Drama of Nonviolence," *Midwest Quarterly,* VII (1965), 29–41; Spalek, J. M., "E. T.: The Need for a New Estimate," *GQ,* XXXIX (1966), 581–98

OTTO MANN

TOLSTOI, Aleksei Nikolayevich

Soviet-Russian novelist, short-story writer, poet, and dramatist, b. 10 Jan. 1883, Saratov province; d. 23 Feb. 1945, Moscow

T. came from an aristocratic family and was distantly related to both Lev Tolstoi (q.v.) and Ivan Turgenev (1818–83). He studied engineering at the Technological Institute in Leningrad and made his literary debut as a "decadent" poet and a short-story writer. In 1911, he published *Za sinimy rekami,* a collection of imitative symbolist poems, which in later years he sought to buy up and destroy.

T.'s attention soon turned to the theater and to the realistic novel, of which his early *Khromoi barin* (1912; The Lame Prince, 1950) is probably the best example. During World War I he was a war correspondent, and when the revolution broke out he fought against the bolsheviks as an officer in the White army. In 1919 he left Russia and settled in France, where he became a contributor to the *émigré* review *Sovremenniya zapiski.*

During this period of exile T. wrote his first historical novels and plays. In 1920 he published *Detstvo Nikity* (Nikita's Childhood, 1945), a novel about his own youth in rural Russia. A member of Smena Vekh, a group of exiles who as Russians sought to establish identification with the new Russia, he returned to the Soviet Union in 1923.

That same year he wrote *Aelita,* a science fiction novel in the manner of Wells (q.v.), which tells of a Soviet expedition to Mars. It was followed by *Giperboloid inzhenera Garina* (1925; The Death Box, 1934), a science fiction thriller about an attempt to establish fascism in Europe, and a variety of similar potboilers and popular historical plays. His novel *Chernoye zoloto* (1931) satirized Russian *émigrés.*

In 1929, T. published the first volume of his historical trilogy *Piotr pervyi* (Peter the Great, 1936); the final and still uncompleted volume was issued in 1945, the year of his death. Written in the best realist tradition, the book enjoyed widespread popularity, and

some critics saw in it flattering parallels between Peter the Great and Stalin. Be this as it may, there is no doubt that in his novel *Khleb* (1937) T. followed the party line by presenting an interpretation of Stalin's decision to defend Tsaritsyn (later renamed Stalingrad).

During his exile in France, T. began work on the second of his great trilogies, *Khozhdeniye po mukam* (1921–41; The Road to Calvary, 1946). Dealing with the attempts of the Russian intelligentsia to cope with the changes brought about by the revolution, the book took T. twenty years to complete. In the final version, earlier portions were revised to bring the work into line with party policy.

In 1942 T. received the Stalin Prize. Among his last important works was the play *Ivan Groznyi* (1943), a modern reinterpretation of events surrounding the rule of Ivan the Terrible.

In the pre-World War II period the works of T. rivaled those of Sholokhov (q.v.) in their popularity with Russian readers, and between them the two men dominated the Soviet literary scene.

FURTHER WORKS: *Dni voiny* (1915); *Novozhdeniye* (1919); *Smert' Dantona* (1919); *Kitaiskiya teni* (1922); *Lyubov kniga zolotaya* (1922); *Gorki tzvet* (1922); *Lunnaya syrost* (1923); *Bunt mashin* (1924); *Golubyye goroda* (1925); *Azef* (1926); *Drevnyi put* (1927); *Izbrannyye povesti i rasskazy* (1932); *Emigranty* (1940); *Pyesy* (1940); *Sobraniye sochinenii* (1958–61). **Selected English translations:** *Daredevils, and Other Stories* (1942); *My Country* (1943); *The Making of Russia* (1945); *Selected Stories* (1949); *A Week in Turenevo, and Other Stories* (1958)

BIBLIOGRAPHY: Vekster, I., *A. N. T.* (1947); Ščerbina, B., *A. N. T.* (Russian, 1951; German, 1959); Rühle, J., *Literatur und Revolution* (1960); Krestinsky, J. A., *A. N. T.* (1960); Junger, H., "Die Ursprünge des Realismus A. N. Ts.," *Zeitschrift für Slawistik,* IX (1964), 540–50; Pertsov, V., "Two Novels about Nineteen-Eighteen: A. T. and Mikhail Bulgakov," *Soviet Literature,* I (1968), 158–62

GEORGE LUCKYJ

TOLSTOI, Lev Nikolayevich

Russian novelist, playwright, and moral philosopher, b. 9 Sept. 1828, Yasnaya Polyana, Tula Province; d. 22 Nov. 1910, Astapovo

T. was born into a family of Russian rural

aristocrats. Orphaned at an early age, he was brought up by other members of the family. His aunt, Tatyana Yergol'skaya, inspired in him the striving for universal happiness and brotherly love that characterizes so many of his writings. From Jean Jacques Rousseau (1712–78) he took the idea that men close to nature are better than men of culture and civilization.

In 1844 T. entered the University of Kazan, but he left in 1847 without graduating. He settled down on his estate and attempted to better the lot of his peasants. In 1851 he went to the Caucasus and joined the army. There he wrote his first novella, *Detstvo* (1862; Childhood, in *Childhood, Boyhood, and Youth*, 1954), which appeared in the review *Sovremennik* in 1852 and was highly praised by prominent Russian writers and critics. In 1854 T. was transferred to the Danube Front and later to Sevastopol. On the basis of his personal experiences and observations during the Crimean campaign, he wrote his *Sevastopol'skiye rasskazy* (1855–56; Sevastopol Sketches, 1887), which was hailed as an outstanding contribution to Russian fiction. After the fall of Sevastopol in 1855, T. went to Leningrad, where he frequented the circle of *Sovremennik* —Ivan Turgenev (1818–83), Dimitri Grigorovich (1822–1900), Nikolai Nekrasov (1821–78), Ivan Panayev (1812–62), Aleksandr Ostrovski (1823–86). In 1857 and again between 1860 and 1861, T. traveled abroad and made the acquaintance of Pierre Joseph Proudhon (1809–1865), Berthold Auerbach (1812–82), and Aleksandr Herzen (1812–70).

He returned to Russia with a pronounced dislike for Western European civilization. On his estate, Yasnaya Polyana, he opened a school for peasant children and compiled for them a model ABC book. In 1862 he married Sofia Behrs, member of an aristocratic Moscow family, and settled on his estate. *Voina i mir* (1869; War and Peace, 1886) was followed, in 1877, by *Anna Karenina* (Eng., 1886). These two masterpieces brought T. universal recognition and fame.

War and Peace, a *roman fleuve* in its essence, recreates the elemental stream of life: birth, growth and maturity, marriage, childbirth, old age, death; war and peace; defeat and victory; anxiety and tranquillity. It is a family chronicle, a historical novel, and a richly philosophical work which presents T.'s views on religion, ethics, and history. One of the greatest novels in world literature, it is an affirmation of life. Man can achieve his happiness in this life, without living in dream or illusion. *Anna Karenina* is the magnificent, elaborate, psychological study of the gradual spiritual disintegration of the beautiful adulteress Anna Karenina, the brilliant wife of a Leningrad official. T.'s own moral philosophy, less optimistic and more puritanical than in *War and Peace,* is diffused throughout the novel. The work is indicative of T.'s personal spiritual crisis, which ultimately brought him to his "conversion."

Increasingly engrossed in the search for meaning in life and dreading the approach of death, he developed his own ethical and religious ideas. Moral self-perception became, from now on, his aspiration. Surrounding himself with Bibles and Gospels, he wrote *Ispoved* (1879; A Confession, 1885); *Kritika dogmaticheskovo bogosloviya* (1880; A Criticism of Dogmatic Theology, 1905), which attacked official Christianity; *Soyedineniye i perevod chetyriokh evangelii* (1881; A Union and Translation of Four Gospels, 1896); and *V chiom moya vera* (1884; What I Believe, 1885), his personal interpretation of Christ's message. The censor permitted none of these works to be published in Russia at the time. They were followed by many other pamphlets, letters, and treatises on religion. In 1901 T. was excommunicated by the Holy Synod for advocating a Christianity purged of priesthood, church organization, and religious ritual. More important than these, T. felt, was brotherly, Christian love.

T. also published several moral tracts, sociological essays, and articles on topics of current interest and on occasion even criticized the Russian government. All these writings share the moral and didactic purpose of the religious and theological essays with which they are contemporaneous. Even after T.'s so-called spiritual conversion some further literary masterpieces came from his pen: *Smert Ivana Il'icha* (1886; The Death of Ivan Ilyich, 1887), the peasant drama *Vlast' tmy* (1886; The Power of Darkness, 1888), "Khozyain i rabotnik" (1895; Master and Man, 1895), "Otetz sergii" (1898; Father Sergius, 1911), "Hadji Murad" (1904; Eng., 1912), and "Falshivyi kupon" (1905; The False Coupon, 1911). His last long novel, *Voskreseniye* (1899; Resurrection, 1900), is much inferior to his other works. In these works, T. contrasted the life of the soul and the life of the body, depicting the latter as evil.

T. expounded his outlook on art in his famous essay "Chto takoye iskusstvo?" (1897;

LEV TOLSTOI

What Is Art?, 1898): art should convey only religious, moral, and valuable social experiences, and do so in clear, simple language accessible to everybody. Art is excellent if it "infects" all people regardless of their social, intellectual, and cultural distinctions. He denounced art for art's sake, and condemned many of the world's greatest artists. Truth and simplicity are characteristic of T.'s plays. Though powerful works, they are, however, not produced today, for they are too explicitly concerned with the sociological problems of T.'s time.

From 1891 to 1892 T. participated in organizing famine relief. He continued to preach brotherly love and the harmonious life and insisted on denouncing private property as evil. Since his wife repudiated his teachings, their relationship deteriorated, especially after 1900. In 1910, estranged from his family, T. left his estate for the South, accompanied by his daughter, Aleksandra, who shared his beliefs. En route he caught pneumonia and died at Astapovo.

All his life T. was concerned with insoluble questions about God, ultimate reality, truth, life, and death. Convinced of the infallibility of reason as a guide in human life, he identified the good with a manner of living that is purely rational; his ethical deductions represent the triumph of rationalism. With all his works, he wanted to instruct the reader about a rational and constructive life.

Always observing and analyzing even his most spontaneous reactions, T. often rejected and condemned them and expected the same rigorous response from the reader. A guilt complex and a longing for perfection remained T.'s moral stimuli and a source for his varied activities throughout life. Essentially an individualist and an anarchist, he believed neither in government nor in any human institutions, and he always reacted against the opinions of the crowd.

T. took up arms against the achievements of culture and civilization, as well as against scientific and technical progress, and ended by rejecting the Russian government and its social and religious institutions. Critical of orthodox Christianity, he attempted to make religion rationalistic. He eliminated from the Gospel all mysticism and took from it only the Sermon on the Mount, which he reduced to five negative statements: be not angry, do not lust, never take oaths, resist not evil by force, be no man's enemy. T.'s system of ethics was thus anarchistic and opposed to any organized society. Later, however, he formulated a new social and economic order, agrarian and primitive in its nature, a type of patriarchal Christian communism.

T. firmly believed that if men followed his five points of Christianity in their individual lives, then the "Kingdom of God on Earth" would immediately be established. Through brotherly love man's individual consciousness would then disappear, leaving only the consciousness of the group.

Pursued by the specter of death, T. was only too eager to find his personal salvation in his "Christian love" and in Rousseauism. Plato, Buddha, Schopenhauer, and science failed to alleviate T.'s tormenting doubts concerning life and death. He found peace in the Russian patriarchal peasantry, in whom he saw an instinctive belief in the significance and fullness of life, an inherent submissiveness and meekness, a deeply felt faith in God, and, above all, a tranquil frame of mind, which he wished to make his own. "God's law, humility, and love" was his ethical and religious credo. T.'s unique emphasis on spiritual and moral reawakening won him numerous disciples and followers.

T. exercised great influence on the *roman fleuve* not only in Russia, but also in the West. Such writers as Hauptmann, Thomas and Heinrich Mann, Zola, Rolland, G. B. Shaw, Galsworthy, Dreiser (qq.v.), and Anna Seghers (b. 1900) owe much of their realistic method to him.

FURTHER WORKS: *Utro pomeshchika* (1856); *Semeinoye shchastye* (1859); *Kazaki* (1863; The Cossacks, 1962); *Polikushka* (1863); *Plody prosveshcheniya* (1889; Fruits of Enlightenment, 1911); *Kreitzerova Sonata* (1890; The Kreutzer Sonata, 1924); *Tzarstvo Boshiye vnutri vas* (1893); *Khristiyanstvo i patriotizm* (1894); *Khristiyanskoye ucheniye* (1898); *Zhivoi trup* (1900; The Living Corpse, 1919); *Posle bala* (1903); *O Shekspire i o drame* (1906); *Detstvo; Otrochestvo; Yunost* (1914; Childhood, Boyhood, Youth, 1954); *Polnoye sobraniye sochinenii* (90 vols., 1928 ff.); *Sobraniye khudozhestvennykh proizvedenii* (12 vols., 1948); *Sobraniye sochinenii* (14 vols., 1951 ff.); **Selected English translations:** *The Novels, and Other Works* (22 vols., 1902); *Complete Works* (ed. Leo Wiener; 24 vols., 1904); *The Dramatic Works* (1923); *Plays by L. T.* (1933); *The Short Stories of T.* (ed. Philip Rahv; 1960)

BIBLIOGRAPHY: Lemonnier, C., *Hommage*

à T. (1901); Maude, A., *The Life of T.* (2 vols., 1910); Rolland, R., *T.* (1911); Shestov, L., *T. und Nietzsche* (1923); Fausset, H., *T., the Inner Drama* (1927); Markovitch, M. I., *T. et Gandhi* (1928); Zweig, S., *Adepts in Self-Portraiture* (1928); Tolstoi, A. L., *The Tragedy of T.* (1938); Mann, T., *Adel des Geistes* (1945); Gourfinkel, N., *T. sans tolstoisme* (1946); Farrell, J. T., *Literature and Morality* (1947); Suxotina, T. I., *The T. Home* (1950); Berlin, I., *The Hedgehog and the Fox* (1953); Steiner, G., *T. or Dostoevsky* (1959); Bayley, J., *T. and the Novel* (1966); Simmons, E. J., *Introduction to T.'s Writings* (1968)

TEMIRA PACHMUSS

If in our time people are afraid of death, have such a convulsive fear of it, as no one had ever experienced before, if all of us in the depth of our hearts, in our flesh and blood feel this "cold tremor," a chill piercing to the marrow of our bones, it is T. whom we must chiefly thank for this fear. T. had no doubt, no hesitation, and no uncertainty about death, that it is a "transition into nothingness," a transition devoid of every mystery. His terror was inconsolable, fruitless, senselessly destructive, and calculated to dry up the very springs of life.

Dmitrii Merezhkovskii, *L. T. i Dostoyevski* (1912), pp. 37–38

I often think of him as a man who in the depth of his soul is stubbornly indifferent to people: he is so much above and beyond them that they seem to him like insects, and their activities ridiculous and miserable. . . . This deepest and most evil nihilism, which sprang from the soil of an infinite and unrelieved despair, arose from a loneliness which, probably, no one but he has experienced with such terrifying clearness.

Maksim Gorki, *Vospominaniya o L've Nikolayeviche Tolstom* (1922), pp. 46–47

T.'s works, opinions and precepts, and his school, do in fact contain flagrant contradictions. On the one hand, an artist of genius, who produced not only incomparable pictures of Russian life but also first-class works of world literature; on the other hand, a property owner who plays the fool in Christ. On the one hand, a wonderfully strong, direct and honest protester against the hypocrisy and deceit of society; on the other, a "Tolstoyan," that is to say, a shabby, hysterical whiner, who calls himself a Russian intellectual, beats his breast in public and says: "I am bad, I am disgusting, but I make moral self-perfection my business: I don't eat meat any more and I now live on rice cutlets." On the one hand, he provides ruthless

criticism of capitalistic exploitation, exposure of government atrocities, of the farce of the judicial system, and of public administration, a revelation of the full depth of the anomaly between increased wealth and civilizing achievements and the growth of poverty and the brutalization and suffering of the laboring masses; on the other hand, a demented, rhapsodical advocacy of "renunciation," of violent "resistance to evil." On the one hand, the most somber realism, the stripping off of each and every mask; on the other, the preaching of one of the most contemptible things in the world: religion, the attempt to replace government-servant priests by priests with moral convictions, *i.e.,* the fostering of the subtlest and therefore most particularly odious kind of pietism.

Vladimir Ilich Lenin

He did not become a Christian; he simply misused the word Christianity. The gospel was for him merely one of the doctrines that upheld his own doctrine.

Nikolai Berdyaeff, *"L. T.," Neue Schweizer Rundschau,* XXI (1928), 674

I recall that . . . I first encountered Robert Louis Stevenson and Mrs. Humphry Ward. . . . But best of all up to then, T. in his novelistic phase: *The Kreutzer Sonata* and *The Death of Ivan Ilyich.* I recall it was Sutcliffe who suggested these . . . as stories which painted life truthfully and yet were creating a stir. I was so astounded and thrilled by the pictures of life they presented that it suddenly occurred to me—almost as a new thought—that it would be a wonderful thing to be a novelist. If a man could but write like T. and have all the world listen to him!

Theodore Dreiser, *Dawn* (1931), p. 555

What a monster! Always up on his hind legs, in revolt against his nature, always forcing one to doubt his sincerity, being everything and all men by turns, and never more personal than when he stops being himself; proud even in renunciation; endlessly proud to the point where he cannot bring himself to die simply, like everybody else. But what agony in that final struggle! The struggle of a Titan against God, against destiny.

André Gide, *Pages de journal* (1945), p. 145 f.

Like Goya and Rilke, T. was haunted by the mystery of death. This hauntedness deepened with the years . . . his whole being rebelled against the paradox of mortality. His terrors were not primarily those of the flesh. . . . He suffered from a despair of reason at the thought that men's lives were doomed through illness or violence or the ravenings of time to irremediable extinction.

George Steiner, *T. or Dostoevsky* (1959), p. 251

TOMASI DI LAMPEDUSA, Giuseppe
See Lampedusa, Giuseppe di

TORRES BODET, Jaime
Mexican poet, essayist, and novelist, b. 17 April 1902, Mexico City

T. B. studied law and later philosophy at the National University. His long career of uninterrupted service as an educator and diplomat began in 1921, when he was appointed private secretary to José Vasconcelos, then Chancellor of the National University. From 1922 to 1924, T. B. was in charge of the Department of Libraries of the Ministry of Education. For the next four years he was professor of French literature at the National University. From 1929 to 1964, T. B. served his country in the diplomatic service in Europe and Latin America, as Under Secretary for Foreign Affairs, as Minister of Education, as Minister of Foreign Affairs. In 1948 he succeeded Julian Huxley (b. 1887) as Director General of UNESCO, a post he held until 1952. In 1966 he was awarded Mexico's National Prize for Literature.

The poetry of T. B. may be divided into three distinct cycles: the poems of his youth are contained in the books published between 1918 (*Fervor*) and 1925 (*Biombo*). The poetry of his early works is characterized by great lyrical simplicity, which in later poems of this period becomes more complex and leads to a more symbolic way of interpreting reality.

The volumes *Destierro* (1930) and *Cripta* (1937) belong to the second cycle, that of T. B.'s maturity. *Destierro* marks a break with the kind of poetry T. B. had written up to that time. We no longer find the graceful compositions of his early works, but are confronted with the nebulous world of dreams in which the harsh noises of the 20th c. are mingled. It is a volume of experimentation in which T. B. searches for his identity and that of his times in the dreamlike labyrinth of surrealism (q.v.). T. B.'s preoccupation in his next volume, *Cripta,* is with the solitude of every human being and with time. It contains perhaps the most beautiful verse he has written.

To the third phase of his work, which reveals still greater mastery of substance and form, belong the poems written since the late 1940's. In *Sonetos* (1949), a collection of philosophical verse, T. B. analyzes and ponders on reality. In the volumes that follow *Sonetos*— *Fronteras* (1954) and *Sin tregua* (1957)—T. B.

sees in his own fate a symbol of mankind's suffering. T. B. considers the role of the poet of utmost importance.

T. B.'s work has evolved in accordance with the changes of contemporary poetry without succumbing to the exaggerated styles of any group. For T. B., poetry is a way of life, in its totality.

In addition to being one of Mexico's greatest poets, T. B. is considered to be one of the outstanding masters of Spanish prose. Perhaps the most successful of his six novels from the point of view of technique is his last, *Sombras* (1937). This is the picture of a solitary old woman who has seen her family disintegrate and meet financial ruin. With regard to its style the novel may be compared with the works of Proust and Giraudoux (qq.v.).

T. B.'s memoirs, *Tiempo de arena* (1955), are indispensable reading for anyone interested in the intellectual life of Mexico during the 1920's and 1930's. There is no better explanation of the literary influences at work on the young poets of T. B.'s time, later to be known as the "contemporáneos" group. The second volume, *Años contra el tiempo* (1969), describes T. B.'s experiences during the years 1943 to 1946 when he served as Minister of Education.

Tres inventores de realidad (1955) groups together the lectures T. B. delivered at El Colegio Nacional in 1954 on Stendhal (1783–1842), Fiodor Dostoyevski (1821–81), and Pérez Galdós (q.v.). The three essays on the 19th-c. novel were followed by a study of the world of Balzac (1959), a book on *León Tolstoi: Su vida y su obra* (1965), which reveals Tolstoi's (q.v.) complex personality, and *Tiempo y memoria en la obra de Proust* (1967), which is an unusually perceptive analysis of Proust's art.

T. B. is one of the great minds of our time, a writer who speaks not only for Latin America, but for men everywhere.

FURTHER WORKS: *Canciones* (1922); *El corazón delirante* (1922); *La casa* (1923); *Los días* (1923); *Nuevas canciones* (1923); *Poemas* (1924); *Margarita de niebla* (1927); *Contemporáneos: Notas de crítica* (1928); *Perspectiva de la literatura mexicana actual, 1915–1928* (1928); *La educación sentimental* (1929); *Proserpina rescatada* (1931); *Estrella de día* (1933); *Primero de enero* (1935); *Nacimiento de Venus y otros relatos* (1941); *Educación mexicana: Discursos, Entrevistas, Mensajes* (1944); *Educación y concordia internacional* (1948);

Selección de poemas (ed. X. Villaurrutia; 1950); *Poesías escogidas* (1954); *Trébol de cuatro hojas* (1958); *Doce mensajes educativos* (1960); *Doce mensajes cívicos* (1961); *Obras escogidas* (1961); *Maestros venecianos* (1961); *La voz de México en Bogotá y Los Angeles* (1963); *Poesía de J. T. B.* (1965); *Discursos, 1941–1964* (1965); *Versos y prosas* (ed. S. Karsen; 1966); *Rubén Darío—Abismo y cima* (1966). **Selected English translation:** *Selected Poems of J. T. B.* (1964)

BIBLIOGRAPHY: Abreu Gómez, E., *Clásicos, románticos y modernos* (1934), pp. 181–87; Toussaint, M., "La obra literaria y educativa de J. T. B.," *Memoria de El Colegio Nacional,* II (1953), viii, 119–32; Leal, L., "T. B. y los 'Contemporáneos,' " *Hispania,* XL (1957), 290–96; Karsen, S., *A Poet in a Changing World* (1963); Forster, M. H., *Los "Contemporáneos" 1920–1932* (1964), pp. 24–55; Cowart, B. F., *La obra educativa de T. B. en lo nacional y lo internacional* (1966); Carballo, E., *J. T. B.* (1968)

SONJA KARSEN

TOZZI, Federigo

Italian novelist and short-story writer, b. 1 Jan. 1883, Siena; d. 21 March 1920, Rome

T.'s adolescence was marked by the loss of his mother, his unsatisfactory performance as a student in various vocational and art schools, and his insecure and unhappy relationship with his father—a farmer and the owner of a successful inn. These experiences had a profound impact upon the sensibility of young T., and were to become the major, and recurrent, themes of his strongly autobiographical fiction.

At twenty-four, prodded by his father, T. won a competitive examination for a post with the national railroads and was assigned to a minor clerical position at Pontedera. His experience there may be found in fictionalized form in the brilliant novella *Ricordi di un impiegato* (written in 1910, but published posthumously in 1927), perhaps the one work by T. that most successfully conjures up a Kafkaesque atmosphere of torment, anguish, and absurdity.

The sudden death of his father, in 1908, forced T. to resign from his post and return to his native Siena to administer a small inherited estate. Discouraged by his financial ineptness, T. eventually sold his land and moved his family to Rome, where he hoped to find newspaper work. During World War I, he was a press officer for the Italian Red Cross. After the war, he returned to his career as a journalist and writer, often living under difficult conditions. He died of pneumonia at the age of thirty-seven.

T.'s first publications were poetry collections —*La zampogna verde* (1911) and *La città della vergine* (1913)—that show the obvious influence of d'Annunzio (q.v.). During this same period, he also wrote his first short stories and an unusual collection, *Bestie* (1917), which, after being turned down by several publishers, was finally brought out in 1917, thanks to the intervention of the influential critic Borgese (q.v.).

T.'s fiction, appreciated only by a handful of critics when it began to appear, was not to achieve its just popularity and recognition until after World War II. Much of it shows the profound influence of Verga (q.v.), the master of *verismo,* and of certain Russian writers, notably Fiodor Dostoyevski (1821–81) and Chekhov (q.v.). It was inspired by the primitive, hard life on the farms, a life T. had experienced first hand. But every piece of fiction T. wrote unmistakably recreates the anxieties, the traumatic experiences of his adolescence and childhood, the estrangement he felt when he found himself without maternal love and without understanding and guidance from his father. Hence the hatred, the anger, and the repressed sense of rebelliousness in his fiction.

The foundations of T.'s creative world are egotism, sensuality, and discord, on which he superimposed a longing for serenity, love, and solidarity. Perhaps the most autobiographical of his novels is *Con gli occhi chiusi* (1918). It focuses on a young man's failures as a student and as a son, and the collapse of his youthful dreams of love when he discovers that the girl he wishes to marry, Ghísola, has been seduced and is expecting a child.

Il podere (1921), on the other hand, tells the story of another young man, Remigio Selmi, who finds himself administering a farm inherited from his father. Remigio is unable to cope with the suspicions of his stepmother and the legal maneuvers of his father's mistress, who claims a large share of the property. Eventually, one of his discontented farmhands murders Remigio in what strikes the reader as another example of the workings of an inimical fate.

Tre croci (1920), the last of T.'s completed

novels, is also his least autobiographical. It tells of the slow financial, moral, and physical decay of three brothers, owners of a small bookshop, who are driven to bankruptcy by their gluttony and fraudulence. The novel is written in T.'s characteristically somber, "ungraceful" style that aptly captures the milieu and the characters' moods.

FURTHER WORKS: *Mascherate e strambotti della Congrega dei Rozzi di Siena* (1915); *Santa Caterina da Siena: le cose più belle* (1918); *L'amore* (1920); *Giovani* (1920); *Gli egoisti* (1923); *Novale* (1925); *Realtà di ieri e di oggi* (1928); *L'immagine e altri racconti* (1928); *Nuovi racconti* (1960)

BIBLIOGRAPHY: Tecchi, B, *Maestri e amici* (1934); Cesarini, P., *Vita di T.* (1935); Michaelis, E., *Saggio su F. T.* (1936); Ulivi, F., *F. T.* (1946); Pacifici, S., *A Guide to Contemporary Italian Literature* (1962); Cimmino, N. F., *Il mondo e l'arte di F. T.* (1966)

SERGIO PACIFICI

TRAGEDY

The writings on modern tragedy are as diverse in their conclusions as they are numerous in origin. As yet, modern criticism has been unsuccessful in determining the true nature of modern tragedy, for the simple reason that in no country have playwrights shown a singleness of approach to the problem. The breadth of vision based on commonly accepted philosophical principles that characterized the Greek and Elizabethan theater has given way in modern drama to a diversity of concepts that depends upon the individual writer, the country, and the environment. Thus, there is a complete lack of philosophical unity among the writers, a lack of common ground or "kind of preliminary pact of understanding" between the author and his society.

One by one, Aristotle's guidelines for the plot, character, diction, spectacle, chorus, and music of tragedy have come under increasing attack. Indeed, each word in his definition of tragedy has been so reduced that such terms as "mimesis," "hamartia," and "catharsis" no longer have any significant force among playwrights and critics.

There is no agreement on what tragedy is and represents, on the form it employs, the manner in which it is communicated, or the function it fulfills. It is perhaps for this reason

that F. L. Lucas, in his *Tragedy* has remolded Aristotle's definition of tragedy as follows: "Serious drama is a serious representation by speech and action of some phase of human life. If there is an unhappy ending, we may call it tragedy." All that remains of Aristotle's definition is this bare tautology.

Although there is no longer agreement among writers as to the exact nature of tragedy, or the tragic spirit, Aristotle continues to fascinate those interested in the theory of tragedy. Indeed, the 20th c. has witnessed a continuous stream of new translations of his *Poetics* and of commentaries in which critics have either tried to demonstrate how Aristotle's ideas on tragedy can be applied in the modern day, or to condemn the work as too unrealistic to be appropriate in a world in which there is a growing insistence upon the worth of each individual as a human being. Practically the only fact agreed upon, aside from the belief that the drama must revolve around some serious question, is that there must be a certain nobility in the protagonist himself. Even here, however, there is no common agreement as to the actual nature of this nobility. All that one can say is that of the three divergent views which see it as due to the hero's (1) ancestry in ritual, (2) suffering, or (3) inner quality of soul, the third view is the one that seems to have currently attained the ascendancy. In other words, modern writers have departed from the notion of the "illustrious" man implied in Aristotle. Modern theorists and playwrights, who live in a more or less democratic world where kings and queens are a thing of the past, have placed the idea of nobility in man—any man—as man.

Today the tragic hero must have a faith in himself as a human being, but a faith which pushes him past the bonds or code of his society, so that he ends by setting himself up as the arbiter of what is just and right. He finds answers only within himself, never questioning whether there is an authority higher than himself to which he may owe allegiance and obedience. The tragic hero, in the final analysis, whether he be "noble," in the sense of possessing royal blood, or a man of the people, must believe that his dream is the only correct one for him. His acts stem from this belief. Whether he becomes ennobled in the process, or whether he passes from a comparatively good man to a complete villain, is not the question. He may do either or both. What is of the essence for modern writers is that man believe in his own mode of conduct, that he hold on to his dream until, in the final denouement, he is stripped of this dream, and what he has accomplished is brought home to him in all its force.

Further, just as there is no agreement relative to the hero's "nobility," so the Aristotelian concept that there should be some lack in the hero himself, some type of flaw or "hamartia," does not find common acceptance today. In the works of numerous playwrights the hero may too frequently appear simply as the victim of circumstances. This does not mean that he never does wrong, but that circumstances, environment, forces outside of himself, often drive him into a situation from which he cannot emerge victorious. A. C. Bradley expressed the belief that the tragic flaw, if one wishes to use the term, may be the hero's very faith in himself, his own "nobility." The hero has characteristics which set him apart from his fellow men, and he follows his dream to its end. He sets up his own ego against any and all outside forces, and goes down to defeat because the forces pitted against him are too strong for him to withstand with any hope of success.

One of the interesting phenomena of 20th-c. tragedy, and the treatment of the protagonist, has been the fact that so many playwrights have ignored the existence of Christian beliefs. These writers have forced their heroes to rely entirely upon themselves, to seek the answers to all problems in a tormented world within their own tormented souls. Their world has become a bleak and hopeless one, a pit from which man cannot escape except into death, which inevitably ends all and answers nothing. Perhaps this is one reason why great tragedy has not been written in the 20th c., and why the tragic dramas of our time have so often tended to end in despair. Although the playwrights have by and large been sincere men looking for the absolute, they have not been able to find it because truth, as they saw it, was not immutable; moral relativism pervaded the life of man; there was no such thing as eternal verities; the absolute was a myth invented to delude man. They have more and more tended to see the individual only in terms of his immediate environment, stressing not the obligations of the individual to the society into which he was born, but the obligations of that society to the individual.

Historically, 20th-c. tragedy has based much of its approach upon Ibsen (q.v.), whose best-known plays are set in a contemporary scene; life's little tragedies became the keynote to tragedy in general. Bourgeois tragedy, given impetus in the 18th c. by George Lillo in his *London Merchant,* was brought to full flower by Ibsen, and the "little" man has gradually usurped the place that the "illustrious" man presided over for so many centuries. In addition, 20th-c. tragedy has in a sense been the product of a scientific determinism that has tended to lead the playwright into a world of pessimism where heredity, environment, Freudian motivations, as well as a mechanical and monolithic society, allowed man little if any true freedom of choice.

One of the early 20th-c. dramatists who sought the answer to man and his place in the universe was O'Neill (q.v.), whose dramas were revolutionary in both technique and form. His plays ranged from the Greek-inspired *Mourning Becomes Electra,* to the expressionistic "social problem tragedies" such as *Emperor Jones* and *The Hairy Ape,* and psychological studies such as *The Great God Brown*—in which aspects of personality were suggested by the use of masks—*Strange Interlude,* and *Desire under the Elms.* Although each play may have been different in its approach to the various problems that beset man, the one element they had in common was the concept of man's lack of stability in a world wherein he not only found himself in conflict with the individual, but with the universe itself. To point up this concept of man attempting—in vain, for the most part—to locate himself, and to retain his dignity as a human being, O'Neill drew his protagonists from all walks of life, making a farmer the hero of one, an escaped Negro convict or a ship's stoker the protagonists in others. Generally, O'Neill's heroes grappled with something bigger than themselves, the conflict often being so unequal that the struggle was hopeless from the outset. In his unceasing but fruitless quest to determine man's place in the universe, O'Neill moved from realism to expressionism, from Greek tragedy with modern psychological implications to studies of miscegenation and philosophical symbolism. With such tragedies as *The Emperor Jones, The Hairy Ape, All God's Chillun Got Wings, Desire under the Elms, The Great God Brown, Strange Interlude, Mourning Becomes Electra, The Iceman Cometh,* and *Long Day's Journey into Night,* he strove to realize "the transfiguring nobility of tragedy" as it was conceived by

422

the Greeks, but to do so in modern terms, and in "seemingly the most ignoble and debased lives." What resulted from his valiant attempts, however, was the dogma of pessimism; in his plays, man never does find his true place in the universe.

There can be no doubt that two world wars and the economic depression of the 1930's aided the advance of the dogma of pessimism in a world gripped by suffering. Since the end of World War II tragedies have ranged from the atheistic existentialist dramas of Sartre and Camus (qq.v.), to the bitter farces of Marcel Aymé and Jean Anouilh (qq.v.). Existentialism came to stand for modern disillusionment and the blank despair of playwrights. Just as Ibsen has been credited with bequeathing the "little" man to the modern stage, so the Danish philosopher Kierkegaard—unknown outside his native country until he was translated into German early in this century—has been credited with providing modern-day existentialism with some of its major concepts, primarily the insistence upon the fact of individual existence and despair attendant upon it. Although his philosophy was a somewhat tormented attempt to see man's relation to God, those who used his work, notably philosophers Karl Jaspers (b. 1883) and Martin Heidegger (b. 1889) in Germany, and through them, Sartre in France, evolved a theory of existence that put man at the center without reference to Christ or any traditional religious belief. For Kierkegaard, the self was the ultimate reality, "and this is a wholly subjective truth, immediately and passionately known, but undemonstrable by reason, and self-contradictory from beginning to end. Yet, the whole duty of self is to seek and serve God."

For Sartre the first duty of self is to deny God. As a result, Sartre's world exists without benefit of an omnipotent being, and human nature as an essence is nonexistent. In his work, *L'Existentialisme est un humanisme,* which borrows partly from Heidegger, Sartre stresses the point that since God does not exist, man is nothing other than he makes himself; he is nothing except his life. Further, if God does not exist, everything is permitted. Man is bound neither by laws or orders. In short, man is the sole legislator for himself. This philosophy of nihilism is found in his plays *The Flies, The Devil the Good Lord, Men without Shadows, No Exit, Dirty Hands,* and *The Respectful Prostitute.*

Condemned to be free, man can never attain

absolute freedom, for life is truly "full of sound and fury, signifying nothing." For Sartre the basic irrational fact is the utter meaninglessness of the universe in which man exists. Yet, man must not only attempt to realize himself in this absurd void, he must assume full responsibility for his actions. Thus, he cannot blame a God, since none exists, and he cannot blame his environment, even though it may limit his choices. He alone must assume full responsibility for all of his actions because he is condemned to be free.

Two other prominent playwrights whose works are representative of tragedy in the second half of the 20th c. are the so-called folk tragedians of modern America: Tennessee Williams, and Arthur Miller (qq.v.). Both Williams (who uses symbolism and a nonnaturalistic style) and Miller (who writes in the prose tradition of Ibsen and is a would-be moralist who leans to realistic stage conventions) regard modern society as a materialistic monster that so overwhelms man that all one can do is weep and pity the individual. Williams omits the spiritual nature of man, with the result that only the animal instincts remain active, forcing man to grasp greedily at life before futility draws the curtain. Miller is confused in his so-called moral intentions, because he also omits the spiritual nature of man—that is, man's relation to something outside of himself—and concentrates on man in a godless society.

Basically Williams's plays revolve around neuroticism and sex, with much of the former arising from the unfulfilled drive of the latter. Such are the themes in *A Streetcar Named Desire, Summer and Smoke,* and *Cat on a Hot Tin Roof.* In later plays the physical brutality found in these earlier works is carried a step further, and physical mutilation becomes the dominant theme. Thus, in *Orpheus Descending,* cannibalism takes the form of devouring dogs; in *Suddenly Last Summer,* hungry children devour the son; and in *Sweet Bird of Youth,* castration is the final punishment.

In *All My Sons, Death of a Salesman, A View from the Bridge, The Crucible,* and even in *The Price,* Miller is concerned with direct social conflict and the common man. He sees tragedy as the province of the common man and as growing out of a "man's total compulsion to evaluate himself justly." The tragic effect is reached when a man, under the stress of this compulsion, is ready to lay down his own life, "if need be, to secure one thing—his sense of personal dignity." *Death of a Salesman* does not strive to produce the grandeur of ancient tragedy, but pity for contemporary common man who is befuddled by a materialistic world with which he is unable to cope. What Miller attempts to emphasize—and because of his own confused sense of values he is not always successful—is the idea of human dignity and significance. His tragedies founder on the unresolved problem of whether the protagonist can be a man whose absolute mediocrity, whose willingness to compromise, whose shifting sense of values, give no sense of true "interior nobility." As a result, Miller's plays also lead only to despair.

Such notable writers as Edward Albee (b. 1928) and Pinter (q.v.) tend to follow the same sentimental school of despair: man can find no solution for the terrible burdens unfairly placed upon him in this inexplicable universe. This attitude is to be found in such Albee plays as *The Zoo Story, The Sand Box, Tiny Alice, Who's Afraid of Virginia Woolf,* and *The Delicate Balance.* Pinter's *The Room, The Birthday Party,* and *The Dumbwaiter* continue the trend which inevitably becomes a part of the "theater of the absurd."

Basically the theater of the absurd came into being when writers, in attempting to show the senselessness of the human condition and reason's inability to come to grips with this reality, turned away from the rational. These playwrights see life as totally absurd, and they find that man's sole role or function in this purposeless universe is to wait—without hope.

The summation of the creed of despair, with no religious salvation or hope for man, is to be found in the works of the Nobel Prize winner Samuel Beckett, especially in *Waiting for Godot.* Godot, of course, never arrives and will never arrive; nothing happens; all is nothing. The characters are isolated from life, terrified in their very isolation, with no hope for the future. This is all that man has to look forward to. Beckett's other works in the theater of the absurd, such as *Play, Krapp's Last Tape, Endgame,* and *All That Fall,* tend to reaffirm *Godot's* message, or the lack of message. There is nothing! Lear's words ironically are true: "Nothing will get you nothing."

Ionesco (q.v.) also belongs to the absurdist movement—or to what might be termed the school of absolute nihilism—in such plays as *The Chairs, Rhinoceros, The Bald Soprano,* and *Jack, or The Submission.* In each, the case for humanity is argued and lost. Ionesco has gone one step further than earlier playwrights in that his plays are peopled by abstract characters rather than by flesh and blood individuals. Man is reduced to the subhuman level. Thus, with Ionesco's works the philosophical or political tract has taken over the stage, and the theater becomes a mere vehicle for the tract itself. Aristotle's "action" is more and more reduced to the long debate; nothing happens because nothing is meant to happen, because nothing can happen—because nothing begets nothing.

The theater of the absurd, however, carries within itself the seeds of its own destruction. Dialogue has given way to duologue; motivation is extinct; form is lost; movement is either frenetic or nonexistent; symbols are purely personal, their ultimate meaning confined to the playwright and the character. As a result, whether the playwright sees it or not, the final absurdity is the play itself. Its very formlessness, its concentration on the monotony of existence, its inert subhuman protagonists can, in the long run, induce only boredom.

Although most contemporary attempts at tragedy have been pessimistic—with plays leaning to less action and conflict and more emphasis on esoteric symbolism—there is some reason to believe that successful modern tragedy will only be achieved when playwrights learn to see man as a totality, with his physical and spiritual natures forming the overall personality. Thus, Maxwell Anderson, retaining the traditional approach to tragedy, *i.e.,* going back to the past for his story, as in *Elizabeth Queen,* stated in his *The Essence of Tragedy* that theater at its best is a religious affirmation, an age-old rite restating and reassuring man's belief in his own destiny and ultimate hope. Claudel (q.v.) attempts to show that men experience their tragedies when they detour from the central plan for the world as set up by God. In his *The Satin Slipper,* he explains the apparent absurdity of the world by showing that God uses crooked lines to write straight. Finally, Eliot (q.v.), who wrote *Murder in the Cathedral* to show how salvation is attained through faith, hope, and love, also makes salvation the theme in his *The Family Reunion* and *The Cocktail Party.*

As the 1970's begin, tragedy seems to be marking time, trying to decide whether its direction will continue on the road of despair

—as for example in the new shock theater of graffiti which it helped to spawn—or will return to a theater of hope. The recent trend to revivals may be some indication that the audience, if not the playwright, is eager for a more positive fare.

BIBLIOGRAPHY: Gassner, J., *Form and Idea in Modern Theatre* (1956); Henn, T. R., *The Harvest of Tragedy* (1956); Muller, H. J., *The Spirit of Tragedy* (1956); Myers, H. A., *Tragedy: a View of Life* (1956); Krutch, J. W., *The American Drama Since 1918: an Informal History* (1957); Scott, R. B., ed., *The Tragic Vision and the Christian Faith* (1957); Lucas, F. L., *Tragedy* (1958); Sewall, R. B., *Vision of Tragedy* (1959); Boulton, M., *The Anatomy of Drama* (1960); Cole, T., ed., *Playwrights on Playwriting; the Meaning and Making of Modern Drama from Ibsen to Ionesco* (1960); Donoghue, D., *The Third Voice: Modern British and American Verse Drama* (1960); Dusenbury, W. L. *The Theme of Loneliness in Modern American Drama* (1960); Engel, S. M., *The Problem of Tragedy* (1960); Raphael, D. D., *The Paradox of Tragedy* (1960); Esslin, M., *The Theatre of the Absurd* (1961); Steiner, G., *The Death of Tragedy* (1961); Hathorn, R. Y., *Tragedy, Myth, and Mystery* (1962); Taylor, J. R., *Anger and After* (1962); Brustein, R., *The Theatre of Revolt: An Approach to the Modern Drama* (1964); Chiari, J., *Landmarks in Contemporary Drama* (1965); Williams, R., *Modern Tragedy* (1966); Calcareo, N. J., *Tragic Being* (1968)

CARL J. STRATMAN, C.S.V.

TRAKL, Georg

Austrian poet, b. 3 Feb. 1887, Salzburg; d. 4 Nov. 1914, Cracow, Poland

T. was the son of a prosperous hardware storekeeper. The family lived in a house full of art treasures and renaissance and baroque furniture. T.'s mother collected antique glass and possessed a distinct artistic sense, which influenced her children. Yet literature meant little to the family. At an early age T., feeling that his parents did not understand him, developed an attachment to his sister Margarethe, a pianist. His affection for her inspired him to sketch her in many guises: as *Jünglingin* ("youth-maiden") and *Fremdlingin* ("stranger-maiden"). He wrote about her in his early poetry and in his last poem, "Grodek,"

where "the sister's shadow" appears before the eyes of dying soldiers.

At the age of eighteen T. failed at the gymnasium. As a result he turned to pharmacy, getting three years of practical training in Salzburg and then studying in Vienna (1908–1910). During this period he became addicted to drugs. From 1910 to 1911 he was in the pharmacy corps of the Austrian army.

In 1912 T., now a civilian, became a pharmacy assistant in the military hospital in Innsbruck. That same year he became one of the group of writers whose center was the periodical *Der Brenner,* edited by Ludwig von Ficker. At Mühlau near Innsbruck he made the acquaintance of Karl Kraus (q.v.) and the architect Alfred Loos.

T.'s life became increasingly restless. In 1913 he took a position as clerk in the department of labor in the Vienna he so detested, but left after three days; a second attempt also ended in flight to the Tyrol. In 1914 he rushed to Berlin to see his critically ill sister Margarethe. While there he met Else Lasker-Schüler (1876–1945), who was close to him in spirit.

At the outbreak of World War I, T. was drafted into the medical corps. He took part in the battle of Grodek, where, with inadequate equipment, he was responsible for caring for ninety seriously wounded men. The sight of their terrible suffering deranged him, and he tried to take his own life. After this he was sent to the military hospital at Cracow for psychiatric observation, where he died of a drug overdose—whether deliberately or accidentally has never been ascertained.

T.'s work consists mainly of poetry and poetic prose sketches. During his pharmacy apprenticeship he made some attempts at drama writing, hoping to make up for his scholastic and social failures by success in the theater. *Totentag* (1906) and *Fata Morgana* (1906) were produced at the Salzburg Theater. The goodwill of the audience made the first play a success, but the second was a total failure. Both are horror plays full of morbid monstrosities and blood lust, shifting back and forth between naturalism and symbolism (qq.v.).

T.'s early lyrical works were published in *Der Brenner.* He was originally influenced by Charles Baudelaire (1821–67) and later by Jean Rimbaud (1854–91). T. was attracted to Baudelaire by Baudelaire's milieu of the degraded, his sympathy with weak, impotent mankind, his interest in prostitutes, his descriptions of the search of the depraved for God. T. was impressed with Rimbaud's glowing imagery and his capacity for departing to unexplored, vibrant realms. (In 1912, encouraged by Rimbaud's journey to Abyssinia, T. considered emigrating to Borneo.) Finally T. found in Paul Verlaine (1844–96) the echoes of muted sorrow to which his own soul was attuned.

At an early age T. had been seized by a feeling of the world's inexorable disintegration and by an all-enveloping loneliness. In his poetry, T. invoked decline and death, which he sensed ominously behind all life. This obsession with decline contains echoes of Nietzsche's (q.v.) cultural pessimism. Combining man and nature in a unified image of decline, T. liked to evoke autumn or winter landscapes, moods of dying life. His language, however, is always concentrated, clear and structured, never expressionistically fragmented. He had a particular fondness for the cold colors—blue, silver, purple, green, and black—which he used for effects of synesthesia. His obsession with color led to a very personal fusing of his Salzburg baroque heritage with the delight in color typical of decadence.

About 1911 T. moved on from confessional poetry to the modern poem of symbolic imagery. "The rewritten poem (*Klagelied*) is better than the original version to the extent that it is now impersonal and full to bursting of movement, of visions. I am convinced that in this universal form and manner it will say and mean more than it did in the limited personal way of the first draft," he wrote to Erhard Buschbeck. In his later poems T. abandoned rhyme and came closer to a hymnal free rhythm like that of the Psalms (in three- or four-line verses). These poems have no rationally comprehensible content; they present "lost signatures" of terror and derangement. Images and words are interchangeable, recurring again and again, with constant shifts and changes of order.

This abandonment of logical connections within the poem in favor of autonomous combinations of images made T. the first and only poet of his kind in the German language. For him the paramount factor is not the unequivocal meaning of the line but its musical harmony and the intensity of its mental impact. The landscape, objects, and living creatures that he frequently invokes in his poems, though in ever new combinations, have no "deeper" symbolic significance, but stand in their own

right as elements of a subjective world, changing like pictures in a kaleidoscope, yet always maintaining their fixed structure.

T.'s feeling of rootlessness—"Es ist die Seele ein Fremdes auf Erden" ("The soul is something alien on earth")—evoked in T. the image of a disembodied spirit wandering back to the realm of a guiltless childhood, a fresh start, where happiness and world unity are to be found. The fragmentation that troubled him in the world as it is known through the senses finds its linguistic correlative in the paratactic syntax of his poetry.

FURTHER WORKS: *Gedichte* (1913); *Sebastian im Traum* (1914); *Die Dichtungen* (1917); *Der Herbst des Einsamen* (1920); *Gesang der Abgeschiedenen* (1933); *Aus goldenem Kelch* (1939); *Die Dichtungen* (3 vols., 1939–49); *Offenbarung und Untergang* (1947); *Gesammelte Werke* (3 vols., 1948 ff.); *Nachlaß und Biographie* (1949); *Nachgelassene Gedichte* (1958). **Selected English translations:** *Decline* (1952); *Twenty Poems* (1961); *Selected Poems* (1968)

BIBLIOGRAPHY: Ritzer, W., *T. Bibliographie* (1956); Ficker, L., and Zangerle, I., *Erinnerungen an G. T.* (2nd ed., 1959); Werner, B., *Erlösungsmotive in der Dichtung G. Ts.* (1961); Magnuson, K., "Consonant Problems in the Lyrics of G. T.," *GR*, XXXVII (1962), 263–81; Bleisch, E. G., *G. T.* (1964); Casey, T. J., *Manshape That Shone: An Interpretation of G. T.* (1964); Basil, O., *G. T. in Selbstzeugnissen und Bilddokumenten* (1965); Brown, R. E., "Attribute Pairs in the Poetry of G. T.," *MLN*, LXXXII (1967), 439–45

GEORGES SCHLOCKER

TRAUSTI, Jón

(pseud. of *Guðmundur Magnússon*), Icelandic novelist, short-story writer, and poet, b. 12 Feb. 1873, Rif; d. 18 Nov. 1918, Reykjavík

T.'s father's death left him at the hands of parish charity when he was five. As a boy he lived through the last great famine winter in Icelandic history, which resulted in thousands of Icelanders emigrating to America. Later he described what things were like in his story "Vorharðindi." Though T. was a great lover of books as a boy, he never received any formal education. In his youth he worked as a farmhand and on fishing boats. In 1893 he learned the printing trade, which was to be his chief source of income for the rest of his life.

Though T. wrote a good deal of poetry, some of which is excellent, his reputation rests most securely on three major novels.

The first of these, *Halla* (1906), and its long sequel *Heiðarbýlið* (4 vols., 1908–1911), are generally acknowledged as his masterpiece. An important trail-blazer in modern Icelandic literature, it is the first large-scale portrait of an entire district and its inhabitants. It is the kind of work that was later to be done so superbly by Halldór Laxness (q.v.). The narrative is held together by its heroine, Halla, whose wasted and unhappy life is chronicled with sympathy and power.

Leysing (1907), the most coherent and best-structured of T.'s novels, is the one of which he was proudest. In this he expertly sustains the narrative pace, and suspense is unusually well maintained.

Borgir (1909) is a well-plotted and effective story about the conflict between the Icelandic state church and the Free Church movement.

In all these novels the characters are psychologically convincing and skillfully and distinctively drawn, though most of them are not very complex. They draw heavily on the personalities, scenes, and situations of T.'s childhood and youth. Like the works of most other Icelandic writers of the period, the novels are strongly steeped in tradition and nationalism. T. admires nothing more than strength of character and heroic individualism. He almost invariably extols the old-fashioned, conservative virtues, even while paying lip service to more progressive ideas. Though T. is theoretically a realist, all these books show strong romantic tendencies in characterization, style, and narrative patterns.

After 1911, T. turned from his often half-hearted "realism" to unabashed romanticism, in a series of historical novels and novellas. This is a genre that he introduced into Icelandic literature. These frequently exciting chronicles of the Icelandic past—mostly from the 14th through the 18th c.'s—contain a number of striking reconstructions of scenes and situations, plotted and narrated in the grand style.

Sögur frá Skaftáreldi (1912–13), the longest and most ambitious of the group, deals with the tragic consequences of the eruption of the volcano Laki in the late 18th c. Perhaps the best of this group is the novella "Anna frá Stóruborg," from *Góðir stofnar* (1914–15). This is the story of a strong-willed woman of the 16th c. who carries on a love affair with her shepherd despite the determined and militant opposition of her overly class-conscious brother.

In 1918, T. turned to contemporary reality in his last novel, *Bessi gamli*. This portrait of life in Reykjavík is a bitter attack on what T. conceived to be its shortcomings. For T. it is unusually conservative in political spirit. Unfortunately T.'s rural background and outlook made him an unsatisfactory chronicler of urban life.

Along with his novels T. produced a number of short stories, both realistic and historical-romantic, and many of these are of high quality. Among the best are: "Einyrkjan," "Keldan," "Tvær systur," the exquisite "Á fjörunni," and "Blái dauðinn."

FURTHER WORKS: *Heima og erlendis* (1899); *Íslandsvísur* (1903); *Teitur* (1903); *Ferðaminningar* (1905); *Sigurbjörn Sleggja* (1908); *Smásögur* (2 vols., 1909–1912); *Dóttir Faraós* (1914); *Tvær gamlar sögur* (1916); *Samtíningur* (1920); *Kvæðabók* (1922); *Ferðasögur* (1930); *Ritsafn* (ed. Stefán Einarsson; 1939–46)

BIBLIOGRAPHY: Einarsson, S., ed., *Ritsafn* (1939–46): Vol. I, pp. 7–38, biographical and critical sketch; Vol. VIII, pp. 621–40, bibliography

RICHARD N. RINGLER

TRAVEN, B.

(possibly pseud.), of unknown nationality and dates

Certain Mexican sources claim that T. was born and bred in the United States and that his original manuscripts were written in English. A textual analysis shows, however, that the American and English editions are translations from German and that the author's frame of reference is consistently German and European. The German editions contain jokes and familiar sayings that cannot easily be translated into English and thus the American editions contain fragments that are quite meaningless to those who read them. T.'s occasional use of unidiomatic and incorrect German even deepens the mystery surrounding his background. The many conflicting statements made by people in Mexico concerning T.'s identity, the numerous representations or misrepresentations involving the author's works (which the idealist T. would not have sanctioned), and the puzzling situation of copyright ownerships seem to indicate that the author has been dead for some years and was not Hal Croves, or Traven Torsvan, who died in 1969.

T.'s works were first published in German by the socialist *Büchergilde Gutenberg* in Germany between 1926 and 1932, and in Switzerland and Holland after 1933. New titles appearing after 1940 are either parts of earlier works with new titles—*Der Banditendoktor* (1957) and *Der dritte Gast* (1958)—or works probably falsely attributed to T.—*Marcario* (1950) and *Aslan Norval* (1960).

T.'s novels have been very popular in Europe and Mexico and have been translated into more than twenty languages. T. is best known in America for the film based on *The Treasure of the Sierra Madre* (1934; *Der Schatz der Sierra Madre,* 1927).

The recurring theme of T.'s novels is the exploitation and oppression of the proletariat. In *Das Totenschiff* (1926; The Death Ship, 1934) the experiences of a countryless seaman, sailing on a doomed ship, reflect the fate of the victims of bureaucracy and capitalist business practices.

This theme in varied forms reappears in the works that deal with the lives of the Mexican Indians. The central characters may be helpless Indians uprooted from their homes by bigbusiness enterprises, mahogany cutters working in a state of bondage, cattle drivers struggling to maintain their livelihood, or Indians in revolt against their exploiters. While the characters have distinct individuality, their portrayal and development are of less importance than is their fate as representatives of their class, and as such they are not idealized or romanticized.

T. makes no attempt to dazzle his readers with a polished and sophisticated style or with involved philosophical reflections. Content takes precedence over form. His works are directed not at the literati but at the broad reading public. The language is simple and direct, yet powerful. It is used effectively in brutally realistic scenes depicting the plight of the victims of oppression as well as in scenes filled with tenderness and compassion. Biting, down-to-earth humor is used frequently to relieve or even to intensify the depressive atmosphere.

Future generations undoubtedly will use T.'s works as source material for studies on social

and political criticism as it appears in the works of authors of the first half of the 20th c. Distrusting the socialists and communists as much as the capitalists, T. was committed to no party line. He may be considered a political primitivist.

FURTHER WORKS: *Das Land des Frühlings* (1928); *Die Baumwollpflücker* (1929; The Cottonpickers, 1956); *Die Brücke im Dschungel* (1929; The Bridge in the Jungle, 1938); *Die weiße Rose* (1929; The White Rose, 1964); *Der Busch* (1930); *Der Karren* (1931; The Carreta, 1935); *Die Regierung* (1931; Government, 1935); *Der Marsch ins Reich der Caoba* (1933; March to Caobaland, 1961); *Sonnenschöpfung* (1936); *Die Rebellion der Gehenkten* (1936; The Rebellion of the Hanged, 1952): *Die Troza* (1936); *Ein General kommt aus dem Dschungel* (1940)

BIBLIOGRAPHY: Hagemann, E. R., "A Checklist of the Work of B. T. and the Critical Estimates and Bibliographical Essays on Him; Together with a Brief Biography," *Papers of The Bibliographical Society of America,* LIII (First Quarter 1959); Jannach, H. "B. T.—An American or German Author," *GQ,* XXXVI (Nov. 1963); Recknagel, R., *B. T.: Beiträge zur Biographie* (1966); Humphrey, R., "B. T.: An Examination of the Controversy over His Identity with an Analysis of His Major Works and His Place in Literature," *DA,* XXVII (1967), 3049A–50A

HUBERT JANNACH

TRAYANOV, Teodor V.

Bulgarian poet, b. 30 Jan. 1882, Pazardzhik; d. 15 Jan. 1945, Sofia

After studying mathematics and physics at Sofia University, T. enrolled in the Polytechnic School in Vienna. He lived there for many years, subsequently becoming an official of the Bulgarian embassy. He became deeply interested in German and French symbolism and expressionism (qq.v.) and felt a close relationship with such writers as George, Hoffmannsthal, Romains, and Duhamel (qq.v.).

After World War I, T. returned to Sofia and became one of the leading representatives of symbolism in Bulgaria. He founded and edited the magazine *Hyperion* (1921–23) and for it wrote articles and reviews, in which he turned against the realistic, socially engaged, and nationalistic tradition in Bulgarian literature. Like his fellow modernists Peyu Yavorov

(1877–1914), Nikolai Liliev (1885–1961), Emanuil Popdimitrov (1885–1943), Demcho Debelyanov (1887–1916), and Khristo Yasenov (1889–1925), T. wrote "lyrics of universal sadness," in which he concentrated on the mysterious and morbid aspects of life, and on death and darkness. Along with international symbolist clichés, T.'s poems contain individualistic, idiosyncratic images, unusual associations, and obscure ideas, all of which give some of his lyrics a rather hermetic character. There is a rhetorical, pathetic tone in many of his poems. Notwithstanding his theories against *engagé* literature, he reveled in high-pitched, patriotic, even chauvinistic verse (especially in the *Bŭlgarski Baladi*, 1921). In the volume *Panteon* (1934), however, he endeavors to transcend this narrow patriotism and to find a synthesis of the Slavic and the western European spirit.

T. is one of the great Bulgarian poets and greatly contributed to the enrichment of the Bulgarian poetic language.

FURTHER WORKS: *Regina mortua* (1909); *Himni i baladi* (1912); *Pesen na pesnite* (1923); *Romantichni pesni* (1926); *Osvobodeniyat chovek* (1929)

BIBLIOGRAPHY: Benaroya, M., *T. T.* (1926); Shishmanov, D., *A Survey of Bulgarian Literature* (1932); Manning, C. A., and Smal-Stocki, R., *The History of Modern Bulgarian Literature* (1960); Tzenkov, B., "T. T.," *Ezik i Literatura*, XX (1965), iii, 21–34

THOMAS EEKMAN

TRENEV, Konstantin Andreyevich

Soviet-Russian playwright and short-story writer, b. 3 June 1876, Romashovo, Ukraine; d. 19 May 1945, Moscow

Son of a peasant and former serf, T. grew up in poverty in a Ukrainian village, was educated in various parochial schools, and completed his formal education by graduating from a theological seminary as well as from the archaeological institute in Leningrad in 1903. He became the editor of a Ukrainian newspaper and later a teacher. After 1917 he reentered the university and studied agronomy in Simferopol. He lived there until 1931 when he moved to Moscow.

T. began to publish naturalist (*see* naturalism) stories and sketches on rural life in 1898 in the vein of Gorki (q.v.), who encouraged his

work. In his stories T. depicts the hardships of peasant life, police oppression, the hypocrisy of the clergy, and the greediness of kulaks and merchants. He liked to write dialogues and lyrical passages on the beauty of the steppe landscape, and he dwelt with special sympathy on characters that are passive, introspective sufferers, valuing them for their purity, meekness, and lack of avarice.

After the Russian Revolution T. became famous for his play *Lyubov Yarovaya* (staged 1926, pub. 1927; Lyubov Yarovaya, 1946). This has become a classic in Soviet repertory and was the only Soviet play presented in 1937 at the Paris International Exhibition. This folk-heroic epic, as Soviet criticism calls it, deals with an episode during the Civil War in a small southern Russian town in which leading communists who had been captured and destined for execution are freed mainly through the initiative and under the leadership of the title heroine, a schoolteacher and communist sympathizer. Her personal drama is closely linked with her political activity because on this crucial day she discovers that her deeply loved husband, presumably killed during World War I, has reappeared as a White officer. In the ensuing conflict between her love and her political commitment, Lyubov finally decides to sacrifice her husband by preventing his escape, thus insuring his liquidation by the Reds. This gives her the right to say at the end of the play to Koshkin, the exemplary Red commissar, that from now on only can she be considered his *true* comrade.

This melodramatic conflict is, however, only a pretext for holding the play together, which is designed to present a spectacle of revolution and counterrevolution. Criticism of the play led T. to revise it somewhat, and the version now used (also that of the English translation) is that of 1940 (see Surkov's comparison of the various versions in his biography of T.).

The play remains important as one of the first Soviet dramas, after Vladimir Bill-Belotzerkovski's (b. 1885) *Shtorm* (1925), to establish the pattern for the typical bolshevik propaganda play, which was supposed to educate as well as entertain. Its mass scenes, its clearly outlined antagonistic class representatives and ideologies, and its basic technique —that of refracting the revolution in a pseudo-realistic melodrama where psychology is subordinated to ideology—have influenced many Soviet dramatists.

Lyubov Yarovaya's enormous success on the

Soviet stage derives from its unusual features: an effective double plot of personal and political intrigue; juxtaposition of humor (often farcical) with grim ruthlessness; the didactic contrast between old-time bourgeois egotism and the new communist morality and devotion. The terse dialogue, pointed repartee, and individualized speech of many characters contribute to the vividness, pace, and colorfulness of the play.

FURTHER WORKS: *Doroginy* (1912); *Vladyka* (1914); *Mokraya balka* (1916); *Pugachevshchina* (1924); *Zhena* (1928); *Yasnyi log* (1931); *Gimnazisty* (1936); *Na beregu Nevy* (1937); *Anna Luchinina* (1941); *Polkovodetz* (1944); *Izbrannyye Proizvedeniya* (1955). **Selected English translation:** *In a Cossack Village, and Other Stories* (1946)

BIBLIOGRAPHY: Surkov, Y., *K. A. T.* (1955); Gorchakov, N. A., *The Theater in Soviet Russia* (1957); Diyev, V. A., *Tvorchestvo K. A. T.* (1960); Slonim, M., *Russian Theater* (1961); Fainberg, R. I., *K. A. T.* (1962)

WOLFGANG HIRSCHBERG

TRILUSSA

(pseud. of *Carlo Alberto Salustri*), Italian satirical poet, b. 26 Oct. 1873, Rome; d. there, 21 Dec. 1950

When T. was three, his father died and the child was brought up in poverty. Though he attended elementary school, T. was largely self-educated and began to write poetry almost as soon as he could write at all. He was only fourteen when his first collection of poems, *Stelle de Rome* (1887), was published. Unlike most of his works, which were in the gutsy dialect of Rome, these poems were written in standard Tuscan; they attracted little attention. They were, however, instrumental in opening to him the doors of various publications, and soon his articles on everything from the theater to folklore were appearing in *Rugantino, Don Chisciotte,* etc.

T.'s next volume of verse, *Er mago de Borgo* (1890), launched a popular career in the dialect tradition represented by such great poets as G. G. Belli (1791–1863). His reputation increased with each succeeding volume and reached its acme in the decade preceding World War II.

Casting a cold eye on the world around him,

T. drew his subject matter from both the public and private aspects of life, often providing the most penetrating, though indirect, criticism of the follies and brutalities of fascism. His poems developed two classical traditions: the satire and the Aesopian fable as established in Italy by Phaedrus (15 B.C.–50 A.D.). Though he originally imitated and parodied the animal fable, he soon introduced into it a new technical virtuosity and unusual subject matter.

A moralist whose often mordant effects were highlighted by his brilliant use of popular speech, T. was able to etch a character or a situation in a few penetrating lines and expose the underlying elements of the comic and the grotesque. Though he castigated human folly and corruption he believed that the tonic effect of laughter could—temporarily—shame man into goodness.

FURTHER WORKS: *Quaranta sonetti romaneschi* (1895); *Favole romanesche* (1900); *Caffè concerto* (1901); *El serrajo* (1903); *Sonetti* (1906); *Ommini e bestie* (1908); *Nove poesie* (1910); *Le storie* (1915); *La vispa Teresa allungato* (1918); *Le finzioni della vita* (1918); *Lupi e agnelli* (1919); *Le favole* (1920); *A tozzi e bocconi* (1921); *Le cose* (1922); *La gente* (1922); *Nove poesie* (1922); *La porchetta bianca* (1930); *Giove e le bestie* (1931); *Compionario* (1931); *Cento favole* (1935); *Il libro muto* (1935); *Duecento sonetti* (1937); *Lo specchio e altre poesie* (1938); *Acqua e vino* (1944); *Libro no. 9* (1946); *Tutte le poesie* (1951). **Selected English translation:** *Roman Satirical Poems* (1945)

BIBLIOGRAPHY: D'Amico, S., *T.* (1925); De Falco, M., *T.* (1935); "Belli e T.," *Il Ponte,* 4 (1951); Addamiano, N., *T.* (1952); Dell'Arco, M., "Volti di T.," *Studi Romani* (1957)

* * * *

TRIOLET, Elsa

(pseud. of *Elsa Blick*), French novelist and short-story writer (writing in French and Russian), b. ca. 1896, Moscow; d. 16 June 1970, Paris

Elsa T.'s earliest books were written in Russian and aroused Gorki's (q.v.) interest. In 1928 she met Aragon (q.v.) in Paris and later married him. In his poetry, prose, and critical pronouncements, Aragon acknowledges her profound influence on his work. In her own right, Elsa T. proved a most imaginative and powerful novelist, a translator of Russian fiction and poetry, and a subtle critic. She introduced to France the poems and plays of her brother-in-law Mayakovski (q.v.), as well as many of Chekhov's (q.v.) dramas.

Of seismographic sensitivity toward changing moods in French society, Elsa T. wrote novels and short stories dealing with man's isolation in the crowd, with uprooted people, and with love hard-won and often unrequited.

"What can man do for others?" she often asks, and her answer is patiently courageous action. Such is the theme of *Le Cheval Blanc* (1943; The White Charger, 1946), in which we are introduced to an intriguingly complex hero, Michel. The search for identity is the primary concern of Elsa T.'s heroes and—especially—heroines.

During the German occupation, Elsa T. and her husband went into hiding but continued their writing and their patriotic activities. She helped found the clandestine literary magazine *Les Lettres Françaises,* which has continued publication to this day. A number of Elsa T.'s stories first appeared under the penname of Laurent Daniel. A collection of these stories, *Le Premier Accroc coûte deux cents francs* (1945; A Fine of 200 Francs, 1947), was the first book to be awarded the Goncourt Prize after the liberation.

Problems of postwar readaptation, visions of a world after a nuclear war (*Le Cheval roux, ou Les Intentions humaines,* 1953), but also fanciful tales of a poetic invention, animate Elsa T.'s impressive novelistic production, which she has on the whole kept free from doctrinaire involvement. Her most significant contribution to literature is to be found in *Mille Regrets* (1942), *Qui est cet Étranger qui n'est pas d'ici?* (1944), and in novels of passion and reflection, such as *Personne ne m'aime* (1946), *Les Fantômes armés* (1946), and *L'Inspecteur des ruines* (1948; The Inspector of Ruins, 1953).

Elsa T.'s novels are permeated by a blend of melancholy and whimsical imagination that recalls the fairy tales of E. T. A. Hoffman or Hans Christian Anderson. The special quality of her work lies in the strange mixture of epic Russianity and of vividly Gallic dialogue.

FURTHER WORKS: *Tahiti* (in Russian, 1925); *Fraise des bois* (in Russian, 1926); *Camouflage* (in Russian, 1928); *Bonsoir Thérèse* (1938); *Maïakovski, Poète Russe, Souvenirs* (1939); *Yvette* (1944); *Ce n'était

qu'un passage de ligne (1945), *Six entre autres* (1945); *L'Écrivain et le livre, ou La Suite dans les idées* (1948); *L'Histoire d'Anton Tchekhov, sa vie, son œuvre* (1954); *Le Rendez-vous des étrangers* (1956); *Le Monument* (1957); *L'Age de Nylon* (1959–63; I, *Roses à crédit,* 1959; II, *Luna-Park,* 1959; III, *L'Âme,* 1963); *Manigances–Journal d'une egoïste* (1962); *Le Grand jamais* (1965); *Écoutez-voir* (1968); *La Mise en mots* (1969); *Le Rossignol se tait à l'aube* (1970)

BIBLIOGRAPHY: Stirling, M., "E. T.," *Atlantic Monthly,* CLXXXIV, iii; *Elsa T. choisie par Aragon* (1960); Bieber, K., "Ups and Downs in Elsa T.'s Prose," *YFS,* No. 27 (1961); Madaule, J., *Ce que dit Elsa* (1961); Pflaum-Vallin, M.-M., "Elsa T. and Aragon: Back to Lilith," *YFS,* No. 27 (1961)

KONRAD BIEBER

TROYAT, Henri

(pseud. of *Lev Tarassov*), French novelist and biographer, b. 1 Nov. 1911, Moscow

T.'s family, forced to flee Russia during the 1917 revolution, finally settled in Paris after three years of extreme hardship in Central Asia and the Middle East. After completing his studies, T. worked in the Préfecture de la Seine, but left this post in 1940. He had already begun publishing by that time, with some success even at the beginning.

In 1959 T. was elected to the French Academy.

Faux jour (1935), a novel about a son in rebellion against his father, was awarded the Prix Populiste. *L'Araigne* (1938) won the Prix Goncourt and brought T. to public attention for its careful study of evil in human relationships. The word "spider" in the title applies to the young protagonist, a venomous character who torments his mother and three sisters.

The work for which T. is best known is a trilogy made up of the following: *Tant que la terre durera* (1947; My Father's House, 1951); *Le Sac et le cendre* (1948; Am., The Red and the White; Eng., Sackcloth and Ashes, 1956); and *Étrangers sur la terre* (1950; Am., Strangers on Earth, 1958; Eng., Strangers in the Land, 1958). In this long novel, T. studies the political and social struggles in Russia during approximately the half-century before 1917. Following the pattern of other French *romans-fleuve,* T. focuses on the members of a middle-class family resembling his own. Through the experiences of the many characters, T. presents a fairly complete picture of the prerevolutionary and revolutionary periods.

La Neige en deuil (1952; The Mountain, 1953), the best of T.'s briefer works, is closer to the traditional French psychological novel, in which two or three characters and their setting emerge with total clarity. In this novel two mountaineer brothers engage in a search for a plane that crashed in the Alps. The motivation of one is humanitarian, but he is constantly frustrated by his younger brother, whose search is motivated by greed.

T. will be remembered for his well-documented, lively biographies, which are psychological and literary studies of major Russian writers: *Dostoïevsky* (1940; Firebrand: The Life of Dostoievsky, 1946); *Pouchkine* (1946; Pushkin: A Biography, 1950); *L'Étrange destin de Lermontov* (1952). His *Tolstoï* (1965; Tolstoy, 1967) was widely acclaimed, especially in the United States.

FURTHER WORKS: *Le Vivier* (1935); *Grandeur nature* (1936; One Minus Two, 1938); *La Clef de voûte: Monsier Citrique* (1937); *Les Vivants* (1940); *Judith Madrier* (1940; Judith Madrier, 1941); *Le Jugement de Dieu* (1941); *Le Mort saisit le vif* (1942); *Le Signe du taureau* (1944); *Du Philanthrope à la rouquine* (1945); *Les Ponts de Paris* (1946); *La Case de l'oncle Sam* (1948); *Sébastien* (1948); *La Tête sur les épaules* (1951); *Les Semailles et les moissons* (5 vols., 1952–58; I, *Amélie*, 1952 [Amelie in Love, 1956]; II, *Amélie et Pierre*, 1955 [Amelie and Pierre, 1957]; III, *La Grive*, 1956 [Elizabeth, 1958]; IV, *Tendre et violente Élisabeth*, 1957 [Tender and Violent Elizabeth, 1960]; V, *La Rencontre*, 1958 [The Encounter, 1962]); *Brésil* (1955); *De Gratte-ciel en cocotier* (1955); *La Maison des bêtes heureuses* (1956); *Sainte Russie* (1956); *La Vie quotidienne en Russie* (1959; Daily Life in Russia under the Last Tsar, 1961); *La Lumière des justes* (5 vols., 1959–63; I, *Les Compagnons du Coquelicot*, 1959 [The Brotherhood of the Red Poppy, 1961]; II, *La Barynia*, 1960 [The Baroness, 1961]; III, *La Gloire des vaincus*, 1961; IV, *Les Dames de Sibérie*, 1962; V, *Sophie*, 1963); *Une Extrême Amitié* (1963; Am., An Extreme Friendship, 1968; Eng., An Intimate Friendship, 1968); *Le Geste d'Eve* (1964); *Les Éygletière* (3 vols., 1965–67; I, *Les Eygletière*, 1965; II, *La Faim*

des Lionceaux, 1966; III, *La Malandre*, 1967); *Les Héritiers de l'avenir* (2 vols., 1968–69; I, *Le Cahier*, 1968; II, *Cent un coups de canon*, 1969)

BIBLIOGRAPHY: Kemp, R., "H. T. à la recherche du pays perdu," *Revue de Paris*, Aug. 1950; Bourdet, D., *Brèves Rencontres* (1963); Gannes, G., *Messieurs les best-sellers* (1966)

CHARLES G. HILL

TURKISH LITERATURE

Turkish literature in the 20th c. is a product of a social milieu marked by upheavals and transformation. The Ottoman Empire entered the century on the brink of collapse. In 1908 the Young Turk revolution introduced constitutional government. Defeat in World War I brought foreign occupation. In their War of Independence (1919–22), under the leadership of Mustafa Kemal Atatürk, the Turks freed themselves from their autocratic ruler. In 1923 Atatürk founded the Turkish Republic. He launched far-reaching legal, political, social, and cultural reforms. A process of modernization patterned on European models was the general aim of government programs. One revolutionary change was that Turkey adopted the Latin alphabet to replace the Arabic. This broke the hold of Islam, and of Arabo-Persian culture, on Turkey. Since World War II, Turkey has made the transition from autocratic one-party rule to the multiparty system. The country experienced an army coup (1960). The military regime restored the multiparty system based on a new constitution with the widest freedoms in Turkish history.

Modern Turkey has witnessed the clash and fusion of many ideologies: nationalism, Islam, secularism, European influence, democracy, traditionalism, capitalism, socialism, and communism. Turkish literature reflects the impact of these credos and of the social tensions they have created. It has also served as a vehicle of criticism and propaganda.

Since the middle of the 19th c., the principal concern of Turkish literature has been to modernize itself. Political and legal reforms, collectively known as Tanzimat, were initiated in 1839. They gave impetus to Westernization in education, technology, and culture. The new orientation led to the emergence of forms, styles, and a language antithetical to the fundamentals of classical Turkish literature. New genres, such as the novel, play, essay, were introduced. Writers began to utilize literature for the dissemination of the concepts of freedom, democracy, justice, nationalism. At the end of the 19th c., the literary movement known as Wealth of Knowledge (Servet-i Fünun) consolidated the European orientation. The early decades of the 20th c. gave rise to the National Literature movement (Millî Edebiyat), which stressed autochthonous traditions. But the Arabo-Persian influences lingered, and the more recent impact of Europe continued.

After the republic was established, Turkish literary figures, on the whole, renounced the classical heritage and sought full-scale entry into the mainstream of European literature. In the 1940's and later, a government-sponsored program of translations of close to a thousand European classics increased European influence. The language-reform movement, which had been gaining momentum since the establishment of the semi-official Turkish Language Society in 1932, brought about a radical change in the idiom and styles of modern literature. In the 1960's Turkish authors felt more confident in their use of newly adopted forms and themes. Many were coming to terms with the heritage of Turkish literature. As a result, a new synthesis of national and international elements was in the making.

Poetry

Poetry has dominated Turkish literature and art since the 8th c. Early oral epic tradition nurtured folk poetry, which continued as an integral part of popular culture and exerted a wide impact on many leading modern poets. Between the 9th and 12th c.'s the Turks became converted to Islam. They assimilated the forms and substance of Arabo-Persian literatures. During the Ottoman Empire, there was not only growth of the folk tradition, but of an elitist classical poetry. This conventional verse, often called "divan," used rigid forms, substantial borrowings from Arabic and Persian vocabulary, and stereotyped images and metaphors. Abstraction and euphony were among its basic features.

As Westernization gained momentum in Turkey in the second half of the 19th c., classical verse was in its death throes. İbrahim Şinasi (1826–71), Ziya Pasha (1825–80), Namık

Kemal (1840–88) and others heralded the Tanzimat poetry. It focused on aesthetic innovations and social commitment. Recaizade Ekrem (1847–1914) objected to the concept of the social and utilitarian function of literature. He defended "art for art's sake." His European orientation and his use of new formal and thematic devices came under vehement attacks from the traditionalists, led by Muallim Naci (1850–93). Abdülhak Hamit Tarhan (1852–1937), well versed in European literature, exerted a major modernizing influence by virtue of his metaphysical, pastoral, and elegiac poems. He helped to promote romantic themes of life and death as well as numerous innovations of form and prosody.

In the closing years of the 19th c. a group of poets initiated the Wealth of Knowledge movement, which rallied around the influential magazine of the same name. The leaders of the movement were Tevfik Fikret (1867–1915) and Cenap Şehabettin (1870–1934). They produced post-romantic, parnassian, and occasionally symbolist poetry. They gained popularity by means of fresh imagery and mellifluous virtuosity. Tevfik Fikret also made a substantial contribution as a crusading poet. He denounced injustice and the sultan's authority and spoke for democracy, progress, and humanism.

Satire, a time-honored tradition in classical and folk poetry, became a potent weapon of invective against the Ottoman establishment in the work of Eşref (1846–1912).

Nationalism was the paramount ideology of Turkish society in the 20th c. Its proponents in poetry sought to create a mystique of Turkish consciousness. They stressed the importance of folk poetry as the source of indigenous themes, forms, and meters as well as the spoken language of the people. They were against the use of traditional prosody—"aruz," a quantitative system of meters which the Turks had adopted from Arabo-Persian verse—as being ill-suited to the sound structure of Turkish.

Mehmet Emin Yurdakul (1869–1944), a leading nationalist poet, composed all his poems in the syllabic meters ("hece vezni") and used the vernacular without stylistic artifices. The influential social thinker Ziya Gökalp (1875–1924) produced many simple didactic poems, also in syllabic verse, to disseminate his ideas of Turkish nationalism. Rıza Tevfik Bölükbaşı (1869–1949) refined the formal structure and themes of popular folk poetry.

The influence of folk literature culminated in the work of five syllabist poets (beş hececiler). They are Faruk Nafiz Çamlıbel (b. 1898), Orhan Seyfi Orhon (b. 1890), Enis Behiç Koryürek (1891–1949), Halit Fahri Ozansoy (b. 1891), and Yusuf Ziya Ortaç (1896–1967). In addition, the influence of folk literature shaped the aesthetics of Kemalettin Kamu (1901–1948), Ömer Bedrettin Uşaklı (1904–1946), and Behçet Kemal Çağlar (1908–1969). Among the poets of stature born in the 20th c., very few have not come under the impact of the substance, forms, and meters of folk poetry.

Three eminent poets kept many basic features of classical poetry alive, although they introduced changes: Ahmet Haşim (1884–1933), Mehmet Âkif Ersoy (1873–1936), and Yahya Kemal Beyatlı (1884–1958). Haşim, under the influence of the French symbolists, combined a striking fiery imagery with melancholy sonal effects to create his lyrics of spiritual exile. Mehmet Âkif, a master of the heroic diction and the "aruz" tradition, devoted much of his verse to the dogma and the passion of Islam. It was his hope that religion might bring a new moral force to Turkish society and save the Ottoman Empire. His nationalism had a strong Islamic content, evident in the lyrics of the Turkish national anthem that he wrote. His most significant poems are those depicting the life of common people in the city of Istanbul. Beyatlı was a much-acclaimed neoclassicist. He produced meticulous lyrics of love, Ottoman grandeur, and Istanbul's natural attractions.

In the 1920's and 1930's young talents explored life's meaning in philosophical terms or gave voice to simple sentiments in tidy lyric poems. Among these, Ahmet Hamdi Tanpınar (1901–1962), Ahmet Kutsi Tecer (1901–1966), Necip Fazıl Kısakürek (b. 1905), Ahmet Muhip Dranas (b. 1909), Cahit Sıtkı Tarancı (1910–56), and Ziya Osman Saba (1910–57), achieved notable success.

The most dedicated revolutionary in modern Turkish poetry was Nâzım Hikmet Ran (1902–1963). He launched and popularized free verse under the influence of Mayakovski (q.v.). Nâzım Hikmet was a communist who spent many years in Turkish jails; he died an exile in the Soviet Union. His work has been translated into many languages. He has been compared to Garcia Lorca, Brecht, Neruda, and Artaud (qq.v.). Many of Nâzım Hikmet's best poems are mellifluous lyrics that lament social injustice, disenfranchisement, and oppression of the masses. They yearn for revolutionary change. (English translations of Nâzım Hikmet's poems appear in the following books:

Poems, 1954; *Selected Poems*, 1967; and *Moscow Symphony*, 1970.)

In 1941 three young poets—Orhan Veli Kanık (1914–50), Oktay Rifat (b. 1914), and Melih Cevdet Anday (b. 1915)—published their poems in a slim volume entitled *Garip* (Strange). Their volume also contained a manifesto proposing that poetry should address itself to the man in the street and must be written in simple colloquial language without any artificial devices. This view, sometimes referred to as "poetic realism," dominated Turkish verse in the 1940's and early 1950's. It served to divest poetry of embellishments. It heralded the common man as its hero, glorified the concrete, and introduced a bittersweet humor as well as an epigrammatic approach. (English translations of Orhan Veli Kanık's selected poems are published in *I Am Listening to Istanbul*, 1971.)

Inspired by the Kanık-Rifat-Anday movement, Bedri Rahmi Eyüboğlu (b. 1913) produced colorful populist poetry. Orhon Murat Arıburnu (b. 1918) wrote satiric epigrams. Metin Eloğlu (b. 1927) poked fun at the inequities of urban life. Nevzat Üstün (b. 1924) protested injustice in Turkey and abroad.

In the 1950's a strong reaction set in against the simple themes and formulations of poetic realism. İlhan Berk (b. 1916), Cemal Süreya (b. 1931), Edip Cansever (b. 1928), and others continued from where a pioneer surrealist, Asaf Halet Çelebi (1907–1958), had left off. They offered a brand of neosurrealism that they called "the second new movement." They defined it as "meaningless poetry." This obscurantist verse, dominant by the end of the 1950's, gained momentum in the 1960's. Even Anday and Rifat started writing in the same vein. Turgut Uyar (b. 1926), Ece Ayhan (b. 1931), and Ülkü Tamer (b. 1937) expanded the scope of neosurrealistic techniques.

Upholding the tradition of social *engagement*, some leading poets wrote denunciations of social ills. They included Ceyhun Atuf Kansu (b. 1919), Necati Cumalı (b. 1921), Ömer Faruk Toprak (b. 1920), Halim Yağcıoğlu (b. 1919), Hasan Hüseyin (b. 1927), Talip Apaydın (b. 1926), and Mehmet Başaran (b. 1926).

A major independent poet who probes the subtleties of reality is a highly accomplished craftsman named Behçet Necatigil (b. 1916). In the late 1960's Attilâ İlhan (b. 1925)—who has gone through neoromantic and obscurantist phases—started a synthesis of various traditional modes and molds, including classical and early 20th-c. features. Özdemir Asaf (b. 1923) is notable for his aphoristic poems.

The leading poet of Turkey in the post-World War II period is Fazıl Hüsnü Dağlarca (b. 1914). His work represents many of the trends and accomplishments of modern poetry. He has produced a vast body of verse ranging from simple love lyrics to long epics, from metaphysical speculations to angry attacks on social problems, from the harsh realities of the Anatolian countryside to the war in Vietnam. In form and substance, he has been a major force and influence on contemporary Turkish poetry. (Dağlarca's principal poems appear in a bilingual volume entitled *Fazıl Hüsnü Dağlarca: Selected Poems, 1969.*)

Fiction

Classical Turkish literature produced long narrative poems and romances about historical, religious, and secular topics. At the same time, the folk tradition gave rise to legends, popular stories, and public narrations by the *meddah* (storyteller). The advent of fiction (in the European sense) dates from the second half of the 19th c., when translations from Fenelon, Hugo, Defoe, Chateaubriand, Voltaire, Lamartine, and Dumas stirred interest in the genre. The first native work of fiction was published in 1870 by Ahmet Mithat Efendi (1844–1912). Following the trends in French fiction, Turkish novelists went through phases of romanticism, realism, and naturalism (q.v.).

Prominent among the 19th-c. novels were *İntibah* (1876), a sentimental work about love and crime, and *Cezmi* (1880), about a 16th-c. heroic episode. Both were written by Namık Kemal (1840–88). Other important novels include: *Sergüzeşt* (1889) by Sami Paşazade Sezai (1860–1936); *Araba Sevdası* (1889), a satire on aristocrats caught in the East-West conflict, by Recaizade Ekrem; and *Kara Bibik* (1890) a novella of rural Turkey by Nabizade Nâzım (1862–93), who was influenced by Zola and Daudet (qq.v.).

Several titles can be named for the best-written novels of the 19th and early 20th c.'s. *Mai ve Siyah* (1897) is a romantic depiction of a young writer beset by frustrations. *Aşk-ı Memnu* (1900) is a colorful account of the life of wealthy Istanbul families. *Kırık Hayatlar* (1924) is a realistic depiction of suffering people. All three titles were written by Halit

Ziya Uşaklıgil (1866–1945). Among the earliest best sellers were *Eylül* (1900) by Mehmet Rauf (1875–1931) and *Zavallı Necdet* (1902) by Saffet Nezihî (1871–1939). Both were sentimental novels about star-crossed lovers who perish together.

Realism produced some of its best specimens in the works of Hüseyin Rahmi Gürpınar (1864–1944) and Ahmet Rasim (1864–1932), authors of humorous fiction about life in Istanbul. Another realist, Ebubekir Hâzım Tepeyran (1864–1947), wrote the first "village novel."

Spurred by the periodical *Genç Kalemler* (Young Pens), which started publication in 1911 in Salonika, the National Literature movement, stressed the use of the vernacular. This movement also emphasized the principle of "halka doğru" (going to the people) and the need to dwell on concrete reality and themes of social significance. In fiction, these views were utilized with success by Ömer Seyfettin (1844–1920). His novellas and short stories have become perennial favorites for their barbs aimed at human foibles and their social satire.

Among the leading novelists in the early decades of the century was Halide Edib Adıvar (1884–1964). She is the author of psychological novels, sagas of the Turkish War of Independence, and city scenes and characters. Her novelistic art culminated in *Sinekli Bakkal* (1936), which she had originally published in English under the title of *The Clown and His Daughter* (1935).

Yakup Kadri Karaosmanoğlu's (b. 1889) *Kiralık Konak* (1920) recounts the disintegration of an old family. His *Nur Baba* (1922) exposes the sybaritic life among the followers of an antiorthodox Islamic sect. *Hüküm Gecesi* (1927), by the same author, is based on actual events. It features many prominent political figures in the 1910's and offers a tense account of party strife.

Karaosmanoğlu's *Yaban* (1932) depicts the conflicts of the urban intellectual and the poverty-stricken peasant.

Reşat Nuri Güntekin (1889–1956) is the author of an all-time popular novel called *Çalıkuşu* (1922; The Autobiography of a Turkish Girl, 1949). It is a picaresque novel about a young schoolteacher. He also wrote *Yeşil Gece* (1928) on the ill effects of fanaticism on Turkish social progress, and *Miskinler Tekkesi* (1946), the story of a band of beggars.

Refik Halit Karay (1888–1965) depicted life in Anatolian towns and villages in carefully

435

constructed, simple stories, which he collected in several volumes. His most influential collection, *Memleket Hikâyeleri,* came out in 1919. The psychological novel found its champion in Peyami Safa (1899–1961), whose *Fatih-Harbiye* (1931) delineates the clash of Turkish traditional society and European influences. His *Matmazel Noraliya'nın Koltuğu* (1949) is a mosaic of psychopathological analyses.

Memduh Şevket Esendal (1883–1952) and Osman Cemal Kaygılı (1890–1945) wrote stories of common people in urban and rural areas. Sadri Ertem (1900–1943) recorded the plight of people beset by unemployment, displacement, and injustice in a novel entitled *Çıkrıklar Durunca* (1931).

An early master of "protest" fiction, Sabahattin Ali (1906–1948), depicted in several volumes of short stories—*Değirmen* (1935), *Kağnı* (1936), *Ses* (1937), *Yeni Dünya* (1943)—the tragic existence of the Anatolian man. In *Sırça Köşk* (1947), Sabahattin Ali offered scathing criticism of Turkish society.

His contemporary, Sait Faik Abasıyanık (1906–1954), published scores of short stories set in the city of Istanbul. Sait Faik's meditative, rambling, romantic fiction is full of intriguing insights into the human soul. It captures the pathos and the bathos of urban life in a style unique for its poetic flair. Abdülhak Şinasi Hisar (1888–1963) and Ahmet Hamdi Tanpınar (1901–1962) are masters of polished style. They produced some of the most impressive character studies in Turkish fiction.

Novels about the predicament of the Anatolian peasant who lives amid the deprivations of his village or who grapples with the mercilessness of the urban areas where he seeks employment evolved into the best achievement of Turkish prose. The leading figure of the genre is Yaşar Kemal (q.v.). He is the only Turkish novelist with an international reputation. His *İnce Memed* (1955; Memed, My Hawk, 1961) and *Orta Direk* (1960; The Wind from the Plain, 1962) blend forceful plots with a poetic diction in depicting the tragic life of the Turkish peasant.

Orhan Kemal (1914–70) is equally famous as a novelist and short-story writer. He captures the suffering of the *lumpenproletariat.* Among the major novelists who concentrate on the crass realities of Turkish villages and small towns are Samim Kocagöz (b. 1916), Talip Apaydın (b. 1926), Kemal Bilbaşar (b. 1910), and İlhan Tarus (1907–1967). Fakir Baykurt's

(b. 1929) *Yılanların Öcü* (1959) is a masterpiece of the village novel.

Halikarnas Balıkçısı (b. 1886) is a chronicler of the daily lives of the common people on the Aegean coast. Orhan Hançerlioğlu (b. 1916) and Oktay Akbal (b. 1923) are expert storytellers who portray city people in crisis. Kemal Tahir (b. 1910), a major writer of the village novel, published a long historical romance in 1967 about the emergence of the Ottoman state in the late 13th c.: *Devlet Ana.* As history and as fiction, it has caused more critical controversy than any other Turkish novel.

Satire and humor dominate the fiction of Haldun Taner (b. 1916) and Rıfat Ilgaz (b. 1911). The leading satirist of modern Turkey is Aziz Nesin (b. 1915), who lambastes the bourgeoisie and the bureaucracy. Nesin's stories have been translated into many languages.

Since the late 1950's a new generation of novelists, under the influence of Joyce, Faulkner (qq.v.), and the exponents of the French anti-novel movement, have been using the stream of consciousness techniques. The most successful practitioners of this type of fiction are Feyyaz Kayacan (b. 1919), Nezihe Meriç, Bilge Karasu (b. 1930), Sevim Burak, Demir Özlü (b. 1935), and Ferit Edgü (b. 1936).

Criticism and the Essay

Articles in newspapers and journals have played a significant role in the intellectual life of Turkey in the 20th c. At the turn of the century, Ahmet Şuayip (1876–1910) formulated the basic principles of literary modernization as conceived by the Wealth of Knowledge movement. Ziya Gökalp (1876–1924) expounded his social philosophy in several prose works. The most influential was *Türkçülüğün Esasları* (1923; The Foundations of Turkish Nationalism, 1950).

Fuat Köprülü (1890–1966) led a revival in the writing of Turkish literary history. Two leading poets—Ahmet Haşim (1884–1933) and Yahya Kemal Beyatlı (1884–1958)—were the early masters of the literary essay. Ruşen Eşref Ünaydın (1892–1959) and Yakup Kadri Karaosmanoğlu wrote prose poems. Hüseyin Cahit Yalçın (1874–1957) and Falih Rıfkı Atay (b. 1894) were journalists who gave lead editorials a literary dimension.

In the 1940's and later, an intellectual movement, which may be described as Turkish humanism, was expounded in the essays of Hasan Âli Yücel (1897–1961) and Orhan Burian (1914–53). Humanist views continued in the essays of Sabahattin Eyüboğlu (b. 1908), Vedat Günyol (b. 1912), and Melih Cevdet Anday (b. 1915). These three also incorporated the tenets of socialism into their writings.

The most influential literary critic in the 1940's and 1950's was Nurullah Ataç (1898–1957). His lucid critical evaluations helped the careers of the poetic realists and their successors. He also spurred the widespread use of "pure" Turkish, divested of Persian and Arabic borrowings.

In 1950 Mahmut Makal (b. 1933), a village teacher in his teens, published *Bizim Köy* (A Village in Anatolia, 1954). This was the first literary reportage on village life written by a peasant. It became a *cause célèbre* and accelerated the emergence of a large body of village literature.

Since the 1950's the influential essayists and literary critics have been Suut Kemal Yetkin (b. 1903), Yaşar Nabi Nayır (b. 1908), Mehmed Kaplan (b. 1915), Asım Bezirci (b. 1927), Memet Fuat (b. 1926), Nermi Uygur (b. 1925), and Cemal Süreya (b. 1931).

Drama

Traditional Turkish theater consisted of *Karagöz* (the shadow play), *Orta Oyunu* (Turkish *Commedia dell'arte*), village plays, and one-man *meddah* (storyteller) shows. European-style legitimate theater started in 1858. The first significant Turkish play, *Şair Evlenmesi*, was written in 1859 by İbrahim Şinasi (1826–71). Adaptations of Molière—particularly the ingenious versions by Ahmet Vefik Pasha (1823–91)—and the major works of Shakespeare, Goldoni, Dumas, Schiller, and others enjoyed popular success. Two Armenian producers, Güllü Agop (1840–1902) and Mardiros Mınakyan (1837–1920), staged most of the translations as well as many plays by the native playwrights.

In 1873 a patriotic play entitled *Vatan Yahut Silistre* by Namık Kemal (1840–88) prompted an antigovernment demonstration, whereupon the sultan exiled the famous poet-playwright. Dramatic writing in the following decades concerned itself mainly with historical and legendary themes, family melodramas, and light comedies. Abdülhak Hamit Tarhan (1852–1937) wrote historical tragedies in verse and prose. Among these, *Eşber* (1880) and

Finten (1916) were moderately successful attempts at tragedy in the grand manner. They show the influences of Corneille, Racine, and Shakespeare.

The final decades of the Ottoman Empire were marked by orientation and groping in dramatic writing and play production. Ali Haydar (1836–1914), Âlî Bey (1844–99), Tahsin Nahit (1887–1918), İzzet Melih Devrim (1887–1966), Ahmet Mithat Efendi (1844–1912), Recaizade Ekrem, and others wrote comedies and melodramas which helped popularize the theater.

In 1914 the city of Istanbul established a subsidized theater called "house of the arts" (*Darülbedayi*). The French director André Antoine acted as consultant. In its early years, this theater produced popular plays. They included *Baykuş* by Halit Fahri Ozansoy (b. 1891); *Kısmet Değilmiş* by İbnürrefik Ahmet Nuri (1874–1935); *Kâbus* by Halit Ziya Uşaklıgil (1866–1945); and *Hançer* and *Taş Parçası* by Reşat Nuri Güntekin (1889–1956).

Since the inauguration of the republic in 1923, theatrical activity has flourished in major cities. The audiences and the number of productions reached unprecedented magnitude in the 1960's. The City Theater of Istanbul, which stages as many as ten plays concurrently, has contributed to the upsurge since the 1920's. The so-called People's Houses, or community centers, spurred wide interest in the theater in the 1930's and 1940's. Since the late 1940's, Turkish theater has received new impetus from the state theater in Ankara and from the emergence of several dozens of private independent theaters. A major force in these developments was the pioneer actor-director-producer Muhsin Ertuğrul (b. 1892), who served as director-general of Istanbul's City Theater, Ankara's State Theater, and two independent theaters.

Turkish playwrighting has taken impressive strides since the 1920's. Among the most popular early plays were satires of Ottoman life and government by Musahipzade Celâl (1870–1959) and by İbnürrefik Ahmet Nuri. Also popular were melodramas by Mahmut Yesari (1895–1945) and Reşat Nuri Güntekin; and patriotic plays by Faruk Nafiz Çamlıbel (b. 1898).

Bir Adam Yaratmak by Necip Fazıl Kısakürek (b. 1905) was about a man's mental disintegration. It enjoyed a vogue in the 1930's when the avant-garde plays of Nâzım Hikmet Ran—*Kafatası* and *Unutulan Adam*—introduced thematic and technical innovations. Vedat Nedim Tör (b. 1897) and Ahmet Muhip Dranas (b. 1909) wrote psychological dramas. Ahmet Kutsi Tecer (1901–1966) dramatized the life of the legendary folk hero, Köroğlu, also delineated the daily joys and sorrows of the common people in Istanbul in *Köşebaşı* (1947; The Neighbourhood, 1964).

In the 1960's the spectrum of the themes and concerns of Turkish dramatic writing broadened. For the first time plays about the stark realities of village life reached the stage. Among the significant village plays were *Pusuda* and *Sultan Gelin* by Cahit Atay and *Nalınlar* and *Susuz Yaz* by Necati Cumalı (b. 1921). Others include *Pembe Kadın* by Hidayet Sayın; *İsyancılar* by Recep Bilginer (b. 1922); *Teneke* by Yaşar Kemal (q.v.); and *Kurban* by Güngör Dilmen (b. 1930).

Ottoman history inspired *Hürrem Sultan* by Orhan Asena (b. 1921) and the verse tragedy *Deli İbrahim* by A. Turan Oflazoğlu (b. 1932). Numerous plays drew upon non-Turkish history or mythology. Orhan Asena recast the Gilgamesh epic in *Tanrılar ve İnsanlar*. Other plays of this type include *Midas'ın Kulakları* (1965; The Ears of Midas, 1967) by Güngör Dilmen and *Büyük Jüstinyen* by Refik Erduran (b. 1928).

Many dramas and comedies of social criticism have attracted wide interest since the 1950's. The leading practitioners of this genre are Cevat Fehmi Başkut (b. 1905), Haldun Taner, Orhan Kemal, Nazım Kurşunlu (b. 1911), and Refik Erduran. Two major plays in the early 1960's reveal the influence of Brechtian drama: Haldun Taner's *Keşanlı Ali Destanı* and *Ayak Bacak Fabrikası* by Sermet Çağan (d. 1970).

Among plays with universal topics and settings are works by Aziz Nesin (b. 1915), Sabahattin Kudret Aksal (b. 1920), Oktay Rifat, Turgut Özakman (b. 1930), Yıldırım Keskin (b. 1932), and Güngör Dilmen. Melih Cevdet Anday is the leading playwright of the theater of the absurd.

BIBLIOGRAPHY: *Anthologie des écrivains turcs d'aujourd'hui* (1935); Saussey, E., *Prosateurs turcs contemporains* (1935); Yücel, H. A., *Ein Gesamtüberblick über die türkische Literatur* (1943); Spies, O., *Die türkische Prosaliteratur der Gegenwart* (1943); Patmore, D., *The Star and the Crescent* (1946); Arzık, N., *Anthologie des poètes turcs contemporains* (1953); Bombaci, A., *Storia della letteratura* *turca* (1956); Special Turkish issue, *The Literary Review*, IV (1960–61) ii; And, M., *A History of Theatre and Popular Entertainment in Turkey* (1963–64); Arzık, N., *Anthologie de la poésie turque* (1968); Halman, T. S., *Modern Turkish Poetry* (1971); "Turkish Literature in the 1960s," *The Literary Review*, 1971

TALAT SAIT HALMAN

TUTUOLA, Amos

Nigerian novelist, b. 1920, Abeokuta

T. had six years of formal education in mission schools, worked as a coppersmith and messenger, and is currently a stock clerk with the Nigerian Broadcasting Corporation in Ibadan.

In all his books he uses the same basic narrative pattern. A hero (or heroine) with supernatural powers or access to supernatural assistance sets out on a journey in quest of something important but suffers incredible hardships before successfully accomplishing his mission. He ventures into unearthly realms, performs arduous tasks, fights with fearsome monsters, endures cruel tortures, and narrowly escapes death. Sometimes he is accompanied by a relative or by loyal companions; sometimes he wanders alone. But he always survives his ordeals, attains his objective, and usually emerges from his nightmarish experiences a wiser, wealthier man. The cycle of his adventures—involving a Departure, Initiation, and Return—resembles that found in myths and folktales the world over.

T.'s first book, *The Palm-Wine Drinkard and His Dead Palm-Wine Tapster in the Dead's Town* (1952), which describes a hero's descent into an African underworld in search of a dead companion, was greatly influenced by Yoruba oral tradition and the Yoruba novels of D. O. Fagunwa. Written in a curiously expressive idiom that Dylan Thomas (q.v.) termed "naive English," this unusual story delighted European and American critics who tended to look upon its author as an extraordinarily imaginative native genius. However, it offended many educated Nigerian readers who recognized T.'s borrowings, disapproved of his bad grammar, and felt he was being lionized abroad by condescending racists.

T.'s reputation is now secure both at home and abroad, for he has come to be accepted as a unique phenomenon in world literature, a writer who bridges two narrative traditions and two cultures by translating oral art into literary art.

FURTHER WORKS: *My Life in the Bush of Ghosts* (1954); *Simbi and the Satyr of the Dark Jungle* (1955); *The Brave African Huntress* (1958); *Feather Woman of the Jungle* (1962); *Ajaiyi and His Inherited Poverty* (1967)

BIBLIOGRAPHY: Moore, G., *Seven African Writers* (1962), pp. 39–57; Obiechina, E. N., "A. T. and the Oral Tradition," *Présence Africaine*, No. 65 (1968), pp. 85–106; Collins, H. R., *A. T.* (1969); Anozie, S. O., "A. T.: littérature et folklore, ou le problème de la synthèse," *Cahiers d'Etudes Africaines*, No. 38 (1970), pp. 335–51; Lindfors, G., "A. T.: Debts and Assets," *Cahiers d'Etudes Africaines*, No. 38 (1970), pp. 306–34

BERNTH LINDFORS

TUWIM, Julian
Polish poet, b. 13 Sept. 1894, Łódź; d. 27 Dec. 1953, Zakopane

The son of a white-collar worker, T. studied law in Warsaw before turning to writing.

T.'s work can be divided into three phases. The first, from 1918 to 1930, is marked by his faith in the new Polish state, while social criticism is not yet much in evidence. Characteristic of the second phase, from 1930 to 1939, are two features: the growth of satirical elements and a more pronounced socially critical aggressiveness, notably in *Bal w operze* (1936). This book, which attacked the government, was temporarily confiscated. In the third phase, which coincides with his years of exile in France and America, he wrote his greatest work, the *Kwiaty polskie* (1948).

A lyrical epic poem of almost nine thousand lines, *Kwiaty polskie* is reminiscent in many ways of Pushkin's (1799–1837) *Evgeni Onegin* and Juliusz Słowacki's (1809–49) *Beniowski*. Ranging from the most intimate lyricism to satire and polemics, it incorporates almost all types of poetry. T. utilized satire and polemics both for political diatribes and for attacks on the Poles in exile. T.'s longing for his homeland is the keynote of the whole work.

After returning to Poland in 1946, T. wrote hardly any original poetry worthy of note. Instead he devoted himself to translations and to studies in Polish literature. His two transla-

tions of the Old Russian *Song of Igor, Słowo o wyprawie Igora* (1928 and 1950), deserve special mention.

T. was the most distinctive poet of the *Skamander* (*see* Polish literature) group, which he helped to found. His early work was influenced by Leopold Staff (1878–1957), but unlike Staff he managed to "democratize" his poetry and make it dynamic by his use of topical themes and by his stylization of colloquial speech. Technically he is indebted to some extent to futurism (q.v.).

FURTHER WORKS: *Czyhanie na Boga* (1918); *Wiosna w mieście* (1918); *Sokrates tańczący* (1920); *Siódma jesień* (1922); *Wierszy tom czwarty* (1923); *Słowa we krwi* (1926); *Treść gorejąca* (1926); *Rzecz czarnoleska* (1929); *Jarmark rymów* (1929); *Biblia cygańska* (1933); *Cztery wieki fraszki polskiej* (1935); *Polski słownik pijacki* (1935); *Lokomotywa* (1938); *Wybór pism* (New York, 1942); *Wybór poezji* (1948); *Dzieła* (6 vols., 1955–59); *Cicer cum caule czyli groch z kapustą* (2 vols., 1958–59). **Selected English translation:** *The Dancing Socrates, and Other Poems* (1968)

BIBLIOGRAPHY: Dembowski, P., "J. T.," in *Canadian Slavistic Papers* (Vol. I, 1958), pp. 17–24; Stradecki, J., *T. Bibliografia* (1959); Wróblewska, E., *J. T.* (1965)

HEINRICH KUNSTMANN

TWAIN, Mark
(pseud. of *Samuel Longhorne Clemens*), American novelist, short-story writer, and journalist, b. 30 Nov. 1835, Florida, Missouri; d. 21 April 1910, Redding, Connecticut

T.'s boyhood was spent largely in the Mississippi river town of Hannibal, Missouri. Although his father was an agnostic, his mother was a fervent Calvinist, and an echo of the religious training he received as a child can perhaps be heard in his later contempt for the "damned human race" and his seriocomic conviction that God had made man because he was "disappointed in the monkey."

Upon the death of his father, at the age of twelve T. left school and became a journeyman printer and later a Mississippi steamboat pilot. When the Civil War temporarily put a halt to river traffic, he served for a few weeks in the Confederate army, but though a born Southerner he had strong convictions against slavery and eventually fled to Nevada. There he took part as a miner in the feverish search for gold and eventually worked as a reporter on the Virginia City *Enterprise*. His talents as a writer were quickly recognized locally, and in his own words he was soon "one of the Comstock features it was proper to see, along with the Ophir and Gould and Curry mines." Later, T. worked as a reporter in San Francisco, where he met Bret Harte (1836–1902), who encouraged him as a writer of "tall tales" in a manner distinct to the American West. After planning to collaborate on a book of sketches, Harte and T. quarreled over a play they were working on together.

Though T. had begun publishing short pieces in eastern newspapers and even in the prestigious *Saturday Evening Post* as early as 1851, it was not until the humorist Artemus Ward (1834–67) urged him to submit "Jim Smiley and His Jumping Frog" to an eastern publisher that he gained something of a national reputation. T. began a lucrative and successful career as a humorous lecturer, and two years later his first important story was published as the title piece of *The Celebrated Jumping Frog of Calaveras County, and Other Sketches* (1867).

Called by William Dean Howells (1837–1920) one of T.'s "most stupendous inventions," the story relates how a cocksure and inveterate bettor gets his comeuppance when a stranger loads his prize jumping frog with buckshot. Rather than an "invention," it was in all likelihood a brilliantly retold version of one of the yarns dear to the western mining camps. "The humorous story is American," T. wrote in *How to Tell a Story* (1897), "the comic story is English, the witty story is French. The humorous story depends for its effect upon the *manner* of telling; the comic story and the witty story upon the matter."

In 1866, T. had traveled to Hawaii to report on the American sugar planters there. Now in 1867 he signed on as a passenger on the *Quaker City*, a ship that was to make a 19th-c. version of a luxury tour of Europe and the Holy Land. He financed his journey by writing travel letters for publication in the *Alta California*, but on his return to San Francisco he "squeezed some of the wind and water" out of his reports from abroad and published his first important book, *The Innocents Abroad* (1869).

His hilarious, often philistine account delighted American readers with its relentless debunking of the glories of European civilization that so intimidated the fledgling nation and dominated the perception of "the best society." As a "man from Missouri," T. was determined to respond only to what he *saw* rather than to what he had been told to expect. What he *saw* was a decayed culture and a civilization that struck him as petty and pretentious when compared with the generous and uncorrupted America he believed in. A miner loose in the Louvre, he "galloped" with hosts of tired and bored tourists through the galleries, defiantly preferring brightly painted copies to the old masters themselves. The stately monuments and the ancient ruins of Italy failed to impress him, and alongside the glories of the American landscape even Europe's mountains, rivers, and lakes seemed puny. The Holy Land, for which training and inclination had better prepared him, was understandably the high point of the journey.

T.'s pen name—derived from a Mississippi boatman's term meaning "two fathoms"—was now nationally known, and in spite of some eastern hesitation at his upstart western manners and views, his literary reputation was firmly established. In 1870 he married Olivia Langdon, the daughter of an Elmira, New York, businessman and four years later settled into a newly built mansion in Hartford, Connecticut.

The influence of his wife in "taming" the frontier journalist—and thereby weakening his fresh, satiric approach to American life—has been the subject of literary controversy ever since the publication of Van Wyck Brooks's *The Ordeal of M. T.* (1920), in which this influential American critic pointed up the stifling effects on T. of his new close contact with the proprieties of polite eastern society and the financial machinations on which it was based. T. would, however, seem to have been a divided soul from the very beginning. His impatient but consistent longing for "acceptance" had made him for a time docilely submit to a variety of mentors, beginning with Bret Harte. "There has always been somebody in authority over my manuscript and privileged to improve it," he complained to a publisher in 1900. But the privilege, Brooks noted in a later work, "had always emanated from M. T. himself."

T.'s ambivalence toward his talent, his goals, the "sivilization" that Huck Finn was to flee —having "been there before"—was to be reflected over the years in story after story that

MARK TWAIN

GEORG TRAKL

dealt with strangely bound twins, mistaken identity, and children switched in the cradle.

Roughing It (1872) presented episodes from T.'s westward trip during the 1860's to the Nevada gold mines, San Francisco, and eventually the Sandwich Islands. A treasure house of vanished frontier customs, sights, and slang—the story of "Buck Fanshawe's Funeral" is a prime example of the latter—it was followed by many books of travel including *A Tramp Abroad* (1880), *Following the Equator* (1897), and the posthumous *Europe and Elsewhere* (1923).

T.'s first attempt at a full-scale novel was *The Gilded Age* (1874), which was written in collaboration with Charles Dudley Warner (1873–1900). Howells, who considered the book a failure, was nevertheless so taken with the character of Colonel Sellers, whom he considered "*the* American character," that he later collaborated with T. on a play about the colonel. A southern gentleman whose fortunes declined after the Civil War, Colonel Sellers is never without a get-rich-quick plan. "I've got the biggest scheme on earth—and I'll take you in; I'll take in every friend I've got that's ever stood by me, for there's enough for all, and to spare." Though T. laughed at this cornpone, homegrown visionary, he was himself time and time again to be drawn into financially ruinous endeavors that kept him tied to the lecture platform in a determined effort to pay off the debts he thereby accumulated or that were accumulated in his name. Sellers was to appear again in *The American Claimant* (1887), one of T.'s least successful works.

The Adventures of Tom Sawyer (1876) was the first of the two immortal "boys'" novels on which T.'s reputation is founded. A fond and somewhat idealized recollection of his boyhood in Hannibal, the book gave T. an international reputation that was equal to that of the two leading novelists of the time: Rudyard Kipling (q.v.) and Charles Dickens (1812–70). It showed a boy often at odds with the pieties and falsehoods of the adult world, but Tom, like T., had already accepted in his heart many of the strictures that he seemed to be struggling against.

The book's success led T. to attempt two somewhat forced sequels—*Tom Sawyer Abroad* (1894) and *Tom Sawyer, Detective, and Other Stories* (1896)—but its true companion piece is *The Adventures of Huckleberry Finn* (1885). T.'s finest work, this book took him more than eight years to complete, often being set aside with seeming indifference to its fate or reluctance to finish it.

T. referred to it as "another boys' book," but it was entirely different in substance and nature from the charmingly inoffensive story of Tom Sawyer. In his account of Huck's attempts to help the slave Jim escape to a free state, T. casts an acid eye on accepted American morality. Though Tom was hardly the model boy of the sentimental novel, Huck is an outsider caught in the conflict between his felt sense of truth and the morality he has been taught to accept. Tom is essentially respectful of the falseness that will eventually turn him into a respectable adult mindlessly perpetuating the injustice and brutality around him; Huck finds within himself the courage to break with the morality he has been taught, to take his chances on eternal damnation rather than betray Jim. It was a decision that was to cause the book to be banned in many libraries as subversive to public morality.

Through the heart of *The Adventures of Huckleberry Finn* flows the majestic Mississippi on which floats the raft of Huck and Jim, each in his own way in search of freedom. As the life-giving river bears them on and Huck witnesses and participates in scenes that contrast sharply with the idyllic version in *The Adventures of Tom Sawyer*, the strength of his inborn convictions increases. (T. has noted that the waters of the Mississippi are so nutritious that a man who had drunk of them could grow corn in his belly if he were so inclined.)

T.'s attitude toward his career as a writer was ambivalent, and he as often as not saw it merely as a means to gain fame and financial security. In *Life on the Mississippi* (1883) he noted, however, that he had always loved being a pilot and that that profession was "far better than any I have followed since." This remarkable book, which captures the sights, sounds, and enthusiasms of ante-bellum steamboat life, began in 1875 as a series of magazine articles. It caught the essentials of T.'s frontier vision and was instrumental—along with T.'s two "boys' books"—in shifting the focus of American literary attention to the vast country stretching beyond the confines of New England and the Hudson River valley.

Travel and frequent residence abroad—some thirteen years, all in all—stimulated T.'s lively interest in history and resulted in the historical novels *The Prince and the Pauper* (1882)—like his later trenchant satire of the American scene, *The Tragedy of Pudd'nhead Wilson* (1894), it deals with mistaken identity—and *A Connecticut Yankee in King Arthur's Court* (1889). In both, T. holds up to ridicule the laws and customs of former times, seemingly accepting as all but ideal the "enlightened" civilization of his own day. In his attempts to reform medieval England, T.'s Connecticut Yankee, Hank Morgan, a hardheaded American mechanic and one of literature's earlier travelers in time, often echoes the materialistic standards that T. had satirized in *The Gilded Age*.

The "other" T. also makes his appearance in *Personal Recollections of Joan of Arc* (1896), a carefully researched panegyric in which T. freely indulges in all the Victorian sentimentalities he mocks in his major books. Aware perhaps of the work's lack of merit—he claimed, however, that he feared to disappoint readers who looked upon him only as a humorist—T. published it as an account written by Joan's page and "translated by Jean François Alden."

T.'s career reached its apogee in the 1870's and 1880's. In the 1890's, the elaborate financial structure that he had built up around his own publishing company and a number of inventions and speculations crumbled. He avoided bankruptcy only by a strenuous international lecture tour. The aging writer was further embittered by the death of his favorite daughter and of his wife.

These events unleashed his innate Calvinistic pessimism and its related preoccupation with determinism. The results were *The Man That Corrupted Hadleyburg* (1900), a corrosive attack on small-town greed, and the anonymously published *What Is Man?* (1906), in which he gives the somewhat adolescent philosophical basis for his rigidly mechanistic beliefs.

Born in the year Halley's Comet appeared in the skies, T. often mystically felt that he was perhaps a mysterious and supernatural visitor from another planet. His later mysticism and pessimism are combined in that unusual posthumously published story "The Mysterious Stranger" (1916). In it he successfully cast his philosophic beliefs in an historic tale set in medieval Austria. To a group of boys, who in some ways recreate the childhood T. knew and loved in Hannibal, Satan appears and eventually succeeds in convincing them that everything—himself as well—is nothing but "the

silly creation of an imagination that is not conscious of its freaks."

Honored during his lifetime in spite of his unevenness as a writer and thinker, T. succeeded in creating a body of work that has had a lasting influence on American literature. Critics have credited him with a signal achievement in capping the long tradition of southwestern humor and preserving it in books of timeless significance. For Hemingway (q.v.) *The Adventures of Huckleberry Finn* was the source of all modern American writing. Surely, by the re-creation of the frontier world T. knew as a child, by his juxtaposition of its anarchic ways with the relentless restrictions of civilization, T. pointed the way for many who were to follow.

FURTHER WORKS: *M. T.'s (Burlesque) Autobiography and First Romance* (1871); *Sketches, New and Old* (1875); *A True Story and the Recent Carnival of Crime* (1877); *Ah, Sin* (with Bret Harte; 1877); *Punch, Brothers, Punch!* (1878); *1601* (1880); *The Stolen White Elephant* (1882); *The American Claimant* (with William Dean Howells; 1887); *Merry Tales* (1892); *Writings* (1899–1910); *English as She Is Taught* (1900); *Edmund Burke on Croker and Tammany* (1901); *A Double Barrelled Detective Story* (1902); *My Debut as a Literary Person* (1903); *A Dog's Tale* (1904); *Extracts from Adam's Diary* (1904); *King Leopold's Soliloquy: A Defense of His Congo Rule* (1905); *Eve's Diary* (1906); *The $30,000 Bequest* (1906); *Christian Science* (1907); *A Horse's Tale* (1907); *Is Shakespeare Dead?* (1909); *Extracts from Captain Stormfield's Visit to Heaven* (1909); *Speeches* (1910); *Letters* (1917); *The Curious Republic of Gondour* (1919); *The Mysterious Stranger, and Other Stories* (1922); *Europe and Elsewhere* (1923); *Writings* (1923–25); *M. T.'s Autobiography* (2 vols., 1924); *Sketches of the Sixties* (with Bret Harte; 1926); *The Adventures of Thomas Jefferson Snodgrass* (1928); *Works* (1929); *M. T.'s Notebooks* (1935); *Slovenly Peter* (1935); *The Washoe Giant in San Francisco* (1938); *Letters from the Sandwich Islands* (1938); *Letters from Honolulu* (1939); *Travels with Mr. Brown* (1940); *M. T. in Eruption* (1940); *Letters to Will Bowen* (1941); *Republican Letters* (1941); *Letters in the Muscatine Journal* (1942); *Washington in 1868* (1943); *Business Man* (1946); *The Letters of Quintius Curtius Snodgrass* (1946); *M. T. in Three Moods* (1948); *M. T. to Mrs. Fairbanks*

(1949); *The Love Letters of M. T.* (1949); *Report from Paradise* (1952); *M. T.–Howells Letters* (1960); *Letters from the Earth* (1962); *The Adventures of Colonel Sellers by S. L. Clemens* (ed. C. Neider; 1966)

BIBLIOGRAPHY: Howells, W. D., *My M. T.* (1911); Paine, A. B., *M. T.: A Biography* (3 vols., 1912); Rourke, C., "Facing West from California's Shores," *American Humor* (1931); Johnson, M., *A Bibliography of the Works of M. T.* (1935); De Voto, B., *M. T. at Work* (1942); Ferguson, D., *M. T.: Man and Legend* (1943); Brooks, V. W., "M. T. in the West," *The Times of Melville and Whitman* (1947); Branch, E. M., *The Literary Apprenticeship of M. T.* (1950); Trilling, L., "Huckleberry Finn," *The Liberal Imagination* (1950); *An End to Innocence* (1952); Wecter, D., *Sam Clemens of Hannibal* (1952); Scott, A. L., ed., *M. T.: Selected Criticism* (1955); Blair, W., *M. T. and Huck Finn* (1960); Fiedler, L., *Love and Death in the American Novel* (1960); Solomon, R. B., *M. T. and the Image of History* (1961); Stone, A. E., Jr., *The Innocent Eye* (1961); Covici, P., Jr., *M. T.'s Humor* (1962); Kaplan, J., *Mr. Clemens and M. T.* (1966)

* * * *

TZARA, Tristan

(born *Sami Rosenstock*), French poet and essayist, b. 14 April 1896, Moinesti, Romania; d. 24 Dec. 1963, Paris

The son of middle-class Romanian parents, T., officially enrolled at the University of Zurich as of 1915, spent the greater part of World War I in Switzerland writing pacificistic appeals. Attracted to literature, but repelled by the bellicose attitude of the major writers of the wartime period, T., the artist Hans Arp (q.v.), and a handful of friends established what was to be the grandfather of all 20th-c. avant-garde movements: dadaism (q.v.).

In the periodical of the same name (July 1917–21, though in typical dadaist fashion the title sometimes varies), an international group of writers gathered around T. developed a doctrine sufficiently iconoclastic to make even the enterprising Apollinaire (q.v.) hesitate to be associated with it. However, Breton (q.v.), the future founder of surrealism (q.v.), was fascinated by T.'s 1918 Manifesto, and was delighted to join forces with him in Paris, where T. arrived penniless in January 1920. There T., the avant-garde painter Picabia, Breton,

and friends set themselves the task of renovating language, literature, and ultimately society. As early as T.'s *Première Aventure céleste de Monsieur Antipyrine* (1916) we have a poem with neither beginning nor end, a tale with no discernible intrigue, yet nonetheless— or perhaps because of that—as fascinating as it is scandalous.

T. believed that literature can be more than that which is seen through the traditional grid of plot, characters, and clever rhymes. For T. literature was a "happening," long before that word had been coined. He saw it as one of the many pretentious masks people wear. It is this conception of literature that he mocks in his *Sept Manifestes Dada* (1924; Seven Dada Manifestoes, 1951, in Robert Motherwell's dada anthology) and in his ground-breaking, mind-boggling poetry from *Vingt-cinq poèmes* (1918) through *L'Homme approximatif* (1931), *L'Antitête* (1933), and the anthology *De la coupe aux lèvres: choix de poèmes 1939–1961* (1961).

Among 20th-c. French poets T. is one of the two or three most gifted image makers and, with Prévert (q.v.), surely the most joyous to read. Though he joined the French Communist Party along with Aragon (q.v.) and others in the 1930's, he was never a doctrinaire ideologue. There was no significant shift in attitudes or style when he moved politically left: the *Deuxième Aventure céleste de M. Antipyrine* (1938) is no more a political tract than is the fanciful *Indicateur des chemins de coeur* (1928).

Tinguely's "self-destructing" machines; the ambivalent contexts of the films of Resnais, Godard, and Fellini; the deliberate pointlessness of the "new novel", the extravagance of William Burroughs (b. 1914); the visual play of *lettrisme* and concrete poetry—all these would be far less likely without T. And his influence has clearly not run its course. All the more pity he has been so little translated.

FURTHER WORKS: *Cinéma calendrier du coeur abstrait* (1920); *Le Coeur à gaz* (1922); *De nos oiseaux* (1923); *Mouchoir de nuages* (1924); *L'Arbre des voyageurs* (1930); "Memoirs of Dadaism," appendix in E. Wilson's *Axel's Castle* (1931); *Où boivent les loups* (1932); "Max Ernst and His Reversible Images" (1934); *Grains et issues* (1935); *La Main passe* (1935); *Sur le champ* (1935); *Ramures* (1936); *Vigies* (1937); *Midis gagnés* (1939); *Une Route seul soleil* (ca. 1944); *ça va* (ca. 1945); *Vingt-cinq-et-un poèmes* (1946); *Le Signe de vie* (1946); *Terre sur terre* (1946); *Entre-temps* (1947); *Morceaux choisis* (1947); *La Fuite* (1947); *Le Surréalisme et l'après-guerre* (1948); *Picasso et les chemins de la connaissance* (1948); *Phases* (1949); *Sans coup férir* (1949); *Parler seul* (1950); *Le Poids du monde* (1951); *De mémoire d'homme* (1951); *La Première Main* (1952); *La Face intérieure* (1953); *L'Égypte face à face* (1954); *Le Temps naissant* (1955); *Miennes* (1955); *La Bonne heure* (1955); *À haute flamme* (1955); *Le Fruit permis* (1956); *Frère bois* (1957); *La Rose et le chien, poème perpétuel* (designed and illustrated by Picasso, 1958); *Juste présent* (1961); *Propos sur Bracelli* (1963); *Lampisteries précédées de sept manifestes Dada* (1963); *Les Premiers Poèmes* (1965)

BIBLIOGRAPHY: *Bibliographie des œuvres de T. T. 1916–1950* (1951); Motherwell, R., *The Dada Painters and Poets: An Anthology* (1951); Hugnet, G., *L'Aventure Dada* (1957); Verkauf, W., Janco, M., and Bollinger, H., *Dada: Monograph of a Movement* (1957); Lacôte, R., and Haldas, G., *T. T.* (1960); Sanouillet, M., *Dada à Paris* (1965); Gershman, H. S., *The Surrealist Revolution in France* (1969); Caws, M. A., "T. T.," in *The Poetry of Dada and Surrealism* (1970)

HERBERT S. GERSHMAN

TZVETAYEVA, Marina Ivanovna

Russian poet and prose writer, b. 2 Sept. 1892, Moscow; d. 31 Aug. 1941, Yelabuga

Marina T.'s father was an art historian, philologist, and museum director. As a child she traveled abroad a great deal with her parents and attended school in Switzerland, Germany, and France. Considered something of a prodigy, she is said to have begun writing when she was six, and her first collection of verse, *Vechernii al'bom* (1910), was published when she was only eighteen. It attracted considerable attention and was followed two years later by *Volshebnyi fonar'*.

Basically unsympathetic to the Bolshevik Revolution, she left Russia in 1922 and thereafter lived in Berlin, Prague, and Paris. In 1939, the imminence of war and the pressures of poverty and homesickness led Marina T. and her husband—S. Efron, a former White Russian officer—to return to Russia. During the German invasion she was evacuated to Yelabuga, where, depressed by the arrest and death of her husband, the arrest of her daughter, and the death of her son, who was killed in action, she hanged herself.

Though distinctly modernist in tone, Marina T.'s poetry shows the influence of the German romantics—especially Goethe (1749–1842) and Novalis (1772–1801)—and Russian folk poetry. Her compressed lyrical style often led to charges that her diction was perfunctory and that she was stylistically careless. In retrospect these features are seen as the poetic devices of a mind extremely sensitive to the sensuousness of sound and the communicative power of strong rhythms. Able to assimilate in poetry even the harshest aspects of reality, she showed a fondness for abrupt colloquialisms often mingled with stately archaisms.

During the Stalinist period her poems were unavailable, but many of them were circulated in manuscript. Those of her works that were published during the "thaw" (*see* Russian literature) had a considerable influence on contemporary poets, and Pasternak (q.v.) considered her the greatest Russian poet of the 20th c.

FURTHER WORKS: *Iz dvukh knig* (1913); *Versty I* (1922); *Stikhi k Bloku* (1922); *Razluka* (1922); *Psikheya* (1922); *Tzar'-Devitza* (1922); *Molodetz* (1924); *Remeslo* (1923); *Posle Rossii* (1928); *Proza* (1953); *Lebedinyi stan* (1958)

BIBLIOGRAPHY: Pasternak, B., *An Essay in Autobiography* (1959), pp. 104–10; Slonim, M., *From Chekhov to the Revolution: Russian Literature, 1900–1917* (1962); Struve, G., "The Transition from Russian to Soviet Literature," in *Literature and Revolution in Soviet Russia, 1917–1962,* eds. M. Hayward and L. Labetz (1963), pp. 1–27; Karlinsky, S., *M. Cvetaeva: Her Life and Art* (1966)

* * * *

UKRAINIAN LITERATURE

The beginnings of Ukrainian literature date from the 11th c., when Kiev became the cultural center of all Russians. Although these early works were written in Church Slavonic (a language, the basis of which was a Bulgarian dialect, introduced among the Slavs by Saints Cyril and Methodius), they show a clear cultural and national distinctiveness.

A special place in Kievan literature is occupied by the *Tale of Igor's Campaign* (Slovo o polku Igoreve), an anonymous epic poem (1187) that describes the unhappy military expedition of Igor, the prince of Novgorod-Seversk, against a nomadic tribe of the steppes in 1185. Deeply rooted in contemporary oral literature, the poem is a work of genius. Full of poetic symbolism and striking imagery, complex in construction, this poem points to the existence of a rich secular folk literature of which very little has been preserved.

In addition, some splendid examples of oral literature in the vernacular survived into the 19th c. when they were first recorded. One example of such folk literature, this one dating from the 16th c., is the *Dumy,* the collection of Cossack lyric-epic songs. These anonymous folk poems deal with the fate of Cossack captives in Turkey, and with the life of the Cossacks in peace and in war. Some of them contain masterful descriptions of nature and subtle characterizations.

The 18th c. provided, somewhat unexpectedly, a stimulus for the creation of a literature in the Ukrainian vernacular. One of the humbler classical literary genres, the burlesque, lent itself to the use of popular speech, and it led, in the Ukraine, to the first

use of the Ukrainian language in a literary work. This task was magnificently carried out by Ivan Kotlyarevs'kyi (1769–1838), who, in 1798, published the first part of his travesty *Eneyida,* based on Osipov's burlesque of Virgil. This long poem, written in syllabo-tonic verse, marked the birth of modern Ukrainian literature.

Ukrainian romanticism began with the publication of collections of Ukrainian folk songs and ethnographic material in the 1820's. It reached its peak in the poetry of Taras Shevchenko (1814–61). Born a serf, he became the greatest poet of the Ukraine and the prophet of her national rebirth. His first collection of poems was *Kobzar* (1840; The Kobzar of Ukraine, 1922). Motivated by a deep love of his people and by a sense of the historical destiny of his country, Shevchenko was also preoccupied with the idea of universal justice and liberty. A late romantic, Marko Vovchok (1834–1907) combined an interest in ethnography with a realistic portrayal of peasant life.

Interest in social problems predominated in the age of realism at the end of the 19th c. Much of the Ukrainian writing of this period was published after a long delay because of the strict tzarist censorship and the so-called *ukaz* of Ems of 1876, which banned nearly all kinds of literature. Thus, for example, Anatol' Svydnytz'kyi's novel *Lyuboratzki,* written in 1862, was not published until 1898. The leading Ukrainian realists were Oleksander Konys'kyi (1836–1900), Ivan Nechui-Levytz'kyi (1838–1918), Panas Myrnyi (1849–1920), Ivan Franko (1856–1916), and Borys Hrinchenko (1863–1910).

Of special significance is the work of Ivan

Franko, a Galician whose many-sided talent made him the greatest figure in western-Ukrainian letters. In the Ukrainian drama and theater, Mykhailo Starytz'kyi (1840–1904), Marko Kropyvnytz'kyi (1840–1910), and Ivan Tobilevych (1845–1907) closely followed the romantic and ethnographic traditions. Of great importance to the development of Ukrainian literature in the second half of the 19th c. was the growth of literary criticism and social and political thought, as represented by Mykhailo Drahomanov (1841–95), Ivan Franko, and Panteleimon Kulish (1819–97).

The relaxation of censorship after 1905 and the development of new aesthetic ideas brought fresh stimulus to Ukrainian letters, leading to the period of modernism. The Ukrainian modernists, influenced by the western-European trends of symbolism (q.v.) and art for art's sake, reappraised two perennial subjects of Ukrainian literature: village life and the role of the intelligentsia. Without turning aside from these subjects they devoted all their attention to the search for a new form, often with great success.

The greatest short-story writer and novelist of this group was Mykhailo Kotzyubyns'kyi (1864–1913), the author of *Fata Morgana* (1904), *Intermezzo* (1908), and *Tini zabutykh predkiv* (1913). Vasyl' Stefanyk (1877–1936) was a great master of miniature studies of peasant life. Among other modernist prose writers were Ol'ha Kobylyans'ka (1865–1942), Les' Martovych (1871-1916), Marko Cheremshyna (1874–1927), Katrya Hrynevych (1875–1947), Hnat Khotkevych (1877–1942), Stepan Vasyl'chenko (1878–1932), and Volodymyr Vynnychenko (1880–1951).

The poets of this period, mostly members of the eastern-Ukrainian group Ukrayins'ka khata or of the western-Ukrainian Moloda Muza, were: Ahatanhel Kryms'kyi (1871–1942), Mykola Voronyi (1871–193?), Vasyl' Pachovs'kyi (1878–1942), Oleksander Oles' (1878–1944), and Bohdan Lepkyi (1872–1941). The latter also wrote historical novels. The most significant work in drama was by Lesya Ukrayinka (1871–1913), the author of *Vavylons'kyi polon* (1903; The Babylonian Captivity, in *Five Russian Plays,* 1916), *Kaminnyi hospodar* (1912), *Lisova pisnya* (1912), *Orhiya* (1913), and many other plays and dramatic poems.

In the early 1920's the process of "Europeanization," begun in Ukrainian literature long before the 1917 Revolution, appeared to be successfully nearing completion. Ukrainian writers no longer felt compelled to emphasize the national and folk aspects of their art in order to emancipate themselves from Russian political and cultural domination. This domination, however, soon reappeared as a factor in Ukrainian affairs. Indeed, the large measure of political and cultural independence granted to the Ukraine in 1919 after the downfall of the national republic was merely a temporary concession dictated by expediency rather than awarded on principle. Ukrainian literature and culture were encouraged solely as a means of strengthening socialist and communist ideology among the masses.

As soon as the bolsheviks realized that Ukrainian literature was becoming independent, they applied firm controls, branding it "nationalistic." After 1928, the problem of "nationalism" in Soviet Ukrainian literature became a major issue, which finally led to the complete subjection of this literature to the Communist Party. The development of literature from this point on must be viewed as a contest between the various literary groups and the party.

Apart from the symbolists (*see* symbolism), futurists (*see* futurism), neoclassicists, and the "fellow-traveler" group Lanka, none of which was in the least nationalistic, two other groups were prominent: Pluh, an organization of peasant writers, and VAPLITE, an organization of proletarian writers that can be classified as nationalistic-communistic. VAPLITE was led by the fiery and gifted writer Mykola Khvyl'ovyi (1893–1933), who openly expressed the feeling of many Ukrainian communists at that time. Impatient with the attitude of the Soviet government toward the development of Ukrainian culture, he claimed the right of the Ukrainian communists to govern their own affairs and called on his countrymen to turn away from Moscow. Although Khvyl'ovyi and VAPLITE were criticized by the government and subjected to severe castigation by Stalin (1926), Khvyl'ovyi continued to organize an effective resistance to party control.

In the Ukraine, the period of the first five-year plan (1928–32) was marked by the most violent purges of cultural and literary organizations. These purges resulted in a severe struggle between the regime, which was intent on achieving conformity and obedience at any price, and the Ukrainian writers and scholars, who forcefully resisted the dictates of the party.

In the 1930's the Soviet purge of Ukrainian writers claimed more than one hundred victims. Among them were Khvyl'ovyi, who shot himself in 1933, and many other writers of the first rank. Those who were not destroyed submitted to party controls The leading supporters of the party in the Ukrainian branch of the Writers' Union—those who had been instrumental in the antinationalistic purges—were themselves later removed in accordance with Stalin's policy of "purging the purgers."

Against this background of literary politics, Ukrainian literature showed great vitality in the 1920's. The early work of the poet of the Ukrainian revolution, Pavlo Tychyna (1891–1967), including *Sonyashni klyarnety* (1918) and *Pluh* (1919), provides the best example of complete emancipation of modern Ukrainian literature. This Ukrainian symbolist, writing about the revolution in the Ukraine as an event of universal, almost cosmic significance, succeeded in creating images of rhythmical beauty through the blending of folk song and poetry. Tychyna's early poems stand in sharp contrast to his later Stalinist panegyrics. Other symbolists were Dmytro Zahul (1890–1938), Yakiv Savchenko (1890–1937), Oleksa Slisarenko (1891–1934), and Mykola Tereshchenko (b. 1898).

A great contribution to Ukrainian poetry in the first decade after the revolution was made by the neoclassicists, including Mykhailo Drai-Khmara (1889–1938); Mykola Zerov (1891–1941); Pavlo Fylypovych (1891–1935?); Oswald Burghardt (1891–1947; he later wrote under the pseudonym of Yurii Klen); and Maksym Ryl's'kyi (1895–1964). The latter, generally regarded as the greatest of the neoclassicists, was an unsurpassed master of contemplative lyrics and a brilliant translator.

Zerov was the chief theorist of the neoclassicists. A distinguished literary critic and professor of literature, he published translations of Roman classical and French parnassian poets. Although he was a lesser talent than Ryl's'kyi, some of his poems, in particular his sonnets, are the most classically perfect ever written in Ukrainian. Zerov's aesthetic and literary beliefs are contained in his essays *Do dzherel* (1926).

The most prominent Ukrainian futurist was Mykhailo Semenko (1892–1939), whose poetry was highly experimental. Though his work shows strong socialist tendencies, Semenko was considered a nationalist and was exiled in the 1930's.

Several poets of the 1920's were not associated with any definite school. Among them were: Todos' Os'machka (1895–1962), whose poems show some expressionistic tendencies; the lyricist Yevhen Pluzhnyk (1898–1936); the intellectual Mykola Bazhan (b. 1904); and Oleksa Vlyz'ko (1908–1934). Among other prominent independent writers were the brilliant parodist Kost' Burevii (1888–1934) and the popular humorist Ostap Vyshnya (1889–1956).

The so-called proletarian writers—members of such organizations as Hart, VAPLITE, VUSPP, Prolitfront, Molodnyak—were in a group by themselves. The poems of Vasyl' Chumak (1900–1919), Vasyl' Ellan-Blakytnyi (1893–1925), and Volodymyr Sosyura (1898–1965), along with the prose of Khvyl'ovyi, Oles' Dosvitnii (1891–1934), and the plays of Mykola Kulish (1892–1942) and Yurii Yanovs'kyi (1902–1954), were the best products of this school. Kulish had an able associate in the producer and director of the Berezil' Theater, Les' Kurbas. The creator of modern Ukrainian theater, Kurbas also died in the purges. Several of Kulish's plays, although topical (*Narodnii Malakhii*, 1929; *Myna Mazailo*, 1929; *Patetychna sonata*, 1931), are masterpieces of modern Ukrainian drama. The arrest and deportation of Kulish was the single greatest loss to Soviet Ukrainian literature.

The Soviet Ukrainian novel showed little achievement. Among the nonproletarian prose writers, however, Valeriyan Pidmohyl'nyi (1901–1941), in the novel *Misto* (1928), gave a powerful portrayal of the contrast between the village and the city under the new regime, and Yurii Yanovs'kyi's *Chotyry shabli* (1929) is revolutionary romanticism at its best. Yurii Smolych (b. 1900) at one time showed signs of becoming a writer of good adventure stories. Andrii Holovko (b. 1897; *Maty*, 1931) and Petro Panch (b. 1891; *Holubi eshelony*, 1927) were also novelists of some note. A most original short-story writer, Hryhorii Kosynka (b. 1899), the author of *V zhytakh* (1926), was executed in 1934.

After the establishment of the Soviet Writers' Union in 1934, the only avenue left open to Soviet writers was that of the party-sponsored "socialist realism" (q.v.) school. A good exponent of this approach is playwright Oleksander Korniichuk (b. 1910), author of *Zahybel' eskadry* (1934), *Platon Krechet* (1936), *Bohdan Khmel'nytzkyi* (1939), *Front* (1943), and *Kryla* (1954; The Wings, 1959). *Maistry chasu* (1934; Masters of Time, in *Four Soviet Plays*, 1937) by Ivan Kocherha was a provocative work. Several novelists refashioned their works to suit the demands of socialist realism (Holovko's *Buryan,* Panch's *Obloha nochi*), while others glorified socialist constructivism (Mykytenko's *Ranok,* 1937). The period of the late 1930's unquestionably marks a sharp decline in artistic achievement.

During World War II writers were allowed and even encouraged to extol Ukrainian patriotism as a means of rallying the people in the struggle against the Germans, although such expressions of national sentiment inevitably had to be tempered by an acknowledgment of the "friendship of the Soviet peoples." The consequences of this brief national revival (1941–45) and of the temporary relaxation of controls were alarming to the party. In 1946 the party condemned the very literature it had encouraged a few years earlier. Ryl's'kyi, Yanovs'kyi (*Zhyva voda*), and Sosyura (*Lyubit' Ukrayinu*) had to admit their deviations in the direction of Ukrainian nationalism. The campaign against nationalism in literature, coupled with the violent denunciation of the West (Malyshko's *Za synim morem*) and the propagation of Soviet messianism (Honchar's *Praporonostzi*), continued until Stalin's death.

The so-called thaw in the 1950's led in the Ukraine to a partial rehabilitation of the works of some writers liquidated in the 1930's (Dosvitnii, Mykola Kulish, Mykytenko). Of considerable literary merit were the novels *Zacharovana Desna* (1954) by the well-known film producer Oleksander Dovzhenko (1894–1956), and *Dykyi med* (1962) by Leonid Pervomais'kyi (b. 1908), and the poetry written by the "young poets" Lina Kostenko (b. 1930), Ivan Drach (b. 1936), Vitalii Korotych (b. 1937), and Mykola Vinhranovs'kyi (1936). In the late 1960's, the best representatives of the most up-to-date brand of "socialist realism" were: Mykhailo Stel'makh (b. 1912), Andrii Malyshko (b. 1912), Platon Voron'ko (b. 1913) and Oles' Honchar (b. 1918). For a short time beginning in 1939, the western Ukraine was brought under Soviet control, and in 1944 it was incorporated into the Soviet Union. But from 1919 to 1939, the western Ukraine was part of Poland, and its literature therefore followed a different course from that in the Soviet Ukraine. Free from political and ideological control, western-Ukrainian literature exhibited a variety of tendencies and styles. On the other hand, Polish chauvinistic and reactionary policies in matters of Ukrainian culture often forced writers to seek refuge in nationalism.

A forum for extreme nationalism was provided by the magazine *Visnyk.* One of its contributors was the émigré poet Yevhen Malanyuk (b. 1897), whose fine poems offer a definite interpretation of Ukrainian history. Different, but equally skillful was the work of the lyric poet Bohdan Antonych (1909–1937).

Three other western-Ukrainian poets— Bohdan Kravtziv (b. 1904), Svyatoslav Hordyns'kyi (b. 1906), and Yurii Kosach (b. 1909)—deserve mention. Kosach also excels as a writer of short stories. The most prominent western-Ukrainian novelist was Ulas Samchuk (b. 1905), whose trilogy *Volyn'* (1932–37), dealing with peasant life in Volhynia, is by now a classic. Natalena Koroleva (b. 1888), Iryna Vil'de (b. 1907), and Halyna Zhurba were leading women novelists.

Between the two world wars two centers of Ukrainian life in Europe, outside the Ukraine, made important contributions to literature. One was in Prague (Yurii Darahan, Oleksa Stefanovych, Oksana Lyaturyns'ka, Oleh Ol'zhych, Leonid Mosendz, Olena Teliha). The other was in Warsaw (Natalya Livtz'ka-Kholodna, Yurii Lypa). As a result of World War II many Ukrainian writers, from both east and west, exiled themselves in western Europe, the United States, and Canada. Among them were Viktor Domontovych, Dokya Humenna (b. 1904), Ivan Bahryany (1907–1963), and Vasyl' Barka (b. 1908). A radical departure from traditional themes and styles may be seen in the works of the modernist group in New York (Bohdan Boichuk, Bohdan Rubchak, Yurii Tarnavs'kyi, Emma Andiyevs'ka, Yevhenya Vasyl'kivs'ka).

BIBLIOGRAPHY: Yefremov, S., *Istoriya ukrayins'koho pys'menstva* (1919–23); Manning, C., *Ukrainian Literature* (1944); *Istoriya ukrayins'koyi literatury* (1954–55); Luckyj, G., *Literary Politics in the Soviet Ukraine, 1917–34* (1956); Lavrinenko, I., *Rozstrilyane vidrodzhennya* (1959); "Literature," in *Ukraine: A Concise Encyclopaedia* (1963); Andrusyshen, C. H., and Kirkconnell, W., *The Ukrainian Poets, 1189–1962* (1963); Koshelivetz', I., *Suchasna literatura v URSR* (1964); Boichuk, B., and Rubchak, B., eds., *Koordynaty* (2 vols., 1969)

GEORGE LUCKYJ

MARINA TZVETAYEVA

MIGUEL DE UNAMUNO Y JUGO

UNAMUNO Y JUGO, Miguel de

Spanish philosopher, novelist, essayist, poet, and dramatist, b. 29 Sept. 1864, Bilbao; d. 31 Dec. 1936, Salamanca

In the essays that U. first published in 1895 in the journal *La España Moderna* and then collected in 1902 under the title *En torno al casticismo* there could already be detected that new spirit that later, with the Generation of '98, marked the beginning of a new interpretation of the Spanish spirit. By concentrating on "interior history" U. opposed the reformist ideas of the earlier *regeneracienismo* movement, which were predominantly politically and economically oriented. Though he had originally upheld the necessity of Spain's Europeanization, by 1906, in *Sobre la europeización,* he supported the counterdemand for the hispanization of Europe, opposing a concept of subjective moral truth to the dominant ideals of positive science.

Through his own longing for personal immortality U. came to regard the striving for eternal life as the basic problem of life and philosophy; he hoped that his work would keep him alive in the memory of others.

U.'s work and personality were marked by the deeply felt conflict between religious and rational thought. As a professor and later as rector of the University of Salamanca, his constant critical opposition to all forms of dogmatism brought him into conflict with all the dominant parties and resulted in political persecution (he was exiled from 1924 to 1930 during the dictatorship of Primo de Rivera) and condemnation by the Church.

Every literary form U. used—essay, newspaper article, novella, novel, drama, and poetry—became a vehicle for his transcendental interpretation of life. Even the historical novel *Paz en la guerra* (1897), the story of the bombardment of Bilbao in 1874 during the last Carlist war, in which U. served, fits this interpretation. The description of the daily life of the city disrupted by war reveals the immutability of "interior history" in the face of historical events.

U.'s next novel, *Amor y pedagogía* (1902), a somewhat contrived satire, focused on the impossibility of regulating life according to scientific rationalism.

Both *Vida de Don Quijote y Sancho* (1905; The Life of Don Quixote and Sancho, 1927) and *Del sentimiento trágico de la vida en los hombres y en los pueblos* (1913; The Tragic Sense of Life, 1921) showed the common source of U.'s basic criticism and themes. The interpretation of Quixote as a messianic champion of faith against reason contained within it U.'s criticism of contemporary tendencies and his fervid religious longing for a solution to the antithesis between faith and science. From this longing springs U.'s "tragic sense of life," which underlies the humor of Cervantes's epic novel. As U. saw it, because man's innate desire for immortality finds no rational confirmation, and because reason is incapable of designating man's ultimate goal, the intellectual and emotional needs of every "man of flesh and blood" are locked in tragic conflict.

Though he rejected dogmatic theology, U. accepted popular Spanish Catholicism because he felt it contained this irrational belief in immortality. Through his own painful experience of the "tragic conflict" he eventually arrived at the concept of compassionate love.

These major essays and many minor ones bear witness to a personal spiritual struggle—a struggle fired by politics, by his reading, and by his visionary response to the Spanish landscape, especially that of Castile. His many-faceted, first-hand knowledge of the literature and philosophy of classical antiquity, England, Denmark (Kierkegaard [1813–55]), and Germany (Nietzsche [q.v.]), as well as that of Italy (Pirandello [q.v.]), France, and Portugal, served to reinforce his opinions and beliefs and resulted in extremely personal literary criticism.

U. had been writing poetry ever since his first collection, *Poesías,* was published in 1907. It forms a significant addition to his work, both because of its range and—despite the frequent criticism that it lacks musicality—its literary qualities. In it he was able to express with complete directness a spirit inspired by both religious longings, *i.e., El Cristo de Velázquez* (1920; The Christ of Velasquez, 1951), and human love, *i.e., Teresa* (1923) and *Rimas de dentro* (1923). That same spirit was equally capable of both evoking in suggestive images the Spanish landscape that inspired its emotions, *i.e., Andanzas y visiones españolas* (1922), and of working itself up into a fury of political satire.

Because of their extreme concentration on fundamental human problems, *Sombras de sueño* (1930), *El otro* (1932), *El hermano Juan o el mundo es teatro* (1934), and other plays gain in intellectual tension, but because of

449

U.'s failure to translate these problems into vivid action, dramatic interest is sacrificed.

From a literary point of view U.'s most successful works are his novels. Their lack of realistically described settings or characters— for example, in *Niebla* (1914; Mist, 1929)— was a complete departure from conventional novel techniques. U.'s manipulation of his protagonists demonstrates his belief in the ambiguous nature of human personality and existence. Life is seen as a dream—and a desire for perpetuation.

U.'s attempt in *Abel Sánchez, Una historia de pasión* (1917; Abel Sanchez, 1947) and *Tres novelas ejemplares y un prólogo* (1920; Three Exemplary Novels: The Marquis of Lumbria, Two Mothers, Nothing Less Than a Man, 1956) to unlock the secret of personality leads to a psychological analysis of the dominating passions. But the characters remain isolated within the circle described around them by the problems U. depicts. The same holds true of *La tía Tula* (1921) and *San Manuel bueno, mártir* (1931; Saint Manuel Bueno, Martyr, 1954), in which U. examines the social framework that determines men's lives.

U.'s profound but diffuse influence in Spain originates in the metaphysical unrest that radiates from his works and protects his philosophical individualism, political liberalism, and new concept of national consciousness.

FURTHER WORKS: *Paisajes* (1902); *De mi pais* (1903); *Por tierras de Portugal y España* (1911); *Rosario de sonetas líricos* (1911); *Contra esto y aquello* (1912); *El espejo de la muerte* (1913); *Ensayos* (1916–18); *Dos madres* (1920); *Raquel* (1921); *Fedra* (1921); *La agonía del Cristianismo* (1925; The Agony of Christianity, 1928); *Todo un hombre* (1926); *¿Como se hace una novela?* (1927); *Romancero del destierro* (1928); *Ensayos completos* (1941, 1943); *Obras completas* (8 vols., 1951 f.); *Cancionero* (1953); *Cartas a Pedro Jiménez Ilundain* (1955); *Cincuenta poesías inéditas* (1958); *Teatro completo* (1959). **Selected English translations:** *Essays and Soliloquies* (1925); *M. de U.: Selections* (1939); *Perplexities and Paradoxes* (1945); *M. de U.: Poems* (1952); *Selected Works* (3 vols., 1967)

BIBLIOGRAPHY: Ferrater Mora, J., *U.* (1944); Curtius, E. R., *Kritische Essays zur europäische Literatur* (1950); Marías, J., *M. de U.* (1953); Alberès, R. M., *U.* (1957); Ortega y Gasset, J., *Monodiálogos de don M. de U.* (1958); Sánchez Barbudo, A. *Estudios sobre U. y Machado* (1959); Rudd, M., *The Lone Heretic: A Biography of M. de U.* (1963); Valdés, M., *Death in the Literature of U.* (1964); Young, H. T., *The Victorious Expression: . . . U., Machado, Jiménez, Lorca* (1964); Bleiberg, G., and Fox, E. I., *Spanish Thought and Letters in the Twentieth Century* (1966); Barcía, J., and Zeitlin, M., eds., *U.: Creator and Creation* (1967); Basdekis, D., *U. and Spanish Literature* (1967); Boudreau, C. W., "Dialectical Elements in the Ontology of U.'s Fiction and Drama," *DA*, XXVIII (1967), 1812A; Ruiz, M. E., "An Inquiry into the Metaphysical Process of M. de U., *DA*, XVIII (1967–68), 4645A–46A

HORST BAADER

UNDER, Marie
Estonian poet, b. 15 March 1883, Tallinn

The daughter of a schoolteacher, Marie U. studied modern European languages in her youth. Until she was over thirty, she published little, and absorbed in herself, she avoided taking part in public affairs. Originally a dominant force among the highly individualistic poets known as the Siuru group, in later years she turned from romantic self-concentration to a sympathetic concern for the plight of her people. In 1944, when Estonia was reabsorbed into the Soviet sphere, she fled to Sweden.

Marie U. made her literary debut with *Sonetid* (1917), a collection of graceful and naïvely erotic love sonnets that surprised the critics by their vitality and their mature command of form. *Verivaila* (1921) and *Pärisosa* (1923), however, revealed a new expressionist (*see* expressionism) orientation in which she broke with her previously conventional poetics. Their vehemence and gloom reflected a state of mind that brought on a long serious illness. By the time she published *Hääl varjust* (1927) and *Rõõm ühest ilusast päevast* (1928), Marie U. had developed a highly personal medium for expressing her inner conflicts, which seem to have found a philosophical resolution in *Kivi südamelt* (1935). In the intervening years she had published *Õnnevarjutus* (1929), a collection of ballads.

The upheavals of World War II forced Marie U. to turn her attention to the sufferings endured by the Estonians. In *Mureliku suuga* (1942) and in the later books written in exile—

Sädemed tuhcs (1954) and *Ääremail* (1963)—she voiced her fierce indignation and became their spokesman.

Responsible for having translated into Estonian works by such major 20th-c. poets as Rilke, Pasternak, and Hcfmannsthal (qq.v.), Marie U. emerged in her own right as the leading Estonian poet of the interwar years.

FURTHER WORKS: *Eelõitseng* (1918); *Lageda taeva all* (1930); *Ja liha sai sõnaks* (1936); *Kogutud teosed* (3 vols., 1940); *Sõnasild* (1945); *Valitud uuuletused* (1958); *Kogutud luuletused* (1958). **Selected English translation:** *Child of Man* (1955)

BIBLIOGRAPHY: H. Visnapuu, "M. U. luuletajana," *Looming* (1928); Stock, H., Introduction to German translation of M. U., *Stimme aus dem Schatten* (1949); Matthews, W. K., Introduction to *Child of Man* (1955); Oras, A., *M. U.* (1963)

* * * *

UNDSET, Sigrid

Norwegian novelist, b. 20 May 1882, Kalundborg, Denmark; d. 10 June 1949, Lillehammer

The daughter of archaeologist Ingvald Undset (1853–93), Sigrid U. at an early age developed a love for Norwegian history, especially that of the Middle Ages. The death of her father forced her to earn her living as a clerk, but the commercial success of her first novel, *Fru Marta Oulie* (1907), the story of a contemporary Oslo marriage, enabled her to devote herself to writing.

Viga Ljot og Vigdis (1909; Gunnar's Daughter, 1936) was Sigrid U.'s first attempt at a medieval subject. It was strongly influenced by the Icelandic family sagas. In *Jenny* (1911; Eng., 1939), the novel that established her literary reputation, she returned to contemporary themes with the story of a young woman's spiritual search and her disastrous romance with an older man. Daring in its day, the novel's treatment of its heroine's erotic life would now be considered simply "sensitive." To some extent it reflects Sigrid U.'s romance with the painter A. C. Svarstad, whom she married in 1912 and divorced in 1925, the same year in which she converted to Catholicism.

Vaaren (1914), *Fru Hjelde* (1917; Images in a Mirror, 1938), *Fru Waage* (1917), the novella collection *Splinten av troldspeilet* (1917), *De kloke jomfruer* (1918), and *Varskyer* (1918) all show increasing concern with the question of woman's role in marriage and in the complex contemporary world.

In the years following World War I, Sigrid U.'s historical and religious interests made her turn again to the Catholic Middle Ages in Norway. Between 1920 and 1922 she published the novels that make up her trilogy *Kristin Lavransdatter,* probably the single most important work of historical fiction in all Norwegian literature. The action of the story spans some fifty years, the first volume, *Kransen* (The Bridal Wreath, 1923), telling of Kristin's girlhood, the next, *Husfrue* (Mistress of Husaby, 1925), describing her life as a married woman, and the final volume, *Korset* (The Cross, 1927), relating her struggle through to the realization that "one must seek God rather than men." Though Kristin marries and bears eight sons, her basic longing and desire is directed toward submissive, disinterested service of God. The trilogy's sustaining motif is the contrast between Kristin's rich, passionate, and earthly life and the solitude of her longing and final novitiate.

Kristin Lavransdatter established Sigrid U. as a writer of international importance. In 1922 she was voted a writer's pension by the Norwegian legislature. *Olav Audunssøn i Hestvikken* (1925) and its sequel, *Olav Audunssøn og hans børn* (1927; published in one volume as The Master of Hestvikken, 1934), further enhanced her reputation and won her the Nobel Prize for Literature in 1928. Like her great trilogy it was set in medieval Catholic Norway, this time during the period of the Black Death. In line with Sigrid U.'s increased involvement in Catholicism, it is a probing description of the anguish and remorse that pursue Olav after he secretly murders his beloved's seducer. Like all Sigrid U.'s novels, it is cast in realistic form. Nevertheless, it can also be read as a symbolic account of man's struggle to escape the domination by God. This combination of realism and symbolism is in many ways reminiscent of Ibsen's (q.v.) *The Master Builder* and *When We Dead Awaken*.

After these major historical works, Sigrid U. returned to contemporary themes, but her creativity had passed its peak. *Gymnadenia* (1929; The Wild Orchid, 1931), *Den braendende busk* (1930; The Burning Bush, 1932), *Ida Elisabeth* (1932; Eng., 1933), and *Den trofaste hustru* (1936; The Faithful Wife, 1937) describe contemporary life in Norway from the viewpoint of a practicing Catholic. *Madame Dorothea* (1929; Eng., 1940) is set in 18th-c.

Norway. During these years, one of Sigrid U.'s most successful books was *Elleve aar* (1934; The Longest Year, 1937), a largely autobiographical description of children's life.

Early in the 1930's Sigrid U. had taken a strong stand against communism and Nazism. After the German occupation of Norway in 1940, she was forced to flee to Sweden and then to the United States, where she worked tirelessly on behalf of her occupied homeland. Two of her books first appeared in English during this period of exile—*Return to the Future* (1942; Atter mod fremtiden, 1943) and *Happy Days in Norway* (1943; Lykkelige dager i Norge, 1943). After the liberation of Norway, she returned home. Her last days were spent working on her posthumously published *Caterina av Siena* (1951; Catherine of Sienna, 1954).

FURTHER WORKS: *Den lykkelige alder* (1908); *Ungdom* (1910); *Fattige skjæbner* (1912); *Fortællinger om Kong Artur* (1915); *Tre søstre* (1917); *Hellig Olav* (1918); *Et kvindesynspunkt* (1919); *Katolsk Propaganda* (1927); *Tre sagaer om Islaendinger* (1927); *Osten fra solen og vestern fra maana* (1930); *Den hellige Angela Merici* (1933); *Etapper: ny række* (1933; Stages on the Road, 1934); *Norske helgener* (1937); *Selvportretter og landskapsbilleder* (1938; Men, Women and Places, 1939); *Samlede romaner fra nutiden* (10 vols., 1949); *Middelalder-Romaner* (10 vols., 1949); *Artikler og taler fra krigstiden* (1952). **Selected English translations:** *Saga of Saints* (1934); *True and Untrue, and Other Norse Tales* (1945); *Four Stories: Selma Brøder, Thjodolf, Miss Smith-Tellefsen, Simonson* (1959)

BIBLIOGRAPHY: Bing, J., *S. U.* (1924); Flaskamp, C., *S. U.* (1934); Jaspers, K., *Die Antwort an S. U.* (1947); Winsnes, A. H., *S. U.* (1949); Baldus, A., *S. U.* (1951); Brady, C. A., "An Appendix to the Sigridssaga," *Thought*, XL (1965), 73–130; Deschamps, N., *S. U. ou la morale de la passion* (1966); Dunn, M. M., "*The Master of Hestvikken*: A New Reading," *SS*, XXXVIII (1966), 281–94, and continued in XL (1968), 210–24

NIELS C. BRØGGER

UNGARETTI, Giuseppe

Italian poet, b. 10 Feb. 1888, Alexandria, Egypt; d. 1 June 1970, Milan

The son of Italian settlers who had emigrated to Egypt from Lucca, in Tuscany, U. spent the first twenty-four years of his life in Alexandria. This crucial, formative period not at all surprisingly had a great impact on the development of his poetry. One of the constantly recurring themes in his work—the desert—is in fact the result of his direct contact with the Sahara.

For U., the desert means distance, light, freedom, sensuousness, the piercing melancholy of Bedouin songs. Above all, it means dreams, mirages—the dreams and mirages of the nomad, who becomes for U. the symbol of the poet in his perennial wanderings in search of innocence, happiness, and love.

In 1912 U. left Egypt for Paris. He enrolled at the Sorbonne, studied under famed professors, such as Henri Bergson (1859–1941), and frequented some of the leading exponents of the literary and artistic avant-garde: Salmon, Jacob, Cendrars, and especially Apollinaire (qq.v.), Pablo Picasso, Georges Braque, and Fernand Léger.

U. remained in France until the outbreak of World War I, at which time he went to Italy and enlisted as an infantry private. It was out of that conflict that his first major poetry was born, although it would be inaccurate to label any of his lyrics "war poems." "In my poems there is no trace of hatred for the enemy, or for anyone," said U., "there is simply an acute awareness of the human condition, of the brotherhood of men in their suffering, and of the extreme precariousness of human life."

In the trenches, during lulls between battles, or at night in his tent, U. wrote what he was later to call his "diary" on scraps of paper that he would stuff into his pack. A literary-minded lieutenant, Ettore Serra, one day discovered them by accident and in 1916 published them at his own expense in an eighty-copy edition. The slender volume—U.'s first book of verse—was called *Il porto sepolto* and revolutionized Italian poetry. Most of the poems were short, the lines were not regular, there was no rhyme, no punctuation, and no attempt at the grandiloquence associated with D'Annunzio (q.v.); the general versification represented a complete break with tradition. Yet those lyrics had a freshness, an intensity, a regenerating strength that was and remains uncannily captivating and moving.

Il porto sepolto was incorporated into a larger collection of poems, *Allegria di naufragi* (1919). Echoing the celebrated last line of Giacomo Leopardi's (1798–1837) "L'infinito"—

SIGRID UNDSET

"E il naufragar m'è dolce in questo mare" ("And to shipwreck is sweet for me in this sea")—the title indicates, as later poems revealed, that U. was then already seeking to get back into the mainstream of Italian lyric tradition (Leopardi had been, with Stéphane Mallarmé [1842–98], the poet who had presided over his youth in Egypt), and that he was rediscovering for himself the meters of the old Italian masters, especially the hendecasyllabic line and the septenary. It was a new "season"—to use the word U. adopted for each progressive stage in his poetic development—that culminated in the publication of *Sentimento del tempo* (1933), the book of summer and sensuality, and, in its second part, of a tormenting religious crisis.

Beginning in the mid-1930's, U. worked on a book in which he intended to reflect the autumn of his life, "an autumn," he wrote, "which bids farewell to the last signs of earthly youth, the last carnal appetites." But the publication of this work, to be called *La terra promessa*, was delayed until 1950. Supervening tragic events—the death in 1939 of his nine-year-old son in Brazil, where U. had taken a post as professor of Italian literature, followed by the horrors of World War II—led instead to the publishing in 1947 of *Il dolore*, which includes some of U.'s most powerful poems.

During the last two decades of his life, U. published four additional volumes of collected verse: *Un grido e paesaggi* (1952), which includes "Monologhetto," a lyric chronicle of some of the most significant moments in his life, as well as new poems for Antonietto, his dead son; *Il taccuino del vechhio* (1960), a collection of poems in the metaphysical vein of *La terra promessa*; and *Morte delle stagioni* (1967), which many thought was his swan song. However, in 1968, when he was eighty, he published *Dialogo*, a love dialogue of dazzling verbal virtuosity and youthful confidence. In an interview shortly before his death, U. observed: "I believe that in the poems of old age the freshness and illusion of youth are gone; but I also believe that they encompass so much experience that if one succeeds in finding the right words, they represent the highest form of poetry one may leave."

In a real sense U. is to be considered the father of contemporary Italian poetry, a master who, by daring to explore anew the hidden meanings as well as the most secret potentialities of the Italian language, was the first to revitalize a lyric tradition that had threatened to become stagnant. Clearly, however, the significance of his work reaches beyond the confines of Italy. The impact of his poetry—his sparing use of words, his capacity to bring language to unusual heights of lyric tension, his power to create illuminating images—makes it rank among the most conspicuous literary achievements of the 20th c.

FURTHER WORKS: *L'allegria* (1942); *Poesie disperse* (1945); 40 *sonetti di Shakespeare* (1946); *Da Gongora e da Mallarmé* (1948); *Il povero nella città* (1949); *Fedra di Jean Racine* (1950); *Il deserto e dopo* (1961); *Visioni di William Blake* (1965); *Innocence et mémoire* (1969); *Vita d'un uomo: Tutte le poesie* (1969). **Selected English translation:** *Life of a Man* (1958)

BIBLIOGRAPHY: Cavalli, G., *U.* (1958); Rebay, L., *Le origini della poesia di G. U.* (1962); Portinari, F., *G. U.* (1967); Cambon, G., *G. U.* (1968); Special U. issue, *BA*, Autumn 1970

LUCIANO REBAY

UPDIKE, John Hoyer

American novelist, short-story writer, essayist, and poet, b. 18 March 1932, Shillington, Pennsylvania

U., the only child of a high-school teacher, grew up in the small, impoverished Pennsylvania Dutch community of Shillington. While attending Harvard, he became editor of the *Harvard Lampoon* for which he both wrote and drew. After graduating in 1954, U. spent the following year at the Ruskin School of Drawing and Fine Arts in Oxford. On his return home he became a staff member of *The New Yorker* for which he did stories, poems, and pieces for "The Talk of the Town" column. U.'s career as a writer has been exceptionally prolific and successful. For his third novel, *The Centaur* (1963), he received the National Book Award for Fiction and in the same year he was also elected to the National Institute of Arts and Letters. He now lives in the small New England town of Ipswich, Massachusetts.

U. has himself noted that a "submerged thread" of autobiography runs through most of his work. Shillington and Ipswich are the barely disguised Olinger and Tarbox of U.'s fiction and represent the extreme poles of his fluctuating interest.

Small towns in southeastern Pennsylvania supply the background for many of his short stories and for his first four novels, notably *The Centaur*. In this controversial book the Greek myth of the centaur Chiron, who died to liberate his son Prometheus, is used as a fictional device to enhance the significance of the relationship between George Caldwell, high-school teacher, and his son Peter. It aptly demonstrates U.'s merits as well as his weaknesses as a writer by offering passages with some of his most intensely realized experiences of childhood in juxtaposition with an overly clever display of verbal and structural ingenuity.

Both *Rabbit, Run* (1960) and *Of the Farm* (1965) can also be seen as based on reactions toward the haunting recollections of childhood. Whereas *The Centaur* is constructed around the figure of the father, *Of the Farm* is dominated by the overpowering image of a widowed mother. The latter's demands on her son—symbolically conveyed by her request that he return to the farm and mow the big field, just as his father did—threaten to disrupt his second marriage. The mother's eventual agreement to sell the farm and the son's acknowledgment of it as their common responsibility leaves unresolved the protagonist's basic dilemma of having to be both son and husband, his mother's and his wife's beloved.

Rabbit, Run, which shares with *The Centaur* the central image of flight and escape, is probably U.'s best performance novel. Once more the thematic focus is nostalgia for childhood and youth: Harry "Rabbit" Angstrom's happiest times were his high-school years when he was the county's best basketball player. As an adult saddled with a growing family, a sloppy wife, and a boring job, he cannot reconcile himself to being "second-best" and seeks comfort in a flight from a confrontation with the facts of his life. He flees maturity and responsibility, but he also tries to escape society's discouragement of those striving for the unusual, of those who have their own standards of excellence. Rabbit's consolation, that "there can be achievement even in defeat," neatly pinpoints the essence of U.'s ethical tenets as manifest in his work.

The romantic vision of childhood, the search for the true self through an evocation of the past, and the concern with basic human issues, are counterbalanced by U.'s "Tarbox" side, that of the sophisticated, elegant, urbane wit who expresses his interest in the trivia of life in adroit Joycean puns that testify to his capacity for observation and amused wonder. Both the people who inhabit Tarbox in *Couples* (1968) and many of the protagonists of his short stories—especially those of his first collection *The Same Door* (1959)—are the nervously worldly-wise of the urban middle class. Their struggle to overcome little daily embarrassments masks the much more fundamental danger that loss of convictions will strip their lives of meaning.

In his most recent book, *Bech: A Book* (1970), U. faces squarely this problem—that of a life stripped of meaning. By means of a group of short stories, U. presents Henry Bech, a Jewish writer in his mid-fifties who functions as a moderate celebrity though he is no longer able to write. Sympathetically, U. offers a moving, funny, sad portrait of a man without wife or child, without fulfilling work, without convictions that matter, one who has even lost his "real self," ironically looking at his terror and the *nada* of his life as he goes through the motions of surviving as best as he can. The "Bulgarian Poetess," which reveals convincingly the alienated man who can no longer act, no longer treat his emotions seriously, is a fully realized achievement of a remarkably talented short-story writer.

U.'s verse—although there is a marked increase of serious poems in *Midpoint* (1969)—falls into the same light-dark pattern as his fiction. Although much of it is trivial and overprecious, such unobtrusive little masterpieces as "Omega" or "A Wooden Darning Egg," from *The Carpentered Hen, and Other Tame Creatures* (1958), reveal in their exquisite and tender stylistic touches the artist's conviction that excellence in the smallest matters may be a standard of culture.

U. has been justly praised as the novelist and the poet who reveals the mythic dimension of people and things that is ordinarily hidden from us. His style and his objective yet sympathetic vision reveal many of the essential concerns of our time.

FURTHER WORKS: *The Poorhouse Fair* (1959); *The Magic Flute* (1962); *Pigeon Feathers* (1962); *Telephone Poles, and Other Poems* (1963); *The Ring* (1964); *Olinger Stories: A Selection* (1964); *A Child's Calendar* (1965); *Verse* (1965); *Assorted Prose* (1965); *Three Texts from Early Ipswich: A Pageant* (1968)

BIBLIOGRAPHY: Ward, J. A., "J. U.'s

Fiction," *Crit,* V (1962), 27–40; Hicks, G., "Generations of the Fifties: Malamud, Gold, and U.," in *The Creative Present,* ed. N. Balakian and C. Simmons (1963), pp. 213–38; Mizener, A., "The American Hero as High-School Boy: Peter Caldwell," in *The Sense of Life in the Modern Novel* (1964), pp. 247–66; Podhoretz, N., "A Dissent on U.," in *Doings and Undoings* (1964), pp. 251–57; Brenner, G., "*Rabbit, Run*: J. U.'s Criticism of the 'Return to Nature,'" *TCL,* XII (1966), 3–14; Galloway, D., "The Absurd Man as Saint," in *The Absurd Hero in American Fiction* (1966), pp. 21–50; Harper, H. M., "J. U.—The Intrinsic Problem of Human Existence," in *Desperate Faith: A Study of Bellow, Salinger, Mailer, Baldwin and U.* (1967), pp. 162–90; Taylor, C. C., *J. U.: A Bibliography* (1968); Samuels, C., *J. U.* (University of Minnesota Press Pamphlets; 1969); Hamilton, A. and K., *The Elements of J. U.* (1970)

BRIGITTE SCHEER-SCHAEZLER

USIGLI, Rodolfo

Mexican dramatist, essayist, critic, poet, and novelist, b. 17 Nov. 1905, Mexico City

Born into a family of Italian and Polish origin, U. made his first stage appearance at the age of twelve and has dedicated most of his life to the theater. In 1935 he received a grant from the Rockefeller Foundation to study dramatic composition at Yale University after which he returned to Mexico City and began the most productive period of his career. He has taught theatrical history and technique at the University of Mexico and held diplomatic posts in France, Lebanon, and Norway.

The bulk of U.'s theater can be divided into two broad categories, the first consisting of social or political satire and the second dealing primarily with abnormal psychological problems. *El gesticulador* (1943) and *Corona de sombra* (1943; Crown of Shadows, 1947) are generally considered his best works. The former, a deft portrayal of an impecunious history professor named César Rubio who assumes the identity of a deceased revolutionary hero in order to gain fortune and political power, rails against the betrayal of revolutionary ideals as well as the fraud prevalent on all levels of Mexican life.

Corona de sombra treats the attempt by Maximilian and Carlota to establish an empire in Mexico in the 1860's. An imaginative interpretation rather than an historical account of this well-known episode, the play depicts Maximilian as a necessary victim in the course of Mexico's struggle for liberty and her emergence as a truly sovereign nation. The initial action takes place in 1927 in the demented Carlota's bedroom on the day of her death, but dimensions are expanded by skillfully manipulated flashbacks evoking critical moments from the distant past.

U.'s two greatest box-office hits are *El niño y la niebla* (1950), an emotion-packed naturalistic tragedy of congenital insanity, and *Jano es una muchacha* (1952), which caused a scandal due to its candid treatment of prostitution and sexual hypocrisy.

U.'s realistic portayal of urban, middle-class mores and his caustic analysis of the national character have made him a controversial figure in intellectual and political circles alike. A master of dialogue, he is more convincing when he abandons psychopathology for social satire, particularly in his exploration of domestic problems and his exposure of false values espoused by the opportunistic *nouveaux riches*.

Although U.'s plots are usually tightly structured, they are occasionally marred by contrived situations. For example, in *El gesticulador* a youthful North American professor of Mexican history fortuitously appears at the door of César Rubio and announces his intention to research the life of a revolutionary figure with the same name as that of his host.

Greater success has been enjoyed by U. outside Mexico—several of his dramas have been translated and staged abroad—than by any other 20th-c. Mexican playwright. The author of two critical volumes on the Mexican theater and of one on dramatic theory, he admits to having been influenced by George Bernard Shaw (q.v.), whom he met in England during World War II and some of whose plays he has translated into Spanish along with works by, among others, Galsworthy, Rice, Schéhadé (qq.v.), and S. N. Behrman (b. 1893).

U. may well be remembered as the creator of the modern Mexican theater and as one of the outstanding Latin American dramatists of his day.

FURTHER WORKS: *El apóstol* (1931); *México en el teatro* (1932); *Caminos del teatro en México* (1933); *Conversación desesperada* (1938); *Medio tono* (1938); *La crítica de "La mujer no hace milagros"* (1940); *Itinerario del autor dramático* (1940); *La familia cena en casa* (1942); *Ensayo de un crimen* (1944); *Otra primavera* (1947); *La última puerta* (1948); *Vacaciones I* (1948); *La mujer no hace milagros* (1949); *Sueño de día* (1949); *Los fugitivos* (1951); *La función de despedida* (1951); *Aguas estancadas* (1952); *Vacaciones II* (1954); *Mientras amemos* (1956); *Una día de éstos* (1957); *Antonio Ruiz et l'art dangereux de la peinture* (1960); *La exposición* (1960); *Alcestes* (1963); *Estado de secreto* (1963); *Falso drama* (1963); *Noche de estío* (1963); *El presidente y el ideal* (1963); *Quatre chemins* (1963); *Teatro completo* (2 vols., 1963–66); *Corona de luz* (1965); *Anatomía del teatro* (1966); *Corona de fuego* (1966); *La diadema* (1966); *Dios, Batidillo y la mujer* (1966); *El encuentro* (1966); *Las madres* (1966); *Un navío cargado de . . .* (1966); *El testamento y el viudo* (1966)

BIBLIOGRAPHY: Howatt, C., "R. U.," *BA,* XXIV (1950), 127–30; Beck, V. F., "La fuerza motriz en la obra dramática de R. U.," *RI,* XVIII (1953), 369–83; Gates, E. J., "U. As Seen in His Prefaces and Epilogues," *Hispania,* XXXVII (1954), 432–37; Magaña Esquivel, A., *Breve historia del teatro mexicano* (1958), pp. 132–35; Ragle, G., "R. U. and His Mexican Scene," *Hispania,* XLVI (1963), 307–11; Solórzano, C., *El teatro latinoamericano en el siglo XX* (1964), pp. 132–35; Jones, W. K., *Behind Spanish American Footlights* (1966), pp. 502–04

GEORGE R. MCMURRAY

V

VAIČIULAITIS, Antanas
Lithuanian novelist, short-story writer, and critic, b. 23 June 1906, Vilkaviškis

V. studied Lithuanian and French literatures at the Lithuanian State University, Kaunas, before attending the University of Grenoble and the Sorbonne. After a number of years spent as a high-school teacher and university lecturer, in 1940 V. joined the staff of the Lithuanian embassy in Rome. Shortly afterward, he emigrated to the United States and later became associated with the Voice of America and the United States Information Agency.

A careful, unhurried artist, V. creates his artistic designs from the texture of day-to-day reality, but he is interested in nuances of human experience that often seem peripheral to the central concerns of most men. For example, in his stories people so identify with the human significance of things rendered obsolete by time that they prefer to follow them into oblivion, the sight of a yellow leaf falling in the autumn sunshine can be an emotionally overwhelming experience, and an illegitimate child personally accepts her mother's guilt and allows her own life to plunge toward tragedy.

V.'s one novel, *Valentina* (1936), depicts a woman's retreat from love into the arms of death. The story is told from the viewpoint of her lover, Antanas, who became a medium for the author's personal sad and gentle visions. Valentina's fragile inner world collapses under the pressure of exterior reality when she is forced to choose between a man she loves and a strong, vulgar man to whom she is morally indebted. Unable to decide, she drowns herself

in a lake during a summer storm. Since Antanas's love for her is essentially based on the ideal vision he has created, Valentina's death is the death of love itself to him, and the novel comes to an abrupt halt.

V. strives for symmetrical correspondence between emotional states and his characters' concrete environment; material reality therefore acquires a symbolic and prophetic significance. This is especially true of the world of nature—the principal medium through which V.'s protagonists become aware of the intensity and meaning of their personal emotions and relationships. In one of his best stories, the autumn floods create a tragic atmosphere in which a desperate love affair, in conflict with the established societal norms, ineluctably speeds to an unhappy end.

In V.'s writing, inanimate phenomena seem to acquire a life independent of natural laws. V. has experimented with genres that verge on fairy tales, even though nothing at all miraculous happens in these stories. He has also written true fairy tales, some of which are "prose fables," in which human passions are conveyed through animal protagonists, and legends of other times and places. He often expresses his moral and aesthetic concerns by using artists, saints, and philosophers as protagonists.

V. is one of the best Lithuanian prose stylists. Though in his work features of objective reality are made indeterminate by emotion, everything remains precise, and his tales retain a classical sense of proportion, order, and clarity.

FURTHER WORKS: *Vakaras sargo namely* (1932); *Vidudienis kaimo smuklėj* (1933; Noon at a Country Inn, 1965); *Mūsų mažoji sesuo* (1936); *Pelkių takas* (1939); *Kur bakūžė*

457

samanota (1947); *Pasakojimai* (1955); *Auksinė kurpelė* (1957); *Gluosnių daina* (1968)

BIBLIOGRAPHY: Šilbajoris, R. R., "A. V. —the Gentle Master of Design," in *Perfection of Exile: 14 Experimental Lithuanian Writers* (1970)

RIMVYDAS ŠILBAJORIS

VALA, Katri Wadenström

(pseud. of *Karin Alice Heikel*), Finnish poet, b. 11 Sept. 1901, Muonio; d. 28 May 1944, Eksjö, Sweden

Katri V. was the daughter of an official of the National Forest Services and spent her early childhood in various faraway places where her father was posted. After his death when she was eleven, the family had a difficult life in Porvoo, southern Finland. After graduation from a teachers' college, she worked as an elementary-school teacher, again at isolated country places.

Katri V.'s first poems are traditional. In 1922, however, she came in contact with a literary group in Helsinki, whose leading personality was Olavi Paavolainen. His influence on her work was not totally desirable, for he admired at that time a rather artificial and outmoded exoticism derived from the work of Loti (q.v.) and Anna-Elisabeth de Noailles (1876–1933) among others.

Kaukainen puutarha (1924) was well received. The free, unrhymed form of Katri V.'s poetry led some critics to speak of expressionism (q.v.), but she said herself that she could only have absorbed such an approach from the air because she knew little about contemporary poets before 1922.

In 1925 in Viipuri, she met the young poets who formed the group called Tulenkantajat. They published an anthology, *Hurmioituneet kasvot* (1925), the most typical product of the Tulenkantajat manner, which also contains Katri V.'s most exotic poems. The poems in *Sininen ovi* (1926) were in the same vein.

Paavolainen's influence can also be seen in Katri V.'s *Maan laiturilla* (1930). He had by then turned toward a romanticism of modern times; accordingly, cars, trains, and airplanes appear also in Katri V.'s poems, though not always with the best results.

Meanwhile Katri V. had married and was living with her husband in rather difficult conditions in a poor part of Helsinki, where she experienced and saw the sufferings produced by the Great Depression. Her brother Erkki Vala was publishing at that time a politically oriented and radically leftist periodical called *Tulenkantajat*. Through it and the periodical *Kirjallisuuslehti,* for which she worked, she came to adopt leftist views. They are reflected in the collection *Paluu* (1934), which prompted the founding of the literary group Kiila. The reviews, which described the collection as still more political than it was, did not make her life easier, for the official trend in Finnish literature was at that time conservative and aesthetic.

During World War II, the tuberculosis she had contracted in 1928 compelled Katri V. to move to Sweden, where she died in a sanatorium.

Katri V. was twice misrepresented in her life: first as a poet preoccupied with exotic motifs; and then as a purely political writer. Especially noticeable in her first works is her passionate although basically chaste worship of life, alternating at times with more quiet, dreamy, and melancholic moods, and enlivened by touches of humor. When, in the 1930's, she wrote essays on socialism, she was defending 19th-c. utopian theories, rather than 20th-c. Marxism. Her criticism of fascistic intolerance and brutality was expressed in poems about the fairy Si-si-dus who would not obey the ugly little men who told her to stop being friendly to everybody.

Fully aware of the tragic aspects of life, Katri V. wonders in a poem how she can bring a child into a world where bombs might start falling at any moment. She also writes of a tree with a burning nest on its branches and of the birds circling it, which sing but not lament a hard song of battle, and she expresses her belief in the ultimate victory of good over evil in images taken from the Book of Revelations. The range and variety of her style and motifs demonstrate that she expressed her feelings and convictions in a way that was her own.

FURTHER WORKS: *Pesäpuu palaa* (1942); *Henki ja aine eli yksinäisen naisen pölynimuri* (1945); *Kootut runot* (1945). **Selected English translations:** selections in *Voices from Finland* (ed. E. Tompuri; 1947); selections in *Singing Finland* (ed. K. V. Ollilainen; 1956)

BIBLIOGRAPHY: Enäjärvi, E., "Nuoren Voiman lyyrikoita," *Tulenkantajat,* No. 1 (1924), pp. 22–48; Ljungdell-Erlandsson, R., "K. V.," in *Ord och Bild* (1945), pp. 223–28; Viljanen, L., "K. V. och modernismens genom-

RODOLFO USIGLI

PAUL VALÉRY

brott i finsk lyrik," in *Nordisk Tidskrift* (1945), pp. 516–24; Paavolainen, O., ed., *K. V.—tulipatsas* (1946); Kupiainen, U., "K. V.," in *Suomalainen lyriikka Juhani Siljosta Kaarlo Sarkiaan* (1948)

JAAKKO A. AHOKAS

VALÉRY, Paul

French poet and essayist, b. 30 Oct. 1871, Sète; d. 20 July 1945, Paris

V., the author of "Le Cimetière marin," can rightly be considered the foremost French poet of the first half of the 20th c. and one of the most rigorous explorers of the mind's activity. Since he did not consider himself a writer but strove to reduce everything to its essence, his literary output—consisting mainly of poems, Socratic dialogues, essays, aphorisms, and poetic theory—was relatively limited.

Born in Sète, of an Italian mother and a Corsican father, V. had a sensibility impregnated with the images, atmosphere, light and sounds of a Mediterranean port, and this was reinforced by vacations spent in Genoa with his mother's family. He first attended the local Sète school overlooking the sea and, after his family moved to Montpellier in 1884, the *lycée* of that city, where he loathed the terroristic methods of his teachers.

Drawn to architecture, painting, and poetry, he spent most of his free time in the Bibliothèque Fabre studying the plates in Eugène Emmanuel Viollet-le-Duc's (1814–79) architectural *Dictionary* and Owen Jones's (1809–1874) *The Grammar of Ornament*. Not knowing "where to go" after he had obtained his *baccalauréat* in 1888, he entered law school at the University of Montpellier.

Until then, V. had mostly admired Théophile Gautier (1811–72), Charles Baudelaire (1821–67), and Victor Hugo (1802–1885), but during his military service at Montpellier (1889–90), he read Joris Karl Huysmans's (1848–1907) *A Rebours* and discovered the poets of decadence —particularly Paul Verlaine (1844–96) and Stéphane Mallarmé (1842–98). At the same time he was fascinated by the mechanics of military theory as well as by the laconic style of the *Army Regulations*. His interest in mathematics, physics, and music, especially that of Richard Wagner (1813–83), also dates from this time. The influence of Edgar Allan Poe's (1809–1849) literary doctrine, *i.e.*, the application of scientific principles to poetry, was para-

mount in his intellectual development, and he saw its realization in Mallarmé, whose work he considered the highest state of poetic perfection. By 1890 V. had already written a great number of poems, one of which had the characteristic line, "*Et je jouis sans fin de mon propre cerveau.*"

On the occasion of the University of Montpellier's 600th anniversary, V. met the young Parisian poet Pierre Louÿs (1875–1925), who oriented him toward personal contact with Mallarmé, Gide (q.v.), and other contemporary poets. Gide, who visited V. in Montpellier in December 1890, was to become his lifelong friend. Through these Parisian connections, V. soon began to have some of his poems published in avant-garde reviews, mainly in *La Conque,* founded by Louÿs.

As the result of a sentimental crisis one night in Genoa, 4–5 October 1892 ("*la nuit de Gênes*), V. resolved to renounce all "idols," including literature, which he judged "impure," and to devote himself with the utmost intellectual rigor to the elucidation of his own mind. He also decided to leave Montpellier for Paris, where he settled in March 1894. He regularly attended Mallarmé's famous "Tuesdays" (*les mardis de la rue de Rome*) and became his favorite disciple. From then on his intellectual quest is to be found mostly in his two prose works, *Introduction à la méthode de Léonard de Vinci* (1895 in *La Nouvelle Revue*; Introduction to the Method of Leonardo da Vinci, 1929) and *La Soirée avec Monsieur Teste* (1896 in *La Centaure*; An Evening with Monsieur Teste, 1925). He continued, however, to write poems occasionally until the death of Mallarmé in 1898—"a great intimate blow." He had also begun the daily practice of rising at dawn to take notes on the process of consciousness. The notebooks he compiled in this way over fifty-one years—meditations, observations, drawings, mathematical formulas, etc. —fill 257 *Cahiers*, which were posthumously published from 1957 to 1961.

In 1895 V. successfully competed for a post in the War Department, where he worked until 1900. In May 1900 he married Jeannie Gobillard, the niece of the impressionist painter Berthe Morisot (1841–95) and an intimate friend of Mallarmé's daughter Geneviève. That same year he became the private secretary of André Lebey, one of the directors of the news bureau Agence Havas. This association proved most stimulating and lasted over twenty years.

V.'s marriage furthered his contacts with the

459

world of painting and music, and his new position gave him ample time for his own introspections. His investigations, however, were not of a literary nature, and his reputation as a poet seemed to have come to an end.

In the winter 1912–13 Gide approached V. with the idea of having the publishing house Gallimard (N.R.F.) reissue his early scattered poems. After initially rejecting the suggestion, V. became reconciled to the idea, revised his poems, and decided to add some thirty lines of a "musical and abstract" nature. This poem, on which he labored over four years, became ultimately the dense five hundred lines of *La Jeune Parque,* which was published separately in 1917. Although extremely hermetic, it was immediately acclaimed by an elite; critic Paul Souday (1869–1929) gave it an enthusiastic review in *Le Temps* and John Middleton Murry (1889–1957) did the same in the London *Times.*

About the time he was working on *La Jeune Parque,* and shortly afterward, V. composed a number of other poems, most of which were concerned with the process of creativity and written in a strict classical form. The most famous, "Le Cimetière marin" (1920 in *La Nouvelle Revue Française*; The Graveyard by the Sea, 1932), the poet's meditation at the cemetery of Sète, appeared in 1920 along with the *Album der vers anciens, 1890–1900* and *Odes. Monsieur Teste* was reprinted in 1921, followed in 1922 by *Charmes,* a complete collection of the poems V. had composed between 1917 and 1922. Both "La Jeune Parque" and "Le Cimetière marin" were republished in it. The 1926 edition of *Charmes* also included the three "Fragments du Narcisse." Two Socratic dialogues in highly poetic prose, *L'Âme et la danse* and *Eupalinos ou l'Architecte* (Eupalinos or the Architect, 1932), published together in 1923, dealt with the role of art and artistic creation. Although V. was still occasionally tempted by verse forms— *Amphion* (1931), *Semiramis* (1943), *Cantate du Narcisse* (1938)—his great second lyrical period came actually to an end with the publication of *Charmes.*

By 1921 V. had already been voted the foremost contemporary French poet in a referendum conducted by the magazine *Connaissance.* In 1925 he was elected to the seat previously occupied by Anatole France (q.v.) in the Académie Française. Ironically enough for one who had refused to be "a man of letters," almost overnight V. had become the official

literary figure of France. As such he was constantly asked to deliver lectures and speeches, to write prefaces, and to contribute to magazines. The greatest part of these commissioned writings, dealing with literature, art, philosophy, politics, civilization, myth, poetics, etc., were gradually published in the five volumes of *Variété* (1924–44; Variety, 1927 ff.), which contains among other things his famous essays "Une Conquête méthodique" and "La Crise de l'ésprit." Some essays appeared separately in *Regards sur le monde actuel* (1933), *Pièces sur l'art* (1934), *Tel Quel* (1941 and 1943), etc.

Among V.'s many official activities were the participation in the administration of the Mediterranean University Center at Nice, the presidency of the P.E.N. Club and of the League of Nations Committee for International Cooperation, and a specially created professorship in poetics at the Collège de France (1937–44). During the German occupation V. used silence and work as a weapon against the Nazis. However his funeral oration at the Académie Française in praise of philosopher Henri Bergson (1859–1941) was considered an act of resistance. Following the liberation of France, V. presided over the Comité National des Écrivains.

From 1940 until almost his death, V. worked on a projected drama, *Mon Faust,* a sort of intellectual autobiography, fragments of which were published posthumously in 1946. V. was accorded national funeral observances in Paris, but he was buried in the *cimetière marin* of Sète, according to his own wish.

The majority of V.'s early verses collected in *Album de vers anciens* reflect the atmosphere of the decadent or symbolist poets. While Mallarmé's influence is particularly evident in poems like "Le Bois amical," "Les Vaines Danseuses," "La Fileuse," "Baignée," and "Valvins," such poems as "Narcisse parle" and "Profusion du soir" already announce Valerian themes. Also, V. had at this early period already started to reflect on problems of literary technique.

After his 1892 crisis, *la nuit de Gênes,* V. turned toward the central concern of his life: the analysis of consciousness and the cultivation of his intellectual powers. Henceforth he became more interested in the mental labor of producing a work than in the work itself.

Both *Léonard de Vinci* (augmented in 1919 by *Note et Digression,* and in 1929 by *Léonard et les philosophes*) and *Monsieur Teste* express his ideal. He saw in Leonardo the greatest example of a universal mind that had mastered all the arts and sciences by turning them into tools of his power. V. therefore endeavored to discover Leonardo's method, the secrets of his creative process, or rather, through Leonardo's example, his own.

Monsieur Teste, a monster of intelligence, willpower, and solitude, who has eliminated everything likely to interfere with the pursuit of perfecting his potential, is the incarnation of the absolute freedom of the intellect. He barely lives; he thinks. It is enough for him to know himself master of a method. Thus *Monsieur Teste* announces another dominant theme of V.'s speculations: the gap between being and knowing, between thinking and acting. Other aspects of Teste's behavior and thoughts were added much later, a few coming directly from the *Cahiers: Lettre de Madame Émilie Teste* (1924)—in which Mme. Teste sees her husband as "a mystic without God"— *Lettre d'un ami* (1924), *Extraits du log-book de M. T.* (1925), *Promenade avec M. T., Dialogue, Pour Un Portrait de M. T., Quelques Pensées de M. T., Fin de M. T.* (posthumous, 1946).

The chief concepts and quests incarnated in V.'s two "heroes" recur in all his later writings. Whether he wrote verse or prose, whether he pondered over the origin of poetry or Greek geometry, his concern was always with some method or situation of the mind, with the mind's conscious or unconscious processes. "Whenever I wrote my poems, I observed myself doing it," he confided to his notebook. In fact, when V. labored over *La Jeune Parque* he considered it as an exercise and an application of his intellectual method. Although he would reluctantly admit that "surprises and accidents of the mind" occasionally had a part in the composition of poetry, he strongly and constantly rejected the idea of inspiration. The role of the poet, according to him, is to awaken a poetic state in the reader, and this requires that the poet have a completely lucid mastery of his craft.

While observing a rigorously classical, often Racinian, prosody, V. used all the resources of language and music—metrical combinations, assonance, alliteration, ellipses, rich sensuous imagery, mysterious suggestions. Structure was most important to him: a poem had to be built. He contended that it was often the form, or even a rhythm, that created and directed the ideas in his poetry.

V. drew a sharp distinction between poetry and prose. As he saw it, the purpose of prose is to impart information, to convey a message as clearly and directly as possible—and V.'s style in his essays is indeed clear and direct; the sole function of poetry, he insisted, is to create delight. Nevertheless, the poems of V.'s maturity contained in *Charmes* are highly speculative compositions. V.'s mastery consists precisely in his unrivaled ability to convey abstract spirituality in a supremely ornate and musical language. *La Jeune Parque* is a mysteriously beautiful monologue dealing with a young woman's various phases of consciousness. In "Le Cimetière marin"—V.'s pathetic though lucid and bitter soliloquy inspired by the scintillating Mediterranean and the tombs in the cliffside cemetery at Sète—the conflict between the spiritual and the sensual is resolved in a grandiose hymn to the *élan vital.* A similar conflict—the tragic impossibility of capturing one's absolute self—is expressed in the elegiac, melancholy "Fragments du Narcisse," while the majority of the pieces of *Charmes* are concerned with the nature and origin of poetry, with its stages and maturation, with the poet's consciousness and his creative power.

V.'s dialogues belong to the same richly creative period as *Charmes.* In *L'Âme et la danse* Socrates assigns to dance, a symbol of poetry, the function of an antidote to the boredom of living. *Eupalinos ou L'Architecte* is the praise of the artist's capacity to assemble, organize, and *construct* a masterpiece by combining intellectual and sensuous experience.

Mon Faust, V.'s last and incomplete major work, is written in a relaxed dialogue form. Faust (and V. can indeed be considered a modern Faust), like Leonardo and Teste, is another and more personal projection of V. himself. While rejecting the immortality of the soul and using Mephistopheles as a tool of research in his *magnum opus,* Faust asserts himself as an individual who has attained the limits of man's intellectual power but is also destroyed by it.

The *Cahiers* are the final evidence of V.'s amazing consistency and constancy. From 1892 on there is hardly any deviation from his intellectual investigations and the mathematical discipline he applied to them.

Because of his tireless explorations of the mind's labyrinth, his agnosticism, his emphasis on the poet as a technician, and his masterly blending of intellectual speculation and sensuous imagery, V. reflects the present self-conscious, rationalistic century. The critic C. M. Bowra (b. 1888) stated that V.'s work "is representative of the age in which it was written, scientific and sceptical of transcendental hypotheses . . . ," and T. S. Eliot (q.v.) wrote that "of all the poets, in any language, of the last thirty years, it is he who will remain for posterity the representative poet, the symbol of the poet, of the first half of the 20th c.—not Yeats, not Rilke [qq.v.], not anyone else."

FURTHER WORKS: *Lettres à quelques-uns* (1952); *André Gide—P. V.: Correspondance, 1890–1942* (1955); *P. V.—Gustave Fourment: Correspondance, 1887–1933* (1957); *Œuvres* (ed. J. Hytier; 2 vols., 1957–60). **Selected English translation:** *The Collected Works of P. V.* (ed. J. Mathews; 1957 ff.)

BIBLIOGRAPHY: Thibaudet, A., *P. V.* (1923); Eliot, T. S., *A Brief Introduction to the Method of P. V.* (1924); Rauhut, F., *P. V.: Geist und Mythos* (1930); Larbaud, V., *P. V.* (1931); Berne-Joffroy, *Présence de P. V.* (1944); Eigeldinger, M., ed., *P. V.: Essais et témoignages inédits* (1945); "P. V. vivant," *CS* (1946); Pommier, J., *P. V. et la création littéraire* (1946); Special V. issue, *Quarterly Review of Literature*, III (1947), iii; Gide, A., *P. V.* (1947); Mondor, H., *Les Premiers Temps d'une amitié: André Gide et P. V.* (1947); Bémol, M., *P. V.* (1949); Bémol, A., *La Méthode critique de P. V.* (1949); Henry, A., *Language et poésie chez P. V.* (1952); Sewell, E., *P. V.: The Mind in the Mirror* (1952); Hytier, J., *La Poétique de V.* (1953); La Rochefoucauld, E. de, *P. V.* (1954); Scarfe, F., *The Art of P. V.* (1954); Suckling, N., *P. V. and the Civilized Mind* (1954); Nadal, O., *P. V., la Jeune Parque* (1957); Mondor, H., *Propos familiers de P. V.* (1957); Noulet, E., *Suite valérienne* (1959); Berne-Joffroy, A., *V.* (1960); Lang, R., *Rilke, Gide et V.* (1960); Blüher, *Strategie des Geistes, P. V.s Faust* (1961); Ince, W. N., *The Poetic Theory of P. V.* (1961); Duchesne-Guillemin, J., *Études pour un P. V.* (1964); Davey, C., *Words in the Mind* (1965); Thomson, A. W., *V.* (1965); Hartman, G. H., *The Unmediated Vision* (1966); Perche, L., *V.: Les Limites de l'humain* (1966); Rouart-Valéry, A., *P. V.* (1966); Grubbs, H. A., *P. V.* (1968); Tauman, L., *P. V., ou Le Mal de l'art* (1969)

RENÉE B. LANG

What I admire most in V. is perhaps indeed his constancy. Incapable of real sympathy, he never let his line of conduct be broken, never let himself be distracted from himself by anyone else.

A. Gide, *The Journals* (8 May 1927), p. 401

One is confronted by a pure intellect that has achieved integrity through a tortuous sequence of distinctions and relationships. One is filled with the need to penetrate and to participate in its austere isolation.

The intellect resists this invasion by every subterfuge of abstraction. Then, one by one, the antagonist captures the keys to its high place. And when one has traversed a certain distance, the other doors open of themselves, and one beholds, in the writings of P. V., a miraculous calm and assured awareness of those hidden motives of the modern mind which others have lacked the hardihood to interrogate.

W. A. Drake, *Contemporary European Writers* (1928), pp. 230–31

Mallarmé is always a painter, usually a watercolorist. . . . whereas V.'s genius is sculptural rather: these mythological poems have a density of cloud-shapes heavily massed—if they were not clouds, we should call them marmoreal. He gives us figures and groups half disengaged—and he runs to effects less of color than of light; the silvery, the sombre, the sunny, the translucent, the crystalline. . . . V. is, indeed, a sort of masculine of an art of which Mallarmé is the feminine.

E. Wilson, *Axel's Castle* (1931), pp. 71–72

V. . . . chose the intellectual side. His ambition resembled that of T. S. Eliot's early days: he was obsessed by the idea of always moving through and "going beyond." Each poem could be translated into a problem capable of solution, capable of supplying a principle which could then be applied to the writing of other poems. . . . Always he was driven further, to attack new problems, discover new principles. And, at a certain point in the process, it became evident that literature itself was a problem capable of solution, and was therefore only an intermediate goal, a stage to be passed through and left behind.

M. Cowley, *New Republic* (1934), p. 219

The mind as it works, loves, knows, suffers in man, lives in science, myth, the arts, or becomes Europe, "brain of the earth's body"; consciousness as it ranges from the lower limits of bodily death or sleep through stages of waking and knowing to the extreme limits of judgment; every gesture, every intermediate throe, spark, or step of the mind as it rises from the rich muck of the unconscious to the complex structures or the artistic or mathematical imagination; the human and historical condition of consciousness, the drama of consciousness, that is the subject of all V.'s work. He called it the Intellectual Comedy.

J. Mathews, Introduction to
Monsieur Teste (1947), pp. x–xi

His poetry, in agreement with his theories, relies on sensations for its primary contact with the reader—the aural sensation of the sound of the verse, the evocation of physical sensations through imagery—while revealing on examination the existence of an intellectual process running through, or behind the physical texture. This is precisely the manner and order in which a live human being presents himself to us: the physical presence first, and afterwards the intellectual or spiritual *persona*. It distinguishes V. from his master, Mallarmé, who strikes us as an intelligence without an adequate, or with a contrived physical presence.

G. Bereton, An Introduction to the French
Poets (1956), p. 260

There is, in the mind and work of V., a curious paradox. He presents himself to the reader, not only as a tireless explorer of the labyrinths of philosophical speculation, but also under the aegis of Leonardo da Vinci, as a man of specific temper, fascinated by the problems of method; a ranging and restless mind; a dilettante of science but a specialist in a science of his own invention —the science of poetry. Yet, when we peruse the list of titles of his essays, we find a remarkably limited subject matter, with no evidence of omnivorous reading, or of the varied interests of a Coleridge or a Goethe. He returns perpetually to the same insoluble problems. It would almost seem that the one object of his curiosity was— himself. He reminds us of Narcissus gazing into the pool, and partakes of the attraction and the mystery of Narcissus, the aloofness and frigidity of that spiritual celibate.

T. S. Eliot, in the introduction to The Art of
Poetry (1958), pp. xxii–xxiii

The readiness to wait until one is sure of the value of what is to be said, and the willingness to be silent once it has been said; the understanding that even the finest poetry is no more than a marginal illustration of the workings of the mind: this it is which sets V. apart from so many of his contemporaries, and the claim of this great poet, to have loved only perfection, will not be disallowed.

A. W. Thomson, V. (1965), p. 114

VALLE-INCLÁN, Ramón María del

Spanish novelist, poet, and dramatist, b. 28 Oct. 1869, Puebla de Caramiñal; d. 5 Jan. 1936, Santiago de Compostela

Born into a family of impoverished Galician aristocrats, in 1885 V. began his young manhood conventionally enough by studying law at the University of Santiago. However, he showed little aptitude for legal studies, which he soon abandoned, and was content to spend his time wandering about Galicia accumulating local legends. In 1892 he announced his intention of settling in Madrid, but much to everybody's surprise he was next heard from as a reporter in Vera Cruz and Mexico City.

The following year V. was back in Spain. After the publication of *Femeninas* (1895), a collection of six somewhat morbidly erotic tales that were later included in *Corte de amor* (1902) and *Jardín umbrío* (1903), V. finally went to Madrid, where he was soon employed in a government agency. V.'s dramatic appearance and deliberately bizarre behavior initially attracted more attention than his writing, which was very much in the *fin-de-siècle* vein of Jules-Amédée Barbey d'Aurevilly (1808– 1889) and Huysmans (q.v.). "Modernistic" in tone, his prose was heavy with sensuous beauty and strove for subtle musical effects that recalled the poetry of Darío, D'Annunzio (qq.v.), and the French symbolists (*see* symbolism).

To this same literary style belong the four novellas that definitively established his reputation: *Sonata de otoño* (1902), *Sonata de estío* (1903), *Sonata de primavera* (1904), and *Sonata de invierno* (1905)—accounts of the libertine adventures of the Marquis de Bradomín, a man as "cynical, unbelieving, and gallant as a Renaissance cardinal." The "sonatas" were later collected as *Memorias del Marqués de Bradomín* (The Pleasant Memoirs of the Marquis de Bradomín, 1925). The same protagonist also appears in *El Marqués de Bradomín* (1907), one of the best of a series of poetic dramas that includes *Cuento de abril* (1910), *Voces de gesta: Tragedia pastoril* (1912), and *La Marquesa Rosalinda: Farsa sentimental y grotesca* (1913).

Over the years a new orientation had begun to appear in V.'s work. The novella *Flor de Santidad* (1904), which focuses on the life of a young girl in Galicia, had already shown V.'s interest in the customs and traditions of his native province, whose atmosphere he admirably evoked. His first collection of poetry, *Aromas de leyenda* (1907), while still reflecting the symbolist influence, draws heavily for inspiration on Spanish history, folklore, and mythology. The same influences predominate in the prose plays known as *comedias bárbaras*—

463

Aguila de blasón (1907), *Romance de lobos* (1908), and *Cara de Plata* (1922)—a dramatic trilogy dealing with events in Spanish history. V.'s Carlist sympathies also led him to write the novelistic trilogy *La guerra Carlista,* which includes *Los cruzados de la causa* (1908), *El resplandor de la hoguera* (1909), and *Gerifaltes de antaño* (1909). More poetic than realistic, these novels depict the defeat of the campaign to re-establish Spain's pre-Bourbon monarchy.

With the poems in *La pipa de Kif* (1919), a new stylistic emphasis—to some extent foreshadowed by the insistence in the *comedias bárbaras* on the crude, the primitive, and the barbarous—begins to dominate V.'s writing in the various genres. While in his youth he had carefully eliminated the nonaesthetic from his work in a self-conscious cultivation of the beautiful, he now seemed to delight in the distorted, the grotesque, and the horrible.

Most representative of this new phase are the dramas V. called *esperpentos* (scarecrows). In them the world seemed to be reflected in a funhouse mirror and his protagonists often had the pre-expressionistic awkwardness of puppets. Horror and mockery mingled in the "village tragicomedy" *Divinas palabras* (1920), and a caustic wit transforms famous historical figures in *Farsa y licencia de la reina castiza* (1920). Other dramas in this new mood include *Los cuernos de Don Friolera* (1921), *Luces de Bohemia* (1924), and *El retablo de la lujuria, la avaricia y la muerte* (1927).

In 1922 V. revisited Mexico and from this stay came one of the best novels of his later years, *Tirano Banderas* (1926; The Tyrant, 1929), an account of a revolution in an imaginary South American country. The Latin American locale and the fictitious protagonists failed to hide the fact that the novel was a statement of V.'s Carlist opposition to Miguel Primo de Rivera, who was dictator of Spain from 1923 to 1929.

La corte de los milagros (1927) and *Viva mi dueño* (1927) are the first two volumes of *El ruedo ibérico,* an unfinished series of novels in which V. intended to examine the social forces that had molded Spanish history in the latter half of the 19th c.

This final evolution in V.'s style and thinking brought him closer to the approach of the Generation of '98 (*see* Spanish literature). Temporarily imprisoned during the last year of Primo de Rivera's dictatorship, V. was showered with honors during the short-lived Spanish republic. He remains one of the most imaginative and representative writers of modern Spain.

FURTHER WORKS: *Epitalamio* (1897); *Cenizas* (1899); *El yermo de las almas* (1908); *Opera omnia* (30 vols., 1909 ff.); *La lámpara maravillosa* (1916); *El pasajero* (1920); *Claves liricas* (1930); *Obras completas* (22 vols., 1944). **Selected English translation:** *V.-I.: Autobiography, Aesthetics, Aphorisms* (1966)

BIBLIOGRAPHY: Ortega y Gasset, J., *Sonata de estío* (1904); Salinas, P., *Literatura española del siglo XX* (1941); Gómez de la Serna, R., *Don R. M. de V.* (1948); Zamora Vicente, A., *Las "Sonatas" de R. de V.* (1951); Callan, R. J., "Satire in the *Sonatas* of V.," *MLQ,* XXV (1964), 330–37; Greenfield, S. M., "Madrid in the Mirror," *Hispania,* XLVIII (1965), 261–66; Special V. issue, *Insula,* XXI (1966), ccxxxvi–ccxxxvii; Boudreau, H. L., "The Circular Structure of V.-I.'s *Ruedo ibérico," PMLA,* LXXXII (1967), 128–35; Zahareas, A. N., et al., *R. de V.-I.: An Appraisal of His Life and Works* (1968)

* * * *

VALLEJO, César

Peruvian poet, b. 16 March 1892, Santiago de Chuco; d. 15 April 1938, Paris

V.'s early life reflects the hardships of the *mestizo* in a society still under the influence of its colonial heritage. He studied at the University of Trujillo and wrote an essay on *El Romanticismo en la poesía castellana* (1915). Toward the end of 1917, V. went to Lima where he taught school.

In 1920, he was imprisoned several months for alleged political activities, an experience that is reflected in his book of short stories, *Escalas melografiadas* (1923), which was published shortly before he left Peru to settle permanently in Paris. There, he and Juan Larrea (b. 1895) founded the short-lived review *Favorables-Paris-Poema* (1926).

Trips to Russia and Spain reflected V.'s restless search for a better social order. V. joined the Communist Party in 1931, the same year he published the novel *El Tungsteno,* and *Rusia en 1931: Observaciones al pie del Kremlin,* an account of his trip to the Soviet Union. V.'s poetry, however, transcends ideological lines; he cannot be claimed by any political faction.

V. supported himself meagerly by writing

RAMÓN DEL VALLE-INCLÁN

CÉSAR VALLEJO

articles on art, literature, and politics for European and Latin-American reviews. He died in poverty.

V.'s first published work, a volume of poetry entitled *Los heraldos negros* (1918), initiates themes that were to remain constant in his work. It also records the transformation of his poetic style and shows how the opulent rhetoric of *modernismo* increasingly gave way to the postmodernist tendency toward indigenous themes and prosaic vignettes of daily or family life related in popular speech patterns that are transformed by the emotional intensity of the poet.

The Indian is seen as a universal symbol of mankind, which is unable to realize its potential because of injustice and oppression. Love is foredoomed by the conditions of human existence. Man is an orphan abandoned by God to seek hope in a world devoid of meaning. Childhood memories become painfully nostalgic, and the mother emerges as the primordial symbol of love.

Trilce (1922) shatters all traditions and inaugurates a new period in Peruvian poetry. This iconoclastic series of seventy-seven poems, bearing only numbers for titles, appeared a year before Breton's (q.v.) *Surrealist Manifesto* (1924) and three years before Neruda's (q.v.) surrealistic *Tentativa del hombre infinito* (1925). Although independent of any particular literary school, it is truly contemporary in its irrational and hermetic expression.

In it V. discards traditional logic and attempts to instill a new life into words. His major themes remain those of an existential search for love and permanent values in an ever-changing, absurd world. Bitter irony and black humor give even the most inaccessible poems a sense of immediacy and urgency, as the poet gropes to express his private vision. The syntax reflects his often violent interior struggle to isolate through language the ultimate spiritual resources of the human animal.

V. published few additional poems during his lifetime, but continued to write and revise, especially during the final months of his life. The posthumously published *Poemas humanos* (1939; Poemas humanos/Human Poems, 1968 —a bilingual edition) reveals a style and unity that characterize V. at the height of his powers. From the self-absorption of *Trilce*, V. emerges to identify with the poor and oppressed everywhere, and through their redemption he seeks his own. As his gaze is directed

outward, his language becomes more accessible, although still dictated by its interior logic. Echoes of Biblical prophets mingle with fervent pleas for social justice and universal love. Daily objects are infused with spiritual values reflecting their significance in the poet's emotional odyssey.

In the group of fifteen poems entitled "España, aparta de mí este cáliz," V. calls for the salvation of mankind through fraternal love and mutual self-sacrifice, best exemplified in the death of the anonymous Republican partisans of the Spanish Civil War. The agony of "Mother Spain" becomes a microcosm of the human predicament.

Poemas humanos achieves a stylistic balance that eliminates both the derivative aspects of *Los heraldos negros* and the often excessive difficulties of *Trilce*. As in the latter work, V. employs all the resources of Spanish, including learned or archaic words and scientific and technical terms, but he is less inclined to syntactical distortion, neologisms, and typographic and orthographic peculiarities. Strong rhythms and irrational, often private images are successfully employed to express the most fundamental and universal of human emotions.

The poems begin and end abruptly, as though forming fragments of one long poem, V.'s final statement concerning his compassion, anguish, and hopes for his fellow man. The result is a work of sustained originality and intensity—a major contribution to world literature.

The publication of V.'s total poetic production, *Obra Poética Completa* (1968), shows how the poet reflected the changing literary fashions of his time without muffling his own voice.

V.'s considerable journalistic production, much of it still uncollected, promotes specific social and cultural reforms he deemed essential to the progress of mankind. But his poetry, shunning all dogmas, embraces the intrinsic dilemmas of the human condition and seeks their solution in a radical change in human nature itself. Within the last decade V. has finally been recognized as one of the most important and original contemporary poets of Latin America.

FURTHER WORKS: *Fabula Salvaje* (1923); *Artículos olvidados* (1960); *Novelas y cuentos completos* (1967). **Selected English translations:** *Twelve Spanish-Speaking Poets* (1943); *Twenty Poems of C. V.* (1962)

BIBLIOGRAPHY: Monguió, L., *C. V.–Vida y obra* (1952); Abril, X., *V., ensayo de aproximación crítica* (1958); Coyné, A., *C. V. y su obra poética* (1958); Larrea, J., *C. V. o Hispanoamérica en la cruz de su razón* (1958); Meo Zilio, G., *Stile e poesía in C. V.* (1960); Paoli, R., *Poesie, di C. V.* (1964); Higgins, J., "The Conflict of Personality in C. V.'s *Poemas humanos*," *BHS*, XLIII (1966), 47–55; McDuffie, K. A., "C. V.: Profile of a Poet," in *Proceedings: Pacific Northwest Conference on Foreign Languages*, ed. J. L. Mordaunt (1968), pp. 135–43; "Homenaje a C. V., Visión del Perú," *Revista de Cultura*, IV (July 1969); Neale-Silva, E., "The Introductory Poem in V.'s *Trilce*," *Hispanic Review*, XXXVIII (1970), i, 2–16; "Homenaje a C. V.," *RI*, XXXVI (April–June 1970), lxxi

KEITH A. MCDUFFIE

VANČURA, Vladislav

Czech novelist, b. 23 June 1891, Háje; d. 1 June 1942, Prague

V. practiced medicine in Zbraslav near Prague. During the Nazi occupation of Czechoslovakia, he was killed.

V.'s first published books were collections of short stories, *Amazonský proud* (1923) and *Dlouhý, Široký a Bystrozraký* (1924). Through the years, V. wrote dramas, but inadequate structure and characterization as well as a lack of dynamic action make his dramatic works less significant than his novels.

V. was especially fond of portraying social outcasts—halfwits, eccentrics, crooks, and vagabonds. In the early novel *Pekař Jan Marhoul* (1924), for example, his hero is a kind of Czech Don Quixote. This interest can also be seen in his antiwar novel *Pole orná a válečná* (1925), in *Poslední soud* (1925), and in *Hrdelní pře anebo Přísloví* (1930). In the historical novel *Markéta Lazarová* (1931)—in which the outcasts are robber-knights and highwaymen—as well as in *Poslední soud* and in *Hrdelní pře anebo Přísloví*, V. examined the problems of unsolved and unexpiated crimes. Gamblers and adventurers play the leading roles in *Konec starých časů* (1934), an adaptation of the Baron Pfašil story about an émigré Russian prince.

It was the virtuosity of language in *Pekař Jan Marhoul* that first brought him to attention. V. delighted in formal and stylistic experimenting, in which the influence of dada-

ism (q.v.) and cubism is obvious. This can be seen in his tendency to reintroduce archaic-sounding language and his use of different functional levels of speech, such as slang and vulgarisms. Sometimes this is done at the expense of the novel's structural and narrative unity. Thus V.'s less ambitious works, such as the short story "Luk královny Dorotky" (1932), seem structurally more integrated than the novels.

V. began to change direction in *Útěk do Budína* (1932), in which contemporary national questions come to the fore. *Tři řeky* (1936), with its more intensified action, prepares the way for V.'s abandonment of linguistic experiments and outcast types. This becomes more marked in *Rodina Horvatová* (1938), the first part of the uncompleted, broad-scale chronicle of several generations, *Koně a vůz*.

V. collaborated with Czech historians on *Obrazy z dějin národa českého* (1939–40). This series of scenes in prose from Czechoslovakia's past concentrates on themes drawn from mythology and the period of the Przemysl dynasty.

V. ranks among the outstanding Czech prose writers of the interwar period.

FURTHER WORKS: *Učitel a žák* (1927); *Nemocná dívka* (1928); *Alchymista* (1932); *Jezero Ukereve* (1935); *Josefína* (1941); *Spisy* (15 vols., 1951–59). **Selected English translation:** *The End of the Old Times* (1965)

BIBLIOGRAPHY: Kundera, M., *Umění románu* (1960); Rechcigl, M., Jr., ed., *The Czechoslovak Contribution to World Culture* (1964); Sturm, R., *Czechoslovakia: A Bibliographic Guide* (1968)

HEINRICH KUNSTMANN

VAZOV, Ivan Minchov

Bulgarian poet, novelist, and short-story writer, b. 27 June 1850, Sopot; d. 22 Sept. 1921, Sofia

Born into a family of small shopkeepers, V., in his youth, avidly read the Russian classics, Homer, Horace, the 19th-c. French poets, and Greek and Turkish anacreontic poetry. He fought in the Russo-Turkish war (1877–78) and then devoted himself to the service of his country as a journalist, man of letters, writer, politician, and government minister.

V.'s interest in Bulgarian folksongs drew him to national themes, as for example in *Pryeporetz i gusla* (1876). Later, in poetry that closely captures the tone of popular ballads, he somberly and austerely highlighted the heroic aspect of the struggle against Turkish domination. The revolt and war are described in the *Epopeya na zabravenite* cycle (1879), which he dedicated to the "apostles" of the uprising. Like many of his contemporaries, V. extolled the privations endured by those who fought for liberation. Some of V.'s poetry emulated European models such as Heinrich Heine (1797–1856) and Nikolai Nekrasov (1821–77), but it lost in originality as its formal facility increased. *Lyuleka mi zamirisa* (1919), a collection of melancholy poetry, is V.'s most important late work.

In 1880 V. began to write novellas that were to be of great significance in Bulgarian literature. The sharply realistic *Chichovtzi* (1885) gives a humorous sketch of the narrow-minded, old Balkan bourgeoisie. Later novellas castigate social injustice and corruption, but the basic tone remains optimistic, humanitarian, and intimately human. A typical example is *Ide li?* (1895), a moving description of a mother waiting for her son, who has been killed in action.

One of V.'s most important works is *Pod igoto* (1889; Under the Yoke, 1894), the first large-scale Bulgarian novel. The story weaves together three themes: the patriarchal small town and its types; the love of a liberation fighter for a village schoolteacher; and the struggle against the Turks and the Bulgarian collaborators, which ends with the tragic death of the lovers. His style is simple and vivid, his descriptions romantic and picaresque. Hugo's *Les Misérables* and Lev Tolstoi's (q.v.) *War and Peace* were lasting influences on him.

All V.'s works proclaim an idealistic belief in progress. He was a creative and stimulating force in every genre: the love lyric, contemplative and patriotic poetry, narrative verse, historical fiction and the contemporary novel of social criticism, drama, the novella, and the sketch. Often called the Bulgarian Victor Hugo, he is today generally regarded as his country's classic writer and the "father" of modern Bulgarian literature.

FURTHER WORKS: *Tugite na Bŭlgariya* (1877); *Gramada* (1880); *Gusla* (1881); *Mitrofan i Dormidolski* (1881); *Zagorka* (1883); *Nemili nedragi* (1883); *Ruska* (1883);

Polya i gori (1884); *Italiya* (1884); *Slivovitza* (1886); *Velikata Rilska pustinya* (1892); *V nedrata na Rodopite* (1892); *Zvokuve* (1893); *Chŭshove* (1894); *Draski i sharki* (1895); *Nova zemya* (1896); *Skitnishki pesni* (1899); *Pod nasheto nebe* (1900); *Videno i chuto* (1901); *Pastar svyat* (1902); *Kazalarskata tzaritza* (1903); *Sluzhbogontzi* (1903); *Utro v Banki* (1905); *Ivan Aleksandŭr* (1907); *Svetoslav Terter* (1907); *Legendi pri Tzarevetz* (1910); *Kŭm propast* (1910); *Borislav* (1910); *Ivailo* (1911); *Pod grŭma na probedite* (1914); *Pesni za Makedoniya* (1916); *Novi ekove* (1917); *Ne shte zagine* (1919); *Sŭchineniya* (28 vols., 1921 ff.); *Izbrani sŭchineniya* (12 vols., 1940 ff.); *Nepublikovani pisma* (1935); *Sabrani sŭchineniya* (20 vols., 1955 ff.)

BIBLIOGRAPHY: Christophorov, P., *I. V.* (1938); Damiani, E., *I. V.* (1947); Gesemann, W., *Die Romankunst I. Vs.* (1966)

WOLFGANG GESEMANN

VENÉZIS, Ilías

(pseud. of *Ilías Mellos*), Greek novelist and short-story writer, b. 4 March 1904, Aivali, Asia Minor

V.'s major literary work deals with the simple joys and sufferings of his people before, during, and after the Greco-Turkish War (1921–22), when the Greeks were uprooted from Asia Minor. In his personal life he showed the Anatolian's unusual ability to adapt and prosper after experiences that would stifle or silence others. Successful as a writer early in his career, he also rose to an important position in the Bank of Greece. He was elected to the Academy of Athens in 1957

In 1922, V. was taken prisoner by the Turks and placed in a slave-labor battalion. This horrendous experience, which lasted fourteen months, was the subject of an autobiographical novel, *To Noúmero 31,328* (1931), an undisputed classic in Greek narrative literature. V. had previously demonstrated his literary skill with *Manólis Lékas* (1928), a collection of short stories, but "the chronicle of slavery" established him as an important writer of the group that was to be known as the "Generation of the Thirties." Viewed retrospectively, *To Noúmero 31,328* is the forerunner of the concentration camp fiction that was to become an important European literary genre after World War II.

Galíni (1939) showed the difficult adjustment of Asia Minor refugees in the barren areas of Attica, in a Greece that was both fatherland and foreign to them. In *Eolikí yi* (1943; Beyond the Aegean, 1955) V. returned to his childhood, to the years before World War I. In lyrical retrospective he recounts a life that seems to resemble dream and folk tale more than everyday reality.

Much of V.'s longer fiction suffers from a lack of structure and an attempt to provide narrative direction by the simple literary device of a recounted journey. As a result his novels are often a mosaic of lyrical or tragic observations loosely unified by the forward thrust of a migration. *Éxodos* (1950), an account of World War II refugees retreating southward to Athens, clearly founders in melodrama and depends for structure on a confusing mythology. *Okianós* (1956), a chronicle of a Greek ship's voyage from Leghorn to Baltimore, is a series of individual portraits rather than a unified novel whose theme rises from the inherent tensions of its protagonists.

V.'s major achievements are his short stories, which are among the best in modern Greek literature. *To Eyéon* (1941), *Ánemi* (1944), *Óra polémou* (1946), and *I nikiméni* (1954) show him to be a careful stylist whose compassion and sensitivity, channeled into the short-story form, are given the compression and purpose his novels seem to lack. His most successful characters are "primitives" or children who are unable to resolve the conflict between their sense of freedom and justice and the responsibilities that society places upon them. In most of V.'s stories, the central characters are made to confront a world whose moral complexity is beyond their ability to grasp and understand.

FURTHER WORKS: *Block C* (1945); *Fthinóporo stin Italía* (1950); *O Arhiepískopos Damáskinos* (1952); *Hronikó tis trápezas tis Eládos* (1955); *Amerikanikí yi* (1955); *I Argonáftes* (1962); *Imanouíl Tsouderós* (1965)

BIBLIOGRAPHY: Panayotópoulos, I. M., *Ta prósopa ke ta kímena* (1943); Hatzínis, Y., *Eliniká kímena* (1955); Sahínis, A., "The Fiction of I. V.," *The Charioteer*, I (Autumn 1960); Karandónis, A., *Pezográfi ke pezografímata tis yeneás tou triánda* (1962); Karaníkas, A. and H., *I. V.* (1969)

THOMAS DOULIS

VERCORS

(pseud. of *Jean Bruller*), French novelist, playwright, and essayist, b. 26 Feb. 1902, Paris

Trained as an engineer, previous to World War II, V. was known to a small public for the satirical drawings published under his real name, Jean Bruller. During the German occupation, he helped found *Les Éditions de Minuit,* and one of the first publications of this originally clandestine press was his novella *Le Silence de la mer* (1942; The Silence of the Sea, 1945), which made his pseudonym, chosen after a mountain range in southeastern France, world-famous.

In this novel, Werner von Ebrennac, a young German officer who sincerely believes in the benefits of Franco-German solidarity—even if it has to be achieved by force—is billeted with a French landowner and his daughter. He enthusiastically pours out his love of France in a long monologue, which they, though not unimpressed, meet with patriotic, stony silence. When Ebrennac realizes the true nature of his Nazi masters, he volunteers for service on the Russian front, where his death is almost certain.

La Marche à l'étoile (1943; The Guiding Star, 1946), which was also published clandestinely, focuses on an eastern-European immigrant to France and his gradual disillusionment with the country he had chosen out of love.

A strong humanitarian message pervades all V.'s books. For a number of years after 1945 V.'s novels, essays, and stories dealt with dilemmas of conscience. In *La Puissance du jour* (1951), he traces the gradual emotional healing of a repatriated war prisoner who owes his survival to the involuntary killing of a fellow prisoner. The essays in *Plus ou moins homme* (1949) probe the limit beyond which man can no longer retain his pride and dignity.

Les Animaux dénaturés (1952; Am., You Shall Know Them, 1953; Eng., Borderline, 1954) deals with the discovery of a new human species and points up our inadequate definition of what constitutes a man. V. adapted it for the stage as *Zoo, ou L'Assassin philanthrope* (1965; Zoo, or The Philanthropic Assassin, 1968). *Sylva* (1961; Eng., 1961) presents the remarkable transformation of a fox into a woman and the simultaneous degradation of a woman drug addict. More recent novels confirm V.'s abiding interest in exploring the subconscious.

Committed to social justice, V. never belonged to any political party and has often been called on to moderate in debates between opposing points of view, as is evidenced in *Morale chrétienne et morale marxiste* (1960). His wartime memoirs, *La Bataille du silence* (1967; The Battle of Silence, 1968), were hailed as an extraordinary account of a tragic time.

A versatile writer of diverse interests, a calm and earnest voice in turbulent times, V. occupies a unique position on the French intellectual scene.

FURTHER WORKS: *Le Sable du temps* (1945); *Les Armes de la nuit* (1946); *L'Imprimerie de Verdun* (1947); *Les Yeux et la lumière* (1948); *Les Pas dans le sable* (1954); *Colères* (1956; The Insurgents, 1956); *Les Divagations d'un Français en Chine* (1956); *Pour Prendre Congé* (1957; For the Time Being, 1957); *Goetz* (1958); *Sur ce rivage* (1958–60; I, *Le Périple*; II, *Monsieur Prousthe*; III, *La Liberté de décembre*); *Les Chemins de l'être* (with P. Misraki, 1965); *Quota* (with P. S. Coronel, 1966; Eng., 1966); *Œdipe-Roi* (1967); *Le Radeau de la Méduse* (1969); *Le Fer et le Velours* (1969). **Selected English translations:** *Three Short Novels by V.* (1947; includes *Guiding Star, Night and Fog*, and *The Verdun Press*); *Paths of Love* (1961; includes *December's Freedom* and *M. Prousthe*)

BIBLIOGRAPHY: Bieber, K., in *L'Allemagne vue par les écrivains de la Résistance Française* (1954); Brodin, P., *Présences contemporaines*, Vol. I (1954); Moeller, C., in *Littérature du XXᵉ siècle et Christianisme*, Vol. III (1957); Chavardès, M., *L'Écrivain dans le siècle* (1959); Konstantinović, R., *V.: Écrivain et dessinateur* (1969)

KONRAD BIEBER

VERGA, Giovanni

Italian novelist, short-story writer, and dramatist, b. 31 Aug. 1840, Catania; d. there, 27 Jan. 1922

Like many 19th-c. Italian writers, V. began his literary career in the tradition of Alessandro Manzoni's (1785–1873) *I promessi sposi* with a historical novel, *I Carbonari della montagna* (1862). The atmosphere of this work shows the influence of Ugo Foscolo (1778–1827), Byron (1788–1824), and Dumas *père* (1802–1870). In V.'s next novel, *Una peccatrice* (1866), the artist Pietro Brusio wins a previously unattainable *femme fatale*. The provin-

cial-bred V. managed to make this languishing, voluptuous lady, whom he places in ambiguous situations, attractive to readers whose tastes ran to lady-of-the-camellias types. The sentimentality of *Storia di una capinera* (1871), which deals with the tribulations of a nun, made V. more widely known. Hot-blooded, high-flown passion is again the subject of *Eva* (1873), whose hero fights a duel for a dancer and later dies of tuberculosis in his native land.

In *Eros* (1875), the last novel of his youthful period, V. carried to absurdity the pseudo-aesthetic attitude of his society ladies and men-about-town. He thus paved the way for a new literary departure, which, although it owed some of its impetus to the naturalistic theories introduced into Italy by novelist Luigi Capuana (1839–1915), was in an entirely personal style.

V.'s masterpieces were, in part, the result of his decision to leave the sophisticated, literary world of Milan and Florence and to return both physically and emotionally to his native Sicily. In most of the books that followed, the desires and instincts of his "Sicilian primitives," which erupt as elementally as lightning, form the core of his work. *Nedda* (1874), a "Sicilian sketch," is characteristic of V.'s later *verismo* (*see* Italian literature) style. The simplicity of the protagonist, a woman farmhand, and her almost animal behavior anticipate the female characters in V.'s novellas collected in *Vita dei campi* (1878).

In addition to the famous "Cavalleria rusticana" (in Cavalleria Rusticana, and Other Stories, 1928), this collection included "La Lupa" (in The She-Wolf, and Other Stories, 1958), a story extremely characteristic of V.'s mature talent. In it a woman of primitive passion falls in love with her daughter's husband and drives him into axing her to death. The story unfolds in an almost mythical atmosphere, and the arid landscape provides a cruelly indifferent setting for the tale of human passion. Both of the above stories were reworked in dramatic form (published 1884) by V. and were influential in introducing naturalism (q.v.) to the Italian stage.

The main characteristics of the novel *I Malavoglia* (1881; The House by the Medlar Tree, 1890) are to be found in the sketch "Fantasticheria." The book highlights V.'s admiration of the fishermen of a small coastal town for their "brave submission in a trouble-ridden life" and for their "family religion, which is reflected in their occupation, their houses, and the rocky hills which surround them." It was V.'s ambition, in accordance with the tenets of Flaubert (1821–80) and the naturalists, to write this novel in a completely impersonal style. "The artist's hand will remain totally invisible, and the novel will bear the stamp of actual events; the work of art will seem to have created itself." Besides this impersonal style, V. also made use of the rich fund of Sicilian folk wisdom, which, like the choral sections in classical tragedy, provides a commentary on the action—the misfortunes of a family—and places it in its timeless context. V. intended *I Malavoglia* to be the prelude to a five-volume cycle, whose title *I vinti* expressed its author's heroic pessimism.

The *Novelle rusticane* (1883; Little Novels of Sicily, 1925) was essentially a continuation of the first novella collection, but fell below its standard. It is worth noting, however, that in the story "Gli orfani," the humorously depicted despair of Compare Meno, twice a widower within three years, resembles current-day southern Italian writing. "La roba" anticipates the theme of V.'s second novel in *I vinti; Mastro don Gesualdo* (1889; Don Gesualdo, 1923). In the short story, an old man, obsessed by the property he has acquired through iron tenacity of purpose, falls into despair at the end of his life when he realizes he must abandon his possessions.

First published in the *Nuova Antologia* (July–December 1888), *Mastro don Gesualdo* is an all-embracing view of life in a small Sicilian town. Its upstart hero remains a slave to his compulsion to work even after he has become a great landowner. With a mastery reminiscent of Balzac (1799–1850), V. enlarges on his protagonist from one scene to the next, until Don Gesualdo dominates everything like a nightmare. In this novel, translated into English by D. H. Lawrence, V. emerges as a sardonic observer of Sicilian society, whose members pursue a personal illusion until fate ineluctably overtakes them.

The Milan novellas collected in *Per le vie* (1883) have a less significant place in V.'s work. Here he applied his veristic technique to a milieu he had lived in for many years, but identification with the feelings and language of his characters is missing.

La duchessa di Leyra, a veristic novel in which V. hoped to recreate the sophisticated, northern Italian world of his early books, never got beyond the first few pages.

L'onorevole Scipioni and L'uomo di lusso, which were to have completed the *I vinti* cycle, were never even begun.

V. is now considered the greatest Italian novelist since Manzoni, but for many years his importance was slighted.

FURTHER WORKS: *Sulle lagune* (1863); *Tigre reale* (1873); *Primavera, e altri racconti* (1876); *Il marito di Elena* (1883); *Drammi intimi* (1884); *Vagabondaggio* (1887); *I ricordi del Capitano d'Arce* (1891); *Don Candeloro e C.* (1894); *La lupa, In portineria, Cavalleria rusticana* (1896); *La caccia al lupo; La caccia alla volpe* (1902); *Dal tuo al mio* (1906); *Opere complete* (1930 ff.); *Teatro* (1952); *Tutte le novelle* (2 vols., 1955); *Lettere al suo traduttore* (1954); *Lettere a Dina* (1963). **Selected English translations:** *Under the Shadow of Etna* (1896); *Pane Nero, and Other Stories* (1962)

BIBLIOGRAPHY: Russo, L., *G. V.* (6 eds., 1919–66); Momigliano, A., *G. V. narratore* (1923); Santangelo, G., *Storia della critica verghiana* (1954); Ragusa, O., *V.'s Milanese Tales* (1964); Testa, J., "The Novels of V. and Zola: Contrasts and Parallels," *DA*, XXV (1965), 7279–80; Erickson, J., "A Milanese Tale by G. V.," *Symposium*, XX (1966), 7–13; Cecchetti, G., *Il V. maggiore* (1968)

JOHANNES HÖSLE

VERHAEREN, Émile

Belgian poet and dramatist (writing in French), b. 21 May 1855, Sainte-Armand-les-Puers; d. 27 Nov. 1916, Rouen

Among V.'s fellow students at the Jesuit Collège Sainte-Barbe in Ghent were Maeterlinck (q.v.) and Georges Rodenbach (1855-98). After studying law at Louvain, V. became associated with the Brussels lawyer and writer Edmond Picard (1836–1924) and contributed to his journal, *Art Moderne*. In 1883, Lemmonier, the Belgian publisher of Zola's (q.v.) works, brought out V.'s first collection of poetry, *Les Flamandes*. The earthy portrayals recall the paintings of Pieter Brueghel and Jordaens.

In 1886, V.'s second volume of poetry, *Les Moines,* was published. Written after a stay of three weeks at the monastery of Forges, these poems sketch portraits of monks and proclaim the poet's mystical mission as a be-

GIOVANNI VERGA

ÉMILE VERHAEREN

lated successor to the "seekers of sublime chimeras."

In the 1880's V. was overcome by severe neurosis. Close to madness, he set down his hallucinations with soul-stirring force in *Les Soirs* (1887), *Les Débâcles* (1888), and *Les Flambeaux noirs* (1890).

After his health was restored, V. wrote three volumes of poetry—*Les Campagnes halluc-inées* (1893), *Les Villes tentaculaires* (1895), and *Les Villages illusoires* (1895). They asserted V.'s naively robust faith in man's social progress. Here a rhapsodic admiration for modernity, science, technology, and industrialization goes hand in hand with a deep sympathy for rural people who have moved to the cities.

V.'s poetry reached full maturity in *Les Visages de la vie* (1899), *Les Forces tumult-ueuses* (1902), and *La Multiple Splendeur* (1906). His belief in the brotherhood of man—now heightened to the point of pantheism—and his faith in the redeeming power of human endeavor were shaken but not broken by World War I.

The traditional meters V. used in his early poetry gradually gave way to free verse. V.'s poetry, with its delight in color, bears the stamp of the word painter. He was attacked for his baroque, emotional imagery, but his worth was recognized by Stéphane Mallarmé (1842–98) and Stefan Zweig (q.v.). V. achieved a reputation around the turn of the century as a "20th-century poet"—a reputation which, however, did not last. His plays, like his poems, are hymns of praise to the forces of nature and human energy, especially man's power over nature.

FURTHER WORKS: *Contes de minuit* (1885); *Les Apparus dans mes chemins* (1891); *Au Bord de la route* (1891); *Trilogie: Les Heures claires* (1896); *Les Aubes* (1898; *Dawn,* 1898); *Le Cloître* (1900; *The Cloister,* 1915); *Philippe II* (1904); *Toute la Flandre* (5 vols., 1904–1911); *Rembrandt* (1905); *Les Heures d'après-midi* (1905; *Afternoon,* 1917); *Hélène de Sparte* (1909); *Les Rhythmes souverains* (1910); *P.-P. Rubens* (1910); *Les Heures du soir* (1911); *Les Blés mouvants* (1912); *Œuvres* (9 vols., 1912–36); *La Belgique sanglante* (1915; *Belgium's Agony,* 1915); *Parmi des cendres* (1916); *Les Ailes rouges de la guerre* (1916); *Les Flammes hautes* (1917); *Choix de poèmes* (1917); *Chants dialogués* (1926); *E. V. à Marthe V., lettres inédites 1889–1916*

(1937). **Selected English translations:** *Poems of E. V.* (1915); *The Love Poems of E. V.* (1916); *The Plays of E. V.: The Dawn, The Cloister, Philip II, Helen of Sparta* (1916); *Five Tales by E. V.* (1924)

BIBLIOGRAPHY: Zweig, S., *É. V.* (3rd ed., 1913); De Smet, J., *É. V.* (2 vols., 1920, 1922); Mockel, A., *É. V.* (3rd ed., 1933); Mansell-Jones, P., *É. V.* (2nd ed., 1957); Sussex, R. T., "Some Unpublished Manuscript Poems of *É. V.*," *Australian Modern Language Association,* XXVI (1966), 185–97

KURT WEINBERG

VERMEYLEN, August

Belgian essayist and novelist (writing in Flemish), b. 12 May 1872, Brussels; d. 10 Jan. 1945, Ukkel

V. became a professor at the University of Brussels in 1901 and at the University of Ghent in 1923. A cofounder and director of the journal *Van Nu en Straks,* he was influential in Belgian intellectual life during the first half of the 20th c.

In various essays which have become classics, collected in *Verzamelde Opstellen* (2 vols., 1904–1905) and *Beschouwingen* (1942), V analyzed the ideological trends of his time, fought regionalism, and argued for "more brains" in literature.

Closely related to V.'s essayistic work is his allegorical-philosophical novel, *De wandelende Jood* (1906). This is an intellectual novel containing excellent characterizations. The protagonist is a seeker for truth who finally arrives at what Lissens called "a rationalism with an idealistic cast." V.'s later novel *Twee Vrienden* (1943) never breaks entirely free of the essay approach.

FURTHER WORKS: *Leven en werken van Jonker Jan van der Noot* (1899); *Geschiedenis der Europeesche plastick en schilderkunst* (3 vols., 1921); *Van Gezelle tot Timmermans* (1923); *Verzameld werk* (6 vols., 1951–55)

BIBLIOGRAPHY: Teirlinck, H., *A. V.* (1958); Westerlinck, A., *De levensbeschouwing van A. V.* (1958); Weisgerber, J., *Formes et domaines du roman flamand* (1963); Venstermans, J., *A. V.* (1965); Brachin, P., *Anthologie de la prose néerlandaise: Belgique I 1893–1940* (1966)

JORIS TAELS

VERWEY, Albert

Dutch poet, dramatist, and critic, b. 15 May 1865, Amsterdam; d. 8 March 1937, Noordwijk

V. played a leading role in the literary life of the Netherlands. He was editor of *Nieuwe Gids* from 1885 to 1894, then editor of the *Tweemaandelijksch Tijdschrift* from 1894 to 1902. (The latter magazine later changed its name to *De XXste Eeuw*.) As editor of *De Beweging* from 1905 to 1920, he set the tone of that journal, in which many writers of the 1910 generation made their debut. From 1925 to 1935 V. was professor of Dutch literature in Leiden. He kept in touch with German literature, partly through his association with Stefan George (q.v.), his friend for many years.

The characteristic feature of V.'s poetry is the predominance of intellect. He strove to depict not just an event that happened but the idea behind appearances. His poems were often written not singly but as a series of continuous observations. The vision of the world behind them was a Spinozistic pantheism with a mystical tinge.

FURTHER WORKS: *Persephone en andere gedichten* (1885); *Van het leven* (1888); *Verzamelde gedichten* (1889); *Aarde* (1896); *De nieuwe tuin* (1898); *Johan van Oldenbarnevelt* (1899); *Het brandende braambosch* (1899); *Dagen en daden* (1901); *Stille toernooien* (1901); *Jacoba van Beieren* (1902); *Luide toernooien* (1903); *Het leven van Potgieter* (1903); *De kristaltwijg* (1903); *Uit de landen bij de zee* (1904); *De oude strijd* (1905); *Droom en tucht* (1908); *Verzamelde gedichten* (3 vols., 1911 ff.); *Het eigen rijk* (1912); *Het zichtbar geheim* (1915); *Het zwaardjaar* (1916); *Goden en grenzen* (1920); *Proza* (10 vols., 1921 ff.); *De weg van het licht* (1922); *De maker* (1924); *Rondom mijn werk* (1925); *Lachende raadsel* (1925; Songs of Ultimate Understanding, 1927); *De legende van de ruimte* (1926); *De getilde last* (1927); *Vondel herdacht* (1929); *De figuren van de sarkofaag* (1930); *Ritme en metrum* (1931); *De ring van leed en geluck* (1932); *Mijn verhouding tot Stefan George* (1934); *In de koorts van het kortstondige* (1936); *De dichter in het derde rijk* (1936); *Oorsprondelijk dichtwerk* (2 vols., 1938)

BIBLIOGRAPHY: Vestdijk, S., *A. V. en de idee* (1940); Gielen, J. J., *De dichter V.* (1942); Hanot, M., *A. Vs. literaire Kritiek* (1957); Pauw, W. de, *De vriendschap van A. V. en*

Stefan George (1960, with summary in French); Pannwitz, R., *A. V. und Stefan George* (1965); Anon., "Across a Frontier," *TLS,* 21 April 1966, p. 346; Baxter, B. M., "A. V. and Shelley: Imitation, Influence or Affinity?" in *Proceedings of the IVth Congress of the International Comparative Literature Association,* ed. F. Jost, Vol. II (1966), pp. 868–74

KAREL REIJNDERS

VESAAS, Tarjei

Norwegian novelist, poet, and dramatist, b. 20 Aug. 1897, Vinje; d. 15 March 1970, Vinje

Except for periods of travel in Scandinavia and on the European continent, V. spent his whole life in the farm community of Vinje in Telemark. He wrote about rural Norwegians, interpreting their actions by means of images from the Telemark landscape. But V. is far more than a regional writer. His travels and readings brought him into contact with modern European thought, and his works, written in a highly polished, lyrical style, deal with general human problems. Although V. wrote in Norway's second language, New Norse, he was well-known, admired, and beloved by his countrymen. Translations into Swedish and Danish won him a wide Scandinavian audience. His position in Norwegian letters has been compared to that of Pär Lagerqvist (q.v.) in Sweden and Martin A. Hansen (1909–1955) in Denmark.

One of V.'s main themes is the struggle for self-knowledge combined with the necessity of finding one's place in life. The most successful solution to these problems appears in *Det store spelet* (1934; The Great Cycle, 1967). The protagonist of this novel is Per Bufast, the oldest son of a farm family whose duty it is to take over the farm when his father dies. From his earliest childhood, Per is told that this is his destiny, but he rebels against it, trying to excel at school so that he can escape. He dreams of the excitement and pleasures in store for him in the wide world, but gradually he finds himself being pulled into the rural cycle of work and life and death. Finally he realizes the truth of his father's words that he will live on the farm all of his days and that the farm will give him all he needs.

In contrast to Per, Mattis, the hero of the novel *Fuglane* (1957; The Birds, 1969), is an outsider who is doomed to loneliness. A poor

Simple Simon with wonderful dreams, he is unfit for any kind of work, but he struggles vainly to understand and to solve his problems. Mattis forgives easily and is grateful for small acts of kindness, but others simply do not know what to do with him. When the sister he lives with falls in love with a lumberman he has brought home, Mattis drowns himself "feeling he has brought happiness like the birds and, like them, must die." *Fuglane* may be interpreted as a plea for understanding and acceptance of eternal children like Mattis.

The problem of communication is central to V.'s works. Many of his characters seem to be driven by daimonic forces. Sometimes they work themselves to death; sometimes they struggle under the weight of fear and guilt. Often the solution to their problems is simply the process of growing up, of learning. The basis of maturing is mutual help: a word, a look, a gesture, may be enough to save a person from disaster. Intuition is perhaps more important for V. than direct communication. Like children, his characters sense reality even when they cannot adequately express what they know. The silences between people can weigh more than their conversations.

V.'s works also reflect the tragedy of World War II. His novels of the 1930's hint of the strange and threatening world beyond the small farm communities and of impending destruction.

In *Kimen* (1940; The Seed, 1965) V. explores the nature of violence, the desire for revenge that it evokes, and finally the resulting self-examination and search for atonement. Violence, which is insane, self-perpetuating, and against the natural order, must be countered by calm, reflection, and an attempt to bring the communal mind back to itself.

The subject of *Huset i mørkret* (1945) is the problem of Norway under the German occupation. V. is concerned here with the decision to resist or not, and with the effects of this decision on human relationships. Loneliness and the need for friendship play no small part in one's decision to collaborate or to rebel.

Although V.'s early works were often romantic, religious, and sentimental, he gradually began to emphasize human development, acceptance of responsibility, understanding, and cooperation. After World War II his style became more and more terse and abstract. His last work, *Båten om kvelden* (1968), contains much autobiographical material and reviews those themes that had fascinated him through-

out his life. It stresses the need for self-fulfillment and right action, and suggests that when one has lived properly, one is not afraid of death.

FURTHER WORKS: *Menneskebonn* (1923); *Sendemann Huskuld* (1924); *Guds bustader* (1925); *Grindegard: Morgonen* (1925); *Grindekveld, eller Den gode engelen* (1926); *Dei svarte hestane* (1928); *Klokka i haugen* (1929); *Fars reise* (1930); *Sigrid Stallbrokk* (1931); *Dei ukjende mennene* (1932); *Sandeltreet* (1933); *Ultimatum* (1934); *Kvinnor ropar heim* (1935); *Leiret og hjulet* (1936); *Hjarta høyrer sine heimlandstonar* (1938); *Kjeldene* (1946); *Bleikeplassen* (1946); *Morgonvinden* (1947); *Leiken og lynet* (1947); *Tårnet* (1948); *Lykke for ferdesmenn* (1949); *Signalet* (1950); *Vindane* (1952); *Løynde eldars land* (1953); *Vårnatt* (1954; Spring Night, 1965); *Ver ny, vår draum* (1956); *Ein vakker dag* (1959); *Brannen* (1961); *Is-slottet* (1963; The Ice Palace, 1966); *Bruene* (1966; The Bridges, 1970)

BIBLIOGRAPHY: Skrede, R., "T. V.," *Norseman*, XI (1953), 206–09; McFarlane, J. W., "T. V.," in *Ibsen and the Temper of Norwegian Literature* (1960), pp. 182–87; Dale, J. A., "T. V.," *American-Scandinavian Review*, LIV (1966), 369–74; Naess, H. S., Introduction to *The Great Cycle* (1967); Stendahl, B. K., "T. V., a Friend," *BA*, XLII (1968), 537–39; Chapman, K. G., *T. V.* (1969)

WALTER D. MORRIS

VIAN, Boris

French dramatist, novelist, and poet, b. 10 March 1920, Ville-d'Avray; d. 23 June 1959, Paris

The son of a Provençal father and a Parisian mother, V. had a quiet childhood in a middle-class Parisian suburb. When he was twelve, a severe case of rheumatic fever developed into the cardiac condition he was to die of twenty-seven years later. He nevertheless managed to continue his schooling. In 1939 he began to study engineering at the École Centrale des Arts et Manufactures.

During the gloomy war years, V. unenthusiastically worked as an engineer. However, by the end of 1944 he was playing a vital role in the existentialist intellectual life of post-liberation Paris. A jazz enthusiast, V. became a trumpeter at the Tabou, one of the Saint Germain-des-Prés *caves* (nightclubs) favored by the young. At the same time he began contributing to the magazines *Jazz Hot* and Sartre's (q.v.) *Les Temps modernes.*

In 1946, V.'s novel *J'irai cracher sur vos tombes* was an immediate *succès de scandale* that was to overshadow his entire literary career. V. pretended that he was only the translator of the novel and that the real author was an American, Vernon Sullivan. Violent and erotic, the book shocked readers and had to be withdrawn. V. and the publisher were fined, and the critics—particularly those who had reviewed the novel enthusiastically—never forgave V. when he announced that he was Vernon Sullivan and that the book, written in ten days as a joke, had no literary value whatsoever.

One of V.'s striking traits was his versatility. He was often simultaneously an engineer, a lecturer, a novelist, a translator (of Algren and Strindberg, qq.v.), a playwright, a poet, an inventor of mechanical gadgets, a jazz critic, a song writer, a singer, a stage director and actor, and a librettist. V. was genuinely interested and successful in all these media.

Of far greater importance than the four "translations" he published as Vernon Sullivan is his other fiction, including his early work. *Vercoquin et le plancton* (1946) gives a picture of French youth at the end of the war—a world of dances and surprise parties. V.'s comic vein is already at its best here, reminding one of François Rabelais (1494–1553) or Jarry (q.v.). Though *L'Écume des jours* (1947; Mood Indigo, 1969) is a rather banal love story, V. manages, through the moving and pathetic character of Chloé, to convey a number of his philosophical ideas, his love of life, his passion for justice, his hatred for what is cruel and artificial in society.

V.'s plays were not successful during his lifetime but are now frequently revived. They are pointed satires of middle-class values and often take as a special target the military. *Les Bâtisseurs d'empire* (1959; The Empire Builders, 1967), probably V.'s best play, goes beyond the superficial satire of social institutions; with a weirdness reminiscent of Ionesco's (q.v.) plays, it points up the fundamental absurdity of life.

Most of V.'s poetry is as yet unpublished; however, his biting and brilliant song lyrics remind one of Prévert (q.v.): the fanciful and the poetic are laced with social criticism.

During his lifetime V. was an object of scandal, and for years after his death he was ignored. Critics have now begun to reevaluate his work, and literary snobbery has contributed to his current popularity in France. Once considered an existential playboy, the court jester of Saint Germain-des-Prés, V. is now viewed by some critics as the most relevant writer of the 1950's. A fair evaluation probably lies somewhere between the two extremes.

FURTHER WORKS: *L'Automne à Pékin* (1947); *Les Morts ont tous la même peau* (1947); *Barnum's Digest* (1948); *Et on tuera tous les affreux* (1948); *Elles se rendent pas compte* (1948); *Les Fourmis* (1949); *L'Herbe rouge* (1950); *Cantilènes en gelée* (1950); *L'Équarissage pour tous* (1950; The Knacker's ABC, 1968); *L'Arrache-coeur* (1953); *En avant la Zizique . . . et par ici les gros sous* (1958); *Fiesta* (1958); *Le Goûter des généraux* (1962; General's Tea Party, 1967); *Les Lurettes fourrées* (1962); *Je voudrais pas crever* (1962); *Le Dernier des métiers* (1965); *Textes et chansons* (1966); *Trouble dans les Andains* (1966)

BIBLIOGRAPHY: *B. V.* (*Cahiers du Collège de Pataphysique*, 1960); Noakes, D., *B. V.* (1964); De Vrée, F., *B. V.* (1965); Arnaud, N., *Les Vies parallèles de B. V.* (1966); Baudin, H., *B. V.: La Poursuite de la vie totale* (1966); Clouzet, J., *B. V.* (1967)

JEAN-CLAUDE MARTIN

VIDAL, Gore

American novelist, dramatist, journalist, and critic, b. 3 Oct. 1925, West Point, New York

The grandson of a senator, V. traveled widely as a child, studied at Phillips Exeter Academy, and spent World War II as a maritime warrant officer in the army. While still in the service, he wrote his first novel, *Williwaw* (1946), which focuses on a group of men aboard an army freighter caught in an Aleutian storm. A scrupulously realistic account with terse dialogue and little character analysis, it was well received by critics.

With the publication of *The City and the Pillar* (1948), V. became a noted—and, to some, notorious—figure. A popular success because of its frank treatment of a male prostitute who is fixated on the memory of his first homosexual affair, the novel was greeted with critical hostility. V. revised and improved it in 1965 by eliminating the melodramatic murder at the end and by deleting much of the philosophizing on the nature—and naturalness—of homosexuality.

V.'s next novels were more ambitious in theme, structure, and style. *The Judgment of Paris* (1952) is a modern version of the Greek myth: an American traveling in Europe encounters three forceful women and finally chooses his Aphrodite from among them. The book is filled with satirical thrusts at modern conceptions of the absolute power of love. In it V. best develops his vision of a world without a moral center.

Failing to obtain through novel-writing the financial rewards he desired, V. turned to the theater, films, and television. His play *The Best Man* (1960), the study of a presidential campaign, was an immediate popular success. Staged while V. was himself a candidate for Congress (unsuccessful), the play examines two ambitious rivals who destroy each other's chances for office. Unfortunately, its mild political comments and hints of the rivals' future reconciliation make it rather intellectually bland.

After his success in the theater and on television, V. turned once more to the novel. The immediate result was *Julian* (1964), his most ambitious effort. An extensively documented study of the 4th-c. Roman emperor who unsuccessfully attempted to stem the Christian tide, the novel is narrated by two old scholars who are as intent on their personal rivalries as on the object of their research. In this work V. achieves his most successful balance of the comic and the serious.

The preponderantly comic *Myra Breckinridge* (1968) is a much more limited success. Published during a time of more relaxed sexual standards, this novel tries its best to duplicate the shock of *The City and the Pillar.* It stresses the dominant influence of Hollywood on all American culture and is content with obvious but amusing jokes.

V.'s most successful achievements are his essay collections—*Rocking the Boat* (1962) and *Reflections upon a Sinking Ship* (1969)—in which his wit is most assured. An acknowledged devotee of George Bernard Shaw (q.v.), he best approaches the brilliance of his master when undistracted by the necessities of plotting and characterization. His less perishable topical essays may well be remembered when his other works—with the exception of *The Judgment of Paris* and *Julian*—are forgotten. By and large, it is V.'s extreme sensitivity to the time we live in that animates his best work.

FURTHER WORKS: *A Search for the King* (1950); *Dark Green, Bright Red* (1950); *Visit to a Small Planet, and Other Television Plays* (1956); *A Thirsty Evil* (1956); *Romulus, A Comedy* (1962); *Three Plays* (1962); *Weekend* (1968); *Two Sisters* (1970)

BIBLIOGRAPHY: Aldridge, J. W., "America's Young Novelists," *SRL*, XXXII (12 Feb. 1949), 6–8, 36–37, 42; Walter, E., "Conversations with G. V.," *Transatlantic Review*, No. 4 (Summer 1960), pp. 5–17; Marcus, S., "A Second Look at Sodom," *New York Herald Tribune Book Week*, 20 June 1965, p. 5; White, R. L., *G. V.* (1968)

RICHARD PEARSE

VIITA, Lauri Arvi

Finnish poet and novelist, b. 17 Dec. 1916, Pirkkala; d. 22 Dec. 1965, Helsinki

The son of a construction worker, V. went to work as a carpenter and construction worker before completing high school. He continued, however, to read widely and was especially interested in modern science.

V.'s first collection of poems, *Betonimylläri* (1947), was well received, and the second, *Kukunor* (1949), confirmed his fame, although its whimsical elements bewildered many critics. His success encouraged other writers in his native city to form a literary club that consisted mostly of working men, except for A. Matson, an older critic and essayist, who guided the discussions. In 1948, V. married Aila Meriluoto, a well-known poet; they were divorced in 1956.

V.'s novel *Moreeni* (1950) showed him to be a good realistic writer, but poetry continued to be his chief field of endeavor. His next volume of verse, *Käppyräinen* (1954), less whimsical than *Kukunor*, was again a success. About this time he developed a severe neurosis and had to be temporarily hospitalized. A new collection of poems, *Suutarikin, suuri viisas,* appeared in 1961, and V. was planning a novelistic trilogy, of which only the first volume, *Entäs sitten, Leevi* (1965), was published when he was killed in an automobile accident.

Conscious of his working-class origin, in his first collection V. occasionally assumed an aggressive social stance, but he soon discarded it, and at no time did he project a definite social or political message. The novel *Moreeni* is set in a working-class neighborhood at the beginning of this century, and though the Civil

War of 1918 is briefly described, V. is obviously more interested in the personal lives of his characters than in social events.

As a poet, V. made skillful use of many verse forms: regularly rhymed poems, poems in the traditional Finnish meter (for example, in the *Kalevala* epic), and unrhymed, free-form poems. The title poem in *Betonimylläri* describes the dreams of an "average" construction worker during a lunch break, but some aspects of these dreams are convincing only if one imagines a construction worker like V. himself. The poems in this collection are often violently satirical and aggressive, but V.'s protest is not specifically directed against social or political evils. He was more concerned with moral and philosophical questions; though in rebellion against the human condition, he believed in man's spiritual capacity to free himself of limitations and to reshape the world.

Kukunor is rather unique in Finnish literature. It is a playful and slightly nonsensical adult fairytale about a troll and a fairy who fall in love. Finding an old atlas, they choose for themselves the most appealing names in it: Kukunor (a lake in Central Asia) and Kalahari (a desert in South Africa). Interwoven with the delightful nonsense are serious symbolic themes, such as the possibility of making the desert—representing human life—bloom again. *Käppyräinen* was better received, as it is more immediately accessible. V.'s humor and satire are mellower in it, and his barbs are directed against pretentiousness. He shows great skill in presenting and ultimately combining contrasts. It is in this last collection that V. showed his greatest formal proficiency. The work includes several love poems that indicate a new freedom in personal expression. An almost absurd kind of humor is employed to hide the poet's anguish due to his recognition of evil in the world, but this humor is simultaneously a protest and an expression of ultimate hope.

V. belongs to those authors who, though they broke with pre-World War II literary traditions, did not follow the young modernists of the 1950's. Difficult to classify, he is a poet whose consummate formal skill and earnestness of purpose made all fashions and trends irrelevant.

FURTHER WORK: *Kootut teokset* (1966)

BIBLIOGRAPHY: Oinonen, Y., "Vaikutelmia kuluneen vuoden runoudesta," in *Työläisopiskelija* (1947), pp. 215–16; Kupiainen, U., "Kukunor," in *Näköala* (1949), pp. 314–21; Groundstroem, N., "Ur fjolårets finska prosa," in *Nya Argus* (1952), pp. 154–57; Kaasalainen, M., "Johdanto," in *L. V., Kootut runot* (1966); Viljanen, L., "Esipuhe," in *L. V., Kootut runot* (1966); Vuotila, L., *Kirjailija ja omatunto. Pekkanen, Linna, Siippainen ja V. eettisinä kirjailijoina* (1967)

JAAKKO A. AHOKAS

VILLAESPESA, Francisco
Spanish poet and dramatist, b. 14 Oct. 1877, Laujar, Almería; d. 9 April 1936, Madrid

For a time V. studied law at the University of Granada. From 1897 until his death—in poverty—he lived a bohemian life in Madrid. V. was a follower of Darío (q.v.) and a friend of J. R. Jiménez (q.v.), the Machado brothers (q.v.), and Ramón Pérez de Ayala (q.v.). He contributed to literary journals and was a member of the modernist movement.

Year after year V. published new volumes of poetry, poems in which he made inventive use of new meters and tonalities to describe the morbid and the decadent. He showed a preference for themes of sensuality, disgust with life, and death; yet at the same time his poetry was rich in imagination and feeling. It revealed the influence of José Zorrilla (1817–93) and Salvador Rueda (1857–1933). Above all it clearly professed V.'s faith in the aesthetic theories of D'Annunzio and Eugénio de Castro (qq.v.), whom he translated into Spanish.

V.'s plays, mostly treating Oriental themes, such as *El alcázar de las perlas* (1912) and his modern version of the historic episode of *Aben Humeya* (1912), have the same faults and qualities as his poetry. In their time they were very successful.

FURTHER WORKS: *Intimidades* (1898); *Luchas* (1899); *La copa del rey de Thule* (1900); *La musa enferma* (1901); *Tristitiae rerum* (1906); *El jardín de las quimeras* (1909); *Los remansos del crepúsculo* (1911); *El rey Galaor* (1913); *Ajimeces de ensueño* (1914); *Judith* (1914); *Los nocturnos del Generalife* (1915); *La leona de Castilla* (1915); *Sonetos espirituales* (1917); *Los conquistadores* (1925); *La gruta azul* (1927); *Obras completas* (12 vols., 1927, 1954); *Teatro escogido* (1951); *Novelas completas* (1952); *Poesías completas* (2 vols., 1953)

BIBLIOGRAPHY: Alvarez Sierra, J., V.

XAVIER VILLAURRUTIA

ANDREI VOZNESENSKI

(1949); Siebenmann, G., *Die moderne Lyrik in Spanien* (1965); Ilie, P., *The Surrealist Mode in Spanish Literature* (1968)

GONZALO SOBEJANO

VILLAURRUTIA, Xavier

Mexican poet, playwright, novelist, and critic, b. 27 March 1903, Mexico City; d. there, 25 Dec. 1950

During the 1920's and early 1930's V. collaborated in various vanguard movements to renew Mexican literature and make its appeal universal. In 1935 he received a Rockefeller Foundation grant to study dramatic composition at Yale Universty. After he returned to his native land, V. taught literature at the University of Mexico and wrote some of his best-known plays and poems.

Most critics consider V. a poet first and a dramatist second. His poetry may be divided into three phases, the first of which is represented by *Reflejos* (1926). In this collection, impressionistic reflections of external reality are depicted in precise, metaphoric language shaded by tones of melancholy and solitude.

V.'s second poetic phase is exemplified by *Nostalgia de la muerte* (1938), generally viewed as his masterpiece. Here the author denies the objective world and, turning to solipsism, seeks in vain to discover a deeper, more intimate reality hidden within his own conscience. Death emerges as the central theme in this significant work, melancholy turning to anguish and solitude to fear of impending disaster. For example, in "Nocturno de la estatua" the poet describes a surrealistic dream in which his attempts at communication are reduced to echoes, and a nearby wall is transformed into a mirror reflecting an image of death. In "Décima muerte," V.'s most famous poem and a classic in Mexican poetry, death is no longer dreaded but welcomed as an *amada* evoked through sensuous baroque imagery.

V.'s last volume of verse, *Canto a la primavera y otros poemas* (1948), marks an abrupt thematic shift from death to unbridled amorous passion. In spite of its technical excellence, it fails to sustain the originality and depth of *Nostalgia de la muerte*.

During the 1930's V. produced five experimental one-act plays, which, published in 1943 under the title *Autos profanos,* constitute the most significant portion of his theater. Ironic in tone, they dramatize the human condition as embodied in weak, puppetlike characters torn by indecision, frustrated by their inability to communicate, and ultimately condemned to loneliness. The poetic style and subtle, philosophic nature of these works create a timeless, ivory-tower atmosphere and oblige the spectator (or reader) to grapple with abstract ideas removed from the realm of immediate reality.

In the final decade of his life, V. wrote and successfully staged a number of three-act plays of wider popular appeal because of their well-structured plots and situations bordering on the melodramatic. Generally speaking, however, they lack the literary merit of *Autos profanos,* the only exception being *Invitación a la muerte* (1944). Because of this play's portrayal of a youth's metaphysical anguish, it is considered a modern Mexican *Hamlet* and V.'s most profound and universal dramatic composition.

V. was well acquainted with several foreign literatures, possible influences on his works including William Blake (1757–1827), Charles Baudelaire (1821–67), Martin Heidegger (b. 1889), Rilke, and Jiménez (qq.v.). As a translator he introduced to the Mexican stage dramas by Lenormand, Romains, Chekhov, and Pirandello (qq.v.).

Although the best of his literary production has been understood and acclaimed by only a limited public, V.'s impeccable style and highly sensitive treatment of existentialist themes have made him one of the most original, significant, and, one might add, disquieting Mexican writers of his generation.

FURTHER WORKS: *Dama de corazones* (1928); *Dos nocturnos* (1931); *Nocturnos* (1931); *Parece mentira* (1933); *¿En qué piensas?* (1934); *Ha llegado el momento* (1934); *Sea Ud. breve* (1934); *Nocturno de los ángeles* (1936); *El ausente* (1937); *Nocturno mar* (1937); *Textos y pretextos* (1940); *Décima muerte y otros poemas no coleccionados* (1941); *La hiedra* (1941); *La mujer legítima* (1942); *La mulata de Córdoba* (1944); *El yerro candente* (1944); *El solterón* (1945); *El pobre Barba Azul* (1946); *La tragedia de las equivocaciones* (1950); *Juego peligroso* (1953); *Poesía y teatro completos de X. V.* (1953); *Cartas de V. a Novo, 1935–1936* (1966)

BIBLIOGRAPHY: Beck, V. F., "X. V., dramaturgo moderno," *RI*, XVIII (1952), 27–39; Dauster, F., "La poesía de X. V.," *RI*, XVIII (1953), 345–59; Lamb, R. S., "X. V. and the Modern Mexican Theatre," *Modern Language Forum*, XXXIX (1954), 108–44;

Leiva, R., *Imagen de la poesía mexicana contemporánea* (1959), pp. 151–63; Moreno, A., "X. V.: The Development of His Theater," *Hispania*, XLIII (1960), 508–14; Shaw, D., "Pasión y verdad en el teatro de V.," *RI*, XXVIII (1962), 337–46; Forster, M. H., *Los contemporáneos* (1964), pp. 83–91

GEORGE R. MCMURRAY

VIRZA, Edvarts

(pseud. of *Edvarts Lieknis*), Latvian poet, b. 27 Dec. 1883, Billites, Salgale; d. 1 March 1940, Riga

V. was born and grew up on the fertile plain of Zemgale in southern Latvia. The ancient patriarchal Zemgale homestead was to recur as the protagonist in several of his works. He later studied in Moscow and Paris. In his youthful search for a personal style, he went from Russian to French symbolism (*see* symbolism). With other writers, he initiated a Latvian symbolist movement that his opponents labeled decadent. His first collection of verse (*Biķeris*, 1908) exhibits characteristic symbolist traits—exclusive concern with personal experience, abundance of sensuous motifs, predominance of symbolist imagery.

During World War I, V.'s mother was killed by a stray German bullet while fleeing her country. This sad event effected a close bond between V. and the fate of his people. The first result of this identification was his work as a war correspondent. After 1918 he helped to shape the ideology of the newly founded Latvian state as an editor and a cultural leader.

V.'s Latvian translations of French poetry of the Renaissance and the 19th c. (*Franču renesanses lirika*, 1930; *Franču lirika XIX gadu simtenī*, 1921) helped him to achieve his own poetic style. As a result, his poems may strike readers as too closely bound to its Gallic models. He discovered a spiritual kinsman in the Belgian poet Verhaeren (q.v.), whose homeland—Flanders—is similar to the landscapes of V.'s Zemgale. (V.'s translations of Verhaeren's poems were published in 1936 as *Verharna dzeja*).

V. searched intensely for new sources of inspiration for Latvian poetry, wishing to free it from what he believed to be the crippling grip of German and Russian influences. France became his second homeland. For several years he was director of the Latvian press bureau in Paris. Through his efforts and through his work with French poetry, he was able to bring

about a neoclassicist concern with form in Latvian letters.

V. was deeply attracted by the age-old peasant ethos and made the yearly cycle of a 19th-c. Zemgale farm the subject of his novel-length poem in prose *Straumēni* (1933). The timeless peasant way of life that we find canonized in Latvian folksongs intertwines in this work with Christian elements, creating a synthesis that is rare in European literature. People and events are subordinate to the main protagonist—the old farm and its spirit—that inescapably determines the course of their lives. The narrative style is biblical and solemn. *Straumēni* is deficient in plot and action, yet the reader is swept along by its ecstatic emotional power, by the directness and limpidity of its narrative as well as the occasional aphoristic flashes that reveal its essence.

Among the subjects of V.'s epic poems are romanticized portraits of historic personalities —the Latvian king Nameitis and Duke Jacob of Kurland (*Poēmas*, 1924)—and aspects of Latvian peasant life (*Dievi un zemnieki*, 1939).

V. also published essays on literature, cultural life, and politics. Possessing the same heightened literary style as *Straumēni*, they tend to present conclusions in the form of striking aphorisms.

V. is a major Latvian poet and a master of classically strict poetic form. This is evident in *Dievišķīgās rotaļas* (1919), *Laikmets un lira* (1923), *Skaidrība* (1927), *Dzejas un poēmas* (1933), and *Pēdējās dzejas* (1942). The mature balance and clarity of his love and nature poetry contrasts with the intense pathos of his widely known patriotic verse.

FURTHER WORKS: *Zaļā Zemgale* (1917); *La litterature lettonne depuis le reveil national* (1925); *Lauku balsis* (1927); *Laikmeta dokumenti* (1930); *Zem karoga* (1935); *Kārlis Ulmanis* (1935); *Jaunā junda* (1936); *Hercogs Jēkabs* (1937); *Kopoti raksti* (1939–40); *Virzas sarakste ar V. Dambergu* (1954); *Kopoti raksti* (4 vols., 1956–66)

BIBLIOGRAPHY: Andrups, J., and Kalve, V., *Latvian Literature* (1954); Matthews, W. K., *A Century of Latvian Poetry* (1957)

JĀNIS ANDRUPS

VITTORINI, Elio

Italian novelist, critic, and essayist, b. 23 July 1908, Syracuse; d. 14 Feb. 1966, Milan

The son of a minor railway employee, V.

spent most of his childhood in remote towns in various parts of Sicily. As a youth he left for the north, working on construction gangs and later as a proofreader for a Florentine newspaper. Around 1927 he began writing fiction, some of which he contributed to the antifascist Florentine review *Solaria*. He was almost totally self-educated.

In 1931, V. published a collection of tales under the title *Piccola borghesia*. His first novel, *Il garofano rosso* (written, 1932–33; The Red Carnation, 1948), was suppressed by the fascist government and published only after the war in 1948. Meanwhile V. had begun a parallel career as a translator and critic of American literature. During the 1930's he translated Faulkner, Steinbeck, Caldwell (qq.v.), and several 19th-c. authors, including Edgar Allan Poe (1809–1849).

All this early work, however, was only preparatory to the central novel of his career, *Conversazione in Sicilia* (1941; In Sicily, 1949). One difficulty with *Il garofano rosso* had been that it dealt with a middle-class and intellectual background that was not V.'s own; another was that it was relatively conventional in technique and showed no striking originality. In *Conversazione in Sicilia* V. struck out boldly into an original vein that is his chief and important contribution to modern literature. His intention, he explained, had been to create an "operatic novel" in which "*something* would do . . . what music does for the opera," *i.e.*, release the narrative from the necessity of realistic or logical sequence.

This "something" was a highly organized, rhythmic, allusive, richly imagistic prose resembling poetry more than it does the novel of the realistic tradition. The action in *Conversazione in Sicilia* is negligible. The narrator, Silvestro, a Milan typographer, is disturbed by the "abstract furies" that shout at him from newspaper headlines, and he sets out on a kind of pilgrimage to his Sicilian homeland. There he encounters various persons, some of them fascist, some antifascist, some non-politicized human beings such as his mother. In a kind of reversal of the Jungian night journey, he travels from darkness into light.

In the climactic scene, Silvestro conducts a dialogue with the ghost of his brother Liborio, evidently killed in the Abyssinian War. This encounter is a moving, strange, and original passage. It is followed by a kind of epilogue in which the mother washes the feet of a stranger who turns out to be the father: a prodigal father greeted by a forgiving son. But even this rather banal piece of allegory is saved by the oblique and poetic manner of its presentation.

With the end of World War II and the collapse of fascism, V. entered a period of crisis. It became evident that he had defined himself not so much as an antifascist writer but as a writer in opposition, a clandestine writer, a writer of highly poetic code. It also became evident that this personal poetic formation had at least partly incapacitated him for writing in a climate of freedom. He produced three more novels and several other volumes of fiction and miscellaneous writings after the war, but all this material is derivative of, and secondary to, *Conversazione in Sicilia*. The most important of these are *Uomini e no* (1945), a Resistance novel set in wartime Milan, and *Le donne di Messina* (1949; rev., 1964), a massive epic of postwar Italy, which fails largely because it lacks a central focus or aesthetic unity. During the late 1940's, V. edited the independent leftist review *Il Politecnico,* and toward the end of his life he and Italo Calvino (b. 1923) edited the literary quarterly *Il Menabò*. In addition, as a reader and editor for one of Italy's leading publishers, V. was influential in introducing many young authors.

FURTHER WORKS: *Viaggio in Sardegna* (1936); *Il Sempione strizza l'occhio al Frejus* (1947; The Twilight of the Elephant, 1951); *Erica e i suoi fratelli: La Garibaldina* (1956; The Dark and the Light, 1960); *Diario in pubblico* (1957); *Le due tensioni: appunti per una ideologia della letteratura* (1967)

BIBLIOGRAPHY: Pacifici, S., "Understanding V. 'Whole,'" *IQ*, I (1958), 95 ff.; Lewis, R. W. B., "E. V.," *IQ*, IV (1961), 55 ff.; Cambon, G., "E. V.: Between Poverty and Wealth," *WSCL*, III (1962), 20 ff.; Heiney, D., *Three Italian Novelists* (1968)

DONALD HEINEY

VOICULESCU, Vasile

Romanian poet, dramatist, novelist, and short-story writer, b. 27 Nov. 1884, Pîrscov; d. 26 April 1963, Bucharest

A physician by profession, V. first began publishing verse in *Convorbiri literare* and *Luceafărul*. His first volumes of poetry—*Poezii* (1916), *Din țara zimbrului* (1918), and *Pîrgă*

(1921)—revealed his talent for depicting local color and peasant life. Initially employing conventional and highly regular meter that echoes earlier Romanian poets, V. slowly develops originality and mastery of rhythms. *Din ţara zimbrului* won the Romanian Academy Prize; *Pîrgă,* more polymetric and relaxed, shows the influence of French *vers libre.*

His association in 1921 with the newly founded Cluj journal *Gîndirea* brought V. into contact with Romania's most distinguished interbellum literary group, whose leader was first Cezar Petrescu (q.v.) and later (1926) Nichifor Crainic (b. 1889). Other members included the great philosopher-poet Blaga (q.v.), Ion Pillat (1891–1945), and Adrian Maniu (1891–1968).

This group founded the *Gîndirism* movement, which looked to Romanian village life and Orthodox Christianity as the true sources of a national literature. The movement was characterized by both mysticism and fierce patriotism, which eventually led to the charge that it was fascist. The members drew upon colorful Romanian folk materials and Byzantine iconography.

V.'s masterpiece, *Poeme cu îngeri* (1927), winner of the Premiul Societăţii Scriitorilor, is the work of a mature poet. Here the mystic emerges fully. The dominant conceit is the angel, who pervades the entire universe in various guises—as a cloud, as a bee ("frantic angel"), as an airplane ("iron archangel"). Through these "angels" man finds his identity with God. The first poems in this collection are polymetric, but others are in a *vers libre* form that nonetheless retains end-on rhymes.

In *Urcuş* (1937, later published as *Suire*) and *Intrezăriri* (1939), V. returns to traditional metrics and the quatrain, redisciplining his lines to the old forms but profiting from his previous experimentation with free verse to produce double rhythms and an enrichment of traditional prosody. The poems show the influence on V. of the symbolists (*see* symbolism).

In line with *Gîndirism's* stress on the complementary function of the arts, especially poetry and drama, in 1930 V. had made his first attempt at a dramatic poem, *La pragul minunii.* His first play, *Fata ursului,* appeared the same year, and he continued writing plays until World War II—*Umbra* (1935) and *Demiurgul* (1943). Though the theater was closed to him after this, he left other plays in manuscript: the comedies *Gimnastică sentimen-*

tală and *Trandafir agăţător,* the historical drama *Pribeaga,* and the radio play *Darul domnişoarei Amalia.* V.'s talents lay chiefly in poetry; however, *Pribeaga,* an experimental play dealing with the early Wallachian history of the Byzantine period, will doubtless survive as one of V.'s major works.

After the war, V. maintained a literary silence until a year or two before his death when he published some short stories and new verse in *Steaua.*

The posthumously published verse in *Ultimele sonete închipuite ale lui Shakespeare în traducere imaginară de V. V.* (1964) reveals the same sensuous robustness and metrical felicity as his earlier work: a similar mingling of free-verse cadence and traditional meter and rhyme. More than just whimsy, these poems—the title literally means "Last Sonnets of Shakespeare as Imagined and Translated by V."—also celebrate in the Renaissance spirit V.'s thirst for spiritual completeness.

V.'s prose tales in *Povestiri* (1966; I, *Capul de zimbru*; II, *Ultimul Berevi*), *Zahei orbul* (1968), and *Viscolul* (1969) once again reveal his love of peasant life, his use of folklore for its philosophical implications, and his undiminished vitality.

V. is one of the interbellum writers recently rediscovered by the current generation of Romanian poets and critics. In search of a national identity and a faith for modern times, these young writers find special meaning in V.'s religious expression, which though derived from Orthodox Christianity is also mystically rooted in peasant feeling and lore—in what has been called his "autochthonous spirituality." They also admire V.'s craftsmanship: his subtle adaptations of new rhythms to old prosody and his adaptation of form to matter, as he blends the past with the future.

FURTHER WORKS: *Destin* (1933); *Duhul pămîntului* (1943); *Poezii* (1944); *Poezii* (1966); *Poezii* (2 vols., 1968); *Căprioara din vis* (1969); *Iubire magică* (1970). **Selected English translations:** Selections in *Anthology of Contemporary Romanian Poetry* (ed. R. MacGregor-Hastie; 1969)

BIBLIOGRAPHY: Munteanu, B., *Panorama de la littérature roumaine contemporaine* (1938); Panaitescu, D., and Pillat, I., *Panoramă a liricii româneşti* (1938); Panaitescu, D., Introduction to *Ultimele sonete închipuite ale lui Shakespeare în traducere imaginară de V. V.* (1964); Streinu, V., *Versificaţia modernă* (1966), pp. 220–22; Martin, A., "V. V.," in *Poeţi contemporani* (1967); Pop, I., "V. V. şi tentaţia mitului," *Luceafărul*, 1 April 1967, p. 7, and 8 April 1967, p. 7; Anghel, P., "Lumea lui V.," in *Arhivă sentimentală* (1968); Lazar, M., "Motivul tainei in proza lui V. V.," *Revista de istorie şi teorie literară*, XVII (1968), 303–11; Rau, A., "Poezia lui V. V.," Introduction to *Poezii* (2 vols., 1968); Bercus, C. I., "Activitatea medicală a poetului V. C. V. (1884–1963)," *Pagini din trecutul medicinii* (1970)

THOMAS A. PERRY

VOJNOVIĆ, Ivo
Croatian dramatist, poet, and short-story writer, b. 9 Nov. 1857, Dubrovnik; d. 30 July 1929, Belgrade

V., who was born into an aristocratic family, studied in Vienna and Zagreb, was a civil servant, and, after 1907, director of the Zagreb Theater.

V.'s literary career began with realistic short stories that recounted the lives of simple people set in a landscape described with originality (*Geranium*, 1880).

V.'s best dramatic works are *Ekvinocij* (1895), the tragedy of a mother who sacrifices herself to her son's happiness, and *Dubrovačka trilogija* (1901; Trilogy of Dubrovnic, 1968), which is a sequence of three one-act plays dealing with the glory and decline of the once-patrician free state of Ragusa. *Gospodja sa suncokretom* (1912) is set in the fashionable world of Venice. *Imperatrix* (1914) is a symbolic pacifist play. V.'s last dramatic work, *Prolog nenapisane drame* (1929), deals with the unconscious element in a writer's work.

The influence of Flaubert (1821–80) and Ibsen (q.v.) can be seen in V.'s writing, which reveals an unusual concern for purity of style.

FURTHER WORKS: *Ksanta* (1886); *Psyche* (1889); *Lapadski soneti* (1892–98); *Suton* (1900); *Allons enfants* (1901); *Na taraci* (1903); *Smrt majke Jugovića* (1907); *Vox clamans* (1910); *Lazarevo vaskresenje* (1913); *La Dalmatia* (1917; Dalmatia and the Jugoslav Movement, 1920); *Maškerate ispodkuplja* (1925); *Sabrana dela* (4 vols., 1939)

BIBLIOGRAPHY: Wenzelides, A., *V.* (1917); Gobalek, J., *V.* (1932); Balota, B. J. A., *V.* (1935); Batušić, S., "Problèmes et crises pendant la formation du théâtre national croate,"

Revue de l'histoire du théâtre, XVI (1964), 138–40; Special issue on Serbo-Croatian literature, *Europe*, Nos. 435–36 (1965)

EMIL ŠTAMPAR

VOLOSHIN-KIRIYENKO, Maksimilian Aleksandrovich
Soviet-Russian poet, b. 28 May 1877, Kiev; d. 11 Aug. 1932, Koktebel', Crimea

On his father's side V. was descended from a Cossack family from Zaporozhe in the Ukraine; his mother's family was German. V. was said to be French by education, Russian by language and temperament, and German by blood.

Returning to czarist Russia after several years in Paris, he joined the symbolists (*see* symbolism), became a member of the literary and philosophical circle of V. I. Ivanov (q.v.), and made his literary debut in the symbolist journal *Apollon* with translations of modern French poets including Claudel and Verhaeren (qq.v.). Before the outbreak of World War I, V. lived in Germany and Switzerland, where he was strongly influenced by German philosophy and by the anthroposophist Rudolf Steiner (1861–1925), who taught that knowledge of the spiritual world could be obtained through a system of self-discipline.

The poetry V. wrote before 1915 combines the formal clarity he learned from French poets, such as José-Maria de Hérédia (1842–1905), and the melodious, romantic subjectivity of Russian symbolism with a strikingly fresh evocation of the Greek myths, which were ever-present and meaningful to him.

Under the disastrous impact of war and revolution V. turned to prophecy and to visionary interpretations of the present. Russian religiosity, traditionally concerned with ultimate ends, gained the upper hand in V.'s writings. In *Stikhi o terrore—Putyami Kaina* (1923) in particular, he tried to discover a religious, ethical meaning in the revolutionary apocalypse. After 1924, V. was unable to publish anything, and he died forgotten and destitute.

FURTHER WORKS: *Stikhotvoreniya* (1910); *Anno mundi ardentis* (1916); *Iverni* (1918); *Demony glukhonemyye* (1919); *Verkharn. Sudba, tvorchestvo* (1919); *Stikhi* (1922)

BIBLIOGRAPHY: Slonim, M., *From Chekhov to the Revolution* (1962); Slonim, M.,

481

Soviet Russian Literature: Writers and Problems (1967); Maguire, R. A., *Red Virgin Soil: Soviet Literature in the 1920's* (1968); Pomorska, K., *Russian Formalist Theory and Its Poetic Ambiance* (1968)

HEINRICH STAMMLER

VOZNESENSKI, Andrei Andreyevich

Soviet-Russian poet, b. 12 May 1933, Moscow

V.'s father was an engineering professor and his mother a teacher of Russian literature. His childhood, including the years of World War II, was spent in Vladimir and Kurgan. He began writing poetry while studying at the Institute of Architecture in Moscow (1951–57). *Mozaika* and *Parabola,* his first volumes of verse, appeared in 1960, and in that same year he became a member of the Union of Soviet Writers.

Like his fellow poet Yevtushenko (q.v.), V. has attracted a large, enthusiastic audience of young people by his public poetry readings. He has traveled widely in western Europe and visited the United States on several occasions.

In Russia V. has been publicly rebuked for his "nihilistic" attitude toward the revolutionary traditions of Soviet literature. In June 1967 Soviet authorities refused to allow him to participate in an arts festival held in New York. Three years later they closed for "revision" an evening of theatrical entertainment built around V.'s poems and Vladimir Vysotzki's songs.

V.'s art can be traced to Russian poetry of the 1920's, above all to Pasternak (q.v.), with whom he was personally acquainted. However, his relationship to Pasternak is not that of a pupil indebted to his teacher, but rather that of a continuer and developer of an approach to poetry established by the older poet.

What distinguishes V. from the poets of his own generation and links him to the traditions of the 1920's is his tight, image-packed construction, experiments with language, and intellectualism—in a 1967 essay on Pasternak he deplored the impoverishment of intellectual poetry in Soviet Russia. His meter, rhythm, and stresses also seem closer to the tradition of the immediate postrevolutionary period than to the work of his contemporaries. Though he generally writes in iambics, he often employs blank verse.

The most immediately apparent feature of V.'s work is an emphasis on alliteration, asso-

nance, and puns. His poetry (which he considers experimental) is rich in bold imagery, startling verbal pictures, and sounds that recall jazz melodies. He also makes abundant use of colloquialisms and even slang, and has a remarkable ear for idiomatic language. Although V. once declared that rhyme was now obsolete, he himself employs various rhyme schemes, showing a preference for assonances.

V.'s political position is generally overestimated in the United States and is really no more than "legal opposition." His basic concern as a citizen is for freedom of expression. The principal motifs of his poetry are enthusiasm for man's creative endeavors, a horror of war, a lyrical appreciation of the Russian landscape, and disillusionment with middle-class conceptions of progress. This disillusionment is counterbalanced by the poet's humanistic ideals (*Oza,* 1964) and a cautious admiration for certain facets of Western life and culture.

Probably some of V.'s best poems were inspired by his travels in the United States, where though he found much that fascinated him he was often disturbed by an indifference —or hostility—to humanistic values and a preoccupation with material progress.

Though it is too early to evaluate V.'s poetry, the significance of his attempt to revive modernistic experimentation in Soviet poetry should not be underestimated. In a world that emphasizes a spurious ideal of progress, V. insists on the free expression and value of human personality.

FURTHER WORKS: *Pishetsya kak lyubitsya* (1962); *Treugolnaya grusha* (1962); *Antimiry* (1964; Antiworlds, 1967); *Akhillesovo serdtze* (1966); *Stikhi* (1967); *Ten zvuka* (1970). **Selected English translations:** *Selected Poems* (1964); Selections in *The New Russian Poets, 1953–1966* (1966); *Antiworlds, and The Fifth Ace* (1967)

BIBLIOGRAPHY: Reeve, F. D., "The Work of Russian Poetry Today," *KR,* XXVI (1964), 533–53; Blake, P., and Hayward, M., eds., Introduction to *Antiworlds, and The Fifth Ace* (1967)

M. KLIMENKO

VRCHLICKÝ, Jaroslav

(pseud. of *Emil Frída*), Czech poet, dramatist, essayist, and translator, b. 17 Feb. 1853, Louny; d. 9 Sept. 1912, Domažlice

A poor merchant's son, V. first intended to

prepare for the priesthood but then switched to the study of history. After traveling in Italy as a tutor, he obtained an administrative post in the Czech Institute of Technology. In 1879 he married a niece of the novelist Karolina Světlá (1830–99), but after a brief happy period the couple became estranged and finally separated in 1892. The following year V. was appointed professor of comparative literature at the University of Prague. His prolific literary output came to a sudden halt when in 1908 he was physically paralyzed by the mental illness that indirectly caused his death four years later.

V.'s best early poetry is to be found in the collection *Epické básně* (1876) and the epic cycles *Duch a svět* (1878), *Myty* (2 vols., 1879–88), and *Zlomky epopeje* (1886). In these works, his vast knowledge of French, Italian, and English literatures led him to break with the dominant German influences and look for new models. He was particularly attracted by the French romantics Charles Leconte de Lisle (1818–94) and Victor Hugo (1802–1885), whose *La Légende des siècles* pointed the way for V.'s own epic poems.

In later years a diffuseness and rhetoric that often marred V.'s lyrics gave way to a pruned and concise style perhaps best exemplified in *Meč Damoklův* (1912). Written during his last illness, it focuses on the essential tragedy of life with a stark simplicity for which he was able to find a correspondingly clear form that heightens the emotional power of these poems.

Though beginning in 1886, V. wrote thirty-five plays—*Dramatické dila* (33 vols., 1886–1912)—which, with the exception of his charming comedy *Noc na Karlštejně* (1884), were wooden imitations of classical and romantic dramas. Of far greater importance are his translations and literary criticism, which kept Czech literature in touch with literary trends in western Europe. Even those critics who are inclined to dismiss V.'s poetry as overblown and imitative acknowledge the Czech language's debt to his meticulous translations that introduced new forms and ideas as well as a

flexibility and maturity seldom previously attained. His translations include not only standard European classics by Hugo, Leconte de Lisle, Lord Byron (1788–1824), Alfred de Vigny (1797–1863), Giacomo Leopardi (1798–1837), Robert Browning (1812–89), and Giosuè Carducci (1835–1907), but poems by the American poets Edgar Allan Poe (1809–1849) and Walt Whitman (1819–92). They brought to a literary culture remote from the modern mainstream an amazing breadth of interest accompanied by verbal brilliance.

Though the reputation of V.'s poetry has declined since his death, he remains one of the single most important influences on 20th-c. Czech literature.

FURTHER WORKS: *Z hlubin* (1875); *Sny o štěstí* (1876); *Eklogy a písně* (1880); *Dojmy a rozmary* (1880); *Nové epické básně* (1881); *Pouti k Eldorádu* (1882); *Hilarion* (1882); *Smrt Odyssea* (1882); *Sfinx* (1883); *Perspektivy* (1884); *Jak táhla mračna* (1885); *Sonety Samotáře* (1885); *Twardowski* (1885); *Julian Apostata* (1885); *Hudba v duši* (1886); *Soud lásky* (1886); *Dědictví Tantalovo* (1887); *Barevné střepy* (1887); *È morta* (1889); *Hořká jádra* (1889); *Hlasy v poušti* (1890); *Hippodamie* (1891); *Fresky a gobeliny* (1891); *Život a smrt* (1892); *Nové barevné střepy* (1892); *Moje sonata* (1893); *Okna v bouři* (1894); *Sebrané spisy* (65 vols., 1895–1912); *Nové zlomky epopeje* (1895); *Pisně poutnika* (1897); *Skvrny na slunci* (1897); *Bar Kochba* (1897); *Rok basnikův* (1900); *Votivní desky* (1902); *Duše mimosa* (1903); *Piseň o Vinetě* (1906); *Strom života* (1910); *Básnické spisy* (19 vols., 1949 ff.). **Selected English translations:** *Satanella* (1932); Selections in *The Soul of a Century* (ed. R. A. Ginsberg; 1942), and in *A Century of Czech and Slovak Poetry* (ed. P. Selver; 1946)

BIBLIOGRAPHY: Weingart, M., *J. V.* (1920); Tichý, V., *J. V.* (1947); Páleníček, L., *J. V.* (1949); Součková, M., *The Parnassian: J. V.* (1964); Bukáček, J., *V. a Dante* (1965)

* * * *

W

WAIN, John Barrington

English novelist, poet, and critic, b. 14 March 1925, Stoke-on-Trent, Staffordshire

W. was educated at St. John's College of Oxford University, where he was a Fereday Fellow (1946–49). He lectured in English literature at the University of Reading from 1947 to 1955, when he resigned to become a freelance author and critic.

Hurry on Down (1953; Am., Born in Captivity, 1954), W.'s first novel, gained immediate attention and linked its writer with Kingsley Amis (q.v.), John Osborne (q.v.), Keith Waterhouse, and others popularly referred to at the time as Angry Young Men. Charles Lumley, hero (or antihero) of the novel, is a young, Oxford-schooled bourgeois who tries to escape from his rigidly stratified society and become neutral and classless. Many of his efforts are grimly comical, and there is fine irony in his ultimate achievement of the social position for which he was originally destined. The importance of the novel derives from W.'s insistence on Charles's personal identity as a product of his own struggles rather than the dictates of society. It is his own efforts, finally, that shape his life and bring him necessary insight into the moral value of the humane and personal.

W.'s next three novels, a volume of poems, and a collection of short stories followed in quick succession. The novels were deemed by some to be flawed by haste, repetitions, and sentimentality; they continue W.'s fundamental assertion of the dignity of the human being, limited and vulgar though he frequently may be.

Though characterized initially as "new-

academic" and somewhat superficial, W.'s poetry shows the consistent touch of the craftsman. *Wildtrack: A Poem* (1965), a set of variations on "the theme of human interdependence," is an uneven and somewhat diffuse work, but at the same time a wide-ranging and interesting contemplation of the dilemma of modern man.

Poetry and literary criticism have come to occupy more and more of W.'s time, attested by his extensive publications of both editions and original works. An extremely hard-working man possessed of a high degree of competence, W. seems most accurately characterized as a general man of letters, rare in an era devoted to specialization.

FURTHER WORKS: *Living in the Present* (1955); *A Word Carved on a Sill* (1956); *Preliminary Essays* (1957); *The Contenders* (1958); *A Travelling Woman* (1959); *Gerard Manley Hopkins: An Idiom of Desperation* (1959); *Nuncle, and Other Stories* (1960); *Weep Before God* (1961); *Strike the Father Dead* (1962); *Sprightly Running: Part of an Autobiography* (1962; rev., 1965); *Essays on Literature and Ideas* (1963); *The Living World of Shakespeare: A Playgoer's Guide* (1964); *The Young Visitors* (1965); *Death of the Hind Legs, and Other Stories* (1966); *Arnold Bennett* (1967); *The Smaller Sky* (1967)

BIBLIOGRAPHY: Wain, J., "My Nineteen-Thirties," *Evergreen Review*, No. 9 (Summer 1960), pp. 76–89; Bluestone, G., "J. W. and John Barth: The Angry and the Accurate," *Massachusetts Review*, I (1960), 582–89; Van O'Connor, W., "J. W.: The Will to Write," *Wisconsin Studies in Contemporary Literature*, I (Winter 1960), 35–49; Gindin, J., *Postwar*

British Fiction (1962); Karl, F., *The Contemporary English Novel* (1962); Martz, L., "Recent Poetry: Roethke, Warren and Others," *Yale Review*, LVI (Winter 1967), 274–84

VERGENE F. LEVERENZ

WALSCHAP, Gerard

Flemish novelist, playwright, and essayist, b. 9 July 1898, Londerzeel, Belgium

The son of a Brabant café owner, W. studied Thomist philosophy at the University of Louvain. After 1923 he contributed to various Flemish periodicals and quickly established his reputation. He won the Beernaert prize of the Royal Flemish Academy of Literature in 1930. Six years later he was made an Academy member, resigning in 1962 in protest against domination of the group by Catholic rightists.

Though W.'s plots are often laced with brutal passion and fate-ridden Flemings beset by overt or hidden violence, they generally end on a note of affirmation. "There's always new life, new gladness, and we're pushed aside," he wrote. His narratives concentrate on life's emotional high points and are unconcerned with questions of "good taste." Disdainful of anything that detracts from the psychological action, he avoids descriptions of nature and local color, focusing on man and society in a direct, functional, and sometimes sloppy prose that shows the influence of his journalistic writing. His stand on Catholicism was foreshadowed in his earlier works and has evolved into his present recognition that religious faith can "coexist" with his own paganism.

W.'s first major novel, *Adelaide* (1929), deals with a woman's desperate struggle against hereditary factors that lead from sensuality to madness. It was followed by *Eric* (1931) and *Carla* (1933), and in 1939 these works were published as *De Familie Roothoofd*, a masterful psychoanalytic trilogy that illustrates the literary tenets of W.'s "new objectivity."

Celibaat (1934) is a tale of gothic horror whose protagonist is the last and evil descendant of a Flemish aristocratic line. In direct, sober prose the author contrasts moving love scenes with ugly descriptions of his anti-hero's pathological behavior. Upon a special royal grant, the novel was combined with the earlier *Trouwen* (1933) and issued in a single-

volume English translation as *Ordeal and Marriage* (1963).

Determined to examine human egoism, cruelty, and hypocrisy without restraints, W. came into open conflict with his fellow Catholics, who were offended by his bold criticism of religion in *Sybille* (1938). *Bejegening van Christus* (1940) heralds his final divorce from the Church. Having shed the notion of sin, in *Houtekiet* (1940), generally considered W.'s masterpiece, he portrays the Dionysiac pagan he himself "would like to be," and he attempts to establish harmony between man and nature.

Denise (1942) recounts the emotional and moral crises of a tormented woman in her relationships with a wide variety of social types. W.'s distinctive, compressed writing here powerfully serves a tumultuous plot replete with strange coincidences. In a stylistic device he made his own, he manages to faithfully capture Flemish folk-speech and expertly integrate his dialogue within sentences of indirect construction.

The moral conflicts generated by World War II and the Nazi occupation of Belgium are analyzed in *Zwart en Wit* (1948). In *Oproer in Congo* (1952) W. turns his attention to the problems of Belgian colonialism.

The best of W.'s plays is *De Spaansche Gebroeders* (1937), in which he uses the rivalry of two siblings as a means of examining the factors that led to the Spanish Civil War (1936–39). *Muziek voor twee Stemmen of Wereld en Geloof* (1965) contains complex and difficult essays on epistemology and teleology, as well as accounts of W.'s indignant encounters of clerical interference in art and education. In sweepingly angry prose, W. calls for tolerance and forces his readers to come to grips with crucial ethical problems.

A strong, tormented mind that favors a rough and honest approach to problems, W. is a prestigious figure in contemporary Flemish literature. Despite his wide erudition, he stays centered on a strip of Flemish earth that bears, he says, "motivations that are equally valid for members of a sports-club, the storekeeper in his street, the villager, the city dweller, the Belgian, the foreigner, and the stateless man."

FURTHER WORKS: *Waldo* (1928); *Volk* (1930); *De Dood in het Dorp* (1930); *Jan-Frans Cantré* (1932); *De Vierde Koning* (1935); *Een Mensch van goeden Wil* (1936); *Het Kind* (1939); *Vaarwel dan* (1940); *Soo Moereman*

(1941); *De Consul* (1943); *Genezing door Aspirine* (1943); *Ons Geluk* (1946); *Moeder* (1950); *Zuster Virgilia* (1951); *Het kleine meisje en ik* (1953); *De Graaf* (1953); *Manneke Maan* (1954); *Reynaert de Vos* (1954); *Salut en Merci* (1955); *Janneke en Mieke in de Oorlog* (1955); *De Française* (1957); *De verloren Zoon* (1958); *De ongelooflyke avonturen van Timan Armenaas* (1960); *Nieuw Deps* (1961); *Alter Ego* (1964); *Dossier W.* (1966); *Het gastmaal* (1966); *Het avondmaal* (1968); *De kulturele repressie* (1969). **Selected English translations:** *Heart of Europe* (1943); *Harvest of the Low-lands* (1945)

BIBLIOGRAPHY: Elebaers, K., *De roman-kunst van G. W.* (1924); Goris, J. A., *Belgian Letters* (1946); Jonckheere, K., *Belgian Literature* (1958); Van Vlierden, B. F., *G. W.* (1958); Brandt Corstius, J. C., *G. W.* (1960); Brachin, P., ed., *Anthologie de la prose néerlandaise: Belgique I 1893–1940* (1966)

HENRI KOPS

WALSER, Martin

German novelist, dramatist, and critic, b. 24 March 1927, Wasserburg-on-the-Lake of Constance

W. studied the humanities at the University of Tübingen (1945–51), earning his Ph.D. with a dissertation on Kafka (q.v.). After a few years as a radio producer he became a free-lance writer. He has won wide recognition at home and abroad, the evidence of which is the many literary prizes he has been awarded. He now lives at Nussdorf/Überlingen-on-the-Lake of Constance.

Ein Flugzeug über dem Haus (1955), W.'s first collection of stories, made clear that W. had forged a style of his own though it is evident that he was under the influence of Kafka while writing the stories. They contain the themes that will form the basis of future works. W.'s primary concern is the struggle of the individual against the dehumanized mechanisms of society. Seldom able to escape, the protagonist gradually (often unknowingly) succumbs.

Observing and narrating from a distance, W. holds up a mirror to postwar society (he does not confine himself to Germany) and lets it recognize itself. Skillful and disciplined, he satirizes society clearly and convincingly. Although the final sentence in *Ein Flugzeug über dem Haus* is "I cannot change all this,"

W. knows well that change *is* his aim. He is a moralist, intending to shock people out of their complacency—which is the first step to change.

Ehen in Philippsburg (1957) centers on the institution of marriage as it is lived by several couples. One couple is the wealthy, socially powerful Volkmanns, who are unable to sustain a close marital relationship. Mrs. Volkmann, who gives lavish parties and attends them in low-cut gowns, betrays her husband only with "respected men." A young journalist is considered to have met the requirements only after he has become the lover of the clumsy, good-natured Anne Volkmann. All are either exploiters or victims—either in business or in love.

"Philippsburg" is the setting for all of W.'s works. For him this imaginary yet real town in the Germany of the *Wirtschaftswunder* could be any middle-sized German town. One of its inhabitants, Anselm Kristlein, is the central figure in *Halbzeit* (1960) and *Das Einhorn* (1966). In *Halbzeit* he is a successful traveling salesman and is estranged from his wife. He moves around frantically behind a pleasant façade. In *Das Einhorn* he is a writer who tries to experience and express love, but is able only to record the story of how futile this endeavor is. In both novels W. debunks cherished middle-class concepts. The epitaph for the tombstone of one character—"War is the Father of all Things"—might well apply to all of W.'s works.

W.'s plays also deal with different types of warfare. *Eiche und Angora* (1962; The Rabbit Race, 1963), which takes us to Philippsburg in 1945, 1950, and 1960, focuses on *engagement*, guilt, and suffering. As Parisian critics observed and the German audience felt, it puts contemporary Germany on trial. So does *Überlebensgroß Herr Krott* (1963), the subject of which is ruthless business rivalry. This is also true of *Der schwarze Schwan* (1964), a Hamlet-like play in which a man represses his activities during the Nazi period until his son uncovers his guilt.

Die Zimmerschlacht (1967) is a masterpiece on the war between the sexes. An inferno of lies, indifference, communication breakdowns, and hostility, it is strongly reminiscent of the vivisections of "conjugal love" of Strindberg, Updike (qq.v.), and Edward Albee (b. 1928).

W. is a formidable, ironical social observer and critic who studies social change by means of analysis of the individual. Though he maintains distance from his content, he is never abstract. His portrayals, vivid and immediate, reveal that he is an explorer who wishes to discover "the still-unknown land" of the human mind.

FURTHER WORKS: *Beschreibung einer Form: Franz Kafka* (1961); *Der Abstecher* (1961); *Lügengeschichten* (1964); *Erfahrungen und Leseerfahrungen* (1965); *Heimatkunde; Aufsätze; Reden* (1968); *Fiction* (1970)

BIBLIOGRAPHY: Hartlaub, G., "Ich sprach mit M. W.," *Westermanns Monatshefte,* CVIII (1967), ix, 56–61; Tindermans, C., "M. W.: De onmacht van het schrijven," *Dietsche Warande en Belfort,* CXII (1967), 458–65

ANNA OTTEN

WALSER, Robert

Swiss novelist, short-story writer, poet, and writer of prose poems, b. 15 April 1878, Biel; d. 25 Dec. 1956, Herisau

After working as a clerk in Switzerland and Germany, W. spent seven years in Berlin, living on the closest terms with his brother, the painter and stage designer Karl Walser (1877–1943). After this he lived in Biel and Bern, devoting himself to writing. For the last thirty years of his life he was mentally ill.

W.'s novel *Geschwister Tanner* (1907) stands in the intellectual tradition of Hesse's (q.v.) *Peter Camenzind;* here "the younger generation jauntily comes forward."

His masterpiece, *Jakob von Gunten* (1908; Eng., 1970), is a dreamlike diary recording events at a training school for servants as seen through Jakob's own special vision. It is whimsical and delightful as well as disturbing and elusive.

A large part of W.'s work consists of poetic prose pieces, partly romantic, playfully ironic descriptions of actual happenings, partly products of the imagination—small prose works of a filigree delicacy. A delight in storytelling, a quiet enjoyment of the here and now, and a sudden horror at the moral and spiritual decline of modern man all fuse in W. The serenity, the buoyancy, and also the enigmatic quality of W.'s language led Kafka (q.v.) to sense in him a kindred spirit.

W. is the most important representative of German-Swiss prose since Gottfried Keller (1819–90), C. F. Meyer (1825–98), and Carl Spitteler (q.v.).

FURTHER WORKS: *Fritz Kochers Aufsätze* (1904); *Der Gehülfe* (1907); *Gedichte* (1909); *Aufsätze* (1913); *Geschichten* (1914); *Kleine Dichtungen* (1914); *Kleine Prosa* (1917); *Der Spaziergang* (1917); *Poetenleben* (1918); *Seeland* (1920); *Gedichte* (1921); *Die Rose* (1924); *Große Kleine Welt* (1937); *Vom Glück des Unglücks und der Armut* (1944); *Gedichte* (1944); *Dichtungen in Prosa* (5 vols., 1953–59); *Unbekannte Gedichte* (1958); *Kleine Wanderung* (1963); *Gesamtausgabe* (1964 ff.); *Festzug* (1966); *Phantasien: Prosa aus der Berliner und Berner Zeit* (1966); *Olympia: Prosa aus der Bieler Zeit, 1925–26* (1967); *Maskerade: Prosa aus der Berner Zeit, 1927–28* (1968); *Der Europäer: Prosa aus der Berner Zeit, 1928–33* (1968). **Selected English translation:** *The Walk, and Other Stories* (1957)

BIBLIOGRAPHY: Seelig, C., *Wanderungen mit R. W.* (1957); Bänziger, H., *Heimat und Fremde* (1958); Waidson, R. M., "R. W.," in *German Men of Letters,* ed. A. Natan, Vol. II (1963), pp. 175–96; Pestalozzi, K., "Nachprüfung einer Vorliebe: Franz Kafkas Beziehungen zum Werk R. Ws.," *Akzente,* XIII (1966), 322–44

CARL SEELIG

WALTARI, Mika Toimi

Finnish novelist, short-story writer, and dramatist, b. 19 Sept. 1908, Helsinki

The son of a secondary-school teacher, W. published his first novel in 1925, graduated from high school in 1926, and achieved fame in 1928 with his novel *Suuri illusioni.* Since then he has written more than one hundred literary pieces of all kinds, including translations, film scripts, criticism, detective stories, and light fiction under various pseudonyms. He was elected to the Finnish Academy in 1957.

W.'s first works deal with the young people of the gay 1920's in Helsinki and reveal some of his basic qualities and defects: an elegant and witty style; an interest in topical subjects, which are treated with apparent boldness though from a fundamentally conservative point of view; and a somewhat superficially pessimistic philosophy of life. In his first books he introduces a character that continues to appear through his *œuvre:* a timid, idealistic, and slightly naïve young or middle-aged man who suffers from the evil in the world but cannot do anything to mitigate it and who

487

is inevitably made to suffer by women. W.'s women are almost always fickle, cunning, and calculating.

In the 1930's, W., realizing that the elegant and frivolous life of the 1920's was no longer fashionable, searched for new writing subjects. Among the works of this period was a trilogy on the growth of Helsinki as seen through the eyes of a family (I, *Mies ja haave,* 1933; II, *Sielu ja liekki,* 1934; III, *Palava nuoruus,* 1935; published together as *Isästä poikaan,* 1942).

In 1936, W. started a bitter controversy by charging two leading liberal critics with being communists. During World War II he worked for the government information service and published a book on Soviet espionage in Finland as well as wrote novels on Finnish history and on wartime life. Like many other members of the Finnish middle class, he saw the outcome of World War II as the victory of the Soviet Union and, consequently, the defeat of civilization by barbarism.

This view is reflected in the huge and colorful historical novels that W. wrote from 1945 on, such as *Sinuhe, egyptiläinen* (Am., The Egyptian, 1949; Eng., Sinuhe the Egyptian, 1949). They increased his fame in Finland and made him known abroad (his works have been translated into eighteen languages). In them he describes violent historical periods and wars in which great empires are overthrown. His subjects were Italy and Turkey in 1527 A.D. in *Mikael Karvajalka* (1948; Am., The Adventurer, 1950; Eng., Michael the Finn, 1950) and *Mikael Hakim* (1949; Am., The Wanderer, 1951; Eng., The Sultan's Renegade, 1951). He turned to the Etruscans and Romans in *Turms, kuolematon* (1955; Am., The Etruscan, 1956, abridged; Eng., The Etruscan, 1957) and to Byzantium in *Johannes Angelos* (1952; The Dark Angel, 1953). The protagonist is the same sensitive man W. had introduced in his early novels.

W.'s short stories and novellas contain the same kind of characters that appear in the historical narratives, but they lack the adventures and colorful settings. *Felix Onnellinen* (1958; The Tongue of Fire, 1959) and *Valtakunnan salaisuus* (1959; The Secret of the Kingdom, 1960) are on religious motifs. *Fine van Brooklyn* (1942), *Kultakutri* (1948; Moonscape, and Other Stories, 1954), and *Neljä päivänlaskua* (1949; A Nail Merchant at Nightfall, 1954) present variations on the theme of the relations between the sexes, seen in W.'s usual manner.

W., a skillful, elegant, and entertaining writer, is by far the best-known and most translated Finnish author.

FURTHER WORKS: *Jumalaa paossa* (1925); *Kuolleen silmät* (1926); *Sinun ristisi juureen* (1927); *Valtatiet* (with O. Paavolainen; 1928); *Yksinäisen miehen juna* (1929); *Dshinnistanin prinssi* (1929); *Muukalaislegioona* (1929); *Jättiläiset ovat kuolleet* (1930); *Siellä missä miehiä tehdään* (1931); *Appelsiininsiemen* (1931); *Keisarin tekohampaat* (with Armas J. Pulla; 1931); *Kiinalainen kissa* (1932); *Punainen madonna* (with Armas J. Pulla; 1932); *Älkää ampuko pianistia* (with Armas J. Pulla; 1932); *Yö yli Euroopan* (1933); *Aiotko kirjailijaksi?* (1935); *Surun ja ilon kaupunki* (1936); *Suomalainen lauantaiehtoo* (1936); *Judean yö* (1936); *Akhnaton, auringosta syntynyt* (1937); *Helsinki kautta vuosisatojen* (1937); *Kuriton sukupolvi* (1937); *Mies rakasti vaimoaan* (1937); *Toimittaja rakastaa* (1937); *Ihmeellinen Joosef* (1938); *Ihmeellinen Joosef eli elämä on seikkailu* (1938); *Jälkinäytös* (1938); *Kuka murhasi rouva Skrofin?* (1939); *Hämeenlinnan kaunotar* (1939); *Antero ei enää palaa* (1940); *Komisario Palmun erehdys* (1940); *Hankala kosinta* (1941); *Maa on ikuinen* (1941); *Kotikaupunkimme Helsinki* (with A. Blomberg; 1941); *Totuus Virosta, Latviasta ja Liettuasta* (1941); *Tulevaisuuden tiellä* (1941); *Yövuorossa* (1941); *Ei koskaan huomispäivää* (1942); *Fine van Brooklyn* (1942); *Hyvin harkittu — puoleksi tehty. Rationalisointi aseena tuotantotaistelussa* (1942); *Kaarina Maununtytär* (1942); *Neuvostovakoilun varjossa* (1942); *Novelleja* (1943); *Paracelsus Baselissa* (1943); *Rakkaus vainoaikaan* (1943); *Yövieras* (1943); *Jokin ihmisessä* (1944); *Tanssi yli hautojen* (1944); *Unohduksen pyörre* (1945); *Gabriel, tule takaisin* (1945); *Runoja* (1945); *Rakas lurjus* (1946); *Elämän rikkaus* (1947); *Noita palaa elämään* (1947); *Omena putoaa* (1947); *Portti pimeään* (1947); *Osakeyhtiö Weilin & Göös Aktiebolag 1872–1947* (with Niilo Hentola; 1947); *Kutsumaton* (1948); *Lähdin Istanbuliin* (1948); *Myöhästynyt hääyö* (1948); *Huhtikuu tulee* (1949); *Leikkaus* (1952); *Kuun maisema* (1953); *Vallaton Waltari* (1957); *Koiranheisipuu ja neljä muuta pienoisromaania* (1961); *Tähdet kertovat, komisario Palmu* (1962); *Keisari ja senaattori* (1963); *Ihmiskunnan viholliset*

MIKA WALTARI

HUGO WAST

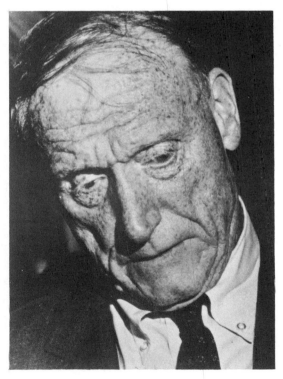

ROBERT PENN WARREN

(1964); *Pöytälaatikko, muistoja ja muistiinpanoja* (1967)

BIBLIOGRAPHY: Mazzucchetti, L., *Prefazione a M. W., Il podere* (1942); Hünger, H., "M. W.s literarisches Schaffen," in *M. W., Karin Magnustochter* (1943); Sauvageot, A., *Préface à M. W., Un inconnu vint à la ferme* (1944); Hakulinen, L., "Sinuhe egyptiläinen," in *Virittäjä* (1946), p. 99; Waltari, M., in *SatR*, XXXII (1949), 10; Van Hoek, K., "W. of Finland," *John O'London's Weekly*, XL (1951), pp. 917–18; Vallinkoski, J., "M. W. teosten käännökset," in *Bibliophilos* (1954), pp. 41–47; Hartwijk, H., "Turms, de onsterselijke door M. W., *De Nieuwe Gids*, No. 4591 (1956); Randel, W., "This Man W.," *BA*, XXX (1956), 165–67; *M. W. juhlakirja* (1958); Orta, M., "M. W. o el desdén frente al mundo," in *M. W., Obras completas* (1958); Velkoborsky, J. P., "Synteza wielkich iluzyj," in *M. W., Egipcjanin Sinuhe* (1967); Heino, Aarre, "Huomioita eräiden Waltarin pienoisromaanien kertojista," *Acta Universitatis Tamperensis*, XXXVI (series A, 1970)

JAAKKO A. AHOKAS

WARREN, Robert Penn

American poet and novelist, b. 24 April 1905, Guthrie, Kentucky

At fifteen W. received an appointment to Annapolis, but before he could undertake his studies for a naval career, he was blinded in the left eye in a freak accident. He therefore went to Vanderbilt University instead, intending to become an electrical engineer. However, he soon came under the influence of John Crowe Ransom, Allen Tate (qq.v.), and the other members of the Vanderbilt literary elite who would (with W.) some day be named "the Fugitives," after the magazine they published in the mid-1920's. A Rhodes scholar, W. has taught at several universities, including Louisiana State, where he helped found the influential *Southern Review*. In 1944–45, he was poetry consultant to the Library of Congress. Since 1950, he has been at Yale. W. married the novelist and essayist Eleanor Clark in 1952.

W. may be the most versatile man of letters writing in the English language today. The only man ever to win the Pulitzer Prize in both fiction and poetry, W. enjoys a literary reputation that would alone have been secure on the basis of his perceptive and clear-spoken

contributions to the "new criticism," (*see* literary criticism) or of his various literary textbooks and essays.

In fiction, W. launched a series of complex and carefully wrought philosophical novels with *Night Rider* (1939), a nightmare vision of flux and violence that, like nearly all W.'s art, draws upon W.'s native South for raw material. This was followed in 1943 by *At Heaven's Gate,* a richly multi-layered story of a search for identity by characters trapped on every side by falsehood, delusion, and betrayal. In 1946, W. published what many critics consider his masterpiece, *All the King's Men* (Pulitzer Prize for fiction, 1947). This novelistic inquiry into the meaning of history is famous partly because of its fictionalized portrait of Louisiana governor Huey Long as a main character.

A collection of short stories, *Circus in the Attic* (1948), was followed by five novels— *World Enough and Time* (1950), *Band of Angels* (1955), *The Cave* (1959), *Wilderness* (1961), and *Flood* (1964)—and by some distinguished writing in nonfiction, including social analyses such as *Segregation: The Inner Conflict in the South* (1956) and *Who Speaks for the Negro?* (1965).

Over the years W. has also published six major volumes of poetry: *Selected Poems, 1923–1943* (1944), which includes most of his two earlier collections, *Thirty-Six Poems* (1935) and *Eleven Poems on the Same Theme* (1942); *Brother to Dragons* (1953), a widely acclaimed narrative poem about murder and sadism in Thomas Jefferson's family; *Promises* (1957), a collection of lyrics dedicated to his infant son and daughter that won the Pulitzer Prize for poetry in 1958; *You, Emperors, and Others* (1960); *Selected Poems, New and Old, 1923–1966* (1966); and *Incarnations, Poems 1966–1968* (1968).

W.'s predominant theme in all his writing is self-definition, or a quest for identity that is usually set off against such false modes of identity as social climbing, money-making, sexual prowess, fame, or adherence to a philosophical, religious, or political sect. True self-definition ultimately requires what W. calls an "osmosis of being" between the self and the entirety of time and nature to which man owes his existence. It is this osmosis of being that requires Jack Burden in *All the King's Men* to accept responsibility for history; that causes Thomas Jefferson in *Brother to Dragons* to accept complicity in a sadistic murder committed without his knowledge; that leads a long series of W. characters in all his novels toward acceptance of a father figure, however shabby or unappealing; and that awakens a character in *Promises* to the recognition that "all Time is a dream, and we're all one Flesh, at last."

In addition to exploring and accepting the outer world of time and history and other people, the W. protagonist must also probe the dim caverns of his own psyche to find his true identity. Here, deeply below the level of name and conscious ego, and holding the secret of ultimate identity, W.'s equivalent to the Freudian id or Jungian shadow awaits the reluctant embrace of the surface ego.

This concept of an undiscovered self deep in the psyche—a permanent, broader self resembling Jung's collective unconscious—is set forth in a long series of animal images extending through decades of W.'s writing, both in prose and poetry. It is probably most brilliantly rendered in *Brother to Dragons*, whose title implies the darker self within. At this deeper level of being, there is a collective guilt and bestiality that is part of "original sin," or our heritage in being human. In man's subconscious being, however, in the realm of dream or animal intuition, W. also finds, paradoxically, a sense of order and permanence transcending the existential anxieties of the conscious ego.

The basic movement in W.'s art, then, is toward unification of self, through reconciling conscious and unconscious parts of the psyche, and toward relating the unified psyche to society, to time and nature, and to God. Full self-realization, W. believes, can be achieved only by thus connecting the self to its total environment, and subordinating the self to a larger being or process that goes on and on.

FURTHER WORKS: *John Brown: The Making of a Martyr* (1929); *An Approach to Literature* (with Cleanth Brooks and John T. Purser; 1936); *Understanding Poetry* (with Cleanth Brooks; 1938); *Modern Rhetoric* (with Cleanth Brooks; 1949); *Selected Essays* (1958); *The Legacy of the Civil War* (1961); *Audubon: A Vision* (1969)

BIBLIOGRAPHY: Bentley, E., "The Meaning of R. P. W.'s Novels," *KR*, X (Summer 1948), 407–24; Bradbury, J. A., *The Fugitives: A Critical Account* (1958); Casper, L., *R. P. W.: The Dark and Bloody Ground* (1960);

Strandberg, V., *A Colder Fire: The Poetry of R. P. W.* (1965); Longley, J. L., ed., *R. P. W.: A Collection of Critical Essays* (1965)

VICTOR H. STRANDBERG

WASSERMANN, Jakob

German novelist and short-story writer, b. 10 March 1873, Fürth; d. 1 Jan. 1934, Alt-Aussee, Austria

W., the son of a merchant in Bavaria, had an impoverished childhood. In Munich he became secretary to Ernst von Wolzogen (1855–1934), novelist and founder of cabaret Überbrettl. Through his help W. joined the staff, as associate editor, of the literary magazine *Simplicissimus*. After 1893, W. devoted himself entirely to writing, living first in Vienna and later in Alt-Aussee. Among his friends were Hofmannsthal, Schnitzler, Thomas Mann (qq.v.), and the statesman Walter Rathenau (1867–1922). W. was particularly influenced by Dostoyevski (1821–81), by psychoanalysis, and, in his later writings, by the studies of the Russian neurologist Constantin von Monakov. Before 1897 he wrote touchingly plaintive poems.

Caspar Hauser (1909; Eng., 1929), which is based on the life of the famous foundling, became in W.'s hands a bitter indictment of the "inertia of the heart" since Caspar in his helpless innocence becomes a victim of the calculating, wholly selfish, and rationalistic lack of understanding in his environment.

The hero of *Christian Wahnschaffe* (2 vols., 1919; expanded, 1932; The World's Illusion, 1922–23) is the son of an industrial magnate who abandons his family and property in order to experience poverty—the source of injustice and confusion. This novel, a critical exposé of the most important contemporary problems written in the style of Dostoyevski, was considered W.'s major work until the appearance of the Kerkhoven trilogy.

The first volume of the Kerkhoven trilogy, *Der Fall Maurizius* (1928; The Maurizius Case, 1929), inspired by a criminal case against a man named Hau, is the tragic story of a miscarriage of justice brought to light by young Etzel Andergast. In *Etzel Andergast* (1930) W. presented a penetrating psychological analysis of post-World War I youth, its problems and its precarious position. The story is continued (with many autobiographical elements) in *Joseph Kerkhovens dritte Existenz*

(1934; Kerkhoven's Third Existence, 1934), in which Kerkhoven, a doctor, frees himself from all earthly vanities in the spirit of Monakov's teachings.

As a novelist W. was a typical representative of the neoromantic style, striving to combine subtle psychology with the ethics of redemption, formal artistry with the claims of humanity. His social criticism and use of characters *à clef* were intended to lend realistic touches to his narratives. In his work the old form of the strongly plotted novel (q.v.) reaches one of its last peaks before the emergence of the modern novel (of what W. rejected as "non-story-telling"), as developed by Joyce, Proust, and Musil (qq.v.).

FURTHER WORKS: *Melusine* (1896); *Die Juden von Zirndorf* (1897; The Dark Pilgrimage, 1953); *Schläfst du, Mutter?* (1897); *Die Schaffnerin* (1897); *Hockenios oder Die Lügenkomödie* (1898); *Die Geschichte der jungen Renate Fuchs* (1901); *Der Moloch* (1903); *Der nie geküßte Mund* (1903); *Die Kunst der Erzählung* (1904); *Alexander in Babylon* (1905; Eng., 1949); *Die Schwestern* (1906); *Die Masken Erwin Reiners* (1910); *Der Literat* (1910); *Der goldene Spiegel* (1911); *Die ungleichen Schalen* (1912); *Faustina: Ein Gespräch über die Liebe* (1912); *Der Mann von vierzig Jahren* (1913); *Deutsche Charaktere und Begebenheiten* (2 vols., 1915); *Das Gänsemännchen* (1915; The Goose Man, 1922); *Der Wendekreis* (4 vols., 1920–24; 1, *Der unbekannte Gast, Adam Urbas, Golowin, Lukardis, Ungnad, Jost*; II, *Oberlins drei Stufen* [Oberlin's Three Stages, 1926]; *Sturreganz*; III, *Ulrike Woytich* [Gold, 1924]; IV, *Faber oder Die verlorenen Jahre* [Faber, or the Lost Years, 1925]); *Mein Weg als Deutscher und Jude* (1921; My Life as German and Jew, 1933); *Das Gold von Caxamalca* (1923); *Der Geist des Pilgers* (1923); *Laudin und die Seinen* (1925; Wedlock, 1926); *Der Aufruhr um den Junker Ernst* (1926; The Triumph of Youth, 1927); *Lebensdienst* (1928); *Christoph Columbus* (1929; Christopher Columbus, 1930); *Hofmannsthal, der Freund* (1930); *Bula Matari* (1932; Bula Matari: Stanley, Conqueror of a Continent, 1933); *Selbstbetrachtungen* (1933); *Tagebuch aus dem Winkel* (1935); *The Letters of J. W. to Frau Julie Wassermann* (1935); *Olivia* (1937); *Briefe an seine Braut und Gattin Julie, 1900–29* (1940); *Gesammelte Werke* (7 vols., 1944–48); *Geliebtes Herz: Briefe an eine Unbekannte* (1949);

Bekenntnisse und Begegnungen (1950). **Selected English translation:** *World's End: Five Stories by J. W.* (1927)

BIBLIOGRAPHY: Bing, S., *J. W.* (2nd ed., 1933); Karlweis, M., *J. W.* (1935); Blankenagel, J. C., *The Writings of J. W.* (1942); Regensteiner, H., "J. W. in Retrospect," *Revue des Langues Vivantes*, XXX (1964), 590–601

JOSEF STRELKA

WAST, Hugo

(pseud. of *Gustavo Martínez Zuriría*), Argentinian novelist, b. 23 Oct. 1883, Córdoba; d. 28 March 1962, Buenos Aires

W.'s family resettled in Santa Fe, where he attended the National University. During his long and active life, he was a newspaper editor, lawyer, professor, rancher, deputy in the National Congress, provincial governor, and for twenty-three years director of the National Library. In addition he traveled extensively throughout Europe.

For several years after World War I, W. was the most popular novelist in Latin America. Sales of his top three novels alone totaled over half a million copies and his books were translated into thirteen languages. His extraordinary success may be attributed in large part to his ability to devise exciting plots. He once observed: "*Robinson Crusoe*, Stevenson's *Treasure Island* and Pereda's *Sotileza* are the books of imagination I have read oftenest. They are simple, human, popular and eternal."

The works of Sir Walter Scott (1771–1832) and Jules Verne (1828–1905) also fired W.'s imagination and helped to shape his novelistic style. His embattled heroes and heroines are constantly involved in complicated intrigue, dangerous situations, and hairbreadth escapes. One exciting incident follows hard on the heels of another, frequently in melodramatic fashion.

Another major portion of W.'s appeal lies in the skill with which he depicts rural types and the picturesque background against which they move. He shows a clearcut kinship with José María de Pereda (1833–1906) in his sympathetic portrayal of country people and country life. Some of his best scenes reflect his brief experience as a cattle raiser—gauchos riding the range, roundups, country dances, maté drinking. His deep religious feeling, great moral integrity, and profound concern for his fellowman convey a basic humanity that for a vast reading public more than compensates for a stylistic oversimplification and lack of artistic polish that have incurred critical disfavor.

W.'s first novel, *Alegre,* appeared in 1906, but it was not until the publication of *Flor de durazno* (1911; Peach Blossom, 1929) that he caught the public eye. This sentimental story of the trials of an unwed mother, reminiscent of Jorge Isaac's (1837–95) *María* in its poetic blending of human emotion and breathtaking natural beauties, was W.'s most popular work, passing through thirty-three editions. *La casa de los cuervos* (1916; The House of Ravens, 1924) is possibly his best novel from a technical standpoint. It is a story of love and adventure in a historical setting of revolutionary activities in Sante Fe in 1877.

A novel described by W. as the one he most wanted to write was *Desierto de piedra* (1925; A Stone Desert, 1928), winner of Argentina's national prize for literature. In it the emphasis is more on atmosphere and character than on action. It contains one of W.'s finest characterizations, a delightful old tippler who owns the ranch around which the action of the story revolves. W. demonstrated his versatility in *Pata de zorra* (1924), a hilarious farce about the complications that arise when a university student decides that the only way he can graduate is to marry the spinster sister of his professor of Roman law.

Many of W.'s works lack a proper regard for artistic concerns, and he has consequently been given short shrift by contemporary critics. But at his best he is a gifted storyteller with proven universal appeal and as such cannot be overlooked in any serious consideration of the 20th-c. novel.

FURTHER WORKS: *Rimas de amor* (1904); *Novia de vacaciones* (1907); *Fuente sellada* (1914); *Valle negro* (1918; Black Valley, n.d.); *Ciudad turbulenta, ciudad alegre* (1919); *La corbata celeste* (1920); *Los ojos vendados* (1921); *El vengador* (1922); *La que no perdonó* (1923); *Una estrella en la ventana* (1924); *Las espigas de Ruth* (1926); *Myriam la conspiradora* (1926); *El jinete de fuego* (1926); *Tierra de jaguares* (1927); *Sangre en el umbral* (1927); *Lucía Miranda* (1929; The Strength of Lovers, 1930); *15 días sacristán* (1930); *El camino de las llamas* (1930); *Vocación de escritor* (1931); *Don Bosco y su tiempo* (1931); *Oro* (1935); *El Kahal* (1935); *Naves, oro, sueños* (1936); *El sexto sello* (1941); *Juana Tabor* (1942); *666*

(1942); *Esperar contra toda esperanza* (1944); *Lo que Dios ha unido* (1945); *Aventuras del padre Vespignani* (1948); *Morir con las botas puestas* (1952); *Estrella de la tarde* (1955); *Le tiraría usted la primera piedra?* (1955); *Año X* (1960)

BIBLIOGRAPHY: Hespelt, E. H., "H. W. —Argentine Novelist," *Hispania,* VII (1924), 360–67; Samperio, J. M., "An Author Whose Books Have Appealed to Thousands," *Inter-America,* VIII (1925), 535–39; Sedgwick, R., *The Novels of H. W.* (1925); Sedgwick, R., "H. W., Argentine's Most Popular Novelist," *Hispanic American Historical Review,* IX (1929), 116–26; Moreno, J. C., *Gustavo Martínez Zuviría* (1962)

KENNETH WEBB

WATKINS, Vernon Phillips
Welsh poet, b. 27 June 1906, Maesteg

W. was educated at Swansea Grammar School, Repton, and Cambridge. He claims to have passed through a highly derivative phase, and it seems likely that the influence of Yeats (q.v.) was strong. W. emerged with a poetic voice that is hieratic in quality and distinguished by its verbal melody and sure sense of form. His subjects often belong to the Gower peninsula, where he lives.

The title poem of his first collection, *The Ballad of the Mari Lwyd, and Other Poems* (1941), was inspired by the Glamorganshire custom of carrying a model of a horse's head from door to door on New Year's Day. "I found myself," he writes, "imagining a skull ... followed and surrounded by all kinds of drunken claims and holy deceptions." His feeling for the supernatural is again communicated in *The Lady with the Unicorn* (1948). This volume, like *The Death Bell, and Other Poems* (1954), indicates the author's preoccupation with Christian as well as pre-Christian themes.

W.'s gift of conjuring up atmosphere and personality was shown early in "Elegy on the Heroine of Childhood" and in his portrait of Yeats in *The Lamp and the Veil* (1945).

Affinities (1962), contains several poems of this kind, including those dedicated to Charles Williams and T. S. Eliot (qq.v.).

As the friend and adviser of Dylan Thomas (q.v.), W. edited Thomas's *Letters to Vernon Watkins* (1957). He also brought out translations of Heinrich Heine (1797–1856) in *The North Sea* (1951).

W.'s power of conveying spiritual and imaginative experience has been compared (particularly in its images of light) with Henry Vaughan's (1622–95).

FURTHER WORKS: *Selected Poems* (1948); *Cypress and Acacia* (1959)

BIBLIOGRAPHY: Raine, K., "V. W.: Poet of Tradition," *Anglo-Welsh Review*, XIV (1965), 20–38; Raine, K., "Intuition's Lightning: The Poetry of V. W.," *Poetry Review*, LXIV (1968), 47–54

CECIL PRICE

WAUGH, Evelyn

English novelist, b. 28 Oct. 1903, London; d. 10 April 1966, Taunton, Somerset

Four years after W., son of publisher Arthur Waugh, graduated from Oxford, his first satirical romance appeared. *Decline and Fall* (1928) was an hilarious assault on Oxford, public schools, the smart set, modern architecture, and prison reformers. W.'s most significant indebtedness in this satire, and in others, was to Firbank (q.v.), whose kaleidoscopic shifting of scene and objective manner inspired W.'s counterpoint technique and pose of ironic detachment.

W. was converted to Roman Catholicism in 1930. In that same year, *Vile Bodies* (1930) revealed that he could create a world, that of the Bright Young People, and give brilliant expression to his sense of the futility of modern experience. The "happy ending," which leaves his antihero on "the biggest battlefield in the history of the world," raised fantasy to the level of prophecy. Another wasteland satire, *A Handful of Dust* (1934), was a masterpiece of poised irony; in this account of adultery, W. revealed the baseness underlying the surface gloss of the fashionable world and also the spiritual inadequacy of Tony Last's devotion to the past. Fleeing the present and seeking an illusory "Gothic" city in the Brazilian jungle, Tony is imprisoned by a halfbreed and forced to read Dickens aloud, over and over. W.'s appalling irony is that Tony is treated no worse by the half-savage than he was by the near-savage in England.

Constantly on the move during the 1930's but responsive to political developments, W. produced, among other travel books, *Remote People* (1931) and *W. in Abyssinia* (1936), which leaned so far to the right that they obscured his actual allegiance to an ideal of the aristocratic life. The African journey inspired *Black Mischief* (1932), a devastating burlesque of the attempted modernization of an African kingdom, and *Scoop* (1938), a spoof on varieties of imperialism and the excesses of the press. Both satires ridiculed the "civilizing" of the barbaric and the barbarism of "modernism." In *Black Mischief*, for instance, natives devour the boots distributed to them, and the amoral Basil Seal unwittingly eats his mistress at a cannibal feast.

Unlike these destructive satires, *Put Out More Flags* (1942) moved toward affirmation, for in it Basil Seal and other 1930's types are caught up in the spirit of the "Churchillian renaissance."

After World War II short pieces of the early outrageous manner appeared. *Scott-King's Modern Europe* (1947) exposed a seedy Balkan dictatorship. *The Loved One* (1948) exploited the decadence of mortuary customs in California. *Love among the Ruins* (1953) followed Huxley and Orwell (qq.v.) into the totalitarian future, protesting things as they are by predicting things to come.

Although *Brideshead Revisited* (1944) affirmed W.'s Catholicism, its narrator so mingled social and religious values in his nostalgic memories of Brideshead and its aristocrats that the intended religious theme was overwhelmed. In *Helena* (1960), W. imbued a saint's legend with rationalistic Catholicism and satire, making it a vehicle for Catholic apologetics.

The distinguished trilogy *Men at Arms* (1952), *Officers and Gentlemen* (1955), and *Unconditional Surrender* (1961) revealed the adjustment of W.'s religion, conservatism, and satire to the conventions of the novel. (In 1965, W. issued a one-volume "recension" of these novels under the title *Sword of Honour*.) Tracing the World War II career of his first actual hero, artfully modulating from burlesque to irony, W. portrayed Guy Crouchback's discovery that his crusade against the modern age was an illusion, that in an ambiguous world good never comes from public causes, but that it may result from individual acts of charity. Disillusioned the story of Guy Crouchback may be, but in it, W. struck the deepest note of his career.

In *The Ordeal of Gilbert Pinfold* (1957), a self-mocking short novel, W. suggested that though the major writers of the century are gone, "a generation notable for elegance and variety and contrivance" survives. His statement suggested the graces of such impeccable biographies as *Edmund Campion* (1935) and *Ronald Knox* (1959) and the wit and urbanity of *A Little Learning* (1964), the first volume of an unfinished autobiography, but it did not quite suggest the seriousness of W.'s wittiest fiction nor his right to be spoken of as the most accomplished English satirist of his time.

FURTHER WORKS: *Rosetti: His Life and Works* (1928); *Labels* (1930); *Ninety-two Days* (1934); *Mr. Loveday's Little Outing, and Other Sad Stories* (1936); *Robbery under Law* (1939); *Work Suspended* (1942); *When the Going Was Good* (abridged reprint of *Labels, Remote People, Ninety-two Days,* and *W. in Abyssinia;* 1946); *The Holy Places* (1953); *Tactical Exercise* (1954); *Tourist in Africa* (1960); *Basil Seal Rides Again* (1963)

BIBLIOGRAPHY: Linklater, E., *The Art of Adventure* (1947); Wilson, E., *Classics and Commercials* (1950); O'Faolain, S., *The Vanishing Hero* (1951); O'Donnell, D., *Maria Cross* (1952); Spender, S. *The Creative Element* (1953); Hollis, C., *E. W.* (1954); De Vitis, A. A., *Roman Holiday* (1956); Stopp, F. J., *E. W.* (1958); Carens, J. F., *The Satiric Art of E. W.* (1967); Davis, R. M., ed., *E. W.* (1969); Doyle, P. A., *E. W.* (1969); *E. W. Newsletter* (founded 1967)

JAMES F. CARENS

WAZYK, Adam

(pseud. of *Adam Wagmann*), Polish poet, novelist, and essayist, b. 17 Nov. 1905, Warsaw

A member of the apolitical Warsaw avant-garde group *Nowa Sztuka* (New Art), W. turned to politics only after fascism and economic depression threatened his country. As an outspoken socialist critic of his government's policies he was repeatedly imprisoned during 1931–39. After the outbreak of World War II, W. fled to Russia, where he joined the Polish unit of the Russian army.

In the army, W was one of the co-founders of the weekly *Kuźnia* (The Anvil), which was the first Polish literary magazine to follow the requirements of socialist realism. From 1950 to 1954, he edited *Twórczość*, the official publication of the Polish Writers Union. W. received the prestigious State Literary Award in 1952, but by 1957 disputes with governmental

censors culminated in the banning of his projected international journal *Europa,* and he resigned from the Polish Communist Party.

Influenced by Charles Baudelaire (1821–67), Paul Verlaine (1844–96), Arthur Rimbaud (1854–91), Apollinaire, and Éluard (qq.v.), W.'s first two volumes of poetry, *Semafory* (1924) and *Oczy i usta* (1925), are mannered but highly original in rhyme and rhythm. Neither volume sold well and the critics labeled W. an obscurantist. Though *Wiersze zebrane* (1934) shows a turn to the language of socialist realism, W.'s interest in early 20th-c. French poetry has never lapsed, as is evident in his *Od Rimbauda do Eluarda* (1964).

. . . *Serce granatu* (1943) contains his first "party poetry." Exhortative, bitter, raw, and easily intelligible, the volume became the spiritual handbook of the Red Polish unit as it advanced toward its homeland. As the title suggests, the poems were meant to be the heart of the grenades.

After the publication in 1930 and 1933 of two surrealistic novels, W.'s prose efforts were confined to literary criticism. *W stronę humanizmu* (1949) and *Mickiewicz i wersylikacja narodowa* (1951) are highly regarded contributions to Marxist literary scholarship. Appearing in the midst of post-World War II social and economic upheaval, these volumes were replete with party terminology; they sought to reaffirm artistic commitment to socialist realism and to prevent deviation from it.

During the height of Soviet influence in Poland, W. translated Mayakovski's (q.v.) poetry (1949) and Aleksandr Pushkin's (1799–1837) *Eugene Onegin* (1954). He was growing increasingly disenchanted with Stalinism, and in August 1955, on the front page of Poland's most important literary journal, *Nowa Kultura,* W. published his "Poemat dla dorosłych" ("A Poem for Adults," in *News from behind the Iron Curtain,* V, Sept. 1956), a bitter assessment of the human costs of Poland's industrialization and of Soviet control of Polish thinking. A *cause célèbre* in both the East and West, the poem, one of the most expressive statements of the short-lived communist literary "thaw," is credited with paving the way for Władysław Gomułka's rise to power.

Though W. later modified his views in a poetic critique of his own poem, the party never forgave his attack on the official optimism of socialist realism. Without the protection of party membership, W. returned to the strict lyricism of his youth. He translated Apollinaire and

EVELYN WAUGH

FRANK WEDEKIND

wrote a long, melancholic verse-fable, *Wagon* (1963). His most recent criticism, *Kwestia gustu* (1966), limited itself to strictly literary matters.

W.'s introspective lyricism and his zealous advocacy and practice of the socialist realist credo are indications of his extraordinary range. Whether he be viewed as a renegade or party ideologue, in both verse and literary criticism, he ranks among his nation's best in the 20th c.

FURTHER WORKS: . . . *Stary dworek* (1945); *Mity rodzinne* (1947); *Widziałem Kraine srod ka* (1953); *Labirynt* (1961); *Epizoa* (1961); *Esej o wierszu* (1964)

BIBLIOGRAPHY: Ziffer, B., 'A Poem for Adults," *PolR*, I (1956), 56–64; Hartmann, K., "Das literarische Schaffen in Polen seit 1944," *Zeitschrift für Ostforschung*, V (1956), 181–232; Krynski, M., "Polish Literature and the 'Thaw,'" *The American Slavic and East European Review*, XVIII (1959), 394–417; MacGregor-Hastie, P., "Profile of A. W.," *The Twentieth Century*, CLXVI (1959), 175–78

STANLEY J. PACION

WEDEKIND, Frank

German dramatist, short-story writer, and poet, b. 24 July 1864, Hanover; d. 9 March 1918, Munich

W. spent his youth in Switzerland and later traveled extensively in France and England. Though he studied law, he decided upon a writing career and was variously employed as a journalist, an advertising agent, and secretary to a circus. In the late 1890's he was for several years associated with *Simplizissimus,* the Munich satirical magazine. Later he worked as a cabaret entertainer, actor, and stage director, chiefly in Leipzig, Berlin, and Munich. In 1906 he married actress Mathilde Newes, who appeared with him in many of his plays.

In his first play, *Frühlings Erwachen* (1891; Spring's Awakening, 1909), a tragedy involving children, W. demonstrated an original dramatic style modeled on that of Jakob Lenz (1751–92) and Georg Büchner (1813–37). It was characterized by an emphasis on the sensuous impact of individual scenes rather than a strict regard for balanced composition and rigorous construction. W.'s "realism" called for the action to be stripped to its essentials.

Contemporary naturalism (q.v.) influenced both the choice of the play's theme—the psychological troubles of young people awakening to physical maturity—and a view in which man was seen as caught between the forces of environment and instinct. In addition, certain characteristics of expressionism (q.v.) are anticipated by W. in his tendency to stylize and distort his characters, and in his general fondness for exaggerated, abstract, and surrealistic (*see* surrealism) elements.

W. had a Nietzschean contempt for middle-class society's "domestication" of man, whom he saw as thereby caught in a fundamental conflict between the spirit and the flesh. This view is the basis for the two-part drama *Der Erdgeist* (1895; republished as *Lulu,* 1903; Earth Spirit, 1932) and *Die Büchse der Pandora* (1904; Pandora's Box, 1914), which reflects W.'s radicalism and cynical pathos. The tragedy of the plays' central protagonist, Lulu—a "soulless creature" whose unbridled sexuality and daemonic impulses claim numerous victims—is marked by strident contrasts, by ironically tragic scenes of horror, and sometimes by low dramatic effects. Despite its stylistic unevenness and somewhat monotonous subject matter, the work—especially the first part—was to be W.'s greatest success. This was largely due to the pungency and economy of the dialogue, to a language that lets fly at the audience with expressionistic vehemence, and to a colorful variety of sometimes exaggerated and grotesque characters.

Elements of the grotesque and the absurd, inherent in most of W.'s work as an expression of life's irreconcilable contradictions, are emphasized in *Der Marquis von Keith* (1900; Eng., 1957). Returning to themes dealt with previously in *Frühlings Erwachen,* W. focuses on two possible responses to life. His over-scrupulous, brooding character comes to grief, while his amoralist lets himself be carried along in a reckless, sensual pursuit of pleasure. W.'s uncompromisingly radical social criticism and his attempt to impose a positive meaning on the apparent futility of human existence are here carried to absurdity. The two antithetical monomaniac types who are the play's protagonists are indications of the relativization of W.'s nihilism and of the tragic-idealistic outlook that is also to be seen in *König Nicolo, oder So ist das Leben* (1901; Such Is Life, 1912) and *Franziska* (1911).

Der Marquis von Keith is the first in the series of "confessional plays" in which W. confronts an anonymous audience and the censor with his internal debate and reflections.

In addition to sexuality, another fundamental problem dealt with in W.'s dramas is the misunderstanding and social rejection of the nonconformist, particularly the artist. The best examples of this theme are to be found in the tragicomedy *König Nicolo, oder So ist das Leben,* an enigmatic story of a king without a country, and *Hidalla, oder Sein und Haben* (1904; republished as *Carl Hettmann, der Zwergriese,* 1905), in which W. combines his Dionysian "morality of beauty" with his war on conventional morality. Set in a brothel, the cynically pessimistic *Totentanz* (1906; republished as *Tod und Teufel,* 1909; Death and Devil, 1952) is a thesis play marred by intellectual stiffness and unconvincing, overdrawn characters. Even more clearly than the Lulu plays it shows a limited world view in its chaotic representation of the horror of permanently unsatisfied sensuality. *Die Zensur* (1908), "theodicy in one act," deals with the artist's relation to his public.

The plays written after 1910 present no significant thematic variations and are even weaker in artistic expression. W. placed greater importance on the statement of his ideas than on their dramatic treatment. This is particularly evident in the three-act fantasy *Schloß Wetterstein* (1910; Castle Wetterstein, 1952), which reexamines themes previously dealt with in the Lulu plays. *Franziska,* "a modern mystery play," also centers on the relations between the sexes. Employing an unconvincing and trivial plot, W. attempts to measure man's erotic drives against a scale of social values. In *Simson, oder Scham und Eifersucht* (1914) and *Herakles* (1917)— both partially written in verse—W. deals with time-honored subjects but shows himself incapable of breaking away from his subjectivism and consequent nihilism.

W.'s novellas such as *Feuerwerk* (1906) are notable for a style that is sometimes rich and colorful, sometimes taut and restrained in its economical suggestion of background. They highlight a conception in which the unrestrained expression of natural instincts is seen as the meaning of life and the will of God. W.'s views on education are set forth in "Mine-Haha, oder Über die körperliche Erziehung der jungen Mädchen" (1903).

The poetry collected in *Die vier Jahreszeiten* (1905) and *Lautenlieder* (1920) consists of ballads of city life written in traditional ballad style, cabaret songs, and verses that are as much influenced by contemporary journalism as by Heinrich Heine's (1797–1856) sentimentality and irony.

FURTHER WORKS: *Die Fürstin Russalka* (1897; Princess Russalka, 1919); *Die junge Welt* (1898); *Der Kammersänger* (1899; The Court Singer, 1913); *Der Liebestrank* (1899; The Solar Spectrum, 1959); *Oaha* (1908); *Musik* (1908); *Der Stein der Weisen* (1909); *Gesammelte Werke* (9 vols., 1912–21); *Bismarck* (1915); *Ein Genußmensch* (1924); *Rabbi Esra* (1924; Eng., 1931); *Gesammelte Briefe* (2 vols., 1924); *Prosa, Dramen, Verse* (1954); *Prosa, Dramen, Verse II* (1964)

BIBLIOGRAPHY: Mann, H., *Erinnerungen an F. W.* (1929); Gundolf, F., *F. W.* (1954); Kutscher, A., *F. W.* (1954; rev. ed., 1964); Emrich, W., "Die Lulutragödie," in *Das Deutsche Drama,* Vol. II (1958); Natan, A., "F. W.," in *German Men of Letters,* Vol. II (1963), 103–29; Lemp, R., ed., *F. W. zum 100. Geburtstag* (1964); Sokel, W. H., "The Changing Role of Eros in W.'s Drama," *GQ,* XXXIX (1966), 201–07; Ude, K., *F. W.* (1966); Westervelt, W. O., "F. W. and the Search for Morality," *DA,* XXVII (1967), 3886A; Maclean, H., "W.'s *Der Marquis von Keith*: An Interpretation Based on the Faust and Circus Motifs," *GR,* XLIII (1968), 163–87; Rothe, F., *F. Ws. Dramen* (1968)

ULRICH MELZER

WEINHEBER, Josef

Austrian poet and novelist, b. 9 March 1892, Vienna; d. 8 April 1945, Kirchstetten

Born into a working-class family, W. lost his father when he was a child, and in 1901 his mother was forced to place him in an orphanage. He received a good liberal education at the gymnasium associated with the orphanage but was dropped in 1909 after failing in mathematics. W.'s orphanage life is depicted in the autobiographical novel *Das Waisenhaus* (1924). From 1911 to 1923, he was a postal employee. After 1923 he devoted himself entirely to his writing.

W.'s novels and poems met with only minor success until *Adel und Untergang* (1934), a collection of verse, won him the Mozart Prize. With the prize money he bought a farm at Kirchstetten, and from then on he divided his time between the farm and Vienna. Though he apparently had serious reservations about the Nazis, they heaped honors and distinctions upon him for his propagandist poetry. In what may have been an accidental death, he died of an overdose of sleeping pills as the allied armies arrived.

W.'s personal life was a perpetual battle against wine and worry, and his poetry helped to keep him on an even keel. Accompanying himself on the guitar, he established a reputation as a great folksinger, and indeed the folksong element is strong in much of his poetry.

Describing himself as a "word artist" (*Wortkünstler*) rather than a poet, W. was a remarkable verbal technician in almost every form and style. *Wien wörtlich* (1935) employs the humorous dialect vernacular to draw a fondly satirical picture of Vienna and the Viennese; *O Mensch, gib acht* (1937) is an "almanac" of poems on familiar subjects and popular themes; *Zwischen Göttern und Dämonen* (1938), a collection of odes in classical meters, was conceived of as a challenge to Rilke's (q.v.) *Duineser Elegien.*

Musical and architectural poems are most characteristic of W.'s work. "Variationen auf eine hölderlinische Ode," included in *Adel und Untergang,* is a remarkably successful attempt to transpose a musical theme and its variations into poetry. The poems in *Kammermusik* (1939) are musical in both subject matter and technique. "Heroische Trilogie" is an architecturally symmetrical poem of three 210-line sections. The first and last sections form individual sonnet cycles, and the central section, in *terza rima,* is subdivided into three parts of seventy lines each.

W.'s poetry is essentially one of statement rather than implication. It is marked by a basic stoicism tempered by a lyrically hedonistic appreciation of all that the world has to offer. Because little of his work has been translated, W. is almost unknown in the English-speaking world.

FURTHER WORKS: *Der einsame Mensch* (1920); *Von beiden Ufern* (1923); *Boot in der Bucht* (1926); *Der Nachwuchs* (1928); *Vereinsamtes Herz* (1935); *Späte Krone* (1936); *Hier ist das Wort* (1944); *Über die Dichtkunst* (1949); *Sämtliche Werke* (5 vols., 1953–56)

BIBLIOGRAPHY: Bergholz, H., "The W. Controversy," *GL&L,* III (1949–50), 50–59; Finke, E., *J. W.: Der Mensch und das Werk* (1950); Zillich, H., ed., *Bekenntnis zu J. W.* (1950); Waldinger, E., "A Propos J. W.," *BA,* XXVI (1952), 248–50; Bergholz, H., *J. W. Bibliographie* (1953); Wassermann, F. M.,

"Between Gods and Demons: J. W., the Man and the Poet," *GL&L,* VI (1953), 81–87: Nadler, J., and Weinheber, H., *J. W. und die Sprache* (1955); Ibel, R., *Mensch der Mitte: George—Carossa—W.* (1962)

CALVIN S. BROWN

WEISS, Konrad

German poet, dramatist, and prose writer, b. 1 May 1880, Rauenbretzingen; d. 4 Jan. 1940, Munich

Born into a Swabian peasant family, W. studied theology, philosophy, art history, and German literature in Tübingen, Munich, and Freiburg im Breisgau. In 1905 he became editor of the Catholic monthly *Hochland.* For a time he joined those around Carl Muth (1867–1944) who were working for a Christian-German cultural revival, but his anticlassical and antiaesthetic ideas caused him to break with Muth in 1920. From then until his death W. was the art critic of the *Münchener Neueste Nachrichten.*

During his lifetime W. was best known for his writings on art, history, and religion contained in *Zum geschichtlichen Gethsemane* (1919), *Das gegenwärtige Problem der Gotik* (1927), and *Der christliche Epimetheus* (1933) —an attempt to establish Christian-German historical development. Over the years, however, he slowly produced a small but important body of poetic works composed of poem cycles, prose poems, and dialogues. Although these aroused the enthusiasm of Borchardt, Hofmannsthal (qq.v.), Carl Schmitt (b. 1888), and Josef Pieper (b. 1904), because of W.'s secluded life and his failure to emphasize his poetry, it was only with the posthumous publication of his *Prosadichtungen* (1948) and *Gedichte* (2 vols., 1948–49) that he became known to a wider audience.

W. originally planned to become a priest, and he saw his literary vocation as a "mediation" between God and man. His images, metaphors, rhymes, assonances, etc., are therefore not poetic devices as much as they are immediate expressions of his theme: man's salvation. The beauty of his lyrics and his metalogical conclusions can only be understood through meditation on his mystical use of language, which renders his poetry and poetic prose undecipherable by logical, causal reasoning.

W.'s first volume of poems, *Tantum dic verbo*

(1918), a title that reveals its liturgical inspiration, contains the essential theme of all his future poetry. Aware of his human imperfection, the poet seeks the "one word," the "basis," the revealing *Inbild* ("intrinsic image"). It cannot be seized; it can merely be represented by the symbolic images orbiting around it. He conceives of poetry as "the universal history of the missing word before the pure image." Man's existence and his salvation are determined by "inadequacy" and *Inbild,* key words in W.'s poetry.

The poem cycles revolve around the "one word" and lead logically from *Die cumäische Sibylle* (1921), later included in the *Das Herz des Wortes* (1929) cycle, to Mary, in whose laps sits the Son of God, the "word" made flesh. The theme of the last complete poem cycle, *Das Sinnreich der Erde* (1929), is the incarnation of the "word," the realization of the soul's redemption. Compared to the previous cycles, the last volume contains more supple formal elements that are sometimes songlike, modeled on medieval religious poetry. It also offers simple pictures of nature.

Die kleine Schöpfung (1926) unfolds W.'s basic Christian theme with the simplicity of a storybook. Singable quatrains relate a day in the life of a child and his playmates—a cock, a dove, and a lamb—and reflect in miniature man's existence on earth and his journey in exile. Here religious poetry finds a perfect intimate form in which a "childlike spirit" overcomes the discontinuity and harshness of W.'s usual verse language.

In his tragedy *Konradin von Hohenstaufen* (1938) W. traces the tragic destiny of the young Staufen king. Terrestrial history is shown to be a "wound" and human existence a "blindness" measurable only in its distance from the *Inbild.* W. was no romantic. In reaching beyond the classics and orienting his concept of history and his feeling for art toward medieval Germany, he thought he could find the essence of German character in the religious background of the period's culture. By going back to the beginning, he hoped to grasp the present.

W.'s prose poems and meditations on history and travel repeat the themes of his poetry cycles in a different form. In the posthumously published *Deutschlands Morgenspiegel* (2 vols., 1950) and *Wanderer in den Zeiten* (1958), he seeks "the lost incarnation of our essential German nature" in old German landscapes, their changing history and their medieval monuments. He was drawn to the Gothic

because of its "ultimate urgency . . . in which the German spirit seeks and finds itself as though in a portrait."

In each of his creative phases W. was essentially a religious poet, probably the greatest in 20th-c. German literature. His mystical use of language opened up new avenues of expressiveness. It cannot be understood without a knowledge of Christian symbolism and liturgy, and it often remains dense and metaphorically obscure. However, his verbal mysticism relates the mythic and natural world to both the drama of salvation and its religious basis.

FURTHER WORKS: *Die Löwin* (1928); *Karl Caspar* (1929); *Tantalus* (1929); *Das kaiserliche Liebesgespräch* (1934); *Dichtungen und Schriften* (1961)

BIBLIOGRAPHY: Ruf, G., *Das dichterische Geschichtsbild bei K. W.* (1953); Kunisch, H., "Das Sinnreich der Erde," *Hochland,* II (1954); Lahnstein, P., *Bürger und Poet: Dichter aus Schwaben als Menschen ihrer Zeit* (1966)

EBERHARD HORST

WEISS, Peter
German dramatist, novelist, and essayist, b. 8 Nov. 1916, Nowawes

W. emigrated from Germany to England in 1934. He moved to Czechoslovakia in 1936, to Switzerland in 1938, then to Sweden in 1939. There he became a citizen in 1945. W. has painted, worked in documentary and experimental cinema, and translated Strindberg's (q.v.) *Miss Julie* and *A Dream Play* into German. He received the Charles Veillon Award in 1963 and the Lessing Prize in 1965.

After inauspicious beginnings as a writer in Swedish (*Från ö till ö,* 1947), W. became an influential figure in German letters with the "micro-novel" *Der Schatten des Körpers des Kutschers* (1960). In it, he minutely delineates some insignificant events at a country boardinghouse. Yet there is no mania for description; W.'s perspective is quite selective. Some of the occurrences recorded are common, others inexplicable. Speech is rendered only in fragments. Other phenomena are reproduced in conventional, even complex syntax.

The book manifests the wide-ranging awareness typical of the modern novel, yet it is not excessively reflective; it is free of coyness and vanity. The prose structure is highly experimental. It utilizes the film techniques of mon-tage, time retardation and acceleration, blow-up, and light and shadow. Living in a non-German-speaking country seems to have given W. the outsider's advantage of detachment. Shunning colloquialisms, his language has a quality of serenity and pristine sobriety.

Two autobiographical novels, *Abschied von den Eltern* (1961; Leave-taking, 1966) and *Fluchtpunkt* (1962; Vanishing Point, 1966), reveal in starkly honest terms the background of W.'s detachment. While the odyssey of the refugee W. is a story of loneliness, withdrawal, and anxiety, it is also a process of self-realization and triumph. Rootlessness and wandering are a gain in objectivity, in honesty, and above all in intellectual freedom.

W.'s nonideological individualism turns to *engagement* in his drama *Die Verfolgung und Ermordung Jean Paul Marats dargestellt durch die Schauspielgruppe des Hospizes zu Charenton unter Anleitung des Herrn de Sade* (1964; The Persecution and Assassination of Jean-Paul Marat as Performed by the Inmates of the Asylum of Charenton under the Direction of the Marquis de Sade, 1965). The play was an international success. Although critics are divided as to its literary merits, they are unanimous in their tribute to its theatrical brilliance.

Marat/Sade has been recognized as a major contribution to the theater of revolt. It owes much to Brecht (q.v.) and also to Artaud's (q.v.) theater of cruelty. Marat's murder is reenacted some fifteen years after his death. The revolution has failed. Therefore, W. intimates, revolutionary efforts must be renewed.

However, he alerts us to the dangers involved. The confrontation between Sade and Marat reveals the paradox of the simultaneously destructive and humanist aspects of the revolutionary mind. The result is an indictment of both the anarchistic individualism of Sade and the stifling collectivism inherent in Marat's views.

Marat/Sade is also an example of theater of participation. There is no separation of actors and audience. They share their roles as asylum inmates, madmen, and social misfits. The players do not merely act, but actually live the revolution as time and again they confuse their acting with their own emotions of revolt.

More objectively historical, though less brilliant, is the play *Die Ermittlung* (1965; The Investigation, 1966). It is a distillation of the actual transcripts made during the Frankfurt trials of those responsible for Auschwitz. The accused constantly fall into the idiom of the Nazi era. There is in them no repentance, no recognition of guilt, and heinous euphemisms serve to screen brutality and murder. As didactic theater the play bares man's bestiality and indicts a world that, having failed to regenerate after Hitler, is seemingly impervious to any cure save revolt.

In *Viet Nam Diskurs* (1968; Viet Nam Discourse, 1970), W. protests against American intervention in the Vietnam war and attacks America's military-industrial complex. In *Trotzki im Exil* (1970), W. focuses on the terrors of Stalinism.

FURTHER WORKS: *De besegrade* (1948); *Duellen* (1953); *Das Gespräch der drei Gehenden* (1963); *Der Turm* (1963); *Nacht mit Gästen* (1963); *Der Gesang vom lusitanischen Popanz* (1967; Song of the Lusitanian Bogey, 1970); *Die Versicherung* (1967); *Wie dem Herrn Mockinpott das Leiden ausgetrieben wird* (1968); *Rapporte* (1968)

BIBLIOGRAPHY: Krolow, K., "Porträt strenger Isoliertheit; Bemerkungen zu drei Büchern von P. W.," *DRs*, LXXXIX (1963), vi, 61–67; Roloff, M., "An Interview with P. W.," *PR*, XXXII (1965), ii, 220–32; Sontag, S., "Marat/Sade/Artaud," *PR*, XXXII (1965), ii, 210–19; Moeller, H. B., "German Theater 1964: W.'s Reasoning in the Madhouse," *Symposium*, XX (1966), 163–73; Freed, D., "P. W. and the Theatre of the Future," *DramS*, XII (1967), ii, 119–71; Rischbieter, H., *P. W.* (1967); White, J. J., "History and Cruelty in P. W.'s *Marat/Sade*," *MLR*, LXIII (1968), 437–48

ERHARD FRIEDRICHSMEYER

WELLS, Herbert George

English novelist, historian, and essayist, b. 21 Sept. 1866, Bromley, Kent; d. 13 Aug. 1946, London

W.'s father was an impecunious small shop-keeper and his mother a former lady's maid who returned to service later as housekeeper. He left school at thirteen and was put to work in a succession of dreary drapers' and chemists' shops, continuing his education with difficulty between intervals of employment.

In these years Plato's *Republic*, Henry George's (1839–97) *Progress and Poverty*, and some acquaintance with science stirred W.'s mind to dream of a planned society. In 1884 he won a scholarship to the Royal College of Science at South Kensington as a teacher in training. There he studied zoology under T. H. Huxley (1825–95) and did work in physics and geology. In addition, he read widely, was active in debating utopian socialism, and contributed to the college magazine.

Continuing his studies, in 1890 W. received a B.S. degree from London University, and the following year he was made a Fellow. That same year he married his cousin, Isabel Mary Wells, later divorcing her and marrying one of his students in 1895.

While teaching at Henley House School, W. wrote a *Text-Book of Biology* (1893). He began sending contributions to *The Saturday Review*. When his early scientific romances had established him as author, he became a member and critic of the Fabian Society, a publicist, and a world traveler. In later years, he was a friend of many famous men, and in 1933 he made world-publicized visits to both Franklin Roosevelt and Stalin. To trace his intellectual development, W. wrote *Experiment in Autobiography* (1934). He continued actively promoting his ideas until his death.

Besides numerous pieces in magazines, W. published about one hundred books. He began with science fiction, an interest that resulted from his studies under Huxley. Though not the first author in this genre, he gave it a new dimension by his genuine understanding of biology.

The Time Machine (1895) presents a pessimistic *fin-de-siècle* interpretation of both Darwinian and Marxist thought. A traveler into the future discovers that humanity has evolved into two races: the Eloi, softened by their conquest of nature and the consequent cessation of struggle, and the Morlocks, predatory descendants of an abused proletariat.

The Island of Dr. Moreau (1896) satirizes the temporarily successful efforts of a mad genius to "evolve" animals into men through surgery and psychological conditioning. *The Invisible Man* (1897) advances the idea that unchecked amoral power is self-destructive.

In *The War of the Worlds* (1898) W. studies the collapse of an aimless social system when highly evolved intelligences from Mars invade the earth. *When the Sleeper Wakes* (1899) projects social and economic trends of the 1890's into a crass, mechanized, and utterly materialistic 22nd c. *The First Men in the Moon* (1901) discovers an "anthill" society in

500

which functional specialization is carried to a grotesque extreme.

W.'s basic viewpoint is expressed by the comment in *When the Sleeper Wakes* that "we were making the future . . . and hardly any of us troubled to think what future we were making." His conviction that society needs planned guidance toward a goal led him into utopian sociology and prophecy.

In *The War in the Air* (1908) W. prophesied that aircraft warfare would bring about complete social collapse, and in *The World Set Free* (1914) he foresaw atomic warfare destroying the world's major cities—after which lesson mankind had the intelligence to establish a World State.

W. wrote also realistic novels that drew upon his youthful experiences and served as vehicle for his social and political ideas. *Love and Mr. Lewisham* (1900) reflects W.'s experiences as a biology teacher and focuses on the conflict between youthful passion and the shackles of convention. *Kipps* (1905), echoing W.'s experiences in a draper's shop, presents humorous pictures of the limitations of middle-class life. *Ann Veronica* (1909) scandalized many by its treatment of a modern woman's struggle for rights in politics, love, and marriage. In *Tono-Bungay* (1909) W. made use of his experiences in a chemist's shop to satirize commercial promotional methods and to detail the rise and fall of a patent medicine. Throughout these novels, W.'s interest is largely in the intellectual and social growth of his characters.

W.'s fiction led to his writings as a publicist and social prophet. Believing that "there is a hitherto undreamt-of fullness, freedom and happiness within reach of our species," W. urged a scientific approach to the creation of order in a disorderly world. His doctrine varied from year to year, but it always included the belief that "an adequately implemented Liberal Socialism" in a planned World State could provide men with incentives for limitless self-development.

Anticipations (1901) examines the processes of change brought about by scientific and industrial progress and advocates the reconstruction of traditional political and social patterns. *The Food of the Gods* (1904) is an allegory of the conflict between the "rare new big-scale way of living" and the "teeming small-scale life of the earth."

A Modern Utopia (1905) rejects the older, static visions of utopia and presents a dynamic, ever-progressing society. It proposes a division

H. G. WELLS

FRANZ WERFEL

of mankind into the poietic (creative), the kinetic (active), the dull, and the base, ruled by a "samurai" of self-sacrificing kinetics helped by the imaginative poietics. In *The World of William Clissold* (1926) the author disguises himself as a retired industrialist and urges that the creative minds of the world cooperate in planning a World State. W.'s ideas are further developed in *The Work, Wealth, and Happiness of Mankind* (1931) and *The Shape of Things to Come* (1933).

To spread interest in world-planning, W. turned to writing history interpreted as biological-social preparation for a future now inevitably being shaped for better or worse. *The Outline of History* (1920) sought to show that political, social, and economic life all tended toward world federation. The same ideas characterize *A Short History of the World* (1922) and *The Science of Life* (with W.'s son G. P. Wells, and Julian Huxley; 1929), a biological handbook for the lay reader.

W. exercised an enormous influence on his own generation and is often credited with having "educated" many of those who now consider his ideas outmoded.

FURTHER WORKS: *The Wonderful Visit* (1895); *The Wheels of Chance* (1896); *The Discovery of the Future* (1902); *The Sea Lady* (1902); *Mankind in the Making* (1903); *In the Days of the Comet* (1906); *The Future in America* (1906); *First and Last Things* (1908); *The History of Mr. Polly* (1910); *The New Machiavelli* (1911); *Marriage* (1912); *The Wife of Sir Isaac Harman* (1914); *The War That Will End War* (1914); *Bealby* (1915); *The Peace of the World* (1915); *Boon* (1915); *The Research Magnificent* (1915); *Mr. Britling Sees It Through* (1916); *God the Invisible King* (1917); *The Soul of a Bishop* (1917); *Joan and Peter* (1918); *Russia in the Shadows* (1920); *The Secret Places of the Heart* (1922); *Men Like Gods* (1923); *The Dream* (1924); *Cristina Alberta's Father* (1925); *Mr. Blettsworthy on Rampole Island* (1926); *Meanwhile* (1927); *The Open Conspiracy* (1928); *The Autocracy of Mr. Parham* (1930); *The Bulpington of Blup* (1933); *The New America* (1935); *The Anatomy of Frustration* (1936); *Brynhyld* (1937); *Star-Begotten* (1937); *Apropos of Dolores* (1938); *The World Brain* (1938); *The Fate of Homo Sapiens* (1939); *The Common Sense of War and Peace* (1940); *The New World Order* (1940); *The Rights of Man* (1940); *All Aboard for Ararat* (1941); *Guide

to the New World* (1941); *The Happy Turning* (1942); *The Conquest of Time* (1942); *Mind at the End of Its Tether* (1945)

BIBLIOGRAPHY: Crawford, A. H. G., *The Religion of H. G. W.* (1909); Beresford, J. D., *H. G. W.* (1915); Guyot, E., *H. G. W.* (1920); Hopkins, R. T., *H. G. W.* (1922); Dark, S., *The Outline of H. G. W.* (1922); Brown, I. J. C., *H. G. W.* (1923); Wells, G. H., *The Works of H. G. W.* (1926); West, G., *H. G. W.* (1932); Mattick, H., *H. G. W. als Sozialreformer* (1935); Lang, H.-J., *H. G. W.* (1948); Nicholson, N. C., *H. G. W.* (1950); Vallentin, A., *H. G. W.* (1950); Brome, V., *H. G. W.* (1951); Belgion, M., *H. G. W.* (1953); Meyer, M. M., *H. G. W. and His Family* (1956); Bergonzi, B., *The Early H. G. W.: The Scientific Romances* (1961); Wagar, W. W., *H. G. W. and the World State* (1961); Costa, R. H., *H. G. W.* (1967); Hillegas, M., *The Future as Nightmare: H. G. W. and the Anti-Utopians* (1967); Dickson, L., *H. G. W.* (1969)

J. O. BAILEY

WELSH LITERATURE

LITERATURE IN THE WELSH LANGUAGE

Welsh literature has developed and flourished in the 20th c. in daunting social circumstances and in spite of influences that have increasingly blurred the outlines of Welsh distinctness. Among these influences are the close economic integration of Wales and England, increased social mobility between the two countries, the growth of urbanization in a society once predominantly rural in character, the merging of political loyalties in the wider British context, and the effects of the mass media, especially in recent times. In 1901 the number of people in Wales who could read and speak Welsh was about fifty percent of a total population of one and three-quarter million. By 1961 it was twenty-six percent of two and a half million.

There does, however, exist today a considerable popular awareness of Welsh nationality. Though some of it is expressed in political terms, the predominant expression is cultural and has been so since the turn of the century. The 19th c. had witnessed the publication of writing in Welsh that far exceeded that of any previous or subsequent period. Only a small proportion of this, however, is considered as high quality by present-day literary critics. The uncertainty and confusion created by social change was reflected in literary standards. The traditional function of the poet had been undermined. "The old classical tradition," it has been maintained, "degenerated into a hampering traditionalism, and the newer influences from without found no sufficiently favorable soil for full development, while the language was corrupted by pseudo-scholarship, the influence of English, and a loss of the instinct for its own idioms." At the same time Welsh prose was tending to become artificial, stylistic, and ponderous. Toward the close of the century, however, there were signs of a literary renascence.

Welsh cultural life was to derive lasting benefit from the completion of a national education system in 1893, when a charter incorporating the federal University of Wales was granted. Well-grounded in the history of Wales, its antiquities and language, the graduates and teachers of the university succeeded in laying scholarly foundations. The literary awakening that followed owed its character both to their guidance and to the artistic contributions that they themselves made.

1. Poetry

Sir John Morris-Jones (1864–1929) is a key figure in any consideration of Welsh literature in the 20th c. A scholar, poet (*Caniada*, 1907), and critic, he has been called "the interpreter of the awakening and the protagonist of the new ideas." He was the medium by means of which fresh ideas permeated Welsh literature and the instigator of a lively controversy over the function of the Welsh poet in the changed social circumstances of his day. Through the *eisteddfod* (the annual competition festival of poets, musicians, and orators) and the press, however, he also reaffirmed the essential of the Welsh poetic tradition by his criticism and influence. His monumental Welsh grammar (1913) was a strong influence in restoring purity of diction to written Welsh. In *Cerdd Dafod* (1925) he analyzed the native poetic meters, while writing his own poetry in both strict meter and free verse.

Modern Welsh poetry in strict meter is composed not by accent but by the number of syllables and by *cynghanedd*, a developed Welsh form of internal rhyme and close, accentuated alliteration within a line. The most

highly regarded Welsh bardic composition is the *awdl*, which is a poem of some length written in *cynghanedd* and in one or more of the "24 strict meters." The "chair" at the National Eisteddfod is awarded only for an *awdl*. In 1902 it was won by Thomas Gwynn Jones (1871–1949) for his *Ymadawiad Arthur*. Though a youthful work, this poem was the harbinger of a new epoch in the history of Welsh poetry. Jones's mastery of strict meter and *cynghanedd*, combined with a dignity and purity of diction, delighted Morris-Jones. The romantic escapism of the poem's theme may be said to have more in common with the spirit of 19th-c. poetry.

As he matured Gwynn Jones achieved greatness as a poet. He experimented successfully in the application of *cynghanedd* to accentual free verse, revealing many new possibilities. In his last volume of poetry, *Y Dwymyn* (1944), all but one of the poems exhibit this use of *cynghanedd*.

Robert Williams Parry (1884–1956), a disciple of Gwynn Jones, was a poet with an acute social consciousness. It was for his poetry written in free verse that he achieved pre-eminence in Wales, but he also incorporated alliterative effects that sprang from his basic mastery of *cynghanedd*. Williams Parry's feeling for nature is unsurpassed among modern Welsh poets as is his almost magical felicity of language. Two volumes of his work have been published: *Yr Haf a Cherddi Eraill* (1924) and *Cerddi'r Gaeaf* (1952).

The main interest of poet William John Gruffydd (1881–1954) was in the wonder of human life and rebellion against narrow Victorian morality. His early poems appeared in *Telynegion* (1900), a volume written jointly with his friend Robert Silyn Roberts (1871–1930). *Telynegion* was followed by *Caneuon a Cherddi* (1906), *Ynys yr Hud a Chaneuon Eraill* (1923), and *Caniadau* (1932).

Sir Thomas Herbert Parry-Williams (b. 1887) made a sensational impact on Welsh literary circles as a young man. His early poetry, like that of his contemporaries, has youthful romantic overtones, but he developed his technique to become the acknowledged master of two forms of Welsh poetry: the sonnet and *rhigymau* (rhymes), a deceptively loose meter of informal style, sometimes a mere short series of couplets. Writing in a highly individual style, with cynical humor and controlled use of colloquialisms, he meditates on life and death, suffering and evil, and the decay of old loyalties recalled in his memories of home in the mountain fastness of Snowdonia in north-western Wales.

Saunders Lewis (b. 1893) is one of the most important personalities in the life and literature of contemporary Wales. A dramatist, novelist, literary critic, scholar, essayist, journalist, politician, and poet, he is the most European of all modern Welsh writers. His poetry conveys his solicitude for Welsh national unity, which is often implied rather than stated openly in his scathing satires of contemporary Welsh society or in his nonromantic attachment to the aristocratic ideals of medieval Wales. Some of his poems are collected in *Byd a Betws* (1941) and *Siwan a Cherddi Eraill* (1955), and he incorporated much of his verse in his dramas.

A marked Welsh patriotism, religion, and a reaction against the ravages of industrialization are the recurring motifs in the poetry of David Gwenallt Jones (1899–1968). He is considered in many ways to have been the most accomplished poet of his generation. He showed a progressive mastery of various meters—from the *englyn* and the *cywydd* (two categories of strict meter) to various forms of the sonnet and free verse—and was noted for the originality of his conceptions and for his strength of phrase. Three volumes of his poetry have been published: *Ysgubau'r Awen* (1939), *Cnoi Cil* (1942), and *Eples* (1951).

Other poets who have enriched the Welsh literary heritage during the century are: I. D. Hooson (1880–1948), especially noted for his ballads; D. Emrys James (1881–1952); E. Prosser Rhys (1901–1945); and T. Rowland Hughes (1903–1949). Many contemporary Welsh poets are deeply influenced by English and continental ideas, and others are still going through an experimental stage in the development.

2. Prose

The new standards of linguistic usage that became apparent at the beginning of the 20th c. had their effect on Welsh prose. Of the men who may be said to have anticipated these standards Sir Owen M. Edwards (1858–1920) was one of the most outstanding. A contemporary of Morris-Jones, Edwards was an author, historian, and educator. He developed a personal style in his writing that was at once simple and direct yet strong in its feeling for native idioms. His influence was manifested through the many periodicals he edited and to which he encouraged many writers to contribute their work. His numerous published books and his contact with schools during his tenure of office (1907–1920) as Chief Inspector for Wales to the Welsh Department of the Board of Education also helped to establish his influence.

The Welsh prose tradition is one of style rather than of genre. The novel, the short story, and the *ysgrif* (short essay) are examples of prose forms that have been developed, to some extent, during the 20th c.

Though there is no lack of mastery over the prose medium or a scarcity of themes in contemporary society, attempts at novel-writing at the turn of the century were few. Daniel Owen (1836–95), a novelist of merit, was one of the few whose works cannot be fairly labeled as mediocre. The length of the novel alone seems to have been a discouraging prospect to 20th-c. Welsh writers, for most of whom writing is usually only an avocation. Instead, prose talent has been channeled into the shorter forms. A substantial number of young writers, however, are now becoming interested in the novel. The most promising of these is Islwyn Ffowc Elis, whose first novel, *Cysgod y Cryman* (1953), won recognition from the critics. Still, it may be claimed with some justification that many Welsh novels are in reality extended short stories.

The conscious development of the short story as a literary genre in Welsh dates from about 1913, when R. Hughes Williams began to publish his stories in the monthly periodical *Cymru*. He later published a collection of his stories, *Storïau Richard Hughes Williams* (1932), the settings of which are in the slate-quarrying districts of northern Wales. It was also a native of northern Wales, Kate Roberts (b. 1891), who mastered the short-story form. Her stories are collected in three volumes: *O Gors y Bryniau* (1925), *Rhigolau Bywyd* (1929), and *Ffair Gaeaf* (1937).

Other short-story writers of standing are D. J. Williams (1885–1970), who published *Storïau'r Tir Glas* (1936), *Storïau'r Tir Coch* (1941), and *Storïau'r Tir Du* (1949), and John Gwilym Jones, noted for his *Y Goeden Eirin* (1946). Many fine short stories are collected in the anthology *Ystorïau Heddiw* (1938).

The *ysgrif*, an essay written in an intimate, personal style, was originated in its modern form by Sir Thomas Parry-Williams. His essays appear in *Ysgrifau* (1928), *Olion* (1935),

Synfyfyrion (1937), *O'r Pedwar Gwynt* (1938), and *Lloffion* (1942). Like his *rhigymau* in verse, the essays have a deceptively casual air, but they are the writings of a cultivated personality and a keen, reflective mind. Their apparent informality conceals a consummate art and a disciplined, powerful economy of expression.

The *ysgrif* has become a very popular prose form. Among its more successful exponents are: R. T. Jenkins (1881–1970), an historian whose vocation naturally influenced his themes; T. J. Morgan; Ffransis Payne; J. O. Williams; and Islwyn Ffowc Elis.

Welsh prose in the 20th c. has proved to be an adequate medium for a large variety of purposes. Essays and criticism in fields ranging from literature and history to scientific and technical interests are many. Historical and literary research is, and has long been, published in Welsh, as have memoirs, biographies, autobiographies, social criticism and comment, travel literature, theology, popular fiction of various kinds, and books for children. There have even been commendable efforts at translating the European classics. Script material for radio and television programs have also been adapted for publication. Not all of this can be considered literature, but the standard of writing of the more serious works is generally high.

3. Drama

Wales has never possessed a national theater. Larger towns, such as Cardiff and Swansea, where theaters do exist, have become too anglicized to provide audiences for more than the occasional production of Welsh plays. Because professional theater companies cannot be maintained on this basis, Welsh plays are usually produced by amateurs in makeshift circumstances. The advent of Welsh-language radio and television, however, is having salutary effect on the present state of drama.

Original Welsh plays vary greatly in artistic merit. Though dramatic literary standards have not been particularly high, there are notable exceptions. Preeminent among modern playwrights is Saunders Lewis, who frequently used blank verse and free verse in his earlier plays *Blodeuwedd* (begun in 1923), *Buchedd Garmon* (1936), and *Amlyn ac Amig* (1940). John Gwilym Jones has published two of his best plays, "Lle Mynno'r Gwynt" and "Gwr Llonydd," in a volume entitled *Dwy Ddrama* (1957). Thomas Parry is noted in drama for

his historical play *Llywelyn Fawr* (1951), written in a strong but flexible blank verse, and his translation of T. S. Eliot's (q.v.) *Murder in the Cathedral* (*Lladd wrth yr Allor,* 1949).

Welsh linguists have translated the plays of the Greek tragedians, Shakespeare, Molière (1622–73), Nikolai Gogol (1809–1952), Ibsen, Anouilh, Chekhov, Priestley, T. S. Eliot (qq.v.), and others.

BIBLIOGRAPHY: Lewis, S., *An Introduction to Contemporary Welsh Literature* (1926); Parry, T., *Hanes Llenyddiaeth Gymraeg hyd 1900* (1944); Parry, T., *Llenyddiaeth Gymraeg 1900–1945* (1945); Williams, D., *A History of Modern Wales* (1950); Parry, T., *A History of Welsh Literature,* tr. H. I. Bell (1955); *The Dictionary of Welsh Biography Down to 1940* (1959); Parry, T., ed., *The Oxford Book of Welsh Verse* (1962); The Council of Wales and Monmouthshire, *Report on the Welsh Language Today* (1963)

GWYNEDD O. PIERCE

ANGLO-WELSH LITERATURE

Anglo-Welsh is the description given to English-writing authors who were either born in Wales or of declared Welsh origins, and to writers who wish to be specifically associated with Wales. The majority of them come from South Wales and Monmouthshire (western England), the urban and industrial areas, where the process of anglicization has been most thorough. Many were raised in Welsh-speaking homes, and some of these authors themselves speak Welsh (*e.g.,* Caradoc Evans, Emlyn Williams, Wyn Griffiths, Jack Jones, Glyn Jones, Huw Menai, Keidrych Rhys, Emyr Humphreys, R. S. Thomas, Idris Davies, Menna Gallie).

Many Anglo-Welsh writers are the products of late 19th-c. Welsh education, which was conducted in the English language. They emerged as a definite school of writers in the late 1920's and early 1930's, when industrial South Wales was a depressed area of unemployment and when rural Wales (the more predominantly Welsh-speaking section of the principality) was struggling toward a national identity. The consequent rapid development of the native Welsh literature has diverted many potential English-writing authors. It seemed in the late 1940's that Anglo-Welsh writing would lose the distinctly Welsh flavor so characteristic of the 1930's, and that Welsh self-determination would fade out. It now seems likely that Anglo-Welsh and Welsh-language writers will continue to exist side by side. Though divided by their use of two languages, they will be united by their common interest in interpreting Welsh life to their compatriots and to an English-reading public.

Anglo-Welsh literature can claim outstanding short-story writers, good novelists, and a few famous poets. But there is only a very small group of dramatists, and the professional (as opposed to the amateur) theater has declined disastrously in Wales between 1920 and 1970. There has been no successful Welsh publisher for Anglo-Welsh literature, and despite the increased patronage of the Arts Council, Anglo-Welsh writers have had to rely for publication on English publishing houses.

The emergence of a distinct school of Anglo-Welsh short-story writers in the 1930's was closely linked with the publication of a large number of small literary periodicals. The virtual disappearance of those periodicals accounts for the recent decline of short-story writing. Four attempts have been made to found Welsh journals devoted to creative writing in English: *The Welsh Outlook* (1914–27), devoted chiefly to social affairs; *Wales* (1937–50, 1958–59); *The Welsh Review* (1939, 1944–48); and *The Anglo-Welsh Review* (1949–57), published with a subsidy from the Arts Council in Wales. *The Anglo-Welsh Review* has a strong literary-criticism section and attracts many young poets. Three new magazines— *Poetry Wales, Mabon,* and *The Planet*—show future promise.

Anglo-Welsh literature can best be discussed by placing it into three periods. In the first period (1900–1920), the writers were less consciously Welsh and often worked outside Wales, writing largely for an English audience. The second period (1920–45), the so-called flowering period, was dominated by short-story writers and fostered by two Welsh-centered literary journals, sharing a common interest in portraying the decaying industrial and rural life of South Wales and the border counties. The third period (1946 to the present) witnessed the emergence of new writers from all parts of Wales. These writers are less conscious of their industrial heritage, more aware of their links with the English literary world, strongly influenced by—or averse to—the work of Dylan Thomas (q.v.) and R. S. Thomas (b. 1915), and shaped to some extent by both the demands of radio and television audiences and the recent rapid growth of university education.

1. 1900–1920

Machen, born in Caerleon, Monmouthshire, was translator, novelist, journalist, short-story writer, and literary critic. The collection of criticism *Hieroglyphics* (1902), the fantasies *The Hill of Dreams* (1907), *The Three Imposters* (1895), *The London Adventure* (1928), *The Cosy Room* (1936), and *The House of Souls* (1936), and the two autobiographies *Things Near and Far* (1923) and *Far Off Things* (1926) are among his best works.

Davies, born in Newport, Monmouthshire, was best-known as a poet. But he also became an active prose writer and man of letters. His collected poems appeared in a series (1916–40), but *The Complete Poems of W. H. Davies* (1962) includes over a hundred poems previously omitted. His best prose works are the vivid accounts of his life as a tramp and beggar —*The Autobiography of a Super-Tramp* (1908), *Beggars* (1909), *A Poet's Pilgrimage* (1918), and *Later Days* (1925).

The London Welshman Edward Thomas (1878–1917), a man of letters and a poet, maintained throughout his life close links with Wales and used Welsh themes in his prose. Some of his best works include *Horae Solitariae* (1902) and *Rose Acre Papers* (1904), *Celtic Stories* (1902), *The Happy-Go-Lucky Morgans* (1913), *Beautiful Wales* (1905), and *The Childhood of Edward Thomas* (written, 1913; published, 1938).

Caradoc Evans (1878–1945), a London journalist who was born in Cardigan in western Wales, was widely acclaimed as the true father of Anglo-Welsh literature. His satiric portraits of rural Calvinistic Wales were written in a concocted, highly personal dialect that was half-Welsh and half-English. These portraits— *My People* (1915), *Capel Sion* (1917), *My Neighbours* (1919), *Wasps* (1933), *Morgan Bible* (1943)—and his play of Welsh village life, *Taffy* (1923), were bitterly resented in Wales.

The dramatist J. O. Francis (b. 1882) was brought up in Merthyr, South Wales, which had direct links with the traveling theaters of 19th-c. industrial Wales. Francis's humorous interpretations of Welsh life have been popular with the native amateur dramatic movement. His best plays include: *John Jones* (1910), *The Poacher* (1914), *The Bakehouse* (1927), *Birds* of a Feather (1927), King of the River (1943), Change (1913), The Dark Little People (1922), Little Village (1930), and Tares in the Wheat (1943).

Three other Welsh writers belong to this early period both in literary intention and in their attitude to Wales. One of these is Eliot Crawshay-Williams (b. 1879), a prolific novelist—The Gutter and the Stars (1918), The Booby Trap (1928), Hywel and Gwyneth (1945), The Wolf from the West (1947). He also wrote dramas: Five Grand Guignol Plays (1924).

Huw Menai (1887–1961) was chiefly known for his poetry—e.g., Through the Upcast Shaft (1920), Back in the Return (1933), and The Simple Vision (1945). A writer and broadcaster, Wyn Griffith (b. 1890) has written poems (Branwen, 1934; The Barren Tree, 1945), novels (Spring of Youth, 1935; Wooden Spoon, 1937), and essays on Welsh life (Word from Wales, 1941; The Welsh and Their Country, 1947; The Welsh, 1950).

2. 1920–1945

Rhys Davies (b. 1903), born in Rhondda in southeastern Wales, was a friend of D. H. Lawrence (q.v.). He continued the earlier tradition of living outside of Wales but with a slight difference: he was tied like Antaeus to his native valley for inspiration. Some of Davies's superb short stories are collected in Selected Stories (1945), The Collected Stories of Rhys Davies (1955), The Darling of Her Heart (1958), and The Chosen One (1967). In addition to his short stories, he has written over sixteen novels—e.g., The Withered Root (1927), Jubilee Blues (1938), A Time to Laugh (1941), Tomorrow to Fresh Woods (1941), Black Venus (1944), The Dark Daughters (1947), Marianne (1957), and Girl Waiting in the Shade (1960). Other important works by Davies include the autobiography Print of a Hare's Foot (1969), a biography of the Danish adventurer Jörgen Jörgensen (Sea Urchin, 1940), My Wales (1936), and The Story of Wales (1943).

Geraint Goodwin (1903–1941) worked for a while as a journalist in London, where he wrote his Conversations with George Moore (1929). After returning in 1935 to his native Montgomeryshire, he wrote three powerful "border" novels—Call Back Yesterday (1935), The Heyday in the Blood (1936), Watch for the Morn-

ing (1938)—and many Laurentian short stories (The White Farm, and Other Stories, 1937).

Almost all the works of Hilda Vaughan, wife of novelist Charles Morgan (1894–1958), are based on the rural life of the Welsh border counties. Among her novels are: The Battle to the Weak (1925), Her Father's House (1930), Harvest Home (1930), Iron and Gold (1948), and The Candle and the Light (1954). Her three plays—She Was Too Young (produced, 1938), The Soldier and the Gentlewoman (produced, 1933), and Forsaking All Others (produced, 1950)—have not yet been published.

The authentic voice (and English dialect) of South Wales emerged in the prolific works of Jack Jones (1884–1970). His realistic works, which recall a vanished industrial life, have been very popular. Among his best-known novels are: Rhondda Roundabout (1934), Black Parade (1935), Off to Philadelphia in the Morning (1947), River out of Eden (1951), and Journey into Death (1956). He also wrote two plays (Land of My Fathers, 1937; Transatlantic Episode, 1947), three autobiographical works (Unfinished Journey, 1937; Me and Mine, 1946; Give Me Back My Heart, 1950), and an idealized biography of the British statesman and prime minister David Lloyd George (The Man David, 1944).

Gwyn Jones (b. 1907) is a professor of English and in the 1940's was the editor of The Welsh Review. As the acknowledged leader of the second period of Anglo-Welsh literature, he is still today a powerful influence in Welsh literary, artistic, and dramatic life. His well-sustained short stories are collected in: The Buttercup Field (1945), The Still Waters (1948), and Shepherd's Hey (1953). He is also acknowledged as a fine novelist (Richard Savage, 1935; Times Like These, 1936; Green Island, 1947; The Walk Home, 1962) and an exponent of Anglo-Welsh writing (The First Forty Years, 1957). His translation (in collaboration with T. Jones) of the famous The Mabinogion, an anonymous collection of Celtic sagas originating about the middle of the 11th c., was published in 1948, and some of the collections of stories that he has compiled and edited contain translations of Welsh-language writers.

Richard Llewellyn (b. 1906), who wrote the ever-popular How Green Was My Valley (1939) and the play Poison Pen (1937), has not returned to Welsh subjects since World War II. Some of his postwar works include A Few Flowers for Shiner (1950), Mr. Hamish

Gleaves (1956), and the play *Noose* (1947). Llewellyn belongs to a group of Welsh-born writers who have devoted only a small portion of their work to native subjects.

One of the group, the painter David Jones (b. 1895), is known for his two autobiographical studies *In Parenthesis* (1937) and *The Anathemata* (1952). Another, Richard Hughes (b. 1900), has published the first part of his autobiography *The Fox in the Attic* (1961) and is well-known for his novels of the sea (*A High Wind in Jamaica*, 1926; and *In Hazard*, 1938).

Others of this group include: Goronwy Rees (b. 1909), *A Bundle of Sensations* (1961); Alex Cordell, who has published the best-selling novels *The Rape of the Fair Country* (1959) and *Song of the Earth* (1969); Eluned Lewis; and Margiad Evans (1909–1956).

In addition to Dylan Thomas, six Welsh poets were active between the world wars. Idris Davies (1910–50) wrote bitter satires of decayed mining towns. Alun Lewis (1915–44) was widely praised as a war poet and short-story writer. India was the theme of some of his works (*e.g.*, *Letters from India*, 1943). Glyn Jones (b. 1905), in addition to his activity as a poet, has written exquisite short stories (*The Blue Bed*, 1937; *The Water Music*, 1944), humorous novels (*The Valley, the City, the Village*, 1956; *The Learning Lark*, 1960), and criticism (*The Dragon Has Two Tongues*, 1968).

Vernon Watkins (1906–1967), a friend of Dylan Thomas, emerged as a significant post-World War II traditional poet. He is also to be credited for his translations of the poetry of Heinrich Heine (1797–1856).

Though also an active poet of this second period—*The Van Pool* (1941), *Storms and Landscapes* (1950), *Poems and Ballads* (1950)—Keidrych Rhys (b. 1915) is better known as the founder of the lively magazine *Wales* and as an anthologist.

Henry Treece (1921–66) has written four unpublished broadcast plays in verse, two novels, and criticism (*e.g.*, *How I See Apocalypse*, 1946; *Dylan Thomas*, 1946; *Herbert Read*, 1944).

The drama of the second period continued, to some extent, the South Wales amateur drama tradition of J. O. Francis. Eynon Evans (b. 1904), actor and dramatist, was instrumental in carrying this tradition on to the professional theater with his one-act play *Prize Onions* (1937) and his full-length plays

Cobbler's Wax (1937), *Wishing Well* (1947), *All Through the Night* (1950), *Bachelor Brothers* (1953), and *Bless This House* (1954).

The somewhat more sophisticated actor-dramatist Emlyn Williams (b. 1905) has drawn largely on themes of North Wales for many of his London stage successes—*The Late Christopher Bean* (1933), *Night Must Fall* (1935), *The Corn Is Green* (1938), *The Druid's Rest* (1944), *The Wind of Heaven* (1945), *The Collected Plays* (1961)—and for his autobiography *George* (1960).

3. 1945–1970

Gwyn Thomas (b. 1912, Rhondda), a widely read Welsh novelist, has reinterpreted Welsh industrial life with a powerful comic style in the novels *The Dark Philosophers* (1946), *Where Did I Put My Pity?* (1947), *The Alone to the Alone* (1947), *All Things Betray Thee* (1949), *Now Lead Us Home* (1952), *The Love Man* (1958), and in the collection *Gazooka, and Other Short Stories* (1957). His play *The Keep* (1962), as well as a few of his nonfiction works (*e.g.*, *A Welsh Eye*, 1967; *A Few Selected Exits*, 1969), is written in the same vein.

Emyr Humphreys (b. 1919, North Wales), whose audience extends beyond Wales, has written eight novels with an ever-widening canvas. In a number of his novels, such as the early *Little Kingdom* (1946) and the recent *The House of Baal* (1968), he shows a deep understanding of Protestant ethics. He has also written radio plays—which have not been collected—poems, and short stories.

More recently Richard Vaughan has completed his *Black Mountain* trilogy—*Moulded in Earth* (1951), *Who Rideth So Wild?* (1952), *All Through the Night* (1957). Menna Gallie (b. 1915) has written of mining and university life, with a delightful ear for comic Welsh dialogue, in the realistic novels such as *Strike for a Kingdom* (1959).

Ron Berry, James Hanley (b. 1901), and John Parker have broken away from the Anglo-Welsh nostalgic themes of the pre-World War II writers in order to concentrate on contemporary social and industrial topics.

The poetry of R. S. Thomas, an Anglican minister, has rural themes and is written in taut verse. Cardiff-born Dannie Abse (b. 1924), a medical doctor, is also popular in England for his poems and his plays (*Three Questor Plays*, 1968).

507

Other poets closely connected with the magazine *The Anglo-Welsh Review* are: its editor, Roland Mathias; Raymond Garlick; Gloria Evans-Davies; Anthony Conran (*Metamorphoses,* 1963); and those writers represented in the anthologies *Dragons and Daffodils* (1960), *Welsh Voices* (1967), *This World of Wales* (1968), and *The Lilting House* (1969).

Alun Owen, originally from Liverpool, and Elaine Morgan are two representative dramatists of the third period. Both have turned from writing for radio and television to writing for the legitimate stage.

The most interesting sampling of Welsh short stories since World War II was published in the anthology *Welsh Short Stories* (1959), edited by G. E. Evans.

BIBLIOGRAPHY: Megroz, R. L., *Rhys Davies: A Critical Sketch* (1932); Lewis, S., *Is There an Anglo-Welsh Literature?* (1938); Bates, H. E., *The Modern Short Story: A Critical Survey* (1941); Jones, G., "Note on Welsh Short-Story Writers," *Life and Letters,* Sept. 1942 and March 1943; Adam, G. F., *Three Contemporary Anglo-Welsh Novelists* (1948); "Idris Davies," *Poetry and Drama Magazine,* IX (1957), ii; Thomas, R. G., "The Poetry of R. S. Thomas," *A Review of English Literature,* III (1962); Thomas, R. G., "R. S. Thomas," *Writers and Their Works,* No. 166 (1964); Garlick, R., *An Introduction to Anglo-Welsh Literature* (1970)

R. GEORGE THOMAS

WELTY, Eudora
American novelist, short-story writer, and critic, b. 13 April 1909, Jackson, Mississippi

Eudora W. grew up in Jackson, Mississippi, graduated from the University of Wisconsin in 1929, then studied advertising at Columbia University. Since 1931 she has lived in Jackson except for brief stints as a visiting professor and writer in residence, and as a staff reviewer for *The New York Times.* In 1936 *Manuscript* published a story, "Death of a Traveling Salesman," and after several acceptances from the *Southern Review* and *Prairie Schooner,* she made writing her career.

In 1941 Eudora W. won (for her story, "A Worn Path") the first of her six O. Henry Memorial Contest awards and published her first collection, *A Curtain of Green.* Her second, *The Wide Net* (1943), soon followed.

Both were critical successes. These stories, the setting of which is Mississippi as is true of most of her work, are characteristic of her fiction. They range from a pitilessly ironic study of human vulgarity ("Petrified Man") to a bittersweet account of a young wife's emotional rebirth upon the death of her aging, patriarchal husband ("Livvie"). Their major themes concern the mysteries of the inner life and the "changing and pervading" mystery of relationship: man's primal isolation, his groping attempts—only fleetingly successful—to understand and surmount it, his undeniable moments of joy. The stories also display Eudora W.'s readiness to experiment with unexpected, subtly shifting points of view and startling but usually "right" images. If a few stories are obscure, most reveal her remarkable talent for conveying the most tenuous aspects of human response and sensitivity through a slight gesture, an illuminating image from the natural and community life associated with the "place" of the story, or a daring verb metaphor.

During the 1940's, while continuing to publish critically acclaimed short stories, Eudora W. experimented with longer forms. Using a shifting point of view, *Delta Wedding* (1946), a full-length novel, develops a major theme from the early stories, the human need for love and separateness. It reveals a plantation family's reactions to the approaching marriage of a daughter and the overseer. It also suggests both virtues and shortcomings in a complacent, self-contained but doomed family-community —implications overlooked by some critics, who deplored its lack of social comment.

The Golden Apples (1949) is a textually complex book of interrelated short stories about a small Mississippi town, whose characters and events convey mythic overtones. Recurring characters, imagery, and symbolism develop a unifying theme: the endless human search, at once personal and universal, for fulfillment in a world where joy and despair, beauty and horror, love and separateness, coexist.

The Ponder Heart (1954), a wildly funny monologue-novella, confirms the comic sense and unerring ear for Southern speech already evident in Eudora W.'s stories. It won the American Academy of Arts and Letters medal for the most distinguished American fiction for 1950–55.

For the next fifteen years, Eudora W. published little: three new stories, a children's book, and some perceptive criticism, notably "Henry Green: A Novelist of the Imagination" (1961) and "Must the Novelist Crusade?" (1965).

Then, in 1970, came an impressive new work, *Losing Battles,* a long, vibrant, serio-comic novel, set in rural Mississippi in the 1930's, about a large family of semiliterate hill people who face imminent impoverishment. In technical daring and major theme it is characteristic. Confined to a two-day reunion celebrating the grandmother's ninetieth birthday and written mostly in dialogue, with limited external narration, it subtly juxtaposes the family's past and present to develop the love-and-separateness theme in a new and expanded context. Touching, funny, unsparingly honest, it reveals how a pervasive family love has provided strength that enabled the family to survive but also obscured its members' view of reality and acerbated their relationships with nonfamily people. With *Losing Battles,* Eudora W. became, in addition to being a major writer of short fiction, a novelist of stature.

FURTHER WORKS: *The Robber Bridegroom* (1942); *Short Stories* (1950); *The Bride of the Innisfallen, and Other Stories* (1955); *Place in Fiction* (1957)

BIBLIOGRAPHY: Warren, R. P., "The Love and Separateness in Miss W.," *KR,* VI (1944), 246–59; Hardy, J. E., "*Delta Wedding* as Region and Symbol," *SR,* LX (1952), 397–417; Daniel, R., "E. W.: The Sense of Place," in *South: Modern Southern Literature in Its Cultural Setting* (1961); Vande Kieft, R., *E. W.* (1962); Eisenger, C. E., "E. W. and the Triumph of the Imagination," in *Fiction of the Forties* (1963); Appel, A., Jr., *A Season of Dreams: The Fiction of E. W.* (1965)

W. U. MCDONALD, JR.

WEÖRES, Sándor

Hungarian poet, b. 22 June 1913, Szombathely

W. attended the University of Pécs, from which he received a doctorate for his dissertation entitled *A vers születése,* published in 1939. Between 1941 and 1950 he worked as a librarian, and later he coedited the Pécs literary review *Sorsunk.* W. twice won the Baumgarten Award, and in 1970 he was awarded the prestigious Kossuth Prize.

W. began writing poetry as a child, and as a very young man he was encouraged by the distinguished poet Babits (q.v.), who published W.'s poems in the literary review *Nyugat.* W.'s first collection of poems, *Hideg van* (1934), showed those qualities that were to become characteristic of his poetry: a definite philosophical bent, an awareness of the human predicament and the tragic antinomies of life, an extraordinary mimetic talent, and an urge to speak through different personae and play elaborate games with the language.

His second book of poetry, *A kö és az ember* (1935), focused on new themes but showed little qualitative change. The depth and breadth of W.'s poetic vision was seen for the first time in *A teremtés dicsérete* (1938). The sudden creative growth is probably traceable to the fact that during these years W. paid short visits to India and Malaya, studied Eastern religions and philosophies, and worked on a translation of the Sumerian epic poem of the legendary hero Gilgamesh.

W.'s great interest in mythology resulted in his long dramatic poem *Theomachia* (1941), which deals with the castration and dethronement of Kronos by Zeus. The mystery of creation and human self-creation is a recurring theme in W.'s poetry, for example, in poems such as "A teremtés," "Elsö emberpár," "Fü, fa, füst." His philosophy is basically religion- and myth-oriented, stressing man's painful alienation from God and reacting skeptically to sweeping claims of scientific and political progress.

W.'s pessimistic credo was first formulated in the poem "De profundis" (1942) and forcefully reiterated in two great poems: "A reménytelenség könyve" (1944) and "XX. századi freskó" (1945). These poems and the prose gnomes and axioms in *A teljesség felé* (1945) advocated individual self-perfection rather than social revolution. They therefore aroused the hostility of communist critics. W. was branded an "escapist" and a "nihilist." Though the publication of his *A Fogak Tornáca* (1947) was one of the outstanding literary events of the short-lived Hungarian democracy, between 1948 and 1955 W. was unable to publish a new book of poems. During these years he translated many foreign classics —Šotho Rustaveli (1182–1212), Taras Shevchenko (1814–61)—and wrote *Bóbita* (1955), a still-popular book of children's verse.

At the time of the "thaw" (*see* Russian literature) W. published a large collection of poems,

A hallgatás tornya (1956), that firmly established his reputation. This volume includes the brilliant cycle of epigrams "Orbis Pictus," the great descriptive poem "Az elveszett napernyö," and the ironic collage "Le Journal," perhaps the most devastating critique in verse of Stalinist Hungary. Two more books of poetry published since 1956 indicate a simultaneous development toward the grotesque and the sublime. In these collections, W.'s catastrophic visions gave way to a more hopeful view of the future. It was no longer his politics that shocked conservative critics but his masterful descriptive handling of the theme of physical love.

W.'s collected translations were published in *A lélek idézese* (1958) and his two plays in the volume *Hold és Sárkány* (1967).

Though he is criticized for his lack of national and social concern, W.'s fertile imagination and supreme linguistic skill single him out as a master of Hungarian verse unequaled in this century.

FURTHER WORKS: *Hideg van* (1934); *A vers születése* (1939); *Bolond Istók* (1943); *Medúza* (1944); *A szerelem ábécéje* (1946); *Elysium* (1946); *Gyümölcskosár* (1946); *Tarka forgó* (with A. Károlyi; 1958); *Tüzkút* (1964); *Merülö Saturnus* (1968); *Egybegyüjtött irások* (2 vols., 1970). **Selected English translation:** selections in *New Writing of East Europe* (ed. G. Gömöri, and C. Newman; 1968)

BIBLIOGRAPHY: Reményi, J., "S. W., Contemporary Hungarian Poet," *MLJ*, XXXIII (April 1949), iv, 302–08; Szabó, L. C., "Conversation with W.," in *New Writing of East Europe*, eds. G. Gömöri and C. Newman (1968), pp. 63–67; Gömöri, G., "S. W.: Unity in Diversity," *BA*, XLIII (Winter 1969), i, 36–41

GEORGE GÖMÖRI

WERFEL, Franz

Austrian novelist, short-story writer, poet, dramatist, and essayist, b. 10 Sept. 1890, Prague; d. 26 Aug. 1945, Beverly Hills, California

W. was the son of a prosperous merchant in Prague. While still a student in Prague, he became a friend of Brod and Kafka (qq.v.). After further studies at Leipzig and Hamburg, he worked for a while in a shipping firm in Hamburg. From 1911 to 1914 he was an editor,

and in 1913 he helped to found the literary series *Der Jüngste Tag*. During World War I he served in the Austrian army at the eastern front. After the war he settled in Vienna, where he later married Alma Mahler, the widow of composer Gustav Mahler. During the 1920's W. traveled in Italy, Egypt, and Palestine. In 1938, after the Nazi Anschluss with Austria, he was forced to leave Vienna, coming to the United States in 1940.

W.'s voluminous literary works comprise short stories, novellas, sketches, poems, essays, plays, and ten novels plus the unfinished *Die schwarze Messe* and *Cella, oder die Überwinder*. His writing is closely bound up with the places in which he lived. The majority of his short stories and some of his novels take place in Vienna and Prague. Many of his poems are on themes from the cities and landscapes of his native region. His stay in Turkey led to the novel *Die vierzig Tage des Musa Dagh* (1933; The Forty Days of Musa Dagh, 1934). As a result of his travels in Italy, he wrote the novels *Verdi* (1924; Verdi: A Novel of the Opera, 1947), *Die Geschwister von Neapel* (1931; The Pascarella Family, 1932), and *Der veruntreute Himmel: Geschichte einer Magd* (1939; Embezzled Heaven, 1939), as well as some short stories.

W.'s European journeys as a refugee after 1938 may be traced by the settings of the works he conceived during that period. In France he wrote sketches of life in Paris and decided to write the novel *Das Lied von Bernadette* (1941; The Song of Bernadette, 1942), the action of which takes place in France. Spain is the scene of *Die arge Legende vom gerissenen Galgenstrick* (1948), while America is the recognizable setting for the posthumously published utopian novel *Stern der Ungeborenen* (1946; Star of the Unborn, 1946).

W.'s late work, however, is noticeably marked by a certain loss of a geographical base of reference. In the narrative *Eine blaßblaue Frauenschrift* (1941) Vera, a Jewish woman on the point of emigration, has a conversation in which someone says to her that Montevideo is terribly far. To this she asks, "Far from where?" W. then added: "This was a reference to a melancholy joke current among the exiles who had lost their geographical center of gravity." The reporter F. W. in *Stern der Ungeborenen* is such a character.

The "astro-mental" world of *Stern der Ungeborenen* is likewise curiously faceless: it has no vegetation to characterize it, no mountains, there are no active means of traversing its space. It is true that the latter peculiarity is supposed to be a mark of astro-mental civilization, the purpose of which is "to abolish the contradiction between man's boundless inner capacity for experience and his earthly and physical limitations." Therefore, "astromentalism may be defined as the art of giving body to the infinitely mobile mental images of our psyche and setting them in space and time." But no doubt it was only W.'s situation as an exile that prompted him to conceive such a "reality." The annexation of what is spatially remote by means of "sharply focused wishes" corresponds exactly to the process by which the exile brings to mind his homeland and in memory walks about the place from which he is barred.

W.'s work was quite unmistakably characterized by his ties with Austria—not so much in the settings of his plots, but rather with regard to its characteristic intellectuality—and with his Jewishness. His Jewish conflicts may be reduced to two main strands, namely, Judaism as an historical phenomenon and as a metaphysical problem. The two are inextricably linked in W.'s mind, as indeed he never isolated human destinies from a metaphysical frame of reference in the shape either of private or of historical and political events. W. was particularly concerned with the relationship between Judaism and Christianity. Although he repeatedly declared himself a Jew, Christian thought is traceable throughout his work. Along with the Old Testament prophets we find the 19th-c. Saint Bernadette among the characters of his books, while piety is seen as an essential element of the human soul that has nothing to do with organized religion.

Nevertheless, W. saw in the special position of Israel its specific religious role. In his novel *Die wahre Geschichte vom wiederhergestellten Kreuz* (1942) he refers expressly to Romans 11: 25: "Obduracy has gripped part of Israel until the full number of heathens has come in." The rabbi interprets this passage as follows: "And then, what would happen if all the Jews in the world were baptized? Israel would disappear. And with it the only real witness to God's revelation would vanish from the world. The holy scriptures, which, through our existence, are a documented truth, would become a vapid, impotent legend like any of the Greek myths. Does the church not see this danger?

We belong together, Reverend, but we are not one. In the Epistle to the Romans it is written that the communion of Christ is based on Judaism. I am convinced that, so long as the church exists, Israel will exist, but also that the church must fall if Israel falls." Also in *Stern der Ungeborenen* the "Jew of the Age" believes, in line with divine ordainment, that he is linked in an indissoluble union with Christianity.

W.'s own attitude seems to have been like that of his characters. It may be for that reason that he never converted to the Christian faith.

W. was deeply interested in the forces of contemporary change—in technology, psychology, and social problems—as well as in the relation of the individual to the state, but he remained all his life an individualist. All the collectivist manifestations of the 20th c. were suspect to him. In his writings he dwelled on human communities, *e.g.*, on family life.

W.'s particular affection went out to those who serve, who sacrifice themselves. In sacrifice and self-abandonment man's value as a person remains inviolate. Traditional, humanistic ideas of self-sacrifice are linked by W. with religious orientation. Since one's metaphysical destiny is fixed, one's integrity is inalienable.

W. saw the development of the cosmos as a whole from the same point of view. He was, above all, suspicious of progress. In his last novel, *Stern der Ungeborenen,* he shows that astro-mental civilization cannot solve man's existential problems.

Even infinitely refined civilization contains the seeds of revolution, decline, destruction. In *Stern der Ungeborenen* the archbishop makes this crucial observation: "The other half of truth is very simple, my son: we not only depart from God through time, but we also approach God through time, inasmuch as we move away from the beginning of all things and toward the end of all things."

W. first became known as a lyric poet. His early volumes, particularly those of poems up to 1920, were among the most important products of expressionism (q.v.). Even the titles of his best-known books of poetry, *Der Weltfreund* (1911), *Wir sind* (1913), and *Einander* (1915), express his fraternal affection for others, his sympathy with men and all living things, his universal love that, despite its awareness of transience, again and again soars up to the Creator in intoxicated rejoicing.

While many of W.'s poems are in conventional form (he sometimes used the simple quatrains of folk song), there are others that tear apart syntax with their ecstatic, hymnlike outbursts, placing all the emphasis on a few words and sacrificing the clarity of the image to associations loaded with emotion. An example is the poem "Lächeln Atmen Schreiten," which is one of the most effective that young W. wrote.

The aim of the early poems is not to provide a meditative summary or to make a statement, but to call out a proclamation. Even though no actual "character" poems are to be found in W.'s poetry, it is clear that there is an intention of dialogue. In addressing himself, the poet appeals at the same time to the reader or listener and thus, with persuasive and dynamic purpose, continually addresses an imaginary interlocutor.

It is not surprising therefore that W. wrote such effective stage works as *Euripides: Die Troerinnen* (1915; an adaptation of Euripides's *Trojan Women*), *Spiegelmensch* (1920), *Juarez und Maximilian* (1924; Eng., 1926), *Paulus unter den Juden* (1926; Paul among the Jews, 1928), and *Jacobowsky und der Oberst* (1944; Jacobowsky and the Colonel, 1944). *Das Reich Gottes in Böhmen* (1930) ranks with Franz Grillparzer's (1791–1872) *Ein Bruderzwist im Hause Habsburg* and Hofmannsthal's (q.v.) *Der Turm* as one of the great Austrian historical dramas on the problem of power and the vanity of action.

In his early years W. wrote prose pieces and sketches, but it was not until about 1926 that he began to publish technically developed stories and novels. In these he usually followed traditional narrative methods—a continuous line of action, told chronologically in the first or third person, often enclosed within a framework. In his middle and later periods, a metaphysical interpretation of the characters replaced the psychological approach that was frequent in his early work. Characteristic of his style are a wealth of imagery and a predilection for symbolic allusions in which the setting is brought into close connection with the action.

W.'s criticism of himself is often incorporated in the fictitious character of a literary man to whom he attributes shortcomings for which he himself has been reproached—intellectual trifling, an undisciplined tendency to write too much, carelessness in expression, a liking for baroque exaggeration and operatic finales.

FURTHER WORKS: *Die Versuchung* (1913); *Gesänge aus den drei Reichen* (1917); *Der Gerichtstag* (1919); *Die Mittagsgöttin* (1919);

Der Besuch aus dem Elysium (1920); *Nicht der Mörder, der Ermordete ist schuldig* (1920; Not the Murderer, 1937); *Spielhof* (1920); *Bocksgesang* (1921; Goat Song, 1926); *Schweiger* (1922; Eng., 1926); *Arien* (1922); *Gesammelte Gedichte* (1927); *Der Snobismus als geistige Weltmacht* (1927); *Der Tod des Kleinbürgers* (1927; The Man Who Conquered Death, 1927); *Geheimnis eines Menschen* (1927; Saverio's Secret, 1937); *Gesammelte Werke* (8 vols., 1927 ff.); *Der Abituriententag* (1928; Class Reunion, 1929); *Barbara oder die Frömmigkeit* (1929; The Pure in Heart, 1931); *Dramatische Dichtungen* (1929); *Kleine Verhältnisse* (1931; Poor People, 1937); *Die Kämpfe der Schwachen* (1933); *Schlaf und Erwachen* (1935); *Der Weg der Verheißung* (1935; Eternal Road, 1936); *Höret die Stimme* (1937; under the title *Jeremias*, 1956; Hearken unto the Voice, 1938); *Von der reinsten Glückseligkeit des Menschen* (1938); *Gedichte aus dreißig Jahren* (1939); *Zwischen Gestern und Morgen* (1942); *Gedichte aus den Jahren 1908–1945* (1945; Poems from the Years 1908–1945, 1945); *Zwischen Oben und Unten* (1946; Between Heaven and Earth, 1944); *Erzählungen aus zwei Welten* (3 vols., 1948–54); *Gesammelte Werke* (13 vols., 1948 ff.); *Die Dramen* (2 vols., 1959); *Das Reich der Mitte* (1961); *Das lyrische Werk F. W.* (1967). **Selected English translations:** *Twilight of the World: Eight Novels* (1937); *Poems by F. W.* (1947)

BIBLIOGRAPHY: Klarmann, A. D., *Musikalität bei F. W.* (1931); Grenzmann, W., *Dichtung und Glaube* (1950); Puttkamer, A. v., *F. W.* (1952); Klarmann, A. D., "Das Weltbild F. Ws.," in *Wissenschaft und Weltbild* (1954); Foltin, L. B., *F. W.* (1960); Fox, W. H., "F. W.," in *German Men of Letters,* ed. A. Natan, Vol. III (1964), 107–25; Lea, H. A., "Prodigal Sons in W.'s Fiction," *GR,* XL (1965), 41–54; Foltin, L. B., "The F. W. Archives in Los Angeles," *GQ,* XXXIX (1966), 55–61; Zahn, L., *F. W.* (1966); Blumenthal, W., "Sin and Salvation in the Works of F. W.," *DA,* XVIII (1968), 2674A

ANNELIESE KUCHINKE-BACH

WEST AFRICAN LITERATURE: ENGLISH LANGUAGE

When the British formally withdrew their administration from the West African colonies, the English language was woven into the educational and administrative organization of these regions. At independence the former British territories of Gambia, Sierra Leone, Ghana, and Nigeria did not attempt to eliminate the English language, because a second language gave the new countries many significant advantages. Not only did English provide them with an international medium, but its use offset inherently centrifugal tendencies in countries established through the arbitrary decisions of colonial powers, often without regard to racial linguistic cohesion. Many writers from this area of Africa have chosen to use English for their works just as their neighbors have chosen to utilize the French language of their old rulers. A few African writers, such as the novelist Fagunwa (who writes in Yoruban) or the dramatist Duro Ladipo, have chosen to write in the vernacular.

This decision actually makes for some rather complex readjustments in the delicate balance between writer and reader. Although some writers, such as the Nigerians Cyprian Ekwensi (b. 1921) and Chinua Achebe (b. 1930), have fairly extensive African sales, the fact that such writing is published in London and has a large part of its readership abroad cannot but influence the writer. He must recognize that a major part of his audience comprehends none of the cultural assumptions that he takes for granted. This is the reason for the rather excessive amount of anthropological information in some African novels intended for a non-African audience. Perhaps, too, the writer, when he plans his story, may remember the desire of a European publisher for evidence of the more exotic aspects of Africa expected by the public. Such characteristics, however, may be only temporary. The growth of education in Africa has increased the audience for African books; a further increase of works directed primarily toward African readers may be expected through the publication of cheap paperback editions and through the development of local African publishers.

A factor that accelerates the distinction between English literature as a whole and African writing in English is the use that African writers have made of the extreme adaptability of the English language. The diction used by Africans is not a dull replica of the English idiom. English teachers did not, like their French counterparts, succeed in instilling a sense of the model nature of their European tongue. English in Africa is changing, lively, local, taking a new color and resilience from the local idioms, and molded by the pressure of the first-language vernaculars into a variety of forms that may approach separate dialects but that are always vivid, new, and expressive.

This new African literature in English appears to owe little to the devices of oral traditions in Africa. When discussing the poetry of Christopher Okigbo (b. 1935) one mentions the influence of Pound (q.v.) rather than recitations of tribal bards. This new and eclectic literature owes much in its technique to Western models, but in theme and subject it is at the same time deeply rooted in the African situation. This attempt at a synthesis distinguishes it from other 20th-c. writing in England and America. The genres are European: the novel, the drama, poetry, and the short story. They have only a remote ancestry in African folk tales, heroic praise poems, or the dramatic patterns of tribal ritual. Such forms, however, have been developed so characteristically by African writers that they almost cease to resemble the corresponding genres in American and European literature; they become African in an entirely new sense.

Although African writing in English began later than that in French, it seems at present the livelier of the two literatures. Little was written by British West Africans except for the work produced by missionary presses. When English-language writing did begin, however, it was not bound to any partisan school such as the principle of négritude devised by the French-speaking Césaire and Senghor (qq.v.). The result was writing that did not bow to over-all policy or attitude. Even today, in a survey of the notable African literature of the last ten years, few writers can be linked in categories other than those of personal friendship and nationality.

Significantly, the work that served as a catalyst to literary activity in Nigeria was not a charged manifesto but the exotic and ghostly folk tale *The Palm Wine Drinkard and His Dead Palm-Wine Tapster in the Dead's Town* (1952) of Tutuola (q.v.). Written in a style that was taken by European critics, including the poet Dylan Thomas (q.v.), to be a new primitive "poetry," it was criticized by Nigerians as incompetent and illiterate. Since the publication of this work, Tutuola has written other books in the same eccentric style. Although his prose is not as wayward as his detractors would suggest, it has not served as a model for other writers. His works, however, did help to establish Nigeria as the dominant country in neo-African literature.

1. The Novel

Among the writers who have helped to foster the novel in Nigeria are Cyprian Achebe, Chinua Ekwensi, and Onuora Nzekwu (b. 1930), who remain the most significant Nigerian novelists, despite the large number of first novels recently published by their compatriots.

Achebe has been the most highly praised, and certainly his writings have that high seriousness, that moral purpose, often lacking in African prose. Much of his success, however, may be attributable to his strong sense of the African tradition, as well as to his recognition of the challenges inherent in the transition of his country from a tribal colony to a mature modern nation. His works, moreover, exhibit a literary excellence that recalls Hardy or Conrad (qq.v.) and the other masters of the English novel.

Achebe's major work is a tetralogy, which by the end of the 1960's had been carried along as far as the novels *Things Fall Apart* (1958), *No Longer at Ease* (1960), and *Arrow of God* (1964). These books all present a tragic outlook, although the second, dealing with contemporary events, seems less burdened than the others by a sense of human misfortune. The first and third novels, adopting an historical approach, describe the first impact of British missionaries and administrators on Nigerian tribal society at the beginning of the 20th c.

In these works Achebe portrays two heroes of tragic dimensions, Okonkwo and Ezeulu, who refuse to compromise with the forces of social and religious change that confront them. These forces, however, eventually overcome the men of heroic stature, leading to a victory only for the weak, the compromisers, those who greedily join in the opportunities to exploit their own people. As the old certainties are broken down, the social order and the conservatism inherent in village tribal life are destroyed.

Achebe's conclusions are pessimistic; he cannot accept the simplistic view that change is identical with progress. He is concerned, moreover, with the plight of the restless and alienated young people who, lacking the old security, drift to the widening slums of the proliferating cities. Some are lost in the amoral urban environment; others abandon themselves to the mindless hedonism of the town.

The members of this new class, the fast-living transients of Lagos, are the characters in Ekwensi's three major novels, *People of the City* (1953), *Jagua Nana* (1961), and *Beautiful Feathers* (1964). Ekwensi is Achebe's opposite in every way. His protagonists are not tribal priests with their ritual—they are cheap whores in shoddy nightclubs. They are not men seeking to renew a sense of certainty in their lives—but those initiating and exploiting change by every form of gross political and financial manipulation.

The differences in the subjects of the two novelists are reflected by the contrast in their styles. Achebe's style is slow-moving, profound, sometimes heavy. Ekwensi's is brittle, slick, even superficial. The influence of movies and popular paperback thrillers is revealed in his violent, melodramatic plots.

Ekwensi thus becomes contemporary in a way that more cautious writers avoid. No one has so powerfully caught the world of corruption and sensuality of the modern African city; no other writer has dared to expose the politicians in a series of caricatures as magnificently comic as they are hugely bitter. Uncle Taiwo, Brother Jacob, and the Minister of Consolation, who resembles a number of characters in novels by Waugh (q.v.), all reveal an approach to political satire that may yet form the substance of a major work.

Nzekwu, in his *Wand of Noble Wood* (1961) and *Blade among the Boys* (1962), manifests one of the major difficulties for the African writer—the necessity of providing an anthropological explanation of his subject. In his books pages, even chapters, seem to have been written less for a literary purpose than to allow Nzekwu to provide information about the traditional customs of bride price, secret societies, and local ritual. When not preoccupied with such subjects he depicts the African scene with considerable skill; no one has exposed the nature of missionary beliefs and education more sardonically than Nzekwu.

Although many other novelists are active in Nigeria, most have published only a single work, usually one centered on a single picturesque (and picaresque) character, or on purely autobiographical material with only the slightest concession to the requirements of objective narration. Thus the novel *One Man One Matcher* (1964) by Thomas M. Aluko (b. 1918), although largely concerned with the need to chop down diseased cocoa trees, is enlivened by a memorably satiric figure, Mr. Bejamin Bejamin, demagogue, opportunist, and rogue.

514

Equally successful is *Danda* (1964), a novel by Nkem Nwanko (b. 1926) and later a successful play. Danda wanders through his land playing his flute, outraging the pompous, delighting those who enjoy the discomfiture of the notables.

Wind versus Polygamy (1964), a first novel by Obi Egbuna, debates in court the charge of polygamy against Chief Ozuomba, who, although illiterate, is knowledgeable and shrewd; he delights in flustering the pompous prosecuting counsel. Each of these figures has a universal larger-than-life stature, but they also display unique and dramatically effective characteristics through which they emerge as memorable individuals.

The autobiographical form so characteristic of many African novels may be either a direct account of the author's experiences or a narrative in which the author and his principal character are so similar that the latter virtually ceases to be a fictional creation. Recent examples of such works include *Toads for Supper* (1965) by Chukwuemeka Ike (b. 1937) and *Second Round* (1965) by Lenrie Peters (b. 1932). The plots of both novels draw heavily on material from the authors' own lives.

The use of such material, however, raises certain artistic problems, particularly in regard to the resolution of the conflicts presented in the plot. Indeed, to presume that such issues can be resolved artistically at all is to suggest that life is amenable to a purely aesthetic organization. The resulting difficulty in adjusting situations taken from life to the requirements of a narrative may account for many of the flaws in these novels—the sudden twists of plot, the melodramatic conclusion that disconcerts a reader.

Thus, in the novel by Ike, the problem of whether the protagonist can marry a woman from another tribe is conveniently solved by her suicide, which the author suddenly reveals to be the result of an inherited homicidal mania. In a less violent denouement, Peters's doctor, unable to solve his problems in love and medicine, walks off into the sunset, as in a film, to serve in some remote part of the country.

The classic example of such a termination is found in *The African* (1961) by the Sierra Leone writer William Conton (b. 1925). After early scenes of notable honesty and warmth, as his childhood is lovingly re-created, Conton has his hero seek revenge against an enemy in South Africa. When the man is found drunk in a wet gutter the hero in an excess of charity carries him home in his arms.

Two recent and completely different novels, however, suggest significant developments; both were written by poets. One of these works, *The Voice* (1964) by Gabrial Okara (b. 1921), may be of limited importance, or it may offer a new potential in African writing. Its theme is commonplace, the quest for enlightenment— the search for "IT," as Okara, with disappointing vagueness, describes the object of his quest. Although the style is said to be a direct translation into English of the Ijaw idiom, the novel clearly shows the effects of a highly evocative poetic sensibility in its imagery and diction.

Okara writes with exotic repetitions, inversions, and metaphors created by using concrete terms for inner qualities—the townsfolk observe of the hero, "Okolo had no chest." This new and vivid manipulation of the English language may influence the style of other novelists in Africa, or it may, like *Finnegans Wake* by Joyce (q.v.), constitute a fascinating performance, which does not invite other writers to follow in its wake.

The second influential novel of contemporary Africa is *The Interpreters* (1965) by Wole Soyinka (q.v.). More orthodox than Okara's work, it is another record of modern Lagos society. It treats it, however, not in a commonplace manner but by analyzing its subject with all the skill and sensibility of a major writer. Such a treatment clearly marks a significant phase in the maturation of the African novel.

These two widely different books show the range and vitality of the African novel in English. They also suggest the possible areas of development, indicating a movement away from the melodramatic and the merely exotic. Such experiments in language and form show the sophistication that may result when able writers manipulate their material with subtlety and confidence.

2. The Short Story

The short-story form has been largely and unexpectedly neglected in West Africa. Collections such as *Modern African Stories,* edited by Ellis Komey and Ezekiel Mphahlele, suggest a range of work, but only Abioseh Nicol has as yet offered a volume of stories by a single author. This relative dearth of activity in the short-story form, which may be partially explained by the general lack of opportunities for publication in this genre, is especially striking when contrasted with the predominance of the form among African writers in South Africa (*see* South African literature).

3. Drama

In drama West African writers have perhaps encountered fewer problems than in other genres. In the novel, for example, no precise connection can be established between ancient traditional storytelling and the contemporary fictional narrative, which, with certain modifications, has been imported from Europe. The drama, however, has been rather firmly established in local traditions, although this indigenous drama usually has little in common with many of the traditional concepts of the Western theater. Thus, African dramatists know and may draw on much that is unique to their environment—the drumming, dancing, and mime through which tribal ritual often comes to resemble a dramatic performance that is meaningful for the entire society. In addition, the difficulties of obtaining a production of a play in the European mode for a European or American audience often dissuade African dramatists from even attempting such a production. Their works, often performed only in semiprofessional productions, are directed primarily toward African audiences and therefore emphasize the author's African characteristics.

For this reason, at least, part of the distinction between writer and audience is eliminated in African drama. The dramatist, more concerned with his distinctly African audience than the novelist with his potential European and American readers, need not provide detailed cultural and anthropological explanations that in any case would be incompatible with the requirements of dramatic form. The resulting works will therefore certainly be rather difficult for American readers, especially when removed from the visual context of their production. In this regard, however, the suggestion by Soyinka that "African drama is more than dancers with bare breasts" becomes especially pertinent, and indeed the reader of African drama may be better able than the spectator to distinguish between the truly original characteristics of a particular dramatic work and the merely exotic aspects of its stage production.

The published drama of West Africa— usually, like the novel, written in English— can be divided into two principal classifications.

First are the works of playwrights who, remaining comfortably within the structure of the British middle class, draw on the English tradition that is marked by the sentimental comedy of Barrie (q.v.), the sophistication of Coward (q.v.), and the problem plays of Terence Rattigan (b. 1911). Others, more ambitious, emulate the tradition of the experimental poetic theater, such as the works of the Irish playwrights Behan and Yeats (qq.v.) and the plays of Eliot (q.v.). The plays of this second category are generally more successful than those of the first, perhaps because the African tradition of drama as ritual makes stage poetry less self-conscious and artificial than in some recent American attempts.

The more conventional dramatists, although they may avoid the inexactness of vague symbolism in their concern with a coherent development of their plots, base their work on a tradition that, even in Great Britain, is virtually depleted. Their middle-class concerns with trivial and contrived domestic situations, their attempts to reproduce dialogue in the manner of Wodehouse (q.v.), and their British character stereotypes are all doubly incongruous in stories set in Africa and played with African characters. Thus, despite the apparent success of some of these plays, they basically lack true life.

One of the best of the conventional plays is *Dear Parent and Ogre* (1961) by the Sierra Leone writer R. Sharif Easmon. As the title suggests, the father depicted in the play can manage his political and business affairs competently, but encounters difficulties in dealing with his engaging and lively family. Following a similar tradition is *Sons and Daughters* (1964) by the Ghanaian playwright Joe de Graft (b. 1930). In a stock situation common to the American theater, a *nouveau riche* and materialistic businessman attempts to oppose the artistic leanings of his children, who prefer painting and music to a professional occupation representative of their standing in the community. James Henshawe's best play, *Medicine for Love*, is very similar, although the energy of its complex plotting gives it an impression of greater liveliness. Other such plays have been published for school production.

More impressive than the plays in this tradition have been those derived from the great world tradition of tragic poetic drama. Two important Nigerian dramatists stand apart in their achievement, John Pepper Clark (b. 1935) and Soyinka. Their plays may prove the most substantial achievement in African writing to date.

Clark's most impressive work is *Song of a Goat* (1962), which expresses a theme of profound and tragic grandeur in speeches of brooding poetry. Its very title, recalling the origin of the word "tragedy" (from the Greek for "goat song"), suggests the origin of tragic ritual in the sacrifice of a scapegoat. Like all of Clark's plays it describes the inexorable conflict between man and the external pressures that are always pitted against him either by society or by the very order of the world itself. *The Masquerade* ends in violent and bloody murder. In *The Raft* men are destroyed by forces of nature that are too ferocious and powerful to be resisted or understood.

Recalling in his plays the tortured protagonists of O'Neill (q.v.), Clark seems even more strongly influenced by Synge (q.v.) and especially by the latter's impassioned play *Riders to the Sea*.

In *Song of a Goat* Zifa's wife is barren because of her husband's impotence; she suffers the shame reserved for the childless wife in Africa. Driven to despair she seduces Zifa's younger brother. When this comes out into the open both men commit suicide, admitting that they have sinned against the standards by which a man must live. As powerful and inexorable as the plots of Clark's plays are, his dramas produce their greatest impact through his vigorous language, which although it frequently recalls Eliot's dramatic verse, takes on a new and distinctively African significance, as in the lines where Clark likens the barrenness of the woman to the African seasons:

> She has waited too long already,
> Too long in the harmattan. The
> rains are here once more and the
> forest getting moist.

Even more significant than Clark is Soyinka, generally regarded as the most powerful figure in West African drama. A complete man of the theater—actor, producer, director, writer— he was responsible for the formation of the first permanent theater group in Africa, known as 1960 Masks. This group, recently named Orisun Players, has established the foundation of professional theater in Africa.

Soyinka has written six plays to date, each touching on the conflict between tribal cohesion and Western disintegration, or between customs and progress—a theme that haunts all African writing, in drama as in the novel. Seeking a source of stability after the destruction of the old certainties, Soyinka treats this subject both comically and tragically. In *The Trials of Brother Jero* (1963) he portrays an African variant of the universal charlatan, a wandering evangelist and rogue, swindling those who come to him in their search for religious reassurance.

Soyinka's most popular play, *The Lion and the Jewel* (1963), depicts the competition between a reactionary old chief and the young progressive schoolmaster for the hand of the village beauty, Sidi, who becomes famous when her photograph appears on a magazine cover. The conventional situation is delightfully reversed when the maiden is won not by the feeble follies of the teacher, but by the tough wiles of the leonine old chief. Progress, hints Soyinka, has its own follies.

Other plays, in a more tragic vein, are *The Strong Breed* (1963) and *The Swamp Dwellers* (1963). These plays record the dark elements in the tribal tradition: the corrupting misery of superstitious belief in pagan gods, the violence and persecution in the ritual, the deprivation that comes with agriculture without competence. In such a world poverty and priestly greed create a mood of despair. Both the absurdity and the strength of the past are described in Soyinka's fifth and most ambitious play, *A Dance of the Forests* (1963). This work, while mocking the pretensions of ritual, acknowledges the power of the old to dominate new generations.

4. Poetry

Like the drama, poetry in West Africa varies in style according to its mixture of African and European elements. The former are particularly strong because of the continuing use of poetic heroic recitation, as recorded by the oral traditions of the tribe. This poetry, however, is not the only influence on modern African poetry in English. The new African poets are not tribal bards but sophisticated young men who, like young poets everywhere using English, respond to the influence of such major Western poets as Pound, Eliot, and Dylan Thomas, while maintaining their African subjects and attitudes. Their poetry thus represents an attempt to synthesize these two disparate elements into a new and meaningful style.

African poetry in English, like other genres, does not fit conveniently into any school or movement, showing no equivalent to the cult of *négritude* (*see* neo-African literature) that inspires the poetry of Senghor. The British colonial authorities never called for an assimilation of black peoples such as was proposed by the French. The Nigerians and Ghanaians therefore did not require a brave assertion of *négritude* as a means of guarding against the dangers of assimilation. In ignoring it they escaped some of the less desirable aspects of this movement, such as the virtual dictation of appropriate themes and concepts that restricted poetry to declamatory rhetoric. Spared this tension, the writers in the former British colonies satirized the French attitudes, as in the remark of Soyinka that a tiger does not have to proclaim his "tigritude"; why then should a Negro announce his *négritude*? More importantly for the development of poetry, Soyinka and his compatriots answered *négritude* with poetry that was personal, precise, pragmatic, intimate rather than appealing to a cult.

Soyinka's poetry is urbane, sometimes sardonic, while Okara writes cryptic and evocative verse. The last two lines of his poem "Piano and Drums" indicate the whole dualism in the world of the African poet using his Western techniques. Okara finds himself within two worlds, "Wandering in the mystic rhythm of jungle drums and the concerto."

The poetry of Peters (q.v.) records a similar dualism. On the one hand his poems deal with conventional themes that are perhaps as much universal as Western: time and changing seasons, love and rejection; these themes, however, are used in a specifically African context. He writes of "cannibals' ghosts" and, with a wry comment on European artists borrowing from Africa, of seeing the world "wearing the Modigliani face." Even within a single poem his imagery draws on this double source.

George Awoonor-Williams is the most significant poet of Ghana. His collection is entitled *Rediscovery* (1964). Perhaps that title in itself is indicative of his attempt to draw on African concepts, but with the attitude of a man versed in Western writing. More confidently than most Africans, he achieves a sense of identity with this tradition. Although new education and sophistication may greatly extend his experience, "there shall linger the communion we forged/the feast of oneness we partook of." This oneness allows him to evoke the imagery and style of his mother tongue, Togo. Such lines as the following with

their balance and repetition are derived from African rather than European elements; they use the devices of the oral tradition of poetry:

> My people, I have been somewhere
> If I turn here, the rain beats me
> If I turn there the sun burns me.

Even though these lines contain a hint of the Bible and more remotely of the line repetitions of Eliot, the vision that they express is always clearly African.

Christopher Okigbo (b. 1935), an important young Nigerian poet, has to attempt his own variant of this always necessary synthesis; in a manner different from that of Awoonor-Williams, however, he endeavors to join his African ideas with European technique— Pound is frequently mentioned as an influence —while Awoonor-Williams attempts to focus on more universal themes in an African idiom. The religious inheritance of two continents is brought, by Okigbo, within a single urgent and universal appeal—the dualism inherent in the beginning of *Heavensgate* (1962). It begins with the African symbol "Before you, mother Idoto, naked I stand." Immediately another echo is heard, of the Christian memory: "watchman, for the watchword at heavensgate, Out of the depths my cry." Although his second volume, *Limits* (1964), owes much to Pound's *Cantos,* his single most renowned image is, and not accidentally, purely African in inspiration.

The most substantial African poet in English is undoubtedly J. P. Clark, known for his *Collected Poetry.* At first reading his work seems notably eclectic, containing lines that recall the Dylan Thomas of "doped out of the deep/ I have bobbed up bellywise." Sometimes the poets are deliberately emulated through various devices, as in "Variation on Hopkins": "Ama are you gall bitter pent?/ Have paltry pittance spent?" Similar but less obvious echoes appear elsewhere. Another clear association with Gerard Manley Hopkins (1844–89) in both idea and style occurs in the sonnet "Of Faith": "Faith can move mountains, will move whole mountains." Despite such external allusions, however, Clark is African as are his themes; his impressions of the continent are recorded with loving and exact precision. In many poems a vein of tenderness appears; it is warm without being maudlin. This can be seen in "For Granny (From Hospital)" with its memory of childhood and "Night Rain" with its evocation of the leaking roof and the vivid African image of "the run of water / that like ants filing out of wood / will scatter and gain possession of the floor." Perhaps his technique can be seen best in the almost haikulike brevity of his little descriptive lyric "Ibadan." The metaphors are colorful, vivid, unexpected but utterly apt:

> Ibadan,
>   running splash of rust
> and gold—flung and scattered
> among seven hills like broken
> china in the sun.

Clark seems the most promising of the African poets. Simultaneously exact and evocative, exploring the African experience with a technique of the most subtle sophistication, he deserves a place among the most impressive of contemporary poets.

West Africa is clearly producing a new literature marked by a literary initiation such as Americans achieved almost unknowingly about a century ago, and such as Australia has suddenly acknowledged. Certainly the new writing must undergo a good deal of experimentation, in which promising writers may not fulfill their potential, producing no novels after their first and turning to nonliterary careers. At this moment, on the other hand, some young student may be publishing his early efforts in a college magazine, beginning a lifetime of significant work. When local publishers become more prominent, African writers will flourish as never before. Even now a new national literature is being developed—one worthy to stand beside other contemporary writing in English.

BIBLIOGRAPHY: Maphalele, E., *The African Image* (1962); Moore, G., *Seven African Writers* (1962); Gleason, J., *This Africa* (1964), Povey, J., and Ekwensi, C., *Crit* (Fall 1965), pp. 63–70; Soyinka, W., *Triquarterly* (Dec. 1965), pp. 129–37; Tibble, A., *African English Literature* (1965); Povey, J., "Contemporary West African Writing in English," *BA*, XL (1966), 253–60; Press, J., ed., *Commonwealth Literature: Unity and Diversity in a Common Culture* (1966); *Journal of Commonwealth Literature* (founded, 1966); Abrash, B., comp., *Black African Literature in English Since 1952: A Bibliography* (1968); Jahn, J., *A History of Neo-African Literature: Writing in Two Continents* (1968); Shelton, A. J., *The African Assertion: A Critical Anthology of African Literature* (1968)

JOHN POVEY

WEST, Nathanael

(pseud. of *Nathan W. Weinstein*), American novelist, b. 17 Oct. 1903, New York City; d. 22 Dec. 1940, El Centro, California

An indifferent student, W. was able to gain admission to Brown University only thanks to a registrar's confusion of names. His prosperous immigrant family was hard hit by the depression, and during the 1930's W. had to work as a night manager in a small New York hotel. In 1933, in a desperate attempt to conserve money so that he could continue his writing, W. withdrew to a lonely New Jersey farm. Two years later, however, he was forced to take a job as a Hollywood scriptwriter. In April 1940, W. married Eileen McKenney, who had served as the model for Ruth McKenney's (b. 1911) popular book and play *My Sister Eileen*. Less than a year later, W. and his wife were killed in an automobile accident.

In his first novel, *The Dream Life of Balso Snell* (1931), W. wrote a comic treatment of the repulsiveness of body and soul in the story of a poet who travels through the intestines of the Trojan Horse.

Miss Lonelyhearts (1933), W.'s most tragic and best-formed book, no doubt profits from some of the pathetic human dramas that W. must have been witness to in his job as hotel manager. In this moving novel, a newspaper reporter assigned to handle the "agony column" so lovingly identifies himself with his tortured correspondents that he eventually becomes a Christ figure who is grotesquely martyred.

A Cool Million (1934) satirizes conservative American virtues by showing the progressive dismemberment of a "poor but honest" super-patriot—a theme of considerable contemporary relevance.

W.'s most ambitious novel is *The Day of the Locust* (1939), an apocalyptic exposé of the emptiness and terror at the heart of Hollywood, America's "dream-dump." In his carefully etched gallery of grand guignol types and in his treatment of the mobs of hostile, cheated people who had "come to California to die," W. presented one of the most powerful expressions of depression despair in American literature.

W.'s style was brilliantly epigrammatical, nervously metaphorical, bitterly ironic, and expressive of intense though absurd suffering. Though highly considered by such writers as Edmund Wilson and Farrell (qq.v.), his four short, surrealist novels were little read during his lifetime. They have since received critical acclaim, and W. is often acknowledged as a forerunner of the post-World War II "black humorists."

FURTHER WORK: *The Complete Works of N. W.* (1957)

BIBLIOGRAPHY: Light, F., *N. W.: An Interpretive Study* (1961); Hyman, S. E., *N. W.* (1962); Comerchero, W., *N. W., The Ironic Prophet* (1964); Martin, J., *N. W.: The Art of His Life* (1970)

MORGAN GIBSON

WEST, Rebecca

(pseud. of *Cicily Isabel Fairfield*), English journalist, novelist, and critic, b. 25 Dec. 1892, County Kerry, Ireland

The daughter of a talented musician and an army officer turned war correspondent, Rebecca W. was educated first in Edinburgh and later in London, briefly at an academy of drama. Her short time on the stage is notable only because to it she owes her penname, taken from Ibsen's (q.v.) heroine in *Rosmersholm*. She became a reviewer for *Freewoman* in 1911, and joined the staff of *The Clarion* in 1912 as a political writer. Her chief interest at this time was feminism, and she was active in the fight for women's suffrage.

Rebecca W.'s first book was a lively study of *Henry James* (1916). Her first novel, *The Return of the Soldier* (1918), is an early example of the influence of Freudian psychology in the English novel. *The Judge* (1922), similar in its psychological orientation, won critical praise for her richly textured, highly colored prose. "Her style," said Raymond Mortimer (*Dial*, Oct. 1922), "reflects her subjects like a metal mirror varying with their colours, but burnishing them all to an ardent, almost truculent, loveliness."

Although the variety of her work makes it impossible to seek a "typical" book, Rebecca W. has grown increasingly to focus upon the beauty and necessity of order as a counter to the forces of violence in society. In her later fiction, *e.g., The Thinking Reed* (1936), she seems to equate order with a female principle and disorder with a male principle. The story of an American girl married to an enormously wealthy French businessman conveys vividly a sense of corruption and moral isolation as the accompaniment of riches.

Illness and a journey undertaken in recuperation provided the impetus to one of her most successful books, *Black Lamb and Gray Falcon* (1941), a superb rendering of her observations of the people and folkways of Yugoslavia. During and after World War II her writing was primarily journalistic, and she won international acclaim for her reporting of the trial of "Lord Haw Haw," and the Nuremberg trials. Many of her essays are gathered in *The Meaning of Treason* (1949) and *A Train of Powder* (1955).

In 1957, Rebecca W. produced a highly original work of literary criticism, *The Court and the Castle,* in which she investigates man's relations with the political power of the state and the religious content of his universe. Using this moral view so long developing in her own mind, she elaborates unusual aspects of the works of numerous writers (Shakespeare, Proust (q.v.), James (q.v.), Kipling (q.v.), Trollope, Kafka (q.v.), and others).

The same year saw the publication of another novel, Rebecca W.'s first in twenty years. *The Fountain Overflows* (1957) is the first of a projected series detailing the life of the Aubrey family in London at the turn of the century. It is a novel rich in wit and wisdom and written with great subtlety, proving that Rebecca W.'s gifts are as yet undiminished.

Called one of the few really great reporters of our time, Rebecca W.'s wide-ranging interests and cultivated intellect have permitted her to achieve worthily in almost every variety of prose writing.

FURTHER WORKS: *The Strange Necessity* (1928); *Lions and Lambs* (with David Low; 1928); *Harriet Hume* (1929); *The War Nurse* (1930); *D. H. Lawrence: an Elegy* (1930); *Arnold Bennett Himself* (1931); *Ending in Earnest, a Literary Log* (1931); *A Letter to a Grandfather* (1933); *St. Augustine* (1933); *The Harsh Voice* (1935); *The Event and Its Images* (1962); *The Vassall Affair* (1963); *The New Meaning of Treason* (1964); *The Birds Fall Down* (1966)

BIBLIOGRAPHY: Swinnerton, F., *The Georgian Literary Scene* (1951); Beaton, C., and Tynan, K., *Persona Grata* (1954); Hutchens, J., "R. W.," *New York Herald-Tribune Book Review,* 22 April 1956; Nichols, L., "A Talk with R. W.," *New York Times Book Review,* 9 Dec. 1956; Orlich, M., Sr., "The Novels of R. W.: A Complex Unity,"

DA, XXVII, 2540A; Ellmann, M., "The Russians of R. W.," *Atlantic Monthly*, CCXVIII (Dec. 1966), 68–71

VERGENE F. LEVERENZ

WHARTON, Edith Newbold Jones

American novelist and short-story writer, b. 23 Jan. 1862, New York City; d. 11 Aug. 1937, St. Brice-sous-Forêt, France

A descendant of New York's old merchant families, Edith W. spent much of her girlhood in Europe. Her informal education under a succession of governesses was supplemented by the lonely hours passed in her father's library. She began writing at eleven, but her debut in society and her marriage at twenty-three to Edward W., a neurasthenic Boston aristocrat, put a temporary halt to any attempt at a literary career. However, unhappy in her marriage and bored with her life as a lady of leisure, she returned to writing. Her rebellion against the social role assigned her and her consequent feeling of isolation explain a great deal about the themes and tones of her fiction.

It was not until she began publishing stories in the periodicals of the 1890's that Edith W. was able to form friendships with other writers, notably Henry James and Bourget (qq.v.). She and James were products of the same background and had a common social outlook, which they shared with Bourget. However, it was James particularly, along with other novelists of manners such as Honoré de Balzac (1799–1850) and William Makepeace Thackeray (1811–63), who influenced her development.

Though their home was in Newport, Rhode Island, and later in Lenox, Massachusetts, Edith W. and her husband spent much of their time in England, France, and Italy. After 1907 they settled permanently in France, where she was to live for the rest of her life. In 1912 she was separated from her husband, and the following year they were divorced.

Edith W.'s first book was *The Decoration of Houses* (1897), on which she collaborated with the architect Ogden Codman. The book's popular and innovative idea was that homes should represent the personalities of those who live in them.

Following the success of two short-story collections—*The Greater Inclination* (1899) and *Crucial Instances* (1901)—Edith W. wrote her first novel, *The Valley of Decision* (1902), a scholarly two-volume romance of 18th-c. Italy. Her first major novel was *The House of Mirth* (1905), which powerfully described the tragic defeat at the hands of a corrupt, materialistic society of Lily Bart, a well-born but penniless young lady whose ambitions bring her into conflict with the social code of her world.

Edith W.'s best work appeared between 1905 and 1920. Critical approval has centered on *The Reef* (1912), her most Jamesian novel; *The Custom of the Country* (1913), in which she traced the destructive career of Undine Spragg, a ruthless social climber; and the Pulitzer Prize-winning *The Age of Innocence* (1920), a bitter-sweet re-creation of the New York of Edith W.'s girlhood. Somewhat of a departure from her themes is the novella *Ethan Frome* (1911), a grimly realistic study of New England farm life, whose structure was suggested by Balzac's *La Grande Bretèche*.

After 1920, Edith W.'s fiction often conformed too closely to the demands of popular women's magazines, which paid her well to rehearse in superficial accents the themes of her earlier successes. Worthy of mention, however, are *Hudson River Bracketed* (1929) and its sequel, *The Gods Arrive* (1932), which contrast American and European cultural values.

Particularly useful for an understanding of Edith W.'s work are *French Ways and Their Meaning* (1919), a small collection of essays; *The Writing of Fiction* (1925), which points up the influence of James on her novels; and *A Backward Glance* (1934), a memoir.

Edith W.'s work is marked by a deep concern for the moral significance of her subjects; by its careful attention to problems of form; by its wittily metaphorical and ironic style; and by its preoccupation with the decay of conservative standards under the corrosive influence of materialism. An influence on her that is generally disregarded is that of the evolutionists—chiefly Charles Darwin (1809–1882), Herbert Spencer (1820–1903), and T. H. Huxley (1825–95)—whom she acknowledged as the greatest formative influences of her youth, and who may help account for the insistent note of determinism in her fiction.

Though deeply attached to the patrician milieu into which she was born, Edith W. was able to depict its decline and decadence with precision and irony. Possibly because she dealt with a narrow society and wrote in a tone generally hostile to democratic pretensions, her influence has not been extensive. It may be seen, however, in the work of lesser novelists such as Katherine Fuller Gerould (1879–1944) and Louis Auchincloss (b. 1917).

FURTHER WORKS: *The Touchstone* (1900); *Sanctuary* (1903); *The Descent of Man* (1904); *Italian Villas and Their Gardens* (1904); *Italian Backgrounds* (1905); *The Fruit of the Tree* (1907); *Madame de Treymes* (1907); *The Hermit and the Wild Woman* (1908); *A Motor-flight through France* (1908); *Artemis to Actaeon* (1909); *Tales of Men and Ghosts* (1910); *Fighting France from Dunkerque to Belfort* (1915); *Xingu* (1916); *Summer* (1917); *The Marne* (1918); *In Morocco* (1920); *The Glimpses of the Moon* (1922); *The Son at the Front* (1923); *Old New York: False Dawn, The Old Maid, The Spark, New Year's Day* (1924); *The Mother's Recompense* (1925); *Here and Beyond* (1926); *Twelve Poems* (1926); *Twilight Sleep* (1927); *The Children* (1928; republished as *The Marriage Playground,* 1930); *Certain People* (1930); *Human Nature* (1933); *The World Over* (1936); *Ghosts* (1937); *The Buccaneers* (1938); *The Best Short Stories* (1959); *The E. W. Reader* (1965); *Collected Short Stories* (1968)

BIBLIOGRAPHY: Lovett, R. M., *E. W.* (1929); Brown, E. K., *E. W.* (1935); Lubbock, P., *Portrait of E. W.* (1947); Nevius, B., *E. W.: A Study of Her Fiction* (1953); Coolidge, O., *E. W., 1862–1937* (1965); Kellogg, G., *The Two Lives of E. W.* (1965); Brenni, J. V., *E. W.: A Bibliography* (1966); Tuttleton, J. W., "E. W.: Form and the Epistemology of Artistic Creation," *Criticism,* X (1968), 334–51

* * * *

WHITE, Patrick Martindale

Australian novelist, short-story writer, dramatist, b. 28 May 1912, London

Coming from a well-established Australian land-owning family, W. had experience as a "jackeroo" on pastoral properties in New South Wales before going to Cambridge in 1932 to complete his education, and to travel in Europe and the United States. His early writings—stories, poems, dramatic sketches—belong to the London of the 1930's and have no Australian reference.

Happy Valley (1939), W.'s first published novel, marks his confrontation with Australia as a subject. It has a documentary interest as a "country town" novel, as precise in record-ing the Race Week Ball among the potted palms at the School of Arts as in tracing the jealousies and frustrations of a small community isolated in the snow country of New South Wales. *Happy Valley* indicates W.'s preoccupation with the solitariness of human beings, the epigraph (from Gandhi) presenting "the law of suffering" as the "indispensable condition of our being."

The concern for unfulfilled lives extends into *The Living and the Dead* (1941), set in Bloomsbury in the 1930's and focused on Elyot Standish as a "Prufrock" figure, an outcast from life's feast. Eden, his dark intense sister, tries to throw off the malaise by compulsively entering into love affairs and going off to the Spanish Civil War, but this is no more a solution than the life of desperately brittle elegance pursued by Catherine Standish, her mother. No one achieves the "intenser form of living" that they seek.

These perplexities disappear in *The Aunt's Story* (1948). Theodora Goodman, a sallow spinster, is the first of W.'s characters to attain a visionary awareness. She resists the pressures of conformity and lives in the moments of insight she shares with others, or in the rare states when she feels her personality dissolving in the created world. The novel presents a character advancing towards the extinction of self—"that desirable state . . . which resembles nothing more than air or water." When Theodora is taken off to the asylum at the end, her integrity unimpaired, it is the values of the sane that are in question.

The theme of alienation persists through the series of major novels that followed W.'s return to Australia after World War II. *The Tree of Man* (1955) seemed to revive the Australian pioneering saga, tracing the life of one man and one woman who establish a holding in the wilderness and endure flood, drought, and bushfire as their shack becomes part of a wider settlement. The deeper theme is the struggle of Stan and Amy Parker for some fulfillment, some enlightenment that seems always withheld. Although there is a Lawrentian insistence on Stan's absorption in his peasantlike activities, he achieves his "illumination" finally in transcending this workaday world, and is then isolated as never before.

The way of transcendence is examined in *Voss* (1957). A German explorer leads an expedition across the Australian continent in order to mortify and exalt himself by suffer-

EDITH WHARTON

ing, as though in rivalry with Christ, to prove that man may become God. Voss's tortures in trying to sustain his selfhood—scourging himself for momentarily yielding to human relationships or to the beauty of the natural world —make this the most compelling of W.'s novels. The defeat of Voss's aspiration—the simplicity and humility to which he comes— reveals the underlying values that would be revealed in W.'s later work.

These values are further, by means of the personalities, explored in the four visionaries of *Riders in the Chariot* (1961). Miss Hare, Himmelfarb, Mrs. Godbold, and Alf Dubbo are all stuides in alienation, inasmuch as they are people whom a bourgeois society would despise or ignore. Although the chariot of which they have differing visions is a symbol of transcendence, the emphasis falls more strongly on the concept of "loving kindness" shown in human terms in the later chapters— flawed as it is by the aversion shown to those outside the visionary circle, and by the sometimes suffocating quality of "loving kindness" in Mrs. Godbold.

The Solid Mandala (1966) deals with the twins Waldo and Arthur Brown. One of them belongs to the world of "tidiness and quick answers, of punctuality and unbreakable rules." The other is an abnormal child who peers into the fathomless depths of four marbles that are his cherished possessions, his solid mandalas. Although the mandala, like the chariot, is a symbol of perfection, the idea of transcendence is now diminished further. Arthur eventually manages to painfully articulate his vision in the uncertain world of human relationships, and dies as a failed visionary, while communicating to others their need to find "somebody to worship," to find liberation from the self in love.

The audacity of conception in W.'s work is matched by a daring in style and method, and is joined to a perceptiveness and compassion that makes him the leading contemporary Australian novelist.

FURTHER WORKS: *The Ploughman, and Other Poems* (1935); *The Burnt Ones* (1964); *Four Plays* (1965); *The Vivisector* (1970)

BIBLIOGRAPHY: Dutton, G., *P. W.* (1961); Brissenden, R. F. *P. W.* (1966); Argyle, B., *P. W.* (1967); Wilkes, G. A., *Ten Essays on P. W.* (1970)

G. A. WILKES

WIECHERT, Ernst Emil

German novelist and short-story writer, b. 18 May 1887, Forsthaus Kleinort, East Prussia; d. 24 Aug. 1950, Uerikon, Switzerland

The son of a chief forester, W. was raised in a remote Masurian area whose natural beauty was to have a deep influence reflected in his later writings. After attending the University of Königsberg, he taught secondary school in Königsberg and Berlin, except for the period of World War I, when he served as an army officer. After 1933, he retired to rural Bavaria and devoted himself solely to his writing.

In the 1930's W. spoke out against the Nazi regime in public readings from the manuscript of *Der weiße Büffel*—an obviously anti-Nazi allegory that was not to be published until 1946. In those years he was an active supporter of Pastor Martin Niemöller (b. 1892), an anti-Nazi Protestant theologian. In 1938, after he lectured at the University of Munich on "Der Dichter und die Zeit" (1945; The Poet and His Time, 1948), W. was imprisoned for several months in the concentration camp at Buchenwald. This experience is described in *Der Totenwald* (1946; Forest of the Dead, 1947). After his release he maintained a political silence.

W. was generally expected to become the moral and literary spokesman for a new Germany after World War II. His attempts to fulfill this expectation led to embitterment on all sides, and the final years of his life were spent in Switzerland in self-imposed exile. In *Jahre und Zeiten* (1949; Tidings, 1959) W. gives his version of events during this period.

W.'s narratives are extremely conservative, closely akin to the "blood and soil" school. He preaches a chthonic religion, which he sometimes loosely terms "primitive Christianity"; he idealizes the primitive, feudal, Eastern world of his childhood as opposed to the corrupt modern city, the organized Christian church, and the Western rational tradition.

W.'s style shows little variety or development after 1928. His frequent landscape descriptions are laden with emotional mysticism and obvious symbolism. His morally good characters are at one with nature; his villains are alienated from it, as in the stories collected under the title *Die Flöte des Pan* (1930). Allegedly aiming to edify and console the common man, W. writes with a mannered, equivocal simplicity.

Das einfache Leben (1939; The Simple Life,

1954), W.'s best-known novel, is typical of his work. Its hero, Captain von Orla, flees from city, family, and himself to an island on a Masurian lake. At the expense of action, the book describes at length Orla's inconclusive struggle to find spiritual rest through manual labor and agnostic resignation. His broodings are reflected in stock secondary characters: clergymen, Prussian nobles, an ancient wise fisherman, and a woman who hates God for having let her son die. *Die Jerominkinder* (2 vols., 1945–47; The Earth Is Our Heritage, 1950) seeks to justify Orla's escapism as a positive ethic not unlike Albert Schweitzer's (1875–1965) reverence for life. But W.'s last novel, *Missa sine nomine* (1950; Eng., 1953), is clearly an expression of the death wish.

W.'s most balanced works appeared 1928–35. Two short novels—*Die Magd des Jürgen Doskocil* (1932; The Girl and the Ferryman, 1947) and *Die Majorin* (1934; The Baroness, 1936)—established his reputation throughout Europe. The themes are no different, but W. does less preaching. The same holds for certain tales, of which *Hirtennovelle* (1935) is the finest. It tells of the growth, temptation, resignation, and heroic—but all too allegorical—death of a young village herdsman. Other well-written narratives are the title stories in the collections *Der silberne Wagen* (1928) and *Der Todeskandidat* (1934), as well as "Tobias" in *Atli der Bestmann* (1938).

FURTHER WORKS: *Die Flucht* (1916); *Der Wald* (1922); *Der Totenwolf* (1924); *Die blauen Schwingen* (1925); *Der Knecht Gottes Andreas Nyland* (1926); *Die kleine Passion* (1929); *Jedermann* (1931); *Das Spiel vom deutschen Bettelmann* (1933); *Der verlorene Sohn* (1935); *Wälder und Menschen* (1936); *Das heilige Jahr* (1936); *Totenmesse* (1945); *Demetrius* (1945); *Märchen* (1946); *Okay, oder Die Unsterblichen* (1946); *Sämtliche Werke* (1957 ff.)

BIBLIOGRAPHY: Workman, J. D., "E. W.'s Escapism," *Monatshefte*, XXXV (1943), 23–33; Morgan, B. Q., "E. W.'s 'Hirtennovelle': Versuch einer Stilanalyse," *GQ*, XIX (1946), 274–82; Stegemann, H., "E. W.," *DRs*, LXXI (April 1948), 44–49; Hollmann, W., "Ethical Responsibility and Personal Freedom in the Works of E. W.," *GR*, XXV (1950), 37–49; Puknat, S. B., "God, Man and Society in the Recent Fiction of E. W.," *GL&L*, III (1950), 221–30; David, C., "Un Écrivain d'arrière-garde: E. W.," *Crit*, XLVI (1951),

199–211; Chick, E. M., "E. W. and the Problem of Evil," *Monatshefte*, XLVI (1954), 181–91; Chick, E. M., "E. W.'s Flight to the Circle of Eternity," *GR*, XXX (1955), 282–93; Petersen, C., "E. W.," in *Christliche Dichter der Gegenwart* (1955); Kirshner, S., "A Bibliography of Critical Writing about E. W.," *Librarium*, VII (1964), 3–11

EDSON M. CHICK

WIERZYŃSKI, Kazimierz

Polish poet, short-story writer, and essayist, b. 27 Aug. 1894, Drohobycz; d. 13 Feb. 1969, London

W. was the son of a railroad-station agent in the foothills of the Carpathians. During his school years W. belonged to a secret organization devoted to the liberation of Poland. He served with the Polish Legion of the Austrian army in World War I. After 1918 he settled in Warsaw.

W.'s entry into Warsaw literary life began with his membership in the artistic cabaret Pod Pikadorem (1918–19), which functioned as a platform for the leading members of the future Skamander (*see* Polish literature) group of poets—Tuwim, Iwaszkiewicz (qq.v.), Jan Lechoń (1899–1956), and Antoni Słonimski (b. 1895). A poem entitled *1863*, published in a local daily (1913), marks the beginning of W.'s prolific career. He began publishing his poetry in the monthly *Skamander*—of which he was also cofounder (1920)—the expressionist biweekly *Zdrój*, and then regularly in such weeklies as *Wiadomości Literackie* and *Cyrulik Warszawski*.

After the outbreak of World War II, W. resided variously in France, Portugal, Brazil, the United States (1941–61), Italy, and England. His émigré writings appeared primarily in the London-based weekly *Wiadomości* and the Paris monthly *Kultura*.

W.'s early collections of poems, *Wiosna i wino* (1919) and *Wróble na dachu* (1921), were willfully euphoric, passionately optimistic, intoxicating in their youthful exuberance, and firmly anchored to life's biological manifestations. His aim was to demonstrate that poetry, although set within the bounds of classical meter and syntax, could become saturated with a new creative force free of sociopolitically influenced aesthetic norms that frequently resulted in a moral unction objectionable to the Skamander poets. As theoretical justification of his views, W. wrote numerous manifestoes cloaked in stanzas and rhymes. The poem *Manifest* (1919) is one such example.

Pieśni fanatyczne (1929) and *Wolność tragiczna* (1936) show a poet by now socially and politically engaged and passionately concerned with public issues. In the 1940's patriotic, martial, and religious themes were appearing in W.'s deeply personal, contemplative lyric poetry. Beginning with *Tkanka ziemi* (1960) W. abandoned traditional meters and stanzaic patterns in favor of more contemporary devices.

W.'s best-known work of prose is a collection of seven short stories entitled *Granice świata* (1933; Patrol, 1958). These naturalistic descriptions of war atrocities are now and then relieved by notes of lyricism and of irony. Economy in structure and in the factual, at times even terse, prose enhances the poet's vision of the world gone amuck.

W garderobie duchów (1938) deals with the theater, and *O Bolesławie Leśmianie* (1939), delivered on the occasion of W.'s admittance into the Polish Academy of Literature, is representative of his literary criticism. In *Współczesna literatura polska na emigracji* (1943) W. discussed émigré literature. In *The Life and Death of Chopin* (1949)—written in English—W. portrays Chopin with poetic insight and sensitivity.

In the last decade of his life W. drew closer in style to the young Polish poets. Form and content, matter and manner, fused spontaneously in a poetic idiom unencumbered by traditional meter, rhyme, and stanza. Many critics consider the poems he wrote in the 1960's to be his best.

FURTHER WORKS: *Wielka niedźwiedzica* (1923); *Pamiętnik miłości* (1925); *Laur olimpijski* (1927); *Rozmowa z puszczą* (1929); *Gorzki urodzaj* (1933); *Kurhany* (1938); *Barbakan warszawski* (1940); *Ziemia wilczyca* (1941); *Róża wiatrów* (1942); *Ballada o Churchillu* (1944); *Pobojowisko* (1944; Eng., The Forgotten Battlefield, 1944); *Podzwonne za kaprala Szczapę* (1945); *Krzyże i miecze* (1946); *Korzec maku* (1951); *Siedem podków* (1954); *Kufer na plecach* (1964); *Cygańskim wozem* (1966); *Moja prywatna Ameryka* (1966); *Czarny polonez* (1968); *Sen mara* (1969). **Selected English translations:** Selections in *Ten Contemporary Polish Stories* (ed. E. Ordon; 1958); *Selected Poems* (ed. C. Mills, and L. Krzyżanowski; 1959)

BIBLIOGRAPHY: Scherer-Virski, O., *The Modern Polish Short Story* (1955), pp. 222–24; Kridl, M., *A Survey of Polish Literature and Culture* (1956), pp. 486–87; Davie, D., Introduction to *Selected Poems* (1959); "K. W.: A Symposium," *The Literary Review*, Spring 1960, pp. 401–15; Gillon, A., and Krzyżanowski, L., *Introduction to Modern Polish Literature: An Anthology of Fiction and Poetry* (1965), p. 394; Miłosz, C., *Postwar Polish Poetry: An Anthology* (1965), p. 17; Miłosz, C., *The History of Polish Literature* (1969), pp. 395–96

JADWIGA ZWOLSKA SELL

WIESEL, Elie

American novelist (writing in French), b. 1928, Sighet, Romania

W. and his family fell victim to the Nazi holocaust. Uprooted from a quiet Orthodox Jewish life, he lived the nightmare of first Auschwitz and then Buchenwald, where his parents and sister died. After the war he made his way to Paris. As a foreign correspondent, he has lived since in Israel and the United States.

Perhaps for no other writer of comparable stature do biographical facts play so important a role in his art. W.'s writing has a single subject: the experience of Nazi terror, its effect on Jewish identity, and the ensuing personal crisis of the individual Jew. In W.'s work, fact becomes indistinguishable from fiction. Past merges with present. His characters, generally recalled from his childhood, reappear in novel after novel; sometimes even their names remain the same.

In *La Nuit* (1958; Night, 1960), a memoir-novel, W. comes closest to relating his actual experiences. He captures the peaceful Orthodox Jewish life in a small Rumanian village in 1941. He details the inhabitants' unwillingness to believe in the reported atrocities, their optimistic faith that accompanies them through deportation and even into the concentration camps. With grim reality W. records the breakdown in personal relationships—friendship betrayed, parental ties severed, men dehumanized.

L'Aube (1960; Dawn, 1961) is ostensibly set in another period, but when its hero, an Israeli freedom fighter assigned to execute a British officer, is awaiting the designated moment, the past overcomes the present. Victims of Nazi terror—family and friends—haunt the very at-mosphere around him, their ghosts raising questions of love and hate and posing prob-lems of conscience for the victim turned ex-ecutioner. W.'s hero inevitably destroys some of his own moral sense when he finally pulls the trigger.

In *Le Jour* (1961; The Accident, 1962) W. uses a similar technique to narrate the story of an Auschwitz survivor, struck by a taxicab in New York, who recalls his ordeal under the Nazis. But the flashback technique in *La Ville de la chance* (1962; The Town beyond the Wall, 1964) more interestingly unites past and present experiences. To withstand tortures designed to make him betray a friend, W.'s hero, whose homeland is now an iron-curtain country, mentally escapes to the past, reliving his childhood experiences under Nazi persecu-tion. Various time-levels merge; the sense of the present wrought through physical discom-fort blends with the mental anguish of recall-ing the Nazi horror, the postwar hopelessness, and the despair of uprootedness.

Les Portes de la forêt (1964; The Gates of the Forest, 1966), too, joins past and present in its description of the adventures of a young Jew who has escaped from the Nazis. As he takes refuge, first in the forest, then with a former servant, and finally with a group of resistance fighters, he relives his earlier com-fortable years and the Nazi takeover. The novel goes beyond this experience, however, and covers the hero's postwar life in America —his search for identity in a Hassidic community, his inability to come to terms with reality until he discovers the value of his own inner self.

In *Le Mendiant de Jerusalem* (1968; A Beggar in Jerusalem, 1970), W. combines his customary impressionistic technique and those of the *anti-roman*. Using the Six-Day War and the mystical relationship of his narrator to a mysterious friend (seemingly killed in the war) as an ambiguous narrative core, W. tells his story on three interwoven time levels: the post-Six-Day-War period, the war itself, and the earlier European Jewish tragedy. Parables drawn out of Jewish tradition contribute fur-ther to W.'s merging of past and present. But ultimately, W.'s purpose remains the same: trying to make sense of the senseless; seeking identity; and pointing to the need for survival and the affirmation of life.

Winner of the Prix Rivarol (1963), the Jew-ish Heritage Award (1968), and the Prix

Medici (1969), W. writes impassioned lyrical prose that conveys the depth of his personal feeling. It would be difficult to reject the pathos and emotion of his art, which he has aptly described as a "desire to carve words on a tombstone: to the memory of a town forever vanished, to the memory of a childhood in exile, to the memory of all those I loved and who, before I could tell them I loved them, went away."

FURTHER WORKS: *Les Juifs du silence* (1966; The Jews of Silence, 1966); *Le Chant des morts* (1966; Legends of Our Time, 1968); *Zalmen, ou La Folie de dieu* (1968)

BIBLIOGRAPHY: Mitgang, H., "An Eye for an Eye," *New York Times Book Review,* 16 July 1961, p. 23; On *The Gates of the Forest*—Alter, R., *Book Week* 29 May 1966, p. 2; Goldstein, L., "Survivor's Heritage," *The Nation,* 17 Oct. 1966, pp. 390–92; Simon, P.-H., "E. W., Prix Rivarol 1963," in *Diagnostic des lettres françaises contemporaines* (1966), pp. 287–91; On *A Beggar in Jerusalem* —Stern, D., *Book World,* 18 Jan. 1970, p. 1

ROBERT D. SPECTOR

WILDE, Oscar

English poet, novelist, and dramatist, b. 16 Oct. 1854, Dublin; d. 30 Nov. 1900, Paris

W. was born into a family at once distin-guished and notorious. His mother achieved some fame as a minor writer of patriotic prose and verse. His father, although knighted for his skill as an eye and ear surgeon, was an indefatigable rake and a party to one of the most scandalous libel suits of the day.

At the age of ten W. entered Portora Royal School; he remained an indifferent student till his final year, when his interest in classical literature was aroused. At Trinity College, Dublin, where he studied from 1871 to 1874, he earned the Berkley Gold Medal for Greek and a scholarship to Magdalen College, Oxford. There he became a disciple of Ruskin (1819–1900), who stimulated his taste for beauty, and of Walter Pater (1839–94), in whose work W. saw a doctrine of aesthetic hedonism that ultimately shaped the core of his own thought. His memories of his travels in Italy produced "Ravenna," the poem that won him the Newdigate Prize in 1878, his last year at Oxford.

In London W. quickly established a reputation as a wit and a champion of art and beauty as opposed to the crassness and ugliness of Victorian life. To further both his cause and his career he occasionally appeared in an "aesthetic" costume, consisting in part of silk stockings, knee breeches, and a velvet jacket.

Poems (1881), a volume of lushly imitative poetry, did little for either his reputation or his finances. As a result, W. was glad to accept an offer for a lecture tour of the United States. As a lecturer he functioned as a kind of advance publicity for Gilbert and Sullivan's *Patience,* which satirized the aestheticism with which W. was associated. The tour brought W. some money and, in 1883, a disastrous New York production of his melodrama *Vera, or the Nihilists.*

In 1884, after lecturing for a time in the English provinces, W. married Constance Lloyd, the daughter of a prosperous Dublin family.

The birth of two sons, Cyril and Vivian, in the early years of the marriage further strained the already delicate finances of the household. In 1887 W. took a job as editor of *Woman's World,* a journal devoted to fashions and home furnishings, at which he worked conscientiously and efficiently for the next two years. In 1888 he published *The Happy Prince, and Other Tales,* the gracious and melancholy fairy tales that are still among his most attractive writings.

In 1890 the Victorian literary world was startled, as W. intended it to be, by the appearance of *The Picture of Dorian Gray,* a novel which owed something to J. K. Huysmans (q.v.) and a good deal to the tradition of the Gothic romance. The story of the young aristocrat whose outward beauty concealed an inward corruption that appeared only in his portrait undoubtedly reflected W.'s personal life, for he had already begun the course of homosexual conduct that eventually led to his trial and disgrace.

In 1891, W. gathered together his critical essays and published them as *Intentions,* which is one of his most significant works. In these graceful essays and dialogues he presented the view that the beauty of a work of art stems from the perfection of its form and that social or moral considerations are irrelevant to it. As an aesthetician W. is the most extreme English representative of the doctrine of the autonomy of art ("art for art's sake"), first postulated by Théophile Gautier (1811–72).

From the beginning of his literary career W. was ambitious to succeed as a playwright. Aside from his early melodramas, however, he had produced only the morbidly exotic biblical tragedy *Salomé* (1893), a much overwrought expression of the theme of infamous passion.

Now W. turned to the commercial theater and produced in quick succession *Lady Windermere's Fan* (1893), *A Woman of No Importance* (1894), and *An Ideal Husband* (1895). These immensely successful combinations of well-made plots and witty dialogue expressed in their sentimental moments W.'s sense of guilt and alienation, and in their brilliant conversation W.'s aesthetic theories, now converted into a kind of elegant code of life. In *The Importance of Being Earnest* (1895), his one genuine masterpiece, W. projected an almost unflawed vision of a world of perfect form, amoral and exquisite.

Meanwhile his personal life was becoming more and more irregular. He made little effort to conceal his homosexuality, but what was to matter more was that he had contracted a friendship with Lord Alfred Douglas, younger son of the Marquess of Queensberry, that so enraged Douglas's father that he persecuted W. with threats and accusations. W. sued Queensberry for criminal libel but was forced to drop the suit at the trial when the Marquess presented evidence substantiating his claims. W. was arrested; at his first trial, the jury disagreed; at the second, he was convicted and sentenced to two years of hard labor. In prison he wrote a long, self-justifying letter to Alfred Douglas, later published as *De Profundis* (1905), and after his release in 1897, he wrote "The Ballad of Reading Gaol"—but his literary career was over. His last years, spent largely in France, were difficult but not nearly so poverty-stricken or degraded as legend has sometimes suggested.

Although the number of W.'s genuinely significant writings is small, both they and his flamboyant life are suggestive of the position of many modern writers, exiles from ordinary society without socially adequate replacement for the traditional views of life that they have rejected.

FURTHER WORKS: *The Harlot's House* (1885); *The Canterville Ghost* (1887); *The Duchess of Padua* (1891); *Lord Arthur Savile's Crime, and Other Stories* (1891); *The House of Pomegranates* (1891); *The Sphinx* (1894); *Love of the King* (1894); *A Florentine Tragedy* (1895)

BIBLIOGRAPHY: Winwar, F., *O. W. and the Yellow Nineties* (1940); Pearson, H., *The Life of O. W.* (1946); Roditi, E., *O. W.* (1947); Merle, R., *O. W.* (1948); Ervine, S. J., *O. W.: A Present Time Appraisal* (1952); Reinert, O., "Satiric Strategy in *The Importance of Being Earnest*," *College English* (Oct. 1956) pp. 14–18; Ganz, A., "The Divided Self in the Society Comedies of O. W.," *Modern Drama*, III (Summer 1960), 16–23; Hyde, H. M., *O. W.: The Aftermath* (1963); MacLiammóir, M., *The Importance of Being O.* (1963); Toliver, H. E., "W. and the Importance of 'Sincere and Studied Triviality,'" *Modern Drama*, V (Spring 1963), 389–99; Mason, S., *Bibliography of O. W.* (1967); San Juan, E., *The Art of O. W.* (1967); Wilde, T., *The Parents of O. W.* (1967)

ARTHUR GANZ

WILDER, Thornton Niven

American dramatist and novelist, b. 17 April 1897, Madison, Wisconsin

W. attended elementary school in California and in China, where his father was a consul general from 1905 to 1909. He finished high school in California and later attended Oberlin and then Yale, interrupting his studies during World War I for service in the Coast Artillery. After receiving his B.A. in 1920, he spent the following year auditing courses in archaeology and art at the American Academy in Rome. He afterward taught French at the Lawrenceville School (1921–28) and during this time wrote his first novel, *The Cabala* (1926). He received a master's degree from Princeton in 1925. During World War II, W. served as an intelligence officer in the U.S. Air Force.

W. first achieved success with the publication of *The Bridge of San Luis Rey* (1928). Derived in part from Prosper Mérimée (1803–1870), Proust, and Conrad (qq.v.), this novel won him popular and critical acclaim and his first Pulitzer Prize. Though it flouted the growing trend of the realistic American novel, its imaginary Peru was so real that some Peruvians felt called upon to point out that the novel was fiction and not history.

The Woman of Andros (1930), W.'s third novel, was suggested by a theme in Terence (190?–159? B.C.). *Heaven's My Destination* (1935) combines farcical and serious adventures in the life of young George Brush, a book salesman seeking religious truth.

W.'s best novel to date is *The Ides of March* (1948), which presents a strong character study of Caesar through the medium, not of narration, but of fragmentary documents, notes, and letters.

The Eighth Day (1967), another commercial success for this most uncommercial of writers, predictably delighted hosts of readers, while puzzling many critics. Ostensibly an old-fashioned whodunit—saintly John Ashley of Coaltown, Illinois, wrongly convicted of murder, mysteriously rescued, disappears into the interior of Peru, etc.!—this long novel quickly settles down into another W. series of allegorical snapshots from the family album of man. Appearances, as usual, deceive: people of all times and places are the same; only the weather changes and "Coaltown is everywhere." "History is one tapestry," and the eighth seamless day (after Creation) has hardly begun, much less ended. W. remains largely unintimidated by other notions of man's destiny.

Much of W.'s current reputation rests on his achievements as a playwright. In 1928, he brought out *The Angel That Troubled the Waters*, a set of three-minute plays. *The Long Christmas Dinner, and Other Plays* (1931), anticipates his later dramaturgy.

"I am not an innovator," W. once said, "but a rediscoverer of forgotten goods, and I hope a remover of obtrusive bric-a-brac." As a remover of bric-a-brac, he succeeded admirably in *Our Town* (1938)—for which he won another Pulitzer Prize—in which he eliminated all but the bare stage, a few props, and the characters manipulated by a chorus-like narrator. For plot he substituted episodes from the rites of passage (love–marriage–death) and thus telescoped time and space into a casual flow of daily living anywhere and always. His techniques shook if they did not demolish the cardboard naturalism of much American theater. And they had their influence. Certainly W.'s old-new methods helped eventually to create such modern classics as Tennessee Williams's (q.v.) *The Glass Menagerie* and Arthur Miller's (q.v.) *The Death of a Salesman*, works which, following W., also reject the rigidity of the realistic play.

In 1939 came *The Merchant of Yonkers*—freely inspired by Johann Nestroy's (1801–1862) *Einen Jux will er sich machen*, which in turn was out of John Oxenford's (1812–77) English farce, *A Well-Spent Day*. Slightly revised as *The Matchmaker* (1955), the play owed a scene and the important character of

OSCAR WILDE

THORNTON WILDER

Mrs. Dolly Levi to Molière's (1622–73) *L'Avare*. In it W. self-consciously ameliorates hard farce by the use of sentiment. *Hello, Dolly!*, the American musical, was successfully adapted from his judicious cross-fertilization of sources.

The allegorical *Skin of Our Teeth* (1942), a redaction of Joyce's (q.v.) cyclical *Finnegans Wake,* precipitated a wild controversy over its originality but still won W. his third Pulitzer Prize in 1943. The play takes the Antrobus family through the ice age, the deluge, and war—natural and man-made disasters. Like *Our Town,* it has proved internationally popular.

The experimental techniques W. exploited in it have since become the clichés of the avant-garde theater of the absurd. To this work are most directly indebted the anti-play and play-within-a-play devices; the frequent interruptions of stage reality to force audience participation; the ubiquitous producer-manager narrators; and, most of all, the audacious and cheeky mixture of the comic and tragic. No doubt W. "rediscovered" some of these elements in European expressionists like Pirandello and Brecht (qq.v.), or in Greek drama, or in Chinese plays, or even in American vaudeville; but he assimilated such "borrowings" and produced an entirely original drama.

W.'s last full-length play is *The Alcestiad,* adapted from Euripides (480?–406? B.C.) and acted in the round at the 1955 Edinburgh Festival as *A Life in the Sun.* As an opera by Louise Talma, the play had its premiere at Frankfurt, Germany (1962), but neither version has yet been published in English, except for the satyr play, "The Drunken Sisters," in *Atlantic* magazine (November 1957). Three one-act plays (*Plays for Bleecker Street*) were presented in 1962 off-Broadway. These fragments are from his works in progress: *The Seven Ages of Man* and *The Seven Deadly Sins.* One of them, "Childhood," was published in *Atlantic* (November 1960).

Now in his mid-seventies W. has become a great sentimental favorite of three generations of world readers and playgoers. Though he sometimes shows a tendency to palliate harsh realities and to substitute interesting episodic techniques for sustained narrative and conflict, his strength as an artist comes from a profound sympathy with all civilized men—regardless of their eras—his knowledge of both

world literature and culture, his joyous though elegant writing, and his great comic verve.

BIBLIOGRAPHY: Kehler, D., "T. W.," *EJ,* XXVIII (Jan. 1939) 1–11; Wilson, E., "The Antrobuses and the Earwickers," *The Nation,* CXVI (30 Jan. 1943), 167–68; Firebaugh, J., "The Humanism of T. W.," *The Pacific Spectator,* IV (Autumn 1950), 426–28; Cowley, M., Introduction to *A T. W. Trio* (1956); Fergusson, F., "Three Allegorists: Brecht, W. and Eliot," *SR,* LXIV (Fall 1956), 544–73; Edelstein, J. M., *A Bibliographical Checklist of the Writings of T. W.* (1959); Modic, J., "The Eclectic Mr. W.," *Ball State Forum,* I (Winter 1960–61), 55–61; Burbank, R., *T. W.* (1961); Kosok, H., "T. W.: A Bibliography of Criticism," *TCL,* IX (1963), 93–100; Goldstein, M., *The Art of T. W.* (1965); Haberman, D., *The Plays of T. W.* (1967); Papajewski, H., *T. W.* (1968)

JOHN L. MODIC

WILLIAMS, Charles Stansby

English novelist, poet, playwright, and critic, b. 20 Sept. 1886, London; d. 15 May 1945, Oxford

W. studied for two years at the University of London before lack of money forced him to give up school. After a few years in a small publishing office, he joined the editorial staff of the Oxford University Press, where he remained until his death. During his years as an editor, he also taught, lectured, and published nearly forty books and more than two hundred shorter pieces. An eloquent speaker, a gifted conversationalist, and an extremely personable man, he numbered among his friends Auden, Eliot, and C. S. Lewis (qq.v.), all of whom have written enthusiastically about him and his work. Though his novels were widely read in England during the 1930's, they were little known in the United States until the publication here of *All Hallows' Eve* in 1948. Within two years all of his novels were available in American editions, and since then serious critical interest in W. has grown.

W.'s novels, popularly described as "supernatural thrillers," are on the simplest level stories of high adventure involving manifestations of other-worldly powers. Fascinating as mere adventure stories, they also are dramatizations of W.'s conception of the spiritual laws governing man's relation to himself, to others, and to the powers that W. generally designates as Love.

Typically, the temptation faced by W.'s characters is to desire power, or the images in which it is manifested, for their own possession or use. In *War in Heaven* (1930), the source of power is the Holy Grail, which has turned up in an obscure English church. Power in *Many Dimensions* (1931) is manifested in a stone inscribed with the Tetragrammaton and capable of transporting the holder through space and time. In *The Greater Trumps* (1932), the Tarot cards and a set of dancing figures—archetypes of the dance of life—give the user power over the forces of nature. Power in the abstract, and ultimately power over life and death, is sought by Nigel Considine in *Shadows of Ecstasy* (1933). In *All Hallows' Eve* (1945) Simon Leclerc seeks through sorcery to become the ruler of the world.

In all of these novels the alternative and saving response to the temptation of power is self-surrender, the offering up of oneself to be an instrument of supernatural love.

W.'s poetry, while less well known than his novels, is considered by some critics to be among the most original poetry of our time. His most important works in this genre are the two books of Grail poems: *Taliessin Through Logres* (1938) and *The Region of the Summer Stars* (1944). These are collections of lyrics touching on the failure of Arthur and his knights to create an ordered and righteous kingdom in Logres (Arthurian Britain) so that the Grail might come to Logres and usher in the Parousia, the second coming of Christ. Rich in symbolism and myth, metaphysical and allusive, the Grail poems deal with many of the same themes treated in the novels.

W.'s plays are significant examples of modern religious verse drama. Often commissioned for religious festivals, they are mannered, formal works that show the influence of Elizabethan drama and the morality play. They include *Thomas Cranmer of Canterbury* (1936), *Judgement at Chelmsford* (1939), and *Seed of Adam, and Other Plays* (1948).

In his best novels, *e.g., Descent into Hell* (1937), W. has an almost poetic clarity of style, and his lofty manner often transforms his quite ordinary characters as they become involved with the higher powers of his fictional worlds.

W. was a devout Anglican, and religious themes and concerns recur in all the genres in which he wrote. As a fiction writer, his pri-

mary achievement lies in the power and imagination with which he was able to transform his theological insights into dramatic form.

FURTHER WORKS: *The Silver Stair* (1912); *Poems of Conformity* (1917); *Divorce* (1920); *Windows of the Night* (1924); *The Masque of the Manuscript* (1927); *A Myth of Shakespeare* (1928); *The Masque of Perusal* (1929); *Heroes and Kings* (1930); *Poetry at Present* (1930); *Three Plays* (1931); *The English Poetic Mind* (1932); *The Place of the Lion* (1932); *Bacon* (1933); *Reason and Beauty in the Poetic Mind* (1933); *James I* (1934); *Rochester* (1935); *Queen Elizabeth* (1936); *Henry VII* (1937); *Stories of Great Names* (1937); *He Came Down from Heaven* (1938); *The Descent of the Dove; A Short History of the Holy Spirit in the Church* (1939); *Witchcraft* (1941); *The Forgiveness of Sins* (1942); *The Figure of Beatrice: A Study in Dante* (1943); *The House of the Octopus* (1945); *Flecker of Dean Close* (1946)

BIBLIOGRAPHY: Eliot, T. S., Introduction to *All Hallows' Eve* (1948); Lewis, C. S., *Arthurian Torso* (1948); Parsons, G., "The Spirit of C. W.," *Atlantic Monthly*, Nov. 1949, pp. 77–79; Winship, G. P., Jr., "This Rough Magic; The Novels of C. W.," *YR*, XL (Winter 1951), 285–96; Auden, W. H., "C. W.," *Christian Century*, 2 May 1956, pp. 552–54; Crowley, C. P., "The Grail Poetry of C. W.," *UTQ*, July 1956, pp. 484–93; Hadfield, A. M., *An Introduction to C. W.* (1959); Shideler, M. M., *The Theology of Romantic Love* (1962); Huttar, C. A., "C. W., Novelist and Prophet," *Gordon Review*, Winter 1967, pp. 51–75

DOROTHY TUCK MCFARLAND

WILLIAMS, Tennessee

American dramatist and novelist, b. 26 March 1911, Columbus, Mississippi

W. was the son of a minister's daughter and a footloose father. In his work, W. has consistently explored the tension between "Puritan" and "Cavalier," which was his inheritance. He spent his early childhood in the Episcopalian rectory of his maternal grandfather and grew to troubled manhood in a tenement flat in St. Louis. His father traveled as a shoe salesman, played poker, and drank immoderately; his mother endured an ill-concealed martyrdom. The tension of their conflict was transmitted to W. and his sister Rose. She resolved her conflicts by retreating into insanity; he managed to forge his experiences into art.

W.'s first dramatic success, *The Glass Menagerie* (1945), came out of the circumstances of his life in St. Louis. The play has since become a classic of the American theater.

An earlier venture, *Battle of Angels* (1940), had closed in Boston; the play was later rewritten and finally reached Broadway as *Orpheus Descending* (1957). W.'s second success, *A Streetcar Named Desire* (1947), is considered by many critics one of the great achievements in American drama. The play not only established W.'s reputation as a playwright of sex and violence, but also gave to actors and audiences two unforgettable characters, Blanche DuBois and Stanley Kowalski. Neither Clifford Odets nor Eugene O'Neill nor Arthur Miller (qq.v.) has produced such a stunning combination of poetic speech, earthy action and dialogue, and psychological insight.

In rapid succession came *Summer and Smoke* (1948), *The Rose Tattoo* (1951), *Camino Real* (1953), *Cat on a Hot Tin Roof* (1955), *Suddenly Last Summer* (1957), *Sweet Bird of Youth* (1959), *Period of Adjustment* (1960), *Night of the Iguana* (1962), *The Milktrain Doesn't Stop Here Anymore* (1964), and *Slapstick Tragedy* (1967). The plays were uneven in artistic achievement and audience popularity. W. often seemed divided between the seriousness of his themes and a desire to shock playgoers—as in *Suddenly Last Summer*.

Although W. has made excursions into both fiction and poetry, his imagination has been essentially dramatic; his short stories are often prose drafts of the plays that later emerge. W.'s work consistently reveals his compassion for the outcast and the alienated. Drunks, bums, whores, and homosexuals expose their failures, their frustrations, and their aching humanity. Even though they are often victimized and brutalized, frequently destroyed, they usually gain a paradoxical victory by demonstrating greater understanding and sensitivity than those who condemn them. Despite appearances, they are capable of love and a moral austerity that eludes their destroyers.

W. has often been misunderstood because he uses sexual material as metaphors of contemporary conditions. The search for individuality and the loss of clear moral standards appear to be his major themes; he often employs Christian symbolism to clarify and buttress these themes. As a technician of drama, W. has been highly experimental. Except for his comedies, he generally avoids straightforward realism in favor of poetic and symbolic expressionism.

The limited popularity of W.'s recent work has produced the criticism that his powers are declining. This pessimistic view has been arrived at prematurely perhaps, yet W.'s latest plays have done little to counter the charge. However, the contributions he has already made to the theater assure him a position of respect in the history of American drama. Few will deny the theatrical power and thematic significance of his best work.

FURTHER WORKS: *27 Wagons Full of Cotton* (1945); *You Touched Me* (with D. Windham; 1946); *One Arm, and Other Stories* (1948); *American Blues: Five Short Plays* (1948); *The Roman Spring of Mrs. Stone* (1950); *Hard Candy, and Other Stories* (1954); *In the Winter of Cities* (1955); *Baby Doll* (1956); *The Knightly Quest* (1967); *Kingdom of Earth* (1968)

BIBLIOGRAPHY: Falk, S., *T. W.* (1961); Nelson, B., *T. W.: The Man and His Work* (1961); Donahue, F., *The Dramatic World of T. W.* (1964); Jackson, E. M., *The Broken World of T. W.* (1965); Maxwell, G., *T. W. and Friends* (1965); Weales, G., *T. W.* (1965); Fedder, N., *The Influence of D. H. Lawrence on T. W.* (1966)

CLIFFORD WARREN

WILLIAMS, William Carlos

American poet, b. 17 Sept. 1883, Rutherford, New Jersey; d. there, 4 March 1963

Educated at New York's Horace Mann High School and the medical college of the University of Pennsylvania, where he formed a lasting friendship with Pound (q.v.), W. combined the practice of medicine and poetry during a lifetime in a small suburban New Jersey city.

Abandoning traditional rhyme and meter for free verse, he early developed a style characterized by precise, vivid imagery and distinctive breath-spaced metrical patterns. Like Walt Whitman (1819–92), W. prized local experience and celebrated the "American idiom" as the source of fresh poetic rhythms. Finding Whitman's long line unsuited to the tempo of modern life, he sought for himself a sparer line to express his vibrant, empathic responses to immediate experience.

Although his work is often identified with modernist movements such as imagism and objectivism, W. was concerned for the interaction of image and idea in the poetic process. The intellectual (but antidoctrinaire) and reflective qualities of his verse became increasingly apparent in his later work, including the five books of *Paterson* (1946–58).

Paterson represents W.'s ambitious effort to write an epic or culture poem comparable to Eliot's (q.v.) *The Waste Land* or Pound's *Cantos*. It is typical of W., however, that he made use of native American—and especially local—materials in his attempt to define himself and his culture in poetry. The river of the poems is the "filthy Passaic," but it is also the stream of life, of time, of the common language from which W. selected his own idiom. *Paterson* represents not only the poet himself and the New Jersey city he has known, but the city of man, imaginatively conceived, in all its trivial actualities and limitless possibilities.

W.'s shorter poems are most fully represented in *The Complete Collected Poems* (1938), *Collected Later Poems* (1950), and *Collected Earlier Poems* (1951). He listed and commented upon his many individual books of verse in *I Wanted to Write a Poem* (1958), an autobiographical-bibliography edited by Edith Heal. *Pictures from Breughel* (1962), his last volume of verse, received the Pulitzer Prize for poetry.

Sympathetic with avant-garde movements in literature and painting, W.'s was an active contributor to many "little magazines." As editor of *Contact* (1920–23; new series, 1932), he advanced his own views and his "faith in the existence of native artists who are capable of having, comprehending, and recording extraordinary experience."

FURTHER WORKS: *The Great American Novel* (1923); *In the American Grain* (1925); *A Voyage to Pagany* (1928); *White Mule* (1937); *In the Money* (1940); *Autobiography* (1951); *The Build-Up* (1952); *Selected Essays* (1954); *Selected Letters* (ed. J. C. Thirlwall; 1957); *Yes, Mrs. Williams* (1959); *The Farmers' Daughters: Collected Stories* (1961); *Many Loves: Collected Plays* (1962)

BIBLIOGRAPHY: Koch, V., *W. C. W.* (1950); Martz, L. L., "The Unicorn in Paterson: W. C. W.," *Thought*, XXXV (1960), 537– 54; Sutton, W., "Dr. W.'s *Paterson* and the Quest for Form," *Criticism*, II (1960), 242–59; Wagner, L. W., *The Poems of W. C. W.* (1964); Miller, J. H., ed., *W. C. W.: A Collection of Critical Essays* (1966); Engels, J., ed., *A Checklist of W. C. W.* (1969)

WALTER SUTTON

WILSON, Angus

English novelist, short-story writer, critic, and essayist, b. 11 Aug. 1913, Bexhill, Sussex

W. studied medieval history at Oxford and was alternately a caterer, restaurant manager, and social organizer before joining the staff of the British Museum in 1937. After suffering a nervous breakdown during the war, he became interested in writing and achieved immediate recognition as an important social commentator with the publication of his first collection of short stories, *The Wrong Set* (1949).

In his early fiction W. satirically inveighs against middle-class liberal humanism and its blindly narcissistic efforts to solve the problems of 20th-c. England. His heroes and heroines are those who can recognize their own personal limitations and exist with courage and humility in a world of disintegrating values and dizzying technological change.

In W.'s first novel, *Hemlock and After* (1952), a famous writer willingly meets his death after acknowledging how evil has infiltrated his most cherished utopian project—a commune for promising young writers—and the heart of his civilized self. The novelist is moralist here, as a Dickensian sense of character and drama is employed in exposing the more sensational and grotesque elements in the night-worlds—criminal and theatrical—of English life.

In *Anglo-Saxon Attitudes* (1956) a variety of traditional techniques convey the emotional awakening of a scholar who had lost motivation. Here the hero's academic brilliance is ironically contrasted with his inability to perceive the moral sources of his personal and professional failures. And though he rediscovers his way, behind him a complexly interrelated world—of television entertainers, politicians, and scholars—is seen in a continual process of spiritual self-destruction.

The Middle Age of Mrs. Eliot (1958) gently parodies two simplistic approaches to the problems of social evil—interpersonal involvement and escapist quietism—but also suggests that

WILLIAM CARLOS WILLIAMS

P. G. WODEHOUSE

the will to live, in a world where one is constantly confronted by the ludicrous and absurd, is in itself a sign of ultimate wisdom.

W.'s later fiction is less harsh in its condemnation of English liberalism and continues to present an impressive display of technical virtuosity as well as a deepened poetic sense of life. In *Late Call* (1964) W.'s belief in the life-potential of those in socially obscure positions is affirmed as an ex-hotel manageress transcends her age and a variety of meddling do-gooders to find personal joy in the contemporary world. And though middle-class ambitions, "worthy" projects, and modern inventiveness are again ridiculed, their kinship to a truer goodness is discernible. In a most ambitious display of stylistic resourcefulness and literary showmanship, *No Laughing Matter* (1967), the individual members of an eccentric and error-prone family are seen to triumph during fifty years of Britain's social, political, and ethical confusions. In this effusive mock chronicle, W. takes a definitive stand on the side of classical humanism and old-fashioned cults of the individual against the progressive and communal tendencies of modern life.

As a critic and essayist W. has written prolifically and on a variety of topics, but he has focused his major attention on Victorian and contemporary literature. His most important works of criticism, *Émile Zola: An Introductory Study of His Novels* (1952) and *The Wild Garden, or Speaking of Writing* (1963), make use of Freudian methodology in trying to understand the workings of the literary imagination.

W. has been justly criticized for overly mechanical plots and for sensational and gimmicky effects, but although he has exploited established techniques rather than developing new ones, he has done so masterfully and has analyzed the contemporary social scene with subtlety and depth. He admirably carries on in the tradition of the great Victorian novelists such as Charles Dickens (1812–70) and George Eliot (1819–80), in portraying the tragicomic struggles of a culture trying to reconstruct itself before dying.

FURTHER WORKS: *Such Darling Dodos, and Other Stories* (1950); *For Whom the Cloche Tolls: A Scrap-book of the Twenties* (with P. Jullian; 1953); *The Mulberry Bush* (1956); *A Bit off the Map, and Other Stories* (1957); *The Old Men at the Zoo* (1961); *The*

Seven Deadly Sins (1962); *Tempo* (1964); *Death Dance: Twenty-five Stories* (1969); *The World of Charles Dickens* (1970)

BIBLIOGRAPHY: Cockshut, A. O. J., "Favored Sons: The Moral World of A. W.," *EIC*, IX (1959), 50–60; Gindin, J., "A. W.'s Qualified Nationalism," in *Postwar British Fiction: New Accents and Attitudes* (1962), pp. 145–64; Halio, J. L., "The Novels of A. W.," *MFS*, VIII (1962), 171–81; Cox, C. B., "A. W.: Studies in Depression," in *The Free Spirit: A Study of Liberal Humanism in the Novels of George Eliot, Henry James, E. M. Forster, Virginia Woolf, and A. W.* (1963), pp. 117–57; Edelstein, A., "A. W.: The Territory Behind," in *Contemporary British Novelists*, ed. C. Shapiro (1965), pp. 144–61; Rabinovitz, R., "A. W.," in *Reaction against Experiment in the English Novel: 1950–60* (1967), pp. 64–96; Shaw, V. A., "*The Middle Age of Mrs. Eliot* and *Late Call*: A. W.'s Traditionalism," *CritQ*, XII (1970), pp. 9–26

LEO ZANDERER

WILSON, Edmund

American critic, journalist, playwright, poet, and novelist, b. 8 May 1895, Red Bank, New Jersey

W.'s career is one of the most varied as well as prolific in American letters. Since 1922 he has published some forty books, mainly collections of essays, articles, and reviews. Although he started out as a reporter for the *New York Evening Sun* in 1916, he left newspaper work after less than a year to enlist in the army. During much of his career since World War I, he has been associated with various magazines, notably the *New Republic* and *The New Yorker*.

W.'s reputation as a man of letters rests mainly on his criticism, even though for thirty years he has been more interested in history and biography. However, in the 1920's when he wrote the first American review of Hemingway's *Three Stories and Ten Poems* and *In Our Time* (1924), he was primarily interested in literature. One of the first critical examinations of the symbolist influence, his *Axel's Castle* (1931) is still an important—and certainly the best-written—evaluation of Yeats, Valéry, Eliot, Proust, Joyce, Gertrude Stein (qq.v.), and Rimbaud. But even early in W.'s career, analysis, explication, and evaluation did not content him.

W.'s ultimate concern was for the human significance of literature, which, he said later in "The Historical Interpretation of Literature" (1938), is "an attempt to give a meaning to our experience—that is, to make life more practicable." Although he derided both the politico-social formulas of the Marxists and the moral proscriptions of the new humanists, he nevertheless shared with both groups a concern for the value of literature in human reform. In *Axel's Castle* he had deplored the artist's isolation from actual life. To W. imaginative literature should above all be a meaningful articulation of human problems, and his approach to literature has scarcely ever been theoretical.

By the time W. published *The Triple Thinkers* (1938; rev. and enlarged ed., 1948), a notable collection of literary and personal essays, his major interest was in literature as a revelation of its authors' personalities. In the revised and enlarged 1948 edition, the two most ambitious essays offer psychobiographical portraits of Henry James and Ben Jonson.

In his next group of literary essays, *The Wound and the Bow* (1941), W. adopted the theory that artistic ability may be a kind of compensation for a psychological wound and that, therefore, the literary work can be adequately understood only in terms of the emotional profile of its author. Unfortunately, this approach obstructs W.'s genuine criticism, particularly in "Dickens: The Two Scrooges" and "The Kipling That Nobody Read." But his strengths as a critic are nevertheless apparent: summary, paraphrase, comparison, survey, taste.

W.'s most impressive critical work, *Patriotic Gore: Studies in the Literature of the Civil War* (1964), is his most historical and biographical. Like his famous study of European revolutionists, *To the Finland Station* (1940), it satisfies the definition of literary criticism that he had learned from his Princeton mentor, Christian Gauss, and to which he referred in his dedication of *Axel's Castle* to Gauss: "a history of man's ideas and imaginings in the setting of the conditions which have shaped them." In *Patriotic Gore*, W. discusses over thirty authors of the Civil War era and shows what their writings reveal of the moral and political confusion of the times. Few of these authors are major literary figures; indeed, most of them are not even "creative" writers but are memoirists, polemicists, orators, and letter writers.

The book's main contribution to literary criticism appears in two chapters. "The Myth of the Old South" establishes the *literary* origin of the idea of Southern chivalry and then traces its development, especially in the poetry of Sidney Lanier. "The Chastening of American Prose Style" explains the change from the turgid writing earlier in the century to a plain, economical style as deriving from the "plain" man (Lincoln), journalism, military writing, and the machine age.

W.'s major interest in *Patriotic Gore* is not literary but historical and polemical. He wishes to define and understand the issues of the Civil War and to suggest how the decline of republican America and the rise of a powerful, centralized government lay in their resolution. Thus, the states-rights question is one of exercising power, through force if necessary, and today it is directly related, in W.'s view, to "the exactions of centralized bureaucracies of both the state and federal authorities."

The individual's relation to an increasingly powerful government has concerned W. throughout his career and is the major theme in his reporting, of which the best example is *The American Earthquake: A Documentary of the Jazz Age, the Great Depression, and the New Deal* (1958). A collection of excellent articles, this work is characterized by a sometimes grim view of American life.

From New York and "the follies" of the 1920's, W. moves across the country during the "earthquake" year of 1930–31, dispassionately recording strikes, trials, and other public events that point up the severe racial, social, economic and moral stresses on American life. Finally he concentrates on the New Deal years of 1932–34 in Washington, D. C., and expresses his dissatisfaction with the implications of its uneasy politics. *The American Earthquake* is a personal book, imbued with a humane consciousness that observes clearly and yet is alienated from the America embraced in its vision. As his later "protest," *The Cold War and the Income Tax* (1963), shows, W. is distressed by the exploitative, big-government America that has emerged since the Civil War.

Yet, personal as W.'s reporting is, it does not exhort as much as his plays, whose major failing as drama is their tendency to preach. Only two of his eight published plays have been produced. *The Crime in the Whistler Room* (1924), like several of W.'s early stories, attacks pre-World War I morality as stifling and cruel. *The Little Blue Light* (1950) warns against political apathy, selfishness, and materialism. His best play, which was not produced professionally, is *Cyprian's Prayer* (1954), the account of a 15th-c. youth who learns black magic so that he may employ its power in elevating the life of the peasant. But Cyprian discovers that intellectual power and self-reliance are superior to any power outside oneself and that human reform cannot be hurried.

W.'s lyric poetry, which he formally abandoned with *Poets, Farewell!* (1929), is undistinguished. He excels, however, in parodistic and satirical verse, of which both *Poets, Farewell!* and *Night Thoughts* (1961) contain examples.

W.'s most interesting imaginative writing is his prose fiction, which relates to most of his other work in its theme of the intellectual's attempts to accept and contribute to the world of actuality. Although he has published only two novels and fourteen stories, several of the stories are superior, and his loosely constructed *Memoirs of Hecate County* (1946) ranks among the better novels of our time. An account of a young scholar's struggles to love, work, and keep his sanity in an environment of despair, its sometimes graphic sexual descriptions caused its suppression at the time of its original publication. With *To the Finland Station, The American Earthquake* and *Patriotic Gore,* it is one of W.'s finest books.

Considered together, W.'s writings form a record of 20th-c. America's intellectual and moral life, scrutinized by an intelligence that is rational, sympathetic, and scrupulous.

FURTHER WORKS: *The Undertaker's Garland* (with John Peale Bishop, 1922); *Discordant Encounters* (1926); *I Thought of Daisy* (1929); *The American Jitters* (1932); *Travels in Two Democracies* (1936); *This Room and This Gin and These Sandwiches* (1937); *The Boys in the Back Room* (1941); *Note-books of Night* (1942); *The Shock of Recognition* (1943); *Europe without Baedeker* (1947; rev. ed., 1966); *Classics and Commercials* (1950); *The Shores of Light* (1952); *Eight Essays* (1954); *Five Plays* (1954); *The Scrolls from the Dead Sea* (1955); *A Piece of My Mind* (1956); *Red, Black, Blond and Olive* (1956); *A Literary Chronicle: 1920–1950* (1956); *Apologies to the Iroquois* (1959); *O Canada* (1965); *The Bit between My Teeth* (1965); *Galahad, and I Thought of Daisy* (1967); *A Prelude* (1967); *The Fruits of the MLA* (1969); *The Duke of Palermo, and*

Other Plays (1969); *The Dead Sea Scrolls: 1947–1969* (1969)

BIBLIOGRAPHY: Warren, R. P., "E. W.'s Civil War," *Commentary,* XXXIV (Aug. 1962), 151–58; Paul, S., *E. W.: A Study of Literary Vocation in Our Time* (1965); Gilman, R., "E. W., Then and Now," *New Republic,* CLV (2 July 1966), 23–8; Berthoff, W., *E. W.* (1968); Ramsay, D., *E. W.: A Bibliography* (1969); Frank, C. P., *E. W.* (1970)

CHARLES FRANK

WINTERS, Yvor

American poet and critic, b. 17 Oct. 1900, Chicago

W. spent most of his childhood in southern California and as a young man taught school in the Southwest. In 1928 he became an instructor at Stanford University, where he taught until he was appointed professor emeritus in 1966.

W. began his literary career as a poet, publishing his first book of verse, *The Immobile Wind,* in 1921. Initially he worked in free and accentual verse forms, and was influenced by Pound, Marianne Moore, and William Carlos Williams (qq.v.). After 1927 he turned to more traditional forms, which he has continued to use. Rhymed and metrically regular, his mature poetry is intellectual, controlled, precise, and subtle. His *Collected Poems* (revised edition, 1960) was awarded the Bollingen Prize in 1961.

W. first set forth his critical principles in *Primitivism and Decadence: A Study of American Experimental Poetry* (1937). As a critic, W. is an uncompromising judge. A believer in absolute values and in the moral relevance of literature, he regards poetry as a moral discipline. As W. sees it, in the act of writing a poem the poet thus makes a moral judgement about experience. It is the task of the critic to evaluate how successfully the poet has communicated his perception and judgment.

W. is primarily concerned with the functional relationship between content and form —between the paraphrasable rational statement and the emotion appropriate to it, which is conveyed by the connotations of the words, the meter, and other structural elements. For a poem to achieve perfection, there must be a balanced and harmonious relationship between subject and form. In his criticism of the poetry of Gerard Manley Hopkins (1844–89), for instance, W. objects that the emotion is excessive and the motive, or subject of the emotion, is not clear. This fault, according to W., is typical of romanticists, who are given to self-expression rather than to the understanding and evaluation of their subjects.

W. has taken his fellow critics severely to task for their failure to define absolute standards of literary judgment. Similarly, he has applied his strict yardstick of excellence to many famous poets and found them lacking. His intransigence and the occasional stridency of his arguments have earned him enmity from many quarters, and his pointing out of defects in the work of Dante, T. S. Eliot (q.v.), Milton, Pound, Shakespeare, and others has sometimes been misinterpreted to mean that he finds the imperfect work totally without value. Many of his critical pronouncements, *e.g.,* that the novel is nearly dead, or that the romantic tradition is an obvious disaster in both art and life, have occasioned hostility, as have his critical judgments on the superiority of the poetry of T. Sturge Moore, Robert Bridges (q.v.), and Elizabeth Daryush.

As both a poet and a critic W. demonstrates a sound knowledge of literary tradition, precision of judgment, and an undeviating stance in the face of opposition. His poems have been admired for their integrity and quiet compassion. Though they have the strength of their virtues, they also tend to be narrow in scope and sometimes dour. However unorthodox his critical judgments, his methods have brought a new and often stimulating light to bear on literature and the principles of criticism.

FURTHER WORKS: *The Magpie's Shadow* (1922); *The Bare Hills* (1927); *The Proof* (1930); *The Journey* (1931); *Before Disaster* (1934); *Maule's Curse: Seven Studies in the History of American Obscurantism* (1938); *Poems* (1940); *The Anatomy of Nonsense* (1944); *Giant Weapon* (1944); *Edward Arlington Robinson* (1946); *In Defense of Reason* (1947); *Collected Poems* (1952); *The Function of Criticism* (1957); *On Modern Poets* (1957); *Forms of Discovery: Critical and Historical Essays on the Forms of the Short Poem in English* (1967)

BIBLIOGRAPHY: McKean, K., "Y. W. and the Neo-Humanists," *University of Kansas City Review,* XXII (1955), 131–33; Elman, R. M., "A Word for Y. W.," *Commonweal,* LXXIV (1961), 401–3; Lowell, R., "Y. W.: A Tribute," *Poetry,* April 1961, pp. 40–42; Kimbrough, R., "Discipline the Saving Grace," *Renascence,* XV (1963), 62–67; Ramsey, P., "Some Abstractions against Abstraction," *SR,* LXXIII (1965), 451–64

DOROTHY TUCK MCFARLAND

WITTLIN, Józef

Polish poet, novelist, and essayist, b. 17 Aug. 1896, Dmytrow

Of Jewish parentage, W. was educated in Lwów and served in the Austrian infantry during World War I. This experience made so deep an impression on him that he later gave it artistic expression in his only novel *Sól ziemi.* In addition he was a dedicated pacifist for the decade after the war. In 1928, however, in the face of the growing menace of fascism, W. publicly denounced pacifism. A few days before the outbreak of World War II, he fled Warsaw for a retreat near Paris. In 1941 he emigrated to the United States, where he now lives.

W.'s first published writings were some poems that appeared in the literary periodical *Zdrój,* then the organ of expressionism (q.v.) in Poland. He is, however, usually identified with the all-inclusive Skamander group (*see* Polish literature).

Bare, hard, showing a crisp break with traditional Polish romanticism, W.'s first collection of poetry, *Hymny* (1920), was a strong protest against nationalism, militarism, and mechanized warfare. The volume received excellent critical notices. Since then, though individual poems have intermittently appeared in various journals—the beautiful patriotic lyric "Stabat Mater" (1943) deserves special mention—W. has never published another volume of poetry, nor is there an edition of his collected poetic works.

W. next turned to translating Homer's *Odyssey* (1924), and his rendition is generally regarded as the best available in Polish. Despite his advocacy of pacifism at the time, this work and an elegy to Homer written in the same year show a strong fascination with those aspects of war that bring heroic individual qualities to the fore. His other translations include Carlo Collodi's (1826–90) *Pinocchio* (1946) and Benét's (q.v.) "The Ballad of the Duke's Mercy," which appeared in the Cracow magazine *Twórczość* in 1946.

Wojna, pokój, i dusza poetry (1925), a collection of essays and speeches on war, peace, and the poetic spirit, was W.'s first volume of prose. While in the same spirit as his early poetry, these pieces particularly decry the brutal dehumanization of the 20th c., a theme that marks all his prose. For W., the 20th-c. world has become a nightmare of bureaucratization, gas-chamber slaughter, and urban decay. "Poe in the Bronx" (1959), an essay in English, is a good example of his general attitudes. Though W.'s style is too elaborate for some tastes, it clearly conveys a sense of horror, disgust, and the macabre.

Sól ziemi (1935; Salt of the Earth, 1941), the first book of an intended trilogy about a humble, obscure infantryman, brought W. international fame and has been translated into many languages. The military life of Piotr Niewiadomski, W.'s naïve, barely literate, unheroic hero—whose surname means "son of an unknown father"—is presented as the biography of the Unknown Soldier.

Painstakingly crafted, based on scrupulous research, the novel took ten years to write. It is a unique perception of what happens to a human being caught in the rules, orders, counterorders, and other bureaucratic machinery of modern warfare. Written in a simple, clear, and detached style that has been likened to biblical prose, it fully expresses W.'s belief that human love and dignity are to be found even in the midst of war, horror, and exile.

W.'s opus has remained disappointingly slim, and his long exile would seem to have extracted a heavy price. Nevertheless his highly regarded poetry, essays, translations, and first volume of the never-completed trilogy have assured him an important place in modern Polish literature.

FURTHER WORKS: *Mój Lwów* (1946); *Orfeusz w piekle xx wieku* (1963)

BIBLIOGRAPHY: Coleman, A. P., "Recent Novels by Polish Writers," *The New York Times Book Review,* 5 July 1936, pp. 4–5; Coleman, A. P., "J. W.," *SatR,* XXIV (2 Aug. 1941), 10–11; Folejewski, Z., "The Creative Path of J. W.," *PolR,* IX (1964), 67–72

STANLEY J. PACION

WODEHOUSE, Pelham Grenville

English novelist, short-story writer, and dramatist, b. 15 Oct. 1881, Guildford

W. attended Dulwich College in London, after growing up in Surrey. In 1902 he published a children's book, *The Pothunters,* and in 1903 began to contribute humor pieces to the *London Globe.* That same year he published a collection of short stories, *A Prefect's Uncle.* W.'s prolific output of light romance and farcical novels followed.

Psmith in the City (1910) launched W.'s Psmith series, which was received favorably. In *The Man with Two Left Feet* (1917), W. introduced perhaps his most important character, Bertie Wooster. Bertie's butler Jeeves soon became a title figure (*My Man Jeeves,* 1919). The Jeeves series include *Very Good, Jeeves* (1930), *Thank You, Jeeves* (1934), and *Stiff Upper Lip, Jeeves* (1963). W. has lived many years in the United States. During World War II, he was interned by the Germans and made five pro-German broadcasts, which compromised him when the war was over.

W.'s plots are outlandish, complex, and ingenious. His style is an original mixture of slang, formal diction, quotation, fantastic metaphor, and conscious cliché. Always in command of his incongruous materials, he has been praised by Belloc and Waugh (qq.v.) as a master of English prose. Though laid in the 20th c., his novels scarcely touch upon its realities. For W., time seemingly stopped in the reign of Edward VII. The characters (after the early juvenile fiction) are adults, but the point of view is that of boyhood, at once raffish and innocent.

Over the years he has repeatedly returned to favorite settings and characters: for instance, to Blandings Castle, which he invented in *Something Fresh* (1915). As a result, he has produced a kind of comic mythology. In a grim era, W.'s world is an engaging place, a comic Arcadia.

FURTHER WORKS: *Love among the Chickens* (1906); *Mike* (1909); *The Man Upstairs* (1914); *Piccadilly Jim* (1918); *Leave It to Psmith* (1923); *Ukridge* (1924); *Meet Mr. Mulliner* (1927); *Blandings Castle* (1935); *The Code of the Woosters* (1938); *Uncle Fred in the Springtime* (1939); *Joy in the Morning* (1947); *Uncle Dynamite* (1948); *Pigs Have Wings* (1952); *Performing Flea* (1953; Am., *Author! Author!,* 1962); *Over Seventy* (1957; Am., *America, I Like You,* 1956); *Jeeves in the Offing* (1960); *The Girl in Blue* (1971)

BIBLIOGRAPHY: Hayward, J., "P. G. W.," *Saturday Book 1941–1942* (1941), pp. 372–89; Orwell, G., "In Defense of P. G. W.," *Dickens, Dali and Others* (1946), pp. 222–43; Aldridge, J. W., "P. G. W.: The Lesson of the

Young Master," *New World Writing 13* (1958), pp. 181–92; Usborne, R., *W. at Work* (1961); Voorhees, R. J., "The Jolly Old World of P. G. W.," *South Atlantic Quarterly*, LXI (Spring 1962), 213–22; Hall, R. A., "P. G. W. and the English Language," *Annali Istituto Universitario Orientale, Napoli, Sezione Germanica*, VII (1964), 103–21; Hall, R. A., "Incongruity and Stylistic Rhythm in P. G. W.," *Annali Istituto Universitario Orientale, Napoli, Sezione Germanica*, XI (1968), 135–44

RICHARD J. VOORHEES

WOESTIJNE, Karel Van de

Belgian poet, short-story writer, and essayist (writing in Flemish), b. 10 March 1878, Ghent; d. 24 Aug. 1929, Zwijnaarde

W. studied philology for a time before working as a journalist and a government employee. In 1921 he became professor of Netherlands literature at the University of Ghent.

In his first volumes of poetry—*Het vaderhuis* (1903), *De boomgaard der vogelen en der vruchten* (1905), and *De gulden schaduw* (1910)—which were influenced by French symbolism (q.v.), individual emotional experiences of his youth are lyrically described in musical language rich in images. The monumental *Interludiën* (2 vols., 1912–14) and *Zon in den rug* (1924) treat classical subjects in an epic-lyrical form.

W.'s poetry reaches its peak in the synthesis of the trilogy *De modderen man* (1920), *God aan zee* (1926), and *Het bergmeer* (1928), published posthumously in 1942 in a single volume entitled *Wiekslag om de kim*. Here he depicts the conflict between spirit and sensuality as well as a yearning for God that is carried to the point of ascetic detachment from terrestrial considerations.

W.'s personal problems also lie at the heart of his prose works. The impressionistic *Laethemsche brieven over de lente* (1904) belongs to the same period as the early volumes of poetry. In powerful language stylistically reminiscent of Spain's Góngora (1561–1627), W. later treated classical subjects, parables, and legends of the saints (*Janus met het dubbele voorhoofd*, 1908; *Afwijkingen*, 1910; *De bestendige aanwezigheid*, 1918; *Goddelijke verbeeldingen*, 1918). He wrote some excellent symbolic short stories: "De heilige van het getal" and "Christophorus" (1926), and espe-

cially "De boer die sterft," which deals with the life of Flemish peasants.

W.'s essays tend to shed more light on his own personality than on the subjects they deal with, and his work in general can be seen as a symbolic autobiography revealing his own tormented spiritual life. Along with Guido Gezelle (1830–99), he is considered the greatest representative in Flemish writing of "autumnal," world-weary *fin de siècle* literature.

FURTHER WORKS: *De Vlaamse primitieven* (1903); *Verzen* (1905); *De vrouw van Kandaules* (1908); *Kunst en geest in Vlaanderen* (1911); *Substrata* (1924); *Beginselen der Chemie* (1925); *Het zatte hart* (1926); *De leemen torens* (with H. Teirlinck; 2 vols., 1928); *De schroeflijn* (2 vols., 1928); *De nieuwe Esopet* (1933); *Over schrijvers en boeken* (2 vols., 1933); *Nagelaten gedichten* (1942); *Verzameld Werk* (8 vols., 1948–50); *Verzamelde Gedichten* (1953)

BIBLIOGRAPHY: Gijsen, M., *W.* (1920); Teirlinck, H., *W.* (1958); Westerlinck, A., *W.* (2nd ed., 1960); Kazemier, G., *In de voorhof der poezie: Inleiding tot het Nederlands vers* (1965)

JORIS TAELS

WOLFE, Thomas Clayton

American novelist, b. 3 Oct. 1900, Asheville, North Carolina; d. 15 Sept. 1938, Baltimore, Maryland

W.'s fame rests upon four autobiographical novels—two of them published posthumously —constituting virtually one *roman fleuve* that transmutes the experiences of three decades into an American legend. An epic scope in time and space and a variety of matter and styles distinguish his work from the many developmental novels.

The first twenty years of W.'s life are paralleled by Eugene Gant's story in *Look Homeward, Angel* (1929). The youngest child of a Pennsylvania tombstone maker and a North Carolina schoolteacher, W. was all his life to suffer from the heritage due to his eccentric and incompatible parents. Within him warred the North and the South, hunger for experience versus lust for the accumulation of property, passion for rhetoric and inexhaustible memory.

Dominated by his mother's possessive love, W. was deprived of a normal family life

THOMAS WOLFE

VIRGINIA WOOLF

because she ran a boarding house. Though unconventional in their lives, his parents accepted middle-class conventions and sent W. to a private school—where his nascent talent was recognized—and then to the University of North Carolina. His sense of isolation and alienation from his family increased, but it was not until the death of his favorite brother, Ben, in 1918, that W. felt free to begin his voyage of self-discovery. His lyric account of Ben's death in *Look Homeward, Angel* is one of those matchless episodes that are W.'s most characteristic and distinguished achievements. In 1920, the same year his father died of cancer, W. left Asheville, only to re-create it in fiction as Altamont and give it a permanent place in American literary geography.

The fictionalized autobiography in *Of Time and the River* (1935) begins with the departure of Eugene-Thomas for Harvard to pursue, in George Pierce Baker's (1866–1935) famous 47 Workshop, the misdirected attempts at playwriting that were to absorb W. until 1925. Baker's influence ultimately proved less seminal than that of another teacher, John Livingston Lowes (1867–1945).

W. taught briefly at New York University, 1924–25, before leaving on the first of several trips to Europe. It was during this voyage abroad that W. decided that his native tradition provided rich resources for fiction.

In *The Web and the Rock* (1939), W. replaced Eugene Gant with a new hero, George Webber, but the change is unimportant since Book IV begins where *Of Time and the River* ended, with the hero's shipboard encounter with Esther. The novel offers a fictionalized account of the tempestuous liaison between W. and Aline Bernstein, the original of Esther. Mrs. Bernstein, a talented scene designer many years W.'s senior, was to him a mother substitute, a mistress, and a literary patron. The formless manuscript that was to be *Look Homeward, Angel* was written between 1926 and 1927, when financial aid from Mrs. Bernstein allowed W. to stop teaching. He resumed teaching again in September 1927, after a brief trip to Europe. On his fourth trip abroad, in 1928, he was injured at the Munich Oktoberfest—an incident reflected in the end of *The Web and the Rock*. Shortly after his recovery, W. got news that Maxwell Perkins, the famous editor of Scribner's publishing company, was interested in his hitherto luckless manuscript. For the next eight months, W. and Perkins worked together to trim the manuscript to its final form.

What Body told Spirit at the end of *The Web and the Rock* is the title of W.'s last novel: *You Can't Go Home Again* (1940). The two preceding novels had dealt with W.'s struggles as a fledgling author; the fourth and final novel deals with the penalties of success and the continuing agonies of creation. Fictionalized in it are W.'s visit to Asheville in September 1929; the subsequent success of *Look Homeward, Angel* and the indignant furor in Asheville; his experiences in the New York literary world; his break with Aline Bernstein; his year abroad on a Guggenheim grant (1930–31); his association with Perkins as his editor, friend, and father figure; and his lonely life in Brooklyn from 1931 to 1935 while writing *Of Time and the River*, much of his last two novels, and the short stories that supplemented his novels.

W.'s break with Perkins in 1936 marked his independence as a writer and thinker and his maturity as a person. On his last trip abroad, W. saw the terrors of the Nazi regime in Germany and turned to America for hope in the future.

In December 1937, W. signed a contract with Harper's publishing company. Several months before he died of a tuberculosis infection of the brain, he delivered a huge manuscript to his editor, Edward Aswell. Full responsibility for the two posthumous novels therefore rested upon Aswell, and the last years of W.'s life are not presented in his own final literary version.

W.'s evolution as an artist is marked by his progress from lyrical romanticism to satirical realism, from reactionary provinciality to cosmopolitan liberalism, from self-centered nostalgia to concern for others and faith in the future. *Look Homeward, Angel* deals with the discovery of the buried life; it shows the young artist in conflict with himself, his family, and society. The angel of creativity, the ghost of the lonely spirit, the stone of the solid earth, the leaf of transient beauty, the door of fellowship, and the train of wandering and exile are the dominant symbols.

In *Of Time and the River*, the quest of self-discovery also becomes the quest for a father and an exploration of America and Europe. Eugene Gant is the Protean hero of legend: Orestes, Young Faustus, Telemachus, Jason. The river is the river of life and the rivers of America. In this second and possibly best novel, W. most successfully interwove the themes and motifs also used in his other works. It also presents most fully the insatiable Faustian hunger and the Renaissance exuberance that generated his luxuriant style and abundant subject matter.

As W. explained in *The Story of a Novel* (1936), an analysis of the creative process, *Of Time and the River* represents a cycle of wandering and hunger, and *The Web and the Rock* —then a work in progress—begins a cycle of "greater certitude" and "a single passion." The "web" is the web of human life, the "rock" is the fabulous city. The struggle to create involves also the struggle between town and city, man and woman, Gentile and Jew, naiveté and sophistication. W.'s satire on the New York literary world matches his treatment of the Harvard drama school in *Of Time and the River*.

Greater objectivity is finally achieved in *You Can't Go Home Again*, in which W.'s immersion in the consciousness of others and his concern with social ills show growing objectivity. Nevertheless, the novel ends on a wholly personal note: the letter to Foxhall Edwards (Maxwell Perkins) and a "Credo," in which W. affirms his faith in the future and expresses a premonition of his death.

W. did not live to outgrow the faults of a youthful writer, but in fiction that combines poetry and realism, he portrayed the young man as artist, and he created a myth of America.

FURTHER WORKS: *From Death to Morning* (1935); *A Note on Experts: Dexter Vespasian Joyner* (1939); *The Face of a Nation* (1939); *The Hills Beyond* (1941); *T. W.'s Letters to His Mother* (1943); *A Stone, A Leaf, A Door* (1946); *The Portable T. W.* (1946); *Mannerhouse* (1948); *A Western Journal* (1951); *The Correspondence of T. W. and Homer Andrew Watt* (1954); *The Letters of T. W.* (1956); *The Short Novels of T. W.* (1961); *The Notebooks of T. W.* (1970)

BIBLIOGRAPHY: Beach, J. W., *American Fiction, 1920–1940* (1941); Kazin, A., *On Native Grounds* (1942); Preston, G. R., *T. W.: A Bibliography* (1943); Muller, H., *T. W.* (1947); Perkins, M., "T. W.," *Harvard Library Bulletin*, I (1947); Johnson, P. H., *Hungry Gulliver* (1948); Walser, R., ed., *The Enigma of T. W.: Biographical and Critical Selections* (1953); Gelfant, B. H., *The American City Novel* (1954); Rubin, L. D., *T. W.: The*

Weather of His Youth (1955); Cowley, M., "T. W.," *Atlantic Monthly*, CC (1957); Watkins, F., *T. W.'s Characters* (1957); Johnson, E. D., *T. W.: A Bibliography, with a Character Index of His Works* (1959); Holman, C. H., *T. W.* (1960); Nowell, E., *T. W.* (1960); Walser, R., *T. W.: An Introduction and Interpretation* (1961); Wheaton, M. W., and Blythe, L., *T. W. and His Family* (1961); Kennedy, R. S., *The Window of Memory* (1962); Fisher, V., *T. W. as I Knew Him* (1963); McElderry, B. R., *T. W.* (1964); Special W. issue, *MFS*, XI (1965), iii; Raynolds, R., *T. W.* (1965); Turnbull, A., *T. W.* (1967); Austin, N. F., *A Biography of T. W.* (1968); Field, L., ed., *T. W.: Three Decades of Criticism* (1968); Johnson, E. D., *T. W.: A Checklist* (1970)

ELIZABETH M. KERR

WOLKER, Jiří

Czech poet, playwright, and short-story writer, b. 29 March 1900, Prostějov; d. there, 3 Jan. 1924

The son of a bank clerk, W. acquired a sound education in the classical and modern languages. As a youth, he was first attracted to painting and music. While studying law at the University of Prague he attended lectures given in the faculty of arts, mainly those of the famous critic F. X. Šalda (q.v.). W. contracted tuberculosis during the course of his studies and died before his twenty-fourth birthday.

Inspired by Victor Hugo (1802–1885), at fourteen W. wrote a poetic drama entitled *Zrádce*. His initial adult works were strongly influenced by Fráňa Šrámek (1887–1952) and, to a lesser extent, by S. K. Neumann (1875–1947) and Hora (q.v.), but he soon found an individual poetic voice in which his personal gentleness merged with revolt against social injustice.

W.'s first collection of poems, *Host do domu* (1921), expressed his love of life and his sense of fraternity with the oppressed. These poems carried on the tradition of pre-World War I Czech poets who wanted to introduce everyday events into the world of poetry. Drawing their strength from childhood reminiscences, the poems showed the dawning of a social conscience. Their realism and sincerity immediately established W. as a popular poet.

W.'s long poem "Svatý Kopeček," originally published separately in 1921 but later added to *Host do domu*, is a semi-epic that illustrates

W.'s increasing attraction toward the social themes that were more fully developed in a book of poems entitled *Těžká hodina* (1922). This collection's humanitarian compassion for the exploited established W. as the chief representative of postwar "proletarian poetry." It contains some of W.'s most powerful poems— "Tvář za sklem," "Jaro," "Moře," and "Mirogoj"—and ballads. The best known of the latter, "Balada o očích topičových" ("The Eyes of the Stoker," 1958) most aptly expresses W.'s celebration of the exploited working classes and his dramatization of the struggle for social justice.

In his posthumously published poems, W.'s eroticism and personal joy is increasingly overshadowed by his awareness of social inequality and his presentiment of death. These themes are developed most powerfully in the poem "U roentgenu" (written in 1923).

Although primarily a poet, W. also wrote three one-act plays (1923), but they are of documentary rather than artistic interest. However, his posthumously published *Povídky a pohádky* (1925), in which he focuses on social and moral themes, is one of the few important attempts in Czech literature to modernize fairy tales.

W. is sometimes described as the poet of the young because his verse is permeated by strong, youthful emotions and lends itself to recitation. Powerful imagery and moving expressions of social compassion give his poetry a lasting appeal that influenced many poets of the interwar period.

FURTHER WORKS: *Spisy* (4 vols., 1924–54); *Listy příteli* (1950); *Korespondence s rodiči* (1952); *Listy dvou básníků* (1953). **Selected English translations:** Selections in *An Anthology of Czechoslovak Literature* (ed. P. Selver; 1929); *Modern Czech Poetry* (ed. E. Osers and J. K. Montgomery; 1945); *Hundred Towers* (ed. F. C. Weiskopf; 1945); *A Handful of Linden Leaves* (ed. E. Pargeter; 1958); *A Book of Czech Verse* (ed. A. French; 1958)

BIBLIOGRAPHY: Šalda, F. X., Introduction to *Spisy* (1924); Nezval, V., *W.* (1925); Kalista, A., *Kamarád W.* (1933); Wolkerová, A., *J. W. ve vzpomínkách své matky* (1937); Píša, A. M. et al., *J. W., příklad naší poesie* (1954); Soldán, F., *J. W.* (1964); French, A., *The Poets of Prague: Czech Poetry between the Wars* (1969), pp. 21–28

B. R. BRADBROOK

WOOLF, Virginia
English novelist and critic, b. 25 Jan. 1882, London; d. 28 March 1941, Lewes

Virginia W., daughter of the biographer and critic Sir Leslie Stephen (1832–1904), owed to her parents two things which, she later said, are the prerequisites of any literature: culture and money. Her parents also gave her entrée into a society of "highbrows," who, as she noted, were the only people capable of talking about human activities since they themselves did not do things and stood "between the acts" as spectators.

After her father's death Virginia W. began to contribute to the *Times Literary Supplement.* ("I made one pound ten and six by my first review; and I bought a Persian cat with the proceeds. Then I grew ambitious.... I must have a motor car. And thus it was that I became a novelist.") Her first novel, *The Voyage Out* (1915), appeared three years after her marriage to the critic and economist Leonard Woolf (b. 1880).

In 1917 the Woolfs founded the Hogarth Press, and the offices of their publishing house soon became a meeting place for young writers. Around the Woolfs gathered a society that included Roger Fry (1866–1934), Elizabeth Bowen, Forster, Garnett, Rosamond Lehmann, Spender, and Strachey (qq.v.), writers who became known as the Bloomsbury group (*see* English literature). T. S. Eliot (q.v.) called Virginia W. "the centre, not of a circle of initiates, but of London literary life." But this life exhausted her physically and mentally. World War I heightened her exhaustion to depression, and in 1918 Virginia W.'s fear of mental illness led to an emotional crisis. In 1941, during World War II, a similar crisis led to suicide by drowning.

From 1919 on Virginia W. was in revolt against traditional novel technique and its chief English representatives, Bennett, Wells, and Galsworthy (qq.v.), on the grounds that these writers "told stories" to which they attached philosophical theories. But human life, she claimed, escapes their well-ordered plots and their didactic rules. "Examine for a moment an ordinary mind on an ordinary day. The mind receives myriad impressions—trivial, fantastic, evanescent, or engraved with the sharpness of steel. From all sides they come, an incessant shower of innumerable atoms; and as they fall, as they shape themselves into the life of Monday or Tuesday... [they form] no plot, no comedy, no tragedy, no love interest or catastrophe in the accepted style. . . . Life is not a series of gig lamps symmetrically arranged; life is a luminous halo, a semitransparent envelope surrounding us from the beginning of consciousness to the end."

According to Virginia W., the writer's task is to "record the atoms as they fall upon the mind in the order in which they fall" and to convey this order and with it man's "unknown and uncircumscribed spirit." Thus the novel becomes a series of sensuous impressions, perceptions, musings, and reflections. To Virginia W. the scene of action is always the mind, the only principle that of time in John Locke's (1632–1704) sense of an "idea of succession." Her novels therefore reject the literary tradition of rationalistic narratives with a specific "thesis." Instead, they hark back to the philosophical tradition of Anglo-Saxon empiricism, and not, as some have argued, to the metaphysics of Henri Bergson (1859–1941), whose works she had never read.

In about 1914 such writers as D. H. Lawrence, Dorothy Richardson (qq.v.), Forster, and above all Joyce (q.v.) began to take up where David Hume's (1711–76) thought and Laurence Sterne's (1713–68) art had left off. Virginia W. said that what she was doing in *Jacob's Room* (1922) was "probably being better done by Mr. Joyce." In 1922 she read Proust's (q.v.) *À La Recherche du temps perdu* and collaborated on a translation of Fiodor Dostoyevski (1821–81): two writers whose works, she said, are examples of a literature "composed purely and wholly of the stuff of the soul," which "is about nothing at all."

Virginia W.'s conception of the novel has its analogue in the approach of those stage directors who sought to "dramatize" the theater, or in the technique of those painters who respected the surface on which they painted. Like Cézanne, Gauguin, Van Gogh, and Picasso, Virginia W. was also seeking an "equivalent of life." The painters tried to create a new reality that would be a correlative of their canvas and their colors; Virginia W.'s aim was to create forms of human existence through the discovery of an appropriate language. Since she wanted to capture the phenomena of consciousness, she was forced to break away from traditional prose because it was ill-suited to her purpose. Since she also wanted to depict characters who experience these phenomena she had to liberate herself from an "egoistic" subjective poetry.

Virginia W. experimented with the widest variety of styles; she blended prose and poetry, trying in this way to avoid violating either language or the nature of the novel. Here she anticipated to some extent what philosophical semantics and neopositivism later attempted. Her art taught 20th-c. writers the same lesson that Joyce and the Swiss novelist Ramuz (q.v.) did: that art is a series of craftsmanlike undertakings.

In 1921 Virginia W. published eight novellas collected in *Monday or Tuesday* (1921; reissued as *A Haunted House,* 1944), in which she departed from the relatively traditional technique of her first novels. These eight novellas present eight "moments of existence," eight bunches of impressions and ideas held together by the momentary mood of the mind that produces the events. Reflections on other writers' styles led to the sophisticated stylistic forms of the collection *The Common Reader* (1925). Here literary criticism assumes the novella form to such a degree that, in the three volumes that her husband published after her death—*The Death of the Moth* (1942), *The Captain's Death Bed* (1950), and *The Moment* (1947)—he placed novellas and essays side by side.

Virginia W., for the first time and in an exemplary manner, accomplished the task of fusing a series of "moments" into a novel in *Mrs. Dalloway* (1925). A June day in London, split up into segments of time by the striking of Big Ben, is peopled by characters acting contemporaneously with Mrs. Dalloway or in past or future times that she invokes in thought. Similarly, a single day is the subject of the first part of *To the Lighthouse* (1927): The Ramsay family and their guests during a prewar September afternoon in the Hebrides.

In Part II it is night. It is also a period during the war. "Time passes" over the deserted house. In Part III it is morning. The surviving characters return and complete the actions proposed in the first part. The symbolic framework of one day is revealed to contain several years.

After *Orlando* (1928), a parody of the classical story, came *A Room of One's Own* (1929), a sharp critique of woman's past and present situation. In *The Waves* (1931) Virginia W. compressed all the years of a human life into a time structure similar to the one used in *To the Lighthouse*. Through its style, *The Waves* gives final form to the theme of loneliness treated in her preceding books. One after

RICHARD WRIGHT

WILLIAM BUTLER YEATS

another, six characters, separated from one another and from their former selves, reveal themselves in monologues. The six lives of the six friends are represented by a series of atomistic roles suggesting Pirandello.

In *The Years* (1937) the history of English society from 1880 to 1936 is represented by a caravan of people who pass before us as in the process of living and dying they act out the comedy of death. This somewhat social novel was complemented by *Three Guineas* (1938), which attacked tyranny in all its forms.

Virginia W.'s working title for the latter publication was "The Next War," a title that might well have applied to *Between the Acts* (1941) in which the war is already perceptible. Beginning far back in time and leading up to the present, the latter novel evokes not only the history of English society but that of all mankind. It epitomizes Virginia W.'s lifework not only because, like *Mrs. Dalloway*, it symbolizes thousands of years in a single July day, or because it unites all her various styles, but because here the major literary problems to which she addressed herself harmoniously coalesce in the form of a novel.

In *Between the Acts* Virginia W. seems to be trying to end twenty-five years of experimentation by creating a microcosm to represent the characteristic world of the artist, the particular world of the English, and the world common to all men—a broken world, a world in tatters, ruins, and fragments. She wanted to take a risk, to change, to keep her eyes and her mind open. She refused to be stamped and stereotyped, as she once said to her critics.

FURTHER WORKS: *Two Stories* (with Leonard Woolf; 1917); *The Mark on the Wall* (1917); *Night and Day* (1919); *Kew Gardens* (1919); *An Unwritten Novel* (1920); *Mr. Bennett and Mrs. Brown* (1924); *Beau Brummel* (1930); *On Being Ill* (1930); *Street Haunting* (1930); *The Common Reader: 2nd Series* (1932; Am., The Second Common Reader, 1932); *A Letter to a Young Poet* (1932); *Flush* (1933); *Walter Sickert: A Conversation* (1934); *The Roger Fry Memorial Exhibition Address* (1935); *Reviewing* (1939); *Roger Fry* (1940); *A Writer's Diary* (ed. Leonard Woolf; 1953); *Virginia W. and Lytton Strachey: Letters* (eds. Leonard Woolf and James Strachey; 1958); *Granite and Rainbow* (1958); *Contemporary Writers* (1965); *Nurse Lugton's Golden Thimble* (1966); *Collected Essays* (ed. Leonard Woolf; 4 vols., 1966)

BIBLIOGRAPHY: Holtby, W., *V. W.* (1932); Forster, E. M., *V. W.* (1942); Bennett, J., *V. W.* (1945; rev. ed., 1965); Daiches, D., *V. W.* (1945; rev. ed., 1963); Auerbach, E., "The Brown Stocking," in *Mimesis* (1953); Chambers, R., *The Novels of V. W.* (1947); Pippet, A., *The Moth and the Star, A Biography of V. W.* (1953); Kirkpatrick, B. J., *A Bibliography of V. W.* (1957); Woodring, C., *V. W.* (1966); Woolf, L., *Downhill All the Way: An Autobiography of the Years 1919–1939*, Vol. I (1967), and *The Journey, Not the Arrival, Matters*, Vol. II (1970)

MAXIME CHASTAING

And the problem before her—the problem that she has set herself, and that certainly would inaugurate a new literature if solved—is to retain her own wonderful new method and form, and yet allow her readers to inhabit each character with Victorian thoroughness. Think how difficult this is. If you work in a storm of atoms and seconds, if your highest joy is "life; London; this moment in June" and your deepest mystery "here is one room; there another," then how can you construct your human beings so that each shall be not a movable monument but an abiding home, how can you build between them any permanent roads of love and hate? There was continuous life in the little hotel people of *The Voyage Out* because there was no innovation in the method. But Jacob in *Jacob's Room* is discontinuous, demanding—and obtaining—separate approval for everything he feels or does. And *Mrs. Dalloway?* There seems a slight change here, an approach towards character-construction in the Tolstoyan sense; Sir William Bradshaw, for instance, is uninterruptedly and embracingly evil. Any approach is significant, for it suggests that in future books she may solve the problem as a whole. She herself believes it can be done, and, with the exception of Joyce, she is the only writer of genius who is trying. All the other so-called innovators are (if not pretentious bunglers) merely innovators in subject matter and the praise we give them is of the kind we should accord to scientists. . . . But they do not advance the novelist's art. Virginia W. has already done that a little, and if she succeeds in her problem of rendering character, she will advance it enormously.

E. M. Forster, *Abinger Harvest* (1936), pp. 110–11

Virginia W. seemed to have the worst defect of the Mandarin style, the ability to spin cocoons of language out of nothing. The history of her literary style has been that of a form at first simple, growing more and more elaborate, the content lagging far behind, then catching up, till, after the falseness of *Orlando*, she produced a masterpiece in *The Waves*.

Her early novels were not written in an elaborate style. Her most significant early book is *Monday or Tuesday* (1921) and demonstrates the rule that Mandarin prose is the product of those who in their youth were poets. In short it is romantic prose. Not all poets were romantic prose writers (e.g. Dryden) but most romantic prose writers have attempted poetry.

The development of Virginia W. is the development of this lyrical feeling away from E. M. Forster, with his artlessness and simple, poetical, colloquial style, into patterns of her own. The reveries of a central character came more and more to dominate her books. In *The Waves* she abandoned the convention of the central figure and described a group of friends, as children, as young people and finally in late middle age. In a series of tableaux are contrasted the mystery of childhood, the promise of youth, the brilliance of maturity and the complex, unmarketable richness of age. If *The Years* seems an impressionist gallery with many canvases, landscapes, portraits, and conversation pieces, then *The Waves* is a group of five or six huge panels which celebrate the dignity of human life and the passage of time. It is one of the books which comes nearest to stating the mystery of life and so, in a sense, nearest to solving it.

Cyril Connolly, *Enemies of Promise* (1948), p. 49

The distinguishing feature of Virginia W.'s apprehension of life lies precisely in its passivity; and furthermore, she subscribed unwittingly . . . to a view of life which placed a primary emphasis upon the object. . . .

This sort of initial inward inertia at once obviates the very possibility of meaning, which cannot conceivably subsist inherently in the world of objects. Virginia W.'s search for "significance" on the primitive level of primary sensational perceptions, therefore, was chimerical from the beginning. And indeed, it is a typical feature of the characters in her novels to be altogether lacking in the capacity for discriminating within experience. They are passively caught up in the stream of events, of "life," of their own random perceptions. The furthest Virginia W. could move in the direction of a positive act of belief was towards the undiscriminating and finally pointless embracing of everything, which is featured in *Mrs. Dalloway*—a comprehensive gesture which itself obviated the very possibility of order achieved through discrimination, since it was precisely discrimination which was repudiated. This very gesture, when its perpetuation became impossible—resulted in an inevitable surrender to eventual explicit meaninglessness.

Derek S. Savage, *The Withered Branch* (1950), p. 95

Mrs. Dalloway walking down Regent Street was aware of the glitter of shop windows, the smooth passage of cars, the conversation of shoppers, but it was only a Regent Street seen by Mrs. Dalloway that was conveyed to the reader: a charming whimsical rather sentimental prose poem was what Regent Street had become: a current of air, a touch of scent, a sparkle of glass. But, we protest, Regent Street too has a right to exist; it is more real than Mrs. Dalloway, and we look back with nostalgia towards the shop houses, the mean courts, the still Sunday streets of Dickens.

Graham Greene, *The Lost Childhood and Other Essays* (1951), p. 70

Mrs. W.'s particular kind of refinement of life led eventually to the emergence of one theme which dominates all her fiction, from *Mrs Dalloway* to *The Years*. This is a theme characteristically abstract, characteristically philosophical, to which action, character, and commentary are alike subordinated; the theme of time, death, and personality and the relations of these three to each other and to some ultimate which includes them all. Significance in events is increasingly judged in terms of these three factors. It is not so much the quality of the observation of life which makes her points, but reflection after observation. A twofold process of rarification goes on. First, life is refined before it is observed with the artist's eye; second, the results of observation are meditatively chewed on as they are being presented to the reader. A certain lack of body in her work is the result.

David Daiches, "Virginia Woolf," in *Critiques and Essays on Modern Fiction 1920–1951* (1952), p. 492

She undoubtedly wanted to discover a new technique for the novelist which would make it possible to portray the inner reality very truthfully; she wanted to show, moreover, that this reality could be only an inner one. Unlike Sartre, Virginia W., in her maturity, did not judge; unlike Lawrence, she did not preach. She was concerned simply to offer the reader a fresher and newer view of life, to open his eyes, to enable him to discover, under surface events, the bare perceptible movements of thoughts and emotions.

André Maurois, *Points of View* (1968), p. 377

WOUK, Herman

American novelist and playwright, b. 27 May 1915, New York City

The son of Russian-Jewish immigrant parents and the grandson of a rabbi, W. has adhered to the traditions of Orthodox Judaism. After his graduation from Columbia College in 1934, he worked for a time as a radio gagwriter, and though he achieved considerable social and financial success in the radio/show-business world, he found both the work and the environment unsatisfying. He enlisted in the navy after the Japanese attack on Pearl Harbor and spent three years as an officer on a destroyer-minesweeper in the Pacific. Much of *Aurora Dawn* (1947), first novel of the New York advertising world, was written while W. was in the service.

The Caine Mutiny (1951), which grew out of W.'s navy experience during World War II, won the Pulitzer Prize and was phenomenally popular both here and abroad. A vivid narrative of life aboard a destroyer-minesweeper commanded by the severe and arbitrary Captain Queeg, *The Caine Mutiny* deals with the problem of responsible and mature action under extreme circumstances. W. clearly suggests that though Queeg is a tyrant and a coward, the true villain is Keefer, a self-centered intellectual who instigates the mutiny, although he is careful not to become involved in it. W. adapted the last section of the book into a successful Broadway play, *The Caine Mutiny Court-Martial* (1954).

Marjorie Morningstar (1955) implicitly contrasts the stability and values of Jewish tradition with the seemingly attractive but ultimately sterile world of the deracinated, Jewish pseudo-intellectual. *Youngblood Hawke* (1962) is the story of a powerful young Southern novelist who markedly resembles Thomas Wolfe (q.v.).

At its best, W.'s writing has narrative clarity and vividness of description and characterization. An admirer of Dickens and Lev Tolstoi (q.v.), W. is a traditional realist in style and a philosophical moralist in outlook. Many critics find him bourgeois and anti-intellectual. While the didacticism of his writing is sometimes too apparent, he is nevertheless capable of stating perennial moral problems in dramatic and realistic situations, using the moral education of his protagonists to compel that of his readers.

FURTHER WORKS: *The City Boy* (1948); *The Traitor* (1949); *This Is My God* (1959); *Don't Stop the Carnival* (1965)

BIBLIOGRAPHY: *Time*, 5 Sept. 1955; Horchler, R. T., "Marjorie Morningstar," *Commonweal*, 4 Nov. 1955; Carpenter, F. I., "H. W.," *College English*, XVII (Jan. 1956); Cohen, J., "W.'s Morningstar and Hemingway's Sun," *South Atlantic Quarterly*, LVIII (Spring 1959); McElderry, B. R., Jr., "The Conservative as Novelist," *Arizona Quarterly*, XV (Spring 1959); On *Youngblood Hawke*—Smith, W. J., *Commonweal*, 29 June 1962; On *Don't Stop the Carnival*—Buitenhuis, P., *New York Times Book Review*, 14 March 1965

DOROTHY TUCK MCFARLAND

WRIGHT, Richard

American novelist, short-story writer, and essayist, b. 4 Sept. 1908, Natchez, Mississippi; d. 28 Nov. 1960, Paris

The son of a Negro country school teacher whose sharecropper husband deserted the family, W. had an impoverished, violent, and nomadic childhood. He was raised by various relatives whose religious and social strictures he vigorously resisted. Frequently transferred from one segregated school to another; brought up as a Seventh Day Adventist in a culture whose dominant religion was Baptist; isolated from the folk culture of Southern Negroes when he had to learn how to survive on the streets of Memphis, W. always felt himself to be an outsider among his own race. His struggle to grow into manhood, to forge an adult identity for himself, was to provide him with the central theme of his fiction.

The vocationally decisive events of W.'s youth were his discovery of Mencken's (q.v.) *Book of Prefaces*—which inspired in him a passion for literature that was deeply involved with his passionate resolve to escape from the South—and his conversion to Marxism. From 1932, when he joined the John Reed Club in Chicago, until the early 1940's, when he broke with the communists, the party was a "home" that provided him not only with "the first sustained relationships in my life" but with the "ideological equivalent" of his experience.

In 1935, W. landed a job on the Writers' Project of WPA as a result of having published a few poems with titles such as "I Am a Red Slogan." Two years later, he moved from Chicago to New York, where he became Harlem editor of the *Daily World* and a frequent contributor to other left-wing periodicals. His literary apprenticeship ended in 1938 when his first book, a collection of four novellas called *Uncle Tom's Children*, won the $500 prize offered by *Story* for the best work of fiction by a writer on WPA.

Uncle Tom's Children traces the growth of the race from adolescence to maturity, from sonship to fatherhood, from gang life to political leadership. Most importantly, it depicts a coherent process of revolt, of which each novella represents a distinct phase. Big Boy's impulsive act of self-defense and retaliation will, in the final novella, undergo the discipline of Taylor's maturity and become an organized protest. Mann—his name, like Big Boy's, declares the mythic design that connects the novellas—has fantasies of escaping his doom by slaughtering his white enemies, but his deed, like his child, never comes to birth; he is checked by a Christian passivity. In Silas, these fantasies become articulate; and, by discovering his great rage, he becomes aware of his relation to white society and to himself.

In *Uncle Tom's Children*, W. showed himself to be a master story-teller. Plot is the soul of each novella; and all the plots are concentrated into a single day and night of terror and violence that frees or dooms the protagonist.

Although W.'s fiction has, with justice, been called "protest realism," his characters struggle for survival in a world of romance, a precarious and irrational world threatened by flood, fire, mountains, bogs, wild animals, Chicago snowstorms. In *Native Son* it is "a world of magic whiteness without sound," a terrifying dreamscape.

In W.'s work, white society is always symbolically associated with some great and destructive force of nature. A "white blur"—nameless, ghostly, all-pervasive—paralyzes the will and terrifies the imaginations of the blacks. The person whose very presence irrevocably condemns the hero might appear at any moment. The white woman surprising Big Boy at a swimming hole; Mr. Heartfield shining his light on Mann; blind Mrs. Dalton, in white robes, entering the bedroom where Bigger Thomas stands over Mary—all catch the Negro in a forbidden situation. And W.'s protagonists, whose lives have been spent in a desperate effort of self-concealment, are suddenly compelled to declare themselves: they murder, and they are hunted down. W.'s books are about fugitives, and he always writes powerfully when describing the nightmare of their flight.

Native Son (1940) is one of the most important and celebrated novels about Negro life in America. It opened up an uncharted region for the novel: the environment and the psyche of a young Negro who, by force of circumstance, becomes a heroic embodiment of the American myth of the "bad nigger." Governed by Bigger's point of view, the novel brilliantly

presents his inner life by means of dramatic imagery. It succeeds as a radical indictment of white America in the first two sections, where the sources of Bigger's compulsive violence are vividly apprehended. But, in the final section, where W. offers an ideological explanation of Bigger's acts, the narrative loses its concentration and power.

Bigger's "supreme and meaningful act" is his murder of Mary Dalton, a young communist whose friendliness arouses the shame and dread and hate that he has been struggling to suppress. His killing of her, which he experiences as an act of self-creation, fills him with the pride and the sense of competence that come with the discovery of one's vocation; and it initiates a series of epiphanies by which he comes into conscious possession of his life.

The themes of self-concealment and self-discovery, of paralysis and violent self-assertion, provide the dramatic center of W.'s autobiography, *Black Boy* (1945). It is a book of battles, a record of a boy's struggle against a world of adults who all share the great secret of race and who participate, as mediators of a social code that stifles every positive impulse the boy feels, in a fierce and religious war to break his spirit, to make him accept his role as a "nigger." It is also a cultural document of great value because of W.'s faithfulness to his experience of poverty and oppression; and because, in the magnificent portraits of his Dickensian grandparents, his paralyzed mother, his coworker Shorty, and his various white employers, W. portrays the sickness and suffering of a whole society.

After 1946, when W. moved permanently to Paris, his creative powers underwent a marked decline. He wrote three books of distinguished journalism, lectured on "The Psychological Reactions of Oppressed People," and, having repudiated the South and the Communist Party, wrote two bad novels—*The Outsider* (1953) and *Savage Holiday* (1954)—in which he was groping for a new subject and a new philosophy.

In *The Long Dream* (1958), W. returned to his primary sources. Cogently depicting the sociological arrangements between the black and white communities of a Southern town and presenting a remarkable portrayal of the relation between a Negro father and son, W.'s last novel broadened and deepened his imaginative world.

W.'s way of mastering white racism, which insisted that he conceal his thoughts and his emotions, even from himself, was to dedicate his life to discovering and telling the truth about his growing up and to forge the experience of his race into the central myth that governs his finest works. His novels, which fuse the naturalism of the traditional *Bildungsroman* and the nightmare-symbols of Gothic romance, were the first novels of considerable power to present the meaning of Negro experience in America.

FURTHER WORKS: *Twelve Million Black Voices* (1941); *Black Power* (1954); *The Color Curtain* (1956); *Pagan Spain* (1957); *White Man, Listen!* (1957); *Eight Men* (1961); *Lawd Today* (1963)

BIBLIOGRAPHY: Embree, E. R., *Thirteen against the Odds* (1944), pp. 25–46; Ellison, R., "R. W.'s Blues," *Antioch Review,* V (June 1945), pp. 198–211; Gloster, H. M., *Negro Voices in American Fiction* (1948), pp. 222–34; Baldwin, J., "Many Thousands Gone," in *Notes of a Native Son* (1955); Baldwin, J., "Alas, Poor Richard," in *Nobody Knows My Name* (1961); Margolies, E., *The Art of R. W.* (1969); McCall, D., *The Example of R. W.* (1969)

MARC KAMINSKY

WYSPIAŃSKI, Stanisław

Polish dramatist and painter, b. 15 Jan. 1869, Cracow; d. there, 28 Nov. 1907

W. is of particular significance as a dramatist because he destroyed 19th-c. realistic conventions to make way for bold, imaginative experiments. At the same time he renewed the tradition of the Polish romantic theater, combining it with elements of Greek drama. This is especially evident in the tragedy *Klątwa* (1899), which concerns a priest's guilt and atonement. National legends and historical events often provided W.'s themes, which he then related to contemporary problems. Symbolic figures and beings drawn from the indefinite realm between a dream world and reality are often employed alongside realistically drawn characters.

W.'s best-known work is his play *Wesele* (1901), which is not without a certain amount of patriotic rhetoric. Here he uses the technique of the *szopka,* the Christmas puppet play of Poland. The legendary-historical drama *Bolesław Śmiały* (1903) deals on one level with King Bolesław the Bold's murder of a bishop and on a deeper level with the conflict between secular and ecclesiastical power. *Wyzwolenie* (1903) is a patriotic fantasy play done in the *commedia dell'arte* manner.

W.'s verse is deliberately crude, and its rhythmic diversity is well suited to the clear expression of complicated themes. His works introduce a new trend, which Leon Schiller, the leading Polish stage director of the first half of this century, called "monumental theater." A similar tendency is found in the plays of Rostworowski (q.v.).

FURTHER WORKS: *Legenda* (1897); *Meleager* (1898; Eng., 1933); *Warszawianka* (1898); *Protesilas i Laodamia* (1899); *Lelewel* (1899); *Legjon* (1900); *Kazimierz Wielki* (1900); *Bolesław Chrobry* (1900); *Achilleis* (1903); *Piast* (1903); *Akropolis* (1904); *Noc listopadowa* (1904); *Skałka* (1907); *Powrót Odysa* (1907; The Return of Odysseus, 1966); *Sędziowie* (1907); *Daniel* (1907); *Dzieła* (8 vols., 1924–32); *Dzieła zebrane* (16 vols., 1958 ff.)

BIBLIOGRAPHY: Marković, Z., *Der Begriff des Dramas bei W.* (1915); Krakowski, E., *Charles Péguy et S. W.* (1937); Backvis, C., *Le dramaturge S. W.* (1952); Natanson, W., *S. W.* (1965)

* * *

X

XENÓPOULOS, Grigóris
Greek novelist, dramatist, and critic, b. 9 Dec. 1867, Constantinople; d. 14 Jan. 1951, Athens

One of the leading Greek literary figures for close to six decades, X. grew up on the island of Zante, which was to provide him with the social milieu for his most successful novels and theatrical works. Like many others of the "Generation of 1880," X. began writing in *katharévousa,* the priest language of the Greek kingdom, but he soon accepted demotic, popular speech as a literary tool.

Although he wrote scores of novels and dramatic works, X. was equally important as a critic, journalist, and editor. In 1894 he took over *I diáplasis ton pédon,* a highly important children's periodical that he edited until his death. In 1927, X. founded *Néa Estía,* which was to be Greece's longest-lived literary periodical. He was elected to the Academy of Athens in 1931.

Like his contemporaries, X. turned to the Greek people for theme and mood, but for historical reasons Zante society was much different from that of the rest of Greece. Whereas the mainland, the Peloponnesus, Crete, and the Aegean Islands had been plundered and brutalized by four centuries of Ottoman rule, the Ionian islands had developed a dense and complex society under the Venetians and the British. X.'s fiction and drama, therefore, focus on a many-leveled social world and the relationships between aristocrats—whether wealthy or impoverished—the ambitious middle class, and the peasants.

Critics agree that the most significant achievement in X.'s prolific production is the

ambitious and uncharacteristic "social trilogy" composed of *Ploúsyi ke ftohí* (1919), *Tímyi ke átimi* (1921–22), and *Tiherí ke átihi* (1924). Related by theme rather than commonly shared protagonists, the "trilogy" is often cited as proof of X.'s awareness of the flaws in a society he loved.

Unlike X.'s other works, these three novels are convincing expressions of a somber view of life. They contain none of the artistic compromises—star-crossed lovers, "picturesque" Zantean customs, etc.—with which X. achieved his initial goal of popularity and financial independence. (X. was the first modern Greek literary man to live solely on his income as a writer—a feat few others have been able to duplicate.)

X.'s work in the theater is significant because it provides a link (in a dramatic repertory almost devoid of continuity) between Antonio Matesis's *Vasilikós* (1829–30) and Christomanos's *Néa Skiní,* with which Modern Greek theater can be said to begin. A prolific and popular dramatist, X. was also important as an astute critic.

Though few of X.'s works, tailored as they were for the sentimental audiences of his time, have borne the test of time, his historical importance cannot be questioned. He played an important role in convincing the general public of the literary worth of demotic Greek. In addition, he was instrumental in establishing a theater that focused on contemporary social problems.

FURTHER WORKS: *Nikólaos Sigálos* (1890); *Margaríta Stéfa* (1893); *I mitriá* (1897; The Stepmother, 1897); *Stélla Violánte* (1901); *Diiyímata* (3 series, 1901–1907); *To mistikó tis Kontésas Valérenas* (1903); *O kókinos vráhos* (1905); *Fotiní Sánti* (1908); *Láoura* (1917); *O pólemos* (1919); *Teréza Várma Dacósta* (1926); *Thíon óniron* (1951); *Ta ápanda* (10 vols., 1958). **Selected English translation:** *Divine Dream* (in *Introduction to Modern Greek Literature,* ed. M. Gianos; 1969)

BIBLIOGRAPHY: Special Christmas issue, "Afiéroma ston X.," *Néa Estía,* XIII (1951), dxcvii, 167–96; Karandónis, A., "Ta mithistorímata tou X.," *Elinikí dimiuryía,* VII (1951); Sahínis, A., *To néo Elinikó mithistórima* (1958); Mélas, S., "G. X.," in *Modern Greek Literature* (1962); Thrílos, A., "G. X.," in *Morfés tis Elinikís pezografíás* (1963)

THOMAS DOULIS

XHOSA LITERATURE

One of the most important of the Bantu languages of South Africa, Xhosa is also the earliest to have undergone the literary impact of the West. The first known work is a Christian hymn that was composed orally by a preliterate convert named Ntsikana (ca. 1873–ca. 1920) during the early years of the 19th c. Until the conquest of Xhosaland in 1877, the composition of hymns was the main literary activity there. Scattered poems in the vernacular press during the last quarter of the century testify to increasing doubts about the beneficence of the white man's intervention.

The first prominent Xhosa author was S. E. K. Mghayi (1875–1945), whose career began with *Ityala CamaWele* (1914), a play in defense of the traditional manner of administering justice. A prolific writer and a highly esteemed praise-poet, Mghayi also published several biographical works, including his own autobiography (1939), and a utopian novel, *U-Don Jadu,* that projects the ideal future he envi-sioned for Africa. Henry M. Ndawo (d. 1949) and Enoch S. Guma, his less-gifted contemporaries, composed edifying novelettes such as the latter's *Nomalizo* (1918; Eng. 1928). Mghayi's generation also included the first Xhosa female writer, L. Kakaza, whose only novel appeared in 1914.

With the next generation Xhosa literature came into its own. Guybon B. Sinxo (1902–1962) introduced the theme of native exploitation in the industrial city with a series of outspokenly realistic novels that described the misery and the moral degradation of slum life. In 1936, James J. R. Jolobe (b. 1902) published *Omyezo* (Poems of an African, 1946), a volume of deeply Christian poems that introduced lyrical descriptive motives unknown to the Xhosa tradition of praise-poetry. Some poems focused on important events in the past of the Xhosa nation, others provided an oblique criticism of South African racism. Jolobe's *Amathunzi obomi* (1958), the first original play composed in Xhosa, deals with Bantu urban life.

The most ambitious Xhosa novel is *Ingqumbo yeminyanya* (1940), a masterpiece and the only work of Archibald C. Jordan (b. 1906). A breathtaking story of social and cultural change in some of the Xhosa people, it is a perceptive and genuinely tragic treatment of two of the major themes of modern African literature: the conflict between traditional misoneism and the need for modernization; and the rejection of clan authority by the educated young in favor of individual choice in matters of love and marriage.

Since World War II, there has been a vast increase in the production of Xhosa literature, but because vernacular writing is now aimed mainly at schoolchildren and because of the interdiction against treating basic political, social, and racial topics, there has been no correspondent growth in quality.

ALBERT S. GÉRARD

Y

YAMAMOTO Yūzō

Japanese dramatist and novelist, b. 27 July 1887, Tochigi

In 1915 Y. graduated from Tokyo Imperial University with a degree in German, having written his graduation thesis on Strindberg (q.v.). He then tried his hand at writing and stage-managing for a theatrical troupe. In two short years, however, financial considerations led him to accept a teaching position at Waseda University as an instructor in the German language. This academic involvement resulted in the publication of his translations of the works of Strindberg and Schnitzler (qq.v.).

The appearance of *Inochi no Kammuri* (1920; Crown of Life, 1935), based upon a trip to Sakhalin almost ten years earlier, brought Y.'s dramatic efforts to the serious attention of the public. The hero of this play places his foreign financial commitment above the more practical, and Confucian, responsibilities to his family. Here Y. raises the issue of conflicting loyalties in the modern world and resolves the conflict by affirming the further removed as opposed to the familiar and immediate. This progressive position is a continuing characteristic of his works.

In 1920 Y., together with Kikuchi Kan and Akutagawa Ryūnosuke, helped to found The Association of Dramatists (Gekisakka-kyokai). Six years later he was instrumental in uniting this association with the Association of Novelists (Shōsetsuka-kyokai) to form The Association of Writers (Bungeika-kyokai). In all such endeavors his aim was to raise the position and protect the rights of writers. During the 1920's he served as editor of the briefly influential

journal *Engeki Shinchō* ("New Tides of Drama").

In 1926 Y. turned his attention to the writing of fiction. With characteristic enthusiasm he immersed himself both stylistically and thematically in the social issues of his day. In style he strove to establish a middle ground between the pulp fiction and the aesthetic prose of the period. As a champion of this *chūkanshōsetsu* (midway fiction) he wrote long, carefully written serialized novels designed to reach an audience that lacked a ready command of the large number of Chinese characters demanded by the more erudite writers.

In his choice of themes Y. has taken particular interest in the struggle by women for equality. In *Onna no isshō* (1932–33; "The Life of a Woman"), which appeared serially in the *Asahi Shimbun*, he presented the dilemma of a woman caught between her wish to pursue a career in medicine and the pressure to assume a more traditional role within society. Her final decision was to seek fulfillment in her profession.

Sensitive treatment of Y.'s heroines is also to be found in his dramatic works. In the feudal setting of *Sakazaki Dewa-no-kami* (1921; Sakazaki, Lord Dewa, 1935) and in his portrayal of the putative mistress of the American consul general Townsend Harris in *Nyonin aishi* (1930; The Story of Chink Okichi, 1935), Y. offers a sympathetic view of female suffering in a traditional society.

As a consequence of his desire to elevate popular literature, Y. has played a leading role in the effort to simplify the Japanese writing system. Even before World War II he served on several national committees who wished to limit the number of Chinese characters in general use. Immediately after the war he became politically active as the leader of the Ryokufu-kai (Green Breeze Society), whose platform contained programs directed at making Japan's literary heritage more readily available to the general public.

Setting an independent course between the doctrinaire realists and the idealistic Shirakaba-ha (White Birch Society), Y., with his intellectual capacities and humane spirit, has established himself as an important influence in Japan.

FURTHER WORKS: *Eijigoroshi* (1920; "Infanticide"); *Iki to shi ikeru mono* (1926; "All Living Things"); *Nami* (1928; "Waves"); *Kaze* (1930; "Wind"); *Shinjitsu ichiro* (1935–36; "The One Road to Truth"); *Robō no ishi* (1937; "The Stone by the Roadside"); *Yamamoto Yūzō zenshū* (1939–41; "The Complete Works of Yamamoto Yūzō)

BIBLIOGRAPHY: Kokusai Bunka Shinkōkai, *Introduction to Contemporary Literature* (1939); Morrison, J., *Modern Japanese Fiction* (1955); Shaw, G., *Three Plays by Yamamoto Yūzō* (1957); Yamagiwa, J., *Japanese Literature of the Showa Period* (1959)

RICHARD L. SPEAR

YÁÑEZ, Agustín

Mexican novelist, short-story writer, and critic, b. 1904, Guadalajara

Y. holds degrees in both law and philosophy and has during his active life taught literature at the National University and served in several government capacities. At various times he collaborated on leading Mexican literary magazines and is at present associated with *Cuadernos Americanos*.

A thorough study of leading European philosophers and social theoreticians gave him a dynamic and ethical concept of society that is reflected in his works. A pervading moral tone and an underlying educational and didactic purpose—he has played an increasingly important role in Mexican education—characterize Y.'s novels. But though he portrays the saga of contemporary Mexican manners and morals with the intent of political, social, and ethical reform, he is also a literary descendant of the great Spanish tradition represented in our time by Valle-Inclán and Unamuno (qq.v.). In addition, his novels, like those of Honoré de Balzac (1799–1850) and Proust (q.v.), are

not only literary works but also social and political documents.

Y.'s ethnographically realistic and psychological novel *Al filo del agua* (1947; The Edge of the Storm, 1963) inaugurated a new trend in contemporary Mexican fiction by assimilating to it modern stylistic techniques. The novel's scene is a remote village in the Archdiocese of Guadalajara inhabited by *mestizos* and dominated by a rigid, inquisitorial, Spanish-type Roman Catholic Church ceaselessly toiling to mold the characters of the parishioners. Spanish traditions mixed with indigenous influences, governmental and theocratic oppression, and an atmosphere of fear, superstition, and sexual repression combine to depict a passionate and pessimistic panorama of Mexico on the eve of the Revolution of 1910. A sustained musical and verbal rhythm, intense lyricism, a copious vocabulary, and a baroque quality distinguish Y.'s prose.

In *La creación* (1959), a novel that fuses the real and the fantastic, the protagonist devotes his life to raising the cultural standard of the national music to the level of universality. Unfortunately, the novel suffers somewhat from the degree to which Y. allows his theories of artistic creation to interfere with the vividness of his characterization.

Ojerosa y pintada (1960) is an incisive document, reminiscent of Zola (q.v.) and Balzac, portraying the people of metropolitan Mexico —the ethical and the unethical, the wealthy and the destitute, the patriotic and the snobs. By means of the device of having representatives from many segments of society use the same taxicab and letting them talk, Y. reveals the complex social structure.

The luxuriant coastal jungle stretching along Jalisco is the setting of *La tierra pródiga* (1960) in which tensions and conflicts erupt among *caciques* (local leaders), and between the *caciques* and the federal government. The protagonist—whose attempts to build a tourist resort are frustrated by the government— appears to be modeled on Max Weber's (1864–1920) psychological and sociological interpretation of the charismatic leader who plays the role of catalyst for social change.

Las tierras flacas (1962; The Lean Lands, 1968) realistically details the persistence of myth, sorcery, witchcraft, and religion as organic aspects of a patriarchal society under the impact of a complex industrial economy promoted by the centralized government. A dynamic use of animal imagery serves as a major characterization device, and a remarkable profusion of proverbs enlivens and lends authenticity to the speech of the rancheros by introducing a poetic and aphoristic element into the dialogue.

Y. employs such contemporary fiction techniques as contrapuntal arrangement of themes, cinematographic devices, a fragmented chronological scheme, interior dialogue, musical effects, simultaneity, etc., to create a vast panoramic view that forms an essential basis for an interpretation of the Mexican ethos. He ranks among the foremost Spanish-American writers.

FURTHER WORKS: *Espejismo de Juchitán* (1940); *Fray Bartolomé de las Casas: El conquistador conquistado* (1942); *Flor de juegos antiguos* (1942); *Genio y figuras de Guadalajara* (1942); *Pasión y convalescencia* (1943); *Don Juan va a tener un hijo* (1943); *Archipiélago de mujeres* (1943); *El contenido social de la literatura ibero-americana* (1944); *Fichas mexicanas* (1945); *Esta es mala suerte* (1945); *Alfonso Gutiérrez Hermosillo y algunos amigos* (1945); *El clima espiritual de Jalisco* (1945); *Melibea, Isolda y Alda en tierras cálidas* (1946); *Poesias y estudio general sobre don Justo Sierra, su vida, sus ideas y su obra* (1948); *Informes del estado de la Administración Pública en Jalisco* (1954–59); *Discursos por Jalisco* (1958); *Discursos por la Reforma* (1958); *La formación política* (1962); *Los sentidos del aire* (1964); *Tres cuentos* (1964)

BIBLIOGRAPHY: Delgado, J., "La novela mexicana de A. Y.," *Cuadernos Americanos,* XVI (1953), 249–55; Schade, G. D., "Augury in *Al filo del agua,*" *Texas Studies in Literature and Language,* 1960, pp. 78–87; Paz, O., "Novela y provincia: A. Y.," in *México en la cultura* (1961); Vázquez Amaral, J., "La novelística de A. Y., II," *Cuadernos Americanos,* CXXXVIII (1965), 218–39; Brushwood, J. S., *Mexico in Its Novel* (1966); Sommers, J., *After the Storm* (1968); Flasher, J., *México contemporáneo en las novelas de A. Y.* (1969); Van Conant, L. M., *A. Y.: Intérprete de la novela mexicana moderna* (1969)

JOHN FLASHER

YAŞAR KEMAL
(often Anglicized as *Yashar Kemal*), Turkish novelist, short-story writer, and essayist, b. 1922, Adana

Y. K., Turkey's most famous novelist, was

born in southern Turkey, where he was exposed to the squalor, brutality, and injustices of village life. At five, he saw his father killed, while the latter was praying in a mosque. Having lost one eye in early childhood, he did not begin school until he was nine, and he never went beyond the eighth grade.

In the ensuing years, Y. K. worked at a variety of jobs—cotton-picker, construction foreman, farm hand, clerk, cobbler's helper, and substitute teacher—and these youthful experiences brought him closer to both the deprivations and the dauntless spirit of the laboring classes. During this same period, he also developed an interest in Turkish folklore.

Among Y. K.'s first publications were some poems and several surveys of Anatolian folklore. His first book, *Ağıtlar* (1943), was a compilation of folk elegies.

In 1951, Y. K. joined the staff of the leading Istanbul daily, *Cumhuriyet,* as a roving reporter, later becoming a columnist and special-feature writer. He also wrote the scenarios for several successful Turkish films based on Anatolian legends and themes.

Y. K.'s journalistic writing—utilizing a colloquial and lyrical style—set a new trend in reportage. His travelogues, interviews, and feature stories have been collected in *Yanan Ormanlarda Elli Gün* (1955), *Çukurova Yana Yana* (1955), *Peri Bacaları* (1957), and *Taş Çatlasa* (1961).

In 1963, Y. K. left *Cumhuriyet* to devote himself to his own writing and to campaign for the leftist Turkish Labor Party. He is one of the founders and owners of *Ant,* which publishes Turkey's most influential leftist weekly.

Y. K. first attracted literary attention with *Sarı Sıcak* (1952), a collection of short stories, and *Teneke* (1955), a novella, but it was not until the publication of *İnce Memed* (1955; Memed, My Hawk, 1960) that he was catapulted to national literary fame. This action-filled novel presents as a folk hero a bandit who—somewhat like Robin Hood—takes up arms against the exploiters of the poor. It was followed by *Orta Direk* (1960; The Wind from the Plain, 1964), a moving saga of destitute peasants fighting for survival, which further enhanced Y. K.'s literary reputation as a master of the Turkish "village novel."

Yer Demir Gök Bakır (1963), *Akçasazın Ağaları* (serialized in 1967), and *Ölmez Otu* (1968) depict the tragic life of the Anatolian peasant as well as his indomitable spirit in the face of natural disasters and the injustices perpetrated by privileged landowners. These themes are central in the second volume of *Ince Memed* (1969), which can be read as an independent novel, though it continues the story of Y. K.'s original protagonist. In 1970 Y. K.'s novella *Ağrı Dağı Efsanesi* appeared. It is a simple and moving story about a pair of lovers in the Mount Ağrı region of eastern Turkey. This book is perhaps the most lyrical of all Y. K.'s novels.

Bütün Hikâyeleri (1967) includes several new short stories as well as material that appeared in earlier collections. It was followed by *Üç Anadolu Efsanesi* (1967), which includes three Anatolian legends in new lyrical versions.

Y. K.'s early novella *Teneke* was successfully adapted to the stage in 1965. Later, Y. K.'s drama *Yer Demir Gök Bakır* (1967) shared the award for first prize at the Nancy International Theater Festival.

Y. K.'s popularity and stature stem from his dynamic, streamlined plots, a narrative style that blends coarse descriptions with lyric formulations, a skillful use of myths and local color, and vivid peasant characters of universal interest.

Selected English translation: *Anatolian Tales* (1968)

TALAT SAIT HALMAN

YEATS, William Butler

Irish poet, dramatist, and essayist, b. 13 June 1865, Dublin; d. 28 Jan. 1939, Cap Martin, France

Y. altered the techniques of the symbolist (*see* symbolism) movement for his own use, combined some of the intellectual resources of modern philosophy with those of occultism, and evolved a powerful poetry characterized by passion, loftiness, and subtlety. He drew into being an Irish national theater and wrote many of its plays. He justified and completed his life and work in a series of autobiographical books and essays that shape, more than they reflect, the thought of his time. In spite of eccentric training and interests, he stands at the center of contemporary literature in English.

Y. was born into a middle-class Protestant family. His grandfather and great-grandfather were rectors of the Church of Ireland, but his father, the portrait-painter John Butler Yeats, broke away from this tradition. He

prepared himself for the bar but in late youth suddenly shifted from law to art. J. B. Yeats's study of painting in London, and his shortage of money, made it necessary for him to keep his family for a few years with his wife's relatives at Sligo, a port town in the west of Ireland. It was here and at Rosses Point nearby that Y. spent much of his childhood, and the landscape remained his favorite. He liked to talk with the fishermen and to hear fairy and folk tales from the old peasants.

In 1874 the family moved to London, but the boy disliked the city and longed to return to Sligo. Six years later, in 1880, they came back to Dublin, where Y. attended high school. His interests—up to this time chiefly scientific, and influenced by his father's admiration for the rationalism of John Stuart Mill—abruptly shifted now to the study of occult phenomena. This was to be a lifelong preoccupation, although it was always tinged with a reluctant skepticism. Finishing high school, Y. attended art school from 1884 to 1886, intending to become a painter, but in 1886 he suddenly left the school and threw himself into poetry.

Even at this stage Y. thought all art should be national, and under the influence of John O'Leary, an old Fenian leader who returned to Dublin from exile in 1885, he bent his energies toward the establishment of a national culture for Ireland. His movement gained ground slowly at first, but the disgrace and death of the Irish leader Charles Stuart Parnell in 1891 enabled Y. to turn Irish political passions toward literature. He formed nationalist literary societies in Dublin and London; young writers began to make use of Irish sagas and poems, which were becoming more available in translation; and by 1894 an "Irish literary revival" was already the subject of a book.

Meanwhile, Y. lived a good deal in London from 1889 on, and in spite of his truculent provincialism attracted the notice of the leading literary men. He came to know William Morris (1834–96), whose medievalism with socialist coloring helped to shape Y.'s own rather aristocratic political theories. Another friend was Oscar Wilde (q.v.), whose theory of the necessity of artifice to make life bearable was deepened by Y., with the aid of Nietzsche (q.v.) and William Blake (1757–1827), into his own theory of self and antiself.

In 1890 Y. helped to organize a group of the younger writers, including Arthur Symons (1865–1945), Lionel Johnson (1867–1902), and Ernest Dowson (1867–1900), as the Rhymers'

Club. The group was one of the last important manifestations of *fin de siècle* literature; most of its members scorned ideas and cultivated only impressions, compensating for broken lives with skill and dignity in art, and depending vaguely on French symbolism for their support.

Y. sympathized with their aestheticism, but his boundless energy, national ambitions, and interest in theories of personality and philosophy, kept him—though their founder—from being one with them. A more important influence on him was Blake, whose works he and Edwin Ellis, a minor artist and poet, edited in 1893. In attempting to work out Blake's symbolism, Y. developed his own. He was also affected by Blake's powerful character.

In 1889, in London, Y. fell in love with a young Irishwoman named Maud Gonne, who was to become the subject of most of his love poems. She was the daughter of an officer in the British garrison in Dublin, and had grown up in the atmosphere of the viceregal court. But she too, like Y. under O'Leary's influence, became a passionate nationalist. Her development as a nationalist gradually diverged from Y.'s; she preferred political and even military action to his notion of more gradual change.

After flirting with Irish revolutionary activities Y. gradually found his work elsewhere, convinced that Ireland must become better as well as free. Although Maud Gonne allowed him to think that one day she might marry him, in 1903 she abruptly married an Irish soldier of fortune, Major John MacBride. Y.'s feelings changed from love to anger and then, as her marriage broke up, to pity. The violent passions she aroused sweep through his poetry from beginning to end.

During this entanglement Y. began with Lady Gregory (1852–1932), G. Moore (q.v.), and Edward Martyn (1859–1923) the theatrical movement that was to culminate in the work of the Abbey Theatre. By 1899 they were producing a few plays, and by 1904 they had found a patron in Miss Annie Horniman.

Under the management of Y. and Lady Gregory, the theater became world-famous. Rejecting the melodramas and social comedies that were usually brought to Dublin by English companies, they presented plays on Irish subjects. Besides those of Y. and Lady Gregory, these included the works of Synge and O'Casey (qq.v.).

In spite of its nationalist orientation, the theater met with a good deal of opposition from its Irish audience, which complained of blasphemy, obscenity, and unconventionality. The theater steered a course between chauvinists to whom anything but arrant patriotism was an act of treason, and antinationalists to whom the idea of a national theater was merely grotesque. Y. demonstrated his ability to exercise control by the force of his personality and the skill of his diplomacy, and he was able to vindicate the cause of artistic freedom. But because of the strain, he felt for a time estranged from his fellow countrymen.

This attitude of isolation gave way in 1916, as a result of the abortive but magnificent Easter Rebellion, to an acceptance of his country's troubles and defects as well as of her future hopes.

In 1917 Y. married Georgie Hyde-Lees, an Englishwoman, and they lived chiefly in Dublin and in an old Norman tower, Thoor Ballylee, in the west of Ireland. As husband and then as father of a son and daughter, Y. expressed in his poems his strong sense of belonging to a community. Certain occult experiences of his wife, chiefly "automatic" writing, supplied him with hints that he used to frame his experience into a kind of symbology. His mind seemed to unfold all its possibilities in these later years. When in 1922 the Irish Free State was founded, Y. became a senator. In 1923 he received international recognition by the award of the Nobel Prize for Literature.

Y.'s last years were marked by a series of violent efforts to renew himself both mentally and physically. His poetry increased in gusto and humor, without any loss of tragic understanding. He spent much time with Eastern thought, translating ten Upanishads with Shri Purohit Swami, and suggesting in verse and prose where the cultures might meet and where they must conflict.

In 1937 Y. published the second edition of *A Vision,* in which his symbology becomes clear. This book, notwithstanding its strange appearance, has many connections with contemporary thought. Its cyclical theory is often like that of Oswald Spengler (1880–1936), though arrived at independently. Its theory of "antiself" or "mask" is close to Nietzsche. Its philosophical implications about reality are at many points, as Y. noted, like those of modern philosophers such as A. N. Whitehead (1861–1947). Finally, its attempts to control the universe with a system of metaphors and symbols suggests Ernst Cassirer (1874–1945).

After some preliminary work in which he had not yet found his Irish setting or his personal tone, Y. published in 1889 *The Wanderings of Oisin, and Other Poems.* Except for an insistent symbolism, the work is in keeping, in its color and melody, with that of the preraphaelite poets. The title poem is Y.'s first extended use of Irish legend and he continued to use similar material steadily until after writing his play *Deirdre* in 1907, when he began to favor Greek myths.

In his next book, *The Countess Kathleen, and Various Legends and Lyrics* (1892), Y. shows the dramatic interest that was to produce not only his plays but his dramatic later lyrics. *The Countess Kathleen* is a "Celtic twilight" version of Faust in which a countess sells her soul to the devil so as to feed starving peasants, and is saved because God considers her intention as well as her action. The lyrics in the book are ostentatiously symbolical, the heart of the symbolism being the rose and the cross. Under this symbolic pressure the beloved becomes more of a transcendent principle than a woman. In this book, and even more prominently in the next, *The Wind among the Reeds* (1899), Y.'s early manner reaches its culmination. The rhythms are slow and stately, words are steadily repeated, images are kept dreamy and indistinct, so that the effect is like that of preraphaelite tapestries.

In the 20th c., as Y. wrote later, "everyone got down off his stilts," and there is an infusion of masculine force and passion into the volumes *In the Seven Woods* (1903) and *The Green Helmet, and Other Poems* (1910), as well as into the plays in prose and verse that Y. wrote for the Abbey Theatre. Hearing his lines spoken by actors encouraged him not only to stiffen his diction in new work, but also to revise old work, and for the rest of his life he continued to revise indefatigably—almost always for the better—as he sought to give the effect of an actual man speaking and feeling.

While critics differ as to where his late work begins, there are certainly signs of it in 1903, and it becomes stronger in *Responsibilities* (1916) and in *The Wild Swans at Coole* (1917). These celebrate spontaneity in personality, individual dignity, and passion; they also begin to deal more intensely with the theme of old age, which is treated in Y.'s later poems with such magnificence.

During the next fifteen years Y. reached his greatest heights in *Michael Roberts and the Dancer* (1921), *The Tower* (1928), and *The Winding Stair* (1933). He deals prophetically with the rise and fall of civilizations, with his horror of totalitarian and egalitarian movements, with old age and—with great originality—with love.

This verse is not without its tone of lament, a characteristic of all Y.'s work, but it is grief confronted and mastered. The speaker of Y.'s poems is no less emotional, but his attitudes are witty and complex, and he speaks more directly to his audience. This power is maintained in Y.'s final volume, *Last Poems and Plays,* published posthumously in 1941, where, without surrendering any of his control, he gives an impression of extravagance in language, technique, and thought, and he penetrates his old themes with renewed candor.

Y.'s work is held together by a faith in imagination, nobility, and passion, and by a constant awareness of the forces that reduce imagination's power and mitigate passion and nobility. Holding fast to these qualities, Y. seeks to present the human mind as fully as he can; his poetry can be read as a series of moods that compose an intricate whole.

The structure of Y.'s work is elaborate and condensed; its force comes from his dealing so passionately with three basic drives. The first is to be in the midst of things, to live with the delight, ebullience and versatility of a Renaissance man. Running counter to this is a second drive, which is to emerge from the melee, to contemplate rather than to act, to sift the stuff of life.

There is a third drive that Y. repudiates, although he gives it expression, and this is the drive to seek goodness alone, to become as disembodied as possible now, and utterly bodiless in a pure heaven later. This, however, is the way of the saints, and when faced with it Y. prefers to stand with the pagans, with, as he says, "Homer and his unchristened heart."

In spite of his interest in religious experience, Y. stands basically on the side of the secular, skeptical mind. A. MacLeish (q.v.) has pointed out how Y., unlike most of his immediate predecessors or contemporaries, attains a "public" poetry. Edmund Wilson (q.v.) has said that with all Y.'s symbolical machinery, his "sense of reality" was "inferior to that of no man alive." Eliot (q.v.) has referred to him as "the greatest poet of our time—certainly the greatest in this language, and so far as I am able to judge, in any language."

FURTHER WORKS: *Mosada* (1886); *Irish Fairy Tales* (1892); *The Celtic Twilight* (1893); *The Land of Heart's Desire* (1894); *Poems* (1895); *The Secret Rose* (1897); *The Tables of the Law, The Adoration of the Magi* (1897); *The Shadowy Waters* (1900); *Cathleen ni Houlihan* (1902); *Where There Is Nothing* (1902); *The Hour-Glass and Other Plays* (1903); *Ideas of Good and Evil* (1903); *The King's Threshold and On Baile's Strand* (1904); *The Pot of Broth* (1904); *Stories of Red Hanrahan* (1904); *Poems, 1899–1905* (1906); *The Poetical Works* (2 vols., 1906–1907); *Discoveries* (1907); *The Golden Helmet* (1908); *The Unicorn from the Stars* (with Lady Gregory; 1908); *Poetry and Ireland* (with Lionel Johnson; 1908); *Synge and the Ireland of His Time* (1911); *Plays for an Irish Theatre* (1911); *The Cutting of an Agate* (1912); *Poems Written in Discouragement* (1913); *Reveries over Childhood and Youth* (1915); *Per Amica Silentia Lunae* (1918); *Two Plays for Dancers* (1919); *Four Plays for Dancers* (1921); *Later Poems* (1922); *Trembling of the Veil* (1922); *Plays and Controversies* (1923); *The Cat and the Moon, and Certain Poems* (1924); *Essays* (1924); *The Bounty of Sweden* (1925); *Early Poems and Stories* (1925); *Autobiographies* (1926); *October Blast* (1927); *The Death of Synge* (1928); *Fighting the Waves* (1929); *A Packet for Ezra Pound* (1929); *St. Patrick's Breast-plate* (1929); *Stories of Michael Robartes and His Friends* (with *The Resurrection*; 1931); *Words for Music Perhaps* (1932); *The Winding Stair* (1933); *Collected Poems* (1933); *The King of the Great Clocktower* (1934); *Wheels and Butterflies* (1934); *Letters to the New Island* (1934); *Collected Plays* (1934; enlarged, 1952); *A Full Moon in March* (1935); *Dramatis Personae* (1935); *Modern Poetry* (1936); *Essays, 1931–1936* (1937); *The Herne's Egg* (1938); *New Poems* (1938); *The Autobiography* (1938); *Last Poems and Two Plays* (1939); *On the Boiler* (1939); *Letters on Poetry to Dorothy Wellesley* (1940); *If I Were Four-and-Twenty* (1940); *Pages from a Diary* (1944); *Tribute to Thomas Davis* (1947); *The Poems* (2 vols., 1949); *The Collected Poems* (1950); *Diarmuid and Grania* (with George Moore; 1951); *The Collected Plays* (1952); *W. B. Y. and T. S. Moore: Their Correspondence* (ed. Ursula Bridge; 1953); *Letters to Katharine Tynan* (ed. Roger McHugh; 1953); *Letters* (ed. Allan Wade; 1954); *Complete Poems* (Variorum edition, ed. P. Alt and R. K. Alspach; 1957); *Mythologies* (1959); *Essays and Introductions* (1960); *Explorations* (1962); *Selected Criticism* (ed. A. Norman Jeffares; 1964); *Plays* (Variorum edition, ed. P. Alt and R. K. Alspach; 1965)

BIBLIOGRAPHY: Ellis-Fermor, U., *The Irish Dramatic Movement* (1939); MacNeice, L., *The Poetry of W. B. Y.* (1941); Ure, P., *Toward a Mythology* (1946); Ellmann, R., *Y.: The Man and the Masks* (1948); Jeffares, A. N., *W. B. Y.: Man and Poet* (1949); Henn, T. R., *The Lonely Tower* (1950; 2nd ed., 1965); Ellmann, R., *The Identity of Y.* (1954); Adams, H., *Blake and Y.* (1955); Wade, A., *A Bibliography* (2nd ed., 1958); Unterecker, J., *A Reader's Guide to W. B. Y.* (1959); Stock, A. G., *W. B. Y., His Poetry and His Thought* (1961); Melchiori, G., *The Whole Mystery of Art* (1961); Ure, P., *Yeats the Playwright* (1963); Engelberg, E., *The Vast Design* (1964); Ure, P., *W. B. Y.* (1964); Centenary tribute volumes, 1965—(1) Donoghue, D., and Mulryne, J., eds., (2) Jeffares, A. N., and Cross, K. G., eds., (3) Skelton, R., and Saddlemyer, A., eds., (4) Maxwell, D., and Bushrui, S. B., eds.; Clark, D. R., *W. B. Y. and the Theatre of Desolate Reality* (1965); Ishibashi, H., *Y. and the Noh* (1965); Ellmann, R., *Eminent Domain: Y. among Wilde, Joyce, Pound, Eliot and Auden* (1967); Orel, H. K., *The Development of W. B. Y.: 1885–1900* (1968)

RICHARD ELLMANN

Mr. Y. is the only one among the younger English poets who has the whole poetical temperament, and nothing but the poetical temperament. He lives on one plane, and you will find in the whole of his work, with its varying degrees of artistic achievement, no unworthy or trivial mood, no occasional concession to the fatigue of high thinking. It is this continuously poetical quality of mind that seems to me to distinguish Mr. Y. from the many men of talent, and to place him among the few men of genius. . . . And that, certainly, is the impression which remains with one after a careful reading of the revised edition of Mr. Y.'s collected poems and of his later volume of lyrics, *The Wind among the Reeds.* . . .

Arthur Symons, in *Studies in Prose and Verse* (1900), pp. 230, 234–35

The Y. of the Celtic twilight . . . uses Celtic folklore almost as William Morris uses Scandinavian folklore. His longer narrative poems bear the mark of Morris. Indeed, in his pre-Raphaelite phase, Y. is by no means the least of the pre-Raphaelites . . .

I think that the phase in which he treated Irish

legend in the manner of Rossetti or Morris is a phase of confusion. He did not master this legend until he made it a vehicle for his own creation of character—not, really, until he began to write the *Plays for Dancers*. The point is, that in becoming more Irish, not in subject-matter but in expression, he became at the same time universal.

> T. S. Eliot, "The Poetry of W. B. Y.," in *The Southern Review*, VII (1941–1942), p. 447 f.

He had morals and he had his ritual; but, as in primitive religions, the two were unrelated . . . In Y., religion returns to its pre-Christian and indeed pre-monotheistic character: the search for knowledge of the unseen and gnostic power . . .

Y. needed religion less as a man than as a poet, and his need was epistemological and metaphysical: he needed to believe that poetry is a form of knowledge and power, not of amusement . . .

> Austin Warren, "Religio Poetae," in *The Southern Review*, VII (1941–1942), p. 637 f.

Y. commonly hovered between myth and philosophy, except for transcending flashes, which is why he is not of the greatest poets. His ambition was too difficult for accomplishment; or his gift too small to content him. His curse was not that he rebelled against the mind of his age, which was an advantage for poetry, considering that mind, but that he could not create, except in fragments, the actuality of his age, as we can see Joyce and Mann and it may be Eliot, in equal rebellion, nevertheless doing. Y., to use one of his own lines, had "to wither into the truth." That he made himself into the greatest poet in English since the seventeenth century, was only possible because in that withering he learned how to create fragments of the actual, not of his own time to which he was unequal, but of all time of which he was a product.

To create greatly is to compass great disorder. Y. suffered from a predominant survival in him of that primitive intellect which insists on asserting absolute order at the expense of the rational imagination; hence his system, made absolute by the resort to magic and astrology, which produced the tragic poetry appropriate to it.

> R. P. Blackmur, 'Between Myth and Philosophy," in *The Southern Review*, VII (1941–1942), p. 424 f.

Y. . . . made a "religion" of art, which means in effect that he neutralized religion . . . The effort to bring actual life into the radius of the ultimate implies the possibility of correspondence between the supernatural and the natural worlds; through which the life of man is given meaning and purpose. It is therefore interesting to find, in Y., the predication of a supernatural realm, the world of Faery, of the "Ever Living," which, however, exists in an antithetical relationship to the world of humanity. This means that for him human life is

lived in a closed circle, a purposeless efflorescence denied the significance which can be given it only by an integral relationship with the absolute, while the supernatural world is such another closed circle. This is a perfect theological justification for aestheticism! In middle life he approached nearer humanity, but because of his view of the separation of the two worlds he wrote poetry of disenchantment, was not able to take human life seriously, and in his old age fell back on the de-spiritualized natural world and celebrated the brutal, sensual life of the blood. There is something inhuman, or soulless, about Y. all the way through.

> Derek S. Savage, "Y.," in *The Kenyon Review* (1944)

At first sight the Irish Renaissance, so venomously featured by George Moore in his *Hail and Farewell*, seems inextricably tangled with the Magic and Symbolism. But actually it played a conflicting rôle in his work, directing it towards the Irish legends and the Celtic Twilight, whereas the Magic and Symbolism became essentially part of his approach to the world around him. One also has to distinguish between the Symbolism which had to do with the Magic and the Symbolism which was part of the symbolist movement in poetry. This close connexion between the mystery of magical symbols and the literary movement of H. D., Ezra Pound and their followers, is typical of Y. However mysterious and shadowy it is, his poetry has always the stamp of success, and his magic invocations always have a slightly public air.

> Stephen Spender, *The Destructive Element* (1953), pp. 119–21

The received opinion among readers of Y. is that the classic poems are in *The Tower* and *The Winding Stair*. And yet by comparison with *The Wild Swans at Coole* the human image in those spectacular books is curiously incomplete; remarkably intense, but marginal; a little off-centre. Does this matter? Yes, it does; intensity is not enough. It matters greatly that *The Wild Swans at Coole* is at the very heart of the human predicament, groping for values through which man may define himself without frenzy or servility.

This book is concerned with the behaviour of man in the cold light of age and approaching death. The ideal stance involves passion, self-conquest, courtesy, and moral responsibility. Y. pays the tribute of wild tears to many personages and to the moral beauty which they embody; the entire book is crammed with moral life. Most of the poems were written between 1915 and 1919, and it is significant that those were the years in which Y. was perfecting his dance-drama; because the dancer was the culmination of the efforts which Yeats made in *The Wild Swans at Coole* to represent the fullness of being as a dynamic action.

> Denis Donoghue, *The London Magazine* (Dec. 1961), pp. 59–60

YEHOASH

(pseud. of *Solomon Blumgarten*), Yiddish poet, b. 16 Sept. 1872, Verballen, Lithuania; d. 10 Jan. 1927, New York City

After intensive studies in Hebrew, Y. turned his attention to modern languages and world literature. Although Peretz (q.v.) praised his early poetry and his translations from Lord Byron (1788–1824), Y. decided against a literary career, and in 1890 he emigrated to New York City, where he planned to go into business. The onset of tuberculosis in 1900 caused him to enter the Denver Hebrew Sanitarium, and during the eight years he remained there he resumed his preoccupation with poetry and Hebrew scholarship. After touring the United States in behalf of the Jewish Consumptive Society, he recorded his impressions of the country's physical beauty and grandeur in a number of sensitive lyrics.

Returning to New York in 1909, Y. began writing for the various Yiddish periodicals. Five years later he decided to settle in Palestine, but the upheavals caused by World War I forced him to return to New York in 1915. The poetic impressions and experiences of his travels are recorded in *Fun New York biz Rekhovos un Tzurik* (3 vols., 1917; condensed as The Feet of the Messenger, 1923).

Y.'s early poems are more interesting for their experimental groping than for their aesthetic beauty or inner depth. During this same period he also translated many English and American poems and began translating portions of the Old Testament.

The first volume of *In Geveb* (1919) contained the poems Y. had written during the previous six years, and it was followed in 1921 by a second volume of later poem. Together they established Y. as a leading Yiddish poet. Reisen (q.v.) wrote of him that he "deepened Yiddish poetry, bringing into it new ideas, thoughts, images, and forms."

Though Y. continued to write poems of increasing lyrical beauty, the last decade of his life was devoted to completing his felicitous Yiddish translation of the Old Testament and compiling accompanying annotations and commentaries. It is considered one of the major works in Yiddish.

FURTHER WORKS: *Neie Shriften* (1910); *Yiddish Verterbukh, enthalt alle Hebreyishe un Khaldishe Verter* (with C. D. Spivak; 1911); *Fablen* (1912); *Fun der Velt un Yener* (1913);

In Zoon un Nebel (1913); *Shloime's Ring* (1916); *Gezamelte Lieder* (1917). **Selected English translation:** *Poems of Y.* (ed. I. Goldstick; 1952)

BIBLIOGRAPHY: Roback, A. A., *The Story of Yiddish Literature* (1940); Rivkin, B., *Yiddishe Dikhter in Amerika* (1947); Glatstein, A., *In Tokh Genumen* (1956); *Lexicon fun der Neier Yiddisher Literatur*, Vol. 4 (1961); Green, B., *Yiddishe Shreiber in Amerika* (1963); Liptzin, S., *The Flowering of Yiddish Literature* (1963); Madison, C. A., *Yiddish Literature* (1968)

CHARLES A. MADISON

YESENIN, Sergei
See Esenin, Sergei

YEVTUSHENKO, Yevgeni
See Evtushenko, Evgeny

YIDDISH LITERATURE

Although the Yiddish language dates back to the 9th c., it was long disdained as a serious literary medium and used only for translations of popular secular tales or for pious stories designed for the edification of women, who by and large could not understand the Hebrew of basic religious texts. In the 19th c., however, emancipated intellectuals attacking the superstition and dogmatism that characterized eastern-European Jewish life began to write in Yiddish as a way to reach the widest possible audience of their coreligionists. Plays, stories, and propaganda manuals exposing religious and social problems and extolling the virtues of 19th-c. enlightenment began to appear, but for decades this agitation had little effect. Only the more exciting stories, such as the romances of I. M. Dick (1807–1893) and Shomer (pseudonym of N. M. Shaikevitch; 1844–1905), had wide appeal.

During the latter half of the 19th c. economic changes and tzarist repression brought about what the early intellectual reformers had failed to achieve. The move to the cities and the need to adapt to modern industrial conditions forced a loosening of medieval piety. To ease this difficult transition, a new generation of Jewish intellectuals provided a didactic literature that served to justify the religious liberalization and to help Jews adapt to the hazards of urban existence.

The most effective of these reformers was Mendele Mokher Sforim (pseudonym of Sholom Jacob Abramovitch; 1835?–1917), a writer of exceptional literary brilliance. Originally didactic in intent, the novels, stories, and plays he wrote beginning in 1864 were to earn him the distinction of being known as the "grandfather" of modern Yiddish literature. Mendele's artistic zeal—particularly in his later years when he revised many of his works—enabled him to take an undeveloped folk language and give it the scope, fluidity, and dignity of a literary medium capable of expressing the subtlest thought and deepest emotion. Among his best-known works are *Dos Vinchfingerl* (1865), *Fishke der Krumer* (1869; *Fishke the Lame*, 1960), *Kitzur Maasois Binjamin Hashlishi* (1875; The Travels and Adventures of Benjamin the Third, 1949), *Di Klatche* (1873; The Nag, 1954), and *Shloime Reb Khaim's* (1899).

It is, however, Sholom Aleichem (q.v.) who is generally considered the "father" of contemporary Yiddish literature. This great modern humorist—his pen name is the common Hebrew greeting meaning "peace be with you"—began his career with a genial short story entitled "The Pocketknife" (1883), a milestone in Yiddish literature.

After an unsuccessful business career, Sholom Aleichem turned to writing stories, novels, monologues, and plays that delighted his contemporaries and that have proved to be a continuing source of pleasure in recent translations. His tales always dealt with some intimately observed aspect of Jewish life either in the still medievally oriented *shtetl* (small town) or in the bustling big city. The infectious and sympathetic laughter of his simple stories teased from his readers a smiling awareness and acknowledgment of their own foibles and foolishness.

Among Sholom Aleichem's immortal creations are Motel, the personification of youth's wide-eyed amazement and amusement at the world around it; Reb Yozefel, the octogenarian rabbi blessed with good sense and actuated by deep altruism; Menakhem Mendel, the citified *luftmensche,* a pathetic and somewhat grotesque dreamer, the product of centuries of struggle to survive under adverse and abject conditions; and Tevieh the Dairyman, a traditionally religious, rustic Jew who embodies Sholom Aleichem's highest humor and truest philosophy of life in his struggles to maintain and protect his family in tzarist

Russia. The Tevieh stories were to provide the basis for the recent musical comedy *Fiddler on the Roof.*

I. L. Perez (q.v.) is the third in the triumvirate of writers who provided the foundation and the impulse for the flowering of Yiddish literature in the 20th c. Even his early work, which focused with a reformer's didacticism on Jewish poverty and suffering, sparkles with flashes of the artistry that he was to polish to a gemlike sheen in his later folkloric and Hasidic stories that reveal the spiritual depths of Jewish piety with loving sympathy. One need only read "Bontche Shveig," "Oib Nit Hekher," or "Drei Matones" to perceive his technical mastery and his profound human insight. Both were to be most tellingly combined in his great poetic drama *Di Goldene Keyt* (1907). As a poet, Peretz was a persistent experimenter with forms, rhythms, rhymes, and meters. Devoted to his people and to Yiddish literature, he encouraged and sponsored dozens of young writers.

In the decades following the 1890's the center of Yiddish literary activity shifted from eastern Europe to the United States. Young men who in earlier days would have steeped themselves in religious study and perhaps written a commentary on some previous exegesis of the Talmud now felt impelled to express their freshly excited emotions and new ideas in verse and fiction. Though almost all first wrote in Hebrew, they soon turned to Yiddish and strove to give this new literature the body and spirit of the other modern literatures that were often reflected in their work. Writers such as Sholom Aleichem, Pinski, Yehoash, Asch, and Hirschbein (qq.v.) settled in New York, where they found a ready audience for their novels, stories, poetry, and plays in the millions of eastern European Jews who had emigrated to this country. Morris Rosenfeld (1862–1923) depicted life in the sweatshops with lyrical protest and poignancy. H. D. Nomberg (1876–1927) on visits here enchanted audiences and readers with hunting verses in which he portrayed the moods and dreams of Yeshiva students. Often the work of newly arrived authors first appeared in Yiddish magazines and newspapers, giving the latter a literary flavor absent from American dailies and providing financial support for fledgling writers.

Inspired by leading European writers, Pinski wrote stories, novels, and plays with a socialistic emphasis. Though many are excellent, some of his work suffers from unevenness. His play *Der Oitzer* (1906), however, won him international fame.

Yehoash wrote poems of Byronic beauty. But in his early verse he was too much the intellectual groper to create the lyric spontaneity he later achieved. His literary permanence is perhaps best established in his felicitous Yiddish translation of the Old Testament. To the end of his life Reisen (q.v.) wrote simple, authentic lyrics and stories of folkloric informality, each stamped with the humor and pathos of his native talent.

Influenced by Maeterlinck and Andreyev (qq.v.), Hirschbein floundered for a time in misty and mystical drama until he discovered a rich vein of comedy in the rustic life of his boyhood. A world traveler, he wrote several perceptive books based on his visits to various parts of the world. He was less successful as a novelist, and his best writing is to be found in *Kinder Yoren* (1932), a beautiful recollection of childhood and adolescence.

The most esteemed of these writers who made their home in America was Asch. He gained an international reputation following the Berlin production, by Max Reinhardt, of his play *Der Gott fun Nekomo* (1907). Among his important early novels are *Mottke der Ganef* (1916; Mottke the Thief, 1935), *Kiddush Hashem* (1919), and *Der Tilim Yid* (1934; Salvation, 1934). *Drei Shtet* (1929–32; Three Cities, 1932) is a masterly treatment of the background of the Russian revolution. After 1939 Asch became a highly controversial figure among his Jewish readers because of Christological novels —*Der Man fun Notzeres* (1943; The Nazarene, 1939), *Paulus* (1943; The Apostle, 1943), and *Maria* (1949; Mary, 1949)—however, they were an international success in translation. Highly readable but of less literary significance are his Old Testament novels *Moishe* (1951; Moses, 1951) and *Der Novi* (1955; The Prophet, 1955).

Outstanding among those who began their literary career in the United States are Opatoshu and Leivick (qq.v.). From 1914 until his death forty years later Opatoshu contributed hundreds of short stories to the New York Yiddish newspaper *Der Tog*. Many of them are beautifully written cameo insights into human folly. His first major novel, *Di Poilishe Velder* (1921; The Polish Woods, 1938), was hailed as a masterpiece and translated into many languages. *A Tog in Regensburg* (1933; A Day in Regensburg (1933; A Day in Regensburg, 1968) is a short novel that treats of Jewish ghetto life in the 16th c. with freshness and gusto.

Opatoshu's last major work, a two-volume historical novel, *Der Letzter Oifshtand* (1948–54; I, The Story of Rabbi Akiba, 1952; II, Bar Kokhba, 1955), portrays life in 2nd-c. Israel, focusing on the efforts of Rabbi Akiba to stimulate Bar Kokhba's revolt against the Romans.

Leivick's poetry lyrically reflects the pain and pathos of his life. A Siberian exile in his teens, he was never to recover either physically or emotionally from the experience of his years of imprisonment. It was, however, to inspire his great poetic drama *Der Golem* (1920; The Golem, 1928), a messianic work rich in symbolic and mystical intimations. Leivick was to return to the Golem theme in later works that probed into Jewish messianism. He was also deeply attracted and disturbed by the story of Isaac's sacrifice, a recurring theme in his work. In addition to poetic dramas, Leivick wrote many lyrics charged with simply expressed but intense emotion.

I. J. Singer (q.v.) and his younger brother, I. B. Singer (q.v.), came to New York from Poland in the 1930's. The elder had since 1922 became a regular contributor to Abraham Cahan's (1860–1951) New York Yiddish daily *Forverts,* and it was there that in 1932 his first major novel, *Yoshe Kalb* (The Sinner, 1933), began to appear in serial form. The following year it was adapted for the stage and its haunting treatment of the superstitious pieties of Hasidic life was hailed the world over. His first work written in this country was *Di Brieder Ashkenazi* (1936; The Brothers Askenazi, 1936), an epic treatment of Polish industrial development and its effect on Jewish life. *Khaver Nakhman* (1938; East of Eden, 1939) reflects his disillusionment with Soviet communism, and *Di Mishpokhe Karnovsky* (1943; The Family Carnowsky, 1969) deals with the plight of Jews in Nazi Germany.

I. B. Singer's stories show a fondness for mystical exoticism, often couched in somewhat whimsical terms. His first major work was *Soten in Goray* (1935; Satan in Goray, 1955), the story of 17th-c. religious degeneracy in the wake of devastating massacres and false messianism. *Di Familie Moskat* (1950; The Moskat Family, 1950), the first of his books to be published in English, depicts the break-up of traditional Jewish life in Poland. Its popularity and critical reception established Singer as a leading American novelist. All his subsequent works have been translated as soon as the Yiddish manuscript is available.

Mention should be made of the host of other talented Yiddish writers who appeared on the literary scene in the early decades of the 20th c. Among them were A. Liessin (1872–1938), H. Roisenblatt (1878–1956), L. Shapiro (1878–1948), J. Rolnik (1879–1958), Y. Rosenfeld (1880–1944), I. Raboy (1882–1944), S. Niger (1883–1958), Mani-Leyb (1884–1953), Moishe Nadir (1885–1943), D. Ignatov (1885–1954), M. L. Halpern (1886–1932), I. I. Trunk (1887–1961), M. Boreisho (1888–1949), A. Glantz-Leyeles (1889–1966), E. Auerbach (b. 1892), M. Ravitch (b. 1893), Kadia Molodovsky (b. 1894), J. Glatstein (b. 1896), A. Zeitlin (b. 1898), I. Manger (1901–1958), and K. Grade (b. 1910), most of whom eventually settled in the United States.

Yiddish was, of course, written wherever Jews had settled in sizable numbers. In Poland, nearly all Yiddish writers were killed during the Nazi occupation of their country in World War II. In Russia, Yiddish writing flourished briefly after the revolution in 1917. Among the more prominent authors were Bergelson (q.v.) and Der Nister (1884–1950), both novelists of exceptional merit. Others of note include Leyb Kvitko (1893–1952), Peretz Markish (1895–1952), Moshe Kulbak (1896–1952), Itzik Kharik (1898–1937), and Itzik Fefer (1900–1952). After 1935 the artistic freedom of these men began to be restricted, and following the pre-World War II purges many were exiled or executed. In the 1948 upsurge of Stalin-inspired anti-Semitism, many talented Yiddish writers were arrested and executed. For more than a decade Yiddish was in effect proscribed. At present there are no Yiddish newspapers in Russia and only one magazine. Very few books are published in Yiddish.

The establishment of Israel favored the Yiddish writers who settled there. In 1949 they started *Di Goldene Keyt*, which rapidly became the most prestigious Yiddish literary periodical. The editor of that quarterly, A. Sutskever (b. 1913), is a poet who writes with brilliance and poignant intensity of the events of the World War II holocaust. Most books published in Yiddish today are put out by the Peretz Verlag in Tel Aviv. Indeed, if Yiddish is to continue as a written medium, its best chance of survival seems to be in Israel.

BIBLIOGRAPHY: Niger, S., *Ueber Yiddishe Shreiber* (1922); Merkin, Z., *Sholem Asch* (1931); Niger, S., *Mendele Mokher Sforim* (1936); Samuel, M., *The World of Sholom Aleichem* (1943); Mayzel, N., *Forgeyers un Nokhgeyers* (1946); Rivkin, B., *Grund-Tendentzen in der Amerikaner Yiddisher Literatur* (1948); Roback, A. A., *The Story of Yiddish Literature* (1948); Samuel, M., *Prince of the Ghetto* (1948); Trunk, I. I., *Yiddish Proze in Poilen Tzvishen Beyde Velt Milkhomes* (1949); Rivkin, B., *Unsere Prozayiker* (1951); Baal Makhshoves, *Geklibene Verk* (1953); *Lexixon fun der Neier Yiddisher Literatur* (7 vols, 1956–68); Bickel, S., *Shreiber fun Mein Dor* (2 vols., 1958–65); Niger, S., *Sholem Asch* (1960); Liptzin, S., *The Flowering of Yiddish Literature* (1963); Madison, C. A., *Yiddish Literature* (1968)

CHARLES A. MADISON

YOURCENAR, Marguerite

(pseud. of *Marguerite de Crayencour*), French novelist, short-story writer, essayist, dramatist, and poet, b. 8 June 1903, Brussels

Marguerite Y. was the only child of a French father and a Belgian mother, who died shortly after her daughter's birth. Marguerite Y. was educated privately under the guidance of her father, a man of broad literary culture, and later traveled extensively in Europe and Asia Minor, studying and writing. In 1939 she left France for the United States, where she taught from 1942 to 1953. She lives on Mount Desert Island off the coast of Maine.

Marguerite Y. creates literature in which she blends the cultural with the sensual and the past with the present. She is concerned with a certain vision of truth, beauty, and lucidity, with the attempts of men and women caught in the circumstances of their age and private destiny, with distinguishing fact from fiction and ineluctable suffering from unnecessary injustice. The ambience may be: Mussolini's Rome (*Denier du rêve*, 1934); the aftermath of World War I and the Russian Revolution (*Le Coup de grâce*, 1939; Coup de Grâce, 1957); Hadrian's Rome (*Mémoires d'Hadrien*, 1951; Memoirs of Hadrian, 1954); the aftermath of the Trojan War (*Electre, ou La Chute des Masques*, 1954); or the upheavals of 16th-c. Europe (*L'Œuvre au noir*, 1968). Her passion for precise knowledge concerning all manifestations of the human presence contributes to the perfection and scope of her writing. Her extraordinary culture and audacious clarity, her persistent reworking of the same material, her notes that contain scholarly comment and critical appraisal, place

561

her at a significant distance from many of her less learned and more dogmatic contemporaries.

Because certain periods of the past are an integral part of Marguerite Y.'s consciousness, her effort as a writer is directed toward a constant synthesis of what was once and what is now. The past imposes a distance; the distance imposes a discipline in method and sensibility. To retell the story of Theseus, to rewrite her own *Denier du rêve,* to translate into French Virginia Woolf, Henry James, Constantin Cavafy (qq.v.), and American Negro spirituals (*Fleuve profond* and *Sombre Rivière,* 1964), are related activities.

The *Mémoires d'Hadrien,* unanimously acclaimed as the *summum* of a singularly erudite and sensitive mind, is a microcosm of Marguerite Y.'s total publications. Hadrian, like Zeno in *L'Œuvre au noir,* thinks and feels as far as the limits of his time and place, scrupulously documented, will allow him to. The domain of his memoirs is his lucid and intense attention to all aspects of his experience: hunting, loving, learning, traveling, governing, and dying. He is given to excesses and yet to the exercise of tolerance; he is a hedonist and an ascetic, capable both of action in the world and contemplation of it. Hadrian is an exemplary hero who maintains a delicate equilibrium between the chaotic elements of human life and the order his commanding voice imposes on them. He belongs to an avant-garde of humanity —those who are aware of their superiority, those who are aware of the limits imposed on human endeavors by the fact of mortality and the inevitable disturbances, brought about by desire and disease, of the mind and the body. Between Hadrian's 2nd c. A.D. and our 20th c. the implicit analogies are numerous: a similar eclecticism, a similar skepticism; a civilization that is, like Hadrian himself, dying.

In Marguerite Y.'s universe the finality of death is always accompanied by a triumph of the outstanding individual who stubbornly retains, until the very end, his particular identity. Marguerite Y.'s compelling voice is one of the most carefully pitched of the 20th c. It joins the past to the present in a lucid and lyrical celebration of the mysterious human adventure.

FURTHER WORKS: *Le Jardin des chimères* (1921); *Le Dieux ne sont pas morts* (1922); *Alexis, ou Le Traité du vain combat* (1929); *La Nouvelle Eurydice* (1931); *Pindare* (1932); *La Mort conduit l'attelage* (1934); *Feux* (1936); *Nouvelles Orientales* (1938); *Les Songes et les*

sorts (1938); *Les Charités d'Alcippe* (1956); *Présentation critique de Constantin Cavafy* (1958); *Sous Bénéfice d'inventaire* (1962); *Le Mystère d'Alceste* and *Qui n'a pas son Minotaure?* (1963); *Présentation critique d'Hortense Flexner* (1969)

BIBLIOGRAPHY: Houston, J., "The Memoirs of Hadrian," *YFS,* No. 27 (1961); *Biblio,* No. 5 (May 1964); *Cahiers des Saisons,* No. 38 (1964); Blot, J., "M. Y.," *NRF,* Nov. 1968; Boisdeffre, P. de, *Une Histoire vivante de la littérature d'adjourd'hui* (1968)

ELAINE MARKS

YUGOSLAV LITERATURE

When in the 7th c. the migrating southern Slavs settled in the regions of present-day Yugoslavia, they were already divided into tribally differentiated and ethnically distinct groups. This, and a host of political adversities in the new homeland prevented them from uniting for some thirteen c.'s, during which they drifted even further apart through religious fragmentation (Greek Orthodoxy, Roman Catholicism, Islam), foreign cultural influences (Austro-Hungarian, Italian, Russian), the divergence of their respective languages (Serbo-Croat, Slovenian, Macedonian), the growth of distinctly regional dialects (Čakavian, Kajkavian, Štokavian), and the adoption of two separate alphabets (Latin in the north and Cyrillic in the south). A mere half c. of a precarious political unity since 1918 has not been enough to erase deep social, cultural, and linguistic differences among regions separated for two-thirds of a millennium, and thus the term "Yugoslav literature" remains primarily an overall geographical designation for a cluster of several related but distinct literatures of the south Slav peoples.

Among them the literatures of the Serbs and the Croats are both quantitatively and qualitatively the most prominent. They are written in the same language (though not in the same alphabet), but differ in their historical development, cultural orientation, and dialectal shadings. Next comes the literature of the Slovenes, whose language forms a bridge between the languages of the western and southern Slavs, and that of the Macedonians, whose language provides a link between Serbo-Croatian and Bulgarian. The literatures of Montenegro and the region of Vojvodina are historically and linguistically within the Serbian literary tradition, while that of Bosnia and Herzegovina is oriented toward either the Serbian or Croatian tradition depending on the origin, linguistic heritage, and cultural inclination of each author.

SERBIAN LITERATURE

The 20th-c. development of Serbian literature can be divided into three periods, all separated and influenced by significant historical events. The first lasted from the overthrow of the Obrenović dynasty in 1903 to the end of World War I, the second from the unification of the Yugo-Slavs in 1918 to the end of World War II, and the third from the emergence of socialist Yugoslavia in 1945 until the present.

After the turn of the c. the traditional Russian influence on Serbian literature declined in favor of the French, primarily because ever greater numbers of Serbs went to France and Switzerland in quest of higher education. The new trend affected poetry strongly. Prose continued to be dominated by regionalism and nostalgia for the simple patriarchal past.

The leading Serbian poet at the turn of the c. was the Herzegovinian Dučić (q.v.). A preoccupation with form and verbal elegance dominates his work, especially in the sonnet form, for which he early demonstrated a pronounced affinity. His favorite subjects were the vanished worlds of the gay and frivolous Dubrovnik aristocracy and the mystically austere Serbian medieval nobility. His treatment of love often betrays an attitude of cool, ironic detachment, a predilection for the anticlimactic and paradoxical in the encounters of lovers, and a basically skeptical view of human nature.

Of the poets from Serbia proper the most prominent was Milan Rakić (1876–1938), who, like Dučić, studied in Paris and later joined the diplomatic corps. The sixty poems that constitute his lifelong poetic effort prove that he possessed an exceptional sense for the rhythm and sonority of the written line. Except for his patriotic Kosovo cycle of seven poems, all of his verse is profoundly somber and pessimistic.

The opposite is true of Milutin Bojić (1892–1917), who died in World War I, his poetic talent not yet fully developed. His two books of verse, *Pesme* (1914) and *Pesme bola i ponosa* (1917), are full of buoyant optimism, vigorous sensuality, and poignant patriotic fervor;

because he wrote hastily, however, they also occasionally display traces of declamatory rhetoric and verbosity. These weaknesses are more apparent in his verse plays *Kraljeva jesen* (1918) and *Uroševa ženidba* (1920), both on themes from medieval Serbian history.

In prose fiction the most notable author of this period was Borisav Stanković (1876–1927). His three volumes of stories—*Iz starog jevanđelja* (1899), *Božji ljudi* (1902), and *Stari dani* (1902)—the play *Koštana* (1902), and the novel *Nečista krv* (1911), all resurrect the colorful ambience of his native Vranje, in which the human spirit was perennially torn between the turgid eruptions of its oriental sensuality and the rigid social code of conventional patriarchalism. His strong-willed individuals, some of the most memorable of them women, usually begin by trampling on the unwritten laws of society and end as beings broken because of their defiance. Stanković's style often suffered from turgidity and repetition, but his imaginary world is replete with colorful situations, striking characters and explosive atmosphere.

An equally significant regionalist was Petar Kočić (1877–1916). Born in Bosnia and educated in Belgrade and Vienna, he remained throughout his literary career a champion of the hardy Bosnian peasant, who, although oppressed by poverty and foreign domination, was sly and full of resilience and earthy wit. Among Kočić's characters most striking are the volatile deacon Simeun, whose imaginary, brandy-aided fantastic exploits are presented in a number of Kočić's stories, and the cunning peasant David Štrbac, who in the play *Jazavac pred sudom* (1904) brings a badger to court to ridicule the stuffiness and bureaucracy of the Austrian occupiers of Bosnia. Although much of his work was left in sketchy form, Kočić was an author of great descriptive power, exceptional simplicity, and rare directness of style.

The leading dramatist of this period (and of the next one as well) was Nušić (q.v.), author of two dozen witty comedies. Despite his keen wit and a sharp eye for the ludicrous, however, he was not a profound social satirist; he wrote rapidly and aimed primarily to entertain.

The most notable literary critics of this time were Bogdan Popović (1863–1944) and Jovan Skerlić (1877–1914). Popović founded the most important Serbian literary journal, *Srpski književni glasnik,* and published an authoritative anthology of Serbian poetry that greatly contributed to the recognition of a score of younger poets. In his numerous critical essays and reviews Popović emphasized matters of form and seldom discussed content. His disciple, Skerlić, who later studied in Lausanne, Munich, and Paris, was much more sociologically oriented. Influenced by the thought of the French poet and philosopher Marie Jean Guyau (1854–1888), the critical concepts of Russian and French sociological critics, and the political ideas of the 19th-c. Serbian socialist Svetozar Marković (1846–1875), he became the champion of ethical positivism in art, and dismissed some of the more radical modernist trends in Serbian literature as worthless. His most significant works are *Omladina i njena književnost 1848–1871* (1906), *Srpska književnost u XVIII veku* (1909), and *Istorija novije srpske književnosti* (1914). Although occasionally paternalistic and narrow in his critical judgments, Skerlić remains one of the most significant literary minds in the entire history of Serbian letters.

In the interwar period following the unification of the Yugo-Slavs, Serbian poetry continued to develop under a strong French influence. Its past divorce from prose fiction became less pronounced, because a number of new authors distinguished themselves in both media, but on the whole prose fiction retained much of its regionalist flavor, despite the noticeable growth of general and stylistic sophistication among its practitioners.

The most outstanding poet of this era is Rastko Petrović (1898–1949). Educated in France and later employed in the foreign service, he early fell under the spell of Apollinaire, Éluard, and Cocteau (qq.v.). His best collection of poems, *Otkrovenje,* was considered sensationalist and blasphemous by the conservatives and the clergy, but it also established him as the most promising Serbian poet of his time. Like Éluard, Petrović sought poetry in real life and favored spontaneous poetic outbursts, unhampered by contemplation and revision. This attitude occasionally robbed his verse of structure and meaning, but it also enhanced its pure verbal magic. The stylistic originality, simplicity of expression, and acuteness of observation found in his lesser-known novels *Burleska gospodina Peruna boga groma* and *Dan šesti,* the chronicle *Ljudi govore,* and a travelogue *Afrika,* further prove that his creative talent was of rare complexity and strength.

Desanka Maksimović (b. 1898) studied in Belgrade and Paris and subsequently taught in a number of Yugoslav schools. Although she produced a score of prose works, poetry remained her *forte* throughout her creative life. The most significant collections of her verse are *Pesme, Zeleni vitez, Pesnik i zavičaj, Otadžbino tu sam, Miris zemlje,* and *Tražim pomilovanje*. Her poetic expression—rich in rhythmic melodiousness, freshness of imagery, and fluidity of thought—slips at times into mawkish sentimentality and generalization. Some of her earlier poems about her illusions and disappointments in love are by far among her best.

Of those authors from this period who contributed to poetry and prose, the most notable is the Belgrade-educated Vojvodinian Miloš Crnjanski (b. 1893), who for a long period during and after World War II lived as a political exile in England. In his two collections of verse, *Lirika Itake* (1919) and *Odabrani stihovi* (1954), he presented a distinctly personal, emotionally intense, and often elegiac view of the contemporary human scene. His greatest prose work is *Seobe* (1929), a historical novel in two parts that depicts the 18th-c. Serbian exodus into Austrian lands. A profoundly pessimistic work, it underscores the endlessness and futility of the human quest for peace, a better life, and domestic tranquillity. Although in this novel Crnjanski's prose frequently appears obscure and antiquated, it bears a highly personal stamp that greatly heightens the elemental intensity of his poetic vision and the contrapuntal broadness of his historical perspective.

Another writer of this era who excelled in more than one genre was Stanislav Vinaver (1891–1955). Educated in France and influenced by Valéry (q.v.), he produced an ethereal poetry unrestricted by space or time. The most important collections of his poems are *Varoš zlih volšebnika, Čuvari sveta,* and *Evropska noć.* His verse, though rich in rhythmic melodiousness, is often rendered difficult by his ceaseless stylistic experimenting. Vinaver's essays *Živi okviri, Čardak ni na nebu ni na zemlji,* and *Jezik naš nasušni* show his immense linguistic versatility as well as his love of polemic and literary ridicule.

Among the prose writers of this period the most distinguished is the Bosnian Andrić (q.v.), the only Yugoslav ever to receive the Nobel Prize for Literature. The three volumes of his short stories published in the interwar years introduce a peculiarly Bosnian milieu and characters that will dominate Andrić's later major works *Travnička hronika* (1959) and *Na Drini ćuprija* (1959). Although rooted in the Serbian realist tradition, Andrić is such an acute observer of inner life, such a subtle psychologist and stylist, that he stands above ordinary classifications.

A Bosnian of Jewish origin and Viennese education, Isak Samokovlija (1899–1955) excelled primarily in the short story. His best collections, *Od proljeća do proljeća, Nosač Samuel, Đerdan,* and *Priča o radostima,* are distinguished by a mixture of heroic and ludicrous, tragic and humorous, lyrical and naturalist details. Like Babel (q v.), Samokovlija showed a great affinity for poor but picturesque characters and used an archaic language of biblical flavor with many Yiddish and obscure expressions.

Born in Banat and educated mainly abroad, Isidora Sekulić (1877–1958) devoted herself primarily to the short story and literary criticism. Her best story collections, *Saputnici, Iz prošlosti,* and *Hronika palanačkog groblja,* reveal her strong romantic affinities and a frequent preoccupation with the dichotomy of human nature. Her essays *Njegošu—knjiga duboke odanosti* and *Mir i nemir* prove that she was an imaginative and stimulating analyst of literary texts albeit a subjective and occasionally inaccurate one.

The final notable prose writer of this era, Branimir Ćosić (1903–1934), is remembered chiefly for his last novel, *Pokošeno polje* (1934), a largely autobiographical work and the only one in this period that successfully depicted the contemporary Serbian urban milieu. Ćosić has also written two other novels of lesser importance, some stories, and two collections of essays.

The leading literary critic of this time, whose career continued well into the postwar years, was Milan Bogdanović (1892–1964). His best essays from both eras are collected in *Kritike* and the four volumes of *Stari i novi.* Influenced by the French critic Jules Lemaitre (1853–1915) and by Skerlić, he emphasized in all his work that literature should be *engagé* and relevant to the reality of its time. This belief prompted him to deny the modernist notions of absolute artistic freedom. His style was distinguished by its fluidity and polish, and his critical judgment was notable for its harmonious blend of ethical and aesthetic considerations.

The fundamental sociopolitical changes that occurred in Yugoslavia at the end of World War II profoundly affected Serbian literature throughout its third and last period of development. In the first postwar decade an attempt was made to replace the traditional Western influence with Soviet-patterned socialist realism (q.v.). In the second, because of the growing independence of Yugoslavia from the Eastern bloc and because of fewer restrictions on artistic expression, the modernists gradually regained lost ground.

At the outset of the socialist period the Belgrade literary scene was dominated by a group of authors who, after championing a largely unsuccessful movement toward surrealism (q.v.) movement in the 1930's, joined the communist cause. The most notable among them are Milan Dedinac (b. 1902), Dušan Matić (b. 1898), Aleksandar Vučo (b. 1897), and Oskar Davičo (b. 1909), all from Serbia proper, all educated in Belgrade and Paris, and all involved in their formative years primarily with poetry.

Dedinac is the least prolific of the four. The best of his literary output comprises three collections of verse, *Javna ptica, Pesme iz dnevnika zarobljenika broj 60211,* and *Od nemila do nedraga.* From the dream world of abstractions similar to those of Breton (q.v.), striking metaphors, and symbolic visions prevalent in his early poetry, Dedinac has gradually shifted to the level of socially relevant expression, although he still tends to overintellectualize his subject matter.

In the prewar years Matić and Vučo collaborated on the poem *Marija Ručara* and the novel *Gluho doba* (1940), both of which were failures. After the war Matić published the collections of verse, *Javna ptica, Pesme iz, Anina balska haljina,* and the novel *Kocka je bačena.* As a prose writer and essayist Matić is urbane and erudite but seldom gripping; as a poet he has produced some significant compositions in the last few years.

Vučo's best verse appeared in the collections *Krov nad prozorom* and *Ako se još jedrom setim,* and his best prose in two novels, *Raspust* and *Mrtve javke.* His poetry is characterized by its black humor and his prose by its erudite complexity.

Davičo is both the most prolific and the most modernist author of this group. His best works are three collections of verse, *Višnja za zidom, Hana* (1951), and *Nastanjene oči* (1954); three novels, *Pesma* (1952), *Beton i svici,* and *Ćutnje;* and a significant essay, *Poezija i otpori*

(1952). Davičo is an original author with a fertile imagination, but his expression often lacks proportion. In his poetry he frequently resorts to irrational constructions, exaggerated metaphors, and vague verbosity. His best novel, *Pesma,* depicts the actions and dilemmas of a young and overimpulsive resistance fighter in occupied Belgrade. This work, regarded as a bold modernist experiment when it appeared, is carelessly structured and full of excessive soliloquizing and fantasy.

Quite different from the above circle is that of the socialist realists, which in the postwar period largely adhered to subject matter from the liberation struggle and the socialist reconstruction of the country.

The most established member of this group is Branko Ćopić (b. 1915), whose career began in the prewar era with three collections of stories that deplored the plight of the poor in his native Bosnia. While serving as a partisan fighter in the war, he turned out a number of patriotic and propagandistic poems of great popular appeal; after the liberation he returned to prose. His most notable works are the collections of stories *Odabrane ratne pripovijetke* and *Doživljaji Nikoletine Bursaća* (1955), and the novels *Prolom* (1952) and *Gluvi barut* (1957), all of which depict, both humorously and solemnly, events and characters from the war. A master of the anecdote and humor, Ćopić occasionally tends to neglect depth of characterization and psychology. His language, however, is lively and colorful and his narrative imbued with a rare vitality and optimism. He has also written a number of very successful books for children.

The Montenegrin Mihailo Lalić (b. 1914) also matured during the war while fighting on the partisan side. In his numerous stories and novels, such as *Svadba, Zlo proljeće, Raskid,* and *Lelejska gora* (1967), he concentrated exclusively on his dark memories of the fratricidal partisan-chetnik war encounters. His characters are masterfully drawn, their conflicts documentarily authentic, and their expression both virile and rich. The singularity of his preoccupation with war, suffering, and destruction, however, gives plots a certain monotony.

Similar to Lalić in background and experiences but greater in talent is Dobrica Ćosić (b. 1921). After his first war novel, *Daleko je sunce* (1951), won wide acclaim for its objectivity and artistic vigor, Ćosić produced an even better one, *Koreni* (1954), in which his penetrating portrayal of life in a rich Serbian peasant family at the turn of the century successfully evoked the overall sociopolitical atmosphere of the time. His last and best endeavor, *Deobe* (1961), a novel in three volumes, follows a descendant of the same family through the ordeals of World War II. Its plot focuses almost exclusively on the Serbian chetniks and the stagnancy and decline of their ill-defined political movement. Ćosić is an exceptionally keen psychologist and an unsurpassable connoisseur of the Serbian peasant mind. The authenticity of his plots, the vibrancy and boldness of his nature sketches, and the free flow of his straightforward, colloquially pungent expression clearly reveal that he is an author of rare potentiality and distinction.

The most representative Serbian postwar literary critics are Marko Ristić (b. 1902) and Velibor Gligorić (b. 1899). Ristić developed within the Belgrade surrealist group and is at present one of the leading supporters of the modernist tendencies in Serbian literature. Of his numerous collections of essays the most notable are *Književna politika* (1952), *Krleža* (1954), and *Od istog pisca—umesto estetike* (1957). Ristić's work is difficult to interpret, because his pronouncements often meander between aestheticism and political pamphleteering. He is more significant as one of the pivotal figures in the current literary skirmish between modernists and socialist realists than for his critical brilliance.

Gligorić is, and has consistently been since the beginning of his career, a champion of socialist realism (q.v.). He denied any literary merit to some of the most prominent modernist poets of the interwar era and steadily encouraged those postwar authors who defended the social aims of literature and its materialistic foundation. His most significant studies are *Kritike, Matoš-Dis-Ujević, Pozorišne kritike, Srpski realisti,* and *Ogledi i studije.* In his early work Gligorić was a stubborn polemicist who frequently expounded extremely one-sided views. In the postwar era he has mellowed considerably, especially as a literary historian. His articles, however, are still impressionistically composed and without annotation.

MACEDONIAN LITERATURE

Because neither the Macedonian language nor the nationality achieved self-determination until after World War II, the Macedonian literature of the 20th c. has had only about twenty-five years of autonomous growth, during which time it has largely followed

Serbian literary trends. The national and cultural awakening, however, has produced a number of authors whose contemporary literary activity shows much promise. Of these the most notable in poetry are Blaže Koneski (b. 1921), Aco Šopov (b. 1923), Mateja Matevski (b. 1929), and Gane Todorovski (b. 1929), and in prose, Slavko Janevski (b. 1920), Jovan Boškovski (b. 1920), and Vlado Maleski (b. 1919).

CROATIAN LITERATURE

Like its Serbian counterpart, Croatian literature went through three separate stages in the 20th c. The first, known as Croatian "Moderna" (from the German *Die Moderne*), extended from 1895 to the end of World War I; the second covered the interwar years 1918–1941, and the third, those of World War II and its socialist aftermath.

Championed by Croatian youth who, while educated in Vienna, Prague, and Munich, absorbed the modernist ideas of the Viennese Secessionists, Moderna was a distinctly anti-traditionalist movement that demanded absolute creative freedom, spontaneity, and classlessness in all artistic endeavor.

The first poet to follow these precepts was the Dalmatian Begović (q.v.), whose early collection of verse *Knjiga Boccadero* (1900), with its Bacchanalian eulogies of the pleasures of the flesh, instantly became the artistic manifesto of the younger generation. Later, in the interwar period, Begović shifted to drama and prose fiction.

The second prominent modernist poet, Vladimir Vidrić (1875–1909), was educated in Zagreb and Vienna and died very young, leaving behind only a handful of poems. The exceptional quality of these, however, is indisputable; the innovative freshness of his style, the plasticity of his imagery, and the vividness of his sketches of nature greatly influenced both his contemporaries and the younger generation.

Also influential was the impoverished nobleman Dragutin Domjanić (1875–1933), whose best verse was so melodiously rich that a number of his poems were later set to music. Although his earlier collection of verse, *Pjesme* (1909), is steeped in the then fashionably decadent pessimism and languidity, his later one, *Kipci i popevke* (1917), written in the popular *kaj* dialect, reveals that beneath his decadent postures he retained a healthy affinity for the peasant masses of his country.

Nazor (q.v.) developed during the Moderna period, but remained on the periphery of its influence. In his early collection of verse *Slavenske legende* (1900), he forcefully exulted old Croat kings and heroes. After a long interwar retreat into Catholic religiosity, shown in his collection *Pjesme o četiri arhanđela*, he returned to contemporary materialist reality with his *Pjesme partizanke*. He also left a significant short-story collection in *Istarske priče* (1913), composed during his early stay in this Italian-occupied region and greatly influential in the national awakening of the Istrian Slavs.

A prominent playwright of this era outside the Moderna mainstream was the Zagreb-educated Dubrovnik nobleman, Vojnović (q.v.). Of his numerous plays the most significant are *Ekvinocij* (1895), set among the sturdy people of the Dalmatian littoral, and *Dubrovačka trilogija* (1900), which depicts the decline of the Republic of Dubrovnik and the gradual degeneration of its once proud and powerful nobility. Vojnović's occasional lapse into oratory and pathos is more than counterbalanced by his exceptional exuberance, lyricism, and a refined diction reminiscent of D'Annunzio (q.v.).

The last independent prose author of note to appear during this period was another Dalmatian, Dinko Šimunović (1873–1933), who excelled in the short story and novel. His best works include three collections of stories, *Mrkodol* (1905), *Đerdan* (1914) and *Sa Krke i sa Cetine* (1930), and the novels *Tuđinac* (1911) and *Porodica Vinčić* (1923), all concerned with the energetic people of the rugged Dalmatian hinterlands.

One of the most committed supporters of the Moderna movement in literary criticism was Milan Marjanović (1879–1955), who, after studying abroad, became the leading Croatian popularizer of the ideas of such critics as Saint Beuve (1807–1889), Hippolyte Taine (1829–93), and Brandes (q.v.). His best-known works are *Savremena Hrvatska*, written on the eve of World War I and published in Serbia, and *Hrvatska Moderna*, completed at the end of his literary career.

A more reliable witness to this age was Vienna-educated Milutin Cihlar-Nehajev (1880–1931), one of the most sophisticated Croatian literary critics, and also a writer of fiction. His short stories, collected in *Veliki grad* (1902), and his novel *Bijeg* (1909), steeped in decadent gloom and despondency, are considered most typical of the Moderna style. In his historical novel *Vuci* (1928), however,

Cihlar-Nehajev abandoned his modernist mournfulness in favor of a stoic acceptance of calamity.

By far the best literary critic of this era was Matoš (q.v.), who spent a good part of his productive life as an exile in Belgrade, Geneva, and Paris. An eclectic and cosmopolitan poet, prose writer, and musician, he not only successfully popularized the great Western authors, but managed to bring Croatian and Serbian literatures closer together. He was above all a national educator and cultural seer whose taste left an indelible imprint on this entire era.

By the beginning of World War I the ideals of the Moderna period had become outdated. The war years both intensified the struggle for a national, realistic literature and prepared writers for the appearance of expressionism (q.v.), which dominated Croatian literature throughout its interwar development.

One of the earliest propagators of German expressionism in Croatia, the Herzegovinian Antun Branko Šimić (1898–1925), excelled primarily in poetry. The prevalent themes in his two important collections of verse, *Preobraženja* and *Pjesme* (1950), reveal that he was almost exclusively concerned with the destinies of the poor and their social problems. He was a staunch defender of free verse who arranged his poems symmetrically, deliberately neglected rules of punctuation, and insisted on a meticulous purity of expression.

The most significant Croatian poet of this era, the Dalmatian Tin Ujević (1891–1955), was educated in Zagreb and later lived for long periods in Paris and Belgrade. His best verse appeared in the collections *Lelek sebra* (1920), *Kolajna* (1926), *Ojađeno zvono* (1933), and *Žedan kamen na studencu* (1954), all of which revealed his rare combination of erudition and sensitivity. Ujević's other work includes two collections of essays, *Ljudi za vratima gostionice* (1938) and *Skalpel Kaosa* (1938), a volume of prose poems, *Mudre i lude djevice,* and translations from several languages.

Even more diverse and prolific is Krleža (q.v.), generally considered the most important Croatian author and one of the very best in all southern Slav literatures. Krleža's style is characterized by its exuberance, abundance of imagery, and structural antithesis. His poetry combines the straightforwardness of commonplace expression with the sonorous lyricism of emotionally exalted utterance. His prose is renowned for its pungency, verbal bravado and a certain vehement, almost irresistible rhythm. In his short stories Krleža largely depicts the world of the Croat common folk, abused in both peace and war by domestic and foreign upper classes; in his plays and novels, he turns to the decadence and moral ambiguities of the Croat and Hapsburg bourgeoisie and gentry struck by the sudden sociopolitical changes of the interwar epoch. In all these spheres Krleža proved an acute observer and impeccable stylist with the creative virility and temperament of a truly great writer.

Unlike Krleža's, the expression of Gustav Krklec (b. 1899) is one of gentle and lilting repose. Born in Lika and educated in Prague and Vienna, Krklec early manifested a gift for poetry, which is quite reminiscent of that of Rilke (q.v.). His best verse is found in the collections *Srebrna cesta* (1921), *Tamnica vremena*, and *Žubor života*, and his most notable essays in the books *Lica i krajolici* and *Pisma Martina Lipnjaka* (1956). Aglow in the brightness and luminosity of his special optimism, Krklec's verse seems to suggest inspiration and encouragement even when it is sentimental and mournful. His essays, which often accompany his excellent translations from German and Slovene, are also imbued with that light, radiant lyricism that is so characteristic of his poetic style.

Of the Croatian poets that came into prominence in the 1930's, the most notable are Dobriša Cesarić (b. 1902) and Dragutin Tadijanović (b. 1905). The first has produced only some hundred short poems, the best of which are collected in his *Lirika* (1931). Recurrent motifs in his earlier poetry involve love, the landscape of his native Slavonia, and the pain of social injustice; those of his later verse point to his inner world of perception and the contemplation of the hereafter. His style is chiefly characterized by its limpid musicality and vivid imagery.

Tadijanović is far more prolific, though stylistically quite similar. His best collections of verse include *Sunce nad oranicama* (1933), *Pepeo srca* (1936), *Blagdan žetve*, and *Prsten*. Intensely subjective, most of Tadijanović's poetry refers to his small world of rural tranquillity. His language flows so gracefully that his verse vignettes glow with warmth and tenderness.

The most significant literary critic of this era, Antun Barac (1894–1955), is noted for both his productivity and his discriminating taste. In addition to a score of excellent monographs on prominent Croatian authors, Barac wrote essays dedicated to general literary problems. His major works, *Hrvatska književna kritika, Jugoslavenska književnost,* and above all *Književnost Ilirizma,* are distinguished by their systematic presentation and calm objectivity.

The most recent period of Croatian literature began with the outbreak of World War II, which greatly affected both those writers whose work had matured before the disaster struck, and those who developed in the midst of the conflict. In the works of both groups the war is prominent, but although the former can treat it systematically and realistically, the latter were never able to synthesize completely the horrors of their most impressionable years.

The leading poet of the older group is Ivan Goran Kovačić (1913–43), whose prewar output includes a collection of verse and one of short stories, both descriptive of the life and people in his native Gorski Kotar. His chief accomplishment, however, is the long poem in ten cantos, *Jama* (1944), written after he joined the partisan resistance and shortly before he was killed. With majestic serenity, classical measure, and an exceptional stylistic verve, *Jama* recounts the sensations of a blinded survivor of a gruesome massacre of the civilian population. A significant part of the poem's greatness lies in its not naming the guilty; it simply unveils the horror of mankind's inhumanity.

The literary career of the Dalmatian-born Vjekoslav Kaleb (b. 1905) also began shortly before the war with the appearance of his collection of short stories *Na kamenju* (1940), and it continued after the war, which the author spent with the partisans, with two novels, *Ponižene ulice* (1950) and *Bijeli kamen* (1955), and the long story *Divota prašine* (1954). Although Kaleb's mature work is thoroughly permeated with his war experiences, it is marked by objectivity, brevity, and composure. He is particularly noted for the terseness of his line, a keen sense of understatement, and a tight control of subject matter.

The third prominent member of this group is another Dalmatian, Ranko Marinković (b. 1913), who drew attention to his talent with his prewar play *Albatros,* but whose best prose work, two collections of stories, *Proza* (1948), and *Ruke* (1953), appeared in the postwar years. Externally marinković depicts life on his native island Vis, but beneath the surface he is usually concerned with basic questions of the human condition. Stylistically, he is both a realist and a modernist. His expression, although occasionally colored by bitter humor and skepticism, is clear, profound, and rich in themes of timeless validity.

Of the younger generation that matured during the war, the most promising are the poets Jure Kaštelan (b. 1919) and Vesna Parun (b. 1922). Kaštelan's experiences in the partisan struggle still seem to haunt his poetic expression. His best verse appeared in the collections *Pjetao na krovu* and *Biti ili ne,* both of which reveal his visceral dread that mankind may again descend into the abyss of war.

In her first verse collection, *Zore i vihori,* the Dalmatian poetess Vesna Parun also pondered the horrors of war and man's destructiveness, but in her subsequent ones, *Crna maslina, Vidrama vjerna,* and *Ropstvo,* she shifted to a subtler, more personal expression. Certain of her poems, such as "Ti koja imaš nevinije ruke," are so extraordinary, so self-contained, and so emotionally effective that they more than compensate for the sentimentalism and monotony of the rest, and decisively prove her uncommon poetic gifts.

SLOVENIAN LITERATURE

Three main stages also mark the development of 20th-c. Slovenian literature: the pre-World War I Slovenian Moderna, the interwar rivalry of expressionist and socialist realist trends, and the complex ferment of the World War II years and the contemporary socialist reality.

The Slovenian Moderna, like its Croatian counterpart, combined aesthetic demands for new modes of expression, new poetic vision, and new concepts of form with practical concern for national survival, social reform, and political independence.

The leading spirit of the new movement was one of the most versatile Slovenian authors, Cankar (q.v.), whose literary activity included poetry, prose, drama, and literary criticism. In poetry he introduced new verse forms, simplified rhythms, and fresh metaphors, while in prose and drama he combined his psychological insight into the true nature of human conflicts with a burning concern for the betterment of social conditions and an inborn flare for the unmasking of hypocrisy and injustice.

Cankar's contemporary and friend Župančič (q.v.) was the greatest representative of Slovenian Moderna in poetry. Renowned for his opposition to traditionalism, involvement in social questions, and faith in the spirit of the people, Župančič enriched Slovenian poetry with smoother rhythms, streamlined and more melodic verse structure, and greater subtlety in revealing personal feelings.

Throughout the interwar period the Slovenian literary scene was the meeting ground of the continuing psychological and socialist realist (*see* socialist realism) tendencies and those of the newly emerging expressionism.

The most notable representative of the psychological realist trend is Bevk (q.v.), whose vast literary output in verse, prose, drama, travelogues, and memoirs makes him the most prolific of all Slovenian writers. An imaginative spinner of plots and a keen psychologist, Bevk drew a multitude of sharply outlined characters in situations that force them to bare their innermost instincts for survival, power, love, and gratification. His combination of terse accuracy and simplicity of description with keen insight into the workings of the human psyche enriched his style with rare authenticity and economy of expression.

The most notable Slovenian expressionists of this era were Anton Vodnik (1901–1965), Miran Jarc (1900–1942), and Anton Podbevšek (b. 1898). Vodnik's best collections of verse, *Žalostne roke, Virgilije,* and *Srebrni rog,* reveal that his poetry is fragile, alienated from everyday reality, wrought with ethereal visions, and ascetically pure, with much of its imagery derived from the Catholic Mass and the Bible.

Although Jarc wrote some prose and criticism, his major literary accomplishment is found in the collections of verse *Človek in noč, Novembrske pesmi,* and *Lirika.* His expression is on the whole less cosmic and more personal than Vodnik's, although he too used expressionistic devices to highlight the quests of modern man imprisoned in an insensitive, decaying social order.

Podbevšek's poetry, best represented by his verse collection *Človek z bombami,* concentrates on the spiritually bankrupt postwar man tormented by the gruesome memories of the war and lost in the deafening clatter of modern technology. Stylistically, Podbevšek appears to be strongly influenced by the American poet Walt Whitman (1819–92) and by futurism (q.v.).

The interwar socialist realist circle produced in the 1930's the powerful prose writer Prežihov (q.v.), who had little formal education but had traveled widely. Socially *engagé,* he joined the Communist Party early, for which he

was later greatly persecuted by the royalists and the German invaders. Because of his clear-cut political commitment his work is notable for its distinctly pronounced class point of view.

With epic force and terse language Prežihov's stories and novels depicted the life of hardy and tenacious Slovenian mountaineers, dominated in war and peace by their domestic and foreign oppressors. Prežihov's language is picturesque and full of dialectal expressions. His characters are convincingly drawn, imbued with animal vitality, and fiercely independent.

Similar to Prežihov in both life experiences and literary style is Ciril Kosmač (b. 1910), who specialized in fiction. His principal accomplishments are the short-story collection *Sreča in kruh,* the novelette *Pomladni dan,* and the film scenario *Na svojoj zemlji.* Kosmač is a dynamic realist and a meticulous craftsman with a particular flair for colloquially authentic dialogue and psychologically accurate character delineation.

The partisan struggle of World War II inspired the work of Bor (q.v.), who began as a poet but later also wrote in prose. From the buoyantly optimistic, aggressive partisan themes prevalent in his early war poetry, Bor progressed to the measured, intimate, personal expression of a mature artist notable for his stylistic embellishments and wit. His novel *Dlajave* (1961) is one of the most modernistically constructed and cosmopolitan works of postwar Slovenian prose.

The leading Slovenian literary critic in the early decades of this c., and the first Slovenian practitioner of the modern psychological-impressionist critical method, was Ivan Prijatelj (1876–1937), who left a number of important scholarly studies dealing with the Slovenian phase of the Protestant Reformation, the literary renaissance, the Illyrian movement, and the struggles for the establishment of a literary language. In addition he wrote monographs on the most prominent Slovenian authors of the 19th and 20th c.'s, and equally significant essays on Russian and Polish literary movements and masters. His most important works, however, were his numerous essays in the realm of general aesthetics and literary theory, because they introduced the standards that brought Slovenian literature closer to the European cultural mainstream.

Prijatelj's dicta were both accepted and applied by Josip Vidmar (b. 1895), who founded the first Slovenian critical periodical,

Kritiko, and fought in it for the autonomy of art and its liberation from market and business considerations. In addition to his excellent studies on Slovenian writers, his work includes the book *Kulturni problem slovenstva,* and three collections of essays, *Literarne kritike, Meditacije,* and *Polemike.* In his evaluation of literary material Vidmar went through both ethical and aesthetic considerations before determining the larger sociological value of a given work. A meticulous and cosmopolitan judge of excellence, he freely compared Slovenian authors with those of greater world literatures, and thus contributed to the widening of Slovenian literary horizons and the retirement of old, narrow, provincial critical standards.

BIBLIOGRAPHY: Urbani, U., *Scrittori Jugoslavi* (1936); Barac, A., *History of Yugoslav Literature* (1955); Cronia, A., *Storia della letteratura serbo-croata* (1956); Kadić, A., *Contemporary Croatian Literature* (1960); Maver, G., *Letteratura serbo-croata* (1960); Maver, G., *Letteratura slovena* (1960); Czuka, Z., *A Jugoslav nepek irodalmanak fortenete* (1963); Kadić, A., *Contemporary Serbian Literature* (1964); Janež, S., and Ravbar, M., *Pregled slovenske književnosti* (1966); Lukić, S., *Savremena jugoslovenska literatura* (1968)

NICHOLAS MORAVCEVICH

Z

ZABOLOTZKI, Nikolai Alekseyevich

Soviet-Russian poet, b. 7 May 1903, Kazan; d. 14 Oct. 1958, Moscow

The son of an agronomist, Z. studied philology in Moscow and later in Leningrad, where he worked in a publishing house directed by S. J. Marshak (1877–1964) and specializing in children's books. In 1937 or 1938 he was arrested and exiled, but during World War II he was released, and new poems and translations began to appear in various magazines and in comparatively limited editions.

Z.'s first collection of verse, *Stolbtzy* (1929), which is a bibliographical rarity now, uses surrealistic (*see* surrealism) imagery and adapts techniques from cubism. In it Z. depicts Leningrad's slums, markets, and places of popular entertainment. He mixes "high" and "low" diction, verse, and prose rhythms, parodying earlier poets and freely employing nonsense elements. The book was severely criticized by the authorities.

The same fate was met by his long poem "Torzhestvo zemledeliya" (1938), which, while seeming to be an apologia for modern mechanized Soviet agriculture, is actually a utopian portrait with pantheistic overtones. It is presented in a manner that recalls primitive painting. In it the influence of Khlebnikov's (q.v.) style and ideas is strongly felt.

The theme of Z.'s *Vtoraya kniga* (1937) is nature and modern biology, and some of the poems show the beginnings of a conformist approach in their topics and style.

After Z.'s return from exile, he published a number of translations among which was the adaptation of *Slovo o polku Igoreve* (1946), an early Ukrainian prose poem describing the campaign of Prince Igor against a nomadic Polovtzki tribe. *Stikhotvoreniya* (1948), in which Z. praises the building of socialism in parnassian manner, shows a continuing tendency toward conventionalism.

Forgotten for many years, Z. has been rediscovered by readers and critics alike and emerged as the most original poet of the Soviet postrevolutionary generation, especially in his nonconformist early poems.

FURTHER WORK: *Izbrannoye* (1960)

BIBLIOGRAPHY: Hayward, M., and Labenz, L., eds., *Literature and Revolution in Soviet Russia, 1917–62* (1963); Chukovski, N., "Vstrechi's Zabolotzkim," *Neva*, No. 9 (1965), pp. 186–91; Muchnic, H., "Three Inner Emigrés: Anna Akhmatova, Osip Mandelstam, N. Z.," *Russian Review*, XXVI (1967), 13–25; Karlinsky, S., "Surrealism in Twentieth Century Russian Poetry: Churilin, Z., Poplavski," *SlavR*, XXVI (1967), 605–17

VLADIMIR MARKOV

ZAMYATIN, Yevgenii Ivanovich

Russian novelist, short-story writer, dramatist, editor, and critic, b. 1 Feb. 1884, Lebedyan, Tambov Province; d. 10 March 1937, Paris

Z. was the son of a teacher, and a naval engineer by training. His first important work was the satirical novella *Uyezdnoye* (1913; A Provincial Tale, 1967). For his second novella, *Na Kulichkakh* (1914), which satirized the life of a provincial garrison town, the czarist authorities brought Z. to trial on charges of maligning the officer corps. Exonerated by the court, he was later sent to England, where he spent two years, during World War I, designing and supervising the building of icebreakers for Russia. On his return he wrote two satires on English life, the novella *Ostrovityane* (1918) and the story *Lovetz chelovekov* (1922). The former was later dramatized as *Obshchestvo pochetnykh zvonariov* (1926; The Society of Honorary Bell-ringers, 1971).

A bolshevik during his student years, repeatedly arrested and exiled from Leningrad, Z. was also persecuted under the communist regime for his outspoken criticism of the regimentation of literature and his insistence on creative freedom. "In art," he wrote in *Novaya russkaya proza* (1923; The New Russian Prose, 1970), "the surest way to destroy is to canonize one given form and one philosophy." He rejected the crude realism of "proletarian literature" and urged the use of the "real," the familiar, merely as a springboard to the realities of being, to philosophy, to the fantastic. Life itself, he felt, "has lost its plane reality: it is projected, not along the old fixed points, but along the dynamic coordinates of Einstein, of revolution. In this new projection, the best-known formulas become displaced, fantastic, familiar–unfamiliar." In his essay *O literature, revolutzii, entropii i prochem* (1924; On Literature, Revolution, and Entropy, 1962), he wrote: "What we need today are vast philosophic horizons; we need the most ultimate, the most fearsome, the most fearless 'Why?' and 'What next?' "

A consummate craftsman, witty, original, and merciless to cant, Z. was the guiding spirit of the Serapion Brothers, a group that included some of the most talented young writers of the 1920's, who, like their teacher, insisted on experiment, innovation, and the artist's right to his own individual vision.

Z.'s famous anti-utopian novel *My* (1952, New York; We, 1925), written in 1920 but never published in Soviet Russia, is a savage satire on the dehumanized society he saw emerging as a result of current trends. It is said to have influenced Huxley's (q.v.) *Brave New World* and Orwell's (q.v.) *1984*. One of the basic ideas of *My* is that there is no final revolution—each revolution is only one in an infinite series that make up the flow of history.

Among his best stories are the balladlike "Sever" (1918; The North, 1967), "Rus" (1922; In Old Russia, 1967), and "Navodneniye" (1929; The Flood, 1967), which probe profoundly into human passions. *Rasskaz o samom glavnom* (1923; A Story about the Most Important Thing, 1967) is a surrealistic, many-faceted commentary on contemporary life. *O tom kak istzelen byl inok Erazm* (1920; The Healing of the Novice Erasmus, 1967) is a tongue-in-cheek ribald tale. *Iks* (1926; X, 1967) combines ribaldry, comic invention, and satire on revolutionary mores.

Z.'s first play, *Ogni Svyatovo Dominika* (1922; The Fires of Saint Dominic, 1971), dealing with the Spanish Inquisition, strongly suggests his condemnation of the inquisition-like policies of the Soviet regime. *Blokha* (1926; The Flea, 1971), a folk play in the tradition of the *commedia dell'arte*, was based on Nikolai Leskov's (1831–95) story *Levsha*. It was performed with great success by the Moscow Art Theater. Atilla (1950, New York; Attila, 1971), written in 1925–27, is a moving poetic tragedy about the death of Attila. In 1928 it was passed by the censors and accepted by the Leningrad Bolshoi Dramatic Theater for production. When it was already in rehearsal and announced in posters, permission to produce it was suddenly withdrawn.

Throughout the 1920's Z. had been violently attacked by party-line critics. Now he was subjected to a particularly vicious campaign of vilification, which used as a pretext the unauthorized appearance in 1927 of excerpts from *My* in *Volya Rossii*, an *émigré* journal published in Prague. Z. was expelled from his editorial positions and denied all access to publication. In 1931 he wrote a moving and forthright letter to Stalin, asking permission to leave Russia until "it becomes possible in our country to serve great ideas in literature without cringing before little men," until "there is at least a partial change in the prevailing view concerning the role of the literary artist." Helped by the intervention of Gorki (q.v.), Z. was allowed to go abroad. He settled in France, where he lived until his death in 1937.

In Russian literature, Z. belongs to the tradition of Gogol, Leskov, Belyi (q.v.), and Remizov (q.v.)—a tradition marked by wit, stylistic inventiveness, and great verbal mastery. A hallmark of this tradition is the refusal to be bound by literal fact, and the blending of reality and fantasy in forms that are often grotesque, oblique, but always true to the writer's original vision.

Z. was one of the most brilliant and influential Soviet writers in the 1920's. He has never been granted even partial "rehabilitation" in

Soviet Russia and is still virtually unknown to the Russian readers.

FURTHER WORKS: *Kryazhi* (1918); *Gerbert Uells* (1922; H. G. Wells, 1970); *Ostrovityane; povesti i rasskazy* (1922); *Robert Mayer* (1922); *Bolshim Detyam Skazki* (1922); *Na Kulichkakh; povesti i rasskazy* (1923); *Fonar* (1926); *Nechestivyye rasskazy* (1927); *Sobraniye sochinenii* (4 vols., 1929); *Zhitiye blokhi* (1929); *Bich Bozhyi* (1939); *Litza* (1955); *Povesti i rasskazy* (1963). **Selected English translations:** *The Dragon: Fifteen Stories* (1967); *A Soviet Heretic: Essays* (1970); *Five Plays* (1971)

BIBLIOGRAPHY: Kozmin, B. P., *Pisateli sovremennoi epokhi,* Vol. I (1928), pp. 131–33; Voronski, A., *Literaturnyye portrety,* Vol. I (1928), pp. 76–110; Eastman, M., *Artists in Uniform* (1934), pp. 82–93; Hayward, M., "Pilnyak and Z.," *Survey,* No. 36 (1961), pp. 85–91; Richards, D. J., *Z.: A Soviet Heretic* (1962); Alexandrova, V., *A History of Soviet Literature* (1963), pp. 84–96; Brown, E. J., "Z. and English Literature," in *American Contributions to the Fifth International Congress of Slavists,* Vol. II (1964), pp. 21–40; Annenkov, J., *Dnevnik Moikh Vstrech* (1966), pp. 246–86; Collins, C., "Z., Wells and the Utopian Literary Tradition," *SEER,* XLIV (July 1966), ciii, 351–60; Collins, C., "Z.'s *We* as Myth," *SEEJ,* X (Summer 1966), ii, 125–33; Shane, A. M., *The Life and Works of E. Z.* (1968)

MIRRA GINSBURG

ZANGWILL, Israel

English novelist, short-story writer, essayist, and dramatist, b. 21 Jan. 1864, London; d. 1 Aug. 1926, Midhurst, Sussex

Born of immigrant parents in the Whitechapel ghetto, Z. was educated at the Jews' Free School and London University. He later taught at the Jews' Free School, resigning in 1888 to devote his time to writing. In 1895 he became active in the Zionist movement but broke with it in 1905 to form the Jewish Territorial Organization, which was dedicated to founding a Jewish national homeland within the British Empire. In 1903 Z. married novelist Edith Ayrton.

Z.'s literary career began in 1882, when he collaborated with Louis Cowen on *Motza Kleis,* a description of market day in Whitechapel. His first novel, *The Premier and the Painter*

(1888), also written in collaboration with Cowen, appeared under the pseudonym "J. Freeman Bell." Subsequently Z. edited a humorous paper, *Ariel* (1890–92), and contributed to *The Jewish Standard, Pall Mall Magazine,* and numerous other journals.

Popular success came with his *The Bachelors' Club* (1891), a series of humorous sketches reminiscent of Charles Dickens's (1812–70) *Pickwick Papers,* and with *The Big Bow Mystery* (1891), a somewhat satirical detective story that has several times been made into a movie. However, it was *Children of the Ghetto* (1892), a realistic novel of Jewish life in Whitechapel, that established Z.'s reputation. The book's interest is not simply in the sympathetically drawn characters or in the revelation of a world foreign to most readers; in its depiction of the conflict between the older, orthodox generation of Jews and the young, skeptical and "emancipated" generation, it develops a theme of universal application. Though Z.'s subsequent novels, short stories, and essays received a friendly critical reception—he was less successful when he tried his hand at poetry—he never again achieved the artistic level of *Children of the Ghetto,* except perhaps in *The King of Schnorrers* (1894), a delightful satire with an audacious confidence-man hero in the tradition of Ben Jonson's (1573–1637) Alchemist.

After the turn of the century, Z. devoted himself to writing plays. Though his drama—ill-received by critics—at times contains melodramatic scenes, stock characters, awkward dialogue, and inflated diction, it is a serious and often forceful treatment of important social themes. *The Melting Pot* (1909), his best-known play, deals with racial assimilation; *The War God* (1911), with the horror and futility of violence; *The Next Religion* (1912), with the attempt to replace outdated creeds with a new religion; *The Cockpit* (1921), with the Machiavellian ethics of statesmanship, and *The Forcing House* (1922), with the failure of state socialism.

Like George Bernard Shaw (q.v.), whom he in some way resembles, Z. worked for social reform—he was a feminist, a pacifist, a territorialist, and an internationalist. A socialist of sorts, he believed that "Society is sacred, not Property." Though his reputation has declined in recent years, the humor, warmth, and intelligence of his best works continue to deserve attention.

FURTHER WORKS: *The Old Maids' Club*
(1892); *Ghetto Tragedies* (1893); *The Master*
(1895); *Without Prejudice* (1896); *Dreamers of
the Ghetto* (1898); *The Celibates' Club, Being
the United Stories of the Bachelors' Club, and
The Old Maids' Club* (1898); *The That Walk
in Darkness* (1899); *The Mantle of Elijah*
(1900); *The Grey Wig: Stories and Novelettes*
(1903); *Blind Children* (1903); *Merely Mary
Ann* (1904); *The Serio-comic Governess*
(1904); *Ghetto Comedies* (1907); *Italian
Fantasies* (1910); *Plaster Saints: A High
Comedy in Three Movements* (1914); *The War
for the World* (1916); *Chosen Peoples: The
Hebraic Ideal "Versus" the Teutonic* (1918);
Jinny the Carrier (1919); *The Voice of
Jerusalem* (1920); *Watchman, What of the
Night?* (1923); *Too Much Money: A Farcical
Comedy in Three Acts* (1924); *We Moderns:
A Post-War Comedy in Three Movements*
(1925)

BIBLIOGRAPHY: Harris, L, "Mr. I. Z. Inter-
viewed," *The Bookman*, XIII (1898), 145–48;
Spire, A., *Israël Zangwill* (1909); Freund, M.,
I. Z.'s Stellung zum Judentum (1927); Leftwich,
J., *I. Z.* (1957); Peterson A., "I. Z. (1864–
1926): A Selected Bibliography," *Bulletin of
Bibliography and Magazine Notes*, XXIII
(1961), 136–40; Wohlgelernter, M., "*I. Z.: A
Study* (1964)

ELSIE B. ADAMS

ZAWIEYSKI, Jerzy

Polish dramatist and novelist, b. 2 Oct. 1902,
Radogoszcz; d. 18 June 1969, Warsaw

After graduating from a Cracow drama school
in 1926, Z. went to work as an actor in the
famous Reduta group, later accompanying
them to France (1929–32). Upon his return to
Poland, Z. began his literary career as a novelist and dramatist.

During World War II, Z. played an important role in the underground cultural life, later
emerging as a major author and a spokesman
for the Roman Catholic intellectual movement.
In 1949 he won an award of the Polish
Episcopate. In 1956 he was elected the vice-
president of the Union of Polish Writers and,
in 1957, became a deputy to the Diet from the
Catholic group Znak. In 1968 he was made a
member of the State Council.

Z.'s interest in moral and social problems
is evident in one of his early dramas, *Powrót
Przełęckiego* (1937).

The suffering, moral anguish, and intellectual
confusion of World War II and its aftermath
provided Z. with themes for his dramas
Rozdroże miłości (1947), *Ocalenie Jakuba*
(1947; The Deliverance of Jacob, 1952), and
Wysoka ściana (1956). Z. often used biblical
and classical motifs to present moral problems
facing modern man. The most characteristic of
these are *Socrates* (1950) and *Tyrtaeus* (1956).
His plays were collected in two volumes,
Dramaty (1957) and *Dramaty współczesne*
(1962).

Z.'s Catholicism is more strongly evident in
his short stories and novels, which offer a
Catholic view of history, morals, and contemporary society. Although he often depicted his
protagonists as helpless victims of historical
circumstances, he saw human suffering and
God's grace as the way to eternal salvation.
His last two novels, *Konrad nie chce zejść ze
sceny* (1966) and *Wawrzyny i cyprysy* (1966),
dealt with Polish history in terms of individual
heroism and freedom of choice.

Strong moral convictions and deep religious
faith underlie his dramas, which gradually
evolved toward modern experimental techniques. He is an important representative of
the contemporary attempt of Polish Catholic
writers to combine religious philosophy and
social ideas.

FURTHER WORKS: *Gdzie jesteś, przy-
jacielu?* (1932); *Człowiek jest niepotrzebny*
(1934); *Daleko do rana* (1934); *Dyktator Faust*
(1934); *Portret Łukasza* (1937); *Prawdziwe
życie Anny* (1939); *Masław* (1945); *Mąż
doskonały* (1945); *Droga do domu* (1946);
Dzień sądu (1947); *Miłość Anny* (1948); *Owoc
swego czasu* (1949); *Niezwyciężony Herakles*
(1952); *Lament Orestesa* (1953); *Pokój głębi*
(1956); *Notatnik liryczny* (1956); *Maski Marii
Dominiki* (1957); *Próby ognia i czasu* (1958);
Brzegiem cienia (1960); *Romans z ojczyzną*
(1963); *W alei bezpożytecznych rozmyślań*
(1966). **Selected English translations:** Selections
in *10 Contemporary Polish Stories* (ed. E.
Ordon; 1958); *Contemporary Polish Short
Stories* (ed. A. Kijowski; 1960); *Polish Plays in
English Translations* (ed. B. Taborski, 1968;
includes four dramas translated and available
in manuscript)

BIBLIOGRAPHY: Starowieyska-Morstinowa,
Z., *Kalejdoskop literacki* (1955); Sadkowski,
W., *Literatura katolicka w Polsce* (1963);
Ziomek, J., *Wizerunki polskich pisarzy*

katolickich (1963); Biernacki, A., "A Word about Ż.," *Polish Perspectives,* IX (1966), v, 25–27

JERZY R. KRZYŻANOWSKI

ŻEROMSKI, Stefan

(pseuds: *Maurycy Zych, Józef Katerla*), Polish novelist, short-story writer, and dramatist, b. 1 Nov. 1864, Strawczyna, d. 20 Nov. 1925, Warsaw

Born into an impoverished noble family, Ż. lost his parents while still in school but was able to continue his studies with the help of relatives and by tutoring fellow students. Having failed to graduate from the Kielce high school, he enrolled in the School of Veterinarians in Warsaw in 1886, only to abandon it a year later and to resume tutoring in the homes of Polish landed gentry. In 1892 he left Poland and worked as a librarian in the Polish Museum in Rapperswil, Switzerland. He returned in 1896 and was employed by the Zamoyski Library in Warsaw until 1904. After World War I he took up permanent residence in Warsaw.

While still a high-school student, Ż. published translations of Mikhail Lermontov's (1814–41) poems and his own poetry in the weekly magazines *Tygodnik Mód i Powieści* and *Przyjaciel Dzieci*. His first short stories appeared in the periodicals *Tygodnik Powszechny* and *Głos* in 1889. Collected in 1895 under the title *Rozdziobią nas kruki i wrony,* they depict the tragic fight of the Polish insurgents and patriots against the Russian oppressors. Ż.'s first novel, *Syzyfowe prace* (1898; republished as *Andrzej Radek,* 1910), is autobiographical in character and reflects the resistance of Polish youth to the Russian attempts to break its spirit and eradicate its national feelings.

The short stories and tales in *Opowiadania* (1895) and *Utwory powieściowe* (1898) deal with Polish social problems, and some—*e.g.,* "Siłacka" and "Doktor Piotr"—offer well-realized characterizations of young idealists. The novel *Ludzie bezdomni* (1900) is both a touching rendering of a doctor's desperate and self-sacrificing fight against social injustice and an emotional and savagely realistic presentation of social evil.

In his great historical epic *Popioły* (1904; The Ashes, 1928), Ż. focuses on the horrors of war and presents a broad picture of Polish national life during the Napoleonic wars.

Dzieje grzechu (1906) portrays contemporary ethical and social problems by recounting a young woman's gradual disintegration in an atmosphere of hopelessness and crime. The trilogy *Walka z Szatanem* (1916–19; I., *Nawracanie Judasza*; II., *Zamieć*; III., *Charitas*) once again deals with crime and passionate love. The 1863 rebellion provides a dramatic background for the love story at the heart of the novel *Wierna rzeka* (1913; The Faithful River, 1943). In his last novel, *Przedwiośnie* (1924), Ż. contrasts the revolutionary turmoil in Russia and the precarious position of the newly independent Poland, torn by local problems and social unrest.

Ż. wrote a number of plays, but they lack dramatic focus. The best of them, *Uciekła mi przepióreczka w proso* (1924), portrays the conflict between personal happiness and devotion to an ideal.

Ż. was the foremost prose writer of the neoromantic "Young Poland" literary movement. He created a gallery of memorable characters —particularly women—whose emotions he subtly and convincingly expressed. His originally structured novels contain nature descriptions unsurpassed in Polish literature, combining deeply felt lyrical passages with minutely detailed and frighteningly realistic scenes. Ż.'s language is rich and precise, emotional and graphic, ranging from dialect to polished poetic prose.

FURTHER WORKS: *Do swego Boga* (1894); *Aryman mści się: Godzina* (1904); *Echa leśne* (1905); *Sen o rycerskiej szpadzie* (1905); *Powieść o Udałym Walgierzu* (1906); *Duma o hetmanie* (1908); *Słowo o Bandosie* (1908); *Róża* (1909); *Sułkowski* (1909); *Uroda życia* (1912); *Sen o szpadze i sen o chlebie* (1916); *Wisła* (1918); *Wszystko i nic* (1919); *Inter arma* (1920); *Ponad śnieg bielszym się stanę* (1921); *Biała rękawiczka* (1921); *Wiatr od morza* (1922); *Turoń* (1923); *Miedzymorze* (1924); *Elegie i inne pisma literackie i społeczne* (1928); *Dziennik podróży* (1933); *Grzech* (1950); *Dzienniki z lat 1882–1890* (1964)

BIBLIOGRAPHY: Dyboski, R., "Ż., and Reymont," *SlavR,* IV (1926); Gatto, E. L., *S. Ż.: Studio critico* (1926); Borowy, W., "Ż.," *SEER,* XIV (1935–36); Kridl, M., *A Survey of Polish Literature and Culture* (1956), pp. 421–35; Hutnikiewicz, A., *S. Ż.* (1960); Kasztelowicz, J., and Eile, S., *S. Ż., Kalendarz życia i twórczości* (1961); Vitt, M., *S. Ż.* (1961)

MARK LIWSZYC

ZILAHY, Lajos
Hungarian novelist, playwright, poet, and essayist, b. 27 March 1891, Nagyszalonta

Son of a well-to-do family of the lesser nobility of the Austro-Hungarian empire, Z. was publishing poetry in Budapest literary magazines by the time he was sixteen. He studied law at the University of Budapest. During World War I, Z. fought on the Russian front and was wounded in 1915. Convinced that Hungary was Germany's cat's-paw in the war, Z. became a pacifist and deserted the army. His first book, *Versek* (1915), a volume of pacifist poems, appeared while he was recovering from his wounds.

After the war Z. turned to journalism, and his essays, poems, and stories were widely published in Hungary. *Halálos tavasz*, his first novel, appeared in 1922. At this time he also began writing plays and quickly achieved national popular success. His fame became international with his third novel, *Két fogoly* (1927; Two Prisoners, 1931). The protagonist, a junior bank employee whose aspirations and desires are suggested by his job, is separated from his wife, having been drafted at the outbreak of World War I and then captured by the Russians. Complex political circumstances and love affairs prevent husband and wife from being reunited; they are "two prisoners" caught in a network of forces released by the war.

A szökevény (1930; The Deserter, 1932), another novel set during the war, detailed the social and personal turmoil in an Hungarian context. Its success added to Z.'s reputation, which continued to grow during the 1930's.

During World War II, while Hungary was allied to Germany but not yet occupied, Z. gave his entire fortune to the Hungarian nation to found the Zilahy Institute for world peace and service to humanity. After the German occupation in 1944, orders were issued for Z.'s arrest. He managed, however, to survive the battle of Budapest, only to be labeled a traitor by the post-war communist government.

In 1947, Z. brought his family to New York. His ninth novel, *Ararát* (1947; The Dukays, 1949), was published at that time. With the possible exception of *Két fogoly*, this long novel —written in the grand style with an impressive control of main and sub plots, a great number and variety of characters, and a broad spectrum of themes and social concerns—is Z.'s finest work. It deals with a wealthy aristocratic family—the Dukays—during the decline of the Austro-Hungarian empire and of traditional European society in general. The fates of various members of two generations of Dukays during the first decades of this century provide the book's central focus, but the novel's basic theme is man's struggle for justice on both the personal and social planes.

The Angry Angel (1953), published only in translation, is a sequel to *Ararát*. In this novel, which ends in 1950, Z. highlights the impact of World War II on the Dukays and their world. *Century in Scarlet* (1965), also published only in translation, concerns the Dukay family in the 19th c., after the fall of Napoleon. Like Z.'s previous works it is rich in characters, panoramic action, and pageantry.

Z.'s style is direct and realistic, yet it has something of a romantic flavor. Idealistic rather than ideological, his stance is that of a concerned, somewhat sardonic observer of the disintegration of middle- and upper-class life in central Europe between the two world wars. His appeal has been broad and humanitarian, and he has remained in the best sense of the term an important popular writer.

FURTHER WORKS: *Szépapám szerelme* (1923); *Süt a nap* (1924); *A fehér szarvas* (1927); *Valamit visz a víz* (1928); *A tábornok* (1928); *Összegyüjtött Munkái* (10 vols., 1929); *A tésasszony* (1930); *Leona* (1930); *A lélek kialszik* (1932); *A tizenkettedik óra* (1932); *Tüzmadár* (1932); *A kisasszony* (1932); *Fatornyok* (1934); *Fehér hajó* (1935); *Az utolsó szerep* (1935); *Fegyverek vissanéznek* (1936); *Úrilány* (1936); *A szüz és a gödölye* (1937); *A földönfutóváros* (1939); *Gyümölcs a fán* (1939); *Csöndes élet, és egyéb elbeszélések* (1941); *Krisztina és a király* (London, 1953)

BIBLIOGRAPHY: Hankiss, J., *Panorama de la littérature hongroise contemporare* (1930); Klaniczay, T., *History of Hungarian Literature* (1964), p. 233; Remenyi, J., *Hungarian Writers and Literature* (1964), pp. 414–23

CONNY NELSON

ZĪVERTS, Mārtiņš
Latvian dramatist, b. 5 Jan. 1903, Mežmuiža parish

Z. studied philosophy at the University of Latvia. He later worked as an editor. He then became stage director for the National and Dailes theaters in Riga, for which he also wrote dramas. Since 1944 he has lived in Sweden and

577

has often been invited to direct stage productions in Denmark, England, Germany, and Australia.

Z. began his career as a writer by attacking the formless stage adaptations in vogue during the 1930's, as questions of form are of central importance in his work. However, even after one of his plays, *Nafta* (1931), had been produced at the National Theater, Z. could find little support for his attempt to renew serious drama. He then had to stage his works in suburban theaters.

In *Tīreļpurvs* (1936) he stripped the form of his play to basic essentials, employing a single set and limiting himself to three characters. All external effects and peripheral plot were avoided, and there was the utmost concentration on the inner experiences of his characters. The play was eventually a triumph and has since been translated into Russian, Finnish, and Estonian. It paved the way for the analytic chamber plays that Z. was to develop later.

Representative of plays written during Z.'s first period are *Āksts* (1938)—whose protagonist is Shakespeare—*Trakais Juris* (1938), and *Minchauzena precības* (1941). In them the construction is episodic, the central conflict developing before the audience's eyes and leading to a climax and a denouement.

Though this form had the advantage of holding audience interest by means of colorful and varied action, Z. felt it lacked the discipline necessary to probe his characters in depth. He therefore turned to analytic chamber plays in which the audience is presented with a dramatic conflict that has arisen before the curtain is lifted. In this tightly disciplined form, the main lines of the denouement are contained in the exposition, and the action of the play concentrates on the unraveling of the threads tangled by life.

Kīnas vāze (1940), a comedy, is an effective realization of the chamber play, and because of its universal character it has been able to maintain itself on the Latvian stage through several changes in the national political situation. Other examples of Z.'s chamber plays are: *Nauda* (1943), *Kāds, kura nav* (1947), *Cilvēks grib dzīvot* (1948), *Lielo Grēcinieku iela* (1953), *Smilšu tornis* (1954), and *Durnā merga* (1965). After *Tīreļpurvs*, Z. returned to the episodic play only when the subject matter demanded it, as for example in *Rūda* (1954; The Ore, 1968).

However, even the analytic chamber play failed to satisfy Z., who felt that its psycho-logically and logically determined denouement was still dependent on stock theatrical devices, whereas it should be determined by the very nature of the dramatic genre. He has worked at developing an ideal form in which the uninterrupted action would continuously rise in intensity (in contrast to classical drama in which a climax is reached at one of several points in the play). Constructing his plays in a one-act form, he has specified that when their length requires an intermission the curtain can be dropped at any point—even in the middle of a sentence.

An example of this ideal form is *Vara* (1944), which focuses on the nature of political power. In line with Z.'s belief that every play is built around a so-called grand scene, the heart of this play is a monologue in which the King Mindaugas of Lithuania justifies his ruthlessness as being in the best interests of the state.

The most important Latvian playwright of our time, Z. has written some fifty plays, many of which were staged but never published. Often accused of exalting technique over artistic content, he feels that the task of the playwright is not to provide a finished literary work but only the "raw materials" for a theatrical production.

FURTHER WORKS: *Katakombas* (1926); *Lietuvēns* (1927); *Hasana harems* (1927); *Cilvēks bez galvas* (1931); *Kropļi* (1933); *Zelta zeme* (1933); *Jaunā demokratija* (1934); *Pavēste* (1934); *Galvu augšā* (1935); *Kolka* (1937); *Melngalvji* (1938); *Cilvēks grib dzīvot* (1939); *Partizāni* (1939); *Nauda* (1943); *Karatavu komēdija* (1945); *Rakte* (1945); *Kaklatiesa* (1945); *Trīs skeči* (1946); *Zaļā krūze* (1949); *Tvans* (1950); *Cenzūra* (1951); *Meli meklē meli* (1952); *Pēdējā laiva* (1956); *Raķete* (1958); *Fiasko* (1959); *Fiksā ideja* (1960); *Kā zaglis naktī* (1961); *Kurpurru* (1962); *Durnā merga* (1963); *Nekā nav tumšāka par gaismu* (1964); *Kaļostro Vilcē* (1965); *Rīga dimd* (1966); *Totems* (1968); *Pedeja laiva* (1970)

BIBLIOGRAPHY: Andrups, J., and Kalve, V., *Latvian Literature* (1954); Johansons, A., *Latviešu literātura* (1953/54)

JĀNIS ANDRUPS

ZOLA, Émile

French novelist and journalist, b. 2 April 1840, Paris; d. there, 29 Sept. 1902

After the death of Z.'s father, an Italian engineer working on a project in Aix-en-

Provence, the family, which had moved from Paris, suffered greatly from poverty. Z. had many friends in Aix, one of whom was Cézanne.

In 1858, Z. and his mother returned to Paris. After failing his baccalaureate examination, he went to work as a clerk, first on the Paris docks and later at the Hachette publishing house. By this time, 1861, he was writing poetry and reading widely in Dante, Shakespeare, Montaigne, Stendhal, Balzac and Flaubert. In addition, thanks to Cézanne, he had met many of the young painters of the day.

Recognizing that the novel was better suited than poetry to his talents, his century and his financial needs, Z. had already been publishing fiction when he left Hachette in 1866. Escape from poverty was slow, however, and he supported himself for several years by journalism, mainly art and drama criticism. His famous defense of Manet and the impressionists was published in a collection of essays entitled *Mes Haines* (1866). In later years, his "J'accuse" (1898; The Dreyfus Case, 1898), a blistering editorial defense of Captain Dreyfus, was to lead to the eventual exoneration of this Jewish army officer falsely convicted of treason.

Z.'s first important novel was *Thérèse Raquin* (1867; Eng., The Devil's Compact, 1892), an early naturalistic work that bears an epigraph from Taine: "Vice and virtue are products like vitriol and sugar." Thérèse's adultery, the murder of her weak husband by her lover, her marriage to the latter, and their eventual double suicide are, Z. tells us in an 1868 preface that emphasizes the scientific aims of the naturalists, all due to the "nerves and blood" of the two "soulless" protagonists.

About this time, Z. conceived the idea of writing a series of novels tracing the history of a single family. The cycle was to be based on "scientifically" accurate observation of concrete reality and to illustrate the theories of heredity and environment that Z. had learned from Darwin, Taine, Prosper Lucas, and Claude Bernard. *La Fortune des Rougon* (The Rougon Family, 1879), the first of twenty novels that make up *Les Rougon-Macquart: histoire naturelle et sociale d'une famille sous le Second Empire*, appeared in 1871.

Z. dreamed of doing for the Second Empire (1851–70) what Balzac had done in *La Comédie humaine* for the Restoration. Like Balzac he was to create a huge cyclical work in which characters reappear in a number of novels. Unlike Balzac, however, he worked from a preconceived general plan and forged ahead, issuing a novel almost every year until the series was completed in 1893. In *Le Roman expérimental* (1880; The Experimental Novel, 1894) and other essays he explained the theories of "scientific naturalism" on which the Rougon-Macquart series was based. He saw the novelist as an experimenter whose fictional creations were "determined" by a combination of hereditary and environmental factors that were stronger than their individual wills. He insisted, however, that "determinism" was not "fatalism," since environmental factors could be changed and that it was indeed the novelist's duty to work through his art toward "the best society.'

By carrying his fictitious family through several generations, Z. was able to "demonstrate" the working out of various hereditary factors in different segments of society. *La Curée* (1872 In the Whirlpool, 1882) dealt with corruption in the world of high finance. The brutal and brutalized lives of those employed in Les Halles, the central Paris food market, were the subject of *Le Ventre de Paris* (1873; The Markets of Paris, 1879). Unhealthy religious mysticism was the focus of *La Faute de l'abbé Mouret* (1875; The Abbé Mouret's Sin, 1957). *Son excellence Eugène Rougon* (1876; Eugène Rougon, 1876) delved into political corruption. The destructive force of sex and the demimonde were underlined in *Nana* (1880; Eng., 1880). Middle-class adultery was the theme of *Pot-Bouille* (1882; Piping Hot, 1889). The foundation of one of Paris' first department stores was described in *Au Bonheur des Dames* (1883; The Ladies' Paradise, 1883). The world of artists provided the center of interest in *L'Œuvre* (1884; The Masterpiece, 1950). A horrifying portrait of French peasant life was offered in *La Terre* (1887; Earth, 1890)—it caused several of Z.'s disciples to break with him and issue the famous "Manifeste des Cinq." Railroads as a dehumanizing force provided the background for *La Bête humaine* (1890; The Human Brutes, 1890). And the disaster of the Franco-Prussian War was the subject of *La Débâcle* (1892; The Downfall, 1892).

The greatest novels of the series are *L'Assommoir* (1877; Gervaise, 1879), which brought Z. the wealth and fame he had long worked for, and *Germinal* (1885; Eng., 1901), perhaps Z.'s crowning achievement. Both deal with the working classes.

The "assommoir" of the first title is the "gin mill" that leads to the downfall of the three principal characters: Gervaise Macquart, Lantier (her former lover and Nana's father), and her husband, Coupeau. Z. focuses on the young laundress, whose will to succeed against the pressures of industrial Paris is undermined and finally broken by her own congenital weaknesses, the backbreaking work, and the weakness and alcoholism of both her husband and Lantier. Her life ends in the total degradation of alcoholism and prostitution. Z.'s powerful picture of working-class life is presented with depressing accuracy, but also with great sympathy.

Germinal is the story of a miners' strike led by Gervaise's son Étienne Lantier in northern France. It is also Z.'s picture of class warfare and his prophecy of hope for the future. Both Christian and pagan myths of the underworld contribute to Z.'s "hell" of the mines. The catastrophes he describes with such power suggest not only the necessary end of a world controlled by inhuman natural and industrial forces, but also the germination (as the title indicates) of a new era, a new society, and perhaps a new kind of earthly paradise.

Consistently attacked during his lifetime and considerably neglected by critics in the generation following his death, Z. nevertheless exercised a strong influence on many "naturalistic" writers: Romains and Martin du Gard (qq.v.) in France; Chekhov and Gorki (qq.v.) in Russia; Dreiser, Steinbeck, and Dos Passos (qq.v.) in the U.S.

Only in the last twenty years has Z. achieved the critical acclaim he deserves. Contemporary critics have shifted attention from the scientific pretensions of his naturalism to the grandeur of his mythic patterns in novels like *Germinal,* in which the forceful, evocative, and poetic quality of his imagery combines with exact description and conveys to the reader Z.'s genuine compassion for his creations. As Z. himself said in a letter to Céard in 1885: "On the springboard of exact observation, we leap into the stars."

FURTHER WORKS: *Contes à Ninon* (1864); *La Confession de Claude* (1865; Claude's Confessions, 1882); *Le Voeu d'une morte* (1866); *Les Mystères de Marseille* (1867; The Mysteries of Marseilles, 1882); *Madeleine Férat* (1868; Eng., 1880); *Nouveaux contes à Ninon* (1874); *La Conquête de Plassans* (1874; The Conquest of Plassans, 1879); *Une Page d'amour* (1878; Hélène; 1878); *Théâtre* (1878); *Documents littéraires* (1881); *Le Naturalisme au théâtre* (1881); *Les Romanciers naturalistes* (1881); *Nos auteurs dramatiques* (1881); *Le Capitaine Burle* (1882); *Une Campagne* (1882); *La Joie de vivre* (1884; Life's Joy, 1884); *Naïs Micolin* (1884); *Le Rêve* (1888; The Dream, 1888); *L'Argent* (1891; Money, 1891); *Le Docteur Pascal* (1893; Doctor Pascal, 1883); *Les Trois Villes* (1894–98; I, *Lourdes,* 1894 [Eng., 1894]; II, *Rome,* 1896 [Eng., 1896]; III, *Paris,* 1898 [Eng., 1898]); *Nouvelle campagne* (1897); *Les Quatre Evangiles* (1899–1903; I, *Fécondité,* 1899 [Fruitfulness, 1900]; II, *Travail,* 1901 [Work, 1901]; III, *Vérité,* 1903 [Truth, 1903]; *Justice,* unfinished); *La Vérité en marche* (1901); *Poèmes lyriques* (1921); *Correspondance* (2 vols., 1928); *Madame Sourdis* (1929; Eng., 1929); *La République en marche* (1956); *Salons* (1959); *Lettres inédites à Henri Céard* (1959); *L'Atelier de Z.* (1963); *Lettres de Paris* (1963); *Pages d'exil* (1964)

BIBLIOGRAPHY: Brown, C. S., *Repetition in Z.'s Novels* (1952); Lanoux, A., *Z.* (1955); Lapp, J. C., *Z. before the Rougon-Macquart* (1964); Wilson, A., *É. Z.* (1965); Grant, E. M., *É. Z.* (1966); Hemmings, F. J. W., *É. Z.* (1966); Bédé, J.-A., *É. Z.* (1968); Walker, P. D., *É. Z.* (1968)

CHARLES G. HILL

ZOLLA, Elémire

Italian novelist and critic, b. 9 July 1926, Turin

Z.'s early years were spent in England, his mother's native land, and in France. He was educated in Italy, however, and shortly after receiving a doctorate in jurisprudence from the University of Turin, he began writing critical essays on contemporary Italian literature. In 1956, having settled in Rome to devote himself to writing, he published his first novel, *Minuetto all'inferno.*

Z.'s importance as a critic of the contemporary novel was established by *Eclissi dell' intellettuale* (1959), a collection of essays exploring two crises confronting the Italian literary world: the decline of the true intellectual and the emergence of the industrial north as a new source of inspiration for the novelist. Z. contends that the true intellectual has become a casualty of the post-World War II Italian industrial revolution, which created a new society that demands of man that he be nothing more than a cog in the complex wheel of industry. Mesmerized by the "hard sell" of big business, Z. affirms, man becomes a slave to machines, to public relations programs, to advertising media—to everything that seeks to reduce him to a conforming nonentity.

Attempts made by big business and by government agencies (still another form of big business, according to Z.) to broaden the cultural life of the masses, have only led to a "cultural" industry that in democratic countries is manipulated by economic groups and in totalitarian nations by the state. Thus man becomes what Z. calls *l'uomo massa*, a conforming member of the masses, whose greatest enemy is the intellectual.

As Z. sees it, only the intellectual can redeem the evil in the world: "Art is today the road that leads us to contemplation that loosens the chains of the ego and of society and disposes us to give perfect attention to reality. . . ."

Calling on novelists to focus on the proper social role of the intellectual, Z. urges them to combat the tendency to create in order to satisfy the greed of those who control the destiny of the masses, or to satisfy their own greed for fame and wealth. Creation must come only from inspiration, from a desire to redeem social evils.

Z. pointed the way for others with his exemplary "industrial novel," *Cecilia o la disattenzione* (1961). In it biting satire, irony, and the jargon of the advertising world are used to arouse the reader's distaste for both the giants of the industrial society and himself—*uomo massa*. A prototype of future "industrial novels," this major work is to all intents and purposes a long essay continuing his *Eclissi dell'intellettuale*.

FURTHER WORKS: *I moralisti moderni* (1959); *La psicanalisi* (1961). *Emily Dickinson* (1961); *Le Marquis de Sade* (1961); *Volgarità e dolore* (1962); *Le origini del transcendentismo* (1963); *I mistici* (1963); *La storia del fantasticare* (1964); *La potenza dell'anima* (1968); *I letterati e lo sciamano* (1969)

BIBLIOGRAPHY: Mauro, W., *Inchiesta sul romanzo italiano* (1960), pp. 9–10, 38–39; Pacifici, S., *A Guide to Contemporary Italian Literature* (1962), pp. 117–309, 321; Barilli, R., *La barriera del naturalismo* (1964), pp. 232–41; Laggini, J. E., "E. Z. and the Industrial Novel," *Italica*, June 1966, pp. 300–306

JOSEPH E. LAGGINI

ZOSHCHENKO, Mikhail Mikhailovich

Soviet-Russian short-story writer, novelist, and dramatist, b. 10 Aug. 1895, Poltava; d. 22 July 1958, Leningrad

The son of a Ukranian painter, Z. was studying law at the University of Saint Petersburg (Leningrad) when World War I broke out. He volunteered for the army and was eventually made a lieutenant in a regiment of grenadiers. After the October Revolution he joined the Red Army.

Deciding against a return to a legal career, during the 1920's Z. began writing for various newspapers and periodicals. His name was soon associated with the literary group known as the Serapion Brothers (*see* Russian literature), among those leaders were the satirist Zamyatin (q.v.) and the critic Viktor Shklovski (b. 1893). Like them Z. felt that the creative instinct must be free to follow its own bent and remain independent of political commitment.

Z.'s first book, *Rasskazy Nazara Ill'cha Sinebryukhova* (1922), immediately established him as a leading Soviet humorist and showed a taste for the fanciful and occasionally the grotesque that ill-suited the growing puritanism of sober-minded party militants. It recounts the funny, fantastic, and often humiliating adventures of a romantic corporal who vainly pursues his awkward attempts to imitate a way of life that had been definitively swept out of existence by the revolution. In his first-person narratives, Z. established a linguistic style that was soon to be associated with his name. A reflection of the language of the man-in-the-street, it is an hilarious and absurd mixture of sharp colloquialisms, malapropisms, badly assimilated party slogans, and half-digested elegancies that reproduce the intellectual confusion of his protagonists as they pit their unregenerated desires against the reconstructed values of the time.

In the following years Z.'s brilliant use of Russian vernacular showed him to be a stylist in the tradition of Nikolai Gogol (1809–1852), Nikolai Leskov (1831–95), and the émigré writer Remizov (q.v.). Adapting the colloquial monologues of Rozanov (q.v.) to his own purposes, he further developed the *skaz*—a short, first-person sketch—adding comic anecdotes in which the pretensions and fraud underlying the veneer of Soviet idealism are laid bare with malice and precision. By zeroing in on the humdrum aspects of daily Soviet life, he exposed the crudity and grayness of the New

Economic Policy period (1921–28). Though readers laughed, Soviet authorities grew increasingly uncomfortable as in story after story Z. pilloried Soviet philistinism, slippery-fingered and incapable bureaucrats, and a citzenry stubbornly insistent on pursuing personal goals behind a public smokescreen of idealistic slogans.

In an early pseudo-biographical sketch, Z. had ridiculed demands for close adherence to party ideology and pointed out that it was only because the Bolsheviks came "closer" to his point of view than other groups that he was "willing to bolshevik around with them." In the still somewhat liberal aftermath of the revolution he noted, "I'm not a communist (or rather not a Marxist), and I think I never shall be."

During the 1930's, however, Z. made fitful attempts to restrain the "negative" aspects of his art that were so at odds with official insistence on the "positive" features of life conceived according to a new ideal. In addition, sensitive to criticism of the fragmentary nature of his hundreds of short tales, Z. resolved to attempt the novel form. One result was *Vozvrashchionnaya molodost'* (1933), a loosely connected series of episodes focusing on an aged professor who successfully achieves rejuvenation, but resigns himself to old age after a turbulent marriage to a young woman. In *Golubaya kniga* (1935), however, Z. returned to a mockingly pseudo-historical collection of anecdotes about famous persons and places. His intention, he noted, was to produce a sort of "cultural film" on Rusian life.

For a time Z. next devoted himself to biography, history, and popular science: *Cherni printz* (1937) dealt with a 19th-c. sunken treasure; *Kerenski* (1937) was a lampoon on the man who had attempted to establish bourgeois democracy in the wake of tzarism. These and similar works failed to carry ideological conviction. Though after the German invasion of the U.S.S.R. during World War II Z. was decorated for his part in the defense of Leningrad, he was still being reproached for a lack of patriotism. Serialization of *Pered voskhodom solntza* (1943; Before the Sunrise, 1961), an autobiographical work in which Z. attempted to probe the sources of his growing melancholy, was suspended, and the editors of *Oktober* declared themselves in "ideological error."

In 1946 Andrei Zhdanov (1888–1948), the party's literary ideologue and champion of socialist realism (q.v.), launched a blistering attack on poet Anna Akhmatova (q.v.) and Z. for their "bourgeois formalism' and "servile cosmopolitanism." His wrath had been particularly aroused by *Priklyucheniya obezyany* (1946), a satiric fable on the new Soviet man. Z. was expelled from the Union of Soviet Writers and loaded with epithets in a manner that recalls the later treatment of Pasternak (q.v.). Though he was eventually allowed to publish colorless, uncharacteristic pieces in periodicals, Z.'s career was over.

Shortly before his death Z. was rehabilitated to some extent, and "selected," bowdlerized editions of his early stories were reissued. Even in these he shows himself a brilliant satirist, capable of synthesizing everyday reality, fantasy, and social criticism.

FURTHER WORKS: *Koza* (1923); *Mudrost* (1925); *O chem pel solovyei* (1925); *Strasnaya noch* (1925); *Veseloye priklyucheniye* (1927); *Nervnyye lyudi* (1927); *Dni nashei zhizni* (1929); *Siren tzvetiot* (1930); *Mikhail Sinyagin* (1930); *Istoriya odnoi zhizni* (1934); *Lichnaya zhizn* (1934); *Fedot da ne tot* (1939); *Taras Shevchenko* (1939); *Rasskazy i povesti 1923–1956* (1959); *Rasskazy, feletony, komedii* (1963). **Selected English translations:** *Russia Laughs* (1935); *The Wonderful Dog, and Other Tales* (1942); *Scenes from the Bathhouse, and Other Stories* (1961); *Nervous People, and Other Satires* (1963)

BIBLIOGRAPHY: McLean, H., Introduction to *Nervous People, and Other Satires* (1963); Mihailovich, V., "Z.'s 'Adventures of a Monkey' as an Allegory," *Satire Newsletter,* IV (1967), 84–89; Von Wiren-Garczynski, V., "Z.'s Psychological Interests," *SEEJ,* XI (1967), 3–22, "The Russian Language in the Immediate Post-Revolutionary Period (1919–28) and Its Literary Stylization in the Fiction of M. Z.," *DA,* XXVIII (1967), 1411A–12A, and "Language and Revolution: The Russian Experience of the 1920's," *Canadian Slavic Studies,* II (1968), 192–207

* * * *

ZUCKMAYER, Carl

German dramatist and novelist, b. 23 Dec. 1896, Nackenheim, Hesse

Z. was born into a well-to-do family of manufacturers. After a happy childhood and youth he voluntarily enlisted in the German artillery in 1914. He saw service on the French front, where he was seriously wounded in 1918. After the war he studied the humanities and biology at the University of Heidelberg, but systematic study toward a degree did not appeal to him. There, however, he did gain deep insight into the intellectual life of post-war Germany.

Like his fellow Hessian the dramatist Georg Büchner (1813–37), Z. is deeply conscious of his roots in the Hessian people and their dialect. After some unsuccessful attempts at writing for the theater he achieved great success with *Der fröhliche Weinberg* (1925), which won him the prestigious Kleist Prize. After turbulent years in Berlin, Z. moved to Henndorf, an idyllic small town in the Austrian province of Salzburg. A decisive incident in Z.'s literary development was his acquaintance with Gerhart Hauptmann (q.v.), whom he first met on the Baltic island of Hiddensee in 1926. Both men were deeply conscious of their affinity; Hauptmann considered Z. his spiritual heir, and Z. completed an unfinished play of Hauptmann, *Herbert Engelmann*, in 1952. When Hitler overran Austria in 1938, Z. emigrated to the United States. He soon tired of Hollywood and started life again as a farmer in the rugged mountains of Vermont. After the war he returned to his homeland and worked on German reeducation, but again he felt drawn to the mountains and finally settled in Saas Fee in the Swiss canton of Valais.

Schinderhannes (1927) is a dramatization of the story of a popular figure from the Rhineland at the time of the Napoleonic wars; like Robin Hood he robbed the rich and gave to the poor. He became a national hero when he got involved in a private war with the French conquerors, was caught and publicly executed. The cast of Rhenish characters is strongly reminiscent of those in the dramas of Büchner.

The colorful world of the wandering circus, with which Z. has been familiar since childhood, is portrayed realistically in *Katharina Knie* (1929). Katharina, a member of a famous circus family, renounces a romance that would cause her to leave the circus; instead, she follows the call of the road. This is a naturalistic drama written in the broad dialect of Z.'s homeland. Despite disparaging reviews the public loved the play. Katharina's father, the patriarch of the circus (Vater Knie), became one of the famous roles of the great actor, Albert Bassermann.

Der Hauptmann von Köpenick (1930; The Captain of Köpenick, 1932) is based on a true incident. Z. gives a realistic account of Prussian military bureaucracy and the universal respect that an officer's uniform commanded in Germany before World War I. There is a strong element of the grotesque (q.v.) in the scenes in which an unemployed shoemaker is respected and obeyed because he is disguised as an army officer. Scenes of earthy realism alternate with scenes of exquisite tenderness. The latter justify the subtitle "A German Fairy Tale" (Ein deutsches Märchen).

It is remarkable that *Des Teufels General* (1946), a play giving an inside view of the Nazi high command, was written on a Vermont farm during World War II at a time when Z. had no contact with Germany. The hero of the play, General Harras, struggles between carrying out his duties as an officer and his opposition to everything Hitler stands for. The conflict cannot be resolved, and Harras goes up in a plane he knows to be defective and crashes. The play is a memorial to Z.'s friend, Udet, a German flyer who died mysteriously in 1941 in the crash of a newly developed airplane.

Although Z.'s reputation rests primarily on his dramatic writings, he is also a novelist of stature. *Salware, oder Die Magdalena von Bozen* (1936) is a naturalistic novel set in the rugged Dolomite Alps. The narrator is torn between his love for Mega, a simple peasant girl, and his love for Magdalena, the aristocratic and mysterious chatelaine of Castle Salvare. The rumors of witchcraft involving Magdalena's ancestors and the gruesome end of Magdalena and her brother, both found dead in an icy gorge near the castle, are reminiscent of the Gothic novels of the 18th c.

Z. believes that our time is undergoing an intellectual and spiritual crisis—"*die Denk-und-Glaubenskrise der Gegenwart.*" In this crisis he stands on the side of human freedom and responsibility. To him nothing seems more symptomatic of the critical state of our world than its defection from nature. He believes that full and undistorted perception of nature is the source of artistic creation. Like Lawrence Durrell (q.v.), Z. believes firmly in the influence of the landscape on human behavior and thought.

Z.'s autobiography, *Als wär's ein Stück von mir* (1968; A Part of Myself, 1970), shows that unpleasant episodes never depressed him but enabled him to find and emphasize the positive sides of life. He was never bitter. Trench warfare in World War I did not turn him against the military. During World War II, unlike most émigrés who sought refuge in the big cities, Z. chose to work as a farmer. In spite of having been exposed to Prussian militarism and Nazi totalitarianism, Z. never lost his innate love for the simple German people.

Z.'s place in world literature rests firmly on his realistic dramas. *Der Hauptmann von Köpenick* is generally acknowledged as one of the few great comedies in German literature.

FURTHER WORKS: *Kreuzweg* (1921); *Pankraz erwacht, oder Die Hinterwäldler* (also published as *Kiktahan oder Die Hinterwäldler*, 1925); *Der Baum* (1926); *Die Geschichte eines Bauern aus dem Taunus* (1927); *Kakadu-Kakada* (1930); *Die Affenhochzeit* (1932); *Eine Liebesgeschichte* (1934); *Der Schelm von Bergen* (1934); *Ein Sommer in Österreich* (1937); *Herr über Leben und Tod* (1938); *Lebensgeschichte* (1938); *Bellmann* (1938; republished as *Ulla Windblad*, 1953); *Second Wind* (1940); *Der Seelenbräu* (1945); *Die Deutschen Dramen* (1947); *Gesammelte Werke* (4 vols., 1947 ff.); *Die Brüder Grimm* (1948); *Gedichte 1916–1948* (1948); *Nach dem Sturm* (1949); *Barbara Blomberg* (1949); *Der Gesang im Feuerofen* (1950); *Komödie und Volksstück* (1950); *Entscheidung vor Morgengrauen* (1952); *Die Geschichte von einer Entenjagd* (1952); *Kaninchentod* (1952); *Die langen Wege* (1952); *Die Erzählungen* (1952); *Engele von Loewen* (1955); *Weihnachtsgeschichte* (1956); *Der trunkene Herkules* (1958); *Die Fastnachtsbeichte* (1959); *Gesammelte Werke* (4 vols., 1960); *Die Uhr schlägt eins* (1961); *Ein voller Erdentag* (1962); *Geschichten aus vierzig Jahren* (1963); *Das Leben des Horace A. W. Tabor* (1964)

BIBLIOGRAPHY: Jacobius, A. J., *Das Schauspiel C. Z.'s* (1956); Meinharz, P., *C. Z.* (1960); Rooke, S., "C. Z.," in *German Men of Letters,* ed. A. Natan, Vol. III (1964), 209–33; Glade, H., "C. Z.'s *The Devil's General* as Autobiography," *MD,* IX (1966), 54–61; Speidel, E., "The Stage as Metaphysical Institution: Z.'s Dramas *Schinderhannes* and *Der Hauptmann von Köpenick,*" *MLR,* LXIII (1968), 425–36

WALTER FLEISCHMANN

ŻUKROWSKI, Wojciech

Polish novelist and short-story writer, b. 14 April 1916, Cracow

Z.'s personality as a man and artist was molded by his Catholic upbringing and his participation in the events in Poland during World War II.

In 1946 Z. made his literary debut with the publication of *W kraju milczenia,* a collection of short stories on the 1939 campaign, life under German occupation, and the Polish underground. In spite of their starkly realistic rendition of suffering and death, the stories arouse neither horror nor despair. Z.'s soldiers and partisans see war much as did Sienkiewicz's (q.v.) 18th-c. knights: a man's job, an unusual and fascinating experience. Death to them, as to the inmates of labor camps, comes in God's own appointed time. This unsophisticated, matter-of-fact, pious *Weltanschauung* constitutes one of Z.'s two principal creative veins.

In Z.'s second collection of short stories, *Piórkiem flaminga* (1947)—which carries a subtitle meaning "contrary tales"—Z. develops and broadens his second creative vein, which he had begun to work with in the grotesque novel *Porwanie w Tiutiurlistanie* (1946).

In these stories Z. develops a precarious balance between everyday reality, greedily absorbed through the five senses, and a certainty maintained through the sensitive antennae of fantasy and faith, of man's mysterious ties with another invisible reality. In this vein Z. combines devices of folktales and animated cartoons with those of Edgar Allan Poe (1809–1849), E. T. A. Hoffmann (1776–1822), and Kafka (q.v.). "Żona" is most characteristic of this side of Z.'s writing.

The novels—except for *Mądre zioła* (1951), a dutiful tribute to short-lived Polish socialist realism—usually deal with the World War II and its aftermath. They are not very outstanding, even though two of them—*Dni klęski* (1952) and *Skąpani w ogniu* (1961)—won several state literary prizes. Possibly, Z.'s eagerness to capture reality in all its intensity enhances the vitality and tempo of his short stories but overburdens the novels. For example, in the huge *Kamienne tablice* (1966), which turns upon a Polish diplomat's love affair in India, the vastness, colorfulness, and noise of the crowded country dwarf the characters and obscure the plot. There is, moreover, too much passion, despair, and soul-searching, as the hero faces the moral laws of the Decalogue, the "stone tablets" of the title.

In 1969, Z. won another state prize—for his contribution to Poland's art and culture over almost a quarter of a century. His fictional world has not undergone change during that period. It continues to be the product of personal experience; it is occasionally disturbed by Ż.'s ebullient spirit and the resulting lapses from artistic discipline. Emotional rather than rational elements still prevail in his later writing, as do the impressionism and fantasy of his earlier "contrary tales."

Ż. possesses powers of observation, a zest for life, a puckish humor, and a simple, comfortable belief in a presence guiding man's steps, in life beyond death—even in apparitions. Conceivably, Ż.'s success stems at least partly from his being well attuned to traditional Polish literary values.

FURTHER WORKS: *Wiersze* (1948); *Ręka ojca* (1949); *Córeczka. Opowiadania o dzieciach i zwierzętach* (1952); *Dom bez ścian* (1954); *W kamieniołomie i inne opowiadania* (1954); *Ognisko w dżungli. Opowieście i baśnie z Wietnamu* (1955); *Wybór opowiadań* (1956); *Kantata. Pierwsze opowiadania* (1957); *Okruchy weselnego tortu* (1958); *Wędrowki z moim Guru* (1960); *W królestwie miliona słoni* (1961); *Nieśmiały narzeczony* (1964)

BIBLIOGRAPHY: Wyka, K., *Pogranicze powieści* (1948); Wittlin, J., "A Quarter Century of Polish Literature," *BA*, XXX (1956), 5–12; Sowinski, Y., "Two Polish Bestsellers," *Canadian Slavonic Papers*, IV (1959), 213–17; Kuncewicz, M., ed., *The Modern Polish Mind: An Anthology* (1962); Lichniak, Z., *Dokoła Wojtka* (1963); Bartelski, L., *W kręgu bliskich* (1967); Kijowski, A., "Twenty Years—1946–66: Contemporary Polish Writing," *Literary Review*, No. 10 (1967), pp. 412–30

XENIA GASIOROWSKA

ZULU LITERATURE

The Zulu people, who make up much of the population of Natal, South Africa, were not finally brought under colonial rule until the beginning of this century. Literacy therefore lagged, and unlike the Xhosa and Sotho peoples (*see* Xhosa literature and Sotho literature), the Zulus did not start producing a written literature until the early 1920's, when some one-act plays dramatizing folktales were published in the Natal *Native Teachers' Journal*.

The first Zulu writer of note was John L. Dube (1871–1946). Although he belonged to the same generation as the Sotho novelist

Thomas Mofolo (1876–1948) and the Xhosa author S. E. K. Mghayi (1875–1945), he did not embark on imaginative writing until 1931, when he published the first Zulu novel, *Insila ka Shaka* (Jege, the Body Servant of King Shaka, 1951), a lively story dealing with Shaka, an early 19th-c. Zulu conqueror. In *Ushembe* (1936) Dube told the life story of Shembe, the founder of a dissident African church. A distinguishing feature of Zulu literature is that much of it consists of more or less fictionalized biographies of past and present leaders.

While Dube was the only author of his own generation, a number of gifted and ambitious younger writers now came on the scene. R. R. R. Dhlomo (b. 1901) began his literary career with a novella in English, *An African Tragedy* (1928), which not only gave a somber picture of native life in city slums, but also offered some cogent criticism of such traditional customs as the bride-price. Dhlomo's following books were written in Zulu and were biographical accounts of such 19th-c. chiefs as Dingane (1936), Shaka (1937), Mpande (1938), and Cetshwayo (1952). With *Indlela yababi* (1948), a dramatic novel of Zulu life in the native townships of Johannesburg, he reverted to his early inspiration.

His younger brother, H. I. E. Dhlomo (1905–1956), wrote only in English. After publishing a number of articles on Bantu literature, he wrote the first play in English by an African writer, *The Girl Who Killed to Save* (1936), an account of a crisis that almost destroyed the Xhosa nation in 1857. *The Valley of a Thousand Hills* (1941), a long elegiac novel in the romantic-victorian manner, contrasted the harmony of nature and the cruelty of colonial society.

Benedict W. Vilakazi (1906–1947), the best Zulu poet, was a linguist and a student of traditional Zulu poetry. After some experiments with European poetic forms, he returned to African forms in two poetry collections: *Inkondlo kaZulu* (1935) and *Amal'ezulu* (1945). Of his two novels, the best is *Nje nempela,* published posthumously in 1955, which deals with the 1906 Zulu uprising.

The 1930's saw the appearance of the first Zulu woman writer, Violet Dube, and the emergence of vernacular drama with *UGubudele namazimu* (1937) by Nimrod Ndebele. More recently, C. L. S. Nyembezi (b. 1919) has given considerable impetus to the novel. *Mntanami! Mntanami!* (1950), a novel about city life—a theme almost obsessional with native African writers—evinces a grasp of individual character that is unusual in African writing. Critics agree that it is the best Zulu work in the novel form.

ALBERT S. GÉRARD

ZUNZUNEGUI, Juan Antonio de

Spanish novelist, b. 21 Dec. 1901, Portugalete (near Bilbao)

Z., the son of a wealthy industrialist, was educated at Deusto and Salamanca. He later studied briefly in Tours and at the University of Perugia and traveled throughout western Europe. After the death of his father he abandoned a career in business. Since about 1940 he has dedicated himself exclusively to writing. He now lives in Madrid. A member of the Real Academia Española since 1957, he has won six of the major literary prizes offered in his country, including the prestigious Premio Fastenrath and the Premio Nacional de Literatura. His works have been translated into French, Italian, Portuguese, German, Dutch, Russian, and Finnish, but never into English.

Z.'s voluminous production encompasses two distinct worlds: Bilbao and Madrid. His first novels portray life in Bilbao in the first third of the century, when Bilbao was the banking and industrial center of Spain. Many of the plots and characters are based on actual episodes of machinations in the realm of high finance. Z.'s authentic knowledge of the material he treats and his scrupulous documentation of historical events lend an air of authenticity to these works, which many consider his best.

The Madrid novels, usually set in the post-1950 capital, depict all social strata from the underworld to the upper middle class. While some of the characterization and plots are well realized, these works lack the solid documentation and intimate knowledge of the milieu so evident in the Bilbao novels. There is a certain artificiality in the Madrid Z. portrays.

Z. follows closely the technique of his admitted models, the 19th-c. giants of the realist school: Pérez Galdós (q.v.), Gustave Flaubert (1821–80); Fiodor Dostoyevski (1821–81), and José Maria Eça de Queiroz (1846–1900). His lengthy works are marked by detailed descriptions of the physical environment, numerous characters, complicated plot elements, by a broad ranging in time and space, and a slow pace. In occasional whimsical departures, he interpolates humorous metaphors of the van-

guardista type similar to those of Gómez de la Serna (q.v.).

Z.'s forte is characterization. He builds his novels around the life story of one or more central figures. In the Bilbao works he uses the lineal technique, following the life of one or two characters over a period of years, while in the Madrid novels he presents a large number of figures in parallel and interweaving plots. He analyzes their psychological processes skillfully, although his work suffers from his tendency to impose his own narrative voice, making their development seem less natural. His creation of a gallery of minor characters in humorous vignettes is admirable.

The best of the Bilbao works are *El chiplichandle* (1940) and *La quiebra* (1946). *El chiplichandle* is a modern-day picaresque novel in which Z. traces the rise of an unscrupulous opportunist from dock bum and swindler to governor of a province by means of a series of brilliantly narrated adventures. The structure of the work is loose and the delineation of the main character not so profound as in later novels, but the work is successful because of the fluidity and humor of the numerous episodes depicting life in the dock area of pre-civil-war Bilbao as seen through the eyes of various flamboyant figures from all social classes.

Considered by many Z.'s best effort, *La quiebra,* against a broad panorama of Bilbao society from 1914 to 1931, is centered around an actual incident: the collapse of a famous bank, El Crédito de la Unión Minera, during the Great Depression. Z. documented this novel thoroughly, studying the trial transcript and consulting lawyers involved in the case; he also knew personally two officials of the bank. The greatest merit of the work is the psychological study of the two principal characters: Ramón, a brilliant but lethargic and unstable young banker who abandons a promising career for a life of debauchery, only to lose his sanity when bankruptcy wipes out his fortune; and Bea, his mistress, who rises from a poor seamstress to a millionaire businesswoman, yet remains frustrated because she has not found true love.

Z. is considered by such critics as Ilie, Alborg, and Sainz de Robles to be one of the most important contemporary Spanish novelists. He is possibly the most widely read writer in Spain today. Despite the limitations of a rather dated technique, he achieves some of the most powerful characterizations seen in the novel in recent years. His masterful portrayal of certain segments of Spanish society makes him the worthy heir of Pérez Galdós and the realist tradition.

FURTHER WORKS: *Vida y paisaje de Bilbao* (1926); *Chiripi* (1931); *Tres en una, o la dichosa honra* (1935); *Dos hombres y dos mujeres en medio* (1941); *!Ay . . . estos hijos!* (1942); *El barco de la muerte* (1945); *La úlcera* (1947); *Las ratas del barco* (1950); *El supremo bien* (1950); *Esta oscura desbandada* (1951); *La vida como es* (1954); *El hijo hecho a contrata* (1956); *El camión justiciero* (1957); *Mis páginas preferidas* (1958); *Los caminos del Señor* (1959); *Una mujer sobre la tierra* (1959); *El mundo sigue* (1960); *La poetisa* (1961); *El premio* (1961); *El camino alegre* (1962); *Don Isidoro y sus límites* (1963); *El trabajo y la vida o la muerte* (1963); *Todo quedó en casa* (1964); *Un hombre entre dos mujeres* (1965); *Bajo mi cielo metalúrgico* (1967); *El don más hermoso* (1969)

BIBLIOGRAPHY: Tamayo, J. A., Introduction to *Dos hombres y dos mujeres en medio* (1944); Dowling, J. C., "'J. A. de Z.: a Biographical Note," *Hispania*, XXV (Nov. 1952), 425–27; Ilie, P., "Z. y la nueva moral española," *Cuadernos Americanos*, XVI (Jan. 1957), i, 217–34; Sainz de Robles, C. F., *La novela española en el siglo XX* (1957); Dowling, J. C., "The fleet of J. A. de Z.," *BA*, No. 32 (1958), pp. 243–47; Alborg, J. L., *Hora actual de la novela española*, Vol. II (1962); Nora, E., *La novela española contemporánea* (1962); Biddle, W. H., "Novelistic Technique in Representative Works of J. A. de Z.," Ph.D. Dissertation, Rutgers University, 1967

WILLIAM H. BIDDLE

ŽUPANČIČ, Oton

Slovene poet, b. 23 Jan. 1878, Vinica; d. 11 June 1949, Ljubljana, Yugoslavia

After studying history at the University of Vienna from 1896 to 1901, Ž. spent several years in Paris, Vienna, and Germany before returning to Slovenia in 1912 to become the director of the National Theater. In 1914 he was chief editor of the *Slovan*; from 1917 to 1920 he edited the *Ljubljanski Zvon*. In 1945 Ž. became director of the Institute of Slovene Language of the Academy of Sciences in Ljubljana.

The psychological essence of modern man is the major theme of Ž.'s poetry, which brought fresh inspiration to Slovene literature. Freeing himself from traditional metric patterns, he used free verse and invented a new lyrical symbolic language.

Ž.'s youthful poetry was influenced by the French "decadents," but he soon made new departures. His early range of themes—the erotic and the profession of poetry—was enlarged to include love of country and social problems. After 1904 his poetry took two separate directions: on the one hand, he wanted to investigate the meaning of life intuitively through a visionary, cosmic lyricism; on the other hand, he tried to take a position on questions of the day such as the emigration and proletarianization of the rural population, the development of the working class in his native Slovenia, or the political destiny of the Slovenes and of all the peoples of Yugoslavia. Shortly before World War I, Ž. was associated with expressionism (q.v.). During and after World War II his poetry extolled the ideal of national self-determination.

Along with Cankar (q.v.), Ž. is the chief representative of "modernist" Slovene poetry. In addition, through his numerous translations from European literatures he contributed significantly to the development of modern Slovene prose language.

FURTHER WORKS: *Čaša opojnosti* (1899); *Pisanice* (1900); *Čez plan* (1904); *Samagovori* (1908); *Lajkih nog nao krog* (1913); *Ciciban in še kaj* (1915); *Sto ubank* (1915); *Mlada pota* (1919); *V zarje Vidove* (1920); *Veronika Desoniška* (1924); *Slehernik* (1934); *Djela* (5 vols., 1936–50); *Zimzelen pod snegom* (1945); *Veš, poet, svoj dolg* (1948); *Sto pésmi* (1948); *Zbrano delo* (1956 ff.). **Selected English translation:** *A Selection of Poems* (1967)

BIBLIOGRAPHY: Tesnière, L., *Oton Joupantchitch, poète slovène: L'Homme et l'œuvre* (1931); Mahnič, J., *O. Ž.* (1955); Kumbatovič, F. K., "Deux Tendances fondamentales dans l'histoire du théâtre slovène," *Revue de L'Histoire du Théâtre*, XVI (1964), 141–45; Kumbatovič, F. K., "Das slowenische Theater als mitteleuropäisches Problem," *Maske und Kothurn*, XII (1966), 228–35

FRAN PETRÈ

ZWEIG, Arnold

German novelist, poet, dramatist, and journalist b. 10 Nov. 1887, Glogau; d. 26 Nov. 1968, East Berlin

After studying literature, modern languages,

philosophy, and history at various universities, Z. served in the German army during World War I. From 1918 to 1923, he was a writer in Munich before moving to Berlin to edit the *Jüdische Rundschau.*

A Zionist and a pacifist, in 1933 Z. emigrated to Palestine via Czechoslovakia, England, and France, contributing to various *émigré* journals. From 1942 to 1943 he was coeditor of the Haifa journal *Orient,* and in 1948 he returned to settle in the East Berlin zone of the German Democratic Republic. A member of the Volkskammer (parliament), Z. participated in the 1949 World Peace Congress in Paris, and he served as president of the East German Academy of Arts (1950–53). He was awarded several prestigious literary prizes, including the Lenin Peace Prize (1958).

A prolific writer, Z. is perhaps best known for a group of novels entitled *Der große Krieg der weißen Männer,* an epic united by the recurring and somewhat autobiographical figure of Werner Bertin, a middle-class Jewish writer whose experiences are representative of those of many German intellectuals of the time. Taking World War I as the focal point, Z. analyzed the psychological effects of war and in these novels provided a literary document tracing the social developments leading from imperialism to socialism. *Die Zeit ist reif* (1959) was written retrospectively to chronicle the years 1913–15. Through the example of the intellectual and indigent Bertin, who meets with social disapproval while courting Leonore Wahl, the daughter of a rich banking family, Z. indicates his opposition to middle-class stratification.

Junge Frau von 1914 (1931; Young Woman of 1914, 1932) a warm love story, shows Leonore's many disappointments (she aborts her illegitimate pregnancy) and problems before marrying Bertin. In stirring passages, Z. traces her maturation from a complacent, middle-class young woman into a vigorous opponent of war. In *Erziehung vor Verdun* (1935; Education before Verdun, 1936), as a soldier, Bertin observes and experiences the effects of rampant militarism and is converted to pacifism.

The breakdown of justice is the theme of Z.'s best-known novel, *Der Streit um den Sergeanten Grischa* (1927; The Case of Sergeant Grischa, 1928), which Z. had written as a play in 1921. In violation of all legal principles, the high command of the German army has a Russian war prisoner executed as an example to those German soldiers who are

drawn to Russian revolutionary ideology. Z. appealed to the conscience of the world in this indictment of militarism. The novel's controversial theme, the author's skill in building a dramatic situation and in clearly characterizing both major and minor figures, and the meticulous analysis of various social points of view contributed to the book's international success. The dramatic version was first performed in 1930.

Die Feuerpause (1954), one of Z.'s weakest works, is an example of Z.'s work under the influence of editors who urged him toward socialist realism. After the armistice and the treaty of Brest Litovsk, Bertin unconvincingly changes from a liberal idealist to a militant socialist. *Einsetzung eines Königs* (1937; The Crowning of a King, 1938) focuses on a German officer who is eventually drawn into the social, economic, political, and military intrigues surrounding the Lithuanian throne in 1918. Z. meant to round out the novelistic series with a work entitled *Das Eis bricht,* which was to describe the dilemma of a country whose social basis is built on militaristic ideals and war industry.

Z.'s novellas and short stories prove him to be a skilful writer who is able to depict the fate of middle-class intellectuals, and who is both sympathetic to their plight and sensitively ironic in dealing with their foibles. As a follower of Freud, in his early works Z. was able to convey psychological dilemmas successfully, but the books of his later years failed because they tended to be the ideological products of a Marxist social scientist.

In a Germany deeply divided by politics and ideologies, Z. stood out as a pacifist whose works emphasize harmony, optimism, and a deep appreciation of human nature. He must increasingly be regarded as the conscience or a disinherited majority.

FURTHER WORKS: *Gedichte* (1908); *Vorfrühling* (1909); *Gedichte* (1909); *Der englische Garten* (1910); *Aufzeichnungen über eine Familie Klopfer: Das Kind* (1911); *Die Novellen um Claudia* (1912; Claudia, 1930); *Abigail und Nabal* (1913); *Ritualmord in Ungarn* (1914); *Geschichtenbuch* (1916); *Benarône* (1918); *Die Bestie* (1919); *Drei Erzählungen* (1920); *Entrückung und Aufruhr* (1920); *Zweites Geschichtenbuch* (1923); *Söhne* (1923); *Gerufene Schatten* (1923); *Frühe Fährten* (1925); *Regenbogen* (1925); *Die Umkehr des Abtrünnigen* (1925); *Der Spiegel des großen*

Kaisers (1926); *Pont und Anna* (1928); *Laubheu und keine Bleibe* (1930); *Die Aufrichtung der Menorah* (1930); *Knaben und Männer* (1931); *Mädchen und Frauen* (1931); *De Vriendt kehrt heim* (1932; De Vriendt Goes Home, 1936); *Spielzeug der Zeit* (1933; Playthings of Time, 1935); *Subjection* (1935); *Signale* (1935); *Versunkene Tage* (1938); *Bonaparte in Jaffa* (1939); *Ha Kardon shel Wandsbek* (Haifa, 1943; Am., The Axe of Wandsbek, 1947; Stockholm, *Das Beil von Wandsbek*, 1948); *Austreibung 1744, oder Das Weihnachtswunder* (1946); *Ein starker Esser* (1947); *Allerleirauh* (1949); *Stufen* (1949); *Über den Nebeln* (1950); *Der Elfenbeinfächer* (1952); *Ausgewählte Novellen* (1953–55); *Der Regenbogen* (1955); *Soldatenspiele* (1956); *Fünf Romanzen* (1958); *Novellen 1907–1955* (1961); *Traum ist teuer* (1962); *Jahresringe* (1964). **Selected English translation:** *A Bit of Blood, and Other Stories* (1959)

BIBLIOGRAPHY: "A.–Z.-Bibliographie," *A. Z. zum siebzigsten Geburtstag* (1957); Rühle, J., "Die Kunst des inneren Vorbehalts," *Die Schriftsteller und der Kommunismus in Deutschland* (1960); Ballusek, L. V., "A. Z.," *Dichter im Dienst* (1963); Reich-Ranicki, M., "Der preussische Jude A. Z.," *Deutsche Literatur in West und Ost* (1963); Kaufmann, E., *A. Z.'s Weg zum Roman: Vorgeschichte und Analyse des Grischaromans* (1967); Hilscher, E., *A. Z.: Leben und Werk* (1968)

STEFAN GRUNWALD

ZWEIG, Stefan

Austrian novelist, biographer, dramatist, and essayist, b. 28 Nov. 1881, Vienna; d. 22 Feb. 1942, Petropolis, Brazil

The son of an upper-middle-class Jewish family, Z. was free to follow his inclination toward literature and travel. He studied in both Vienna and Paris, where he met Verhaeren and Rolland (qq.v.), who were to be important influences on his life. World War I, its exacerbated nationalism and pointless suffering, was to convert him to lifelong pacifism and make him ever after suspicious of the moral values of a dying culture. In the final year of the war he managed to get to Switzerland, where his antimilitarist tragedy *Jeremias* (1917; Jeremiah, 1922) had been produced. There he joined Rolland in efforts to promote an early peace.

After 1918 Z. lived in Salzburg, and in 1934 he visited England to do research for his biography *Maria Stuart* (1935; The Queen of Scots, 1950). Political turmoil made him reluctant to return to Austria, and following the *Anschluss* with Nazi Germany (1938) he settled temporarily in England and became a British citizen. However, he soon found his adopted country too insular. Travel, which had been the joy of Z.'s young manhood, became the ironic necessity of his last years. He went first to the United States and finally to Brazil. There, exhausted and discouraged, Z. and his second wife committed suicide by taking poison.

Z.'s earliest literary efforts were translations of Verhaeren that successfully reproduced the intense lyricism of the Belgian symbolist. *Silberne Saiten* (1901) and *Die frühen Kränze* (1906), the first collection of his own poems, show the influence of the French symbolists (*see* symbolism) and the German poets Hofmannsthal and Rilke (qq.v.). *Verhaeren* (1910), a monograph on his friend and poetic mentor, was the forerunner of many historical biographies that were to be largely responsible for Z.'s literary success.

"My main interest in writing," he noted, "has always been the psychological representation of personalities and their lives, and this was also the reason which prompted me to write various essays and biographical studies of well-known personalities." His friendship with Sigmund Freud (1856–1939) led to his being one of the earliest writers to apply the insights afforded by psychoanalysis. Over the years he wrote illuminating short studies of Honoré de Balzac (1799–1850), Friedrich Hölderlin (1770–1843), Stendhal (1783–1842), Heinrich von Kleist (1777–1811), Nietzsche, Lev Tolstoi (qq.v.), and many others. Some of these were republished in 1935 under the collective title *Baumeister der Welt* (Master Builders: A Typology of the Spirit, 1939). Of perhaps special interest are *Heilung durch den Geist* (1931; Mental Healers, 1932) and longer, somewhat romanticized biographies such as *Joseph Fouché* (1929; Eng., 1948) and *Marie Antoinette* (1932; Eng., 1933). *Triumph und Tragik des Erasmus von Rotterdam* (1934; Erasmus of Rotterdam, 1934) and *Castellio gegen Calvin* (1936; The Right to Heresy: Castellio against Calvin, 1936) are strong defenses of individual intellectual freedom written at a time when ideology backed by terror was on the rise.

Throughout his youth in Vienna, Z. had assiduously attended the theater, which was then dominated by the works of Hermann Sudermann (1857–1928) and Gerhart Hauptmann (q.v.). He naturally enough tried his own

589

hand at the drama, but with the exception of his free adaptation of Ben Jonson's (ca. 1573–1637) *Volpone* (1925; Eng., 1928) and his libretto for Richard Strauss's opera *Die schweigsame Frau* (1935), his work for the theater met with little success.

Of greater interest are his novellas, which reveal the same psychoanalytic orientation as Z.'s historical studies. Among the best of these is the famous *Amok* (1922; Eng., 1931), the story of a doctor in the tropics who is driven mad by his love for an arrogant woman. *Die Liebe der Erika Ewald* (1904) and *Erstes Erlebnis* (1911) explore the impact of initial sexual experiences, while *Angst* (1920) focuses on the fears of an adulterous wife. *Der Zwang* (1920) deals with the war, and an unusual collection entitled *Verwirrung der Gefühle* (1927) offers three studies of people in the grip of a strong emotion. In *Schachnovelle* (1941; Royal Game, 1945), a game of chess is used to symbolize the disintegration and dehumanization of contemporary human values.

Z.'s posthumously published autobiography, *Die Welt von gestern* (1944; first published in English, The World of Yesterday, 1943), describes the autumnal glories of a European culture whose disappearance he chose not to survive.

FURTHER WORKS: *Verlaine* (1905); *Das Haus am Meer* (1912); *Der verwandelte Komödiant* (1913); *Fahrten* (1919); *Legende eines Lebens* (1919); *Drei Meister: Balzac, Dickens, Dostojevskij* (1920); *Marceline Desbordes-Valmore* (1920); *Romain Rolland* (1921); *Die Augen des ewigen Bruders* (1922); *Frans Masereel* (1923); *Die gesammelten Gedichte* (1924); *Der Kampf mit dem Dämon: Hölderlin, Kleist, Nietzsche* (1925); *Der Flüchtling* (1927); *Die Flucht zu Gott* (1927); *Abschied von Rilke* (1927); *Sternstunden der Menschheit* (1927; Tide of Fortune, 1955); *Drei Dichter ihres Lebens: Casanova, Stendhal, Tolstoi* (1928; Adepts in Self-Portraiture, 1952); *Quiproquo* (1928); *Kleine Chronik* (1929); *Das Lamm der Armen* (1929); *Die schweigsame Frau* (1935); *Arturo Toscanini* (1936); *Gesammelte Erzählungen* (2 vols., 1936); *Begegnungen mit Menschen, Büchern, Städten* (1937); *Der begrabene Leuchter* (1937; Buried Candelabra, 1944); *Kaleidoskop* (1938; Kaleidoscope, 2 vols., 1949–51); *Magellan* (1938); *Ungeduld des Herzens* (1938; Beware of Pity, 1953); *Brasilien, ein Land der Zukunft* (1941); *Amerigo* (Eng., 1942; German, Amerigo: Die Geschichte eines historischen Irrtums, 1944); *Legenden* (1945; Stories and Legends, 1955); *Balzac* (1946; Eng., 1946); *Zeit und Welt, Aufsätze und Vorträge, 1904–1940* (1943); *Briefwechsel 1912–1942: S. Z.—Friederike Zweig* (1957; S. Z. and Friederike Zweig: Their Correspondence 1912–42, 1954); *Briefwechsel Richard Strauss-S. Z.* (1957); *Europäisches Erbe* (1960); *Gesammelte Werke* (12 vols., 1960 ff.); *Die Dramen* (1964); *Unbekannte Briefe aus der Emigration an eine Freundin* (1964)

BIBLIOGRAPHY: Zech, P., *S. Z.* (1943); Hellwig, H., *S. Z. Ein Lebensbild* (1948); Zweig, F., *S. Z.* (1948); Arens, H., *S. Z.* (1949); Zohn, H., ed., *S. Zs. Freundeskreis* (1953); Arens, H., ed., *Der große Europäer S. Z.* (1956); Lucas, W. I., "S. Z.," in *German Men of Letters*, ed. A. Natan, Vol. II (1963), 227–48; Klawiter, R. J., *S. Z.: A Bibliography* (1965); Dumont, R., *S. Z. et la France* (1967); Zohn, H., "Jewish Themes in S. Z.," *Journal of the International Arthur Schnitzler Research Association*, VI (1967), ii, 32–38

* * * *

JUAN ANTONIO DE ZUNZUNEGUI

STEFAN ZWEIG